Adam Nathan

101 Win ps,
VOLUME I:

SAMS | 800 East 96th Street, Indianapolis, Indiana 46240 USA

101 Windows® Phone 7 Apps, Volume I
Copyright © 2011 by Adam Nathan

ISBN-13: 978-0-672-33552-5
ISBN-10: 0-672-33552-2

Library of Congress Cataloging-in-Publication Data

Nathan, Adam, 1977-
  101 Windows phone 7 apps / Adam Nathan.
    v. cm.
  Includes index.
  Contents: v. 1. Developing apps 1-50.
  ISBN-13: 978-0-672-33552-5 (v. 1)
  ISBN-10: 0-672-33119-5 (v. 1)
  1. Application software—Development. 2. Windows phone (Computer file) 3. Smartphones—Programming. 4. Mobile computing. I. Title. II. Title: One hundred one Windows phone 7 apps.
  QA76.76.A65N378 2011
  004.165—dc22

                        2011010335

Printed in the United States of America

First Printing April 2011

Trademarks

Warning and Disclaimer

Bulk Sales

Sams Publishing offers excellent discounts on this book when ordered in quantity for bulk purchases or special sales. For more information, please contact

U.S. Corporate and Government Sales
1-800-382-3419
corpsales@pearsontechgroup.com

For sales outside of the U.S., please contact

International Sales
international@pearsoned.com

EDITOR-IN-CHIEF
Greg Wiegand

EXECUTIVE EDITOR
Neil Rowe

DEVELOPMENT EDITOR
Mark Renfrow

MANAGING EDITOR
Kristy Hart

PROJECT EDITOR
Betsy Harris

SENIOR INDEXER
Cheryl Lenser

PROOFREADER
Apostrophe Editing Services

TECHNICAL EDITOR
Dave Relyea

PUBLISHING COORDINATOR
Cindy Teeters

BOOK DESIGNERS
Gary Adair
Adam Nathan

COMPOSITOR
Bronkella Publishing LLC

contents at a glance

part III   storing & retrieving local data

part IV   pivot, panorama, charts, & graphs

part V   audio & video

part VI   microphone

table of contents

About the Author

Adam Nathan is a principal software development engineer for Microsoft, a best-selling technical author, and arguably the most prolific developer for Windows Phone. Adam previously cofounded Popfly, Microsoft's first product built on Silverlight, named one of the 25 most innovative products of 2007 by *PCWorld* magazine. He is also the founder of PINVOKE.NET, the online resource for .NET developers who need to access Win32.

Adam has created several top apps in the Windows Phone Marketplace that have been featured on Lifehacker, Gizmodo, ZDNet, ParentMap, and various Windows Phone enthusiast sites. Many of them are identical to or based on apps in this book. Chapter 36's Sound Recorder app was featured on MSDN's first Channel 9 "Hot Apps" show. With the purchase of this book, the same app is now yours to tweak and sell!

Adam's books have been considered required reading by many inside Microsoft and throughout the industry. Adam is the author of *Silverlight 1.0 Unleashed* (Sams, 2008), *WPF Unleashed* (Sams, 2006), *WPF 4 Unleashed* (Sams, 2010), and *.NET and COM: The Complete Interoperability Guide* (Sams, 2002); a coauthor of *ASP.NET: Tips, Tutorials, and Code* (Sams, 2001); and a contributor to books including *.NET Framework Standard Library Annotated Reference,* Volume 2 (Addison-Wesley, 2005), and *Windows Developer Power Tools* (O'Reilly, 2006). You can find Adam online at www.adamnathan.net or @adamnathan on Twitter.

Dedication

To Lindsay, Tyler, and Ryan.

Acknowledgments

Behind most authors is either an incredibly understanding spouse or, perhaps more likely, an ex-spouse. I'm fortunate to say that I've still got the former. My wonderful and beautiful wife, Lindsay Nathan, has not only been inhumanly patient and understanding during the whole book-writing process, but she's practically my coauthor in this book series. She came up with many of the app ideas, read significant portions of the book (despite having no previous programming experience!), found many errors, and suggested tremendous improvements to the book as well as the apps.

Lindsay constantly surprises me—and everyone around her—with her incredible talent and ability to excel at absolutely anything she tries. As a result of her involvement, she has even become a registered Windows Phone developer! You can search for "Lindsay Nathan" in the Windows Phone Marketplace to see some of her handiwork.

While I was preoccupied with writing for far too long, Lindsay made sure that our life didn't fall apart. More than that, she even enabled things to run smoothly. She's an incredible mother, wife, and friend and has made more sacrifices for her family than she'll ever get credit for. I literally could never have done this or any other book without her. You, the reader, may have gotten 101 apps out of this book series, but Lindsay has given me 101 new reasons to love her as much as I do. Thank you, Lindsay.

Although Lindsay is the reason this book is in your hands, this book also came together because of the work of several talented and hard-working people who aren't married to me. I'd like to take a moment to thank them as well, with the risk of accidentally omitting some people.

I owe huge thanks to Dave Relyea, the development lead for the Silverlight for Windows Phone team and the most knowledgeable Silverlight developer on the planet, for being a truly fantastic technical editor. Dave actually learned C# when writing the forensic DNA analysis software used to identify the 9/11 World Trade Center attack victims. After that, he started working for Microsoft on WPF 3.0, then Silverlight versions 1–4, and then the Silverlight for Windows Phone Toolkit, before becoming the lead for Silverlight for Windows Phone. He personally developed many of Silverlight's (and the toolkit's) features described in this book, so having his insight captured in these pages is invaluable.

Dave's feedback on my drafts was so thorough, the book is far better because of him. He also did a fantastic job tracking down the right experts to answer questions or add more depth to a number of topics. As a result, many of the topics covered in this book have been reviewed by the developer who implemented the corresponding features. Having that level of scrutiny is priceless. Dave was the technical editor for my first Silverlight book which, at 250 pages, was much less of a time commitment than editing this book! I'm grateful he agreed to devote so much time to this book to make me look better and make you more successful. I hope he's still up for reviewing Volume II!

I thank Jeff Wilcox, David Anson, Andi Fein, and Austin Lamb, who each did an excellent job reviewing a chapter. I also thank Peter Torr, Stefan Wick, Joao Guberman Raza, Ashu Tatake, Shane Guillet, and Edward Sumanaseni for their assistance. I really appreciate it.

Matt Cavallari deserves many thanks for his tremendous and timely help. If it weren't for his assistance during the early days, this book would probably have been released much later.

I'd like to thank Tim Rice, James Lissiak, Ben Anderson, Patrick Wong, Andy Sterland, Tim Wagner, Emily Basalik, Anjali Acharya, Chris Brumme, Eric Rudder, Brandon Watson, Jason Zander, Gus Perez, and Paramesh Vaidyanathan, who helped in a number of ways. As always, I thank my family for having the foresight to introduce me to Basic programming on our IBM PCjr when I was in elementary school.

I sincerely thank the folks at Sams, especially Neil Rowe, Betsy Harris, and Gary Adair, who are always a pleasure to work with. I couldn't have asked for a better publishing team. Perhaps against their better judgment, they gave me complete freedom to run with my crazy idea of a two-part book series on 101 apps. They even enabled me to customize the design of the books inside and out, which was a lot of fun. They have never complained about my insistence on full-color printing or numerous nit-picky requests. Amazingly, with all the pressures publishers face, they didn't even rush me. This benefits you greatly in terms of quality and the coverage of developments after the launch of Windows Phone 7, so please thank them as well. I hope the risks that they've taken on these books work out for them as much as I hope it works out for me.

Finally, I thank *you* for picking up a copy of this book! I don't think you'll regret it!

We Want to Hear from You!

As the reader of this book, *you* are our most important critic and commentator. We value your opinion and want to know what we're doing right, what we could do better, what areas you'd like to see us publish in, and any other words of wisdom you're willing to pass our way.

You can email or write me directly to let me know what you did or didn't like about this book—as well as what we can do to make our books stronger.

Please note that I cannot help you with technical problems related to the topic of this book, and that due to the high volume of mail I receive, I might not be able to reply to every message.

When you write, please be sure to include this book's title and author as well as your name and phone or email address. I will carefully review your comments and share them with the author and editors who worked on the book.

E-mail: feedback@samspublishing.com

Mail: Neil Rowe
Executive Editor
Sams Publishing
800 East 96th Street
Indianapolis, IN 46240 USA

Reader Services

Visit our website and register this book at informit.com/register for convenient access to any updates, downloads, or errata that might be available for this book.

introduction

Many people dream about making millions by selling smartphone apps. Some people have even succeeded. Sure, as Scott Adams so humorously points out, earning *millions* from apps is a long shot. But with a little creativity, artistic skill, and programming skill, could you earn *thousands*? You bet. Do I think you, as a reader of this book, should be able to earn more than you paid for it? I do (although I make no guarantees)!

All kidding aside, there has never been a better time for hobbyist programmers to make good money doing what they love. I remember releasing a few shareware games in junior high school and asking for $5 donations to be sent to my home address. I earned $15. One of the three donations was from my grandmother, who didn't even own a computer! These days, however, adults and kids alike can make money on simple apps and games without relying on kind and generous individuals going to the trouble of mailing a check! The painless distribution and automatic payment systems enabled by app stores and marketplaces is the best thing to happen to developers in a really long time.

As a new platform at the time of this writing, Windows Phone 7 is in a unique spot of having a rapidly growing user base (expected to accelerate with the addition of Nokia Windows Phones) yet a relatively small number of developers. Your apps have a pretty good chance of standing out in the still-young Windows Phone Marketplace.

So let's get started building some apps! I've been writing programming books for a long time, but I've never been more excited about the topic than I am for Windows Phone 7. I feel that it deserves a different kind of treatment unlike any I've seen. This book is not just app-focused, but focused on the things that *really* matter when building apps.

I wrote this book with the following goals in mind:

→ To be insanely practical, with examples that you can credibly ship as complete apps

→ To provide a solid grounding in the underlying concepts in an approachable fashion

→ To answer the questions most people have when learning Windows Phone development and to show how commonly desired tasks are accomplished

→ To be an authoritative source, thanks to input from many members of the Windows Phone team who designed, implemented, and tested the technology

→ To help you write apps that look great and follow Windows Phone design guidelines

→ To help you follow best practices but not shy away from hacks if they're needed to get the job done

→ To not limit the book to the functionality that ships with Windows Phone, but to also include interesting open source libraries

→ To optimize for concise, easy-to-understand code rather than enforcing architectural patterns that can be impractical or increase the number of concepts to understand

→ To be fun to read!

To elaborate on the second-to-last point: You won't find examples of patterns such as Model-View-ViewModel (MVVM) in this book. I *am* a fan of applying such patterns to code, but I don't want to distract from the core lessons in each chapter. You are certainly free to apply such patterns as you make changes to these apps for your own needs, although I personally find that it can be overkill given the limited size and scope of some apps.

Who Should Read This Book?

This book is for software developers of all skill levels who want to write apps for Windows Phone. It is certainly *not* just a book for beginners; even developers who are Silverlight pros and/or Windows Phone pros should be able to get a lot out of it.

This book does not teach you how to program, nor does it teach the basics of the C# language. However, it is designed to be understandable even for folks who are new to the .NET Framework and does not require previous experience with Silverlight or with Windows Phone.

As my wife will attest, even nonprogrammers can follow along to some degree and tweak the apps in this book. If you've got a knack for graphic design and you have some good ideas for ways to re-theme the apps in this book, you could be quite successful in the Windows Phone Marketplace!

 If you're thinking about tweaking some apps in this book and wondering how to get the most bang for your buck, you might consider searching for "Adam Nathan" in the Windows Phone Marketplace (or visiting http://adamnathanapps.com) to examine the relative popularity of this book's apps. Although I've enhanced some of my apps in the marketplace compared to what is in this book, many of them are identical.

I'm really interested to see what apps you publish based on apps in this book! Send me a tweet with details, and I might highlight your apps. I'm @adamnathan on Twitter.

Choosing a Technology

Windows Phone supports two primary programming models: Silverlight and XNA.

Silverlight, originally designed as a plugin for Web browsers, enables the rapid development of rich applications. It emphasizes declarative UI with powerful support for animation, data binding, vector graphics, and controls that can be easily composed and themed. The current version of Silverlight used by Windows Phone is effectively the same as version 3 used by Windows and Mac, but with some irrelevant features removed and other phone-specific features and performance tuning added.

XNA, originally designed for Xbox but also available for Windows and Zune HD (as well as Windows Phone), enables high-performance games, whether 2D sprite-based games or games with full 3D graphics. Windows Phone supports the same XNA 4.0 Reach profile that is supported on Xbox and just about all modern PCs, except it does not support shaders.

XNA Does Not Stand for Anything

However, it is commonly stated that it's actually an acronym for "XNA is Not an Acronym."

The typical advice for developers is, "Use Silverlight for apps and XNA for games." The reality is a little more subtle.

Building Games with Silverlight

You can certainly create fantastic games with Silverlight, as games are apps, too! Chapter 40, "Darts," is a great example of this. Shortly after I released a version of this app in the Windows Phone Marketplace, it was ranked as the #11 paid app, sitting among many Xbox LIVE games that use XNA. Games written in Silverlight have several advantages at the time of this writing, such as easy integration with services such as Facebook and Twitter, as well as the ability to use all the standard Silverlight controls (perhaps re-themed) for menus, scoreboards, and more.

On the other hand, trying to create complex games with Silverlight can be infeasible performance-wise. 3D games are also out of the question. Xbox LIVE features are only available for XNA games, but you need to be a specially designated Xbox LIVE developer to take advantage of these features anyway.

Building Apps with XNA

You could write a nongame app with XNA, but that would be a strange thing to do. Besides being a lot more work to re-create basic controls such as buttons and list boxes, XNA apps are not currently able to take advantage of the user's phone theme, the application bar, the web browser control, and more. Several third-party control libraries exist for XNA, however, that can make your job much easier. See http://bit.ly/xnalibs1 and http://bit.ly/xnalibs2.

Mixing Silverlight with XNA

An app can mix and match functionality from Silverlight and XNA. Although all 50 apps in this book are Silverlight apps, several take advantage of XNA functionality: using the microphone, playing sound effects, and so on. And although XNA apps cannot embed a web browser, they can use Silverlight's networking classes to make web requests. The only limitation is that, at the time of this writing, you cannot mix Silverlight user interface rendering with XNA user interface rendering. From the perspective of the user interface, an app can only be one or the other.

 **Marketplace certification enforces that Silverlight and XNA are not improperly mixed!**

Even if you find some way of using XNA user interface pieces in a Silverlight app that seems to work, your app will not be approved for inclusion in the Windows Phone Marketplace at the time of this writing. As long as you avoid referencing `Microsoft.Xna.Framework.Game.dll` and `Microsoft.Xna.Framework.Graphics.dll` in a Silverlight app, you should be fine.

The relationship between Silverlight and XNA is more confusing than it needs to be, caused by the goal of Silverlight for Windows Phone to be mostly compatible with Silverlight for Windows and Mac, and by the goal of XNA for Windows Phone to be mostly compatible with XNA for Xbox, Windows, and Zune HD. The result is some duplication of functionality and arbitrary distinctions between technologies. For example, although Windows Phone has a single class for interacting with the microphone, it is an XNA feature (and lives in an XNA assembly) simply because it's compatible with what earlier versions of XNA have already exposed to developers.

HTML, CSS, and JavaScript

A final subtlety is that there's really a third development model you can use for Windows Phone apps: the combination of HTML, CSS, and JavaScript. Technically, such an app would be a Silverlight app that hosts the web browser control, but inside that control you could provide an entire app's experience with HTML, CSS, and JavaScript that is either locally hosted or resides on a Web server. With a little bit of C# glue code in the app hosting the web browser, you could even cause pieces of your HTML user interface to trigger phone-specific actions, such as initiating a phone call.

Can I write an app with HTML5 for Windows Phone?

Not at the time of this writing, but you will be able to by the end of 2011. Microsoft has announced that Internet Explorer 9 will be available on Windows Phone by this time. This not only adds great HTML5 support to the Internet Explorer app, but to the web browser control available to developers as well.

Can I write a game for Windows Phone with OpenGL?

No. Your best bet is to use XNA.

Software Requirements

This book targets Windows Phone 7 (all phone models running Windows Phone OS 7.0) and the corresponding Windows Phone Developer Tools.

Other than the desktop operating system you use for development (which can be Windows Vista or later, but not Windows Server), getting the most out of this book doesn't require anything other than free software:

→ The Windows Phone Developer Tools, a free download at http://developer.windowsphone.com, includes

  → Visual Studio 2010 Express for Windows Phone, used for developing Silverlight apps

  → Expression Blend 4 for Windows Phone, which can optionally be used for designing Silverlight-based vector graphics, animations, and control templates

  → XNA Game Studio 4.0, used for developing XNA apps

  → Windows Phone Emulator, used for running and testing your apps on a PC rather than a real phone

  This book has been tested with the January 2011 update of the tools, which adds copy/paste support to the emulator's version of the Windows Phone operating system (version 7.0.7338.0).

→ The Silverlight for Windows Phone Toolkit, a free download at http://silverlight.codeplex.com, which contains numerous controls and important features missing from the Windows Developer Power Tools. This book has been tested with the February 2011 version. Later versions are not guaranteed to be backwards compatible, so be careful if you decide to try a later version.

→ The Silverlight Toolkit, a free download also available at
http://silverlight.codeplex.com, which contains additional controls that can be used
on Windows Phone, such as charts and graphs.

→ PAINT.NET, a free download at http://getpaint.net, used for creating and editing
graphics.

Throughout the book, links to other resources are given as they are needed.

If you already use a more powerful edition of Visual Studio, you don't have to use the
Express edition included in the Windows Developer Power Tools; installing the tools also
adds the Windows Phone-specific functionality to other editions. Any differences between
Visual Studio Express and paid editions of Visual Studio have nothing to do with
Windows Phone; the differences are in developer productivity features, application lifecy-
cle management tools, and so on.

The current version of the Windows Phone Developer Tools, and this book, only supports
programming with C# and XAML. However, you can download an extension to Visual
Studio Professional or higher that enables the use of Visual Basic instead of C# when
creating Silverlight apps for Windows Phone. See
http://go.microsoft.com/fwlink/?LinkId=206790.

If you choose to use Visual Basic instead
of C#, you should still be able to use this
book. After all, the concepts, APIs, and
XAML are identical. The only thing you
miss out on is the ability to directly
copy/paste from the vast amount of
code accompanying this book, at least
without a C#-to-VB conversion tool.

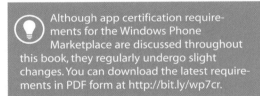

Although app certification requirements for the Windows Phone
Marketplace are discussed throughout
this book, they regularly undergo slight
changes. You can download the latest requirements in PDF form at http://bit.ly/wp7cr.

Several Windows Phone development tools exist that are *not* free. Two worth mentioning
are

→ Silverlight Spy (http://firstfloorsoftware.com/silverlightspy), which enables you to inspect
and tweak your app's element tree and even inspect its isolated storage contents

→ Runtime Intelligence for Windows Phone (http://preemptive.com/windowsphone7),
which enables obfuscation, optimizations, and analytics

Hardware Requirements

You're going to need a computer that can run the software listed in the preceding section.
In addition, although technically not required, I recommend testing any apps you submit
to the Windows Phone Marketplace on a real phone.

(?) As a developer, what phone should I purchase for testing my apps?

The beauty of Windows Phone 7 is that it shouldn't matter. Despite the variety of form factors, the functionality exposed to developers is consistent. For example, although some models have better cameras than others, the way you interact with the camera doesn't know or care. (The downside of this consistency, of course, is that you cannot write an app that takes advantage of the unique hardware features of a specific phone, unless you are the manufacturer of the phone.)

The most obvious difference between phone models is the existence of (and placement of) a hardware keyboard. Although I did some testing on a model with a hardware keyboard, it was no longer necessary once I learned how it worked. And I share that information with you in Chapter 3, "In Case of Emergency." So don't feel that you need to buy a phone with a hardware keyboard solely for testing purposes! The emulator also does a good job of emulating a portrait slide-out hardware keyboard.

As time goes on and phones become increasingly differentiated by processing power, testing your apps on the least powerful phone could become interesting for ensuring they run quickly enough.

Although the screen resolution (480x800 pixels) is common among all Windows Phone 7 phones, the physical size of the screen may vary slightly. Keep this in mind for anything that relies on physical measurements (as with the Ruler app in Chapter 5). The solution for this is to ensure that you provide calibration so the user can adjust your app to their device accordingly. All the apps in this book were tested on a Samsung Focus.

The emulator that comes with the Windows Phone Developer Tools is very good for most things, but there are many things it doesn't emulate. For example:

You can purchase a Windows phone without a voice or data contract at http://www.zones.com/windowsphonedeveloperpurchase.

→ It doesn't provide a good way to test accelerometer data.

→ It doesn't provide a way to emulate multi-touch gestures unless you have a multi-touch PC or use techniques such as the one described at http://bit.ly/multitouchemulator.

→ You can't test consuming pictures from the camera, although it does provide some built-in photos you can use with the photo chooser.

→ It doesn't expose full functionality when launching external actions such as composing an email.

→ It doesn't expose the built-in apps, which are handy to examine for matching the style and conventions expected of Windows Phone apps.

→ It doesn't provide a way to test the FM radio tuner.

With the emulator, you can't predict the performance of your application when it runs on a physical device!

Sometimes an app runs faster on the emulator and sometimes it can actually run more slowly, based on a number of factors. Although you certainly use it to test *relative* performance improvements you make, there is absolutely no substitute for running it on a real phone.

That said, if you try to gauge performance while running in the emulator with frame rate counters enabled (see Chapter 13, "Metronome"), the *fill rate* value is the best predictor of device rendering performance.

For me, running apps on a phone is helpful for ensuring that touch targets are not too small, too close together, or too close to the edge of the screen. When I created a pool game, I didn't realize that the user's finger would block important information on the screen until I tested it on a real phone. The bottom line is that submitting apps to the Windows Phone Marketplace that you've only tested on the emulator is risky.

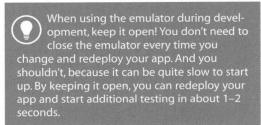

When using the emulator during development, keep it open! You don't need to close the emulator every time you change and redeploy your app. And you shouldn't, because it can be quite slow to start up. By keeping it open, you can redeploy your app and start additional testing in about 1–2 seconds.

For the most part, using the emulator is straightforward, but there are a few keyboard shortcuts that are good to know about:

→ The F1 key is a keyboard shortcut for the hardware Back button.

→ The F2 key (or Windows key) is a keyboard shortcut for the hardware Home button.

→ The Pause key toggles the hardware keyboard. When it is activated, you can type with your computer's keyboard rather than clicking keys on the screen (which can be excruciating). You can also use Page Up to enable the hardware keyboard and Page Down to switch back to the on-screen keyboard.

The emulator has many other keyboard shortcuts, most of which aren't supported by the limited version of the Windows Phone operating system that currently ships with the emulator. See http://bit.ly/emulatorshortcuts for more details.

Code Examples

The source code for examples in this book can be downloaded from www.informit.com/title/9780672335525. You must register your book before you can access the source code.

How This Book Is Organized

This unconventional book contains 50 chapters, one for each complete app in the available source code. Although each chapter is focused on building a specific app, the goal of each one is to teach you about new features and/or approaches that you can apply to unique apps that you want to build.

This book obviously encourages jumping to a specific chapter if all you want to do is build a similar app. However, I've designed it to be read (or at least skimmed) *sequentially*, due to the gradual introduction of features that build on earlier chapters, and the inclusion of sidebars throughout that are generally applicable. So even if you have no interest in building the Tally app from Chapter 1, you should still flip through it to make sure you don't miss something important, like what to do about your app's icons and capabilities list. Although you probably don't care about building the Flashlight app from Chapter 2, it contains vital lessons regarding the application bar and advanced tips such as using XNA to customize the buttons on a standard message box.

If you find the app-focused organization of this book frustrating for finding out how to do a specific task, then Appendix A, "Lessons Index," should be your starting point. It contains a concise index of the lessons from all the chapters. For example, are you wondering how to use a toggle switch? Appendix A reveals that Chapter 20, "Alarm Clock," is the place to find your answer.

This book is arranged in eight main parts, from essentials such as Silverlight and Windows Phone basics, animated effects, and data management (the first three parts) to specific topics that are only interesting for certain types of apps (such as using the phone's microphone or accelerometer). The following sections provide a summary of each part. The most important lesson(s) from each chapter are included in parentheses. The full list of each chapter's lessons appears on the first page of that chapter.

Part I: Getting Started

Although the first part of the book is given the humble title of "Getting Started," it could almost be a complete book on Silverlight on its own! By the end of Part I, you learn about controls, layout, events, vector graphics, data binding, resources, restyling and retemplating controls, dynamic XAML, enhancing your productivity with the Silverlight for Windows Phone Toolkit, and more.

Special attention is given to areas of Silverlight that are unique to Windows Phone, such as the navigation scheme and the application lifecycle (best known for its *tombstoning* behavior). Many essential phone topics are also examined: orientation, the on-screen and hardware keyboards, the application bar and status bar, phone themes, vibration, running while the phone is locked, preventing auto-lock, and customizing the behavior of the hardware Back button.

This first part of the book not only has the most chapters, but its chapters are generally longer than the ones in the rest of the book simply because there's so much background material to cover. If you were only going to read one part of this book sequentially, Part I should be it.

Chapters in this part:

 1   Tally (App Basics)

 2   Flashlight (Application Bar)

 3   In Case of Emergency (Orientation & Keyboards)

 4   Stopwatch (Grid & User Controls)

 5   Ruler (Canvas & Vector Graphics)

 6   Baby Sign Language (Page Navigation & Data Binding)

 7   Date Diff (Silverlight for Windows Phone Toolkit)

 8   Vibration Composer (Vibration & Running While Locked)

 9   Fake Call (Resources & Styles)

 10   Tip Calculator (Application Lifecycle & Control Templates)

 11   XAML Editor (Dynamic XAML & Popup)

Part II: Transforms & Animations

Animations are a huge part of a typical Windows Phone app's experience. Part II provides a comprehensive tour of Silverlight's animation system, which supports a variety of complex behavior in a relatively simple fashion. It also covers the typical targets of any animation: 2D and 3D transforms that can be applied to just about anything. Compared to Part I, this part's apps tend to be smaller, more focused on a single lesson, and sillier.

Chapters in this part:

 12 Silly Eye (Intro to Animation)

 13 Metronome (Intro to 2D Transforms)

 14   Love Meter (Keyframe Animations)

 15 Mood Ring (Color, Object & Point Animations)

 16 Lottery Numbers Picker (Sharing Animations)

 17 Pick a Card Magic Trick (3D Transforms)

 18 Cocktails (Quick Jump Grid)

 19 Animation Lab (Custom Controls & VSM)

Part III: Storing & Retrieving Local Data

Almost every app needs to store and later retrieve some data, even if it's just a user setting or some state that the app should remember the next time it is launched. The main technology covered by this section is something called *isolated storage*, although it also explains techniques for shipping initial data with your apps.

This part covers a wide range of scenarios: storing and retrieving settings, state, text files, and photos. It even demonstrates how to use a local SQL database, something that isn't currently included in the core development platform.

Chapters in this part:

 20 Alarm Clock (Settings, Toggle Switch, Custom Font)

 21 Passwords & Secrets (Encryption & Observable Collections)

 22 Notepad (Reading & Writing Files)

23 Baby Milestones (Reading & Writing Pictures)

   24 Baby Name Eliminator (Local Databases & Embedded Resources)

   25 Book Reader (Pagination & List Picker)

Part IV: Pivot, Panorama, Charts, & Graphs

Part IV focuses on some specialized controls that can make your apps stand out. The pivot and panorama controls enable you to create user interfaces that match Windows Phone's signature style. The unique panorama, with its parallax scrolling, enables an experience like the phone's built-in hubs. For many people, the panorama defines the Windows Phone experience. The pivot control is a popular way to provide filtered views over data, as done by the Mail app.

This part also shows you how to use rich charts and graphs in your apps by repurposing functionality from the Silverlight Toolkit (which was not originally meant for Windows Phone).

Chapters in this part:

   26 TODO List (Pivot & Context Menu)

   27 Groceries (Panorama)

   28 Alphabet Flashcards (Filmstrip-Style Swiping)

   29 Weight Tracker (Charts & Graphs)

Part V: Audio & Video

This part examines how to include audio and video in your apps, as well as using the built-in FM radio tuner that all Windows Phones contain. There are plenty of gotchas and limitations in this area, especially when it comes to performance and passing certification for the Windows Phone Marketplace.

Chapters in this part:

 30 Cowbell (Sound Effects)

 31 Trombone (Sound Manipulation)

 32 Local FM Radio (Radio Tuner)

 33 Subservient Cat (Video)

Part VI: Microphone

Although clearly an audio feature, use of the phone's microphone is given its own part in this book. The microphone is one of the features that is only exposed through XNA, but fortunately Silverlight apps can still take advantage of it.

Chapters in this part:

 34 Bubble Blower (Sound Detection)

 35 Talking Parrot (Recording & Playing)

 36 Sound Recorder (Saving Audio Files & Playing Sound Backwards)

Part VII: Touch & Multi-Touch

Although most apps limit their interaction to simple finger taps or scrolling gestures built into controls such as list box and panorama, there are many uses for custom gestures that may involve multiple fingers simultaneously. Part VII demonstrates how to implement all kinds of custom touch and multi-touch behavior, and how the Silverlight for Windows Phone Toolkit makes it easy to support several standard gestures such as flicking, pinching, stretching, dragging, rotating, double-tapping and more.

Chapters in this part:

 37 Reflex Test (Single Touch)

 38 Musical Robot (Multi-Touch)

Part VIII: Accelerometer Tricks

All Windows phones have an accelerometer, which is basically a 3D motion sensor. Accelerometers in phones have ushered in a new era of mobile gaming, but they are also useful for a wide variety of gimmicks. This final part of the book demonstrates how to use the accelerometer to detect a variety of complex gestures, such as a throwing motion, walking motion, shaking, turning the phone upside-down, and of course determining the angle of the phone. Determining the angle is the foundation for one of the canonical apps for any smartphone: a level.

Chapters in this part:

Conventions Used in This Book

Various typefaces in this book identify new terms and other special items. These typefaces include the following:

Typeface	Meaning
Italic	Italic is used for new terms or phrases when they are initially defined and occasionally for emphasis.
Monospace	Monospace is used for screen messages, code listings, and filenames. In code listings, `italic monospace type` is used for placeholder text.
	Code listings are colorized similarly to the way they are colorized in Visual Studio. `Blue monospace type` is used for XML elements and C# keywords, `brown monospace type` is used for XML element names and C# strings, `green monospace type` is used for comments, `red monospace type` is used for XML attributes, and `teal monospace type` is used for type names in C#.
Bold	When appropriate, bold is used for code directly related to the main lesson(s) in a chapter.

Throughout this book, and even in this introduction, you'll find a number of sidebar elements:

What is a FAQ sidebar?

A Frequently Asked Question (FAQ) sidebar presents a question you might have about the subject matter in a particular spot in the book—and then provides a concise answer.

Digging Deeper Sidebars •••

A Digging Deeper sidebar presents advanced or more detailed information on a subject than is provided in the surrounding text. Think of Digging Deeper material as something you can look into if you're curious but can ignore if you're not.

A tip offers information about design guidelines, shortcuts or alternative approaches to produce better results, or something that makes a task easier. This is the most common type of sidebar used throughout the book.

Warning!

A warning alerts you to an action or a condition that can lead to an unexpected or unpredictable result—and then tells you how to avoid it.

chapter 1 lessons

TALLY

> If you're like me, you probably skipped over this book's "Introduction" section. If so, please go back and at least skim it, as it explains how to get started with the development tools, gives you tips for using the Windows Phone Emulator, and describes how this book works.

How many times have you wanted to count something and felt that your fingers and concentration alone were not enough for the task? Perhaps you've needed to count for a friend who is swimming laps or lifting weights. Perhaps you've wanted to keep track of something over a long period of time, such as how many times your spouse annoyed you with something she constantly says or does. In the past, I haven't been able to count how many times my wife has asked me, "Do I look fat?" With the Tally app, now I can.

The Tally app that we'll create in this chapter increments a counter every time you tap the screen. It has a "reset" button to clear the count. It remembers your current count indefinitely—until you either press the "reset" button or uninstall the app.

Despite my sales pitch, I must admit that Tally is not the most compelling application imaginable. However, it is simple enough to provide a good introduction to developing for Windows Phone. Compared to other chapters, this chapter is much less about the app itself and more about understanding the structure and basic features of a Windows Phone project in Visual Studio.

Why do Windows Phone apps often look so plain?

It's an artistic choice. Windows Phone and its apps are designed to communicate relevant information quickly and clearly, much like signs in an airport, train station, bus terminal, or subway. Microsoft appropriately calls this design *Metro*. Proper Metro-styled apps favor white-space over clutter and place heavy emphasis on typography with, at times, simple monochromatic icons. The main "wow" factor from Windows Phone apps usually does not come from their static visuals, but rather from rich animations that encourage exploration.

Therefore, the style of Windows Phone is definitely not meant to be like iPhone, which emphasizes shiny, gradient-filled visuals. Another subtle difference between the intended design of Windows Phone apps and iPhone apps is that iPhone encourages the use of literal real-world visuals (such as a Notes app that looks like a physical paper notepad) whereas Windows Phone encourages user interfaces that *don't* mimic the real world so closely. Instead, excluding games and novelty apps, the experience should be "authentically digital." Some of the Metro guidelines, especially around capitalization, are nonintuitive and take getting used to, but this book reinforces the guidelines throughout.

Why do Windows Phone apps predominantly use white text on a black background?

It's also an artistic choice. However, black is not only meant to be fashionable, but also power-conscious. Most Windows Phones use *organic light-emitting diode* (OLED) screens. Such screens can be great for power consumption (because they don't require a backlight), but the amount of power consumed varies based on the color and brightness of the screen. On such screens, white text on a black background consumes significantly less power than black text on a white background!

You can get detailed information about the Windows Phone design system (Metro), Photoshop template files, and more at http://go.microsoft.com/fwlink/?LinkID=190696.

Deconstructing a "Windows Phone Application" Visual Studio Project

When you create a new "Windows Phone Application" project in Visual Studio, you get a complete app that you can instantly compile into a .xap file and deploy to the emulator or a physical phone. The app doesn't actually *do* anything other than display some text on the screen, but it sets up a lot of infrastructure that would be difficult and tedious to create from scratch. Before creating the Tally app, let's understand the main pieces of any new "Windows Phone Application" project:

→ The application manifest

→ Images

→ XAML code: `MainPage.xaml` and `App.xaml`

→ C# code: `MainPage.xaml.cs`, `App.xaml.cs`, and `AssemblyInfo.cs`

The Application Manifest

The file called `WMAppManifest.xml` (where WM oddly stands for the outdated "Windows Mobile" term) is an *application manifest*. It describes your app to the operating system—its name, what it looks like, how it starts, what it's allowed to do, and more. Listing 1.1 shows what Visual Studio generates inside this file when you create a new project and name it "Tally." You can find this file in your project's "Properties" folder.

Visual Studio provides a few types of Windows Phone projects for more complex applications, based on the control that populates the main screen: a databound (list) application, a panorama application, and a pivot application. Almost all of the applications in this book were created from the basic "Windows Phone Application" project, as it's relatively easy to manually add a databound list, a panorama control, or a pivot control to a project without having to start with a specialized project type.

`.xap` **Files**

`.xap` files, introduced by Silverlight but also used by XNA apps for Windows Phone, are just `.zip` files. If you rename a `.xap` file and give it a `.zip` extension, you can inspect its contents just like any `.zip` file. A `.xap` file for a Windows Phone app contains several files: compiled DLL(s), manifests, images, and potentially other assets used by your app that aren't embedded into a DLL, such as videos or data files.

LISTING 1.1   `WMAppManifest.xml`—The Initial Application Manifest for the Tally Project

```xml
<?xml version="1.0" encoding="utf-8"?>
<Deployment xmlns="http://schemas.microsoft.com/windowsphone/2009/deployment"
            AppPlatformVersion="7.0">
  <App xmlns="" ProductID="{2f711986-cfb4-40d3-9b7d-64aa37faf338}" Title="Tally"
    RuntimeType="Silverlight" Version="1.0.0.0" Genre="apps.normal"
    Author="Tally author" Description="Sample description" Publisher="Tally">
    <IconPath IsRelative="true" IsResource="false">ApplicationIcon.png</IconPath>
    <Capabilities>
      <Capability Name="ID_CAP_GAMERSERVICES"/>
      <Capability Name="ID_CAP_IDENTITY_DEVICE"/>
      <Capability Name="ID_CAP_IDENTITY_USER"/>
      <Capability Name="ID_CAP_LOCATION"/>
      <Capability Name="ID_CAP_MEDIALIB"/>
      <Capability Name="ID_CAP_MICROPHONE"/>
      <Capability Name="ID_CAP_NETWORKING"/>
      <Capability Name="ID_CAP_PHONEDIALER"/>
      <Capability Name="ID_CAP_PUSH_NOTIFICATION"/>
      <Capability Name="ID_CAP_SENSORS"/>
      <Capability Name="ID_CAP_WEBBROWSERCOMPONENT"/>
    </Capabilities>
    <Tasks>
```

LISTING 1.1   Continued

```
    <DefaultTask Name ="_default" NavigationPage="MainPage.xaml"/>
  </Tasks>
  <Tokens>
    <PrimaryToken TokenID="TallyToken" TaskName="_default">
      <TemplateType5>
        <BackgroundImageURI IsRelative="true" IsResource="false">
          Background.png
        </BackgroundImageURI>
        <Count>0</Count>
        <Title>Tally</Title>
      </TemplateType5>
    </PrimaryToken>
  </Tokens>
</App>
</Deployment>
```

The application manifest is a strange file, because most of it gets overwritten by the Windows Phone Marketplace certification process. Therefore, the application manifest inside your app that can be downloaded from the marketplace will be different than the manifest inside your private copy of your app that you manually deploy.

The App element contains a ProductID Globally Unique Identifier (GUID) that uniquely identifies your app, and a RuntimeType value that indicates this is a Silverlight app rather than an XNA app. The value for Title is displayed with your installed app (either in the normal app list or the Games hub). The other four attributes are only applicable for listing your app in the marketplace, but these values (as well as Title) get overwritten by the data you enter on the marketplace website (the App Hub).

The Genre value affects where your app gets installed on the phone. If you use apps.normal, it gets placed in the normal app list. If you instead use apps.games, it gets placed inside the Games hub. (Yes, Silverlight apps can do this; the Games hub is not limited to apps created with XNA.) You must choose one of the two locations; your app cannot be installed in both. Leaving this as apps.normal is much more convenient at development-time, because the emulator does not expose the Games hub. When submitting an app to the marketplace, this value also

The text overlaid on a tile is defined by the Title element inside the PrimaryToken element. This means that you can use something different than your app name. Although it is best to use your app name to avoid user confusion, shortening it is a good idea when your app name is too long for the tile.

You can leave the title element empty to produce a text-free tile (as done by the Facebook app), although the marketplace might reject such a submission unless you provide justification. The marketplace wants to ensure that users are not confused about which tile belongs to which app.

gets overwritten by the category you choose on the website.

The `IconPath` element points to your icon image file, the `Tasks` element points to the main Silverlight page where your app begins running, and the `Tokens` element contains information about your tile (seen by users who pin your app to their start screen). These parts are rarely changed, but these values are preserved when your app is published in the marketplace.

> **The Other Manifest**
>
> Visual Studio projects contain a second manifest in the "Properties" folder called `AppManifest.xml`. This is needed by Silverlight infrastructure, but you do not need to touch this file.

Capabilities

The most interesting part of `WMAppManifest.xml` is the list of capabilities inside the `Capabilities` element. These are special permissions for actions that users might not want certain apps to perform, whether for privacy concerns or concerns about data usage charges. The Visual Studio-generated manifest requests all available capabilities. You can restrict this list to test what happens when your app tries to perform an action for which it does not have permission, but that's a moot point. With one exception described later, the marketplace certification process automatically detects what capabilities your app needs and overwrites your list in the application manifest with the minimal set of required capabilities.

In the marketplace, users are told what capabilities your app will be granted before they decide whether to download it. Each capability has a user-friendly name, so `ID_CAP_LOCATION` in Listing 1.1 is called "location services" in the marketplace, and `ID_CAP_NETWORKING` is called "data connection." The user approval is an implicit part of the action of downloading your app. The location services capability, however, requires *explicit* consent by the user. The marketplace prompts users to agree to the sending of location data before they download the app.

 Once your app is running, you do not need to check if you've been granted any of your requested capabilities. (There's not even an API to do so!) If your app is running, then all requested capabilities have been granted. They cannot be revoked.

The key point is that there's no need for your app to obtain permission from the user for any capability, nor do you have to worry about whether your app has been granted certain capabilities. Just remember:

➔ If your app is running, it has been granted all the capabilities listed in its manifest.

 `ID_CAP_NETWORKING` **is the one capability you must manually request!**

There's one huge exception to the idea that you can let the marketplace certification process worry about the capabilities list for you. Although it can figure out everything else, marketplace certification cannot reliably figure out whether your app needs the phone's networking capability. If `ID_CAP_NETWORKING` is present in your manifest, it will be granted even if you don't need it, and if it is not present, it might *not* be granted even if you *do* need it!

→ If your app has been downloaded from the marketplace, its manifest automatically lists all the capabilities it needs and no more (except for ID_CAP_NETWORKING, as described in the warning sidebar).

You want to restrict the set of capabilities requested by your app, because it is a competitive advantage. For example, users might decide not to buy your Tip Calculator app if it wants permission to use the phone's data connection! Therefore, be sure to remove the ID_CAP_NETWORKING capability if you don't need it. Otherwise, your marketplace listing will say that your app "requires access to your data connection."

Although ID_CAP_NETWORKING is currently the only capability to be careful about, the best practice is to use the Windows Phone Capability Detection Tool that ships with the Windows Phone Developer Tools starting with the October 2010 release. This runs the same automatic capability detection done by the marketplace certification process and then tells you what to put in your manifest. Before submitting your app to the marketplace, you should replace your requested capabilities with this minimal set (and, if appropriate, ignore the ID_CAP_NETWORKING capability that is usually falsely reported by the tool).

Why can I no longer debug my app on a physical phone after updating its capabilities?

That pesky ID_CAP_NETWORKING capability is to blame. Without ID_CAP_NETWORKING, the debugger is unable to communicate with the attached phone. So keep it there during development, but be sure to remember to remove this capability before submitting your app to the marketplace if your app does not require it!

How can I write a game that uses Xbox LIVE features?

Some capabilities are for specific developers such as mobile operators and phone manufacturers; not for mere mortals like you and me. ID_CAP_GAMERSERVICES is one such capability that does not work for everyone. It grants access to Xbox LIVE APIs, but only to games approved by Microsoft. You can peruse the Xbox LIVE functionality by looking at the Microsoft.Xna. Framework.GamerServices assembly with Visual Studio's Object Browser, if you want to know what you're missing. Most of the functionality inside throws a NotSupportedException unless you are a registered Xbox LIVE developer and have gone through a specific process to enable your game for Xbox LIVE.

If you believe you've developed a game worthy of the ID_CAP_GAMERSERVICES capability (so you can integrate with Xbox LIVE achievements, leaderboards, and more), you can email wpgames@microsoft.com for more information. Just keep in mind that the standards are very high! Look at the current set of Xbox LIVE games in the marketplace to get an idea of the kind of games that have been approved.

Of course, anybody can write a great game for Windows Phone without the ID_CAP_GAMERSER-VICES capability, and they can do so in XNA or Silverlight. Volume II of this book series shows plenty of examples of Silverlight games. You'll even see how to take advantage of Xbox LIVE avatar images without needing any kind of special access or arrangement with Microsoft.

Images

The project generated by Visual Studio includes three images, shown in Figure 1.1:

→ **ApplicationIcon.png**—The main icon, used wherever the app is installed. For normal apps (placed in the phone's app list), the icon should be 62x62 pixels to avoid scaling. For games (placed in the Games hub), the icon should instead be 173x173 pixels.

→ **Background.png**—The tile icon (173x173) used when the user pins the application to the phone's start screen, whether the app came from the app list or the Games hub. This poorly named file is named as such because it's technically the *background* for the tile. The Title in the application manifest is automatically overlaid on the tile's bottom-left corner, so care must be taken in the image to leave room for the text.

→ **SplashScreenImage.jpg**—The splash screen (480x800) shown while the application is loading.

ApplicationIcon.png

Background.png

SplashScreenImage.jpg

FIGURE 1.1   The three standard images included in a Visual Studio "Windows Phone Application" project.

You can change the name and location of the first two images, and they can be either JPEG or PNG files. Just remember to update your application manifest accordingly.

To create an icon that fits in with the Windows Phone built-in apps, it should usually have a transparent background and the drawing inside should:

→ be completely white

→ be composed of simple geometric shapes

→ reuse iconography already used by the phone if possible

→ use an understandable real-world metaphor

The drawing for the 62x62 icon should generally have a 12-pixel margin around all sides. (In other words, the actual content should fit in a 38x38 box centered in the image.) The drawing for the 173x173 icon should generally fit in a 73x73 almost-centered box. It should be nudged 3 pixels higher than center, giving a 47-pixel margin on top, 53-pixel margin on bottom, and 50-pixel margin on the sides.

For drawings significantly longer in one dimension, you may want to leave less of a margin. In most cases, the drawing inside Background.png should be the same as the one in ApplicationIcon.png, just larger. As with all user interface guidelines, games are generally exempt from these guidelines.

Creating these types of images requires some practice and patience. You'll want to use tools such as PAINT.NET, mentioned in this book's "Introduction" section. A few of the characters from the Wingdings and Webdings fonts can even be used to help create a decent icon!

These are not strict guidelines or even official guidelines from Microsoft, nor does it match what the initial image files contain; it just tends to look right for most cases. Of course, apps with their own strong branding (such as the Facebook, eBay, and iMDb apps) usually do *not* follow these guidelines, as being consistent with their own identity outweighs being consistent with Windows Phone. In addition, it often makes sense to deviate from this style if you want your app to stand out in the marketplace.

 How can my icon get the user's theme accent color as its background, as with the built-in apps?

Each tile icon is rendered on top of an accent-colored square when pinned to Start, so using a transparent background color in your PNG file is all you need to do. Unfortunately, each third-party app icon in the app list is always rendered on top of a dark grey square, so there's no way to get the same effect in the app list. Nothing prevents you from using one of the standard theme colors as a hard-coded background inside your image file, but you shouldn't do this unless it happens to be a color associated with your brand. That's because it will never change and there-fore look out-of-place to users who switch their accent color.

Icons for your marketplace listing have different guidelines than your app's real icons!

Whereas using a transparent background is encouraged for your tile icon, it should be avoided for the separate set of icons you upload to the marketplace. The phone's Marketplace app renders icons on black squares, which looks odd under the dark theme when the icon has transparency. Even worse, the marketplace section of the Zune program leaves its default white background underneath the icon. For typical Windows Phone app icons, the result is a completely invisible icon due to the white-on-white effect!

To avoid this, you must choose a background color for your marketplace icons. It's a good idea to use this same background for your app icon, even if your tile icon uses transparency to fit in with the user's theme.

Leveraging the built-in splash screen support by supplying the `SplashScreenImage.jpg` file can be useful for boosting the perceived load time of your app. A desirable approach is to make the image look like what your app will look like once fully loaded, perhaps with disabled-looking controls and without text. This gives the appearance of your app being instantly "there," but not fully loaded. The text is normally omitted from the image because even if you localize your app for multiple languages, you can still only have the single image file per app.

Unfortunately, due to the single-file nature of the splash screen support, it's only worthwhile for apps that use hard-coded colors and support only a single orientation. That's because a typical Windows Phone app looks radically different under the dark versus light theme (or in a portrait versus landscape orientation), so no single image can provide a seamless experience for one case without being jarring for the other cases. In addition, I'm a big believer in making apps feel the same as the built-in apps unless there's a good reason not to, and none of the built-in apps use a perceivable splash screen.

The good news is that the phone already produces a built-in animated "Loading…" or "Resuming…" user interface when an app is launched or reactivated. If yours is not fast to load, I'd recommend addressing the core issue (such as delaying computationally expensive work) rather than using a sub-standard splash screen. In this book, none of the apps use a splash screen. To remove the splash screen from your app, simply remove `SplashScreenImage.jpg` from your project.

Many apps in the marketplace (such as the Facebook and Twitter apps) *do* use a splash screen, but not to improve the perceived loading time. They simply use it to help customize the loading process with their own branding.

> **(!)** **The icon and splash screen images must have a build action set to** Content!
>
> If you replace any of the three image files with your own, be sure to set each file's **Build Action** in Visual Studio to **Content**, rather than the default **Resource**, as shown in Figure 1.2. This correctly places the files directly inside your .xap file rather than embedded inside your DLL. Note that the value of **Copy to Output Directory** does not matter. Even if the file is not copied to the output directory, it still gets copied to the correct place inside the resultant .xap file.

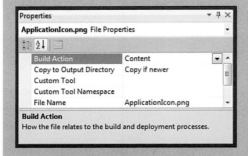

FIGURE 1.2   The three image files discussed in this section must be given a build action of Content in Visual Studio's Properties window.

MainPage.xaml

Every app consists of one or more pages. New projects are given a single page called MainPage. This page defines what the user sees once your app has loaded. It is implemented across two files: MainPage.xaml contains the user interface, and MainPage.xaml.cs contains the logic, often called the *code-behind*. Listing 1.2 shows the initial contents of MainPage.xaml, and Figure 1.3 shows what this XAML produces when you run the app.

>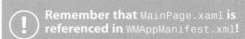
>
> **Remember that** MainPage.xaml **is referenced in** WMAppManifest.xml!
>
> If you want to rename this file, you must also change its name inside your application manifest; otherwise your app will stop working.

LISTING 1.2   MainPage.xaml—The Initial Markup for the App's Main Page

```
<phone:PhoneApplicationPage
  x:Class="Tally.MainPage"
  xmlns="http://schemas.microsoft.com/winfx/2006/xaml/presentation"
  xmlns:x="http://schemas.microsoft.com/winfx/2006/xaml"
  xmlns:phone="clr-namespace:Microsoft.Phone.Controls;assembly=Microsoft.Phone"
  xmlns:shell="clr-namespace:Microsoft.Phone.Shell;assembly=Microsoft.Phone"
  xmlns:d="http://schemas.microsoft.com/expression/blend/2008"
```

LISTING 1.2   Continued

```xml
    xmlns:mc="http://schemas.openxmlformats.org/markup-compatibility/2006"
    FontFamily="{StaticResource PhoneFontFamilyNormal}"
    FontSize="{StaticResource PhoneFontSizeNormal}"
    Foreground="{StaticResource PhoneForegroundBrush}"
    SupportedOrientations="Portrait" Orientation="Portrait"
    mc:Ignorable="d" d:DesignWidth="480" d:DesignHeight="768"
    shell:SystemTray.IsVisible="True">

    <!--LayoutRoot contains the root grid where all other page content is placed-->
    <Grid x:Name="LayoutRoot" Background="Transparent">
      <Grid.RowDefinitions>
        <RowDefinition Height="Auto"/>
        <RowDefinition Height="*"/>
      </Grid.RowDefinitions>

      <!--TitlePanel contains the name of the application and page title-->
      <StackPanel x:Name="TitlePanel" Grid.Row="0" Margin="24,24,0,12">
        <TextBlock x:Name="ApplicationTitle" Text="MY APPLICATION"
                   Style="{StaticResource PhoneTextNormalStyle}"/>
        <TextBlock x:Name="PageTitle" Text="page name" Margin="-3,-8,0,0"
                   Style="{StaticResource PhoneTextTitle1Style}"/>
      </StackPanel>

      <!--ContentPanel - place additional content here-->
      <Grid x:Name="ContentGrid" Grid.Row="1">
      </Grid>
    </Grid>

    <!-- Sample code showing usage of ApplicationBar
...
    -->
</phone:PhoneApplicationPage>
```

At a quick glance, this file tells us:

→ This is a class called MainPage (in the Tally namespace) that derives from the PhoneApplicationPage control.

→ It is marked to only support the portrait (vertical) orientation.

→ It contains two text blocks with boilerplate text that are meant to be the application name and an appropriate page title.

→ The page leverages `Grid` and `StackPanel` controls to arrange the current text blocks, and additional content is meant to be placed in the grid named `ContentGrid`.

→ For such a simple page, there are a lot of things in here!

We'll examine the following two aspects of this file more deeply:

→ The XML namespaces used at the top of the file

→ Phone theme resources, referenced as "`{StaticResource XXX}`"

Orientation is an interesting and important topic, but we'll save that for Chapter 3, "In Case of Emergency." This page also gives an example of how you might use an application bar (inside a comment at the end of the file), but this chapter's apps is one of the few that doesn't use an application bar. Therefore, we'll cover this in the next chapter.

XML Namespaces

`MainPage.xaml` contains most of the XML namespaces you'll see in this book. Table 1.1 explains them. Although some look like URLs that you can view in a Web browser, they are not. They all map to .NET namespaces in specific assemblies.

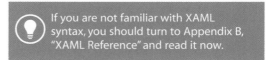

FIGURE 1.3   The initial `MainPage.xaml`.

If you are not familiar with XAML syntax, you should turn to Appendix B, "XAML Reference" and read it now.

TABLE 1.1   The Common Namespaces in Windows Phone XAML Files

Namespace	Typical Prefix	Description
`http://schemas.microsoft.com/ winfx/2006/xaml/presentation`	(none)	The standard Silverlight namespace. Contains elements such `Grid`, `Button`, and `TextBlock`.
`http://schemas.microsoft.com/ winfx/2006/xaml`	x	The XAML language namespace. Contains keywords such as `Class`, `Name`, and `Key`.
`clr-namespace:Microsoft.Phone. Controls;assembly=Microsoft.Phone`	phone	The namespace for phone-specific Silverlight controls such as `PhoneApplicationPage`.

TABLE 1.1   Continued

Namespace	Typical Prefix	Description
`clr-namespace:Microsoft.Phone.Shell;` `assembly=Microsoft.Phone`	`shell`	The namespace for parts of the phone outside your root Silverlight element: the status bar and application bar.
`http://schemas.microsoft.com/` `expression/blend/2008`	`d`	A namespace for design-time information that helps tools like Expression Blend and Visual Studio show a proper preview.
`http://schemas.openxmlformats.org/` `markup-compatibility/2006`	`mc`	A markup compatibility namespace that can be used to mark other name-spaces/elements as ignorable. Normally used with the design-time namespace, whose attributes should be ignored at run-time.

The first three namespaces are almost always used in Windows Phone apps. The `shell` namespace is only needed when a page uses an application bar via the `ApplicationBar` class, or when it enables the status bar by setting `SystemTray.IsVisible` to `True`. The *status bar* is the top area of the phone that displays the time and, based on various factors, signal strength, battery charge, and more. As a developer, you can't do anything with the status bar other than show or hide it.

The last two namespaces, and the corresponding `mc:Ignorable`, `d:DesignWidth`, and `d:DesignHeight` attributes that are plopped in every page, add a lot of clutter, so many examples in this book remove them. This can negatively affect the design views in Visual Studio and Expression Blend, so if you find yourself in such a situation with the code in this book, you can add these namespaces and attributes back. Visual Studio even (annoyingly) adds these back when you make certain kinds of edits to your page.

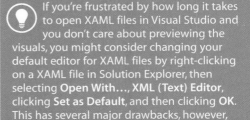

If you're frustrated by how long it takes to open XAML files in Visual Studio and you don't care about previewing the visuals, you might consider changing your default editor for XAML files by right-clicking on a XAML file in Solution Explorer, then selecting **Open With…**, **XML (Text) Editor**, clicking **Set as Default**, and then clicking **OK**. This has several major drawbacks, however, such as losing Intellisense support.

• • •

You're Not Supposed to Call the Status Bar the "System Tray"

Microsoft has generally frowned upon people using the term "system tray" to describe what is officially known as the "status bar" in Windows Phone (or the "notification area" in Windows). And yet, the class representing the system's status bar is called `SystemTray`! So I don't blame you if you use that term.

Phone Theme Resources

Rather than hardcoding fonts, font sizes, and colors, `MainPage.xaml` makes use of several phone-specific resources using `StaticResource` syntax. Windows Phone defines several resources to make it easy for apps to get a look-and-feel consistent with guidelines and with the user's chosen theme. Appendix C, "Theme Resources Reference," lists them all and demonstrates what they look like for both user themes (light and dark). These resources not only contain individual colors, brushes, fonts, font sizes, and thicknesses (for borders and margins/padding) but also contain a bunch of styles for text blocks that package individual resources together.

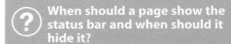

When should a page show the status bar and when should it hide it?

Every page should show the status bar unless it is trying to provide an immersive, full-screen experience as with a game or a panorama-based application such as the People, Pictures, and Music+Videos hubs. Otherwise, your users might not appreciate having to lock their phone or exit your app (or looking at their watch!) in order to see what time it is.

The resources used by this initial page are

→ **PhoneFontFamilyNormal**—Segoe WP

→ **PhoneFontSizeNormal**—20 px (15 pt)

→ **PhoneForegroundBrush**—A solid color brush that is white in the dark theme and black in the light theme

→ **PhoneTextNormalStyle**—The previous three resources combined: a FontFamily of PhoneFontFamilyNormal, FontSize of PhoneFontSizeNormal, and Foreground of PhoneForegroundBrush

→ **PhoneTextTitle1Style**—A FontFamily of PhoneFontFamilySemiLight (Segoe WP Semilight), FontSize of PhoneFontSizeExtraExtraLarge (72 px, which is 54 pt), and Foreground of PhoneForegroundBrush.

FIGURE 1.4   The initial `MainPage.xaml`, shown under the light theme.

This explains how Listing 1.2 produces the result from Figure 1.3 when the user's theme is dark. Figure 1.4 shows the same page when the phone uses the light theme.

Avoid using hardcoded colors, especially if they are mixed in with theme colors!

You should try to respect the user's theme (and the Windows Phone style guidelines) as much as possible. If you want complete control over your color palette, beware of accidentally letting theme colors sneak in. For example, using hard-coded white text on the default background looks fine in the dark theme, but invisible in the light theme. Using a standard button on top of a dark photograph might look fine in the dark theme (because the button text and border are white) but hard to see in the light theme (because the button text and border are black).

Outlook always uses the light theme and Internet Explorer always uses the dark theme, regardless of user settings. Can my app also choose which theme to use?

Not quite. You could certainly ignore or override the theme resources with your own colors, but you cannot change the colors used by the status bar. You can, however, hide the status bar.

The Segoe WP font, and variations of it, is specifically made for Windows Phone and used everywhere in the operating system and apps. Unless there's a compelling reason—as when creating a game or a book/document reader—using any other font in a Windows Phone app would look strange.

MainPage.xaml.cs

Listing 1.3 shows the initial contents of `MainPage.xaml.cs`, the code-behind file for `MainPage.xaml`. Because this app does not yet do anything, it only contains the required call to `InitializeComponent` that constructs the page with all the visuals defined in the XAML file. The class is marked with the `partial` keyword because its definition is shared with a hidden C# file that gets generated when the XAML file is compiled.

LISTING 1.3   `MainPage.xaml.cs`—The Initial Code-Behind for the App's Main Page

```
using System;
using System.Collections.Generic;
using System.Linq;
using System.Net;
using System.Windows;
using System.Windows.Controls;
using System.Windows.Documents;
using System.Windows.Input;
using System.Windows.Media;
using System.Windows.Media.Animation;
using System.Windows.Shapes;
using Microsoft.Phone.Controls;
```

LISTING 1.3   Continued

```
namespace Tally
{
  public partial class MainPage : PhoneApplicationPage
  {
    // Constructor
    public MainPage()
    {
      InitializeComponent();
    }
  }
}
```

 Never remove the call to InitializeComponent **in the constructor of your code-behind class!**

InitializeComponent is what associates your XAML-defined content with the instance of the class at run-time.

App.xaml and App.xaml.cs

App.xaml is a special XAML file that doesn't define any visuals, but rather defines an App class that can handle application-level tasks. Usually the only reason to touch this XAML file is to place new application-wide resources, such as custom styles, inside its Application.Resources collection. Many apps in this book do just that. You'll see examples of this starting with Chapter 9, "Fake Call."

The most notable job of App.xaml.cs, the code-behind file with a lot of plumbing, is handling the application lifetime events of Launching, Activated, Deactivated, and Closing. We'll examine these events in Chapter 10, "Tip Calculator."

AssemblyInfo.cs

This file is not worth showing in this book. It contains a bunch of attributes where you *can* put a title, description, company name, copyright, and so on, that get compiled into your assembly. But setting these is unnecessary because all of the information used by the marketplace is separately managed. Still, the AssemblyVersion and AssemblyFileVersion attributes, typically set to the same value, can be useful for you to keep track of distinct versions of your application:

```
[assembly: AssemblyVersion("1.0.0.0")]
[assembly: AssemblyFileVersion("1.0.0.0")]
```

By using *-syntax, such as "1.0.*", you can even let the version number auto-increment every time you rebuild your app.

Modifying the Project to Create "Tally"

Now that we understand what is in a newly created Visual Studio project, we can modify it to create Tally. First, we can remove all capabilities in the application manifest, but temporarily leave ID_CAP_NETWORKING so we can debug the app on a phone:

```
<Capabilities>
  <!-- None needed -->
  <!-- TODO: This is only for debugging on a device: -->
  <Capability Name="ID_CAP_NETWORKING" />
</Capabilities>
```

We can also change the two icon images and remove the splash screen image from the project. Now we're ready to change MainPage.xaml and MainPage.xaml.cs.

 Visual Studio gives a bogus warning when a project's capabilities list is empty!

At the time of this writing, Visual Studio complains when opening a project that lists no capabilities. It states, "You are using a project created by previous version of Windows Phone Developer Tools CTP. Your application may not run properly."

You can safely ignore this warning. This is regrettable, because it is completely valid to have a project that requires no special capabilities.

Updating the User Interface

Listing 1.4 contains the XAML needed to create Tally, which produces the result shown at the beginning of this chapter.

LISTING 1.4   MainPage.xaml—The User Interface for Tally

```
<phone:PhoneApplicationPage
  x:Class="Tally.MainPage"
  xmlns="http://schemas.microsoft.com/winfx/2006/xaml/presentation"
  xmlns:x="http://schemas.microsoft.com/winfx/2006/xaml"
  xmlns:phone="clr-namespace:Microsoft.Phone.Controls;assembly=Microsoft.Phone"
  xmlns:shell="clr-namespace:Microsoft.Phone.Shell;assembly=Microsoft.Phone"
  FontFamily="{StaticResource PhoneFontFamilyNormal}"
  FontSize="{StaticResource PhoneFontSizeHuge}"
  Foreground="{StaticResource PhoneForegroundBrush}"
  SupportedOrientations="Portrait"
  shell:SystemTray.IsVisible="True">
  <Grid>
    <Grid.RowDefinitions>
      <RowDefinition Height="Auto"/>
      <RowDefinition Height="*"/>
      <RowDefinition Height="Auto"/>
    </Grid.RowDefinitions>

    <!-- Row 0: The Header -->
    <StackPanel Grid.Row="0" Margin="24,24,0,12">
      <TextBlock Text="TALLY" Style="{StaticResource PhoneTextNormalStyle}"/>
```

LISTING 1.4   Continued

```
      <TextBlock Text="tap to count" Margin="-3,-8,0,0"
                 Style="{StaticResource PhoneTextTitle1Style}"/>
    </StackPanel>

    <!-- Row 1: The text block containing the count -->
    <TextBlock x:Name="CountTextBlock" Grid.Row="1" TextAlignment="Center"
               Text="0"/>

    <!-- Row 2: The reset button -->
    <Button x:Name="ResetButton" Grid.Row="2" Click="ResetButton_Click"
            Content="reset"/>
  </Grid>
</phone:PhoneApplicationPage>
```

Notes:

→ Unnecessary attributes have been removed, the two text blocks in the header have been updated, and the old `ContentGrid` has been replaced with a text block and a button. A third row has been added to the grid to hold the button. The behavior of the `Grid` control is examined further in Chapter 4, "Stopwatch."

→ The text block and reset button have been assigned names (`CountTextBlock` and `ResetButton`, respectively) so they can be referenced easily in the code-behind file.

→ The page's font size has been changed to `PhoneFontSizeHuge` (186.667 px, which is 140 pt). This value is inherited by `CountTextBlock` only, because the other text blocks have their own styles explicitly set and the text inside `ResetButton` doesn't inherit page-level text properties.

→ The reset button has a `Click` event, and it is assigned to a handler called `ResetButton_Click` that must be defined in the code-behind file.

• • •

How x:Name **Works**

The XAML compiler generates an internal field in the root class (MainPage in this case) for each named element, using the element name as the field name. Therefore, Tally's MainPage has a field called CountTextBlock and a field called ResetButton that can be used in the code-behind file. You can look inside the hidden C# file that gets generated by the XAML compiler in the obj\Debug or obj\Release folder (MainPage.g.cs, where the g stands for *generated*) to see how this is done inside the implementation of InitializeComponent:

```
    public void InitializeComponent() {
      if (_contentLoaded) {
        return;
      }
      _contentLoaded = true;
```

```
      Application.LoadComponent(this, new
        Uri("/Tally;component/MainPage.xaml", UriKind.Relative));
      this.CountTextBlock = (TextBlock)this.FindName("CountTextBlock");
      this.ResetButton = (Button)this.FindName("ResetButton");
    }
```

The FindName method defined on many Silverlight elements recursively searches the element's children for an element marked with a matching x:Name. Once you obtain an instance to the named element, you can do anything you want with it: set properties, attach event handlers, call methods, and so on.

Many elements have a Name property that you can set in XAML *without* using the x: prefix, but the x:Name keyword works in more scenarios, so that is what this book uses consistently. This book also generally only names an element if it needs to be accessed in the code-behind file.

Updating the Code-Behind

Listing 1.5 contains all the logic needed to make Tally work.

LISTING 1.5   MainPage.xaml.cs—The Code-Behind for Tally

```csharp
using System.Windows;
using System.Windows.Input;
using System.Windows.Navigation;
using Microsoft.Phone.Controls;
using WindowsPhoneApp; // For the Setting class

namespace Tally
{
  public partial class MainPage : PhoneApplicationPage
  {
    int count = 0;
    // Remember what the user typed, for future app activations or launches
    Setting<int> savedCount = new Setting<int>("SavedCount", 0);

    public MainPage()
    {
      InitializeComponent();
    }

    // Handle a tap anywhere on the page (other than the Button)
    protected override void OnMouseLeftButtonDown(MouseButtonEventArgs e)
    {
      base.OnMouseLeftButtonDown(e);
      this.count++;
      this.CountTextBlock.Text = this.count.ToString("N0");
```

LISTING 1.5   Continued

```
    }

    // Handle a tap on the button
    void ResetButton_Click(object sender, RoutedEventArgs e)
    {
      this.count = 0;
      this.CountTextBlock.Text = this.count.ToString("N0");
    }

    protected override void OnNavigatedFrom(NavigationEventArgs e)
    {
      base.OnNavigatedFrom(e);
      // Persist state when leaving for any reason (Deactivated or Closing)
      this.savedCount.Value = this.count;
    }

    protected override void OnNavigatedTo(NavigationEventArgs e)
    {
      base.OnNavigatedTo(e);
      // Restore persisted state
      this.count = this.savedCount.Value;
      this.CountTextBlock.Text = this.count.ToString("N0");
    }
  }
}
```

> **(?) Why do Windows Phone apps use mouse events such as**
> **MouseLeftButtonDown? You can't use a mouse with your phone!**
>
> This is one of several weird artifacts stemming from compatibility with desktop Silverlight.
> Although touch and multi-touch specific events do exist (covered in Part VII, "Touch &
> Multi-Touch"), simple single-finger motion is also exposed through mouse events such as
> MouseLeftButtonDown, MouseMove, and MouseLeftButtonUp. It turns out that these events are
> easier to work with than the touch events, so most apps use these strange-sounding events
> instead. Just think of your finger as the mouse pointer, and the screen as the mouse left button!

Notes:

→ Often, a class that exposes an event *XXX* also exposes an On*XXX* method that
    subclasses can override rather than attaching a handler to the event. By
    overriding OnMouseLeftButtonDown, this code effectively handles the page's
    MouseLeftButtonDown event, which gets raised for any tap on the page *except* for
    taps on the button—exactly the condition we want for incrementing the count and
    updating the TextBlock's Text property accordingly. This method conveniently

doesn't get called on button taps because buttons internally handle this event (as well as the `MouseLeftButtonUp` event) in order to provide special behavior, preventing it from bubbling up to the page.

➔ `"N0"` formatting is used whenever the count is turned into a string. This basically means "show it as a natural number (with the thousands separator)." The thousands separator is a comma for United States English but it automatically varies based on the phone's "region & language" settings.

➔ `Button` has its own event for a tap, called `Click`, which should be handled instead of its `MouseLeftButtonDown` event. One reason is that this event gets suppressed, as you'll see in Chapter 10. Another reason is that a button is not supposed to invoke its action when it is *tapped*; it should invoke it when it is *released*. A button highlights itself when a finger presses it (`MouseLeftButtonDown`, internally) and unhighlights itself while raising the separate `Click` event when the finger is removed (`MouseLeftButtonUp`). This button's `Click` event handler—`ResetButton_Click`— simply resets the count and updates the `TextBlock` accordingly.

➔ The `Setting` member called `savedCount`, along with the `OnNavigatedFrom`/`OnNavigatedTo` methods, provide a simple way for the count to be remembered whenever the user leaves the app and restored whenever the user comes back to it (even if the user reboots the phone). The two methods are discussed in Chapter 6, "Baby Sign Language," and the `Setting` class is implemented and explained in Chapter 20, "Alarm Clock."

➔ Remembering to update `TextBlock.Text` every time count changes can be error-prone, especially for larger apps. A more robust approach would be to turn `count` into a *dependency property* that can be data-bound to the text block's `Text` property, enabling the display to update automatically whenever the value is changed. We're keeping things simple for Chapter 1, however, so this approach will be used in some of the later chapters.

 Why does `Click` correspond to *lifting* a finger from the screen rather than *pressing* a finger on it?

Although it might sound strange it first, this is actually standard behavior seen in just about every desktop and phone platform. A benefit of this behavior is that it gives the user a chance to change their mind (if they pressed the wrong button, for example) by dragging their finger off the button instead of simply releasing it.

Buttons *do* support two other modes of clicking, however. If you set a button's `ClickMode` property to `Press`, `Click` gets raised when a finger initially presses it. If you set a button's `ClickMode` property to `Hover`, `Click` gets raised when a finger drags over it. You should avoid using these modes, however, as the resulting behavior can be quite confusing.

The Finished Product

The initial app
appearance

After tapping once

After tapping again

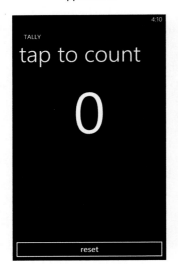

When you submit an app to the marketplace, you must provide at least one screenshot. You can save yourself a lot of time by using the Snipping Tool program that ships with Windows 7. If you select "Window Snip" from the tool's drop-down list, you can then click on the Windows Phone Emulator screen to instantly capture an appropriate 480x800 image. Just be sure that the zoom level of the emulator is set to 100%.

chapter 2 lessons

FLASHLIGHT

A flashlight app is one of the canonical simple apps that anybody can create. The idea is that the app makes the screen completely white, so the screen itself becomes a decent flashlight when it's dark. (Another variation would be a "mirror" app that makes the screen completely black!) Certainly a "blank white screen" app is even simpler to implement than the Tally app. But this chapter's Flashlight app is no ordinary flashlight! It supports custom colors, flashing SOS in Morse code, and even a strobe light mode!

> **? Can my app turn on the phone camera's flash and use that as a *real* flashlight?**
>
> No, this is not currently supported. Leveraging the light from the screen is the best you can do.

Creating this multi-mode application gives a good opportunity to understand and use the *application bar*, a central part of the Windows Phone experience. The application bar is used by almost all of the apps in this book.

The Application Bar

The application bar is the 72-pixel-thick strip of buttons docked on the edge of the screen adjacent to the hardware buttons. Figure 2.1 shows a two-button application bar from the built-in Alarms app in a variety of situations.

Portrait (dark theme): docked on bottom

Portrait (light theme): docked on bottom

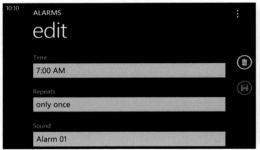

Landscape left (dark theme): docked on right

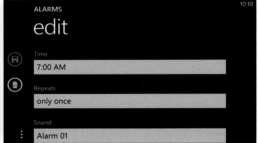

Landscape right (dark theme): docked on left

FIGURE 2.1   An application bar in action, seen in the dark and light themes and in all orientations.

Each button represents a common action relevant to the current content, such as the "save" and "delete" actions relevant to the current alarm shown in Figure 2.1. Sometimes it makes sense for actions to be disabled, such as "save" in Figure 2.1. In this example, the current alarm has not been modified so there are no changes to save.

Every application bar button has an icon and text label, although the labels can only be seen when you tap or drag the ellipsis (or left margin), as shown in Figure 2.2. This controversial idea minimizes clutter, consistent with one of the Metro mottos, "content, not chrome," also expressed as "the content is the interface." Although users might not know what each button does the first time they see them, they will probably remember in the future after peeking at the labels once or twice. Of course, this design places major importance on using understandable icons. (Although my sons have never seen a real floppy disk, even *they* recognize it as a save icon!)

FIGURE 2.2   The application bar from Figure 2.1 with its "save" and "delete" text labels showing.

> ⓘ **The application bar is designed to act differently than the iPhone tab bar!**
>
> In an iPhone tab bar, pictured in Figure 2.3 for the iPhone Clock app, each button typically switches to a different page, and each button has a selection state to communicate which page you're currently looking at. Buttons on the Windows Phone application bar, however, do not have any notion of being selected. Often, the action each one triggers does not involve taking you to a different page. And if it does, the new page likely has a different application bar (or none at all). In such cases, the user is expected to return to the previous page using the hardware Back button. This difference in how the two mechanisms are designed means that a proper Windows Phone app often has a much different navigation flow than a proper iPhone app. Chapter 6, "Baby Sign Language," examines best practices for navigation, which influences when you should use an application bar and what you should put in it.

FIGURE 2.3   The tab bar on the iPhone looks similar to the Windows Phone application bar, but behaves much differently.

Before we build Flashlight, the rest of this section examines:

→ The application bar menu

→ Creating button icons

→ Using an application bar in your app

 **The application bar can only fit four buttons!**

The actions that occupy these limited slots must therefore be carefully chosen. Additional actions can be placed in the application bar menu, which has no limit on the number of items.

The Application Bar Menu

The application bar menu is an unbounded list of text-only items that can appear below the application bar buttons when the user taps or flicks the ellipsis or left margin (the same gestures used to show the button text labels). These items are meant to be used for a few different types of actions:

→ Advanced and/or infrequent actions.

→ Actions that are hard to convey with an icon.

→ Actions that simply won't fit as buttons on the application bar because all four slots are already being used.

Figure 2.4 shows an application bar menu used by Internet Explorer 7. (IE9, due for release on Windows Phone by the end of 2011, uses a modified application bar menu.)

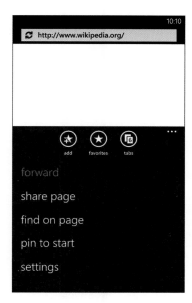

FIGURE 2.4   The main application bar menu used by Internet Explorer contains five menu items.

Do not jam as many buttons as you can onto an application bar just because there is room for them. Instead, save them only for commonly used actions—even if there are only one or two such actions (or *no* such actions)—and consider using an application bar menu for the rest.

For example, most apps place links to their settings and about pages on an application bar menu even if there is room for them as buttons, despite the fact that they are very easily represented as icons. Because accessing settings should be rare (and accessing an about page even more rare), adding them to an application bar would add a lot of unnecessary clutter. The Pictures hub uses an application bar with several menu items *but no buttons* when viewing an individual picture. And of course, Internet Explorer 7 only uses three buttons despite having several menu items, as seen in Figure 2.4.

Many users may never discover your menu items, especially if the meaning of each icon button is obvious! That's because there's no visual indication that menu items exist until the user taps the ellipsis (which is always present even if there are no menu items). Therefore, it does not make sense to rely on an application bar menu for primary navigation, such as a main menu.

To avoid the need for the user to scroll the menu, the design guidelines recommend using no more than five menu items. However, for some apps—such as Flashlight—using additional menu items is better than many alternatives.

Creating Button Icons

Icons for application bar buttons should be all white with a transparent background. (The white will automatically appear black instead when the light theme is used.) The image *file* should be 48x48, although the drawing inside should approximately fit in a 22x22 area in the center (leaving a 13-pixel margin on all sides). The drawing should be composed of simple geometric shapes and be recognizable without further explanation. Except for the sizing, these guidelines should sound familiar, as they are the same as the guidelines for creating app icons. In some rare cases, a little bit of color can be appropriate (such as in a red-circle "record" icon), but you should generally avoid using anything other than white.

 Text in an application bar menu gets cut off if it is too long!

Although the menu scrolls vertically when there are more than five items, it never scrolls horizontally. The amount of characters that fit varies based on the letters used, although the available width remains consistent for both portrait and landscape orientations. Using trial and error, take care to keep the labels short enough to avoid truncation.

 Image files used for application bar button icons should *not* include the outer circle. The application bar automatically places the circle around each icon.

 To avoid a low-quality result, be sure that every image file used for an application bar button icon is 48x48 pixels.

The Windows Phone Developer Tools includes a set of white-on-transparent icons for common application bar buttons installed in the Program Files\Microsoft SDKs\Windows Phone\v7.0\Icons\dark folder. Figure 2.5 shows some of them—but in black so they show up on these white pages—along with their meaning.

✚	✏	💾	🗑	✔	✖
Add	Edit	Save	Delete	Done	Cancel
⚙	🔍	📷	🎥	★	⭐
Settings	Search	Camera	Video	Favorites	Add to Favorites
⏮	⏸	▶	⏭	🔄	?
Rewind	Pause	Play	Fast Forward	Refresh	Help
⬇	⬆	■	🎁	←	→
Download	Upload	Folder	Share	Previous	Next

FIGURE 2.5 Some icons installed with the Windows Phone Developer Tools.

Using an Application Bar in Your App

You can give any page an application bar by setting its `ApplicationBar` property to an instance of an `ApplicationBar` object. It can contain up to four `ApplicationBarIconButton` children, and it also has a separate `MenuItems` collection that can be filled with as many `ApplicationBarMenuItems`

> The Program Files\Microsoft SDKs\Windows Phone\v7.0\Icons includes black icons in addition to white icons, and other files that can be useful for prototyping or for contexts other than the application bar, such as the outer circle that gets automatically placed on each button. It also includes a vector-based file with all the icons, so you can tweak the existing icons to create new ones.

as you want. The following XAML shows the application bar used by Flashlight, shown at the beginning of this chapter:

```
<phone:PhoneApplicationPage …>
  <phone:PhoneApplicationPage.ApplicationBar>
    <!-- The ApplicationBar object: -->
    <shell:ApplicationBar Opacity=".5">
      <!-- Two buttons: -->
      <shell:ApplicationBarIconButton Text="sos" IconUri="Images/sos.png"
                                      Click="SosButton_Click"/>
      <shell:ApplicationBarIconButton Text="strobe" IconUri="Images/strobe.png"
                                      Click="StrobeButton_Click"/>
      <!-- Eight menu items: -->
      <shell:ApplicationBar.MenuItems>
        <shell:ApplicationBarMenuItem Text="red"/>
        <shell:ApplicationBarMenuItem Text="orange"/>
        <shell:ApplicationBarMenuItem Text="yellow"/>
        <shell:ApplicationBarMenuItem Text="green"/>
        <shell:ApplicationBarMenuItem Text="cyan"/>
        <shell:ApplicationBarMenuItem Text="purple"/>
        <shell:ApplicationBarMenuItem Text="gray"/>
        <shell:ApplicationBarMenuItem Text="white"/>
      </shell:ApplicationBar.MenuItems>
    </shell:ApplicationBar>
  </phone:PhoneApplicationPage.ApplicationBar>
  …
</phone:PhoneApplicationPage>
```

The two buttons enable switching the flashlight's mode to SOS or strobe, and the menu items change the color of the flashlight from white to one of seven other colors (and back). Note that this follows the guideline of not using all four application bar buttons just because we can. (It would not be appropriate to have "red" and "orange" be two more buttons on the application bar with the rest of the colors as menu items, for example.)

The resultant application bar is the exact same control used by the built-in phone apps, complete with buttons and menu items that tilt when pressed and many other animations: menu items and buttons that slide in and out, buttons that rotate when the orientation changes, and so on. It would be ill-advised to work around application bar limitations by creating your own control that mimics it, considering all the subtle behaviors it contains.

> Each application bar belongs to an indi-vidual page, so every page can have a different one. (The application bar really should have been called the *page* bar.) You cannot use the same application bar across multiple pages. Even if you give multiple pages an identical-looking application bar, the new buttons still animate onto the bar when the page transition occurs.

ApplicationBar

The ApplicationBar object exposes the following read/write properties:

→ **BackgroundColor** and **ForegroundColor**—Enables customizing both colors used by the application bar. (ForegroundColor is used by the button icons, button labels, menu items, and ellipsis.) Apps should not override these colors except for special circumstances.

→ **IsVisible** (true by default)—Enables showing and hiding the application bar.

→ **IsMenuEnabled** (true by default)—When set to false, the application bar behaves as if there are no menu items. The user can still tap the ellipsis to reveal the labels under each button.

→ **Opacity** (1 by default)—Adjusts the opacity of the background color. When Opacity is 1, the page is not given the space underneath the application bar. (In the portrait orientation, for example, the page's actual height is reduced by 72 pixels when the application bar is visible.) When Opacity is any value less than 1, the page is given the space underneath so it can place content underneath the translucent or trans-parent background.

ApplicationBar also defines a StateChanged event that is raised when-ever the menu is shown or hidden, in case an app wants to adjust the page content when this happens.

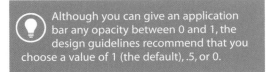

> Although you can give an application bar any opacity between 0 and 1, the design guidelines recommend that you choose a value of 1 (the default), .5, or 0.

ApplicationBarIconButton and ApplicationBarMenuItem

The ApplicationBarIconButton object used for each button has two mandatory proper-ties: IconUri, a URI pointing to the image file to be used for the icon, and Text, the string to be used for the label. The string used for Text should be short—ideally one word. If the string is too long, the resulting label will be ellipsized. As with a normal button, ApplicationBarIconButton's Click event is used to react to the button being tapped.

`ApplicationBarIconButton` also defines an `IsEnabled` property (`true` by default) for enabling/disabling it, and a corresponding (and poorly-named) `Changed` event that gets raised when `IsEnabled` changes. When an application bar button is disabled it becomes translucent ("faded out") and unclickable, as seen with the save button back in Figures 2.1 and 2.2.

The `ApplicationBarMenuMenuItem` object that represents each menu item has all the same properties and events as `ApplicationBarIconButton`, except for `IconUri`, naturally, because menu items cannot have icons.

 Why doesn't my icon show up on my application bar? I get an "X" icon instead!

This happens when the image file's build action is not set to **Content** (assuming you have already included the image file in your project and have set `IconUri` to the correct path and file). This is a very easy mistake to make because Visual Studio chooses a default build action of **Resource** when you add an image file to your project. You can change this in Visual Studio's Properties window, as shown in the preceding chapter.

Marking items in an application bar with x:Name **does not work!**

Although using x:Name on an application bar button or menu item causes the XAML compiler to generate a field for the item, the field will always be `null` at run-time. This is because the `FindName` method (used inside `InitializeComponent`) is unable to find these items, as they are not Silverlight UI elements inside the page's visual tree. They are special phone shell elements that happen to be exposed via convenient .NET APIs.

The fact that the application bar and its contents are not true Silverlight UI elements has further implications. You cannot use data binding with any of its properties, you cannot apply styles, animations, and/or transforms, and so on. For the most part, this isn't a big deal. (Even if you could have, you should not use custom animations or alternate styles with an application bar anyway.) The lack of data binding, however, means that you cannot use some common coding practices that Silverlight developers have gotten accustomed to.

Don't rely on relative button placement in the application bar for communicating information. When the orientation changes, the rotated buttons can effectively appear in the reverse order (when scanning from top-to-bottom compared to left-to-right). You can see this phenomenon back in Figure 2.1. In the landscape left orientation, the delete button appears to be placed before the save button.

The User Interface

Listing 2.1 contains the very simple user interface for Flashlight, which uses the application bar shown previously and places only a grid inside the page. The result is shown in Figure 2.6, with the menu visible.

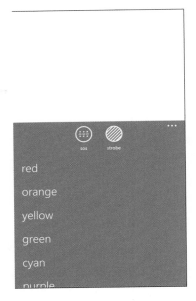

FIGURE 2.6   The Flashlight user interface, with the menu showing.

LISTING 2.1   MainPage.xaml—The User Interface for Flashlight

```
<phone:PhoneApplicationPage
  x:Class="WindowsPhoneApp.MainPage"
  xmlns="http://schemas.microsoft.com/winfx/2006/xaml/presentation"
  xmlns:x="http://schemas.microsoft.com/winfx/2006/xaml"
  xmlns:phone="clr-namespace:Microsoft.Phone.Controls;assembly=Microsoft.Phone"
  xmlns:shell="clr-namespace:Microsoft.Phone.Shell;assembly=Microsoft.Phone"
  SupportedOrientations="PortraitOrLandscape">

  <phone:PhoneApplicationPage.ApplicationBar>
    <!-- The ApplicationBar object: -->
    <shell:ApplicationBar Opacity=".5">
      <!-- Two buttons: -->
      <shell:ApplicationBarIconButton Text="sos" IconUri="Images/sos.png"
                                      Click="SosButton_Click"/>
      <shell:ApplicationBarIconButton Text="strobe" IconUri="Images/strobe.png"
                                      Click="StrobeButton_Click"/>
      <!-- Eight menu items: -->
      <shell:ApplicationBar.MenuItems>
        <shell:ApplicationBarMenuItem Text="red"/>
        <shell:ApplicationBarMenuItem Text="orange"/>
        <shell:ApplicationBarMenuItem Text="yellow"/>
        <shell:ApplicationBarMenuItem Text="green"/>
```

LISTING 2.1   Continued

```
        <shell:ApplicationBarMenuItem Text="cyan"/>
        <shell:ApplicationBarMenuItem Text="purple"/>
        <shell:ApplicationBarMenuItem Text="gray"/>
        <shell:ApplicationBarMenuItem Text="white"/>
      </shell:ApplicationBar.MenuItems>
    </shell:ApplicationBar>
  </phone:PhoneApplicationPage.ApplicationBar>

  <!-- No content other than a solid background: -->
  <Grid x:Name="BackgroundGrid" Background="White"/>

</phone:PhoneApplicationPage>
```

Notes:

→ This app—and the remaining apps in this book—all use a .NET namespace of simply `WindowsPhoneApp`. This is done for easy code sharing. Several controls, pages, and other classes are shared among apps in this book series simply by linking the common source files into the relevant projects. The one such class already seen is the `Setting` class referenced in the preceding chapter.

→ The page supports all orientations because there is no reason not to; the application bar and its menu handle every orientation as expected.

→ A grid is placed inside the page with the hard-coded white background because setting the page's background has no effect.

→ The application bar is given an opacity of .5 rather than 0 so the icons and text appear in all conditions, avoiding white-on-white and black-on-black. The application bar foreground is either black or white based on the user's theme, and the app background periodically becomes black when SOS or strobe modes are used.

→ Although the two buttons have handlers for their `Click` event assigned in XAML, the handler for the `Click` event on each menu item is assigned in the code-behind seen in the next section.

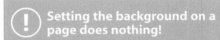
Setting the background on a page does nothing!

Despite having a Background property, a page's background always appears as the theme-specific PhoneBackgroundBrush (black for the dark theme or white for the light theme). The workaround for this confusing behavior is simply to set the background on a child element that consumes the entire space of the page.

The Code-Behind

Listing 2.2 contains the code-behind, which must handle all the special features of this flashlight—strobe mode, SOS mode, and various colors.

LISTING 2.2   `MainPage.xaml.cs`—The Code-Behind for Flashlight

```
using System;
using System.Reflection;
using System.Windows;
using System.Windows.Media;
using System.Windows.Threading;
using Microsoft.Phone.Controls;
using Microsoft.Phone.Shell;

namespace WindowsPhoneApp
{
  public partial class MainPage : PhoneApplicationPage
  {
    // Members for the two application bar buttons:
    IApplicationBarIconButton sosButton;
    IApplicationBarIconButton strobeButton;

    // For the two special modes:
    SolidColorBrush onBrush;
    SolidColorBrush offBrush = new SolidColorBrush(Colors.Black);
    DispatcherTimer strobeTimer = new DispatcherTimer();
    DispatcherTimer sosTimer = new DispatcherTimer();
    int sosStep;

    // Remember the chosen color, for future app activations or launches:
    Setting<Color> savedColor = new Setting<Color>("SavedColor", Colors.White);

    // The current mode (Solid, Sos, or Strobe)
    FlashlightMode mode = FlashlightMode.Solid;

    public MainPage()
    {
      InitializeComponent();

      // Assign application bar buttons to member fields, because this cannot be
      // done by InitializeComponent:
      this.sosButton = this.ApplicationBar.Buttons[0]
        as IApplicationBarIconButton;
      this.strobeButton = this.ApplicationBar.Buttons[1]
        as IApplicationBarIconButton;
```

LISTING 2.2   Continued

```
  // Initialize the timer for strobe mode
  this.strobeTimer.Interval = TimeSpan.FromSeconds(.1); // Not too fast!
  this.strobeTimer.Tick += StrobeTimer_Tick;

  // Initialize the timer for SOS mode
  this.sosTimer.Interval = TimeSpan.Zero;
  this.sosTimer.Tick += SosTimer_Tick;

  // Attach the same Click handler to all menu items in the application bar
  foreach (IApplicationBarMenuItem menuItem in this.ApplicationBar.MenuItems)
    menuItem.Click += MenuItem_Click;

  // Restore persisted color
  this.onBrush = new SolidColorBrush(this.savedColor.Value);
  this.BackgroundGrid.Background = onBrush;
}

// The menu item Click handler that changes the flashlight color
void MenuItem_Click(object sender, EventArgs e)
{
  // Grab the text from the menu item to determine the desired color
  string chosenColor = (sender as IApplicationBarMenuItem).Text;

  // Use reflection to turn the color name (e.g. "red") into an actual Color
  Color c = (Color)typeof(Colors).GetProperty(chosenColor,
      BindingFlags.Public | BindingFlags.Static | BindingFlags.IgnoreCase).
      GetValue(null, null);
  // Persist this choice and set the background color
  this.savedColor.Value = c;
  this.onBrush = new SolidColorBrush(this.savedColor.Value);
  this.BackgroundGrid.Background = onBrush;
}

// The Click handler for the strobe button
void StrobeButton_Click(object sender, EventArgs e)
{
  // First, reset the current state to solid mode
  FlashlightMode mode = this.mode;
  RestoreSolidMode();

  // If we were already in strobe mode, then this click
  // cancels it and we are done
  if (mode == FlashlightMode.Strobe)
    return;
```

LISTING 2.2   Continued

```
  // Show a warning
  MessageBoxResult result = MessageBox.Show("Strobe lights can trigger " +
    "seizures for people with photosensitive epilepsy. " +
    "Are you sure you want to start the strobe light?",
      "Warning!", MessageBoxButton.OKCancel);

  // If the user agreed, change to strobe mode
  if (result == MessageBoxResult.OK)
  {
    // Change the button icon, the mode, and start the timer
    (sender as IApplicationBarIconButton).IconUri =
      new Uri("Images/cancel.png", UriKind.Relative);
    this.mode = FlashlightMode.Strobe;
    this.strobeTimer.Start();
  }
}

void StrobeTimer_Tick(object sender, EventArgs e)
{
  // Toggle the background on every tick
  if (this.BackgroundGrid.Background == this.onBrush)
    this.BackgroundGrid.Background = this.offBrush;
  else
    this.BackgroundGrid.Background = this.onBrush;
}

// The Click handler for the SOS button
void SosButton_Click(object sender, EventArgs e)
{
  // First, reset the current state to solid mode
  FlashlightMode mode = this.mode;
  RestoreSolidMode();

  // If we were already in SOS mode, then this click
  // cancels it and we are done
  if (mode == FlashlightMode.Sos)
    return;

  // Change to SOS mode
  // Change the button icon, the mode, a counter, and start the timer
  (sender as IApplicationBarIconButton).IconUri =
    new Uri("Images/cancel.png", UriKind.Relative);
  this.mode = FlashlightMode.Sos;
  this.sosStep = 0;
```

LISTING 2.2   Continued

```csharp
    this.sosTimer.Start();
}

void SosTimer_Tick(object sender, EventArgs e)
{
  // Toggle the background, but also adjust the time between each tick in
  // order to make the dot-dot-dot-dash-dash-dash-dot-dot-dot pattern
  switch (this.sosStep)
  {
    case 1: case 3: case 5:          // Each dot in the first S
    case 13: case 15: case 17:       // Each dot in the second S
      this.BackgroundGrid.Background = this.onBrush;
      this.sosTimer.Interval = TimeSpan.FromSeconds(.2); // A short value
      break;
    case 7: case 9: case 11:         // Each dash in the O
      this.BackgroundGrid.Background = this.onBrush;
      this.sosTimer.Interval = TimeSpan.FromSeconds(1); // A long value
      break;
    case 18:                         // The space between the end of one SOS
                                     // and the beginning of the next one
      this.BackgroundGrid.Background = this.offBrush;
      this.sosTimer.Interval = TimeSpan.FromSeconds(1);
      break;
    default:                         // The space between each dot/dash
      this.BackgroundGrid.Background = this.offBrush;
      this.sosTimer.Interval = TimeSpan.FromSeconds(.2);
      break;
  }

  // Cycle from 0 - 18
  this.sosStep = (this.sosStep + 1) % 19;
}

// Reset the state associated with mode switches
void RestoreSolidMode()
{
  this.strobeTimer.Stop();
  this.sosTimer.Stop();
  this.BackgroundGrid.Background = onBrush;
  this.sosButton.IconUri = new Uri("Images/sos.png", UriKind.Relative);
  this.strobeButton.IconUri = new Uri("Images/strobe.png", UriKind.Relative);
  this.mode = FlashlightMode.Solid;
}
```

LISTING 2.2   Continued

```
    // All three modes
    enum FlashlightMode
    {
      Solid,
      Sos,
      Strobe
    }
  }
}
```

Notes:

→ The sosButton and strobeButton fields are explicitly assigned by referencing items in the application bar's Buttons collection because the XAML naming approach is not supported for items in the application bar, as described in an earlier warning. Assigning such member variables right after InitializeComponent is a nice practice to avoid hardcoded indices scattered throughout your code.

→ Two DispatcherTimers are used to perform the SOS and strobe on/off patterns. This technique is described in an upcoming sidebar.

→ Rather than setting all eight menu item Click event handlers in XAML, the constructor loops through the MenuItems collection and assigns MenuItem_Click to each item. This shortcut works nicely in this case because the same handler is able to work for all menu items.

→ Once again, an instance of the Setting class (implemented in Chapter 20, "Alarm Clock") is used to remember the user's color preference for subsequent usage of the app. Because BackgroundGrid's background is set in the code-behind, the "White" setting in XAML in Listing 2.1 is actually unnecessary.

→ To work for every menu item, the MenuItem_Click handler must figure out which color has just been selected. To do this, it retrieves the label from the menu item that was just tapped (passed as the sender) then uses a .NET reflection trick to turn the string into an instance of the Color class. This works thanks to the static Colors class that contains named properties for several color instances. Note that this trick only works for the small set of colors represented by this class. You could define your own Colors class with a different set of properties, however, if you wanted to do this with different colors.

> **(!) Using .NET reflection is slow!**
>
> Although Listing 2.2 uses reflection as a trick to avoid writing a little more code, it is a slow way to get the job done. Although the poor performance is negligible in this case, you should generally avoid reflection unless there is absolutely no alternative. A better approach for this app would be to use the menu text as a key for a resource dictionary filled with brushes. Resource dictionaries are covered in Chapter 9, "Fake Call."

→ In this app, the chosen color setting is persisted as soon as a new one is selected (inside MenuItem_Click). This is unlike the previous app, in which this action was only done when the page was about to be departed (inside OnNavigatedFrom).

→ The sender in MenuItem_Click is cast to IApplicationBarMenuItem (an interface implemented by ApplicationBarMenuItem) rather than directly to ApplicationBarMenuItem. A similar thing is done in later event handlers with IApplicationBarIconButton when the sender is an ApplicationBarIconButton. The Windows Phone team prefers that code references the interfaces rather than the concrete classes to allow for future flexibility, although this is only important for class libraries that don't also instantiate the concrete button and menu item instances (as this app does in its XAML).

→ The strobe button Click handler, StrobeButton_Click, shows a standard message box to guard against accidental activation of strobe mode and to educate the user about the danger of strobe lights. Message boxes are discussed further at the end of this chapter.

→ The Tick event handler for the strobe timer simply toggles the background between the "on" brush (white, unless the user changed the color) and the "off" brush (black). Once the strobe timer has been started, this is called every .1 seconds, as configured in this page's constructor. Although you could certainly make this toggle more frequently, I would strongly caution against it. When I tried a value of .05 seconds instead, I got a bad headache after a quick test!

→ Both button Click handlers temporarily change the button's icon to a cancel image because a subsequent click to the button returns the flashlight to solid mode. They use the sender to access the tapped button just for demonstration, as they could have easily used the strobeButton and sosButton fields instead.

→ The Tick event handler for the SOS timer is more complicated than the handler for the strobe timer, as it has to repeatedly produce the Morse code pattern for the SOS distress signal (dot-dot-dot-dash-dash-dash-dot-dot-dot). It dynamically adjusts the timer's interval to achieve this effect.

→ The capitalization of Sos in the code follows a .NET Framework coding guideline of avoiding more than two consecutive capital letters, even for a well-known abbreviation. You can see this practice throughout the .NET Framework APIs, with terms such as Uri, Xml, Xaml, and so on. Note that this guideline does not apply to labels inside user interfaces!

Don't forget UriKind.Relative **(or** UriKind.RelativeOrAbsolute**) when using a relative URI in code!**

Programming for Windows Phone often involves constructing relative URIs in C# code, whether they are URIs for image files, pages, or other items. A common coding mistake is to use the simple overload of the Uri constructor that accepts only a string rather than the overload that accepts a string *and* a value from the UriKind enumeration (Absolute, Relative, or RelativeOrAbsolute). Using the simple constructor fails with a relative URI because the default value of UriKind used by the simple constructor overload is Absolute rather than the more forgiving RelativeOrAbsolute!

> Most Silverlight properties that appear to be set to a color are actually set to a *brush* instead. Usually, this distinction is unimportant because the most commonly used brush— the *solid color brush* seen in Listing 2.2—acts the same as the simple color it represents. However, more advanced brushes exist: a linear gradient brush, a radial gradient brush, and an image brush. These fancy brushes can generally be used as any element's foreground/background/stroke/fill, even as the foreground for text!

•••
`DispatcherTimer` **and Other Time-Based Approaches for Executing Code**

`DispatcherTimer`, used by Flashlight, is the most natural timer to use in a Silverlight app. You can start and stop it at any time, customize its frequency with its `Interval` property, and handle its `Tick` event to perform work at the chosen interval. Event handlers for `Tick` are guaranteed to be called on the UI thread, so code inside these handlers can manipulate elements on the page the same way this is done everywhere else. `DispatcherTimer` is not the only timer available, however.

The `System.Threading` namespace has a `Timer` class that provides similar functionality, but the callback you provide does *not* get called on the UI thread. With this mechanism, you need to partition any logic that updates the UI into a different method and use the page's dispatcher to invoke it on the UI thread. Here's an example:

```
void TimerCallback(object state)
{
  // Call the DoTheRealWork method on the UI thread:
  this.Dispatcher.BeginInvoke(DoTheRealWork);
}
```

Unless your timer-based code has no need to update the UI, you should stick to using `DispatcherTimer` instead of `Timer`.

The Reactive Extensions for .NET also includes a mechanism for creating a sequence that produces each value at a timed interval (`Microsoft.Phone.Reactive.Observable.Timer`) but the apps in this book series avoid using Reactive Extensions for the sake of having easily-understood code.

Any of these timers can work great for the needs of Flashlight and apps like it, but they should not be used for animations. These timers are not in sync with the screen's refresh rate, nor are they in sync with the Silverlight rendering engine. Instead, many animations should use the animations classes covered throughout Part II, "Transforms & Animations." These classes could even be used in Flashlight instead of a timer.

Complex animations (such as physics-based animations) can use a static `CompositionTarget.Rendering` event that gets raised on every frame, regardless of the exact timing. This event is first demonstrated in Chapter 30, "Cowbell."

Message Boxes

Flashlight uses a message box to show a standard warning that enables the user to cancel the action. On most platforms, using a message box to communicate information is indicative of a lazy programmer who doesn't want to create a nicer-looking user interface. On Windows Phone, however, a message box is not only appropriate for many situations, but it has a lot of niceties that are hard to create on your own! As with the phone's built-in apps, it animates in and out (with a flip), it dims and disables the rest of the screen (including the application bar), its buttons tilt when pressed, it automatically shows the status bar with a background that matches the message box background (regardless of the app's `SystemTray.IsVisible` setting), it makes a pleasant sound, and it vibrates. Naturally, it also respects the user's theme and the phone's orientation.

`MessageBox` contains two overloads of its static `Show` method. With one, you simply pass a single piece of text:

```
MessageBox.Show("This is the message.");
```

As shown in Figure 2.7, the resultant message box shows the message with a single OK button. It looks odd because it has no caption, so apps should not use this overload of `Show`.

The more functional overload of `Show`, used by Flashlight, enables you to set the text *and* caption, plus choose what buttons you want with a value from the `MessageBoxButton` enumeration: `OK` (a single OK button) or `OKCancel` (two buttons—OK and cancel). Figure 2.8 shows the message box created back in Listing 2.2.

FIGURE 2.7   The standard message box with no caption and a single OK button.

Both overloads of `Show` return a `MessageBoxResult` enumeration value that indicates which button, if any, was tapped. The only supported values are `OK` and `Cancel`. The latter is returned if the user taps the cancel button *or* if the user simply dismisses the message box with the hardware Back button.

Unfortunately, `MessageBox.Show` does not support custom labels for the two buttons. The "ok" and "cancel" labels are all you get. Built-in phone apps, on the other hand, often customize the "ok" label to be more specific to the task at hand, such as "call" versus "don't call" or "delete" versus "cancel."

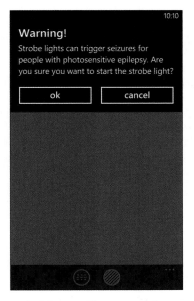

FIGURE 2.8   The message box used by Flashlight, shown in the context of the entire page.

You *can* actually customize the text on the two message box buttons, but not with the MessageBox class. Instead, this functionality is hidden in an odd place—the `Microsoft.Xna.Framework.GamerServices` assembly! The `Guide` class in the `Microsoft.Xna.Framework.GamerServices` namespace provides a pair of static methods that any app (XNA or Silverlight) can use without any special capabilities—`BeginShowMessageBox` and `EndShowMessageBox`. `BeginShowMessageBox` can be used as follows:

```
Guide.BeginShowMessageBox("Title",
  "This is the message.",
  new string[] { "button 1", "button 2" }, // 2 buttons with custom labels
  0,                                        // Button index that has focus
                                            // (irrelevant for the phone)
  MessageBoxIcon.None,                      // This is ignored
  new AsyncCallback(OnMessageBoxClosed),    // Callback to process result
  null                                      // Custom state given to callback
);
```

The `OnMessageBoxClosed` callback, which uses `EndShowMessageBox`, can look as follows:

```
void OnMessageBoxClosed(IAsyncResult result)
{
  // See which button was tapped (if any)
  int? buttonIndex = Guide.EndShowMessageBox(result);
  if (buttonIndex == 1)
    // Perform action #1
  else if (buttonIndex == 2)
    // Perform action #2
  else
    // Message box was dismissed with the hardware back button
}
```

Despite the fact that you pass an arbitrary list of button labels to `BeginShowMessageBox`, only one or two labels are supported because you can only have one or two buttons.

When using your own labels, be sure to follow design guidelines by putting the positive OK-style button on the left and the negative cancel-style button on the right.

The Finished Product

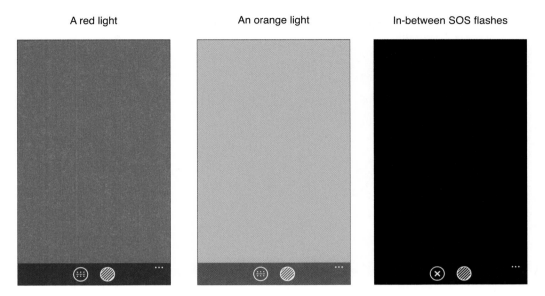

A red light   An orange light   In-between SOS flashes

chapter 3 lessons

IN CASE OF EMERGENCY

The "In Case of Emergency" app is meant to help save your life in the event you become a victim of a serious accident. The idea is that if someone finds you in a state in which you are unable to communicate, that person might check your phone for important information about yourself. (Hopefully this is done after calling 911!) If this person launches the "In Case of Emergency" app, they will see an emergency contact whom he/she can call, as well as any important medical information that the paramedics should know.

To help this Good Samaritan stumble upon your "In Case of Emergency" app, its app icon and tile icon are bright red, as shown in Figure 3.1. Basically, this app is for super-prepared people who don't password-protect their phones! As ridiculous as this might sound, there is a market for this type of app.

Although the "In Case of Emergency" title fits (barely) in the app list, it does not fit on the tile. Therefore, this app modifies the default token title in the application manifest (as described in Chapter 1, "Tally") to simply "ICE," a somewhat-common abbreviation for "In Case of Emergency." (Some people store a contact on their phone named "ICE," in case their rescuer is familiar with this convention.)

This is the first app that must do work to support multiple orientations and the first app that involves typing, so before creating it we will explore the following three topics:

> → Orientation

> → The On-Screen Keyboard

> → The Hardware Keyboard

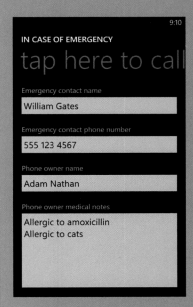

FIGURE 3.1   The tile for "In Case of Emergency" clearly stands out (unless the user's theme accent color is red).

Orientation

As shown in the preceding chapter, Windows phones support three orientations:

→ Portrait (vertical, with the screen above the hardware buttons)

→ Landscape Left (horizontal, with the screen to the left of the hardware buttons)

→ Landscape Right (horizontal, with the screen to the right of the hardware buttons)

What is the difference between a page's SupportedOrientations **and** Orientation **properties?**

SupportedOrientations is the only one you should worry about. Most of the apps in this book remove the confusing Orientation property, so it made its only appearance so far inside the initial contents of MainPage.xaml in Chapter 1. Orientation is for design-time use only, so Visual Studio and Expression Blend display the page in the desired orientation. Setting Orientation has no effect at run-time.

To support orientations other than portrait, you can change the value of a page's SupportedOrientations property to Landscape to only support the two landscape orientations, or to PortraitOrLandscape to support all three. You cannot choose to support only *one* of the landscape orientations; if your app works with one of the landscape orientations then it must work for both of them. Therefore, do not assume which side of the screen the application bar resides for a landscape page. As seen in the preceding chapter, it can appear on either the left or right side.

? What orientation(s) should my app support?

If users never need to do any typing inside your app, it's okay for it to be portrait-only. After all, many built-in phone experiences (such as Start and the app list) are portrait-only, and auto-rotation can sometimes be more annoying than helpful. When I'm lying down in bed and trying to use my phone, automatic rotation to landscape is frustrating! Therefore, I recommend that apps that support all orientations consider providing an "orientation lock" feature. Chapter 4, "Stopwatch," shows how to do this.

For apps that involve typing, however, supporting landscape orientations is practically mandatory (unlike with iPhone). The reason for this is that some phones have a landscape-oriented hardware keyboard, and typing on it would not be a great experience if its orientation doesn't match the screen's orientation.

Supporting *only* landscape is okay for some games and novelty apps, but weird for anything else. Of course, if such an app involves typing (such as typing a user name for a high score), those parts should support the portrait orientation for the sake of phones with a *portrait*-oriented hardware keyboard!

When you set SupportedOrientations to PortraitOrLandscape, the page automatically rotates to the proper orientation at the appropriate times (based on the angle the user holds their phone and whether a hardware keyboard is activated). This rotation is instant; your content is not animated. System-provided components, such as the status bar, application bar, message boxes and other notifications, adjust automatically as well, but with animations.

? How can I get orientation changes to animate, as seen in built-in apps such as Internet Explorer, Messaging, and Outlook?

Animated orientation changes are one of many nice touches that are not exposed to third-party apps. With transitions from the Silverlight for Windows Phone Toolkit, described in Chapter 19, "Animation Lab," you can easily perform animated orientation changes similar to the built-in apps.

? What are the screen dimensions given to my app?

All Windows phones currently have Wide Video Graphics Array (WVGA) screens that are 480 pixels wide and 800 pixels tall. Your app can consume all of this space if you are not showing the status bar or application bar. In the portrait orientation, the status bar consumes 32 pixels of height and a fully-opaque application bar consumes 72 pixels of height. In the landscape orientations, the status bar and application bar each consume 72 pixels of *width* because they don't move from their original locations, as seen in the preceding chapter.

Another consideration when designing your user interfaces is that toast notifications, when they appear, temporarily cover the top 60 pixels of the screen. If your app is used in the midst of a phone call, a bar with call information covers the top 64 pixels of the screen. When the user adjusts the phone's volume or interacts with the audio transport controls, the resulting volume control covers the top 93 pixels. This is one of the reasons that the standard page design of showing the application name at the top works out nicely, as only that gets covered in these cases.

That said, it's best to avoid depending on the specific screen dimensions. Future phones will undoubtedly have different dimensions. You can dynamically discover the resolution with the following two properties:

```
(Application.Current.RootVisual as FrameworkElement).ActualWidth
(Application.Current.RootVisual as FrameworkElement).ActualHeight
```

or:

```
Application.Current.Host.Content.ActualWidth
Application.Current.Host.Content.ActualHeight
```

You can also discover the current *page's* dimensions (minus the status bar and application bar, if applicable) by checking the page instance's `ActualWidth` and `ActualHeight` properties.

If you wish to perform a custom action when the orientation changes, such as a full-screen animation or custom rearranging of elements, you can leverage a page's `OrientationChanged` event.

The On-Screen Keyboard

The on-screen keyboard is the primary mechanism for typing on a Windows phone. For many models, it is the *only* way. It is sometimes called the *software input panel* (SIP). When it appears, it covers the bottom 339 pixels of the screen in the portrait orientation or the bottom 259 pixels in the landscape orientations. (In landscape, its keys expand horizontally but shrink vertically.) It occupies an additional 62 pixels when text suggestions are given, or when copy/paste has been used.

There are no APIs for interacting with the on-screen keyboard. Instead, it automatically slides up when a text box or password box gets focus (normally from a user tapping on it) and it automatically slides down when the text box or password box loses focus (normally from a user tapping on something else or pressing the hardware Back button). There is no way to leverage the on-screen keyboard in your app without using a text box or password box.

 Can I force the on-screen keyboard to appear without requiring the user to tap on a text box or password box?

Yes, but you still need a text box or password box to get focus and receive the keystrokes. Therefore, you can accomplish this by programmatically giving it focus. This can be done by calling its Focus method, although this call can fail (and return `false`) under certain conditions. For example, you cannot set focus on a control from a page's constructor; it's too early. You can, however, call it from a page's Loaded event.

The design guidelines recommend automatically showing the on-screen keyboard when navigating to a page only when doing so does not obscure other parts of the page. So for "In Case of Emergency," this behavior is not appropriate.

The most interesting aspect of the on-screen keyboard, and what gives it a big advantage over a hardware keyboard, is its ability to change its display depending on the context. For example, it can show a ".com" button when it knows you need to type a URL, or a phone keypad when it knows you need to type a phone number.

The on-screen keyboard can currently appear in 11 different modes. You can choose which one to use by marking the relevant text box with an appropriate *input scope*. An input scope is basically a pre-defined label that can be assigned to a text box's InputScope property. Some examples are Default, Url, and PhoneNumber. It can be assigned in XAML as follows:

```
<TextBox InputScope="PhoneNumber"/>
```

The list of allowed input scopes is provided by the InputScopeNameValue enumeration. The confusing thing about input scopes, however, is that there are *62* valid values despite there being only *11* distinct keyboard modes!

Can I force the on-screen keyboard to *disappear* without requiring the user to tap on something else?

Yes, by programmatically giving focus to a control other than the text box or password box. This is commonly done in response to the user tapping the Enter key, because this key otherwise does nothing except for multiline text boxes. This chapter's app demonstrates this technique.

Marking a text box with an input scope as specific as possible (such as TelephoneAreaCode) is a good idea even if it has no effect compared to a more generic choice. Consider it as extra documentation for any developer who reads your code. Plus, because you're communicating your intent to the operating system, one day a future version might provide a better experience for your chosen context. (For TelephoneAreaCode, you could imagine a future experience where you can see the geographic name corresponding to the chosen area code, or where you can even search for area codes geographically.)

So how do 62 values map into 11 modes? Some values are simply synonyms for the same concept, such as Numbers versus Digits. Some values express different intent, but there is no meaningful way for the keyboard to show distinct displays, such as PersonalGivenName versus PersonalMiddleName versus PersonalSurname. Some values would ideally produce different displays (and might in a future release) but are currently lumped together, such as CurrencyAmount versus CurrencyAmountAndSymbol. Many other values are simply not implemented and produce the default display instead, such as Password, CurrencyChinese, and Bopomofo. Table 3.1 lists all 62 values grouped into the 11 distinct modes and shows the resulting on-screen keyboard.

TABLE 3.1   The Valid Values for a Text Box's Input Scope and the Resulting Keyboard Display

Name	Description	Result
Default AlphanumericFullWidth AlphanumericHalfWidth Bopomofo CurrencyChinese EnumString FileName FullFilePath Hanja Hiragana KatakanaFullWidth KatakanaHalfWidth LogOnName NumberFullWidth OneChar Password PhraseList RegularExpression Srgs Yomi	The default mode. It starts on a page with letter keys, and has a "&123" button to switch to a page with number and symbol keys.	
Number Digits AddressStreet CurrencyAmount CurrencyAmountAndSymbol DateDay DateMonth DateYear PostalAddress PostalCode Time TimeHour TimeMinorSec	"Numeric mode." This is still the default keyboard, but it starts on the page with number and symbol keys. You can switch to the page of letter keys by pressing the "abcd" button.	
TelephoneNumber TelephoneAreaCode TelephoneCountryCode TelephoneLocalNumber	Used for entering a phone number. Shows a keypad that looks similar to the Phone app's keypad. Adds an extra column of keys for backspace, space, comma, and period. The latter two are there in case you want to use this mode as a better "numeric mode."	

TABLE 3.1   Continued

Name	Description	Result
Url	Used for entering a URL. Shows a ".com" button instead of a comma and restyles the Enter key. (The comma still appears on the numbers and symbols page.) I wish the enter key always looked like this, because I sometimes confuse the default one with the backspace key!	
EmailNameOrAddress EmailSmtpAddress EmailUserName	Used for entering an email address. Shows a ".com" button and duplicates the @ key from the numbers and symbols page for quick access. Unlike for Url, the @ and ".com" buttons are present on both pages of keys.	
NameOrPhoneNumber	"SMS mode," for entering a recipient of an SMS message. Like the default mode, but the comma key is replaced with an @ key and a semicolon key. (The semicolon is useful for delimiting consecutive names/numbers.) Note that there is a "123" button instead of the usual "&123" button. This brings up a phone-style numeric keypad that only has numbers and a backspace key.	

TABLE 3.1   Continued

Name	Description	Result

`AddressCity`
`AddressCountryName`
`AddressCountryShortName`
`AddressStateOrProvince`
`Date`
`DateDayName`
`DateMonthName`
`PersonalFullName`
`PersonalGivenName`
`PersonalMiddleName`
`PersonalNamePrefix`
`PersonalNameSuffix`
`PersonalSurname`
	"Capitalized mode." Like the default mode, but with shift depressed to make the first letter capital. The keyboard returns to lowercase after the first letter is typed.	

`Text` `Chat`	Like the default mode, but with a bar of text suggestions and an emoticons button that gives access to two pages of common emoticons. (The first page of emoticons is pictured to the right.) It also starts out with shift depressed so the first letter is capitalized. Although one could imagine that `Chat` mode would use a dictionary with slang and abbreviations (LOL, ROFL, brb, …) whereas `Text` mode could use a "proper" dictionary, these two modes are actually identical and use the same dictionary. As shown in the picture, this dictionary indeed includes several slang terms and abbreviations that would make your English teacher weep.	 

TABLE 3.1   Continued

Name	Description	Result
Maps ApplicationEnd	Matches the keyboard used by the Maps app (and Bing app). Adds the text suggestions bar to the default mode, but with the restyled Enter key and no emoticons button. Again, although you can imagine a customized dictionary that only includes terms relevant for a map, this mode uses the same dictionary as every mode with the text suggestions bar.	
Search	Like the default mode, but with a restyled enter key. Oddly, this is not the keyboard used by the Bing app because there are no text suggestions. Instead, the Maps value matches what Bing uses.	
Private	This mode should not be used. It is exactly like the default mode, but with a text suggestions bar that is always empty.	

> **⚠ Do not use the Password input scope!**
>
> Because this input scope is no different than Default, it does not provide the proper password-entering experience (which shows a dot for each letter). To get this experience, you should use a password box (the PasswordBox control) instead of a text box. Note that password boxes do not support input scopes; you can only get the default on-screen keyboard with them.

? How do I make the keyboard show only number keys and nothing else?

You can't. The `TelephoneNumber` input scope is the closest thing to a pure-number keyboard, but even that has some non-numeric keys. Also, the phone keypad styling is not very desirable for contexts that have nothing to do with a phone number. An app that wants this behavior, such as the Tip Calculator app in Chapter 10, is usually better off creating its own grid of numeric buttons.

? How do I restrict what gets typed into a text box (such as only allowing numbers)?

You must write code that manually filters out unwanted characters; input scopes do not help in this regard. For most input scopes, the user can still find a way to type every possible character via the on-screen keyboard. And even when an input scope with a limited on-screen keyboard is used, such as `TelephoneNumber`, users with a hardware keyboard can still type every character possible! Input scopes are about providing convenience to the user; they are not about restricting or validating input.

Unfortunately, you can't reliably restrict input in all cases. Instead, you can only reliably remove characters after the fact with a `TextChanged` event handler. The following code *should* enable the rejection of non-digit keystrokes, but it currently does work due to a bug that causes the pressing of Shift to not be reported:

```
void TextBox_KeyDown(object sender, KeyEventArgs e)
{
  switch (e.Key)
  {
    case Key.D0: case Key.D1: case Key.D2: case Key.D3: case Key.D4:
    case Key.D5: case Key.D6: case Key.D7: case Key.D8: case Key.D9:
        if ((Keyboard.Modifiers & ModifierKeys.Shift) == ModifierKeys.Shift)
        {
          // Shift is reported as being pressed! (This doesn't currently happen
          // due to a bug.) That means we just caught a !, @, #, $, %, ^, &, *,
          // (, or ) pretending to be a digit!
          // This is not allowed. Swallow the keystroke!
          e.Handled = true;
        }
        else
        {
          // This is allowed. There's nothing more to do!
        }
        break;
    default:
        // This is not allowed. Swallow the keystroke!
        e.Handled = true;
        break;
  }
}
```

Can I supply a custom context-specific dictionary for the text suggestions bar?

No. The XAML Editor app in Chapter 11 deals with this limitation by mimicking the text suggestions bar with its own set of words.

The on-screen keyboard has several nice behaviors that you might not be aware of. For example, you can hold down or double-tap the shift key to turn on Caps Lock and tap it later to turn it off. You can also hold down many keys to get alternatives related to that key. Figure 3.2 shows a few examples of this.

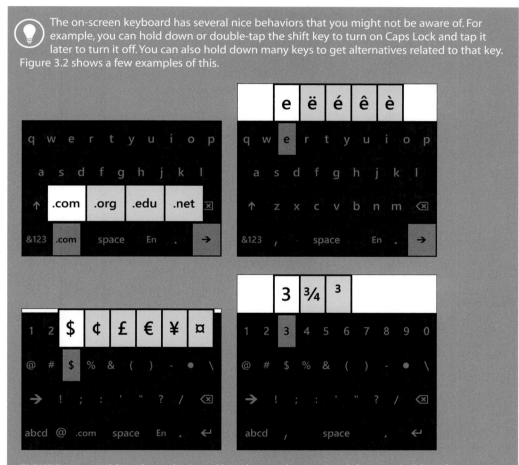

FIGURE 3.2 Holding down the ".com" key shows other top-level domains, holding down a vowel shows variations with accents, holding down the dollar sign shows other units of currency, and holding down 1, 2, or 3 shows fractions and exponents.

•••

Setting an Input Scope in C#

Although setting the `InputScope` property in XAML is simple, setting it in C# is more compli-cated than you probably expect. That's because `InputScope` doesn't really accept a simple string; XAML just makes it look that way thanks to a *type converter*. (Type converters are explained in Appendix B, "XAML Reference.") Here is how you can set a text box's input scope to `Url` in C#:

```
// Create the input scope
InputScope inputScope = new InputScope();
inputScope.Names.Add(new InputScopeName { NameValue=InputScopeNameValue.Url });
// Assign it to a text box
this.TextBox.InputScope = inputScope;
```

You can use an equivalent verbose approach in XAML as follows, rather than using the short syntax shown earlier:

```
<TextBox x:Name="TextBox">
  <TextBox.InputScope>
    <InputScope>
      <InputScope.Names>
        <InputScopeName NameValue="Url"/>
      </InputScope.Names>
    </InputScope>
  </TextBox.InputScope>
</TextBox>
```

The only real benefit of doing it this way is that you get Intellisense to help you out when typing the value of the `NameValue` property. When you set `InputScope` to a simple string value, Intellisense does not kick in.

The Hardware Keyboard

Although you probably have a Windows phone for testing your apps, you may very well not have a model with a hardware keyboard. Don't worry—as long as you support both orientations for any page involving typing, your app should work just fine on such a device without further testing. Still, it is helpful to understand how the hardware keyboard works.

A Windows phone can have a hardware keyboard in a number of different configurations. It could slide out, flip out, swivel out, or just be stationary. It could be placed anywhere, and be oriented for either portrait, landscape left, or landscape right.

When a non-stationary keyboard is tucked away, the phone acts as if there is no hardware keyboard, and the on-screen keyboard behaves as it always does. When a non-stationary hardware keyboard is pulled/flipped/swiveled out, the screen's orientation automatically changes to match the orientation of the keyboard (if the current page is marked as supporting this orientation). This happens regardless of the phone's physical orientation, so it may temporarily produce a sideways screen. However, the user will presumably rotate the phone appropriately before using the keyboard.

When the hardware keyboard is activated, the on-screen keyboard goes away (if it was visible at the time) and stays away, except for a few special circumstances. Pressing the symbol (SYM) key on the hardware keyboard invokes the on-screen keyboard with pages of numbers and symbols. Pressing the emoticons key on the hardware keyboard invokes the on-screen keyboard with pages of emoticons. Pressing the accent key after typing certain letters automatically cycles through the accented variations, but it also shows the accented variations as on-screen keyboard buttons. Text suggestions, when used by the current input scope, also appear on the screen. And so on. The last two circumstances are demonstrated in Figure 3.3 inside the built-in Alarms app.

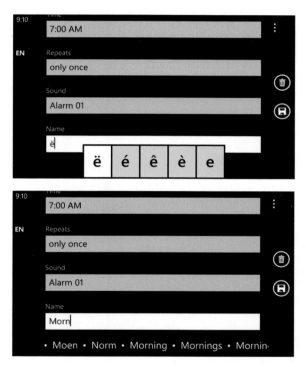

FIGURE 3.3 Two examples of small on-screen supplements for an activated hardware keyboard, displayed at the edge of the screen adjacent to the keyboard.

The most important thing to understand about the hardware keyboard is what it is and isn't intended for. It is meant to provide an alternate way to type text into a text box. And that is it. It should never be used for any kind of navigation (scrolling, panning, changing control focus)—even for a game. Although it may have arrow keys for moving the caret within a text box, those arrows should be used for any other purpose. The hardware number keys can't even be used with the built-in Calculator app, because that is not the same thing as typing into a text box!

Although these restrictions make the hardware keyboard less compelling than it could have been, it frees developers from having to worry about exploiting such optional features. It also protects users from the existence of apps that only work well with a hardware keyboard. Windows Phone and its apps are clearly optimized for touch screen usage, and users without a hardware keyboard should not feel like they are missing out on anything other than arguably easier typing.

 You can mimic the use of a hardware keyboard with the Windows Phone Emulator. The Pause key on your computer's keyboard toggles between having an on-screen keyboard and a hardware keyboard. To use the hardware keyboard, simply use your computer's keyboard! This mimics the behavior of a portrait slide-out keyboard, as pages always stay in the portrait orientation (if they support it).

The emulation is not perfect, however. Custom logic that processes keystrokes might not work in the emulator due to some keys not being reported correctly. For example, on my laptop, the Enter key appears as Key.Unknown inside a KeyDown event handler rather than Key.Enter.

Is there a way to know when the user has activated (e.g. slid out) a hardware keyboard?

No. There are no APIs specific to hardware keyboards.

Is there a way to know when the user has typed something on the hardware keyboard?

Not reliably. You *can* attach a KeyDown and/or KeyUp event handler to Silverlight elements other than a text box or password box, and this can sometimes be exploited in strange ways that aren't guaranteed to continue working. For example, if a scroll viewer—even an empty one—has focus (e.g. the user has tapped it), its KeyDown and KeyUp events get raised when keys on the hardware keyboard are pressed and released! (This does not happen for other elements, such as a grid.) Inside such event handlers, you know that the source must have been the hardware keyboard, because no on-screen keyboard could have possibly been involved.

Is there a way to know if the current phone even has a hardware keyboard?

Not reliably. You can possibly infer this information after checking the values of DeviceManufacturer and/or DeviceName from the static Microsoft.Phone.Info. DeviceExtendedProperties class (which requires the ID_CAP_IDENTITY_DEVICE capability).

The User Interface

Listing 3.1 contains the XAML for "In Case of Emergency," which consists of the standard header, four text boxes, and four corresponding text blocks. The resulting user interface is shown in Figure 3.4.

FIGURE 3.4   The "In Case of Emergency" user interface, shown in the dark theme and themes.

LISTING 3.1   `MainPage.xaml`—The User Interface for "In Case of Emergency"

```xml
<phone:PhoneApplicationPage x:Class="WindowsPhoneApp.MainPage"
    xmlns="http://schemas.microsoft.com/winfx/2006/xaml/presentation"
    xmlns:x="http://schemas.microsoft.com/winfx/2006/xaml"
    xmlns:phone="clr-namespace:Microsoft.Phone.Controls;assembly=Microsoft.Phone"
    xmlns:shell="clr-namespace:Microsoft.Phone.Shell;assembly=Microsoft.Phone"
    FontFamily="{StaticResource PhoneFontFamilyNormal}"
    FontSize="{StaticResource PhoneFontSizeNormal}"
    Foreground="{StaticResource PhoneForegroundBrush}"
    SupportedOrientations="PortraitOrLandscape"
    shell:SystemTray.IsVisible="True">
  <Grid>
    <Grid.RowDefinitions>
      <RowDefinition Height="Auto"/>
      <RowDefinition Height="*"/>
    </Grid.RowDefinitions>
```

LISTING 3.1   Continued

```xml
    <!-- The standard header, with some tweaks -->
    <StackPanel Grid.Row="0" Margin="24,16,0,12">
      <TextBlock Text="IN CASE OF EMERGENCY" Margin="-1,0,0,0"
                 FontFamily="{StaticResource PhoneFontFamilySemiBold}"
                 FontSize="{StaticResource PhoneFontSizeMedium}" />
      <TextBlock Text="tap here to call" Foreground="Red" Margin="-3,-10,0,0"
                 FontFamily="{StaticResource PhoneFontFamilySemiLight}"
                 FontSize="{StaticResource PhoneFontSizeExtraExtraLarge}"
                 MouseLeftButtonUp="TapHereToCall_MouseLeftButtonUp" />
    </StackPanel>

    <!-- Scrollable pane (for the sake of the landscape orientation) -->
    <ScrollViewer Grid.Row="1">
      <!-- Four text block / text box pairs stacked vertically -->
      <StackPanel>
        <TextBlock Text="Emergency contact name" Margin="24,17,24,-5"
                   Foreground="{StaticResource PhoneSubtleBrush}" />
        <TextBox x:Name="ContactNameTextBox" InputScope="PersonalFullName"
                 Margin="{StaticResource PhoneHorizontalMargin}"
                 GotFocus="TextBox_GotFocus" KeyDown="TextBox_KeyDown" />

        <TextBlock Text="Emergency contact phone number" Margin="24,17,24,-5"
                   Foreground="{StaticResource PhoneSubtleBrush}" />
        <TextBox x:Name="PhoneNumberTextBox" InputScope="TelephoneNumber"
                 Margin="{StaticResource PhoneHorizontalMargin}"
                 GotFocus="TextBox_GotFocus" KeyDown="TextBox_KeyDown" />

        <TextBlock Text="Phone owner name" Margin="24,17,24,-5"
                   Foreground="{StaticResource PhoneSubtleBrush}" />
        <TextBox x:Name="OwnerNameTextBox" InputScope="PersonalFullName"
                 Margin="{StaticResource PhoneHorizontalMargin}"
                 GotFocus="TextBox_GotFocus" KeyDown="TextBox_KeyDown" />

        <TextBlock Text="Phone owner medical notes" Margin="24,17,24,-5"
                   Foreground="{StaticResource PhoneSubtleBrush}" />
        <!-- A multiline text box -->
        <TextBox x:Name="MedicalNotesTextBox" InputScope="Text"
                 AcceptsReturn="True" MinHeight="236" TextWrapping="Wrap"
                 Margin="{StaticResource PhoneHorizontalMargin}" />
      </StackPanel>
    </ScrollViewer>
  </Grid>
</phone:PhoneApplicationPage>
```

Notes:

→ This page supports all orientations due to its use of typing. However, because its contents are too long to fit on the screen in a landscape orientation, a scroll viewer is used to enable scrolling in this situation. Scroll viewers are discussed in the following section.

→ The two text blocks in the standard header are given new margins and explicit font settings that are different from what Visual Studio generates when you create a page. That's because the automatically-generated page unfortunately doesn't do a good enough job of matching the header style of built-in apps. I ignored this annoyance in Chapter 1 (and Chapter 2, "Flashlight," didn't have a header), but from now on, every app goes out of its way to look as good as possible.

→ The "tap here to call" text block is given a hard-coded red foreground to convey the sense of emergency. Fortunately, this looks fine over both possible theme backgrounds, as seen in Figure 3.4.

→ The "tap here to call" text block has a MouseLeftButtonUp event handler for handling a tap to launch the Phone app. (Unlike buttons, text blocks do not have a Click event.) This disobeys a design guideline that page titles should not be interactive, but in this case breaking the rule seems appropriate.

→ Each of the four main text blocks is given a PhoneSubtleBrush foreground and very specific margins to match the style of such labels used by built-in apps. PhoneSubtleBrush is a theme-defined gray color that varies ever so slightly for the dark and light themes.

→ Whereas text *blocks* are static labels, text *boxes* are meant for editable text. Text boxes contain several advanced methods and properties for grabbing chunks of text as well as methods for converting between a character index and a physical region within the control. They also define TextChanged and SelectionChanged events.

→ Each text box is given an explicit theme-defined margin (PhoneHorizontalMargin, which is 12 pixels on the left and right). Text boxes naturally have 12 pixels of space on all sides, but the text boxes used in built-in apps are usually seen with *24* pixels of space on the left and right. Therefore, adding this margin to the existing spacing makes these text boxes match the style of built-in apps. Margins are discussed in an upcoming section.

→ The first three text boxes have handlers for their GotFocus and KeyDown events to enable subtle but important behaviors discussed in the code-behind section.

→ Each text box is marked with an appropriate (and non-default) input scope. The first and third use PersonalFullName, which appropriately auto-capitalizes the first letter and doesn't attempt to offer suggestions as you type someone's name. The second text box uses TelephoneNumber because that is exactly what it wants. The last text box uses Text because text suggestions are appropriate for what you might type in this box. As shown in Figure 3.5, this comes in very handy when attempting to type a long and difficult word like Amoxicillin!

→ The duplication of the margin and foreground settings on each text block is not very satisfactory from a code-maintenance perspective. Property values that are repeatedly applied to elements should usually be abstracted into a custom style to reduce the amount of duplicated code. We will start doing this in Chapter 9, "Fake Call," which explains styles in depth. The same technique will be used to avoid duplicating the new margin and font settings on the standard header in every app.

PersonalFullName   TelephoneNumber   Text

FIGURE 3.5   Listing 3.1 uses three different input scopes to provide the best typing experience.

Figure 3.6 shows the appearance of the first keyboard (and the corresponding focused text box) under the light theme and under a landscape orientation, as this book has not yet shown what these situations look like.

> **(?) How do I create a multiline text box?**
>
> Set its `AcceptsReturn` property to true, as done with the medical notes text box in Listing 3.1. In some cases, depending on the page layout, the text box might also have to be given an explicit height (or explicit minimum height) so multiple lines of text can be seen simultaneously. This is done in Listing 3.1 because a text box in a vertical stack panel is the height of a single line of text by default. If this text box were in a grid, it would stretch to fill its grid cell in both dimensions.
>
> Note that a text box *always* supports multiple lines of text programmatically. If `Text` is set to a string containing newline characters, it displays the multiple lines regardless of the value of `AcceptsReturn`. Also, the multiline support is completely independent from text wrapping. Text wrapping applies only to individual lines of text that are wider than the control.

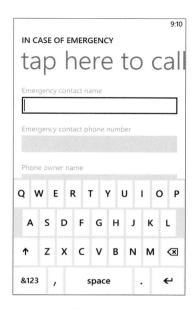

Light theme

Landscape left

FIGURE 3.6   The on-screen keyboard for the first text box, viewed with the light theme and with a landscape orientation.

Now that we're starting to use a lot of text in an app, it's a good time to explain the Windows Phone guidelines for capitalization and punctuation. When looking at "In Case of Emergency," you might wonder, "Why don't the four main text blocks end in colons?" or "Why don't they use title capitalization?" Here is why:

Capitalization guidelines:

→ Use **all capital letters** for the application title, the AM/PM used for time, and occasionally for items in a panorama control. (Panoramas are covered in Part IV, "Pivot, Panorama, Charts, & Graphs.")

→ Use **all lowercase letters** for the page title, button text (or other command labels), list items, list titles, group titles, panorama and pivot control headings, and example text. Proper names, however, should still be capitalized as they normally are.

→ Use **sentence capitalization** in labels for everything else: text boxes, check boxes, radio buttons, toggle switches, and so on. Also use it for progress, notification, status, and explanatory text.

→ **Title capitalization** is almost never used for anything other than proper names, although it is sometimes used for standalone links that aren't part of a sentence (such as the "Privacy Statement" link in Internet Explorer's settings page).

Punctuation guidelines:

→ Never use a **colon** on any labels unless it is directly introducing a value (typically a number) in the same label, such as "Score: 100" or "Carrier: AT&T". Notice that no colons are used in Figure 3.4.

→ Never use an **ellipsis** unless it's at the end of active progress text. Using an ellipsis in a button is common on a PC (such as having a `"Browse..."` button) but is not appropriate for Windows Phone.

→ Do not use **ending punctuation**—*even when using sentence capitalization*—except in instructional text. Question marks are okay for questions, but you should avoid asking a question unless it is a message box title. When using multiple sentences (which should only be for instructional text), you should separate them with one space (not two).

→ Avoid using **parentheses**, but they are okay for acronyms or other short information.

→ When referring to a list of items, they should all be separated by **commas** (including a comma between the last two items).

→ It's okay to use an **ampersand** in labels rather than spelling out "and."

These guidelines are based not just on Microsoft documents (which are sometimes inaccurate) but also on what built-in apps on Windows Phone actually do. They may seem silly and arbitrary (and in some ways they are), but it's important to follow them for consistency with the rest of the phone and its apps.

Scroll Viewer

For user interfaces meant to fit on the screen without scrolling, using a grid as the root element inside a page is the best way to dynamically adjust to different page dimensions. For user interfaces meant to scroll when there is not enough space—such as this app— scroll viewer comes to the rescue.

By wrapping any element in a scroll viewer, the element automatically becomes scrollable when there is not enough space to render it all at once. For this app, the entire stack panel with all eight elements fits on the screen in the portrait orientation, so the scroll viewer

> According to design guidelines, the application and page titles (if present) should never scroll out of view unless the on-screen keyboard pushes them out of the way. By placing the scroll viewer around the stack panel (and not the entire grid), this page complies.

isn't needed. In a landscape orientation, however, the scroll viewer kicks in and enables the page to be swiped up and down. Figure 3.7 shows the page before the user touches it, and then shows it while the user scrolls it about halfway down.

A scroll viewer may only contain a single direct child element, but this child element is typically a complex panel such as a grid or, in this case, a stack panel. A scroll viewer contains several properties and methods for more advanced or programmatic manipulation of scrolling (such as a `ScrollToVerticalOffset` method that can be passed a number of pixels), but its two most important properties are `VerticalScrollBarVisibility` and `HorizontalScrollBarVisibility`. Both of these properties are of type `ScrollBarVisibility`, an enumeration that determines the behavior of its two scroll bars. `ScrollBarVisibility` has four values, but two of them are redundant. The values are

→ **Visible** and **Auto**—Enables scrolling in the relevant dimension. The scroll bar automatically becomes visible while the user is dragging the screen (and the content is long enough to scroll in that dimension).

→ **Disabled** and **Hidden**—Disables scrolling in the relevant dimension.

Before any scrolling

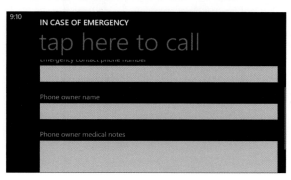

Scrolled about half the total distance, with scroll bar visible

FIGURE 3.7   The scroll viewer ensures that the entire page is accessible in a landscape orientation even though it can't all be seen at once.

The default value for `VerticalScrollBarVisibility` is `Auto`, and the default value for `HorizontalScrollBarVisibility` is `Disabled`, to match the scrolling behavior used by almost all apps. If you were to mark the scroll viewer in Listing 3.1 with `HorizontalScrollBarVisibility="Auto"` and manually set the `Width` property on one of the text boxes to a large enough value, you would be able to scroll the page horizontally.

When the on-screen keyboard appears, the text box with focus might need to be scrolled upward in order to remain in view above the keyboard. Fortunately, this happens automatically, *even when no scroll viewer is used*. Notice that in the last image in Figures 3.5 and 3.6, the entire page has been magically scrolled, even the normally unscrollable header! When the keyboard is dismissed, the page returns to its normal state.

Controlling the Size of Elements

Silverlight elements tend to *size to their content*, meaning that they try to be large enough to fit their content and no larger. This size can be influenced via several straightforward properties.

Elements have simple `Height` and `Width` properties (of type `double`), and they also have `MinHeight`, `MaxHeight`, `MinWidth`, and `MaxWidth` properties that can be used to specify a range of acceptable values. Any or all of these can be easily set on elements in C# or in XAML.

An element naturally stays as small as possible, so if you use `MinHeight` or `MinWidth`, it is rendered at that height/width unless its content forces it to grow. In addition, that growth can be limited by using `MaxHeight` and `MaxWidth` (as long as these values are larger than their `Min` counterparts). When using an explicit `Height` and `Width` at the same time as their `Min` and `Max` counterparts, `Height` and `Width` take precedence as long as they are in the range from `Min` to `Max`. The default value of `MinHeight` and `MinWidth` is `0`, and the default value of `MaxHeight` and `MaxWidth` is `Double.PositiveInfinity` (which can be set in XAML as simply `"Infinity"`).

To complicate matters, elements also contain `ActualHeight` and `ActualWidth` properties. Unlike the other six properties that are *input* to the layout process, however, these are read-only properties representing *output* from the layout process.

`ActualHeight` and `ActualWidth` represent the final size of an element after layout

> ### ! Avoid setting explicit sizes!
> Giving controls explicit sizes opens up the risk of cutting off text when content is dynamic or if you decide to localize your app for other languages. Therefore, you should avoid setting explicit sizes unless absolutely necessary. Fortunately, setting explicit sizes is rarely necessary, thanks to the panels described in the next chapter.
>
> Notice that the medical notes text box in Listing 3.1 uses `MinHeight="236"` rather than `Height="236"`, but for a different reason. Although a multiline text box supports some amount of internal scrolling if the text doesn't fit, this is hard to do. (It involves holding your finger down to reveal the caret, then dragging the caret.) Instead, because the text box already resides inside a scroll viewer, allowing it to grow as a user adds more lines of text results in an interface that is much easier to use.

> ### The Special "Auto" Length
> An element's `Height` and `Width` have a default value of `Double.NaN` (where NaN stands for *not a number*), meaning that the element will be only as large as its content needs it to be. This setting can also be explicitly specified in XAML using `"NaN"` (which is case sensitive) or the preferred `"Auto"` (which is not case sensitive), thanks a type converter associated with these properties. To check if one of these properties is autosized, you can use the static `Double.IsNaN` method.

is complete. That's right: Whether an element specified an explicit size, specified a range of acceptable sizes, or didn't specify anything at all, the behavior of other elements can alter an element's final size on the screen. These three properties are, therefore, useful for advanced scenarios in which you need to programmatically act on an element's size. The values of all the other size-related properties, on the other hand, aren't very interesting to base logic on. For example, when not set explicitly, the value of `Height` and `Width` are `Double.NaN`, regardless of the element's true size.

Margins and Padding

Silverlight elements have a `Margin` property that gives you control over how much extra space gets placed around the outside edges of the element. Many elements also have a `Padding` property that gives you control over how much extra space gets placed around the inside edges of the element. Margins are used very often to get an appropriate-looking user interface. Padding is normally not used, nor should it be used with standard elements, because they are already given default padding that gives them a consistent look with the rest of the phone.

Both `Margin` and `Padding` are of type `Thickness`, an interesting class that can represent one, two, or four values. Here is how the values are interpreted when set in XAML:

→ When set to a list of **four values**, as done many times with `Margin` in Listing 3.1, the numbers represent the left, top, right, and bottom edges, respectively.

→ When set to a list of **two values**, the first number is used for the left and right edges and the second number is used for the top and bottom edges. So `"12,24"` is a shortcut way of specifying `"12,24,12,24"`.

→ When set to a **single value**, it is used for all four sides. So `"12"` is a shortcut way of specifying `"12,12"`, which is a shortcut for `"12,12,12,12"`.

→ Negative values may be used for margins (and often are), but are not allowed for padding.

→ The commas are optional. You can use spaces instead of, or in addition to, commas. `"12,24"` is the same as `"12 24"` and `"12, 24"`.

When creating a `Thickness` in C#, you can use its constructor that accepts either a single value or all four values:

```
this.TextBox.Margin = new Thickness(12);          // Margin="12" in XAML
this.TextBox.Margin = new Thickness(12,24,12,24); // Margin="12,24" in XAML
```

Note that the handy two-number syntax is a shortcut only available through XAML. `Thickness` does not have a two-parameter constructor.

By default, text boxes have a padding of 2 (on all sides). Figure 3.8 demonstrates how explicitly setting different values affects their appearance, done with the following XAML:

```
<StackPanel>
  <TextBox Text="padding = 0" Padding="0"/>
  <TextBox Text="padding = 2 (default)"/>
  <TextBox Text="padding = 10" Padding="10"/>
  <TextBox Text="padding = 40,2" Padding="40,2"/>
</StackPanel>
```

The first text box has two fewer pixels of space around the text than the default one, and the third text box has eight more pixels of space around the text. When the text boxes are stacked like this, these two settings also change the overall height of each text box but not the width (because the text boxes are getting stretched horizontally to the width of the parent page). The final text box keeps the default padding on the top and bottom, but gets 40 pixels of padding on the left and right.

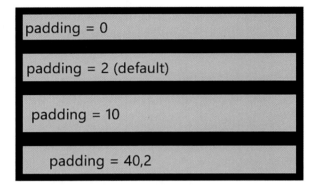

FIGURE 3.8   The effect of `Padding` on four text boxes.

> Although done here for demonstration purposes, you should avoid overriding the padding on standard controls. The default padding values were carefully chosen to match design guidelines. A valid place to use padding would be in the design of your own custom control, or a control with special-purpose content that already makes it appear non-standard.

The Code-Behind

Listing 3.2 contains the code-behind, which is pretty short, especially compared to the preceding chapter. Its job is to persist what the user has typed in, launch the Phone app, and provide a few subtle text box behaviors.

LISTING 3.2   `MainPage.xaml.cs`—The Code-Behind for "In Case of Emergency"

```
using System.Windows;
using System.Windows.Controls;
using System.Windows.Input;
using System.Windows.Navigation;
using Microsoft.Phone.Controls;
using Microsoft.Phone.Tasks;

namespace WindowsPhoneApp
{
  public partial class MainPage : PhoneApplicationPage
  {
    // Remember what is typed in the text boxes, otherwise this app is pointless!
    Setting<string> savedContactName = new Setting<string>("ContactName", "");
```

LISTING 3.2   Continued

```csharp
Setting<string> savedPhoneNumber = new Setting<string>("PhoneNumber", "");
Setting<string> savedOwnerName = new Setting<string>("OwnerName", "");
Setting<string> savedMedicalNotes = new Setting<string>("MedicalNotes", "");

public MainPage()
{
  InitializeComponent();
}

protected override void OnNavigatedTo(NavigationEventArgs e)
{
  base.OnNavigatedTo(e);
  // Restore saved text box contents when entering this page
  ContactNameTextBox.Text = this.savedContactName.Value;
  PhoneNumberTextBox.Text = this.savedPhoneNumber.Value;
  OwnerNameTextBox.Text = this.savedOwnerName.Value;
  MedicalNotesTextBox.Text = this.savedMedicalNotes.Value;
}

protected override void OnNavigatingFrom(NavigatingCancelEventArgs e)
{
  base.OnNavigatingFrom(e);
  // Persist text box contents when leaving this page for any reason
  this.savedContactName.Value = ContactNameTextBox.Text;
  this.savedPhoneNumber.Value = PhoneNumberTextBox.Text;
  this.savedOwnerName.Value = OwnerNameTextBox.Text;
  this.savedMedicalNotes.Value = MedicalNotesTextBox.Text;
}

void TapHereToCall_MouseLeftButtonUp(object sender, MouseButtonEventArgs e)
{
  // Launch the Phone app with the contact name and phone number
  PhoneCallTask phoneLauncher = new PhoneCallTask();
  phoneLauncher.DisplayName = this.ContactNameTextBox.Text;
  phoneLauncher.PhoneNumber = this.PhoneNumberTextBox.Text;

  if (phoneLauncher.PhoneNumber.Length == 0)
    MessageBox.Show("There is no emergency contact phone number to call.",
      "Phone", MessageBoxButton.OK);
  else
    phoneLauncher.Show();
}

void TextBox_GotFocus(object sender, RoutedEventArgs e)
```

LISTING 3.2   Continued

```
  {
    // Select all text so it can be cleared with one keystroke
    (sender as TextBox).SelectAll();
  }

  void TextBox_KeyDown(object sender, KeyEventArgs e)
  {
    if (e.Key == Key.Enter)
    {
      if (sender == this.ContactNameTextBox)
        this.PhoneNumberTextBox.Focus();
      else if (sender == this.PhoneNumberTextBox) // hardware keyboard only
        this.OwnerNameTextBox.Focus();
      else if (sender == this.OwnerNameTextBox)
        this.MedicalNotesTextBox.Focus();

      e.Handled = true;
    }
  }
 }
}
```

Notes:

→ The four `Setting` members and the `OnNavigatedTo`/`OnNavigatedFrom` methods exist to remember what the user has typed in the four text boxes for subsequent uses of the app.

→ The tap event handler for the "tap here to call" label (`TapHereToCall_ MouseLeftButtonUp`) uses the *phone launcher* (the `PhoneCallTask` class) to make a phone call with whatever phone number has been typed into `PhoneNumberTextBox` (and whatever display name has been typed into `ContactNameTextBox`). It's okay if the display name is an empty string, but if the phone number is an empty string then the call to `Show` silently does nothing. Therefore, we check for this error condition and explain to the user why the phone wasn't launched. The full set of Windows Phone launchers are examined in Volume II of this book series, but you can see the phone launcher is straightforward to use. Note that users are prompted before any phone call is made, and they have the power to cancel the phone call. This prompt is shown at the end of the chapter.

> The phone launcher is one of many features that do not work in the emulator. Instantiating `PhoneCallTask` throws an exception that is not handled by this app. If you care to write code that guards against such problems when running in the emulator, you can check the value of the static `Microsoft.Devices.Environment. DeviceType` property. This is set to either `Device` or `Emulator`.

→ The `GotFocus` event handler shared by the first three text boxes (`TextBox_GotFocus`) selects (highlights) all the text inside it, as shown in Figure 3.9. This is done by most text boxes in Windows Phone apps (such as the URL box in Internet Explorer) so the user can delete all the text by pressing backspace once, or by simply starting to type something new. For the rare case of the user wanting to *append* text to the existing text, the user must first tap the text box to remove the selection. When the text box is empty, the call to `SelectAll` has no effect, which is exactly the behavior we want. This handler is not attached to the multiline text box, because it's more likely that the user would tap on it to append text rather than replace it all.

→ The `KeyDown` event handler (`TextBox_KeyDown`) provides another convenient behavior: moving focus to the next text box when the Enter key is pressed. (Otherwise, pressing Enter in a single-line text box does nothing, which is a weird experience.) To do this, it determines which text box raised the event so it knows which one to give focus. Setting `KeyEventArgs.Handled` to `true` is important to prevent the keystroke from getting processed any further. Without this, when `MedicalNotesTextBox` is given focus, it would also receive the Enter keystroke (even though it was pressed when `OwnerNameTextBox` had focus) and an unwanted newline would appear in it.

→ For the sake of navigation, pressing Enter when the last text box has focus would ideally dismiss the on-screen keyboard. However, because it's a multiline text box, it is not appropriate to take any custom action when Enter is pressed. That is why we didn't attach `TextBox_KeyDown` to `MedicalNotesTextBox`'s KeyDown event in Listing 3.1.

→ Navigating from the first to last text box via the Enter key doesn't entirely work with the on-screen keyboard because it doesn't have an Enter key when `PhoneNumberTextBox` has focus (due to its use of the `PhoneNumber` input scope)! With a hardware keyboard, this is not an issue, so the focus can keep moving without getting "stuck," thanks to the logic inside `TextBox_KeyDown`.

FIGURE 3.9 When one of the first three text boxes has existing text and gets focus, its text becomes selected thanks to the implementation of `TextBox_GotFocus`.

> For consistency and convenience, every single-line text box should be used with an event handler that selects the text when it gets focus, unless you believe that appending text is a more common action than replacing it in your scenario. Every single-line text box should also be used with code that acts upon the Enter key, such as moving focus to the next text box, submitting the entered data, and/or dismissing the on-screen keyboard.

> If you want to remove focus from a text box but you don't have any other focusable controls on the page, you can call Focus on the page itself. Just make sure that the page's IsTabStop is true (as it is by default) to ensure that it's focusable also.

The Finished Product

Changing the phone number in a landscape orientation

The prompt seen when invoking the phone launcher

The phone launcher prompt when the display name is an empty string

STOPWATCH

The Stopwatch app enables you to time any event with a start/stop button and a reset button. When running, the reset button turns into a "lap" button that adds an intermediate time to a list at the bottom of the page without stopping the overall timing. This is a common stopwatch feature used in a number of sporting events.

Stopwatch displays an interesting bar toward the top that visualizes the progress of the current lap compared to the length of the preceding lap. (During the first lap, the bar is a solid color, as it has no relative progress to show.) With this bar and the start/stop button, this app shows that you can use a bit of color and still fit in with the Windows Phone style. Not everything has to be black, white, and gray!

Stopwatch supports all orientations, but it provides an "orientation lock" feature on its application bar that enables users to keep it in portrait mode when holding the phone sideways, and vice versa. This is a handy feature that other apps in this book share. The main downside is that if future phones have a built-in orientation lock feature, this functionality will be redundant for those phones.

The orientation lock is a neat trick, but this app does something even more slick. It provides the illusion of running in the background. You can start the timer, leave the app (even reboot the phone!), return to it 10 minutes later, and see the timer still running with 10 more minutes on the clock. Of course, Stopwatch, like all third-party apps at the time of writing, is unable to actually run in the back-

ground. Instead, it remembers the state of the app when exiting—including the current time—so it can seamlessly continue when restarted and account for the missing time.

This app takes advantage of previously unseen stack panel and grid features to produce a relatively-sophisticated user interface that looks great in any orientation. Therefore, before building Stopwatch, this chapter examines how Silverlight layout works and describes the features provided by stack panel and grid.

Controlling Layout with Panels

Sizing and positioning of elements in Silverlight is often called *layout*. A number of rich layout features exist to create flexible user interfaces that can act intelligently in the face of a number of changes: the screen size changing due to an orientation change, elements being added and removed, or elements growing or shrinking—sometimes in ways you didn't originally anticipate, such as later deciding to translate your app's text into a different language.

One piece to the layout story is a number of properties on individual elements: the size properties discussed in the preceding chapter (`Width`, `MinWidth`, `MaxWidth`, `Height`, `MinHeight`, and `MaxHeight`) and some alignment properties introduced later in this chapter. The other piece is a handful of elements known as *panels*, whose job is to arrange child elements in specific ways. Windows Phone 7 ships with five panels:

→ Stack Panel

→ Grid

→ Canvas

→ Virtualizing Stack Panel

→ Panorama Panel

Both the stack panel and grid have already been used many times, but we'll discuss them formally now. Canvas is for placing items at specific (x,y) coordinates, and is discussed in the next chapter.

The virtualizing stack panel is just like a stack panel, but with performance optimizations for databound items (delaying the creation of off-screen elements until they are scrolled onto the screen and recycling item containers). This panel is used as an implementation detail for controls such as a list box, and is normally not used directly unless you are designing your own list control. The panorama panel is also an implementation detail of the panorama control discussed in Part IV of this book, "Pivot, Panorama, Charts, & Graphs," and is not meant to be used directly.

The Silverlight for Windows Phone Toolkit, introduced in Chapter 7, "Date Diff," adds another handy panel to the list, called a wrap panel. The wrap panel is demonstrated in Chapter 8, "Vibration Composer," and Chapter 45, "Coin Toss."

You can arbitrarily nest panels inside each other, as each one is just a Silverlight element. You can also create your own custom panels by deriving from the abstract `Panel` class, although this is not a common thing to do.

Stack Panel

The stack panel is a popular panel because of its simplicity and usefulness. As its name suggests, it simply stacks its children sequentially. Although we've only seen it stack its children vertically, you can also make it stack its children horizontally by setting its `Orientation` property to `Horizontal` rather than the default `Vertical`.

Figure 4.1 renders the following XAML, which leverages a horizontal stack panel to provide a hypothetical user interface for entering a social security number (three groups of digits separated by dashes):

```
<StackPanel Orientation="Horizontal">
  <TextBox Width="80"/>
  <TextBlock Text="-" VerticalAlignment="Center"/>
  <TextBox Width="65"/>
  <TextBlock Text="-" VerticalAlignment="Center"/>
  <TextBox Width="80"/>
</StackPanel>
```

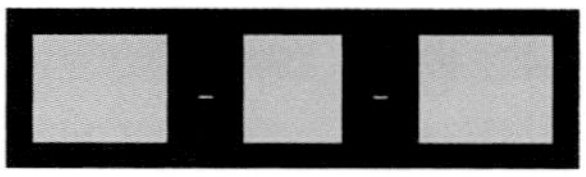

The `VerticalAlignment` property is discussed later, in the "Alignment" section.

FIGURE 4.1   Five elements stacked in a horizontal stack panel create a form for entering a Social Security number.

Grid

Grid is the most versatile panel and the one apps use most often for the root of their pages. (Apps that don't use a grid tend to use a canvas, which is good for games and certain novelty apps.) Grid enables you to arrange its children in a multirow and multi-column fashion, with many features to control the rows and columns in interesting ways. Working with grid is a lot like working with a table in HTML.

When using a grid, you define the number of rows and columns by adding that number of `RowDefinition` and `ColumnDefinition` elements to its `RowDefinitions` and `ColumnDefinitions` properties. (This is a little verbose but handy for giving individual rows and columns distinct sizes.) By default, all rows are the same size (dividing the height equally) and all columns are the same size (dividing the width equally). When you don't explicitly specify any rows or columns, the grid is implicitly given a single cell.

You can choose a specific cell for every child element in the grid by using `Grid.Row` and `Grid.Column`, which are zero-based indices. When you don't explicitly set `Grid.Row` and/or `Grid.Column` on child elements, the value 0 is used. Figure 4.2 demonstrates the appearance of the following grid:

```
<Grid>
  <Grid.RowDefinitions>
```

```xml
    <RowDefinition/>
    <RowDefinition/>
  </Grid.RowDefinitions>
  <Grid.ColumnDefinitions>
    <ColumnDefinition/>
    <ColumnDefinition/>
  </Grid.ColumnDefinitions>
  <Button Content="0,0"/>
  <Button Grid.Column="1" Content="0,1"/>
  <Button Grid.Row="1" Content="1,0"/>
  <Button Grid.Row="1" Grid.Column="1" Content="1,1"/>
</Grid>
```

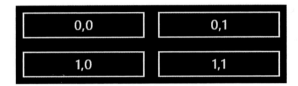

FIGURE 4.2   Four buttons in a 2x2 grid.

Grid.Row and Grid.Column are called *attachable properties* because although they are *defined* by the Grid class, they can be *attached* to other elements in XAML. (Any XAML attribute whose name includes a period is an attachable property. The identifier to the left of the period is always the class defining the property named to the right of the period.)

Using Attachable Properties in C#

Attachable properties are a special convention enabled by XAML when a class defines certain static Get/Set methods. C# doesn't have the concept of such properties, so you just call the underlying static methods directly. In C#, you can get the value of Grid.Row on a button assigned to a button variable as follows:

```csharp
int row = Grid.GetRow(button);
```

You can set the value of Grid.Column as follows:

```csharp
Grid.SetColumn(button, 2);
```

Note that the size of the grid and the appearance of its contents, which usually stretch in both dimensions to fill each cell, depends on the grid's parent element (or size-related properties on the grid itself). Figure 4.3 shows what the same grid from Figure 4.2 looks like if it is used to fill an entire page.

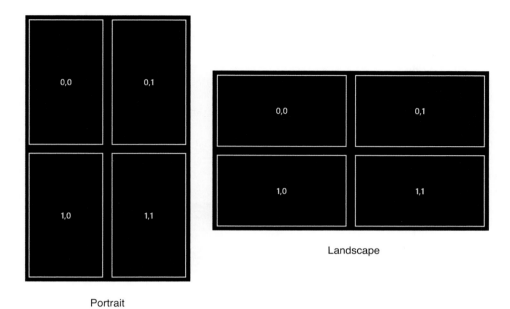

Portrait

Landscape

FIGURE 4.3   The grid from Figure 4.2, used to fill an entire page.

Multiple Elements in the Same Cell

Grid cells can be left empty, and multiple elements can appear in the same cell. In this case, elements are simply rendered on top of one another according to their ordering in XAML. (Later elements are rendered on top of earlier elements.) You can customize this order, often called the *z order* or *z index*) by setting the `Canvas.ZIndex` attachable property on any element—even though this example has nothing to do with a canvas!

> In a page that supports multiple orientations, using a grid is the easiest way to arrange its user interface in a way that can look nice in both portrait and landscape views without having to manually rearrange elements when the orientation change happens.

`Canvas.ZIndex` is an integer with a default value of 0 that you can set to any number (positive or negative). Elements with larger values are rendered on top of elements with smaller values, so the element with the smallest value is in the back, and the element with the largest value is in the front. If multiple children have the same value, the order is determined by their order in the grid's collection of children, as in the default case. Figure 4.4 shows what the following XAML produces, which contains empty cells and cells with multiple elements:

```
<Grid>
  <Grid.RowDefinitions>
    <RowDefinition/>
    <RowDefinition/>
```

```
  </Grid.RowDefinitions>
  <Grid.ColumnDefinitions>
    <ColumnDefinition/>
    <ColumnDefinition/>
  </Grid.ColumnDefinitions>
  <!-- These are both in cell 0,0 -->
  <Button Canvas.ZIndex="1" Foreground="Aqua" Content="on top"/>
  <Button Content="on bottom"/>
  <!-- These are both in cell 1,1 -->
  <Button Grid.Row="1" Grid.Column="1" Content="on bottom"/>
  <Button Grid.Row="1" Grid.Column="1" Foreground="Red" Content="on top"/>
</Grid>
```

The button with blue text is on top only because of its `Canvas.ZIndex` setting. The button with the red text is on top because it appears after the other button in the XAML file. Of course, making one visible button completely overlap another doesn't make much sense, as only the topmost one can be tapped. But

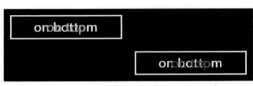

FIGURE 4.4   Four buttons in a 2x2 grid, demonstrating overlap and the use of `Canvas.ZIndex`.

there can be many reasons to overlap (completely or partially) all sorts of items. Even this chapter's app finds a good reason to overlap buttons in the same grid cell, as you'll see later.

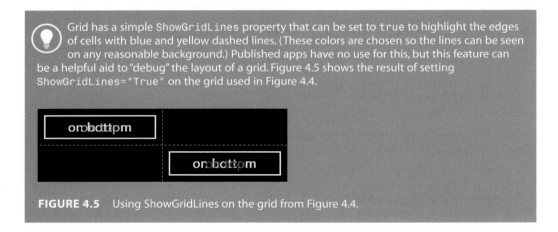

Grid has a simple `ShowGridLines` property that can be set to `true` to highlight the edges of cells with blue and yellow dashed lines. (These colors are chosen so the lines can be seen on any reasonable background.) Published apps have no use for this, but this feature can be a helpful aid to "debug" the layout of a grid. Figure 4.5 shows the result of setting `ShowGridLines="True"` on the grid used in Figure 4.4.

FIGURE 4.5   Using ShowGridLines on the grid from Figure 4.4.

Spanning Multiple Cells

Grid has two more attachable properties—`Grid.RowSpan` and `Grid.ColumnSpan`, both 1 by default—that enable a single element to stretch across multiple consecutive rows and/or columns. (If a value greater than the number of rows or columns is given, the element simply spans the maximum number that it can.) Therefore, the following XAML produces the result in Figure 4.6:

```
<Grid ShowGridLines="True">
  <Grid.RowDefinitions>
    <RowDefinition/>
    <RowDefinition/>
    <RowDefinition/>
  </Grid.RowDefinitions>
  <Grid.ColumnDefinitions>
    <ColumnDefinition/>
    <ColumnDefinition/>
    <ColumnDefinition/>
  </Grid.ColumnDefinitions>
  <Button Grid.ColumnSpan="3" Content="0,0 - 0,2"/>
  <Button Grid.Row="1" Grid.RowSpan="2" Content="1,0 - 2,0"/>
  <Button Grid.Row="1" Grid.Column="1" Grid.RowSpan="2" Grid.ColumnSpan="2"
          Content="1,1 - 2,2"/>
</Grid>
```

Customizing Rows and Column Sizes

Unlike a normal element's `Width` and `Height` properties, `RowDefinition`'s and `ColumnDefinition`'s corresponding properties do not default to `Auto`. Also, they are of type `GridLength` rather than `double`, enabling grid to uniquely support three different types of sizing:

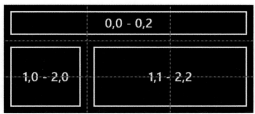

FIGURE 4.6   Using `Grid.RowSpan` and `Grid.ColumnSpan` to make elements expand beyond their cell.

→ **Absolute sizing**—Setting `Width` or `Height` to a number of pixels. Unlike the other two types of sizing, an absolute-sized row or column does not grow or shrink as the size of the grid or size of the elements changes.

→ **Autosizing**—Setting `Width` or `Height` to `Auto`, which gives child elements the space they need and no more. For a row, this is the height of the tallest element, and for a column, this is the width of the widest element.

→ **Proportional sizing (sometimes called *star sizing*)**—Setting `Width` or `Height` to special syntax to divide available space into equal-sized regions or regions based on fixed ratios. A proportional-sized row or column grows and shrinks as the grid is resized.

Absolute sizing and autosizing are straightforward, but proportional sizing needs more explanation. It is done with *star syntax* that works as follows:

→ When a row's height or column's width is set to *, it occupies all the remaining space.

→ When multiple rows or columns use *, the remaining space is divided equally between them.

→ Rows and columns can place a coefficient in front of the asterisk (like 2* or 5.5*) to take proportionately more space than other columns using the asterisk notation. A column with width 2* is always twice the width of a column with width * (which is shorthand for 1*) *in the same grid*. A column with width 5.5* is always twice the width of a column with width 2.75* *in the same grid*.

The "remaining space" is the height or width of the grid minus any rows or columns that use absolute sizing or autosizing. Figure 4.7 demonstrates these different scenarios with simple columns in four different grids.

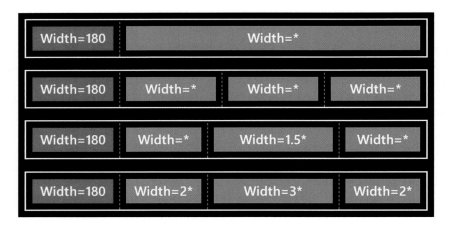

FIGURE 4.7   Proportional-sized grid columns in action.

The default height and width for grid rows and columns is *, *not* Auto. That's why the rows and columns are evenly distributed in Figures 4.2 through 4.6.

 RowDefinition defines MinHeight/MaxHeight properties, and ColumnDefinition defines MinWidth/MaxWidth properties. This can be handy for ensuring that proportional-sized rows and columns do not end up truncating elements or stretching them to ridiculous proportions when undergoing the drastic layout change from portrait to landscape and vice versa.

Why doesn't grid provide built-in support for percentage sizing, like in an HTML table?

The most common use of percentage sizing in HTML—setting the width or height of an item to 100%—is already handled by setting an element's `HorizontalAlignment` or `VerticalAlignment` properties described in the next section. For more complicated scenarios, grid's proportional sizing effectively provides percentage sizing, but with a syntax that takes a little getting used to. For example, to have a column always occupy 25% of a grid's width, you can mark it with * and ensure that the remaining columns have a total width of 3*.

Microsoft chose this syntax so developers wouldn't have to worry about keeping the sum of percentages equal to 100 as rows or columns are dynamically added or removed. In addition, the fact that proportional sizing is specified relative to the remaining space (as opposed to the entire grid) makes its behavior more understandable than an HTML table when mixing proportional rows or columns with fixed-size rows or columns.

How can I give grid cells background colors, padding, and borders, as with cells of an HTML table?

There is no intrinsic mechanism to give grid cells such properties, but you can simulate them pretty easily, thanks to the fact that multiple elements can appear in any cell. To give a cell a background color, you can plop in a `Rectangle` element with the desired `Fill` brush, which stretches to fill the cell by default. To give a cell padding, you can use autosizing and set the margin on the appropriate child element. For borders, you can again use a `Rectangle` element but set its `Stroke` property to the desired brush, or you can use a `Border` element instead.

Just be sure to add such rectangles or borders to the grid *before* adding any of the other children (or explicitly mark them with `Canvas.ZIndex`), so their Z order puts them behind the main content.

• • •

Using `GridLength` in C#

In C#, you can use one of two constructors to construct the appropriate `GridLength` structure. The key is a `GridUnitType` enumeration that identifies which of the three types of values you're creating.

For absolute sizing, you can use the constructor that takes a simple double value (such as 180):

```
GridLength length = new GridLength(180);
```

or you can use another constructor that accepts a `GridUnitType` value:

```
GridLength length = new GridLength(180, GridUnitType.Pixel);
```

In both examples, the length is 180 pixels.

`Double.NaN` isn't a supported value for the `GridLength` constructors, so for autosizing you must use `GridUnitType.Auto`:

```
GridLength length = new GridLength(0, GridUnitType.Auto);
```

The number passed as the first parameter is ignored. However, the preferred approach is to simply use the static `GridLength.Auto` property, which returns an instance of `GridLength` just like the one created by the preceding line of code. For proportional sizing, you can pass a number along with `GridUnitType.Star`:

```
GridLength length = new GridLength(2, GridUnitType.Star);
```

This example is equivalent to specifying 2* in XAML. You can pass 1 with `GridUnitType.Star` to get the equivalent of *.

The User Interface

Listing 4.1 contains the XAML for Stopwatch, which uses a seven-row, two-column grid to arrange its user interface in a manner that works well for both portrait and landscape orientations. Figure 4.8 shows the user interface in two orientations, and with grid lines showing to help you visualize how the grid is being used.

FIGURE 4.8   The Stopwatch user interface with grid lines showing.

LISTING 4.1   `MainPage.xaml`—The User Interface for Stopwatch

```
<phone:PhoneApplicationPage
    x:Class="WindowsPhoneApp.MainPage"
    xmlns="http://schemas.microsoft.com/winfx/2006/xaml/presentation"
    xmlns:x="http://schemas.microsoft.com/winfx/2006/xaml"
    xmlns:phone="clr-namespace:Microsoft.Phone.Controls;assembly=Microsoft.Phone"
    xmlns:shell="clr-namespace:Microsoft.Phone.Shell;assembly=Microsoft.Phone"
```

LISTING 4.1 Continued

```xml
      xmlns:local="clr-namespace:WindowsPhoneApp"
      FontFamily="{StaticResource PhoneFontFamilyNormal}"
      FontSize="{StaticResource PhoneFontSizeNormal}"
      Foreground="{StaticResource PhoneForegroundBrush}"
      SupportedOrientations="PortraitOrLandscape"
      shell:SystemTray.IsVisible="True">

  <!-- Application bar containing the orientation lock button -->
  <phone:PhoneApplicationPage.ApplicationBar>
    <shell:ApplicationBar>
      <shell:ApplicationBarIconButton Text="lock screen"
        IconUri="/Shared/Images/appbar.orientationUnlocked.png"
        Click="OrientationLockButton_Click"/>
    </shell:ApplicationBar>
  </phone:PhoneApplicationPage.ApplicationBar>

  <Grid>
    <!-- This grid has 6 rows of varying heights -->
    <Grid.RowDefinitions>
      <RowDefinition Height="Auto"/>
      <RowDefinition Height="Auto"/>
      <RowDefinition Height="Auto"/>
      <RowDefinition Height="4*"/>
      <RowDefinition Height="Auto"/>
      <RowDefinition Height="3*"/>
    </Grid.RowDefinitions>
    <!-- This grid has 2 equal-width columns -->
    <Grid.ColumnDefinitions>
      <ColumnDefinition/>
      <ColumnDefinition/>
    </Grid.ColumnDefinitions>

    <!-- Row 0: The standard header, with some tweaks -->
    <StackPanel Grid.Row="0" Grid.ColumnSpan="2" Margin="24,16,0,12">
      <TextBlock Text="STOPWATCH" Margin="-1,0,0,0"
                 FontFamily="{StaticResource PhoneFontFamilySemiBold}"
                 FontSize="{StaticResource PhoneFontSizeMedium}"/>
    </StackPanel>

    <!-- Row 1: "current lap" text block -->
    <TextBlock Grid.Row="1" Grid.ColumnSpan="2" Text="current lap"
               HorizontalAlignment="Right"
               Style="{StaticResource PhoneTextSubtleStyle}"/>
```

LISTING 4.1   Continued

```xml
<!-- Row 2: current lap time display -->
<local:TimeSpanDisplay x:Name="CurrentLapTimeDisplay" Grid.Row="2"
                       Grid.ColumnSpan="2" DigitWidth="18"
                       HorizontalAlignment="Right" Margin="0,0,12,0"
                       FontSize="{StaticResource PhoneFontSizeLarge}"/>

<!-- Row 3: total time display and progress bar -->
<local:TimeSpanDisplay x:Name="TotalTimeDisplay" Grid.Row="3"
                       Grid.ColumnSpan="2" DigitWidth="67"
                       HorizontalAlignment="Center"
                       FontFamily="Segoe WP Black" FontSize="108" />
<ProgressBar x:Name="LapProgressBar" Grid.Row="3" Grid.ColumnSpan="2"
             VerticalAlignment="Top" />

<!-- Row 4: the buttons:
            Column 0: start and stop
            Column 1: reset and lap -->
<Button Name="StartButton" Grid.Row="4" Content="start" Margin="12,0,0,0"
        Foreground="White" BorderBrush="{StaticResource PhoneAccentBrush}"
        Background="{StaticResource PhoneAccentBrush}"
        Click="StartButton_Click" local:Tilt.IsEnabled="True" />
<Button Name="StopButton" Grid.Row="4" Content="stop" Margin="12,0,0,0"
        Foreground="White" BorderBrush="#E51400" Background="#E51400"
        Click="StopButton_Click" local:Tilt.IsEnabled="True"
        Visibility="Collapsed"/>
<Button Name="ResetButton" Grid.Row="4" Grid.Column="1" Content="reset"
        IsEnabled="False" Margin="0,0,12,0" Click="ResetButton_Click"
        local:Tilt.IsEnabled="True" />
<Button Name="LapButton" Grid.Row="4" Grid.Column="1" Content="lap"
        Margin="0,0,12,0" Click="LapButton_Click" local:Tilt.IsEnabled="True"
        Visibility="Collapsed"/>

<!-- Row 5: the list of laps -->
<ScrollViewer Grid.Row="5" Grid.ColumnSpan="2"
              FontSize="{StaticResource PhoneFontSizeLarge}">
  <StackPanel x:Name="LapsStackPanel" />
</ScrollViewer>
  </Grid>
</phone:PhoneApplicationPage>
```

Notes:

→ The auto-sized rows are important not just for sequential stacking behavior at the top, but to ensure that the contents in those rows are never clipped. With the remaining space, the row with the total elapsed time is given 33% more height than the row with the list of laps (4* versus 3*). This was chosen to ensure that there's enough room for the total elapsed time in a landscape orientation.

→ On my first attempt at creating this user interface, I used a text block for both time displays (in rows 2 and 3), but realized there is a problem with this approach. Segoe WP (and its related fonts) are proportional-width fonts, so the time displays jiggle as the values change. Windows Phone ships one fixed-width font—Courier New—but using this font looked out-of-place. Therefore, this page instead uses a `TimeSpanDisplay` user control that is able to display time values in a fixed-width (non-jiggly) fashion, even with a proportional-width font like Segoe WP. This difference is demonstrated in Figure 4.9, involving the most narrow digit (1) and the widest digit (4). You'll see how this user control was created at the end of this chapter.

0:11.4   Courier New (Bold) doesn't jiggle thanks to fixed-width characters, but it doesn't have a great aesthetic.

0:11.4   Segoe WP Black looks appropriate but jiggles due to changing number widths.

0:11.4   `TimeSpanDisplay` places each digit in a fixed-width container, regardless of font.

FIGURE 4.9   Three potential display options for the same time span.

→ The line that shows the current lap progress compared to the previous lap is implemented with a progress bar in row 3. Progress bars are discussed in the upcoming "Progress Bars" section.

→ In row 4, the start/stop button on the left is actually two different buttons, with only one visible at a time. The same is true for reset and lap on the right. This makes the code-behind a bit nicer, but the primary motivation for this is that the start and stop buttons have different background colors. If they were combined into a single button, we would need to change its background dynamically, and this is harder than you would expect. (This is explained in an upcoming FAQ sidebar.)

→ Unlike the application bar and status bar that are special shell controls, normal Silverlight elements do not have a Boolean `IsVisible` property. Instead, they have a `Visibility` property that can be set to either `Visible` or `Collapsed` (`Visibility.Visible` or `Visibility.Collapsed` in C#). This oddity comes from

Silverlight's roots in Windows Presentation Foundation (WPF), which defines a third possible value for `Visibility`.

→ The buttons are given outer margins to make the space on their outer edges match the space between the left and right buttons (24 pixels). The stop button is given a red background, but it uses the value `#E51400` rather than simply `red` because the former is the official red color available as one of the theme accent color choices. (Silverlight's definition of `red`, on the other hand, is the standard `#FF0000`.)

→ Now that you're familiar with attachable properties, you should recognize that the tilt effect applied to the buttons is a class called `Tilt` with an attachable property called `IsEnabled`. `Tilt.IsEnabled` is used throughout this book. The code for this class is included with this book's source code.

→ Although the bottom row starts out empty, a new item gets dynamically added to the stack panel from the code-behind each time `LapButton` is tapped. The stack panel is wrapped in a scroll viewer so it can scroll when the list is taller than the grid row.

→ The `PhoneAccentBrush` theme resource is used as the background (and border) of `StartButton`. This refers to the accent color from the user's current theme. Combined with the fact that the progress bar automatically uses the same color, this app conforms to user preferences nicely. Figure 4.10 shows how the appearance changes when the light theme is used with a pink accent color.

FIGURE 4.10   The progress bar and customized start button use the accent color from the user's theme.

Two aspects of this user interface deserve a deeper look: its use of alignment properties, and its use of a progress bar.

Alignment

Often, elements are given more space than they need. How they use this space depends on their values of HorizontalAlignment and VerticalAlignment. Just about any sophisticated user interface will have some occasions to customize the alignment of elements. Indeed, Listing 4.1 uses these properties on a few elements to override the default behavior that would cause them to stretch and fill their grid cell. Each property has a corresponding enumeration with the same name, giving the following options:

→ **HorizontalAlignment**—Left, Center, Right, and Stretch

→ **VerticalAlignment**—Top, Center, Bottom, and Stretch

Stretch is the default value for both properties, although some elements implicitly override this setting. The effects of HorizontalAlignment can easily be seen by placing a few buttons in a vertical stack panel and marking them with each value from the enumeration:

```
<StackPanel>
  <Button HorizontalAlignment="Left" Content="Left" Background="Red"/>
  <Button HorizontalAlignment="Center" Content="Center" Background="Orange"/>
  <Button HorizontalAlignment="Right" Content="Right" Background="Green"/>
  <Button HorizontalAlignment="Stretch" Content="Stretch" Background="Blue"/>
</StackPanel>
```

The rendered result appears in Figure 4.11.

These alignment properties are useful only on an element whose parent has given it more space than it needs. For example, adding VerticalAlignment values to the buttons in Figure 4.11 would make no difference, as each element is already given the exact amount of height it needs (no more, no less). In a horizontal stack panel, VerticalAlignment has an effect but HorizontalAlignment does not. In a grid, both alignments have an effect. For

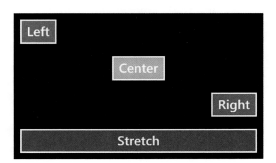

FIGURE 4.11 The effects of HorizontalAlignment on buttons in a stack panel.

example, back in Listing 4.1, the top-aligned progress bar and the center-aligned total time display share the same two grid cells.

This differing behavior of parent panels can sometimes cause surprising results. For example, if the text boxes inside the horizontal stack panel back in Figure 4.1 did not have explicit widths, they would start out extremely narrow and grow as the text inside them grows (occupying as much space as each needs but no more). If you were to place a grid inside a vertical stack panel, it would no longer stretch vertically, and even its proportional-height rows would collapse to nothing if they were left empty!

Content Alignment

In addition to `HorizontalAlignment` and `VerticalAlignment` properties, elements deriving from `Control` also have `Horizontal`**Content**`Alignment` and `Vertical`**Content**`Alignment` properties. These properties determine how a control's *content* fills the space within the control, *if* there is extra space. (Therefore, the relationship between alignment and content alignment is somewhat like the relationship between margins and padding.)

> **Interaction Between** `Stretch` **Alignment and Explicit Sizes**
>
> When an element uses `Stretch` alignment (horizontally or vertically), an explicit `Width` or `Height` setting still takes precedence. `MaxWidth` and `MaxHeight` can overrule stretching, but only when their values are *smaller* than the natural stretched size. Similarly, `MinWidth` and `MinHeight` overrule stretching only when their values are *larger* than the natural stretched size. When `Stretch` is used in a context that constrains the element's size (such as using a hard-coded `Width` or `Height`), it acts like an alignment of `Center` (or `Left` if the element is too large to be centered in its parent).

The content alignment properties are of the same enumeration types as the corresponding alignment properties, so they provide the same options but with different default values. The default value for `HorizontalContentAlignment` is `Left`, and the default value for `VerticalContentAlignment` is `Top`. However, some elements implicitly choose different defaults. Buttons, for example, center their content in both dimensions by default.

Figure 4.12 demonstrates the effects of `HorizontalContentAlignment`, simply by taking the previous XAML snippet and changing the property name as follows:

```
<StackPanel>
  <Button HorizontalContentAlignment="Left" Content="Left" Background="Red"/>
  <Button HorizontalContentAlignment="Center" Content="Center"
        Background="Orange"/>
  <Button HorizontalContentAlignment="Right" Content="Right" Background="Green"/>
  <Button HorizontalContentAlignment="Stretch" Content="Stretch"
        Background="Blue"/>
</StackPanel>
```

The last button in Figure 4.12 probably does not appear as you expected. Internally, it uses a text block to display the "Stretch" string, and that text block is technically stretched. However, text blocks do not support stretching their text in this manner, so the result looks no different than a

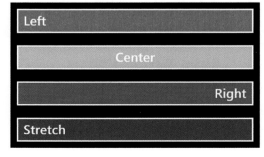

FIGURE 4.12 The effects of `HorizontalContentAlignment` on buttons in a stack panel.

HorizontalContentAlignment of Left. For other types of content, Stretch can indeed have the intended effect.

Progress Bars

This app's use of a progress bar is definitely unorthodox, but appropriate in this author's opinion. A progress bar has three basic properties: Value (0 by default), Minimum (0 by default), and Maximum (100 by default). As progress is being made (whatever that means for your app), you can update Value until it matches Maximum, which should mean that the work being measured is complete. You can choose different values of Minimum and Maximum if it's more convenient for you to work on a scale different than 0–100.

In addition, progress bars have two properties for customizing their appearance:

→ **IsIndeterminate**—When set to true, this turns the bar into the standard "dancing dots" progress animation that runs as long as the progress bar is visible, making the values of Value, Minimum, and Maximum irrelevant. This is meant for times when you have no clue how long something will take, such as when you're waiting for a network request to complete.

→ **Orientation**—This is set to Horizontal by default but can be set to Vertical to make progress go from bottom to top rather than left to right. Vertical progress bars are unusual, however, and the design guidelines recommend only using horizontal ones.

> (!) **Indeterminate progress bars can hurt your app's performance!**
> See Chapter 18, "Cocktails," for more details.

The Code-Behind

Listing 4.2 contains the code-behind for MainPage, which must perform all the timer logic in response to the four main buttons, implement the orientation lock feature, and persist/restore the app's state across multiple uses.

LISTING 4.2   MainPage.xaml.cs—The Code-Behind for Stopwatch

```
using System;
using System.Collections.Generic;
using System.Windows;
using System.Windows.Controls;
using System.Windows.Navigation;
using System.Windows.Threading;
using Microsoft.Phone.Controls;
using Microsoft.Phone.Shell;

namespace WindowsPhoneApp
{
```

LISTING 4.2   Continued

```
public partial class MainPage : PhoneApplicationPage
{
  // Use a Setting for each "normal" variable, so we can automatically persist
  // the values and easily restore them
  Setting<TimeSpan> totalTime =
    new Setting<TimeSpan>("TotalTime", TimeSpan.Zero);
  Setting<TimeSpan> currentLapTime =
    new Setting<TimeSpan>("CurrentLapTime", TimeSpan.Zero);
  Setting<TimeSpan> previousLapTime =
    new Setting<TimeSpan>("PreviousLapTime", TimeSpan.Zero);
  Setting<List<TimeSpan>> lapList =
    new Setting<List<TimeSpan>>("LapList", new List<TimeSpan>());
  Setting<DateTime> previousTick =
    new Setting<DateTime>("PreviousTick", DateTime.MinValue);

  // Two more pieces of state that we only use so we can return to the page
  // in the same state that we left it
  Setting<SupportedPageOrientation> savedSupportedOrientations =
    new Setting<SupportedPageOrientation>("SavedSupportedOrientations",
      SupportedPageOrientation.PortraitOrLandscape);
  Setting<bool> wasRunning =
    new Setting<bool>("WasRunning", false);

  // A timer, so we can update the display every 100 milliseconds
  DispatcherTimer timer =
    new DispatcherTimer {Interval = TimeSpan.FromSeconds(.1) };

  // The single button on the application bar
  IApplicationBarIconButton orientationLockButton;

  public MainPage()
  {
    InitializeComponent();
    this.orientationLockButton =
      this.ApplicationBar.Buttons[0] as IApplicationBarIconButton;
    this.timer.Tick += Timer_Tick;
  }

  protected override void OnNavigatedTo(NavigationEventArgs e)
  {
    base.OnNavigatedTo(e);

    // Update the time displays and progress bar with the data from last time
    // (which has been automatically restored)
```

LISTING 4.2   Continued

```
  ShowCurrentTime();

  // Refill the lap list with the data from last time
  foreach (TimeSpan lapTime in this.lapList.Value)
    InsertLapInList(lapTime);

  // If we previously left the page with a non-zero total time, then the reset
  // button was enabled. Enable it again:
  if (this.totalTime.Value > TimeSpan.Zero)
    this.ResetButton.IsEnabled = true;

  // Restore the orientation setting to whatever it was last time
  this.SupportedOrientations = this.savedSupportedOrientations.Value;

  // If the restored value is not PortraitOrLandscape, then the orientation
  // has been locked. Change the state of the application bar button to
  // reflect this.
  if (this.SupportedOrientations !=
    SupportedPageOrientation.PortraitOrLandscape)
  {
    this.orientationLockButton.Text = "unlock";
    this.orientationLockButton.IconUri = new Uri(
      "/Shared/Images/appbar.orientationLocked.png", UriKind.Relative);
  }

  // If the page was left while running, automatically start running again
  // to give the illusion of running in the background. The time will
  // accurately reflect the time spent away from the app, thanks to the saved
  // values of totalTime, currentLapTime, and previousTick.
  if (this.wasRunning.Value)
    Start();
}

void Timer_Tick(object sender, EventArgs e)
{
  // Determine how much time has passed since the last tick.
  // In most cases, this will be around 100 milliseconds (but not exactly).
  // In some cases, this could be a very large amount of time, if the app
  // was exited without stopping the timer. This is what gives the illusion
  // that the timer was still running the whole time.
  TimeSpan delta = DateTime.UtcNow - this.previousTick.Value;
```

LISTING 4.2   Continued

```
    // Remember the current time for the sake of the next Timer_Tick call
    this.previousTick.Value += delta;

    // Update the total time and current lap time
    this.totalTime.Value += delta;
    this.currentLapTime.Value += delta;

    // Refresh the UI
    ShowCurrentTime();
  }

  void ShowCurrentTime()
  {
    // Update the two numeric displays
    this.TotalTimeDisplay.Time = this.totalTime.Value;
    this.CurrentLapTimeDisplay.Time = this.currentLapTime.Value;

    // Update the progress bar (and ensure its maximum value is consistent
    // with the length of the previous lap, which occasionally changes)
    this.LapProgressBar.Maximum = this.previousLapTime.Value.TotalSeconds;
    this.LapProgressBar.Value = this.currentLapTime.Value.TotalSeconds;
  }

  void StartButton_Click(object sender, RoutedEventArgs e)
  {
    // Reset previousTick so the calculations start from the current time
    this.previousTick.Value = DateTime.UtcNow;
    Start();
  }

  void StopButton_Click(object sender, RoutedEventArgs e)
  {
    Stop();
  }

  void ResetButton_Click(object sender, RoutedEventArgs e)
  {
    Reset();
  }

  void LapButton_Click(object sender, RoutedEventArgs e)
  {
    // Add a new entry to the list on the screen
    InsertLapInList(this.currentLapTime.Value);
```

LISTING 4.2   Continued

```csharp
        // Add the new piece of data to the list of values
        this.lapList.Value.Add(this.currentLapTime.Value);

        // This is the start of a new lap, so update our bookkeeping
        this.previousLapTime.Value = this.currentLapTime.Value;
        this.currentLapTime.Value = TimeSpan.Zero;
    }

    void Start()
    {
      this.ResetButton.IsEnabled = true;

        // Toggle the visibility of the buttons and the progress bar
        this.StartButton.Visibility = Visibility.Collapsed;
        this.StopButton.Visibility = Visibility.Visible;
        this.ResetButton.Visibility = Visibility.Collapsed;
        this.LapButton.Visibility = Visibility.Visible;

        // Start the timer
        this.timer.Start();

        // Remember that the timer was running if the page is left before stopping
        this.wasRunning.Value = true;
    }

    void Stop()
    {
        // Toggle the visibility of the buttons and the progress bar
        this.StartButton.Visibility = Visibility.Visible;
        this.StopButton.Visibility = Visibility.Collapsed;
        this.ResetButton.Visibility = Visibility.Visible;
        this.LapButton.Visibility = Visibility.Collapsed;

        // Stop the timer
        this.timer.Stop();

        // Remember that the timer was stopped if the page is left
        this.wasRunning.Value = false;
    }

    void Reset()
    {
      // Reset all data
      this.totalTime.Value = TimeSpan.Zero;
```

LISTING 4.2   Continued

```
    this.currentLapTime.Value = TimeSpan.Zero;
    this.previousLapTime.Value = TimeSpan.Zero;
    this.lapList.Value.Clear();

    // Reset the UI
    this.ResetButton.IsEnabled = false;
    this.LapsStackPanel.Children.Clear();
    ShowCurrentTime();
}

void InsertLapInList(TimeSpan timeSpan)
{
    int lapNumber = LapsStackPanel.Children.Count + 1;

    // Dynamically create a new grid to represent the new lap entry in the list
    Grid grid = new Grid();

    // The grid has "lap N" docked on the left, where N is 1, 2, 3, ...
    grid.Children.Add(new TextBlock { Text = "lap " + lapNumber,
      Margin = new Thickness(24, 0, 0, 0) });

    // The grid has a TimeSpanDisplay instance docked on the right that
    // shows the length of the lap
    TimeSpanDisplay display = new TimeSpanDisplay { Time = timeSpan,
      DigitWidth = 18, HorizontalAlignment = HorizontalAlignment.Right,
      Margin = new Thickness(0, 0, 24, 0) };
    grid.Children.Add(display);

    // Insert the new grid at the beginning of the StackPanel
    LapsStackPanel.Children.Insert(0, grid);
}

// The "orientation lock" feature
void OrientationLockButton_Click(object sender, EventArgs e)
{
    // Check the value of SupportedOrientations to see if we're currently
    // "locked" to a value other than PortraitOrLandscape.
    if (this.SupportedOrientations !=
      SupportedPageOrientation.PortraitOrLandscape)
    {
      // We are locked, so unlock now
      this.SupportedOrientations = SupportedPageOrientation.PortraitOrLandscape;

      // Change the state of the application bar button to reflect this
```

LISTING 4.2   Continued

```
      this.orientationLockButton.Text = "lock screen";
      this.orientationLockButton.IconUri = new Uri(
        "/Shared/Images/appbar.orientationUnlocked.png", UriKind.Relative);
    }
    else
    {
      // We are unlocked, so lock to the current orientation now
      if (IsMatchingOrientation(PageOrientation.Portrait))
        this.SupportedOrientations = SupportedPageOrientation.Portrait;
      else
        this.SupportedOrientations = SupportedPageOrientation.Landscape;

      // Change the state of the application bar button to reflect this
      this.orientationLockButton.Text = "unlock";
      this.orientationLockButton.IconUri = new Uri(
        "/Shared/Images/appbar.orientationLocked.png", UriKind.Relative);
    }

    // Remember the new setting after the page has been left
    this.savedSupportedOrientations.Value = this.SupportedOrientations;
  }

  bool IsMatchingOrientation(PageOrientation orientation)
  {
    return ((this.Orientation & orientation) == orientation);
  }
  }
}
```

Notes:

→ To keep the app in the state it was previously left in, and to provide the illusion of running in the background, this app has many Setting members. But rather than keeping a separate set of variables and copying the values to/from the corresponding Settings, as done in all previous apps, this app uses each Setting as the primary storage. This simplification doesn't damage the performance of the app, despite the fact that several of these values are updated with every tick of the timer (10 times a second)! That's because the Setting mechanism adds very little overhead. (Internally, the values aren't actually persisted until the app is exiting.)

→ DispatcherTimer is the natural choice for doing the core work of the stopwatch, for the reasons discussed in Chapter 2, "Flashlight."

→ TimeSpans are used throughout this code whenever a length of time is needed, which is a natural choice. TimeSpan not only has many convenient methods for doing calculations and setting or extracting individual components of the time (such as minutes versus seconds), but it also happens to be what gets returned to you when you subtract one `DateTime` from another.

➜ Inside `OnNavigatedTo`, various pieces of the UI are updated to match the current values of the `Settings`. This is not needed for the first run of the app; it is done for the sake of subsequent runs. This includes automatically restarting the timer if it was running when the app was previously left.

➜ No `OnNavigatedFrom` method is needed for this app because all the `Setting` persistence is handled by keeping those members up-to-date at all times.

➜ The timer's `Tick` event handler (`Timer_Tick`) figures out how much time has elapsed so it can update the UI appropriately. Even though the handler is *supposed* to be called every 100 milliseconds, it's important that the code checks to see how much time *actually* elapsed because the exact timing of the event varies. Also, this behavior enables the illusion of running in the background, because when returning to this app, the time of the last tick may have been several minutes ago!

➜ `DateTime.`**`Utc`**`Now` is used to track the elapsed time rather than `DateTime.Now`. This is important for ensuring that the app works correctly if the user changes time zones while the timer is running (or pretending to run in the background). This might not be as far-fetched as it sounds. For example, perhaps a user wishes to time the duration of a cross-country flight.

➜ `ShowCurrentTime`, called from a few places, refreshes both time displays and the progress bar to match the current values. To set the progress bar's `Value` and `Maximum` values, `TimeSpan`'s `TotalSeconds` property is used to get a simple numeric representation of the length of time. `TotalSeconds` is of type `double`, so it has no problem representing a fractional number of seconds. (The choice of seconds is arbitrary. `TotalMinutes`, `TotalHours`, and so on, could have been used instead.)

➜ The `Start` and `Stop` methods not only start and stop the timer, but toggle the visibility of the buttons so "stop" and "lap" are seen when running whereas "start" and "reset" are seen when stopped.

➜ `InsertLapInList` is interesting because this is the first time we've created new UI elements on-the-fly. Every time the lap button is pressed, this is called to add a new single-cell grid to the laps stack panel at the bottom of the page. (Grid is used because it is the easiest way to get the desired display. This takes advantage of the fact that a grid in a vertical stack panel stretches horizontally but stays as small as it can vertically.) The grid is given two children: a text block providing the lap number, and another instance of a `TimeSpanDisplay` to display the corresponding lap time. Again, this `TimeSpanDisplay` could have been just another text block instead if we didn't care about having a proportional-width time display. Although both elements are added to the same (one and only) grid cell, `HorizontalAlignment` is used to right-align the lap time so it doesn't visually overlap the lap number. This new grid is equivalent to the following grid defined in XAML, for a lap number of 1 and a time of `0:14.2`:

```
<Grid>
  <TextBlock Text="lap 1" Margin="24,0,0,0"/>
  <local:TimeSpanDisplay Time="0:14.2" DigitWidth="18"
                         HorizontalAlignment="Right" Margin="0,0,24,0"/>
</Grid>
```

→ Although both elements are added to the new grid's `Children` collection inside `InsertLapInList`, nothing actually gets added to the page until the grid is placed in the stack panel's `Children` collection. Notice that `Insert` is called with an index of 0, rather than the simpler `Add` method. That's because `Add` places the new child at the *end* of the collection, but we want each new lap to appear at the *beginning*.

→ `OrientationLockButton_Click` and the `IsMatchingOrientation` helper method handle the implementation of orientation lock, discussed in the next section.

Orientation Lock

The idea behind the orientation lock is simple. When "unlocked," the page's `SupportedOrientations` property should be set to `PortraitOrLandscape`. When "locked," the property should be updated to match whatever the current orientation is, so it stops responding to future orientation changes until "unlocked." The implementation, however, is not quite that simple. `SupportedOrientations` can only be set to one of the three values in the `SupportedPageOrientation` enumeration, whereas the page's `Orientation` property is actually a different enumeration type called `PageOrientation`.

`PageOrientation` defines *seven* values: `Landscape`, `LandscapeLeft`, `LandscapeRight`, `Portrait`, `PortraitUp`, `PortraitDown`, and `None`. However, a page's `Orientation` property will only ever report one of three values: `LandscapeLeft`, `LandscapeRight`, or `PortraitUp`. `PortraitDown` (an upside-down portrait mode) is not supported and `None` is a dummy value. The reason the generic `Landscape` and `Portrait` values are in the list is that `PageOrientation` is a bit-flags enumeration. This enables you to either check for an exact orientation (like `LandscapeLeft`) or a group of orientations (which would only apply to `Landscape`). Therefore, to reliably check for a specific value *or* a group of values, you should perform a bit-wise AND with the desired value. This is exactly what is done by the `IsMatchingOrientation` method.

This orientation lock implementation has a weakness!

Because setting the page's `SupportedOrientations` property to Landscape does not distinguish between landscape left and landscape right, the "locked" app will still switch between these two orientations as you rotate the phone accordingly. Fortunately, the main motivation for locking the orientation is to avoid portrait/landscape switches, which this technique handles just fine. Also, it's pretty hard to accidentally rotate the phone from one landscape orientation to another, so most users will probably never realize that this limitation exists.

Figure 4.13 shows the result of locking to the portrait orientation and then tilting the phone sideways.

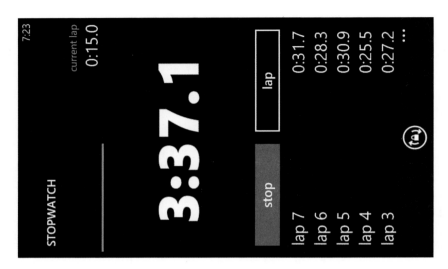

FIGURE 4.13   Locked to the portrait orientation, even when the phone is held in a landscape position.

Although the orientation lock button initially has text "lock screen," the code toggles this text to "unlock" and back. Ideally it would have said "lock orientation" and "unlock orientation"—or at least a symmetric "lock screen" and "unlock screen"—but these options are too long to fit.

In each case, the icon represents the current state rather than the result of the action (e.g. the button for locking shows an *unlocked* icon and vice versa), as shown in Figure 4.14. This seems like the more appropriate choice, much like a mute/unmute button that shows a muted state even though clicking it would *unmute* the speaker.

FIGURE 4.14   The two states of the orientation lock button.

The `TimeSpanDisplay` **User Control**

To show the numbers in a time display like a fixed-width font, even when the font is *not* a fixed-width font, a horizontal stack panel can do the trick. The idea is to add each character of the string as an individual element. The key is to give each element displaying a number a uniform width that's wide enough for every digit. The nonnumeric parts of the text (the colon and period) should be left at their natural width, to prevent the display from looking odd. For the best results, each digit should be centered inside the space allocated to it. Figure 4.15 demonstrates this idea.

FIGURE 4.15   To prevent jiggling from changing digits, each character is added to a horizontal stack panel, and each digit is given a fixed width.

A single-row grid could also work, but a stack panel is easier to work with when you've got an unbounded number of children.

Because Stopwatch needs this same kind of time display in multiple places (one for the total time, one for the current lap time, and one for each previous lap time), it makes sense to encapsulate the UI and logic for this display into a control that can be used multiple times, just like a button or a text box.

> Although a grid is the most powerful panel, a stack panel is often a better choice when dealing with an indeterminate number of child elements. Generally speaking, a stack panel also provides better performance than grid because its layout algorithm is not as complex.

Silverlight provides two mechanisms for creating your own control. One approach produces what is often called a *custom control*, and the other approach produces a *user control*. User controls have some constraints that custom controls don't have, but they are also much easier to create. In addition, creating a user control is usually good enough, especially if your motivation is reuse of the control among your own apps. For the most part, creating a custom control is unnecessary unless you're planning on broadly releasing it as part of a library for others to use.

Don't get confused by the *user control* term; it's a long-standing term used by Microsoft to refer to custom controls that are easy to create. Think of it like "user-created control," where the user is actually you, the developer. Therefore, this app's `TimeSpanDisplay` class is a user control, and this section shows how it is created. Custom controls are covered in Chapter 19, "Animation Lab."

To add a new user control to a Visual Studio project, you can right-click on the project in Solution Explorer and select Add, New Item…, Windows Phone User Control. Give it a filename other than the default `WindowsPhoneControl1.xaml`—such as `TimeSpanDisplay.xaml` in this case—and press OK. This generates two new files in your project: `TimeSpanDisplay.xaml` and its corresponding code-behind file, `TimeSpanDisplay.xaml.cs`. These two files work the same way as the two files for any page.

The initial contents of `TimeSpanDisplay.xaml` are as follows:

```xml
<UserControl x:Class="WindowsPhoneApp.TimeSpanDisplay"
    xmlns="http://schemas.microsoft.com/winfx/2006/xaml/presentation"
    xmlns:x="http://schemas.microsoft.com/winfx/2006/xaml"
    xmlns:d="http://schemas.microsoft.com/expression/blend/2008"
    xmlns:mc="http://schemas.openxmlformats.org/markup-compatibility/2006"
    mc:Ignorable="d"
    FontFamily="{StaticResource PhoneFontFamilyNormal}"
    FontSize="{StaticResource PhoneFontSizeNormal}"
    Foreground="{StaticResource PhoneForegroundBrush}"
    d:DesignHeight="480" d:DesignWidth="480">

    <Grid x:Name="LayoutRoot" Background="{StaticResource PhoneChromeBrush}">

    </Grid>
</UserControl>
```

This defines a `TimeSpanDisplay` class that derives from `UserControl`. The `PhoneChromeBrush` background and the 480x480 design-time dimensions are completely arbitrary, and are often replaced with something completely different.

The `TimeSpanDisplay.xaml.cs` code-behind file contains the constructor that makes the required `InitializeComponent` call, as follows (omitting the using statements for brevity):

```csharp
namespace WindowsPhoneApplication3
{
  public partial class TimeSpanDisplay : UserControl
  {
    public TimeSpanDisplay()
    {
      InitializeComponent();
    }
  }
}
```

With this in our project, we can now change the contents of both files to create the control that is needed by the rest of the app. Listing 4.3 contains the updated XAML file.

LISTING 4.3   `TimeSpanDisplay.xaml`—The User Interface for the `TimeSpanDisplay` User Control

```xml
<UserControl x:Class="WindowsPhoneApp.TimeSpanDisplay"
    xmlns="http://schemas.microsoft.com/winfx/2006/xaml/presentation"
    xmlns:x="http://schemas.microsoft.com/winfx/2006/xaml"
    VerticalAlignment="Center">
  <StackPanel x:Name="LayoutRoot" Orientation="Horizontal"/>
</UserControl>
```

The XAML got a lot simpler! Unnecessary attributes were removed and the grid was replaced with a horizontal stack panel that gets filled from the code-behind.

 It's often a good idea to remove the font and foreground settings that are placed on an auto-generated user control. By doing so, you enable individual instances of the control to inherit these settings from wherever they end up getting used. Note that this will make the design-time preview in Visual Studio look a bit unusual, because its default fonts and colors do not represent the actual appearance of the control at run-time.

Listing 4.4 contains the updated code-behind file.

LISTING 4.4   TimeSpanDisplay.xaml.cs—The Code-Behind for the TimeSpanDisplay User Control

```
using System;
using System.ComponentModel;
using System.Globalization;
using System.Windows;
using System.Windows.Controls;

namespace WindowsPhoneApp
{
  public partial class TimeSpanDisplay : UserControl
  {
    int digitWidth;
    TimeSpan time;

    public TimeSpanDisplay()
    {
      InitializeComponent();

      // In design mode, show something other than an empty StackPanel
      if (DesignerProperties.IsInDesignTool)
        this.LayoutRoot.Children.Add(new TextBlock { Text = "0:00.0" });
    }

    public int DigitWidth {
      get { return this.digitWidth; }
      set
      {
        this.digitWidth = value;
        // Force a display update using the new width:
        this.Time = this.time;
```

LISTING 4.4   Continued

```
      }
    }

  public TimeSpan Time
  {
    get { return this.time; }
    set
    {
      this.LayoutRoot.Children.Clear();

      // Carve out the appropriate digits and add each individually

      // Support an arbitrary # of minutes digits (with no leading 0)
      string minutesString = value.Minutes.ToString();
      for (int i = 0; i < minutesString.Length; i++)
        AddDigitString(minutesString[i].ToString());

      this.LayoutRoot.Children.Add(new TextBlock { Text = ":" });

      // Seconds (always two digits, including a leading zero if necessary)
      AddDigitString((value.Seconds / 10).ToString());
      AddDigitString((value.Seconds % 10).ToString());

      // Add the decimal separator (a period for en-US)
      this.LayoutRoot.Children.Add(new TextBlock { Text =
        CultureInfo.CurrentUICulture.NumberFormat.NumberDecimalSeparator });

      // The Remainder (always a single digit)
      AddDigitString((value.Milliseconds / 100).ToString());

      this.time = value;
    }
  }

  void AddDigitString(string digitString)
  {
    Border border = new Border { Width = this.DigitWidth };
    border.Child = new TextBlock { Text = digitString,
      HorizontalAlignment = HorizontalAlignment.Center };
    this.LayoutRoot.Children.Add(border);
  }
  }
}
```

Notes:

→ In addition to the Time property for updating the display, this control defines a DigitWidth property so the consumer can customize how wide the slot for each digit should be. This is necessary because the app author can choose the font family, size, and weight, and different values require different widths. When DigitWidth is set, the code in the Time property setter is invoked to be sure that the display respects the new width instantly. Without this, the control would not work properly if the consumer happened to set Time before DigitWidth (which is actually done inside InsertLapInList back in Listing 4.2). Proper properties should be able to be set in any order and behave identically.

→ Inside the Time property, various digits are extracted from the TimeSpan one-by-one leveraging its Minutes, Seconds, and Milliseconds properties. Unlike the TotalMinutes, TotalSeconds, and TotalMilliseconds properties, these are integers and produce only the relevant slice of the time value. (For example, Seconds is 5 for both TimeSpan values of 1:05.1 and 2:05.9.) Note that this code clears the stack panel and recreates all the child elements each time. A more efficient approach would reuse existing elements instead.

→ This code supports an arbitrarily-long number of minutes, despite the fact that the app as-is would have trouble displaying a total time of 100 minutes or more in portrait mode unless the font size is reduced.

→ Rather than hardcoding a period after the seconds value, this code uses the NumberDecimalSeparator property. This ensures a proper display for the phone's current region and language settings.

→ The AddDigitString method is responsible for adding each digit element to the stack panel. Each digit is not just a text block, however. In order to be properly horizontally centered inside the allocated width, it is wrapped inside a simple element called Border. (Text blocks have no HorizontalContentAlignment property, and recall that HorizontalAlignment is meaningless on an element directly inside a horizontal stack panel.) The border is given the appropriate DigitWidth, so the presumably narrower text block inside can be centered with the HorizontalContentAlignment marking. Because of this extra wrapping, the digits would not be aligned with the colon and period text blocks if it weren't for the VerticalAlignment setting placed on the XAML file in Listing 4.3.

→ The constructor leverages the static DesignerProperties.IsInDesignTool property to provide a reasonable display at design-time inside Visual Studio and Expression Blend. Without this code, the instances of the control wouldn't be visible on the design surface of MainPage.xaml because each one starts out as an empty stack panel. With this code, however, they are visible, as shown in Figure 4.16.

FIGURE 4.16 In the Visual Studio designer for `MainPage.xaml`, both instances of
`TimeSpanDisplay` appear as "0:00.0" thanks to the logic inside the control's constructor.

> The Visual Studio and Expression Blend designers invoke the constructor of each element it
> needs to render at design-time, including the constructors of your own user controls. You
> can use the `DesignerProperties.IsInDesignTool` property from the
> `System.ComponentModel` namespace in your constructor (or code called from your constructor)
> to provide special design-time behavior. Although `TimeSpanDisplay` uses this to add extra
> design-time behavior, this property is instead often used to avoid doing unnecessary work at
> design-time.

The Finished Product

When first starting, the progress bar is completely filled.

After pressing the lap button, the progress bar compares the ongoing lap to lap 1.

When the timer is stopped, you can restart where you left off or reset everything.

chapter 5

RULER

As with a flashlight, a ruler is something that is really handy to have on rare occasions, yet something that you almost never have when you need it. With the Ruler app, you can measure anything on-the-go with the phone already in your pocket!

Ruler shows a standard display of inches (divided into 16ths) and centimeters (divided into millimeters) and enables you to tap and drag on its surface to place a marker line that reveals the precise measurement at that point. Of course, unless you're measuring something shorter than your phone's screen, you'll need some way to move to later sections of the ruler. This is done with left and right buttons. Therefore, the best approach to measure something long is as follows:

1. Align the starting edge of the object with the starting edge of the phone screen.

2. Tap the screen toward the end of the visible ruler to place the marker line on the screen.

3. Place an available finger on the object and align it with the marker line (to remember that precise location).

4. Tap the right button to advance the ruler. This moves the marker line (along with the rest of the ruler) toward the start of the screen.

5. Slide your phone so the new position of the marker line is aligned with your finger that remembered the old position.

6. Repeat steps 2–5 until you've reached the end of the object.

Ruler also has a calibration button for adjusting the space between its lines, as not all Windows Phone screens are the same size.

There are several notable things about this app. Among other things, it is the first landscape-only app in this book, it is the first one to use a canvas, and the first to use some vector graphics (albeit simple ones). This chapter examines canvas and vector graphics features before proceeding to the Ruler app.

The physical size of the phone's screen varies between different Windows Phone models!

Despite the fact that all Windows Phone screens are currently 800x400 pixels, different screens have different pixel density. Therefore, any app that depends on translating pixels into real-world measurements should have a way for the user to adjust the calculation. The Ruler app defaults to an assumed screen length of 2.97 inches, but has a "calibration mode" for adjusting to a wide range.

Canvas

Canvas is the most basic panel. It doesn't have any features for automatically arranging its child elements, such as stretching or stacking them. Instead, it only supports the classic notion of positioning elements with explicit (x,y) coordinates.

You can position elements in a canvas by using its two attachable properties: `Canvas.Left` and `Canvas.Top`. `Canvas.Left` represents the distance between the left edge of the canvas and the left edge of the child element, and `Canvas.Top` represents the distance between the two top edges. When not specified, a value of 0 is assumed, so an element placed in a canvas without any explicit positioning gets rendered in the top-left corner of the canvas. Figure 5.1 demonstrates how the following three buttons render inside the following blue canvas:

```
<Canvas Background="Blue">
  <Button Content="(0,0)"/>
  <Button Canvas.Left="120" Content="(120,0)"/>
  <Button Canvas.Left="30" Canvas.Top="30" Content="(30,30)"/>
</Canvas>
```

As with the other panels, you can use `Canvas.ZIndex` to override the natural ordering of which elements get placed on top of others.

Setting `Canvas.Left` and/or `Canvas.Top` is no different than giving each element an equivalent margin. For example, the following XAML produces the exact same result as seen in Figure 5.1:

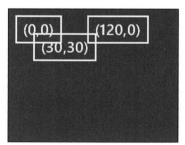

FIGURE 5.1   Three buttons placed in a blue canvas.

```
<Canvas Background="Blue">
  <Button Content="(0,0)"/>
  <Button Margin="120,0,0,0" Content="(120,0)"/>
```

```
    <Button Margin="30,30,0,0" Content="(30,30)"/>
</Canvas>
```

If you use `Canvas.Left` and/or `Canvas.Top` *and* set a margin, the values are added together to produce a combined offset from the top-left corner.

Elements in a canvas are given the exact amount of space they need, so the alignment properties (including any default stretching behavior) never have any effect on such elements. And unlike in a stack panel and grid, elements in a canvas have no layout interaction; one element can never "push" another element. Therefore, putting a right and/or bottom margin on such an element has no effect.

Apps usually use a canvas for arranging images or vector graphics in specific locations. Due to the static layout inside a canvas, such apps also tend to only support one orientation unless the use of canvas is restricted to a small portion of the whole page.

Although the behavior of canvas described so far is straightforward, it has two subtle behaviors related to its size and hit testing, examined next.

Canvas Size

The size of a canvas is irrelevant when it comes to rendering its children. If there is room on the screen, child elements are happily rendered outside of the canvas's bounds. Figure 5.2 demonstrates this for the following updated blue canvas XAML:

```
<Canvas Background="Blue" Width="50" Height="50">
    <Button Content="(0,0)"/>
    <Button Canvas.Left="120" Content="(120,0)"/>
    <Button Canvas.Left="30" Canvas.Top="30" Content="(30,30)"/>
</Canvas>
```

Keep in mind that buttons have 12 pixels of space around their border, which is why each one appears to be shifted down and to the right 12 pixels too far.

Furthermore, the default size of a canvas is effectively 0 pixels tall and 0 pixels wide! This detail normally doesn't matter—if you place a canvas directly inside a page or a grid, it gets stretched to fill the space given to it (as long as it doesn't have explicit width/height

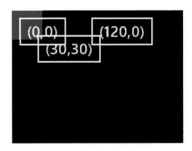

FIGURE 5.2 The blue canvas from Figure 5.1, constrained to 50x50 pixels.

values). But if you place it inside a stack panel, you see the subtle behavior caused by this fact. Figure 5.3 shows the rendered result of the following XAML, which places the canvas from Figure 5.1 between two buttons in a stack panel:

```
<StackPanel>
    <Button Content="above" Background="Orange"/>
```

```
<Canvas Background="Blue">
  <Button Content="(0,0)"/>
  <Button Margin="120,0,0,0" Content="(120,0)"/>
  <Button Margin="30,30,0,0" Content="(30,30)"/>
</Canvas>
<Button Content="below" Background="Red" Opacity=".5"/>
</StackPanel>
```

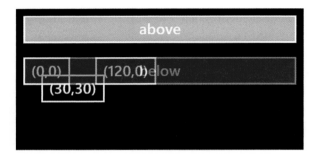

FIGURE 5.3   The blue canvas from Figure 5.1, stacked between two buttons.

Most people would expect to see the "above" button above the canvas *and* the "below" button below it. But because the canvas has a height of 0, the "below" button gets stacked immedi-

Just like the application bar, any Silverlight UI element can be given an opacity anywhere from 0 to 1.

ately below the "above" button, overlapping the canvas and its contents. (The "below" button is given a reduced opacity so you can see the two buttons that are completely obscured.) You also see none of the canvas's blue background because of its size.

To avoid the overlapping behavior, the canvas needs to be given an explicit height, for example:

```
<StackPanel>
  <Button Content="above" Background="Orange"/>
  <Canvas Background="Blue" Height="100">
    <Button Content="(0,0)"/>
    <Button Margin="120,0,0,0" Content="(120,0)"/>
    <Button Margin="30,30,0,0" Content="(30,30)"/>
  </Canvas>
  <Button Content="below" Background="Red" Opacity=".5"/>
</StackPanel>
```

The result of doing this is shown in Figure 5.4. Notice that we didn't need to give the canvas an explicit width. That's because the vertical stack panel is stretching it horizontally, as with the buttons.

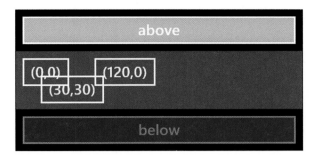

FIGURE 5.4   The blue canvas from Figure 5.1, stacked between two buttons and given an explicit height of 100 pixels.

Hit Testing

Hit testing refers to the detection of taps, drags, and other gestures on an element. A canvas can detect gestures (e.g. raise `MouseLeftButtonDown` and other events) within its own area as well as within the area of its children, *even when these children are outside of the canvas's bounds.* Because the size of the canvas is not always intuitive, the resulting hit testing area can be just as unintuitive when the canvas does not have a visible background color.

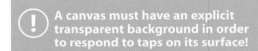

A canvas must have an explicit transparent background in order to respond to taps on its surface!

The default `null` value for a canvas's Background property is like an open window; there is nothing to tap on. Setting the background to `Transparent` is like closing the window. You can still see through the window, but you can now tap anywhere on it.

Another subtlety is that the default background for canvas is not transparent, but rather `null`. A `null` background looks no different than a transparent background, but it does not detect any gestures. (Gestures on its children are still detected.) An explicit transparent background, on the other hand, detects taps on its surface.

Vector Graphics

Both Silverlight and XNA support using images in your user interface, but Silverlight also supports vector graphics. Vector graphics bring a number of benefits, such as the ability to stay crisp at any zoom level and the ability to easily make dynamic tweaks to the content. Such tweaks can include morphing the shapes, changing the thickness of strokes, and changing colors.

For Windows Phone apps, the ability to change colors in vector graphics is extremely helpful for having graphical content that can match the current theme colors. The Ruler app takes advantage of this: Its ruler lines are rendered with the current theme's foreground brush, and the marker line is rendered with the current theme's accent brush. The end of this chapter shows the Ruler app under the light theme, which gives it more of a real-world ruler look compared to its dark-theme appearance.

You can create vector graphics based on six different shapes (usually precisely placed within a canvas):

→ Rectangle

→ Ellipse

→ Line

→ Polyline

→ Polygon

→ Path

These shapes have many of the members that other elements have, such as the width/height properties, alignment properties, and all the mouse events. Instead of Foreground and Background properties, however, these shapes have Fill and Stroke properties, which can also be set to any brush. They also have a StrokeThickness property, a double value that is 1 by default.

Rectangle

The Rectangle element can be used to draw a rectangle, whether you give it an explicit width and height or allow it to stretch and fill an area. Interestingly, you can set RadiusX and RadiusY properties (of type double) on a rectangle to give it rounded corners. Figure 5.5 shows the following stacked rectangles with various values of RadiusX and RadiusY:

```
<StackPanel>
  <Rectangle Height="100" Fill="Orange" Margin="4"
    Stroke="{StaticResource PhoneForegroundBrush}" StrokeThickness="10"/>
  <Rectangle Width="200" Height="100" RadiusX="10" RadiusY="30"
    Fill="Orange" Stroke="{StaticResource PhoneForegroundBrush}"
    StrokeThickness="10" Margin="4"/>
  <Rectangle Height="100" RadiusY="50" RadiusX="50"
    Fill="Orange" Stroke="{StaticResource PhoneForegroundBrush}"
    StrokeThickness="10" Margin="4"/>
  <Rectangle Width="200" Height="100" RadiusX="100" RadiusY="50"
    Fill="Orange" Stroke="{StaticResource PhoneForegroundBrush}"
    StrokeThickness="10" Margin="4"/>
</StackPanel>
```

The first and third rectangles are allowed to stretch to fill the stack panel's width because they are not given an explicit width. RadiusX can be at most half the Width of the Rectangle, and RadiusY can be at most half the Height. Setting them any higher makes no difference.

 You must explicitly set Stroke **or** Fill **for a shape to be seen!**

Both Stroke and Fill are set to null by default. Therefore, shapes are completely invisible (and not hit-testable) unless you set one or both of these properties.

Both RadiusX and RadiusY must be nonzero for either one to have an effect.

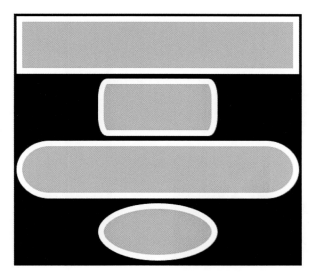

FIGURE 5.5   Four rectangles with different values for RadiusX and RadiusY.

Ellipse

After discovering the flexibility of the Rectangle element and realizing that it can be made to look like an ellipse (or circle), you'd think that a separate Ellipse element would be redundant. And you'd be right! All Ellipse does is make it easier to get an elliptical shape. It simply fills its rectangular region with the largest possible elliptical shape.

The following ellipse could replace the last rectangle in the previous XAML snippet, and Figure 5.5 would look identical:

```
<Ellipse Width="200" Height="100" StrokeThickness="10" Margin="4"
        Fill="Orange" Stroke="{StaticResource PhoneForegroundBrush}"/>
```

The only change is replacing the element name and removing the references to RadiusX and RadiusY.

Line

The Line element, the one shape used by the Ruler app, defines four double properties to represent a line segment connecting points ($x1$,$y1$) and ($x2$,$y2$). These properties are called X1, Y1, X2, and Y2.

The values of Line's properties are not absolute coordinates. They are relative to the space given to the Line element by its parent. For example, the following stack panel contains three lines, and is rendered in Figure 5.6:

FIGURE 5.6   Three lines in a stack panel, demonstrating that their coordinates are relative.

```
<StackPanel>
  <Line X1="0" Y1="0"   X2="100" Y2="100" Margin="4"
        Stroke="{StaticResource PhoneForegroundBrush}" StrokeThickness="10"/>
  <Line X1="0" Y1="0"   X2="100" Y2="0"    Margin="4"
        Stroke="{StaticResource PhoneForegroundBrush}" StrokeThickness="10"/>
  <Line X1="0" Y1="100" X2="100" Y2="0"    Margin="4"
        Stroke="{StaticResource PhoneForegroundBrush}" StrokeThickness="10"/>
</StackPanel>
```

Notice that each line is given the space needed by its bounding box, so the horizontal line gets only 10 units (for the thickness of its stroke) plus the specified margin. Lines inherit a `Fill` property from their base `Shape` class, but it is meaningless because there is never any area to fill.

Of course, when lines or any other shapes are placed in a canvas (as they usually are), they are allowed to overlap. By simply replacing the stack panel in the previous XAML snippet with a canvas, the result in Figure 5.7 is produced.

FIGURE 5.7   The same three lines in Figure 5.6, but with the parent stack panel replaced by a canvas.

Polyline

A `Polyline` element represents a sequence of lines, expressed in its `Points` property. The following four polylines are rendered in Figure 5.8:

```
<StackPanel>
  <Polyline Points="0,0 100,100" Margin="4"
    Stroke="{StaticResource PhoneForegroundBrush}" StrokeThickness="10"/>
  <Polyline Points="0,0 100,100 200,0" Margin="4"
    Stroke="{StaticResource PhoneForegroundBrush}" StrokeThickness="10"/>
  <Polyline Points="0,0 100,100 200,0 300,100" Margin="4"
    Stroke="{StaticResource PhoneForegroundBrush}" StrokeThickness="10"/>
  <Polyline Points="0,0 100,100 200,0 300,100 100,100" Margin="4"
    Stroke="{StaticResource PhoneForegroundBrush}" StrokeThickness="10"/>
</StackPanel>
```

FIGURE 5.8   Four polylines, ranging from 2 to 5 points.

As with margin and padding syntax, the placement of spaces and commas for value of `Points` is flexible. (You can place commas between any two values or use no commas at all.)

Figure 5.9 demonstrates what happens when each of the four polylines' `Fill` property is set to `{StaticResource PhoneAccentBrush}`. It's a neat trick; polylines pretend that a line segment exists to connect the first and last points, and then fills it accordingly.

Polygon

Just as `Rectangle` makes `Ellipse` redundant, `Polyline` makes `Polygon` redundant. The only difference between the `Polyline` and `Polygon` elements is that `Polygon` automatically adds a line segment connecting the first and last points. If you take each polyline from Figure 5.9 and simply change each element name to `Polygon`, you get the result shown in Figure 5.10.

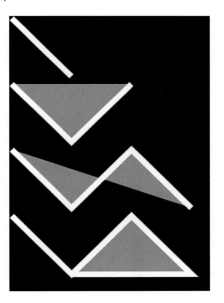

FIGURE 5.9   The same polylines from Figure 5.8, but with an explicit fill.

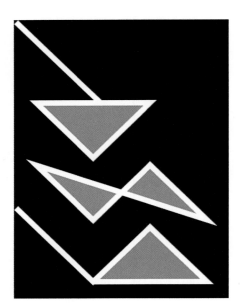

FIGURE 5.10   Polygons are just like polylines, except that they always form a closed shape.

Notice that the initial line segment in the first and last polygons in Figure 5.10 is quite a bit longer than in Figure 5.9, which even causes the first polygon to overlap the second one. This is because of the miter joint applied to every corner. Because the angle between the first and last line segments is 0° in these cases (as they share the same coordinates), the corner would be infinitely long if not for the StrokeMiterLimit property limiting it to 10 units by default. If you don't want miter joints, you can set the StrokeLineJoin property to Round or Bevel instead of the default Miter value. The three options are demonstrated in Figure 5.11. Both StrokeLineJoin and StrokeMiterLimit properties are available on all shapes.

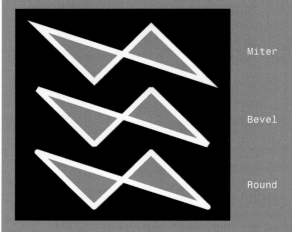

FIGURE 5.11   The values of StrokeLineJoin applied to the same polygon.

Path

The Path element is the most powerful shape. It can do everything done by the previous five shapes and much, much more. When you draw with a pen or pencil in a tool like Expression Blend, it generates corresponding Path elements. The characteristics of a path are determined by its Data property. In XAML, you can set this to a string that you are unlikely to craft by hand but rather let a tool like Expression Blend create for you. For example, the following path is shown in Figure 5.12:

FIGURE 5.12   Paths enable the expression of complex shapes.

```
<Path Stroke="{StaticResource PhoneForegroundBrush}" StrokeThickness="10"
  Fill="{StaticResource PhoneAccentBrush}"
  Data="M0,0 L0,100 C0,100 150,50 150,250 C300,100 50,150 250,250"/>
```

The information given to Data represents a *geometry*. The string can be fairly human-readable for people familiar with the syntax. For example, the "M0,0 L0,100" at the beginning means, "move to position (0,0) and draw a line to position (0,100)." Geometries, including this string syntax, are covered in Appendix E, "Geometry Reference."

Stroke Customization

Besides its brush, thickness, and line join behavior, you can customize a stroke's edges with custom *line caps*, and make it a dotted and/or dashed line.

Custom Line Caps

Whereas StrokeLineJoin customizes the appearance of joints, you can customize the endpoints of any *open* line segment by setting StrokeStartLineCap and/or StrokeEndLineCap to Flat (the default),

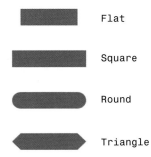

FIGURE 5.13   Each type of line cap applied to lines.

Square, Round, or Triangle. Figure 5.13 shows each of the values applied to a line's StartLineCap and EndLineCap properties. The Ruler app makes use of Triangle start and end line caps for the line that marks a precise measurement.

> **(?) What's the difference between applying Flat versus Square to a line cap?**
>
> A Flat line cap ends exactly on the endpoint, whereas a Square line cap extends beyond the endpoint. Much like the Round line cap, you can imagine a square with the same dimensions as the stroke thickness centered on the endpoint. Therefore, the line ends up extending *half* the length of the line segment's stroke thickness.

Dotted and Dashed Lines

You can make a shape's stroke dotted, dashed, or any combination in-between with its `StrokeDashArray` property. You can set this property to a pattern of numbers where the odd values represent the lengths of the dot/dash (relative to the stroke thickness) and the even values represent the lengths of the space between them (also relative to the stroke thickness). Whatever pattern you choose is then repeated indefinitely.

You can also customize the shape of each dot/dash with the `StrokeDashCap` property, which works just like `StartLineCap` and `EndLineCap`. You can even adjust where the pattern begins by setting the `StrokeDashOffset` property.

Figure 5.14 demonstrates several `StrokeDashArray` values applied to ellipses as follows:

```
<StackPanel Margin="100,100,0,0" >
  <Ellipse Width="200" Height="100" StrokeThickness="10" Margin="4"
           StrokeDashArray="1,1" Stroke="Red"/>
  <Ellipse Width="200" Height="100" StrokeThickness="10" Margin="4"
           StrokeDashArray="1,2" Stroke="Orange"/>
  <Ellipse Width="200" Height="100" StrokeThickness="10" Margin="4"
           StrokeDashArray="2,1" Stroke="Yellow"/>
  <Ellipse Width="200" Height="100" StrokeThickness="10" Margin="4"
           StrokeDashArray="1,1,4,2" Stroke="Lime"/>
  <Ellipse Width="200" Height="100" StrokeThickness="10" Margin="4"
           StrokeDashArray="0,1" StrokeDashCap="Round" Stroke="Aqua"/>
  <Ellipse Width="200" Height="100" StrokeThickness="10" Margin="4"
           StrokeDashArray="0,1" StrokeDashCap="Triangle" Stroke="Magenta"/>
</StackPanel>
```

The confusing thing about using a `StrokeDashCap` other than the default value of `Flat` is that the cap itself adds 1 to the odd values in `StrokeDashArray`. This is why the last two values use 0 rather than 1 for the first number in the array.

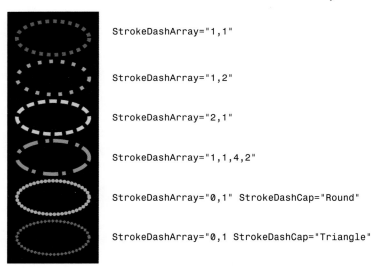

FIGURE 5.14   Various dotted and dashed lines applied to ellipses.

The User Interface

Listing 5.1 contains the XAML for Ruler's page. Its root grid contains a single cell with five elements layered on top of each other. These layers are visualized in Figure 5.15. Although `Canvas.ZIndex` could be used to control what layer is on top of what other layer, this XAML file relies on their natural ordering.

Canvas.ZIndex only affects the relative ordering of elements within the same panel!

The `Canvas.ZIndex` value is relative to sibling elements (with the same direct parent element) only. No value on an element inside Ruler's bottom layer could ever make it render on top of an element inside Ruler's top layer.

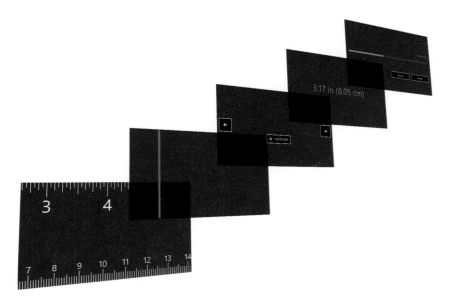

FIGURE 5.15   Ruler's user interface is composed of five layers.

LISTING 5.1   `MainPage.xaml`—The User Interface for Ruler

```
<phone:PhoneApplicationPage
    x:Class="WindowsPhoneApp.MainPage"
    xmlns="http://schemas.microsoft.com/winfx/2006/xaml/presentation"
    xmlns:x="http://schemas.microsoft.com/winfx/2006/xaml"
    xmlns:phone="clr-namespace:Microsoft.Phone.Controls;assembly=Microsoft.Phone"
    xmlns:shell="clr-namespace:Microsoft.Phone.Shell;assembly=Microsoft.Phone"
    xmlns:local="clr-namespace:WindowsPhoneApp"
    FontFamily="{StaticResource PhoneFontFamilyNormal}"
    FontSize="{StaticResource PhoneFontSizeNormal}"
    SupportedOrientations="Landscape" Orientation="Landscape">
```

LISTING 5.1   Continued

```xml
<!-- The root 1x1 grid holds several overlapping panels in the same cell -->
<Grid x:Name="LayoutRoot">

  <!-- Holds the lines and their labels -->
  <Canvas x:Name="RulerCanvas"/>

  <!-- Interactive canvas listening for taps and drags -->
  <Canvas Background="Transparent" MouseMove="InteractiveCanvas_MouseTapOrDrag"
          MouseLeftButtonDown="InteractiveCanvas_MouseTapOrDrag">
    <!-- The marker line that gets dragged -->
    <Line x:Name="ExactMeasurementLine" Y1="7" Y2="473" StrokeThickness="12"
          Stroke="{StaticResource PhoneAccentBrush}" Opacity=".8"
          StrokeEndLineCap="Triangle" StrokeStartLineCap="Triangle"/>
  </Canvas>

  <!-- Contains buttons (separate so button taps don't move marker line) -->
  <Canvas x:Name="ButtonsCanvas">
    <!-- right -->
    <Button Canvas.Left="698" Canvas.Top="189" Click="LeftOrRightButton_Click"
            Padding="12" Background="Black" local:Tilt.IsEnabled="True">
      <Image Source="Shared/Images/appbar.right.png"/>
    </Button>

    <!-- left -->
    <RepeatButton x:Name="LeftButton" Canvas.Left="0" Canvas.Top="189"
                  Padding="12" Click="LeftOrRightButton_Click"
                  Background="Black" Visibility="Collapsed"
                  local:Tilt.IsEnabled="True">
      <Image Source="Shared/Images/appbar.left.png"/>
    </RepeatButton>

    <!-- calibrate -->
    <Button Canvas.Top="270" Canvas.Left="305" Click="CalibrateButton_Click"
            Padding="0" Background="Black" local:Tilt.IsEnabled="True">
      <StackPanel Orientation="Horizontal">
        <Image Source="Shared/Images/appbar.settings.png"/>
        <TextBlock Foreground="White" Text="calibrate" Padding="0,4,12,0"/>
      </StackPanel>
    </Button>
  </Canvas>

  <!-- A direct child of the grid so it's easily centered -->
  <TextBlock x:Name="ExactMeasurementTextBlock" FontSize="60" Margin="0,0,0,8"
             HorizontalAlignment="Center" VerticalAlignment="Center"
```

LISTING 5.1   Continued

```xml
                    IsHitTestVisible="False"
                    Foreground="{StaticResource PhoneSubtleBrush}"/>

      <!-- The UI for "calibration mode" -->
      <Grid x:Name="CalibrationPanel" Background="Transparent"
            Visibility="Collapsed">
        <!-- Explanation of slider -->
        <TextBlock Text="Adjust scale" Margin="24" Padding="0,0,0,134"
                    VerticalAlignment="Center" HorizontalAlignment="Right"
                    Foreground="{StaticResource PhoneSubtleBrush}"/>
        <!-- The slider that adjusts the line spacing -->
        <Slider x:Name="SpacingSlider" Minimum="12" Maximum="24" LargeChange=".2"
                VerticalAlignment="Center" Margin="{StaticResource PhoneMargin}"
                ValueChanged="SpacingSlider_ValueChanged" />
        <!-- A pair of done & reset buttons in the bottom-right corner -->
        <StackPanel Orientation="Horizontal" Margin="0,0,12,88"
                    VerticalAlignment="Bottom" HorizontalAlignment="Right">
          <Button Content="done" MinWidth="200" local:Tilt.IsEnabled="True"
                  Background="Black" Foreground="White"
                  Click="CalibrationDoneButton_Click"/>
          <Button Content="reset" MinWidth="200" local:Tilt.IsEnabled="True"
                  Background="Black" Foreground="White"
                  Click="CalibrationResetButton_Click"/>
        </StackPanel>
      </Grid>
    </Grid>
  </phone:PhoneApplicationPage>
```

Notes:

➔ The `Orientation` property is set to `Landscape` in addition to the usual `SupportedOrientations` property to avoid an annoying design-time behavior. The default value of the design-time `Orientation` property is `Portrait`, so if you set `SupportedOrientations` to `Landscape` without setting `Orientation` to match, the Visual Studio designer complains, "This page does not support the current orientation." So although this setting is not needed at run-time, it is present to improve the design-time experience.

➔ This page does not show the status bar, as it is not appropriate for this style of app (and would reduce the on-screen ruler length).

➔ The second layer (the canvas with the line) is given an explicit transparent background so it can respond to taps and drags anywhere on its surface. Notice that the events for both tapping (`MouseLeftButtonDown`) and dragging (`MouseMove`) are attached to the same event handler.

➜ The left button is not a normal button; it is a *repeat button*. A repeat button is just like a normal button but it has two unique behaviors. It raises its `Click` event when pressing your finger down (instead of waiting for your finger to be released). Also, after the first `Click` (and an initial delay), it repeatedly raises more `Click`

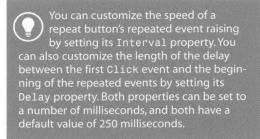

You can customize the speed of a repeat button's repeated event raising by setting its `Interval` property. You can also customize the length of the delay between the first `Click` event and the beginning of the repeated events by setting its `Delay` property. Both properties can be set to a number of milliseconds, and both have a default value of 250 milliseconds.

events as long as your finger is held down. This matches the behavior of scrollbar buttons typically seen on a PC. The left button uses this behavior because the user might want a quick way to return to the beginning of the ruler after measuring something long. There is no button for going back to the beginning, so instead the user can hold their finger down on the left button. The right button does not act this way because proper measuring involves advancing slowly, one section at a time.

➜ Notice that the three buttons in the third layer don't contain text! The first two contain an image, and the last one contains a stack panel with its own children! There's a reason that buttons have a `Content` property rather than a property called `Text`; it can be set to any object, including a whole tree of elements! You can set `Content` to an arbitrary object using *property element* syntax:

```
<Button …>
  <Button.Content>
    <Image Source="Shared/Images/appbar.right.png"/>
  </Button.Content>
</Button>
```

However, because `Content` is designated as a *content property*, you can omit the `Button.Content` tags, as is done in Listing 5.1. Appendix B, "XAML Reference," discusses property element syntax, content properties, and more.

Buttons get their `Content` property from a base class called `ContentControl`, so it is one of many controls referred to as a *content control*. Other content controls include repeat buttons, check boxes, radio buttons, and even scroll viewers! All content controls can have their content set to arbitrary objects.

 Although you *can* set the content of buttons to something other than text, you rarely *should*.

By convention, Windows Phone buttons should contain only a word or two of text. However, there are occasionally situations in which it might be appropriate to have more complex content in a button, such as in the Ruler app. Still, putting non-text content in a button has one big drawback: it doesn't automatically change to the appropriate color when the button is being pressed or when the button is disabled.

If you put vector graphics in a button, you could manually change the stroke/fill of the content when appropriate. If you put an image in a button, you could manually swap it with a different image when appropriate. The Ruler app takes a simpler approach: it uses white images and gives the buttons a hard-coded black background. It also avoids disabling any of the buttons. (When the left button is not valid to use, it gets hidden rather than disabled.) This is not ideal, as the pressed state of these buttons looks like a solid white rectangle under the dark theme, but it is acceptable.

→ The right, left, and calibrate buttons are given explicit padding for two reasons. One is that it makes sense for the right and left buttons to be a bit larger than normal so they are easier to tap. If the user tries to tap one but misses, they will end up repositioning the marker line instead, and that would be a frustrating experience. The other reason is that buttons have an asymmetrical default padding (`"10,3,10,5"`). Although this works well for text, it does not look good for other content.

→ `ExactMeasurementTextBlock` is placed above the canvas with the marker line to ensure its numbers don't get covered by the line. This centered text suffers from the same jiggling problem described in the

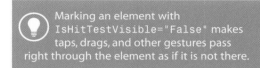

Marking an element with `IsHitTestVisible="False"` makes taps, drags, and other gestures pass right through the element as if it is not there.

preceding chapter, but it seems acceptable in this case because the text only changes while the user is moving the marker line. To prevent it from blocking tapping and dragging on the canvas underneath, it is marked with `IsHitTestVisible="False"`.

→ The topmost layer, `CalibrationPanel`, is given an explicit transparent background so it blocks the usual tap and drag processing to move the marker line when it is shown. It starts out invisible (`Collapsed`), and it's shown when the calibrate button is tapped.

→ `CalibrationPanel` contains a *slider* control to enable the user to adjust the spacing of the ruler lines. It is given a vertical alignment of `Center` to avoid accidental taps. Although it looks no different with its default `Stretch` vertical alignment, a stretched slider would respond to taps anywhere on the screen.

→ `CalibrationPanel`'s two buttons are given explicit foreground and background brushes, but not because they need them. This is simply done to match the other buttons used by this app.

Sliders

In Listing 5.1, the slider is used for the exact purpose for which it was designed—adjusting a numeric value within a finite (usually small) range. It looks like a progress bar, but it is interactive. The user can slide the value back and forth, or tap-and-hold to the left or right of the current value to make it repeatedly jump a fixed amount lower or higher.

Like a progress bar, a slider is primarily customized with three properties: Minimum (0 by default), Maximum (10 by default), and Value (0 by default). It has a LargeChange property (1 by default) that determines how much the value moves up or down each time during the tap-and-hold gesture. (It also has a SmallChange property, but it has no effect.)

In this Ruler app, the value of the slider represents the number of pixels between each 16th-of-an-inch line, so a smaller value fits more of the ruler on the screen. The minimum value of 12 makes just over 4 inches fit on the screen, and the maximum value of 24 makes just over 2 inches fit on the screen. The default value (set in code-behind) matches the size of my phone's screen, which fits just under 3 inches. LargeChange is set to .2 because the typical amount of adjustment is typically very small, and tapping a slider to change its value is easier than dragging it. Figure 5.16 shows CalibrationPanel when it is visible, when the slider has three different values. The logic that adjusts the ruler's lines as a reaction to the slider's value changing is done in the code-behind, triggered by the ValueChanged event handler (SpacingSlider_ValueChanged).

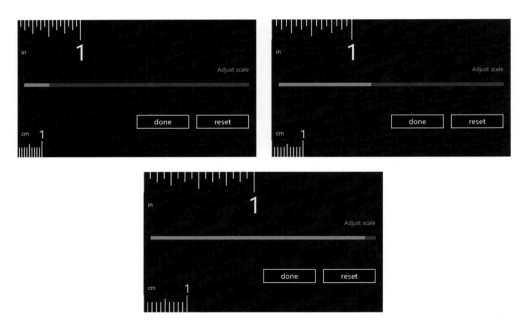

FIGURE 5.16   Changing the slider's value changes the spacing of the ruler lines.

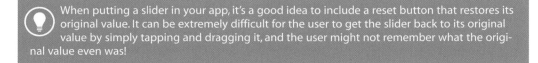

When putting a slider in your app, it's a good idea to include a reset button that restores its original value. It can be extremely difficult for the user to get the slider back to its original value by simply tapping and dragging it, and the user might not remember what the original value even was!

> The edges of a slider's bar should not get closer than 24 pixels to the edge of the screen. Otherwise, it's too difficult for the user to tap/drag the value to its minimum and/or maximum value. By default, the bar inside a slider is given only 12 pixels of space on either side. This is why Listing 5.1 gives the slider an extra 12-pixel (PhoneMargin) margin.

The Code-Behind

Listing 5.2 contains the code-behind for MainPage. Most of the code is related to the main task of drawing the on-screen portion of the ruler.

LISTING 5.2   MainPage.xaml.cs—The Code-Behind for Ruler

```
using System;
using System.ComponentModel;
using System.Windows;
using System.Windows.Controls;
using System.Windows.Input;
using System.Windows.Media;
using System.Windows.Navigation;
using System.Windows.Shapes;
using Microsoft.Phone.Controls;

namespace WindowsPhoneApp
{
  public partial class MainPage : PhoneApplicationPage
  {
    // Remember the calibration setting
    Setting<double> inch16thSpacing = new Setting<double>(
      "Inch16thSpacing", Constants.DEFAULT_INCH_16TH_SPACING);

    // Two more settings to remember the current state
    Setting<double> exactMeasurementPosition =
      new Setting<double>("ExactMeasurementPosition", 0);
    Setting<double> horizontalOffset =
      new Setting<double>("HorizontalOffset", 0);

    // State to restore after exiting the temporary calibration mode
    double preCalibrationScrollOffset;
    double preCalibrationSpacing;

    public MainPage()
    {
      InitializeComponent();
    }
```

LISTING 5.2   Continued

```
protected override void OnNavigatedTo(NavigationEventArgs e)
{
  base.OnNavigatedTo(e);

  // Refresh the UI based on the persisted settings
  DrawRuler();
  if (this.horizontalOffset.Value > 0)
    this.LeftButton.Visibility = Visibility.Visible;
  this.ExactMeasurementLine.X1 = this.exactMeasurementPosition.Value;
  this.ExactMeasurementLine.X2 = this.exactMeasurementPosition.Value;
  UpdateExactMeasurementText();
  this.SpacingSlider.Value = this.inch16thSpacing.Value;
}

protected override void OnNavigatedFrom(NavigationEventArgs e)
{
  base.OnNavigatedFrom(e);

  // Undo the offset change from calibration mode and save the original one
  if (this.CalibrationPanel.Visibility == Visibility.Visible)
    this.horizontalOffset.Value = this.preCalibrationScrollOffset;
}

// Override the behavior of the hardware Back button
protected override void OnBackKeyPress(CancelEventArgs e)
{
  base.OnBackKeyPress(e);

  if (this.CalibrationPanel.Visibility == Visibility.Visible)
  {
    // "Click" the done button
    CalibrationDoneButton_Click(null, null);
    // Cancel exiting the app
    e.Cancel = true;
  }
}

void SpacingSlider_ValueChanged(object sender,
  RoutedPropertyChangedEventArgs<double> e)
{
  // Guard against null when raised from within InitializeComponent
  if (this.SpacingSlider != null)
  {
    this.inch16thSpacing.Value = this.SpacingSlider.Value;
    DrawRuler();
```

LISTING 5.2   Continued

```
    }
  }

  void LeftOrRightButton_Click(object sender, RoutedEventArgs e)
  {
    double delta;
    if (sender == this.LeftButton)
    {
      // Scroll left, and don't go below 0
      delta = -1 * Math.Min(Constants.DEFAULT_SCROLL_AMOUNT,
                            this.horizontalOffset.Value);
    }
    else
    {
      // Scroll right
      delta = Constants.DEFAULT_SCROLL_AMOUNT;
      // If the line appears to be used, ensure it moves close to the start
      if (this.ExactMeasurementLine.X1 > 20)
        delta = this.ExactMeasurementLine.X1 - 20;
    }

    // Perform the virtual scrolling
    this.horizontalOffset.Value += delta;

    // Keep the line in the correct (now shifted) position
    this.ExactMeasurementLine.X1 -= delta;
    this.ExactMeasurementLine.X2 -= delta;
    this.exactMeasurementPosition.Value -= delta;

    if (this.horizontalOffset.Value == 0)
      this.LeftButton.Visibility = Visibility.Collapsed;
    else
      this.LeftButton.Visibility = Visibility.Visible;

    DrawRuler();
  }

  void CalibrateButton_Click(object sender, RoutedEventArgs e)
  {
    // Hide non-calibration pieces of UI and show the calibration panel
    this.ButtonsCanvas.Visibility = Visibility.Collapsed;
    this.ExactMeasurementTextBlock.Visibility = Visibility.Collapsed;
    this.ExactMeasurementLine.Visibility = Visibility.Collapsed;
    this.CalibrationPanel.Visibility = Visibility.Visible;
```

LISTING 5.2   Continued

```
  // Draw the ruler in "calibration mode" with fewer lines & a fixed position
  this.LayoutRoot.Background =
    Application.Current.Resources["PhoneChromeBrush"] as Brush;
  // Save the current position and spacing
  this.preCalibrationScrollOffset = this.horizontalOffset.Value;
  this.preCalibrationSpacing = this.inch16thSpacing.Value;
  this.horizontalOffset.Value = 0;
  DrawRuler();
}

void CalibrationDoneButton_Click(object sender, RoutedEventArgs e)
{
  // Restore the non-calibration pieces of UI and hide the calibration panel
  this.ButtonsCanvas.Visibility = Visibility.Visible;
  this.ExactMeasurementTextBlock.Visibility = Visibility.Visible;
  this.ExactMeasurementLine.Visibility = Visibility.Visible;
  this.CalibrationPanel.Visibility = Visibility.Collapsed;

  // Enter "normal mode"
  this.LayoutRoot.Background = null;

  if (this.inch16thSpacing.Value == this.preCalibrationSpacing)
  {
    // The spacing hasn't changed, so restore the UI to its previous state
    this.horizontalOffset.Value = this.preCalibrationScrollOffset;
  }
  else
  {
    // The spacing has changed, so keep the offset at 0 and reset the UI
    UpdateExactMeasurementText();
    this.LeftButton.Visibility = Visibility.Collapsed;
  }

  DrawRuler();
}

void CalibrationResetButton_Click(object sender, RoutedEventArgs e)
{
  // This invokes CalibrationSlider_ValueChanged,
  // which does the rest of the work
  this.SpacingSlider.Value = this.inch16thSpacing.DefaultValue;
}

void InteractiveCanvas_MouseTapOrDrag(object sender, MouseEventArgs e)
{
```

LISTING 5.2 Continued

```csharp
    // Get the finger position relative to the landscape-oriented page
    double x = e.GetPosition(this).X;

    // Move the line and save this position
    this.ExactMeasurementLine.X1 = x;
    this.ExactMeasurementLine.X2 = x;
    this.exactMeasurementPosition.Value = x;

    UpdateExactMeasurementText();
  }

  void UpdateExactMeasurementText()
  {
    double inches = (this.horizontalOffset.Value + this.ExactMeasurementLine.X1)
                    / (this.inch16thSpacing.Value * 16);
    double cm = inches * Constants.CONVERT_IN_TO_CM;
    this.ExactMeasurementTextBlock.Text = inches.ToString("0.00") + " in ("
                                  + cm.ToString("0.00") + " cm)";
  }

  void DrawRuler()
  {
    // Remove all elements and draw everything over again
    this.RulerCanvas.Children.Clear();

    double mmSpacing = this.inch16thSpacing.Value
                       * Constants.CONVERT_INCH_16TH_SPACING_TO_MM_SPACING;

    // By default, draw until we reach the end of the screen
    double inch16thXLimit = Constants.SCREEN_WIDTH + Constants.LINE_WIDTH;
    double cmXLimit = Constants.SCREEN_WIDTH + Constants.LINE_WIDTH;

    if (this.CalibrationPanel.Visibility == Visibility.Visible)
    {
      // In "calibration mode", only draw up to 1 inch and 2 cm, which gives
      // better performance while dragging the slider
      inch16thXLimit = 16 * this.inch16thSpacing.Value - Constants.LINE_WIDTH;
      cmXLimit = 10 * mmSpacing - Constants.LINE_WIDTH;
    }

    // Note: Behaves badly when horizontalOffset becomes unrealistically huge
    int inch16thLineIndex = (int)(this.horizontalOffset.Value /
                              this.inch16thSpacing.Value);
    int mmLineIndex = (int)(this.horizontalOffset.Value / mmSpacing);
```

LISTING 5.2   Continued

```
    // Render each inch number label
    double x = 0;
    int index = inch16thLineIndex;
    while (x < inch16thXLimit)
    {
      x = DrawNumber(index / 16, true);
      index += 16;
    }

    // Render each centimeter number label
    x = 0;
    index = mmLineIndex;
    while (x < cmXLimit)
    {
      x = DrawNumber(index / 10, false);
      index += 10;
    }

    // Render each 16th-of-an-inch line
    double inchLineX = -Constants.LINE_WIDTH;
    while (inchLineX <= inch16thXLimit)
    {
      inchLineX = Draw16thInchLine(inch16thLineIndex);
      inch16thLineIndex++;
    }

    // Render each millimeter line
    double mmLineX = -Constants.LINE_WIDTH;
    while (mmLineX <= cmXLimit)
    {
      mmLineX = DrawMillimeterLine(mmLineIndex);
      mmLineIndex++;
    }
  }

  double Draw16thInchLine(int lineIndex)
  {
    // Determine the correct horizontal position from the line index
    double x = (lineIndex * this.inch16thSpacing.Value)
               - this.horizontalOffset.Value;

    // Create and position the line, and add it to the canvas
    Line line = new Line {
      Stroke = Application.Current.Resources["PhoneForegroundBrush"] as Brush,
      StrokeThickness = Constants.LINE_WIDTH };
```

LISTING 5.2   Continued

```csharp
    Canvas.SetLeft(line, x);
    this.RulerCanvas.Children.Add(line);

    // Vary the length based on whether it's a whole inch, half inch, ...
    if (lineIndex % 16 == 0)
      line.Y2 = Constants.INCH_LINE_LENGTH;
    else if (lineIndex % 8 == 0)
      line.Y2 = Constants.INCH_HALF_LINE_LENGTH;
    else if (lineIndex % 4 == 0)
      line.Y2 = Constants.INCH_4TH_LINE_LENGTH;
    else if (lineIndex % 2 == 0)
      line.Y2 = Constants.INCH_8TH_LINE_LENGTH;
    else
      line.Y2 = Constants.INCH_16TH_LINE_LENGTH;

    return x;
  }

  double DrawMillimeterLine(int lineIndex)
  {
    // Determine the correct horizontal position from the line index
    double x = (lineIndex * this.inch16thSpacing.Value *
                Constants.CONVERT_INCH_16TH_SPACING_TO_MM_SPACING)
                - this.horizontalOffset.Value;

    // Create and position the line, and add it to the canvas
    Line line = new Line { Y1 = Constants.SCREEN_HEIGHT,
      Stroke = Application.Current.Resources["PhoneForegroundBrush"] as Brush,
      StrokeThickness = Constants.LINE_WIDTH };
    Canvas.SetLeft(line, x);
    this.RulerCanvas.Children.Add(line);

    // Vary the length based on whether it's a whole cm, half cm, ...
    if (lineIndex % 10 == 0)
      line.Y2 = Constants.SCREEN_HEIGHT - Constants.CENTIMETER_LINE_LENGTH;
    else if (lineIndex % 5 == 0)
      line.Y2 = Constants.SCREEN_HEIGHT - Constants.CENTIMETER_HALF_LINE_LENGTH;
    else
      line.Y2 = Constants.SCREEN_HEIGHT - Constants.MILLIMETER_LINE_LENGTH;

    return x;
  }

  double DrawNumber(int num, bool isInch)
  {
```

LISTING 5.2   Continued

```csharp
    // Determine the correct horizontal position of the line
    // corresponding to the inch or cm number
    double x;
    if (isInch)
      x = (num * 16 * this.inch16thSpacing.Value)
          - this.horizontalOffset.Value;
    else
      x = (num * 10 * this.inch16thSpacing.Value *
            Constants.CONVERT_INCH_16TH_SPACING_TO_MM_SPACING)
          - this.horizontalOffset.Value;

    if (num == 0)
    {
      // Don't actually render a "0"... put an "in" or "cm" label instead
      TextBlock textBlock = new TextBlock();
      textBlock.Text = isInch ? "in" : "cm";
      Canvas.SetTop(textBlock, isInch ? 98 : 382);
      Canvas.SetLeft(textBlock, x + Constants.LABEL_X);
      this.RulerCanvas.Children.Add(textBlock);
    }
    else
    {
      // Use a content control to enable centering the number on the line
      ContentControl container = new ContentControl {
        Width = this.inch16thSpacing.Value * 16, // Wide enough both in and cm
        HorizontalContentAlignment = HorizontalAlignment.Center };

      // This left position centers the content control on x
      Canvas.SetLeft(container, x - container.Width / 2);
      Canvas.SetTop(container, isInch ? 56 : Constants.SCREEN_HEIGHT - 110);
      this.RulerCanvas.Children.Add(container);

      // Add the text block to the content control, which centers its content
      TextBlock textBlock = new TextBlock { Text = num.ToString(),
                                            FontSize = isInch ? 80 : 40 };
      container.Content = textBlock;
    }

    return x;
  }
 }
}
```

Notes:

→ To make the calibration mode act like a dialog, it dismisses when the user presses the hardware Back button (and changes the background to use the PhoneChromeBrush resource used by message boxes and other dialogs). In order to accomplish this, we must detect when the button is pressed, then close the dialog and cancel exiting the app, *but only when CalibrationPanel is showing.* This is done by overriding the page's OnBackKeyPress method. Yes, this method can be exploited to prevent your app from ever exiting, but don't think that such an app will get approved by the marketplace! Apps are only meant to provide custom behavior for the hardware Back button in order to dismiss a dialog-like UI, just like in this app.

→ To move the marker line to the appropriate spot when the screen is tapped/dragged, we must figure out where the finger is making contact. This can be done with the GetPosition method on the MouseEventArgs instance passed to any mouse event handlers (InteractiveCanvas_ MouseTapOrDrag, in this case). The returned position is relative to whatever element is passed to the method. In InteractiveCanvas_MouseTapOrDrag, the page (this) is passed to GetPosition to get the page-relative location.

→ When the calibration slider is moved, the change is applied instantly. This is in accordance with design guidelines, which dictate that settings should take effect instantly and not require any sort of "apply" button.

Can I override the behavior of the other two hardware buttons (Start and Search)?

No, you can only override the behavior of the hardware Back button. A future version of Windows Phone may enable overriding the hardware Search button for enabling app-specific search, but the hardware Start button will always remain off-limits to apps. This gives users a reliable way to instantly leave an app.

 When setting a slider's minimum value to greater than 0 in XAML, its ValueChanged event gets raised within InitializeComponent!

This is significant, because it happens before the relevant field is assigned to the instance of the slider (if the slider was given a name). This is why SpacingSlider_ValueChanged must check to see if SpacingSlider is null in Listing 5.2. When the event is raised from this initialization, it can simply be ignored.

Be careful what you pass to MouseEventArgs.GetPosition!

When Silverlight is used on the web, it is common to pass null to GetPosition to get the position relative to the root element. On Windows Phone, passing null gives the screen-relative position, but it always treats the screen as if it's in the portrait orientation. Therefore, for a landscape-orientated page such as Ruler's, passing null to GetPosition always gives inverted values.

→ `DrawRuler` and its helper methods, `Draw16thInchLine`, `DrawMillimeterLine`, and `DrawNumber`, draw the on-screen slice of the ruler according to the

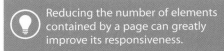

Reducing the number of elements contained by a page can greatly improve its responsiveness.

current value of `horizontalOffset`. At any point, only the on-screen elements exist because performance would suffer if too many off-screen elements were kept in memory.

→ Rather than setting the `X1` and `X2` values of each ruler line created in `Draw16thInchLine` and `DrawMillimeterLine`, the code sets `Canvas.Left` via a call to `Canvas.SetLeft`. Both approaches are equivalent, but the approach chosen saves one line of code.

→ Although it would appear that the ruler can be infinitely long, the largest supported measurement is 84,546,599.99 inches (22,726,125,279 pixels under the default calibration setting) due to limitations in the math and casting from `double` to `int`. Considering that this about half the distance from New York to Los Angeles, and considering that the user can only advance the ruler a few inches at a time, this app doesn't worry about this limit! (Also, the display of the numbers breaks down far before this limit due to space constraints.)

To access a phone theme resource in C#, you can use the `Application.Current.Resources` dictionary using a key that matches the name used with `StaticResource` syntax in XAML. This is done in Listing 5.2 to set the foreground of each ruler line to `ForegroundBrush` and the background of `LayoutRoot` to `PhoneChromeBrush` during calibration mode. For example:

```
this.LayoutRoot.Background =
    Application.Current.Resources["PhoneChromeBrush"] as Brush;
```

The code-behind file uses several constants. They are defined as follows in a separate file (`Constants.cs`):

```
namespace WindowsPhoneApp
{
  public static class Constants
  {
    // Screen
    public const int SCREEN_WIDTH = 800;
    public const int SCREEN_HEIGHT = 480;

    // Conversions
    public const double CONVERT_INCH_16TH_SPACING_TO_MM_SPACING = (50d / 127d)
                                                                * (16d / 10d);
```

```
public const double CONVERT_IN_TO_CM = 127d / 50d;

// Misc measurements
public const int DEFAULT_SCROLL_AMOUNT = 750;
public const int LABEL_X = 15;
public const int LINE_WIDTH = 3;
public const double DEFAULT_INCH_16TH_SPACING = 16.8;

// Lines on the inches side
public const int INCH_LINE_LENGTH = 70;
public const int INCH_HALF_LINE_LENGTH = 58;
public const int INCH_4TH_LINE_LENGTH = 47;
public const int INCH_8TH_LINE_LENGTH = 35;
public const int INCH_16TH_LINE_LENGTH = 23;

// Lines on the centimeter side
public const int CENTIMETER_LINE_LENGTH = 58;
public const int CENTIMETER_HALF_LINE_LENGTH = 46;
public const int MILLIMETER_LINE_LENGTH = 35;
    }
}
```

The Finished Product

Using Ruler with the light theme and an orange accent color

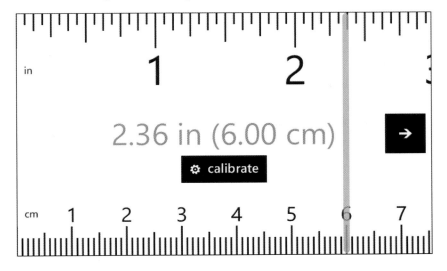

chapter 6

BABY SIGN LANGUAGE

These days, it's quite common for parents to teach their babies a limited amount of sign language before they are old enough to talk. This ability to communicate simple wishes like "eat" or "milk" at an early age can reduce their frustration and, according to some experts, even accelerate their language skills. Of course, to teach a baby sign language, the parent must learn some! That's where this app comes in.

The Baby Sign Language app explains how to do eight common signs that are helpful for a baby to learn by showing an illustration and written instructions for each one. The signs are organized in a two-level list—the first level contains three categories, and the second level contains the subset of signs belonging to the chosen category.

This project is similar to the auto-generated project you would get by creating a "Windows Phone Databound Application" project in Visual Studio. Both feature a main page with a list box, and a details page for displaying details about the selected item from the list. Both also leverage data binding.

This app has two significant firsts for this book—it is the first app to use more than one page, and it is the first app to use data binding. It certainly won't be the last to use these very-common features. The topic of navigating between multiple pages is explored first, before examining the code for the Baby Sign Language app. Data binding is covered at the end of the chapter.

Page Navigation

Although Visual Studio projects are given a single page by default, you can add more pages by right-clicking the project in Solution Explorer and then selecting Add, New Item…, Windows Phone Landscape Page or Windows Phone Portrait Page. (The two choices simply set the `SupportedOrientations` and `Orientation` properties differently on the generated pages. You can choose either option and easily switch the property values later to make it behave however you want.) The generated page looks just like the initial contents of `MainPage.xaml` but with whatever name you chose in the Add New Item dialog. If you add a new page called `DetailsPage`, two files get generated to define the `DetailsPage` class: `DetailsPage.xaml` and `DetailsPage.xaml.cs`.

The Baby Sign Language app uses three different pages: the main page, a details page, and an about page. Figure 6.1 maps out the possible paths of forward navigation through these pages. On any page, pressing the hardware Back button goes to the previous page (or exits the app when you're on the initial page).

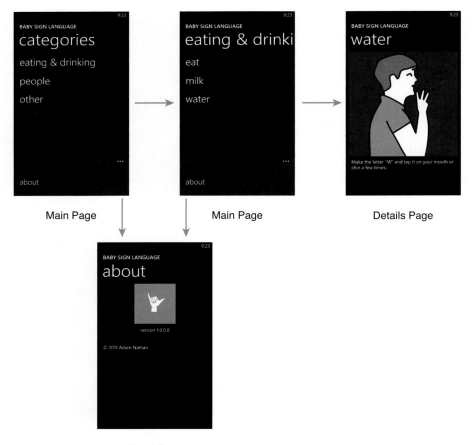

Main Page   Main Page   Details Page

About Page

FIGURE 6.1   The navigation structure of the multi-page Baby Sign Language app.

Notice that the main page is used for *both* levels of the categorized list! When an instance of MainPage is the first page of the app, it shows the three categories of signs. When you tap any of the three categories, the app navigates to a new instance of MainPage that instead shows the list of signs in the chosen category. From one of these instances, tapping a sign navigates to DetailsPage to explain the specific sign.

Every instance of MainPage has a link to an about page in its application bar menu. Pressing the hardware Back button from the about page goes back to whichever instance brought you there.

This section describes how to implement this or any other page navigation scheme. It examines

→ Pages, their frame, and their navigation service

→ Navigating forward and back

→ Passing data between pages

→ Designing a proper navigation scheme

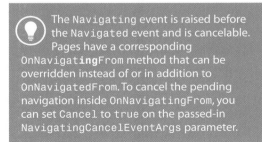

For the current set of data used by this app (eight signs spread across three categories), using two levels of list navigation is overkill; a single list with all eight signs would be more appropriate. Or displaying the information inside a panorama or pivot control (covered in Part IV, "Pivot, Panorama, Charts, & Graphs," of this book) would be a slick alternative. But it's instructive to see how you can construct arbitrarily deep nestings of lists, in case you decide to add more data to this app or have a different app in mind that needs nested lists.

Pages, Their Frame, and Their Navigation Service

Although it's natural to think of a page as the root element of an app (especially for single-page apps), all pages actually are contained in something called a *frame*. (The frames discussed in this book are technically instances of a class called PhoneApplicationFrame, just as pages are instances of a class called PhoneApplicationPage.)

The frame provides several members to enable page-to-page navigation, most importantly a method called Navigate. It also defines Navigating and Navigated events, among others. You rarely need to interact with the frame directly, however, because its navigation methods, properties, and events are exposed via a property on every page called NavigationService (of type NavigationService). Furthermore, pages already have OnNavigatedTo and OnNavigatedFrom methods (seen in the previous chapters) that are called in response to the relevant Navigated event. Using these methods and the NavigationService property is preferable over interacting with the frame directly, as it makes your code less intertwined.

The Navigating event is raised before the Navigated event and is cancelable. Pages have a corresponding OnNavigat**ing**From method that can be overridden instead of or in addition to OnNavigatedFrom. To cancel the pending navigation inside OnNavigatingFrom, you can set Cancel to true on the passed-in NavigatingCancelEventArgs parameter.

Frame Interaction inside `App.xaml.cs`   •••

Inside the `App.xaml.cs` code-behind file (which we haven't needed to touch for the apps so far), you can find code that interacts with the app's frame. The App class (derived from `System.Windows.Application`) is given a `RootFrame` property to expose the frame to the rest of the app:

```
// Easy access to the root frame
public PhoneApplicationFrame RootFrame { get; private set; }
```

However, this is not really necessary because the frame is also set as the base `Application` class's *root visual* later in the file. Therefore, code anywhere in your app has two ways to access the frame:

```
PhoneApplicationFrame frame = (Application.Current as App).RootFrame;
```

or

```
PhoneApplicationFrame frame =
  Application.Current.RootVisual as PhoneApplicationFrame;
```

Navigation occurs asynchronously, so handling some navigation events can be important. If you attempt navigate to a bogus page, the attempt fails with no explanation unless you handle the `NavigationFailed` event. Fortunately, this is already done inside `App.xaml.cs`, with an implementation that halts the debugger (but does nothing when the app runs normally) to give you, the developer, a chance to see what went wrong:

```
// Code to execute if a navigation fails
void RootFrame_NavigationFailed(object sender, NavigationFailedEventArgs e)
{
  if (System.Diagnostics.Debugger.IsAttached)
  {
    // A navigation has failed; break into the debugger
    System.Diagnostics.Debugger.Break();
  }
}
```

This file has a similar handler for unhandled exceptions in your app.

Navigating Forward and Back

To navigate from one page to another, you call the navigation service's `Navigate` method with a URI pointing to the destination page. For example, tapping an "instructions" button on an application bar can navigate to an instructions page if it has the following event handler attached to its `Click` event:

```
void InstructionsButton_Click(object sender, EventArgs e)
{
  this.NavigationService.Navigate(new Uri("/InstructionsPage.xaml",
    UriKind.Relative));
}
```

The URI refers to the XAML file compiled into your project, and its path represents the folder path in your source code. If `InstructionsPage.xaml` were placed in a Pages\Instructions subfolder, the URI should be `"/Pages/Instructions/InstructionsPage.xaml"`.

> **URIs pointing to pages must start with a forward slash!**
>
> Unlike with the URIs seen in Chapter 2, "Flashlight," for application bar button images, the URIs for pages must start with a forward slash, otherwise `Navigate` fails with an `ArgumentException`.

Just like a web browser, the navigation service maintains a back stack and a forward stack. In addition to the `Navigate` method, the navigation service exposes `GoBack` and `GoForward` methods. Table 6.1 explains the behavior of these three methods and their impact on the back and forward stacks.

TABLE 6.1   Navigation Effects on the Back and Forward Stacks

Action	Result
Navigate	Pushes the current page onto the back stack, empties the forward stack, and navigates to the desired page
GoBack	Pushes the current page onto the forward stack, pops a page off the back stack, and navigates to it
GoForward	Pushes the current page onto the back stack, pops a page off the forward stack, and navigates to it

GoBack fails when the back stack is empty (which means you're currently on the app's initial page), and `GoForward` fails when the forward stack is empty. If a piece of code is not certain what the states of these stacks are, it can check the Boolean `CanGoBack` and `CanGoForward` properties first.

Although the `GoBack` and `GoForward` methods enable you to put back and forward buttons in your user interface, do not do this! With small exceptions explained in the warning on the next page, Windows Phone and its apps do not put such buttons or links on the screen. Going back is handled with the hardware Back button, and going forward to a page on the forward stack is not usually done. (The user can start a *new* forward navigation to the same

> When navigating from one page to another, there is no "page-flip" animation as seen with the phone's built-in apps; the transition is instantaneous. I find this behavior unacceptable. Not only is the animation used consistently in the built-in apps, but also it is an important visual cue to let the user know that navigation just occurred.
>
> Therefore, the apps in this book use a custom frame control (an `AnimatedFrame` class that derives from `PhoneApplicationFrame`) that automatically provides the correct forward or back page-flip animation when navigation occurs. The custom frame is swapped in by changing one line of code inside `App.xaml.cs`. Chapter 19, "Animation Lab," shows this, as well as the source code for this custom control. Alternatively, you could use animated transitions provided by the Silverlight for Windows Phone Toolkit, also demonstrated in that chapter.

destination by tapping whatever button or link caused the original forward navigation.) Consider that even the Internet Explorer app does not have a back button on the screen!

Not only is adding such buttons against design guidelines, it also is extra clutter for users who understand the navigation model of the phone.

> ⓘ **Do not put a back button on your pages!**
>
> This is worth repeating because the temptation to do so is huge for a newcomer to Windows Phone. Whenever I show a multi-page app to someone who doesn't own a Windows phone, the first question after navigating to a new page is always, "How do I get back?" Questions like this make it tempting to add a back button to your own apps. But don't. Anyone who owns a Windows phone learns how to go back from any page *very* quickly, as the lack of a software back button permeates the experience.
>
> There are two exceptions to this rule (sort of). Some pages provide a pair of done/cancel buttons (or variations of done and cancel) that are really no different than a software back button except that one of them involves extra behavior of saving/deleting state. For example, the implementation of a cancel button Click handler is usually just a call to GoBack. Figure 6.2 shows examples of such buttons from various built-in apps.
>
>
>
> **FIGURE 6.2**   A cancel button, and related buttons such as done, save, and delete, are often not much different from having a back button, but are acceptable to use in a Windows Phone app.
>
> The other exception is that it's considered acceptable to have *previous* and *next* buttons to enable switching between items on the same page, such as photos in the same album or email messages in the same folder. Of course, the implementation of such buttons does not involve the navigation service. The built-in Mail app has such buttons, called *newer* and *older*. As shown in Chapter 2, the button icons in the Windows Phone Developer Tools include images for previous and next.

If you want an underlined text link, like the kind you see in HTML, you can use a `HyperlinkButton` control as follows:

```
<HyperlinkButton NavigateUri="/DetailsPage.xaml" Content="details" />
```

Not only does this give you the automatic formatting, it also automatically navigates to the specified `NavigateUri` when tapped, so you don't have to write any C# code for this.

That said, these are rarely used, partly because they are harder to tap than a normal button or application bar button/menu item. When this style of hyperlink is used, it is often to launch the Internet Explorer app for a specific website. This has nothing to do with the navigation features in this chapter, but you can accomplish this with `HyperlinkButton` by setting its `TargetName` to `_self` or `_blank` and setting its `NavigateUri` to the URL.

Multiple Instances of the Same Page   •••

When you navigate to a page by calling `Navigate` (or using a `HyperlinkButton`), you get a brand new instance of it, regardless of whether you've previously visited it. (Calling `GoBack` or `GoForward`, on the other hand, retrieves the existing instance.) No special relationship exists between two instances of a page other than the fact that they happen to come from the same source code. The Baby Sign Language app leverages this behavior in order to reuse `MainPage` for the first two levels of list navigation. However, if you want every instance of the same page to act as if it's really the same page (and "remember" its data from the previously seen instance), then you need to manage this yourself, perhaps with static members on the relevant page class.

Passing Data Between Pages

Often, when you navigate to a page, you need to communicate some information to it. In the Baby Sign Language app, when you tap on an item in the list, the next page needs to know what item you just tapped so it can display the appropriate data. Other apps have times when the user must navigate to a new page to select something or fill out a form, and that data needs to be communicated *back* to the original page when the new page is dismissed.

Passing data forward can be handled the same way as on the Web—by passing parameters in a query string. A query string is simply a ? appended to the URI string followed by one or more name/value pairs in a format such as *name1=value1&name2=value2*.

The Baby Sign Language app leverages such query parameters in several places. For example, it uses a generic about page shared by many of the apps in this book. This page customizes its display for whatever app is using it by enabling the app's name to be passed in the query string as an `appName` parameter:

```
this.NavigationService.Navigate(new Uri(
  "/Shared/About/AboutPage.xaml?appName=Baby Sign Language",
  UriKind.Relative));
```

When we examine the rest of this app's code, you'll see how the destination page is able to retrieve the query string so it can act on such name/value pairs.

For some types of data, encoding it as a string to pass within the URI can be cumbersome or impractical. Also, using a query string doesn't help in the scenario of passing data *back* to the previous page. For these cases, you can just find a shared place to store the data where both pages know to look. For example, this could be your own static member on one of your classes. This chapter's app uses a mixture of the query string approach and the static member approach.

 Page instances are kept alive as long as they are on the back and forward stacks. This is good, because they keep all of their state without having to be reinitialized. This can cause bad behavior, however, if a page is doing unnecessary work even though it is no longer visible (such as having code running on a timer). Such pages can use the OnNavigatedFrom method to pause its processing and the OnNavigatedTo method to resume it.

Designing a Proper Navigation Scheme

Figuring out the best way to organize your app into separate pages and figuring out the best way for pages to link to each other isn't always easy; it can take practice. Sometimes the most straightforward structure causes unwanted effects, especially when it comes to managing the back stack.

Due to the asynchronous nature of navigation, you cannot call GoBack or GoForward (or Navigate) repeatedly in a loop. Invoking a new navigation action while navigation is already in progress causes an InvalidOperationException to be thrown. Instead, you could navigate forward or backward multiple times

How do I programmatically exit my app from any page?

You can't, unless you force your app to exit by throwing an unhandled exception to make it crash! (And this is definitely not recommended.) Only the user has the power to gracefully exit your app by pressing the hardware Back button from your app's initial page. There's a common misconception that calling GoBack from the initial page exits your app. This is true, but only because of the unhandled exception that gets thrown by attempting to access an empty back stack! Chapter 9, "Fake Call," discusses programmatic app-exiting in a bit more depth, as it has a valid scenario for wishing to do so.

in a row by having a listener to the frame's Navigated event continually make the next GoBack or GoForward call once the in-progress navigation has completed. Besides being messy, however, this can produce unwanted delays and visual effects.

Because you can't programmatically exit the app from any page, or even go back more than one page at a time very easily, care must be taken to not to make the back stack grow too large. Your users will likely get annoyed if they have to go back through several pages in order to exit your app. (Yes, they can always leave instantly by pressing the hardware Start button, but that doesn't count because it doesn't completely close your app, as discussed in Chapter 10, "Tip Calculator." Many users might be reluctant to exit your app in this fashion.)

Figure 6.3 demonstrates a hypothetical page structure and navigation flow for one of the games created in Volume II of this book series. The game has several logical screens, including a main menu (seen when launching the app), the game itself (seen after tapping "play"), and a scoreboard. It's natural to make each logical screen be a distinct page. However, if your desire is to automatically navigate to the scoreboard when the game ends (perhaps to record a new high score), this causes a problem: What should happen when the user presses the hardware Back button while on the scoreboard page? Ideally, the user would return to the main menu, but the game page is still on the back stack!

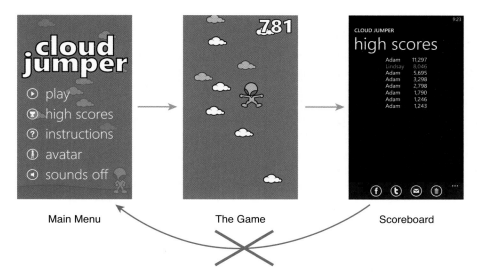

Main Menu   The Game   Scoreboard

FIGURE 6.3 A common problem with a navigation scheme for a game.

We know that instantly navigating back two pages is not an option. After the hardware Back button takes the user from the scoreboard page to the game page, the game page could detect this situation and call GoBack to trigger a new navigation to the main menu, but this has the same problems of delays and unwanted visual effects mentioned earlier. (It's effectively the same technique as using the frame's Navigated event.)

The solution chosen for such games in Volume II is to merge the main menu and game page into two different modes of the same page. Navigating to and from the scoreboard page then works as desired, as long as this combined page knows when it should show the menu

If you find yourself wanting to perform "fake" navigation such as programmatically going forward or back more than one page at a time or simulating a back navigation by going *forward* to a new instance of the previous page, then you're doing something wrong. Rethink your page structure, and try to avoid having more than 1 or 2 pages in the back stack at any time. A "hub and spoke" model works well, in which the initial page may have many offshoot pages, but they're always a single step away.

and when it should be actively running the game. (This structure happens to be more convenient for additional reasons, such as the behavior of pausing and unpausing the game.)

The Main Page

Now that we've covered page navigation in depth, it's time to see how the Baby Sign Language app is implemented. Starting with MainPage, we'll look at its user interface, the definition of the data used by the app, and its code-behind. You'll also learn about a powerful Silverlight feature known as *data templates*.

The User Interface

Listing 6.1 contains the XAML for MainPage, the page with the list of items. As indicated in Figure 6.1, this page can appear with four different sets of data: the list of categories, and the lists of signs for each of the three categories.

LISTING 6.1   MainPage.xaml—The Primary User Interface for Baby Sign Language

```
<phone:PhoneApplicationPage x:Class="WindowsPhoneApp.MainPage"
    xmlns="http://schemas.microsoft.com/winfx/2006/xaml/presentation"
    xmlns:x="http://schemas.microsoft.com/winfx/2006/xaml"
    xmlns:phone="clr-namespace:Microsoft.Phone.Controls;assembly=Microsoft.Phone"
    xmlns:shell="clr-namespace:Microsoft.Phone.Shell;assembly=Microsoft.Phone"
    xmlns:local="clr-namespace:WindowsPhoneApp"
    FontSize="{StaticResource PhoneFontSizeNormal}"
    Foreground="{StaticResource PhoneForegroundBrush}"
    SupportedOrientations="PortraitOrLandscape"
    shell:SystemTray.IsVisible="True">

  <!-- An application bar with an "about" menu item and no buttons -->
  <phone:PhoneApplicationPage.ApplicationBar>
    <shell:ApplicationBar>
      <shell:ApplicationBar.MenuItems>
        <shell:ApplicationBarMenuItem Text="about" Click="AboutMenuItem_Click"/>
      </shell:ApplicationBar.MenuItems>
    </shell:ApplicationBar>
  </phone:PhoneApplicationPage.ApplicationBar>

  <Grid x:Name="LayoutRoot">
    <Grid.RowDefinitions>
      <RowDefinition Height="Auto"/>
      <RowDefinition Height="*"/>
    </Grid.RowDefinitions>
```

LISTING 6.1   Continued

```xml
  <!-- The standard header, with some tweaks -->
  <StackPanel Margin="24,16,0,12">
    <TextBlock Text="BABY SIGN LANGUAGE" Margin="-1,0,0,0"
               FontFamily="{StaticResource PhoneFontFamilySemiBold}"
               FontSize="{StaticResource PhoneFontSizeMedium}"/>
    <TextBlock x:Name="PageTitle" Text="categories" Margin="-3,-10,0,0"
               FontFamily="{StaticResource PhoneFontFamilySemiLight}"
               FontSize="{StaticResource PhoneFontSizeExtraExtraLarge}"/>
  </StackPanel>

  <Grid Grid.Row="1" Margin="{StaticResource PhoneHorizontalMargin}">
    <ListBox x:Name="ListBox" SelectionChanged="ListBox_SelectionChanged">
      <ListBox.ItemTemplate>
        <!-- The data template controls how each item renders -->
        <DataTemplate>
          <!-- The text block displays value of the
               current item's Name property -->
          <TextBlock Text="{Binding Name}"
                     Margin="{StaticResource PhoneMargin}"
                     Style="{StaticResource PhoneTextExtraLargeStyle}"
                     local:Tilt.IsEnabled="True"/>
        </DataTemplate>
      </ListBox.ItemTemplate>
    </ListBox>
  </Grid>
 </Grid>
</phone:PhoneApplicationPage>
```

Notes:

→ This page has a button-less application bar with just a single menu item for navigating to the about page. Viewing an about page is not an important-enough action to warrant a button.

→ Although the page title is initialized to "categories," the code-behind updates this text when this page is used to display the other three lists.

→ Whereas Chapter 4, "Stopwatch," uses a stack panel in a scroll viewer for its list of items, this page uses a list box. A list box is a lot like a stack panel in a scroll viewer, but it supports additional behaviors related to item selection and data binding.

→ The list box is empty (to be filled by the code-behind), but its ItemTemplate property is set to an instance of a *data template* that gives each item in the list a specific appearance. Data templates are examined in the upcoming "Data Templates" section.

→ The list box has a `SelectionChanged` event that is raised when a new item is tapped (or selected programmatically). A handler is attached to this, which we'll examine in the code-behind.

The Data

Before looking at the code-behind for `MainPage`, we should see how the categorized data is represented in code. This project defines a `Category` class that contains a name and a list of signs that belong to the category:

```
public class Category
{
  public string Name { get; private set; }
  public IList<Sign> Signs { get; private set; }

  public Category(string name, IList<Sign> signs)
  {
    this.Name = name;
    this.Signs = signs;
  }
}
```

`Sign` is defined as follows, storing a name, a path to an image, and a description:

```
public class Sign
{
  public string Name { get; private set; }
  public Uri ImageUri { get; private set; }
  public string Description { get; private set; }

  public Sign(string name, Uri imageUri, string description)
  {
    this.Name = name;
    this.ImageUri = imageUri;
    this.Description = description;
  }
}
```

The actual data (three categories and eight signs) is represented in a static `Data.Categories` array that defines everything inline, leveraging the constructors for `Category` and `Sign`:

```
public class Data
{
  public static readonly Category[] Categories = {
    new Category("eating & drinking",
      new Sign[] {
```

```
        new Sign("eat", new Uri("Images/eat.png", UriKind.Relative), "…"),
        new Sign("milk", new Uri("Images/milk.png", UriKind.Relative), "…"),
        new Sign("water", new Uri("Images/water.png", UriKind.Relative), "…")
      }),
    new Category("people",
      new Sign[] {
        new Sign("daddy", new Uri("Images/daddy.png", UriKind.Relative), "…"),
        new Sign("mommy", new Uri("Images/mommy.png", UriKind.Relative), "…")
      }),
    new Category("other",
      new Sign[] {
        new Sign("all done", new Uri("Images/alldone.png",
                              UriKind.Relative), "…"),
        new Sign("more", new Uri("Images/more.png", UriKind.Relative), "…"),
        new Sign("play", new Uri("Images/play.png", UriKind.Relative), "…")
      })
  };
}
```

Therefore, `Data.Categories` is a three-element array, and each of its elements has a `Signs` property that is a two- or three-element array.

There are many alternative approaches for representing this data, such as defining it in a file that is read when the app is initialized and dynamically constructing all the `Category` and `Sign` instances corresponding to the file contents. Part III, "Storing & Retrieving Local Data," discusses such options. However, defining the data in a C# file, as done here, works just fine.

The Code-Behind

Listing 6.2 contains the code-behind for `MainPage`, which is responsible for determining which of the four lists it should be showing and then showing the correct data.

LISTING 6.2   `MainPage.xaml.cs`—The Main Code-Behind for Baby Sign Language

```
using System;
using System.Windows;
using System.Windows.Controls;
using System.Windows.Navigation;
using Microsoft.Phone.Controls;

namespace WindowsPhoneApp
{
  public partial class MainPage : PhoneApplicationPage
  {
    int categoryIndex = -1;
```

LISTING 6.2   Continued

```
public MainPage()
{
  InitializeComponent();
  this.Loaded += MainPage_Loaded;
}

void MainPage_Loaded(object sender, RoutedEventArgs e)
{
  if (this.ListBox.Items.Count > 0)
    return; // We already added the data.
            // (We must be navigating back to this page.)

  if (this.categoryIndex == -1)
  {
    // This is the root page. Fill the list box with the categories.
    foreach (Category category in Data.Categories)
      this.ListBox.Items.Add(category);
  }
  else
  {
    // This is a page for a specific category.
    // Fill the list box with the category's items.
    foreach (Sign sign in Data.Categories[this.categoryIndex].Signs)
      this.ListBox.Items.Add(sign);
  }
}

void ListBox_SelectionChanged(object sender, SelectionChangedEventArgs e)
{
  if (this.ListBox.SelectedIndex == -1)
    return; // The selection was cleared, so do nothing

  if (this.categoryIndex == -1)
  {
    // This is the root page, so the selection is a category. Navigate to a
    // new instance of this page initialized with the chosen category.
    this.NavigationService.Navigate(new Uri("/MainPage.xaml?categoryIndex=" +
      this.ListBox.SelectedIndex, UriKind.Relative));
  }
  else
  {
    // We're already on the page for a specific category, so the selection is
    // a sign. Navigate to the details page for this sign.
    this.NavigationService.Navigate(new Uri(
      "/DetailsPage.xaml?categoryIndex=" + this.categoryIndex +
```

LISTING 6.2   Continued

```
          "&signIndex=" + this.ListBox.SelectedIndex, UriKind.Relative));
    }

    // Clear the selection so the same item can be selected
    // again on subsequent visits to this page
    this.ListBox.SelectedIndex = -1;
  }

  protected override void OnNavigatedTo(NavigationEventArgs e)
  {
    base.OnNavigatedTo(e);
    if (this.NavigationContext.QueryString.ContainsKey("categoryIndex"))
    {
      // This is the page for a specific category.
      // Remember its index and display its name.
      this.categoryIndex = int.Parse(
        this.NavigationContext.QueryString["categoryIndex"]);
      this.PageTitle.Text = Data.Categories[this.categoryIndex].Name;
    }
  }

  void AboutMenuItem_Click(object sender, EventArgs e)
  {
    this.NavigationService.Navigate(new Uri(
      "/Shared/About/AboutPage.xaml?appName=Baby Sign Language",
      UriKind.Relative));
  }
}
```

Notes:

→ This page uses a `categoryIndex` member to determine which list to show. A value of -1 means no category has been selected, so this is the initial page that must show the categories. Any other value means that a category has been chosen, and that value represents the chosen category's index in the `Data.Categories` list (0, 1, or 2).

 The Loaded **event is raised after every navigation to the page!**

Unlike the constructor, which only runs once for each instance of the page, the Loaded event is raised every time the page is visited (after OnNavigatedTo is called). If MainPage_Loaded did not return early when the list box is already filled, the list of items would keep growing every time the user navigates back to the page!

→ Inside the page's `Loaded` event handler (`MainPage_Loaded`), the list box's items are filled based on the value of `categoryIndex`. Notice that whereas panels have a

`Children` collection, list box's collection is called `Items`. The index of each item in the list box's `Items` collection ends up matching the index in the original list, a fact that is leveraged in the rest of the app.

→ Inside the list box's `SelectionChanged` event handler (`ListBox_SelectionChanged`), a navigation is performed in response to one of the items in the list being tapped. Which page it navigates to, and the data passed to it, depends on which item was tapped and the current value of `categoryIndex`. If `categoryIndex` is -1, the code navigates to a new instance of `MainPage` but passes along a new `categoryIndex` in the query string that indicates which category was just selected. (Without passing this value, this would navigate to an identical-looking instance and the user would be trapped in a loop.) List boxes have a `SelectedIndex` property that keeps track of the selected item's index, so we can simply use this as the value of `categoryIndex` for the new `MainPage` instance. If `categoryIndex` is already nonnegative, the code navigates to `DetailsPage` instead and passes along two pieces of data: the existing `categoryIndex`, and the index of the selected sign inside that category. The latter is again available to us from the list box's `SelectedIndex` property.

→ At the end of `ListBox_SelectionChanged`, `SelectedIndex` is reset to -1 (meaning no item is selected). This is important to ensure that the page acts as expected when the user navigates back to it. A list box only raises its `SelectionChanged` event when the selected item *changes*, meaning that tapping on the same item multiple times in a row has no effect after the first time.

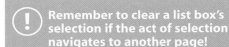

Remember to clear a list box's selection if the act of selection navigates to another page!

Forgetting to do this is a common mistake and can result in confusing behavior that you might not uncover in testing. For example, if a user selects "people" on the initial page to navigate to that category, later presses the hardware Back button to get back to the initial page, and then taps on "people" again, nothing would happen if you don't reset `SelectedIndex` because the item would still be selected! This is especially subtle because the visualization given to each item in Baby Sign Language does not look any different when it is selected.

→ The implementation of `OnNavigatedTo` reveals how the `categoryIndex` member gets set to the value of the `categoryIndex` from the query string. Nothing is automatic; the code must explicitly check for any query parameters it expects. The query string can be accessed from any page's `NavigationContext` property. `NavigationContext`'s `QueryString` property exposes the name/value pairs via a convenient dictionary, so you don't have to parse the string to get the individual values. Each value is still a string, however, so this code uses integer's `Parse` method to turn the retrieved `categoryIndex` value into an integer. This code also updates the page's title by fetching the name of the current category.

Uri's properties don't work on relative URIs!

The parameter passed to `OnNavigatedTo` (and related methods) contains a `Uri` parameter that exposes the URI used to navigate to the page. It's reasonable to think that you could use its `Query` property to access the query string. However, attempting to access just about every property throws an `InvalidOperationException` explaining that these properties do not work on relative URIs! (Its `IsAbsoluteUri` property correctly returns `false`, however.) Therefore, you should always use the `NavigationContext` property to access the query string instead, as done in Listing 6.2.

Instead of calling `ContainsKey` on the `QueryString` dictionary and then separately retrieving the value, you can use the dictionary's `TryGetValue` method. With this approach, you perform only one dictionary lookup instead of two.

Data Templates

In Listing 6.2, notice that `Category` and `Sign` objects were added directly to the list box's `Items` collection. This is a new concept. In the Stopwatch app, we explicitly created new visual elements (a grid, a text block, and so on) every time we needed to add a new item to the stack panel. Panels require that its children are classes that derive from `UIElement` (visual objects that have their own rendering behavior), but list boxes enable us to add arbitrary data objects to its contents.

But what does it mean visually to add `Category` and `Sign` objects to a list box? Figure 6.4 shows what the initial instance of `MainPage` would look like if the list box's `ItemTemplate` property setting was removed from the XAML in Listing 6.1, as well as what the next instance would look like after tapping the first category.

FIGURE 6.4   The appearance of two `MainPage` instances when no data template is applied.

By default, each item is rendered as a plain text block whose text is whatever gets returned by each object's `ToString` method (and by default, this is the namespace-qualified class name). In this state, the app still "works"—you can tap items to get to the proper details page (which renders completely correctly). Notice that the second page instance in Figure 6.4 still has the correct title, because that is fetched directly from the data source based on its index, regardless of how the items in the list box actually render.

Of course, this rendering is not satisfactory. You could override the `ToString` method on `Category` and `Sign` and have them return the value of their `Name` property, but this is still pretty limiting. For example, the default margin and font size seen in Figure 6.4 is not satisfactory, and the items do not tilt when you press them. And what if you wanted to customize the rendering even further?

That's where data templates come in. A data template is a visual element that can be applied to nonvisual objects. (And this visual element could be a panel containing a complex tree of elements.) When used as the value for a list box's `ItemTemplate` property, the template is used for each item in the list.

Figure 6.5 shows what the initial page of this app would look like if you replaced the data template in Listing 6.1 with the following one:

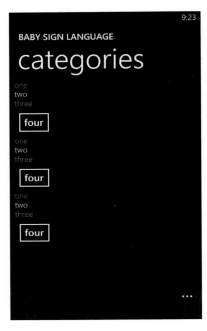

FIGURE 6.5   The appearance of the initial `MainPage` instance when a silly data template is applied.

```xml
<ListBox …>
  <ListBox.ItemTemplate>
    <!-- The data template controls how each item renders -->
    <DataTemplate>
      <StackPanel>
        <TextBlock Text="one" Foreground="Red"/>
        <TextBlock Text="two" Foreground="Aqua"/>
        <TextBlock Text="three" Foreground="Magenta"/>
        <Button Content="four"/>
      </StackPanel>
    </DataTemplate>
  </ListBox.ItemTemplate>
</ListBox>
```

Besides being a silly data template, each visual item has nothing to do with the data item it's supposed to represent. Each item looks identical!

A proper data template needs a way to access the data object so it can customize its display appropriately. This can be done with special data binding syntax of the form {Binding *XXX*}, where *XXX* is a property of the source data object.

In Listing 6.1, the data template successfully used by this app's list box is

```
<DataTemplate>
  <!-- The text block displays value of the
       current item's Name property -->
  <TextBlock Text="{Binding Name}"
             Margin="{StaticResource PhoneMargin}"
             Style="{StaticResource PhoneTextExtraLargeStyle}"
             local:Tilt.IsEnabled="True"/>
</DataTemplate>
```

It's just a text block whose text is automatically set to the value of each item's Name property. The neat thing about this is that the same data template works for both Category and Sign objects because they both happen to have a property called Name. If you were to change the value to {Binding Description} instead, it would show the description of each Sign, but the text block would be empty for each Category because it doesn't have a Description property.

Various controls expose properties of type DataTemplate to enable the separation of data and visual appearance. For example, content controls define a ContentTemplate property for customizing the rendering of their Content property.

The Details Page

The details page used by Baby Sign Language contains the information that the user is looking for at the end of the navigation chain. It displays the three properties of the chosen Sign object: its name, image, and description. Listing 6.3 contains the XAML for this page.

LISTING 6.3 DetailsPage.xaml—The User Interface for the Baby Sign Language Details Page

```
<phone:PhoneApplicationPage x:Class="WindowsPhoneApp.DetailsPage"
    xmlns="http://schemas.microsoft.com/winfx/2006/xaml/presentation"
    xmlns:x="http://schemas.microsoft.com/winfx/2006/xaml"
    xmlns:phone="clr-namespace:Microsoft.Phone.Controls;assembly=Microsoft.Phone"
    xmlns:shell="clr-namespace:Microsoft.Phone.Shell;assembly=Microsoft.Phone"
    FontSize="{StaticResource PhoneFontSizeNormal}"
    Foreground="{StaticResource PhoneForegroundBrush}"
    SupportedOrientations="PortraitOrLandscape"
    shell:SystemTray.IsVisible="True">
```

LISTING 6.3   Continued

```
<Grid>
  <Grid.RowDefinitions>
    <RowDefinition Height="Auto"/>
    <RowDefinition Height="*"/>
  </Grid.RowDefinitions>

  <!-- The standard header, with some tweaks -->
  <StackPanel Margin="24,16,0,12">
    <TextBlock Text="BABY SIGN LANGUAGE" Margin="-1,0,0,0"
               FontFamily="{StaticResource PhoneFontFamilySemiBold}"
               FontSize="{StaticResource PhoneFontSizeMedium}"/>
    <TextBlock x:Name="PageTitle" Text="" Margin="-3,-10,0,0"
               FontFamily="{StaticResource PhoneFontFamilySemiLight}"
               FontSize="{StaticResource PhoneFontSizeExtraExtraLarge}"/>
  </StackPanel>

  <ScrollViewer Grid.Row="1">
    <StackPanel Margin="{StaticResource PhoneHorizontalMargin}">
      <Image x:Name="ItemImage"/>
      <TextBlock x:Name="ItemTextBlock" Margin="{StaticResource PhoneMargin}"
                 TextWrapping="Wrap"/>
    </StackPanel>
  </ScrollViewer>
</Grid>
</phone:PhoneApplicationPage>
```

Notes:

→ An Image element is used to display the appropriate image, just like the images that Ruler used in the preceding chapter. Its Source property must be set in order for something to be displayed, but this is done in the code-behind.

→ The text block is told to wrap its text to prevent it from going off the right edge of the screen.

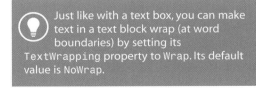

Just like with a text box, you can make text in a text block wrap (at word boundaries) by setting its TextWrapping property to Wrap. Its default value is NoWrap.

→ The stack panel is placed in a scroll viewer, for the sake of the landscape orientations.

Listing 6.4 contains the code-behind for this page.

LISTING 6.4   `DetailsPage.xaml.cs`—The Code-Behind for the Baby Sign Language Details Page

```csharp
using System.Windows.Media.Imaging;
using System.Windows.Navigation;
using Microsoft.Phone.Controls;

namespace WindowsPhoneApp
{
  public partial class DetailsPage : PhoneApplicationPage
  {
    public DetailsPage()
    {
      InitializeComponent();
    }

    protected override void OnNavigatedTo(NavigationEventArgs e)
    {
      // Make sure the two indices are passed along
      if (!this.NavigationContext.QueryString.ContainsKey("categoryIndex") ||
          !this.NavigationContext.QueryString.ContainsKey("signIndex"))
        return;

      // Convert the query string parameters into integers
      int categoryIndex =
        int.Parse(this.NavigationContext.QueryString["categoryIndex"]);
      int signIndex = int.Parse(this.NavigationContext.QueryString["signIndex"]);

      // Fetch the data
      Sign sign = Data.Categories[categoryIndex].Signs[signIndex];

      // Update the UI
      this.PageTitle.Text = sign.Name;
      this.ItemImage.Source = new BitmapImage(sign.ImageUri);
      this.ItemTextBlock.Text = sign.Description;
    }
  }
}
```

This implementation of `OnNavigatedTo` is similar to `MainPage`'s `OnNavigatedTo` method, except that it retrieves two values from the query string instead of one. Once it has both indices, it is able to retrieve the appropriate `Sign` instance from `Data.Categories`, and then it updates three pieces of UI with its three pieces of data.

Images

Although Listing 6.4 shows an image's source being set to an instance of a `BitmapImage` constructed with a URI, in XAML all you need to do is set `Source` to the desired URI. For example:

```
<Image Source="Images/play.png"/>
```

`Image` only supports PNG and JPEG files. Unlike with application bar buttons, the URI used with `Image` can point to a file included in your project with a Build Action of Content *or* Resource. The URI can even point to an image on the Internet:

```
<Image Source="http://adamnathanapps.com/logo.png"/>
```

? Which Build Action should I use with my images: Content or Resource?

Content is usually the best choice. Recall that resource files are embedded in DLL(s) inside the `.xap` file, whereas content files are placed directly inside the `.xap` file. Therefore, each resource increases the size of its DLL. This is important because larger DLLs cause an app to start more slowly, due in part to security checks done by the operating system when loading them. In addition, when an image is loaded from a content file, the work is done asynchronously (although still on the UI thread). When an image is loaded from a resource file, the work is done synchronously (also on the UI thread). There are a few cases where the synchronous behavior of a resource file is desired. See Chapter 27, "Groceries."

If you rotate the phone while an instance of `DetailsPage` is showing, something interesting happens with the image. As shown in Figure 6.6, it gets enlarged to continue filling the width of the page.

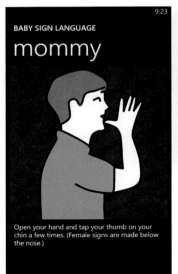

FIGURE 6.6   The image enlarges in a landscape orientation so it remains as wide as possible.

This behavior is caused by the Image element's Stretch property, and this can be customized. Stretch can be set to one of the following values:

→ **None**—The image is always shown at its original dimensions.

→ **Fill**—The image fills the space given to it. Therefore, its aspect ratio may not be preserved.

→ **Uniform** (the default value)—The image is scaled as large as possible while still fitting entirely within the space given to it and preserving its aspect ratio. Therefore, there will be extra space in one dimension if its aspect ratio doesn't match.

→ **UniformToFill**—The image is scaled to completely fill the space given to it while preserving its aspect ratio. Therefore, the content will be cropped in one dimension if its aspect ratio doesn't match.

As with the alignment properties, the result of setting Stretch to these values depends on the space allocated by the element's parent. Because the image in DetailsPage is placed in a vertical stack panel, setting its Stretch property to Fill, Uniform, and UniformToFill all behave identically, producing the result in Figure 6.6. When a smaller image is placed in a grid, however, the difference between all four values can be easily demonstrated, as shown in Figure 6.7.

| None | Fill | Uniform | UniformToFill |

FIGURE 6.7   Each of the four values for Image's Stretch property.

> **URIs pointing to image resources must *not* start with a forward slash!**
> Yes, you read that correctly. Keeping track of all the rules for using or not using a leading slash can be very confusing. Here's a summary that applies to almost all uses of URIs in Silverlight:
> → Navigation URIs must have a leading slash.
> → URIs pointing to a resource file (Build Action = Resource) must not have a leading slash.
> → URIs pointing to a content file (Build Action = Content) work both ways, slash or no slash.
> Furthermore, resource files referenced with a leading slash appear to work in the Visual Studio designer, despite the fact that they do not work at run-time.

The About Page

This app is the first of many to use a shared "about page" that displays something reasonable for any app that uses it, as seen back in Figure 6.1. The page requires the app's name to be passed to it, and it uses hardcoded copyright information, but it uses two tricks to automatically display the app's icon and the version number. Listing 6.5 shows its XAML.

> The Windows Phone Marketplace strongly recommends that apps include support information somewhere (the app's name, version number, and a way to contact the author). For a brief period of time, this was even required. An about page is great for conveying this information, typically via a link on an application bar menu.

LISTING 6.5   AboutPage.xaml—The User Interface for the About Page

```
<phone:PhoneApplicationPage x:Class="WindowsPhoneApp.AboutPage"
    xmlns="http://schemas.microsoft.com/winfx/2006/xaml/presentation"
    xmlns:x="http://schemas.microsoft.com/winfx/2006/xaml"
    xmlns:phone="clr-namespace:Microsoft.Phone.Controls;assembly=Microsoft.Phone"
    xmlns:shell="clr-namespace:Microsoft.Phone.Shell;assembly=Microsoft.Phone"
    FontFamily="{StaticResource PhoneFontFamilyNormal}"
    FontSize="{StaticResource PhoneFontSizeNormal}"
    Foreground="{StaticResource PhoneForegroundBrush}"
    SupportedOrientations="PortraitOrLandscape"
    shell:SystemTray.IsVisible="True">
  <Grid>
    <Grid.RowDefinitions>
      <RowDefinition Height="Auto"/>
      <RowDefinition Height="*"/>
    </Grid.RowDefinitions>

    <!-- The standard header, with some tweaks -->
    <StackPanel Margin="24,16,0,12">
```

LISTING 6.5 Continued

```xml
        <TextBlock x:Name="ApplicationName" Margin="-1,0,0,0"
                   FontFamily="{StaticResource PhoneFontFamilySemiBold}"
                   FontSize="{StaticResource PhoneFontSizeMedium}"/>
        <TextBlock Text="about" Margin="-3,-10,0,0"
                   FontFamily="{StaticResource PhoneFontFamilySemiLight}"
                   FontSize="{StaticResource PhoneFontSizeExtraExtraLarge}"/>
      </StackPanel>

      <!-- A stacked tile icon, version #, and copyright -->
      <ScrollViewer Grid.Row="1">
        <StackPanel>
          <Border Background="{StaticResource PhoneAccentBrush}"
                  HorizontalAlignment="Center">
            <Image Source="/Background.png" Stretch="None"/>
          </Border>
          <TextBlock x:Name="VersionTextBlock" Margin="24,8,24,0"/>
          <TextBlock Margin="24,36,24,0">© 2011 Adam Nathan</TextBlock>
        </StackPanel>
      </ScrollViewer>
    </Grid>
</phone:PhoneApplicationPage>
```

The trick to display the icon is simply to grab the same image used for the tile icon, assuming it is the standard spot (the root of the project) with the standard name (Background.png). The URI starts with a forward slash to ensure that the file is retrieved from the root, even if the page is linked into the project at a nonroot folder. This works because Background.png must be included as a content file in order to work as a tile icon.

Listing 6.6 contains the code-behind for this page.

LISTING 6.6   AboutPage.xaml.cs—The Code-Behind for the About Page

```csharp
using System.Windows.Navigation;
using Microsoft.Phone.Controls;

namespace WindowsPhoneApp
{
  public partial class AboutPage : PhoneApplicationPage
  {
    public AboutPage()
    {
      InitializeComponent();

      // Fill out the version number
      try
```

LISTING 6.6   Continued

```
    {
      string s = typeof(AboutPage).Assembly.ToString();
      if (s != null && s.IndexOf("Version=") >= 0)
      {
        s = s.Substring(s.IndexOf("Version=") + "Version=".Length);
        s = s.Substring(0, s.IndexOf(","));
        this.VersionTextBlock.Text = "version " + s;
      }
    }
    catch { /* Never mind! */ }
  }

  protected override void OnNavigatedTo(NavigationEventArgs e)
  {
    base.OnNavigatedTo(e);
    // Set the application name in the header
    if (this.NavigationContext.QueryString.ContainsKey("appName"))
    {
      this.ApplicationName.Text =
        this.NavigationContext.QueryString["appName"].ToUpperInvariant();
    }
  }
 }
}
```

To display that app's name, `OnNavigatedTo` does the now-familiar technique of grabbing it from the query string.

To display the version number, this code parses it out of the string returned by the current assembly's `ToString` method. This string can look something like this:

```
BabySignLanguage, Version=1.0.0.0, Culture=neutral, PublicKeyToken=null
```

`Assembly` has a `GetName` method that returns an object with a `Version` property, so it would have been better for the code to simply be:

```
VersionTextBlock.Text = "version " +
  typeof(AboutPage).Assembly.GetName().Version.ToString();
```

However, apps do not have permission to call this (it returns more information than what you get from `ToString`), which is why the string parsing technique is used instead.

> You can customize the version number displayed by this about page by changing the value of the `AssemblyVersion` attribute in your project's `AssemblyInfo.cs` file. This version number doesn't materially impact anything else. For example, the marketplace does not care what your assembly version number is, or if it even changes from one version to the next. If you use this about page, however, you should keep this number in sync with the version number you choose on the App Hub website when submitting your app so your page displays the correct information.

Data Binding

Although we've now seen a completely functional implementation of the Baby Sign Language app, the project included with this book has a few tweaks to make the code a bit nicer. It leverages data binding in a few more cases to reduce the amount C# code that needs to be written.

When data binding is used in the `MainPage` list box data template (the `{Binding Name}` string), it is implicitly given the context of the current list item so referencing the `Name` property has meaning. You can use this same data binding technique in other places, too, as long as you explicitly set the context.

Updating the Details Page

For example, the code-behind for `DetailsPage` in Listing 6.4 has this code inside of `OnNavigatedTo`:

```
// Update the UI
this.PageTitle.Text = sign.Name;
this.ItemImage.Source = new BitmapImage(sign.ImageUri);
this.ItemTextBlock.Text = sign.Description;
```

We can move the setting of these three properties from C# to XAML if we change these three lines of code to one that sets the page's `DataContext` property instead:

```
// Update the UI
this.DataContext = sign;
```

`DataContext` is of type `object`, so it can be set to anything. When it is set to the `sign` variable, the special `{Binding XXX}` syntax can be used by any element on the page to refer to properties on this object. Therefore, the XAML for `DetailsPage` in Listing 6.3 can change as follows to leverage this data context:

```
<phone:PhoneApplicationPage …>
  <Grid>
    <Grid.RowDefinitions>
      <RowDefinition Height="Auto"/>
      <RowDefinition Height="*"/>
    </Grid.RowDefinitions>
```

```
<!-- The standard header, with some tweaks -->
<StackPanel Margin="24,16,0,12">
  <TextBlock Text="BABY SIGN LANGUAGE" Margin="-1,0,0,0"
             FontFamily="{StaticResource PhoneFontFamilySemiBold}"
             FontSize="{StaticResource PhoneFontSizeMedium}"/>
  <TextBlock x:Name="PageTitle" Text="{Binding Name}" Margin="-3,-10,0,0"
             FontFamily="{StaticResource PhoneFontFamilySemiLight}"
             FontSize="{StaticResource PhoneFontSizeExtraExtraLarge}"/>
</StackPanel>

<ScrollViewer Grid.Row="1">
  <StackPanel Margin="{StaticResource PhoneHorizontalMargin}">
    <Image x:Name="ItemImage" Source="{Binding ImageUri}"/>
    <TextBlock x:Name="ItemTextBlock" Text="{Binding Description}"
               Margin="{StaticResource PhoneMargin}"
               TextWrapping="Wrap"/>
  </StackPanel>
</ScrollViewer>
</Grid>
</phone:PhoneApplicationPage>
```

Notice that the three elements with databound property values no longer need to be named, as they no longer need to be accessed from code-behind! Although this updated `DetailsPage` behaves identically to the original one, having the details of the data display captured entirely within the XAML file usually enables a more flexible and less error-prone development process compared to keeping things in sync

> The `DataContext` property can be set on any visual element in your page, not just on the page itself. Therefore, you can give the page one overall context, but give different pieces of the page different contexts. An element's context always overrides a context that would have been inherited from an ancestor element, not just for that element but also for any of its descendants.

across a XAML file and its code-behind file. And although the `Binding` syntax takes some getting used to, it usually results in fewer lines of code needing to be written.

Updating the Main Page

`MainPage` can also be updated to take advantage of data binding when filling the list box with its items. Listing 6.2 has the following implementation of the page's `Loaded` event handler:

```
void MainPage_Loaded(object sender, RoutedEventArgs e)
{
  if (this.ListBox.Items.Count > 0)
    return; // We already added the data.
           // (We must be navigating back to this page.)
```

```
if (this.categoryIndex == -1)
{
  // This is the root page. Fill the list box with the categories.
  foreach (Category category in Data.Categories)
    this.ListBox.Items.Add(category);
}
else
{
  // This is a page for a specific category.
  // Fill the list box with the category's items.
  foreach (Sign sign in Data.Categories[this.categoryIndex].Signs)
    this.ListBox.Items.Add(sign);
}
}
```

In addition to its Items property, however, ListBox has an ItemsSource property. This property (of type IEnumerable) can be used instead of Items to assign an entire collection of data in one step, rather than filling its Items collection one-by-one:

```
void MainPage_Loaded(object sender, RoutedEventArgs e)
{
  if (this.ListBox.Items.Count > 0)
    return; // We already added the data.
            // (We must be navigating back to this page.)

  if (this.categoryIndex == -1)
  {
    // This is the root page. Fill the list box with the categories.
    this.ListBox.ItemsSource = Data.Categories;
  }
  else
  {
    // This is a page for a specific category.
    // Fill the list box with the category's items.
    this.ListBox.ItemsSource = Data.Categories[this.categoryIndex].Signs;
  }
}
```

This reduces the amount of code by two lines, but it doesn't buy us much. The advantage of using ItemsSource (and the reason for its existence) is that you can set its value via data binding. The final implementation of MainPage_Loaded sets the page's DataContext property instead of directly setting ItemsSource:

```
void MainPage_Loaded(object sender, RoutedEventArgs e)
{
  if (this.ListBox.Items.Count > 0)
```

```
      return; // We already added the data.
              // (We must be navigating back to this page.)

  if (this.categoryIndex == -1)
  {
    // This is the root page. Fill the list box with the categories.
    this.DataContext = Data.Categories;
  }
  else
  {
    // This is a page for a specific category.
    // Fill the list box with the category's items.
    this.DataContext = Data.Categories[this.categoryIndex].Signs;
  }
}
```

With this in place, the list box in `MainPage.xaml` (Listing 6.1) can be updated to set its `ItemsSource` to the entire `DataContext` object:

```
<ListBox x:Name="ListBox" ItemsSource="{Binding}"
        SelectionChanged="ListBox_SelectionChanged">
  <ListBox.ItemTemplate>
    …
  </ListBox.ItemTemplate>
</ListBox>
```

When the `Binding` syntax is used without any property name, this indicates that the entire object should be used rather than the value of one of its properties.

The advantage of using data binding is not obvious in this case. Setting a list box's `ItemsSource` with data binding enables it to provide performance optimizations when the list of data is large. Data binding also provides a number of convenient behaviors when the underlying data changes (seen in later chapters). Although neither of these is true for this small set of unchanging data, it's a good habit to interact with a list box in this fashion.

 When using `ItemsSource`, **you cannot modify the collection via the** `Items` **property!**

When you set a list box's `ItemsSource`, its `Items` property automatically provides data about the same collection, and it can be accessed in a readonly fashion. (Notice that the modified implementation of `MainPage_Loaded` is still able to check the `Items.Count` property.) Attempting to *modify* the collection via `Items`, however, throws an `InvalidOperationException` if `ItemsSource` is non-null. You should be modifying the underlying collection (such as `Data.Categories`) instead. Depending on the type of collection, the list box gets updated automatically. Chapter 21, "Passwords & Secrets," introduces such *observable* collections.

> The design-time XML namespace (typically used with the d prefix in XAML files) defines a mechanism for using *design-time data*. This mechanism can be used to provide a fake data context at design-time only, so any databound property values on a page can display something meaningful in the Visual Studio or Expression Blend designer. If you create a "Windows Phone Databound Application" project in Visual Studio, you can see this being used in both `MainPage.xaml` and `DetailsPage.xaml`:
>
> ```
> d:DataContext="{d:DesignData SampleData/MainViewModelSampleData.xaml}"
> ```
>
> The design-time collection of fake data is actually defined in a XAML file. (XAML can be useful for representing data as well as UI!)

The Finished Product

Navigating from one page to another performs the "page flip" animation

Viewing the details of the "eat" sign

Viewing the details of the "play" sign

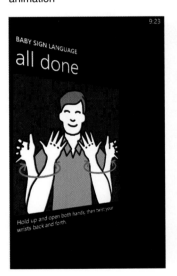

chapter 7 lessons

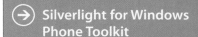 **Silverlight for Windows Phone Toolkit**

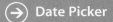 **Date Picker**

DATE DIFF

Date Diff, named after the T-SQL DATEDIFF function, tells you how many days or weeks apart two dates are. This app requires very little code, thanks to the Silverlight for Windows Phone Toolkit.

The Silverlight for Windows Phone Toolkit, available at http://silverlight.codeplex.com, contains lots of rich controls and functionality leveraged throughout this book. It's open source, so you can even tweak it relatively easily! This app makes use of its date picker control, which matches the date picker used by the phone's built-in apps. It starts out looking like a text box, but it presents a rich full-page interface when tapped.

> To use the Silverlight for Windows Phone Toolkit, download it from http://silverlight.codeplex.com. You can either install the `.msi` file or get the source code `.zip` file and compile it yourself. Once you have taken one of these actions, you can reference the `Microsoft.Phone.Controls.Toolkit` assembly in your projects.

Future releases of the Silverlight for Windows Phone Toolkit may not be compatible with earlier releases!

The goal of the toolkit, besides providing developers with handy functionality, is to rapidly iterate on features that might become a part of the official Windows Phone Developer Tools in the future. Therefore, the team is not shy about making changes that can break code compiled against a previous version. Also, when features from the toolkit are added to the Windows Phone Developer Tools, they will likely be *removed* from the toolkit.

As long as you continue to use the same version of the toolkit in your apps, future changes should not cause you any trouble. The only thing to be careful about is upgrading the toolkit and recompiling your apps without thoroughly testing them. The apps in this book use the February 2011 release of the toolkit.

The Main Page

Date Diff's only page (other than the page automatically presented by the date picker) is pictured in Figure 7.1. The user can customize the date in each date picker instance and then see the difference below.

Before dates are chosen   After Date #2 is changed

FIGURE 7.1   The main page enables the selection of two dates and then shows the difference.

Listing 7.1 contains the XAML for this page.

LISTING 7.1   `MainPage.xaml`—The User Interface for Date Diff's Main Page

```xaml
<phone:PhoneApplicationPage x:Class="WindowsPhoneApp.MainPage"
    xmlns="http://schemas.microsoft.com/winfx/2006/xaml/presentation"
    xmlns:x="http://schemas.microsoft.com/winfx/2006/xaml"
    xmlns:phone="clr-namespace:Microsoft.Phone.Controls;assembly=Microsoft.Phone"
    xmlns:shell="clr-namespace:Microsoft.Phone.Shell;assembly=Microsoft.Phone"
    xmlns:toolkit="clr-namespace:Microsoft.Phone.Controls;
➥assembly=Microsoft.Phone.Controls.Toolkit"
    xmlns:local="clr-namespace:WindowsPhoneApp"
    FontFamily="{StaticResource PhoneFontFamilyNormal}"
    FontSize="{StaticResource PhoneFontSizeNormal}"
    Foreground="{StaticResource PhoneForegroundBrush}"
    SupportedOrientations="PortraitOrLandscape"
    shell:SystemTray.IsVisible="True">
  <Grid>
    <Grid.RowDefinitions>
      <RowDefinition Height="Auto"/>
      <RowDefinition Height="*"/>
    </Grid.RowDefinitions>

    <!-- The standard header, with some tweaks -->
    <StackPanel Margin="24,16,0,12">
      <TextBlock Text="DATE DIFF" Margin="-1,0,0,0"
                 FontFamily="{StaticResource PhoneFontFamilySemiBold}"
                 FontSize="{StaticResource PhoneFontSizeMedium}"/>
      <TextBlock Text="pick two dates" Margin="-3,-10,0,0"
                 FontFamily="{StaticResource PhoneFontFamilySemiLight}"
                 FontSize="{StaticResource PhoneFontSizeExtraExtraLarge}"/>
    </StackPanel>

    <StackPanel Grid.Row="1">
      <!-- Date #1 -->
      <TextBlock Text="Date #1" Margin="24,17,24,-5"
                 Foreground="{StaticResource PhoneSubtleBrush}"/>
      <toolkit:DatePicker x:Name="DatePicker1" Margin="12,0"
        local:Tilt.IsEnabled="True" ValueChanged="DatePicker_ValueChanged"/>

      <!-- Date #2 -->
      <TextBlock Text="Date #2" Margin="24,17,24,-5"
                 Foreground="{StaticResource PhoneSubtleBrush}"/>
      <toolkit:DatePicker x:Name="DatePicker2" Margin="12,0"
        local:Tilt.IsEnabled="True" ValueChanged="DatePicker_ValueChanged"/>

      <!-- The result -->
      <TextBlock x:Name="ResultTextBlock" Margin="24,0"
```

LISTING 7.1   Continued

```
                    FontSize="{StaticResource PhoneFontSizeExtraLarge}"/>
    </StackPanel>
  </Grid>
</phone:PhoneApplicationPage>
```

Notes:

→ Although `DatePicker` is in the same `Microsoft.Phone.Controls` namespace as other controls, it resides in the `Microsoft.Phone.Controls.`**`Toolkit`** assembly, so this XAML file requires a separate XML namespace declaration. By convention, apps in this book use the `toolkit` prefix for this namespace/assembly.

→ The two date pickers automatically show today's date by default, and when tapped they invoke the full-screen picker interface shown at the beginning of this chapter. The tilt effect applied to each date picker only affects the inline display; not the full-screen picker.

> (!) **The date picker requires two specific images to be included in your project!**
>
> The page shown by the date picker uses an application bar with the standard "done" and "cancel" buttons. However, *you* are responsible for including the two icon images in your project (and marking them with a **Build Action** of **Content**) with the proper names and location. If you fail to do this, you'll see the standard error icons in their place.
>
> The two icons must be named `ApplicationBar.Check.png` and `ApplicationBar.Cancel.png`, and they must be placed in a folder called `Toolkit.Content` in the root of your project. These image files are included with the Silverlight for Windows Phone Toolkit (as well as the source code for this chapter).
>
> This requirement is caused by the application bar's limitation of only working with images marked as *content*.

Listing 7.2 contains the code-behind for the main page.

LISTING 7.2   `MainPage.xaml.cs`—The Code-Behind for Date Diff's Main Page

```
using System;
using Microsoft.Phone.Controls;

namespace WindowsPhoneApp
{
  public partial class MainPage : PhoneApplicationPage
  {
    public MainPage()
    {
      InitializeComponent();
```

LISTING 7.2   Continued

```csharp
      }

      void DatePicker_ValueChanged(object sender, DateTimeValueChangedEventArgs e)
      {
        // Do the calculation
        TimeSpan span = this.DatePicker2.Value.Value - this.DatePicker1.Value.Value;

        // Format the result
        int days = span.Days;
        int wholeWeeks = days / 7;
        int remainder = days % 7;

        string result = days + (Math.Abs(days) == 1 ? " day" : " days");
        if (Math.Abs(days) > 14)
        {
          result += "\n(" + wholeWeeks + " weeks";
          if (remainder != 0)
            result += ", " + remainder
                          + (Math.Abs(remainder) == 1 ? " day" : " days");
          result += ")";
        }

        // Display the result
        this.ResultTextBlock.Text = result;
      }
    }
}
```

Notes:

→ Each date picker's date can be retrieved via its `Value` property, which is a nullable `DateTime` that has its own `Value` property. The nullability is handy because it enables each picker to express the concept of no date being selected. However, it also results in awkward-looking `Value.Value` property accesses. Because `Value` can only become `null` programmatically, this code can safely access each `Value` subproperty without checking for `null`.

→ Most of the code is concerned with formatting the string, which takes a few different forms depending on how far apart the two dates are.

The Finished Product

An ending date
before the starting date

A whole number of
weeks between the dates

An ending date only one
day after the starting date

chapter 8

VIBRATION COMPOSER

Vibration Composer is probably the strangest app in this part of the book. A cross between a musical instrument and a handheld massager, this app provides an interesting way to create your own custom vibrating patterns.

Users can do some fun things with this app:

→ Create a solid vibration to use it like a massager app.

→ Set the phone on a table while it vibrates and watch it move!

→ Play music from the Music + Videos hub and then use this app to accompany it with vibrations.

> This app requires the running-while-the-phone-is-locked capability (automatically granted during the market-place certification process). Therefore, this app's market-place listing will contain the awkward phrase, "This app makes use of your phone's RunsUnderLock." (The exact phrase depends on whether you look in Zune or the phone's Marketplace app, and may change in the future.)

The Main Page

Vibration Composer's main page represents time in square chunks. Each chunk lasts 1/10th of a second. You can tap any square to toggle it between an activated state and a deactivated state. When you press the app's start button, it highlights each square in sequence and makes the phone

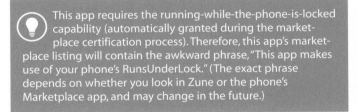

vibrate when an activated square is highlighted. Once it reaches the last activated square, it repeats the sequence from the beginning. Therefore, although the page contains 90 squares (enabling the unique pattern to be up to 9 seconds long), the user is in control over the length of the segment to be repeated. Figure 8.1 demonstrates three simple vibration patterns.

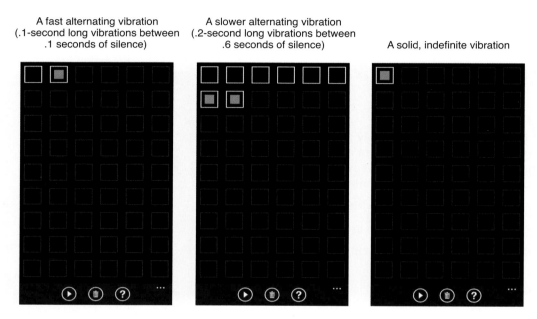

A fast alternating vibration (.1-second long vibrations between .1 seconds of silence)

A slower alternating vibration (.2-second long vibrations between .6 seconds of silence)

A solid, indefinite vibration

FIGURE 8.1   The pattern to be repeated is automatically trimmed after the last activated square.

The User Interface

Listing 8.1 contains the XAML for the main page.

LISTING 8.1   `MainPage.xaml`—The User Interface for Vibration Composer's Main Page

```
<phone:PhoneApplicationPage
  x:Class="WindowsPhoneApp.MainPage"
  xmlns="http://schemas.microsoft.com/winfx/2006/xaml/presentation"
  xmlns:x="http://schemas.microsoft.com/winfx/2006/xaml"
  xmlns:phone="clr-namespace:Microsoft.Phone.Controls;assembly=Microsoft.Phone"
  xmlns:shell="clr-namespace:Microsoft.Phone.Shell;assembly=Microsoft.Phone"
  xmlns:toolkit="clr-namespace:Microsoft.Phone.Controls;
➥assembly=Microsoft.Phone.Controls.Toolkit"
  SupportedOrientations="PortraitOrLandscape">

  <!-- The application bar, with three buttons and five menu items -->
```

LISTING 8.1   Continued

```xml
<phone:PhoneApplicationPage.ApplicationBar>
  <shell:ApplicationBar>
    <shell:ApplicationBarIconButton Text="start"
      IconUri="/Shared/Images/appbar.play.png" Click="StartStopButton_Click"/>
    <shell:ApplicationBarIconButton Text="delete"
      IconUri="/Shared/Images/appbar.delete.png" Click="DeleteButton_Click"/>
    <shell:ApplicationBarIconButton Text="instructions"
      IconUri="/Shared/Images/appbar.instructions.png"
      Click="InstructionsButton_Click"/>
    <shell:ApplicationBar.MenuItems>
      <shell:ApplicationBarMenuItem Text="solid"/>
      <shell:ApplicationBarMenuItem Text="alternating fast"/>
      <shell:ApplicationBarMenuItem Text="alternating slow"/>
      <shell:ApplicationBarMenuItem Text="sos"/>
      <shell:ApplicationBarMenuItem Text="phone ring"/>
    </shell:ApplicationBar.MenuItems>
  </shell:ApplicationBar>
</phone:PhoneApplicationPage.ApplicationBar>

<ScrollViewer>
  <Grid>
    <!-- A wrap panel for containing the 90 buttons -->
    <toolkit:WrapPanel x:Name="WrapPanel"/>
    <!-- A separate rectangle for tracking the current position -->
    <Rectangle x:Name="CurrentPositionRectangle" Visibility="Collapsed"
               Width="56" Height="56" Margin="12" Opacity=".8"
               HorizontalAlignment="Left" VerticalAlignment="Top"
               Fill="{StaticResource PhoneForegroundBrush}"/>
  </Grid>
</ScrollViewer>

</phone:PhoneApplicationPage>
```

Notes:

→ The first application bar button starts and stops the vibration sequence playback, the second button clears the sequence, and the third button navigates to an instructions page. Each of the menu items, shown in Figure 8.2, fills the page with a predefined pattern to help familiarize users with the app and give them ideas for getting interesting results.

→ This page uses a panel from the Silverlight for Windows Phone Toolkit known as a *wrap panel* to contain each of the squares. (The squares are added in code-behind.) A wrap panel stacks its children from left to right, and then wraps them from top to bottom when it runs out of room. (Or you can change the wrap panel's Orientation property to Vertical to make it stack its children from top to bottom and then wrap them from left to right.)

Figure 8.3 demonstrates how the wrap panel changes the layout of the squares based on the current orientation. In the portrait orientation, 6 squares fit in each row before wrapping to the next row. In the landscape orientations, 9 squares fit before wrapping. The reason this app uses a total of 90 squares is that it happens to be divisible by 6 and 9, avoiding a partial row of squares at the end.

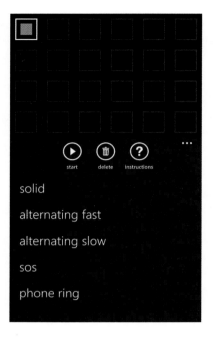

FIGURE 8.2   The application bar menu provides access to five predefined patterns.

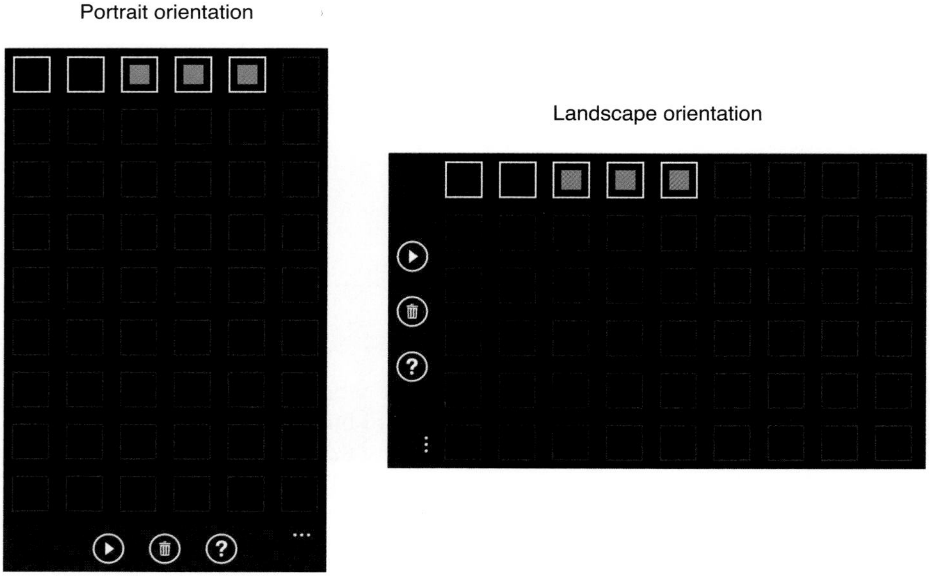

Portrait orientation

Landscape orientation

FIGURE 8.3   The wrap panel reflows the squares based on the current orientation.

→ The wrap panel is placed in a grid so a rectangle tracking the current position can be moved by code-behind to overlap each square when appropriate. This grid is placed inside a scroll viewer, so the user can access all 90 squares.

The Code-Behind

Listing 8.2 contains the code-behind for the main page.

LISTING 8.2   `MainPage.xaml.cs`—The Code-Behind for Vibration Composer's Main Page

```
using System;
using System.Collections.Generic;
using System.Windows;
using System.Windows.Controls;
using System.Windows.Media;
using System.Windows.Navigation;
using System.Windows.Shapes;
using System.Windows.Threading;
using Microsoft.Phone.Controls;
using Microsoft.Phone.Shell;
using Microsoft.Devices;

namespace WindowsPhoneApp
{
  public partial class MainPage : PhoneApplicationPage
  {
    // The squares
    Button[] buttons = new Button[90];

    // Remember the current sequence
    Setting<IList<bool>> savedSequence = new Setting<IList<bool>>("Sequence",
      new List<bool>());

    DispatcherTimer timer = new DispatcherTimer();
    int sequencePosition;
    int sequenceEndPosition = -1;
    bool isRunning = false;

    IApplicationBarIconButton startStopButton;

    public MainPage()
    {
      InitializeComponent();
      this.startStopButton = this.ApplicationBar.Buttons[0]
        as IApplicationBarIconButton;
```

LISTING 8.2   Continued

```
  // Initialize the timer
  this.timer.Interval = TimeSpan.FromSeconds(.1);
  this.timer.Tick += Timer_Tick;

  // Attach the same Click handler to all menu items in the application bar
  foreach (IApplicationBarMenuItem menuItem in this.ApplicationBar.MenuItems)
    menuItem.Click += MenuItem_Click;

  // Fill the wrap panel with the 90 buttons
  for (int i = 0; i < this.buttons.Length; i++)
  {
    this.buttons[i] = new Button {
      // Each button contains a square, invisible (Fill=null) when off and
      // accent-colored when on
      Content = new Rectangle { Margin = new Thickness(0, 7, 0, 5),
                                Width = 30, Height = 30 }
    };
    this.buttons[i].Click += Button_Click;
    this.WrapPanel.Children.Add(this.buttons[i]);
  }
  TrimSequence();

  // Allow the app to run (and vibrate) even when the phone is locked.
  // Once disabled, you cannot re-enable the default behavior!
  PhoneApplicationService.Current.ApplicationIdleDetectionMode =
    IdleDetectionMode.Disabled;
}

protected override void OnNavigatedFrom(NavigationEventArgs e)
{
  base.OnNavigatedFrom(e);

  // Persist the current sequence
  this.savedSequence.Value.Clear();
  for (int i = 0; i <= this.sequenceEndPosition; i++)
    this.savedSequence.Value.Add(this.buttons[i].Tag != null);

  // Prevent this from running while instructions are shown
  Stop();
}

protected override void OnNavigatedTo(NavigationEventArgs e)
{
  base.OnNavigatedTo(e);
```

LISTING 8.2   Continued

```
    // Restore the saved sequence, if any
    for (int i = 0; i < this.savedSequence.Value.Count; i++)
    {
      if (this.savedSequence.Value[i])
        TurnOn(this.buttons[i]);
    }
    TrimSequence();
  }

  // Click handler for each of the 90 buttons
  void Button_Click(object sender, RoutedEventArgs e)
  {
    // Toggle the state of this button
    Button b = sender as Button;
    if (b.Tag != null)
      TurnOff(b);
    else
      TurnOn(b);

    TrimSequence();
  }

  void TurnOn(Button b)
  {
    b.Tag = true; // This button is "on"
    (b.Content as Rectangle).Fill =
      Application.Current.Resources["PhoneAccentBrush"] as Brush;
  }

  void TurnOff(Button b)
  {
    b.Tag = null; // This button is "off"
    (b.Content as Rectangle).Fill = null;
  }

  void TrimSequence()
  {
    // Find the end of the sequence (the last "on" button)
    // and make the remaining buttons dim (opacity of .2)
    this.sequenceEndPosition = -1;
    for (int i = this.buttons.Length - 1; i >= 0; i--)
    {
      this.buttons[i].Opacity = 1;
```

LISTING 8.2   Continued

```
      if (this.sequenceEndPosition == -1)
      {
        if (this.buttons[i].Tag == null)
          this.buttons[i].Opacity = .2;
        else
          this.sequenceEndPosition = i;
      }
    }

    if (this.isRunning && this.sequenceEndPosition == -1)
    {
      // Force the playback to stop, because a sequenceEndPosition of -1
      // means that the sequence is empty (all buttons are off)
      StartStopButton_Click(this, EventArgs.Empty);
    }
  }

  void Timer_Tick(object sender, EventArgs e)
  {
    // Find the wrap-panel-relative location of the current button
    Point buttonLocation = this.buttons[this.sequencePosition]
      .TransformToVisual(this.WrapPanel).Transform(new Point(0, 0));

    // Move the current position rectangle to overlap the current button
    this.CurrentPositionRectangle.Margin = new Thickness(
      buttonLocation.X + 12, buttonLocation.Y + 12, 0, 0);

    // Either start or stop vibrating, based on the state of the current button
    if (this.buttons[this.sequencePosition].Tag != null)
      VibrateController.Default.Start(TimeSpan.FromSeconds(.5));
    else
      VibrateController.Default.Stop();

    // Advance the current position, and make it loop indefinitely
    this.sequencePosition = (this.sequencePosition + 1)
                            % (this.sequenceEndPosition + 1);
  }

  void Stop()
  {
    this.timer.Stop();
    VibrateController.Default.Stop();
    this.startStopButton.IconUri = new Uri("/Shared/Images/appbar.play.png",
                                    UriKind.Relative);
```

LISTING 8.2   Continued

```csharp
      this.startStopButton.Text = "start";
      this.CurrentPositionRectangle.Visibility = Visibility.Collapsed;
      this.isRunning = false;
    }

    void Clear()
    {
      for (int i = 0; i < this.buttons.Length; i++)
        TurnOff(this.buttons[i]);
    }

    // Application bar handlers

    void StartStopButton_Click(object sender, EventArgs e)
    {
      if (this.isRunning)
      {
        // Stop and restore all state
        Stop();
        return;
      }

      if (this.sequenceEndPosition == -1)
      {
        MessageBox.Show("The vibration pattern is empty! You must turn at least "
          + "one square on.", "Empty Sequence", MessageBoxButton.OK);
        return;
      }

      // Start
      this.startStopButton.IconUri =
        new Uri("/Shared/Images/appbar.stop.png", UriKind.Relative);
      this.startStopButton.Text = "stop";
      this.CurrentPositionRectangle.Visibility = Visibility.Visible;
      this.sequencePosition = 0;
      this.isRunning = true;
      this.timer.Start();
    }

    void InstructionsButton_Click(object sender, EventArgs e)
    {
      this.NavigationService.Navigate(new Uri("/InstructionsPage.xaml",
                                      UriKind.Relative));
    }
```

LISTING 8.2   Continued

```
void DeleteButton_Click(object sender, EventArgs e)
{
  if (MessageBox.Show("Are you sure you want to clear the whole sequence?",
    "Delete Sequence", MessageBoxButton.OKCancel) == MessageBoxResult.OK)
  {
    Clear();
    TrimSequence();
  }
}

void MenuItem_Click(object sender, EventArgs e)
{
  Clear();

  // Grab the text from the menu item to determine the chosen sequence
  switch ((sender as IApplicationBarMenuItem).Text)
  {
    case "solid":
      TurnOn(this.buttons[0]);
      break;
    case "alternating fast":
      TurnOn(this.buttons[1]);
      break;
    case "alternating slow":
      TurnOn(this.buttons[6]);
      TurnOn(this.buttons[7]);
      break;
    case "sos":
      TurnOn(this.buttons[10]);
      TurnOn(this.buttons[11]);

      …
      break;
    case "phone ring":
      TurnOn(this.buttons[17]);
      TurnOn(this.buttons[21]);

      …
      break;
  }

  TrimSequence();
  }
 }
}
```

Notes:

→ The squares used by this app are actually normal buttons whose content is a rectangle element. These are created in the page's constructor and added to the wrap panel.

→ The setting of `ApplicationIdleDetectionMode` to `Disabled` allows the app to continue running even if the user locks their screen. (This is the only kind of background running your app can do in version 7.0 of Windows Phone. Actual multitasking is coming by the end of 2011.) This enables the phone to be used as, say, a massager, without needing to keep the screen active and worrying about accidentally tapping things.

> `PhoneApplicationService` defines two properties for customizing the behavior of phone locking, but their confusing names make it hard to remember what they do.
>
> When `PhoneApplicationService.Current.ApplicationIdleDetectionMode` is set to `Disabled`, the app continues to run if and when the phone is locked—even when the screen is off. This is useful for apps that track long-term movement via GPS or apps that play music.
>
> While `PhoneApplicationService.Current.UserIdleDetectionMode` is set to `Disabled`, the user's screen time-out setting is ignored so the screen is never automatically dimmed or locked. (If the user presses the Power button, the phone will still lock and the screen will be turned off.) This is meant for apps where the user is likely to go a long period of time without touching the screen, such an app that plays videos, accelerometer-based games, or a turn-by-turn navigation app. This feature is used in the next chapter.

> When you make your app run under the lock screen, consider making it optional by providing a setting that toggles the value of `ApplicationIdleDetectionMode`. Unfortunately, although setting it to `Disabled` takes effect immediately, setting it to `Enabled` once it's in this state does not work. Therefore, you must explain to your users that toggling the run-under-lock feature requires restarting your app, at least in one direction.
>
> For a brief period of time, the Windows Phone Marketplace *required* that any app that sets `ApplicationIdleDetectionMode` to `Disabled` must provide a way for users to set it to `Enabled`. For now, this is no longer a requirement.

→ The state of each button is stored in its `Tag` property. In addition to updating the fill of the rectangle inside the relevant button, `TurnOn` sets the button's `Tag` to true, whereas `TurnOff` sets it to `null`. `Tag` can be set to any object, and it's up to you how you want to use the values. It's just a handy spot to store your own data. Using `Tag` is considered to be a bit of a hack, but it's a simple solution. Instead of using it in this case, many Silverlight developers might use the Visual State Manager, covered in Chapter 19, "Animation Lab," to define two distinct states for each button.

→ A timer keeps track of where we are when playing the sequence of vibrations, much like the timers used in Chapter 2, "Flashlight." The `Tick` event handler, `Timer_Tick`, either starts or stops the phone's vibration with `VibrateController.Default.Start` and `VibrateController.Default.Stop` (from the `Microsoft.Devices` namespace). You can call `Start` with a time span of up to 5 seconds. Although longer time spans aren't supported, using a timer enables you to combine shorter vibrations into an arbitrarily-long one.

Given that the timer interval is 1/10th of a second, a more straightforward implementation of `Timer_Tick` would make the phone vibrate for 1/10th of a second if the current square is on, otherwise do nothing:

```
if (this.buttons[this.sequencePosition].Tag != null)
  VibrateController.Default.Start(TimeSpan.FromSeconds(.1));
else { /* Nothing to do! */ }
```

However, this can cause small gaps of silence when consecutive squares are on. Because I wanted to enable long stretches of vibration with consecutive "on" squares, `Timer_Tick` instead starts the vibration for longer than necessary (half a second) or stops the vibration each tick. (Calling `Start` while the phone is already vibrating is fine; the vibration will simply continue for the length of time specified.)

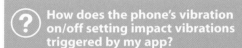

How does the phone's vibration on/off setting impact vibrations triggered by my app?

It has no impact. The phone's vibration setting (found under "ringtones & sounds" in the Settings app) only controls whether incoming phone calls can vibrate. When you use `VibrateController`, it *always* makes the phone vibrate. Furthermore, you have no way to discover the phone's vibration setting, so you can't manually respect this setting even if you want to.

→ Inside `Timer_Tick`, the rectangle that highlights the current position is moved to completely overlap the appropriate button. This is done with the handy `TransformToVisual` method (available on all UI elements), which provides a way to map any point relative to one element into coordinates relative to another element. Previously, we have done this by calling `GetPosition` on a `MouseEventArgs` instance, but we have no such instance at this point in the code. The awkward thing about `TransformToVisual` (in addition to its name) is that it returns an instance of a `GeneralTransform` object. From this object, you must then call `Transform` to map one point to another.

→ The timer is stopped when the user navigates away from this page. This is done to avoid a problem when navigating to the instructions page while the timer is running. The `Timer_Tick` event would continue to be called, but the call to `TransformToVisual` fails when main page is no longer the active page.

The Instructions Page

Listing 8.3 contains the XAML for the simple instructions page shown in Figure 8.4.

Toggle the squares on and off to compose a repeating pattern of vibration. Each square represents 1/10th of a second. Swipe the page to access all 9 seconds of squares.

When you're ready to start the vibration, tap the "play" button. You can edit the sequence while it's playing.

The end of the sequence is always the last "on" square. Therefore, to add silence between each sequence repetition, you must leave empty squares at the beginning.

Tap "..." to access a menu of sample sequences.

FIGURE 8.4   The instructions page used by Vibration Composer.

LISTING 8.3   `InstructionsPage.xaml`—The User Interface for the Instructions Page

```
<phone:PhoneApplicationPage
    x:Class="WindowsPhoneApp.InstructionsPage"
    xmlns="http://schemas.microsoft.com/winfx/2006/xaml/presentation"
    xmlns:x="http://schemas.microsoft.com/winfx/2006/xaml"
    xmlns:phone="clr-namespace:Microsoft.Phone.Controls;assembly=Microsoft.Phone"
    xmlns:shell="clr-namespace:Microsoft.Phone.Shell;assembly=Microsoft.Phone"
    FontFamily="{StaticResource PhoneFontFamilyNormal}"
    FontSize="{StaticResource PhoneFontSizeNormal}"
    Foreground="{StaticResource PhoneForegroundBrush}"
    SupportedOrientations="PortraitOrLandscape" shell:SystemTray.IsVisible="True">
  <Grid>
    <Grid.RowDefinitions>
      <RowDefinition Height="Auto"/>
      <RowDefinition Height="*"/>
    </Grid.RowDefinitions>

    <!-- The standard header, with some tweaks -->
    <StackPanel Margin="24,16,0,12">
      <TextBlock Text="VIBRATION COMPOSER" Margin="-1,0,0,0
                FontFamily="{StaticResource PhoneFontFamilySemiBold}"
                FontSize="{StaticResource PhoneFontSizeMedium}"/>
```

LISTING 8.3   Continued

```
        <TextBlock Text="instructions" Margin="-3,-10,0,0"
                FontFamily="{StaticResource PhoneFontFamilySemiLight}"
                FontSize="{StaticResource PhoneFontSizeExtraExtraLarge}"/>
    </StackPanel>

    <ScrollViewer Grid.Row="1">
      <TextBlock Margin="24,12" TextWrapping="Wrap">
        Tap the squares to toggle them on and off. …
        <LineBreak/><LineBreak/>
        When you're ready to start the vibration, tap the "play" button. …
        <LineBreak/><LineBreak/>
        The end of the sequence is always the last "on" square. …
        <LineBreak/><LineBreak/>
        Tap "..." to access a menu of sample sequences.
      </TextBlock>
    </ScrollViewer>
  </Grid>
</phone:PhoneApplicationPage>
```

→ This page also supports all orientations, and uses a scroll viewer to ensure that all the text can be read regardless of orientation.

→ The code-behind file, `InstructionsPage.xaml.cs`, has nothing more than the call to `InitializeComponent` in the class's constructor.

Listing 8.3 has something new inside its text block: LineBreak elements! You can use LineBreak to insert a carriage return in the middle of a single text block's text. This only works when the text is specified as the inner content of the element. It cannot be used when assigning the Text attribute to a string.

The Finished Product

The current position rectangle shows the playback progress

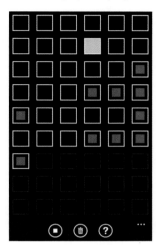

Using the light theme and orange accent color

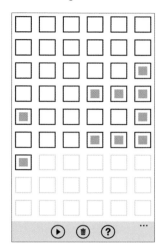

Using the light theme and magenta accent color

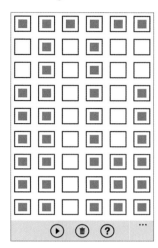

chapter 9

FAKE CALL

The Fake Call app makes your phone appear to receive an incoming call at a time you specify. You can use this as an excuse to get out of a bad date or an otherwise-unpleasant situation. Simply pretend to answer the fake call, make up some plausible story about needing to leave as a result of the phone call, and leave!

This app has three pages:

→ The main page (for your eyes only), which enables you to customize when the fake call will occur and who is fake-calling you—in case the victim of your scheme catches a glimpse of your screen.

→ The incoming-call page, which stays blank until it's time for the incoming call to appear.

→ The call-in-progress page, which mimics the active phone call once you press the "answer" button.

Unlike the preceding app, this intentionally does not use the page transition animation when navigating from one page to another, because that would interfere with the illusion that the real Phone app is being used. In this app, multiple pages are used just as a nice way to structure the code rather than as a metaphor that benefits users.

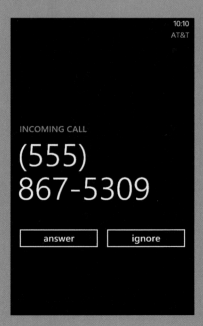

This app provides opportunities for an ambitious reader to add several features. For example, you could add support for

→ Animations that mimic the real Phone app

→ Customizations to mimic the experience when one of your contacts calls you (such as showing their photo in the background)

→ Support for ringtones in addition to the vibrating ring

→ Human speech coming out of the speaker, for extra believability

The Main Page

Fake Call's main page, pictured in Figure 9.1, is extremely similar to the main (and only) page in Chapter 3, "In Case of Emergency." It enables the entry of three pieces of data—the time of the next fake call, the phone number shown in the incoming call display, and the wireless carrier shown in the incoming call display. Unlike "In Case of Emergency," this page also has a button for navigating to the next page (the incoming call page).

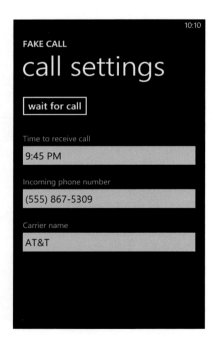

FIGURE 9.1   The main page is a simple form to fill out, much like the main page in the "In Case of Emergency" app.

The User Interface

Listing 9.1 contains the XAML for the main page.

LISTING 9.1   `MainPage.xaml`—The User Interface for Fake Call's Main Page

```xaml
<phone:PhoneApplicationPage
  x:Class="WindowsPhoneApp.MainPage"
  xmlns="http://schemas.microsoft.com/winfx/2006/xaml/presentation"
  xmlns:x="http://schemas.microsoft.com/winfx/2006/xaml"
  xmlns:phone="clr-namespace:Microsoft.Phone.Controls;assembly=Microsoft.Phone"
  xmlns:shell="clr-namespace:Microsoft.Phone.Shell;assembly=Microsoft.Phone"
  xmlns:local="clr-namespace:WindowsPhoneApp"
  xmlns:toolkit="clr-namespace:Microsoft.Phone.Controls;
➥assembly=Microsoft.Phone.Controls.Toolkit"
  FontFamily="{StaticResource PhoneFontFamilyNormal}"
  FontSize="{StaticResource PhoneFontSizeNormal}"
  Foreground="{StaticResource PhoneForegroundBrush}"
  SupportedOrientations="PortraitOrLandscape"
  shell:SystemTray.IsVisible="True">

  <!-- Add some items to the page's resource dictionary -->
  <phone:PhoneApplicationPage.Resources>

    <!-- A margin for the standard header -->
    <Thickness x:Key="PhoneTitlePanelMargin">24,16,0,12</Thickness>

    <!-- The tweaked application title style -->
    <Style x:Key="PhoneTextTitle0Style" TargetType="TextBlock">
      <Setter Property="FontFamily"
              Value="{StaticResource PhoneFontFamilySemiBold}"/>
      <Setter Property="Foreground"
              Value="{StaticResource PhoneForegroundBrush}"/>
      <Setter Property="FontSize" Value="{StaticResource PhoneFontSizeMedium}"/>
      <Setter Property="Margin" Value="-1,0,0,0"/>
    </Style>

    <!-- The tweaked page title style -->
    <Style x:Key="PhoneTextTitle1Style" TargetType="TextBlock">
      <Setter Property="FontFamily"
              Value="{StaticResource PhoneFontFamilySemiLight}"/>
      <Setter Property="Foreground"
              Value="{StaticResource PhoneForegroundBrush}"/>
      <Setter Property="FontSize"
              Value="{StaticResource PhoneFontSizeExtraExtraLarge}"/>
      <Setter Property="Margin" Value="-3,-10,0,0"/>
    </Style>

    <!-- A style for text blocks that act as a label for a text box -->
    <Style x:Key="LabelStyle" TargetType="TextBlock">
```

LISTING 9.1   Continued

```xml
      <Setter Property="Foreground" Value="{StaticResource PhoneSubtleBrush}"/>
      <Setter Property="Margin" Value="24,17,24,-5"/>
  </Style>

</phone:PhoneApplicationPage.Resources>

<Grid>
  <Grid.RowDefinitions>
    <RowDefinition Height="Auto"/>
    <RowDefinition Height="*"/>
  </Grid.RowDefinitions>

  <!-- The standard header, with some tweaks -->
  <StackPanel Grid.Row="0" Margin="{StaticResource PhoneTitlePanelMargin}">
    <TextBlock Text="FAKE CALL" Style="{StaticResource PhoneTextTitle0Style}"/>
    <TextBlock Text="call settings"
               Style="{StaticResource PhoneTextTitle1Style}"/>
  </StackPanel>

  <!-- Scrollable pane (for the sake of the landscape orientation) -->
  <ScrollViewer Grid.Row="1">
    <!-- A button and three text block / text box pairs stacked vertically -->
    <StackPanel>
      <Button Content="wait for call" HorizontalAlignment="Left"
              Margin="12,13,0,18" Click="WaitForCallButton_Click"/>

      <TextBlock Text="Time to receive call"
                 Style="{StaticResource LabelStyle}"/>
      <toolkit:TimePicker x:Name="TimePicker" local:Tilt.IsEnabled="True"
                          ValueChanged="TimePicker_ValueChanged"
                          Margin="{StaticResource PhoneHorizontalMargin}"/>

      <TextBlock Text="Incoming phone number"
                 Style="{StaticResource LabelStyle}"/>
      <!-- Use the Number input scope so we also get parentheses and a dash -->
      <TextBox x:Name="PhoneNumberTextBox" InputScope="Number"
               Margin="{StaticResource PhoneHorizontalMargin}"
               GotFocus="TextBox_GotFocus" KeyDown="TextBox_KeyDown"/>

      <TextBlock Text="Carrier name" Style="{StaticResource LabelStyle}"/>
      <TextBox x:Name="CarrierTextBox" InputScope="PersonalFullName"
               Margin="{StaticResource PhoneHorizontalMargin}"
               GotFocus="TextBox_GotFocus" KeyDown="TextBox_KeyDown"/>
    </StackPanel>
```

LISTING 9.1   Continued

```
    </ScrollViewer>
  </Grid>
</phone:PhoneApplicationPage>
```

Notes:

→ This page supports all orientations for the sake of text entry.

→ This page appropriately uses a time picker rather than a simple text box for choosing the call time. Although it initially looks like a text box, it presents a rich full-page interface when tapped that matches the phone's built-in apps, as pictured in Figure 9.2. The time picker ships with the Silverlight for Windows Phone Toolkit, so you must reference the toolkit's assembly and namespace to use it.

→ The `PhoneNumberTextBox` text box uses the `Number` input scope rather than `TelephoneNumber` because its text is displayed as-is on subsequent pages. This enables the user to type parentheses and a dash to get the optimal display. The `Number` input scope includes these keys, but `TelephoneNumber` does not.

→ The most important aspect of this listing is its use of resources and styles, covered next.

Resources

Windows Phone apps can have two types of resources. One type, often called *binary resources*, consists of things like image files, audio/video files, and font files. Sometimes these are embedded into your DLL (when the Build Action is

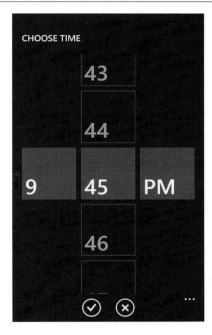

FIGURE 9.2   The time picker makes it easy to choose a time with taps and swipes.

The time picker requires two specific images to be included in your project!

As with the date picker, you must include two images from the Silverlight for Windows Phone Toolkit in your project (and mark them with a **Build Action** of **Content**). These images are `ApplicationBar.Check.png` and `ApplicationBar.Cancel.png`, and they must be placed in a folder called `Toolkit.Content` in the root of your project.

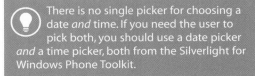
There is no single picker for choosing a date *and* time. If you need the user to pick both, you should use a date picker *and* a time picker, both from the Silverlight for Windows Phone Toolkit.

set to Resource) and sometimes these are placed as loose files inside your .xap file (when the Build Action is set to Content). The choice of how to package binary resources is sometimes dictated by their consumer (such as the application bar requiring loose files), and sometimes dictated by how you wish to localize the resources in order support multiple languages and regions. As you've seen in previous chapters, various elements support referencing binary resources via URIs.

Defining XAML Resources

The XAML files in this app, such as MainPage.xaml in Listing 9.1, make use of the *other* type of resources. They are often called *XAML resources* because they are typically defined in XAML, but this book generally refers to them as simply *resources*, using the term *binary resources* to refer to the other kind.

A resource is an arbitrary object stored in an element's Resources property. Such objects can be anything—a number, a brush, or a complex object such as a style. The first resource defined in Listing 9.1 is a thickness, the data type used by margins and padding:

```
<Thickness x:Key="PhoneTitlePanelMargin">24,16,0,12</Thickness>
```

The point of defining a resource is to separate and consolidate styling information, much like using Cascading Style Sheets (CSS) to control colors and styles in a webpage rather than hard-coding them on individual elements. The Resources property is a dictionary (usually called a *resource dictionary*), so adding a child element is equivalent to adding a new key/value pair to the dictionary in C#. The value is the element, and the key is the string specified via the x:Key attribute. Everything placed in a resource dictionary must have a key.

Referencing XAML Resources

Resources are referenced with the familiar StaticResource syntax. Each resource is often referenced by more than one element, although the thickness resource with the PhoneTitlePanelMargin key happens to be referenced only once:

```
<StackPanel Grid.Row="0" Margin="{StaticResource PhoneTitlePanelMargin}">
  …
</StackPanel>
```

The identifier specified along with StaticResource is the key for the desired resource. Because the object with the PhoneTitlePanelMargin key is the right data type for the Margin property, setting it this way is valid and behaves exactly the same as setting it directly:

```
<StackPanel Grid.Row="0" Margin="24,16,0,12">
  …
</StackPanel>
```

Applying a resource to an element's properties is a one-time action that happens when the element is loaded. If you later change the definition of the resource (for example, adjusting the thickness values from code-behind), elements that have referenced the resource do not automatically get updated.

A Hierarchy of Resource Dictionaries

All visual elements have their own resource dictionary (e.g. a `Resources` property), not just a page. And the `StaticResource` mechanism doesn't simply look in the current page's resource dictionary for the matching key. It starts by checking the current element's resource dictionary, and then it checks the parent element, its parent, and so on until it reaches the root element (the frame containing the current page). After that, it checks a resource dictionary defined on the `Application` object. (There's one more place it checks, but that's only relevant for building custom controls, so that's covered in Chapter 19, "Animation Lab.")

You can see the application-wide resource dictionary in any project, initially empty, in the Visual Studio-generated `App.xaml` file:

```
<Application …>
  <!-- Add a style to the application-wide resource dictionary -->
  <Application.Resources>
  </Application.Resources>
  …
</Application>
```

This means that you can define a top-level set of resources and override them at arbitrary points in the tree of elements (similar to data contexts). Although each individual resource dictionary requires unique keys, the same key can be used in multiple dictionaries. The one "closest" to the element referencing the resource wins.

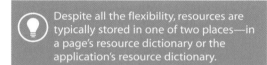

Despite all the flexibility, resources are typically stored in one of two places—in a page's resource dictionary or the application's resource dictionary.

The reason why we've been able to use `StaticResource` to reference phone theme resources such as `PhoneForegroundBrush` and `PhoneBackgroundBrush` is that these resources are automatically injected into the app when it starts. You can see the resource dictionary for each combination of theme and accent color in `ThemeResources.xaml` files under `%ProgramFiles%\Microsoft SDKs\Windows Phone\v7.0\Design`.

If you reference a resource in C#, you need to retrieve it from the exact dictionary containing it, for example:

```
// Get a resource from the page's resource dictionary
this.someElement.Margin = (Thickness)this.Resources["PhoneTitlePanelMargin"];
```

Or as done in the Ruler app:

```
// Get a resource from the application-wide resource dictionary
this.LayoutRoot.Background =
  Application.Current.Resources["PhoneChromeBrush"] as Brush;
```

C# code doesn't have an automatic mechanism to find a resource in multiple locations, like what happens in XAML.

Although the apps in this book always reference phone theme resources from the application-wide resource dictionary, you can actually reference them from *any* element's resource dictionary. They are injected into the app as *global fallback* resources, which is a special mechanism reserved for these specific items.

Styles

A *style* is a pretty simple entity. It collects several property values that could otherwise be set individually. It does this with a collection of setters that each names a property and its value, as with the following style from Listing 9.1:

```
<!-- A style for text blocks that act as a label for a text box -->
<Style x:Key="LabelStyle" TargetType="TextBlock">
  <Setter Property="Foreground" Value="{StaticResource PhoneSubtleBrush}"/>
  <Setter Property="Margin" Value="24,17,24,-5"/>
</Style>
```

Visual elements have a `Style` property that can be directly set to an instance of a style, but the point of using a style is to define it as a resource instead. That way, you get the flexibility of sharing and overriding styles. Styles can be applied just like any other resource:

```
<TextBlock Text="Carrier name" Style="{StaticResource LabelStyle}"/>
```

Notice that styles stored as resources often contain their own references to other resources. A resource can reference earlier resources from the same resource dictionary, or from a parent resource dictionary (such as the application-wide resource dictionary containing `PhoneSubtleBrush` in this example).

Any individual element can override aspects of its style by directly setting a property to a local value. For example, the "carrier name" text block in Listing 9.1 could do the following to retain the margin from `LabelStyle` yet have a red foreground:

```
<TextBlock Text="Carrier name" Style="{StaticResource LabelStyle}"
  Foreground="Red"/>
```

Note that style setters are for properties only. You cannot attach event handlers as part of a style.

The Code-Behind

Listing 9.2 contains the code-behind for the main page.

LISTING 9.2   `MainPage.xaml.cs`—The Code-Behind for Fake Call's Main Page

```csharp
using System;
using System.Windows;
using System.Windows.Controls;
using System.Windows.Input;
using System.Windows.Navigation;
using Microsoft.Phone.Controls;

namespace WindowsPhoneApp
{
  public partial class MainPage : PhoneApplicationPage
  {
    public MainPage()
    {
      InitializeComponent();
    }

    protected override void OnNavigatedTo(NavigationEventArgs e)
    {
      base.OnNavigatedTo(e);
      // Restore saved text box contents when entering this page
      this.PhoneNumberTextBox.Text = Settings.PhoneNumber.Value;
      this.CarrierTextBox.Text = Settings.Carrier.Value;

      // Restore the time if it's in the future, otherwise use the current time
      if (Settings.CallTime.Value > DateTime.Now)
        this.TimePicker.Value = Settings.CallTime.Value;
      else
        this.TimePicker.Value = DateTime.Now;
    }

    protected override void OnNavigatedFrom(NavigationEventArgs e)
    {
      base.OnNavigatedFrom(e);
      // Persist contents when leaving this page for any reason
      Settings.CallTime.Value = this.TimePicker.Value ?? DateTime.Now;
      Settings.PhoneNumber.Value = this.PhoneNumberTextBox.Text;
      Settings.Carrier.Value = this.CarrierTextBox.Text;
    }

    void TextBox_GotFocus(object sender, RoutedEventArgs e)
    {
      // Select all text so it can be cleared with one keystroke
      (sender as TextBox).SelectAll();
    }
```

LISTING 9.2 Continued

```csharp
    void TextBox_KeyDown(object sender, KeyEventArgs e)
    {
      if (e.Key == Key.Enter)
      {
        // Cycle through the text boxes
        if (sender == this.PhoneNumberTextBox)
          this.CarrierTextBox.Focus();
        else if (sender == this.CarrierTextBox)
          this.TimePicker.Focus(); // Cycle back to the beginning

        e.Handled = true;
      }
    }

    void WaitForCallButton_Click(object sender, RoutedEventArgs e)
    {
      // Go to the next page
      this.NavigationService.Navigate(new Uri("/IncomingCallPage.xaml",
UriKind.Relative));
    }

    void TimePicker_ValueChanged(object sender, DateTimeValueChangedEventArgs e)
    {
        // To prevent getting clobbered on way back in
        Settings.CallTime.Value = e.NewDateTime ?? DateTime.Now;
    }
  }
}
```

Notes:

→ Because the three settings used by this app need to be accessed on three different pages, they are defined as public fields on a separate class called `Settings`:

```csharp
public static class Settings
{
  public static readonly Setting<DateTime> CallTime =
    new Setting<DateTime>("CallTime", DateTime.Now);
  public static readonly Setting<string> PhoneNumber =
    new Setting<string>("PhoneNumber", "");
  public static readonly Setting<string> Carrier =
    new Setting<string>("Carrier", "AT&T");
}
```

This pattern is used throughout the rest of the book for settings that need to be shared across multiple pages.

➔ The operation of the time picker causes a small wrinkle with our saving/restoring of settings in `OnNavigatedFrom`/`OnNavigatedTo`. Because changing the time picker's value involves navigating to and from a different page, the following line in `OnNavigatedTo` wipes out the value that the user just chose, replacing it with the previously-saved value:

```
Settings.CallTime.Value = this.TimePicker.Value ?? DateTime.Now;
```

To work around this, Listing 9.2 handles the time picker's `ValueChanged` event (with the `TimePicker_ValueChanged` handler) and saves the new value instantly. This way, when `OnNavigatedTo` is called moments later, the assignment is a no-op.

➔ The `Value` property on the time picker is a nullable `DateTime`, to support a state of no time being chosen. Unlike the date picker, however, a time picker's initial value is `null`. Fake Call chooses to avoid handling this state by initializing it to `DateTime.Now` instead.

The Incoming-Call Page

The incoming-call page has two modes, shown in Figure 9.3 with `ShowGridLines="True"` temporarily set on the page's innermost grid. While waiting for the fake call to arrive, the screen is black to simulate it being off. When the call arrives, the screen mimics the incoming-call experience from the real Phone app. To help the user get used to how the app works, the "waiting mode" also shows a countdown to the call, but this can be hidden by tapping the screen. When using this app for real, the user should hide the countdown to avoid exposing the secret.

FIGURE 9.3   The two modes of the incoming-call page, with some grid lines showing to help explain the layout.

The User Interface

Listing 9.3 contains the XAML file for the incoming-call page.

LISTING 9.3   `IncomingCall.xaml`—The User Interface for Fake Call's Incoming Call Page

```xaml
<phone:PhoneApplicationPage
    x:Class="WindowsPhoneApp.IncomingCallPage"
    xmlns="http://schemas.microsoft.com/winfx/2006/xaml/presentation"
    xmlns:x="http://schemas.microsoft.com/winfx/2006/xaml"
    xmlns:phone="clr-namespace:Microsoft.Phone.Controls;assembly=Microsoft.Phone"
    xmlns:local="clr-namespace:WindowsPhoneApp"
    FontFamily="{StaticResource PhoneFontFamilyNormal}"
    FontSize="{StaticResource PhoneFontSizeNormal}"
    Foreground="{StaticResource PhoneForegroundBrush}"
    SupportedOrientations="Portrait">

  <!-- Add one item to the page's resource dictionary -->
  <phone:PhoneApplicationPage.Resources>

    <!-- A style for the two text blocks in WaitingForCallPanel -->
    <Style x:Key="WaitingTextStyle" TargetType="TextBlock">
      <Setter Property="Foreground" Value="#99FFFFFF"/>
      <Setter Property="FontFamily"
              Value="{StaticResource PhoneFontFamilySemiBold}"/>
      <Setter Property="FontSize" Value="23"/>
    </Style>

  </phone:PhoneApplicationPage.Resources>

  <!-- A 1x1 grid holds two overlapping stack panels -->
  <Grid>
    <!-- The initial panel that can show a countdown to the phone call -->
    <StackPanel x:Name="WaitingForCallPanel" Background="Black">
      <TextBlock x:Name="CountdownTextBlock" Margin="11,120,0,0"
                 Style="{StaticResource WaitingTextStyle}"/>
      <TextBlock x:Name="TapToHideTextBlock" Margin="11,0,0,0"
                 Text="(tap screen to hide)"
                 Style="{StaticResource WaitingTextStyle}"/>
    </StackPanel>
    <!-- The fake "incoming call" user interface -->
    <StackPanel x:Name="IncomingCallPanel" Visibility="Collapsed"
                Background="{StaticResource PhoneChromeBrush}">
      <!-- These two text blocks form the fake status bar -->
      <TextBlock x:Name="CurrentTimeTextBlock"
                 Style="{StaticResource StatusBarTextStyle}"/>
      <TextBlock x:Name="CarrierTextBlock"
```

LISTING 9.3   Continued

```xml
                      Style="{StaticResource StatusBarTextStyle}"
                      Foreground="{StaticResource PhoneSubtleBrush}"/>
      <Grid Margin="12,1,12,0" Height="566">
        <Grid.RowDefinitions>
          <RowDefinition/>
          <RowDefinition Height="Auto"/>
          <RowDefinition Height="Auto"/>
        </Grid.RowDefinitions>
        <Grid.ColumnDefinitions>
          <ColumnDefinition/>
          <ColumnDefinition/>
        </Grid.ColumnDefinitions>
        <!-- "INCOMING CALL" -->
        <TextBlock Grid.ColumnSpan="2" Text="INCOMING CALL" Margin="11,0,0,-10"
                   VerticalAlignment="Bottom" FontSize="23"
                   FontFamily="{StaticResource PhoneFontFamilySemiBold}"
                   Foreground="{StaticResource PhoneAccentBrush}"/>
        <!-- The phone number -->
        <TextBlock x:Name="PhoneNumberTextBlock" Grid.Row="1" Grid.ColumnSpan="2"
                   Margin="6,22,0,51" TextWrapping="Wrap" FontSize="85"
                   LineHeight="91" LineStackingStrategy="BlockLineHeight"
                   FontFamily="{StaticResource PhoneFontFamilySemiLight}" />
        <!-- The answer/ignore buttons -->
        <Button Grid.Row="2" Content="answer" Click="AnswerButton_Click"
                local:Tilt.IsEnabled="True"/>
        <Button Grid.Column="1" Grid.Row="2" Content="ignore"
                Click="IgnoreButton_Click" local:Tilt.IsEnabled="True"/>
      </Grid>
    </StackPanel>
  </Grid>
</phone:PhoneApplicationPage>
```

Notes:

➔ Unlike the main page, this page (and the next one) is portrait-only to match the behavior of the phone app.

➔ This page (and the next one) uses a fake status bar. This enables it to blend in with the `PhoneChromeBrush` background. Although the real Phone app looks this way, third-party apps cannot change the color of the real status bar.

> You should avoid creating a fake status bar in your app, because it cannot behave like the real one (e.g. showing signal strength and other information when the user taps it). It's acceptable for this app only because a number of things are intentionally fake. Note that the main page uses a real status bar to avoid confusing users.

→ The `WaitingTextStyle` style is defined in this page's resource dictionary, but the `StatusBarTextStyle` style is defined in the application-level resource dictionary inside `App.xaml` so it can be shared by two pages:

```
<Application …>
  <!-- Add a style to the application-wide resource dictionary -->
  <Application.Resources>
    <Style x:Key="StatusBarTextStyle" TargetType="TextBlock">
      <Setter Property="HorizontalAlignment" Value="Right"/>
      <Setter Property="Margin" Value="0,0,13,4"/>
    </Style>
  </Application.Resources>
  …
</Application>
```

→ PhoneNumberTextBlock wraps its text by setting its `TextWrapping` property to `Wrap`. This alone doesn't exactly match the real Phone app, because the wrapped lines are too far apart. Therefore, it uses an explicit `LineHeight` setting to better match the tight wrapping, as shown in Figure 9.4.

With LineHeight="91" and
LineStackingStrategy="BlockLineHeight"

Without an explicit LineHeight
and LineStackingStrategy

FIGURE 9.4   The impact of giving a wrapping text block an explicit line height.

→ The layout of this page keeps the answer and ignore buttons in a fixed position even as the length of the phone number text changes. Figure 9.5 shows the appearance of this page when the phone number is left blank, and when the user gets creative with long, custom text.

Use any nonzero value of `LineHeight` to customize the line spacing in a text block. Note that this only works when `LineStackingStrategy` is also set to `BlockLineHeight` rather than the default `MaxHeight`.

FIGURE 9.5   The text grows upward while the buttons remain in a fixed position.

The Code-Behind

Listing 9.4 contains the code-behind for the incoming-call page.

LISTING 9.4   `IncomingCall.xaml.cs`—The Code-Behind for Fake Call's Incoming Call Page

```
using System;
using System.Windows;
using System.Windows.Input;
using System.Windows.Navigation;
using System.Windows.Threading;
using Microsoft.Devices;
using Microsoft.Phone.Controls;
using Microsoft.Phone.Shell;
```

LISTING 9.4   Continued

```csharp
namespace WindowsPhoneApp
{
  public partial class IncomingCallPage : PhoneApplicationPage
  {
    // A timer that ticks once per second to keep track of the time
    DispatcherTimer timer = new DispatcherTimer {
      Interval = TimeSpan.FromSeconds(1)
    };

    // A variable-interval timer that performs the call vibration pattern
    DispatcherTimer vibrationTimer = new DispatcherTimer();

    // Bookkeeping for the vibration pattern used to simulate ringing
    bool isRinging;
    int vibrationStep;

    public IncomingCallPage()
    {
      InitializeComponent();
      this.timer.Tick += Timer_Tick;
      this.vibrationTimer.Tick += VibrationTimer_Tick;
    }

    protected override void OnMouseLeftButtonDown(MouseButtonEventArgs e)
    {
      base.OnMouseLeftButtonDown(e);
      if (this.WaitingForCallPanel.Visibility == Visibility.Visible)
      {
        // Hide the contents of WaitingForCallPanel when the screen is tapped
        this.CountdownTextBlock.Visibility = Visibility.Collapsed;
        this.TapToHideTextBlock.Visibility = Visibility.Collapsed;
      }
    }

    protected override void OnNavigatedTo(NavigationEventArgs e)
    {
      base.OnNavigatedTo(e);

      // Respect the current settings
      this.CarrierTextBlock.Text = Settings.Carrier.Value;
      this.PhoneNumberTextBlock.Text = Settings.PhoneNumber.Value;

      // Start the main timer
      this.timer.Start();
```

LISTING 9.4   Continued

```
    Timer_Tick(null, null); // Force initial update

    // While on this page, don't allow the screen to auto-lock
    PhoneApplicationService.Current.UserIdleDetectionMode =
      IdleDetectionMode.Disabled;
  }

  protected override void OnNavigatedFrom(NavigationEventArgs e)
  {
    base.OnNavigatedFrom(e);

    // Stop the main timer
    this.timer.Stop();

    // Stop ringing (if ringing)
    StopRinging();

    // Restore the ability for the screen to auto-lock when on other pages
    PhoneApplicationService.Current.UserIdleDetectionMode =
      IdleDetectionMode.Enabled;
  }

  void StartRinging()
  {
    // Show IncomingCallPanel and start the vibration pattern
    isRinging = true;
    this.WaitingForCallPanel.Visibility = Visibility.Collapsed;
    this.IncomingCallPanel.Visibility = Visibility.Visible;
    this.vibrationStep = 0;
    this.vibrationTimer.Start();
  }

  void StopRinging()
  {
    // Hide IncomingCallPanel, stop the vibration, and set the next call time
    // to two minutes from now
    isRinging = false;
    this.WaitingForCallPanel.Visibility = Visibility.Visible;
    this.IncomingCallPanel.Visibility = Visibility.Collapsed;
    this.vibrationTimer.Stop();
    Settings.CallTime.Value = DateTime.Now + TimeSpan.FromMinutes(2);
    Timer_Tick(null, null); // Force an update now
  }
```

LISTING 9.4   Continued

```
void Timer_Tick(object sender, EventArgs e)
{
  // Show the current time on the fake status bar
  this.CurrentTimeTextBlock.Text = DateTime.Now.ToString("h:mm");

  TimeSpan delta = Settings.CallTime.Value - DateTime.Now;

  if (delta > TimeSpan.Zero)
  {
    // It's not time to ring yet. Update the countdown in case it is visible.
    this.CountdownTextBlock.Text = "COUNTDOWN: " + (int)delta.TotalHours + ":"
      + delta.Minutes.ToString("00") + ":"
      + Math.Ceiling(delta.Seconds).ToString("00");
  }
  else if (!this.isRinging)
  {
    // It's time to ring
    StartRinging();
  }
}

void AnswerButton_Click(object sender, RoutedEventArgs e)
{
  // Go to the next page
  this.NavigationService.Navigate(new Uri("/CallInProgressPage.xaml",
    UriKind.Relative));
}

void IgnoreButton_Click(object sender, RoutedEventArgs e)
{
  StopRinging();
}

void VibrationTimer_Tick(object sender, EventArgs e)
{
  // Make a short-long-short-long pattern of vibration
  switch (this.vibrationStep % 4) // Cycle from 0 - 3
  {
    case 0:
    case 2:
      VibrateController.Default.Start(TimeSpan.FromSeconds(.1)); // short
      // Leave space between this short and the next long
      this.vibrationTimer.Interval = TimeSpan.FromSeconds(.4);
      break;
```

LISTING 9.4   Continued

```
        case 1:
          VibrateController.Default.Start(TimeSpan.FromSeconds(.4)); // long
          // Leave more space between this long and the next short
          this.vibrationTimer.Interval = TimeSpan.FromSeconds(.8);
          break;
        case 3:
          VibrateController.Default.Start(TimeSpan.FromSeconds(.4)); // long
          // Leave even more space after every other long
          this.vibrationTimer.Interval = TimeSpan.FromSeconds(2.1);
          break;
      }

      this.vibrationStep++;

      // Stop ringing after 20 seconds (6 full cycles of the 4-part pattern)
      if (this.vibrationStep == 24)
        StopRinging();
    }
  }
}
```

Notes:

➔ The implementation of OnNavigatedTo and OnNavigatedFrom ensures that the app's UserIdleDetectionMode property is set to Disabled while this page is active. As explained in the preceding chapter, this prevents the screen from automatically locking while the user waits for the fake phone call to arrive, as this would interfere with its operation. Unlike **Application**IdleDetectionMode, **User**IdleDetectionMode can be changed at any time. Running under the screen lock with ApplicationIdleDetectionMode is not useful for Fake Call, because even though it enables the phone to pretend-ring while it is locked, the user would still need to press the Power button, swipe upward, and enter their password (if the phone is password-protected) before seeing the incoming-call screen!

➔ The processing of the carrier and phone number settings could have been done in the constructor rather than in OnNavigatedTo, but then the main page would have had to override its OnNavigat**ing**From method and set these values there rather than OnNavigat**ed**From to prevent this page from getting stale values. This page is constructed between the previous page's OnNavigatingFrom and OnNavigatedFrom events.

➔ Every time the phone stops ringing (either because the user tapped "ignore" or because they answered the fake call), the CallTime setting is changed to 2 minutes from the current time. This will simulate the person calling again every 2 minutes for as long as you keep the app open.

→ The time on the fake status bar is formatted with an `"h:mm"` string, ensuring that the hour and minutes are displayed without the corresponding AM or PM. This matches the phone's real status bar *except* when it has the 24-hour clock setting turned on.

→ Pieces of the countdown string use the `"00"` format string to ensure that two digits are displayed, even if one is a padded 0. The countdown string has the wiggling problem described in Chapter 4, "Stopwatch," but it is not a big deal for this app, especially because the countdown only updates once per second.

→ The "ringing" is done with a pattern of vibration that mimics the sound of a real incoming call when the ringer is set to vibrate. This is the same vibrating pattern as the "phone call" preset from the preceding chapter.

The Call-In-Progress Page

The final page—the call-in-progress page—is pictured in Figure 9.6 with `ShowGridLines="True"` marked on its second grid.

The User Interface

Listing 9.5 contains this page's XAML file.

FIGURE 9.6   The call-in-progress page, with some grid lines showing to help explain the layout.

LISTING 9.5   `CallInProgress.xaml`—The User Interface for Fake Call's Call-In-Progress Page

```
<phone:PhoneApplicationPage
    x:Class="WindowsPhoneApp.CallInProgressPage"
    xmlns="http://schemas.microsoft.com/winfx/2006/xaml/presentation"
    xmlns:x="http://schemas.microsoft.com/winfx/2006/xaml"
    xmlns:phone="clr-namespace:Microsoft.Phone.Controls;assembly=Microsoft.Phone"
    xmlns:local="clr-namespace:WindowsPhoneApp"
    xmlns:sys="clr-namespace:System;assembly=mscorlib"
    FontFamily="{StaticResource PhoneFontFamilyNormal}"
```

LISTING 9.5 Continued

```
  FontSize="{StaticResource PhoneFontSizeNormal}"
  Foreground="{StaticResource PhoneForegroundBrush}"
  SupportedOrientations="Portrait">

<!-- Add two items to the page's resource dictionary -->
<phone:PhoneApplicationPage.Resources>
  <Thickness x:Key="ButtonMargin">0,41,0,12</Thickness>
  <sys:Int32 x:Key="SmallButtonWidth">88</sys:Int32>
</phone:PhoneApplicationPage.Resources>

<StackPanel Background="{StaticResource PhoneChromeBrush}"
            VerticalAlignment="Top">
  <Grid>
    <!-- The fake signal-strength bars for the fake status bar -->
    <Canvas>
      <!-- Add two styles to this canvas's resource dictionary -->
      <Canvas.Resources>
        <Style x:Key="BarOnStyle" TargetType="Line">
          <Setter Property="Stroke"
                  Value="{StaticResource PhoneForegroundBrush}"/>
          <Setter Property="StrokeThickness" Value="5"/>
          <Setter Property="Y2" Value="26"/>
        </Style>
        <Style x:Key="BarOffStyle" BasedOn="{StaticResource BarOnStyle}"
                                   TargetType="Line">
          <Setter Property="Stroke" Value="{StaticResource PhoneSubtleBrush}"/>
          <Setter Property="Opacity" Value=".3"/>
        </Style>
      </Canvas.Resources>
      <Line Style="{StaticResource BarOnStyle}"
                  X1="16" X2="16" Y1="22"/>
      <Line Style="{StaticResource BarOnStyle}"
                  X1="22" X2="22" Y1="18"/>
      <Line Style="{StaticResource BarOffStyle}"
                  X1="28" X2="28" Y1="15"/>
      <Line Style="{StaticResource BarOffStyle}"
                  X1="34" X2="34" Y1="11"/>
      <Line Style="{StaticResource BarOffStyle}"
                  X1="40" X2="40" Y1="7"/>
    </Canvas>
    <!-- The current time for the fake status bar-->
    <TextBlock x:Name="CurrentTimeTextBlock"
               Style="{StaticResource StatusBarTextStyle}"/>
  </Grid>
```

LISTING 9.5   Continued

```xml
<!-- The carrier for the fake status bar-->
<TextBlock x:Name="CarrierTextBlock"
           Style="{StaticResource StatusBarTextStyle}"
           Foreground="{StaticResource PhoneSubtleBrush}"/>
<Grid Margin="12,1,12,0">
  <Grid.RowDefinitions>
    <RowDefinition Height="Auto"/>
    <RowDefinition Height="Auto"/>
    <RowDefinition Height="Auto"/>
  </Grid.RowDefinitions>
  <Grid.ColumnDefinitions>
    <ColumnDefinition/>
    <ColumnDefinition Width="Auto"/>
    <ColumnDefinition Width="Auto"/>
  </Grid.ColumnDefinitions>

  <TextBlock x:Name="CallDurationTextBlock" Grid.ColumnSpan="3" FontSize="21"
           Margin="12,20,0,0" Foreground="{StaticResource PhoneAccentBrush}"/>

  <TextBlock x:Name="PhoneNumberTextBlock" Grid.Row="1" Grid.ColumnSpan="3"
             Margin="6,-5,0,28" TextWrapping="Wrap" FontSize="68"
             FontFamily="{StaticResource PhoneFontFamilySemiLight}" />

  <!-- The "end call" button -->
  <Button Grid.Row="2" Content="end call" Click="EndCallButton_Click"
          Margin="{StaticResource ButtonMargin}" local:Tilt.IsEnabled="True"
          Background="{StaticResource PhoneAccentBrush}"/>

  <!-- The fake keypad button -->
  <Button Grid.Row="2" Grid.Column="1" Margin="{StaticResource ButtonMargin}"
        Width="{StaticResource SmallButtonWidth}" local:Tilt.IsEnabled="True">
    <Canvas Width="16" Height="18">
      <!-- Add a style to this canvas's resource dictionary -->
      <Canvas.Resources>
        <Style x:Key="SquareStyle" TargetType="Rectangle">
          <Setter Property="Width" Value="4"/>
          <Setter Property="Height" Value="4"/>
          <Setter Property="Fill"
                  Value="{StaticResource PhoneForegroundBrush}"/>
        </Style>
      </Canvas.Resources>
      <Rectangle Style="{StaticResource SquareStyle}"/>
      <Rectangle Canvas.Left="6" Style="{StaticResource SquareStyle}"/>
      <Rectangle Canvas.Left="12" Style="{StaticResource SquareStyle}"/>
```

LISTING 9.5   Continued

```xml
            <Rectangle Canvas.Top="6" Style="{StaticResource SquareStyle}"/>
            <Rectangle Canvas.Left="6" Canvas.Top="6"
                       Style="{StaticResource SquareStyle}"/>
            <Rectangle Canvas.Left="12" Canvas.Top="6"
                       Style="{StaticResource SquareStyle}"/>
            <Rectangle Canvas.Top="12" Style="{StaticResource SquareStyle}"/>
            <Rectangle Canvas.Left="6" Canvas.Top="12"
                       Style="{StaticResource SquareStyle}"/>
            <Rectangle Canvas.Left="12" Canvas.Top="12"
                       Style="{StaticResource SquareStyle}"/>
            <Rectangle Canvas.Left="6" Canvas.Top="18"
                       Style="{StaticResource SquareStyle}"/>
          </Canvas>
        </Button>

        <!-- The fake double-arrow button -->
        <Button Width="{StaticResource SmallButtonWidth}" Grid.Row="2"
                Grid.Column="2" Margin="{StaticResource ButtonMargin}"
                local:Tilt.IsEnabled="True">
          <Path Fill="{StaticResource PhoneForegroundBrush}"
                Data="M0,2 14,2 7,11z M0,13 14,13 7,22" />
        </Button>
      </Grid>
    </StackPanel>
</phone:PhoneApplicationPage>
```

Notes:

→ The `SmallButtonWidth` resource is an integer used as the width of the two small buttons. To create an integer element in XAML, the `Int32` type is referenced from the `System` namespace in the `mscorlib` assembly.

→ This page has a second reason to use a fake status bar—so it can show fake signal-strength bars that mimic the real Phone app experience. The fake bars are created with 5 lines in a canvas (the first two always on and the remaining always off). To avoid repeating several property settings, two styles shared by the lines are placed in the canvas's resource dictionary. There is no need to have the styles in the page's resource dictionary because they are only used in this specific spot.

→ The keypad button contains ten rectangles to produce the appropriate appearance, and the double-arrow button is created with a `Path` shape. See Appendix E, "Geometry Reference," for more

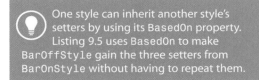
One style can inherit another style's setters by using its BasedOn property. Listing 9.5 uses BasedOn to make BarOffStyle gain the three setters from BarOnStyle without having to repeat them.

information. These buttons don't actually do anything; they are just there to visually match the real Phone app.

→ Unlike the incoming-call page, the content grows downward if the user has chosen long text that wraps, as shown in Figure 9.7.

FIGURE 9.7   The buttons get pushed downward to make room for long text.

The Code-Behind

Listing 9.6 contains the code-behind for this page.

LISTING 9.6   `CallInProgress.xaml.cs`—The Code-Behind for Fake Call's Call-In-Progress Page

```
using System;
using System.Windows;
using System.Windows.Navigation;
using System.Windows.Threading;
using Microsoft.Phone.Controls;
```

LISTING 9.6   Continued

```csharp
using Microsoft.Phone.Shell;

namespace WindowsPhoneApp
{
  public partial class CallInProgressPage : PhoneApplicationPage
  {
    // A timer that ticks once per second to keep track of the time
    DispatcherTimer timer = new DispatcherTimer {
      Interval = TimeSpan.FromSeconds(1) };

    TimeSpan callDuration;

    public CallInProgressPage()
    {
      InitializeComponent();
      this.timer.Tick += Timer_Tick;
    }

    protected override void OnNavigatedTo(NavigationEventArgs e)
    {
      base.OnNavigatedTo(e);

      // Respect the current settings
      this.CarrierTextBlock.Text = Settings.Carrier.Value;
      this.PhoneNumberTextBlock.Text = Settings.PhoneNumber.Value;

      // Start at -1 seconds because Timer_Tick is about to increase it by 1
      this.callDuration = TimeSpan.Zero - TimeSpan.FromSeconds(1);

      // Start the main timer
      this.timer.Start();
      Timer_Tick(null, null); // Force an update now

      // While on this page, don't allow the screen to auto-lock
      PhoneApplicationService.Current.UserIdleDetectionMode =
        IdleDetectionMode.Disabled;
    }

    protected override void OnNavigatedFrom(NavigationEventArgs e)
    {
      base.OnNavigatedFrom(e);

      // Stop the main timer
```

LISTING 9.6   Continued

```
      this.timer.Stop();

      // Set the next call time to two minutes from now
      Settings.CallTime.Value = DateTime.Now + TimeSpan.FromMinutes(2);

      // Restore the ability for the screen to auto-lock when on other pages
      PhoneApplicationService.Current.UserIdleDetectionMode =
        IdleDetectionMode.Enabled;
    }

    void Timer_Tick(object sender, EventArgs e)
    {
      // Show the current time on the fake status bar
      this.CurrentTimeTextBlock.Text = DateTime.Now.ToString("h:mm");

      // Update the call duration display
      this.callDuration = this.callDuration.Add(TimeSpan.FromSeconds(1));
      this.CallDurationTextBlock.Text = (int)this.callDuration.TotalMinutes +
        ":" + this.callDuration.Seconds.ToString("00");
    }

    void EndCallButton_Click(object sender, RoutedEventArgs e)
    {
      // Go back to the incoming call page, which will wait for the next call
      if (this.NavigationService.CanGoBack)
        this.NavigationService.GoBack();
    }
  }
}
```

The code-behind for this page is similar to the code-behind for the previous page, just a bit simpler. Ideally, the app would just exit when the user taps the "end call" button, but there's no good way to accomplish this. Therefore, after the user taps "end call," they can either press the Power button to lock their phone or the Start button to leave this app—if they don't want to be fake-called again in 2 minutes.

Exiting an App Programmatically

To make the app easier to quickly exit, you could merge all of Fake Call's functionality onto one page to avoid filling the back stack. However, this would make the code messier, and the user would still need to press the hardware Back button to exit the app.

Throwing an unhandled exception would force the app to exit, but this has two problems. If you do this, settings won't be properly persisted to disk (because this is internally done during a graceful app shutdown). Also, such behavior would not get past the marketplace certification process. So don't ever attempt to force an app to exit this way!

Another approach would be to call XNA's `Game.Exit` method from the `Microsoft.Xna.Framework.Game` assembly. However, calling anything from this assembly will cause your app to fail marketplace certification. You *might* be able to get away with using .NET reflection to call `Game.Exit` in a way that the certification process doesn't detect, but I wouldn't recommend it.

The Finished Product

An incoming call in the light theme with the purple accent color

Pretending to talk in the dark theme with the red accent color

Pretending to talk in the light theme with the lime accent color

chapter 10 $\rightarrow$

TIP CALCULATOR

This chapter's app is a stylish and effective tip calculator. The basic idea of a tip calculator is that the user enters an amount of money, decides what percentage of a tip he or she wishes to pay, and then the app gives the proper amount of the tip and the total. This can be a timesaver at restaurants or other places where you need to leave a tip, and it can either save you money or prevent you from looking cheap!

A tip calculator is one of the classic phone apps that people attempt to build, but creating one that works well enough for people to use on a regular basis, and one that embraces the Windows Phone style, takes a lot of care. This app has four different bottom panes for entering data, and the user can switch between them by tapping one of the four buttons on the top left side of the screen.

The primary bottom pane is for entering the amount of money. It uses a custom number pad styled like the one in the built-in Calculator app. Creating this is more complex than using the standard on-screen keyboard, but the result is more useful and attractive—even if the on-screen keyboard were to use the Number or TelephoneNumber input scopes. This app's custom number pad contains *only* the keys that are relevant: the 10 digits, a special key for entering two zeros simultaneously, a backspace key, and a button to clear the entire number. (It also enables entering numbers without the use of a text box.)

The three other bottom panes are all list boxes. They enable the user to choose the desired tip percentage,

choose to round the tip or total either up or down, and split the total among multiple people to see the correct per-person cost.

> There are plenty of other calculator apps you could create with the same basic techniques and code from this chapter: a loan calculator, a sale price calculator, a BMI calculator, and so on.

Tip Calculator is the first app to behave differently depending on how it is closed and how it is re-opened, so we'll first examine what is often referred to as the *application lifecycle* for a Windows Phone app. Later, this chapter also examines some significant new concepts, such as control templates and routed events.

Understanding an App's Lifecycle

An app can exit in one of two ways: It can be **closed**, or it can be **deactivated**. Technically, the app is terminated in both cases, but many users have different expectations for how most apps should behave in one case versus the other.

A **closed** app is not only permanently closed, but it should *appear* to be permanently closed as well. This means that the next time the user runs the app, it should appear to be a "fresh" instance without temporary state left over from last time.

The only way for a user to close an app is to press the hardware Back button while on the app's initial page. A user can only re-run a closed app by tapping its icon or pinned tile.

A **deactivated** app should appear to be "pushed to the background." This is the condition for which an app should provide the illusion that it is still actively running (or running in a "paused" state). Logically, the phone maintains a back stack of pages that the user can keep backing into, regardless of which application each page belongs to. When the user backs into a deactivated app's page, it should appear as if it were there the whole time, waiting patiently for the user's return.

Because there's only one way to close an app, every other action deactivates it instead:

→ The user pressing the hardware Start button

→ The screen locking (either user-provoked or due to timeout)

→ The user directly launching another app by tapping a toast notification or answering a phone call that interrupts your app

→ The app itself launching another app (the phone, web browser, and so on) via a launcher or chooser

The user can return to a deactivated app via the hardware Back button, by unlocking the screen, or by completing whatever task was spawned via a launcher or chooser.

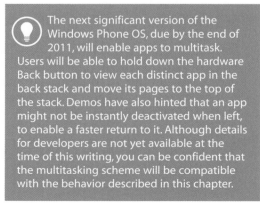

> The next significant version of the Windows Phone OS, due by the end of 2011, will enable apps to multitask. Users will be able to hold down the hardware Back button to view each distinct app in the back stack and move its pages to the top of the stack. Demos have also hinted that an app might not be instantly deactivated when left, to enable a faster return to it. Although details for developers are not yet available at the time of this writing, you can be confident that the multitasking scheme will be compatible with the behavior described in this chapter.

States and Events

An app, therefore, can be in one of three states at any time: running, closed, or deactivated. The PhoneApplicationService class defines four events that notify you when four out of the five possible state transitions occur, as illustrated in Figure 10.1:

→ **Launching**—Raised for a fresh instance of the app.

→ **Closing**—Raised when the app is closing for good. Despite the name, a handler for this event cannot cancel the action (and there is no corresponding "closed" event).

→ **Deactivated**—Raised when the app's pages are logically sent to the back stack.

→ **Activated**—Raised when one of the app's pages is popped off the back stack, making the app run again.

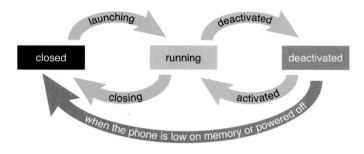

FIGURE 10.1   Four events signal all but one of the possible transitions between three states.

From Figure 10.1, you can see that a deactivated app may never be activated, even if the user wants to activate it later. The back stack may be trimmed due to memory constraints. In this case, or if the phone is powered off, the deactivated apps are now considered to be closed, and apps do not get any sort of notification when this happens (as they are not running at the time). Furthermore, if your app has been deactivated but the user later launches it from its icon or pinned tile, this is a *launching* action rather than a reactivation. In this case, the new instance of your app receives the Launching event—not the Activated event—and the deactivated instance's pages are silently removed from the back stack. (Some users might not understand the distinction between leaving an app via the Back versus Start buttons, so your app might *never* receive a Closing event if a user always leaves apps via the Start button!)

The deactivated state is sometimes referred to as *tombstoned*, and the process of deactivating is sometimes called *tombstoning*. This terminology helps reinforce to developers that a deactivated app is actually dead and technically *not* in some sort of paused state, and that it may never be brought back to life. Note that a deactivated app may be kept in memory as a performance optimization, so activating an app is usually faster than launching it. This helps to preserve the user's illusion that the app is not dead.

An app does not get deactivated when an incoming call obscures the screen; it only gets deactivated if the user taps "answer." A separate pair of events—Obscured and Unobscured, exposed on the frame—enable you to optionally react to this condition. The Obscured event gets raised even when the phone is partially obscured, such as when a toast notification appears or a message box is shown. It also gets raised when the lock screen is shown—right before the Deactivated event is raised.

An Obscured handler cannot know exactly what is obscuring the screen; it can only find out whether it's the lock screen via an IsLocked property on the passed-in event args parameter.

When to Distinguish Between States

Several of the apps in previous chapters have indeed provided the illusion that they are running even when they are not. For example, Tally remembers its current count, Stopwatch pretends to advance its timer, and Ruler remembers the scroll position and current measurement. However, these apps have not made the distinction between being closed versus being deactivated. The data gets saved whether the app is closed or deactivated, and the data gets restored whether the app is launched or activated. Although this behavior is acceptable for these apps (and arguable for Ruler), other apps should often make the distinction between being closed/deactivated and launched/activated. Tip Calculator is one such app.

To decide whether to behave specially for deactivation and activation, consider whether your app involves two types of state:

→ User-configurable settings or other data that should be remembered indefinitely

→ Transient state, like a partially filled form for creating a new item that has not yet been saved

The first type of state should always be saved whether the app is closed or deactivated, and restored whether the app is launched or activated. The second type of state, however, should usually only be saved when deactivated and restored when activated. If the user returns to the app after leaving it for a short period of time (such as being interrupted by a phone call or accidentally locking the screen), he or she expects to see the app exactly how it was left. But if the user launches the app several days later, or expects to see a fresh instance by tapping its icon rather than using the hardware Back button, seeing it in the exact same state could be surprising and annoying, depending on the type of app.

Tip Calculator has data that is useful to remember indefinitely—the chosen tip percentage and whether the user rounded the tip or total—because users likely want to reuse these settings every time they dine out. Forcing users to change these settings from their default values every time the app is launched would be annoying. Therefore, the app persists and restores these settings no matter what.

Tip Calculator also has data that is *not* useful to remember indefinitely—the current amount of the bill and whether it is being split (and with how many people)—as this information should only be relevant for the current meal. So while it absolutely makes sense to remember this information in the face of a short-term interruption like a phone

call or a screen lock, it would be annoying if the user launches the app the
following day and is forced to clear these
values before entering the correct values
for the current meal. Similarly, it makes
sense for the app to remember which of
the four input panels is currently active
to provide the illusion of running-while-
deactivated, but when launching a fresh
instance, it makes sense for the app to
start with the calculator buttons visible.
Therefore, the app persists and restores
this information *only* when it is deactivated and activated.

 **The marketplace certification
process sometimes enforces that
a launched app appears like a
fresh instance!**

According to certification requirement 5.2.2,
"When an application is started after being
closed, …it is recommended that the application appears to be a fresh instance." However,
I have encountered some marketplace testers
who treat this recommendation as a requirement. Therefore, the Ruler app from Chapter 5
can sometimes fail certification due to the
fact that it always remembers the user's previous position.

Implementation

You can attach a handler to any of the four lifecycle events by accessing the current
PhoneApplicationService instance as follows:

```
Microsoft.Phone.Shell.PhoneApplicationService.Current.Activated +=
  Application_Activated;
```

However, a handler for each event is already attached inside the App.xaml file generated
by Visual Studio:

```
<Application …>
  …
  <Application.ApplicationLifetimeObjects>
    <!--Required object that handles lifetime events for the application-->
    <shell:PhoneApplicationService
      Launching="Application_Launching" Closing="Application_Closing"
      Activated="Application_Activated" Deactivated="Application_Deactivated"/>
  </Application.ApplicationLifetimeObjects>

</Application>
```

These handlers are empty methods inside the generated App.xaml.cs code-behind file:

```
// Code to execute when the application is launching (eg, from Start)
// This code will not execute when the application is reactivated
private void Application_Launching(object sender, LaunchingEventArgs e)
{
}


// Code to execute when the application is activated (brought to foreground)
// This code will not execute when the application is first launched
```

```
private void Application_Activated(object sender, ActivatedEventArgs e)
{
}

// Code to execute when the application is deactivated (sent to background)
// This code will not execute when the application is closing
private void Application_Deactivated(object sender, DeactivatedEventArgs e)
{
}

// Code to execute when the application is closing (eg, user hit Back)
// This code will not execute when the application is deactivated
private void Application_Closing(object sender, ClosingEventArgs e)
{
}
```

With these handlers in place, how do you implement them to persist/restore permanent state and transient state?

Permanent state should be persisted to (and restored from) *isolated storage*, a topic covered in Part III, "Storing & Retrieving Local Data." The Setting class used by this book's apps uses isolated storage internally to persist each value, so this class is all you need to handle permanent state.

Transient state can be managed with the same isolated storage mechanism, but there are fortunately separate mechanisms that make working with transient state even easier: *application state* and *page state*.

Application state is a dictionary on the PhoneApplicationState class exposed via its State property, and page state is a dictionary exposed on every page, also via a State property. Application state can be used as follows from anywhere within the app:

```
// Store a value
PhoneApplicationService.Current.State["Amount"] = amount;

// Retrieve a value
if (PhoneApplicationService.Current.State.ContainsKey("Amount"))
  amount = (double)PhoneApplicationService.Current.State["Amount"];
```

Page state can be used as follows, inside any of a page's instance members (where this refers to the page):

```
// Store a value
this.State["Amount"] = amount;

// Retrieve a value
if (this.State.ContainsKey("Amount"))
  amount = (double)this.State["Amount"];
```

But these dictionaries are more than just simple collections of name/value pairs; their contents are automatically persisted when an app is deactivated and automatically restored when an app is activated. Conveniently, these dictionaries are *not* persisted when an app is closed, and they are left empty when an app is launched, even if it was previously deactivated with data in its dictionaries.

Thanks to this behavior, apps can often behave appropriately without the need to even handle the lifetime events.

 Values used in the application state and page state dictionaries must be serializable!

These dictionaries get persisted to disk when an app is deactivated, so all the data types used must support the automatic serialization mechanism. Primitive data types are serializable, but UI elements, for example, are not. If you place a nonserializable object in one of the dictionaries, an `InvalidDataContractException` is raised while the app exits. If you use an instance of your own class with serializable members, be sure that it is marked public, otherwise serialization will fail with a `SecurityException`.

Inside a page's familiar `OnNavigatedTo` and `OnNavigatedFrom` methods, the isolated-storage-based mechanism can be used for permanent data and page state can be used for transient data. The Tip Calculator app does this, as you'll see in its code-behind.

 If you explicitly handle the lifecycle events, make sure that the work done in a handler for `Deactivated` is a superset of the work done in a handler for `Closing`. If there's any data you want to save during `Closing`, you must also save it during `Deactivated`. Remember that, depending on user behavior, your app might never receive the `Closing` event!

The same is true for `Activated` and `Launching`. Whatever data you restore inside `Launching` should also be restored inside `Activated` (potentially in addition to data that is only restored inside `Activated`).

If you store transient data in application state or page state, you need to be okay with the possibility that the data might never get restored.

You can leverage application state or page state as a cache that makes your activation code path faster than the launching code path. For example, if your app makes a network request when launched, consider caching the resultant data and using it instead of a live network request when activated. Databound apps can consider caching the entire data context as a single entry in one of the dictionaries.

You can prevent your app from being deactivated when the screen is locked with the confusingly named `ApplicationIdleDetectionMode` setting briefly mentioned in previous chapters.

When this is set to `Disabled`, your app continues to run, even when the screen is off. There are still a few conditions that can cause your app to be deactivated, however, such as the user activating the camera.

Apps should avoid doing this, however, because it drains the battery in a way that's not obvious to the user. Also, once this kind of deactivation is disabled, it cannot be re-enabled for the same instance of the app.

The User Interface

Figure 10.2 displays the four different modes of Tip Calculator's single page, each with the name of the bottom element currently showing.

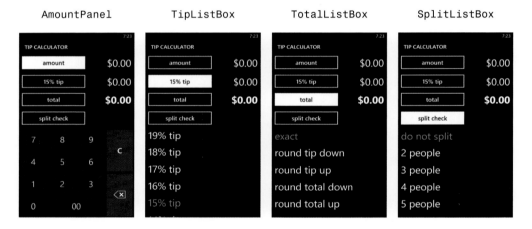

FIGURE 10.2   The bottom input area changes based on which button has been tapped.

The buttons used by this app are not normal buttons, because they remain highlighted after they are tapped. This behavior is enabled by *toggle buttons*, which support the notion of being *checked* or *unchecked*. (You can think of a toggle button like a check box that happens to look like a button. In fact, the `CheckBox` class derives from `ToggleButton`. Its only difference is its visual appearance.)

Tip Calculator doesn't use `ToggleButton` elements, however. Instead, it uses `RadioButton`, a class derived from `ToggleButton` that adds built-in behavior for mutual exclusion. In other words, rather than writing code to manually ensure that only one toggle button is checked at a time, radio buttons enforce that only one radio button is checked at a time when multiple radio buttons have the same parent element. When one is checked, the others are automatically unchecked.

The behavior of radio buttons is perfect for Tip Calculator, but the visual appearance is not ideal. Figure 10.3 shows what the app would look like if radio buttons were used without any customizations. It gives the impression that you must choose only one of the four options (like a multiple-choice question), which can be confusing.

Fortunately, Silverlight controls can be radically restyled by giving them new *control templates*. Tip Calculator uses a custom control template to give its radio buttons the appearance of plain toggle buttons. This gives the best of both worlds: the visual behavior of a toggle button combined with the extra logic in a radio button. The upcoming "Control Templates" section explains how this is done.

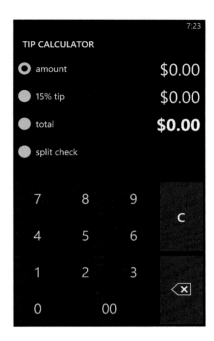

FIGURE 10.3   What Tip Calculator would look like with plain radio buttons.

Listing 10.1 contains the XAML for Tip Calculator's page.

LISTING 10.1   `MainPage.xaml`—The User Interface for Tip Calculator

```
<phone:PhoneApplicationPage
    x:Class="WindowsPhoneApp.MainPage" x:Name="Page"
    xmlns="http://schemas.microsoft.com/winfx/2006/xaml/presentation"
    xmlns:x="http://schemas.microsoft.com/winfx/2006/xaml"
    xmlns:phone="clr-namespace:Microsoft.Phone.Controls;assembly=Microsoft.Phone"
    xmlns:shell="clr-namespace:Microsoft.Phone.Shell;assembly=Microsoft.Phone"
    xmlns:local="clr-namespace:WindowsPhoneApp"
    FontFamily="{StaticResource PhoneFontFamilyNormal}"
    FontSize="{StaticResource PhoneFontSizeNormal}"
    Foreground="{StaticResource PhoneForegroundBrush}"
    SupportedOrientations="Portrait" shell:SystemTray.IsVisible="True"
    Loaded="MainPage_Loaded">

  <phone:PhoneApplicationPage.Resources>

    <!-- Style to make a radio button look like a plain toggle button -->
```

LISTING 10.1   Continued

```
<Style x:Key="RadioToggleButtonStyle" TargetType="RadioButton">
  <!-- Override left alignment of RadioButton: -->
  <Setter Property="HorizontalContentAlignment" Value="Center"/>
  <!-- Add tilt effect: -->
  <Setter Property="local:Tilt.IsEnabled" Value="True"/>
  <!-- The rest is the normal style of a ToggleButton: -->
  <Setter Property="Background" Value="Transparent"/>
  <Setter Property="BorderBrush"
          Value="{StaticResource PhoneForegroundBrush}"/>
  <Setter Property="Foreground"
          Value="{StaticResource PhoneForegroundBrush}"/>
  <Setter Property="BorderThickness"
          Value="{StaticResource PhoneBorderThickness}"/>
  <Setter Property="FontFamily"
          Value="{StaticResource PhoneFontFamilySemiBold}"/>
  <Setter Property="FontSize"
          Value="{StaticResource PhoneFontSizeMediumLarge}"/>
  <Setter Property="Padding" Value="8"/>
  <Setter Property="Template">
    <Setter.Value>
      <ControlTemplate TargetType="ToggleButton">
        <Grid Background="Transparent" >
          <VisualStateManager.VisualStateGroups>
            …
          </VisualStateManager.VisualStateGroups>
          <Border x:Name="EnabledBackground"
                  Background="{TemplateBinding Background}"
                  BorderBrush="{TemplateBinding BorderBrush}"
                  BorderThickness="{TemplateBinding BorderThickness}"
                  Margin="{StaticResource PhoneTouchTargetOverhang}">
            <ContentControl x:Name="EnabledContent" Foreground=
              "{TemplateBinding Foreground}" HorizontalContentAlignment=
              "{TemplateBinding HorizontalContentAlignment}"
              VerticalContentAlignment=
              "{TemplateBinding VerticalContentAlignment}"
              Margin="{TemplateBinding Padding}"
              Content="{TemplateBinding Content}"
              ContentTemplate="{TemplateBinding ContentTemplate}"/>
          </Border>
          <Border x:Name="DisabledBackground" IsHitTestVisible="False"
            Background="Transparent" Visibility="Collapsed"
            BorderBrush="{StaticResource PhoneDisabledBrush}"
            BorderThickness="{TemplateBinding BorderThickness}"
            Margin="{StaticResource PhoneTouchTargetOverhang}">
```

LISTING 10.1   Continued

```
                    <ContentControl x:Name="DisabledContent"
                      Foreground="{StaticResource PhoneDisabledBrush}"
                      HorizontalContentAlignment=
                      "{TemplateBinding HorizontalContentAlignment}"
                      VerticalContentAlignment=
                      "{TemplateBinding VerticalContentAlignment}"
                      Margin="{TemplateBinding Padding}"
                      Content="{TemplateBinding Content}"
                      ContentTemplate="{TemplateBinding ContentTemplate}"/>
                  </Border>
                </Grid>
              </ControlTemplate>
            </Setter.Value>
          </Setter>
        </Style>

        <!-- Style for calculator buttons -->
        <Style x:Key="CalculatorButtonStyle" TargetType="Button">
          <Setter Property="FontSize" Value="36"/>
          <Setter Property="FontFamily"
                  Value="{StaticResource PhoneFontFamilySemiLight}"/>
          <Setter Property="BorderThickness" Value="0"/>
          <Setter Property="Width" Value="132"/>
          <Setter Property="Height" Value="108"/>
        </Style>

        <!-- Style for list box items -->
        <Style x:Key="ListBoxItemStyle" TargetType="ListBoxItem">
          <Setter Property="FontSize"
                  Value="{StaticResource PhoneFontSizeExtraLarge}"/>
          <Setter Property="local:Tilt.IsEnabled" Value="True"/>
          <Setter Property="Padding" Value="12,8,8,8"/>
        </Style>

        <!-- Style for text blocks -->
        <Style x:Key="TextBlockStyle" TargetType="TextBlock">
          <Setter Property="FontSize"
                  Value="{StaticResource PhoneFontSizeExtraLarge}"/>
          <Setter Property="Margin" Value="0,0,12,0"/>
          <Setter Property="HorizontalAlignment" Value="Right"/>
          <Setter Property="VerticalAlignment" Value="Center"/>
        </Style>
```

LISTING 10.1   Continued

```
</phone:PhoneApplicationPage.Resources>

<!-- The root grid with the header, the area with four buttons
     and text blocks, and the bottom input area -->
<Grid>
  <Grid.RowDefinitions>
    <RowDefinition Height="Auto"/>
    <RowDefinition Height="Auto"/>
    <RowDefinition Height="*"/>
  </Grid.RowDefinitions>

  <!-- The header -->
  <StackPanel Grid.Row="0" Style="{StaticResource PhoneTitlePanelStyle}">
    <TextBlock Text="TIP CALCULATOR"
               Style="{StaticResource PhoneTextTitle0Style}"/>
  </StackPanel>

  <!-- The area with four buttons and corresponding text blocks -->
  <Grid Grid.Row="1">
    <Grid.RowDefinitions>
      <RowDefinition/>
      <RowDefinition/>
      <RowDefinition/>
      <RowDefinition/>
    </Grid.RowDefinitions>
    <Grid.ColumnDefinitions>
      <ColumnDefinition Width="1.5*"/>
      <ColumnDefinition Width="*"/>
    </Grid.ColumnDefinitions>

    <!-- The four main buttons -->
    <RadioButton x:Name="AmountButton" Grid.Row="0" Content="amount"
                 Style="{StaticResource RadioToggleButtonStyle}"
                 Checked="RadioButton_Checked"
                 Tag="{Binding ElementName=AmountPanel}"/>
    <RadioButton x:Name="TipButton" Grid.Row="1" Content=" "
                 Style="{StaticResource RadioToggleButtonStyle}"
                 Checked="RadioButton_Checked"
                 Tag="{Binding ElementName=TipListBox}"/>
    <RadioButton x:Name="TotalButton" Grid.Row="2" Content=" "
                 Style="{StaticResource RadioToggleButtonStyle}"
                 Checked="RadioButton_Checked"
                 Tag="{Binding ElementName=TotalListBox}"/>
```

LISTING 10.1   Continued

```xml
<RadioButton x:Name="SplitButton" Grid.Row="3" Content=" "
             Checked="RadioButton_Checked"
             Style="{StaticResource RadioToggleButtonStyle}"
             Tag="{Binding ElementName=SplitListBox}"/>


<!-- The four main text blocks -->
<TextBlock x:Name="AmountTextBlock" Grid.Column="1"
           Style="{StaticResource TextBlockStyle}"/>
<TextBlock x:Name="TipTextBlock" Grid.Row="1" Grid.Column="1"
           Style="{StaticResource TextBlockStyle}"/>
<TextBlock x:Name="TotalTextBlock" Grid.Row="2" Grid.Column="1"
           FontWeight="Bold" Style="{StaticResource TextBlockStyle}"/>
<TextBlock x:Name="SplitTextBlock" Grid.Row="3" Grid.Column="1"
           FontWeight="Bold" Foreground="{StaticResource PhoneAccentBrush}"
           Style="{StaticResource TextBlockStyle}"/>
</Grid>

<!-- The bottom input area, which overlays four children in the same
     grid cell -->
<Grid Grid.Row="2">
  <!-- The calculator buttons shown for "amount" -->
  <Canvas x:Name="AmountPanel" Visibility="Collapsed">
    <Button Style="{StaticResource CalculatorButtonStyle}"
            Background="{Binding CalculatorMainBrush, ElementName=Page}"
            Content="7" Canvas.Left="-6" Canvas.Top="-1"/>
    <Button Style="{StaticResource CalculatorButtonStyle}"
            Background="{Binding CalculatorMainBrush, ElementName=Page}"
            Content="8" Canvas.Left="114" Canvas.Top="-1"/>
    <Button Style="{StaticResource CalculatorButtonStyle}"
            Background="{Binding CalculatorMainBrush, ElementName=Page}"
            Content="9" Canvas.Left="234" Canvas.Top="-1"/>
    <Button Style="{StaticResource CalculatorButtonStyle}"
            Background="{Binding CalculatorMainBrush, ElementName=Page}"
            Content="4" Canvas.Top="95" Canvas.Left="-6"/>
    <Button Style="{StaticResource CalculatorButtonStyle}"
            Background="{Binding CalculatorMainBrush, ElementName=Page}"
            Content="5" Canvas.Top="95" Canvas.Left="114"/>
    <Button Style="{StaticResource CalculatorButtonStyle}"
            Background="{Binding CalculatorMainBrush, ElementName=Page}"
            Content="6" Canvas.Top="95" Canvas.Left="234"/>
    <Button Style="{StaticResource CalculatorButtonStyle}"
            Background="{Binding CalculatorMainBrush, ElementName=Page}"
            Content="1" Canvas.Top="191" Canvas.Left="-6"/>
```

LISTING 10.1   Continued

```xml
<Button Style="{StaticResource CalculatorButtonStyle}"
        Background="{Binding CalculatorMainBrush, ElementName=Page}"
        Content="2" Canvas.Top="191" Canvas.Left="114"/>
<Button Style="{StaticResource CalculatorButtonStyle}"
        Background="{Binding CalculatorMainBrush, ElementName=Page}"
        Content="3" Canvas.Top="191" Canvas.Left="234"/>
<Button Style="{StaticResource CalculatorButtonStyle}"
        Background="{Binding CalculatorMainBrush, ElementName=Page}"
        Content="0" Canvas.Top="287" Canvas.Left="-6"/>
<Button Style="{StaticResource CalculatorButtonStyle}"
        Background="{Binding CalculatorMainBrush, ElementName=Page}"
        Content="00" Width="252" Canvas.Top="287" Canvas.Left="114"/>
<Button Style="{StaticResource CalculatorButtonStyle}" FontSize="32"
        FontFamily="{StaticResource PhoneFontFamilySemiBold}"
        Background="{Binding CalculatorSecondaryBrush, ElementName=Page}"
        Content="C" Height="204" Canvas.Top="-1" Canvas.Left="354"/>
<Button x:Name="BackspaceButton" Height="204"
        Style="{StaticResource CalculatorButtonStyle}"
        Background="{Binding CalculatorSecondaryBrush, ElementName=Page}"
        Canvas.Top="191" Canvas.Left="354">
  <!-- The "X in an arrow" backspace drawing -->
  <Canvas Width="48" Height="32">
    <Path x:Name="BackspaceXPath" Data="M24,8 39,24 M39,8 24,24"
          Stroke="{StaticResource PhoneForegroundBrush}"
          StrokeThickness="4"/>
    <Path x:Name="BackspaceBorderPath" StrokeThickness="2"
          Data="M16,0 47,0 47,31 16,31 0,16.5z"
          Stroke="{StaticResource PhoneForegroundBrush}"/>
  </Canvas>
</Button>
</Canvas>

<!-- The list box shown for "X% tip" -->
<ListBox x:Name="TipListBox" Visibility="Collapsed"
         SelectionChanged="TipListBox_SelectionChanged"/>

<!-- The list box shown for "total" -->
<ListBox x:Name="TotalListBox" Visibility="Collapsed"
         SelectionChanged="TotalListBox_SelectionChanged">
  <ListBoxItem Style="{StaticResource ListBoxItemStyle}"
               Content="exact" Tag="NoRounding"/>
  <ListBoxItem Style="{StaticResource ListBoxItemStyle}"
               Content="round tip down" Tag="RoundTipDown"/>
```

LISTING 10.1   Continued

```xml
      <ListBoxItem Style="{StaticResource ListBoxItemStyle}"
                   Content="round tip up" Tag="RoundTipUp"/>
      <ListBoxItem Style="{StaticResource ListBoxItemStyle}"
                   Content="round total down" Tag="RoundTotalDown"/>
      <ListBoxItem Style="{StaticResource ListBoxItemStyle}"
                   Content="round total up" Tag="RoundTotalUp"/>
    </ListBox>

    <!-- The list box shown for "split check" -->
    <ListBox x:Name="SplitListBox" Visibility="Collapsed"
             SelectionChanged="SplitListBox_SelectionChanged"/>
   </Grid>
  </Grid>
</phone:PhoneApplicationPage>
```

Notes:

→ The page's resources collection contains custom styles for the radio buttons (which contains the custom control template), calculator buttons, list box items, and text blocks.

→ The PhoneTitlePanelStyle and PhoneTextTitle0Style styles, the latter of which was introduced in the preceding chapter, are defined in App.xaml (and not shown in this chapter). This app, and the remaining apps in this book, does this with commonly-used styles so they can be easily shared among multiple pages.

→ For convenience, several elements have their Tag property set. For example, the radio buttons set their Tag to the element that should be made visible when each one is checked. The code-behind retrieves the element reference and performs the work to make it visible.

 When using data binding, you can override the default data source by setting the binding's ElementName property. For example, the following button displays "True" or "False" depending on the value of AmountButton's IsChecked property:

```xml
<Button Content="{Binding IsChecked, ElementName=AmountButton}"/>
```

When using ElementName without a property name, as done in Listing 10.1, the binding returns a reference to the element itself.

→ Because the content of the last three radio buttons is dynamic, the XAML file leaves them blank to avoid a flicker when the code-behind restores their current values. They are set to a string with a space in it to prevent them from initially being too short.

→ `AmountPanel` is a canvas with precisely positioned and precisely sized calculator buttons. This could have been done with a grid instead, although each button would have to be given negative margins, because the desired style of the buttons requires overlapping them a bit so the visible space between them is 12 pixels rather than 24. Because this app only supports the portrait orientation, the hardcoded canvas layout works just fine.

→ The built-in Calculator app that this is modeled after uses two different colors of buttons that are *similar to* but not quite the same as the `PhoneChromeBrush` resource. Therefore, this page defines two custom brushes as properties in its code-behind file— `CalculatorMainBrush` for the digit keys and `CalculatorSecondaryBrush` for the other keys. The calculator buttons use data binding to set each background to the value of the appropriate property. This is why the page is given the name of `"Page"`— so it can be referenced in the data-binding expressions.

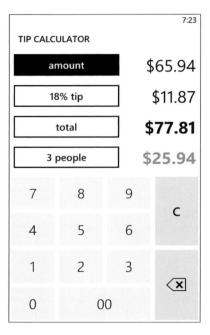

The reason data binding is used is that these two brushes must change for the light theme versus the dark theme. As shown in Figure 10.4, light-themed buttons that match the built-in Calculator app have different colors. If these two custom brushes did not ever need to change, they could have been defined as simple resources on the page and `StaticResource` syntax could have been used to set each button's background.

FIGURE 10.4 The custom brushes dynamically change with the current theme, so Tip Calculator's buttons match the built-in Calculator's buttons in the light theme.

⚠ **You cannot use a databound value in a style's setter!**

Rather than repeating the same background value on 11 out of the 13 calculator buttons, it would have been nice to set it once inside `CalculatorButtonStyle`:

```
<Style x:Key="CalculatorButtonStyle" TargetType="Button">
  <Setter Property="FontSize" Value="36"/>
  <Setter Property="FontFamily"
          Value="{StaticResource PhoneFontFamilySemiLight}"/>
  <Setter Property="BorderThickness" Value="0"/>
```

```
<Setter Property="Width" Value="132"/>
<Setter Property="Height" Value="108"/>
<Setter Property="Background"
        Value="{Binding CalculatorMainBrush, ElementName=Page}"/>
</Style>
```

However, Silverlight does not support using data binding inside a style's setter.

→ The calculator buttons purposely do not use the tilting effect used on the toggle buttons, because this matches the behavior of the built-in Calculator app. The only thing missing is the sound effect when tapping each button!

→ The graphical content for the backspace button is created with two `Path` elements. (See Appendix E, "Geometry Reference," to understand the syntax.) Because the content is vector-based, the code-behind can (and does) easily update its color dynamically to ensure that it remains visible when the button is pressed.

→ Rather than adding text blocks to `TotalListBox`, this code uses instances of a control called `ListBoxItem`. List box items are normally the best kind of element to add to a list box because they automatically highlight their content with the theme's accent color when it is selected (if their content is textual). You can see the automatic highlighting of selected items in Figure 10.2.

Only provide your own mechanism for text input if the input is very limited!

Providing custom buttons for text input, rather than using the built-in keyboard, can be a dangerous undertaking. The built-in keyboard has many behaviors for handling multiple languages and regions, such as convenient ways to add accents to letters. If your custom buttons do not replicate such functionality, your app might be unusable to a significant portion of your audience. Even adding a period button to the calculator would be problematic, because in some regions the decimal point is represented as a comma instead. (The built-in Calculator app changes its period button to a comma depending on the phone's current settings.) Making custom buttons for digits only, as done in this app, is safe to do without worrying about having to morph the keyboard based on current settings.

Control Templates

Much like the data templates seen in Chapter 6, "Baby Sign Language," control templates define how a control gets rendered. Every control has a default control template, but you can override it with an arbitrary element tree in order to completely change its appearance.

A control template can be set directly on an element with its `Template` property, although this property is usually set inside a style. For demonstration purposes, the following button is directly given a custom control template that makes it look like the red ellipse shown in Figure 10.5:

FIGURE 10.5   A normal button restyled to look like a red ellipse.

```
<Button Content="ok">
  <Button.Template>
    <ControlTemplate TargetType="Button">
      <Ellipse Fill="Red" Width="200" Height="50"/>
    </ControlTemplate>
  </Button.Template>
</Button>
```

Despite its custom look, the button still has all the same behaviors, such as a `Click` event that gets raised when it is tapped. After all, it is still an instance of the `Button` class!

This is not a good template, however, because it ignores properties on the button. For example, the button in Figure 10.5 has its `Content` property set to `"ok"` but that does not get displayed. If you're creating a control template that's meant to be shared among multiple controls, you should data-bind to various properties on the control. The following template updates the previous one to respect the button's content, producing the result in Figure 10.6:

FIGURE 10.6   The button's control template now shows its "ok" content.

```
<Button Content="ok">
  <Button.Template>
    <ControlTemplate TargetType="Button">
      <Grid Width="200" Height="50">
        <Ellipse Fill="Red"/>
        <TextBlock Text="{TemplateBinding Content}"
                   HorizontalAlignment="Center" VerticalAlignment="Center"/>
      </Grid>
    </ControlTemplate>
  </Button.Template>
</Button>
```

Rather than using normal `Binding` syntax, the template uses `TemplateBinding` syntax. This works just like `Binding`, but the data source is automatically set to the instance of the control being templated, so it's ideal for use inside control templates. In fact, `TemplateBinding` can *only* be used inside control templates and data templates.

Of course, a button can contain nontext content, so using a text block to display it creates an artificial limitation. To ensure that all types of content get displayed properly, you can use a generic content control instead of a text block. It would also be nice to respect several other properties of the button. The following control template, placed in a style shared by several buttons, does this:

```xml
<phone:PhoneApplicationPage …>
  <phone:PhoneApplicationPage.Resources>
    <Style x:Name="ButtonStyle" TargetType="Button">
      <!-- Some default property values -->
      <Setter Property="Background" Value="Red"/>
      <Setter Property="Padding" Value="12"/>
      <!-- The custom control template -->
      <Setter Property="Template">
        <Setter.Value>
          <ControlTemplate TargetType="Button">
            <Grid>
              <Ellipse Fill="{TemplateBinding Background}"/>
              <ContentControl Content="{TemplateBinding Content}"
                Margin="{TemplateBinding Padding}"
                HorizontalAlignment="{TemplateBinding HorizontalContentAlignment}"
                VerticalAlignment="{TemplateBinding VerticalContentAlignment}"/>
            </Grid>
          </ControlTemplate>
        </Setter.Value>
      </Setter>
    </Style>
  </phone:PhoneApplicationPage.Resources>
  <StackPanel>
    <!-- button 1 -->
    <Button Content="ok" Style="{StaticResource ButtonStyle}"/>
    <!-- button 2 -->
    <Button Background="Lime" Style="{StaticResource ButtonStyle}">
      <Button.Content>
        <!-- The "X in an arrow" backspace drawing -->
        <Canvas Width="48" Height="32">
          <Path x:Name="BackspaceXPath" Data="M24,8 39,24 M39,8 24,24"
                Stroke="{StaticResource PhoneForegroundBrush}"
                StrokeThickness="4"/>
          <Path x:Name="BackspaceBorderPath" StrokeThickness="2"
                Data="M16,0 47,0 47,31 16,31 0,16.5z"
                Stroke="{StaticResource PhoneForegroundBrush}"/>
        </Canvas>
```

```
        </Button.Content>
    </Button>
    <!-- button 3 -->
    <Button Content="content alignment and padding"
            HorizontalContentAlignment="Right"
            Padding="50"
            Style="{StaticResource ButtonStyle}"/>
    <!-- button 4 -->
    <Button Content="5 properties that just work" HorizontalAlignment="Left"
            Height="100" FontSize="40" FontStyle="Italic" Margin="20"
            Style="{StaticResource ButtonStyle}"/>
    </StackPanel>
</phone:PhoneApplicationPage>
```

The result of this XAML is shown in Figure 10.7. By removing the hardcoded width and height from the template, the buttons are automatically given the appropriate size based on their layout properties and the space provided by their parent element. This is why all the buttons now stretch horizontally by default and why the last button is able to get the desired effect when setting its height and alignment. The second button demonstrates that nontext content now works as well as setting a custom background brush. Because the default red brush is moved into the style and the template binds to the current back-ground, the background is now overridable by an individual button while preserving its default appearance. The same is true for the padding, which the third button is able to override. Notice that the five properties (other than `Content` and `Style`) set on the last button automatically work without any special treatment needed by the control template.

When creating a control template inside a style to be shared by many controls, use template binding as much as possible and avoid setting specific property values inside the template. Instead, set specific values in other style setters, so they become override-able default values. You can see this technique put to good use inside the control template for radio buttons in Listing 10.1.

It might seem counterintuitive at first, but the template maps the control's *padding* to the content control's *margin*, and it maps the control's *content* alignment properties to the content control's regular alignment properties. This is a common practice, as the definition of padding is the margin around the inner content, and the definition of the content alignment properties is the alignment of the inner content.

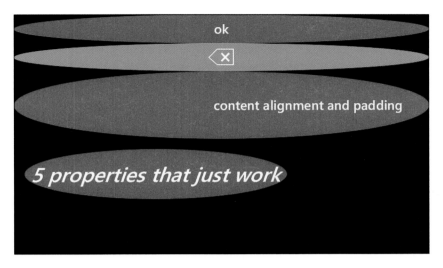

FIGURE 10.7 The custom control template respects many properties that are customized on four different buttons.

Rather than use a content control inside a control template, you should use the lighter-weight `ContentPresenter` element. A *content presenter* displays content just like a content control, but it was designed specifically for use in control templates. A content presenter is a primitive building block, whereas a content control is a full-blown control with its own control template—that contains a content presenter!

In the control template used in Figure 10.7, you can replace the content control with a content presenter simply by swapping the name of the element:

```
<ContentPresenter Content="{TemplateBinding Content}"
  Margin="{TemplateBinding Padding}"
  HorizontalAlignment="{TemplateBinding HorizontalContentAlignment}"
  VerticalAlignment="{TemplateBinding VerticalContentAlignment}"/>
```

Content presenters also have a built-in shortcut. If you omit setting its `Content` to `{TemplateBinding Content}`, it implicitly assumes that's what you want. So, you can replace the preceding element with the following and Figure 10.7 would look identical:

```
<ContentPresenter Margin="{TemplateBinding Padding}"
  HorizontalAlignment="{TemplateBinding HorizontalContentAlignment}"
  VerticalAlignment="{TemplateBinding VerticalContentAlignment}"/>
```

This works only when the control template is given a target type of `ContentControl` or one of its subclasses (such as `Button`).

Still, with all this work, the control template used for Figure 10.7 is not complete because it does not respect the various visual states of the buttons. A button should have a different appearance when it is pressed and a different appearance when it is disabled. To enable this, you must work with the Visual State Manager, and that's a topic saved for Chapter 19, "Animation Lab."

 How do I make small tweaks to an existing control template rather than create a brand-new one from scratch?

There is no mechanism for tweaking existing templates. Instead, you must get the XAML for an existing template, manually modify it, and then apply it as a brand-new template. Fortunately, the Windows Phone Developer Tools installs a XAML file containing all the default styles (and their templates) for the built-in controls: `%ProgramFiles%\Microsoft SDKs\Windows Phone\v7.0\Design\System.Windows.xaml`. Or, in Expression Blend, you can create the appropriate control then choose Edit Template, Edit a Copy… to get a copy of its default style pasted into your XAML.

To create Listing 10.1, I used this technique to grab and tweak the default style of a toggle button. It would be quite a lot of work to come up with that control template on your own!

The Code-Behind

Listing 10.2 contains the code-behind for Tip Calculator's page. It makes use of the following enum defined in a separate file (`RoundingType.cs`):

```
public enum RoundingType
{
  NoRounding,
  RoundTipDown,
  RoundTipUp,
  RoundTotalDown,
  RoundTotalUp
}
```

LISTING 10.2   `MainPage.xaml.cs`—The Code-Behind for Tip Calculator

```
using System;
using System.Windows;
using System.Windows.Controls;
using System.Windows.Input;
using System.Windows.Media;
using System.Windows.Navigation;
using Microsoft.Phone.Controls;

namespace WindowsPhoneApp
{
```

LISTING 10.2   Continued

```csharp
public partial class MainPage : PhoneApplicationPage
{
  // Persistent settings. These are remembered no matter what.
  Setting<RoundingType> savedRoundingType =
    new Setting<RoundingType>("RoundingType", RoundingType.NoRounding);
  Setting<double> savedTipPercent = new Setting<double>("TipPercent", .15);

  // The current values used for the calculation
  double amount;
  double tipPercent;
  double tipAmount;
  double totalAmount;
  int split = 1;
  RoundingType roundingType;

  // Which of the four radio buttons is currently checked
  RadioButton checkedButton;

  // Two theme-specific custom brushes
  public Brush CalculatorMainBrush { get; set; }
  public Brush CalculatorSecondaryBrush { get; set; }

  public MainPage()
  {
    InitializeComponent();

    // A single handler for all calculator button taps
    this.AmountPanel.AddHandler(Button.MouseLeftButtonUpEvent,
      new MouseButtonEventHandler(CalculatorButton_MouseLeftButtonUp),
      true /* handledEventsToo */);

    // Handlers to ensure that the backspace button's vector content changes
    // color appropriately when the button is pressed
    this.BackspaceButton.AddHandler(Button.MouseLeftButtonDownEvent,
      new MouseButtonEventHandler(BackspaceButton_MouseLeftButtonDown),
      true /* handledEventsToo */);
    this.BackspaceButton.AddHandler(Button.MouseLeftButtonUpEvent,
      new MouseButtonEventHandler(BackspaceButton_MouseLeftButtonUp),
      true /* handledEventsToo */);
    this.BackspaceButton.MouseMove += BackspaceButton_MouseMove;
  }
```

LISTING 10.2   Continued

```
protected override void OnNavigatedFrom(NavigationEventArgs e)
{
  base.OnNavigatedFrom(e);

  // Remember transient page data that isn't appropriate to always persist
  this.State["Amount"] = this.amount;
  this.State["Split"] = this.split;
  this.State["CheckedButtonName"] = this.checkedButton.Name;

  // Save the persistent settings
  this.savedRoundingType.Value = this.roundingType;
  this.savedTipPercent.Value = this.tipPercent;
}

protected override void OnNavigatedTo(NavigationEventArgs e)
{
  base.OnNavigatedTo(e);

  // Set the colors of the two custom brushes based on whether
  // we're in the light theme or dark theme
  if ((Visibility)Application.Current.Resources["PhoneLightThemeVisibility"]
                  == Visibility.Visible)
  {
    this.CalculatorMainBrush = new SolidColorBrush(
                               Color.FromArgb(0xFF, 0xEF, 0xEF, 0xEF));
    this.CalculatorSecondaryBrush = new SolidColorBrush(
                               Color.FromArgb(0xFF, 0xDE, 0xDF, 0xDE));
  }
  else
  {
    this.CalculatorMainBrush = new SolidColorBrush(
                               Color.FromArgb(0xFF, 0x18, 0x1C, 0x18));
    this.CalculatorSecondaryBrush = new SolidColorBrush(
                               Color.FromArgb(0xFF, 0x31, 0x30, 0x31));
  }

  // Restore transient page data, if there is any from last time
  if (this.State.ContainsKey("Amount"))
    this.amount = (double)this.State["Amount"];
  if (this.State.ContainsKey("Split"))
    this.split = (int)this.State["Split"];

  // Restore the persisted settings
  this.roundingType = this.savedRoundingType.Value;
```

LISTING 10.2   Continued

```
    this.tipPercent = this.savedTipPercent.Value;

    RefreshAllCalculations();

    // Fill TipListBox and set its selected item correctly
    this.TipListBox.Items.Clear();
    for (int i = 50; i >= 0; i--)
    {
      ListBoxItem item = new ListBoxItem { Content = i + "% tip",
        Tag = (double)i / 100,
        Style = this.Resources["ListBoxItemStyle"] as Style };
      if ((double)item.Tag == this.tipPercent)
        item.IsSelected = true;
      this.TipListBox.Items.Add(item);
    }

    // Fill SplitListBox and set its selected item correctly
    this.SplitListBox.Items.Clear();
    for (int i = 1; i <= 20; i++)
    {
      ListBoxItem item = new ListBoxItem {
        Content = (i == 1 ? "do not split" : i + " people"), Tag = i,
        Style = this.Resources["ListBoxItemStyle"] as Style };
      if ((int)item.Tag == this.split)
        item.IsSelected = true;
      this.SplitListBox.Items.Add(item);
    }

    // TotalListBox is already filled in XAML, but set its selected item
    this.TotalListBox.SelectedIndex = (int)this.roundingType;
  }

  void MainPage_Loaded(object sender, EventArgs e)
  {
    // Restore one more transient value: which radio button was checked when
    // the app was deactivated.
    // This is done here instead of inside OnNavigatedTo because the Loaded
    // event is raised after the data binding occurs that sets each button's
    // Tag (needed by the handler called when IsChecked is set to true)
    if (this.State.ContainsKey("CheckedButtonName"))
    {
      RadioButton button =
        this.FindName((string)this.State["CheckedButtonName"]) as RadioButton;
      if (button != null)
```

LISTING 10.2   Continued

```
      button.IsChecked = true;
  }
  else
  {
    // For a fresh instance of the app, check the amount button
    this.AmountButton.IsChecked = true;
  }
}

// A single handler for all calculator button taps
void CalculatorButton_MouseLeftButtonUp(object sender, MouseButtonEventArgs e)
{
  // Although sender is the canvas, the OriginalSource is the tapped button
  Button button = e.OriginalSource as Button;
  if (button == null)
    return;

  string content = button.Content.ToString();

  // Determine what to do based on the string content of the tapped button
  double digit;
  if (content == "00")
  {
    // Append two zeros
    this.amount *= 100;
  }
  else if (double.TryParse(content, out digit)) // double so division works
  {
    // Append the digit
    this.amount *= 10;
    this.amount += digit / 100;
  }
  else if (content == "C")
  {
    // Clear the amount
    this.amount = 0;
  }
  else // The backspace button
  {
    // Chop off the last digit.
    // The multiplication preserves the first digit after the decimal point
    // because the cast to int chops off what's after it
    int temp = (int)(this.amount * 10);
    // Shift right by 2 places (1 extra due to the temporary multiplication)
```

LISTING 10.2   Continued

```csharp
      this.amount = (double)temp / 100;
    }

    RefreshAllCalculations();
  }

  void TipListBox_SelectionChanged(object sender, SelectionChangedEventArgs e)
  {
    if (e.AddedItems.Count > 0)
    {
      // The item's Tag has been set to the actual percent value
      this.tipPercent = (double)(e.AddedItems[0] as ListBoxItem).Tag;
      RefreshAllCalculations();
    }
  }

  void TotalListBox_SelectionChanged(object sender, SelectionChangedEventArgs e)
  {
    if (e.AddedItems.Count > 0)
    {
      // The item's Tag has been set to a string containg one of the enum's
      // named values. Use Enum.Parse to convert to string to an instance
      // of the RoundingType enum.
      this.roundingType = (RoundingType)Enum.Parse(typeof(RoundingType),
        (e.AddedItems[0] as ListBoxItem).Tag.ToString(), true);
      RefreshAllCalculations();
    }
  }

  void SplitListBox_SelectionChanged(object sender, SelectionChangedEventArgs e)
  {
    if (e.AddedItems.Count > 0)
    {
      // The item's Tag has been set to the split number
      this.split = (int)(e.AddedItems[0] as ListBoxItem).Tag;
      RefreshSplitTotal();
    }
  }

  void RefreshAllCalculations()
  {
    RefreshAmount();
    RefreshTip();
    RefreshTotal();
```

LISTING 10.2   Continued

```
    RefreshSplitTotal();
  }

  void RefreshAmount()
  {
    // Use currency string formatting ("C") to get the proper display
    this.AmountTextBlock.Text = this.amount.ToString("C");
  }

  void RefreshTip()
  {
    // The content of the tip button and text block are impacted by the
    // current rounding setting.
    string buttonLabel = (this.tipPercent * 100) + "% tip";
    switch (this.roundingType)
    {
      case RoundingType.RoundTipDown:
        this.tipAmount = Math.Floor(this.amount * this.tipPercent);
        buttonLabel += " (rounded)";
        break;
      case RoundingType.RoundTipUp:
        this.tipAmount = Math.Ceiling(this.amount * this.tipPercent);
        buttonLabel += " (rounded)";
        break;
      default:
        this.tipAmount = this.amount * this.tipPercent;
        break;
    }
    this.TipTextBlock.Text = this.tipAmount.ToString("C"); // C == Currency
    this.TipButton.Content = buttonLabel;
  }

  void RefreshTotal()
  {
    // The content of the total button and text block are impacted by the
    // current rounding setting.
    string buttonLabel = "total";
    switch (this.roundingType)
    {
      case RoundingType.RoundTotalDown:
        this.totalAmount = Math.Floor(this.amount + this.tipAmount);
        buttonLabel += " (rounded)";
        break;
      case RoundingType.RoundTotalUp:
```

LISTING 10.2   Continued

```
      this.totalAmount = Math.Ceiling(this.amount + this.tipAmount);
      buttonLabel += " (rounded)";
      break;
    default:
      this.totalAmount = this.amount + this.tipAmount;
      break;
  }
  this.TotalTextBlock.Text = this.totalAmount.ToString("C"); // C == Currency
  this.TotalButton.Content = buttonLabel;
}

void RefreshSplitTotal()
{
  if (this.split == 1)
  {
    // Don't show the value if we're not splitting the check
    this.SplitTextBlock.Text = "";
    this.SplitButton.Content = "split check";
  }
  else
  {
    this.SplitTextBlock.Text = (this.totalAmount / this.split).ToString("C");
    this.SplitButton.Content = this.split + " people";
  }
}

// Called when any of the four toggle buttons are tapped
void RadioButton_Checked(object sender, RoutedEventArgs e)
{
  // Which button was tapped
  this.checkedButton = sender as RadioButton;
  // Which bottom element to show (which was stored in Tag in XAML)
  UIElement bottomElement = this.checkedButton.Tag as UIElement;

  // Hide all bottom elements...
  this.AmountPanel.Visibility = Visibility.Collapsed;
  this.TipListBox.Visibility = Visibility.Collapsed;
  this.TotalListBox.Visibility = Visibility.Collapsed;
  this.SplitListBox.Visibility = Visibility.Collapsed;

  // ...then show the correct one
  bottomElement.Visibility = Visibility.Visible;

  // If a list box was just shown, ensure its selected item is on-screen.
```

LISTING 10.2   Continued

```
    // This is delayed because a layout pass must first run (as a result of
    // setting Visibility) in order for ScrollIntoView to have any effect.
    this.Dispatcher.BeginInvoke(delegate()
    {
      if (sender == this.TipButton)
        this.TipListBox.ScrollIntoView(this.TipListBox.SelectedItem);
      else if (sender == this.TotalButton)
        this.TotalListBox.ScrollIntoView(this.TotalListBox.SelectedItem);
      else if (sender == this.SplitButton)
        this.SplitListBox.ScrollIntoView(this.SplitListBox.SelectedItem);
    });
  }

  // Change the color of the two paths inside the backspace button when pressed
  void BackspaceButton_MouseLeftButtonDown(object sender, MouseButtonEventArgs e)
  {
    this.BackspaceXPath.Stroke =
      Application.Current.Resources["PhoneBackgroundBrush"] as Brush;
    this.BackspaceBorderPath.Stroke =
      Application.Current.Resources["PhoneBackgroundBrush"] as Brush;
  }

  // Change the color of the two paths back when no longer pressed
  void BackspaceButton_MouseLeftButtonUp(object sender, MouseEventArgs e)
  {
    this.BackspaceXPath.Stroke =
      Application.Current.Resources["PhoneForegroundBrush"] as Brush;
    this.BackspaceBorderPath.Stroke =
      Application.Current.Resources["PhoneForegroundBrush"] as Brush;
  }

  // Workaround for when the finger has not yet been released but the color
  // needs to change back because the finger is no longer over the button
  void BackspaceButton_MouseMove(object sender, MouseEventArgs e)
  {
    // this.BackspaceButton.IsMouseOver lies when it has captured the mouse!
    // Use GetPosition instead:
    Point relativePoint = e.GetPosition(this.BackspaceButton);
    // We can get away with this simple check because
    // the button is in the bottom-right corner
    if (relativePoint.X < 0 || relativePoint.Y < 0)
      BackspaceButton_MouseLeftButtonUp(null, null); // Not over the button
    else
```

LISTING 10.2   Continued

```
        BackspaceButton_MouseLeftButtonDown(null, null); // Still over the button
    }
  }
}
```

Notes:

→ In the constructor, three out of four handlers are attached to events using a special AddHandler method that works with a type of event called a *routed event*. Routed events are discussed later in this section.

→ Inside OnNavigatedFrom and OnNavigatedTo (and MainPage_Loaded), you can see the separate handling of permanent data stored in Setting objects and transient data stored in page state. Although one of the pieces of information to save in page state is the currently-checked radio button, a reference to the radio button itself cannot be placed in page state because it is not serializable. Instead, the radio button's *name* is put in the dictionary. When this state is restored inside MainPage_Loaded, the page's FindName method is called with the saved name in order to retrieve the correct instance of the radio button.

→ Inside OnNavigatedTo, the trick to set the two custom brushes differently for the light versus dark theme is accomplished by checking the value of the PhoneLightThemeVisibility resource.

→ Unlike with TotalListBox, the items for TipListBox and SplitListBox are created in code-behind because they are much longer lists that can easily be created in a loop. These list box

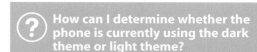

How can I determine whether the phone is currently using the dark theme or light theme?

The reliable way to do this is to check the value of either PhoneLightThemeVisibility or PhoneDarkThemeVisibility, two values defined in any resource dictionary. Each one is set to Visible or Collapsed, as appropriate. If you prefer, you could alternatively check for the value of PhoneLightThemeOpacity or PhoneDarkThemeOpacity, which are either set to 0 or 1, as appropriate.

items also have their Tag property set so the code that processes the selected item has a reliable way to discover the meaning of the selected item without parsing its string content. List box items have a handy IsSelected property that can be set to select an item rather than using the list box's SelectedItem or SelectedIndex property. The two loops make use of this to initially select the appropriate values.

→ In the three list box SelectionChanged event handlers, e.AddedItems[0] is used to reference the selected item rather than the list box's SelectedItem property. This is just done for demonstration purposes, as either approach does the same thing. List boxes can support multiple selections (if their SelectionMode property is set to Multiple), so any time SelectionChanged is raised, you can discover what items have been selected or deselected via the e parameter's `AddedItems` and `RemovedItems` properties. When a list box only supports a single selection, as in this app, `AddedItems` and `RemovedItems` can only have zero or one element.

→ The strings created for the text blocks use *currency formatting* by passing "C" to `ToString`. For the English (United States) region, this is what prepends the dollar signs to the numeric displays. If you change your phone's "Region format" to "French (France)" under the phone's "region & language" settings, the currency formatting automatically adjusts its display, as shown in Figure 10.8.

→ `RadioButton_Checked` has logic to ensure the selected item is not scrolled off-screen when the bottom pane switches to a list box. This is accomplished with list box's

FIGURE 10.8   When the region format is French (France), the euro symbol and comma are automatically used instead of a dollar sign and decimal point.

`ScrollIntoView` method. However, it is called inside in asynchronous callback because it doesn't work when the list box isn't visible, and the setting of its `Visibility` property doesn't take effect instantly. (It happens after the event handler returns and Silverlight updates the layout of the page.) Ideally this logic would have been performed in an event handler for a "visibility changed" event, but no such event exists in Silverlight.

→ Because the background color of buttons invert when pressed, `BackspaceButton_MouseLeftButtonUp` and `BackspaceButton_MouseLeftButtonDown` swap the stroke brushes of the paths inside the backspace button to ensure they remain visible. However, doing the work in these two event handlers isn't quite enough. When the user holds their finger on the button and drags it off *without releasing their finger*, the button colors revert to normal but the `MouseLeftButtonUp` event is not yet raised to revert the path strokes in sync.

To detect this situation, the backspace button's `MouseMove` event is also handled. This event continues to get raised even when the finger is moving outside of the button's bounds because the button "captures" the mouse input when the finger is depressed and doesn't release it until the finger is released. The `MouseMove` handler (`BackspaceButton_MouseMove`) determines whether the finger is outside the bounds of the button, and calls either the `MouseLeftButtonUp` or `MouseLeftButtonDown` handler to adjust the strokes accordingly. As a result, the custom graphics in the backspace button behave appropriately in every situation. Figure 10.9 shows the appearance of the backspace button while a finger is pressing it.

This behavior would be simpler to implement with Visual State Manager animations inside a custom control template for the backspace button. However, it is too early in this book to make use of these features.

Routed Events

Some of the events raised by Silverlight elements, called *routed events*, have extra behavior in order to work well with a tree of elements. When a routed event is raised, it travels up the element tree from the source element all the way to the root, getting raised on each element along the way. This process is called *event bubbling*.

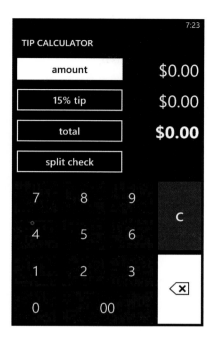

FIGURE 10.9   When the backspace button is pressed, you can always see the inner content, thanks to the code that switches its brush.

Some elements, such as buttons, leverage event bubbling to be able to provide a consistent Click event even if it contents are a complex tree of elements. Even if the user taps an element nested many layers deep, the MouseLeftButtonUp event bubbles up to the button so it can raise Click. Thanks to event bubbling, the button's code has no idea what its contents actually are, nor does it need to.

Some elements, such as buttons, also halt event bubbling from proceeding any further. Because buttons want their consumers to use their Click event rather than listening to MouseLeftButtonUp and/or MouseLeftButtonDown, it marks these events as handled when it receives them. (This is done via an internal mechanism. *Your* code doesn't have a way to halt bubbling.)

Routed Events in Tip Calculator

In Listing 10.2, Tip Calculator leverages event bubbling for convenience. Rather than attaching a Click event handler to each of the 13 buttons individually, it attaches a single MouseLeftButtonUp event handler to their parent canvas using the AddHandler method supported by all UI elements and a static MouseLeftButtonUpEvent field that identifies the routed event:

```
// A single handler for all calculator button taps
this.AmountPanel.AddHandler(Button.MouseLeftButtonUpEvent,
```

```
new MouseButtonEventHandler(CalculatorButton_MouseLeftButtonUp),
true /* handledEventsToo */);
```

This event is chosen, rather than `Click`, because `MouseLeftButtonUp` is a routed event whereas `Click` is not. Although attaching this handler could be done in XAML with the same syntax used for any event, the attaching is done in C# to enable special behavior. By passing `true` as the last parameter, we are able to receive the event even though the button has halted its bubbling! Therefore, the halting done by buttons is just an illusion; the bubbling still occurs, but you must go out of your way to see it.

> Using the `handledEventsToo` parameter to handle routed events that would otherwise not be raised is a very handy and common technique when customizing the behavior of certain elements. The tilt effect used throughout this book also leverages this mechanism to be able to reliably tilt and untilt anything it is applied to.

Tip Calculator also leverages this special behavior to add its brush-changing `MouseLeftButtonDown` and `MouseLeftButtonUp` handlers to the backspace button. Without attaching these handlers in code with the `true` third parameter, it would never receive these events. In contrast, it attaches the `MouseMove` handler with normal += syntax because `MouseMove` is not a routed event. (Alternatively, it could have attached the `MouseMove` handler in XAML.)

Determining Which Events Are Routed Events

You can figure out which Silverlight events are routed in one of three ways:

→ Looking for a corresponding static field of type `RoutedEvent` on the class with the event. For example, all UI elements have a static field called `MouseLeftButtonUpEvent`, among others.

→ Checking if the second parameter of corresponding event handlers derives from `RoutedEventArgs`.

→ Reading the documentation (but that's no fun).

You cannot define your own routed events.

Routed Event Handlers

Handlers for routed events have a signature matching the pattern for general .NET event handlers: The first parameter is an object typically named `sender`, and the second parameter (typically named e) is a class that derives from `EventArgs`. For a routed event handler, the sender is always the element to which the handler was attached. The e parameter is (or derives from) `RoutedEventArgs`, a subclass of `EventArgs` with an `OriginalSource` property that exposes the element that originally raised the event.

Handlers typically want to interact with the original source rather than the sender. Because `CalculatorButton_MouseLeftButtonUp` is attached to `AmountPanel` in Listing 10.2, it uses `OriginalSource` to get to the relevant button:

```
// A single handler for all calculator button taps
void CalculatorButton_MouseLeftButtonUp(object sender, MouseButtonEventArgs e)
{
  // Although sender is the canvas, the OriginalSource is the tapped button
  Button button = e.OriginalSource as Button;
  …
}
```

The Finished Product

When the tip is rounded, the tip button contains a "(rounded)" suffix.

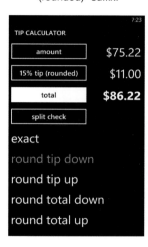

When the total is rounded, the total button contains a "(rounded)" suffix.

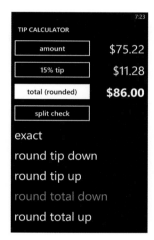

When the amount is split among multiple people, the split button indicates how many people.

chapter 11

XAML EDITOR

XAML Editor is a text editor for XAML, much like the famous XAMLPad program for the Windows desktop. At first, XAML Editor looks like nothing more than a page with a text box, but it is much more for a number of reasons:

→ It renders the XAML you type as live objects (including any interactivity).

→ It provides XAML-specific auto-completion via a custom text suggestions bar (somewhat like Intellisense).

→ It has a menu of samples, to aid in experimentation.

→ It enables you to email your XAML, in case you come up with something you want to save.

→ It shows error information for invalid XAML in an unobtrusive way.

The custom text suggestions bar is vital for making this app usable, as without it common XAML characters like angle brackets, the forward slash, quotes, and curly braces are buried in inconvenient locations. With this bar, users don't normally need to leave the first page of keyboard keys unless they are typing numbers.

On the surface, the main lesson for this chapter seems like the mechanism for reading XAML at run-time and producing a dynamic user interface. However, this is accomplished with just one line of code. The main challenge to implementing XAML Editor is providing a custom text suggestions bar. The real text suggestions bar does not support customization, so XAML Editor provides one with a lot of trickery involving an element known as Popup.

The trickery (or, to be honest, *hacks*) done by this chapter also forms a cautionary tale. In the initial version of Windows Phone 7 (version 7.0.7004.0), the fake suggestions bar was a reasonable replacement for the built-in one, as shown in Figure 11.1. With the addition of the copy/paste feature (starting with version 7.0.7338.0), however, it can no longer act this way. The app had relied on suppressing the real bar by using the default input scope on the text box, but app authors can no longer reliably do this because the bar still appears whenever something can be pasted. Furthermore, there is no way for the fake bar to integrate with the clipboard and provide its own paste button. Therefore, the latest version of XAML Editor treats the fake suggestions bar as a *second* bar on top of the primary one, as pictured on the first page of this chapter.

FIGURE 11.1   Because the Windows Phone copy/paste feature did not yet exist, the first version of XAML Editor could reliably place the fake suggestions bar where the real one would be.

Popup

A *popup* is an element that floats on top of other elements. It was designed for temporary pieces of UI, such as tooltips. However, as in this chapter, is often used in hacky ways to produce behavior that is difficult to accomplish otherwise.

A popup doesn't have any visual appearance by itself, but it can contain a visual element as its single child (and that child could be a complex element containing other elements). By default, a popup docks to the top-left corner of its parent, although you can move it by giving it a margin and/or setting its HorizontalOffset and VerticalOffset properties.

On Top of (Almost) Everything

Figure 11.2 demonstrates the behavior of the popup in the following page:

```
<phone:PhoneApplicationPage
    x:Class="WindowsPhoneApp.MainPage"
    xmlns="http://schemas.microsoft.com/winfx/2006/xaml/presentation"
    xmlns:x="http://schemas.microsoft.com/winfx/2006/xaml"
```

```
    xmlns:phone="clr-namespace:Microsoft.Phone.Controls;assembly=Microsoft.Phone"
    SupportedOrientations="PortraitOrLandscape" Orientation="Landscape">
  <Grid>
    <!-- Inner grid with a button-in-popup and a separate button -->
    <Grid Background="Red" Margin="100">
      <Popup IsOpen="True">
        <Button Content="button in popup in grid" Background="Blue"/>
      </Popup>
      <Button Content="button in grid" Canvas.ZIndex="100"/>
    </Grid>
    <!-- A rectangle that overlaps the inner grid underneath it -->
    <Rectangle Width="200" Height="200" Fill="Lime"
               HorizontalAlignment="Left" VerticalAlignment="Top"/>
  </Grid>
</phone:PhoneApplicationPage>
```

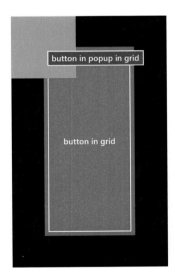

Portrait

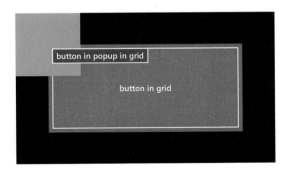

Landscape

FIGURE 11.2   The popup's content doesn't stretch, stays in the top-left corner of its parent, and stays on top of all other elements.

There are three interesting things to note about Figure 11.2:

→ A popup is only visible when its IsOpen property is set to true.

→ The layout inside a popup is like the layout inside a canvas; a child element is only given the exact amount of space it needs.

→ Popups have a unique power: They can render on top of all other Silverlight elements! Although the sibling button in Figure 11.2 has a larger z-index, and although the lime rectangle is a sibling to the popup's *parent* (making it the popup's uncle?), it appears on top of both of them!

 Although a popup's placement is based on its parent element, it is rendered on top of all other elements, regardless of their place in the element tree. Only three things can render on top of a popup:

→ Another popup

→ Shell-provided UI: the application bar, status bar, keyboard, and message boxes

→ UI from outside your app (the same things that cause the Obscured event to be raised): toast notifications, the incoming call screen, and so on

Multiple popups are rendered based solely on where they are placed in tree (with later ones on top of earlier ones); marking them with Canvas.ZIndex has no effect.

Exempt from Orientation Changes

Besides their topmost rendering, popups have another claim to fame: they are able to ignore orientation changes! This happens when you create and show a popup without attaching it to any parent element. In this case, it is implicitly attached to the root frame, which always acts as if it is in the portrait orientation.

The following empty page demonstrates this behavior:

```
<phone:PhoneApplicationPage x:Class="WindowsPhoneApp.MainPage"
    xmlns="http://schemas.microsoft.com/winfx/2006/xaml/presentation"
    xmlns:x="http://schemas.microsoft.com/winfx/2006/xaml"
    xmlns:phone="clr-namespace:Microsoft.Phone.Controls;assembly=Microsoft.Phone"
    SupportedOrientations="PortraitOrLandscape" Orientation="Landscape">
  <Grid x:Name="Grid"/>
</phone:PhoneApplicationPage>
```

In this page's code-behind, two popups are created in the constructor. The first one is attached to the grid, but the second one is implicitly attached to the frame:

```
public MainPage()
{
  InitializeComponent();
  Popup popup1 = new Popup();
  popup1.Child = new Button { Content = "button in popup in grid", FontSize=40 };
  popup1.IsOpen = true;
  this.Grid.Children.Add(popup1); // Attach this to the grid

  Popup popup2 = new Popup();
  popup2.Child = new Button { Content = "button in popup", FontSize=55,
    Foreground = new SolidColorBrush(Colors.Cyan),
    BorderBrush = new SolidColorBrush(Colors.Cyan) };
  popup2.IsOpen = true; // Show without explicitly attaching it to anything
}
```

This page is shown in Figure 11.3. The cyan button (inside popup2) behaves like the whole screen would behave if it were marked as `SupportedOrientations="Portrait"`, whereas the white button (inside popup1) adjusts to remain on the edges of the screen currently acting as the top and the left.

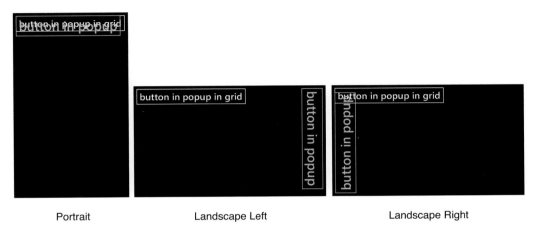

| Portrait | Landscape Left | Landscape Right |

FIGURE 11.3   The popup that isn't attached to the grid stays docked to the physical top and left of the phone for any orientation.

Frame-rooted popups also do not move with the rest of the page when the on-screen keyboard automatically pushes the page upward to keep the focused textbox visible. XAML Editor leverages this fact, as the popup containing the text suggestions bar must always be in the exact same spot regardless of what has happened to the page.

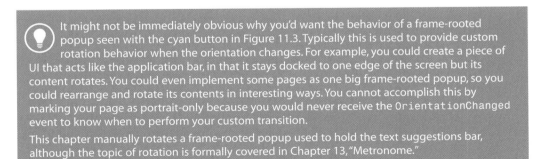

It might not be immediately obvious why you'd want the behavior of a frame-rooted popup seen with the cyan button in Figure 11.3. Typically this is used to provide custom rotation behavior when the orientation changes. For example, you could create a piece of UI that acts like the application bar, in that it stays docked to one edge of the screen but its content rotates. You could even implement some pages as one big frame-rooted popup, so you could rearrange and rotate its contents in interesting ways. You cannot accomplish this by marking your page as portrait-only because you would never receive the `OrientationChanged` event to know when to perform your custom transition.

This chapter manually rotates a frame-rooted popup used to hold the text suggestions bar, although the topic of rotation is formally covered in Chapter 13, "Metronome."

The User Interface

Listing 11.1 contains the XAML for this app's only page, shown at the beginning of this chapter. The page contains a text box on top of a grid used to hold the rendered result from parsing the XAML, and an application bar with four buttons and four menu items.

LISTING 11.1   `MainPage.xaml`—The User Interface for XAML Editor

```xml
<phone:PhoneApplicationPage
    x:Class="WindowsPhoneApp.MainPage"
    xmlns="http://schemas.microsoft.com/winfx/2006/xaml/presentation"
    xmlns:x="http://schemas.microsoft.com/winfx/2006/xaml"
    xmlns:phone="clr-namespace:Microsoft.Phone.Controls;assembly=Microsoft.Phone"
    xmlns:shell="clr-namespace:Microsoft.Phone.Shell;assembly=Microsoft.Phone"
    Loaded="MainPage_Loaded"
    SupportedOrientations="PortraitOrLandscape">

  <!-- Application bar with 3-4 buttons and 4 menu items -->
  <phone:PhoneApplicationPage.ApplicationBar>
    <shell:ApplicationBar>
      <shell:ApplicationBarIconButton Text="view" Click="SwitchViewButton_Click"
                                      IconUri="/Shared/Images/appbar.view.png"/>
      <shell:ApplicationBarIconButton Text="clear" Click="ClearButton_Click"
                                      IconUri="/Shared/Images/appbar.cancel.png"/>
      <shell:ApplicationBarIconButton Text="email" Click="EmailButton_Click"
                                      IconUri="/Shared/Images/appbar.email.png"/>
      <shell:ApplicationBarIconButton Text="error" Click="ErrorButton_Click"
                                      IconUri="/Shared/Images/appbar.error.png"/>
      <shell:ApplicationBar.MenuItems>
        <shell:ApplicationBarMenuItem Text="simple shapes"
                                      Click="SampleMenuItem_Click"/>
        <shell:ApplicationBarMenuItem Text="gradient text"
                                      Click="SampleMenuItem_Click"/>
        <shell:ApplicationBarMenuItem Text="clipped image"
                                      Click="SampleMenuItem_Click"/>
        <shell:ApplicationBarMenuItem Text="controls"
                                      Click="SampleMenuItem_Click"/>
      </shell:ApplicationBar.MenuItems>
    </shell:ApplicationBar>
  </phone:PhoneApplicationPage.ApplicationBar>

  <!-- 1x1 grid containing 2 overlapping child grids -->
  <Grid>
    <!-- where the live XAML goes -->
    <Grid x:Name="ViewPanel"/>

    <!-- The text editor-->
    <Grid x:Name="EditorPanel" Background="{StaticResource PhoneBackgroundBrush}"
          Opacity=".9">
      <ScrollViewer x:Name="ScrollViewer">
        <TextBox x:Name="XamlTextBox" AcceptsReturn="True" VerticalAlignment="Top"
                 Height="2048" TextWrapping="Wrap" InputScope="Text"
```

LISTING 11.1 Continued

```
                    FontFamily="Courier New" FontSize="19" FontWeight="Bold"
                    SelectionChanged="XamlTextBox_SelectionChanged"
                    GotFocus="XamlTextBox_GotFocus" LostFocus="XamlTextBox_LostFocus"
                    TextChanged="XamlTextBox_TextChanged"/>
      </ScrollViewer>
    </Grid>
  </Grid>

</phone:PhoneApplicationPage>
```

Notes:

→ This page supports all orientations for the sake of text entry.

→ Courier New, the phone's only built-in fixed-width font, is used to give the text box a code-editor feel.

→ If the text box were to use the default input scope, then the text suggestions bar may or may not appear based on whether there's something to paste. This would make it impossible to properly place this app's fake suggestions bar directly above the on-screen keyboard because there's no way for an app to detect whether there's currently something on the clipboard. Therefore, the text box is marked with the Text input scope. With the real text suggestions bar always present, the fake one can be reliably placed on top of it. Plus, its standard text suggestions might occasionally be useful while editing XAML.

→ Although the text box supports internal scrolling of its content when the user holds down a finger and drags the caret, it is pretty challenging for users to do this in a satisfactory way. To combat this, the text box is given its maximum supported height and placed in a scroll viewer that enables much more user-friendly scrolling. (It is also marked with word wrapping to avoid the need for horizontal scrolling.) The explicit height is used rather than letting the text box grow on its own because the implementation of the fake suggestions bar requires that part of the text box is always underneath it, and this overlapping would obscure the bottom few lines of text if the text box weren't longer than its text.

Unfortunately, this causes the loss of an important text box feature—the ability to keep the caret visible on the screen while the user is typing. If you knew the current vertical position of the caret, you could scroll the scroll viewer with its ScrollToVerticalOffset method whenever the text changes. Unfortunately, the only caret position exposed by a text box is the character index in the string, and it takes a significant amount of work to calculate coordinates from this. Chapter 25, "Book Reader," demonstrates how this can be done.

Therefore, XAML Editor forces the user to manually scroll the page if the caret goes off-screen or gets hidden under the keyboard.

> ⓘ **Elements have a size limitation!**
>   You should avoid making any Silverlight element larger than 2,048 pixels in any dimension, due to system limitations. Otherwise, a variety of behaviors can be seen, such as forced clipping or even the entire screen going blank! The best workaround for a text box would be to virtualize its contents, e.g. only make it contain the on-screen contents (and perhaps a little more) at any single time. Implementing such a scheme while making sure scrolling and typing works as expected can be complex. XAML Editor simply hopes that users don't type more than approximately 93 lines of XAML!

The Code-Behind

Listing 11.2 contains the code-behind for the main page.

LISTING 11.2   `MainPage.xaml.cs`—The Code-Behind for XAML Editor

```
using System;
using System.Collections.Generic;
using System.ComponentModel;
using System.Windows;
using System.Windows.Controls;
using System.Windows.Controls.Primitives;
using System.Windows.Input;
using System.Windows.Media;
using System.Windows.Navigation;
using System.Windows.Threading;
using Microsoft.Phone.Controls;
using Microsoft.Phone.Shell;
using Microsoft.Phone.Tasks;

namespace WindowsPhoneApp
{
  public partial class MainPage : PhoneApplicationPage
  {
    // Always remember the text box's text, caret position and selection
    Setting<string> savedXaml = new Setting<string>("XAML", Data.SimpleShapes);
    Setting<int> savedSelectionStart = new Setting<int>("SelectionStart", 0);
    Setting<int> savedSelectionLength = new Setting<int>("SelectionLength", 0);

    // The popup and its content are not attached to the page
    internal Popup Popup;
    internal TextSuggestionsBar TextSuggestionsBar;

    // Named fields for two application bar buttons
    IApplicationBarIconButton viewButton;
    IApplicationBarIconButton errorButton;
```

LISTING 11.2 Continued

```csharp
// Remember the current XAML parsing error in case the user wants to see it
string currentError;

// A timer for delaying the update of the view after keystrokes
DispatcherTimer timer =
  new DispatcherTimer { Interval = TimeSpan.FromSeconds(1) };

public MainPage()
{
  InitializeComponent();

  // Assign the application bar buttons because they can't be named in XAML
  this.viewButton = this.ApplicationBar.Buttons[0]
    as IApplicationBarIconButton;
  this.errorButton = this.ApplicationBar.Buttons[3]
    as IApplicationBarIconButton;

  // Initialize the popup and its content
  this.TextSuggestionsBar = new TextSuggestionsBar(this.XamlTextBox);
  this.Popup = new Popup();
  this.Popup.Child = this.TextSuggestionsBar;

  // PopupHelper does the dirty work of positioning & rotating the popup
  PopupHelper.Initialize(this);

  // When the timer ticks, refresh the view then stop it, so there's
  // only one refresh per timer.Start()
  this.timer.Tick += delegate(object sender, EventArgs e)
  {
    RefreshView();
    this.timer.Stop();
  };
}

protected override void OnNavigatedFrom(NavigationEventArgs e)
{
  base.OnNavigatedFrom(e);
  // Remember the text box's text, caret position and selection
  this.savedXaml.Value = this.XamlTextBox.Text;
  this.savedSelectionStart.Value = this.XamlTextBox.SelectionStart;
  this.savedSelectionLength.Value = this.XamlTextBox.SelectionLength;
}

protected override void OnNavigatedTo(NavigationEventArgs e)
```

LISTING 11.2   Continued

```csharp
  {
    base.OnNavigatedTo(e);
    // Restore the text box's text, caret position and selection
    this.XamlTextBox.Text = this.savedXaml.Value;
    this.XamlTextBox.SelectionStart = this.savedSelectionStart.Value;
    this.XamlTextBox.SelectionLength = this.savedSelectionLength.Value;
  }

  void MainPage_Loaded(object sender, RoutedEventArgs e)
  {
    // Make on-screen keyboard instantly appear
    this.XamlTextBox.Focus();
  }

  protected override void OnMouseLeftButtonDown(MouseButtonEventArgs e)
  {
    base.OnMouseLeftButtonDown(e);
    // Send mouse info to the text suggestions bar, if appropriate
    if (PopupHelper.IsOnPopup(e))
      this.TextSuggestionsBar.OnMouseDown(PopupHelper.GetPopupRelativePoint(e));
  }

  protected override void OnMouseMove(MouseEventArgs e)
  {
    base.OnMouseMove(e);
    // Send mouse info to the text suggestions bar, if appropriate
    if (PopupHelper.IsOnPopup(e))
      this.TextSuggestionsBar.OnMouseMove(PopupHelper.GetPopupRelativePoint(e));
  }

  protected override void OnMouseLeftButtonUp(MouseButtonEventArgs e)
  {
    base.OnMouseLeftButtonUp(e);
    // Send mouse info to the text suggestions bar, in case its appropriate
    this.TextSuggestionsBar.OnMouseUp(PopupHelper.IsOnPopup(e));
  }

  void XamlTextBox_GotFocus(object sender, RoutedEventArgs e)
  {
    // Show the popup whenever the text box has focus (and is visible)
    if (this.EditorPanel.Visibility == Visibility.Visible)
      this.Popup.IsOpen = true;
  }
```

LISTING 11.2   Continued

```csharp
void XamlTextBox_LostFocus(object sender, RoutedEventArgs e)
{
  // Hide the popup whenever the text box loses focus
  this.Popup.IsOpen = false;
}

void XamlTextBox_SelectionChanged(object sender, RoutedEventArgs e)
{
  // Update the suggestions based on the text behind the caret location
  string text = this.XamlTextBox.Text;
  int position = this.XamlTextBox.SelectionStart - 1;

  // Initiate the suggestion-picking algorithm on a background thread
  BackgroundWorker backgroundWorker = new BackgroundWorker();

  backgroundWorker.DoWork += delegate(object s, DoWorkEventArgs args)
  {
    // This runs on a background thread
    args.Result = UpdateTextSuggestions(text, position);
  };

  backgroundWorker.RunWorkerCompleted +=
    delegate(object s, RunWorkerCompletedEventArgs args)
  {
    // This runs on the UI thread after BackgroundWorker_DoWork is done

    // Grab the list created on the background thread
    IList<Suggestion> suggestions = args.Result as IList<Suggestion>;
    if (suggestions == null)
      return;

    // Clear the current list
    this.TextSuggestionsBar.ClearSuggestions();

    // Fill the bar with the new list
    foreach (Suggestion suggestion in suggestions)
      this.TextSuggestionsBar.AddSuggestion(suggestion);
  };

  backgroundWorker.RunWorkerAsync();
}

void XamlTextBox_TextChanged(object sender, TextChangedEventArgs e)
{
```

LISTING 11.2   Continued

```csharp
      // Remember the current caret position and selection
      int start = this.XamlTextBox.SelectionStart;
      int length = this.XamlTextBox.SelectionLength;

      // Ensure the text always ends with several newlines so the user
      // can easily scroll to see the very bottom of the text
      if (!this.XamlTextBox.Text.EndsWith(Constants.NEWLINES))
        this.XamlTextBox.Text = this.XamlTextBox.Text.TrimEnd()
                                  + Constants.NEWLINES;

      // Restore the caret position and selection, which gets
      // overwritten if the text is updated
      this.XamlTextBox.SelectionStart = start;
      this.XamlTextBox.SelectionLength = length;

      // Cancel any pending refresh
      if (this.timer.IsEnabled)
        this.timer.Stop();

      // Schedule a refresh of the view for one second from now
      this.timer.Start();
    }

  void RefreshView()
  {
    try
    {
      // Wrap the user's text in a page with appropriate namespace definitions
      string xaml = @"<phone:PhoneApplicationPage
xmlns=""http://schemas.microsoft.com/winfx/2006/xaml/presentation""
xmlns:x=""http://schemas.microsoft.com/winfx/2006/xaml""
xmlns:phone=""clr-namespace:Microsoft.Phone.Controls;assembly=Microsoft.Phone""
FontFamily=""{StaticResource PhoneFontFamilyNormal}""
FontSize=""{StaticResource PhoneFontSizeNormal}""
Foreground=""{StaticResource PhoneForegroundBrush}"">"
        + this.XamlTextBox.Text
        + "</phone:PhoneApplicationPage>";

      // Parse the XAML and get the root element (the page)
      UIElement root = System.Windows.Markup.XamlReader.Load(xaml) as UIElement;

      // Replace ViewPanel's content with the new elements
      this.ViewPanel.Children.Clear();
      this.ViewPanel.Children.Add(root);
```

LISTING 11.2   Continued

```
      // An exception wasn't thrown, so clear any error state
      this.XamlTextBox.Foreground = new SolidColorBrush(Colors.Black);
      this.ApplicationBar.Buttons.Remove(this.errorButton);
    }
    catch (Exception ex)
    {
      // The XAML was invalid, so transition to an error state
      this.XamlTextBox.Foreground = new SolidColorBrush(Colors.Red);
      if (!this.ApplicationBar.Buttons.Contains(this.errorButton))
        this.ApplicationBar.Buttons.Add(this.errorButton);

      // Use the exception message as the error message, but remove the line #
      this.currentError = ex.Message;
      if (this.currentError.Contains(" [Line:"))
        this.currentError = this.currentError.Substring(0,
          this.currentError.IndexOf(" [Line:"));
    }
  }


  IList<Suggestion> UpdateTextSuggestions(string text, int position)
  {
    // The list of suggestions to report
    List<Suggestion> suggestions = new List<Suggestion>();

    if (position == -1)
    {
      // We're at the beginning of the text box
      suggestions.Add(new Suggestion { Text = "<", InsertionOffset = 0 });
      return suggestions;
    }

    char character = text[position];

    if (Char.IsDigit(character))
    {
      // A number is likely a value to be followed by an end quote, or it could
      // be a property like X1 or X2 to be followed by an equals sign
      suggestions.Add(new Suggestion { Text = "\"", InsertionOffset = 0 });
      suggestions.Add(new Suggestion { Text = "=", InsertionOffset = 0 });
    }
    else if (!Char.IsLetter(character))
    {
      // Choose various likely completions based on the special character
      switch (character)
```

LISTING 11.2   Continued

```
      {
        case '<':
          suggestions.Add(new Suggestion { Text = "/", InsertionOffset = 0 });
          break;
        case '/':
          suggestions.Add(new Suggestion { Text = ">", InsertionOffset = 0 });
          suggestions.Add(new Suggestion { Text = "\"", InsertionOffset = 0 });
          break;
        case ' ':
        case '\r':
        case '\n':
          suggestions.Add(new Suggestion { Text = "<", InsertionOffset = 0 });
          suggestions.Add(new Suggestion { Text = "/", InsertionOffset = 0 });
          suggestions.Add(new Suggestion { Text = ">", InsertionOffset = 0 });
          break;
        case '>':
          suggestions.Add(new Suggestion { Text = "<", InsertionOffset = 0 });
          break;
        case '=':
        case '}':
          suggestions.Add(new Suggestion { Text = "\"", InsertionOffset = 0 });
          break;
        case '{':
          suggestions.Add(
            new Suggestion { Text = "Binding ", InsertionOffset = 0 });
          suggestions.Add(
            new Suggestion { Text = "StaticResource ", InsertionOffset = 0 });
          break;
        case '"':
          suggestions.Add(new Suggestion { Text = "/", InsertionOffset = 0 });
          suggestions.Add(new Suggestion { Text = ">", InsertionOffset = 0 });
          suggestions.Add(new Suggestion { Text = "{", InsertionOffset = 0 });
          break;
      }
    }
    else
    {
      // This is a letter

      // First add a few special symbols
      suggestions.Add(new Suggestion { Text = "/", InsertionOffset = 0 });
      suggestions.Add(new Suggestion { Text = ">", InsertionOffset = 0 });
      suggestions.Add(new Suggestion { Text = "=", InsertionOffset = 0 });
      suggestions.Add(new Suggestion { Text = "\"", InsertionOffset = 0 });
```

LISTING 11.2   Continued

```
      suggestions.Add(new Suggestion { Text = "}", InsertionOffset = 0 });

      // Keep traversing backwards until we hit a non-letter
      string letters = null;
      while (position >= 0 && (letters == null ||
                              Char.IsLetter(text[position])))
        letters = text[position--] + letters;

      // Add words from our custom dictionary that match the current text as
      // as prefix
      for (int i = 0; i < Data.Words.Length; i++)
      {
        // Only include exact matches if the case is different
        // (so the user can tap the suggestion to fix their casing)
        if (Data.Words[i].StartsWith(letters,
              StringComparison.InvariantCultureIgnoreCase) &&
           !Data.Words[i].Equals(letters, StringComparison.InvariantCulture))
        {
          suggestions.Add(new Suggestion { Text = Data.Words[i],
                                    InsertionOffset = -letters.Length });
        }
      }
    }

    return suggestions;
  }

  // Application bar handlers

  void ViewButton_Click(object sender, EventArgs e)
  {
    // Switch between viewing the results and viewing the XAML text box
    if (this.EditorPanel.Visibility == Visibility.Visible)
    {
      this.EditorPanel.Visibility = Visibility.Collapsed;
      this.viewButton.IconUri = new Uri("/Images/appbar.xaml.png",
        UriKind.Relative);
      this.viewButton.Text = "xaml";
    }
    else
    {
      this.EditorPanel.Visibility = Visibility.Visible;
      this.viewButton.IconUri = new Uri("/Shared/Images/appbar.view.png",
        UriKind.Relative);
```

LISTING 11.2   Continued

```csharp
      this.viewButton.Text = "view";
      this.XamlTextBox.Focus();
    }
  }

  void ClearButton_Click(object sender, EventArgs e)
  {
    // Clear the text box if the user agrees
    if (MessageBox.Show("Are you sure you want to clear this XAML?",
      "Clear XAML", MessageBoxButton.OKCancel) == MessageBoxResult.OK)
      this.XamlTextBox.Text = "";
  }

  void EmailButton_Click(object sender, EventArgs e)
  {
    // Launch an email with the content of the text box
    EmailComposeTask emailLauncher = new EmailComposeTask {
      Body = this.XamlTextBox.Text, Subject = "XAML from the XAML Editor app" };
    emailLauncher.Show();
  }

  void ErrorButton_Click(object sender, EventArgs e)
  {
    // Show whatever the current error is
    MessageBox.Show(this.currentError, "XAML Error", MessageBoxButton.OK);
  }

  void SampleMenuItem_Click(object sender, EventArgs e)
  {
    if (this.XamlTextBox.Text.Trim().Length != 0 &&
      MessageBox.Show("Are you sure you want to replace the XAML?",
      "Replace XAML", MessageBoxButton.OKCancel) != MessageBoxResult.OK)
      return;

    // Fill the text box with the chosen sample
    switch ((sender as IApplicationBarMenuItem).Text)
    {
      case "simple shapes":
        this.XamlTextBox.Text = Data.SimpleShapes;
        break;
      case "gradient text":
        this.XamlTextBox.Text = Data.GradientText;
        break;
      case "clipped image":
```

LISTING 11.2   Continued

```
        this.XamlTextBox.Text = Data.ClippedImage;
        break;
      case "controls":
        this.XamlTextBox.Text = Data.Controls;
        break;
    }
  }
 }
}
}
```

Notes:

→ The popup's child is set to an instance of a TextSuggestionsBar user control, implemented in the next section, which handles the display and interaction of the bar.

→ A fair amount of code is needed to properly position the popup and report where it is being touched, so this is factored into a separate PopupHelper class examined next.

→ In MainPage_Loaded, the on-screen keyboard is automatically deployed (unless a hardware keyboard is active) because there's no other UI to obscure.

→ Inside the three OnMouse... handlers, the data is being passed along to the text suggestions bar. This highlights the main challenge of implementing this bar—it must never get focus because the on-screen keyboard would go away if the text box loses focus! Therefore, the root of the TextSuggestionsBar user control is marked with IsHitTestVisible="False", and the control exposes its own trio of OnMouse... methods, so it can act like it's being touched when it's really the text box underneath that is receiving these events.

→ The performance of updating the text suggestions bar is important because it happens on every keystroke (or other movement of the caret). Inside XamlTextBox_SelectionChanged, a *background worker* is used to execute the time-consuming work—UpdateTextSuggestions. This only works because UpdateTextSuggestions doesn't interact with any UI or do anything else that requires being run on the UI thread.

With a background worker, you can attach a delegate to its DoWork event, which gets raised on a background thread once RunWorkerAsync is called (done at

For maximum responsiveness in your app, try to offload work to a background worker so the UI thread can spend its time on tasks such as creating/rendering UI elements and processing input. This is normally easier said than done, because many tasks such as interacting with UI elements *must* be done on the UI thread. For code that is algorithmic in nature, however, this is often doable. In addition to this chapter, background workers are used in Chapter 24, "Baby Name Eliminator," to interact with a local database, and in Chapter 25 to perform calculations on a large string.

the end of XamlTextBox_
SelectionChanged). When the
background work has completed,
the RunWorkerCompleted event is
raised on the original (UI) thread.
This enables user interface updates
to occur based on whatever work
was done in the background.
(Alternatively, the background-
thread code could call BeginInvoke
on the page's dispatcher to schedule work on the UI thread.) The
DoWork handler can pass data to
the RunWorkerCompleted handler
via a Result property on the
event-args parameter.

> → XamlTextBox_TextChanged uses
> another technique to improve this
> app's performance. Rather than
> instantly re-render the XAML
> every time it changes, it uses a
> timer to wait one second. That way, it can cancel a pending update if another
> change occurs within that second. This technique, as well as the use of a back-
> ground worker for filling the text suggestions bar, vastly improves the performance
> when the user holds down a repeatable key (the space bar, backspace, or Enter).

> → RefreshView contains the single line of code needed to turn XAML into a tree of
> live objects. The static XamlReader.Load method accepts a XAML string as input and
> returns an object corresponding to the root element in the string. If there's anything
> wrong with the XAML, it throws a XamlParseException. RefreshView captures any
> exception and shows the message to the user if they tap the error button that
> appears on the application bar. This code strips out any line and position informa-
> tion from the message because (a) the surrounding page element throws off the line
> number and (b) it's often not accurate anyway.

Background workers have infrastructure to support cancellation and progress reporting.

You can opt-in to cancellation by setting WorkerSupportsCancellation to true. DoWork handlers must then periodically check the value of CancellationPending (set to true when someone calls CancelAsync on the worker) and return early in order for the cancellation to actually work.

You can opt-in to progress reporting by setting WorkerReportsProgress to true. DoWork handlers can periodically call ReportProgress, resulting in a ProgressChanged event being raised by the worker.

Background workers also support passing data to DoWork handlers via an overload of RunWorkerAsync, but when handlers are anonymous methods, as in Listing 11.2, this is not needed thanks to their ability to capture local variables.

The XAML string must be self-
contained, so its elements cannot
have event handlers assigned, nor
can it have unresolved XML namespace prefixes. RefreshView wraps
the user's XAML in a page element
with the main namespaces so the
user's XAML doesn't need to be
cluttered with this. (This could have been a grid, and the result would look the
same.) Therefore, this code ends up attaching an instance of a page as a child of the
ViewPanel grid. It's weird for a page to contain another page, but it works just fine.

XamlReader.Load can be used to create dynamic user interfaces. Unfortunately, while it enables you to construct a live user interface from a string, there is no corresponding XAML writer that serializes a live user interface into a XAML string.

→ `UpdateTextSuggestions` contains the simple algorithm for providing suggestions based on the text preceding the current caret location. It treats numbers, letters, and symbols differently. Perhaps the most clever thing it does is suggest `"Binding "` and `"StaticResource "` (with the trailing space included) immediately after a {. It makes use of a simple structure defined in `Suggestion.cs` as follows:

```
namespace WindowsPhoneApp
{
  public struct Suggestion
  {
    public string Text { get; set; }
    public int InsertionOffset { get; set; }
  }
}
```

The insertion offset captures how much of the suggestion has already been typed before the caret.

→ The custom dictionary of XAML-relevant words (over 300) is a static string array called `Words` in a static `Data` class. It contains common element names, property names, and some common property values. The XAML samples accessed via the application bar menu are stored as static fields on the same class. The `Data` class is not shown in this chapter, but as with all the apps, you can download the complete source code.

PopupHelper

Listing 11.3 contains the implementation of the `PopupHelper` class used by Listing 11.2. It is directly tied to the main page rather than being any sort of reusable control.

LISTING 11.3   `PopupHelper.cs`—A Class That Manipulates the Popup Containing the Text Suggestions Bar

```
using System;
using System.Windows;
using System.Windows.Input;
using System.Windows.Media;
using Microsoft.Phone.Controls;

namespace WindowsPhoneApp
{
  internal static class PopupHelper
  {
    static MainPage page;
    static bool textSuggestionsBarSlidDown;

    internal static void Initialize(MainPage p)
    {
      page = p;
```

LISTING 11.3   Continued

```
    page.OrientationChanged += Page_OrientationChanged;
    page.TextSuggestionsBar.DownButtonTap += TextSuggestionsBar_DownButtonTap;
    AdjustForCurrentOrientation();
  }

  // Report whether the mouse event occurred within the popup's bounds
  internal static bool IsOnPopup(MouseEventArgs e)
  {
    if (!page.Popup.IsOpen)
      return false;

    Point popupRelativePoint = GetPopupRelativePoint(e);
    return (popupRelativePoint.Y >= 0 &&
           popupRelativePoint.Y < page.TextSuggestionsBar.ActualHeight);
  }

  // Return the X,Y position of the mouse, relative to the popup
  internal static Point GetPopupRelativePoint(MouseEventArgs e)
  {
    Point popupRelativePoint = new Point();

    // We can use the page-relative X as the popup-relative X
    Point pageRelativePoint = e.GetPosition(page);
    popupRelativePoint.X = pageRelativePoint.X;

    // We can't use the page-relative Y because the page can be automatically
    // "pushed" by the on-screen keyboard, whereas the floating popup remains
    // still. Therefore, first get the frame-relative Y:
    Point frameRelativePoint = e.GetPosition(null /* the frame */);
    popupRelativePoint.Y = frameRelativePoint.Y;

    // A frame-relative point is always portrait-oriented, so invert
    // the value if we're currently in a landscape orientation
    if (IsMatchingOrientation(PageOrientation.Landscape))
      popupRelativePoint.Y = frameRelativePoint.X;

    // Now adjust the Y to be relative to the top of the popup
    // rather than the top of the screen
    if (IsMatchingOrientation(PageOrientation.LandscapeLeft))
      popupRelativePoint.Y = -(popupRelativePoint.Y+page.Popup.VerticalOffset);
    else
      popupRelativePoint.Y -= page.Popup.VerticalOffset;

    return popupRelativePoint;
  }
```

LISTING 11.3   Continued

```
static void Page_OrientationChanged(object sender,
                                    OrientationChangedEventArgs e)
{
  // Clear the slid-down setting on any orientation change
  textSuggestionsBarSlidDown = false;
  AdjustForCurrentOrientation();
}

static void TextSuggestionsBar_DownButtonTap(object sender, EventArgs e)
{
  textSuggestionsBarSlidDown = true;
  AdjustForCurrentOrientation();
}

static bool IsMatchingOrientation(PageOrientation orientation)
{
  return ((page.Orientation & orientation) == orientation);
}

static void AdjustForCurrentOrientation()
{
  page.TextSuggestionsBar.ResetScrollPosition();

  if (IsMatchingOrientation(PageOrientation.Portrait))
  {
    // Adjust the position, size, and rotation for portrait
    page.TextSuggestionsBar.MinWidth = Constants.SCREEN_WIDTH;
    page.Popup.HorizontalOffset = 0;
    page.Popup.VerticalOffset = Constants.SCREEN_HEIGHT -
      Constants.APPLICATION_BAR_THICKNESS - Constants.PORTRAIT_KEYBOARD_HEIGHT
      - Constants.TEXT_SUGGESTIONS_HEIGHT*2; // 1 for the real bar, 1 for this
    page.Popup.RenderTransform = new RotateTransform { Angle = 0 };

    if (textSuggestionsBarSlidDown)
      page.Popup.VerticalOffset += Constants.PORTRAIT_KEYBOARD_HEIGHT;
  }
  else
  {
    // Adjust the position, size, and rotation for landscape
    page.TextSuggestionsBar.MinWidth = Constants.SCREEN_HEIGHT -
                                    Constants.APPLICATION_BAR_THICKNESS;

    if (IsMatchingOrientation(PageOrientation.LandscapeLeft))
    {
      page.Popup.RenderTransform = new RotateTransform { Angle = 90 };
```

LISTING 11.3   Continued

```
            page.Popup.HorizontalOffset = 0;
            page.Popup.VerticalOffset = -(Constants.LANDSCAPE_KEYBOARD_HEIGHT +
                                        Constants.TEXT_SUGGESTIONS_HEIGHT*2);
                                        // 1 for the real bar, 1 for this
        }
        else // LandscapeRight
        {
            page.Popup.RenderTransform = new RotateTransform { Angle = 270 };
            page.Popup.Width = Constants.SCREEN_HEIGHT -
                            Constants.APPLICATION_BAR_THICKNESS;
            page.Popup.HorizontalOffset = -page.Popup.Width;
            page.Popup.VerticalOffset = Constants.SCREEN_WIDTH -
                                        Constants.LANDSCAPE_KEYBOARD_HEIGHT -
                                        Constants.TEXT_SUGGESTIONS_HEIGHT*2;
                                        // 1 for the real bar, 1 for this
        }

        if (textSuggestionsBarSlidDown)
            page.Popup.VerticalOffset += Constants.LANDSCAPE_KEYBOARD_HEIGHT;
      }
    }
  }
}
```

→   Due to the manual rotation being done to the popup to make it always match the page's orientation, `GetPopupRelativePoint` must adjust the page-relative mouse position in a number of ways, depending on the current orientation.

→   This app uses a number of constants. They are defined in `Constants.cs` as follows:

```
public static class Constants
{
  public const int SCREEN_WIDTH = 480;
  public const int SCREEN_HEIGHT = 800;
  public const int APPLICATION_BAR_THICKNESS = 72;
  // Part of it is 259px tall, but this is the # we need:
  public const int LANDSCAPE_KEYBOARD_HEIGHT = 256;
  public const int PORTRAIT_KEYBOARD_HEIGHT = 339;
  public const int TEXT_SUGGESTIONS_HEIGHT = 62;
  public const int MARGIN = 12;
  public const int TAP_MARGIN = 14;
  public const int MIN_SCROLL_AMOUNT = 10;
  public static readonly string NEWLINES = Environment.NewLine +
    Environment.NewLine + Environment.NewLine + Environment.NewLine +
    Environment.NewLine;
}
```

→ This code handles an event on the `TextSuggestionsBar` called `DownButtonTap` and moves the position of the popup to the bottom of the screen when this happens. The next section explains what this is about.

The `TextSuggestionsBar` **User Control**

The `TextSuggestionsBar` user control handles the display of the dot-delimited text suggestions and the proper tapping and scrolling interaction. It also contains a workaround for a problem with hardware keyboards.

Ideally, the popup containing this control would automatically position itself above the on-screen keyboard when it is used, but close to the bottom edge of the screen when a hardware keyboard is used instead. Unfortunately, there is no good way to detect when a hardware keyboard is in use, so this app relies on the user to move it. The `TextSuggestionsBar` has an extra "down" button that is hidden under the on-screen keyboard when it is in use, but revealed when a hardware keyboard is used. The user can tap this button to move the bar to the bottom, just above the real text suggestions bar. Figure 11.4 shows what this looks like. Rather than consuming space with a corresponding "up" button, this app only moves the bar back to its higher position when the phone's orientation changes.

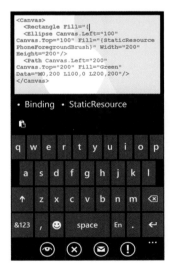

Everything looks great when the on-screen keyboard is used.

When a portrait hardware keyboard is deployed, the bar doesn't move, but a down button is revealed.

Tapping the down button moves the bar to its proper spot.

FIGURE 11.4   The user must manually move the custom text suggestions bar to the appropriate spot when using a hardware keyboard.

Listing 11.4 contains the XAML for this user control, and Listing 11.5 contains the code-behind.

LISTING 11.4   `TextSuggestionsBar.xaml`—The User Interface for the `TextSuggestionsBar` User Control

```xaml
<UserControl x:Class="WindowsPhoneApp.TextSuggestionsBar"
             xmlns="http://schemas.microsoft.com/winfx/2006/xaml/presentation"
             xmlns:x="http://schemas.microsoft.com/winfx/2006/xaml"
             IsHitTestVisible="False">
  <StackPanel>
    <Canvas Background="{StaticResource PhoneChromeBrush}" Height="62">
      <!-- The suggestions go in this stack panel -->
      <StackPanel x:Name="StackPanel" Orientation="Horizontal" Height="62"/>
    </Canvas>
    <!-- The double-arrow "button" (just a border with a path) -->
    <Border Background="{StaticResource PhoneChromeBrush}" Width="62"
            Height="62" HorizontalAlignment="Left">
      <Path Fill="{StaticResource PhoneForegroundBrush}"
            HorizontalAlignment="Center" VerticalAlignment="Center"
            Data="M0,2 14,2 7,11z M0,13 14,13 7,22"/>
    </Border>
  </StackPanel>
</UserControl>
```

LISTING 11.5   `TextSuggestionsBar.xaml.cs`—The Code-Behind for the `TextSuggestionsBar` User Control

```csharp
using System;
using System.Windows;
using System.Windows.Controls;
using System.Windows.Media;

namespace WindowsPhoneApp
{
  public partial class TextSuggestionsBar : UserControl
  {
    // A custom event, raised when the down button is tapped
    public event EventHandler DownButtonTap;

    TextBox textBox;
    double mouseDownX;
    double mouseMoveX;
    Border pressedSuggestionElement;

    int selectionStart;
```

LISTING 11.5   Continued

```
int selectionLength;

public TextSuggestionsBar(TextBox textBox)
{
  InitializeComponent();
  this.textBox = textBox;
}

public void OnMouseDown(Point point)
{
  // Grab the current position/selection before it changes! The text box
  // still has focus, so the tap is likely to change the caret position
  this.selectionStart = this.textBox.SelectionStart;
  this.selectionLength = this.textBox.SelectionLength;

  this.mouseDownX = this.mouseMoveX = point.X;

  this.pressedSuggestionElement = FindSuggestionElementAtPoint(point);
  if (this.pressedSuggestionElement != null)
  {
    // Give the pressed suggestion the hover brushes
    this.pressedSuggestionElement.Background =
      Application.Current.Resources["PhoneForegroundBrush"] as Brush;
    (this.pressedSuggestionElement.Child as TextBlock).Foreground =
      Application.Current.Resources["PhoneBackgroundBrush"] as Brush;
  }
  else if (point.Y > this.StackPanel.Height)
  {
    // Treat this as a tap on the down arrow
    if (this.DownButtonTap != null)
      this.DownButtonTap(this, EventArgs.Empty);
  }
}

public void OnMouseMove(Point point)
{
  double delta = point.X - this.mouseMoveX;
  if (delta == 0)
    return;

  // Adjust the stack panel's left margin to simulate scrolling.
  // Don't let it scroll past either its left or right edge.
  double newLeft = Math.Min(0, Math.Max(this.ActualWidth -
    this.StackPanel.ActualWidth, this.StackPanel.Margin.Left + delta));
```

LISTING 11.5 Continued

```csharp
    this.StackPanel.Margin = new Thickness(newLeft, 0, 0, 0);

    // If a suggestion is currently being pressed but we've now scrolled a
    // certain amount, cancel the tapping action
    if (pressedSuggestionElement != null && Math.Abs(this.mouseMoveX
          - this.mouseDownX) > Constants.MIN_SCROLL_AMOUNT)
    {
      // Undo the hover brushes
      pressedSuggestionElement.Background = null;
      (pressedSuggestionElement.Child as TextBlock).Foreground =
        Application.Current.Resources["PhoneForegroundBrush"] as Brush;

      // Stop tracking the element
      pressedSuggestionElement = null;
    }
    this.mouseMoveX = point.X;
  }

  public void OnMouseUp(bool isInBounds)
  {
    if (this.pressedSuggestionElement != null)
    {
      if (isInBounds)
        InsertText();

      // Undo the hover brushes
      pressedSuggestionElement.Background = null;
      (pressedSuggestionElement.Child as TextBlock).Foreground =
        Application.Current.Resources["PhoneForegroundBrush"] as Brush;

      // Stop tracking the element
      pressedSuggestionElement = null;
    }
  }

  public void ResetScrollPosition()
  {
    this.StackPanel.Margin = new Thickness(0, 0, 0, 0);
  }

  public void ClearSuggestions()
  {
    this.StackPanel.Children.Clear();
    ResetScrollPosition();
```

LISTING 11.5   Continued

```
  }

  // Each suggestion is added to the stack panel as two elements:
  // - A border containing a textblock with a • separator
  // - A border containing the suggested text
  public void AddSuggestion(Suggestion suggestion)
  {
    // Add the • element to the stack panel
    TextBlock textBlock = new TextBlock { Text = "•", FontSize = 16,
      Margin = new Thickness(this.StackPanel.Children.Count == 0 ? 20 : 3, 6, 4,
        0), Foreground = Application.Current.Resources["PhoneForegroundBrush"]
        as Brush, VerticalAlignment = VerticalAlignment.Center };
    Border border = new Border();
    border.Child = textBlock;
    this.StackPanel.Children.Add(border);

    // Add the suggested-text element to the stack panel
    textBlock = new TextBlock { Text = suggestion.Text, FontSize = 28,
      Margin = new Thickness(10, 6, 10, 0),
      HorizontalAlignment = HorizontalAlignment.Center,
      VerticalAlignment = VerticalAlignment.Center,
      Foreground = Application.Current.Resources["PhoneForegroundBrush"]
        as Brush };
    // MinWidth makes single-character suggestions like / easier to tap
    // Stuff the insertion offset into the tag for easy retrieval later
    border = new Border { MinWidth = 28, Tag = suggestion.InsertionOffset };
    border.Child = textBlock;
    this.StackPanel.Children.Add(border);
  }

  void InsertText()
  {
    string newText = (this.pressedSuggestionElement.Child as TextBlock).Text;
    int numCharsToDelete = ((int)this.pressedSuggestionElement.Tag) * -1;
    string allText = this.textBox.Text;

    // Perform the insertion
    allText = allText.Substring(0, this.selectionStart - numCharsToDelete)
      + newText
      + allText.Substring(this.selectionStart + this.selectionLength);
    this.textBox.Text = allText;

    // Place the caret immediately after the inserted text
    this.textBox.SelectionStart = this.selectionStart + newText.Length -
```

LISTING 11.5   Continued

```
        numCharsToDelete;
  }


  // Find the Border element at the current point
  Border FindSuggestionElementAtPoint(Point point)
  {
    Border border = null;

    // Loop through the borders to find the right one (if there is one)
    for (int i = 0; i < this.StackPanel.Children.Count; i++)
    {
      Border b = this.StackPanel.Children[i] as Border;

      // Transform the point to be relative to this border
      GeneralTransform generalTransform = this.StackPanel.TransformToVisual(b);
      Point pt = generalTransform.Transform(point);
      pt.X -= this.StackPanel.Margin.Left; // Adjust for scrolling

      // See if the point is within the border's bounds.
      // The extra right margin ensures that there are no "holes" in the bar
      // where tapping does nothing.
      if (pt.X >= 0 && pt.X < b.ActualWidth + Constants.TAP_MARGIN
          && pt.Y <= this.StackPanel.Height)
      {
        border = b;
        // If this is the • element, treat it as part of the next element
        // (the actual word), so return that one instead
        if ((b.Child as TextBlock).Text == "•")
          border = this.StackPanel.Children[i + 1] as Border;
        break;
      }
    }

    return border;
  }
 }
}
```

Notes:

➔ OnMouseDown takes care of highlighting the tapped suggestion, OnMouseMove performs the scrolling of the bar, and OnMouseUp inserts the highlighted suggestion (if there is one).

→ Inside `FindSuggestionElementAtPoint`, the `TransformToVisual` method introduced in Chapter 8, "Vibration Composer," is used to find the tapped suggestion. Check out Chapter 40, "Darts," for a more efficient approach with a method called `FindElementsInHostCoordinates`.

The Finished Product

Viewing the menu of XAML samples	Viewing the live result underneath the text box	Using the landscape right orientation

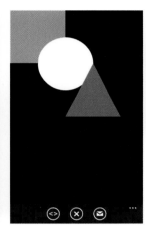

> **?** **Can I write code that interacts with the phone's copy & paste feature?**
>
> No. Copy & paste functionality is automatically supported for any text box, but there is currently no way for a developer to interact with the clipboard, disable the feature, or otherwise influence its behavior.

chapter 12 lessons

SILLY EYE

Silly Eye is a crowd-pleaser, especially when the crowd contains children. This app displays a large cartoonish eye that animates in a funny, frantic way that can't be conveyed on paper. Simply hold it up to your right eye and pretend it's your own silly eye! Figure 12.1 demonstrates how to use this app.

This app introduces some useful new techniques related to creating settings pages and enabling the user to choose custom colors. But most importantly, it's the first app to rely on animation, the main topic for Part II, "Transforms & Animations," of this book.

Introducing Animation

When most people think about animation, they think of a cartoon-like mechanism, where movement is simulated by displaying images in rapid succession. In Silverlight, animation has a more specific definition: varying the value of a property over time. This could be related to motion, such as making an element grow by increasing its width, or it could be something completely different like varying an element's opacity.

There are many ways to change a property's value over time. The classic approach is to use a timer, much like the DispatcherTimer used in previous chapters, and use a method that is periodically called back based on the frequency of the timer (the Tick event handler). Inside this method, you can manually update the target property

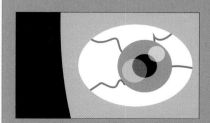

(doing a little math to determine the current value based on the elapsed time) until it reaches the final value. At that point, you can stop the timer and/or remove the event handler.

FIGURE 12.1   Give yourself a silly eye by holding the phone up to your right eye.

However, Silverlight provides an animation mechanism that is much easier to use, more powerful, and performs better than a timer-based approach. It is centered around an object known as a *storyboard*. Storyboards contain one or more special animation objects and apply them to specific properties on specific elements.

Silly Eye uses three storyboards to perform its animations. To understand what story-boards are and how they work, we'll examine each one:

→ The pupil storyboard

→ The iris storyboard

→ The eyelid storyboard

The Pupil Storyboard

Here is the storyboard that Silly Eye applies to the pupil to make it appear to repeatedly grow and shrink:

```
<Storyboard x:Name="PupilStoryboard"
            Storyboard.TargetName="Pupil"
```

```
            Storyboard.TargetProperty="StrokeThickness">
  <DoubleAnimation From="100" To="70" Duration="0:0:.5"
                    AutoReverse="True" RepeatBehavior="Forever">
    <DoubleAnimation.EasingFunction>
      <ElasticEase/>
    </DoubleAnimation.EasingFunction>
  </DoubleAnimation>
</Storyboard>
```

Notes:

→ The `Storyboard.TargetName` attachable property indicates that this animation is being applied to an element on the page named `Pupil`. `Pupil` is an ellipse defined as follows:

```
<Ellipse x:Name="Pupil" Width="238" Height="237" StrokeThickness="100"
         Fill="Black"/>
```

(The brush for its stroke is set in code-behind.)

→ The `Storyboard.TargetProperty` attachable property indicates that `Pupil`'s `StrokeThickness` property is being animated.

→ The `DoubleAnimation` inside the storyboard indicates that `StrokeThickness` will be animated from 100 to 70 over a duration of half a second. The "Double" in `DoubleAnimation` represents the type of the target property being animated. (`StrokeThickness` is a double.)

→ Because `AutoReverse` is set to `true`, `StrokeThickness` will automatically animate back to 100 after reaching the end value of 70. Because `RepeatBehavior` is set to `Forever`, this cycle from 100 to 70 to 100 will repeat indefinitely once the animation has started.

→ The `EasingFunction` property (set to an instance of an `ElasticEase`) controls how the value of `StrokeThickness` is interpolated over time. This is discussed in the upcoming "Interpolation" section.

To begin the animation, the storyboard's `Begin` method is called as follows:

```
this.PupilStoryboard.Begin();
```

The result of this animation is shown in Figure 12.2 in the context of the entire app. The `Pupil` ellipse has been given a light blue stroke via code-behind.

StrokeThickness = 100

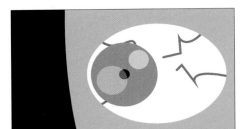

StrokeThickness = 85
(halfway between 100 and 70)

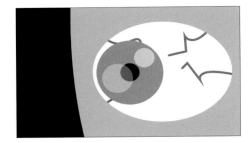

StrokeThickness = 70

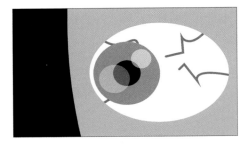

FIGURE 12.2   `PupilStoryboard` makes `Pupil`'s stroke thickness (seen in blue) shrink from 100 down to 70, causing its black fill to appear to grow.

> There is a way to trigger a storyboard entirely in XAML so there's no need for a call to its `Begin` method in code-behind. You can add an *event trigger* to an element's `Triggers` property. This can look as follows:

```
<Grid>
  <Grid.Triggers>
    <EventTrigger RoutedEvent="Grid.Loaded">
      <BeginStoryboard>
        <Storyboard Storyboard.TargetName="Pupil"
                    Storyboard.TargetProperty="StrokeThickness">
          <DoubleAnimation To="70" Duration="0:0:.5" AutoReverse="True"
                           RepeatBehavior="Forever">
            <DoubleAnimation.EasingFunction>
              <ElasticEase/>
            </DoubleAnimation.EasingFunction>
          </DoubleAnimation>
        </Storyboard>
      </BeginStoryboard>
    </EventTrigger>
```

```
    </Grid.Triggers>
    ...
</Grid>
```

Thanks to the special BeginStoryboard element, this internally calls Begin on the storyboard in response to the grid's Loaded event. The Loaded event is the only event supported by event triggers in Silverlight.

Types of Animations

Silverlight provides animation classes to animate four different data types: double, Color, Point, and object. Only double properties are animated in Silly Eye. The rest are demonstrated in Chapter 15, "Mood Ring."

If you want to vary the value of an element's double property over time (such as Width, Height, Opacity, Canvas.Left, and so on), you can use an instance of DoubleAnimation. If you instead want to vary the value of an element's Point property over time (such as a linear gradient brush's StartPoint or EndPoint property), you could use an instance of PointAnimation. DoubleAnimation is by far the most commonly used animation class due to large the number of properties of type double that make sense to animate.

Interpolation

It's important to note that, by default, DoubleAnimation takes care of smoothly changing the double value over time via *linear interpolation*. In other words, for a one-second animation from 50 to 100, the value is 55 when 0.1 seconds have elapsed (10% progress in both the value and time elapsed), 75 when 0.5 seconds have elapsed (50% progress in both the

 You cannot animate *any* property, even if the data type matches the type of animation class used!

Only a special kind of property known as a *dependency property* can be animated with the mechanism discussed in this chapter. Fortunately, most properties on visual elements are dependency properties. Dependency properties are discussed in Chapter 18, "Cocktails."

Similar to determining whether an event is a routed event, you can determine whether a property is a dependency property by looking for a static field named *PropertyName*Property of type DependencyProperty on the class containing the property. If it has such a field, such as ellipse's StrokeThicknessProperty field, then it's a dependency property.

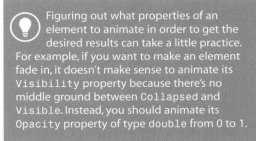 Figuring out what properties of an element to animate in order to get the desired results can take a little practice. For example, if you want to make an element fade in, it doesn't make sense to animate its Visibility property because there's no middle ground between Collapsed and Visible. Instead, you should animate its Opacity property of type double from 0 to 1.

value and time elapsed), and so on. This is why `StrokeThickness` is shown with a value of 85 halfway through the animation in Figure 12.2.

Most animations used in Windows Phone apps are not linear, however. Instead, they tend to "spring" from one value to another with a bit of acceleration or deceleration. This makes the animations more lifelike and interesting. You can produce such nonlinear animations by applying an *easing function*.

An easing function is responsible for doing custom interpolation from the starting value to the ending value. The pupil storyboard uses an easing function called `ElasticEase` to make its behavior much more "silly" than linear. Figure 12.3 graphs how the interpolation from 100 to 70 differs between the default linear behavior and the elastic ease behavior. In this case, the midpoint value of 85 actually isn't reached half-way through the animation, but rather right toward the end.

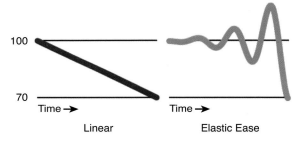

FIGURE 12.3   The `ElasticEase` easing function drastically alters how a `double` value changes from 100 to 70.

Silverlight provides eleven different easing functions, each with three different modes, and several with properties to further customize their behavior. For example, `ElasticEase` has `Oscillations` and `Springiness` properties, both set to 3 by default. Combined with the fact that you can write your own easing functions to plug into animations, the possibilities for custom behaviors are endless. The easing functions used in this app give a wildly different experience than the default linear behavior.

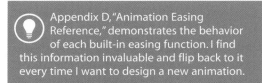

Appendix D, "Animation Easing Reference," demonstrates the behavior of each built-in easing function. I find this information invaluable and flip back to it every time I want to design a new animation.

• • •

Another Way to Produce Nonlinear Animations

Easing functions are not the only way to create a nonlinear animation. *Keyframe animations,* discussed in Chapter 14, "Love Meter," enable you to break up an animation into distinct segments with varied interpolation behavior.

The Iris Storyboard

Silly Eye applies the following storyboard to a canvas called `Iris` to make the eyeball appear to move left and right:

```
<Storyboard x:Name="IrisStoryboard"
            Storyboard.TargetName="Iris"
            Storyboard.TargetProperty="(Canvas.Left)">
  <DoubleAnimation To="543" Duration="0:0:2"
                   AutoReverse="True" RepeatBehavior="Forever">
    <DoubleAnimation.EasingFunction>
      <BounceEase/>
    </DoubleAnimation.EasingFunction>
  </DoubleAnimation>
</Storyboard>
```

Notes:

→ The syntax for `TargetProperty` is sometimes more complex than just a property name. When set to an attachable property such as `Canvas.Left`, it must be surrounded in parentheses.

→ The animation has a different easing function applied that gives the movement a noticeable bounciness. See Appendix D for a graph of `BounceEase` behavior.

> Omitting an explicit `From` setting is important for getting smooth animations, especially when an animation is initiated in response to a repeatable user action. For example, if an animation causes an element to grow whenever it is tapped, rapid tapping would make the size jump back to the explicit `From` value each time. By omitting `From`, however, subsequent taps make the animation continue from its current animated value, keeping the visual smoothness of the effect.

→ The animation is missing a `From` value! This is okay and often recommended. When no `From` is specified, the animation starts with the target property's current value, whatever it may be. Similarly, an animation can specify a `From` but no `To`! This animates the property from the value specified in `From` to whatever its current (pre-animation) value is.

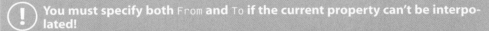

You must specify both `From` **and** `To` **if the current property can't be interpolated!**

If you try to animate the width or height of an auto-sized element with a `From`-less or `To`-less animation, nothing happens. Elements are auto-sized when their width and height are set to `Double.NaN` (not-a-number), and the `DoubleAnimation` can't interpolate between two values when one of them isn't even a number. Furthermore, applying the animation to `ActualWidth` or `ActualHeight` (which is set to the true width/height rather than NaN) isn't an option because these properties are read-only and they are not dependency properties. Instead, you must explicitly set the width/height of the target element for such an animation to work.

As with the pupil storyboard, this storyboard's `Begin` method is called to make it start:

```
this.IrisStoryboard.Begin();
```

The result of this animation is shown in Figure 12.4. The `Iris` canvas contains the `Pupil` ellipse (whose stroke is actually the iris) along with two other ellipses that give the iris its "shine." Because the position of the parent canvas is animated, all these contents move together.

Canvas.Left = 287

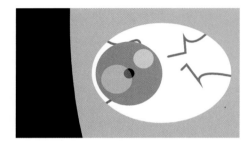

Canvas.Left = 415 (halfway between 287 and 543)

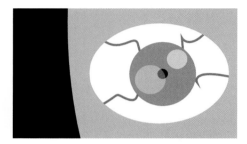

Canvas.Left = 543

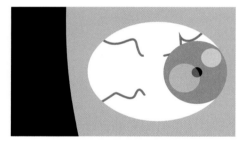

FIGURE 12.4   `IrisStoryboard` moves the `Iris` canvas horizontally from 287 (its initial `Canvas.Left` value) to 543.

 Animations also have a By field that can be set instead of the To field. The following animation means "animate the value by adding 256 to its current value":

```
<DoubleAnimation By="256" Duration="0:0:2"/>
```

Negative values are supported for shrinking the current value.

The Eyelid Animation

The final storyboard used by Silly Eye animates *two* properties on a skin-colored `Eyelid` ellipse to simulate blinking:

```
<Storyboard x:Name="EyelidStoryboard"
            Storyboard.TargetName="Eyelid"
            RepeatBehavior="Forever" Duration="0:0:3">
```

```
<DoubleAnimation Storyboard.TargetProperty="Height"
                 To="380" Duration="0:0:.1" AutoReverse="True"/>
<DoubleAnimation Storyboard.TargetProperty="(Canvas.Top)"
                 To="50" Duration="0:0:.1" AutoReverse="True"/>
</Storyboard>
```

The `Eyelid` ellipse is defined as follows:

```
<Ellipse x:Name="Eyelid" Canvas.Left="73" Canvas.Top="-145"
         Width="897" Height="770" StrokeThickness="200"/>
```

As with the `Pupil` ellipse, the skin-colored brush for its stroke is set in code-behind.

Notes:

→ There's a reason that `Storyboard.TargetName` and `Storyboard.TargetProperty` are attachable properties: They can be set on individual animations to override any storyboard-wide settings. This storyboard targets both the `Height` and `Canvas.Top` properties on the target `Eyelid` ellipse. Therefore, a single target name is marked on the storyboard but separate target properties are marked for each animation.

→ `Canvas.Top` is animated in sync with `Height` so the ellipse stays centered as it shrinks vertically. Transforms, introduced in the next chapter, provide a more convenient way to do this.

→ The two animations both use the default linear interpolation behavior. Their motion is so quick that it's not necessary to try anything more lifelike.

→ A storyboard is more than just a simple container that associates animations with target objects and their properties. This storyboard has its *own* duration and repeat behavior! The two animations only last .2 seconds (.1 seconds to animate from the current value to 380 and 50, and another .1 seconds to animate back to the original values due to the auto-reverse setting). However, because the storyboard is given a duration of 3 seconds, and because it has the auto-reverse setting rather than its children, the animation remains stationery until the 3 seconds are up. At that point, the .2-second long movement occurs again, and the animation will then be still for another 2.8 seconds. Therefore, this storyboard makes the eyelid blink very quickly, but only once every 3 seconds.

The result of this animation is shown in Figure 12.5 (after calling `Begin` in C#). Because the `Eyelid` ellipse is the same color as the background (and intentionally covered on its left side by the black area), you can't see the ellipse itself. Instead, you see the empty space inside it shrinking to nothing once the height of the ellipse (380) is less than two times its stroke thickness (400).

Height = 770, Canvas.Top = -145

Height = 575, Canvas.Top = -47.5
(halfway through)

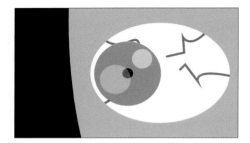 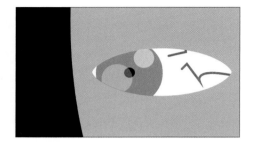

Height = 380, Canvas.Top = 50

FIGURE 12.5   `EyelidStoryboard` compresses the height of the `Eyelid` ellipse and moves it downward to keep it centered.

Storyboard and Animation Properties

You've already seen the `Duration`, `AutoReverse`, and `RepeatBehavior` properties, which can apply to individual animations or an entire storyboard. In total, there are six properties that can be applied to both storyboards and animations:

→ **Duration**—The length of the animation or storyboard, set to 1 second by default.

> **Be careful when specifying a duration!**
>
> The format of a duration string is the same format used by the `TimeSpan.Parse` API:
>
> `days.hours:minutes:seconds.fraction`
>
> Shortcuts are allowed so you don't have to specify every chunk of that string, but the behavior is not what you might expect. The string "2" means 2 *days*, not 2 seconds! The string "2.5" means 2 *days* and 5 *hours*! And the string "0:2" means 2 *minutes*. Given that most animations should be no more than a few seconds long, the typical syntax used is *hours:minutes:seconds* or *hours:minutes:seconds.fraction*. So, 2 seconds can be expressed as "0:0:2", and half a second can be expressed as "0:0:0.5" or "0:0:.5".

→ **BeginTime**—A timespan that delays the start of the animation or storyboard by the specified amount of time, set to 0 by default. A storyboard can use custom BeginTime values on its child animations to make them occur in sequence rather than simultaneously.

→ **SpeedRatio**—A multiplier applied to duration, set to 1 by default. You can set it to any double value greater than 0. A value less than 1 slows down the animation, and a value greater than 1 speeds it up. SpeedRatio does not impact BeginTime.

→ **AutoReverse**—Can be set to true to make an animation or storyboard "play backward" once it completes. The reversal takes the same amount of time as the forward progress, so SpeedRatio affects the reversal as well. Note that any delay specified via BeginTime does *not* delay the reversal; it always happens immediately after the normal part of the animation completes.

→ **RepeatBehavior**—Can be set to a timespan, or a string like "2x" or "3x", or "Forever". Therefore, you can use RepeatBehavior to make animations repeat themselves (or cut themselves short) based on a time cutoff, to make animations repeat themselves a certain number of times (even a fractional number of times like "2.5x"), or to make animations repeat themselves forever (as done in this chapter). If AutoReverse is true, the reversal is repeated as well.

→ **FillBehavior**—Can be set to Stop rather than its default value of HoldEnd, to make the animated properties jump back to their pre-animation values once the relevant animations are complete.

•••

The Total Length of an Animation

With all the different adjustments that can be made to an animation by using properties such as BeginTime, SpeedRatio, AutoReverse, and RepeatBehavior, it can be hard to keep track of how long it will take an animation to finish after it is initiated. Its Duration value certainly isn't adequate for describing the true length of time! Instead, the following formula describes an animation's true duration:

$$\text{Total Length} = \text{BeginTime} + \left(\frac{\text{Duration} \times (\text{AutoReverse ? 2:1})}{\text{SpeedRatio}} \times \text{RepeatBehavior} \right)$$

This applies if RepeatBehavior is specified as a double value (or left as its default value of 1). If RepeatBehavior is specified as a timespan, the total timeline length is simply the value of RepeatBehavior plus the value of BeginTime.

The Main Page

Silly Eye's main page, whose XAML is in Listing 12.1, contains some vector graphics, an application bar, and the three storyboards just discussed. It also contains an "intro pane" that tells the user to tap the screen to begin, as shown in Figure 12.6. This is done so we can initially show the application bar but then hide it while the app is in use, as the buttons on the screen interfere with the effect. The intro pane informs the user that they can bring the application bar back at any time by tapping the screen.

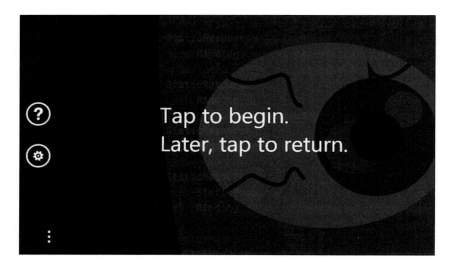

FIGURE 12.6   The application bar is only visible when the "intro pane" is visible.

LISTING 12.1   `MainPage.xaml`—The Main User Interface for Silly Eye

```xml
<phone:PhoneApplicationPage
    x:Class="WindowsPhoneApp.MainPage"
    xmlns="http://schemas.microsoft.com/winfx/2006/xaml/presentation"
    xmlns:x="http://schemas.microsoft.com/winfx/2006/xaml"
    xmlns:phone="clr-namespace:Microsoft.Phone.Controls;assembly=Microsoft.Phone"
    xmlns:shell="clr-namespace:Microsoft.Phone.Shell;assembly=Microsoft.Phone"
    FontFamily="{StaticResource PhoneFontFamilyNormal}"
    Foreground="{StaticResource PhoneForegroundBrush}"
    SupportedOrientations="Landscape" Orientation="Landscape">

  <!-- The application bar, with 2 buttons and 1 menu item -->
  <phone:PhoneApplicationPage.ApplicationBar>
    <shell:ApplicationBar>
      <shell:ApplicationBarIconButton Text="instructions"
              IconUri="/Shared/Images/appbar.instructions.png"
              Click="InstructionsButton_Click"/>
      <shell:ApplicationBarIconButton Text="settings" Click="SettingsButton_Click"
              IconUri="/Shared/Images/appbar.settings.png"/>
      <shell:ApplicationBar.MenuItems>
        <shell:ApplicationBarMenuItem Text="about" Click="AboutMenuItem_Click"/>
      </shell:ApplicationBar.MenuItems>
    </shell:ApplicationBar>
```

LISTING 12.1   Continued

```xml
  </phone:PhoneApplicationPage.ApplicationBar>

  <!-- Three storyboard resources -->
  <phone:PhoneApplicationPage.Resources>
    <!-- Animate the stroke thickness surrounding the pupil -->
    <Storyboard x:Name="PupilStoryboard" Storyboard.TargetName="Pupil"
                Storyboard.TargetProperty="StrokeThickness">
      <DoubleAnimation To="70" Duration="0:0:.5" AutoReverse="True"
                       RepeatBehavior="Forever">
        <DoubleAnimation.EasingFunction>
          <ElasticEase/>
        </DoubleAnimation.EasingFunction>
      </DoubleAnimation>
    </Storyboard>

    <!-- Animate the iris so it moves left and right -->
    <Storyboard x:Name="IrisStoryboard" Storyboard.TargetName="Iris"
                Storyboard.TargetProperty="(Canvas.Left)">
      <DoubleAnimation To="543" Duration="0:0:2" AutoReverse="True"
                       RepeatBehavior="Forever">
        <DoubleAnimation.EasingFunction>
          <BounceEase/>
        </DoubleAnimation.EasingFunction>
      </DoubleAnimation>
    </Storyboard>

    <!-- Animate the eyelid so it blinks -->
    <Storyboard x:Name="EyelidStoryboard" Storyboard.TargetName="Eyelid"
                RepeatBehavior="Forever" Duration="0:0:3">
      <DoubleAnimation Storyboard.TargetProperty="Height"
                       To="380" Duration="0:0:.1" AutoReverse="True"/>
      <DoubleAnimation Storyboard.TargetProperty="(Canvas.Top)"
                       To="50" Duration="0:0:.1" AutoReverse="True"/>
    </Storyboard>
  </phone:PhoneApplicationPage.Resources>

  <!-- A 1x1 grid with IntroPanel on top of EyeCanvas -->
  <Grid>
    <Canvas x:Name="EyeCanvas"
            MouseLeftButtonDown="EyeCanvas_MouseLeftButtonDown">
      <!-- The eyeball -->
      <Ellipse Canvas.Left="270" Canvas.Top="55" Width="503" Height="370"
               Fill="White"/>
      <!-- Four "bloodshot" curvy/angled paths -->
```

LISTING 12.1   Continued

```xml
        <Path Data="M782,252 C648,224 666,270 666,270 L622,212 L604,230" Width="190"
              Height="70" Canvas.Left="588" Canvas.Top="206" Stroke="Red"
              StrokeThickness="8" Stretch="Fill" StrokeEndLineCap="Triangle"/>
        <Path Data="M658,122 C604,176 582,136 582,136 L586,190 L526,204" Width="144"
              Height="94" Canvas.Left="541" Canvas.Top="91" Stretch="Fill"
              Stroke="Red" StrokeThickness="8" StrokeEndLineCap="Triangle"/>
        <Path Data="M348,334 C414,296 386,296 428,314 C470,332 464,302 476,292
              C488,282 498,314 500,306" Width="164" Height="56" Canvas.Left="316"
              Canvas.Top="303" Stretch="Fill" Stroke="Red" StrokeThickness="8"/>
        <Path Data="M324,164 C388,210 434,130 444,178 C454,226 464,226 470,224"
              Width="154" Height="70" Canvas.Left="322" Canvas.Top="115"
              Stretch="Fill" Stroke="Red" StrokeThickness="8"/>
        <!-- The complete iris canvas -->
        <Canvas x:Name="Iris" Canvas.Left="287" Canvas.Top="124">
          <!-- The pupil, whose stroke is the iris -->
          <Ellipse x:Name="Pupil" Width="238" Height="237" StrokeThickness="100"
                   Fill="Black"/>
          <!-- Two "shine" circles -->
          <Ellipse Width="73" Height="72" Canvas.Left="134" Canvas.Top="28"
                   Fill="#8DFFFFFF"/>
          <Ellipse Width="110" Height="107" Canvas.Left="20" Canvas.Top="86"
                   Fill="#5FFFFFFF"/>
        </Canvas>
        <!-- The skin-colored eyelid -->
        <Ellipse x:Name="Eyelid" StrokeThickness="200" Width="897" Height="770"
                 Canvas.Left="73" Canvas.Top="-145"/>
        <!-- The black area on the left side that defines the edge of the face -->
        <Ellipse Stroke="Black" StrokeThickness="300" Width="1270" Height="2380"
                 Canvas.Left="-105" Canvas.Top="-1140"/>
      </Canvas>

      <!-- Quick instructions shown at the beginning -->
      <Grid x:Name="IntroPanel" Opacity=".8"
            Background="{StaticResource PhoneBackgroundBrush}">
        <!-- Enable tapping anywhere except very close to the application bar -->
        <TextBlock x:Name="IntroTextBlock" Width="700" Padding="170"
                   MouseLeftButtonDown="IntroTextBlock_MouseLeftButtonDown"
                   HorizontalAlignment="Left" VerticalAlignment="Stretch"
                   FontSize="{StaticResource PhoneFontSizeExtraLarge}">
          Tap to begin.<LineBreak/>Later, tap to return.
        </TextBlock>
      </Grid>
    </Grid>
</phone:PhoneApplicationPage>
```

Notes:

→ The application bar contains links to a settings page, an instructions page, and an about page. The first two pages are shown in the next two sections. You've already seen the about page in Chapter 6, "Baby Sign Language." The settings item has been deemed worthy of a button on the application bar rather than a menu item, because in this app it should be quite common for users to customize settings. (The application bar also doesn't add any clutter during the app's normal operation, because it gets hidden!)

→ Notice that the three storyboard resources are given names with x:Name rather than keys with x:Key! This is a handy trick that makes using resources from code-behind much more convenient. When you give a resource a name, it is used as the key in the dictionary *and* a field with that name is generated for access from C#!

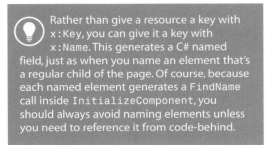
Rather than give a resource a key with x:Key, you can give it a key with x:Name. This generates a C# named field, just as when you name an element that's a regular child of the page. Of course, because each named element generates a FindName call inside InitializeComponent, you should always avoid naming elements unless you need to reference it from code-behind.

→ The explicit From value has been removed from PupilStoryboard's animation because it's not necessary. It was included earlier in the chapter simply to help explain how animations work.

→ IntroTextBlock is the element that listens for taps and hides IntroPanel. It is given a width of 700 rather than the entire width of the page because if it gets too close to the application bar, users might accidentally tap it (and hide the application bar) when actually trying to tap the bar—especially its ellipsis.

Listing 12.2 contains the code-behind for the main page.

LISTING 12.2   MainPage.xaml.cs—The Code-Behind for Silly Eye's Main Page

```
using System;
using System.Windows;
using System.Windows.Input;
using System.Windows.Media;
using System.Windows.Navigation;
using Microsoft.Phone.Controls;

namespace WindowsPhoneApp
{
  public partial class MainPage : PhoneApplicationPage
  {
    public MainPage()
    {
```

LISTING 12.2   Continued

```
    InitializeComponent();

    // Start all the storyboards, which animate indefinitely
    this.IrisStoryboard.Begin();
    this.PupilStoryboard.Begin();
    this.EyelidStoryboard.Begin();

    // Prevent off-screen parts from being seen when animating to other pages
    this.Clip = new RectangleGeometry { Rect = new Rect(0, 0,
      Constants.SCREEN_WIDTH, Constants.SCREEN_HEIGHT) };
  }

  protected override void OnNavigatedFrom(NavigationEventArgs e)
  {
    base.OnNavigatedFrom(e);
    // Remember the intro panel's visibility for deactivation/activation
    this.State["IntroPanelVisibility"] = this.IntroPanel.Visibility;
  }

  protected override void OnNavigatedTo(NavigationEventArgs e)
  {
    base.OnNavigatedTo(e);
    // Respect the saved settings for the skin and eye colors
    SolidColorBrush skinBrush = new SolidColorBrush(Settings.SkinColor.Value);
    this.Eyelid.Stroke = skinBrush;
    this.EyeCanvas.Background = skinBrush;
    this.Pupil.Stroke = new SolidColorBrush(Settings.EyeColor.Value);

    // Restore the intro panel's visibility if we're being activated
    if (this.State.ContainsKey("IntroPanelVisibility"))
    {
      this.IntroPanel.Visibility =
        (Visibility)this.State["IntroPanelVisibility"];
      this.ApplicationBar.IsVisible =
        (this.IntroPanel.Visibility == Visibility.Visible);
    }
  }

  protected override void OnOrientationChanged(OrientationChangedEventArgs e)
  {
    base.OnOrientationChanged(e);
    // Keep the text block aligned to the opposite side as the application bar,
    // to preserve the "dead zone" where tapping doesn't hide the bar
    if (e.Orientation == PageOrientation.LandscapeRight)
```

LISTING 12.2   Continued

```
      this.IntroTextBlock.HorizontalAlignment = HorizontalAlignment.Right;
    else
      this.IntroTextBlock.HorizontalAlignment = HorizontalAlignment.Left;
  }

  void IntroTextBlock_MouseLeftButtonDown(object sender, MouseButtonEventArgs e)
  {
    // Hide IntroPanel and application bar when the text block is tapped
    this.IntroPanel.Visibility = Visibility.Collapsed;
    this.ApplicationBar.IsVisible = false;
  }

  void EyeCanvas_MouseLeftButtonDown(object sender, MouseButtonEventArgs e)
  {
    // Show IntroPanel and application bar when the canvas is tapped
    this.IntroPanel.Visibility = Visibility.Visible;
    this.ApplicationBar.IsVisible = true;
  }

  // Application bar handlers

  void InstructionsButton_Click(object sender, EventArgs e)
  {
    this.NavigationService.Navigate(new Uri("/InstructionsPage.xaml",
      UriKind.Relative));
  }

  void SettingsButton_Click(object sender, EventArgs e)
  {
    this.NavigationService.Navigate(new Uri("/SettingsPage.xaml",
      UriKind.Relative));
  }

  void AboutMenuItem_Click(object sender, EventArgs e)
  {
    this.NavigationService.Navigate(new Uri(
      "/Shared/About/AboutPage.xaml?appName=Silly Eye", UriKind.Relative));
  }
 }
}
```

Notes:

→ The three storyboards are initiated from the constructor by name, thanks to the `x:Name` markings in XAML.

→ The page's `Clip` property is set to a screen-size rectangular region. This is done to prevent the off-screen portions of the vector graphics from being rendered during the animated page-flip transition when navigating to another page. This not only prevents strange visual artifacts, but can be good for performance as well. All UI elements have this `Clip` property that can be set to an arbitrary geometry.

Geometries Used for Clipping   •••

The `Clip` property can be set to geometry objects that are similar to, but distinct from, the shape objects introduced in Chapter 5, "Ruler." You can use a `RectangleGeometry`, `EllipseGeometry`, `LineGeometry`, `PathGeometry`, or a `GeometryGroup` that combines multiple geometries together. Appendix E, "Geometry Reference," discusses geometries.

→ Two persisted settings are used for the skin and eye color, and they are respected in `OnNavigatedTo`. They do not need to be saved in `OnNavigatedFrom` because the settings page takes care of this. The settings are defined in a separate `Settings.cs` file as follows:

```
public static class Settings
{
  public static readonly Setting<Color> EyeColor = new Setting<Color>(
    "EyeColor", (Color)Application.Current.Resources["PhoneAccentColor"]);
  public static readonly Setting<Color> SkinColor = new Setting<Color>(
    "SkinColor", /* "Tan" */ Color.FromArgb(0xFF, 0xD2, 0xB4, 0x8C));
}
```

The default eye color is actually the phone theme's accent color, which happens to give the realistic blue color in this chapter's figures.

→ The visibility of `IntroPanel` (and the application bar) is placed in page state so the page looks the same if deactivated and later activated.

> Whenever a page undergoes a noticeable state change, don't forget to use page state so you can quickly and automatically restore this state in case your app is interrupted then reactivated!

→ The alignment of `IntroTextBlock` is adjusted in `OnOrientationChanged` to keep it on the opposite side of the application bar. Recall that the application bar appears on the left side of the screen for the landscape right orientation, and the right side of the screen for the landscape left orientation.

The Settings Page

Listing 12.3 contains the XAML for this app's settings page, shown in Figure 12.7. It enables the user to choose different colors for the eye and the skin.

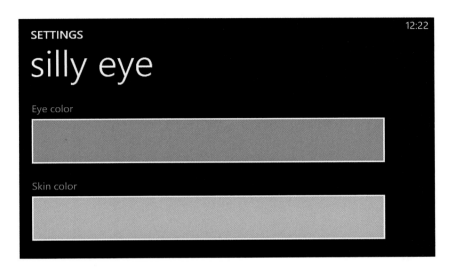

FIGURE 12.7   The settings page enables the user to change both of Silly Eye's color settings.

How can I add a settings page for my app inside the built-in Settings app?

You can't, at least in version 7.0 of Windows Phone. Although the Settings app contains a list of system settings and a list of application settings, the latter is only for built-in apps. Instead, you are supposed to provide your own in-app settings page but make it look like the user magically switched to the Settings app. In other words, your settings page should use "SETTINGS" as the application name in the standard header, and use the app name as the page title, as seen in Figure 12.7.

 For settings page design guidelines, see Chapter 20, "Alarm Clock."

LISTING 12.3   `SettingsPage.xaml`—The User Interface for the Settings Page

```
<phone:PhoneApplicationPage
    x:Class="WindowsPhoneApp.SettingsPage"
    xmlns="http://schemas.microsoft.com/winfx/2006/xaml/presentation"
    xmlns:x="http://schemas.microsoft.com/winfx/2006/xaml"
    xmlns:phone="clr-namespace:Microsoft.Phone.Controls;assembly=Microsoft.Phone"
```

LISTING 12.3   Continued

```
  xmlns:shell="clr-namespace:Microsoft.Phone.Shell;assembly=Microsoft.Phone"
  xmlns:local="clr-namespace:WindowsPhoneApp"
  FontFamily="{StaticResource PhoneFontFamilyNormal}"
  FontSize="{StaticResource PhoneFontSizeNormal}"
  Foreground="{StaticResource PhoneForegroundBrush}"
  SupportedOrientations="PortraitOrLandscape" shell:SystemTray.IsVisible="True">
  <Grid>
    <Grid.RowDefinitions>
      <RowDefinition Height="Auto"/>
      <RowDefinition Height="*"/>
    </Grid.RowDefinitions>

    <!-- The standard settings header -->
    <StackPanel Grid.Row="0" Style="{StaticResource PhoneTitlePanelStyle}">
      <TextBlock Text="SETTINGS" Style="{StaticResource PhoneTextTitle0Style}"/>
      <TextBlock Text="silly eye" Style="{StaticResource PhoneTextTitle1Style}"/>
    </StackPanel>

    <!-- A rectangle (and text block) for each of the two settings -->
    <ScrollViewer Grid.Row="1">
      <StackPanel Margin="{StaticResource PhoneMargin}">
        <TextBlock Text="Eye color" Foreground="{StaticResource PhoneSubtleBrush}"
                   Margin="12,7,12,8"/>
        <Rectangle x:Name="EyeColorRectangle" Margin="12,0,12,18" Height="90"
                   Stroke="{StaticResource PhoneForegroundBrush}"
                   StrokeThickness="3" local:Tilt.IsEnabled="True"
                   MouseLeftButtonUp="EyeColorRectangle_MouseLeftButtonUp"/>
        <TextBlock Text="Skin color"
                   Foreground="{StaticResource PhoneSubtleBrush}"
                   Margin="12,12,12,8"/>
        <Rectangle x:Name="SkinColorRectangle" Height="90"
                   Margin="{StaticResource PhoneHorizontalMargin}"
                   Stroke="{StaticResource PhoneForegroundBrush}"
                   StrokeThickness="3" local:Tilt.IsEnabled="True"
                   MouseLeftButtonUp="SkinColorRectangle_MouseLeftButtonUp"/>
      </StackPanel>
    </ScrollViewer>
  </Grid>
</phone:PhoneApplicationPage>
```

➔   This page leverages the custom header styles from in App.xaml. As with the remaining multi-page apps in this book, the App.xaml.cs code-behind file is also leveraging the custom frame that provides page transition animations, explained in Chapter 19, "Animation Lab."

→ The two clickable regions that display the current colors look like buttons, but they are just rectangles. Their `MouseLeftButtonUp` event handlers take care of invoking the user interface that enables the user to change each color.

> On many pages, such as a settings page, instructions page or about page, it's nice to wrap the content in a scroll viewer even if all the content fits on the page. That way, the user can do a quick swipe and get visual feedback that there's no more content to see (due to the scroll-and-squish behavior of the scroll viewer). This feedback is strangely satisfying. When the screen does nothing in response to a swipe, the user might think that he or she didn't press hard enough, and might even try again to be sure.

→ The main stack panel is placed in a scroll viewer even though the content completely fits on the screen in all orientations. This is a nice extra touch for users, as they are able to swipe the screen and easily convince themselves that there is no more content.

Listing 12.4 contains the code-behind for this settings page.

LISTING 12.4   `SettingsPage.xaml.cs`—The Code-Behind for the Settings Page

```
using System;
using System.Windows.Input;
using System.Windows.Media;
using System.Windows.Navigation;
using Microsoft.Phone.Controls;

namespace WindowsPhoneApp
{
  public partial class SettingsPage : PhoneApplicationPage
  {
    public SettingsPage()
    {
      InitializeComponent();
    }

    protected override void OnNavigatedTo(NavigationEventArgs e)
    {
      base.OnNavigatedTo(e);
      // Respect the saved settings
      this.EyeColorRectangle.Fill = new SolidColorBrush(Settings.EyeColor.Value);
      this.SkinColorRectangle.Fill = new SolidColorBrush(Settings.SkinColor.Value);
    }
```

LISTING 12.4   Continued

```
void EyeColorRectangle_MouseLeftButtonUp(object sender, MouseButtonEventArgs e)
{
  // Get a string representation of the colors we need to pass to the color
  // picker, without the leading #
  string currentColorString = Settings.EyeColor.Value.ToString().Substring(1);
  string defaultColorString =
    Settings.EyeColor.DefaultValue.ToString().Substring(1);

  // The color picker works with the same isolated storage value that the
  // Setting works with, but we have to clear its cached value to pick up
  // the value chosen in the color picker
  Settings.EyeColor.ForceRefresh();

  // Navigate to the color picker
  this.NavigationService.Navigate(new Uri(
    "/Shared/Color Picker/ColorPickerPage.xaml?"
    + "&currentColor=" + currentColorString
    + "&defaultColor=" + defaultColorString
    + "&settingName=EyeColor", UriKind.Relative));
}

void SkinColorRectangle_MouseLeftButtonUp(object sender, MouseButtonEventArgs
e)
{
  // Get a string representation of the colors, without the leading #
  string currentColorString = Settings.SkinColor.Value.ToString().Substring(1);
  string defaultColorString =
    Settings.SkinColor.DefaultValue.ToString().Substring(1);

  // The color picker works with the same isolated storage value that the
  // Setting works with, but we have to clear its cached value to pick up
  // the value chosen in the color picker
  Settings.SkinColor.ForceRefresh();

  // Navigate to the color picker
  this.NavigationService.Navigate(new Uri(
    "/Shared/Color Picker/ColorPickerPage.xaml?"
    + "showOpacity=false"
    + "&currentColor=" + currentColorString
    + "&defaultColor=" + defaultColorString
    + "&settingName=SkinColor", UriKind.Relative));
  }
 }
}
```

To enable the user to change each color, this page navigates to a color picker page pictured in Figure 12.8. This feature-filled page, shared by many apps, is included with this book's source code. It provides a palette of standard colors but it also enables the user to finely customize the hue, saturation, and lightness of the color whether through interactive UI or by simply typing in a hex value (or any string recognized by XAML, such as "red", "tan", or "lemonchiffon"). It optionally enables adjusting the color's opacity.

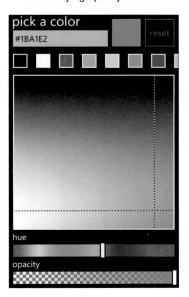
With varying opacity allowed

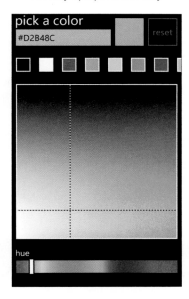
For fully-opaque colors only

FIGURE 12.8   The color picker page provides a slick way to select a color.

The color picker page accepts four parameters via its query string:

→ **showOpacity**—true by default, but can be set to false to hide the opacity slider. This also removes transparent from the palette of colors at the top, and it prevents users from typing in nonopaque colors. Therefore, when you set this to false, you can be sure that an opaque color will be chosen.

→ **currentColor**—The initial color selected when the page appears. It must be passed as a string that would be valid for XAML. If specified as a hex value, the # must be removed to avoid interfering with the URI.

→ **defaultColor**—The color that the user gets when they press the reset button on the color picker page. It must be specified in the same string format as currentColor.

→ **settingName**—A named slot in isolated storage where the chosen color can be found on return from the page. This is the same name used when constructing a Setting instance. The code in Listing 12.4's `OnNavigatedTo` method automatically picks up the new value chosen when navigating back from the color picker page, but only because of the `ForceRefresh` call made before navigating to the color picker. Chapter 20 shows exactly how this works.

Use this book's color picker page (or a page like it) to give users an easy yet powerful way to pick a custom color. The main limitation of this page, in its current form, is that it only supports the portrait orientation. Therefore, typing a color in the text box with a landscape hardware keyboard is not a pleasant experience.

The Instructions Page

Listing 12.5 contains the XAML for the simple instructions page shown in Figure 12.9. Later chapters won't bother showing the XAML for their instructions pages unless there's something noteworthy inside.

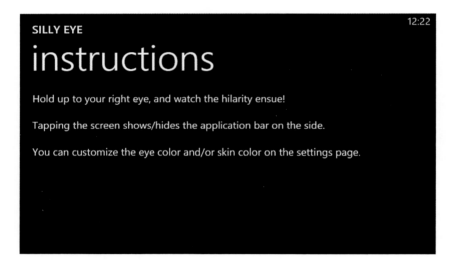

FIGURE 12.9 The instructions page used by Silly Eye.

LISTING 12.5 `InstructionsPage.xaml`—The User Interface for the Instructions Page

```
<phone:PhoneApplicationPage
    x:Class="WindowsPhoneApp.InstructionsPage"
    xmlns="http://schemas.microsoft.com/winfx/2006/xaml/presentation"
    xmlns:x="http://schemas.microsoft.com/winfx/2006/xaml"
    xmlns:phone="clr-namespace:Microsoft.Phone.Controls;assembly=Microsoft.Phone"
    xmlns:shell="clr-namespace:Microsoft.Phone.Shell;assembly=Microsoft.Phone"
    FontFamily="{StaticResource PhoneFontFamilyNormal}"
```

LISTING 12.5   Continued

```xml
      FontSize="{StaticResource PhoneFontSizeNormal}"
      Foreground="{StaticResource PhoneForegroundBrush}"
      SupportedOrientations="PortraitOrLandscape" shell:SystemTray.IsVisible="True">
  <Grid>
    <Grid.RowDefinitions>
      <RowDefinition Height="Auto"/>
      <RowDefinition Height="*"/>
    </Grid.RowDefinitions>

    <!-- The standard header -->
    <StackPanel Style="{StaticResource PhoneTitlePanelStyle}">
      <TextBlock Text="SILLY EYE" Style="{StaticResource PhoneTextTitle0Style}"/>
      <TextBlock Text="instructions"
                 Style="{StaticResource PhoneTextTitle1Style}"/>
    </StackPanel>

    <ScrollViewer Grid.Row="1">
      <TextBlock Margin="24 12" TextWrapping="Wrap">
        Hold up to your right eye, and watch the hilarity ensue!
        <LineBreak/><LineBreak/>
        Tapping the screen shows/hides the application bar on the side.
        <LineBreak/><LineBreak/>
        You can customize the eye color and/or skin color on the settings page.
      </TextBlock>
    </ScrollViewer>
  </Grid>
</phone:PhoneApplicationPage>
```

→ As with the settings page, the main content is placed in a scroll viewer simply to give the user feedback that there is no more content.

→ As with the intro pane on the main page, a single text block makes use of LineBreak elements to format its text.

→ The code-behind file, InstructionsPage.xaml.cs, has nothing more than the call to InitializeComponent in its constructor.

The Finished Product

Translucent orange iris with green skin

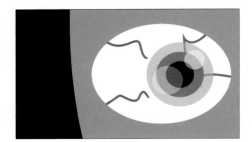

Transparent iris with black skin

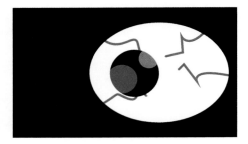

Black iris with pink skin

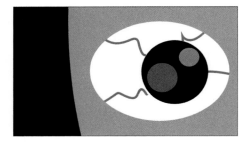

chapter 13

METRONOME

A metronome can be a useful tool for musicians, and this chapter's Metronome app enables this functionality to be with you wherever you go. Metronome features the classic arm with an adjustable weight that swings like a pendulum. It supports a range of 25–200 beats per minute, and it produces sounds to denote each beat as well as the beginning of each measure. Three time signatures are supported: 2/4, 3/4, and 4/4. (If you're not a musician, don't worry about the concepts of time signatures and measures; this only affects the pattern of sounds produced and is not an important part of this chapter.)

The pendulum-swinging style definitely leans toward mimicking the real world rather than providing an "authentically digital" experience like a proper Metro app would, but this novelty app can get away with it. It also provides a perfect opportunity to introduce transforms, as this is what enables the rotation of the arm.

Introducing Transforms

Silverlight contains a handful of 2D transform classes that enable you to morph elements in exotic ways. The 2D transform classes are

→ `RotateTransform`

→ `ScaleTransform`

→ `SkewTransform`

→ `TranslateTransform`

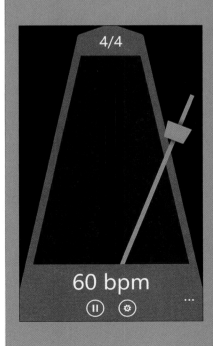

→ Three ways to combine all of the above (`CompositeTransform`, `TransformGroup`, and `MatrixTransform`)

Although it can sometimes be useful to manually rotate/scale/skew/translate an element, these transform classes are typically used as the target of animations. Metronome uses animations targeting `RotateTransform` to enable the swinging pendulum motion of its arm.

RotateTransform

`RotateTransform` rotates an element according to the values of three `double` properties:

→ **Angle**—Angle of rotation, specified in degrees (default value = 0)

→ **CenterX**—Horizontal center of rotation (default value = 0)

→ **CenterY**—Vertical center of rotation (default value = 0)

The default (`CenterX`,`CenterY`) point of (0,0) represents the top-left corner of the element.

To apply `RotateTransform` (or any transform) to an element, you use it as the value of the element's `RenderTransform` property. This is done in a first attempt at Metronome's main page, as follows:

```
<phone:PhoneApplicationPage …>
  <Grid>
    <Image Source="Images/metronome.png" Stretch="None" VerticalAlignment="Top"/>
    <Canvas Margin="0,60,0,0" Width="200" Height="570" Background="#A0A0">
      <Canvas.RenderTransform>
        <RotateTransform Angle="30"/>
      </Canvas.RenderTransform>
      <Image Canvas.Left="94" Source="Images/arm.png"/>
      <Image Canvas.Left="66" Canvas.Top="434" Source="Images/weight.png"/>
    </Canvas>
  </Grid>
</phone:PhoneApplicationPage>
```

The result is shown in Figure 13.1. The canvas being rotated is given a translucent green background, so it's easier to see how it's being rotated.

Of course, using the top-left corner as the center of rotation does not give the desired effect. Instead, we want the canvas to rotate around its bottom middle. Based on the size of this canvas, this could be done by setting `RotateTransform`'s `CenterX` to 100 and `CenterY` to 570, but there's another way to do this that is generally preferred.

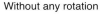
Without any rotation   With 30° rotation applied

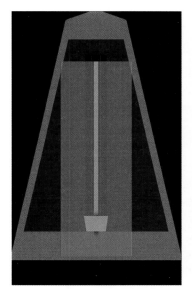

FIGURE 13.1   Rotating the translucent green canvas by 30°.

Every element with a `RenderTransform` property also has a `RenderTransform`**Origin** property that represents the starting point of the transform (the point that remains stationary). For `RotateTransform`, this is the same as specifying the (CenterX,CenterY) point, except that the *x* and *y* values used in `RenderTransformOrigin` are always on a relative scale from 0 to 1. The default origin of (0,0) is the top-left corner, (0,1) is the bottom-left corner, (1,0) is the top-right corner, and (1,1) is the bottom-right corner. You can use numbers greater than 1 to set the origin to a point outside the bounds of an element, and you can use fractional values. Therefore, an origin of (0.5,0.5) can be used to rotate an element around its middle.

Figure 13.2 shows two values of `RenderTransformOrigin` applied to the translucent green canvas. The first one spins it around its middle, and the second one spins it around its bottom-middle (the desired effect for this app), as follows:

```
<phone:PhoneApplicationPage …>
  <Grid>
    <Image Source="Images/metronome.png" Stretch="None" VerticalAlignment="Top"/>
    <Canvas Margin="0,60,0,0" Width="200" Height="570" Background="#A0A0"
            RenderTransformOrigin=".5,1">
      <Canvas.RenderTransform>
        <RotateTransform Angle="30"/>
      </Canvas.RenderTransform>
      <Image Canvas.Left="94" Source="Images/arm.png"/>
```

```
    <Image Canvas.Left="66" Canvas.Top="434" Source="Images/weight.png"/>
  </Canvas>
 </Grid>
</phone:PhoneApplicationPage>
```

Rotated around the middle
(RenderTransformOrigin=".5,.5")

Rotated around the bottom-middle, the desired effect
(RenderTransformOrigin=".5,1")

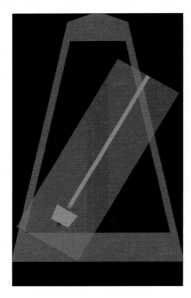
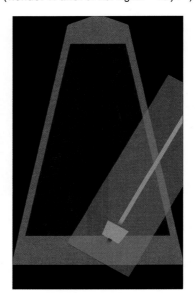

FIGURE 13.2   Customizing the origin of rotation with RenderTransformOrigin.

Positioning a transform's starting point with RenderTransformOrigin is handy because its relative specification automatically scales with the target element. For example, even if an element changes size due to stretch alignment and an orientation change, a RenderTransformOrigin set to ".5,.5" will continue to transform it around its middle. (If you use RenderTransformOrigin at the same time as CenterX and CenterY on RotateTransform, the origin is calculated based on a combination of both.)

How can I rotate an element in 3D?

This can be accomplished with perspective transforms, covered in Chapter 17, "Pick a Card Magic Trick."

ScaleTransform

ScaleTransform enlarges or shrinks an element horizontally, vertically, or in both directions. It works like RotateTransform, except it has ScaleX and ScaleY properties instead of an Angle property. ScaleTransform is used in the next chapter.

SkewTransform

SkewTransform slants an element according to separate AngleX and AngleY properties. This transform is leveraged to create the tilt effect used in most apps.

TranslateTransform

TranslateTransform simply moves an element based on its X and Y properties. RenderTransformOrigin has no effect on this transform (nor does this transform have CenterX and CenterY properties) because no point of the element remains stationary when it is moved horizontally and/or vertically.

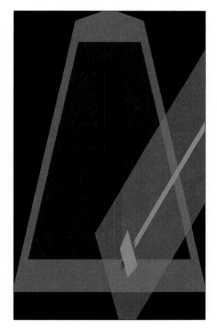

Combining Transforms

If you want to transform an element multiple ways simultaneously, such as rotate *and* scale it, the CompositeTransform class is the easiest way to do so. It has all the properties of the previous four transforms, although some have slightly different names: Rotation, ScaleX, ScaleY, SkewX, SkewY, TranslateX, TranslateY, CenterX, and CenterY.

Figure 13.3 changes the transform used in Figure 13.2 to the following (and uses a RenderTransformOrigin of ".5,1"):

FIGURE 13.3   A skewed and rotated arm and weight created with a CompositeTransform.

```
<Canvas.RenderTransform>
  <CompositeTransform Rotation="30" SkewY="45"/>
</Canvas.RenderTransform>
```

CompositeTransform always applies its transforms in the same order: Scale, skew, rotate, and then translate. If you require a nonstandard order, you can use a TransformGroup instead and then put its child transforms in any order. For example, the following transform reverses the order of the skew and rotation performed in Figure 13.3:

```
<Canvas.RenderTransform>
  <TransformGroup>
    <!-- First rotate, then skew! -->
    <RotateTransform Angle="30"/>
    <SkewTransform AngleY="45"/>
  </TransformGroup>
</Canvas.RenderTransform>
```

The result is shown in Figure 13.4.

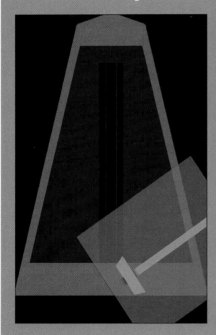

FIGURE 13.4   The arm and weight are now rotated first and then skewed, which creates a different result from Figure 13.3.

Transforms Versus Layout

Transforms are applied *after* the layout process has finished (immediately before the element is rendered). When applying them to elements in a canvas or single-cell grid, this doesn't really matter. But when applying them inside a layout where the positions of other elements are dependent on the transformed element's size and position, this becomes evident. Figure 13.5 demonstrates this with the following stack panel:

```
<phone:PhoneApplicationPage …>
  <StackPanel VerticalAlignment="Center">
    <Button Content="1"/>
    <Button Content="2" RenderTransformOrigin=".5,.5">
      <Button.RenderTransform>
        <CompositeTransform Rotation="45" ScaleY="5" />
      </Button.RenderTransform>
    </Button>
    <Button Content="3"/>
  </StackPanel>
</phone:PhoneApplicationPage>
```

The placement of the third button is based on the original size and position of the second button. This, by the way, is how TranslateTransform differs from giving an element equivalent margins. Adding a margin to button 2 would push down button 3, but translating it would not push down button 3.

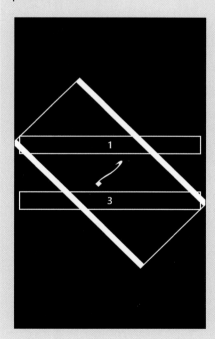

FIGURE 13.5   A rotated and scaled button still occupies its pretransform space as far as layout is concerned.

This also means that nontransformed elements that would get clipped by the parent panel remain clipped the same way, even when a transform makes it possible for more of the element to be rendered inside its parent's bounds.

> **MatrixTransform**   •••
>
> In case you're a linear algebra buff, you can use a low-level `MatrixTransform` to represent all combinations of rotation, scaling, skewing, and translating as an affine transformation matrix. (*Affine* means that straight lines remain straight.) Its `Matrix` property has the following subproperties representing 6 values in a 3x3 matrix:
>
> $$\left\{ \begin{array}{ccc} \texttt{M11} & \texttt{M12} & \texttt{0} \\ \texttt{M21} & \texttt{M22} & \texttt{0} \\ \texttt{OffsetX} & \texttt{OffsetY} & \texttt{1} \end{array} \right\}$$
>
> The final column's values cannot be changed.

The Main Page

Metronome has a main page, a settings page, and the standard about page. The main page contains the metronome, featuring a weight that can be slid up or down to adjust the number of beats per minute, just like on a real swinging-arm metronome. The main page's application bar has links to the two other pages, as well as a button for starting and stopping the metronome.

The User Interface

Listing 13.1 contains the main page's XAML.

LISTING 13.1   `MainPage.xaml`—The User Interface for Metronome's Main Page

```xml
<phone:PhoneApplicationPage x:Class="WindowsPhoneApp.MainPage"
    xmlns="http://schemas.microsoft.com/winfx/2006/xaml/presentation"
    xmlns:x="http://schemas.microsoft.com/winfx/2006/xaml"
    xmlns:phone="clr-namespace:Microsoft.Phone.Controls;assembly=Microsoft.Phone"
    xmlns:shell="clr-namespace:Microsoft.Phone.Shell;assembly=Microsoft.Phone"
    FontFamily="{StaticResource PhoneFontFamilyNormal}"
    FontSize="{StaticResource PhoneFontSizeNormal}"
    Foreground="{StaticResource PhoneForegroundBrush}"
    SupportedOrientations="Portrait">

  <!-- An application bar that acts like the base of the metronome -->
  <phone:PhoneApplicationPage.ApplicationBar>
    <shell:ApplicationBar BackgroundColor="#925E26" ForegroundColor="White">
      <shell:ApplicationBarIconButton Text="start"
                                IconUri="/Shared/Images/appbar.play.png"
                                Click="StartOrPauseButton_Click"/>
      <shell:ApplicationBarIconButton Text="settings"
                                IconUri="/Shared/Images/appbar.settings.png"
                                Click="SettingsButton_Click"/>
      <shell:ApplicationBar.MenuItems>
```

LISTING 13.1   Continued

```xml
        <shell:ApplicationBarMenuItem Text="about" Click="AboutMenuItem_Click"/>
      </shell:ApplicationBar.MenuItems>
    </shell:ApplicationBar>
  </phone:PhoneApplicationPage.ApplicationBar>

  <!-- Two storyboards added to the page's resource dictionary -->
  <phone:PhoneApplicationPage.Resources>

    <!-- A storyboard for swinging back and forth -->
    <Storyboard x:Name="SwingStoryboard"
                Storyboard.TargetName="MetronomeRotation"
                Storyboard.TargetProperty="Angle"
                Completed="SwingStoryboard_Completed">
      <DoubleAnimation x:Name="SwingAnimation" From="-35" To="35">
        <DoubleAnimation.EasingFunction>
          <QuadraticEase EasingMode="EaseInOut"/>
        </DoubleAnimation.EasingFunction>
      </DoubleAnimation>
    </Storyboard>

    <!-- A storyboard for gracefully stopping (and returning upright) -->
    <Storyboard x:Name="StopSwingingStoryboard"
                Storyboard.TargetName="MetronomeRotation"
                Storyboard.TargetProperty="Angle">
      <DoubleAnimation x:Name="StopSwingingAnimation" Duration="0:0:.2" To="0"/>
    </Storyboard>

  </phone:PhoneApplicationPage.Resources>

  <!-- A 1x1 grid with four layers -->
  <Grid>
    <!-- Bottom layer: The metronome image as a background -->
    <Image Source="Images/metronome.png" Stretch="None" VerticalAlignment="Top"/>

    <!-- Middle layer: A Canvas containing the swinging arm and weight -->
    <Canvas VerticalAlignment="Top" Margin="0,146,0,0">
      <Canvas.Clip>
        <!-- Clip the bottom of the arm and weight -->
        <RectangleGeometry Rect="0,0,480,498"/>
      </Canvas.Clip>
      <Canvas x:Name="SliderCanvas" Width="200" Height="570" Canvas.Left="140"
              RenderTransformOrigin=".5,1" Background="Transparent"
              MouseLeftButtonDown="SliderCanvas_MouseLeftButtonDown"
              MouseMove="SliderCanvas_MouseMove">
```

LISTING 13.1   Continued

```
    <Canvas.RenderTransform>
      <RotateTransform x:Name="MetronomeRotation"/>
    </Canvas.RenderTransform>
    <Canvas.Clip>
      <!-- Ensure the weight's top shadow doesn't extend past the arm -->
      <RectangleGeometry Rect="0,0,200,570"/>
    </Canvas.Clip>
    <!-- The arm -->
    <Image Canvas.Left="94" Source="Images/arm.png" IsHitTestVisible="False"/>
    <!-- The weight -->
    <Image x:Name="WeightImage" Canvas.Left="66" Canvas.Top="434"
           IsHitTestVisible="False" Source="Images/weight.png"/>
  </Canvas>
</Canvas>

<!-- Top two layers: Text blocks centered at the top and bottom -->
<TextBlock x:Name="TimeSignatureTextBlock" FontSize="40" Margin="0,14,0,0"
           HorizontalAlignment="Center" VerticalAlignment="Top"
           IsHitTestVisible="False"/>
<TextBlock x:Name="BpmTextBlock" FontSize="60" Margin="0,0,0,0"
           HorizontalAlignment="Center" VerticalAlignment="Bottom"
           IsHitTestVisible="False"/>
  </Grid>

</phone:PhoneApplicationPage>
```

Notes:

→ The combination of being portrait-only and giving the application bar hard-coded colors enables it to act like the base of the metronome, extending the brown color where the background graphic ends. As with the preceding chapter, the settings item feels appropriate as an application bar button rather than tucked away in the application bar menu.

→ SwingStoryboard changes the angle of the rotated arm from –35° (to the left) to 35° (to the right). The code-behind gets notified of the animation's completion thanks to its Completed event, so it can play a sound, reverse the animation, and start it again. QuadraticEase gives the animation a very subtle acceleration and deceleration, and its EaseInOut mode ensures that the interpolation remains symmetrical. See Appendix D, "Animation Easing Reference" for a graph of this behavior.

→ StopSwingingStoryboard is not really needed to stop SwingStoryboard; if you are fine with the arm jumping back to its initial location when the metronome is stopped, the code-behind could just call SwingStoryboard's Stop method at the appropriate time. However, it looks much nicer for the swinging arm to gradually swing back to its vertical resting position, so that's what StopSwingingStoryboard enables.

→ SliderCanvas is placed inside another canvas that clips the bottom of the arm. (This is the same clipping technique used by the preceding chapter, but done in XAML rather than C#.) The clipping prevents the bar and weight from overlapping the bottom of the metronome image when rotated. It also prevents a bottom shadow on the weight image (seen in Figures 13.1 and 13.2) from extending past the bottom of the arm. SliderCanvas also uses clipping to prevent the weight image's top shadow from extending past the top of the bar. Figure 13.6 helps visualize the clipping by coloring SliderCanvas green and its parent canvas pink.

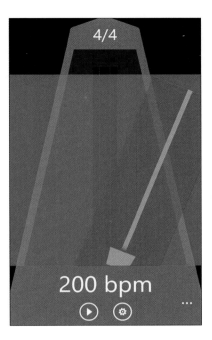

FIGURE 13.6   The canvas shown in pink clips the bottom of the arm and weight, and the canvas shown in green clips the top of the arm and weight.

The clipping done by the pink-tinted canvas in Figure 13.6 is also good for performance, due to its prevention of off-screen elements. If you examine the frame rate counter shown on the screen when running your app under the debugger, you can see that it prevents texture memory usage from doubling at the end of each animation cycle.

See http://www.jeff.wilcox.name/2010/07/counters for a great explanation of the cryptic values shown by the frame rate counter.

→ SliderCanvas is given a RotateTransform so it can be animated by the storyboard. When not animated, it has its default value of 0°, which has no visible effect on the canvas. Note that SliderCanvas requires its explicit width and height for the rotation to work correctly. If left sizeless, RenderTransformOrigin would have no effect because any multiple of a 0x0 square gives the same point on the screen.

→ SliderCanvas has an explicit transparent background, so it responds to taps and slides anywhere on its surface. WeightImage and the arm are also marked IsHitTestVisible="False" so they don't interfere with the canvas events.

The Code-Behind

Listing 13.2 contains the code-behind for the main page.

LISTING 13.2   `MainPage.xaml.cs`—The Code-Behind for Metronome's Main Page

```csharp
using System;
using System.Windows.Controls;
using System.Windows.Input;
using System.Windows.Navigation;
using Microsoft.Phone.Controls;
using Microsoft.Phone.Shell;

namespace WindowsPhoneApp
{
  public partial class MainPage : PhoneApplicationPage
  {
    IApplicationBarIconButton startOrPauseButton;
    bool isActive;
    int beat;

    public MainPage()
    {
      InitializeComponent();
      // Assign the start/pause button because it can't be named in XAML
      this.startOrPauseButton = this.ApplicationBar.Buttons[0]
                                as IApplicationBarIconButton;

      // Initialize the two sound effects
      SoundEffects.Initialize();

      // Allow the app to run (producing sounds) even when the phone is locked.
      // Once disabled, you cannot re-enable the default behavior!
      PhoneApplicationService.Current.ApplicationIdleDetectionMode =
        IdleDetectionMode.Disabled;
    }

    protected override void OnNavigatedFrom(NavigationEventArgs e)
    {
      base.OnNavigatedFrom(e);
      // Remember whether the metronome is running or paused
      this.State["IsActive"] = this.isActive;
    }

    protected override void OnNavigatedTo(NavigationEventArgs e)
    {
```

LISTING 13.2   Continued

```
    base.OnNavigatedTo(e);

    // Respect the persisted settings
    MoveWeight(Settings.WeightPosition.Value);
    this.TimeSignatureTextBlock.Text = Settings.TimeSignature.Value + "/4";

    // Restore any page state
    if (this.State.ContainsKey("IsActive"))
    {
      if ((bool)this.State["IsActive"])
        Start();
      else
        Pause();
    }
  }

  void SliderCanvas_MouseLeftButtonDown(object sender, MouseButtonEventArgs e)
  {
    // Center the weight on the vertical position of the finger
    MoveWeight(e.GetPosition(this.SliderCanvas).Y -
               this.WeightImage.ActualHeight / 2);
  }

  void SliderCanvas_MouseMove(object sender, MouseEventArgs e)
  {
    // Center the weight on the vertical position of the finger
    MoveWeight(e.GetPosition(this.SliderCanvas).Y -
               this.WeightImage.ActualHeight / 2);
  }

  void MoveWeight(double y)
  {
    // Clamp the value to a range of -20 to 434
    double position = Math.Min(434, Math.Max(-20, y));
    Canvas.SetTop(this.WeightImage, position);

    // Remember this position
    Settings.WeightPosition.Value = position;

    // Map the pixel range to a beats-per-minute range of 25-200
    int bpm = (int)Math.Ceiling((position + 85) / 2.6);

    // Update the display and the animation to match
    this.BpmTextBlock.Text = bpm + " bpm";
```

LISTING 13.2   Continued

```
    this.SwingAnimation.Duration = TimeSpan.FromMinutes(1d / bpm);
  }

  void Start()
  {
    isActive = true;
    // Update the application bar button
    this.startOrPauseButton.IconUri = new Uri("/Shared/Images/appbar.pause.png",
                                          UriKind.Relative);
    this.startOrPauseButton.Text = "pause";

    // Stop the stop-swinging storyboard, just in case it's still running
    this.StopSwingingStoryboard.Stop();

    // We want the first run of the animation to start with an angle of 0, the
    // midpoint of the animation. Therefore, give the storyboard a BeginTime of
    // negative 1/2 the duration so it starts halfway through!
    this.SwingStoryboard.BeginTime = TimeSpan.FromSeconds(
      this.SwingAnimation.Duration.TimeSpan.TotalSeconds / -2);

    // Start swinging!
    this.SwingStoryboard.Begin();
  }

  void Pause()
  {
    isActive = false;
    // Update the application bar button
    this.startOrPauseButton.IconUri = new Uri("/Shared/Images/appbar.play.png",
                                          UriKind.Relative);
    this.startOrPauseButton.Text = "start";

    // Start the short stop-swinging storyboard. But first, hand-off the current
    // angle, which gets cleared when SwingStoryboard is stopped.
    this.StopSwingingAnimation.From = this.MetronomeRotation.Angle;
    this.SwingStoryboard.Stop();
    this.StopSwingingStoryboard.Begin();
  }

  void SwingStoryboard_Completed(object sender, EventArgs e)
  {
    // Play a special tone at the beginning of each measure, determined by the
    // chosen time signature. Play a different tone for every other beat.
    if (this.beat % Settings.TimeSignature.Value == 0)
```

LISTING 13.2   Continued

```
      SoundEffects.NewMeasureBeat.Play();
    else
      SoundEffects.Beat.Play();

    this.beat++;

    // Clear the negative BeginTime used for the first run of this storyboard
    // so successive runs are the complete animation
    if (this.SwingStoryboard.BeginTime != TimeSpan.Zero)
      this.SwingStoryboard.BeginTime = TimeSpan.Zero;

    // Reverse the animation
    this.SwingAnimation.To *= -1;
    this.SwingAnimation.From *= -1;

    // Now swing the opposite way
    this.SwingStoryboard.Begin();
  }

  // Application bar handlers

  void StartOrPauseButton_Click(object sender, EventArgs e)
  {
    if (isActive)
      Pause();
    else
      Start();
  }

  void SettingsButton_Click(object sender, EventArgs e)
  {
    this.NavigationService.Navigate(new Uri("/SettingsPage.xaml",
      UriKind.Relative));
  }

  void AboutMenuItem_Click(object sender, EventArgs e)
  {
    this.NavigationService.Navigate(new Uri(
      "/Shared/About/AboutPage.xaml?appName=Metronome", UriKind.Relative));
  }
 }
}
```

Notes:

→ This app uses two sound effects—one for a normal beat and one for the first beat of every measure. The use of sound effects is explained in Part V, "Audio & Video."

→ This app is marked to run while the phone is locked, which can be useful for listening to the metronome beat sounds while playing an instrument. This is done by disabling `ApplicationIdleDetectionMode`, described in Chapter 8, "Vibration Composer."

→ This app uses two persisted settings defined as follows in `Settings.cs`:

```
public static class Settings
{
  public static readonly Setting<int> TimeSignature =
    new Setting<int>("TimeSignature", 4);
  public static readonly Setting<double> WeightPosition =
    new Setting<double>("WeightPosition", 120);
}
```

The pixel position of the weight is remembered rather than the beats-per-minute value it maps to, because more than one pixel value maps to the same beats-per-minute value.

→ Inside `MoveWeight`, the duration of `SwingAnimation` is adjusted to correspond to whatever beats-per-minute value has been chosen.

→ The `Start` method does a neat trick before starting `SwingStoryboard`. Because the resting position of the arm is 0°, we want it to start swinging from there to give a seamless animation from 0° to 35°. However, because the animation is set to start at -35°, we need it to start at its halfway point instead. This is accomplished by giving the storyboard a *negative* `BeginTime` value. With a `BeginTime` of negative one-half of the duration, the animation acts like it has already performed the first half of the animation, so it starts halfway through (at 0°)!

→ Inside `Pause`, `SwingStoryboard` is stopped and `StopSwingingStoryboard` is started. But first, `StopSwingingStoryboard`'s animation must be given an explicit `From` value matching the arm's current angle. Otherwise, stopping `SwingStoryboard` instantly restores the angle to 0° and `StopSwingingStoryboard` would have no effect.

→ Every time `SwingStoryboard` completes, the code in `SwingStoryboard_Completed` plays the appropriate sound, ensures that `BeginTime` is 0 for remaining runs of the animation, reverses the animation, and then starts it again. It would have been nice to reverse the animation by multiplying its `SpeedRatio` by -1, but negative

SpeedRatio values are not supported. Instead, the To and From values are both multiplied by -1 to toggle between -35 and 35.

The Settings Page

The settings page shows the three possible time signatures (2, 3, or 4 beats per measure) in a list of radio buttons, as shown in Figure 13.7. Because the main page is still running on the back stack, the user can hear how each choice effects the pattern of sounds made by the metronome as they tap each one (if the metronome is left running when navigating away).

The User Interface

Listing 13.3 contains the XAML for this settings page.

FIGURE 13.7 The settings page enables the user to switch between three different time signatures.

LISTING 13.3   SettingsPage.xaml—The User Interface for Metronome's Settings Page

```
<phone:PhoneApplicationPage
    x:Class="WindowsPhoneApp.SettingsPage"
    xmlns="http://schemas.microsoft.com/winfx/2006/xaml/presentation"
    xmlns:x="http://schemas.microsoft.com/winfx/2006/xaml"
    xmlns:phone="clr-namespace:Microsoft.Phone.Controls;assembly=Microsoft.Phone"
    xmlns:shell="clr-namespace:Microsoft.Phone.Shell;assembly=Microsoft.Phone"
    xmlns:local="clr-namespace:WindowsPhoneApp"
    FontFamily="{StaticResource PhoneFontFamilyNormal}"
    FontSize="{StaticResource PhoneFontSizeNormal}"
    Foreground="{StaticResource PhoneForegroundBrush}"
    SupportedOrientations="PortraitOrLandscape"
    shell:SystemTray.IsVisible="True">
  <Grid>
    <Grid.RowDefinitions>
      <RowDefinition Height="Auto"/>
      <RowDefinition Height="*"/>
    </Grid.RowDefinitions>
```

LISTING 13.3   Continued

```
<!-- The standard settings header -->
<StackPanel Grid.Row="0" Style="{StaticResource PhoneTitlePanelStyle}">
  <TextBlock Text="SETTINGS" Style="{StaticResource PhoneTextTitle0Style}"/>
  <TextBlock Text="metronome" Style="{StaticResource PhoneTextTitle1Style}"/>
</StackPanel>

<!-- Three radio buttons and their header -->
<ScrollViewer Grid.Row="1">
  <StackPanel Margin="{StaticResource PhoneMargin}"
              HorizontalAlignment="Left">
    <TextBlock Text="Time signature" Margin="12,7,12,8"
               Foreground="{StaticResource PhoneSubtleBrush}"/>
    <RadioButton x:Name="TwoRadioButton" Content="2/4" Tag="2"
                 Checked="RadioButton_Checked" local:Tilt.IsEnabled="True"/>
    <RadioButton x:Name="ThreeRadioButton" Content="3/4" Tag="3"
                 Checked="RadioButton_Checked" local:Tilt.IsEnabled="True"/>
    <RadioButton x:Name="FourRadioButton" Content="4/4" Tag="4"
                 Checked="RadioButton_Checked" local:Tilt.IsEnabled="True"/>
  </StackPanel>
</ScrollViewer>
  </Grid>
</phone:PhoneApplicationPage>
```

The stack panel is left-aligned, so each radio button isn't clickable across the entire width of the page. This is consistent with similar pages in the built-in Settings app, and consistent with design guidelines.

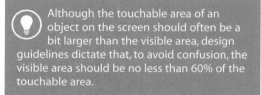

Although the touchable area of an object on the screen should often be a bit larger than the visible area, design guidelines dictate that, to avoid confusion, the visible area should be no less than 60% of the touchable area.

The Code-Behind

Listing 13.4 contains the code-behind for the settings page. When a radio button is checked, the time signature value (2, 3, or 4) is retrieved from the Tag property and stored in the persisted setting.

LISTING 13.4   `SettingsPage.xaml.cs`—The Code-Behind for Metronome's Settings Page

```
using System.Windows;
using System.Windows.Controls;
using System.Windows.Navigation;
using Microsoft.Phone.Controls;

namespace WindowsPhoneApp
{
```

LISTING 13.4   Continued

```csharp
public partial class SettingsPage : PhoneApplicationPage
{
  public SettingsPage()
  {
    InitializeComponent();
  }

  protected override void OnNavigatedTo(NavigationEventArgs e)
  {
    base.OnNavigatedTo(e);
    // Respect the saved setting
    switch (Settings.TimeSignature.Value)
    {
      case 2:
        this.TwoRadioButton.IsChecked = true; break;
      case 3:
        this.ThreeRadioButton.IsChecked = true; break;
      case 4:
        this.FourRadioButton.IsChecked = true; break;
    }
  }

  void RadioButton_Checked(object sender, RoutedEventArgs e)
  {
    // Save the chosen setting
    int timeSignature = int.Parse((sender as RadioButton).Tag.ToString());
    Settings.TimeSignature.Value = timeSignature;
  }
}
```

The Finished Product

Running at the minimum
beats per minute

Paused at the maximum
beats per minute

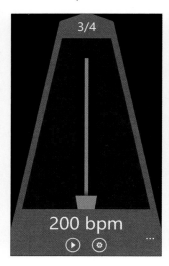

The expanded application bar

chapter 14

LOVE METER

Love Meter is a silly, but fun, novelty app. If you can't decide whether to start or continue a relationship with someone, the Love Meter app can tell you how much chemistry you and your potential mate have. All you need to do is to convince the other person to hold their finger on your phone's screen for about 8 seconds while you do the same. While you do this, Love Meter shows a beating heart and progress bar as it performs its analysis and then reports how much love exists between you two, on a scale from 0 to 100%. A red heart fills a white heart border with the same percentage, to help you visualize the percentage somewhat like a pie chart.

This app demonstrates a new category of animations—keyframe animations. It also demonstrates how `ScaleTransform`, introduced in the preceding chapter, works in practice.

> ! **Love Meter doesn't actually measure anything!**
> It should go without saying, but this app is for entertainment purposes only. Windows phones do not (yet!) have a sensor for measuring human chemistry!

> ! **This app requires multi-touch!**
> Therefore, you cannot test it as-is on the emulator unless your computer supports multi-touch.

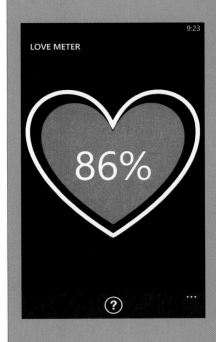

Keyframe Animations

Sometimes the animation behavior you desire cannot be represented by linear interpolation or any of the built-in easing functions. For example, Love Meter performs its heartbeat animation by animating the scale of a vector heart graphic marked with the following `ScaleTransform`:

```
<!-- The solid red heart with a complex geometry -->
<Path …>
  <Path.RenderTransform>
    <!-- The target of the heartbeat and final animations -->
    <ScaleTransform x:Name="HeartScale" ScaleX="0" ScaleY="0"/>
  </Path.RenderTransform>
</Path>
```

To make its scale grow in a heartbeat pattern (with alternating small and large "beats"), you might try to create a multi-animation storyboard as follows (for `ScaleX`, at least):

```
<!-- Horizontal stretching and shrinking -->
<Storyboard x:Name="HeartbeatStoryboard" Storyboard.TargetName="HeartScale"
            Storyboard.TargetProperty="ScaleX" RepeatBehavior="6x">
  <DoubleAnimation BeginTime="0:0:0" To="0"/>
  <DoubleAnimation BeginTime="0:0:.4" To="0"/>
  <DoubleAnimation BeginTime="0:0:.6" To=".5"/>
  <DoubleAnimation BeginTime="0:0:.8" To="0"/>
  <DoubleAnimation BeginTime="0:0:1" To="1"/>
  <DoubleAnimation BeginTime="0:0:1.4" To="0"/>
</Storyboard>
```

However, this fails with an `InvalidOperationException` that explains, "Multiple animations in the same containing Storyboard cannot target the same property on a single element." You could split this up into multiple storyboards and start one when another one ends, but that's cumbersome to manage.

Instead, you can use a *keyframe animation* that supports as many distinct segments as you want. Keyframe animations enable you to specify any number of *keyframes*—specific property values at specific times—rather than being limited to a single `From` value and a single `To` value. For example, the preceding heartbeat animation can be correctly written as follows:

```
<!-- Horizontal stretching and shrinking -->
<Storyboard x:Name="HeartbeatStoryboard" Storyboard.TargetName="HeartScale"
            Storyboard.TargetProperty="ScaleX" RepeatBehavior="6x">
  <DoubleAnimationUsingKeyFrames>
    <LinearDoubleKeyFrame KeyTime="0:0:0" Value="0"/>
    <LinearDoubleKeyFrame KeyTime="0:0:.4" Value="0"/>
    <LinearDoubleKeyFrame KeyTime="0:0:.6" Value=".5"/>
    <LinearDoubleKeyFrame KeyTime="0:0:.8" Value="0"/>
```

```
      <LinearDoubleKeyFrame KeyTime="0:0:1" Value="1"/>
      <LinearDoubleKeyFrame KeyTime="0:0:1.4" Value="0"/>
    </DoubleAnimationUsingKeyFrames>
</Storyboard>
```

This only animates ScaleX, so Love Meter uses an identical keyframe animation for ScaleY as well, to grow and shrink the heart's scale in sync.

The use of keyframes requires a keyframe-enabled animation class. For this case, DoubleAnimation's companion DoubleAnimation**UsingKeyFrames** class is used. The other three animation classes have corresponding keyframe classes as well. The keyframe animation classes have the same properties as their counterparts except for From, To, and By, as that information is represented inside each child keyframe.

Interpolation can be done between each keyframe, and the interpolation can be different between each pair. This is based on which type of keyframe is used, out of the four available:

→ **Linear keyframes**—Perform basic linear interpolation.

→ **Easing keyframes**—Perform interpolation based on the specified easing function.

→ **Spline keyframes**—Perform interpolation based on a spline object that describes the desired motion as a cubic Bézier curve.

→ **Discrete keyframes**—Perform no interpolation; the value jumps to the new value at the appropriate time.

Inside **Double**AnimationUsingKeyFrames, you choose from the four types of keyframes by using a Linear**Double**KeyFrame, Easing**Double**KeyFrame, Spline**Double**KeyFrame, or Discrete**Double**KeyFrame. Inside **Color**AnimationUsingKeyFrames, you choose by using a Linear**Color**KeyFrame, Easing**Color**KeyFrame, Spline**Color**KeyFrame, or Discrete**Color**KeyFrame. And so on.

The type of keyframe chosen affects the interpolation between the *previous* value and its own value. Linear and easing keyframes enable the same familiar capabilities as non-keyframe animations, but on a per-keyframe basis. Spline and discrete behavior is specific to keyframe animations. Figure 14.1 illustrates the motion enabled by applying the following storyboard to a heart on a canvas:

```
<Storyboard x:Name="Figure14_1_Storyboard" Storyboard.TargetName="Heart">
  <!-- Move the heart vertically in a complicated pattern -->
  <DoubleAnimationUsingKeyFrames Storyboard.TargetProperty="(Canvas.Top)">
    <LinearDoubleKeyFrame Value="0" KeyTime="0:0:0"/>
    <LinearDoubleKeyFrame Value="200" KeyTime="0:0:1"/>
    <DiscreteDoubleKeyFrame Value="0" KeyTime="0:0:2"/>
    <LinearDoubleKeyFrame Value="0" KeyTime="0:0:3"/>
    <SplineDoubleKeyFrame Value="200" KeySpline="0,1 1,0" KeyTime="0:0:4"/>
  </DoubleAnimationUsingKeyFrames>
```

```
<!-- Move the heart horizontally (linearly) at the same time -->
<DoubleAnimation Storyboard.TargetProperty="(Canvas.Left)"
        From="0" To="500" Duration="0:0:4"/>
</Storyboard>
```

The type of the first keyframe never matters, as there's no previous value from which to interpolate. In this example, the type of the fourth keyframe is also irrelevant because the keyframe's value (0) is identical to the preceding value.

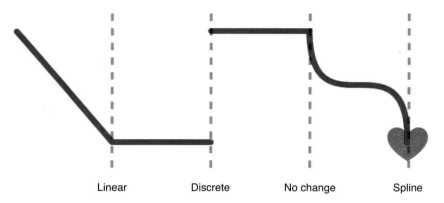

| Linear | Discrete | No change | Spline |

FIGURE 14.1   Motion enabled by a mixture of linear, discrete, and spline keyframes.

•••

Spline Keyframes and Bézier Curves

The spline keyframe classes have a KeySpline property that defines the interpolation as a cubic Bézier curve. Bézier curves (named after engineer Pierre Bézier) are commonly used in computer graphics for representing smooth curves, and are even used by fonts to mathematically describe curves in their glyphs.

The basic idea is that in addition to two endpoints, a Bézier curve has one or more *control points* that give the line segment its curve. These control points are not visible (and not necessarily on the curve itself) but rather are used as input to a formula that dictates where each point on the curve exists. Intuitively, each control point acts like a center of gravity, so the line segment appears to be "pulled" toward these points. The control points specified inside KeySpline are relative, where the start of the curve is 0 and the end is 1.

Finding the right value for KeySpline that gives the desired effect can be tricky and almost certainly requires the use of a design tool such as Expression Blend. But several free tools can be found online that help you visualize Bézier curves based on the specified control points.

The User Interface

Love Meter has a single page besides its instructions and about pages, whose code isn't shown in this chapter. Listing 14.1 contains the main page's XAML.

LISTING 14.1   `MainPage.xaml`—The Main User Interface for Love Meter

```xaml
<phone:PhoneApplicationPage
    x:Class="WindowsPhoneApp.MainPage"
    xmlns="http://schemas.microsoft.com/winfx/2006/xaml/presentation"
    xmlns:x="http://schemas.microsoft.com/winfx/2006/xaml"
    xmlns:phone="clr-namespace:Microsoft.Phone.Controls;assembly=Microsoft.Phone"
    xmlns:shell="clr-namespace:Microsoft.Phone.Shell;assembly=Microsoft.Phone"
    FontFamily="{StaticResource PhoneFontFamilyNormal}"
    FontSize="{StaticResource PhoneFontSizeNormal}"
    Foreground="{StaticResource PhoneForegroundBrush}"
    SupportedOrientations="Portrait" shell:SystemTray.IsVisible="True">

  <!-- The application bar, for instructions and about -->
  <phone:PhoneApplicationPage.ApplicationBar>
    <shell:ApplicationBar>
      <shell:ApplicationBarIconButton Text="instructions"
                IconUri="/Shared/Images/appbar.instructions.png"
                Click="InstructionsButton_Click"/>
      <shell:ApplicationBar.MenuItems>
        <shell:ApplicationBarMenuItem Text="about" Click="AboutMenuItem_Click"/>
      </shell:ApplicationBar.MenuItems>
    </shell:ApplicationBar>
  </phone:PhoneApplicationPage.ApplicationBar>

  <!-- Add three storyboards to the page's resource dictionary -->
  <phone:PhoneApplicationPage.Resources>

    <!-- The storyboard for the heartbeat scale animation (repeated 6 times) -->
    <Storyboard x:Name="HeartbeatStoryboard" Storyboard.TargetName="HeartScale"
                RepeatBehavior="6x">
      <!-- The horizontal stretching and shrinking -->
      <DoubleAnimationUsingKeyFrames Storyboard.TargetProperty="ScaleX">
        <LinearDoubleKeyFrame KeyTime="0:0:0" Value="0"/>
        <LinearDoubleKeyFrame KeyTime="0:0:.4" Value="0"/>
        <LinearDoubleKeyFrame KeyTime="0:0:.6" Value=".5"/>
        <LinearDoubleKeyFrame KeyTime="0:0:.8" Value="0"/>
        <LinearDoubleKeyFrame KeyTime="0:0:1" Value="1"/>
        <LinearDoubleKeyFrame KeyTime="0:0:1.4" Value="0"/>
      </DoubleAnimationUsingKeyFrames>
```

LISTING 14.1   Continued

```xml
    <!-- The vertical stretching and shrinking (in sync) -->
    <DoubleAnimationUsingKeyFrames Storyboard.TargetProperty="ScaleY">
      <LinearDoubleKeyFrame KeyTime="0:0:0" Value="0"/>
      <LinearDoubleKeyFrame KeyTime="0:0:.4" Value="0"/>
      <LinearDoubleKeyFrame KeyTime="0:0:.6" Value=".5"/>
      <LinearDoubleKeyFrame KeyTime="0:0:.8" Value="0"/>
      <LinearDoubleKeyFrame KeyTime="0:0:1" Value="1"/>
      <LinearDoubleKeyFrame KeyTime="0:0:1.4" Value="0"/>
    </DoubleAnimationUsingKeyFrames>

    <!-- Ensure the result text is hidden when beginning -->
    <DoubleAnimationUsingKeyFrames Storyboard.TargetName="ResultTextBlock"
                                   Storyboard.TargetProperty="Opacity">
      <DiscreteDoubleKeyFrame KeyTime="0:0:0" Value="0"/>
    </DoubleAnimationUsingKeyFrames>
  </Storyboard>

  <!-- The storyboard that animates the progress bar -->
  <Storyboard x:Name="ProgressStoryboard"
              Completed="ProgressStoryboard_Completed">
    <!-- Show the progress bar at the beginning and hide it at the end -->
    <DoubleAnimationUsingKeyFrames
            Storyboard.TargetName="ProgressPanel"
            Storyboard.TargetProperty="Opacity">
      <DiscreteDoubleKeyFrame KeyTime="0:0:0" Value="1"/>
      <DiscreteDoubleKeyFrame KeyTime="0:0:8.4" Value="0"/>
    </DoubleAnimationUsingKeyFrames>

    <!-- Animate its value from 0 to 100% -->
    <DoubleAnimation From="0" To="100" Duration="0:0:8.4"
                     Storyboard.TargetName="ProgressBar"
                     Storyboard.TargetProperty="Value"/>
  </Storyboard>

  <!-- A final random animation before displaying the result -->
  <Storyboard x:Name="FinalStoryboard" Storyboard.TargetName="HeartScale">
    <!-- Horizontal stretching and shrinking, set via code-behind -->
    <DoubleAnimationUsingKeyFrames x:Name="FinalAnimationX"
                                   Storyboard.TargetProperty="ScaleX"/>
    <!-- Vertical stretching and shrinking, set via code-behind -->
    <DoubleAnimationUsingKeyFrames x:Name="FinalAnimationY"
                                   Storyboard.TargetProperty="ScaleY"/>
    <!-- Show the result at the end of the animation -->
```

LISTING 14.1   Continued

```xml
<DoubleAnimationUsingKeyFrames Storyboard.TargetName="ResultTextBlock"
                               Storyboard.TargetProperty="Opacity">
  <DiscreteDoubleKeyFrame KeyTime="0:0:1" Value="1"/>
</DoubleAnimationUsingKeyFrames>

</Storyboard>

</phone:PhoneApplicationPage.Resources>

<!-- Transparent background to receive touch input -->
<Grid Background="Transparent">

  <!-- Mini-header -->
  <TextBlock Text="LOVE METER" Margin="24,16,0,12"
             Style="{StaticResource PhoneTextTitle0Style}"/>

  <!-- The progress bar and corresponding text block -->
  <StackPanel x:Name="ProgressPanel" Opacity="0" Margin="0,60,0,0">
    <TextBlock Margin="24,0" Text="Measuring chemistry..."/>
    <ProgressBar x:Name="ProgressBar" VerticalAlignment="Top" Margin="12,24"/>
  </StackPanel>

  <!-- The solid red heart with a complex geometry -->
  <Path Width="436" Stretch="Uniform" Fill="#E51400" Margin="12,0"
        HorizontalAlignment="Center" VerticalAlignment="Center"
        RenderTransformOrigin=".5,.5"
        Data="F1 M 349.267,270.347C 374.787,266.867 401.253,269.427
        425.267,278.92C 453.48,289.173 477.067,309.027 496.333,331.6C
        507.533,345.013 516.68,360 524.547,375.56C 527.587,381.733
        529.893,388.253 533.333,394.24C 537.573,386.76 540.2,378.52
        544.467,371.08C 555.253,351.573 567.667,332.667 583.84,317.173C
        597.32,303.027 613.707,291.773 631.36,283.467C 660.36,269.16
        694.16,265.547 725.76,271.92C 746.72,276.547 766.8,285.627
        783.72,298.92C 799.147,311.693 812.573,327.133 821.52,345.173C
        831.867,366.267 837.827,389.773 837.373,413.333C 838.707,448.413
        829.133,483.093 814.987,514.933C 793.107,563.24 760.693,606.053
        724.373,644.413C 712.653,658 699.253,669.973 686.2,682.213C
        640.48,724.373 590.373,761.52 538.667,795.96C 536.653,797.013
        534.6,798.733 532.213,798.493C 528.067,796.613 524.6,793.573
        520.84,791.067C 468.253,756.28 417.973,717.8 372.107,674.493C
        356,659.96 341.453,643.813 326.933,627.733C 311.28,609.84
        296.267,591.293 283.4,571.28C 265.067,544.44 250.013,515.24
        239.92,484.307C 233.48,462.133 228.32,439.227 229.28,416C
        228.64,403.027 230.867,390.187 233.533,377.547C 241.507,342.733
```

LISTING 14.1   Continued

```
        263.187,311.213 293.16,291.72C 310.107,280.76 329.293,273.32
        349.267,270.347 Z">
    <Path.RenderTransform>
      <!-- The target of the heartbeat and final animations -->
      <ScaleTransform x:Name="HeartScale" ScaleX="0" ScaleY="0"/>
    </Path.RenderTransform>
  </Path>

  <!-- The same heart with no fill and outlined in white or black -->
  <Path Width="456" Stretch="Uniform" StrokeThickness="12" Margin="12,0"
        Stroke="{StaticResource PhoneForegroundBrush}"
        Data="…"/>

  <!-- A text block for displaying the resulting percentage -->
  <TextBlock x:Name="ResultTextBlock" Opacity="0" FontSize="108"
             HorizontalAlignment="Center" VerticalAlignment="Center"/>
  </Grid>

</phone:PhoneApplicationPage>
```

Notes:

➜ HeartbeatStoryboard contains the keyframe animation shown earlier for the horizontal component of the beating visualization (ScaleX), as well as one for the vertical component (ScaleY). With RepeatBehavior on the storyboard, the beat pattern occurs six times.

➜ HeartbeatStoryboard also contains a keyframe animation that "animates" the result text (shown at the end of the whole process) to an opacity of 0. This is done for the benefit of subsequent runs during the same session, because the result text already has an opacity of 0 before the first run. Rather than making the text fade out, the animation instantly sets the opacity to 0 with a single discrete keyframe that takes effect at the start of the storyboard.

➜ The first animation inside ProgressStoryboard uses the same technique to instantly show the progress bar and its text block (inside ProgressPanel) at the start of the storyboard and instantly hide it at the end. The normal DoubleAnimation smoothly and linearly animates the progress bar's value from 0 to 100 over the course of 8.4 seconds, which is how long it takes for HeartbeatStoryboard to finish. The code-behind initiates HeartbeatStoryboard and ProgressStoryboard simultaneously when two fingers touch the screen. The progress UI inside ProgressPanel is shown in Figure 14.2.

→ FinalStoryboard is started by code-behind after HeartbeatStoryboard and ProgressStoryboard finish. It randomly shrinks and stretches the heart for a second before revealing ResultTextBlock. This is done by adding keyframes with random values in code-behind.

→ The grid uses a transparent background, so the fingers can be pressed anywhere on the screen and the appropriate event gets raised.

→ The heart is vector-based, so it can scale to any size and still look crisp. Although not shown here, the outline's Data property is set to the same long string used for the heart's Data property.

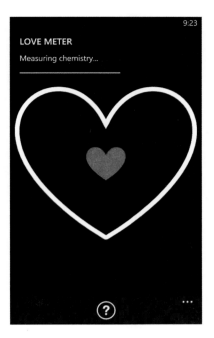

FIGURE 14.2   While the heart beats, the text and progress bar inside ProgressPanel shows how much more time is needed to finish the app's "analysis."

→ On the ScaleTransform, ScaleX is a multiplier for the element's width, and ScaleY is a multiplier for its height. (A ScaleX value of 0.5 shrinks an element's rendered width in half, whereas a ScaleX value of 2 doubles the width.) Their default value is 1, but they are both initialized to 0 in this case, so the red heart is initially invisible.

> The best way to animate the size and location of an element is to attach a ScaleTransform and/or TranslateTransform and animate its properties. Animating ScaleTransform's ScaleX and ScaleY is generally more useful than animating Width and Height because it enables you to change the element size by a percentage rather than a fixed number of units. And animating TranslateTransform is better than animating something like Canvas.Left and Canvas.Top because it works regardless of what Panel contains the element.

How do transforms such as ScaleTransform **affect the values returned by an element's** ActualHeight **and** ActualWidth **properties?**

Applying a transform never changes the values of these properties. Therefore, because of transforms, these properties can "lie" about the size of an element on the screen. For example, the red heart in Love Meter always reports 436 as its ActualWidth value, despite the initial ScaleTransform that makes its actual size 0.

Such "lies" might surprise you, but they're for the best. First, it's debatable how such values should even be expressed for some transforms. More importantly, the point of transforms is to alter an element's appearance without the element's knowledge. Giving elements the illusion that they are being rendered normally enables custom elements to be plugged in and transformed without special handling.

The Code-Behind

Listing 14.2 contains the code-behind for the main page.

LISTING 14.2   MainPage.xaml.cs—The Code-Behind for Love Meter's Main Page

```
using System;
using System.Windows.Input;
using System.Windows.Media.Animation;
using System.Windows.Navigation;
using Microsoft.Phone.Controls;

namespace WindowsPhoneApp
{
  public partial class MainPage : PhoneApplicationPage
  {
    // The secret chemistry-measuring algorithm is just choosing a random number!
    Random random = new Random();

    public MainPage()
    {
      InitializeComponent();
    }

    protected override void OnNavigatedTo(NavigationEventArgs e)
    {
      base.OnNavigatedTo(e);
      // This is application-wide, so only listen while on this page
      Touch.FrameReported += Touch_FrameReported;
    }

    protected override void OnNavigatedFrom(NavigationEventArgs e)
    {
```

LISTING 14.2   Continued

```
      base.OnNavigatedFrom(e);
      // Unhook the handler attached in OnNavigatedTo
      Touch.FrameReported -= Touch_FrameReported;
    }

    void Touch_FrameReported(object sender, TouchFrameEventArgs e)
    {
      TouchPointCollection fingers = e.GetTouchPoints(this);

      // Stop the storyboards if there aren't two fingers currently on the screen
      if (fingers.Count != 2 || (fingers.Count == 2 &&
                                 (fingers[0].Action == TouchAction.Up ||
                                  fingers[1].Action == TouchAction.Up)))
      {
        this.HeartbeatStoryboard.Stop();
        this.ProgressStoryboard.Stop();
      }
      // Start the storyboards if two fingers are in contact and the second one
      // just made contact, AND if the storyboards aren't already running
      else if (fingers.Count == 2 && (fingers[0].Action == TouchAction.Down ||
                                      fingers[1].Action == TouchAction.Down)
            && this.HeartbeatStoryboard.GetCurrentState() != ClockState.Active)
      {
        this.HeartbeatStoryboard.Begin();
        this.ProgressStoryboard.Begin();
      }
    }

    // Called when the progress bar reaches 100%
    void ProgressStoryboard_Completed(object sender, EventArgs e)
    {
      this.FinalStoryboard.Stop(); // So we can clear its keyframes

      // Fill the X & Y animations with 10 random keyframes
      this.FinalAnimationX.KeyFrames.Clear();
      this.FinalAnimationY.KeyFrames.Clear();
      for (int i = 0; i < 10; i++)
      {
        this.FinalAnimationX.KeyFrames.Add(new LinearDoubleKeyFrame {
          KeyTime = TimeSpan.FromMilliseconds(i * 100),
          Value = (double)random.Next(0, 101) / 100 });
        this.FinalAnimationY.KeyFrames.Add(new LinearDoubleKeyFrame {
          KeyTime = TimeSpan.FromMilliseconds(i * 100),
```

LISTING 14.2   Continued

```
            Value = (double)random.Next(0, 101) / 100 });
    }

    // Choose the result
    double finalPercentage = random.Next(0, 101);

    // Ensure that the otherwise-random animations end up at the right value
    this.FinalAnimationX.KeyFrames.Add(new LinearDoubleKeyFrame { KeyTime =
      TimeSpan.FromMilliseconds(1100), Value = finalPercentage / 100 });
    this.FinalAnimationY.KeyFrames.Add(new LinearDoubleKeyFrame { KeyTime =
      TimeSpan.FromMilliseconds(1100), Value = finalPercentage / 100 });

    // Update the text block now, which still has an opacity of 0.
    // It will be shown when FinalStoryboard finishes.
    this.ResultTextBlock.Text = finalPercentage + "%";

    // Start the new random animations
    this.FinalStoryboard.Begin();
  }

  // Application bar handlers

  void InstructionsButton_Click(object sender, EventArgs e)
  {
    this.NavigationService.Navigate(new Uri("/InstructionsPage.xaml",
      UriKind.Relative));
  }

  void AboutMenuItem_Click(object sender, EventArgs e)
  {
    this.NavigationService.Navigate(new Uri(
      "/Shared/About/AboutPage.xaml?appName=Love Meter", UriKind.Relative));
  }
  }
}
```

Notes:

➔ This application has special handling to initiate the first two storyboards only when *two* fingers are simultaneously pressed on the screen, and to stop the storyboards otherwise. This is done with the multi-touch `FrameReported` event and corresponding functionality, covered in Part VII, "Touch & Multi-Touch."

➔ We only want to start the first two storyboards if they aren't already in progress. This is especially important inside the `FrameReported` event handler because it gets called repeatedly while the two fingers are pressed down. To check the status of the storyboards, it calls the `GetCurrentState` method on one of them, which returns either `Active`, `Stopped`, or `Filling`. `Filling` represents the case for which an animation has completed, but the animated property values remain at their post-animation values. This always happens for a completed storyboard until its `Stop` method is called, unless its `FillBehavior` property is set to `Stop` to make it stop automatically on completion.

→ Inside `ProgressStoryboard_Completed`, `FinalStoryboard` is filled with random-value keyframes before revealing the (also-randomly chosen) chemistry value in the final keyframe. Although the final keyframe uses the same value for both `ScaleX` and `ScaleY`, the inter-

FIGURE 14.3   The red heart compresses horizontally and/or vertically during the final random storyboard.

mediate keyframes do not. This produces a more interesting animation that morphs the heart in either dimension, as demonstrated in Figure 14.3.

The Finished Product

Not much love

Unlike in the preceding two chapters, this app respects the light theme.

The instructions page contains instructions and a disclaimer.

chapter 15 lessons

MOOD RING

A *mood ring* is a ring with an element that changes color based on the body temperature of the person wearing it. Some people claim that such temperature changes are able to reveal the wearer's mood, making these rings fun novelty items.

The Mood Ring app captures the essence of a mood ring. Users can press their finger on the screen, and the spot they touch slowly changes color to reveal their mood. In one way, the Mood Ring app is even better that a real mood ring—it explains what the resulting color means. (For example, orange means restless.) In another way, the Mood Ring app is worse than a real mood ring—much like the preceding chapter, it must randomly choose what mood to display rather than base it on your finger's temperature. Windows phones have many sensors, but a thermometer is not one of them!

The preceding three chapters have only used `DoubleAnimations`, but this app makes use of color and object animations. It also provides an excuse to use a radial gradient brush, which rarely has an appropriate use in a Windows Phone app.

Color Animations

The idea of a color animation might sound strange at first. For example, what exactly does it mean to animate a color from red to blue? Internally, each color has floating-point values representing its alpha, red, green, and blue channels.

Therefore, color animations can interpolate those values the same way that
`DoubleAnimation` does for its single value. As a result of this interpolation, an animation
from red to blue appears to change the color from red to deep pink to purple to blue.

Colors (and solid color brushes) can be specified in XAML with several different string
representations:

→ A name, like Red, Khaki, or DodgerBlue. Some (but not nearly all) of these colors appear
as static properties on the Colors class. These color names are the same ones used in
CSS and elsewhere. See http://www.w3schools.com/css/css_colornames.asp for a
complete list.

→ The standard RGB representation #argb, where a, r, g, and b are hexadecimal values for
the alpha, red, green, and blue channels. For example, opaque Red is #FFFF0000, or more
simply #FF0000 (because the alpha channel is assumed to be the maximum 255 by
default). Shortcut syntax is also supported, so #ABC is the same as #AABBCC.

→ The esoteric enhanced RGB color space (scRGB) representation sc#a r g b, where a, r,
g, and b are decimal values for each channel between 0 and 1. In this representation,
opaque Red is sc#1 1 0 0, or more simply sc#1 0 0. Commas are also allowed
between each value. scRGB allows for values outside the 0–1 range, so information isn't
lost if you apply transformations to colors that temporarily push any channel outside its
normal range. scRGB also has increased accuracy compared to standard RGB (sometimes
called sRGB) because it is a linear color space.

The phone theme resources include entries for colors as well as brushes, such as
PhoneForeground**Color**, PhoneBackground**Color**, and PhoneAccent**Color**, as shown in
Appendix C, "Theme Resources Reference."

There aren't many color properties to be directly animated by a color animation. Mood
Ring happens to animate one such property (`Color` on `GradientStop`). Most of the properties that *appear* to be set to colors in XAML (`Foreground`, `Background`, and so on) are actually brush properties. But because solid color brushes have a color property (called `Color`),
color animations can be used on brushes with subproperty syntax like the following:

```
<ColorAnimation From="Red" To="Blue" Storyboard.TargetName="TextBlock"
  Storyboard.TargetProperty="(TextBlock.Foreground).(SolidColorBrush.Color)"/>
```

This assumes the presence of a text block named `TextBlock` as follows:

```
<Grid x:Name="Grid">
  <TextBlock x:Name="TextBlock" Foreground="Red" …/>
</Grid>
```

The value used for `Storyboard.TargetProperty` is called a *property path*. With it, you can
specify a chain of properties and subproperties, where each property is wrapped in parentheses and qualified with its class name. You can even use array syntax, so the following
property path works when the animation target is changed to the parent grid:

```
<ColorAnimation From="Red" To="Blue" Storyboard.TargetName="Grid"
  Storyboard.TargetProperty=
  "(Grid.Children)[0].(TextBlock.Foreground).(SolidColorBrush.Color)"/>
```

> ⓘ **Color animations don't perform as well as other animations!**
>
> When animations do not alter the underlying render surface (also called a *texture*), Silverlight is able to perform the animation on the Graphics Processing Unit (GPU) rather than the Central Processing Unit (CPU), using a thread known as the *compositor thread*. Preventing work from occurring on the UI thread is important for high-performing apps, because the UI thread is needed to handle input, data binding, your app's logic, and more.
>
> Changing an element's color requires changing the underlying surface, so color animations involve a lot of work for the UI thread. Animating an element's opacity (or rotating it, translating it, or scaling it), on the other hand, does not require changing the underlying surface.

> 💡 Although *animating* opacity is more efficient than *animating* a color, it is usually more efficient to use static colors with translucency coming from their alpha channels than to use the `Opacity` property to apply translucency to an otherwise-opaque solid color. If you do animate an element's opacity, you should mark it with `CacheMode="BitmapCache"` to avoid performance problems. See Chapter 19, "Animation Lab," for more information.

Gradient Brushes

Silverlight includes two types of gradient brushes, one for filling an area with a linear gradient and one for filling an area with a radial gradient. Mood Ring uses a radial gradient brush to make the appropriate color radiate from the point where the user's finger touches the screen.

The following radial gradient brush fills a grid's background with the multi-color pattern shown in Figure 15.1:

```
<phone:PhoneApplicationPage …>
  <Grid>
    <Grid.Background>
      <RadialGradientBrush>
        <GradientStop Offset="0" Color="Red"/>
        <GradientStop Offset=".2" Color="Blue"/>
        <GradientStop Offset=".4" Color="Orange"/>
        <GradientStop Offset=".6" Color="Green"/>
        <GradientStop Offset=".8" Color="Purple"/>
        <GradientStop Offset="1" Color="Yellow"/>
      </RadialGradientBrush>
    </Grid.Background>
  </Grid>
</phone:PhoneApplicationPage>
```

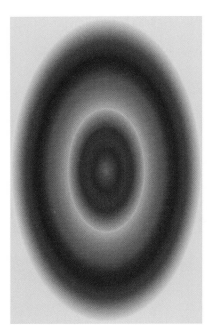

FIGURE 15.1   A radial gradient brush with six color stops.

The brush contains a collection of gradient stops, each of which contains a color and an offset. The offset is a `double` value relative to the bounding box of the area being filled, where 0 is the beginning and 1 is the end. The brush performs linear interpolation between each gradient stop to fill the area smoothly. Both radial gradient brushes and linear gradient brushes define several properties for tweaking their appearance.

> (!) **Gradients do not render smoothly on Windows Phone 7!**
>
> Although gradients render nicely in the emulator (and the figures in this book), the screens on current Windows phones are set to only use 16-bit color depth. Although good for performance, 16-bit color depth is not good enough to show gradients nicely. The result is a "banding" phenomenon where sharp lines are seen between individual colors in the gradient. The closer the colors in the gradient are (and the larger the gradient-filled area is), the more noticeable this problem becomes.
>
> This normally isn't a problem, as using a gradient looks out of place in the flat Metro style of Windows Phone apps. You certainly won't find any gradients in the phone's built-in apps. (By the way, this does not normally affect the display of photos and video, whose inherent noise usually counteracts any noticeable banding.)
>
> Therefore, you should use gradients extremely sparingly. In this book, only the color picker page seen in the preceding chapter uses linear gradients, and only Mood Ring uses a radial gradient. If you insist on using a gradient (which can be appropriate for games), you can get better results by using a gradient-filled image with dithering or other noise built in.

Gradient brushes can be used wherever solid color brushes can be used, such as the stroke of a shape, the border or background of a button, or the foreground for text, such as the following text block shown in Figure 15.2:

```xml
<phone:PhoneApplicationPage …>
  <Grid>
    <TextBlock Text="psychedelic" FontSize="150">
      <TextBlock.Foreground>
        <RadialGradientBrush>
          <GradientStop Offset="0" Color="Red"/>
          <GradientStop Offset=".2" Color="Blue"/>
          <GradientStop Offset=".4" Color="Orange"/>
          <GradientStop Offset=".6" Color="Green"/>
          <GradientStop Offset=".8" Color="Purple"/>
          <GradientStop Offset="1" Color="Yellow"/>
        </RadialGradientBrush>
      </TextBlock.Foreground>
    </TextBlock>
  </Grid>
</phone:PhoneApplicationPage>
```

The gradient stretches to fill the text block's bounding box.

FIGURE 15.2 Creating gradient-filled text is possible, although not recommended.

To get crisp lines inside a gradient brush, you can simply add two gradient stops at the same offset with different colors. The following linear gradient brush does this at offsets .2 *and* .6 to get two distinct lines defining the `PhoneAccentColor` region, shown in Figure 15.3 in blue:

```xml
<phone:PhoneApplicationPage …>
  <Grid>
    <Grid.Background>
      <LinearGradientBrush>
        <GradientStop Offset="0"
                      Color="{StaticResource PhoneBackgroundColor}"/>
        <GradientStop Offset=".2"
                      Color="{StaticResource PhoneForegroundColor}"/>
        <GradientStop Offset=".2" Color="{StaticResource PhoneAccentColor}"/>
        <GradientStop Offset=".4" Color="{StaticResource PhoneAccentColor}"/>
        <GradientStop Offset=".6" Color="{StaticResource PhoneAccentColor}"/>
        <GradientStop Offset=".6"
                      Color="{StaticResource PhoneBackgroundColor}"/>
        <GradientStop Offset=".8"
                      Color="{StaticResource PhoneBackgroundColor}"/>
        <GradientStop Offset="1"
                      Color="{StaticResource PhoneForegroundColor}"/>
      </LinearGradientBrush>
    </Grid.Background>
  </Grid>
</phone:PhoneApplicationPage>
```

FIGURE 15.3   Two crisp lines inside the gradient, enabled by duplicate offsets.

When it comes to gradients, not all transparent colors are equal!

Because all colors have an alpha channel, you can incorporate transparency and translucency into any gradient by changing the alpha channel on any gradient stop's color. The following linear gradient brush uses two blue colors, one fully opaque and one fully transparent:

```
<LinearGradientBrush>
  <GradientStop Offset="0" Color="#FF0000FF"/>
  <GradientStop Offset="1" Color="#000000FF"/>
</LinearGradientBrush>
```

Notice that the second gradient stop uses a "transparent blue" color rather than simply specifying Transparent as the color. That's because Transparent is defined as white with a 0 alpha channel (#00FFFFFF). Although both colors are completely invisible, the interpolation to each color does not behave the same way. If Transparent were used for the second gradient stop, you would not only see the alpha value gradually change from 0xFF to 0, you would also see the red and green values gradually change from 0 to 0xFF, giving the brush more of a gray look. This is demonstrated in Figure 15.4 on top of a black background.

From blue to transparent blue

From blue to the official Transparent color (transparent white)

FIGURE 15.4   Subtly different gradients, caused by different transparent colors.

The User Interface

Mood Ring only has one page other than its instructions and about pages, which aren't shown in this chapter. Listing 15.1 contains its XAML.

LISTING 15.1   `MainPage.xaml`—The Main User Interface for Mood Ring

```xml
<phone:PhoneApplicationPage
    x:Class="WindowsPhoneApp.MainPage"
    xmlns="http://schemas.microsoft.com/winfx/2006/xaml/presentation"
    xmlns:x="http://schemas.microsoft.com/winfx/2006/xaml"
    xmlns:phone="clr-namespace:Microsoft.Phone.Controls;assembly=Microsoft.Phone"
    xmlns:shell="clr-namespace:Microsoft.Phone.Shell;assembly=Microsoft.Phone"
    SupportedOrientations="PortraitOrLandscape">

  <!-- The application bar, for instructions and about,
       forced to be white on the black background -->
  <phone:PhoneApplicationPage.ApplicationBar>
    <shell:ApplicationBar Opacity="0" ForegroundColor="White">
      <shell:ApplicationBarIconButton Text="instructions"
              IconUri="/Shared/Images/appbar.instructions.png"
              Click="InstructionsButton_Click"/>
      <shell:ApplicationBar.MenuItems>
        <shell:ApplicationBarMenuItem Text="about" Click="AboutMenuItem_Click"/>
      </shell:ApplicationBar.MenuItems>
    </shell:ApplicationBar>
  </phone:PhoneApplicationPage.ApplicationBar>

  <phone:PhoneApplicationPage.Resources>

    <!-- The storyboard that reveals the current mood color -->
    <Storyboard x:Name="ShowColorStoryboard" Storyboard.TargetName="GradientStop">

      <!-- Change the gradient stop color to gray and then the mood color
           (set in code-behind) -->
      <ColorAnimationUsingKeyFrames Storyboard.TargetProperty="Color">
        <LinearColorKeyFrame KeyTime="0:0:4" Value="Gray"/>
        <LinearColorKeyFrame x:Name="MoodColorKeyFrame" KeyTime="0:0:8"/>
      </ColorAnimationUsingKeyFrames>

      <!-- Move the gradient stop's initial offset to .5 during the
           second half of the storyboard -->
      <DoubleAnimation BeginTime="0:0:4" To=".5"
                       Storyboard.TargetProperty="Offset" Duration="0:0:4"/>
    </Storyboard>
```

LISTING 15.1   Continued

```xml
<!-- The storyboard that removes the current mood color -->
<Storyboard x:Name="HideColorStoryboard" Storyboard.TargetName="GradientStop">
  <!-- Fade the gradient back to black -->
  <ColorAnimation To="Black" Duration="0:0:1"
                  Storyboard.TargetProperty="Color"/>
  <!-- Move the gradient stop's initial offset back to 0 -->
  <DoubleAnimation To="0" Duration="0:0:1"
                   Storyboard.TargetProperty="Offset"/>
</Storyboard>

<!-- The storyboard that animates the progress bar -->
<Storyboard x:Name="ProgressStoryboard"
            Completed="ProgressStoryboard_Completed"
            Storyboard.TargetName="ProgressBar">

  <!-- Show the progress bar at the beginning and hide it at the end -->
  <ObjectAnimationUsingKeyFrames Storyboard.TargetProperty="Visibility">
    <DiscreteObjectKeyFrame KeyTime="0:0:0" Value="Visible"/>
    <DiscreteObjectKeyFrame KeyTime="0:0:8" Value="Collapsed"/>
  </ObjectAnimationUsingKeyFrames>

  <!-- Animate its value to 100% -->
  <DoubleAnimation To="100" Duration="0:0:8"
                   Storyboard.TargetProperty="Value"/>
</Storyboard>

</phone:PhoneApplicationPage.Resources>

<Grid>
  <!-- Set the background to a gradient (that initially looks solid black) -->
  <Grid.Background>
    <RadialGradientBrush x:Name="GradientBrush">
      <GradientStop x:Name="GradientStop" Offset="0" Color="Black"/>
      <GradientStop Offset="1" Color="Black"/>
    </RadialGradientBrush>
  </Grid.Background>
  <Grid>
    <ProgressBar x:Name="ProgressBar" Visibility="Collapsed"
                 VerticalAlignment="Top" Margin="12,24"/>
    <!-- A drop shadow for MoodTextBlock, created by duplicating the text in
         black and offsetting it 4 pixels to the right and 4 pixels down -->
    <TextBlock x:Name="MoodTextBlockDropShadow" Foreground="Black"
               HorizontalAlignment="Center" VerticalAlignment="Center"
```

LISTING 15.1   Continued

```
                Visibility="Collapsed" FontSize="65" Margin="4,4,0,0"/>
      <TextBlock x:Name="MoodTextBlock" Opacity=".8"
              HorizontalAlignment="Center" VerticalAlignment="Center"
              Visibility="Collapsed" FontSize="65"/>
    </Grid>
  </Grid>

</phone:PhoneApplicationPage>
```

Notes:

→ The application bar is given an opacity of 0 so it doesn't interfere with the color gradient.

→ The color animation in `ShowColorStoryboard` has two keyframes in order to keep users in suspense as they wait for their mood to be revealed. During the first four seconds, the first gradient stop in the page's grid's background (named `GradientStop`) is animated from its initial color of black to gray. For the remaining four seconds, the color is animated from gray to a color chosen in code-behind. The second animation in this storyboard also animates the gradient stop's offset from 0 to .5 to make the chosen color grow into a solid ellipse that ends up occupying half the size of the screen.

> **!** **Gray is darker than DarkGray!**
>
> For historical reasons, as in CSS, the color named Gray is actually a darker shade than the color named DarkGray.

→ In `HideColorStoryboard`, the gradient stop's color is quickly restored to black and its offset is restored to 0.

→ `ProgressStoryboard` works much like `ProgressStoryboard` from the preceding chapter. It smoothly animates the value of a progress bar to 100 (completely filled) over a fixed duration (this time, exactly 8 seconds). However, rather than showing and hiding the progress bar with a `DoubleAnimation` operating on `Opacity`, it uses an *object animation* to animate the progress bar's `Visibility` property from `Visible` to `Collapsed`.

Because animations operating on arbitrary objects cannot possibly perform any kind of interpolation, object animations must be keyframe animations (using the `ObjectAnimationUsingKeyFrames` class) and only discrete keyframes are supported (using the `DiscreteObjectKeyFrame` class). Therefore, object animations enable you to simply set arbitrary properties to arbitrary values at specific times.

Setting `Visibility` **to** `Collapsed` **Versus Setting** `Opacity` **to 0**

Rather than toggling the progress bar's visibility, the first animation inside `ProgressStoryboard` could have been changed to the following and it would produce the same result (assuming the progress bar is initially marked with `Opacity="0"` rather than `Visibility="Collapsed"`):

```
<!-- Show the progress bar at the beginning and hide it at the end -->
<DoubleAnimationUsingKeyFrames Storyboard.TargetProperty="Opacity">
  <DiscreteDoubleKeyFrame KeyTime="0:0:0" Value="1"/>
  <DiscreteDoubleKeyFrame KeyTime="0:0:8" Value="0"/>
</DoubleAnimationUsingKeyFrames>
```

Although an element is invisible whether its `Opacity` is set to 0 or its `Visibility` is set to `Collapsed`, the choice you make has subtle differences. Setting an element's `Visibility` to `Collapsed` makes the layout system ignore it, which conserves memory and stops it from receiving input events. When an element's `Opacity` is set to 0, it still receives input events and, if marked appropriately, its render surface is cached in video memory so it can be later shown again much more efficiently than by toggling `Visibility`. This marking is done with the `CacheMode` property discussed in Chapter 19.

 Object animations (which are always discrete keyframe animations) are useful for setting property values after a delay, or in a regular pattern. For example, the SOS pattern used by Chapter 2, "Flashlight," could have been implemented with an object animation in a more-readable way than the C# code that was used.

→ The text block that displays the chosen mood (`MoodTextBlock`) is given a drop shadow (simulated with `MoodTextBlockDropShadow`) and an opacity of .8 so it is always readable on top of the gradient. The code-behind gives `MoodTextBlock` a foreground color matching the chosen mood color.

The easiest way to give text a drop shadow is to duplicate the text block, offset one of them a bit, and give one a different color. This is done in Listing 15.1 with the `MoodTextBlock` text block and its corresponding `MoodTextBlockDropShadow` text block.

Point Animations

Other than classes for animating `double`, `Color`, and `Object` data types, the only remaining animation classes are for the `Point` data type. There aren't many reasons to use a point animation, as very few dependency properties of type `Point` exist. One such property is `GradientOrigin` on a gradient brush, so you could add the following animation to `ShowColorStoryboard` to create an interesting effect:

```
<PointAnimation Storyboard.TargetName="GradientBrush"
                Storyboard.TargetProperty="GradientOrigin"
                From="0,0" To="1,1" AutoReverse="True"
                RepeatBehavior="Forever"/>
```

The Code-Behind

Listing 15.2 contains the code-behind for the main page.

LISTING 15.2   `MainPage.xaml.cs`—The Code-Behind for Mood Ring's Main Page

```
using System;
using System.Windows;
using System.Windows.Input;
using System.Windows.Media;
using Microsoft.Phone.Controls;

namespace WindowsPhoneApp
{
  public partial class MainPage : PhoneApplicationPage
  {
    Random random = new Random();
    DateTime fingerReleaseTime;
    int moodIndex;

    public MainPage()
    {
      InitializeComponent();
    }

    protected override void OnMouseLeftButtonDown(MouseButtonEventArgs e)
    {
      base.OnMouseLeftButtonDown(e);
      // Move the gradient origin to where the screen was tapped,
      // and begin mood detection
      MoveGradientOrigin(e);
      StartMoodDetection();
    }

    protected override void OnMouseMove(MouseEventArgs e)
    {
      base.OnMouseMove(e);
      // Move the gradient origin to wherever the finger goes
      MoveGradientOrigin(e);
    }

    protected override void OnMouseLeftButtonUp(MouseButtonEventArgs e)
    {
      base.OnMouseLeftButtonUp(e);

      // Stopping the storyboard undoes everything done by it, returning
```

LISTING 15.2 Continued

```
    // the progress bar's value to 0 and hiding it
    this.ProgressStoryboard.Stop();

    // ShowColorStoryboard doesn't need to be stopped, because
    // HideColorStoryboard animates the same properties back to their
    // initial values
    this.HideColorStoryboard.Begin();

    // Remember when this happened
    this.fingerReleaseTime = DateTime.Now;
  }

  void ProgressStoryboard_Completed(object sender, EventArgs e)
  {
    // We've made it to the end, so show the text block and its drop shadow
    this.MoodTextBlock.Visibility = Visibility.Visible;
    this.MoodTextBlockDropShadow.Visibility = Visibility.Visible;
  }

  void MoveGradientOrigin(MouseEventArgs e)
  {
    // Get the finger's point but scale each dimension from 0 to 1
    Point point = e.GetPosition(this);
    point.X /= this.ActualWidth;
    point.Y /= this.ActualHeight;

    // Move both the gradient origin and center to this point
    this.GradientBrush.GradientOrigin = point;
    this.GradientBrush.Center = point;
  }

  void StartMoodDetection()
  {
    // Only change the mood if it has been at least 3 seconds from the last tap
    // (A simple attempt to give the same result when the same user tries
    // tapping many times in a row.)
    if (DateTime.Now - this.fingerReleaseTime > TimeSpan.FromSeconds(3))
      this.moodIndex = random.Next(0, 12); // Randomly choose a mood

    Color currentColor = Colors.Black;
    string currentMood = null;

    switch (this.moodIndex)
    {
```

LISTING 15.2   Continued

```
    case 0:
      currentMood = "tense"; currentColor = Colors.DarkGray;
      break;
    case 1:
      currentMood = "unsettled"; currentColor = Colors.Brown;
      break;
    case 2:
      currentMood = "active";
      currentColor = Color.FromArgb(0xFF, 0, 0xFF, 0); // Lime
      break;
    case 3:
      currentMood = "relaxed"; currentColor = Colors.Cyan;
      break;
    case 4:
      currentMood = "happy"; currentColor = Colors.Blue;
      break;
    case 5:
      currentMood = "frustrated"; currentColor = Colors.White;
      break;
    case 6:
      currentMood = "restless"; currentColor = Colors.Orange;
      break;
    case 7:
      currentMood = "fearful"; currentColor = Colors.Magenta;
      break;
    case 8:
      currentMood = "imaginative"; currentColor = Colors.Yellow;
      break;
    case 9:
      currentMood = "stimulated"; currentColor = Colors.Orange;
      break;
    case 10:
      currentMood = "excited"; currentColor = Colors.Red;
      break;
    case 11:
      currentMood = "romantic"; currentColor = Colors.Purple;
      break;
  }

  // Apply the chosen color to the animation and the text block
  this.MoodColorKeyFrame.Value = currentColor;
  this.MoodTextBlock.Foreground = new SolidColorBrush(currentColor);

  // Apply the name of the mood to the text block and its drop shadow
```

LISTING 15.2   Continued

```
    this.MoodTextBlock.Text = currentMood;
    this.MoodTextBlockDropShadow.Text = currentMood;

    // Hide the text block and its shadow, so it doesn't reveal
    // the current mood until the Completed event is raised
    this.MoodTextBlock.Visibility = Visibility.Collapsed;
    this.MoodTextBlockDropShadow.Visibility = Visibility.Collapsed;

    // Begin the storyboards
    this.ShowColorStoryboard.Begin();
    this.ProgressStoryboard.Begin();
  }

  // Application bar handlers

  void InstructionsButton_Click(object sender, EventArgs e)
  {
    this.NavigationService.Navigate(new Uri("/InstructionsPage.xaml",
      UriKind.Relative));
  }

  void AboutMenuItem_Click(object sender, EventArgs e)
  {
    this.NavigationService.Navigate(new Uri(
      "/Shared/About/AboutPage.xaml?appName=Mood Ring", UriKind.Relative));
  }
 }
}
```

Notes:

→ Inside OnMouseLeftButtonUp, ProgressStoryboard is stopped, so the progress bar's value is restored to its pre-animation value of 0 and it is hidden (in case the storyboard is stopped in the middle). This is why the animation doesn't have (or need) an explicit To value of 0 in XAML. Rather than simply stopping ShowColorStoryboard, however, HideColorStoryboard is started to smoothly return the gradient stop's color and offset to its pre-animation values. The time of this event is remembered, because this app does a little trick of reporting the same mood when the screen is pressed fewer than three seconds after a finger is released.

→ The text block and its drop shadow are manually shown when ProgressStoryboard completes (inside ProgressStoryboard_Completed) and manually hidden inside StartMoodDetection (which is only called inside OnMouseLeftButtonDown). That way, the chosen mood remains visible after the user removes their finger from the screen.

→ MoveGradientOrigin adjusts two properties of the gradient brush—GradientOrigin and Center. When these two properties are not in-sync, interesting effects occur, such as a sharp conical shape. The finger's position is divided by the dimensions of the page so it is scaled from 0 to 1, as the gradient brush's mapping mode is RelativeToBoundingBox by default. You can change the mapping mode to Absolute with the brush's MappingMode property, but this mode doesn't work correctly in Windows Phone 7.

→ StartMoodDetection chooses a random mood (a number from 0 to 11) or reuses the previous one and then adjusts the relevant pieces of UI accordingly before starting the two relevant storyboards.

The Finished Product

Getting "imaginative" as the resulting mood

After lifting your finger, the gradient fades to black, and the mood remains visible.

The instructions page

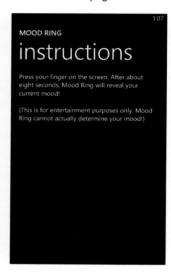

chapter 16 lessons

LOTTERY NUMBERS PICKER

Lottery Numbers Picker helps you choose potentially winning numbers to use when you buy a lottery ticket. First, you can tell it how many numbers it needs to select, what the range of the numbers should be, and whether duplicate numbers are allowed. Then, Lottery Numbers Picker selects the numbers with a fun animation that mimics a machine filled with percolating lottery balls (the kind you see on TV).

The Main Page

Lottery Numbers Picker has a main page, a settings page, and the standard about page.

The User Interface

Listing 16.1 contains the XAML for the main page.

LISTING 16.1   `MainPage.xaml`—The Main User Interface for Lottery Numbers Picker

```xml
<phone:PhoneApplicationPage
    x:Class="WindowsPhoneApp.MainPage"
    xmlns="http://schemas.microsoft.com/winfx/2006/xaml/presentation"
    xmlns:x="http://schemas.microsoft.com/winfx/2006/xaml"
    xmlns:phone="clr-namespace:Microsoft.Phone.Controls;assembly=Microsoft.Phone"
    xmlns:shell="clr-namespace:Microsoft.Phone.Shell;assembly=Microsoft.Phone"
    xmlns:local="clr-namespace:WindowsPhoneApp"
    FontFamily="{StaticResource PhoneFontFamilyNormal}"
    FontSize="{StaticResource PhoneFontSizeNormal}"
    Foreground="{StaticResource PhoneForegroundBrush}"
    SupportedOrientations="Portrait" shell:SystemTray.IsVisible="True">

  <!-- The application bar -->
  <phone:PhoneApplicationPage.ApplicationBar>
    <shell:ApplicationBar>
      <shell:ApplicationBarIconButton Text="pick"
              IconUri="/Shared/Images/appbar.play.png"
              Click="PickButton_Click"/>
      <shell:ApplicationBarIconButton Text="settings"
              IconUri="/Shared/Images/appbar.settings.png"
              Click="SettingsButton_Click"/>
      <shell:ApplicationBar.MenuItems>
        <shell:ApplicationBarMenuItem Text="about" Click="AboutMenuItem_Click"/>
      </shell:ApplicationBar.MenuItems>
    </shell:ApplicationBar>
  </phone:PhoneApplicationPage.ApplicationBar>

  <!-- Add one storyboard to the page's resource dictionary -->
  <phone:PhoneApplicationPage.Resources>
    <!-- This storyboard is applied to each chosen ball, one at a time -->
    <Storyboard x:Name="ChosenBallStoryboard"
              Completed="ChosenBallStoryboard_Completed">
      <!-- Makes the chosen ball "blow" upward from the bottom -->
      <DoubleAnimationUsingKeyFrames Storyboard.TargetProperty="(Canvas.Top)">
        <LinearDoubleKeyFrame KeyTime="0:0:0" Value="728"/>
        <EasingDoubleKeyFrame KeyTime="0:0:1.5" Value="100">
          <EasingDoubleKeyFrame.EasingFunction>
            <ElasticEase Oscillations="1" Springiness="6" EasingMode="EaseOut"/>
          </EasingDoubleKeyFrame.EasingFunction>
        </EasingDoubleKeyFrame>
      </DoubleAnimationUsingKeyFrames>
      <!-- Makes the chosen ball slide to the left, once at the top -->
      <DoubleAnimationUsingKeyFrames Storyboard.TargetProperty="(Canvas.Left)">
        <LinearDoubleKeyFrame KeyTime="0:0:0" Value="424"/>
```

LISTING 16.1   Continued

```xml
        <LinearDoubleKeyFrame KeyTime="0:0:1.2" Value="424"/>
        <EasingDoubleKeyFrame x:Name="FinalLeftKeyFrame" KeyTime="0:0:2">
          <EasingDoubleKeyFrame.EasingFunction>
            <BounceEase EasingMode="EaseOut" Bounces="1" Bounciness="8"/>
          </EasingDoubleKeyFrame.EasingFunction>
        </EasingDoubleKeyFrame>
      </DoubleAnimationUsingKeyFrames>
      <!-- Spins the chosen ball while it moves up and left, and end upright -->
      <DoubleAnimationUsingKeyFrames Storyboard.TargetProperty=
          "(local:LotteryBall.RenderTransform).(RotateTransform.Angle)">
        <LinearDoubleKeyFrame KeyTime="0:0:0" Value="0"/>
        <EasingDoubleKeyFrame KeyTime="0:0:1.2" Value="360">
          <EasingDoubleKeyFrame.EasingFunction>
            <BounceEase Bounces="10"/>
          </EasingDoubleKeyFrame.EasingFunction>
        </EasingDoubleKeyFrame>
        <EasingDoubleKeyFrame KeyTime="0:0:2" Value="0">
          <EasingDoubleKeyFrame.EasingFunction>
            <BounceEase EasingMode="EaseOut" Bounces="1" Bounciness="8"/>
          </EasingDoubleKeyFrame.EasingFunction>
        </EasingDoubleKeyFrame>
      </DoubleAnimationUsingKeyFrames>
    </Storyboard>
  </phone:PhoneApplicationPage.Resources>

  <!-- Prevent off-screen visuals from appearing during a page transition -->
  <phone:PhoneApplicationPage.Clip>
    <RectangleGeometry Rect="0,0,480,728"/>
  </phone:PhoneApplicationPage.Clip>

  <Canvas>
    <!-- Mini-header -->
    <TextBlock Text="LOTTERY NUMBERS PICKER" Margin="24,16,0,12"
               Style="{StaticResource PhoneTextTitle0Style}"/>
    <!-- Chosen balls get dynamically added to this canvas -->
    <Canvas x:Name="ChosenBallsCanvas"/>
    <!-- A canvas filled with percolating plain balls -->
    <Canvas>
      <local:LotteryBall Percolating="True" Canvas.Top="630"/>
      <local:LotteryBall Percolating="True" Canvas.Left="40" Canvas.Top="635"/>
      <local:LotteryBall Percolating="True" Canvas.Left="80" Canvas.Top="630"/>
      <local:LotteryBall Percolating="True" Canvas.Left="120" Canvas.Top="635"/>
      <local:LotteryBall Percolating="True" Canvas.Left="160" Canvas.Top="630"/>
      <local:LotteryBall Percolating="True" Canvas.Left="200" Canvas.Top="635"/>
```

LISTING 16.1   Continued

```xml
        <local:LotteryBall Percolating="True" Canvas.Left="240" Canvas.Top="630"/>
        <local:LotteryBall Percolating="True" Canvas.Left="280" Canvas.Top="635"/>
        <local:LotteryBall Percolating="True" Canvas.Left="320" Canvas.Top="630"/>
        <local:LotteryBall Percolating="True" Canvas.Left="360" Canvas.Top="635"/>
        <local:LotteryBall Percolating="True" Canvas.Left="5" Canvas.Top="650"/>
        <local:LotteryBall Percolating="True" Canvas.Left="45" Canvas.Top="655"/>
        <local:LotteryBall Percolating="True" Canvas.Left="85" Canvas.Top="650"/>
        <local:LotteryBall Percolating="True" Canvas.Left="125" Canvas.Top="655"/>
        <local:LotteryBall Percolating="True" Canvas.Left="165" Canvas.Top="650"/>
        <local:LotteryBall Percolating="True" Canvas.Left="205" Canvas.Top="655"/>
        <local:LotteryBall Percolating="True" Canvas.Left="245" Canvas.Top="650"/>
        <local:LotteryBall Percolating="True" Canvas.Left="285" Canvas.Top="655"/>
        <local:LotteryBall Percolating="True" Canvas.Left="325" Canvas.Top="650"/>
        <local:LotteryBall Percolating="True" Canvas.Left="365" Canvas.Top="655"/>
        <local:LotteryBall Percolating="True" Canvas.Top="670"/>
        <local:LotteryBall Percolating="True" Canvas.Left="40" Canvas.Top="675"/>
        <local:LotteryBall Percolating="True" Canvas.Left="80" Canvas.Top="670"/>
        <local:LotteryBall Percolating="True" Canvas.Left="120" Canvas.Top="675"/>
        <local:LotteryBall Percolating="True" Canvas.Left="160" Canvas.Top="670"/>
        <local:LotteryBall Percolating="True" Canvas.Left="200" Canvas.Top="675"/>
        <local:LotteryBall Percolating="True" Canvas.Left="240" Canvas.Top="670"/>
        <local:LotteryBall Percolating="True" Canvas.Left="280" Canvas.Top="675"/>
        <local:LotteryBall Percolating="True" Canvas.Left="320" Canvas.Top="670"/>
        <local:LotteryBall Percolating="True" Canvas.Left="360" Canvas.Top="675"/>
    </Canvas>
    <!-- The container of balls -->
    <Rectangle Fill="{StaticResource PhoneAccentBrush}" Canvas.Top="153"
            Width="421" Height="600" Opacity=".5"/>
  </Canvas>
</phone:PhoneApplicationPage>
```

Notes:

→ The single storyboard in Listing 16.1 doesn't have Storyboard.TargetName assigned.
That's because this storyboard is dynamically assigned to each new ball that reveals
a lottery number, as you'll see in the code-behind. It contains three animations: one
to move the ball upward along the right side of the screen, one to move it over to
the left, and one to spin it the whole time. The animations are given various easing
functions with various properties set to give a lifelike appearance of each ball being
blown into place.

→ Although the chosen lottery balls are dynamically added to ChosenBallsCanvas, the
percolating balls in the ball machine have been statically added to the next canvas
in hardcoded locations. Each ball is represented by a LotteryBall user control,

shown in the next section. Because their custom `Percolating` property is set to true, these balls bounce erratically.

The Code-Behind

Listing 16.2 contains the code-behind for the main page.

LISTING 16.2   `MainPage.xaml.cs`—The Code-Behind for Lottery Numbers Picker's Main Page

```
using System;
using System.Collections.Generic;
using System.Windows.Controls;
using System.Windows.Media;
using System.Windows.Media.Animation;
using Microsoft.Phone.Controls;

namespace WindowsPhoneApp
{
  public partial class MainPage : PhoneApplicationPage
  {
    Random random = new Random();
    List<int> chosenNumbers = new List<int>();
    LotteryBall mostRecentBall;
    IApplicationBarIconButton pickButton;

    public MainPage()
    {
      InitializeComponent();
      this.pickButton = this.ApplicationBar.Buttons[0]
                        as IApplicationBarIconButton;
    }

    void ShowNewBall()
    {
      // Create a new ball with the correct chosen number.
      // The RotateTransform is there so the spinning animation works.
      this.mostRecentBall = new LotteryBall {
        RenderTransform = new RotateTransform(),
        Number = this.chosenNumbers[this.ChosenBallsCanvas.Children.Count]
      };

      // Assign the storyboard to this new ball
      Storyboard.SetTarget(this.ChosenBallStoryboard, this.mostRecentBall);
```

LISTING 16.2   Continued

```csharp
    // Adjust the final horizontal position of the ball based on which one it is
    this.FinalLeftKeyFrame.Value = this.mostRecentBall.Width *
                                   this.ChosenBallsCanvas.Children.Count;

    // Add the new ball to the canvas
    this.ChosenBallsCanvas.Children.Add(this.mostRecentBall);

    // Start animating
    this.ChosenBallStoryboard.Begin();
  }

  void ChosenBallStoryboard_Completed(object sender, EventArgs e)
  {
    // The storyboard must be stopped before its
    // target is changed again inside ShowNewBall
    this.ChosenBallStoryboard.Stop();

    // Manually position the ball in the same spot where the animation left it
    Canvas.SetTop(this.mostRecentBall, 100);
    Canvas.SetLeft(this.mostRecentBall,
      this.mostRecentBall.Width * (this.ChosenBallsCanvas.Children.Count - 1));

    // Keep going until enough balls have been chosen
    if (this.ChosenBallsCanvas.Children.Count < Settings.NumBalls.Value)
      ShowNewBall();
    else
      this.pickButton.IsEnabled = true;
  }

  // Application bar handlers

  void PickButton_Click(object sender, EventArgs e)
  {
    this.pickButton.IsEnabled = false;

    this.chosenNumbers.Clear();
    this.ChosenBallsCanvas.Children.Clear();

    // Pick all the numbers
    for (int i = 0; i < Settings.NumBalls.Value; i++)
    {
      // If no duplicate numbers are allowed, keep
      // picking until the number is unique
      int num;
```

LISTING 16.2   Continued

```
      do
      {
        num = this.random.Next(Settings.MinNumber.Value,
                         Settings.MaxNumber.Value + 1);
      }
      while (!Settings.AllowDuplicates.Value &&
             this.chosenNumbers.Contains(num));

      this.chosenNumbers.Add(num);
    }

    // Sort the chosen numbers in increasing numeric order
    this.chosenNumbers.Sort();

    // Reveal the first ball
    ShowNewBall();
  }

  void SettingsButton_Click(object sender, EventArgs e)
  {
    this.NavigationService.Navigate(new Uri("/SettingsPage.xaml",
      UriKind.Relative));
  }

  void AboutMenuItem_Click(object sender, EventArgs e)
  {
    this.NavigationService.Navigate(new Uri(
      "/Shared/About/AboutPage.xaml?appName=Lottery Numbers Picker",
      UriKind.Relative));
  }
  }
}
}
```

Notes:

→ Inside `ShowNewBall`, a number is assigned to the new ball from the `chosenNumbers` list that is filled inside `PickButton_Click`. The number of children in `ChosenBallsCanvas` can be used as the list's index *before the new ball is added to the canvas* because the number is 0 for the first ball, 1 for the second ball, and so on.

→ Rather than calling `Storyboard.SetTargetName` (which effectively sets the `Storyboard.TargetName` attachable property), the code calls `Storyboard.SetTarget` to assign the target element to the storyboard. This is easier to use in C#, because you can simply pass it the instance of the element to animate even when it doesn't have a name.

→ The storyboard's `Completed` event
handler (`ChosenBallStoryboad_`
`Completed`) calls `ShowNewBall` to
repeat the creation and animation
of a new ball until the correct
number of balls have been shown.
It must stop the storyboard, rather
than having it remain in a filling
state, because otherwise the next
call to `Storyboard.SetTarget`

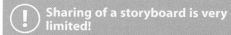

**Sharing of a storyboard is very
limited!**

Although you can reuse the same storyboard
on multiple elements, this can only be done
one element at a time. At any given time,
every animation in a storyboard can only be
assigned to one target element and one
target property. And you can only change
these values when the storyboard is stopped.

inside `ShowNewBall` would fail. You cannot change a storyboard's target unless it is
completely stopped. Because the storyboard is stopped, the just-animated ball is
manually given its ending position. Without this code, the ball would snap back to its
pre-animation position. An alternative approach would be to get the ball's position
before stopping the storyboard and then setting it to that position after stopping it.

The `LotteryBall` User Control

The `LotteryBall` user control used by the main page represents each circle with an
optional number centered on it. The XAML for this user control is shown in Listing 16.3.
The most interesting part of this XAML is that the control uses a `TransformGroup` for its
translation and rotation rather than a `CompositeTransform`. This is because a
`CompositeTransform` performs rotation *before* translation, but the functionality of this
control requires that the rotation happens *after* the translation. Therefore,
`TransformGroup` is used with its `TranslateTransform` child placed before the
`RotateTransform` child.

LISTING 16.3   `LotteryBall.xaml`—The User Interface for the `LotteryBall` User Control

```
<UserControl x:Class="WindowsPhoneApp.LotteryBall"
    xmlns="http://schemas.microsoft.com/winfx/2006/xaml/presentation"
    xmlns:x="http://schemas.microsoft.com/winfx/2006/xaml"
    FontFamily="Segoe WP Black" FontSize="{StaticResource PhoneFontSizeLarge}"
    Width="53" Height="53" RenderTransformOrigin=".5,.5">
  <UserControl.RenderTransform>
    <TransformGroup>
      <TranslateTransform x:Name="TranslateTransform"/>
      <RotateTransform x:Name="RotateTransform"/>
    </TransformGroup>
  </UserControl.RenderTransform>
  <Grid>
    <Ellipse Fill="{StaticResource PhoneForegroundBrush}"/>
    <TextBlock x:Name="NumberTextBlock" Margin="1,0,0,3"
               Foreground="{StaticResource PhoneBackgroundBrush}"
               HorizontalAlignment="Center" VerticalAlignment="Center"/>
  </Grid>
</UserControl>
```

Listing 16.4 contains the code-behind for this user control.

LISTING 16.4   LotteryBall.xaml.cs—The Code-Behind for the LotteryBall User Control

```csharp
using System;
using System.Windows;
using System.Windows.Controls;
using System.Windows.Media.Animation;

namespace WindowsPhoneApp
{
  public partial class LotteryBall : UserControl
  {
    int number;
    bool percolating;
    Storyboard percolatingStoryboard;
    DoubleAnimation percolatingAnimation;
    Random random = new Random();

    public LotteryBall()
    {
      InitializeComponent();
    }

    public int Number
    {
      get { return this.number; }
      set
      {
        this.NumberTextBlock.Text = value.ToString();
        this.number = value;
      }
    }

    public bool Percolating
    {
      get { return this.percolating; }
      set
      {
        this.percolating = value;
        if (this.percolating)
        {
          // Create a new single-animation storyboard
          this.percolatingStoryboard = new Storyboard();
          this.percolatingAnimation = new DoubleAnimation { AutoReverse = true };
          this.percolatingAnimation.EasingFunction = new QuadraticEase {
```

LISTING 16.4   Continued

```
            EasingMode = EasingMode.EaseInOut };
        this.percolatingStoryboard.Children.Add(this.percolatingAnimation);

        // Assign the storyboard to this instance's TranslateTransform and
        // animate its Y property to create a "bounce"
        Storyboard.SetTarget(this.percolatingStoryboard,
                             this.TranslateTransform);
        Storyboard.SetTargetProperty(this.percolatingStoryboard,
                             new PropertyPath("Y"));

        // When the "bounce" completes, choose new random values and start
        // it again. Repeat indefinitely.
        this.percolatingStoryboard.Completed += delegate(object s, EventArgs e)
        {
          Randomize();
          this.percolatingStoryboard.Begin();
        };

        // Choose random values related to the animation
        // and start it for the first time
        Randomize();
        percolatingStoryboard.Begin();
      }
    }
  }

  void Randomize()
  {
    // Vary the distance and duration of the bounce
    this.percolatingAnimation.To = this.random.Next(20, 60) * -1;
    this.percolatingAnimation.Duration = TimeSpan.FromMilliseconds(
                                  this.random.Next(50, 200));
    // Very the angle of the bounce
    this.RotateTransform.Angle = this.random.Next(0, 90) * -1;
  }
 }
}
```

Notes:

➔ This user control exposes two properties: Number, which displays the input number
  on top of the ellipse, and Percolating, which makes the ball bounce erratically
  when set to true. In this app, only Number is set for the chosen balls and only
  Percolating is set for the balls inside the machine.

→ The erratic bouncing of a percolating ball is enabled by a short random bounce storyboard that, when completed, is given new random values before beginning again. This storyboard and animation is created entirely in C#, which has not previously been seen in this book. The code mirrors what you would write in XAML, except that the adding of the animation to the storyboard is more explicit (with a call to `Children.Add`), and the property path used for specifying the target property is also more explicit. As with Listing 16.2, `SetTarget` is used to directly associate the storyboard with the target object.

→ Inside `Randomize`, the length of each bounce is allowed to vary from 20 to 59 pixels upward (in the negative direction), and the duration of the upward motion is allowed to vary from 50 to 199 milliseconds. To prevent each ball from bouncing straight up, the angle of the user control is randomly set to a range of 0 to –90°. Although the angle is not part of the animation, it affects the animation because it changes the meaning of translating upward. This is why it's important that the `RotateTransform` appears after the `TranslateTransform` in Listing 16.3. Although the ball is translated upward from its origin, the whole coordinate space is then rotated, causing the ball to translate at whatever angle has been chosen. (If the rotation happened first, it would have no effect on the symmetric plain circle.) The range of 0 to –90° is chosen so the balls don't ever bounce to the right and break the illusion that they are contained inside the machine.

The Settings Page

The Lottery Numbers Picker app uses the following settings defined in `Settings.cs`:

```
public static class Settings
{
  public static readonly Setting<int> NumBalls =
    new Setting<int>("NumBalls", 5);
  public static readonly Setting<int> MinNumber =
    new Setting<int>("MinNumber", 1);
  public static readonly Setting<int> MaxNumber =
    new Setting<int>("MaxNumber", 56);
  public static readonly Setting<bool> AllowDuplicates =
    new Setting<bool>("AllowDuplicates", false);
}
```

The settings page, shown in Figure 16.1, enables the user to adjust all these settings.

FIGURE 16.1   The settings page contains a check box and three sliders.

The User Interface

Listing 16.5 contains the XAML for the settings page.

LISTING 16.5   `SettingsPage.xaml`—The User Interface for Lottery Numbers Picker's Settings Page

```
<phone:PhoneApplicationPage
    x:Class="WindowsPhoneApp.SettingsPage"
    xmlns="http://schemas.microsoft.com/winfx/2006/xaml/presentation"
    xmlns:x="http://schemas.microsoft.com/winfx/2006/xaml"
    xmlns:phone="clr-namespace:Microsoft.Phone.Controls;assembly=Microsoft.Phone"
    xmlns:shell="clr-namespace:Microsoft.Phone.Shell;assembly=Microsoft.Phone"
    xmlns:local="clr-namespace:WindowsPhoneApp"
    FontFamily="{StaticResource PhoneFontFamilyNormal}"
    FontSize="{StaticResource PhoneFontSizeNormal}"
    Foreground="{StaticResource PhoneForegroundBrush}"
    SupportedOrientations="PortraitOrLandscape" shell:SystemTray.IsVisible="True">
  <Grid>
    <Grid.RowDefinitions>
      <RowDefinition Height="Auto"/>
      <RowDefinition Height="*"/>
    </Grid.RowDefinitions>
```

LISTING 16.5   Continued

```xml
<!-- The standard settings header -->
<StackPanel Grid.Row="0" Style="{StaticResource PhoneTitlePanelStyle}">
  <TextBlock Text="SETTINGS" Style="{StaticResource PhoneTextTitle0Style}"/>
  <TextBlock Text="lottery numbers picker"
             Style="{StaticResource PhoneTextTitle1Style}"/>
</StackPanel>

<ScrollViewer Grid.Row="1">
  <Grid Margin="{StaticResource PhoneMargin}">
    <Grid.RowDefinitions>
      <RowDefinition Height="Auto"/>
      <RowDefinition Height="Auto"/>
      <RowDefinition Height="Auto"/>
      <RowDefinition Height="Auto"/>
      <RowDefinition Height="Auto"/>
      <RowDefinition Height="Auto"/>
      <RowDefinition Height="Auto"/>
    </Grid.RowDefinitions>
    <!-- Allow duplicate numbers -->
    <CheckBox x:Name="AllowDuplicatesCheckBox" HorizontalAlignment="Left"
              Content="Allow duplicate numbers" local:Tilt.IsEnabled="True"/>

    <!-- Number of balls -->
    <TextBlock Grid.Row="1" Text="Number of balls" Margin="12,16,0,8"
               Foreground="{StaticResource PhoneSubtleBrush}"/>
    <TextBlock x:Name="NumBallsTextBlock" Grid.Row="1" Margin="0,16,23,0"
               HorizontalAlignment="Right"
               Text="{Binding Value, ElementName=NumBallsSlider}"/>

    <Slider x:Name="NumBallsSlider" Grid.Row="2" Minimum="1" Maximum="8"
            Tag="{Binding ElementName=NumBallsTextBlock}"
            ValueChanged="Slider_ValueChanged" />

    <!-- Smallest possible number -->
    <TextBlock Grid.Row="3" Text="Smallest possible number" Margin="12,7,0,8"
               Foreground="{StaticResource PhoneSubtleBrush}"/>
    <TextBlock x:Name="MinNumberTextBlock" Grid.Row="3" Margin="0,7,23,0"
               HorizontalAlignment="Right"
               Text="{Binding Value, ElementName=MinNumberSlider}"/>

    <Slider x:Name="MinNumberSlider" Grid.Row="4" Minimum="0" Maximum="98"
            Tag="{Binding ElementName=MinNumberTextBlock}"
            ValueChanged="Slider_ValueChanged" />
```

LISTING 16.5   Continued

```
        <!-- Largest possible number -->
        <TextBlock Grid.Row="5" Text="Largest possible number" Margin="12,7,0,8"
                   Foreground="{StaticResource PhoneSubtleBrush}"/>
        <TextBlock x:Name="MaxNumberTextBlock" Grid.Row="5" Margin="0,7,23,0"
                   HorizontalAlignment="Right"
                   Text="{Binding Value, ElementName=MaxNumberSlider}"/>

        <Slider x:Name="MaxNumberSlider" Grid.Row="6" Minimum="1" Maximum="99"
                Tag="{Binding ElementName=MaxNumberTextBlock}"
                ValueChanged="Slider_ValueChanged" />
      </Grid>
    </ScrollViewer>
  </Grid>
</phone:PhoneApplicationPage>
```

Notes:

→ `AllowDuplicatesCheckBox` is aligned to the left to prevent accidental tapping and over-tilting if the right side of the screen is tapped.

→ `NumBallsSlider` enables a range from 1 to 8, `MinNumberSlider` enables a range from 0 to 98, and `MaxNumberSlider` enables a range from 1 to 99. Each slider has a corresponding text block that binds its text to the slider's current value. This only works appropriately due to logic in code-behind in an event handler for each slider's `ValueChanged` event.

> A slider is not great for choosing a precise number, because most users don't realize that they can simply tap on the left side to decrease the value by a predictable amount (the value of its `LargeChange` property) or tap on the right side to increase the value by the same amount. Instead, users typically try to drag their finger, and getting the desired value this way ranges from hard to impossible.
>
> A *numeric spinner* control that acts like a portion of the date picker or time picker would be much better suited for precise number picking. Dave Relyea from the Silverlight team has demonstrated how to use the `LoopingSelector` control from the Silverlight for Windows Phone Toolkit in such a manner. His project is included with this chapter's source code.

The Code-Behind

Listing 16.6 contains the code-behind for the settings page.

LISTING 16.6   `SettingsPage.xaml.cs`—The Code-Behind for Lottery Numbers Picker's Settings Page

```
using System;
using System.Windows;
using System.Windows.Controls;
using System.Windows.Navigation;
using Microsoft.Phone.Controls;

namespace WindowsPhoneApp
{
  public partial class SettingsPage : PhoneApplicationPage
  {
    bool initialized = false;

    public SettingsPage()
    {
      InitializeComponent();
    }

    protected override void OnNavigatedFrom(NavigationEventArgs e)
    {
      base.OnNavigatedFrom(e);
      // Save the chosen settings
      Settings.AllowDuplicates.Value =
        this.AllowDuplicatesCheckBox.IsChecked.Value;
      Settings.NumBalls.Value = (int)this.NumBallsSlider.Value;
      Settings.MinNumber.Value = (int)this.MinNumberSlider.Value;
      Settings.MaxNumber.Value = (int)this.MaxNumberSlider.Value;
    }

    protected override void OnNavigatedTo(NavigationEventArgs e)
    {
      base.OnNavigatedTo(e);
      // Respect the saved settings
      this.AllowDuplicatesCheckBox.IsChecked = Settings.AllowDuplicates.Value;
      this.NumBallsSlider.Value = Settings.NumBalls.Value;
      this.MinNumberSlider.Value = Settings.MinNumber.Value;
      this.MaxNumberSlider.Value = Settings.MaxNumber.Value;
      this.initialized = true;
    }

    void Slider_ValueChanged(object sender,
                             RoutedPropertyChangedEventArgs<double> e)
    {
```

LISTING 16.6   Continued

```
      Slider slider = sender as Slider;

      // Round the value so it's a whole number even when the slider is dragged
      slider.Value = Math.Round(slider.Value);

      // Don't do anything until all initial values have been set
      if (this.initialized)
      {
        // Don't allow min to be higher than max
        if (this.MinNumberSlider.Value > this.MaxNumberSlider.Value)
          this.MaxNumberSlider.Value = this.MinNumberSlider.Value;

        // If the range is too small, auto-allow duplicates
        if (this.MinNumberSlider.Value >=
              this.MaxNumberSlider.Value - this.NumBallsSlider.Value)
        {
          this.AllowDuplicatesCheckBox.IsChecked = true;
          this.AllowDuplicatesCheckBox.IsEnabled = false;
        }
        else
        {
          this.AllowDuplicatesCheckBox.IsEnabled = true;
        }
      }
    }

    bool IsMatchingOrientation(PageOrientation orientation)
    {
      return ((this.Orientation & orientation) == orientation);
    }
  }
}
```

Slider_ValueChanged forces each slider's value to an integral value, because it could otherwise become fractional when the user drags the slider. (When this Math.Round assignment actually changes the value, it causes Slider_ValueChanged to be called again. When the value is already a whole number, this does not happen, which is important for preventing an infinite loop.) This method also guards against conditions that would cause the app to crash or hang, enforcing a valid relationship between the minimum number and the maximum number.

The Finished Product

Choosing six numbers from
0 to 9 with duplicates allowed
(pink accent color)

Choosing a single number from
0 to 99 (green accent color)

Under the light theme with the
brown accent color

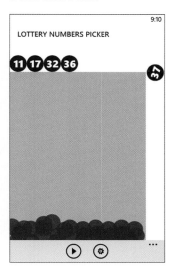

chapter 17 lessons

PICK A CARD MAGIC TRICK

The Pick a Card Magic Trick app enables you to amaze your friends with a slick magic trick that's likely to keep them guessing how it's done even after multiple performances. In this trick, you ask someone in your audience to name any card while the deck of cards is shuffling. After he or she names a card, you press "tap here when ready" to stop the shuffling, shown in Figure 17.1. You then tap the screen to flip over the card, and the card they just named is shown! You can tap the card again to start over.

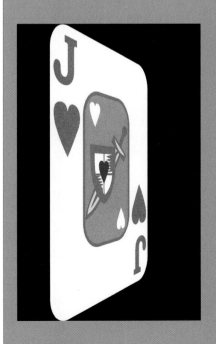

FIGURE 17.1 The deck of cards shuffles in the background while the "tap here when ready" button is showing.

The magician's secret is not revealed in this book; you'll have to run the app (or look at the full source code) that comes with this book in order to see how it is done! (My wife still can't figure it out; she thinks the app is using speech recognition in order to know what card to show.) What *is* shown is the main lesson of this chapter—using 3D transforms to flip the playing cards.

3D Transforms

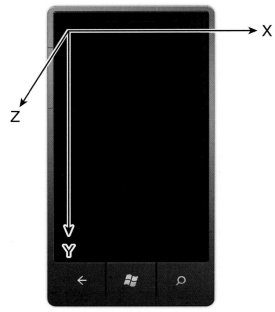

Unlike XNA, Silverlight does not provide a full 3D graphics engine. However, Silverlight enables you to perform the most common 3D effects with *perspective transforms*. These transforms escape the limitations of the 2D transforms by enabling you to rotate and translate an element in any or all of the three dimensions.

Perspective transforms are normally done with a class called `PlaneProjection`, which defines `RotationX`, `RotationY`, and `RotationZ` properties. The X and Y dimensions are defined as usual, and the Z dimension extends into and out of the screen, as illustrated in Figure 17.2. X increases from left-to-right, Y increases from top-to-bottom, and Z increases from back-to-front.

FIGURE 17.2   The three dimensions, relative to the phone screen.

Although plane projections act like render transforms, they are not assigned to an element via the `RenderTransform` property, but rather a separate property called `Projection`. The following plane projections are marked on playing card images, producing the result in Figure 17.3:

```
<phone:PhoneApplicationPage …>
  <StackPanel Orientation="Horizontal">
    <Image Source="Images/CardHA.png" Width="150" Margin="12">
      <Image.Projection>
        <PlaneProjection RotationX="55"/>
      </Image.Projection>
    </Image>
    <Image Source="Images/CardH2.png" Width="150">
      <Image.Projection>
        <PlaneProjection RotationY="55"/>
      </Image.Projection>
    </Image>
```

```
    <Image Source="Images/CardH3.png" Width="150" Margin="36">
      <Image.Projection>
        <PlaneProjection RotationZ="55"/>
      </Image.Projection>
    </Image>
    <Image Source="Images/CardH4.png" Width="150" Margin="48">
      <Image.Projection>
        <PlaneProjection RotationX="30" RotationY="30" RotationZ="30"/>
      </Image.Projection>
    </Image>
  </StackPanel>
</phone:PhoneApplicationPage>
```

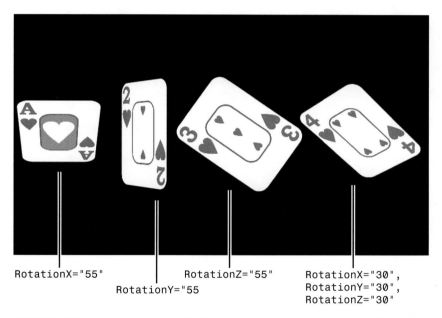

RotationX="55"   RotationZ="55"   RotationX="30",
                                                RotationY="30",
         RotationY="55   RotationZ="30"

FIGURE 17.3   Using a plane projection to rotate the card around the X, Y, and Z axes and then all three axes.

Notice that rotating around only the Z axis is like using a 2D `RotateTransform`, although the direction is reversed.

Although having permanently rotated elements might be interesting for some apps, normally plane projections are used as the target of an animation. Pick a Card leverages a plane projection for its card-flip animation, as well as its card-shuffling animation. Figure 17.4 demonstrates the 3D card flip. After the card back is rotated 90° (to be perpendicular to the screen and therefore temporarily invisible), the image is hidden to reveal the 9 of diamonds card front for the remaining 90° of the animation.

FIGURE 17.4   The 3D card flip is enabled with a plane projection and an animated property.

Much like the 2D transform classes, `PlaneProjection` defines additional properties for changing the center of rotation: CenterOfRotationX, CenterOfRotationY, and CenterOfRotationZ. The first two properties are relative to the size of the element, on a scale from 0 to 1. The `CenterOfRotationZ` property is always in terms of absolute pixels, as elements never have any size in the Z dimension to enable a relative specification. Pick a Card leverages `CenterOfRotationX` in its shuffle animation to make cards flip in from either the left edge of the screen or the right edge of the screen, as demonstrated in Figure 17.5 for the following XAML:

```
<phone:PhoneApplicationPage …>
  <Grid>
    <!-- The card on the left -->
    <Image Source="Images/CardBack.png">
      <Image.Projection>
        <PlaneProjection RotationY="62" CenterOfRotationX="0"/>
      </Image.Projection>
    </Image>
    <!-- The card on the right -->
    <Image Source="Images/CardBack.png">
      <Image.Projection>
```

```
              <PlaneProjection RotationY="-62" CenterOfRotationX="1"/>
            </Image.Projection>
          </Image>
        </Grid>
      </phone:PhoneApplicationPage>
```

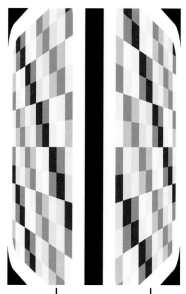

CenterOfRotationX="0"

CenterOfRotationX="1"

FIGURE 17.5 Two playing cards that would normally overlap are given different centers of rotation, so they appear to flip in from opposite edges of the screen.

PlaneProjection defines six properties for translating an element in any or all dimensions. GlobalOffsetX, GlobalOffsetY, and GlobalOffsetZ apply the translation after the rotation, so the offsets are relative to the global screen coordinates. LocalOffsetX, LocalOffsetY, and LocalOffsetZ apply the translation before the rotation, causing the rotation to be relative to the rotated coordinate space.

Matrix3DProjection

One other type of projection exists that can be assigned as to element's Projection property: Matrix3DProjection. This is a low-level construct that enables you to specify the projection as a 4x4 3D transformation matrix. This can be handy if you are already working with 3D transformation matrices, otherwise the simpler PlaneProjection is all you need to use.

The Main Page

Pick a Card's main page doesn't do much; it's a main menu that has two modes—an initial one for teaching you how to use the app, and one that hides the secrets once you have learned how to perform the trick. Both modes are shown in Figure 17.6.

The initial main menu

The main menu, after you've learned how to perform the trick

FIGURE 17.6   The main page in two different modes.

The initial main menu has three buttons: one for instructions, one for performing the trick in a special practice mode, and one for the standard about page. Once the instructions have self-destructed (which can be done by tapping a button on the instructions page), the main menu has a button for performing the trick in its normal mode, and the same about button.

The User Interface

Listing 17.1 contains the XAML for the main page.

LISTING 17.1   `MainPage.xaml`—The User Interface for Pick a Card's Main Page

```
<phone:PhoneApplicationPage
    x:Class="WindowsPhoneApp.MainPage"
    xmlns="http://schemas.microsoft.com/winfx/2006/xaml/presentation"
    xmlns:x="http://schemas.microsoft.com/winfx/2006/xaml"
    xmlns:phone="clr-namespace:Microsoft.Phone.Controls;assembly=Microsoft.Phone"
    xmlns:shell="clr-namespace:Microsoft.Phone.Shell;assembly=Microsoft.Phone"
    xmlns:local="clr-namespace:WindowsPhoneApp"
```

LISTING 17.1   Continued

```
      FontFamily="{StaticResource PhoneFontFamilyNormal}"
      FontSize="{StaticResource PhoneFontSizeNormal}"
      Foreground="{StaticResource PhoneForegroundBrush}"
      SupportedOrientations="Portrait" shell:SystemTray.IsVisible="True">
  <Grid>
    <Grid.RowDefinitions>
      <RowDefinition Height="5*"/>
      <RowDefinition Height="Auto"/>
      <RowDefinition Height="Auto"/>
      <RowDefinition Height="Auto"/>
      <RowDefinition Height="*"/>
    </Grid.RowDefinitions>
    <Rectangle Fill="{StaticResource PhoneForegroundBrush}" Margin="0,0,0,40"
               Width="158" Height="200" VerticalAlignment="Bottom">
      <Rectangle.OpacityMask>
        <ImageBrush ImageSource="Images/logo.png"/>
      </Rectangle.OpacityMask>
    </Rectangle>
    <TextBlock Text="pick a card" Margin="21,16,0,0"
               Style="{StaticResource PhoneTextTitle1Style}"/>
    <Button x:Name="InstructionsButton" Grid.Row="1"
            Content="instructions for the new magician" Height="100"
            local:Tilt.IsEnabled="True" Click="InstructionsButton_Click"/>
    <Button x:Name="BeginButton" Grid.Row="2"
            Content="practice (FOR YOUR EYES ONLY!)" Height="100"
            local:Tilt.IsEnabled="True" Click="BeginButton_Click"/>
    <Button Content="about" Grid.Row="3" Height="100" Click="AboutButton_Click"
            local:Tilt.IsEnabled="True"/>
  </Grid>
</phone:PhoneApplicationPage>
```

Notes:

→ The page is set up for its initial mode. Code-behind transforms it to the other mode.

→ Rather than using an Image element to display the logo, Listing 17.1 uses the logo.png file as an *opacity mask* for a rectangle filled with the phone theme foreground color. This is done to enable the otherwise-white image to appear black under the light theme, as shown in Figure 17.7.

> Any element can be given an opacity mask to clip it to an arbitrary shape and pattern. Any brush can be used as an opacity mask, and its alpha channel is used to determine the opacity of every pixel. In Listing 17.1, an *image brush* is used to set the opacity of each of the rectangle's pixels based on the content of logo.png.

FIGURE 17.7   The opacity mask enables the image to remain the phone theme's foreground color, regardless of the theme.

> **⚠ Opacity masks are often harmful for performance!**
>
> Using an opacity mask with an image brush is a neat trick for enabling nonvector content to respect the phone's current theme. However, be aware that their use can severely hamper the performance of your app, especially when animations are involved. Opacity masks cause animations to be rasterized on the UI thread, even if they otherwise would have been able to completely run on the compositor thread. Therefore, use extreme caution when applying an opacity mask. You can check whether it is impacting your app by examining the frame rate counter with and without the opacity mask applied.

The Code-Behind

Listing 17.2 contains the code-behind for the main page, which consists of straightforward `Click` event handlers for each button and code to morph the main menu after the instructions have been hidden. This is based off of a single setting defined in `Settings.cs`:

```
public static class Settings
{
  public static readonly Setting<bool> PracticeMode =
    new Setting<bool>("PracticeMode", true);
}
```

LISTING 17.2   `MainPage.xaml.cs`—The Code-Behind for Pick a Card's Main Page

```csharp
using System;
using System.Windows;
using System.Windows.Navigation;
using Microsoft.Phone.Controls;

namespace WindowsPhoneApp
{
  public partial class MainPage : PhoneApplicationPage
  {
    public MainPage()
    {
      InitializeComponent();
    }

    protected override void OnNavigatedTo(NavigationEventArgs e)
    {
      base.OnNavigatedTo(e);

      if (!Settings.PracticeMode.Value)
      {
        BeginButton.Content = "begin";
        InstructionsButton.Visibility = Visibility.Collapsed;
      }
    }

    void BeginButton_Click(object sender, RoutedEventArgs e)
    {
      this.NavigationService.Navigate(new Uri("/TrickPage.xaml",
        UriKind.Relative));
    }

    void InstructionsButton_Click(object sender, RoutedEventArgs e)
    {
      this.NavigationService.Navigate(new Uri("/InstructionsPage.xaml",
        UriKind.Relative));
    }

    void AboutButton_Click(object sender, RoutedEventArgs e)
    {
      this.NavigationService.Navigate(new Uri(
        "/Shared/About/AboutPage.xaml?appName=Pick a Card", UriKind.Relative));
    }
  }
}
```

The Trick Page

The "trick page" is used for both phases of the trick—the shuffling and the final card reveal. This same page is used whether the trick is running in "practice mode" or for real.

The User Interface

Listing 17.3 contains the XAML for the trick page.

LISTING 17.3   `TrickPage.xaml`—The User Interface for Pick a Card's Trick Page

```
<phone:PhoneApplicationPage
    x:Class="WindowsPhoneApp.TrickPage"
    xmlns="http://schemas.microsoft.com/winfx/2006/xaml/presentation"
    xmlns:x="http://schemas.microsoft.com/winfx/2006/xaml"
    xmlns:phone="clr-namespace:Microsoft.Phone.Controls;assembly=Microsoft.Phone"
    FontFamily="{StaticResource PhoneFontFamilyNormal}"
    FontSize="{StaticResource PhoneFontSizeNormal}"
    Foreground="{StaticResource PhoneForegroundBrush}"
    SupportedOrientations="Portrait">
  <!-- Prevent off-screen visuals from appearing during a page transition -->
  <phone:PhoneApplicationPage.Clip>
    <RectangleGeometry Rect="0,0,480,800"/>
  </phone:PhoneApplicationPage.Clip>


  <!-- Add two storyboards to the page's resource dictionary -->
  <phone:PhoneApplicationPage.Resources>
    <!-- The flip -->
    <Storyboard x:Name="FlipStoryboard"
                Storyboard.TargetName="ChosenCardProjection"
                Storyboard.TargetProperty="RotationY"
                Completed="FlipStoryboard_Completed">
      <DoubleAnimation By="90" Duration="0:0:.25"/>
    </Storyboard>
    <!-- The shuffle, with separate left and right animations -->
    <Storyboard x:Name="ShuffleStoryboard"
                Storyboard.TargetProperty="RotationY">
      <DoubleAnimation Storyboard.TargetName="NextCardLeftProjection" From="120"
                  To="0" Duration="0:0:.2" RepeatBehavior="Forever"
                  BeginTime="0:0:.1"/>
      <DoubleAnimation Storyboard.TargetName="NextCardRightProjection"
                  From="-120" To="0" Duration="0:0:.2"
                  RepeatBehavior="Forever"/>
    </Storyboard>
  </phone:PhoneApplicationPage.Resources>
```

LISTING 17.3   Continued

```xml
<Grid Background="Black">

  <!-- The card that flips over -->
  <Grid>
    <Grid.Projection>
      <PlaneProjection x:Name="ChosenCardProjection"/>
    </Grid.Projection>
    <Image x:Name="CardFrontImage" RenderTransformOrigin=".5,.5">
      <!-- Reverse, so it looks correct when flipped over -->
      <Image.RenderTransform>
        <ScaleTransform ScaleX="-1"/>
      </Image.RenderTransform>
    </Image>
    <Image x:Name="CardBackImage" Source="Images/CardBack.png"/>
  </Grid>

  <!-- More cards, for shuffling -->
  <Image x:Name="NextCardRightImage" Source="Images/CardBack.png">
    <Image.Projection>
      <PlaneProjection x:Name="NextCardRightProjection" CenterOfRotationX="1"/>
    </Image.Projection>
  </Image>
  <Image x:Name="NextCardLeftImage" Source="Images/CardBack.png">
    <Image.Projection>
      <PlaneProjection x:Name="NextCardLeftProjection" CenterOfRotationX="-1"/>
    </Image.Projection>
  </Image>

  <!-- The "tap here when ready" button and a translucent background-->
  <Grid x:Name="ReadyPanel" Background="#7000">
    <Button Background="{StaticResource PhoneBackgroundBrush}"
            Content="tap here when ready"
            VerticalAlignment="Center"/>
  </Grid>

  <!-- Images for practice mode -->
  <Image x:Name="PracticeImage1" Visibility="Collapsed"
                                 Source="Images/practice1.png"/>
  <Image x:Name="PracticeImage2" Visibility="Collapsed"
                                 Source="Images/practice2.png"/>
</Grid>
</phone:PhoneApplicationPage>
```

Notes:

→ The grid containing the chosen card has a plane projection (ChosenCardProjection) that is animated by FlipStoryboard to perform the 3D flip. This grid contains the image for the card front (chosen by code-behind) and the image for the card back. The card front image is reversed (with a ScaleTransform) so it appears correctly once the grid is flipped around. The animation only rotates the card 90°, because at that point the card back needs to be hidden so the card front can be seen for the remaining 90°. This is handled by the FlipStoryboard_Completed method in code-behind.

→ ShuffleStoryboard performs the shuffling by animating the plane projections on NextCardRightImage and NextCardLeftImage. These are given centers of rotation that make them flip from the outer edges of the screen, as seen back in Figure 17.1. The left image is given a center of −1 rather than 0 to give a more realistic, asymmetric effect.

The Code-Behind

Listing 17.4 contains the code-behind for the trick page, with 61 lines of code omitted that "magically" set the chosenSuit string to C, D, H, or S and the chosenRank string to A, 2, 3, 4, 5, 6, 7, 8, 9, 10, J, Q, or K.

LISTING 17.4   TrickPage.xaml.cs—The Code-Behind for Pick a Card's Trick Page

```
using System;
using System.Windows;
using System.Windows.Controls;
using System.Windows.Input;
using System.Windows.Media.Animation;
using System.Windows.Media.Imaging;
using System.Windows.Navigation;
using Microsoft.Phone.Controls;

namespace WindowsPhoneApp
{
  public partial class TrickPage : PhoneApplicationPage
  {
    string chosenSuit;
    string chosenRank;
    bool flipPart2;
    bool finalPhase;

    public TrickPage()
    {
      InitializeComponent();
```

LISTING 17.4   Continued

```csharp
    this.AddHandler(Page.MouseLeftButtonUpEvent,
      new MouseButtonEventHandler(MainPage_MouseLeftButtonUp),
      true /* handledEventsToo, so we get the button click */);

    InitializeTrick();
}

void InitializeTrick()
{
  if (Settings.PracticeMode.Value)
    this.PracticeImage1.Visibility = Visibility.Visible;

  // Reset everything
  this.ReadyPanel.Visibility = Visibility.Visible;
  this.CardBackImage.Visibility = Visibility.Visible;
  this.NextCardLeftImage.Visibility = Visibility.Visible;
  this.NextCardRightImage.Visibility = Visibility.Visible;
  this.CardFrontImage.Source = null;
  this.flipPart2 = false;
  this.ChosenCardProjection.RotationY = 0;

  // Start shuffling
  this.ShuffleStoryboard.Begin();
}

void MainPage_MouseLeftButtonUp(object sender, MouseButtonEventArgs e)
{
  if (this.ReadyPanel.Visibility == Visibility.Visible)
  {
    // This is a tap on the "tap here when ready" button
    if (Settings.PracticeMode.Value)
    {
      this.PracticeImage1.Visibility = Visibility.Collapsed;
      this.PracticeImage2.Visibility = Visibility.Visible;
    }

    // Hide ReadyPanel and the shuffling deck,
    // leaving the single card back exposed
    this.ReadyPanel.Visibility = Visibility.Collapsed;
    this.NextCardLeftImage.Visibility = Visibility.Collapsed;
    this.NextCardRightImage.Visibility = Visibility.Collapsed;
    this.ShuffleStoryboard.Stop();
    this.finalPhase = true;
  }
```

LISTING 17.4   Continued

```
    else if (this.finalPhase)
    {
      // This is a tap on the card back to flip it over
      if (Settings.PracticeMode.Value)
        this.PracticeImage2.Visibility = Visibility.Collapsed;

      // Show the chosen card image
      this.CardFrontImage.Source = new BitmapImage(new Uri("Images/Card" +
        this.chosenSuit + this.chosenRank + ".png", UriKind.Relative));

      // Perform the first 90° of the flip
      this.FlipStoryboard.Begin();

      this.finalPhase = false;
    }
    else if (this.FlipStoryboard.GetCurrentState() != ClockState.Active)
    {
      // Do it again. (Don't allow this until the flip animation is finished.)
      InitializeTrick();
    }
  }

  void FlipStoryboard_Completed(object sender, EventArgs e)
  {
    if (!this.flipPart2)
    {
      // The card is now perpendicular to the screen. It's time to hide the
      // back and run the animation again so the remaining 90° shows the front
      this.CardBackImage.Visibility = Visibility.Collapsed;
      this.flipPart2 = true;
      this.FlipStoryboard.Begin();
    }
  }

  #region Magician's Secret
  …
  #endregion
  }
}
```

Notes:

➔ A single handler—MainPage_MouseLeftButtonUp—handles the first tap on the "tap here when ready" button, which can actually be anywhere on the screen, the tap on the card back to flip it over, and the tap on the card front to start the trick again. The handler is attached with `true` passed for `handledEventsToo`, so the event is received when the button is tapped.

→ When the card back is tapped (indicated by `finalPhase` being `true` inside `MainPage_MouseLeftButtonUp`), the card front image is set to one of 52 images included in the project. These 52 images are shown in Figure 17.8.

→ Inside `FlipStoryboard_Completed`, the card back is hidden and `FlipStoryboad` is run again to complete the 180° flip. This works because the animation is marked with `By="90"`, so the first run takes it from 0° to 90°, and the second run takes it from 90° to 180°. The card back must be manually hidden because flipping elements over in 3D does not change their Z-order. In other words, unlike in the physical world, the card back remains on top of the card front regardless of the angle of rotation.

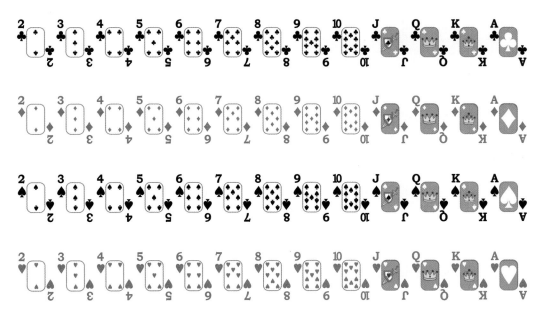

FIGURE 17.8 The 52 card images cover every choice except a Joker.

The Instructions Page

The instructions page, shown in Figure 17.9, contains a button that makes them self-destruct (turning off practice mode and changing the main menu). Once this is done, the instructions never come back unless the app is uninstalled and reinstalled. This is done to prevent nosy audience members from figuring out the secret to the trick. The XAML for this page isn't very interesting (other than the fact that its text reveals the secret to the trick), but Listing 17.5 shows the code-behind, which implements the self-destructing behavior.

The top of the instructions page, with the self-destruct button

A warning to guard against accidental button taps

FIGURE 17.9   The instructions page contains a button that permanently hides the instructions and turns off practice mode.

LISTING 17.5   `InstructionsPage.xaml.cs`—The Code-Behind for Pick a Card's Instructions Page

```
using System.Windows;
using Microsoft.Phone.Controls;

namespace WindowsPhoneApp
{
  public partial class InstructionsPage : PhoneApplicationPage
  {
    public InstructionsPage()
    {
      InitializeComponent();
    }

    void SelfDestructButton_Click(object sender, RoutedEventArgs e)
    {
      if (MessageBox.Show("To protect the secret of this trick, these " +
          "instructions will disappear forever once you turn off practice mode." +
          "  The only way to get them back is to uninstall then reinstall this " +
          "app.  Are you ready to destroy the instructions?",
          "These instructions will self-destruct!", MessageBoxButton.OKCancel)
          == MessageBoxResult.OK)
      {
```

LISTING 17.5   Continued

```
        Settings.PracticeMode.Value = false;
        if (this.NavigationService.CanGoBack)
          this.NavigationService.GoBack();
      }
    }
  }
}
```

To make the instructions self-destruct, Listing 17.5 changes the `PracticeMode` persisted setting to `false` and then navigates back to the main page which hides the instructions button. This setting never changes unless the app is uninstalled because it doesn't provide the user any way to change it back. Because uninstalling an app removes anything it puts in isolated storage, however, reinstalling it restores `PracticeMode`'s default value of `true`.

> To implement a behavior that only happens the first time an app is run (or until the user makes some action to turn it off), simply base it on a value persisted in isolated storage. The `Setting` object used throughout this book internally uses isolated storage to preserve each value until it is either changed by code or deleted by the app being uninstalled.

The Finished Product

Your card is…the Ace of Hearts!   Your card is…the Queen of Clubs!   Your card is…the 10 of Diamonds!

chapter 18

COCKTAILS

At a recent party, I walked up to the bar and asked for a Roy Rogers (Coke with grenadine and a maraschino cherry). The bartender said "Sure," had a quick conversation with the other bartender, hesitated for a moment, whipped out his iPhone, and then swiped around for a bit before finally asking me, "What's a Roy Rogers?"

If this bartender had instead used a Windows phone and this chapter's Cocktails app, he would have found his answer without the embarrassment of admitting his ignorance. (Although ordering a Roy Rodgers was just as embarrassing for me!)

The Cocktails app contains an alphabetized list of over 1,100 cocktails (including nonalcoholic drinks, such as Roy Rodgers). Each one links to a recipe (and other relevant information) from About.com. A list this long requires something more than a simple list box. Therefore, Cocktails uses a *quick jump grid*, the alphabetized list with tiles that jump to each letter that is featured in the People and Music + Videos hubs.

QuickJumpGrid **Versus** LongListSelector

The Silverlight for Windows Phone Toolkit includes a control called LongListSelector that can be used as a quick jump grid. At its core, it's a list box with performance optimizations for large lists of items, complete with smoother scrolling, UI virtualization, *and* data virtualization. In addition, it supports arbitrary grouping of its items with headers that can be tapped to bring up the list of groups. The groups can be anything, as demonstrated in Figure 18.1.

The Cocktails app, however, does not use LongListSelector. Instead, it uses a simpler but more limited user control created in this chapter called QuickJumpGrid. QuickJumpGrid isn't nearly as flexible as LongListSelector, and it only supports alphabetic categorization. If the alphabetic categorization is what you want, however, QuickJumpGrid is simpler to use because you only need to give it a flat list of key/value pairs. (LongListSelector is much more complicated to fill with data, although the Silverlight for Windows Phone Toolkit includes a good sample.) QuickJumpGrid also mimics the behavior of the quick jump grid used by the built-in apps more faithfully with appropriate animations and a grid that doesn't needlessly scroll.

A large portion of this chapter is dedicated to showing how to the

FIGURE 18.1 A hypothetical version of Cocktails that uses LongListSelector to group drinks by descriptive categories.

 Surprisingly, Windows Phone design guidelines dictate that category labels in a quick jump grid should be capitalized unless they are single letters.

QuickJumpGrid control is built, as it helps highlight some of this chapter's lessons. It also leverages the animation features discussed in the previous few chapters.

The Main Page

The Cocktails app's main page, whose XAML is shown in Listing 18.1, contains just the status bar, the app name, and a quick jump grid filled with the list of cocktails. The quick jump grid starts out looking like an alphabetized list box with a header tile for each unique starting letter (and a # for all digits), as seen in Figure 18.2.

Tapping any of the letter tiles (or # tile) animates in the grid shown at the beginning of this chapter. Tapping any of the tiles on this grid jumps to that part of the list. Figure 18.3 shows the main page after the user brings up the grid and taps on the letter v.

FIGURE 18.2   The main page showcases the quick jump grid.

FIGURE 18.3   Jumping to the letter v with the quick jump grid avoids scrolling through over 1,000 previous cocktails!

The User Interface

The XAML for the main page is shown in Listing 18.1.

LISTING 18.1   `MainPage.xaml`—The User Interface for the Cocktails App's Main Page

```
<phone:PhoneApplicationPage
    x:Class="WindowsPhoneApp.MainPage"
    xmlns="http://schemas.microsoft.com/winfx/2006/xaml/presentation"
    xmlns:x="http://schemas.microsoft.com/winfx/2006/xaml"
    xmlns:phone="clr-namespace:Microsoft.Phone.Controls;assembly=Microsoft.Phone"
    xmlns:shell="clr-namespace:Microsoft.Phone.Shell;assembly=Microsoft.Phone"
    xmlns:local="clr-namespace:WindowsPhoneApp"
    x:Name="Page" Loaded="MainPage_Loaded" SupportedOrientations="Portrait"
    shell:SystemTray.IsVisible="True">
  <Grid>
    <Grid.RowDefinitions>
      <RowDefinition Height="Auto"/>
      <RowDefinition Height="*"/>
    </Grid.RowDefinitions>
    <!-- Mini-header -->
    <TextBlock Text="COCKTAILS" Margin="24,16,0,12"
               Style="{StaticResource PhoneTextTitle0Style}"/>
    <!-- Quick jump grid -->
    <local:QuickJumpGrid x:Name="QuickJumpGrid" Grid.Row="1" Margin="24,0,0,0"
                         Page="{Binding ElementName=Page}"
                         ItemSelected="QuickJumpGrid_ItemSelected"/>
  </Grid>
</phone:PhoneApplicationPage>
```

The `QuickJumpGrid` user control must be given an instance of the host page via its `Page` property, so it can automatically hide the status bar and application bar (if the page uses them) when showing the 4x7 grid of alphabet tiles shown at the beginning of this chapter. Otherwise, these would get in the way, as no elements can ever appear on top of them. This page uses data binding to set `Page`.

The Code-Behind

Listing 18.2 contains the code-behind for the main page, which handles the interaction with the `QuickJumpGrid` user control.

LISTING 18.2   `MainPage.xaml.cs`—The Code-Behind for the Cocktails App's Main Page

```
using System;
using System.Collections.Generic;
using System.Net;
using System.Windows;
```

LISTING 18.2   Continued

```
using System.Windows.Controls;
using Microsoft.Phone.Controls;

namespace WindowsPhoneApp
{
  public partial class MainPage : PhoneApplicationPage
  {
    bool listInitialized = false;

    public MainPage()
    {
      InitializeComponent();

      // Add no more than 10 items so the initial UI comes up quickly
      for (int i = 0; i < 10 && i < Data.Cocktails.Length; i++)
        this.QuickJumpGrid.Add(new KeyValuePair<string, object>(
          Data.Cocktails[i].Name, Data.Cocktails[i]));

      // Refresh the list
      this.QuickJumpGrid.Update();
    }

    void MainPage_Loaded(object sender, RoutedEventArgs e)
    {
      if (!this.listInitialized)
      {
        // Now add the remaining items
        for (int i = 10; i < Data.Cocktails.Length; i++)
          this.QuickJumpGrid.Add(new KeyValuePair<string, object>(
            Data.Cocktails[i].Name, Data.Cocktails[i]));

        // Refresh the list
        this.QuickJumpGrid.Update();

        // Only do this once
        this.listInitialized = true;
      }
    }

    void QuickJumpGrid_ItemSelected(object sender, SelectionChangedEventArgs e)
    {
      if (e.AddedItems.Count == 0)
        return;
```

LISTING 18.2   Continued

```
    // Each item in the list is a key/value pair, where each value is a Cocktail
    KeyValuePair<string, object> item =
      (KeyValuePair<string, object>)e.AddedItems[0];

    // Show details for the chosen item
    this.NavigationService.Navigate(new Uri("/DetailsPage.xaml?url=" +
      HttpUtility.UrlEncode((item.Value as Cocktail).Url.AbsoluteUri),
      UriKind.Relative));
  }
 }
}
```

Notes:

→ `QuickJumpGrid` exposes a few simple methods. The ones used here are `Add` and `Update`. These methods are a bit unorthodox for a Silverlight control, but it keeps the code in this chapter simple and performant. `LongListSelector` exposes a more flexible set of APIs.

→ `Add` adds an item to the list as a key/value pair. You cannot specify where to add the item in the list, as it is automatically alphabetized. The `string` key is used for sorting the list (and deciding which letter bucket each item belongs to) and the `object` value can be anything. This app uses `Cocktail` objects defined as follows in `Cocktail.cs`:

```
    public class Cocktail
    {
      public string Name { get; private set; }
      public Uri Url { get; private set; }

      public Cocktail(string name, Uri url)
      {
        this.Name = name;
        this.Url = url;
      }

      public override string ToString()
      {
        return this.Name;
      }
    }
```

The list of over 1,100 `Cocktail` objects is defined as an array in `Data.cs`:

```
public class Data
{
```

```
public static readonly Cocktail[] Cocktails = {
  new Cocktail("#26 Cocktail", new Uri(
    "http://cocktails.about.com/od/cocktailrecipes/r/number_26cktl.htm")),
  new Cocktail("50-50", new Uri(
    "http://cocktails.about.com/od/cocktailrecipes/r/50_50_mrtni.htm")),
  …
  };
}
```

→ Update refreshes the control with its current set of data. Until you call Update, any Add/Remove calls have no visual effect. This is done for performance reasons. In Listing 15.1, Update is called after adding the first 10 items, to make the list appear quickly. It is then called only one more time, after the entire list has been populated. This is all done on the UI thread, as the underlying collection is not thread-safe. However, populating the list is fairly fast because the visuals aren't updated until the end.

→ When an item is selected, this page navigates to the details page, passing along the URL of the details page from About.com. The code calls HttpUtility.UrlEncode to ensure that the About.com URL can be passed as a query parameter to the DetailsPage.xaml URL without its colon and slashes interfering with URL parsing done by the system.

The Details Page

The details page, shown in Figure 18.4 for the Jack-o-Lantern Punch drink, simply hosts a WebBrowser control to show the relevant page from About.com inline. Its XAML is shown in Listing 18.3, and its code-behind is shown in Listing 18.4.

FIGURE 18.4 The details for any cocktail is shown directly from About.com, thanks to the WebBrowser control.

LISTING 18.3 DetailsPage.xaml—The User Interface for the Cocktails App's Details Page

```
<phone:PhoneApplicationPage
    x:Class="WindowsPhoneApp.DetailsPage"
    xmlns="http://schemas.microsoft.com/winfx/2006/xaml/presentation"
    xmlns:x="http://schemas.microsoft.com/winfx/2006/xaml"
    xmlns:phone="clr-namespace:Microsoft.Phone.Controls;assembly=Microsoft.Phone"
```

LISTING 18.3   Continued

```
    xmlns:toolkit="clr-namespace:Microsoft.Phone.Controls;
➥assembly=Microsoft.Phone.Controls.Toolkit"
    SupportedOrientations="PortraitOrLandscape" Background="White">
  <Grid>
    <phone:WebBrowser x:Name="WebBrowser" Navigating="WebBrowser_Navigating"
                      Navigated="WebBrowser_Navigated"/>
    <toolkit:PerformanceProgressBar x:Name="ProgressBar" VerticalAlignment="Top"/>
  </Grid>
</phone:PhoneApplicationPage>
```

LISTING 18.4   `DetailsPage.xaml.cs`—The Code-Behind for the Cocktails App's Details Page

```
using System;
using System.Windows;
using System.Windows.Navigation;
using Microsoft.Phone.Controls;

namespace WindowsPhoneApp
{
  public partial class DetailsPage : PhoneApplicationPage
  {
    public DetailsPage()
    {
      InitializeComponent();
    }

    protected override void OnNavigatedTo(NavigationEventArgs e)
    {
      base.OnNavigatedTo(e);

      // Navigate to the correct details page
      this.WebBrowser.Source = new Uri(this.NavigationContext.QueryString["url"]);
    }

    void WebBrowser_Navigating(object sender, NavigatingEventArgs e)
    {
      this.ProgressBar.Visibility = Visibility.Visible;
      // Avoid a performance problem by only making it indeterminate when needed
      this.ProgressBar.IsIndeterminate = false;
    }

    void WebBrowser_Navigated(object sender, NavigationEventArgs e)
    {
      // Avoid a performance problem by only making it indeterminate when needed
      this.ProgressBar.IsIndeterminate = true;
```

LISTING 18.4   Continued

```
      this.ProgressBar.Visibility = Visibility.Collapsed;
    }
  }
}
```

Notes:

→ In Listing 18.3, the page is given an explicit white background to prevent a jarring experience when the web browser is shown (which is white until a page loads).

→ The web browser's `Source` property is set to the URL passed via the query string, causing the appropriate navigation. Note that `HttpUtility.UrlDecode` did not need to be called, because the query string is automatically decoded when retrieved via `NavigationContext.QueryString`.

→ Because all the state for this page is passed via the query string (just the relevant URL), this page behaves appropriately if deactivated and then reactivated. Because the query string is preserved on reactivation, the page is still populated correctly.

→ A progress bar is shown while the page is still loading. This applies not only to the initial navigation, but any navigation caused by the user clicking links inside the web page.

→ Instead of using the `ProgressBar` control that ships with Silverlight, this page uses a **Performance**`ProgressBar` control that ships with the Silverlight for Windows Phone Toolkit. This fixes some performance problems with the built-in `ProgressBar` control when its indeterminate (dancing dots) mode is used. Whether you use `ProgressBar` or `PerformanceProgressBar`, you should still only set `IsIndeterminate` to true when the progress bar is shown to avoid performance problems.

 Indeterminate progress bars continue to do a lot of work on the UI thread, even when hidden!

When a standard progress bar's `IsIndeterminate` property is set to true, it performs a complicated animation that unfortunately involves significant work on the UI thread. What comes as a shock to most is that this work still happens even when the progress bar's `Visibility` is set to `Collapsed`!

The easiest workaround for this is to set `IsIndeterminate` to false whenever you set `Visibility` to `Collapsed`, and temporarily set it to true when `Visibility` is `Visible`. In addition, if you use `PerformanceProgressBar` from the Silverlight for Windows Phone Toolkit instead of `ProgressBar`, the animation runs on the compositor thread rather than the UI thread.

(!) Some websites are not yet formatted appropriately for Windows Phone 7!

At the time of writing, sites such as About.com present their desktop-formatted pages to a Windows phone rather than their mobile-formatted pages. It may take a while for many websites to recognize the user agent string passed by Internet Explorer on Windows Phone 7, because the platform is so new.

The `QuickJumpGrid` User Control

The `QuickJumpGrid` user control, used in Listing 18.1, internally uses two additional user controls covered later in this chapter.

The User Interface

Listing 18.5 contains the XAML for the `QuickJumpGrid` user control used by the main page.

LISTING 18.5   `QuickJumpGrid.xaml`—The User Interface for the Quick Jump Grid

```
<UserControl x:Class="WindowsPhoneApp.QuickJumpGrid"
    xmlns="http://schemas.microsoft.com/winfx/2006/xaml/presentation"
    xmlns:x="http://schemas.microsoft.com/winfx/2006/xaml"
    xmlns:local="clr-namespace:WindowsPhoneApp">
  <!-- Add two items to the user control's resource dictionary -->
  <UserControl.Resources>
    <!-- An empty storyboard used as a timer from code-behind -->
    <Storyboard x:Name="DelayedPopupCloseStoryboard" Duration="0:0:.15"
            Completed="DelayedPopupCloseStoryboard_Completed"/>

    <!-- A frame-rooted popup shown by code-behind -->
    <Popup x:Name="Popup" Width="480" Height="800">
      <Canvas Width="480" Height="800">
        <Rectangle Fill="{StaticResource PhoneBackgroundBrush}" Opacity=".68"
                Width="480" Height="800"/>
        <Canvas x:Name="QuickJumpTiles"
                MouseLeftButtonUp="QuickJumpTiles_MouseLeftButtonUp">
          <local:QuickJumpTile Text="#" Canvas.Left="24" Canvas.Top="24"/>
          <local:QuickJumpTile Text="a" Canvas.Left="135" Canvas.Top="24"/>
          <local:QuickJumpTile Text="b" Canvas.Left="246" Canvas.Top="24"/>
          <local:QuickJumpTile Text="c" Canvas.Left="357" Canvas.Top="24"/>
          <local:QuickJumpTile Text="d" Canvas.Left="24" Canvas.Top="135"/>
          <local:QuickJumpTile Text="e" Canvas.Left="135" Canvas.Top="135"/>
          <local:QuickJumpTile Text="f" Canvas.Left="246" Canvas.Top="135"/>
          <local:QuickJumpTile Text="g" Canvas.Left="357" Canvas.Top="135"/>
          <local:QuickJumpTile Text="h" Canvas.Left="24" Canvas.Top="246"/>
          <local:QuickJumpTile Text="i" Canvas.Left="135" Canvas.Top="246"/>
          <local:QuickJumpTile Text="j" Canvas.Left="246" Canvas.Top="246"/>
          <local:QuickJumpTile Text="k" Canvas.Left="357" Canvas.Top="246"/>
          <local:QuickJumpTile Text="l" Canvas.Left="24" Canvas.Top="357"/>
          <local:QuickJumpTile Text="m" Canvas.Left="135" Canvas.Top="357"/>
          <local:QuickJumpTile Text="n" Canvas.Left="246" Canvas.Top="357"/>
          <local:QuickJumpTile Text="o" Canvas.Left="357" Canvas.Top="357"/>
          <local:QuickJumpTile Text="p" Canvas.Left="24" Canvas.Top="468"/>
          <local:QuickJumpTile Text="q" Canvas.Left="135" Canvas.Top="468"/>
```

LISTING 18.5   Continued

```
            <local:QuickJumpTile Text="r" Canvas.Left="246" Canvas.Top="468"/>
            <local:QuickJumpTile Text="s" Canvas.Left="357" Canvas.Top="468"/>
            <local:QuickJumpTile Text="t" Canvas.Left="24" Canvas.Top="579"/>
            <local:QuickJumpTile Text="u" Canvas.Left="135" Canvas.Top="579"/>
            <local:QuickJumpTile Text="v" Canvas.Left="246" Canvas.Top="579"/>
            <local:QuickJumpTile Text="w" Canvas.Left="357" Canvas.Top="579"/>
            <local:QuickJumpTile Text="x" Canvas.Left="24" Canvas.Top="690"/>
            <local:QuickJumpTile Text="y" Canvas.Left="135" Canvas.Top="690"/>
            <local:QuickJumpTile Text="z" Canvas.Left="246" Canvas.Top="690"/>
          </Canvas>
        </Canvas>
      </Popup>
  </UserControl.Resources>

  <!-- The list box -->
  <ListBox x:Name="ListBox" SelectionChanged="ListBox_SelectionChanged">
    <ListBox.ItemTemplate>
      <DataTemplate>
        <local:QuickJumpItem Margin="0,6" KeyValuePair="{Binding}"
                            local:Tilt.IsEnabled="True"/>
      </DataTemplate>
    </ListBox.ItemTemplate>
  </ListBox>
</UserControl>
```

Notes:

→ There are two main pieces to the quick jump grid—a list box to contain the alpha-betized items, and a canvas that contains the 27 tiles in a grid formation. The list box makes use of a `QuickJumpItem` user control to render each item (the key/value pairs seen in Listing 18.2) and the canvas uses 27 instances of a `QuickJumpTile` user control. These controls are implemented in the last two sections of this chapter.

→ This control uses a frame-rooted popup, defined as a resource, to contain the canvas with 27 tiles. A popup is used so it is able to cover the entire screen regardless of where the `QuickJumpGrid` is placed on the page. (In this app's main page, for example, the top of the `QuickJumpGrid` is 91 pixels down the page due to the status bar and "COCKTAILS" header, but the popup is able to cover everything.) Recall from Chapter 11, "XAML Editor," that if the popup where placed as a child of one of this control's elements, it would have been placed at its top-left corner, rather than the top-left corner of the screen.

→ The empty storyboard is used from code-behind as a handy way to do delayed work. Once `DelayedPopupCloseStoryboard.Begin` is called, `DelayedPopupCloseStoryboard_Completed` will be called .15 seconds later (the duration of the storyboard).

The Code-Behind

Listing 18.6 contains the code-behind for the `QuickJumpGrid` user control.

LISTING 18.6   `QuickJumpGrid.xaml.cs`—The Code-Behind for the Quick Jump Grid

```
using System;
using System.Collections.Generic;
using System.ComponentModel;
using System.Windows;
using System.Windows.Controls;
using System.Windows.Controls.Primitives;
using System.Windows.Input;
using Microsoft.Phone.Controls;
using Microsoft.Phone.Shell;

namespace WindowsPhoneApp
{
  public partial class QuickJumpGrid : UserControl
  {
    List<KeyValuePair<string, object>> items =
      new List<KeyValuePair<string, object>>();
    bool isPageStatusBarVisible;
    bool isPageAppBarVisible;

    public event SelectionChangedEventHandler ItemSelected;

    public QuickJumpGrid()
    {
      InitializeComponent();
      //
      // HACK: Transfer the popup's content to a new popup to avoid a bug
      //
      // Remove the popup's content
      UIElement child = this.Popup.Child;
      this.Popup.Child = null;
      // Create a new popup with the same content
      Popup p = new Popup { Child = child };
      // Make this the new popup member
      this.Popup = p;
    }

    // Add the item to the sorted list, using the key for sorting
    public void Add(KeyValuePair<string, object> item)
    {
      // Find where to insert it
      int i = 0;
```

LISTING 18.6   Continued

```csharp
    while (i < this.items.Count && string.Compare(this.items[i].Key,
      item.Key, StringComparison.InvariantCultureIgnoreCase) <= 0)
      i++;

    this.items.Insert(i, item);
}

// Remove the items from the list
public void Remove(KeyValuePair<string, object> item)
{
  this.items.Remove(item);
}

// Refresh the list box with the current collection of items
public void Update()
{
  this.ListBox.ItemsSource = GetAllItems();
}

// Return the list of items, with header items injected
// in the appropriate spots
IEnumerable<KeyValuePair<string, object>> GetAllItems()
{
  char currentBucket = '\0';
  foreach (KeyValuePair<string, object> item in this.items)
  {
    char bucket = CharHelper.GetBucket(item.Key);
    if (bucket != currentBucket)
    {
      // This is a new bucket, so return the header item.
      // The key is the letter (or #) and the value is null.
      yield return new KeyValuePair<string, object>(bucket.ToString(), null);
      currentBucket = bucket;
    }

    // Return the real item
    yield return item;
  }
}

// Return a list of only header items
IEnumerable<KeyValuePair<string, object>> GetUsedLetterItems()
{
  char currentBucket = '\0';
```

LISTING 18.6   Continued

```csharp
    foreach (KeyValuePair<string, object> item in this.items)
    {
      char bucket = CharHelper.GetBucket(item.Key);
      if (bucket != currentBucket)
      {
        // This is a new bucket, so return the header item.
        // The key is the letter (or #) and the value is null.
        yield return new KeyValuePair<string, object>(bucket.ToString(), null);
        currentBucket = bucket;
      }
    }
  }

  // A Page dependency property
  public static readonly DependencyProperty PageProperty =
      DependencyProperty.Register("Page",                 // name
        typeof(PhoneApplicationPage),                      // property type
        typeof(QuickJumpGrid),                             // owner type
        new PropertyMetadata(
          null,                                            // default value
          new PropertyChangedCallback(OnPageChanged) // callback
        )
      );

  // A wrapper .NET property for the dependency property
  public PhoneApplicationPage Page
  {
    get { return (PhoneApplicationPage)GetValue(PageProperty); }
    set { SetValue(PageProperty, value); }
  }

  // When Page is set, intercept presses on the hardware Back button
  static void OnPageChanged(DependencyObject d,
                            DependencyPropertyChangedEventArgs e)
  {
    QuickJumpGrid quickJumpGrid = d as QuickJumpGrid;

    if (e.OldValue != null)
      (e.OldValue as PhoneApplicationPage).BackKeyPress -=
        quickJumpGrid.Page_BackKeyPress;

    quickJumpGrid.Page.BackKeyPress += quickJumpGrid.Page_BackKeyPress;
  }
```

LISTING 18.6   Continued

```
void Page_BackKeyPress(object sender, CancelEventArgs e)
{
  // If the popup is open, close it rather than navigating away from the page
  if (this.Popup.IsOpen)
  {
    ClosePopup();
    e.Cancel = true;
  }
}

void ClosePopup()
{
  // Animate each tile out
  foreach (QuickJumpTile tile in this.QuickJumpTiles.Children)
    tile.FlipOut();

  // Close the popup after the tiles have a chance to animate out
  this.DelayedPopupCloseStoryboard.Begin();
}

// Handle item selection from the list box
void ListBox_SelectionChanged(object sender, SelectionChangedEventArgs e)
{
  // Make sure the consumer has set the Page property
  if (this.Page == null)
    throw new InvalidOperationException(
      "The Page property must be set to the host page.");

  if (e.AddedItems.Count != 1)
    return;

  KeyValuePair<string, object> item =
    (KeyValuePair<string, object>)e.AddedItems[0];

  if (item.Value != null)
  {
    // This is a normal item, so raise the event to consumers of this control
    if (this.ItemSelected != null)
      this.ItemSelected(sender, e);
  }
  else
  {
    // This is a header, so show the popup
    foreach (QuickJumpTile tile in this.QuickJumpTiles.Children)
```

LISTING 18.6   Continued

```
    {
      // Start by "disabling" each tile
      tile.HasItems = false;
      // Animate it in
      tile.FlipIn();
    }
    // "Enable" the tiles that actually have items
    foreach (var pair in GetUsedLetterItems())
    {
      char bucket = CharHelper.GetBucket(pair.Key);
      QuickJumpTile tile;
      if (pair.Key == "#")
        tile = this.QuickJumpTiles.Children[0] as QuickJumpTile;
      else
        tile = this.QuickJumpTiles.Children[pair.Key[0] - 'a' + 1]
                  as QuickJumpTile;

      tile.HasItems = true;
      tile.Tag = pair; // Also store the item from the list for later
    }

    // Remember the current visibility of the status bar & application bar
    this.isPageStatusBarVisible = SystemTray.GetIsVisible(this.Page);
    this.isPageAppBarVisible = this.Page.ApplicationBar != null ?
                               this.Page.ApplicationBar.IsVisible : false;

    // Ensure that both bars are hidden, so they don't overlap the popup
    SystemTray.SetIsVisible(this.Page, false);
    if (this.Page.ApplicationBar != null)
      this.Page.ApplicationBar.IsVisible = false;

    // Now open the popup
    this.Popup.IsOpen = true;
  }
  // Clear selection so repeated taps work
  this.ListBox.SelectedIndex = -1;
}

// Handle taps on tiles in the popup
void QuickJumpTiles_MouseLeftButtonUp(object sender, MouseButtonEventArgs e)
{
  QuickJumpTile tile = e.OriginalSource as QuickJumpTile;
  if (tile != null && tile.HasItems)
  {
```

LISTING 18.6   Continued

```csharp
      // Retrieve the header item from the list
      KeyValuePair<string, object> header =
        (KeyValuePair<string, object>)tile.Tag;

      // Scroll to the end, THEN scroll the tile into view,
      // so the tile is at the top of the page rather than the bottom

      // Prevent flicker from seeing the end
      this.ListBox.Opacity = 0;
      // Scroll to the end
      this.ListBox.ScrollIntoView(
        this.ListBox.Items[this.ListBox.Items.Count - 1]);
      this.Dispatcher.BeginInvoke(delegate()
      {
        // Now scroll to the chosen header
        this.ListBox.ScrollIntoView(header);
        this.ListBox.Opacity = 1; // Restore
        ClosePopup();
      });
    }
  }

  void DelayedPopupCloseStoryboard_Completed(object sender, EventArgs e)
  {
    this.Popup.IsOpen = false;
    // Restore the visibility of the status bar and application bar
    SystemTray.SetIsVisible(this.Page, this.isPageStatusBarVisible);
    if (this.Page.ApplicationBar != null)
      this.Page.ApplicationBar.IsVisible = this.isPageAppBarVisible;
  }
 }
}
```

Notes:

➜ Although the popup is defined in Listing 18.5 as a XAML resource, a Silverlight bug causes it to not be showable unless it starts out with IsOpen set to true. Therefore, the constructor performs a workaround of transferring the popup's child to a *new* popup created in C#. This new popup can start out hidden and can be shown correctly when desired.

> ⚠ **Avoid putting UI elements in resource dictionaries!**
>
> In general, UI elements (classes deriving from `UIElement`) cannot be used when they have been placed inside a resource dictionary. You can get away with it in limited cases, such as what is done with the popup inside `QuickJumpGrid`.

→ The `GetAllItems` method, used internally by `Update` for populating the list box, is a C# iterator that returns the true list of items in the list box, including the letter-tile headers that separate each group of real items. The `GetUsedLetterItems` method works the same way, but only returns the letter-tile headers.

→ This control defines its `Page` property as a dependency property, discussed after these notes. As mentioned earlier, `Page` is used to temporarily hide the page's status bar and application bar (if present) so it doesn't overlap the popup. It is also used to enable pressing the hardware back button to dismiss the popup.

→ Inside `ClosePopup`, the empty `DelayedPopupCloseStoryboard` storyboard is leveraged to delay the actual closing of the popup by .15 seconds. This is done to give the content of the popup a chance to animate out.

→ Inside `ListBox_SelectionChanged`, the code checks whether a real item has been selected or a header tile. If it's a header tile, then the popup is shown. Before this is done, however, each tile has its `HasItems` property set appropriately. This enables letters with no items to appear disabled and unclickable, as seen at the beginning of this chapter. In this app, every letter has items except q and x.

→ The code that performs the actual quick-jumping (`QuickJumpTiles_MouseLeftButtonUp`) uses list box's `ScrollIntoView` method to ensure that the passed-in item (the letter-tile header) is on-screen. However, it performs a little trick to provide proper behavior. `ScrollIntoView` scrolls the smallest amount necessary to get the target item on-screen. This means that if the target tile is lower in the list, it will end up at the *bottom* of the list after `ScrollIntoView` is called. We want jumping to a letter to put the letter-tile header at the *top* of the list, however. Therefore, this code first scrolls to the very end of the list, and *then* it scrolls to the target tile. This ensures that it is always on the top (unless only a few number of items remain after the tile).

Dependency Properties

Dependency properties play a very important role in Silverlight. As mentioned in Chapter 12, "Silly Eye," only dependency properties can be animated with a storyboard. Dependency properties are also the only type of property that can be used in a style's setter, and the only type of property that can be used as a target of data binding.

A dependency property is named as such because it *depends* on multiple providers for determining its value at any point in time. These providers could be an animation continuously changing its value, a parent element whose property value propagates down to its children, and so on.

Recall that the main page in Listing 18.1 uses data binding to set the value of QuickJumpGrid's Page property:

```
<local:QuickJumpGrid x:Name="QuickJumpGrid" Grid.Row="1" Margin="24,0,0,0"
                     Page="{Binding ElementName=Page}"
                     ItemSelected="QuickJumpGrid_ItemSelected"/>
```

This is the reason that Listing 18.6 defines Page as a dependency property; to enable consumers to use data binding to set it. If Page were a normal .NET property instead, parsing the XAML file in Listing 18.1 would throw an exception.

Most commonly, a dependency property is created to take advantage of automatic change notification. In this scenario, the dependency property is used as the *source* of a binding and changes to its value are automatically reflected in the target element.

To define a dependency property, you call DependencyProperty.Register and assign its result to a static field, as done in Listing 18.6:

```
// A Page dependency property
public static readonly DependencyProperty PageProperty =
  DependencyProperty.Register("Page",                      // name
    typeof(PhoneApplicationPage),                          // property type
    typeof(QuickJumpGrid),                                 // owner type
    new PropertyMetadata(
      null,                                                // default value
      new PropertyChangedCallback(OnPageChanged) // callback
    )
  );
```

The optional property-changed callback gets called whenever the property's value changes. It must be a static method, but the relevant instance is passed as the first parameter, as seen in the implementation of OnPageChanged in Listing 18.6.

A dependency property's value can be get and set via GetValue and SetValue methods on the class defining the prop-

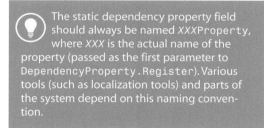

The static dependency property field should always be named *XXX*Property, where *XXX* is the actual name of the property (passed as the first parameter to DependencyProperty.Register). Various tools (such as localization tools) and parts of the system depend on this naming convention.

erty (QuickJumpGrid, in this example). All controls have these methods, inherited from a base DependencyObject class. However, to make things simpler for C# and XAML consumers, it's common practice to define a .NET property that wraps these two methods, as done in Listing 18.6:

```
public PhoneApplicationPage Page
{
  get { return (PhoneApplicationPage)GetValue(PageProperty); }
  set { SetValue(PageProperty, value); }
}
```

.NET properties are ignored at runtime when setting dependency properties in XAML!

When a dependency property is set in XAML, GetValue is called directly. Therefore, to maintain parity between setting a property in XAML versus C#, it's crucial that property wrappers, such as Page in Listing 18.6, not contain any logic in addition to the GetValue/SetValue calls. If you want to add custom logic, that's what the property-changed callback is for.

Visual Studio has a snippet called propdp that automatically expands into a definition of a dependency property and a wrapper .NET property, which makes defining one much faster than doing all the typing yourself! (It also has a snippet called propa for defining an attachable property.) Note that this snippet was originally created for WPF, so it needs a small tweak in order to work for Silverlight. It attempts to construct a class called UIPropertyMetadata for the last parameter of DependencyProperty.Register, but you must change this to PropertyMetadata instead.

The CharHelper **Class**

In Listing 18.6, QuickJumpGrid uses a class called CharHelper to figure out which of the 27 "buckets" each string key belongs in (a-z or #). This class is implemented in Listing 18.7.

LISTING 18.7   CharHelper.cs—A Static Helper Class for Bucketizing Entries

```
using System;
using System.Collections.Generic;

namespace WindowsPhoneApp
{
  public static class CharHelper
  {
    static Dictionary<char, char> accentMap = new Dictionary<char, char>();

    static CharHelper()
    {
      // Map some common accented letters to non-accented letters
      accentMap.Add('à', 'a'); accentMap.Add('á', 'a'); accentMap.Add('â', 'a');
      accentMap.Add('ã', 'a'); accentMap.Add('ä', 'a'); accentMap.Add('à', 'a');
      accentMap.Add('æ', 'a');
      accentMap.Add('è', 'e'); accentMap.Add('é', 'e'); accentMap.Add('ê', 'e');
      accentMap.Add('ë', 'e');
      accentMap.Add('ì', 'i'); accentMap.Add('í', 'i'); accentMap.Add('î', 'i');
      accentMap.Add('ï', 'i');
      accentMap.Add('ò', 'o'); accentMap.Add('ó', 'o'); accentMap.Add('ô', 'o');
      accentMap.Add('õ', 'o'); accentMap.Add('ö', 'o');
```

LISTING 18.7   Continued

```
      accentMap.Add('ù', 'u'); accentMap.Add('ú', 'u'); accentMap.Add('û', 'u');
      accentMap.Add('ü', 'u');
    }

    public static char GetBucket(string s)
    {
      char c = Char.ToLowerInvariant(s[0]);
      if (!Char.IsLetter(c))
        return '#';
      return RemoveAccent(c);
    }

    static char RemoveAccent(char letter)
    {
      if (letter >= 'a' && letter <= 'z')
        return letter;

      if (accentMap.ContainsKey(letter))
        return accentMap[letter];

      // Unknown accented letter
      return '#';
    }
  }
}
```

If it weren't for accented letters, all GetBucket would need to do is check if the first character of the string is a letter and return that letter (in a case-insensitive fashion), otherwise return #. However, this code maps several common accented letters to their non-accented version so strings beginning with such characters can appear where expected. In Cocktails, this enables a drink called Épicé Sidecar to appear in the e list.

The QuickJumpTile User Control

The QuickJumpTile user control, used 27 times in QuickJumpGrid's popup, is implemented in Listings 18.8 and 18.9.

LISTING 18.8   QuickJumpTile.xaml—The User Interface for the QuickJumpTile User Control

```
<UserControl x:Class="WindowsPhoneApp.QuickJumpTile"
    xmlns="http://schemas.microsoft.com/winfx/2006/xaml/presentation"
    xmlns:x="http://schemas.microsoft.com/winfx/2006/xaml"
    Foreground="{StaticResource PhoneForegroundBrush}"
    FontFamily="{StaticResource PhoneFontFamilySemiBold}"
```

LISTING 18.8   Continued

```
    FontSize="49" Width="99" Height="99">
  <!-- Add two storyboards to the user control's resource dictionary -->
  <UserControl.Resources>
    <!-- Flip in -->
    <Storyboard x:Name="FlipInStoryboard" Storyboard.TargetName="PlaneProjection"
                Storyboard.TargetProperty="RotationX">
      <DoubleAnimation From="-90" To="0" Duration="0:0:.8" BeginTime="0:0:.2">
        <DoubleAnimation.EasingFunction>
          <QuinticEase/>
        </DoubleAnimation.EasingFunction>
      </DoubleAnimation>
    </Storyboard>
    <!-- Flip out -->
    <Storyboard x:Name="FlipOutStoryboard" Storyboard.TargetName="PlaneProjection"
                Storyboard.TargetProperty="RotationX">
      <DoubleAnimation From="0" To="90" Duration="0:0:.15"/>
    </Storyboard>
  </UserControl.Resources>

  <Canvas x:Name="Canvas" Background="{StaticResource PhoneChromeBrush}">
    <Canvas.Projection>
      <PlaneProjection x:Name="PlaneProjection" RotationX="-90"/>
    </Canvas.Projection>
    <TextBlock x:Name="TextBlock" Foreground="{StaticResource PhoneDisabledBrush}"
               Canvas.Left="9" Canvas.Top="34"/>
  </Canvas>
</UserControl>
```

LISTING 18.9   `QuickJumpTile.xaml.cs`—The Code-Behind for the `QuickJumpTile` User Control

```
using System.Windows;
using System.Windows.Controls;
using System.Windows.Media;

namespace WindowsPhoneApp
{
  public partial class QuickJumpTile : UserControl
  {
    static SolidColorBrush whiteBrush = new SolidColorBrush(Colors.White);
    string text;
    bool hasItems;

    public QuickJumpTile()
    {
```

LISTING 18.9   Continued

```
    InitializeComponent();
  }

  public string Text
  {
    get { return this.text; }
    set
    {
      this.text = value;
      this.TextBlock.Text = this.text;
    }
  }

  public bool HasItems
  {
    get { return this.hasItems; }
    set
    {
      this.hasItems = value;
      if (this.hasItems)
      {
        // Enable this tile
        this.Canvas.Background =
          Application.Current.Resources["PhoneAccentBrush"] as Brush;
        this.TextBlock.Foreground = whiteBrush;
        Tilt.SetIsEnabled(this, true);
      }
      else
      {
        // Disable this tile
        this.Canvas.Background =
          Application.Current.Resources["PhoneChromeBrush"] as Brush;
        this.TextBlock.Foreground =
          Application.Current.Resources["PhoneDisabledBrush"] as Brush;
        Tilt.SetIsEnabled(this, false);
      }
    }
  }

  public void FlipIn()
  {
    this.FlipInStoryboard.Begin();
  }
```

LISTING 18.9   Continued

```
  public void FlipOut()
  {
    this.FlipOutStoryboard.Begin();
  }
  }
}
```

Notes:

→ The two storyboards animate RotationX on the canvas's plane projection to make each tile flip in when the popup appears and flip out before it disappears. This is shown in Figure 18.5.

Tiles flipping in   Tiles flipping out

FIGURE 18.5   The tiles can flip in and out.

→ FlipInStoryboard uses a slight delay (a BeginTime of .2 seconds) to help ensure that the animation can be seen.

→ The plane projection is placed on the canvas rather than the root user control so it doesn't interfere with the tilt effect (enabled in code-behind when HasItems is true).

→ The text foreground (when HasItems is true) is set to white—*not* PhoneForegroundBrush—to match the behavior of the quick jump grid used by the built-in apps.

The `QuickJumpItem` User Control

The `QuickJumpItem` user control, used to represent every item in `QuickJumpGrid`'s list box, is implemented in Listings 18.10 and 18.11.

LISTING 18.10 `QuickJumpItem.xaml`—The User Interface for the `QuickJumpItem` User Control

```xml
<UserControl x:Class="WindowsPhoneApp.QuickJumpItem"
    xmlns="http://schemas.microsoft.com/winfx/2006/xaml/presentation"
    xmlns:x="http://schemas.microsoft.com/winfx/2006/xaml"
    Foreground="{StaticResource PhoneForegroundBrush}"
    FontFamily="{StaticResource PhoneFontFamilySemiLight}" FontSize="42">
  <StackPanel Orientation="Horizontal" Background="Transparent">
    <Canvas x:Name="Canvas" Width="62" Height="62"
            Background="{StaticResource PhoneAccentBrush}">
      <TextBlock x:Name="TextBlock" Foreground="White" FontSize="49"
                 Canvas.Left="7" Canvas.Top="-3"/>
    </Canvas>
    <ContentPresenter Margin="18,0,0,0" x:Name="ContentPresenter"/>
  </StackPanel>
</UserControl>
```

LISTING 18.11 `QuickJumpItem.xaml.cs`—The Code-Behind for the `QuickJumpItem` User Control

```csharp
using System.Collections.Generic;
using System.Windows;
using System.Windows.Controls;
using System.Windows.Media;

namespace WindowsPhoneApp
{
  public partial class QuickJumpItem : UserControl
  {
    public QuickJumpItem()
    {
      InitializeComponent();
    }

    public bool IsHeader { get; private set; }

    // A KeyValuePair dependency property
    public static readonly DependencyProperty KeyValuePairProperty =
        DependencyProperty.Register("KeyValuePair",              // name
          typeof(KeyValuePair<string, object>),                 // property type
```

LISTING 18.11   Continued

```
      typeof(QuickJumpItem),                              // owner type
      new PropertyMetadata(
        new KeyValuePair<string, object>(),               // default value
        new PropertyChangedCallback(OnKeyValuePairChanged) // callback
      )
    );

  // A wrapper .NET property for the dependency property
  public KeyValuePair<string, object> KeyValuePair
  {
    get { return (KeyValuePair<string, object>)GetValue(KeyValuePairProperty); }
    set { SetValue(KeyValuePairProperty, value); }
  }

  static void OnKeyValuePairChanged(DependencyObject d,
                              DependencyPropertyChangedEventArgs e)
  {
    QuickJumpItem item = d as QuickJumpItem;

    if (item.KeyValuePair.Value != null)
    {
      // Show this as a normal item
      item.Canvas.Background =
        Application.Current.Resources["PhoneChromeBrush"] as Brush;
      item.ContentPresenter.Content = item.KeyValuePair.Value;
      item.TextBlock.Text = null;
    }
    else
    {
      // Show this as a special header tile
      item.Canvas.Background =
        Application.Current.Resources["PhoneAccentBrush"] as Brush;
      item.ContentPresenter.Content = null;
      item.TextBlock.Text = item.KeyValuePair.Key;
      item.IsHeader = true;
    }
  }
 }
}
}
```

Notes:

→ The item consists of a square tile stacked to the left of a content presenter. The content presenter enables an arbitrary element to be rendered inside the item, even though this app uses plain text for each cocktail (which comes from the `Cocktail` class's `ToString` method).

→ As with `QuickJumpTile`, the text foreground inside `QuickJumpItem`'s tile is hard-coded to white to match the built-in quick jump grid.

→ `KeyValuePair` is defined as a dependency property, which is what enables it to be databound to each item in the data template for `QuickJumpGrid`'s list box back in Listing 18.5.

→ The display of this item is updated based on whether the underlying key/value pair is a letter-tile header (indicated by a `null` value) or a normal item. For normal items, the tile is a plain square filled with `PhoneChromeBrush`.

The Finished Product

Jumping to the letter e

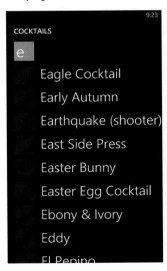

Jumping to the letter l

The grid seen under the light theme with the red accent color

chapter 19

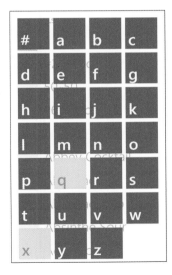

ANIMATION LAB

Animation Lab enables you to experiment with all sorts of transforms and animations. There's nothing like seeing the various easing functions and other settings in action to understand how the topics in this part of the book really work. So Animation Lab is a useful developer education tool.

Although running and interacting with this app is a great way to conclude your journey into Silverlight animations, the app's code is not extremely interesting. It performs the tedious job of applying all the settings chosen by the user to a storyboard that is constantly running and/or a `CompositeTransform` and `Projection` on the image demonstrating the animation behavior. Therefore, unlike all the other chapters, this chapter does not examine the app's code.

Instead, this chapter takes a look at a custom control used by this app and almost every other app in this book: `AnimatedFrame`. This subclass of `PhoneApplicationFrame` is responsible for producing the page-flip animations when navigating between pages. The apps in this book include it by referencing its assembly (AdamNathanAppsLibrary.dll) and then changing one line of code in App.xaml.cs from

```
RootFrame = new PhoneApplicationFrame();
```

to

```
RootFrame = new AdamNathanAppsLibrary.AnimatedFrame();
```

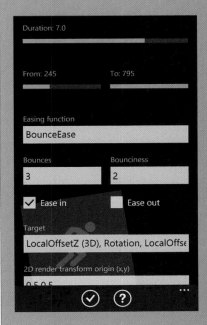

The Silverlight for Windows Phone Toolkit contains slick support for performing a variety of animated page transitions. It defines a new notion of a *transition*, which is like a storyboard but with automatic enabling of bitmap caching and automatic disabling of hit testing while the animation is underway. It includes five built-in transitions: TurnstileTransition (the typical page-flip that is expected for page transitions), RollTransition, SlideTransition, SwivelTransition, and RotateTransition. The last one is intended for animating a change in page orientation.

A transition can be applied to any UI element and can be triggered at any time with a call to its Begin method, so they are quite powerful. However, there are two reasons that the apps in this book do not use transitions for animating page navigation:

1. Proper page-navigation transitions are astoundingly verbose. It involves four distinct transitions (animating in when navigating forward, animating in when navigating backward, animating out when navigating forward, and animating out when navigating backward), and they must be assigned individually. This looks like the following:

```
<phone:PhoneApplicationPage …>
  <toolkit:TransitionService.NavigationInTransition>
    <toolkit:NavigationInTransition>
      <toolkit:NavigationInTransition.Backward>
        <toolkit:TurnstileTransition Mode="BackwardIn"/>
      </toolkit:NavigationInTransition.Backward>
      <toolkit:NavigationInTransition.Forward>
        <toolkit:TurnstileTransition Mode="ForwardIn"/>
      </toolkit:NavigationInTransition.Forward>
    </toolkit:NavigationInTransition>
  </toolkit:TransitionService.NavigationInTransition>
  <toolkit:TransitionService.NavigationOutTransition>
    <toolkit:NavigationOutTransition>
      <toolkit:NavigationOutTransition.Backward>
        <toolkit:TurnstileTransition Mode="BackwardOut"/>
      </toolkit:NavigationOutTransition.Backward>
      <toolkit:NavigationOutTransition.Forward>
        <toolkit:TurnstileTransition Mode="ForwardOut"/>
      </toolkit:NavigationOutTransition.Forward>
    </toolkit:NavigationOutTransition>
  </toolkit:TransitionService.NavigationOutTransition>
  …
</phone:PhoneApplicationPage>
```

Imagine how long this book would be if each page's XAML file contained that!

2. Using transitions for page navigation has the same requirement of replacing one line of code in App.xaml.cs, so using them doesn't save you from that awkwardness. In this case, the new line of code is:

```
RootFrame = new TransitionFrame();
```

Animation Lab also uses a custom control called `PickerBox`, which acts like a full-mode list picker. Although it is more limited than the list picker control in the Silverlight for Windows Phone Toolkit (covered in Chapter 25, "Book Reader"), it has one advantage leveraged by this app: It supports a multiselect mode that follows the Windows Phone design guidelines.

The Silverlight for Windows Phone Toolkit also contains a `TiltEffect` class that is similar to the custom `Tilt` class used by just about every app in this book. Instead of setting `Tilt.IsEnabled` to true, you can set `TiltEffect.IsTiltEnabled` to true. Whereas `Tilt.IsEnabled` must be applied directly to the elements you wish to tilt, `TiltEffect.IsTiltEnabled` searches for any "tiltable" child elements and automatically applies the effect (unless such an element has `TiltEffect.SuppressTilt` set to true). By default, this includes all buttons and list box items, but you can change this behavior by modifying `TiltEffect`'s `TiltableItems` list.

Creating a Custom Control

Silverlight has two schemes for writing your own controls: writing a *user control* (the easier of the two) and writing a *custom control* (the more complicated but also more flexible variety). Although user controls have a distinct `UserControl` base class, what really distinguishes them is the process by which they are created. When you create a new one in Visual Studio, you are given a XAML file and a code-behind file, just like with a page.

Custom controls act more like the built-in Silverlight controls. They can derive from any `Control` subclass (or `Control` itself), but their important distinction is also how they are built. They are implemented with as little dependence on their specific visual representation as possible. Although they provide a default style in a special XAML file, they allow consumers to swap it out with a new style that potentially overhauls the visuals with a new control template.

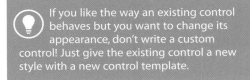 If you like the way an existing control behaves but you want to change its appearance, don't write a custom control! Just give the existing control a new style with a new control template.

Writing a custom control is a two-step process. Step 1 is implementing the class. The following class is just about the simplest possible custom control with no behavior above and beyond what it inherits from its base class:

```
using System.Windows.Controls;
namespace WindowsPhoneApp
{
  public class MyCustomControl : Control
  {
    public MyCustomControl()
    {
```

```
        // Apply a style with the target type of MyCustomControl instead of Control
        this.DefaultStyleKey = typeof(MyCustomControl);
    }
  }
}
```

The assignment of `DefaultStyleKey` is important. Setting it to the type of this control enables a default style to be provided specifically for it. Without setting this, it would pick up the default style for its base class (the most-derived one that assigns `DefaultStyleKey` accordingly).

Don't forget to assign `DefaultStyleKey` when writing a custom control!

This is the most common mistake I see made when someone is trying to determine why their custom control isn't picking up the desired style. Another mistake is setting `DefaultStyleKey` to `this.GetType()`. If you do this, the default style is not found for any subclasses of the control because the type of the subclass is used for the style key.

Step 2 is to place a default style for your control in your project's *generic theme dictionary*. This is a XAML file containing a resource dictionary as its root element. This file must be named `generic.xaml`, it must be in a folder called `Themes` in the root of your project, and it must have a Build Action of Resource. If any of these conditions are not met, your default style will not be found.

The following is an example `generic.xaml` file containing a default style for `MyCustomControl`:

```xml
<ResourceDictionary
   xmlns="http://schemas.microsoft.com/winfx/2006/xaml/presentation"
   xmlns:x="http://schemas.microsoft.com/winfx/2006/xaml"
   xmlns:local="clr-namespace:WindowsPhoneApp">
  <!-- MyCustomControl default style -->
  <Style TargetType="local:MyCustomControl">
    <Setter Property="Foreground" Value="Blue"/>
    <Setter Property="Width" Value="75"/>
    <Setter Property="Height" Value="75"/>
    <Setter Property="Template">
      <Setter.Value>
        <ControlTemplate TargetType="local:MyCustomControl">
          <Ellipse Fill="{TemplateBinding Foreground}"
                   Width="{TemplateBinding Width}"
                   Height="{TemplateBinding Height}"/>
        </ControlTemplate>
      </Setter.Value>
    </Setter>
  </Style>
</ResourceDictionary>
```

With that, the control can now be consumed. The following stack panel contains three instances. The first instance uses its default settings, the second instance customizes its appearance with a few properties (that are fortunately respected in the default control template, otherwise setting them as done below would have no effect), and the third instance has a custom style with a custom control template applied. The result of this is rendered in Figure 19.1.

FIGURE 19.1   A consumer of MyCustomControl can completely change its visual appearance, such as turning the ellipse into a rectangle.

```
<StackPanel>
  <StackPanel.Resources>
    <Style x:Key="CustomStyle" TargetType="local:MyCustomControl">
      <Setter Property="Template">
        <Setter.Value>
          <ControlTemplate TargetType="local:MyCustomControl">
            <Rectangle Fill="{TemplateBinding Foreground}"
                       Width="{TemplateBinding Width}"
                       Height="{TemplateBinding Height}"/>
          </ControlTemplate>
        </Setter.Value>
      </Setter>
    </Style>
  </StackPanel.Resources>

  <local:MyCustomControl/>
  <local:MyCustomControl Foreground="Red" Width="200" Height="100"/>
  <local:MyCustomControl Style="{StaticResource CustomStyle}"/>
</StackPanel>
```

Defining States

A good control has logic that is independent from whatever specific visuals are currently applied (such as the rectangle instead of the ellipse). To help enable controls to keep their logic separated from their appearance, the *Visual State Manager* (VSM) can give control templates more power and expressiveness.

The Visual State Manager enables a control author to formally specify different *states* for their controls, so a consumer creating a custom control template can specify different visuals for each one. Expression Blend takes advantage of this information to provide a nice experience for control template authors.

On the control side, the author can define several named states and then add internal logic to transition to these states at the right times (by calling a static `VisualStateManager.GoToState` method). The states must be grouped into one or more mutually exclusive *state groups*. Table 19.1 lists the states (and their state groups) exposed by five built-in controls.

TABLE 19.1   State Groups and States Used by Five of Silverlight's Built-In Controls

Control	State Group	States
`Button`	`CommonStates`	`Normal,MouseOver,Pressed,Disabled`
	`FocusStates`	`Unfocused,Focused`
`PhoneApplicationFrame`	*(none)*	
`ProgressBar`	`CommonStates`	`Determinate,Indeterminate`
`ScrollViewer`	`ScrollStates`	`Scrolling,NotScrolling`
`TextBox`	`CommonStates`	`ReadOnly,Normal,MouseOver,Disabled`
	`FocusStates`	`Unfocused,Focused`
	`ValidationStates`	`Valid,InvalidUnfocused,` `InvalidFocused`

At any time, a control is in one state *from every group*. For example, a button is `Normal` *and* `Unfocused` by default. This grouping mechanism exists to help prevent a long list of states meant to cover every combination of independent properties (such as `NormalUnfocused`, `NormalFocused`, `DisabledUnfocused`, `DisabledFocused`, and so on). Sometimes a control's states aren't as neatly organized as they ideally would be, such as the ones in text box's `ValidationStates` group that overlap with `FocusStates` when it comes to the notion of having focus.

After the next section, we'll look at code that defines and uses states, as well as a control template that acts upon state changes.

Defining Parts

Sometimes it's hard to avoid writing a control that makes some assumptions about its visual appearance. And that's okay, as long as the control doesn't cause unhandled exceptions when these assumptions aren't valid. When a control wants certain elements to be in its control template, these elements are called *parts*.

Parts are just named elements that the control can retrieve, similar to a page using an element's `FindName` method to retrieve an element by name. In this case, a control can call its inherited (protected) `GetTemplateChild` method, which is able to retrieve an element defined the current control template.

Table 19.2 shows all the parts expected by the same five controls from Table 19.1. These controls apply some logic to these named elements when present in the control template. For example, when a progress bar control template has elements named `ProgressBarIndicator` and `ProgressBarTrack`, the control ensures that the width of `ProgressBarIndicator` remains the correct percentage of the width of `ProgressBarTrack`, based on the progress bar's `Value`, `Minimum`, and `Maximum` properties. For a control template that wishes to look somewhat like a normal progress bar, taking advantage of this support greatly simplifies it (and removes the need for custom code for doing the math).

TABLE 19.2   Named Parts Used by Five of Silverlight's Built-In Controls

Control	Part Name	Part Type
Button	*(none)*	
PhoneApplicationFrame	ClientArea	FrameworkElement
ProgressBar	ProgressBarIndicator	FrameworkElement
	ProgressBarTrack	FrameworkElement
ScrollViewer	HorizontalScrollBar	ScrollBar
	ScrollContentPresenter	ScrollContentPresenter
	VerticalScrollBar	ScrollBar
TextBox	ContentElement	FrameworkElement

The `AnimatedFrame` **Custom Control Code**

With an understanding of how custom controls are defined and the ideas behind Visual State Manager's parts and states model, let's examine how `AnimatedFrame` is implemented.

Listing 19.1 contains the code (not code-*behind*!) for `AnimatedFrame`. This code resides in the AdamNathanAppsLibrary DLL project that builds the DLL shared by almost every app in this book.

LISTING 19.1   `AnimatedFrame.cs`—The Implementation of the `AnimatedFrame` Custom Control

```
using System.Windows;
using System.Windows.Controls;
using System.Windows.Navigation;
using Microsoft.Phone.Controls;

namespace AdamNathanAppsLibrary
{
  // Documentation of parts for tools like Expression Blend
  [TemplatePart(Name="OldContent", Type=typeof(ContentPresenter))]
  [TemplatePart(Name="NewContent", Type=typeof(ContentPresenter))]
  [TemplatePart(Name="ClientArea", Type=typeof(FrameworkElement))]

  // Documentation of states for tools like Expression Blend
  [TemplateVisualState(Name="GoingBack", GroupName="NavigationStates")]
  [TemplateVisualState(Name="GoingForward", GroupName="NavigationStates")]
  [TemplateVisualState(Name="NavigationDone", GroupName="NavigationStates")]

  public class AnimatedFrame : PhoneApplicationFrame
```

LISTING 19.1   Continued

```csharp
{
  bool goingForward = true;
  ContentPresenter oldContentPresenter;
  ContentPresenter newContentPresenter;
  VisualStateGroup stateGroup;

  public AnimatedFrame()
  {
    // Apply a style with the target type of AnimatedFrame
    // instead of PhoneApplicationFrame
    this.DefaultStyleKey = typeof(AnimatedFrame);
    this.Navigating += AnimatedFrame_Navigating;
  }

  public override void OnApplyTemplate()
  {
    base.OnApplyTemplate();

    // Get the two named parts expected to be in the current control template
    this.oldContentPresenter =
      GetTemplateChild("OldContent") as ContentPresenter;
    this.newContentPresenter =
      GetTemplateChild("NewContent") as ContentPresenter;

    // Remove the old handler if this isn't the first template applied
    if (this.stateGroup != null)
      this.stateGroup.CurrentStateChanged -= VisualStateGroup_StateChanged;

    // Retrieve the visual state group from the current control template,
    // if it's there
    this.stateGroup = GetTemplateChild("NavigationStates") as VisualStateGroup;

    // Add a handler for the CurrentStateChanged event
    if (this.stateGroup != null)
      this.stateGroup.CurrentStateChanged += VisualStateGroup_StateChanged;

    // Force a call to OnContentChanged
    if (this.Content != null)
      OnContentChanged(null, this.Content);
  }

  // Changes the content and performs the state change
  protected override void OnContentChanged(object oldContent, object newContent)
  {
```

LISTING 19.1   Continued

```
    base.OnContentChanged(oldContent, newContent);

    if (newContent == null || oldContent == null)
      return;

    // Assign the contents to the correct parts in the current visual tree
    if (this.newContentPresenter != null)
      this.newContentPresenter.Content = newContent;
    if (this.oldContentPresenter != null)
      this.oldContentPresenter.Content = oldContent;

    // Do an instant switch to the GoingForward or GoingBack state
    bool success = VisualStateManager.GoToState(this,   /* control */
      this.goingForward ? "GoingForward" : "GoingBack", /* stateName */
      false                                             /* useTransitions */);

    if (success)
    {
      // Now transition to the NavigationDone state
      if (VisualStateManager.GoToState(this,              /* control */
                                  "NavigationDone", /* stateName */
                                  true              /* useTransitions */))
        return;
    }

    // One of the state changes was not successful
    if (this.oldContentPresenter != null)
      this.oldContentPresenter.Content = null;
  }

  void AnimatedFrame_Navigating(object sender, NavigatingCancelEventArgs e)
  {
    // Record whether we're going forward or back
    this.goingForward = (e.NavigationMode != NavigationMode.Back);
    // Detach the old content
    if (this.oldContentPresenter != null)
      this.oldContentPresenter.Content = null;
  }

  // Removes the old content when the animation is done
  void VisualStateGroup_StateChanged(object sender,
                                  VisualStateChangedEventArgs e)
  {
    // Detach the old content when the transition to NavigationDone is done
```

LISTING 19.1   Continued

```
    if (e.NewState.Name == "NavigationDone" && this.oldContentPresenter != null)
      this.oldContentPresenter.Content = null;
    }
  }
}
```

Notes:

→ Although it has no impact on run-time behavior, a control should document all of its parts with `TemplatePart` attributes and all of its states with `TemplateVisualState` attributes. This information is consumed by tools such as Expression Blend to provide a design-time experience for parts and states.

→ This control expects two content presenters named `OldContent` and `NewContent` that represent the two pages involved in a navigation transition. The third part, `ClientArea`, is not used by this listing but is a requirement of the `PhoneApplicationFrame` base class.

→ This control defines three states in a group called `NavigationStates`. The control first transitions to `GoingBack` or `GoingForward` based on whether a back or forward navigation has occurred, and then it transitions to `NavigationDone`. As you'll see in the next section, this

 Any control template for `PhoneApplicationFrame` or a derived class must include an element (typically the root element) called `ClientArea`!

If you do not include such an element, several bad things happen. For example, the tops of pages get obscured by the status bar (if present), and switching to a landscape orientation causes an unhandled exception! This is a great example of a control that has failed to be resilient in the face of missing parts in its control template.

 Controls should not add any states to state groups already defined by a base class!

New states should be added to new state group(s). Because each state group works independently, new transitions among states in a new state group must not interfere with base class logic. If you add new states to an existing state group, however, there's no guarantee that the base class logic to transition among states will continue operate correctly.

gives control templates the opportunity to define any kind of animated transition they wish, and to distinguish between a backward animation and a forward animation.

→ The default style key is assigned so a default style can be given for the `AnimatedFrame` type.

→ To retrieve specially designated control parts, this listing overrides the `OnApplyTemplate` method inherited from `FrameworkElement`. This method is called any time a template is applied, so it gives you the opportunity to handle dynamic template changes gracefully. To retrieve the instances of elements inside the control template, GetTemplateChild is used. The null checks throughout this listing prevent unhandled exceptions from being thrown even if a control template is applied without elements named OldContent and NewContent.

 Do not assume that OnApplyTemplate will only be called once!

If a control is given a new template at runtime, OnApplyTemplate will get called again with new visuals. Event handlers and references to the old parts should be cleaned up appropriately.

→ Inside OnContentChanged, defined by the ContentControl base class, the old and new pieces of content are assigned to the appropriate content presenters and then the state changes are made. First, an instant state change is made to either GoingForward or GoingBack, based on the value captured in the frame's Navigating event. Then, a state change is made to NavigationDone with transitions enabled. (Transitions are animations that can be defined by the control template.) Just as a control template may omit named parts, they may also omit states. The GoToState method returns false when the target state does not exist in the current control template.

→ Controls typically call GoToState in the following situations:

   → Inside OnApplyTemplate (with useTransitions=false)

   → When the control first loads (with useTransitions=false)

   → Inside appropriate event handlers. In this example, there's no ContentChanged event, but the OnContentChanged override is the sensible spot because the state change is designed to expose this situation.

There is no harm in calling GoToState when the destination state is the same as the current state. (When this is done, the call does nothing.)

Every state must have a unique name, even across different state groups!

Despite any partitioning into multiple state groups, a control must not have two states with the same name. This limitation can be surprising until you've implemented state transitions and realize that VisualStateManager's GoToState method doesn't have the concept of state groups. State groups are really just a documentation tool for understanding the behavior of a control's states and the possible transitions.

Therefore, it's good to double-check the names of states used by your base classes, and to give your states very specific names (*not* names like Default or Normal that are likely already in use).

> **When a control loads, it should explicitly transition to the default state in every state group!**
>
> If a control does not explicitly transition to the default state(s), it introduces a subtle bug for consumers of the control. Before the initial transition for any state group, the control is not yet in *any* of those states. That means that the first transition to a non-default state will not invoke any transition from the default state that consumers may have defined.
>
> When you perform this initial transition, you should pass `false` for `VisualStateManager.GoToState`'s useTransitions parameter to make it happen instantaneously. `AnimatedFrame` does this, although it waits until the first call to `OnContentChanged` to perform that initial transition.

> **Do not call** `GoToState` **in a control's constructor!**
>
> `GoToState` should not be called until all of a control's visuals have been created and references to the parts obtained. Making the first call at the end of `OnApplyTemplate` is appropriate.

> To help manage multiple state groups, most controls define an `UpdateState` method that consolidates all `GoToState` calls. Because it's fine to call `GoToState` when the destination state is the same as the current state, `UpdateState` should update the current state for *every* state group based on current property values. This simplifies the control's logic.

The `AnimatedFrame` Custom Control Default Style

Now we can look at the default style with a control template that leverages `AnimatedFrame`'s parts and states. First, let's examine the outline of the control template, as it's easy to get overwhelmed by the amount of XAML in the full listing. It is structured as follows:

```
<ControlTemplate TargetType="local:AnimatedFrame">
  <Grid x:Name="ClientArea">
    <!-- The visual state groups -->
    <VisualStateManager.VisualStateGroups>
      <!-- Only one group -->
      <VisualStateGroup x:Name="NavigationStates">

        <!-- Specific (and optional) transitions between states -->
        <VisualStateGroup.Transitions>
          <!-- Transition #1 -->
          <VisualTransition From="GoingForward" To="NavigationDone">
            <Storyboard>…</Storyboard>
          </VisualTransition>

          <!-- Transition #2 -->
```

```xml
        <VisualTransition From="GoingBack" To="NavigationDone">
          <Storyboard>…</Storyboard>
        </VisualTransition>
      </VisualStateGroup.Transitions>

      <!-- State #1 -->
      <VisualState x:Name="GoingForward"/>

      <!-- State #2 -->
      <VisualState x:Name="GoingBack"/>

      <!-- State #3 -->
      <VisualState x:Name="NavigationDone"/>
    </VisualStateGroup>
  </VisualStateManager.VisualStateGroups>

  <!-- The visual content -->
  <ContentPresenter x:Name="OldContent" …>
    …
  </ContentPresenter>
  <ContentPresenter x:Name="NewContent" …>
    …
  </ContentPresenter>
</Grid>
</ControlTemplate>
```

To write a control template that takes advantage of states, you set the
VisualStateManager.VisualStateGroups attachable property on the root element in the
template's visual tree to a collection of visual state groups, each of which has a collection
of visual state children. In this case there's only one group.

Each visual state can contain a storyboard that adjusts visual elements based on the state.
These are often used like property setters in a style, "animating" a property to its final
value with a duration of 0, and/or using discrete object animations to change the value of
something that can't be interpolated, such as an element's visibility. You can do any sort
of animation, however; even one that runs indefinitely while the control is in that
specific state.

Each visual state group can also define a collection of visual transitions can automatically
generate smooth animations when transitioning between states. Each VisualTransition
object has To and From string properties that can be set to the names of the source and
target states. You can omit both properties to make it apply to all transitions, specify only
a To to make it apply to all transitions to that state, and so on. When transitioning from

one state to another, the Visual State Manager chooses the most specific VisualTransition that matches the transition. The order of precedence is as follows:

1. A VisualTransition with matching To and From
2. A VisualTransition with a matching To and no explicit From
3. A VisualTransition with a matching From and no explicit To
4. The default VisualTransition, with no To or From specified

If VisualStateGroup's Transitions property isn't set, the default transition between any states is a zero-duration animation.

To specify the characteristics of a VisualTransition, you can set its GeneratedDuration property to control the duration of the generated linear animation. You can also set its GeneratedEasingFunction property to get a nonlinear animation between states. For the most customization, you can even set its Storyboard property to a Storyboard with arbitrary custom animations.

Listing 19.2 contains the complete default style for AnimatedFrame inside the project's generic.xaml file.

LISTING 19.2   generic.xaml—The Generic Theme Dictionary Containing the Default Style for AnimatedFrame

```
<ResourceDictionary
  xmlns="http://schemas.microsoft.com/winfx/2006/xaml/presentation"
  xmlns:x="http://schemas.microsoft.com/winfx/2006/xaml"
  xmlns:local="clr-namespace:AdamNathanAppsLibrary">

  <!-- AnimatedFrame default style -->
  <Style TargetType="local:AnimatedFrame">
    <Setter Property="HorizontalContentAlignment" Value="Stretch"/>
    <Setter Property="VerticalContentAlignment" Value="Stretch"/>
    <Setter Property="Template">
      <Setter.Value>
        <ControlTemplate TargetType="local:AnimatedFrame">
          <Grid x:Name="ClientArea">
            <!-- The visual state groups -->
            <VisualStateManager.VisualStateGroups>
              <!-- Only one group -->
              <VisualStateGroup x:Name="NavigationStates">

                <!-- Specific (and optional) transitions between states -->
                <VisualStateGroup.Transitions>

                  <!-- Transition #1 -->
                  <VisualTransition From="GoingForward" To="NavigationDone">
```

LISTING 19.2   Continued

```xml
                        <Storyboard>
                          <!-- Flip the old content (the current page)
                               out toward the screen -->
                          <DoubleAnimationUsingKeyFrames
                            Storyboard.TargetName="OldContent"
Storyboard.TargetProperty="(UIElement.Projection).(PlaneProjection.RotationY)">
                            <LinearDoubleKeyFrame KeyTime="0" Value="0"/>
                            <EasingDoubleKeyFrame KeyTime="0:0:.8" Value="120">
                              <EasingDoubleKeyFrame.EasingFunction>
                                <PowerEase Power="5"/>
                              </EasingDoubleKeyFrame.EasingFunction>
                            </EasingDoubleKeyFrame>
                          </DoubleAnimationUsingKeyFrames>

                          <!-- Hide the old content (the current page) -->
                          <ObjectAnimationUsingKeyFrames
                            Storyboard.TargetName="OldContent"
                            Storyboard.TargetProperty="Visibility">
                            <DiscreteObjectKeyFrame KeyTime="0" Value="Visible"/>
                            <DiscreteObjectKeyFrame KeyTime="0:0:.8"
                                                    Value="Collapsed"/>
                          </ObjectAnimationUsingKeyFrames>

                          <!-- Show the new content (the next page) -->
                          <ObjectAnimationUsingKeyFrames
                            Storyboard.TargetName="NewContent"
                            Storyboard.TargetProperty="Visibility">
                            <DiscreteObjectKeyFrame KeyTime="0" Value="Collapsed"/>
                            <DiscreteObjectKeyFrame KeyTime="0:0:.2" Value="Visible"/>
                          </ObjectAnimationUsingKeyFrames>

                          <!-- Flip the new content (the next page) in from behind -->
                          <DoubleAnimationUsingKeyFrames BeginTime="0:0:.2"
                            Storyboard.TargetName="NewContent"
Storyboard.TargetProperty="(UIElement.Projection).(PlaneProjection.RotationY)">
                            <LinearDoubleKeyFrame KeyTime="0" Value="-120"/>
                            <EasingDoubleKeyFrame KeyTime="0:0:.6" Value="0">
                              <EasingDoubleKeyFrame.EasingFunction>
                                <PowerEase Power="10"/>
                              </EasingDoubleKeyFrame.EasingFunction>
                            </EasingDoubleKeyFrame>
                          </DoubleAnimationUsingKeyFrames>
                        </Storyboard>
                      </VisualTransition>
```

LISTING 19.2   Continued

```
                        <!-- Transition #2 -->
                        <VisualTransition From="GoingBack" To="NavigationDone">
                          <Storyboard>
                            <!-- Flip the old content (the current page)
                                 out away from the screen -->
                            <DoubleAnimationUsingKeyFrames
                              Storyboard.TargetName="OldContent"
Storyboard.TargetProperty="(UIElement.Projection).(PlaneProjection.RotationY)">
                              <LinearDoubleKeyFrame KeyTime="0" Value="0"/>
                              <EasingDoubleKeyFrame KeyTime="0:0:.8" Value="-120">
                                <EasingDoubleKeyFrame.EasingFunction>
                                  <PowerEase Power="10"/>
                                </EasingDoubleKeyFrame.EasingFunction>
                              </EasingDoubleKeyFrame>
                            </DoubleAnimationUsingKeyFrames>

                            <!-- Hide the old content (the current page) -->
                            <ObjectAnimationUsingKeyFrames
                              Storyboard.TargetName="OldContent"
                              Storyboard.TargetProperty="Visibility">
                              <DiscreteObjectKeyFrame KeyTime="0" Value="Visible"/>
                              <DiscreteObjectKeyFrame KeyTime="0:0:.8"
                                                      Value="Collapsed"/>
                            </ObjectAnimationUsingKeyFrames>

                            <!-- Show the new content (the previous page) -->
                            <ObjectAnimationUsingKeyFrames
                              Storyboard.TargetName="NewContent"
                              Storyboard.TargetProperty="Visibility">
                              <DiscreteObjectKeyFrame KeyTime="0" Value="Collapsed"/>
                              <DiscreteObjectKeyFrame KeyTime="0:0:.2" Value="Visible"/>
                            </ObjectAnimationUsingKeyFrames>

                            <!-- Flip the new content (the previous page) in
                                 from in front of the screen -->
                            <DoubleAnimationUsingKeyFrames BeginTime="0:0:.2"
                              Storyboard.TargetName="NewContent"
Storyboard.TargetProperty="(UIElement.Projection).(PlaneProjection.RotationY)">
                              <LinearDoubleKeyFrame KeyTime="0" Value="120"/>
                              <EasingDoubleKeyFrame KeyTime="0:0:.6" Value="0">
                                <EasingDoubleKeyFrame.EasingFunction>
                                  <PowerEase Power="10"/>
                                </EasingDoubleKeyFrame.EasingFunction>
                              </EasingDoubleKeyFrame>
```

LISTING 19.2   Continued

```xml
                      </DoubleAnimationUsingKeyFrames>
                    </Storyboard>
                  </VisualTransition>
                </VisualStateGroup.Transitions>

                <!-- State #1 -->
                <VisualState x:Name="GoingForward"/>
                <!-- State #2 -->
                <VisualState x:Name="GoingBack"/>
                <!-- State #3 -->
                <VisualState x:Name="NavigationDone"/>
              </VisualStateGroup>
            </VisualStateManager.VisualStateGroups>

            <!-- The visual content -->
            <ContentPresenter x:Name="OldContent" CacheMode="BitmapCache"
                              Visibility="Collapsed">
              <ContentPresenter.Projection>
                <PlaneProjection CenterOfRotationX="0"/>
              </ContentPresenter.Projection>
            </ContentPresenter>
            <ContentPresenter x:Name="NewContent" CacheMode="BitmapCache">
              <ContentPresenter.Projection>
                <PlaneProjection CenterOfRotationX="0"/>
              </ContentPresenter.Projection>
            </ContentPresenter>
          </Grid>
        </ControlTemplate>
      </Setter.Value>
    </Setter>
  </Style>

  <!-- PickerBox default style -->
  <Style TargetType="local:PickerBox">
    …
  </Style>
</ResourceDictionary>
```

Notes:

→ This control template opts for completely custom storyboards for the transitions from `GoingForward` to `NavigationDone` and `GoingBack` to `NavigationDone`, leaving all three states empty. This suppresses the usual automatically generated state-change animations (because there's nothing defined in any state to interpolate), and is the best option here considering the complexity of the animations.

→ Each transition consists of four animations: one to flip out the old content, one to hide it when the flip is done, one to flip in the new content, and one to show it before the flip starts. The direction of the flip varies between the two transitions.

→ The actual content of the control template is simply the two content presenters, one on top of the other, inside a grid.

→ This 3D-flip animation is very similar to the one done in Chapter 17, "Pick a Card Magic Trick." Simple changes can change the effect in interesting ways. For example, removing `CenterOfRotationX="0"` from the plane projection on both content presenters makes the pages flip around their middle instead.

→ All default styles for custom controls in this assembly must be defined in this file, or in a resource dictionary merged into this file with resource dictionary's `MergedDictionaries` property. Therefore, this file also contains the style for the `PickerBox` control.

→ Chapter 9, "Fake Call," mentions that `StaticResource` lookup starts at the current element's resource dictionary, traverses all the way up to the root frame, and then checks the application-wide resource dictionary. After that, however, any relevant generic theme resource dictionary is checked. This is what enables a control's default style to be applied yet overridden.

 The `System.Windows.xaml` file installed by the Windows Developer Power Tools to `%ProgramFiles%\Microsoft SDKs\Windows Phone\v7.0\Design` is a great source of real-world examples of control templates leveraging the Visual State Manager.

Improving Rendering Performance with Bitmap Caching

Notice that both content presenters in Listing 19.2 are marked with `CacheMode="BitmapCache"`. This is done to enable an important performance optimization that every Windows Phone developer should know about.

Vector graphics have a lot of advantages over bitmap-based graphics, but with those advantages come inherent scalability issues. In scenarios where there might be a rapid succession of redrawing, as with an animation, the cost of rendering can significantly impact the resulting user experience.

With the *bitmap caching* feature, also known as *cached composition*, you can automatically cache any UI element, including its tree of subelements, as a bitmap in video memory. In certain circumstances, this enables animations to run entirely on the compositor thread (on the GPU), freeing up the UI thread (and CPU) for other tasks. (The compositor thread, introduced in Chapter 15, "Mood Ring," is sometimes referred to as the *composition thread* or *render thread*.)

To use this feature, set the `CacheMode` property on any element you wish to cache. The type of the `CacheMode` property is the abstract `CacheMode` class, although `BitmapCache` is the only `CacheMode` subclass. Therefore, you can set it on a `Grid` as follows:

```
<Grid …>
<Grid.CacheMode>
  <BitmapCache/>
</Grid.CacheMode>
  …
</Grid>
```

or, thanks to a type converter:

```
<Grid CacheMode="BitmapCache">
  …
</Grid>
```

When a cached element (including any of its children) is updated, BitmapCache automatically generates a new bitmap. This means that you never have to worry about a cached element becoming stale or losing its interactivity, but it also means that you should avoid caching a frequently changing element. Generating a new bitmap is an expensive operation. Fortunately, updates to any parents do not invalidate the cache, nor do updates to most of the element's transforms or opacity.

Bitmap Caching and Animations

Only the following types of animations can run on the compositor thread, and only when the target element does not have a nonrectangular clip applied:

→ Translation

→ Rotation

→ Scaling (if the scale changes by less than 50%)

→ Plane projection

→ Opacity (if not using an opacity mask)

If the target of the animation isn't already marked with BitmapCache, such an animation automatically creates a bitmap cache when the animation begins and discards it when the animation ends. Although this enables the improved performance of running on the compositor thread, this automatic caching can become costly if the animation runs repeatedly. Therefore, for the best results, relevant elements should be explicitly marked with BitmapCache.

That said, Silverlight for Windows Phone effectively marks some elements with BitmapCache automatically so you don't have to:

→ ListBoxItem

→ ScrollViewer

→ MediaElement

→ Any element with a plane projection applied

Because bitmap caching applies to an element's entire tree of subelements, the special treatment on `ScrollViewer` covers a lot of cases.

 BitmapCache is most appropriate for static content that gets animated in one of the ways previously mentioned, to avoid creating a bottleneck in the rendering pipeline due to the CPU-bound work of repeated tessellation and rasterization on every frame. There is a trade-off, however. The more you cache, the bigger the memory consumption will be on the GPU.

For more detailed information about this and other performance considerations, as well as using performance debugging features such as redraw regions and cache visualizations, see http://bit.ly/perftips.

Rendering at a Custom Scale

`BitmapCache` has a `RenderAtScale` property (a double whose value is 1 by default) that can be used to customize the scale of an element when it is rendered to the cached bitmap. This property is especially interesting when you plan on changing the size of the element. If you zoom the element to a larger size, setting `RenderAtScale` to the final scale avoids a degraded result. Setting `RenderAtScale` to a smaller scale improves performance while sacrificing quality.

For demonstration purposes, Figure 19.2 shows the use of `RenderAtScale` with four different values on an entire page, as follows:

```
<phone:PhoneApplicationPage …>
  <phone:PhoneApplicationPage.CacheMode>
    <BitmapCache RenderAtScale="…"/>
  </phone:PhoneApplicationPage.CacheMode>
  …
</phone:PhoneApplicationPage>
```

To set `RenderAtScale`, you must use property element syntax when setting `CacheMode`. Notice that the application bar is not affected in Figure 19.2, as it is not rendered by Silverlight.

RenderAtScale=1   RenderAtScale=.4   RenderAtScale=.1   RenderAtScale=.05

FIGURE 19.2   Using `RenderAtScale` to reduce the resolution of the cached bitmap.

The Finished Product

Adjusting various animation settings

The settings pane can be dismissed to watch the animation more clearly.

Choosing one or more animation targets with the multiselect picker box

ALARM CLOCK

The Alarm Clock app mimics a somewhat-retro digital alarm clock. It pretends to have a fixed display with segments that can be turned on or off as needed. It displays the current time and day of the week, and it enables setting a snoozable alarm. (The alarm only goes off if the app is still running, even if it's under the lock screen.)

Alarm Clock exposes several user-configurable settings related to the color and formatting of the clock and its alarm vibration behavior. It also persists state such as whether the alarm is on and what time it should go off. All of this is done with the Setting class that has been used in almost every app so far. Now, given the topic of Part III, "Storing & Retrieving Local Data," it is time to look into how the Setting class works and understand more about storing and retrieving data.

Setting and Isolated Storage

Isolated storage is a special folder provided to each app where arbitrary data files can be stored. The files in this folder are isolated to the designated app. One app can never access the isolated storage for another app. Even if an app *wants* to share the data in its storage with others, it cannot.

Although you can read and write files from isolated storage, covered in Chapter 22, "Notepad," the Setting class used by most of the apps in this book leverages a simpler mechanism known as *application settings*. This is a static IsolatedStorageSettings.ApplicationSettings dictionary

in the `System.IO.IsolatedStorage` namespace. You can store any serializable object in this dictionary with a string key. When an application exits (whether closed or deactivated), the contents of the `ApplicationSettings` dictionary is automatically serialized to a file in isolated storage. And when an application is launched or activated, the dictionary is automatically populated with any previously persisted data. Listing 20.1 contains the implementation of the generic `Setting` class that wraps the use of the `ApplicationSettings` dictionary.

LISTING 20.1   `Setting.cs`—The `Setting` Class Automatically Persists a Named Value to Isolated Storage

```
using System.IO.IsolatedStorage;

namespace WindowsPhoneApp
{
  // Encapsulates a key/value pair stored in Isolated Storage ApplicationSettings
  public class Setting<T>
  {
    string name;
    T value;
    T defaultValue;
    bool hasValue;

    public Setting(string name, T defaultValue)
    {
      this.name = name;
      this.defaultValue = defaultValue;
    }

    public T Value
    {
      get
      {
        // Check for the cached value
        if (!this.hasValue)
        {
          // Try to get the value from Isolated Storage
          if (!IsolatedStorageSettings.ApplicationSettings.TryGetValue(
              this.name, out this.value))
          {
            // It hasn't been set yet
            this.value = this.defaultValue;
            IsolatedStorageSettings.ApplicationSettings[this.name] = this.value;
          }
          this.hasValue = true;
        }
```

LISTING 20.1 Continued

```
      return this.value;
    }

    set
    {
      // Save the value to Isolated Storage
      IsolatedStorageSettings.ApplicationSettings[this.name] = value;
      this.value = value;
      this.hasValue = true;
    }
  }

  public T DefaultValue
  {
    get { return this.defaultValue; }
  }

  // "Clear" cached value:
  public void ForceRefresh()
  {
    this.hasValue = false;
  }
}
}
```

Although placing items in the `ApplicationSettings` dictionary and retrieving them is straightforward, the `Setting` class cuts down on the amount of code needed by apps compared to using `ApplicationSettings` directly. This is especially true because users of `ApplicationSettings` must be prepared for keys that are not in the dictionary

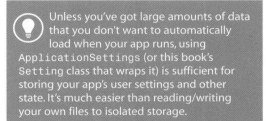

Unless you've got large amounts of data that you don't want to automatically load when your app runs, using `ApplicationSettings` (or this book's `Setting` class that wraps it) is sufficient for storing your app's user settings and other state. It's much easier than reading/writing your own files to isolated storage.

(typically for the first run of the app). The `Setting` class supports the specification of a default value, and it caches its value so it doesn't need to fetch it from the dictionary every time.

The `ForceRefresh` method resolves cases where the underlying dictionary entry is modified from external code. This is leveraged by every app that uses this book's color picker, because the color picker's page updates `ApplicationSettings` directly.

> 💡 Although `IsolatedStorageSettings` defines a `Save` method, you don't need to call it because all contents are automatically saved when your app exits. Your app must *gracefully* exit for this to happen, however. Therefore, the only valid reason to call `Save` manually would be to guard against data loss in case your app crashes before it is closed or deactivated.

> ❓ **What happens to the data in isolated storage when an app is updated or uninstalled?**
>
> When an app is updated to a new version, the data in its isolated storage is preserved. When an app is uninstalled, the data in its isolated storage is deleted. There's no way to recover it after the fact.

> ❓ **How much storage space is each app granted?**
>
> The space is only limited by the phone's capacity. Unlike with Silverlight on the web, no artificial storage limit is imposed on apps.

The Settings Page

Alarm Clock has four pages: a main page, an alarm page, a settings page, and an instructions page (not shown in this chapter). Because settings pages are one of this chapter's lessons, we'll look at Alarm Clock's settings page first. Shown in Figure 20.1, the page's XAML is in Listing 20.2.

FIGURE 20.1   Alarm Clock's settings page exposes several settings.

LISTING 20.2   `SettingsPage.xaml`—The User Interface for Alarm Clock's Settings Page

```xml
<phone:PhoneApplicationPage
    x:Class="WindowsPhoneApp.SettingsPage"
    xmlns="http://schemas.microsoft.com/winfx/2006/xaml/presentation"
    xmlns:x="http://schemas.microsoft.com/winfx/2006/xaml"
    xmlns:phone="clr-namespace:Microsoft.Phone.Controls;assembly=Microsoft.Phone"
    xmlns:shell="clr-namespace:Microsoft.Phone.Shell;assembly=Microsoft.Phone"
    xmlns:toolkit="clr-namespace:Microsoft.Phone.Controls;
          ➥assembly=Microsoft.Phone.Controls.Toolkit"
    xmlns:local="clr-namespace:WindowsPhoneApp"
    FontFamily="{StaticResource PhoneFontFamilyNormal}"
    FontSize="{StaticResource PhoneFontSizeNormal}"
    Foreground="{StaticResource PhoneForegroundBrush}"
    SupportedOrientations="PortraitOrLandscape" shell:SystemTray.IsVisible="True">
  <Grid>
    <Grid.RowDefinitions>
      <RowDefinition Height="Auto"/>
      <RowDefinition Height="*"/>
    </Grid.RowDefinitions>

    <!-- The standard settings header -->
    <StackPanel Grid.Row="0" Style="{StaticResource PhoneTitlePanelStyle}">
      <TextBlock Text="SETTINGS" Style="{StaticResource PhoneTextTitle0Style}"/>
      <TextBlock Text="alarm clock"
                 Style="{StaticResource PhoneTextTitle1Style}"/>
    </StackPanel>

    <ScrollViewer Grid.Row="1">
      <Grid Margin="{StaticResource PhoneMargin}">
        <Grid.ColumnDefinitions>
          <ColumnDefinition/>
          <ColumnDefinition/>
        </Grid.ColumnDefinitions>
        <Grid.RowDefinitions>
          <RowDefinition/>
          <RowDefinition/>
          <RowDefinition/>
          <RowDefinition/>
          <RowDefinition/>
          <RowDefinition/>
        </Grid.RowDefinitions>
        <TextBlock Text="Foreground color" Margin="12,7,12,8"
          Foreground="{StaticResource PhoneSubtleBrush}"/>
        <Rectangle x:Name="ForegroundColorRectangle" Grid.Row="1" Height="90"
          Margin="12,0,12,18" StrokeThickness="3" local:Tilt.IsEnabled="True"
```

LISTING 20.2   Continued

```
        Stroke="{StaticResource PhoneForegroundBrush}"
        MouseLeftButtonUp="ForegroundColorRectangle_MouseLeftButtonUp"/>
      <TextBlock Text="Background color" Grid.Column="1" Margin="12,7,12,8"
        Foreground="{StaticResource PhoneSubtleBrush}"/>
      <Rectangle x:Name="BackgroundColorRectangle" Grid.Row="1" Grid.Column="1"
        Margin="12,0,12,18" Height="90" StrokeThickness="3"
        Stroke="{StaticResource PhoneForegroundBrush}"
        local:Tilt.IsEnabled="True"
        MouseLeftButtonUp="BackgroundColorRectangle_MouseLeftButtonUp"/>
    <toolkit:ToggleSwitch x:Name="DisableScreenLockToggleSwitch" Grid.Row="2"
        Grid.ColumnSpan="2" Header="Disable screen time-out"/>
    <toolkit:ToggleSwitch x:Name="Show24HourToggleSwitch" Grid.Row="3"
        Grid.ColumnSpan="2" Header="24-hour clock"/>
    <toolkit:ToggleSwitch x:Name="ShowSecondsToggleSwitch" Grid.Row="4"
        Grid.ColumnSpan="2" Header="Show seconds"/>
    <toolkit:ToggleSwitch x:Name="EnableVibrationToggleSwitch" Grid.Row="5"
        Grid.ColumnSpan="2" Header="Enable vibration"/>
    </Grid>
  </ScrollViewer>
  </Grid>
</phone:PhoneApplicationPage>
```

This page makes use of several *toggle switch* controls from the Silverlight for Windows Phone Toolkit. Programmatically, a toggle switch acts like a check box. Visually, its default appearance is an on/off sliding switch.

The Windows Phone team publishes several guidelines for how an app's settings page should look and behave:

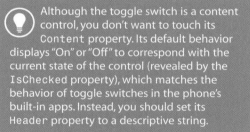

Although the toggle switch is a content control, you don't want to touch its Content property. Its default behavior displays "On" or "Off" to correspond with the current state of the control (revealed by the IsChecked property), which matches the behavior of toggle switches in the phone's built-in apps. Instead, you should set its Header property to a descriptive string.

→ The page should have the standard two-text-block header, and it should never scroll, even if the rest of the page does.

→ The text block that typically shows the application name should say "SETTINGS" instead, as if the user got transported to the phone's Settings app.

→ The text block that typically shows the page title should be the application name, again to match the appearance of pages in the Settings app.

→ When the user changes a setting, it should take effect immediately. There should be no page-level apply/cancel buttons.

→ Specific actions that are irreversible should prompt the user with a message box that gives the opportunity to cancel.

→ Try to keep the settings page as concise as possible.

→ Avoid creating more than one settings page. Making use of scrolling and/or a pivot control (covered in Part IV, "Pivot, Panorama, Charts, & Graphs) is a good way to handle content that won't fit on the screen.

How can my app add a page to the built-in Settings app?

It can't. In the current version of Windows Phone, 3rd-party apps can only expose a settings page inside themselves.

Look at pages in the phone's built-in Settings app for good examples of what settings pages should look like.

The page's code-behind is shown in Listing 20.3. It makes use of the some of the following settings defined in `Settings.cs`:

```csharp
public static class Settings
{
  // Persistent user settings from the settings page
  public static readonly Setting<Color> ForegroundColor = new Setting<Color>(
    "ForegroundColor", (Color)Application.Current.Resources["PhoneAccentColor"]);
  public static readonly Setting<Color> BackgroundColor = new Setting<Color>(
    "BackgroundColor", Colors.Black);
  public static readonly Setting<bool> DisableScreenLock =
    new Setting<bool>("DisableScreenLock", true);
  public static readonly Setting<bool> ShowSeconds =
    new Setting<bool>("ShowSeconds", true);
  public static readonly Setting<bool> Show24Hours =
    new Setting<bool>("Show24Hours", false);
  public static readonly Setting<bool> EnableVibration =
    new Setting<bool>("EnableVibration", true);

  // Persistent user settings from the alarm page
  public static readonly Setting<DateTime> AlarmTime = new Setting<DateTime>(
    "AlarmTime", new DateTime(2010, 1, 1, 8, 0, 0));
  public static readonly Setting<bool> IsAlarmOn =
    new Setting<bool>("IsAlarmOn", false);

  // Persistent state
  public static readonly Setting<SupportedPageOrientation> SupportedOrientations
    = new Setting<SupportedPageOrientation>("SupportedOrientations",
      SupportedPageOrientation.PortraitOrLandscape);
  public static readonly Setting<DateTime?> SnoozeTime =
    new Setting<DateTime?>("SnoozeTime", null);
}
```

LISTING 20.3   `SettingsPage.xaml.cs`—The Code-Behind for Alarm Clock's Settings Page

```csharp
using System;
using System.Windows.Input;
using System.Windows.Media;
using System.Windows.Navigation;
using Microsoft.Phone.Controls;

namespace WindowsPhoneApp
{
  public partial class SettingsPage : PhoneApplicationPage
  {
    public SettingsPage()
    {
      InitializeComponent();
    }

    protected override void OnNavigatedTo(NavigationEventArgs e)
    {
      base.OnNavigatedTo(e);
      // Respect the saved settings
      this.ForegroundColorRectangle.Fill =
        new SolidColorBrush(Settings.ForegroundColor.Value);
      this.BackgroundColorRectangle.Fill =
        new SolidColorBrush(Settings.BackgroundColor.Value);
      this.DisableScreenLockToggleSwitch.IsChecked =
        Settings.DisableScreenLock.Value;
      this.Show24HourToggleSwitch.IsChecked = Settings.Show24Hours.Value;
      this.ShowSecondsToggleSwitch.IsChecked = Settings.ShowSeconds.Value;
      this.EnableVibrationToggleSwitch.IsChecked = Settings.EnableVibration.Value;
    }

    protected override void OnNavigatedFrom(NavigationEventArgs e)
    {
      base.OnNavigatedFrom(e);
      // Save the settings (except the colors, already saved by the color picker)
      Settings.DisableScreenLock.Value =
        this.DisableScreenLockToggleSwitch.IsChecked.Value;
      Settings.Show24Hours.Value = this.Show24HourToggleSwitch.IsChecked.Value;
      Settings.ShowSeconds.Value = this.ShowSecondsToggleSwitch.IsChecked.Value;
      Settings.EnableVibration.Value =
        this.EnableVibrationToggleSwitch.IsChecked.Value;
    }

    void ForegroundColorRectangle_MouseLeftButtonUp(object sender,
      MouseButtonEventArgs e)
```

LISTING 20.3   Continued

```
  {
    // Get a string representation of the colors we need to pass to the color
    // picker, without the leading #
    string currentColorString =
      Settings.ForegroundColor.Value.ToString().Substring(1);
    string defaultColorString =
      Settings.ForegroundColor.DefaultValue.ToString().Substring(1);

    // The color picker works with the same isolated storage value that the
    // Setting works with, but we have to clear its cached value to pick up
    // the value chosen in the color picker
    Settings.ForegroundColor.ForceRefresh();

    // Navigate to the color picker
    this.NavigationService.Navigate(new Uri(
      "/Shared/Color Picker/ColorPickerPage.xaml?"
      + "&currentColor=" + currentColorString
      + "&defaultColor=" + defaultColorString
      + "&settingName=ForegroundColor", UriKind.Relative));
  }

  void BackgroundColorRectangle_MouseLeftButtonUp(object sender,
    MouseButtonEventArgs e)
  {
    // Get a string representation of the colors we need to pass to the color
    // picker, without the leading #
    string currentColorString =
      Settings.BackgroundColor.Value.ToString().Substring(1);
    string defaultColorString =
      Settings.BackgroundColor.DefaultValue.ToString().Substring(1);

    // The color picker works with the same isolated storage value that the
    // Setting works with, but we have to clear its cached value to pick up
    // the value chosen in the color picker
    Settings.BackgroundColor.ForceRefresh();

    // Navigate to the color picker
    this.NavigationService.Navigate(new Uri(
      "/Shared/Color Picker/ColorPickerPage.xaml?"
      + "&currentColor=" + currentColorString
      + "&defaultColor=" + defaultColorString
      + "&settingName=BackgroundColor", UriKind.Relative));
  }
 }
}
```

The color picker page writes the chosen color value directly to the `IsolatedStorageSettings.ApplicationSettings` dictionary, using the passed-in `settingName` as the key. This is how it is able to work with the `Setting` objects used by any app, and why a call to `ForceRefresh` is required before the `Setting` is accessed again.

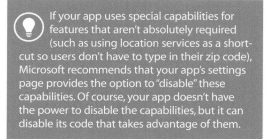 If your app uses special capabilities for features that aren't absolutely required (such as using location services as a short-cut so users don't have to type in their zip code), Microsoft recommends that your app's settings page provides the option to "disable" these capabilities. Of course, your app doesn't have the power to disable the capabilities, but it can disable its code that takes advantage of them.

The Alarm Page

The alarm page, shown in Figure 20.2, is basically a second settings page, but dedicated to turning the alarm on and off, and settings its time. It also has a button for testing the alarm volume, so users can make sure it is loud enough to wake them up.

FIGURE 20.2   The alarm page exposes the most important settings in the app.

Although apps should avoid having more than one settings page, this page is distinct-and important-enough to warrant its own page. A user may wish to visit the alarm page every night to ensure the alarm is set correctly, whereas they may never have the need to visit the settings page. Listing 20.4 contains its XAML and Listing 20.5 contains its code-behind.

LISTING 20.4   `AlarmPage.xaml`—The User Interface for Alarm Clock's Alarm Page

```xml
<phone:PhoneApplicationPage
    x:Class="WindowsPhoneApp.AlarmPage"
    xmlns="http://schemas.microsoft.com/winfx/2006/xaml/presentation"
    xmlns:x="http://schemas.microsoft.com/winfx/2006/xaml"
    xmlns:phone="clr-namespace:Microsoft.Phone.Controls;assembly=Microsoft.Phone"
    xmlns:shell="clr-namespace:Microsoft.Phone.Shell;assembly=Microsoft.Phone"
    xmlns:toolkit="clr-namespace:Microsoft.Phone.Controls;
            ➥assembly=Microsoft.Phone.Controls.Toolkit"
    xmlns:local="clr-namespace:WindowsPhoneApp"
    FontFamily="{StaticResource PhoneFontFamilyNormal}"
    FontSize="{StaticResource PhoneFontSizeNormal}"
    Foreground="{StaticResource PhoneForegroundBrush}"
    SupportedOrientations="PortraitOrLandscape" shell:SystemTray.IsVisible="True">
  <Grid>
    <Grid.RowDefinitions>
      <RowDefinition Height="Auto"/>
      <RowDefinition Height="*"/>
    </Grid.RowDefinitions>

    <!-- The standard settings header -->
    <StackPanel Grid.Row="0" Style="{StaticResource PhoneTitlePanelStyle}">
      <TextBlock Text="ALARM CLOCK"
                 Style="{StaticResource PhoneTextTitle0Style}"/>
      <TextBlock Text="set alarm" Style="{StaticResource PhoneTextTitle1Style}"/>
    </StackPanel>

    <ScrollViewer Grid.Row="1">
      <StackPanel Margin="{StaticResource PhoneMargin}">
        <toolkit:ToggleSwitch x:Name="ToggleSwitch" Header="Alarm"
                              Checked="ToggleSwitch_IsCheckedChanged"
                              Unchecked="ToggleSwitch_IsCheckedChanged"/>
        <toolkit:TimePicker x:Name="TimePicker"
                            ValueChanged="TimePicker_ValueChanged"/>
        <ToggleButton x:Name="TestVolumeButton" Content="test volume"
                      Margin="0,36,0,0" Checked="TestVolumeButton_Checked"
                      Unchecked="TestVolumeButton_Unchecked"
                      local:Tilt.IsEnabled="True"/>
      </StackPanel>
    </ScrollViewer>
  </Grid>
</phone:PhoneApplicationPage>
```

Listing 20.4 leverages two controls from the Silverlight for Windows Phone Toolkit: the toggle switch and the time picker. Toggle switches don't have an `IsCheckedChanged` event, so this listing attaches the `ToggleSwitch_IsCheckedChanged` event handler to two individual events—`Checked` and `Unchecked`.

LISTING 20.5   `AlarmPage.xaml.cs`—The Code-Behind for Alarm Clock's Alarm Page

```
using System;
using System.Windows;
using System.Windows.Navigation;
using System.Windows.Threading;
using Microsoft.Devices;
using Microsoft.Phone.Controls;
using Microsoft.Xna.Framework.Audio; // For SoundEffectInstance

namespace WindowsPhoneApp
{
  public partial class AlarmPage : PhoneApplicationPage
  {
    // For the sound and vibration
    SoundEffectInstance alarmSound;
    DispatcherTimer timer =
      new DispatcherTimer { Interval = TimeSpan.FromSeconds(1) };

    public AlarmPage()
    {
      InitializeComponent();
      this.timer.Tick += Timer_Tick;

      // Initialize the alarm sound
      this.alarmSound = SoundEffects.Alarm.CreateInstance();
      this.alarmSound.IsLooped = true;
    }

    protected override void OnNavigatedTo(NavigationEventArgs e)
    {
      base.OnNavigatedTo(e);
      // Respect the saved settings
      this.ToggleSwitch.IsChecked = Settings.IsAlarmOn.Value;
      this.TimePicker.Value = Settings.AlarmTime.Value;
    }

    protected override void OnNavigatedFrom(NavigationEventArgs e)
    {
      base.OnNavigatedFrom(e);
      // Save the settings (except AlarmTime, handled in TimePicker_ValueChanged)
```

LISTING 20.5 Continued

```
    Settings.IsAlarmOn.Value = this.ToggleSwitch.IsChecked.Value;

    // Stop the vibration/sound effect if still playing
    this.timer.Stop();
    this.alarmSound.Stop();
  }

  void TimePicker_ValueChanged(object sender, DateTimeValueChangedEventArgs e)
  {
    // To prevent getting clobbered on way back in
    Settings.AlarmTime.Value = this.TimePicker.Value.Value;
    Settings.SnoozeTime.Value = null;
  }

  void ToggleSwitch_IsCheckedChanged(object sender, RoutedEventArgs e)
  {
    // If we're currently snoozing, cancel it
    Settings.SnoozeTime.Value = null;
  }

  void TestVolumeButton_Checked(object sender, RoutedEventArgs e)
  {
    // Vibrate, only if its enabled
    if (Settings.EnableVibration.Value)
      this.timer.Start();
    // Play the sound
    this.alarmSound.Play();
  }

  void TestVolumeButton_Unchecked(object sender, RoutedEventArgs e)
  {
    // Stop the sound and vibration
    this.timer.Stop();
    this.alarmSound.Stop();
  }

  void Timer_Tick(object sender, EventArgs e)
  {
    // Vibrate for half a second
    VibrateController.Default.Start(TimeSpan.FromSeconds(.5));
  }
  }
}
```

Notes:

→ To produce the alarm sound, this app uses sound effect APIs covered in Part V, "Audio & Video."

→ As with Chapter 9, "Fake Call," the time picker's `ValueChanged` event is used to apply the new value to the corresponding setting. Without this, the `OnNavigatedTo` code that sets the time picker's value would overwrite the newly chosen value due to the page navigation invoked by the time picker.

The Main Page

The main page is the page that acts like a physical digital alarm clock, with its time display, day-of-the-week display, and alarm information. Its root grid contains many columns, mainly for evenly distributing the seven days of the week. Listing 20.6 contains its XAML, and Figure 20.3 shows this page with its root grid temporarily marked with `ShowGridLines="True"`.

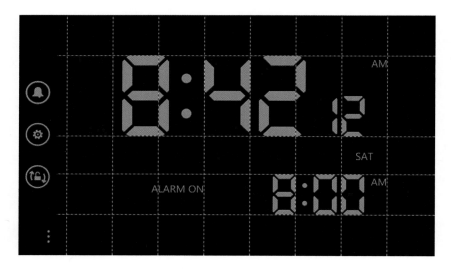

FIGURE 20.3   The main page, with grid lines showing.

LISTING 20.6   `MainPage.xaml`—The User Interface for Alarm Clock's Main Page

```
<phone:PhoneApplicationPage
    x:Class="WindowsPhoneApp.MainPage"
    xmlns="http://schemas.microsoft.com/winfx/2006/xaml/presentation"
    xmlns:x="http://schemas.microsoft.com/winfx/2006/xaml"
    xmlns:phone="clr-namespace:Microsoft.Phone.Controls;assembly=Microsoft.Phone"
    xmlns:shell="clr-namespace:Microsoft.Phone.Shell;assembly=Microsoft.Phone"
    xmlns:local="clr-namespace:WindowsPhoneApp"
```

LISTING 20.6   Continued

```
   FontFamily="{StaticResource PhoneFontFamilyNormal}"
   FontSize="{StaticResource PhoneFontSizeNormal}"
   SupportedOrientations="PortraitOrLandscape">

 <phone:PhoneApplicationPage.Resources>
   <!-- A style shared by SUN,MON,TUE,WED,THU,FRI,SAT -->
   <Style x:Name="DayOfWeekStyle" TargetType="TextBlock">
     <Setter Property="HorizontalAlignment" Value="Center"/>
     <Setter Property="VerticalAlignment" Value="Center"/>
     <Setter Property="Grid.Row" Value="2"/>
   </Style>
 </phone:PhoneApplicationPage.Resources>

 <!-- The application bar, with three buttons and two menu items -->
 <phone:PhoneApplicationPage.ApplicationBar>
   <shell:ApplicationBar Opacity=".95">
     <shell:ApplicationBarIconButton Text="set alarm"
       IconUri="/Images/appbar.alarm.png" Click="AlarmButton_Click"/>
     <shell:ApplicationBarIconButton Text="settings"
       IconUri="/Shared/Images/appbar.settings.png" Click="SettingsButton_Click"/>
     <shell:ApplicationBarIconButton Text="lock screen"
       IconUri="/Shared/Images/appbar.orientationUnlocked.png"
       Click="OrientationLockButton_Click"/>
     <shell:ApplicationBar.MenuItems>
       <shell:ApplicationBarMenuItem Text="instructions"
                                Click="InstructionsMenuItem_Click"/>
       <shell:ApplicationBarMenuItem Text="about" Click="AboutMenuItem_Click"/>
     </shell:ApplicationBar.MenuItems>
   </shell:ApplicationBar>
 </phone:PhoneApplicationPage.ApplicationBar>

 <Grid x:Name="Grid">
   <Grid.RowDefinitions>
     <RowDefinition/> <!-- Top margin -->
     <RowDefinition Height="Auto"/>
     <RowDefinition Height="75"/>
     <RowDefinition Height="Auto"/>
     <RowDefinition/> <!-- Bottom margin -->
   </Grid.RowDefinitions>
   <Grid.ColumnDefinitions>
     <ColumnDefinition x:Name="LeftMargin" Width="0"/>
     <ColumnDefinition/> <!-- SUN -->
     <ColumnDefinition/> <!-- MON -->
     <ColumnDefinition/> <!-- TUE -->
```

LISTING 20.6   Continued

```xml
            <ColumnDefinition/> <!-- WED -->
            <ColumnDefinition/> <!-- THU -->
            <ColumnDefinition/> <!-- FRI -->
            <ColumnDefinition/> <!-- SAT -->
            <ColumnDefinition x:Name="RightMargin" Width="0"/>
        </Grid.ColumnDefinitions>

        <!-- The current time -->
        <local:TimeDisplay x:Name="MainTimeDisplay" Grid.Row="1" Grid.Column="1"
                           Grid.ColumnSpan="7" HorizontalAlignment="Center"/>

        <!-- Two simple labels -->
        <TextBlock x:Name="AlarmOnTextBlock" Grid.Row="3" Grid.Column="1"
                   Grid.ColumnSpan="3" Text="ALARM ON" Margin="0,-24,0,0"
                   HorizontalAlignment="Right" VerticalAlignment="Center"/>
        <TextBlock x:Name="SnoozeTextBlock" Grid.Row="3" Grid.Column="1"
                   Grid.ColumnSpan="3" Text="SNOOZING UNTIL" Margin="0,24,0,0"
                   HorizontalAlignment="Right" VerticalAlignment="Center"/>

        <!-- The alarm/snooze time -->
        <local:TimeDisplay x:Name="AlarmTimeDisplay" ShowSeconds="False"
                           Grid.Row="3" Grid.Column="3" Grid.ColumnSpan="5"
                           HorizontalAlignment="Right"/>
    </Grid>
</phone:PhoneApplicationPage>
```

The XAML uses two instances of a `TimeDisplay` user control, shown in the next section. The code-behind is in Listing 20.7.

LISTING 20.7   `MainPage.xaml.cs`—The Code-Behind for Alarm Clock's Main Page

```csharp
using System;
using System.Windows;
using System.Windows.Controls;
using System.Windows.Input;
using System.Windows.Media;
using System.Windows.Navigation;
using System.Windows.Threading;
using Microsoft.Devices;
using Microsoft.Phone.Controls;
using Microsoft.Phone.Shell;
using Microsoft.Xna.Framework.Audio; // For SoundEffectInstance

namespace WindowsPhoneApp
```

LISTING 20.7 Continued

```
{
  public partial class MainPage : PhoneApplicationPage
  {
    // A timer, so we can update the display every second
    DispatcherTimer timer =
      new DispatcherTimer { Interval = TimeSpan.FromSeconds(1) };

    IApplicationBarIconButton orientationLockButton;
    TextBlock[] dayOfWeekTextBlocks = new TextBlock[7];
    SoundEffectInstance alarmSound;
    bool tappedAlarmOff;

    public MainPage()
    {
      InitializeComponent();
      this.orientationLockButton =
        this.ApplicationBar.Buttons[2] as IApplicationBarIconButton;

      this.timer.Tick += Timer_Tick;
      this.timer.Start();

      // Initialize the alarm sound effect
      SoundEffects.Initialize();
      this.alarmSound = SoundEffects.Alarm.CreateInstance();
      this.alarmSound.IsLooped = true;

      // Add the seven day-of-week text blocks here, assigning them to an array
      this.dayOfWeekTextBlocks[0] = new TextBlock { Text = "SUN",
        Style = this.DayOfWeekStyle };
      Grid.SetColumn(this.dayOfWeekTextBlocks[0], 1);

      this.dayOfWeekTextBlocks[1] = new TextBlock { Text = "MON",
        Style = this.DayOfWeekStyle };
      Grid.SetColumn(this.dayOfWeekTextBlocks[1], 2);

      this.dayOfWeekTextBlocks[2] = new TextBlock { Text = "TUE",
        Style = this.DayOfWeekStyle };
      Grid.SetColumn(this.dayOfWeekTextBlocks[2], 3);

      this.dayOfWeekTextBlocks[3] = new TextBlock { Text = "WED",
        Style = this.DayOfWeekStyle };
      Grid.SetColumn(this.dayOfWeekTextBlocks[3], 4);

      this.dayOfWeekTextBlocks[4] = new TextBlock { Text = "THU",
```

LISTING 20.7   Continued

```
        Style = this.DayOfWeekStyle };
      Grid.SetColumn(this.dayOfWeekTextBlocks[4], 5);

      this.dayOfWeekTextBlocks[5] = new TextBlock { Text = "FRI",
        Style = this.DayOfWeekStyle };
      Grid.SetColumn(this.dayOfWeekTextBlocks[5], 6);

      this.dayOfWeekTextBlocks[6] = new TextBlock { Text = "SAT",
        Style = this.DayOfWeekStyle };
      Grid.SetColumn(this.dayOfWeekTextBlocks[6], 7);

      for (int i = 0; i < this.dayOfWeekTextBlocks.Length; i++)
        this.Grid.Children.Add(dayOfWeekTextBlocks[i]);

      // Allow the app to run (making the alarm sound and vibration)
      // even when the phone is locked.
      // Once disabled, you cannot re-enable the default behavior!
      PhoneApplicationService.Current.ApplicationIdleDetectionMode =
        IdleDetectionMode.Disabled;
    }

    protected override void OnNavigatedFrom(NavigationEventArgs e)
    {
      base.OnNavigatedFrom(e);

      // Restore the ability for the screen to auto-lock when on other pages
      PhoneApplicationService.Current.UserIdleDetectionMode =
        IdleDetectionMode.Enabled;
    }

    protected override void OnNavigatedTo(NavigationEventArgs e)
    {
      base.OnNavigatedTo(e);

      this.tappedAlarmOff = false;

      // Respect the saved settings
      this.Foreground = new SolidColorBrush(Settings.ForegroundColor.Value);
      this.Grid.Background = new SolidColorBrush(Settings.BackgroundColor.Value);
      this.ApplicationBar.ForegroundColor = Settings.ForegroundColor.Value;
      this.ApplicationBar.BackgroundColor = Settings.BackgroundColor.Value;

      // While on this page, don't allow the screen to auto-lock
      if (Settings.DisableScreenLock.Value)
```

LISTING 20.7   Continued

```
      PhoneApplicationService.Current.UserIdleDetectionMode =
        IdleDetectionMode.Disabled;

    // Restore the orientation setting to whatever it was last time
    this.SupportedOrientations = Settings.SupportedOrientations.Value;

    // If the restored value is not PortraitOrLandscape, then the orientation
    // has been locked. Change the state of the application bar button to
    // reflect this.
    if (this.SupportedOrientations !=
      SupportedPageOrientation.PortraitOrLandscape)
    {
      this.orientationLockButton.Text = "unlock";
      this.orientationLockButton.IconUri = new Uri(
        "/Shared/Images/appbar.orientationLocked.png", UriKind.Relative);
    }

    RefreshDisplays();

    // Don't wait for the next tick
    Timer_Tick(this, EventArgs.Empty);
  }

  protected override void OnOrientationChanged(OrientationChangedEventArgs e)
  {
    base.OnOrientationChanged(e);
    RefreshDisplays();
  }

  protected override void OnMouseLeftButtonDown(MouseButtonEventArgs e)
  {
    base.OnMouseLeftButtonDown(e);

    if (this.alarmSound.State == SoundState.Playing)
    {
      // Turn the alarm off
      this.tappedAlarmOff = true;
      this.alarmSound.Stop();

      // Set the snooze time to five minutes from now
      DateTime currentTimeWithoutSeconds = DateTime.Now;
      currentTimeWithoutSeconds =
        currentTimeWithoutSeconds.AddSeconds(-currentTimeWithoutSeconds.Second);
      Settings.SnoozeTime.Value = currentTimeWithoutSeconds.AddMinutes(5);
```

LISTING 20.7   Continued

```csharp
      RefreshDisplays();
    }
    else
    {
      // Toggle the application bar visibility
      this.ApplicationBar.IsVisible = !this.ApplicationBar.IsVisible;
    }
  }


  void RefreshDisplays()
  {
    if (IsMatchingOrientation(PageOrientation.Portrait))
    {
      // Adjust the margins for portrait
      this.LeftMargin.Width = new GridLength(12);
      this.RightMargin.Width = new GridLength(12);
      // Set the font size accordingly
      if (Settings.ShowSeconds.Value)
        this.MainTimeDisplay.FontSize = 182;
      else
        this.MainTimeDisplay.FontSize = 223;
    }
    else
    {
      // Adjust the margins for landscape
      this.LeftMargin.Width = new GridLength(92);
      this.RightMargin.Width = new GridLength(92);
      // Set the font size accordingly
      if (Settings.ShowSeconds.Value)
        this.MainTimeDisplay.FontSize = 251;
      else
        this.MainTimeDisplay.FontSize = 307;
    }

    this.AlarmTimeDisplay.FontSize = this.MainTimeDisplay.FontSize / 2;

    // Respect the settings in the two time displays
    this.MainTimeDisplay.Show24Hours = Settings.Show24Hours.Value;
    this.AlarmTimeDisplay.Show24Hours = Settings.Show24Hours.Value;
    this.MainTimeDisplay.ShowSeconds = Settings.ShowSeconds.Value;
    this.MainTimeDisplay.Initialize();
    this.AlarmTimeDisplay.Initialize();

    if (Settings.IsAlarmOn.Value)
```

LISTING 20.7   Continued

```
  {
    if (Settings.SnoozeTime.Value != null)
    {
      // Show that we're snoozing
      this.AlarmOnTextBlock.Opacity = .1;
      this.SnoozeTextBlock.Opacity = 1;
      this.AlarmTimeDisplay.Time = Settings.SnoozeTime.Value;
    }
    else
    {
      // Show when the alarm will go off
      this.AlarmOnTextBlock.Opacity = 1;
      this.SnoozeTextBlock.Opacity = .1;
      this.AlarmTimeDisplay.Time = Settings.AlarmTime.Value;
    }
  }
  else
  {
    // No alarm, no snooze
    this.AlarmOnTextBlock.Opacity = .1;
    this.SnoozeTextBlock.Opacity = .1;
    this.AlarmTimeDisplay.Time = null;
  }
}

void Timer_Tick(object sender, EventArgs e)
{
  // Refresh the current time
  this.MainTimeDisplay.Time = DateTime.Now;

  // Keep the day of the week up-to-date
  for (int i = 0; i < this.dayOfWeekTextBlocks.Length; i++)
    this.dayOfWeekTextBlocks[i].Opacity = .2;
  this.dayOfWeekTextBlocks[(int)DateTime.Now.DayOfWeek].Opacity = 1;

  // If the alarm sound is playing, accompany it with vibration
  // (if that setting is enabled)
  if (this.alarmSound.State == SoundState.Playing
      && Settings.EnableVibration.Value)
    VibrateController.Default.Start(TimeSpan.FromSeconds(.5));

  if (Settings.IsAlarmOn.Value)
  {
    TimeSpan timeToAlarm =
```

LISTING 20.7   Continued

```
            Settings.AlarmTime.Value.TimeOfDay - DateTime.Now.TimeOfDay;

      // Let the alarm go off up to 60 seconds after the designated time
      // (in case the app wasn't running at the beginning of the minute or it
      // was on a different page)
      if (!this.tappedAlarmOff && this.alarmSound.State != SoundState.Playing
          && timeToAlarm.TotalSeconds <= 0 && timeToAlarm.TotalSeconds > -60)
      {
        this.alarmSound.Play();
        return; // Don't bother with snooze
      }
    }

    if (Settings.SnoozeTime.Value != null)
    {
      TimeSpan timeToSnooze =
        Settings.SnoozeTime.Value.Value.TimeOfDay - DateTime.Now.TimeOfDay;

      // Let the snoozed alarm go off up to 60 seconds after the designated time
      // (in case the app wasn't running at the beginning of the minute or it
      // was on a different page)
      if (this.alarmSound.State != SoundState.Playing
          && timeToSnooze.TotalSeconds <= 0 && timeToSnooze.TotalSeconds > -60)
      {
        this.alarmSound.Play();
      }
    }
  }
}

bool IsMatchingOrientation(PageOrientation orientation)
{
  return ((this.Orientation & orientation) == orientation);
}

// Application bar handlers

void AlarmButton_Click(object sender, EventArgs e)
{
  this.NavigationService.Navigate(new Uri("/AlarmPage.xaml",
    UriKind.Relative));
}

void SettingsButton_Click(object sender, EventArgs e)
{
```

LISTING 20.7   Continued

```
    this.NavigationService.Navigate(new Uri("/SettingsPage.xaml",
      UriKind.Relative));
  }

  // The "orientation lock" feature
  void OrientationLockButton_Click(object sender, EventArgs e)
  {
    // Check the value of SupportedOrientations to see if we're currently
    // "locked" to a value other than PortraitOrLandscape.
    if (this.SupportedOrientations !=
      SupportedPageOrientation.PortraitOrLandscape)
    {
      // We are locked, so unlock now
      this.SupportedOrientations = SupportedPageOrientation.PortraitOrLandscape;

      // Change the state of the application bar button to reflect this
      this.orientationLockButton.Text = "lock screen";
      this.orientationLockButton.IconUri = new Uri(
        "/Shared/Images/appbar.orientationUnlocked.png", UriKind.Relative);
    }
    else
    {
      // We are unlocked, so lock to the current orientation now
      if (IsMatchingOrientation(PageOrientation.Portrait))
        this.SupportedOrientations = SupportedPageOrientation.Portrait;
      else
        this.SupportedOrientations = SupportedPageOrientation.Landscape;

      // Change the state of the application bar button to reflect this
      this.orientationLockButton.Text = "unlock";
      this.orientationLockButton.IconUri = new Uri(
        "/Shared/Images/appbar.orientationLocked.png", UriKind.Relative);
    }

    // Remember the new setting after the page has been left
    Settings.SupportedOrientations.Value = this.SupportedOrientations;
  }

  void InstructionsMenuItem_Click(object sender, EventArgs e)
  {
    this.NavigationService.Navigate(new Uri("/InstructionsPage.xaml",
      UriKind.Relative));
  }
```

LISTING 20.7 Continued

```
void AboutMenuItem_Click(object sender, EventArgs e)
{
  this.NavigationService.Navigate(new Uri(
    "/Shared/About/AboutPage.xaml?appName=Alarm Clock", UriKind.Relative));
}
}
}
```

Notes:

→ Similar to Chapter 4, "Stopwatch," this page uses a timer to continually refresh the current time. It does it once per second, which also happens to be useful for triggering the once-per-second vibration while the alarm is going off.

→ This page also uses the same orientation lock approach from Chapter 4.

→ The seven day-of-the-week text blocks are constructed and added to their parent grid in code-behind rather than in XAML. This is done because having them in an array is convenient for the code that needs to illuminate the appropriate one.

→ This page sets `ApplicationIdleDetectionMode` to `Disabled` so it runs while the screen is locked (and off). This is the most likely what users would want to do, rather than leaving the screen on all night. However, if they wish to do so, this page also sets `UserIdleDetectionMode` to `Disabled` so it won't automatically lock. If the users want to turn off their screen, they must do it manually.

→ This page does something a bit unique; it applies the chosen foreground and background colors to the application bar in addition to the main display. The chosen background color is applied to the grid rather than the page. Recall that setting a page's background color has no effect.

→ If the alarm is going off, tapping the screen snoozes it by five minutes. (This is five minutes from the *beginning* of the current minute, as it would be confusing if the alarm didn't go off at a minute boundary.) Otherwise, tapping the screen toggles the visibility of the application bar. This provides a way for the user to get a more realistic and minimalistic display.

→ The various text blocks are illuminated with an opacity of 1, and they are "turned off" with an opacity of either .1 or .2. (The variation is there just to give more realism.) The code inside of `Timer_Tick` leverages the array of day-of-the-week text blocks, using `DateTime.Now.DayOfWeek` (a number from 0 to 6, inclusive) as the index into the array.

The `TimeDisplay` User Control

What makes this app special is its time display that uses seven-segment digital numerals. There are a few ways to accomplish such a display. For example, you could create vector-based shapes and illuminate the appropriate segments at an appropriate time with their fill settings. This app takes a somewhat-easier approach: using a custom font. Listing 20.8 contains the XAML for the `TimeDisplay` user control that implements the seven-segment display.

> **① Before using a custom font, make sure you have permission!**
>
> Using a custom font is easy. Using it *legally* is another story. Be sure you understand the rules for any specific font you wish to use. The custom font used in Listing 20.8 is called "Pendule Ornamental," created by Scott Lawrence and available at http://fontstruct.fontshop.com/fontstructions/show/200136. It is licensed under a Creative Commons Attribution Share Alike license (http://creativecommons.org/licenses/by-sa/3.0/).

LISTING 20.8   `TimeDisplay.xaml`—The User Interface for the `TimeDisplay` User Control

```xaml
<UserControl x:Class="WindowsPhoneApp.TimeDisplay"
    xmlns="http://schemas.microsoft.com/winfx/2006/xaml/presentation"
    xmlns:x="http://schemas.microsoft.com/winfx/2006/xaml">
  <Grid x:Name="Grid" Background="Transparent">
    <Grid.ColumnDefinitions>
      <ColumnDefinition Width="Auto"/>
      <ColumnDefinition Width="Auto"/>
    </Grid.ColumnDefinitions>

    <!-- The background "off" segments -->
    <TextBlock FontFamily="Fonts/pendule_ornamental.ttf#pendule ornamental"
             Opacity=".1">
      <!-- It's important not to have whitespace between the runs!-->
      <Run x:Name="TimeBackgroundRun">88:88</Run><Run
          x:Name="SecondsBackgroundRun">88</Run>
    </TextBlock>

    <!-- The foreground "on" segments -->
    <TextBlock FontFamily="Fonts/pendule_ornamental.ttf#pendule ornamental">
      <!-- It's important not to have whitespace between the runs!-->
      <Run x:Name="TimeRun"/><Run x:Name="SecondsRun"/>
    </TextBlock>

    <!-- AM / PM -->
    <TextBlock x:Name="AMTextBlock" Grid.Column="1" Text="AM"
```

LISTING 20.8   Continued

```
            FontSize="{StaticResource PhoneFontSizeNormal}"
            HorizontalAlignment="Center" Margin="4,0,0,0"/>
    <TextBlock x:Name="PMTextBlock" Grid.Column="1" Text="PM"
            FontSize="{StaticResource PhoneFontSizeNormal}"
            HorizontalAlignment="Center" Margin="4,24,0,0"/>
  </Grid>
</UserControl>
```

Notes:

→ To use a custom font, simply include the font file in your project (with a Build Action of Content), and then reference it in the FontFamily value on any text block or text box (or element whose font family will be inherited by relevant child elements). The syntax is

pathAndFilename#fontName

You can see the correct value for *fontName* by opening the font file via Windows Explorer.

→ To give the effect of dim "off" segments in each numeral, this user control actually uses two overlapping text blocks. The one in the back has all segments activated at all times (with a value of 88:88 for the hour/minutes and a value of 88 for the seconds), but is given an opacity of .1. The one in the front displays the actual time at full opacity.

→ Each text block contains two *runs*, one for the larger hour/minutes and one for the smaller seconds. (The sizes and values are set in code-behind.) A surprising fact about a text block is that its content property is *not* its Text property, but rather a property called Inlines. Although a type converter enables you to set it to a simple string in XAML, Inlines can be set to a collection of Inline objects. There are two classes that derive from the abstract Inline class: Run and LineBreak. LineBreak was introduced in Chapter 8, "Vibration Composer."

→ On a run, you can set the same formatting properties available on a text block, such as FontFamily, FontSize, FontStyle, FontWeight, Foreground, and TextDecorations. Runs, therefore, provide a convenient way to create text with mixed formatting all inside a single text block.

The white space between Run **elements matters!**

Listing 20.8 takes great care not to have any white space between the two runs inside each text block. Much like in HTML, this would have the effect of putting a single space between the two runs.

Listing 20.9 contains the code-behind for this user control.

LISTING 20.9   `TimeDisplay.xaml.cs`—The Code-Behind for the `TimeDisplay` User Control

```
using System;
using System.Windows;
using System.Windows.Controls;

namespace WindowsPhoneApp
{
  public partial class TimeDisplay : UserControl
  {
    DateTime? time;

    public TimeDisplay()
    {
      InitializeComponent();
      Time = null;
    }

    public void Initialize()
    {
      if (!this.ShowSeconds)
      {
        // Remove the seconds display
        this.SecondsRun.Text = null;
        this.SecondsBackgroundRun.Text = null;
      }

      // Hide AM and PM in 24-hour mode
      this.AMTextBlock.Visibility =
        this.Show24Hours ? Visibility.Collapsed : Visibility.Visible;
      this.PMTextBlock.Visibility =
        this.Show24Hours ? Visibility.Collapsed : Visibility.Visible;

      // The seconds font size is always half of whatever the main font size is
      this.SecondsBackgroundRun.FontSize = this.SecondsRun.FontSize =
        this.FontSize / 2;
    }

    public bool ShowSeconds { get; set; }
    public bool Show24Hours { get; set; }

    public DateTime? Time
    {
      get { return this.time; }
      set
      {
```

LISTING 20.9   Continued

```
      this.time = value;

      if (this.time == null)
      {
        // Clear everything
        this.TimeRun.Text = null;
        this.SecondsRun.Text = null;
        this.AMTextBlock.Opacity = .1;
        this.PMTextBlock.Opacity = .1;
        return;
      }

      string formatString = this.Show24Hours ? "H:mm" : "h:mm";

      // The hour needs a leading space if it ends up being only one digit
      if ((this.Show24Hours && this.time.Value.Hour < 10) ||
          (!this.Show24Hours &&
          (this.time.Value.Hour % 12 < 10 && this.time.Value.Hour % 12 > 0)))
        formatString = " " + formatString;

      this.TimeRun.Text = this.time.Value.ToString(formatString);

      if (this.ShowSeconds)
        this.SecondsRun.Text = this.time.Value.ToString("ss");

      if (!this.Show24Hours)
      {
        // Show either AM or PM
        if (this.time.Value.Hour < 12)
        {
          this.AMTextBlock.Opacity = 1;
          this.PMTextBlock.Opacity = .1;
        }
        else
        {
          this.AMTextBlock.Opacity = .1;
          this.PMTextBlock.Opacity = 1;
        }
      }
    }
  }
}
}
```

The Finished Product

Turning off the seconds display

Portrait orientation with
the application bar hidden

Using the 24-hour clock and
no seconds display

chapter 21

PASSWORDS & SECRETS

Passwords & Secrets is a notepad-style app that you can protect with a master password. Therefore, it's a great app for storing a variety of passwords and other secrets that you don't want getting into the wrong hands. The note-taking functionality is top-notch, supporting

- → Auto-save, which makes jotting down notes fast and easy
- → Quick previews of each note
- → The ability to customize each note's background/foreground colors and text size
- → The ability to email your notes

On top of this, the data in each note is encrypted with 256-bit Advanced Encryption Standard (AES) encryption to keep prying eyes from discovering the data. This encryption is done based on the master password, so it's important that the user never forgets their password! There is no way for the app to retrieve the data without it, as the app does not store the password for security reasons.

To make management of the master password as easy as possible, Passwords & Secrets supports specifying and showing a password hint. It also enables you to change your password (but only if you know the current password).

Why would I need to encrypt data stored in isolated storage? Isn't my app the only thing that can access it?

Barring any bugs in the Windows Phone OS, another app should never be able to read your app's isolated storage. And nobody should be able to *remotely* peer into your isolated storage. But if skilled hackers get physical access to your phone, they could certainly read the data stored on it. Encryption makes it virtually impossible for hackers to make any sense of the stored data.

Basic Cryptography

Silverlight's System.Security.Cryptography namespace contains quite a bit of functionality for cryptographic tasks. This app wraps the necessary pieces of functionality from this namespace in order to expose an easy-to-use Crypto class. This class exposes two simple methods—Encrypt and Decrypt—that accept the decrypted/encrypted data along with a password to use as the basis for the encryption and decryption. Listing 21.1 contains the implementation.

LISTING 21.1   Crypto.cs—The Crypto Class That Exposes Simple Encrypt and Decrypt Methods

```
using System;
using System.IO;
using System.Security.Cryptography;
using System.Text;

namespace WindowsPhoneApp
{
  public static class Crypto
  {
    public static string Encrypt(string data, string password)
    {
      if (data == null)
        return null;

      using (SymmetricAlgorithm algorithm = GetAlgorithm(password))
      using (MemoryStream memoryStream = new MemoryStream())
      using (CryptoStream cryptoStream = new CryptoStream(
        memoryStream, algorithm.CreateEncryptor(), CryptoStreamMode.Write))
      {
        // Convert the original data to bytes then write them to the CryptoStream
        byte[] buffer = Encoding.UTF8.GetBytes(data);
        cryptoStream.Write(buffer, 0, buffer.Length);
        cryptoStream.FlushFinalBlock();
        // Convert the encrypted bytes back into a string
        return Convert.ToBase64String(memoryStream.ToArray());
```

LISTING 21.1   Continued

```
    }
  }

  public static string Decrypt(string data, string password)
  {
    if (data == null)
      return null;

    using (SymmetricAlgorithm algorithm = GetAlgorithm(password))
    using (MemoryStream memoryStream = new MemoryStream())
    using (CryptoStream cryptoStream = new CryptoStream(
      memoryStream, algorithm.CreateDecryptor(), CryptoStreamMode.Write))
    {
      // Convert the encrypted string to bytes then write them
      // to the CryptoStream
      byte[] buffer = Convert.FromBase64String(data);
      cryptoStream.Write(buffer, 0, buffer.Length);
      cryptoStream.FlushFinalBlock();
      // Convert the original data back to a string
      buffer = memoryStream.ToArray();
      return Encoding.UTF8.GetString(buffer, 0, buffer.Length);
    }
  }

  // Hash the input data with a salt, typically used for storing a password
  public static string Hash(string data)
  {
    // Convert the data to bytes
    byte[] dataBytes = Encoding.UTF8.GetBytes(data);

    // Create a new array with the salt bytes followed by the data bytes
    byte[] allBytes = new byte[Settings.Salt.Value.Length + dataBytes.Length];
    // Copy the salt at the beginning
    Settings.Salt.Value.CopyTo(allBytes, 0);
    // Copy the data after the salt
    dataBytes.CopyTo(allBytes, Settings.Salt.Value.Length);

    // Compute the hash for the combined set of bytes
    byte[] hash = new SHA256Managed().ComputeHash(allBytes);

    // Convert the bytes into a string
    return Convert.ToBase64String(hash);
  }
```

LISTING 21.1   Continued

```
public static byte[] GenerateNewSalt(int length)
{
  Byte[] bytes = new Byte[length];
  // Fill the array with random bytes, using a cryptographic
  // random number generator (RNG)
  new RNGCryptoServiceProvider().GetBytes(bytes);
  return bytes;
}

static SymmetricAlgorithm GetAlgorithm(string password)
{
  // Use the Advanced Encryption Standard (AES) algorithm
  AesManaged algorithm = new AesManaged();

  // Derive an encryption key from the password
  Rfc2898DeriveBytes bytes = new Rfc2898DeriveBytes(password,
    Settings.Salt.Value);

  // Initialize, converting the two values in bits to bytes (dividing by 8)
  algorithm.Key = bytes.GetBytes(algorithm.KeySize / 8);
  algorithm.IV = bytes.GetBytes(algorithm.BlockSize / 8);

  return algorithm;
  }
 }
}
```

→ Both Encrypt and Decrypt call a GetAlgorithm helper method (defined at the end of the file) to get started. The returned algorithm can create an *encryptor* or a *decryptor*, which is passed to a crypto stream that is used to drive the encryption/decryption work.

→ In Encrypt, the input string is converted to bytes based on a UTF8 encoding. These bytes can then be written to the crypto stream to perform the encryption. The encrypted bytes are retrieved by using the ToArray method on the underlying memory stream used by the crypto stream. These bytes are converted back to a stream using Base64 encoding, which is a common approach for representing binary data in a string.

→ Decrypt starts with the Base64-encoded string and converts it to bytes to be written to the crypto stream. It then uses the underlying memory stream's ToArray method to convert the decrypted UTF8 bytes back into a string.

→ The Hash function computes a SHA256 (Secure Hash Algorithm with a 256-bit digest) cryptographic hash of the input string prepended with a random "salt." This is sometimes called a *salted hash*. This app calls this method in order to store a salted hash of the password rather than the password itself, for extra security. After all, if a hacker got a hold of the data in isolated storage, the encryption would be pointless if the password were stored along with it in plain text!

→ `GenerateNewSalt` simply produces a random byte array of the desired length. Rather than using the simple `Random` class used in other apps, this method uses `RNGCryptoServiceProvider`, a higher-quality pseudo-random number generator that is more appropriate to use in cryptographic applications. As shown in the next section, this app calls this method only once, and only the first time the app is run. It stores the randomly generated salt in isolated storage and then uses that for all future encryption, decryption, and hashing.

→ `GetAlgorithm` constructs the only built-in encryption algorithm, `AesManaged`, which is the AES symmetric algorithm. The algorithm needs to be initialized with a secret key and an initialization vector (IV), so this is handled by the `Rfc2898DeriveBytes` instance.

→ `Rfc2898DeriveBytes` is an implementation of a password-based key derivation function—PBKDF2. This uses the password and a random "salt" value, and applies a pseudo-random function based on a SHA1 hash function many times (1000 by default). All this makes the password much harder to crack.

→ The default value of `AesManaged`'s `KeySize` property is also its maximum supported value: 256. This means that the key is 256-bits long, which is why this process is called 256-bit encryption.

> **Salt in Cryptography**   • • •
>
> Using salt can provide a number of benefits for slowing down hackers, especially when the salt can be kept a secret. In this app, although a salt must be passed to the constructor of `Rfc2898DeriveBytes`, it doesn't really add value because the salt must be stored along with the encrypted data. The same goes for the salting of the hash inside the `Hash` function. Although this is good practice for a server managing multiple passwords (so dictionary-based attacks must be regenerated for each user, and so users with the same password won't have the same hash), it is done in this app mainly for show.

The `LoginControl` User Control

With the `Crypto` class in place, we can create a login control that handles all the user interaction needed for the app's master password. The `LoginControl` user control used by this app is shown in Figure 21.1. It has three different modes:

→ The *new user* mode, in which the user must choose their master password for the first time

→ The *normal login* mode, in which the user must enter their previously chosen password

→ The ***change password*** mode, in which the user can change their password (after entering their existing password)

New User   Normal Login   Change Password

FIGURE 21.1   The three modes of the `LoginControl` user control in action.

Listing 21.2 contains the XAML for this control.

LISTING 21.2   `LoginControl.xaml`—The User Interface for the `LoginControl` User Control

```
<UserControl x:Class="WindowsPhoneApp.LoginControl"
    xmlns="http://schemas.microsoft.com/winfx/2006/xaml/presentation"
    xmlns:x="http://schemas.microsoft.com/winfx/2006/xaml"
    xmlns:local="clr-namespace:WindowsPhoneApp"
    FontFamily="{StaticResource PhoneFontFamilyNormal}"
    FontSize="{StaticResource PhoneFontSizeNormal}"
    Foreground="{StaticResource PhoneForegroundBrush}">
  <Grid Background="{StaticResource PhoneBackgroundBrush}">

    <!-- A dim accent-colored padlock image -->
    <Rectangle Fill="{StaticResource PhoneAccentBrush}" Width="300" Height="364"
               VerticalAlignment="Bottom" HorizontalAlignment="Right"
               Margin="{StaticResource PhoneMargin}" Opacity=".5">
      <Rectangle.OpacityMask>
        <ImageBrush ImageSource="Images/lock.png"/>
      </Rectangle.OpacityMask>
    </Rectangle>
```

LISTING 21.2   Continued

```xml
<ScrollViewer>
  <Grid>
    <!-- This panel is used for both New User and Change Password modes -->
    <StackPanel x:Name="ChangePasswordPanel" Visibility="Collapsed"
                Margin="{StaticResource PhoneMargin}">

      <!-- Welcome! -->
      <TextBlock x:Name="WelcomeTextBlock" Visibility="Collapsed"
        Margin="{StaticResource PhoneHorizontalMargin}" TextWrapping="Wrap">
      <Run FontWeight="Bold">Welcome!</Run>
      <LineBreak/>
      Choose a password that you'll remember.  There is no way to recover …
      </TextBlock>

      <!-- Old password -->
      <TextBlock Text="Old password" x:Name="OldPasswordLabel"
                 Style="{StaticResource LabelStyle}"/>
      <PasswordBox x:Name="OldPasswordBox" KeyUp="PasswordBox_KeyUp"/>

      <!-- New password -->
      <TextBlock Text="New password" Style="{StaticResource LabelStyle}"/>
      <PasswordBox x:Name="NewPasswordBox" KeyUp="PasswordBox_KeyUp"/>

      <!-- Confirm new password -->
      <TextBlock Text="Type new password again"
                 Style="{StaticResource LabelStyle}"/>
      <PasswordBox x:Name="ConfirmNewPasswordBox" KeyUp="PasswordBox_KeyUp"/>

      <!-- Password hint -->
      <TextBlock Text="Password hint (optional)"
                 Style="{StaticResource LabelStyle}"/>
      <TextBox x:Name="PasswordHintTextBox" InputScope="Text"
               KeyUp="PasswordBox_KeyUp"/>

      <Button Content="ok" Click="OkButton_Click" MinWidth="226"
              HorizontalAlignment="Left" Margin="0,12,0,0"
              local:Tilt.IsEnabled="True"/>
    </StackPanel>

    <!-- This panel is used only for the Normal Login mode -->
    <StackPanel x:Name="NormalLoginPanel" Visibility="Collapsed"
                Margin="{StaticResource PhoneMargin}">
      <TextBlock Text="Enter your password"
                 Style="{StaticResource LabelStyle}"/>
```

LISTING 21.2   Continued

```
        <PasswordBox x:Name="NormalLoginPasswordBox" KeyUp="PasswordBox_KeyUp"/>
        <Button Content="ok" Click="OkButton_Click" MinWidth="226"
                HorizontalAlignment="Left" local:Tilt.IsEnabled="True"/>
      </StackPanel>
    </Grid>
  </ScrollViewer>
 </Grid>
</UserControl>
```

Notes:

→ This control uses a password box wherever a password should be entered. A password box is just like a text box, except that it displays each character as a circle (after a brief moment in which you see the letter you just typed). This matches the behavior of password entry in all the built-in apps. Instead of a Text property, it has a Password property.

→ The opacity mask trick from Chapter 17, "Pick a Card Magic Trick," is used to give an image of a padlock the color of the current theme's accent color. It's also given 50% opacity, so it blends into the background a bit more.

Listing 21.3 contains the code-behind.

LISTING 21.3   LoginControl.xaml.cs—The Code-Behind for the LoginControl User Control

```csharp
using System;
using System.Windows;
using System.Windows.Controls;
using System.Windows.Input;

namespace WindowsPhoneApp
{
  public partial class LoginControl : UserControl
  {
    // A custom event
    public event EventHandler Closed;

    public LoginControl()
    {
      InitializeComponent();

      // Update the UI depending on which of the three modes we're in
      if (Settings.HashedPassword.Value == null)
      {
        // The "new user" mode
```

LISTING 21.3   Continued

```
        this.WelcomeTextBlock.Visibility = Visibility.Visible;
        this.OldPasswordLabel.Visibility = Visibility.Collapsed;
        this.OldPasswordBox.Visibility = Visibility.Collapsed;
        this.ChangePasswordPanel.Visibility = Visibility.Visible;
      }
      else if (CurrentContext.IsLoggedIn)
      {
        // The "change password" mode
        this.ChangePasswordPanel.Visibility = Visibility.Visible;
      }
      else
      {
        // The "normal login" mode
        this.NormalLoginPanel.Visibility = Visibility.Visible;
      }
    }

    void OkButton_Click(object sender, RoutedEventArgs e)
    {
      string currentHashedPassword = Settings.HashedPassword.Value;

      if (currentHashedPassword != null && !CurrentContext.IsLoggedIn)
      {
        // We're in "normal login" mode

        // If the hash of the attempted password matches the stored hash,
        // then we know the user entered the correct password.
        if (Crypto.Hash(this.NormalLoginPasswordBox.Password)
            != currentHashedPassword)
        {
          MessageBox.Show("", "Incorrect password", MessageBoxButton.OK);
          return;
        }

        // Keep the unencrypted password in-memory,
        // only until this app is deactivated/closed
        CurrentContext.Password = this.NormalLoginPasswordBox.Password;
      }
      else
      {
        // We're in "new user" or "change password" mode

        // For "change password," be sure that the old password is correct
```

LISTING 21.3   Continued

```csharp
if (CurrentContext.IsLoggedIn && Crypto.Hash(this.OldPasswordBox.Password)
    != currentHashedPassword)
{
  MessageBox.Show("", "Incorrect old password", MessageBoxButton.OK);
  return;
}

// Now validate the new password
if (this.NewPasswordBox.Password != this.ConfirmNewPasswordBox.Password)
{
  MessageBox.Show("The two passwords don't match.  Please try again.",
                  "Oops!", MessageBoxButton.OK);
  return;
}

string newPassword = this.NewPasswordBox.Password;

if (newPassword == null || newPassword.Length == 0)
{
  MessageBox.Show("The password cannot be empty.  Please try again.",
                  "Nice try!", MessageBoxButton.OK);
  return;
}

// Store a hash of the password so we can check for the correct
// password in future logins without storing the actual password
Settings.HashedPassword.Value = Crypto.Hash(newPassword);

// Store the password hint as plain text
Settings.PasswordHint.Value = this.PasswordHintTextBox.Text;

// Keep the unencrypted password in-memory,
// only until this app is deactivated/closed
CurrentContext.Password = newPassword;

// If there already was a password, we must decrypt all data with the old
// password (then re-encrypt it with the new password) while we still
// know the old password! Otherwise the data will be unreadable!
if (currentHashedPassword != null)
{
  // Each item in the NotesList setting has an EncryptedContent property
  // that must be processed
  for (int i = 0; i < Settings.NotesList.Value.Count; i++)
  {
```

LISTING 21.3   Continued

```csharp
        // Encrypt with the new password the data that is decrypted
        // with the old password
        Settings.NotesList.Value[i].EncryptedContent =
          Crypto.Encrypt(
            Crypto.Decrypt(Settings.NotesList.Value[i].EncryptedContent,
            this.OldPasswordBox.Password),
            newPassword
          );
      }
    }
  }

  CurrentContext.IsLoggedIn = true;
  Close();
}

void PasswordBox_KeyUp(object sender, KeyEventArgs e)
{
  // Allow the Enter key to cycle between text boxes and to press the ok
  // button when on the last text box
  if (e.Key == Key.Enter)
  {
    if (sender == this.PasswordHintTextBox ||
        sender == this.NormalLoginPasswordBox)
      OkButton_Click(sender, e);
    else if (sender == this.OldPasswordBox)
      this.NewPasswordBox.Focus();
    else if (sender == this.NewPasswordBox)
      this.ConfirmNewPasswordBox.Focus();
    else if (sender == this.ConfirmNewPasswordBox)
      this.PasswordHintTextBox.Focus();
  }
}

public void Close()
{
  if (this.Visibility == Visibility.Collapsed)
    return; // Already closed

  // Clear all
  this.OldPasswordBox.Password = "";
  this.NewPasswordBox.Password = "";
  this.ConfirmNewPasswordBox.Password = "";
  this.NormalLoginPasswordBox.Password = "";
```

LISTING 21.3   Continued

```csharp
      this.PasswordHintTextBox.Text = "";

    // Close by becoming invisible
    this.Visibility = Visibility.Collapsed;

    // Raise the event
    if (this.Closed != null)
      this.Closed(this, EventArgs.Empty);
  }
 }
}
```

Notes:

→ This listing makes use of some of the following settings defined in a separate
  Settings.cs file:

```csharp
public static class Settings
{
    // Password-related settings
    public static readonly Setting<byte[]> Salt =
      new Setting<byte[]>("Salt", Crypto.GenerateNewSalt(16));
    public static readonly Setting<string> HashedPassword =
      new Setting<string>("HashedPassword", null);
    public static readonly Setting<string> PasswordHint =
      new Setting<string>("PasswordHint", null);

    // The user's data
    public static readonly Setting<ObservableCollection<Note>> NotesList =
      new Setting<ObservableCollection<Note>>("NotesList",
                                              new ObservableCollection<Note>());

    // User settings
    public static readonly Setting<bool> MakeDefault =
      new Setting<bool>("MakeDefault", false);
    public static readonly Setting<Color> ScreenColor =
      new Setting<Color>("ScreenColor", Color.FromArgb(0xFF, 0xFE, 0xCF, 0x58));
    public static readonly Setting<Color> TextColor =
      new Setting<Color>("TextColor", Colors.Black);
    public static readonly Setting<int> TextSize = new Setting<int>("TextSize",
      22);

    // Temporary state
    public static readonly Setting<int> CurrentNoteIndex =
      new Setting<int>("CurrentNoteIndex", -1);
```

```
public static readonly Setting<Color?> TempScreenColor =
  new Setting<Color?>("TempScreenColor", null);
public static readonly Setting<Color?> TempTextColor =
  new Setting<Color?>("TempTextColor", null);
}
```

The salt required by Rfc2898DeriveBytes used by the Crypto class must be at least 8 bytes. With the call to GenerateNewSalt, this app generates a 16-byte salt.

→ In the normal login mode, the control must determine whether the entered password is correct. But the app doesn't store the user's password. Instead, it stores a salted hash of the password. Therefore, to validate the entered password, it calls the same Crypto.Hash function and checks if it matches the stored hashed value.

→ Although the unencrypted password is not persisted, it is kept in memory while the app runs so it can decrypt the user's saved content and encrypt any new content. This is done with the CurrentContext class, defined as follows in CurrentContext.cs:

```
public static class CurrentContext
{
  public static bool IsLoggedIn = false;
  public static string Password = null;
}
```

→ In the change password mode, something very important must be done before the old password is forgotten. Everything that has been encrypted with the old password must be decrypted then re-encrypted with the new password. Otherwise, the data would become unreadable because the new password cannot be used to decrypt data that was encrypted with the old password!

→ Inside Close, the Password property of each password box is set to an empty string instead of null because the Password property throws an exception if set to null.

→ You can see that LoginControl is not a general-purpose control but rather tailored to this app. (Although it wouldn't be hard to generalize it by providing a hook for the consumer to perform the data re-encryption during the password-change process.) It is used in three separate places, shown in the next three sections of this chapter.

The Change Password Page

The change password page, seen previously in Figure 21.1, is nothing more than a page hosting a LoginControl instance. The user can only reach this page when already signed in, so the control is automatically initialized to the "change password" mode thanks to the code in Listing 21.3. Listings 21.4 and 21.5 contain the simple XAML and code-behind for the change password page.

LISTING 21.4   `ChangePasswordPage.xaml`—The User Interface for Password & Secrets' Change Password Page

```xaml
<phone:PhoneApplicationPage
    x:Class="WindowsPhoneApp.ChangePasswordPage"
    xmlns="http://schemas.microsoft.com/winfx/2006/xaml/presentation"
    xmlns:x="http://schemas.microsoft.com/winfx/2006/xaml"
    xmlns:phone="clr-namespace:Microsoft.Phone.Controls;assembly=Microsoft.Phone"
    xmlns:shell="clr-namespace:Microsoft.Phone.Shell;assembly=Microsoft.Phone"
    xmlns:local="clr-namespace:WindowsPhoneApp"
    FontFamily="{StaticResource PhoneFontFamilyNormal}"
    FontSize="{StaticResource PhoneFontSizeNormal}"
    Foreground="{StaticResource PhoneForegroundBrush}"
    SupportedOrientations="PortraitOrLandscape" shell:SystemTray.IsVisible="True">
  <Grid>
    <Grid.RowDefinitions>
      <RowDefinition Height="Auto"/>
      <RowDefinition Height="*"/>
    </Grid.RowDefinitions>

    <!-- The standard header -->
    <StackPanel Style="{StaticResource PhoneTitlePanelStyle}">
      <TextBlock Text="PASSWORDS &amp; SECRETS"
                 Style="{StaticResource PhoneTextTitle0Style}"/>
      <TextBlock Text="change password"
                 Style="{StaticResource PhoneTextTitle1Style}"/>
    </StackPanel>

    <!-- The user control -->
    <local:LoginControl Grid.Row="1" Closed="LoginControl_Closed"/>
  </Grid>
</phone:PhoneApplicationPage>
```

LISTING 21.5   `ChangePasswordPage.xaml.cs`—The Code-Behind for Password & Secrets' Change Password Page

```csharp
using Microsoft.Phone.Controls;

namespace WindowsPhoneApp
{
  public partial class ChangePasswordPage : PhoneApplicationPage
  {
    public ChangePasswordPage()
    {
      InitializeComponent();
    }

    void LoginControl_Closed(object sender, System.EventArgs e)
```

LISTING 21.5   Continued

```
  {
    if (this.NavigationService.CanGoBack)
      this.NavigationService.GoBack();
  }
 }
}
```

The Main Page

This app's main page contains the list of user's notes, as demonstrated in Figure 21.2. Each one can be tapped to view and/or edit it. A button on the application bar enables adding new notes. But before the list is populated and any of this is shown, the user must enter the correct password. When the user isn't logged in, the `LoginControl` covers the entire page except its header, and the application bar doesn't have the add-note button.

Logged out

Logged in

FIGURE 21.2   A list of notes on the main page, in various colors and sizes.

The User Interface

Listing 21.6 contains the XAML for the main page.

LISTING 21.6   `MainPage.xaml`—The User Interface for Password & Secrets' Main Page

```
<phone:PhoneApplicationPage
    x:Class="WindowsPhoneApp.MainPage"
    xmlns="http://schemas.microsoft.com/winfx/2006/xaml/presentation"
    xmlns:x="http://schemas.microsoft.com/winfx/2006/xaml"
```

LISTING 21.6   Continued

```
  xmlns:phone="clr-namespace:Microsoft.Phone.Controls;assembly=Microsoft.Phone"
  xmlns:shell="clr-namespace:Microsoft.Phone.Shell;assembly=Microsoft.Phone"
  xmlns:local="clr-namespace:WindowsPhoneApp"
  FontFamily="{StaticResource PhoneFontFamilyNormal}"
  FontSize="{StaticResource PhoneFontSizeNormal}"
  Foreground="{StaticResource PhoneForegroundBrush}"
  SupportedOrientations="PortraitOrLandscape" shell:SystemTray.IsVisible="True">

 <phone:PhoneApplicationPage.Resources>
   <local:DateConverter x:Key="DateConverter"/>
 </phone:PhoneApplicationPage.Resources>

 <!-- The application bar, with 3 menu items -->
 <phone:PhoneApplicationPage.ApplicationBar>
   <shell:ApplicationBar>
     <shell:ApplicationBar.MenuItems>
       <shell:ApplicationBarMenuItem Text="show password hint"
                                     Click="PasswordMenuItem_Click"/>
       <shell:ApplicationBarMenuItem Text="instructions"
                                     Click="InstructionsMenuItem_Click"/>
       <shell:ApplicationBarMenuItem Text="about" Click="AboutMenuItem_Click"/>
       <shell:ApplicationBarMenuItem Text="more apps"
                                     Click="MoreAppsMenuItem_Click"/>
     </shell:ApplicationBar.MenuItems>
   </shell:ApplicationBar>
 </phone:PhoneApplicationPage.ApplicationBar>

 <Grid Background="Transparent">
   <Grid.RowDefinitions>
     <RowDefinition Height="Auto"/>
     <RowDefinition Height="*"/>
   </Grid.RowDefinitions>

   <!-- The standard header -->
   <StackPanel Grid.Row="0"
               Style="{StaticResource PhoneTitlePanelStyle}">
     <TextBlock Text="PASSWORDS &amp; SECRETS"
                Style="{StaticResource PhoneTextTitle0Style}"/>
   </StackPanel>

   <!-- Show this when there are no notes -->
   <TextBlock Name="NoItemsTextBlock" Grid.Row="1" Text="No notes"
              Visibility="Collapsed" Margin="22,17,0,0"
              Style="{StaticResource PhoneTextGroupHeaderStyle}"/>

   <!-- The list box containing notes -->
```

LISTING 21.6   Continued

```
    <ListBox x:Name="ListBox" Grid.Row="1" ItemsSource="{Binding}"
            SelectionChanged="ListBox_SelectionChanged">
      <ListBox.ItemTemplate>
        <DataTemplate>
          <StackPanel>
            <!-- The title, in a style matching the note -->
            <Border Background="{Binding ScreenBrush}" Margin="24,0" Width="800"
                    MinHeight="60" local:Tilt.IsEnabled="True">
              <TextBlock Text="{Binding Title}" FontSize="{Binding TextSize}"
                      Foreground="{Binding TextBrush}" Margin="12"
                      VerticalAlignment="Center"/>
            </Border>
            <!-- The modified date -->
            <TextBlock Foreground="{StaticResource PhoneSubtleBrush}"
              Text="{Binding Modified, Converter={StaticResource DateConverter}}"
              Margin="24,0,0,12"/>
          </StackPanel>
        </DataTemplate>
      </ListBox.ItemTemplate>
    </ListBox>


    <!-- The user control -->
    <local:LoginControl x:Name="LoginControl" Grid.Row="1"
Closed="LoginControl_Closed"/>
  </Grid>
</phone:PhoneApplicationPage>
```

Notes:

➔ The ampersand in the app's title is XML encoded to avoid a XAML parsing error.

➔ The `LoginControl` user control is used as a part of this page, rather than as a separate login page, to ensure a sensible navigation flow. When the user opens the app, logs in, and then sees the data on the main page, pressing the hardware Back button should exit the app, not go back to a login page!

➔ `LoginControl` doesn't protect the data simply by visually covering it up; you'll see in the code-behind that it isn't populated until after login. And there's no way for the app to show the data before login because the correct password is needed to properly decrypt the stored notes.

➔ The list box's item template binds to several properties of each note. (The `Note` class used to represent each one is shown later in this chapter.) The binding to the `Modified` property uses something called a *value converter* to change the resultant display. Value converters are discussed next.

Value Converters

In data binding, value converters can morph a source value into a completely different target value. They enable you to plug in custom logic without giving up the benefits of data binding.

Value converters are often used to reconcile a source and target that are different data types. For example, you could change the background or foreground color of an element based on the value of some nonbrush data source, à la conditional formatting in Microsoft Excel. As another example, the toggle switch in the Silverlight for Windows Phone Toolkit leverages a value converter called OnOffConverter that converts the nullable Boolean IsChecked value to an "On" or "Off" string used as its default content.

In Passwords & Secrets, we want to *slightly* customize the display of each note's Modified property. Modified is of type DateTimeOffset, so without a value converter applied, it would appear as follows:

```
12/11/2012 10:18:49 PM -08:00
```

The -08:00 represents the time zone. It is expressed as an offset from Coordinated Universal Time (UTC).

Our custom value converter strips off the time zone information and the seconds, as that's more information than we need. It produces a result like the following:

```
12/11/2010 10:18 PM
```

Even if Modified were a DateTime instead of a DateTimeOffset, the value converter would still be useful for stripping the seconds value out of the string.

(?) What's the difference between the DateTime data type and DateTimeOffset?

Whereas DateTime refers to a logical point in time that is independent of any time zone, DateTimeOffset is a real point in time with an offset relative to the UTC time zone. In this app, DateTimeOffset is appropriate to use for the modified time of each note because users shouldn't expect that point in time to change even if they later travel to a different time zone. The preceding chapter's Alarm Clock, however, appropriately uses DateTime for the alarm time. Imagine that you set the alarm while in one time zone but you're in a different time zone when it's time for it to go off. If you had set your alarm for 8:00 AM, you probably expect it to go off at 8:00 AM no matter what time zone you happen to be in at the time.

For most scenarios, using DateTimeOffset is preferable to DateTime. However, it was introduced into the .NET Framework years after DateTime, so the better name was already taken. (Designers of the class rejected calling it DateTime2 or DateTimeEx). Fortunately, consumers of these data types can pretty much use them interchangeably.

To create a value converter, you must write a class that implements an IValueConverter interface in the System.Windows.Data namespace. This interface has two simple methods—Convert, which is passed the source instance that must be converted to the target instance, and ConvertBack, which does the opposite. Listing 21.7 contains the implementation of the DateConverter value converter used in Listing 21.6.

LISTING 21.7   `DateConverter.cs`—A Value Converter That Customizes the Display of a `DateTimeOffset`

```
using System;
using System.Globalization;
using System.Windows;
using System.Windows.Data;

namespace WindowsPhoneApp
{
  public class DateConverter : IValueConverter
  {
    public object Convert(object value, Type targetType, object parameter,
      CultureInfo culture)
    {
      DateTimeOffset date = (DateTimeOffset)value;
      // Return a custom format
      return date.LocalDateTime.ToShortDateString() + " "
          + date.LocalDateTime.ToShortTimeString();
    }

    public object ConvertBack(object value, Type targetType, object parameter,
      CultureInfo culture)
    {
      return DependencyProperty.UnsetValue;
    }
  }
}
```

The `Convert` method is called every time the source value changes. It's given the `DateTimeOffset` value and returns a string with the date and time in a short format. The `ConvertBack` method is not needed, as it is only invoked in two-way data binding. Therefore, it returns a dummy value.

Value converters can be applied to any data binding with its `Converter` parameter. This was done in Listing 21.6 as follows:

```
<!-- The modified date -->
<TextBlock Foreground="{StaticResource PhoneSubtleBrush}"
  Text="{Binding Modified, Converter={StaticResource DateConverter}}"
  Margin="24,0,0,12"/>
```

Setting this via `StaticResource` syntax requires an instance of the converter class to be defined in an appropriate resource dictionary. Listing 21.6 added an instance with the `DateConverter` key to the page's resource dictionary:

```
<phone:PhoneApplicationPage.Resources>
  <local:DateConverter x:Key="DateConverter"/>
</phone:PhoneApplicationPage.Resources>
```

• • •

Additional Data for Value Converters

The methods of IValueConverter are passed a parameter and a culture. By default, parameter is set to null and culture is set to the value of the target element's Language property. However, the consumer of bindings can control these two values via Binding.ConverterParameter and Binding.ConverterCulture. For example:

```
<!-- The modified date -->
<TextBlock Foreground="{StaticResource PhoneSubtleBrush}"
  Text="{Binding Modified, Converter={StaticResource DateConverter},
         ConverterParameter=custom data, ConverterCulture=en-US}"
  Margin="24,0,0,12"/>
```

The ConverterParameter can be any custom data for the converter class to act upon, much like the Tag property on elements. ConverterCulture can be set to an Internet Engineering Task Force (IETF) language tag (such as en-US or ko-KR), and the converter receives the appropriate CultureInfo object. In DateConverter, the ToString methods already respect the current culture, so there's no need to do anything custom with the culture.

Value converters are the key to plugging any kind of custom logic into the data-binding process that goes beyond basic formatting. Whether you want to apply some sort of transformation to the source value before displaying it or change how the target gets updated based on the value of the source, you can easily accomplish this with a class that implements IValueConverter.

A very common value converter that people create is a Boolean-to-Visibility converter (usually called BooleanToVisibilityConverter) that can convert between the Visibility enumeration and a Boolean or nullable Boolean. In one direction, true is mapped to Visible, whereas false and null are mapped to Collapsed. In the other direction, Visible is mapped to true, whereas Collapsed is mapped to false. This is useful for toggling the visibility of elements based on the state of an otherwise unrelated element, all in XAML. For example, the following snippet of XAML implements a Show Button check box without requiring any procedural code (other than the value converter):

```
<phone:PhoneApplicationPage.Resources>
  <local:BooleanToVisibilityConverter x:Key="BooltoVis"/>
</phone:PhoneApplicationPage.Resources>
…
<CheckBox x:Name="CheckBox">Show Button</CheckBox>
…
<Button Visibility="{Binding IsChecked, ElementName=CheckBox,
  Converter={StaticResource BoolToVis}}"…/>
```

In this case, the button is visible when (and only when) the check box's IsChecked property is true.

The Code-Behind

The code-behind for the main page is shown in Listing 21.8.

LISTING 21.8   `MainPage.xaml.cs`—The Code-Behind for Password & Secrets' Main Page

```csharp
using System;
using System.Windows;
using System.Windows.Controls;
using System.Windows.Navigation;
using Microsoft.Phone.Controls;
using Microsoft.Phone.Shell;

namespace WindowsPhoneApp
{
  public partial class MainPage : PhoneApplicationPage
  {
    IApplicationBarMenuItem passwordMenuItem;

    public MainPage()
    {
      InitializeComponent();
      this.passwordMenuItem = this.ApplicationBar.MenuItems[0]
        as IApplicationBarMenuItem;
    }

    protected override void OnNavigatedTo(NavigationEventArgs e)
    {
      base.OnNavigatedTo(e);

      // The password menu item is "show password hint" when not logged in,
      // or "change password" when logged in
      if (CurrentContext.IsLoggedIn)
      {
        this.passwordMenuItem.Text = "change password";
        // This is only needed when reactivating app and navigating back to this
        // page from the details page, because going back can instantiate
        // this page in a logged-in state
        this.LoginControl.Close();
      }
      else
      {
        this.passwordMenuItem.Text = "show password hint";
      }

      // Clear the selection so selecting the same item twice in a row will
      // still raise the SelectionChanged event
```

LISTING 21.8   Continued

```
    Settings.CurrentNoteIndex.Value = -1;
    this.ListBox.SelectedIndex = -1;

    if (Settings.NotesList.Value.Count == 0)
      this.NoItemsTextBlock.Visibility = Visibility.Visible;
    else
      this.NoItemsTextBlock.Visibility = Visibility.Collapsed;
  }

  void ListBox_SelectionChanged(object sender, SelectionChangedEventArgs e)
  {
    if (ListBox.SelectedIndex >= 0)
    {
      // Navigate to the details page for the selected item
      Settings.CurrentNoteIndex.Value = ListBox.SelectedIndex;
      this.NavigationService.Navigate(new Uri("/DetailsPage.xaml",
        UriKind.Relative));
    }
  }

  void LoginControl_Closed(object sender, EventArgs e)
  {
    // Now that we're logged-in, add the "new" button to the application bar
    ApplicationBarIconButton newButton = new ApplicationBarIconButton
    {
      Text = "new",
      IconUri = new Uri("/Shared/Images/appbar.add.png", UriKind.Relative)
    };
    newButton.Click += NewButton_Click;
    this.ApplicationBar.Buttons.Add(newButton);

    // The password menu item is "show password hint" when not logged in,
    // or "change password" when logged in
    this.passwordMenuItem.Text = "change password";

    // Now bind the notes list as the data source for the list box,
    // because its contents can be decrypted
    this.DataContext = Settings.NotesList.Value;
  }

  // Application bar handlers

  void NewButton_Click(object sender, EventArgs e)
  {
```

LISTING 21.8   Continued

```
      // Create a new note and add it to the top of the list
      Note note = new Note();
      note.Modified = DateTimeOffset.Now;
      note.ScreenColor = Settings.ScreenColor.Value;
      note.TextColor = Settings.TextColor.Value;
      note.TextSize = Settings.TextSize.Value;
      Settings.NotesList.Value.Insert(0, note);

      // "Select" the new note
      Settings.CurrentNoteIndex.Value = 0;

      // Navigate to the details page for the newly created note
      this.NavigationService.Navigate(new Uri("/DetailsPage.xaml",
        UriKind.Relative));
    }

    void PasswordMenuItem_Click(object sender, EventArgs e)
    {
      if (CurrentContext.IsLoggedIn)
      {
        // Change password
        this.NavigationService.Navigate(new Uri("/ChangePasswordPage.xaml",
          UriKind.Relative));
      }
      else
      {
        // Show password hint
        if (Settings.PasswordHint.Value == null ||
            Settings.PasswordHint.Value.Trim().Length == 0)
        {
          MessageBox.Show("Sorry, but there is no hint!", "Password hint",
            MessageBoxButton.OK);
        }
        else
        {
          MessageBox.Show(Settings.PasswordHint.Value, "Password hint",
            MessageBoxButton.OK);
        }
      }
    }

    void InstructionsMenuItem_Click(object sender, EventArgs e)
    {
      this.NavigationService.Navigate(new Uri("/InstructionsPage.xaml",
```

LISTING 21.8   Continued

```
      UriKind.Relative));
  }

  void AboutMenuItem_Click(object sender, EventArgs e)
  {
    this.NavigationService.Navigate(
      new Uri("/Shared/About/AboutPage.xaml?appName=Passwords %26 Secrets",
        UriKind.Relative));
  }
 }
}
```

Notes:

→ The first menu item on the application bar, shown expanded in Figure 21.3, reveals the password hint when the user is logged out and navigates to the change password page when the user is logged in.

FIGURE 21.3   The expanded application bar menu shows "change password" when the user is logged in.

→ As seen earlier, the `NotesList` collection used as the data context for the list box is not just any collection (like `List<Note>`); it's an *observable collection*:

```
public static readonly Setting<ObservableCollection<Note>> NotesList =
  new Setting<ObservableCollection<Note>>("NotesList",
                                  new ObservableCollection<Note>());
```

Observable collections raise a `CollectionChanged` event whenever any changes occur, such as items being added or removed. Data binding automatically leverages this event to keep the target (the list box, in this page) up-to-date at all times. Thanks to this, Listing 21.8 simply sets the page's data context to the list and the rest takes care of itself.

The `INotifyPropertyChanged` Interface

Although the observable collection takes care off additions and deletions being reflected in the list box, each `Note` item must provide notifications to ensure that item-specific property changes are reflected in the databound list box. `Note` does this by implementing `INotifyPropertyChanged`, as shown in Listing 21.9.

LISTING 21.9   `Note.cs`—The Note Class Representing Each Item in the List

```
using System;
using System.ComponentModel;
using System.Windows.Media;

namespace WindowsPhoneApp
{
  public class Note : INotifyPropertyChanged
  {
    public event PropertyChangedEventHandler PropertyChanged;

    // A helper method used by the properties
    void OnPropertyChanged(string propertyName)
    {
      PropertyChangedEventHandler handler = this.PropertyChanged;
      if (handler != null)
        handler(this, new PropertyChangedEventArgs(propertyName));
    }

    string encryptedContent;
    public string EncryptedContent
    {
      get { return this.encryptedContent; }
      set { this.encryptedContent = value;
            OnPropertyChanged("EncryptedContent"); OnPropertyChanged("Title"); }
    }
```

LISTING 21.9   Continued

```
DateTimeOffset modified;
public DateTimeOffset Modified
{
  get { return this.modified; }
  set { this.modified = value; OnPropertyChanged("Modified"); }
}

int textSize;
public int TextSize
{
  get { return this.textSize; }
  set { this.textSize = value; OnPropertyChanged("TextSize"); }
}

Color screenColor;
public Color ScreenColor
{
  get { return this.screenColor; }
  set { this.screenColor = value;
        OnPropertyChanged("ScreenColor"); OnPropertyChanged("ScreenBrush"); }
}

Color textColor;
public Color TextColor
{
  get { return this.textColor; }
  set { this.textColor = value;
        OnPropertyChanged("TextColor"); OnPropertyChanged("TextBrush"); }
}

// Three readonly properties whose value is computed from other properties:

public Brush ScreenBrush
{
  get { return new SolidColorBrush(this.ScreenColor); }
}

public Brush TextBrush
{
  get { return new SolidColorBrush(this.TextColor); }
}

public string Title
{
```

LISTING 21.9   Continued

```
      get
      {
        // Grab the note's content
        string title =
          Crypto.Decrypt(this.EncryptedContent, CurrentContext.Password) ?? "";

        // Don't include more than the first 100 characters, which should be long
        // enough, even in landscape with a small font
        if (title.Length > 100)
          title = title.Substring(0, 100);

        // Fold the remaining content into a single line. We can't use
        // Environment.NewLine because it's \r\n, whereas newlines inserted from
        // a text box are just \r
        return title.Replace('\r', ' ');
      }
    }
  }
}
```

Notes:

→ INotifyPropertyChanged has a single member—a PropertyChanged event. If the implementer raises this event at the appropriate time with the name of each property that has changed, data binding takes care of refreshing any targets.

→ The raising of the PropertyChanged event is handled by the OnPropertyChanged helper method. The event handler field is assigned to a handler variable to avoid a potential bug. Without this, if a different thread removed the last handler between the time that the current thread checked for null and performed the invocation, a NullReferenceException would be thrown. (The event handler field becomes null when no more listeners are attached.)

> Dependency properties automatically implement a change-notification mechanism that acts like (but is distinct from) INotifyPropertyChanged. Therefore, when you use a dependency property, change notification automatically works with data binding with no additional code needed.

→ Notice that some properties, when changed, raise the PropertyChanged event for an additional property. For example, when EncryptedContent is set to a new value, a PropertyChanged event is raised for the readonly Title property. This is done because the value of Title is based on the value of EncryptedContent, so a change to EncryptedContent may change Title.

> •••
>
> INotifyCollectionChanged
>
> Observable collections perform their magic by implementing INotifyCollectionChanged, an interface that is very similar to INotifyPropertyChanged. This interface contains a single CollectionChanged event. It is very rare, however, for people to write their own collection class and implement INotifyCollectionChanged rather than simply using the ObservableCollection class.

The Details Page

The details page, shown in Figure 21.4, appears when the user taps a note in the list box on the main page. This page displays the entire contents of the note and enables the user to edit it, delete it, or email its contents. It also provides access to a per-note settings page that gives control over the note's colors and text size. Listing 21.10 contains this page's XAML.

In viewing mode, with the application bar visible

In edit mode, which hides the application bar

FIGURE 21.4   The details page, shown for a white-on-red note.

LISTING 21.10   DetailsPage.xaml—The User Interface for Passwords & Secrets' Details Page

```
<phone:PhoneApplicationPage
    x:Class="WindowsPhoneApp.DetailsPage"
    xmlns="http://schemas.microsoft.com/winfx/2006/xaml/presentation"
    xmlns:x="http://schemas.microsoft.com/winfx/2006/xaml"
    xmlns:phone="clr-namespace:Microsoft.Phone.Controls;assembly=Microsoft.Phone"
```

LISTING 21.10   Continued

```xml
    xmlns:shell="clr-namespace:Microsoft.Phone.Shell;assembly=Microsoft.Phone"
    xmlns:local="clr-namespace:WindowsPhoneApp"
    FontFamily="{StaticResource PhoneFontFamilyNormal}"
    FontSize="{StaticResource PhoneFontSizeNormal}"
    Foreground="{StaticResource PhoneForegroundBrush}"
    SupportedOrientations="PortraitOrLandscape" shell:SystemTray.IsVisible="True">

  <!-- The application bar, with three buttons -->
  <phone:PhoneApplicationPage.ApplicationBar>
    <shell:ApplicationBar IsVisible="False">
      <shell:ApplicationBarIconButton Text="delete"
                                      IconUri="/Shared/Images/appbar.delete.png"
                                      Click="DeleteButton_Click"/>
      <shell:ApplicationBarIconButton Text="email"
                                      IconUri="/Shared/Images/appbar.email.png"
                                      Click="EmailButton_Click"/>
      <shell:ApplicationBarIconButton Text="settings"
                                      IconUri="/Shared/Images/appbar.settings.png"
                                      Click="SettingsButton_Click"/>
    </shell:ApplicationBar>
  </phone:PhoneApplicationPage.ApplicationBar>

  <phone:PhoneApplicationPage.Resources>

    <!-- A copy of the text box default style with its border removed and
         background applied differently. Compare with the style in Program Files\
         Microsoft SDKs\Windows Phone\v7.0\Design\System.Windows.xaml -->
    …
  </phone:PhoneApplicationPage.Resources>

  <ScrollViewer>
    <Grid>
      <!-- The full-screen text box -->
      <TextBox x:Name="TextBox" InputScope="Text"
               Style="{StaticResource PhoneTextBox}"
               AcceptsReturn="True" TextWrapping="Wrap"
               GotFocus="TextBox_GotFocus" LostFocus="TextBox_LostFocus"/>

      <!-- The user control -->
      <local:LoginControl x:Name="LoginControl" Closed="LoginControl_Closed"/>
    </Grid>
  </ScrollViewer>
</phone:PhoneApplicationPage>
```

The text box that basically occupies the whole screen is given a custom style that removes its border and ensures the desired background color remains visible whether the text box has focus. The style was created by copying the default style from `%ProgramFiles%\Microsoft SDKs\Windows Phone\v7.0\Design\System.Windows.xaml` then making a few tweaks.

Listing 21.11 contains the code-behind for this page.

LISTING 21.11   `DetailsPage.xaml.cs`—The Code-Behind for Passwords & Secrets' Details Page

```csharp
using System;
using System.Windows;
using System.Windows.Navigation;
using Microsoft.Phone.Controls;
using Microsoft.Phone.Tasks;

namespace WindowsPhoneApp
{
  public partial class DetailsPage : PhoneApplicationPage
  {
    bool navigatingFrom;
    string initialText = "";

    public DetailsPage()
    {
      InitializeComponent();
      this.Loaded += DetailsPage_Loaded;
    }

    void DetailsPage_Loaded(object sender, RoutedEventArgs e)
    {
      if (CurrentContext.IsLoggedIn)
      {
        // Automatically show the keyboard for new notes.
        // This also gets called when navigating away, hence the extra check
        // to make sure we're only doing this when navigating to the page
        if (this.TextBox.Text.Length == 0 && !this.navigatingFrom)
          this.TextBox.Focus();
      }
    }

    protected override void OnNavigatedFrom(NavigationEventArgs e)
    {
      this.navigatingFrom = true;
      base.OnNavigatedFrom(e);
```

LISTING 21.11   Continued

```
      if (this.initialText != this.TextBox.Text)
      {
        // Automatically save the new content
        Note n = Settings.NotesList.Value[Settings.CurrentNoteIndex.Value];
        n.EncryptedContent =
          Crypto.Encrypt(this.TextBox.Text, CurrentContext.Password) ?? "";
        n.Modified = DateTimeOffset.Now;
      }
    }

    protected override void OnNavigatedTo(NavigationEventArgs e)
    {
      base.OnNavigatedTo(e);
      if (CurrentContext.IsLoggedIn)
        this.LoginControl.Close();
    }

    void TextBox_GotFocus(object sender, RoutedEventArgs e)
    {
      this.ApplicationBar.IsVisible = false;
    }

    void TextBox_LostFocus(object sender, RoutedEventArgs e)
    {
      this.ApplicationBar.IsVisible = true;
    }

    void LoginControl_Closed(object sender, EventArgs e)
    {
      this.ApplicationBar.IsVisible = true;

      // Show the note's contents
      Note n = Settings.NotesList.Value[Settings.CurrentNoteIndex.Value];
      if (n != null)
      {
        this.TextBox.Background = n.ScreenBrush;
        this.TextBox.Foreground = n.TextBrush;
        this.TextBox.FontSize = n.TextSize;
        this.initialText = this.TextBox.Text =
          Crypto.Decrypt(n.EncryptedContent, CurrentContext.Password) ?? "";
      }
    }

    // Application bar handlers:
```

LISTING 21.11   Continued

```
void DeleteButton_Click(object sender, EventArgs e)
{
  if (MessageBox.Show("Are you sure you want to delete this note?",
    "Delete note?", MessageBoxButton.OKCancel) == MessageBoxResult.OK)
  {
    Settings.NotesList.Value.Remove(
      Settings.NotesList.Value[Settings.CurrentNoteIndex.Value]);

    if (this.NavigationService.CanGoBack)
      this.NavigationService.GoBack();
  }
}

void EmailButton_Click(object sender, EventArgs e)
{
  EmailComposeTask launcher = new EmailComposeTask();
  launcher.Body = this.TextBox.Text;
  launcher.Subject = "Note";
  launcher.Show();
}

void SettingsButton_Click(object sender, EventArgs e)
{
  this.NavigationService.Navigate(new Uri("/SettingsPage.xaml",
    UriKind.Relative));
}
  }
}
```

Notes:

→ This page uses a navigatingFrom flag to check whether the page is in the process of navigating away. That's because the Loaded event gets raised a second time after OnNavigatedFrom, and applying focus to the text box at this time could cause an unwanted flicker from the on-screen keyboard briefly appearing.

> **(!) A page's Loaded event is incorrectly raised when navigating away!**
>
> This is simply a bug in the current version of Windows Phone. To avoid performance problems, potential flickering, or other issues, consider setting a flag in OnNavigatedFrom that you can check inside Loaded, as done in Listing 21.11. That way, you can be sure that your page-loading logic only runs when the page is actually loading.

→ The code for the settings page linked to this page is shown in the next chapter, because it is identical to the one used by this app!

The Finished Product

Running under the light theme
with the red accent color

Showing the password hint

The settings page (covered in
the next chapter)

NOTEPAD

The Notepad app enables fast, efficient note-taking. It boasts the following features:

→ Auto-save, which makes jotting down notes fast and easy

→ Quick previews of each note

→ The ability to customize each note's background/foreground colors and text size

→ The ability to email your notes

Does this sound familiar? It should, because to a user this app behaves exactly like the preceding chapter's Passwords & Secrets app, but without the master password and associated encryption. There is one important difference in its implementation, however, that makes it interesting for this chapter. Because the notes stored by Notepad are expected to be longer than the notes stored by Passwords & Secrets, each note is persisted as a separate file in isolated storage. This enables the app to load a note's contents on-demand rather than loading everything each time the app launches/activates (which is what happens with application settings).

This chapter highlights the differences between the code in Notepad and the code in Passwords & Secrets, and also shows the settings page shared by both.

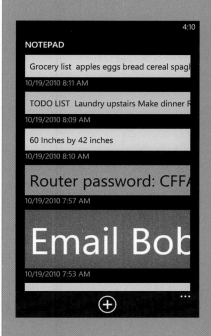

The Main Page

Notepad's main page works just like the previous chapter's main page, but without the LoginControl user control and associated logic. Listing 22.1 contains the XAML for the main page, with differences emphasized.

LISTING 22.1   MainPage.xaml—The User Interface for Notepad's Main Page

```xml
<phone:PhoneApplicationPage
    x:Class="WindowsPhoneApp.MainPage"
    xmlns="http://schemas.microsoft.com/winfx/2006/xaml/presentation"
    xmlns:x="http://schemas.microsoft.com/winfx/2006/xaml"
    xmlns:phone="clr-namespace:Microsoft.Phone.Controls;assembly=Microsoft.Phone"
    xmlns:shell="clr-namespace:Microsoft.Phone.Shell;assembly=Microsoft.Phone"
    xmlns:local="clr-namespace:WindowsPhoneApp"
    FontFamily="{StaticResource PhoneFontFamilyNormal}"
    FontSize="{StaticResource PhoneFontSizeNormal}"
    Foreground="{StaticResource PhoneForegroundBrush}"
    SupportedOrientations="PortraitOrLandscape" shell:SystemTray.IsVisible="True">

  <phone:PhoneApplicationPage.Resources>
    <local:DateConverter x:Key="DateConverter"/>
  </phone:PhoneApplicationPage.Resources>

  <!-- The application bar, with one button and one menu item -->
  <phone:PhoneApplicationPage.ApplicationBar>
    <shell:ApplicationBar>
      <shell:ApplicationBarIconButton Text="new"
        IconUri="/Shared/Images/appbar.add.png" Click="NewButton_Click"/>
      <shell:ApplicationBar.MenuItems>
        <shell:ApplicationBarMenuItem Text="about" Click="AboutMenuItem_Click"/>
      </shell:ApplicationBar.MenuItems>
    </shell:ApplicationBar>
  </phone:PhoneApplicationPage.ApplicationBar>

  <Grid Background="Transparent">
    <Grid.RowDefinitions>
      <RowDefinition Height="Auto"/>
      <RowDefinition Height="*"/>
    </Grid.RowDefinitions>

    <!-- The standard header -->
    <StackPanel Grid.Row="0" Style="{StaticResource PhoneTitlePanelStyle}">
      <TextBlock Text="NOTEPAD" Style="{StaticResource PhoneTextTitle0Style}"/>
    </StackPanel>
```

LISTING 22.1   Continued

```xml
    <!-- Show this when there are no notes -->
    <TextBlock Name="NoItemsTextBlock" Grid.Row="1" Text="No notes"
               Visibility="Collapsed" Margin="22,17,0,0"
               Style="{StaticResource PhoneTextGroupHeaderStyle}"/>

    <!-- The list box containing notes -->
    <ListBox x:Name="ListBox" Grid.Row="1" ItemsSource="{Binding}"
             SelectionChanged="ListBox_SelectionChanged">
      <ListBox.ItemTemplate>
        <DataTemplate>
          <StackPanel>
            <!-- The title, in a style matching the note -->
            <Border Background="{Binding ScreenBrush}" Margin="24,0" Width="800"
                    MinHeight="60" local:Tilt.IsEnabled="True">
              <TextBlock Text="{Binding Title}" FontSize="{Binding TextSize}"
                         Foreground="{Binding TextBrush}" Margin="12"
                         VerticalAlignment="Center"/>
            </Border>
            <!-- The modified date -->
            <TextBlock Foreground="{StaticResource PhoneSubtleBrush}"
               Text="{Binding Modified, Converter={StaticResource DateConverter}}"
               Margin="24,0,0,12"/>
          </StackPanel>
        </DataTemplate>
      </ListBox.ItemTemplate>
    </ListBox>
  </Grid>
</phone:PhoneApplicationPage>
```

The application bar now has the "new" button from the start because there is no mode in which adding new notes is forbidden.

The code-behind for the main page is shown in Listing 22.2.

LISTING 22.2   `MainPage.xaml.cs`—The Code-Behind for Notepad's Main Page

```csharp
using System;
using System.Windows;
using System.Windows.Controls;
using System.Windows.Navigation;
using Microsoft.Phone.Controls;

namespace WindowsPhoneApp
{
  public partial class MainPage : PhoneApplicationPage
```

LISTING 22.2   Continued

```
{
  public MainPage()
  {
    InitializeComponent();
  }

  protected override void OnNavigatedTo(NavigationEventArgs e)
  {
    base.OnNavigatedTo(e);

    // Bind the notes list as the data source for the list box
    if (this.DataContext == null)
      this.DataContext = Settings.NotesList.Value;

    // Clear the selection so selecting the same item twice in a row will
    // still raise the SelectionChanged event
    Settings.CurrentNoteIndex.Value = -1;
    this.ListBox.SelectedIndex = -1;

    if (Settings.NotesList.Value.Count == 0)
      NoItemsTextBlock.Visibility = Visibility.Visible;
    else
      NoItemsTextBlock.Visibility = Visibility.Collapsed;
  }

  void ListBox_SelectionChanged(object sender, SelectionChangedEventArgs e)
  {
    if (ListBox.SelectedIndex >= 0)
    {
      // Navigate to the details page for the selected item
      Settings.CurrentNoteIndex.Value = ListBox.SelectedIndex;
      this.NavigationService.Navigate(new Uri("/DetailsPage.xaml",
        UriKind.Relative));
    }
  }

  // Application bar handlers

  void NewButton_Click(object sender, EventArgs e)
  {
    // Create a new note and add it to the top of the list
    Note note = new Note();
    note.Filename = Guid.NewGuid().ToString();
    note.Modified = DateTimeOffset.Now;
```

LISTING 22.2   Continued

```
      note.ScreenColor = Settings.ScreenColor.Value;
      note.TextColor = Settings.TextColor.Value;
      note.TextSize = Settings.TextSize.Value;
      Settings.NotesList.Value.Insert(0, note);

      // "Select" the new note
      Settings.CurrentNoteIndex.Value = 0;

      // Navigate to the details page for the newly created note
      this.NavigationService.Navigate(new Uri("/DetailsPage.xaml",
        UriKind.Relative));
    }

    void AboutMenuItem_Click(object sender, EventArgs e)
    {
      this.NavigationService.Navigate(new Uri(
        "/Shared/About/AboutPage.xaml?appName=Notepad", UriKind.Relative));
    }
  }
}
```

Notes:

→ The list box is now filled immediately inside `OnNavigatedTo` by setting the page's data context to the list of notes.

→ The `Note` class, shown at the end of this chapter, is slightly different from the preceding chapter in order to accommodate its file-based storage. Inside `NewButton_Click`, you can see that it now has a `Filename` property that points to the file containing its contents. The filename is never shown in this app's user interface; internally, each note just needs to know where to fetch its content. Therefore, when a new note is created, it is given a unique filename thanks to the `Guid.NewGuid` method. This returns a Globally Unique Identifier (GUID) that is unique for all practical purposes.

The Details Page

The details page, just like in Passwords & Secrets, displays the entire contents of the note and enables the user to edit it, delete it, change its settings, or email its contents. The page's XAML is identical to `DetailsPage.xaml` in the preceding chapter, except the application bar is not marked with `IsVisible="False"` because it doesn't need to be hidden while the `LoginControl` is shown. Listing 22.3 contains the code-behind for this page with differences emphasized.

LISTING 22.3   `DetailsPage.xaml.cs`—The Code-Behind for Passwords & Secrets' Details Page

```
using System;
using System.Windows;
using System.Windows.Navigation;
using Microsoft.Phone.Controls;
using Microsoft.Phone.Tasks;

namespace WindowsPhoneApp
{
  public partial class DetailsPage : PhoneApplicationPage
  {
    bool navigatingFrom;
    string initialText = "";

    public DetailsPage()
    {
      InitializeComponent();
      this.Loaded += DetailsPage_Loaded;
    }

    void DetailsPage_Loaded(object sender, RoutedEventArgs e)
    {
      // Automatically show the keyboard for new notes.
      // This also gets called when navigating away, hence the extra check
      // to make sure we're only doing this when navigating to the page
      if (this.TextBox.Text.Length == 0 && !this.navigatingFrom)
        this.TextBox.Focus();
    }

    protected override void OnNavigatedFrom(NavigationEventArgs e)
    {
      this.navigatingFrom = true;
      base.OnNavigatedFrom(e);

      if (this.initialText != this.TextBox.Text)
      {
        // Automatically save the new content
        Note n = Settings.NotesList.Value[Settings.CurrentNoteIndex.Value];

        n.SaveContent(this.TextBox.Text);

        // Update the title now, so each one can be accessed
        // later without reading the file's contents
        string title = this.TextBox.Text.TrimStart();
```

LISTING 22.3   Continued

```csharp
    // Don't include more than the first 100 characters, which should be long
    // enough, even in landscape with a small font
    if (title.Length > 100)
      title = title.Substring(0, 100);

    // Fold the remaining content into a single line. We can't use
    // Environment.NewLine because it's \r\n, whereas newlines inserted from
    // a text box are just \r
    n.Title = title.Replace('\r', ' ');

    n.Modified = DateTimeOffset.Now;
  }
}

protected override void OnNavigatedTo(NavigationEventArgs e)
{
  base.OnNavigatedTo(e);

  // Show the note's contents
  Note n = Settings.NotesList.Value[Settings.CurrentNoteIndex.Value];
  if (n != null)
  {
    this.initialText = this.TextBox.Text = n.GetContent();
    this.TextBox.Background = n.ScreenBrush;
    this.TextBox.Foreground = n.TextBrush;
    this.TextBox.FontSize = n.TextSize;
  }
}

void TextBox_GotFocus(object sender, RoutedEventArgs e)
{
  this.ApplicationBar.IsVisible = false;
}

void TextBox_LostFocus(object sender, RoutedEventArgs e)
{
  this.ApplicationBar.IsVisible = true;
}

// Application bar handlers:

void DeleteButton_Click(object sender, EventArgs e)
{
  if (MessageBox.Show("Are you sure you want to delete this note?",
```

LISTING 22.3   Continued

```
          "Delete note?", MessageBoxButton.OKCancel) == MessageBoxResult.OK)
      {
        Note n = Settings.NotesList.Value[Settings.CurrentNoteIndex.Value];
        n.DeleteContent();
        Settings.NotesList.Value.Remove(n);

        if (this.NavigationService.CanGoBack)
          this.NavigationService.GoBack();
      }
    }

    void EmailButton_Click(object sender, EventArgs e)
    {
      EmailComposeTask launcher = new EmailComposeTask();
      launcher.Body = this.TextBox.Text;
      launcher.Subject = "Note";
      launcher.Show();
    }

    void SettingsButton_Click(object sender, EventArgs e)
    {
      this.NavigationService.Navigate(new Uri("/SettingsPage.xaml",
        UriKind.Relative));
    }
  }
}
```

Notes:

→ In OnNavigatedFrom, the content of the text box is saved to a file via the
SaveContent method shown later in this chapter. The Title property for each note
is set at this point rather than dynamically when the property is accessed because it
enables each title to be shown without reading each file. Otherwise, rendering the
list on the main page would end up reading the contents of every file and take away
the advantage of storing the notes in files!

→ The note's contents are immediately shown inside OnNavigatedTo with the help of a
GetContent method defined on Note.

→ Inside DeleteButton_Click, the note's DeleteContent method ensures that the
backing file doesn't get left behind when a note is deleted.

The Note Class

Listing 22.4 shows the implementation of the modified Note class used by this app, with differences from the preceding chapter emphasized.

LISTING 22.4   Note.cs—The Code-Behind for Passwords & Secrets' Details Page

```csharp
using System;
using System.ComponentModel;
using System.IO;
using System.IO.IsolatedStorage;
using System.Windows.Media;

namespace WindowsPhoneApp
{
  public class Note : INotifyPropertyChanged
  {
    public event PropertyChangedEventHandler PropertyChanged;

    // A helper method used by the properties
    void OnPropertyChanged(string propertyName)
    {
      PropertyChangedEventHandler handler = this.PropertyChanged;
      if (handler != null)
        handler(this, new PropertyChangedEventArgs(propertyName));
    }

    DateTimeOffset modified;
    public DateTimeOffset Modified
    {
      get { return this.modified; }
      set { this.modified = value; OnPropertyChanged("Modified"); }
    }

    int textSize;
    public int TextSize
    {
      get { return this.textSize; }
      set { this.textSize = value; OnPropertyChanged("TextSize"); }
    }

    Color screenColor;
    public Color ScreenColor
    {
      get { return this.screenColor; }
      set { this.screenColor = value;
```

LISTING 22.4   Continued

```
            OnPropertyChanged("ScreenColor"); OnPropertyChanged("ScreenBrush"); }
  }

  Color textColor;
  public Color TextColor
  {
    get { return this.textColor; }
    set { this.textColor = value;
          OnPropertyChanged("TextColor"); OnPropertyChanged("TextBrush"); }
  }

  // Three readonly properties whose value is computed from other properties:

  public Brush ScreenBrush
  {
    get { return new SolidColorBrush(this.ScreenColor); }
  }

  public Brush TextBrush
  {
    get { return new SolidColorBrush(this.TextColor); }
  }

  string title;
  public string Title
  {
    get { return this.title; }
    set { this.title = value; OnPropertyChanged("Title"); }
  }

  public string Filename { get; set; }

  public void SaveContent(string content)
  {
    using (IsolatedStorageFile userStore =
           IsolatedStorageFile.GetUserStoreForApplication())
    using (IsolatedStorageFileStream stream =
           userStore.CreateFile(this.Filename))
    using (StreamWriter writer = new StreamWriter(stream))
    {
      writer.Write(content);
    }
  }
```

LISTING 22.4   Continued

```
  public string GetContent()
  {
    using (IsolatedStorageFile userStore =
           IsolatedStorageFile.GetUserStoreForApplication())
    {
      if (!userStore.FileExists(this.Filename))
        return "";
      else
      {
        using (IsolatedStorageFileStream stream =
               userStore.OpenFile(this.Filename, FileMode.Open))
        using (StreamReader reader = new StreamReader(stream))
          return reader.ReadToEnd();
      }
    }
  }

  public void DeleteContent()
  {
    using (IsolatedStorageFile userStore =
           IsolatedStorageFile.GetUserStoreForApplication())
      userStore.DeleteFile(this.Filename);
  }
}
}
```

Notes:

➔ As implied earlier, the `Title` property is now a normal read-write property rather than a read-only property whose value is determined dynamically.

➔ To save a new file, `SaveContent` first calls `IsolatedStorageFile.GetUserStoreForApplication`. This is the first step in any code that interacts directly with the isolated storage file system. The `IsolatedStoreFile` instance returned contains several methods for creating, enumerating, opening, and deleting files and folders. Once `CreateFile` is called, `SaveContent` uses a `StreamWriter` to easily write the passed-in string to the stream.

➔ `GetContent` and `DeleteContent` work similarly to `SaveContent`, making use of three more methods on `IsolatedStorageFile`: `FileExists`, `OpenFile`, and `DeleteFile`. To keep the UI responsive while interacting with large files, this would be a good place to use `BackgroundWorker`, introduced in Chapter 11, "XAML Editor."

When managing files, it's tempting to simply use the `IsolatedStorageFile.GetFileNames` method to enumerate and perhaps display the files. This approach has problems, however. For example:

→ The isolated storage APIs don't expose any way to discover the created/modified dates of files. Therefore, sorting files by such properties rather than the default alphabetical order requires you to store extra information (stored in the `Note` class in this app).

→ The list includes an extra file if you use any isolated storage application settings. These get persisted in an XML file called `__ApplicationSettings` in the root of your app's isolated storage folder. Although you could manually filter this out, there's no guarantee that there won't be other special files in the future.

→ As in Windows, filenames have restrictions on their characters (such as no colons or question marks). If you use filenames as user-visible and potentially editable labels, you need to make sure you don't introduce invalid characters.

The Settings Page

The settings page, shown in Figure 22.1, enables the customization of any note's foreground color, background color, and text size. Although these settings are only applied to the current note (stored as properties on the `Note` instance), the user can check a check box to automatically apply the chosen settings to any new notes created in the future. Listing 22.5 contains the XAML for this page, and Listing 22.6 contains the code-behind.

FIGURE 22.1   The settings page exposes per-note settings and enables you to apply them to all future notes.

LISTING 22.5   `SettingsPage.xaml`—The User Interface for Notepad's Settings Page

```xml
<phone:PhoneApplicationPage
    x:Class="WindowsPhoneApp.SettingsPage"
    xmlns="http://schemas.microsoft.com/winfx/2006/xaml/presentation"
    xmlns:x="http://schemas.microsoft.com/winfx/2006/xaml"
    xmlns:phone="clr-namespace:Microsoft.Phone.Controls;assembly=Microsoft.Phone"
    xmlns:shell="clr-namespace:Microsoft.Phone.Shell;assembly=Microsoft.Phone"
    xmlns:local="clr-namespace:WindowsPhoneApp"
    FontFamily="{StaticResource PhoneFontFamilyNormal}"
    FontSize="{StaticResource PhoneFontSizeNormal}"
    Foreground="{StaticResource PhoneForegroundBrush}"
    SupportedOrientations="PortraitOrLandscape" shell:SystemTray.IsVisible="True">
  <Grid>
    <Grid.RowDefinitions>
      <RowDefinition Height="Auto"/>
      <RowDefinition Height="*"/>
    </Grid.RowDefinitions>

    <!-- The standard settings header -->
    <StackPanel Grid.Row="0" Style="{StaticResource PhoneTitlePanelStyle}">
      <TextBlock Text="SETTINGS" Style="{StaticResource PhoneTextTitle0Style}"/>
      <TextBlock Text="notepad" Style="{StaticResource PhoneTextTitle1Style}"/>
    </StackPanel>

    <ScrollViewer Grid.Row="1">
      <Grid Margin="{StaticResource PhoneMargin}">
        <Grid.RowDefinitions>
          <RowDefinition Height="Auto"/>
          <RowDefinition Height="Auto"/>
          <RowDefinition Height="Auto"/>
          <RowDefinition Height="Auto"/>
          <RowDefinition Height="Auto"/>
          <RowDefinition/>
        </Grid.RowDefinitions>
        <Grid.ColumnDefinitions>
          <ColumnDefinition/>
          <ColumnDefinition/>
        </Grid.ColumnDefinitions>

        <CheckBox x:Name="MakeDefaultCheckBox" Grid.ColumnSpan="2"
                  Content="Make these the default settings" Margin="0,-4,0,0"
                  Checked="MakeDefaultCheckBox_IsCheckedChanged"
                  Unchecked="MakeDefaultCheckBox_IsCheckedChanged"
                  local:Tilt.IsEnabled="True"/>
```

LISTING 22.5 Continued

```xml
        <!-- The two colors -->
        <TextBlock Grid.Row="1" Text="Screen color"
                   Foreground="{StaticResource PhoneSubtleBrush}" Margin="12,8"/>
        <Rectangle Grid.Row="2" x:Name="ScreenColorRectangle"
                   Margin="{StaticResource PhoneHorizontalMargin}" Height="90"
                   Stroke="{StaticResource PhoneForegroundBrush}"
                   StrokeThickness="3" local:Tilt.IsEnabled="True"
                   MouseLeftButtonUp="ScreenColorRectangle_MouseLeftButtonUp"/>
        <TextBlock Grid.Row="1" Grid.Column="1" Text="Text color"
                   Foreground="{StaticResource PhoneSubtleBrush}" Margin="12,8"/>
        <Rectangle Grid.Row="2" Grid.Column="1" x:Name="TextColorRectangle"
                   Height="90" StrokeThickness="3" local:Tilt.IsEnabled="True"
                   Margin="{StaticResource PhoneHorizontalMargin}"
                   Stroke="{StaticResource PhoneForegroundBrush}"
                   MouseLeftButtonUp="TextColorRectangle_MouseLeftButtonUp"/>

        <!-- Text size -->
        <TextBlock Grid.Row="3" Grid.ColumnSpan="2" Text="Text size"
                   Foreground="{StaticResource PhoneSubtleBrush}"
                   Margin="12,20,12,-14"/>
        <Grid Grid.Row="4" Grid.ColumnSpan="2">
          <Grid.ColumnDefinitions>
            <ColumnDefinition/>
            <ColumnDefinition Width="Auto"/>
          </Grid.ColumnDefinitions>
          <Slider x:Name="TextSizeSlider" Minimum="12" Maximum="100"
                  ValueChanged="TextSizeSlider_ValueChanged"/>
          <Button x:Name="ResetButton" Grid.Column="1" Content="reset"
                  VerticalAlignment="Top" Click="ResetButton_Click"
                  local:Tilt.IsEnabled="True"/>
        </Grid>

        <!-- Sample text -->
        <Rectangle x:Name="SampleBackground" Grid.Row="5" Grid.ColumnSpan="2"
                   Margin="-12,0,-12,-12"/>
        <TextBlock x:Name="SampleTextBlock" Grid.Row="5" Grid.ColumnSpan="2"
                   Text="Sample text." Padding="12"/>
      </Grid>
    </ScrollViewer>
  </Grid>
</phone:PhoneApplicationPage>
```

LISTING 22.6   `SettingsPage.xaml.cs`—The Code-Behind for Notepad's Settings Page

```csharp
using System;
using System.ComponentModel;
using System.Windows;
using System.Windows.Input;
using System.Windows.Media;
using System.Windows.Navigation;
using Microsoft.Phone.Controls;

namespace WindowsPhoneApp
{
  public partial class SettingsPage : PhoneApplicationPage
  {
    public SettingsPage()
    {
      InitializeComponent();
    }

    protected override void OnBackKeyPress(CancelEventArgs e)
    {
      base.OnBackKeyPress(e);

      // Doing this here instead of OnNavigatedFrom, so it's not
      // applied when navigating forward to color picker pages
      if (Settings.MakeDefault.Value)
      {
        // Apply everything as defaults, too
        Note n = Settings.NotesList.Value[Settings.CurrentNoteIndex.Value];
        Settings.ScreenColor.Value = n.ScreenColor;
        Settings.TextColor.Value = n.TextColor;
        Settings.TextSize.Value = n.TextSize;
      }
    }

    protected override void OnNavigatedTo(NavigationEventArgs e)
    {
      base.OnNavigatedTo(e);

      Note n = Settings.NotesList.Value[Settings.CurrentNoteIndex.Value];

      // Apply any color just selected from the color picker
      if (Settings.TempScreenColor.Value != null)
      {
        n.ScreenColor = Settings.TempScreenColor.Value.Value;
        Settings.TempScreenColor.Value = null;
```

LISTING 22.6   Continued

```
    }
    if (Settings.TempTextColor.Value != null)
    {
      n.TextColor = Settings.TempTextColor.Value.Value;
      Settings.TempTextColor.Value = null;
    }

    // Respect the saved settings
    this.MakeDefaultCheckBox.IsChecked = Settings.MakeDefault.Value;
    this.ScreenColorRectangle.Fill = new SolidColorBrush(n.ScreenColor);
    this.TextColorRectangle.Fill = new SolidColorBrush(n.TextColor);
    this.SampleBackground.Fill = this.ScreenColorRectangle.Fill;
    this.SampleTextBlock.Foreground = this.TextColorRectangle.Fill;
    this.TextSizeSlider.Value = n.TextSize;
  }

  void ScreenColorRectangle_MouseLeftButtonUp(object sender,
    MouseButtonEventArgs e)
  {
    // Get a string representation of the colors we need to pass to the color
    // picker, without the leading #
    string currentColorString = Settings.NotesList.Value
      [Settings.CurrentNoteIndex.Value].ScreenColor.ToString().Substring(1);
    string defaultColorString =
      Settings.ScreenColor.Value.ToString().Substring(1);

    // The color picker works with the same isolated storage value that the
    // Setting works with, but we have to clear its cached value to pick up
    // the value chosen in the color picker
    Settings.TempScreenColor.ForceRefresh();

    // Navigate to the color picker
    this.NavigationService.Navigate(new Uri(
      "/Shared/Color Picker/ColorPickerPage.xaml?"
      + "&currentColor=" + currentColorString
      + "&defaultColor=" + defaultColorString
      + "&settingName=TempScreenColor", UriKind.Relative));
  }

  void TextColorRectangle_MouseLeftButtonUp(object sender,
    MouseButtonEventArgs e)
  {
    // Get a string representation of the colors, without the leading #
    string currentColorString = Settings.NotesList.Value
      [Settings.CurrentNoteIndex.Value].TextColor.ToString().Substring(1);
```

LISTING 22.6   Continued

```csharp
      string defaultColorString =
        Settings.TextColor.Value.ToString().Substring(1);

      // The color picker works with the same isolated storage value that the
      // Setting works with, but we have to clear its cached value to pick up
      // the value chosen in the color picker
      Settings.TempTextColor.ForceRefresh();

      // Navigate to the color picker
      this.NavigationService.Navigate(new Uri(
        "/Shared/Color Picker/ColorPickerPage.xaml?"
        + "showOpacity=false"
        + "&currentColor=" + currentColorString
        + "&defaultColor=" + defaultColorString
        + "&settingName=TempTextColor", UriKind.Relative));
    }

    void TextSizeSlider_ValueChanged(object sender,
      RoutedPropertyChangedEventArgs<double> e)
    {
      // Gets called during InitializeComponent
      if (this.TextSizeSlider != null)
      {
        int textSize = (int)Math.Round(this.TextSizeSlider.Value);
        Settings.NotesList.Value[Settings.CurrentNoteIndex.Value].TextSize =
          textSize;
        this.SampleTextBlock.FontSize = textSize;
      }
    }

    void MakeDefaultCheckBox_IsCheckedChanged(object sender, RoutedEventArgs e)
    {
      Settings.MakeDefault.Value = this.MakeDefaultCheckBox.IsChecked.Value;
    }

    void ResetButton_Click(object sender, RoutedEventArgs e)
    {
      int textSize = Settings.TextSize.DefaultValue;
      this.TextSizeSlider.Value = textSize;
      Settings.NotesList.Value[Settings.CurrentNoteIndex.Value].TextSize =
        textSize;
      this.SampleTextBlock.FontSize = textSize;
    }
  }
}
```

To work with the color picker that writes directly to a key in the isolated storage application settings, `TempScreenColor` and `TempTextColor` settings are used. These values are then applied to the current note's properties inside `OnNavigatedTo`.

The Finished Product

Reading a note

Changing one of the two colors in a note

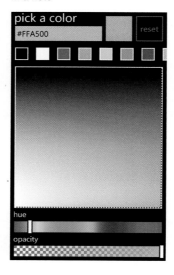

The main page under the light theme

chapter 23 lessons

BABY MILESTONES

Baby Milestones informs parents about typical milestones in a baby's development from birth to the age of 2. This app enables parents to keep track of developmental milestones and ensure that their baby is developing on schedule. It presents month-by-month lists of skills that most babies can accomplish at each age, and enables the parent to record the date that the baby demonstrated each skill. The main page of the app shows a dashboard with the current month-by-month progress.

A little bonus feature in this app happens to be the main reason that it is included in this part of the book. It demonstrates how to store a photo in isolated storage, and later retrieve and display it. Each month's list in this app (from 1 to 24) supports specifying a custom image as the page's background. The idea is that the parent can take a photo of their baby at the appropriate age to provide a bit of nostalgic context to each list.

The Main Page

The main page, shown in Figure 23.1, contains a list box that links to each of the 24 monthly lists. Each label in the list is accompanied with a progress bar that reveals the current progress in each month. Completed months are displayed in the phone's foreground color, whereas incomplete months are displayed in the phone's accent color.

FIGURE 23.1   The progress bars turn an otherwise-simple list box into a useful dashboard view.

Listing 23.1 contains the XAML for this main page, and Listing 23.2 contains the code-behind.

LISTING 23.1   `MainPage.xaml`—The User Interface for Baby Milestones' Main Page

```
<phone:PhoneApplicationPage x:Class="WindowsPhoneApp.MainPage"
    xmlns="http://schemas.microsoft.com/winfx/2006/xaml/presentation"
    xmlns:x="http://schemas.microsoft.com/winfx/2006/xaml"
    xmlns:phone="clr-namespace:Microsoft.Phone.Controls;assembly=Microsoft.Phone"
    xmlns:shell="clr-namespace:Microsoft.Phone.Shell;assembly=Microsoft.Phone"
    xmlns:local="clr-namespace:WindowsPhoneApp"
    FontSize="{StaticResource PhoneFontSizeNormal}"
    Foreground="{StaticResource PhoneForegroundBrush}"
    SupportedOrientations="PortraitOrLandscape"
    x:Name="Page" shell:SystemTray.IsVisible="True">

  <phone:PhoneApplicationPage.Resources>
    <!-- A value converter for the binding of each item's foreground -->
    <local:PercentageToBrushConverter x:Key="PercentageToBrushConverter"/>
  </phone:PhoneApplicationPage.Resources>

  <Grid>
    <Grid.RowDefinitions>
```

LISTING 23.1   Continued

```xml
        <RowDefinition Height="Auto"/>
        <RowDefinition Height="*"/>
    </Grid.RowDefinitions>

    <!-- The standard header -->
    <StackPanel Style="{StaticResource PhoneTitlePanelStyle}">
      <TextBlock Text="BABY MILESTONES"
                 Style="{StaticResource PhoneTextTitle0Style}"/>
    </StackPanel>

    <!-- The list box that fills the page -->
    <ListBox x:Name="ListBox" Grid.Row="1" ItemsSource="{Binding}"
             Margin="{StaticResource PhoneHorizontalMargin}"
             SelectionChanged="ListBox_SelectionChanged">
      <ListBox.ItemTemplate>
        <!-- The data template controls how each item renders -->
        <DataTemplate>
          <!-- The explicit width is only here for the sake of the tilt effect -->
          <StackPanel Orientation="Horizontal" local:Tilt.IsEnabled="True"
                      Width="{Binding ActualWidth, ElementName=Page}"
                      Background="Transparent">
            <ProgressBar Value="{Binding PercentComplete}" Width="120"/>
            <!-- The text block displays the Name property value, colored based
                 on the % complete -->
            <TextBlock Text="{Binding Name}" Margin="{StaticResource PhoneMargin}"
              Style="{StaticResource PhoneTextExtraLargeStyle}"
              Foreground="{Binding PercentComplete, Converter=
                          {StaticResource PercentageToBrushConverter}}"/>
          </StackPanel>
        </DataTemplate>
      </ListBox.ItemTemplate>
    </ListBox>
  </Grid>
</phone:PhoneApplicationPage>
```

LISTING 23.2   MainPage.xaml.cs—The Code-Behind for Baby Milestones' Main Page

```csharp
using System;
using System.Windows;
using System.Windows.Controls;
using Microsoft.Phone.Controls;

namespace WindowsPhoneApp
{
```

LISTING 23.2   Continued

```csharp
public partial class MainPage : PhoneApplicationPage
{
  public MainPage()
  {
    InitializeComponent();
    this.Loaded += MainPage_Loaded;
  }

  void MainPage_Loaded(object sender, RoutedEventArgs e)
  {
    if (this.ListBox.Items.Count > 0)
      return; // We already added the data

    // Fill the list box with the ages
    this.DataContext = Settings.List.Value;

    // Ensure that the most-recently-selected item is scrolled into view.
    // Do this delayed to ensure the list box has been filled
    this.Dispatcher.BeginInvoke(delegate()
    {
      if (this.ListBox.Items.Count > Settings.CurrentAgeIndex.Value)
        this.ListBox.ScrollIntoView(
          this.ListBox.Items[Settings.CurrentAgeIndex.Value]);
    });
  }

  void ListBox_SelectionChanged(object sender, SelectionChangedEventArgs e)
  {
    if (this.ListBox.SelectedIndex >= 0)
    {
      Settings.CurrentAgeIndex.Value = this.ListBox.SelectedIndex;

      // Navigate to the details page for this age
      this.NavigationService.Navigate(new Uri(
        "/DetailsPage.xaml", UriKind.Relative));

      // Clear the selection so the same item can be selected
      // again on subsequent visits to this page
      this.ListBox.SelectedIndex = -1;
    }
  }
}
}
```

Notes:

➔ This app makes use of the following two settings defined in `Settings.cs`:

```
public static class Settings
{
  public static readonly Setting<IList<Age>> List =
    new Setting<IList<Age>>("List", Data.Ages);
  public static readonly Setting<int> CurrentAgeIndex =
    new Setting<int>("CurrentAgeIndex", 0);
}
```

`Data.Ages` represents the list of 24 ages, each of which contains a list of skills:

```
public class Data
{
  public static readonly Age[] Ages = {
    new Age { Name = "1 month",
              Skills = new Skill[] { new Skill("lifts head"),
                new Skill("stares at faces"), new Skill("responds to sound") }
          },
    …
  };
}
```

The `Age` and `Skill` classes are defined in Listings 23.3 and 23.4.

➔ In this page's XAML, the progress bar inside the data template binds directly to each `Age` item's `PercentComplete` property. To give each text block the appropriate foreground brush, however, a custom value converter is used. This app makes use of three value converters, all shown in the next section.

➔ In the code-behind, the `MainPage_Loaded` method ensures that the most recently selected age is scrolled into view, because it would be annoying to constantly scroll the page down once the baby is older than 9 months. This is done via a `BeginInvoke` call, because attempting to scroll the list box immediately after setting the data context would not work. You need to let the binding complete before manipulating the list box in this fashion.

➔ As with most uses of a list box in a Windows Phone app, the `SelectionChanged` event's behavior (only raising when the selection changes rather than on each tap) is undesirable. Therefore, the `ListBox_SelectionChanged` handler clears the just-selected item, so consecutive taps on the same item work as expected.

LISTING 23.3   `Age.cs`—The `Age` Class Used to Represent Each List Box Item

```
using System.Collections.Generic;
using System.ComponentModel;

namespace WindowsPhoneApp
{
  public class Age : INotifyPropertyChanged
  {
    public string Name { get; set; }
    public IList<Skill> Skills { get; set; }
    public string PhotoFilename { get; set; }

    // A readonly property that calculates completion on-the-fly
    public double PercentComplete
    {
      get
      {
        int total = this.Skills.Count;
        int numComplete = 0;
        foreach (Skill s in this.Skills)
          if (s.Date != null)
            numComplete++;

        return ((double)numComplete / total) * 100;
      }
    }

    // Enables any consumer to trigger the
    // property changed event for PercentComplete
    public void RefreshPercentComplete()
    {
      PropertyChangedEventHandler handler = this.PropertyChanged;
      if (handler != null)
        handler(this, new PropertyChangedEventArgs("PercentComplete"));
    }

    public event PropertyChangedEventHandler PropertyChanged;
  }
}
```

LISTING 23.4   `Skill.cs`—The `Skill` Class Used by Each `Age` Instance

```
using System;
using System.ComponentModel;
```

LISTING 23.4   Continued

```
namespace WindowsPhoneApp
{
  public class Skill : INotifyPropertyChanged
  {
    // A default constructor (normally implicit) is required for serialization
    public Skill()
    {
    }

    public Skill(string name)
    {
      this.Name = name;
    }

    public string Name { get; set; }
    public Age Age { get; set; }

    // The only property that raises the PropertyChanged event
    DateTime? date;
    public DateTime? Date
    {
      get { return this.date; }
      set
      {
        this.date = value;
        PropertyChangedEventHandler handler = this.PropertyChanged;
        if (handler != null)
          handler(this, new PropertyChangedEventArgs("Date"));
      }
    }

    public event PropertyChangedEventHandler PropertyChanged;
  }
}
```

Notes:

→ Both Age and Skill implement INotifyPropertyChanged and raise PropertyChanged events for their properties used as the source of data binding. This enables the display on the main page and the details page (shown next) to remain up-to-date without any manual work in those pages.

→ Because Age's PercentComplete property is based on the value of each Date in its Skills list (null means incomplete, whereas any date means complete), raising a PropertyChanged event for PercentComplete at the appropriate time is tricky. The

Age class could have subscribed to the `PropertyChanged` event on each of its `Skill` instances and raise one for `PercentComplete` whenever a date has been changed. Instead, this class simply requires its consumer to call `RefreshPercentComplete` whenever a relevant date has been changed.

→ `Skill` is given an explicit default constructor because this is required for it to be properly serialized to isolated storage. Normally the default constructor is implicitly generated by the C# compiler. However, when a nondefault constructor is defined, as in Listing 23.4, you must explicitly define a default constructor (if you want one).

Serialization and Isolated Storage Application Settings

Every object that gets placed in the `IsolatedStorageSettings.ApplicationSettings` dictionary (or assigned to an instance of the `Settings` class used throughout this book)—including the transitive closure of all of its members—must be serializable. As mentioned in the preceding chapter, the contents of this dictionary get serialized to XML inside a file called `__ApplicationSettings`. If any piece of data is not serializable, none of the dictionary's contents get persisted. This failure can appear to happen silently, unless you happen to catch the unhandled exception in the debugger.

Most of the time, this requirement is satisfied without any extra work. None of the apps in this book (until now) had to take any special action to ensure that their settings were serializable, as all the basic data types (string, numeric values, `DateTime`, and so on), the generic `List` used with such basic data types, and classes with members of those types are all serializable.

Sometimes, however, you need to go out of your way to ensure that the data you persist is represented with serializable data types. This could be as simple as adding an explicit default constructor, as in Listing 23.4, or it could involve more work such as changing your data types or decorating them with custom attributes. The `System.Runtime.Serialization` namespace defines a `DataContract` attribute, along with attributes such as `DataMember` and `IgnoreDataMember` that enable you to customize how your classes get serialized. For example, if a class has a member than can't be serialized (and doesn't need to be serialized), you can mark it with the `IgnoreDataMember` attribute to exclude it.

 Avoid persisting multiple references to the same object!

Although you can store more than one reference to the same object in the isolated storage application settings dictionary, the references will no longer point to the same instance the next time the app runs. That's because when each reference is serialized, its data is persisted as an individual copy. On deserialization, each copy of the data becomes a distinct object instance.

This is why Baby Milestones uses a `CurrentAgeIndex` setting rather than a setting that stores a reference to the relevant Age instance. After serialization and deserialization, the logic in Listing 23.2 to automatically scroll the list box would no longer do anything, because the Age instance would no longer be in the list box.

> You can add custom logic to the serialization and deserialization process by marking a method with one of several custom attributes from the System.Runtime. Serialization namespace: OnSerializing, OnSerialized, OnDeserializing, and OnDeserialized. For your marked methods to be called at the appropriate times, they must be public (or internal with an appropriate InternalsVisibleTo attribute) and have a single StreamingContext parameter.

The Details Page

The details page, shown in Figure 23.2, appears when the user taps an age on the main page. This page displays the age-specific list of skills that can be tapped to record the date the skill was acquired. The tap brings up a date picker initialized to today's date, as shown in Figure 23.3. Listing 23.5 contains this page's XAML.

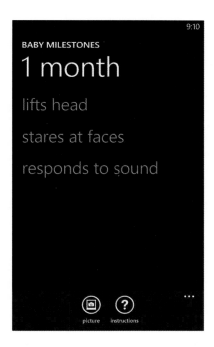

FIGURE 23.2   The details page, shown with the "1 month" list.

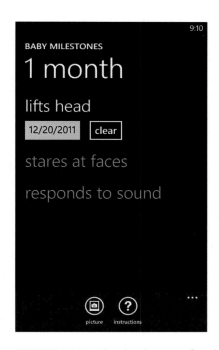

FIGURE 23.3   The details page after the first item is tapped.

LISTING 23.5   DetailsPage.xaml—The User Interface for Baby Milestones' Details Page

```
<phone:PhoneApplicationPage x:Class="WindowsPhoneApp.DetailsPage"
    xmlns="http://schemas.microsoft.com/winfx/2006/xaml/presentation"
    xmlns:x="http://schemas.microsoft.com/winfx/2006/xaml"
    xmlns:phone="clr-namespace:Microsoft.Phone.Controls;assembly=Microsoft.Phone"
```

LISTING 23.5   Continued

```xml
    xmlns:shell="clr-namespace:Microsoft.Phone.Shell;assembly=Microsoft.Phone"
    xmlns:toolkit="clr-namespace:Microsoft.Phone.Controls;
➥assembly=Microsoft.Phone.Controls.Toolkit"
    xmlns:local="clr-namespace:WindowsPhoneApp"
    FontSize="{StaticResource PhoneFontSizeNormal}"
    Foreground="{StaticResource PhoneForegroundBrush}"
    SupportedOrientations="PortraitOrLandscape"
    shell:SystemTray.IsVisible="True">

  <phone:PhoneApplicationPage.Resources>
    <!-- Two value converters -->
    <local:NullableObjectToVisibilityConverter
      x:Key="NullableObjectToVisibilityConverter"/>
    <local:NullableObjectToBrushConverter
      x:Key="NullableObjectToBrushConverter"/>
  </phone:PhoneApplicationPage.Resources>

  <phone:PhoneApplicationPage.ApplicationBar>
    <!-- The application bar, with two buttons -->
    <shell:ApplicationBar>
      <shell:ApplicationBarIconButton Text="picture"
                                      IconUri="/Shared/Images/appbar.picture.png"
                                      Click="PictureButton_Click"/>
      <shell:ApplicationBarIconButton Text="instructions"
                                  IconUri="/Shared/Images/appbar.instructions.png"
                                      Click="InstructionsButton_Click"/>
    </shell:ApplicationBar>
  </phone:PhoneApplicationPage.ApplicationBar>

  <Grid>
    <Grid.RowDefinitions>
      <RowDefinition Height="Auto"/>
      <RowDefinition Height="*"/>
    </Grid.RowDefinitions>

    <!-- The optional background image -->
    <Image x:Name="BackgroundImage" Grid.RowSpan="2" Opacity=".5"
           Stretch="UniformToFill"/>

    <!-- The standard header -->
    <StackPanel Style="{StaticResource PhoneTitlePanelStyle}">
      <TextBlock Text="BABY MILESTONES"
                 Style="{StaticResource PhoneTextTitle0Style}"/>
      <TextBlock Text="{Binding Name}"
                 Style="{StaticResource PhoneTextTitle1Style}"/>
```

LISTING 23.5   Continued

```
      </StackPanel>

      <!-- The list box that fills the page -->
      <ListBox x:Name="ListBox" Grid.Row="1" ItemsSource="{Binding Skills}"
               Margin="{StaticResource PhoneHorizontalMargin}"
               SelectionChanged="ListBox_SelectionChanged">
        <ListBox.ItemTemplate>
          <!-- The data template controls how each item renders -->
          <DataTemplate>
            <!-- The explicit width is only here for the sake of the tilt effect -->
            <StackPanel local:Tilt.IsEnabled="True"
                        Width="{Binding ActualWidth, ElementName=Page}">
              <TextBlock Text="{Binding Name}" TextWrapping="Wrap"
                         Margin="{StaticResource PhoneMargin}"
                         Style="{StaticResource PhoneTextExtraLargeStyle}"
                         Foreground="{Binding Date, Converter=
                           {StaticResource NullableObjectToBrushConverter}}"/>
              <StackPanel Orientation="Horizontal" Margin="0,-12,0,0"
                          Visibility="{Binding Date, Converter=
                            {StaticResource NullableObjectToVisibilityConverter}}">
                <toolkit:DatePicker Value="{Binding Date, Mode=TwoWay}"/>
                <Button Content="clear" Click="ClearButton_Click"/>
              </StackPanel>
            </StackPanel>
          </DataTemplate>
        </ListBox.ItemTemplate>
      </ListBox>
    </Grid>
</phone:PhoneApplicationPage>
```

→ The visibility of each item's date picker and the color of each item's text block are based on the value of the Skill instance's Date property. This is done with two value converters. These two classes, along with the value converter used by the main page, are shown in Listing 23.6.

→ The value for the date picker uses *two-way data binding*, which is useful for any property whose value can be manipulated by the user. Changes to the Skill's Date property are not only automatically reflected in the date picker, but also changes that the user makes via the date picker user interface are automatically reflected back to the Date property.

LISTING 23.6   `ValueConverters.cs`—The Three Value Converters Used by Baby Milestones

```csharp
using System;
using System.Globalization;
using System.Windows;
using System.Windows.Data;

namespace WindowsPhoneApp
{
  // Return Collapsed for null and Visible for nonnull
  public class NullableObjectToVisibilityConverter : IValueConverter
  {
    public object Convert(object value, Type targetType, object parameter,
      CultureInfo culture)
    {
      if (value != null)
        return Visibility.Visible;
      else
        return Visibility.Collapsed;
    }

    public object ConvertBack(object value, Type targetType, object parameter,
      CultureInfo culture)
    {
      return DependencyProperty.UnsetValue;
    }
  }

  // Return the accent brush for null and the foreground brush for nonnull
  public class NullableObjectToBrushConverter : IValueConverter
  {
    public object Convert(object value, Type targetType, object parameter,
      CultureInfo culture)
    {
      if (value != null)
        return Application.Current.Resources["PhoneForegroundBrush"];
      else
        return Application.Current.Resources["PhoneAccentBrush"];
    }

    public object ConvertBack(object value, Type targetType, object parameter,
      CultureInfo culture)
    {
      return DependencyProperty.UnsetValue;
    }
  }
```

LISTING 23.6   Continued

```
  // Return the accent brush for any value other than 100 and
  // the foreground brush for 100
  public class PercentageToBrushConverter : IValueConverter
  {
    public object Convert(object value, Type targetType, object parameter,
      CultureInfo culture)
    {
      if ((double)value == 100)
        return Application.Current.Resources["PhoneForegroundBrush"];
      else
        return Application.Current.Resources["PhoneAccentBrush"];
    }

    public object ConvertBack(object value, Type targetType, object parameter,
      CultureInfo culture)
    {
      return DependencyProperty.UnsetValue;
    }
  }
}
```

Listing 23.7 contains the code-behind for the details page.

LISTING 23.7   `DetailsPage.xaml.cs`—The Code-Behind for Baby Milestones' Details Page

```
using System;
using System.IO;
using System.Windows;
using System.Windows.Controls;
using System.Windows.Navigation;
using Microsoft.Phone;
using Microsoft.Phone.Controls;
using Microsoft.Phone.Tasks;

namespace WindowsPhoneApp
{
  public partial class DetailsPage : PhoneApplicationPage
  {
    public DetailsPage()
    {
      InitializeComponent();
    }

    protected override void OnNavigatedTo(NavigationEventArgs e)
```

LISTING 23.7   Continued

```
  {
    Age age = Settings.List.Value[Settings.CurrentAgeIndex.Value];
    // Update the UI
    this.DataContext = age;

    if (age.PhotoFilename != null)
      this.BackgroundImage.Source =
        IsolatedStorageHelper.LoadFile(age.PhotoFilename);
  }

  void ListBox_SelectionChanged(object sender, SelectionChangedEventArgs e)
  {
    if (this.ListBox.SelectedIndex >= 0)
    {
      // Set the date to today
      (this.ListBox.SelectedItem as Skill).Date = DateTime.Now;
      // Trigger the property changed event that will refresh the UI
      Settings.List.Value[
        Settings.CurrentAgeIndex.Value].RefreshPercentComplete();

      // Clear the selection so the same item can be selected
      // multiple times in a row
      this.ListBox.SelectedIndex = -1;
    }
  }

  void ClearButton_Click(object sender, RoutedEventArgs e)
  {
    Skill skill = (sender as Button).DataContext as Skill;
    if (MessageBox.Show("Are you sure you want to clear the date for \"" +
      skill.Name + "\"?", "Clear Date", MessageBoxButton.OKCancel)
      == MessageBoxResult.OK)
    {
      skill.Date = null;
      Settings.List.Value[
        Settings.CurrentAgeIndex.Value].RefreshPercentComplete();
    }
  }

  // Application bar handlers

  void PictureButton_Click(object sender, EventArgs e)
  {
    Microsoft.Phone.Tasks.PhotoChooserTask task = new PhotoChooserTask();
```

LISTING 23.7   Continued

```
      task.ShowCamera = true;
      task.Completed += delegate(object s, PhotoResult args)
      {
        if (args.TaskResult == TaskResult.OK)
        {
          string filename = Guid.NewGuid().ToString();
          IsolatedStorageHelper.SaveFile(filename, args.ChosenPhoto);

          Age age = Settings.List.Value[Settings.CurrentAgeIndex.Value];
          if (age.PhotoFilename != null)
            IsolatedStorageHelper.DeleteFile(age.PhotoFilename);
          age.PhotoFilename = filename;

          // Seek back to the beginning of the stream
          args.ChosenPhoto.Seek(0, SeekOrigin.Begin);

          // Set the background image instantly from the stream
          // Turn the stream into an ImageSource
          this.BackgroundImage.Source = PictureDecoder.DecodeJpeg(
            args.ChosenPhoto, (int)this.ActualWidth, (int)this.ActualHeight);
        }
      };
      task.Show();
    }

    void InstructionsButton_Click(object sender, EventArgs e)
    {
      this.NavigationService.Navigate(new Uri("/InstructionsPage.xaml",
        UriKind.Relative));
    }
  }
}
```

This listing uses a custom `IsolatedStorageHelper` class to load, save, and delete image files. The images originate from the photo chooser, shown in Figure 23.4, which returns the selected photo as a stream.

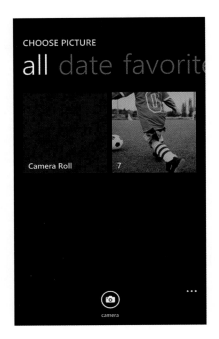

FIGURE 23.4   The photo chooser supports choosing a picture from the media library or taking a new photo from the camera.

`IsolatedStorageHelper` is implemented in Listing 23.8.

LISTING 23.8   `IsolatedStorageHelper.cs`—A Class That Stores and Retrieves Image Files to/from Isolated Storage

```
using System.Collections.Generic;
using System.IO;
using System.IO.IsolatedStorage;
using System.Windows.Media;
using Microsoft.Phone;

namespace WindowsPhoneApp
{
  public static class IsolatedStorageHelper
  {
    static Dictionary<string, ImageSource> cache =
      new Dictionary<string, ImageSource>();

    public static void SaveFile(string filename, Stream data)
    {
      using (IsolatedStorageFile userStore =
        IsolatedStorageFile.GetUserStoreForApplication())
      using (IsolatedStorageFileStream stream = userStore.CreateFile(filename))
```

LISTING 23.8   Continued

```
    {
      // Get the bytes from the input stream
      byte[] bytes = new byte[data.Length];
      data.Read(bytes, 0, bytes.Length);

      // Write the bytes to the new stream
      stream.Write(bytes, 0, bytes.Length);
    }
  }

  public static ImageSource LoadFile(string filename)
  {
    if (cache.ContainsKey(filename))
      return cache[filename];

    using (IsolatedStorageFile userStore =
      IsolatedStorageFile.GetUserStoreForApplication())
    using (IsolatedStorageFileStream stream =
            userStore.OpenFile(filename, FileMode.Open))
    {
      // Turn the stream into an ImageSource
      ImageSource source = PictureDecoder.DecodeJpeg(stream);
      cache[filename] = source;
      return source;
    }
  }

  public static void DeleteFile(string filename)
  {
    using (IsolatedStorageFile userStore =
            IsolatedStorageFile.GetUserStoreForApplication())
      userStore.DeleteFile(filename);
  }
 }
}
```

Notes:

→ The DeleteFile method is identical to the code to delete files in the preceding chapter, and SaveFile is not specific to images but rather generically saves the input stream's bytes to a new file stream. The picture-specific part is in LoadFile, which calls PictureDecoder.DecodeJpeg (in the Microsoft.Phone namespace) to convert the stream into an ImageSource that can be set as the source to any Image or ImageBrush element.

→ The DecodeJpeg method is fairly slow and must be called on the UI thread, so this class caches each ImageSource it creates so it can be instantly returned the next time its filename is passed to LoadFile. (The same ImageSource instance can be shared by multiple UI elements, so there's no danger in reusing one.)

Instead of PictureDecoder. DecodeJpeg, consider using WriteableBitmap.LoadJpeg. The latter can be called on a background thread, avoiding the unresponsiveness caused by decoding a large photo. WriteableBitmap is examined further in Chapter 42, "Jigsaw Puzzle."

LoadFile could use an alternate approach for constructing an ImageSource from an image in isolated storage. It could construct a BitmapImage with its default constructor and then call its SetSource method that accepts a stream with an instance of IsolatedStorageFileStream.

If your app enables saving photos from the camera, it's a good idea to allow the user to save it to the media library. This way, the photo can remain on the phone if your app is deleted. Also, once the photo is in the media library, users can sync it to their computer or easily share it in a number of ways (such as uploading it to Facebook or SkyDrive). You can enable this with a single call to MediaLibrary.SavePicture.

PictureDecoder.DecodeJpeg has a bug!

The overload of DecodeJpeg used in Listing 23.7 has maxPixelWidth and maxPixelHeight parameters that can restrict the size of the produced image for performance reasons. However, when the JPEG is wider than it is tall, DecodeJpeg mixes up the meaning of these two parameters. It uses maxPixelWidth to restrict the height and maxPixelHeight to restrict the width.

The Finished Product

Choosing a date with the date picker

Confirmation is required when you tap one of the clear buttons.

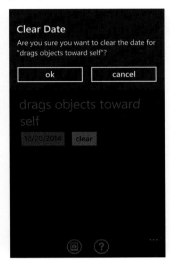

The instructions page

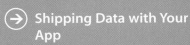

BABY NAME ELIMINATOR

Baby Name Eliminator provides the perfect technique for Type A personalities to name their babies. (It's the technique my wife and I used to name our two sons!) Rather than trying to brainstorm names and worrying that you're missing the perfect one, this app enables you to use the process of elimination to name your baby!

Baby Name Eliminator starts with a massive database of essentially every name ever used in the United States: 36,065 boy names and 60,438 girl names. After you choose a gender, the app enables you to quickly narrow down the list with a variety of filters. These filters are based on the popularity of each name, its starting/ending letter, and the year the name was first in use. Once you've finished filtering the list, you can eliminate names one-by-one until your decision is made.

When naming our sons, we went through several rounds, eliminating names that were obviously bad and leaving names that we had any hesitation about. Once we got down to about 20 names, my wife and I each picked our top 5 choices. With our first son, we only had one name in common, so our decision was made! If you and your spouse both have a Windows phone, independently eliminating names can be a fun way to come up with a final list of candidate names.

So where does this massive database of names come from? The Social Security Administration, which provides data

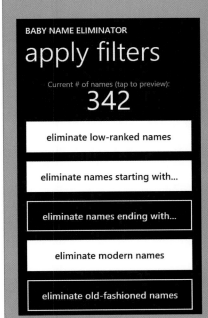

BABY NAME ELIMINATOR

apply filters

Current # of names (tap to preview):

342

eliminate low-ranked names

eliminate names starting with...

eliminate names ending with...

eliminate modern names

eliminate old-fashioned names

about almost every first name used in a Social Security card application from 1880 to the present. There are a few caveats to this list:

→ For privacy reasons, only names used at least five times in any given year are included.

→ One-character names are excluded.

→ Many people born before 1937 never applied for a Social Security card, so data from these years is spotty.

→ Distinct spellings of the same name are treated as different names.

→ The data is raw and uncorrected. Sometimes the sex on an application is incorrect, causing some boy names to show up in the girl names list and vice versa. In addition, some names are recorded as "Unknown," "Unnamed," or "Baby." Restricting your list to the top 1,000 or so names in any year generally gets rid of such artifacts.

To enable its filtering, this app makes use of two local databases—one for boy names and one for girl names.

Working with Local Databases

The lack of local database support in Windows Phone 7 is one of its more publicized shortcomings. Apps are encouraged to work with server-side databases instead, but this adds extra burden for developers and extra hassle for users (latency, a working data connection, and potential data charges). Fortunately, several third-party database options exist. My favorite is an open-source port of SQLite for Windows Phone 7 created by Dan Ciprian Ardelean. You can read about it at http://sviluppomobile.blogspot.com/ 2010/03/sqlite-for-wp-7-series-proof-of-concept.html and get the latest version (at the time of this writing) at http://www.neologics.eu/Dan/WP7_Sqlite_20.09.2010.zip. This includes C# source code and a `Community.CsharpSqlite.WP.dll` assembly that you can reference in your project. It's certainly not bug-free, but it works quite well for a number of scenarios (such as the needs of this app).

SQLite for Windows Phone 7 reads from and writes to database files in isolated storage. If you want to ship a database with your app that's already filled with data, you can include the database file in your project with a Build Action of Content. At run-time, your app can retrieve the file then save it to isolated storage before its first use of SQLite.

 To access a file included in your project as content, you can call `Application.GetResourceStream`. This is demonstrated in Listing 24.1.

How can I create a .db **file that contains the database I want to ship with my app?**

I followed the somewhat-cumbersome approach of writing a Windows Phone app that

1. Uses SQLite to generate the database, executing CREATE TABLE and INSERT commands
2. Retrieves the raw bytes from the .db file saved by SQLite to isolated storage, using the normal isolated storage APIs
3. Copies the bytes from the Visual Studio debugger as a Base64-encoded string and saves them to the needed .db file with a separate (desktop) program that decodes the string

Listing 24.1 contains a DatabaseHelper class used by Baby Name Eliminator that handles all interaction with the two SQLite databases included in the app.

LISTING 24.1   `DatabaseHelper.cs`—A Class That Wraps SQLite

```
using System;
using System.Collections.Generic;
using System.ComponentModel;
using System.IO;
using System.IO.IsolatedStorage;
using System.Windows;
using System.Windows.Resources;
using SQLiteClient;

namespace WindowsPhoneApp
{
  public class DatabaseHelper
  {
    // The name of the file included as content in this project,
    // also used as the isolated storage filename
    public static string DatabaseName { get; set; }

    // "Load" the database. If the file does not yet exist in isolated storage,
    // copy it from the original file. If the file already exists,
    // this is a no-op.
    public static void LoadAsync(Action callback)
    {
      BackgroundWorker worker = new BackgroundWorker();
      worker.DoWork += delegate(object sender, DoWorkEventArgs e)
      {
        if (!HasLoadedBefore)
        {
          StreamResourceInfo info = Application.GetResourceStream(
            new Uri(DatabaseName, UriKind.Relative));
          using (info.Stream)
```

LISTING 24.1   Continued

```
        SaveFile(DatabaseName, info.Stream);
      }
      if (callback != null)
        callback();
    };
    worker.RunWorkerAsync();
  }

  // Retrieve a single value from the database
  public static void ExecuteScalar(string command, Action<object> onSuccess,
    Action<Exception> onError = null)
  {
    BackgroundWorker worker = new BackgroundWorker();
    worker.DoWork += delegate(object sender, DoWorkEventArgs e)
    {
      try
      {
        object result = null;
        using (SQLiteConnection db = new SQLiteConnection(DatabaseName))
        {
          db.Open();
          SQLiteCommand c = db.CreateCommand(command);
          result = c.ExecuteScalar();
        }
        if (onSuccess != null)
          onSuccess(result);
      }
      catch (Exception ex)
      {
        if (onError != null)
          onError(ex);
      }
    };
    worker.RunWorkerAsync();
  }

  // Retrieve a collection of items from the database
  public static void ExecuteQuery<T>(string command,
    Action<IEnumerable<T>> onSuccess,
    Action<Exception> onError = null) where T : new()
  {
    BackgroundWorker worker = new BackgroundWorker();
    worker.DoWork += delegate(object sender, DoWorkEventArgs e)
    {
```

LISTING 24.1   Continued

```
      try
      {
        IEnumerable<T> result = null;
        List<T> copy = new List<T>();
        using (SQLiteConnection db = new SQLiteConnection(DatabaseName))
        {
          db.Open();
          SQLiteCommand c = db.CreateCommand(command);
          result = c.ExecuteQuery<T>();

          // Copy the data, because enumeration only
          // works while the connection is open
          copy.AddRange(result);
        }
        if (onSuccess != null)
          onSuccess(copy);
      }
      catch (Exception ex)
      {
        if (onError != null)
          onError(ex);
      }
    };
    worker.RunWorkerAsync();
  }

  public static bool HasLoadedBefore
  {
    get
    {
      using (IsolatedStorageFile userStore =
        IsolatedStorageFile.GetUserStoreForApplication())
        return userStore.FileExists(DatabaseName);
    }
  }

  // Save a stream to isolated storage
  static void SaveFile(string filename, Stream data)
  {
    using (IsolatedStorageFile userStore =
          IsolatedStorageFile.GetUserStoreForApplication())
    using (IsolatedStorageFileStream stream = userStore.CreateFile(filename))
    {
      // Get the bytes
```

LISTING 24.1   Continued

```
        byte[] bytes = new byte[data.Length];
        data.Read(bytes, 0, bytes.Length);

        // Write the bytes to the new stream
        stream.Write(bytes, 0, bytes.Length);
      }
    }
  }
}
```

Notes:

→ To enable a responsive user interface while expensive database operations are conducted, interaction with SQLite is done on a background thread with the help of `BackgroundWorker`, and success/failure is communicated via callbacks.

→ The command strings passed to `ExecuteScalar` and `ExecuteQuery` can be SQL commands like `SELECT COUNT(*) FROM `*table*.

→ `ExecuteQuery` is a generic method whose generic argument (`T`) must be a class with a property corresponding to each column selected in the query.

 `Application.GetResourceStream` works with files included in your project with a Build Action of Content *or* with a Build Action of Resource. For the latter case, the passed-in URI must have the following syntax:

/dllName;component/*pathAndFilename*

Note that *dllName* can refer to *any* DLL inside the `.xap` file, as long as it contains the requested resource. It should not contain the `.dll` suffix.

For this app, the `DatabaseName` string would look as follows for the database of boy names (`Boys.db`) included in the root of the project as a resource rather than content:

`/WindowsPhoneApp;component/Boys.db`

However, if this were done, Listing 24.1's use of `SaveFile` would have to change, because the `DatabaseName` string would no longer be a valid filename for isolated storage.

`Application.GetResourceStream` Versus `Assembly.GetManifestResourceStream`

You might stumble across the `Assembly.GetManifestResourceStream` API as a way to read files included with your app. This works, but only for files marked with a Build Action of **Embedded Resource** (*not* Resource). Using this in Listing 24.1 instead of `Application.GetResourceStream` would look as follows:

```
if (!HasLoadedBefore)
{
  using (Stream stream = typeof(DatabaseHelper).
```

```
       Assembly.GetManifestResourceStream(DatabaseName))
          SaveFile(DatabaseName, stream);
    }
```

However, the string passed to GetManifestResourceStream has its own unique syntax: *dllName*.*filename*, where *dllName* is the name of the DLL containing the embedded resource. That's because the C# compiler automatically prepends the DLL name (minus the .dll extension) to the filename when naming each embedded resource. (You can see these names by opening a DLL in a tool such as .NET Reflector.) For this app, the two valid strings would be "WindowsPhoneApp.Boys.db" and "WindowsPhoneApp.Girls.db".

There's no significant reason to use this approach rather than the more flexible Application. GetResourceStream. Using GetResourceStream with files included as content is generally preferable compared to *either* scheme with files embedded as resources, because resources increase the size of DLLs, and that can increase an app's load time.

The Filter Page

Rather than examine this app's main page, which you can view in the included source code, we'll examine the filter page that makes use of the DatabaseHelper class. The filter page, shown in Figure 24.1, displays how many names are in your list then enables you to filter it further with several options that map to SQL queries performed on the database. (The choice of boy names versus girl names is done previously on the main page.)

Each button reveals a dialog or other display, shown in Figure 24.2, that enables the user to control each relevant filter. Tapping the count of names reveals the actual list of names, as shown in Figure 24.3. This list doesn't enable interactive elimination, however, as that is handled on the main page.

FIGURE 24.1 The filter page supports five different types of filters.

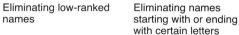

| Eliminating low-ranked names | Eliminating names starting with or ending with certain letters | Eliminating modern names | Eliminating old-fashioned names |

FIGURE 24.2   The result of tapping each button on the filter page.

FIGURE 24.3   Previewing the filtered list of names.

Listing 24.2 contains the XAML for the filter page.

LISTING 24.2   `FilterPage.xaml`—The User Interface for Baby Name Eliminator's Filter Page

```xaml
<phone:PhoneApplicationPage x:Name="Page"
    x:Class="WindowsPhoneApp.FilterPage"
    xmlns="http://schemas.microsoft.com/winfx/2006/xaml/presentation"
    xmlns:x="http://schemas.microsoft.com/winfx/2006/xaml"
    xmlns:phone="clr-namespace:Microsoft.Phone.Controls;assembly=Microsoft.Phone"
    xmlns:local="clr-namespace:WindowsPhoneApp"
    FontFamily="{StaticResource PhoneFontFamilyNormal}"
    FontSize="{StaticResource PhoneFontSizeNormal}"
    Foreground="{StaticResource PhoneForegroundBrush}"
    SupportedOrientations="PortraitOrLandscape">
  <Grid Background="Transparent">
    <Grid.RowDefinitions>
      <RowDefinition Height="Auto"/>
      <RowDefinition Height="*"/>
    </Grid.RowDefinitions>

    <!-- The standard header -->
    <StackPanel Style="{StaticResource PhoneTitlePanelStyle}">
      <TextBlock Text="BABY NAME ELIMINATOR"
                 Style="{StaticResource PhoneTextTitle0Style}"/>
      <TextBlock Text="apply filters"
                 Style="{StaticResource PhoneTextTitle1Style}"/>
    </StackPanel>

    <ScrollViewer Grid.Row="1">
      <Grid Margin="12,0">
        <Grid.RowDefinitions>
          <RowDefinition/>
          <RowDefinition/>
          <RowDefinition/>
          <RowDefinition/>
          <RowDefinition/>
          <RowDefinition/>
        </Grid.RowDefinitions>

        <!-- The current number of names -->
        <StackPanel Background="Transparent" local:Tilt.IsEnabled="True"
                    MouseLeftButtonUp="Preview_Click">
          <TextBlock Text="Current # of names (tap to preview):"
                     HorizontalAlignment="Center"
                     Style="{StaticResource LabelStyle}"/>
          <TextBlock x:Name="NumberTextBlock" Text="0" Margin="0,-16,0,0"
                     HorizontalAlignment="Center"
                     FontSize="{StaticResource PhoneFontSizeExtraExtraLarge}"/>
```

LISTING 24.2   Continued

```
      </StackPanel>

      <!-- Progress indicator while a query is running -->
      <Grid x:Name="ProgressPanel">
        <Rectangle Fill="{StaticResource PhoneBackgroundBrush}" Opacity=".9"/>
        <ProgressBar x:Name="ProgressBar" VerticalAlignment="Top"/>
        <TextBlock x:Name="ProgressText" TextWrapping="Wrap"
                   HorizontalAlignment="Center"
                   VerticalAlignment="Top" Margin="0,60,0,0" Text="Loading"/>
      </Grid>

      <!-- The five filter buttons -->
      <ToggleButton x:Name="RankMaxButton" Grid.Row="1"
                    Content="eliminate low-ranked names"
                    local:Tilt.IsEnabled="True" Click="RankMaxButton_Click"/>
      <ToggleButton x:Name="NameStartButton" Grid.Row="2"
                    Content="eliminate names starting with..."
                    local:Tilt.IsEnabled="True" Click="NameStartButton_Click"/>
      <ToggleButton x:Name="NameEndButton" Grid.Row="3"
                    Content="eliminate names ending with..."
                    local:Tilt.IsEnabled="True" Click="NameEndButton_Click"/>
      <ToggleButton x:Name="YearMaxButton" Grid.Row="4"
                    Content="eliminate modern names"
                    local:Tilt.IsEnabled="True" Click="YearMaxButton_Click"/>
      <ToggleButton x:Name="YearMinButton" Grid.Row="5"
                    Content="eliminate old-fashioned names"
                    local:Tilt.IsEnabled="True" Click="YearMinButton_Click"/>

      <!-- A user control that displays the letter grid in a popup -->
      <local:LetterPicker x:Name="LetterPicker"
                          Page="{Binding ElementName=Page}"
                          Closed="LetterPicker_Closed"/>
    </Grid>
  </ScrollViewer>

  <!-- Eliminate low-ranked names dialog -->
  <local:Dialog x:Name="RankMaxDialog" Grid.RowSpan="2" Closed="Dialog_Closed">
    <local:Dialog.InnerContent>
      <StackPanel>
        <TextBlock Text="…" TextWrapping="Wrap" Margin="11,5,0,-5"/>
        <TextBox MaxLength="5" InputScope="Number"
                 Text="{Binding Result, Mode=TwoWay}"/>
        <TextBlock Text="Enter a number, or leave blank to clear this filter."
                   TextWrapping="Wrap" Margin="11,-10,0,-10"
```

LISTING 24.2   Continued

```
                      Foreground="{StaticResource PhoneSubtleBrush}"/>
    </StackPanel>
  </local:Dialog.InnerContent>
</local:Dialog>

<!-- Eliminate modern names dialog -->
<local:Dialog x:Name="YearMaxDialog" Grid.RowSpan="2" Closed="Dialog_Closed">
  <local:Dialog.InnerContent>
    <StackPanel>
      <TextBlock TextWrapping="Wrap" Margin="11,5,0,-5">
        …
      </TextBlock>
      <TextBox MaxLength="4" InputScope="Number"
               Text="{Binding Result, Mode=TwoWay}"/>
      <TextBlock Text="…" TextWrapping="Wrap" Margin="11,-10,0,-10"
                 Foreground="{StaticResource PhoneSubtleBrush}"/>
    </StackPanel>
  </local:Dialog.InnerContent>
</local:Dialog>

<!-- Eliminate old-fashioned names dialog -->
<local:Dialog x:Name="YearMinDialog" Grid.RowSpan="2" Closed="Dialog_Closed">
  <local:Dialog.InnerContent>
    <StackPanel>
      <TextBlock TextWrapping="Wrap" Margin="11,5,0,-5">
        …
      </TextBlock>
      <TextBox MaxLength="4" InputScope="Number"
               Text="{Binding Result, Mode=TwoWay}"/>
      <TextBlock Text="…" TextWrapping="Wrap" Margin="11,-10,0,-10"
                 Foreground="{StaticResource PhoneSubtleBrush}"/>
    </StackPanel>
  </local:Dialog.InnerContent>
</local:Dialog>

<!-- The list of names shown when tapping the current number -->
<Grid x:Name="PreviewPane" Grid.RowSpan="2" Visibility="Collapsed">
  <Grid.RowDefinitions>
    <RowDefinition Height="Auto"/>
    <RowDefinition Height="*"/>
  </Grid.RowDefinitions>
  <Rectangle Grid.RowSpan="2" Fill="{StaticResource PhoneChromeBrush}"
             Opacity=".9"/>
  <StackPanel Style="{StaticResource PhoneTitlePanelStyle}">
```

LISTING 24.2   Continued

```
        <TextBlock x:Name="PreviewHeader"
                    Style="{StaticResource PhoneTextTitle0Style}"/>
    </StackPanel>
    <ListBox Grid.Row="1" x:Name="PreviewListBox" Margin="24,0,0,0"/>
  </Grid>
 </Grid>
</phone:PhoneApplicationPage>
```

Notes:

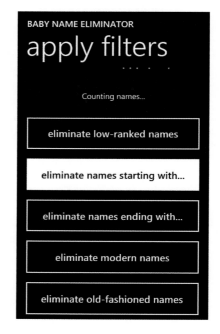

→ The dialogs shown when tapping buttons are created with a Dialog user control included with this app's source code. The grid of letters is created with a LetterGrid user control that is also included. This grid is very similar to the QuickJumpGrid user control from Chapter 18, "Cocktails."

→ The five filter buttons are toggle buttons whose IsChecked state is managed by code-behind. If a filter is active, its corresponding button is checked (highlighted) so the user can see this without tapping every button and double-checking its filter settings.

→ The progress bar and related user interface, shown while a query is executing on a background thread, is shown in Figure 24.4. Because it does not occupy the whole screen,

FIGURE 24.4   Showing progress while a database query executes on a background thread.

it enables the user to continue working if he or she doesn't care to wait for the current count of names.

Listing 24.3 contains the code-behind for the filter page.

LISTING 24.3   FilterPage.xaml.cs—The Code-Behind for Baby Name Eliminator's Filter Page

```
using System;
using System.Collections.Generic;
using System.ComponentModel;
using System.Windows;
```

LISTING 24.3   Continued

```csharp
using System.Windows.Input;
using System.Windows.Navigation;
using Microsoft.Phone.Controls;

namespace WindowsPhoneApp
{
  public partial class FilterPage : PhoneApplicationPage
  {
    public FilterPage()
    {
      InitializeComponent();
    }

    protected override void OnNavigatedTo(NavigationEventArgs e)
    {
      base.OnNavigatedTo(e);
      RefreshCount();
      RefreshButtons();
    }

    protected override void OnBackKeyPress(CancelEventArgs e)
    {
      base.OnBackKeyPress(e);

      // If a dialog, letter picker, or preview pane is open,
      // close it instead of leaving the page
      if (this.RankMaxDialog.Visibility == Visibility.Visible)
      {
        e.Cancel = true;
        this.RankMaxDialog.Hide(MessageBoxResult.Cancel);
      }
      else if (this.YearMaxDialog.Visibility == Visibility.Visible)
      {
        e.Cancel = true;
        this.YearMaxDialog.Hide(MessageBoxResult.Cancel);
      }
      else if (this.YearMinDialog.Visibility == Visibility.Visible)
      {
        e.Cancel = true;
        this.YearMinDialog.Hide(MessageBoxResult.Cancel);
      }
      else if (this.PreviewPane.Visibility == Visibility.Visible)
      {
        e.Cancel = true;
```

LISTING 24.3   Continued

```
      this.PreviewPane.Visibility = Visibility.Collapsed;
    }
  }

  void RefreshCount()
  {
    // Choose one of the included databases: boy names or girl names
    if (Settings.IsBoy.Value.Value)
      DatabaseHelper.DatabaseName = "Boys.db";
    else
      DatabaseHelper.DatabaseName = "Girls.db";

    if (!DatabaseHelper.HasLoadedBefore)
    {
      ShowProgress("Preparing database for the first time...");
      this.RankMaxButton.IsEnabled = false;
      this.NameStartButton.IsEnabled = false;
      this.NameEndButton.IsEnabled = false;
      this.YearMaxButton.IsEnabled = false;
      this.YearMinButton.IsEnabled = false;
    }

    DatabaseHelper.LoadAsync(delegate()
    {
      // The callback is called on a background thread, so transition back
      // to the main thread for manipulating UI
      this.Dispatcher.BeginInvoke(delegate()
      {
        ShowProgress("Counting names...");
        this.RankMaxButton.IsEnabled = true;
        this.NameStartButton.IsEnabled = true;
        this.NameEndButton.IsEnabled = true;
        this.YearMaxButton.IsEnabled = true;
        this.YearMinButton.IsEnabled = true;

        // Execute a query
        DatabaseHelper.ExecuteScalar("SELECT COUNT(*) FROM Names " +
          Settings.BuildQuerySuffix(), delegate(object result)
        {
          // The callback is called on a background thread, so transition back
          // to the main thread for manipulating UI
          this.Dispatcher.BeginInvoke(delegate()
          {
            HideProgress();
```

LISTING 24.3   Continued

```
                this.NumberTextBlock.Text = ((int)result).ToString("N0");
            });
          });
        });
      });
    }

    void RefreshButtons()
    {
      // Check (highlight) any button whose filter is active
      this.RankMaxButton.IsChecked =
        Settings.RankMax.Value != Settings.RankMax.DefaultValue;
      this.NameStartButton.IsChecked =
        Settings.ExcludedStartingLetters.Value.Count > 0;
      this.NameEndButton.IsChecked =
        Settings.ExcludedEndingLetters.Value.Count > 0;
      this.YearMaxButton.IsChecked =
        Settings.YearMax.Value != Settings.YearMax.DefaultValue;
      this.YearMinButton.IsChecked =
        Settings.YearMin.Value != Settings.YearMin.DefaultValue;
    }

    void Preview_Click(object sender, MouseButtonEventArgs e)
    {
      this.PreviewHeader.Text = "LOADING...";
      this.PreviewListBox.ItemsSource = null;
      this.PreviewPane.Visibility = Visibility.Visible;

      // Choose one of the included databases: boy names or girl names
      if (Settings.IsBoy.Value.Value)
        DatabaseHelper.DatabaseName = "Boys.db";
      else
        DatabaseHelper.DatabaseName = "Girls.db";

      DatabaseHelper.LoadAsync(delegate()
      {
        // It's okay to execute this on the background thread
        DatabaseHelper.ExecuteQuery<Record>("SELECT Name FROM Names " +
          Settings.BuildQuerySuffix(), delegate(IEnumerable<Record> result)
        {
          // Transition back to the main thread for manipulating UI
          this.Dispatcher.BeginInvoke(delegate()
          {
            this.PreviewHeader.Text = "PRESS BACK WHEN DONE";
```

LISTING 24.3   Continued

```
          this.PreviewListBox.ItemsSource = result;
        });
      });
    });
  }

  void ShowProgress(string message)
  {
    this.ProgressText.Text = message;
    this.ProgressBar.IsIndeterminate = true;
    this.ProgressPanel.Visibility = Visibility.Visible;
  }

  void HideProgress()
  {
    this.ProgressPanel.Visibility = Visibility.Collapsed;
    this.ProgressBar.IsIndeterminate = false; // Avoid a perf problem
  }

  // A click handler for each of the five filter buttons

  void RankMaxButton_Click(object sender, RoutedEventArgs e)
  {
    if (Settings.RankMax.Value != null)
      RankMaxDialog.Result = Settings.RankMax.Value.Value;
    RankMaxDialog.Show();
  }

  void NameStartButton_Click(object sender, RoutedEventArgs e)
  {
    this.LetterPicker.SetBinding(LetterPicker.ExcludedLettersProperty,
      new Binding { Path = new PropertyPath("Value"),
                    Source = Settings.ExcludedStartingLetters,
                    Mode = BindingMode.TwoWay });
    this.LetterPicker.ShowPopup();
  }

  void NameEndButton_Click(object sender, RoutedEventArgs e)
  {
    this.LetterPicker.SetBinding(LetterPicker.ExcludedLettersProperty,
      new Binding { Path = new PropertyPath("Value"),
                    Source = Settings.ExcludedEndingLetters,
                    Mode = BindingMode.TwoWay });
    this.LetterPicker.ShowPopup();
```

LISTING 24.3   Continued

```csharp
  }

  void YearMaxButton_Click(object sender, RoutedEventArgs e)
  {
    if (Settings.YearMax.Value != null)
      YearMaxDialog.Result = Settings.YearMax.Value.Value;
    YearMaxDialog.Show();
  }

  void YearMinButton_Click(object sender, RoutedEventArgs e)
  {
    if (Settings.YearMin.Value != null)
      YearMinDialog.Result = Settings.YearMin.Value.Value;
    YearMinDialog.Show();
  }

  // Two handlers for the dialog or letter picker being closed

  void LetterPicker_Closed(object sender, EventArgs e)
  {
    RefreshCount();
    RefreshButtons();
  }

  void Dialog_Closed(object sender, MessageBoxResultEventArgs e)
  {
    if (e.Result == MessageBoxResult.OK)
    {
      // Update or clear a setting, depending on which dialog was just closed
      int result;
      if (sender == RankMaxDialog)
      {
        if (RankMaxDialog.Result != null &&
            int.TryParse(RankMaxDialog.Result.ToString(), out result))
          Settings.RankMax.Value = result;
        else
          Settings.RankMax.Value = null;
      }
      if (sender == YearMaxDialog)
      {
        if (YearMaxDialog.Result != null &&
            int.TryParse(YearMaxDialog.Result.ToString(), out result))
          Settings.YearMax.Value = (short)result;
        else
```

LISTING 24.3   Continued

```
            Settings.YearMax.Value = null;
        }
        if (sender == YearMinDialog)
        {
          if (YearMinDialog.Result != null &&
              int.TryParse(YearMinDialog.Result.ToString(), out result))
            Settings.YearMin.Value = (short)result;
          else
            Settings.YearMin.Value = null;
        }

        // Only bother refreshing the count if the dialog result is OK
        RefreshCount();
      }

      // Refresh buttons when the dialog is closed for any reason,
      // to undo automatic check-when-tapped
      RefreshButtons();
    }
  }
}
```

Notes:

→ This project includes two databases (`Boys.db` and `Girls.db`) that have an identical schema. They contain a single table called `Names` with three columns: `Name`, `BestRank` (its best single-year ranking), and `FirstYear` (the first year the name appeared in Social Security data).

→ The query to refresh the count of names is "`SELECT COUNT(*) FROM Names`" with a `WHERE` clause based on settings whose values are determined by the filters. The settings and the `BuildQuerySuffix` method are defined in Listing 24.4.

→ The query to display the list of actual names is "`SELECT` **Name** `FROM Names`" with the same `WHERE` clause. The `Record` class used with `ExecuteQuery` is therefore a class with a single string `Name` property:

```
public class Record
{
  public string Name { get; set; }

  public override string ToString()
  {
    return this.Name;
  }
}
```

The `ToString` method enables the collection of `Records` to be used as the data source for the preview list box without any item template, as the default `ToString`-in-a-text-block rendering is sufficient.

→ Just like the date picker in the preceding chapter, this app leverages two-way data binding with each letter picker.

LISTING 24.4   `Settings.cs`—The `Settings` Class for Baby Name Eliminator

```csharp
using System.Collections.Generic;
using System.Collections.ObjectModel;
using System.Text;
using Microsoft.Phone.Controls;

namespace WindowsPhoneApp
{
  public static class Settings
  {
    // Step 1: Gender
    public static readonly Setting<bool?> IsBoy =
      new Setting<bool?>("IsBoy", null);

    // Step 2: Filters
    public static readonly Setting<int?> RankMax =
      new Setting<int?>("RankMax", null);
    public static readonly Setting<List<char>> ExcludedStartingLetters =
      new Setting<List<char>>("IncludedStartingLetters", new List<char>());
    public static readonly Setting<List<char>> ExcludedEndingLetters =
      new Setting<List<char>>("ExcludedEndingLetters", new List<char>());
    public static readonly Setting<short?> YearMax =
      new Setting<short?>("YearMax", null);
    public static readonly Setting<short?> YearMin =
      new Setting<short?>("YearMin", null);

    // Step 3: Elimination
    public static readonly Setting<ObservableCollection<string>> FilteredList =
      new Setting<ObservableCollection<string>>("FilteredList", null);
    public static readonly Setting<double> ScrollPosition =
      new Setting<double>("ScrollPosition", 0);

    // Orientation lock for the main page
    public static readonly Setting<SupportedPageOrientation>
      SupportedOrientations = new Setting<SupportedPageOrientation>(
        "SupportedOrientations", SupportedPageOrientation.PortraitOrLandscape);

    // Build up a WHERE clause if any filters have been chosen
```

LISTING 24.4   Continued

```csharp
public static string BuildQuerySuffix()
{
  List<string> conditions = new List<string>();

  if (Settings.RankMax.Value != null)
    conditions.Add(" BestRank <= " + Settings.RankMax.Value.Value);

  foreach (char c in Settings.ExcludedStartingLetters.Value)
    conditions.Add(" NOT Name LIKE '" + c + "%'");

  foreach (char c in Settings.ExcludedEndingLetters.Value)
    conditions.Add(" NOT Name LIKE '%" + c + "'");

  if (Settings.YearMax.Value != null)
    conditions.Add(" FirstYear <= " + Settings.YearMax.Value.Value);

  if (Settings.YearMin.Value != null)
    conditions.Add(" FirstYear >= " + Settings.YearMin.Value.Value);

  if (conditions.Count == 0)
    return "";
  else
  {
    StringBuilder whereClause = new StringBuilder("WHERE ");
    whereClause.Append(conditions[0]);
    for (int i = 1; i < conditions.Count; i++)
      whereClause.Append(" AND " + conditions[i]);

    return whereClause.ToString();
  }
}
```

The Finished Product

The main page initially walks the user through the three-step process.

The main page is used to perform the name-by-name elimination once the "start eliminating" button is tapped.

Eliminating several letters with the letter picker

chapter 25 lessons

BOOK READER

This chapter's Book Reader app provides a phone-optimized reading experience for Jane Austen's classic novel, *Pride and Prejudice*. The text for the book comes from Project Gutenberg (www.gutenberg.org), which provides free eBooks in the United States thanks to expired copyrights.

> **(!) If you plan to release an app with content from Project Gutenberg, make sure you understand the Project Gutenberg License.**
>
> See www.gutenberg.org for more details.

To get the best reading experience, this app enables you to customize the foreground and background colors, the text size, and even the font family. Book Reader provides easy page navigation and enables jumping to any chapter or page number.

It might not be immediately obvious, but the biggest challenge to implementing this app is pagination—dividing the book's contents into discrete pages based on the font settings. Avoiding this challenge by placing the entire book's contents in a scroll viewer wouldn't be a great user experience. It also wouldn't be feasible without extra trickery due to the size limitation of UI elements. Therefore, this app shows one page of text at a time. The user can tap the screen to advance the page, or tap a button on the application bar to go back by one page.

Chapter 1

It is a truth universally acknowledged, that a single man in possession of a good fortune, must be in want of a wife.

However little known the feelings or views of such a man may be on his first entering a neighbourhood, this truth is so well fixed in the minds of the surrounding families, that he is considered the rightful property of some one or other of their daughters.

4 / 1,452   ...

The Main Page

The main page, pictured in Figure 25.1 with its application bar expanded, shows the current page and an application bar with a button to go back one page, a button to jump to any chapter or page, and a button to change settings. The application bar area also shows the current page number as well as the total number of pages in the book (based on the current font settings). Listing 25.1 contains this page's XAML.

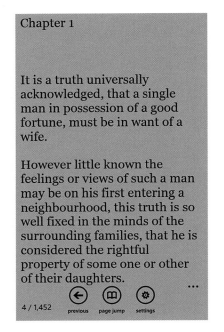

FIGURE 25.1   The main page, with its default Amazon Kindle-inspired color scheme that provides just enough contrast for reading.

LISTING 25.1   MainPage.xaml—The User Interface for Book Reader's Main Page

```
<phone:PhoneApplicationPage x:Class="WindowsPhoneApp.MainPage"
    xmlns="http://schemas.microsoft.com/winfx/2006/xaml/presentation"
    xmlns:x="http://schemas.microsoft.com/winfx/2006/xaml"
    xmlns:phone="clr-namespace:Microsoft.Phone.Controls;assembly=Microsoft.Phone"
    xmlns:shell="clr-namespace:Microsoft.Phone.Shell;assembly=Microsoft.Phone"
    xmlns:local="clr-namespace:WindowsPhoneApp"
    FontFamily="{StaticResource PhoneFontFamilyNormal}"
    FontSize="{StaticResource PhoneFontSizeNormal}"
    Foreground="{StaticResource PhoneForegroundBrush}"
    SupportedOrientations="Portrait">

  <!-- The application bar, with three buttons -->
```

LISTING 25.1   Continued

```xml
<phone:PhoneApplicationPage.ApplicationBar>
  <shell:ApplicationBar Opacity="0">
    <shell:ApplicationBarIconButton Text="previous" IsEnabled="False"
      IconUri="/Shared/Images/appbar.left.png" Click="PreviousButton_Click"/>
    <shell:ApplicationBarIconButton Text="page jump"
      IconUri="/Images/appbar.book.png" Click="JumpButton_Click"/>
    <shell:ApplicationBarIconButton Text="settings" IconUri=
      "/Shared/Images/appbar.settings.png" Click="SettingsButton_Click"/>
  </shell:ApplicationBar>
</phone:PhoneApplicationPage.ApplicationBar>

<Grid x:Name="LayoutRoot">
  <Grid.RowDefinitions>
    <RowDefinition/>
    <RowDefinition Height="56"/>
  </Grid.RowDefinitions>

  <!-- The document that takes up most of the page -->
  <local:PaginatedDocument x:Name="Document" Margin="12"
                           Width="456" Height="720"/>
  <!-- The footer that shows the page number and total page count -->
  <TextBlock x:Name="Footer" Grid.Row="1" Margin="14,0,0,17"
             HorizontalAlignment="Left" VerticalAlignment="Center"/>

  <!-- The full-screen panel with the text box and chapter list -->
  <Grid x:Name="JumpPanel" Grid.RowSpan="2" Visibility="Collapsed">
    <Grid.RowDefinitions>
      <RowDefinition Height="Auto"/>
      <RowDefinition/>
    </Grid.RowDefinitions>
    <Rectangle Grid.RowSpan="2" Fill="{StaticResource PhoneBackgroundBrush}"
               Opacity=".9"/>
    <!-- Enter a page number -->
    <StackPanel Orientation="Horizontal" Margin="12">
      <TextBlock Text="Jump to page:" VerticalAlignment="Center"/>
      <TextBox x:Name="PageTextBox" InputScope="Number" MinWidth="150"
               GotFocus="PageTextBox_GotFocus" KeyUp="PageTextBox_KeyUp"/>
      <Button Content="Go" MinWidth="150" local:Tilt.IsEnabled="True"
              Click="GoButton_Click"/>
    </StackPanel>
    <!-- Choose a chapter from the list box -->
    <ListBox x:Name="ChaptersListBox" Grid.Row="1" Margin="12"
             FontSize="{StaticResource PhoneFontSizeExtraLarge}"
             SelectionChanged="ChaptersListBox_SelectionChanged">

      <!-- This is done so the chapter page numbers are right-aligned -->
```

LISTING 25.1   Continued

```xml
      <ListBox.ItemContainerStyle>
        <Style TargetType="ListBoxItem">
          <Setter Property="HorizontalContentAlignment" Value="Stretch"/>
        </Style>
      </ListBox.ItemContainerStyle>

      <ListBox.ItemTemplate>
        <DataTemplate>
          <Grid local:Tilt.IsEnabled="True">
            <!-- The left-aligned chapter title -->
            <TextBlock Text="{Binding Key}"/>
            <!-- The right-aligned page number -->
            <TextBlock Text="{Binding Value}" HorizontalAlignment="Right"/>
          </Grid>
        </DataTemplate>
      </ListBox.ItemTemplate>
    </ListBox>
  </Grid>
  </Grid>
</phone:PhoneApplicationPage>
```

Notes:

→ This app's pagination magic is handled by a `PaginatedDocument` user control examined at the end of this chapter.

→ The `Footer` text block appears in the application bar area because it is placed underneath its area, and the application bar is marked with an opacity of 0.

→ The list box filled with chapters, shown in Figure 25.2, uses an important but hard-to-discover trick to enable the list box items to stretch to fill the width of the list box. This enables elements of each item (the page number, in this case) to be right-aligned without giving each item an explicit width.

Jump to page: 4	Go
Chapter 1	4
Chapter 2	15
Chapter 3	25
Chapter 4	44
Chapter 5	56
Chapter 6	68
Chapter 7	96
Chapter 8	120
Chapter 9	144
Chapter 10	165
Chapter 11	193
Chapter 12	212

FIGURE 25.2   The list box with chapters uses a `HorizontalContentAlignment` of `Stretch`, so the page numbers can be right-aligned without giving each item an explicit width.

To make the content of list box items stretch to fill the width of the list box, give the list box an `ItemContainerStyle` as follows:

```
<ListBox.ItemContainerStyle>
  <Style TargetType="ListBoxItem">
    <Setter Property="HorizontalContentAlignment" Value="Stretch"/>
  </Style>
</ListBox.ItemContainerStyle>
```

Listing 25.2 contains the code-behind for the main page.

LISTING 25.2   `MainPage.xaml.cs`—The Code-Behind for Book Reader's Main Page

```csharp
using System;
using System.Collections.Generic;
using System.ComponentModel;
using System.IO;
using System.Windows;
using System.Windows.Controls;
using System.Windows.Input;
using System.Windows.Media;
using System.Windows.Navigation;
using System.Windows.Resources;
using Microsoft.Phone.Controls;
using Microsoft.Phone.Shell;

namespace WindowsPhoneApp
{
  public partial class MainPage : PhoneApplicationPage
  {
    IApplicationBarIconButton previousButton;

    public MainPage()
    {
      InitializeComponent();
      this.previousButton = this.ApplicationBar.Buttons[0]
        as IApplicationBarIconButton;
    }

    protected override void OnNavigatedTo(NavigationEventArgs e)
    {
      base.OnNavigatedTo(e);

      // Respect the saved settings
```

LISTING 25.2   Continued

```
  this.ApplicationBar.ForegroundColor = Settings.TextColor.Value;
  this.LayoutRoot.Background = new SolidColorBrush(Settings.PageColor.Value);
  this.Document.Foreground = this.Footer.Foreground =
    new SolidColorBrush(Settings.TextColor.Value);
  this.Document.FontSize = Settings.TextSize.Value;
  this.Document.FontFamily = new FontFamily(Settings.Font.Value);

  if (this.Document.Text == null)
  {
    // Load the book as one big string from the included file
    LoadBook(delegate(string s)
    {
      // This happens on a background thread, but that's okay
      this.Document.Text = s;
      UpdatePagination();
    });
  }
  else if (this.State.ContainsKey("TextSize"))
  {
    if (((int)this.State["TextSize"] != Settings.TextSize.Value ||
      (string)this.State["Font"] != Settings.Font.Value))
    {
      // If the font family or size changed, the book needs to be repaginated
      UpdatePagination();
    }
    else if ((Color)this.State["TextColor"] != Settings.TextColor.Value)
    {
      // If only the color changed, simply re-render the current page
      this.Document.RefreshCurrentPage();
    }
  }

  // Remember the current text settings so we can detect if they
  // were changed when returning from the settings page
  this.State["TextSize"] = Settings.TextSize.Value;
  this.State["Font"] = Settings.Font.Value;
  this.State["TextColor"] = Settings.TextColor.Value;
}

protected override void OnBackKeyPress(CancelEventArgs e)
{
  base.OnBackKeyPress(e);

  // If the page/chapter jump panel is open, make the back button close it
```

LISTING 25.2   Continued

```
    if (this.JumpPanel.Visibility == Visibility.Visible)
    {
      e.Cancel = true;
      CloseJumpPanel();
    }
  }

  protected override void OnMouseLeftButtonUp(MouseButtonEventArgs e)
  {
    base.OnMouseLeftButtonUp(e);

    // Treat any tap as a page advance,
    // unless the page/chapter jump panel is open
    if (this.JumpPanel.Visibility == Visibility.Collapsed)
    {
      this.Document.ShowNextPage();
      RefreshFooter();
    }
  }

  // Retrieve the text from the included text file
  public static void LoadBook(Action<string> callback)
  {
    string s = null;

    BackgroundWorker worker = new BackgroundWorker();
    worker.DoWork += delegate(object sender, DoWorkEventArgs e)
    {
      // Do this work on a background thread
      StreamResourceInfo info = Application.GetResourceStream(
        new Uri("1342.txt", UriKind.Relative));
      using (info.Stream)
      using (StreamReader reader = new StreamReader(info.Stream))
        s = reader.ReadToEnd();

      if (callback != null)
        callback(s);
    };
    worker.RunWorkerAsync();
  }

  void UpdatePagination()
  {
    this.Document.UpdatePagination(delegate()
```

LISTING 25.2 Continued

```csharp
    {
      // Now that the book has been repaginated, refresh some UI
      // on the main thread
      this.Dispatcher.BeginInvoke(delegate()
      {
        // Move to the page we were previously on based on the character index
        // in the string (because the old page numbers are now meaningless)
        this.Document.ShowPageWithCharacterIndex(
          Settings.CurrentCharacterIndex.Value);

        RefreshFooter();

        // Fill the chapters list box based on the current page numbers
        this.ChaptersListBox.Items.Clear();
        for (int i = 0; i < this.Document.Chapters.Count; i++)
        {
          this.ChaptersListBox.Items.Add(new KeyValuePair<string, string>(
            "Chapter " + (i + 1),                  // Title
            this.Document.Chapters[i].ToString("N0") // Page number
          ));
        }
      });
    });
  }

  void RefreshFooter()
  {
    // Because this is called whenever the page is changed, this is a good
    // spot to store the current spot in the book
    Settings.CurrentCharacterIndex.Value = this.Document.CurrentCharacterIndex;
    this.Footer.Text = this.Document.CurrentPage.ToString("N0") + " / " +
                       this.Document.TotalPages.ToString("N0");
    this.previousButton.IsEnabled = (this.Document.CurrentPage > 1);
  }

  void OpenJumpPanel()
  {
    this.JumpPanel.Visibility = Visibility.Visible;
    this.ApplicationBar.IsVisible = false;
    // Fill the text box with the current page number
    // (without thousands separator)
    this.PageTextBox.Text = this.Document.CurrentPage.ToString();
    // Temporarily support landscape hardware keyboards
    this.SupportedOrientations = SupportedPageOrientation.PortraitOrLandscape;
```

LISTING 25.2   Continued

```
  }

  void CloseJumpPanel()
  {
    this.JumpPanel.Visibility = Visibility.Collapsed;
    this.ApplicationBar.IsVisible = true;
    this.SupportedOrientations = SupportedPageOrientation.Portrait;
  }

  void ChaptersListBox_SelectionChanged(object sender,
                                        SelectionChangedEventArgs e)
  {
    if (this.ChaptersListBox.SelectedIndex >= 0)
    {
      // Jump to the selected page
      this.Document.ShowPage(
        this.Document.Chapters[this.ChaptersListBox.SelectedIndex]);

      RefreshFooter();

      // Clear the selection so consecutive taps on the same item works
      this.ChaptersListBox.SelectedIndex = -1;

      // Delay the closing of the panel so OnMouseLeftButtonUp
      // doesn't advance the page
      this.Dispatcher.BeginInvoke(delegate() { CloseJumpPanel(); });
    }
  }

  void PageTextBox_GotFocus(object sender, RoutedEventArgs e)
  {
    this.PageTextBox.SelectAll();
  }

  void PageTextBox_KeyUp(object sender, System.Windows.Input.KeyEventArgs e)
  {
    // Make pressing Enter do the same thing as tapping "Go"
    if (e.Key == Key.Enter)
      GoButton_Click(this, null);
  }

  void GoButton_Click(object sender, RoutedEventArgs e)
  {
    // If the page number is valid, jump to it
```

LISTING 25.2   Continued

```csharp
    int pageNumber;
    if (int.TryParse(this.PageTextBox.Text, out pageNumber))
    {
      this.Document.ShowPage(pageNumber);
      RefreshFooter();
      CloseJumpPanel();
    }
  }

  // Application bar handlers

  void PreviousButton_Click(object sender, EventArgs e)
  {
    this.Document.ShowPreviousPage();
    RefreshFooter();
  }

  void JumpButton_Click(object sender, EventArgs e)
  {
    OpenJumpPanel();
  }

  void SettingsButton_Click(object sender, EventArgs e)
  {
    this.NavigationService.Navigate(new Uri("/SettingsPage.xaml",
      UriKind.Relative));
  }
 }
}
```

Notes:

→ The book is a text file included as content (Build Action = Content), just like the
   database files in the preceding chapter. The filename is `1342.txt`, matching the
   document downloaded from the Project Gutenberg website.

→ This app uses the following settings:

```csharp
public static class Settings
{
  // The current position in the book
  public static readonly Setting<int> CurrentCharacterIndex =
    new Setting<int>("CurrentCharacterIndex", 0);

  // The user-configurable settings
  public static readonly Setting<string> Font =
```

```
    new Setting<string>("Font", "Georgia");
  public static readonly Setting<Color> PageColor =
    new Setting<Color>("PageColor", Color.FromArgb(0xFF, 0xA1, 0xA1, 0xA1));
  public static readonly Setting<Color> TextColor =
    new Setting<Color>("TextColor", Colors.Black);
  public static readonly Setting<int> TextSize =
    new Setting<int>("TextSize", 32);
}
```

The reader's position in the book is stored as a character index—the index of the first character on the current page in the string containing the entire contents of the book. This is done because the page number associated with any spot in the book can vary dramatically based on the font settings. With this scheme, the user's true position in the book is always maintained.

→ The key-value pair added to the chapters list box is a convenient type to use because it exposes two separate string properties that the data template in Listing 25.1 is able to bind to. The "key" is the left-aligned chapter title and the "value" is the right-aligned page number.

The Settings Page

Book Reader's settings page is almost identical to the settings page for Notepad. The difference is a font picker on top of the other controls, shown in Figure 25.3. This font picker is created with the *list picker* control from the Silverlight for Windows Phone Toolkit.

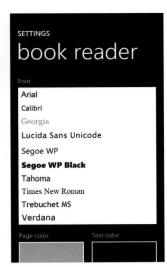

The collapsed font picker   The expanded font picker

FIGURE 25.3   The font picker shows ten fonts in a WYSIWYG picker.

A list picker is basically a combo box. It initially looks like a text box but, when tapped, it enables the user to pick one value out of a list of possible values.

To get the WYSIWYG font list inside the list picker, Book Reader's settings page uses the following XAML:

```
<toolkit:ListPicker x:Name="FontPicker" Header="Font" Grid.ColumnSpan="2"
  SelectionChanged="FontPicker_SelectionChanged" ItemCountThreshold="10">
  <toolkit:ListPicker.ItemTemplate>
    <DataTemplate>
      <TextBlock FontFamily="{Binding}" Text="{Binding}"/>
    </DataTemplate>
  </toolkit:ListPicker.ItemTemplate>
  <sys:String>Arial</sys:String>
  <sys:String>Calibri</sys:String>
  <sys:String>Georgia</sys:String>
  <sys:String>Lucida Sans Unicode</sys:String>
  <sys:String>Segoe WP</sys:String>
  <sys:String>Segoe WP Black</sys:String>
  <sys:String>Tahoma</sys:String>
  <sys:String>Times New Roman</sys:String>
  <sys:String>Trebuchet MS</sys:String>
  <sys:String>Verdana</sys:String>
</toolkit:ListPicker>
```

The data template binds both `FontFamily` and `Text` properties of each text block to display each string in the list.

List pickers support two different ways of presenting their list of items: an *inline mode* and a *full mode*. In the inline mode, the control expands and collapses with smooth animations. This is what is happening in Figure 25.3. In the full mode, the control displays a full-screen popup that presents its list of items. This is pictured in Figure 25.4.

Why does the ComboBox **control look so strange when I try to use it in a Windows Phone app?**

The ComboBox control is a core Silverlight control frequently used on the web, but it was never given a style that is appropriate for Windows Phone. It is not intended to be used. (The control should have been removed to avoid confusion.) If you find yourself wanting to use a combo box, use the list picker instead.

By default, a list picker uses its inline mode if there are five or fewer items; otherwise, it uses full mode. This is consistent with Windows Phone design guidelines. However, you can force either mode by setting the value of `ItemCountThreshold` appropriately. The list picker will stay in its inline mode as long as the number of items is less than or equal to `ItemCountThreshold`. Book Reader chooses to keep the font picker with 10 fonts in inline mode, so it sets this property to 10.

List picker defines a `Header` and corresponding `HeaderTemplate` property, and an `ItemTemplate` property for customizing the appearance of each item in the inline mode. Even if you use full mode, these properties are still important for the appearance of the list picker when the full-screen list isn't showing. For the full-screen list, list picker also defines separate `FullModeHeader` and `FullModeItemTemplate` properties. The full-mode list picker shown in Figure 25.4 takes advantage of these two properties as follows:

FIGURE 25.4   A variation of Book Reader's font picker, configured to use full mode.

```
<toolkit:ListPicker Header="Font" FullModeHeader="FONT">
  <toolkit:ListPicker.ItemTemplate>
    <!-- For displaying the selected item inline -->
    <DataTemplate>
      <TextBlock FontFamily="{Binding}" Text="{Binding}"/>
    </DataTemplate>
  </toolkit:ListPicker.ItemTemplate>
  <toolkit:ListPicker.FullModeItemTemplate>
    <!-- For displaying each item in full mode -->
    <DataTemplate>
      <TextBlock FontFamily="{Binding}" Text="{Binding}" Margin="12"
                 FontSize="{StaticResource PhoneFontSizeExtraLarge}"/>
    </DataTemplate>
  </toolkit:ListPicker.FullModeItemTemplate>
  <sys:String>Arial</sys:String>
  <sys:String>Calibri</sys:String>
  <sys:String>Georgia</sys:String>
  <sys:String>Lucida Sans Unicode</sys:String>
  <sys:String>Segoe WP</sys:String>
  <sys:String>Segoe WP Black</sys:String>
  <sys:String>Tahoma</sys:String>
```

```
  <sys:String>Times New Roman</sys:String>
  <sys:String>Trebuchet MS</sys:String>
  <sys:String>Verdana</sys:String>
</toolkit:ListPicker>
```

If you don't specify a `FullModeItemTemplate`, the full mode will use `ItemTemplate`.

> **(!) List pickers cannot contain UI elements when full mode is used!**
>
> If you directly place UI elements such as text blocks or the toolkit's own `ListPickerItem` controls inside a list picker, an exception is thrown when attempting to display the full-mode popup. That's because the control attempts to add each item to the additional full-screen list, but a single UI element can only be in one place at a time. The solution is to place nonvisual data items in the list picker then use item template(s) to control each item's visual appearance.

> **(!) Avoid putting an inline-mode list picker at the bottom of a scroll viewer!**
>
> List picker behaves poorly in this situation. When it first expands, the view is not shifted to ensure its contents are on-screen. Then, when attempting to scroll to view the off-screen contents, the list picker collapses!

> For the best performance, elements below an inline-mode list picker should be marked with `CacheMode="BitmapCache"`. That's because the expansion and contraction of the list picker animates the positions of these elements.

> • • •
>
> **List Pickers and Picker Boxes**
>
> Although the single list picker control provides two different experiences, some Windows Phone literature refers to a full-mode list picker as a separate *picker box* control, reserving the term *list picker* for the inline experience. This is why the custom control used in Chapter 19, "Animation Lab," is called `PickerBox`.

The `PaginatedDocument` User Control

To determine where page breaks occur, the `PaginatedDocument` user control must measure the width and height of each character under the current font settings. The only way to perform this measurement is to place text in a text block and check the values of its `ActualWidth` and `ActualHeight` properties. Therefore, `PaginatedDocument` uses the following three-step algorithm:

1. Find each unique character in the document. (The *Pride and Prejudice* document contains only 85 unique characters.)

2. Measure the width and height of each character by placing each one in a text block, one at a time. The height of all characters is always the same (as the reported height is the line height, padding and all), so the height only needs to be checked once.

3. Go through the document from beginning to end and, using the precalculated widths of each character, figure out where each line break occurs. With this information, and with the precalculated line height, we know where each page break occurs. Determining line breaks can be a bit tricky due to the need to wrap words appropriately.

The control renders any page by adding a text block for each line, based on the calculated page breaks and line breaks. This is done to ensure that every line break occurs exactly where we expect it to.

Listing 25.3 contains the user control's XAML and Listing 25.4 contains its code-behind.

LISTING 25.3   `PaginatedDocument.xaml`—The User Interface for the `PaginatedDocument` User Control

```xaml
<UserControl x:Class="WindowsPhoneApp.PaginatedDocument"
    xmlns="http://schemas.microsoft.com/winfx/2006/xaml/presentation"
    xmlns:x="http://schemas.microsoft.com/winfx/2006/xaml"
    FontFamily="{StaticResource PhoneFontFamilyNormal}"
    FontSize="{StaticResource PhoneFontSizeNormal}"
    Foreground="{StaticResource PhoneForegroundBrush}">
  <Canvas>
    <!-- Contains the lines of text -->
    <StackPanel x:Name="StackPanel" Margin="0,-6,0,0"/>
    <!-- Used for measurements -->
    <TextBlock x:Name="MeasuringTextBlock"/>
  </Canvas>
</UserControl>
```

LISTING 25.4   `PaginatedDocument.xaml.cs`—The Code-Behind for the `PaginatedDocument` User Control

```csharp
using System;
using System.Collections.Generic;
using System.ComponentModel;
using System.Windows.Controls;

namespace WindowsPhoneApp
{
  public partial class PaginatedDocument : UserControl
  {
    Dictionary<char, double> characterWidths = new Dictionary<char, double>();
    double characterHeight;
```

LISTING 25.4   Continued

```csharp
bool isUpdating;
int currentPageBreakIndex;

List<int> pageBreaks = new List<int>();
List<int> lineBreaks = new List<int>();
public List<int> Chapters = new List<int>();

public PaginatedDocument()
{
  InitializeComponent();
}

public int CurrentPage
{
  get { return this.currentPageBreakIndex + 1; }
}

public int TotalPages
{
  get { return this.pageBreaks.Count - 1; }
}

public string Text { get; set; }

public int CurrentCharacterIndex { get; private set; }

public void UpdatePagination(Action doneCallback)
{
  if (this.Text == null || this.isUpdating)
    throw new InvalidOperationException();

  this.isUpdating = true;

  // Reset measurements
  this.pageBreaks.Clear(); this.lineBreaks.Clear();
  this.pageBreaks.Add(0); this.lineBreaks.Add(0);
  this.Chapters.Clear();
  this.characterWidths.Clear();
  this.characterHeight = -1;

  BackgroundWorker worker = new BackgroundWorker();
  worker.DoWork += delegate(object sender, DoWorkEventArgs e)
  {
    // STEP 1: BACKGROUND THREAD
```

LISTING 25.4   Continued

```csharp
// Build up a dictionary of unique characters in the text
for (int i = 0; i < this.Text.Length; i++)
{
  if (!this.characterWidths.ContainsKey(this.Text[i]))
    this.characterWidths.Add(this.Text[i], -1);
}

// Copy the character keys so we can update the width values
// without affecting the enumeration
char[] chars = new char[this.characterWidths.Keys.Count];
this.characterWidths.Keys.CopyTo(chars, 0);

this.Dispatcher.BeginInvoke(delegate()
{
  // STEP 2: MAIN THREAD
  // Measure the height of all characters
  // and the width of each character

  foreach (char c in chars)
  {
    // The only way to measure the width is to place the
    // character in a text block and ask for its ActualWidth
    this.MeasuringTextBlock.Text = c.ToString();
    this.characterWidths[c] = this.MeasuringTextBlock.ActualWidth;

    // The height for all characters is the same
    // (except for newlines, which are twice the height)
    if (this.characterHeight == -1 && !Char.IsWhiteSpace(c))
      this.characterHeight = this.MeasuringTextBlock.ActualHeight;
  }
  this.MeasuringTextBlock.Text = "";

  double pageWidth = this.Width + 1; // Allow one pixel more than width
  double linesPerPage = this.Height / this.characterHeight;

  BackgroundWorker worker2 = new BackgroundWorker();
  worker2.DoWork += delegate(object sender2, DoWorkEventArgs e2)
  {
    // STEP 3: BACKGROUND THREAD
    // Determine the index of each page break
    int linesOnThisPage = 0;
    double currentLineWidth = 0;
    int lastWordEndingIndex = -1;
```

LISTING 25.4   Continued

```
                // Loop through each character and determine each line
                // break based on character widths and text block wrapping behavior.
                // A line break should then be a page break when the cumulative
                // height of lines exceeds the page height.
                for (int i = 0; i < this.Text.Length; i++)
                {
                  char c = this.Text[i];

                  bool isLineBreak = false;
                  bool isForcedPageBreak = false;

                  if (c == '\n')
                  {
                    if (linesOnThisPage == 0 && currentLineWidth == 0)
                      continue; // Skip blank lines at the start of a page

                    isLineBreak = true;
                    lastWordEndingIndex = i;
                  }
                  else if (c == '\r')
                  {
                    isLineBreak = isForcedPageBreak = true;
                    lastWordEndingIndex = i;
                    // This is the start of a chapter
                    // Add 1 because the page break isn't added yet
                    Chapters.Add(this.pageBreaks.Count + 1);
                  }
                  else
                  {
                    currentLineWidth += this.characterWidths[c];
                    // Check for a needed line break
                    if (currentLineWidth > pageWidth)
                      isLineBreak = true;
                  }

                  if (isLineBreak)
                  {
                    linesOnThisPage++;

                    if (lastWordEndingIndex<=this.lineBreaks[this.lineBreaks.Count-1])
                    {
                      // The last spot where the line can be broken was already
                      // used as a line break. Therefore, we have no choice but to
```

LISTING 25.4   Continued

```
            // force a line break right now.
        }
        else
        {
          // Move back to first character after the actual break, which
          // we may have passed due to word wrapping
          i = lastWordEndingIndex;
        }

        // Reset the width for the next line
        currentLineWidth = 0;

        // Skip the space between split words
        int breakIndex;
        if (i < this.Text.Length - 1 && this.Text[i + 1] == ' ')
          breakIndex = i + 1;
        else
          breakIndex = i;

        this.lineBreaks.Add(breakIndex);

        // See if this is a page break.
        // It is if the NEXT line would be cut off
        bool isNaturalPageBreak = (linesOnThisPage + 1) > linesPerPage;

        if (isForcedPageBreak || isNaturalPageBreak)
        {
          this.pageBreaks.Add(breakIndex);
          // Reset
          linesOnThisPage = 0;
        }
      }
      else if (c == ' ' || c == '-' || c == '--')
        lastWordEndingIndex = i; // This can be used as a line break
                                 // if we run out of space
    }

    // Add a final line break and page break
    // marking the end of the document
    if (this.lineBreaks[this.lineBreaks.Count - 1] != this.Text.Length)
    {
      this.lineBreaks.Add(this.Text.Length);
      this.pageBreaks.Add(this.Text.Length);
    }
```

LISTING 25.4   Continued

```
            // We're done!
            doneCallback();
            this.isUpdating = false;
          };
          worker2.RunWorkerAsync();
        });
      };
    worker.RunWorkerAsync();
}

public void ShowPageWithCharacterIndex(int characterIndex)
{
    if (characterIndex < 0 || characterIndex >= this.Text.Length ||
        this.Text == null)
      return;

    int pageBreakIndex = this.pageBreaks.BinarySearch(characterIndex);
    if (pageBreakIndex < 0)
    {
      // The characterIndex doesn't match an exact page break, but BinarySearch
      // has returned a negative number that is the bitwise complement of the
      // index of the next element that is larger than characterIndex
      // (or the list's count if there is no larger element).
      // By subtracting one, this gives the index of the smaller element, or
      // the index of the last element if the index is too big.
      // Because 0 is in the list, this will always give a valid index.
      pageBreakIndex = ~pageBreakIndex - 1;
    }

    // If the page break index is the last one (signifying the last character
    // of the book), go back one so we'll render the whole last page
    if (pageBreakIndex == this.pageBreaks.Count - 1)
      pageBreakIndex--;

    ShowPage(pageBreakIndex + 1); // 1-based instead of 0-based
}

public void ShowPage(int pageNumber)
{
    if (pageNumber >= this.pageBreaks.Count || this.Text == null)
      return;

    this.currentPageBreakIndex = pageNumber - 1;
    RefreshCurrentPage();
```

LISTING 25.4   Continued

```
  }

  public void ShowPreviousPage()
  {
    if (this.currentPageBreakIndex == 0 || this.Text == null)
      return;

    this.currentPageBreakIndex--;
    RefreshCurrentPage();
  }

  public void ShowNextPage()
  {
    if (this.currentPageBreakIndex >= this.pageBreaks.Count - 2 ||
        this.Text == null)
      return;

    this.currentPageBreakIndex++;
    RefreshCurrentPage();
  }

  public void RefreshCurrentPage()
  {
    // An exact match should always be found
    int firstLineBreakIndex = this.lineBreaks.BinarySearch(
      this.pageBreaks[this.currentPageBreakIndex]);
    int lastLineBreakIndex = this.lineBreaks.BinarySearch(
      this.pageBreaks[this.currentPageBreakIndex + 1]) - 1;

    this.StackPanel.Children.Clear();

    for (int i = firstLineBreakIndex; i <= lastLineBreakIndex; i++)
    {
      // We're guaranteed that lastLineBreakIndex is always less than count - 1
      string line = this.Text.Substring(this.lineBreaks[i],
                        this.lineBreaks[i + 1] - this.lineBreaks[i]);

      line = line.Trim();

      if (line.Length == 0)
        line = " ";

      this.StackPanel.Children.Add(new TextBlock
      {
```

LISTING 25.4   Continued

```
          Text = line,
          Foreground = this.MeasuringTextBlock.Foreground,
          FontSize = this.MeasuringTextBlock.FontSize,
          FontFamily = this.MeasuringTextBlock.FontFamily
        });
    }

    this.CurrentCharacterIndex = this.lineBreaks[firstLineBreakIndex];
    }
  }
}
```

Notes:

→ The index of each line break and page break is stored in respective lists. The list of page breaks is a subset of the list of line breaks, and this relationship is leveraged when a page must be rendered.

→ Inside `UpdatePagination`, as much work as possible is offloaded to a background thread. Because the actual measurement must be done on the UI thread, however, two background workers are used to transition from a background thread to the main thread then back to a background thread.

→ This control makes a few assumptions about the input text, and the *Pride and Prejudice* document included in the project has been preprocessed to make these assumptions true:

   1. A line feed character (\n) denotes a forced line break, which should only occur at the end of a paragraph. (The original text used a fixed line width and therefore places \n characters at regular intervals, which defeats the purpose of the dynamic layout.)

   2. A carriage return character (\r) denotes the beginning of a chapter. This enables the automatic population of the chapters collection, which drives the population of the chapters list box on the main page.

The Finished Product

Using a small font

"But consider your daughters. Only think what an establishment it would be for one of them. Sir William and Lady Lucas are determined to go, merely on that account, for in general, you know, they visit no newcomers. Indeed you must go, for it will be impossible for _us_ to visit him if you do not."

"You are over-scrupulous, surely. I dare say Mr. Bingley will be very glad to see you; and I will send a few lines by you to assure him of my hearty consent to his marrying whichever he chooses of the girls; though I must throw in a good word for my little Lizzy."

"I desire you will do no such thing. Lizzy is not a bit better than the others; and I am sure she is not half so handsome as Jane, nor half so good-humoured as Lydia. But you are always giving _her_ the preference."

"They have none of them much to recommend them," replied he; "they are all silly and ignorant like other girls; but Lizzy has something more of quickness than her sisters."

"Mr. Bennet, how _can_ you abuse your own children in such a way? You take delight in vexing me. You have no compassion for my poor nerves."

6 / 630

Using a large font

mistake me, my dear. I have a high respect for your nerves.

72 / 11,358

Another font and color combination

myself."

The girls stared at their father. Mrs. Bennet said only, "Nonsense, nonsense!"

"What can be the meaning of that emphatic exclamation?" cried he. "Do you consider the forms of introduction, and the stress that is laid on them, as nonsense? I

30 / 2,338

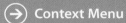

TODO LIST

TODO List enables you to manage tasks in a fast, easy, and attractive way. Mark tasks with colored stars and/or detailed descriptions. Filter them in multiple ways, such as seeing overdue tasks, tasks due today, or tasks with stars. See what you've accomplished in a "done" list, with the ability to undo tasks. Trim the filters to only the ones you care about.

TODO List contains more code than most of the apps in this book, mostly because of list management: viewing items, viewing details for each item, sorting items, adding and deleting items, and editing items. The app has five pages: a main page, a details page, a page for adding or editing an item, a settings page, and an instructions page. The pages and code that enable all of the list management can be trivially adapted to any app that enables the user to manage items.

The main purpose of TODO List, however, is to demonstrate the pivot control. The pivot is one of the two signature user interface paradigms introduced by Windows Phone 7. (The other is the panorama covered by the next chapter.)

The Pivot Control

A pivot is basically a tabbed user interface in which you can swipe horizontally or tap one of the headers to switch to a different tab. This style of user interface is featured prominently in the built-in Mail, Calendar, and Settings

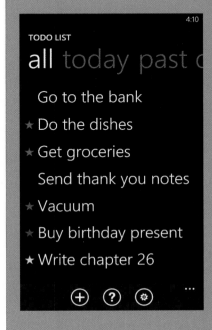

apps, but also used by most of the other built-in apps: Internet Explorer, Maps, Marketplace, Music + Videos, People, and Pictures.

Pivots are designed to provide filtered views over the same set of data (as in the Mail app), distinct views over the same set of data (as in the Calendar app), or to provide easily switchable views over separate sets of data (such as application versus system settings in the Settings app). They are *not* meant to be used to expose sequential steps in a task, such as a wizard-style user interface. They are meant to occupy the entire page except, perhaps, for an application bar and/or status bar.

Just like the list box and list picker, pivot is an items control. Although the `Pivot` class exposes an `Items` collection to which any type of object can be added, only `PivotItem` objects or data objects should be added.

`PivotItem` is a simple content control with `Content` and `Header` properties of type `object`. Although these properties can be set to anything, `Content` is typically set to a panel such as a grid that contains a complex user interface, whereas `Header` is typically set to a string.

The pivot and panorama controls reside in an assembly that isn't referenced by default in "Windows Phone Application" projects!

Although their .NET namespace (`Microsoft.Phone.Controls`) is the same as some commonly used types such as `PhoneApplicationPage`, the pivot and panorama controls are defined in the `Microsoft.Phone.Controls` assembly. (Controls such as `PhoneApplicationPage` are defined in the `Microsoft.Phone` assembly.)

To use these controls, be sure to add a reference to `Microsoft.Phone.Controls.dll`. If you use Visual Studio's "Windows Phone Pivot Application" or "Windows Phone Panorama Application" project templates, this assembly is already referenced by default. Similarly, if you add a "Windows Phone Pivot Page" or "Windows Phone Panorama Page" from Visual Studio's Add New Item dialog, the assembly reference is automatically added to your project.

Here are three pivot design guidelines that apps should—but often don't—obey:

→ Header text should be lowercase, with the exception of proper names.

→ As already mentioned, do not use one to organize sequential tasks that the user must complete.

→ There should be no more than seven pivot items in a single pivot.

• • •

A Pivot without `PivotItems`

Pivots are unusable with any UI elements other than `PivotItem` controls. The pivot attempts to render such elements as each item's header *and* content. Therefore, attempting to use a different type of UI element throws an exception explaining, "Element is already the child of another element." This is not a problem, however, because there's no reason to not use `PivotItems`. They can contain anything, so you can always wrap your desired content with one. You can also add nonvisual data objects to a pivot and then use its `ItemTemplate` and `HeaderTemplate` properties to format them appropriately.

The Main Page

TODO List's main page is the only one that uses a pivot. It contains five pivot items, all shown in Figure 26.1 in their empty states when first launching the app.

FIGURE 26.1   The five pivot items in their initial states.

The User Interface

Listing 26.1 contains the XAML for the main page.

LISTING 26.1   `MainPage.xaml`—The Main User Interface for TODO List

```
<phone:PhoneApplicationPage x:Class="WindowsPhoneApp.MainPage"
    xmlns="http://schemas.microsoft.com/winfx/2006/xaml/presentation"
    xmlns:x="http://schemas.microsoft.com/winfx/2006/xaml"
    xmlns:phone="clr-namespace:Microsoft.Phone.Controls;assembly=Microsoft.Phone"
    xmlns:shell="clr-namespace:Microsoft.Phone.Shell;assembly=Microsoft.Phone"
    xmlns:controls="clr-namespace:Microsoft.Phone.Controls;
➥assembly=Microsoft.Phone.Controls"
    xmlns:toolkit="clr-namespace:Microsoft.Phone.Controls;
➥assembly=Microsoft.Phone.Controls.Toolkit"
    xmlns:local="clr-namespace:WindowsPhoneApp"
    FontFamily="{StaticResource PhoneFontFamilyNormal}"
    FontSize="{StaticResource PhoneFontSizeNormal}"
    Foreground="{StaticResource PhoneForegroundBrush}"
    SupportedOrientations="PortraitOrLandscape" shell:SystemTray.IsVisible="True">

  <!-- The application bar, with 3 buttons and 1 menu item -->
  <phone:PhoneApplicationPage.ApplicationBar>
    <shell:ApplicationBar>
      <shell:ApplicationBarIconButton Text="new"
        IconUri="/Shared/Images/appbar.add.png" Click="AddButton_Click"/>
      <shell:ApplicationBarIconButton Text="instructions"
        IconUri="/Shared/Images/appbar.instructions.png"
```

LISTING 26.1   Continued

```
        Click="InstructionsButton_Click"/>
      <shell:ApplicationBarIconButton Text="settings"
        IconUri="/Shared/Images/appbar.settings.png"
        Click="SettingsButton_Click"/>
      <shell:ApplicationBar.MenuItems>
        <shell:ApplicationBarMenuItem Text="about" Click="AboutMenuItem_Click"/>
      </shell:ApplicationBar.MenuItems>
    </shell:ApplicationBar>
  </phone:PhoneApplicationPage.ApplicationBar>


<phone:PhoneApplicationPage.Resources>
  <!-- A data template shared by the first four list boxes -->
  <DataTemplate x:Key="DataTemplate">
    <StackPanel Orientation="Horizontal" local:Tilt.IsEnabled="True">

      <!-- Add a context menu to the item -->
      <toolkit:ContextMenuService.ContextMenu>
        <toolkit:ContextMenu Opened="ContextMenu_Opened"
                             Closed="ContextMenu_Closed">
          <toolkit:MenuItem Header="mark as done" Click="MarkMenuItem_Click"/>
          <toolkit:MenuItem Header="edit" Click="EditMenuItem_Click"/>
          <toolkit:MenuItem Header="delete" Click="DeleteMenuItem_Click"/>
        </toolkit:ContextMenu>
      </toolkit:ContextMenuService.ContextMenu>

      <!-- The star, with the item-specific color -->
      <Rectangle Fill="{Binding Star}" Width="26" Height="25" Margin="0,0,0,10">
        <Rectangle.OpacityMask>
          <ImageBrush ImageSource="Images/star.png"/>
        </Rectangle.OpacityMask>
      </Rectangle>
      <!-- The title -->
      <TextBlock Text="{Binding Title}" Margin="8,0,0,16"
                 Style="{StaticResource PhoneTextExtraLargeStyle}"/>
    </StackPanel>
  </DataTemplate>
</phone:PhoneApplicationPage.Resources>

<controls:Pivot x:Name="Pivot" Title="TODO LIST">

  <!-- Make the TODO LIST title match built-in apps better -->
  <controls:Pivot.TitleTemplate>
    <DataTemplate>
```

LISTING 26.1   Continued

```xml
        <TextBlock Text="{Binding}" Margin="-1,-1,0,-3"
                  Style="{StaticResource PhoneTextTitle0Style}"/>
      </DataTemplate>
  </controls:Pivot.TitleTemplate>

  <!-- Pivot item #1 -->
  <controls:PivotItem Header="all">
    <Grid>
      <TextBlock x:Name="NoAllTextBlock" Text="No tasks" Visibility="Collapsed"
        Margin="22,17,0,0" Style="{StaticResource PhoneTextGroupHeaderStyle}"/>
      <ListBox x:Name="AllListBox" ItemsSource="{Binding}"
              ItemTemplate="{StaticResource DataTemplate}"
              SelectionChanged="ListBox_SelectionChanged"/>
    </Grid>
  </controls:PivotItem>

  <!-- Pivot item #2 -->
  <controls:PivotItem x:Name="TodayPivotItem" Header="today">
    <Grid>
      <TextBlock x:Name="NoTodayTextBlock" Text="Nothing is due today"
        Visibility="Collapsed" Margin="22,17,0,0"
        Style="{StaticResource PhoneTextGroupHeaderStyle}"/>
      <!-- Show today's date underneath the list box -->
      <TextBlock x:Name="TodayTextBlock" Opacity=".2" Margin="0,0,0,4"
        HorizontalAlignment="Right" VerticalAlignment="Bottom" FontWeight="Bold"
        FontSize="{StaticResource PhoneFontSizeExtraExtraLarge}"/>
      <ListBox x:Name="TodayListBox"
              ItemTemplate="{StaticResource DataTemplate}"
              SelectionChanged="ListBox_SelectionChanged"/>
    </Grid>
  </controls:PivotItem>

  <!-- Pivot item #3 -->
  <controls:PivotItem x:Name="PastDuePivotItem" Header="past due">
    <Grid>
      <TextBlock x:Name="NoPastDueTextBlock" Visibility="Collapsed"
        Text="Nothing is past due. Good job!" Margin="22,17,0,0"
        Style="{StaticResource PhoneTextGroupHeaderStyle}"/>
      <!-- Show a clock underneath the list box -->
      <Rectangle Opacity=".2" Margin="0,0,0,12" VerticalAlignment="Bottom"
                HorizontalAlignment="Right" Width="240" Height="240"
                Fill="{StaticResource PhoneForegroundBrush}">
        <Rectangle.OpacityMask>
          <ImageBrush ImageSource="Images/clock.png"/>
```

LISTING 26.1 Continued

```
        </Rectangle.OpacityMask>
      </Rectangle>
      <ListBox x:Name="PastDueListBox"
             ItemTemplate="{StaticResource DataTemplate}"
             SelectionChanged="ListBox_SelectionChanged"/>
    </Grid>
  </controls:PivotItem>

  <!-- Pivot item #4 -->
  <controls:PivotItem x:Name="StarredPivotItem" Header="starred">
    <Grid>
      <TextBlock x:Name="NoStarredTextBlock" Text="No starred tasks"
        Visibility="Collapsed" Margin="22,17,0,0"
        Style="{StaticResource PhoneTextGroupHeaderStyle}"/>
      <!-- Show a star underneath the list box -->
      <Rectangle Opacity=".2" Margin="0,0,0,12" VerticalAlignment="Bottom"
               HorizontalAlignment="Right" Width="240" Height="240"
               Fill="{StaticResource PhoneForegroundBrush}">
        <Rectangle.OpacityMask>
          <ImageBrush ImageSource="Images/bigStar.png"/>
        </Rectangle.OpacityMask>
      </Rectangle>
      <ListBox x:Name="StarredListBox"
             ItemTemplate="{StaticResource DataTemplate}"
             SelectionChanged="ListBox_SelectionChanged"/>
    </Grid>
  </controls:PivotItem>

  <!-- Pivot item #5 -->
  <controls:PivotItem x:Name="DonePivotItem" Header="done">
    <Grid>
      <TextBlock x:Name="NoDoneTextBlock" Text="Nothing done. Get to work!"
        Visibility="Collapsed" Margin="22,17,0,0"
        Style="{StaticResource PhoneTextGroupHeaderStyle}"/>
      <!-- Show a checkmark underneath the list box -->
      <Rectangle Opacity=".2" Margin="0,0,0,12" VerticalAlignment="Bottom"
               HorizontalAlignment="Right" Width="277" Height="240"
               Fill="{StaticResource PhoneForegroundBrush}">
        <Rectangle.OpacityMask>
          <ImageBrush ImageSource="Images/done.png"/>
        </Rectangle.OpacityMask>
      </Rectangle>
      <ListBox x:Name="DoneListBox" ItemsSource="{Binding}"
             SelectionChanged="ListBox_SelectionChanged">
```

LISTING 26.1   Continued

```xml
<ListBox.ItemTemplate>
  <!-- A separate data template specific to the "done" list box -->
  <DataTemplate>
    <StackPanel Orientation="Horizontal" Background="Transparent"
                local:Tilt.IsEnabled="True">

      <!-- Add a context menu to the item -->
      <toolkit:ContextMenuService.ContextMenu>
        <toolkit:ContextMenu Opened="ContextMenu_Opened"
                             Closed="ContextMenu_Closed">
          <toolkit:MenuItem Header="unmark as done"
                            Click="UnmarkMenuItem_Click"/>
          <toolkit:MenuItem Header="edit" Click="EditMenuItem_Click"/>
          <toolkit:MenuItem Header="delete"
                            Click="DeleteMenuItem_Click"/>
        </toolkit:ContextMenu>
      </toolkit:ContextMenuService.ContextMenu>

      <!-- A checkmark-in-a-circle image -->
      <Rectangle Width="48" Height="48"
                 Fill="{StaticResource PhoneForegroundBrush}">
        <Rectangle.OpacityMask>
          <ImageBrush ImageSource="Shared/Images/normal.done.png"/>
        </Rectangle.OpacityMask>
      </Rectangle>

      <Grid>
        <StackPanel Orientation="Horizontal" Margin="8,0,0,0">
          <!-- The star, with the item-specific color -->
          <Rectangle Fill="{Binding Star}" Width="26" Height="25">
            <Rectangle.OpacityMask>
              <ImageBrush ImageSource="Images/star.png"/>
            </Rectangle.OpacityMask>
          </Rectangle>
          <!-- The title -->
          <TextBlock Text="{Binding Title}" Margin="8,0,0,6"
                     Style="{StaticResource PhoneTextExtraLargeStyle}"
                     HorizontalAlignment="Left" />
        </StackPanel>
        <!-- A horizontal line on top of the title -->
        <Line X1="-2" X2="800" Y1="32" Y2="32" StrokeThickness="2"
              Stroke="{StaticResource PhoneForegroundBrush}"/>
      </Grid>
    </StackPanel>
```

LISTING 26.1   Continued

```
            </DataTemplate>
          </ListBox.ItemTemplate>
        </ListBox>
      </Grid>
    </controls:PivotItem>
  </controls:Pivot>
</phone:PhoneApplicationPage>
```

Notes:

➔ A separate XML namespace is needed for the unique namespace/assembly combination required by the pivot. The conventional prefix for this XML namespace is `controls`.

➔ Because a pivot is meant to be full-screen, the control includes a `Title` property that you can use for your app title rather than the typical page header. The control does a decent job of mimicking what the app title should look like, but the position and font weight are slightly wrong. Fortunately, you can customize the title's appearance however you wish. `Title` is of type object, so you can set it to an arbitrary tree of UI elements rather than a simple string. Or you can use a `TitleTemplate` property to customize its appearance. This page leverages `TitleTemplate` to tweak the appearance of the title string, as shown in Figure 26.2. Future releases of Windows Phone might address this issue, if Silverlight will support the same text kerning done natively by Windows Phone OS. Until such time, applying a custom template is a reasonable workaround.

With no title template applied

With the title template from Listing 26.1

FIGURE 26.2   The custom title template makes subtle changes to the default appearance of the pivot's title.

→ Pivot also exposes a `HeaderTemplate` property for customizing the appearance of each pivot item's header. However, the default headers are perfect for matching the style of the built-in apps, so most apps have no use for this property. If you're doing something custom, however, such as putting text *and* an image in each header, this property enables you to do just that.

→ Each pivot item contains a text block (displayed when that item's list is empty) and a list box in a grid. All but the first item also have a subtle image or text decoration behind the list box.

→ The first four list boxes share the same item template defined as a resource called `DataTemplate`. The list box for the "done" pivot item, however, uses its own template that adds a check mark and a strikethrough effect. This is shown in Figure 26.3.

→ Both templates add a context menu to each item, leveraging the `ContextMenu` element in the Silverlight for Windows Phone Toolkit. To use a context menu, you simply set the `ContextMenuService.ContextMenu` attachable property on the element that should react to the user's touch-and-hold gesture. After one second, the menu is shown with the list of menu items you place inside the context menu. This is demonstrated in Figure 26.4.

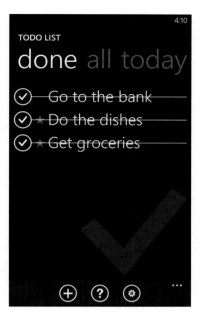

FIGURE 26.3   The separate item template for the "done" list box adds check marks and a strikethrough effect.

FIGURE 26.4   The context menu, shown here for "Do the dishes," exposes three additional actions for each task.

On Windows, it's standard for a context menu to include an item's default on-click action, and even show it in bold. On Windows Phone, context menus should *not* include the default on-tap action. Instead, context menu items should be reserved for additional actions that cannot be invoked by any other means on the page. For example, the context menus in Listing 26.1 do *not* list "view details" as one of the menu items because normal taps on each item already perform that action. Following this guideline not only makes the context menu behavior consistent with the phone's built-in apps, but it also preserves precious screen real estate.

Although none of them are used by TODO List, pivot exposes several events that are useful for dynamic pivot items:

→ `SelectionChanged`—Raised when the pivot item currently occupying the screen has changed

→ `LoadingPivotItem`—Raised right before a pivot item is displayed for the first time

→ `LoadedPivotItem`—Raised right after a pivot item is displayed for the first time

→ `UnloadingPivotItem`—Raised right before a pivot item is removed from the pivot's `Items` collection

→ `UnloadedPivotItem`—Raised right after a pivot item is removed from the pivot's `Items` collection

Pivot already delay-loads items that are more than one swipe away to improve startup time, but many popular apps use these events to improve performance even further with their own pivot-item virtualization scheme.

The Code-Behind

Listing 26.2 contains the code-behind for the main page.

LISTING 26.2   `MainPage.xaml.cs`—The Code-Behind for TODO List's Main Page

```
using System;
using System.Windows;
using System.Windows.Controls;
using System.Windows.Navigation;
using Microsoft.Phone.Controls;

namespace WindowsPhoneApp
{
  public partial class MainPage : PhoneApplicationPage
  {
    bool isNavigatingAway;
    bool isContextMenuOpen;

    public MainPage()
```

LISTING 26.2   Continued

```
  {
    InitializeComponent();
    this.Loaded += MainPage_Loaded;
  }

  protected override void OnNavigatedFrom(NavigationEventArgs e)
  {
    this.isNavigatingAway = true;
    base.OnNavigatedFrom(e);
    // Remember the selected item
    Settings.SelectedPivotItemName.Value =
      (this.Pivot.SelectedItem as PivotItem).Name;

    // Workaround for troubles when pivot items are removed and
    // cause SelectedIndex > Count-1
    this.Pivot.SelectedIndex = 0;
  }

  protected override void OnNavigatedTo(NavigationEventArgs e)
  {
    this.isNavigatingAway = false;
    base.OnNavigatedTo(e);
    this.TodayTextBlock.Text = DateTime.Now.ToShortDateString();

    // If the set of included pivot items were changed
    // on the settings page, refresh them
    int newPivotItemsCount = 1 + (Settings.IsTodayVisible.Value ? 1 : 0) +
                                 (Settings.IsPastDueVisible.Value ? 1 : 0) +
                                 (Settings.IsStarredVisible.Value ? 1 : 0) +
                                 (Settings.IsDoneVisible.Value ? 1 : 0);
    if (this.Pivot.Items.Count != newPivotItemsCount)
    {
      int insertLocation = 1;
      ShowOrHidePivotItem(this.TodayPivotItem,
        Settings.IsTodayVisible.Value, ref insertLocation);
      ShowOrHidePivotItem(this.PastDuePivotItem,
        Settings.IsPastDueVisible.Value, ref insertLocation);
      ShowOrHidePivotItem(this.StarredPivotItem,
        Settings.IsStarredVisible.Value, ref insertLocation);
      ShowOrHidePivotItem(this.DonePivotItem,
        Settings.IsDoneVisible.Value, ref insertLocation);
    }
  }
```

LISTING 26.2   Continued

```csharp
void ShowOrHidePivotItem(PivotItem item, bool show, ref int insertLocation)
{
  // Insert or remove the pivot item, if necessary
  if (show && item.Parent == null)
    this.Pivot.Items.Insert(insertLocation, item);
  else if (!show && item.Parent != null)
    this.Pivot.Items.Remove(item);

  if (show)
    insertLocation++;
}

void MainPage_Loaded(object sender, RoutedEventArgs e)
{
  if (!isNavigatingAway) // Workaround for Loaded-raised-too-often bug
  {
    // Two of the list boxes use data binding
    this.AllListBox.DataContext = Settings.TaskList.Value;
    this.DoneListBox.DataContext = Settings.DoneList.Value;

    // The rest are manually filled by filtering the task list
    RefreshLists();

    // Restore the selected item
    // (done here because OnNavigatedTo is too early)
    PivotItem pivotItem =
      this.FindName(Settings.SelectedPivotItemName.Value) as PivotItem;
    if (pivotItem != null)
      this.Pivot.SelectedItem = pivotItem;
  }
}

void RefreshLists()
{
  DateTime today = DateTime.Now.Date;

  // Fill the three filtered lists
  this.TodayListBox.Items.Clear();
  this.PastDueListBox.Items.Clear();
  this.StarredListBox.Items.Clear();
  foreach (Task item in Settings.TaskList.Value)
  {
    // today
    if (item.DueDate.Date == today)
```

LISTING 26.2   Continued

```
      this.TodayListBox.Items.Add(item);

    // past due
    if (item.DueDate < DateTime.Now)
      this.PastDueListBox.Items.Add(item);

    // starred
    if (item.Star != null && item.Star != "none")
      this.StarredListBox.Items.Add(item);
  }

  // Show/hide the "no tasks" labels
  this.NoAllTextBlock.Visibility = Settings.TaskList.Value.Count == 0 ?
    Visibility.Visible : Visibility.Collapsed;
  this.NoTodayTextBlock.Visibility = this.TodayListBox.Items.Count == 0 ?
    Visibility.Visible : Visibility.Collapsed;
  this.NoPastDueTextBlock.Visibility = this.PastDueListBox.Items.Count == 0 ?
    Visibility.Visible : Visibility.Collapsed;
  this.NoStarredTextBlock.Visibility = this.StarredListBox.Items.Count == 0 ?
    Visibility.Visible : Visibility.Collapsed;
  this.NoDoneTextBlock.Visibility = Settings.DoneList.Value.Count == 0 ?
    Visibility.Visible : Visibility.Collapsed;
}

void ListBox_SelectionChanged(object sender, SelectionChangedEventArgs e)
{
  if (isContextMenuOpen)
  {
    // Cancel the selection
    (sender as ListBox).SelectedIndex = -1;
    return;
  }

  if (e.AddedItems.Count != 1)
    return;

  // Communicate the selected item to the details page
  Settings.CurrentTask.Value = e.AddedItems[0] as Task;

  // Navigate to the details page
  this.NavigationService.Navigate(new Uri("/DetailsPage.xaml",
    UriKind.Relative));

  // Undo the selection so the same item can be tapped again upon return
```

LISTING 26.2   Continued

```csharp
      (sender as ListBox).SelectedIndex = -1;
  }

  // Context menu handlers

  void ContextMenu_Opened(object sender, RoutedEventArgs e)
  {
    this.isContextMenuOpen = true;
  }

  void ContextMenu_Closed(object sender, RoutedEventArgs e)
  {
    this.isContextMenuOpen = false;
  }

  void MarkMenuItem_Click(object sender, RoutedEventArgs e)
  {
    Task task = (sender as MenuItem).DataContext as Task;

    // Move from the task list to the done list
    Settings.TaskList.Value.Remove(task);
    Settings.DoneList.Value.Add(task);

    RefreshLists();
  }

  void UnmarkMenuItem_Click(object sender, RoutedEventArgs e)
  {
    Task task = (sender as MenuItem).DataContext as Task;

    // Move from the done list to the task list
    Settings.DoneList.Value.Remove(task);
    Settings.TaskList.Value.Add(task);

    RefreshLists();
  }

  void EditMenuItem_Click(object sender, RoutedEventArgs e)
  {
    // Communicate the selected item to the add/edit page
    Settings.CurrentTask.Value = (sender as MenuItem).DataContext as Task;

    // Navigate to the add/edit page
    this.NavigationService.Navigate(new Uri("/AddEditPage.xaml",
      UriKind.Relative));
```

LISTING 26.2   Continued

```
    }

    void DeleteMenuItem_Click(object sender, RoutedEventArgs e)
    {
      if (MessageBox.Show(
        "Are you sure you want to permanently delete this task?", "Delete task",
        MessageBoxButton.OKCancel) == MessageBoxResult.OK)
      {
        // The task is only in one of the two lists, but just try deleting from
        // both rather than checking. One call will work, one will be a no-op.
        Settings.TaskList.Value.Remove((sender as MenuItem).DataContext as Task);
        Settings.DoneList.Value.Remove((sender as MenuItem).DataContext as Task);

        RefreshLists();
      }
    }

    // Application bar handlers

    void AddButton_Click(object sender, EventArgs e)
    {
      Settings.CurrentTask.Value = null;
      this.NavigationService.Navigate(new Uri("/AddEditPage.xaml",
        UriKind.Relative));
    }

    void InstructionsButton_Click(object sender, EventArgs e)
    {
      this.NavigationService.Navigate(new Uri("/InstructionsPage.xaml",
        UriKind.Relative));
    }

    void SettingsButton_Click(object sender, EventArgs e)
    {
      this.NavigationService.Navigate(new Uri("/SettingsPage.xaml",
        UriKind.Relative));
    }

    void AboutMenuItem_Click(object sender, EventArgs e)
    {
      this.NavigationService.Navigate(new Uri(
        "/Shared/About/AboutPage.xaml?appName=TODO List", UriKind.Relative));
    }
  }
}
```

Notes:

→ A pivot exposes a `SelectedItem` (and `SelectedIndex`) property that represents which of the pivot items is occupying the screen. TODO List stores the selected item as a persisted setting, but it does so by storing the *name* of the element rather than its index. This is done because this app's settings page enables the user to hide any of the pivot items except the first one, and the hiding is done by removing the pivot item(s) from the pivot's collection.

Setting a pivot's `SelectedItem` or `SelectedIndex` property earlier than the `Loaded` event fails!

It's natural to want to set a pivot's `SelectedItem` or `SelectedIndex` property inside `OnNavigatedTo`, most likely to restore the control's previous state. Unfortunately, due to a bug that hasn't yet been fixed at the time of this writing, doing so throws an exception. Until this is fixed, use the `Loading` event to set the selection, as in Listing 26.2.

Setting a pivot's `SelectedItem` or `SelectedIndex` property always animates the change in selection!

This is extremely irritating for the main scenarios in which I can imagine these properties being used. For example, when an app is activated and you want to restore a pivot to its previous state (providing the illusion that it was running the whole time), you really want it to appear with the user's previous selection instantly visible. A workaround to enable this behavior would be to physically shift the order of the pivot items, so the previous selection is always the 0th item and to not write any code that depends on indices.

Setting a pivot item's visibility has no effect!

Temporarily hiding pivot items would be easy to do if you could simply set its `Visibility` property to `Collapsed`. Unfortunately, because this has no effect, the only way to hide a pivot item—and not have it occupy space—is to remove it from the pivot's `Items` collection.

According to Windows Phone design guidelines, you should avoid removing empty pivot items if the user has some way to add information to it. Instead, you should show the empty pivot page or perhaps put an explanatory message in it, as done with each pivot item in TODO List's main page.

→ In `OnNavigatedTo` (which is called upon return from adjusting the visible set of pivot items on the settings page), pivot items are either added or removed from the pivot based on the current settings.

→ Pivot does not handle the removal of pivot items very gracefully. If pivot items are removed such that the previously selected index is greater than the new last index, an `ArgumentOutOfRangeException` is thrown. This happens even if pivot's `SelectedIndex` property is set to 0 immediately before removing pivot items, presumably due to its animation from the old item to the new item. This is a bug that might be fixed in a future release of Windows Phone.

Therefore, Listing 26.2 works around this problem by setting `SelectedIndex` to 0 in `OnNavigatedFrom`. That way, even if the user visits the settings page, removes pivot items, and returns to the main page extremely quickly, there is still plenty of time for the pivot's animation to complete beforehand. Also, the pivot will only remain on the 0th item if the previously selected item has been removed thanks to the logic in `Loaded` that restores the selected item after `OnNavigatedTo` has executed.

→ The "all" list box databinds to a `TaskList` setting and the "done" list box databinds to a `DoneList` setting. The remaining three list boxes all contain a filtered version of `TaskList`. They are filled manually inside `RefreshLists` because there's no automatic data-binding mechanism that filters a collection.

→ The context menu's `Opened` and `Closed` events are handled simply to enable code to check on-demand whether a context menu is currently open. `ListBox_SelectionChanged` leverages this to ignore a tap on an item when that tap is actually dismissing an open context menu.

 Be careful not to respond to taps in the usual way when the user is simply trying to dismiss a context menu!

Ideally, the system would handle this for you, but it does not. In many situations, you should track when a context menu is open so you can properly ignore certain events during that time. A context menu's `Open` and `Closed` events enable you to do this, as Listing 26.2 demonstrates.

→ Because the same context menu handlers are used for both context menus, the code is written in a way to work for either context. The `sender` passed to these handlers is the `MenuItem` that was tapped, so its `DataContext` property is used to retrieve the source item to which the context menu's item template is applied.

 When handling a context menu item click, how do I retrieve the item that was pressed and held?

This question is usually asked about context menus that are placed inside a data template, because there doesn't appear to be any way to connect the specific menu item instance with the data object. As Listing 26.2 demonstrates, the answer is to use the menu item's `DataContext` property. When people normally think about `DataContext`, they think about *setting* it to a data object (which is also done in Listing 26.2). For cases like this, however, *getting* its value is very useful.

Supporting Data Types

As seen in the preceding section, TODO List manipulates two collections of tasks exposed as settings. This involves three classes that are important to understand for appreciating how this app works. Listing 26.3 shows the implementation of the Task class used to represent each item shown in any of main page's list boxes.

LISTING 26.3   Task.cs—The Type of Every Item in Every List Box

```csharp
using System;
using System.ComponentModel;

namespace WindowsPhoneApp
{
  public class Task : INotifyPropertyChanged
  {
    // The backing fields
    string title;
    string description;
    string star;
    DateTimeOffset createdDate;
    DateTimeOffset modifiedDate;
    DateTimeOffset dueDate;

    // The properties, which raise change notifications
    public string Title {
      get { return this.title; }
      set { this.title = value; OnPropertyChanged("Title"); }
    }
    public string Description {
      get { return this.description; }
      set { this.description = value; OnPropertyChanged("Description"); }
    }
    public string Star {
      get { return this.star; }
      set { this.star = value; OnPropertyChanged("Star"); }
    }
    public DateTimeOffset CreatedDate {
      get { return this.createdDate; }
      set { this.createdDate = value; OnPropertyChanged("CreatedDate"); }
    }
    public DateTimeOffset ModifiedDate {
      get { return this.modifiedDate; }
      set { this.modifiedDate = value; OnPropertyChanged("ModifiedDate"); }
    }
    public DateTimeOffset DueDate {
      get { return this.dueDate; }
      set { this.dueDate = value; OnPropertyChanged("DueDate"); }
    }
```

LISTING 26.3   Continued

```
    void OnPropertyChanged(string propertyName)
    {
      PropertyChangedEventHandler handler = this.PropertyChanged;
      if (handler != null)
        handler(this, new PropertyChangedEventArgs(propertyName));
    }

    public event PropertyChangedEventHandler PropertyChanged;
  }
}
```

Notes:

→ The item templates on main page leverage the value of each task's Title and Star properties. All the properties are displayed on the details and add/edit pages, and the DueDate property is also used for sorting the list of tasks.

→ The CreatedDate and ModifiedDate properties are appropriately of type DateTimeOffset rather than DateTime, and the DueDate property is also a DateTimeOffset to match the others. (One could argue that DueDate should be a DateTime instead, representing a logical point in time that is always expressed in the current time zone, for the same reason that Chapter 20's Alarm Clock app uses DateTime.)

→ The Star value is a string representing the color (like "red" or "yellow"). This is strange from an API perspective, but it happens to work out nicely because the item templates on the main page and a star on the upcoming details page are able to bind directly to the property without needing a value converter.

→ The property-changed notifications ensure that data-bound user interface elements can remain up-to-date. This is leveraged on the main page and the upcoming details page. On the main page, it turns out that this is only needed for the "done" list due to the way item editing works. This is explained in the upcoming "The Add/Edit Page" section.

Listing 26.4 contains the entire set of persisted settings used by TODO List.

LISTING 26.4   Settings.cs—All the Settings Persisted to Isolated Storage

```
using System.Collections.ObjectModel;

namespace WindowsPhoneApp
{
  public static class Settings
  {
    // The selected pivot item, stored by name
```

LISTING 26.4   Continued

```
    public static readonly Setting<string> SelectedPivotItemName =
      new Setting<string>("SelectedPivotItemName", "all");

    // Which pivot items are included in the pivot
    public static readonly Setting<bool> IsTodayVisible =
      new Setting<bool>("IsTodayVisible", true);
    public static readonly Setting<bool> IsPastDueVisible =
      new Setting<bool>("IsPastDueVisible", true);
    public static readonly Setting<bool> IsStarredVisible =
      new Setting<bool>("IsStarredVisible", true);
    public static readonly Setting<bool> IsDoneVisible =
      new Setting<bool>("IsDoneVisible", true);

    // The task currently in the details or add/edit page
    public static readonly Setting<Task> CurrentTask =
      new Setting<Task>("CurrentTask", null);

    // Sorted in chronological order
    public static readonly Setting<SortedTaskCollection> TaskList =
      new Setting<SortedTaskCollection>("TaskList",
        new SortedTaskCollection());

    // Kept in the order tasks get done
    public static readonly Setting<ObservableCollection<Task>> DoneList =
      new Setting<ObservableCollection<Task>>("DoneList",
        new ObservableCollection<Task>());
  }
}
```

Notes:

→ The first five settings maintain the state of the pivot control on the main page, and the next setting (`CurrentTask`) tells the details and add/edit pages which item was just selected on the main page.

→ The most important settings are the last two—the list of unfinished tasks and list of done tasks. Notice that these are two different types of collections. `DoneList` is a basic observable collection of tasks. No sorting is ever done, so the list is always in the order that tasks were finished. (If users want to change the ordering, they would need to "unmark" tasks as done and then mark them again.) `TaskList`, on the other hand, is an observable collection that automatically sorts its tasks in chronological order based on the value of the `DueDate` property. This enables every list box on the main page (except the "done" list) to be sorted in this fashion without any sorting code outside of the collection class itself.

➔ The fact that both lists are observable collections is important, because the main page relies on the collection-changed notifications for keeping its "all" and "done" lists up-to-date as items are added and removed.

Listing 26.5 shows the implementation of this sorted collection class.

LISTING 26.5   `SortedTaskCollection.cs`—Adds Automatic Sorting to an Observable Collection of Tasks

```csharp
using System;
using System.Collections.ObjectModel;
using System.Runtime.Serialization;

namespace WindowsPhoneApp
{
  [CollectionDataContract]
  public class SortedTaskCollection : ObservableCollection<Task>
  {
    protected override void InsertItem(int index, Task item)
    {
      // Ignore the index. Instead, keep the list sorted in chronological order
      int i = 0;
      for (i = 0; i < this.Count; i++)
      {
        DateTimeOffset d = this[i].DueDate;
        if (d > item.DueDate)
          break;
      }
      base.InsertItem(i, item);
    }
  }
}
```

Notes:

➔ All this class needs to do is override `ObservableCollection`'s protected `InsertItem` method that ultimately gets called by both `Add` and `Insert`. It ignores the passed-in index and instead chooses an index that maintains the desired sorting of the list. The result is confusing for someone trying to call the collection's `Insert` method with a specific index (not done by this app), but calling `Add` works seamlessly.

➔ The most subtle part of this collection's implementation is the `CollectionDataContract` attribute. This attribute, defined in the `System.Runtime.Serialization` namespace in the `System.Runtime.Serialization` assembly (which is not referenced by Windows Phone projects by default), is necessary for this app's settings to be serialized successfully. The reason why, however, is obscure. Because `SortedTaskCollection` derives from `ObservableCollection<Task>`, the two classes have the same *data contract name* as far as the built-in serialization process is concerned. However, each type serialized must have a unique data contract name, so the `CollectionDataContract` attribute assigns one to `SortedTaskCollection`. (You don't even need to choose an explicit name for this to work!)

Without this attribute, an exception with the following message is raised when the app is closing or deactivating, due to automatic attempt to serialize this app's settings:

```
Type
'System.Collections.ObjectModel.ObservableCollection`1[WindowsPhoneApp.Task]'
cannot be added to list of known types since another type
'WindowsPhoneApp.SortedTaskCollection' with the same data contract name
'http://schemas.datacontract.org/2004/07/WindowsPhoneApp:ArrayOfTask' is
already present.
```

Note that if *both* lists were of type `SortedTaskCollection`, the serialization would work just fine without the attribute because there would be no conflict. Of course, it's a good idea to make classes you intend to serialize with such attributes to avoid subtle bugs in the future.

In addition to the `CollectionDataContract` attribute designed for collection classes, `System.Runtime.Serialization` exposes a `DataContract` attribute that can be used on regular (non-collection) classes.

Normally, when data fails to serialize to isolated storage or page state, your only indication is that the data does not exist when you next launch or activate the app. To be able to see detailed exception information for the serialization failure, run your app under Visual Studio's debugger but tell it to catch all first-chance .NET exceptions. You can do this by checking the "Thrown" checkbox next to "Common Language Runtime Exceptions" on the Exceptions dialog (found under the Debug, Exceptions… menu item). When doing this, you might encounter several additional exceptions within the .NET Framework that are actually harmless and not related to the problems your app is experiencing. You'll need to continue past those to see the relevant exception.

The Details Page

The details page, shown in Figure 26.5, is a straightforward display of each task's properties. The task's title is used as the page title, and the description and date properties are shown below it. If the item has been given a star, it is shown as well. For convenience, the page's application bar exposes buttons for each of the three actions that the main page exposes as context menu items.

Listing 26.6 contains this page's XAML and Listing 26.7 contains its code-behind.

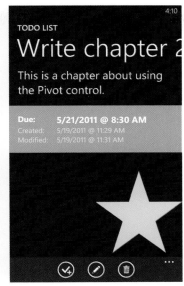

FIGURE 26.5 The details page for an item, before and after it is marked with a yellow star.

LISTING 26.6 `DetailsPage.xaml`—The User Interface for TODO List's Details Page

```
<phone:PhoneApplicationPage x:Class="WindowsPhoneApp.DetailsPage"
    xmlns="http://schemas.microsoft.com/winfx/2006/xaml/presentation"
    xmlns:x="http://schemas.microsoft.com/winfx/2006/xaml"
    xmlns:phone="clr-namespace:Microsoft.Phone.Controls;assembly=Microsoft.Phone"
    xmlns:shell="clr-namespace:Microsoft.Phone.Shell;assembly=Microsoft.Phone"
    xmlns:local="clr-namespace:WindowsPhoneApp"
    FontFamily="{StaticResource PhoneFontFamilyNormal}"
    FontSize="{StaticResource PhoneFontSizeNormal}"
    Foreground="{StaticResource PhoneForegroundBrush}"
    SupportedOrientations="PortraitOrLandscape" shell:SystemTray.IsVisible="True">

  <!-- The application bar, with 3 buttons and a menu item -->
  <phone:PhoneApplicationPage.ApplicationBar>
    <shell:ApplicationBar>
      <shell:ApplicationBarIconButton Text="mark done"
        IconUri="/Images/appbar.markDone.png" Click="MarkUnmarkButton_Click"/>
      <shell:ApplicationBarIconButton Text="edit"
        IconUri="/Shared/Images/appbar.edit.png" Click="EditButton_Click"/>
      <shell:ApplicationBarIconButton Text="delete"
        IconUri="/Shared/Images/appbar.delete.png" Click="DeleteButton_Click"/>
```

LISTING 26.6   Continued

```
    <shell:ApplicationBar.MenuItems>
      <shell:ApplicationBarMenuItem Text="about" Click="AboutMenuItem_Click"/>
    </shell:ApplicationBar.MenuItems>
  </shell:ApplicationBar>
</phone:PhoneApplicationPage.ApplicationBar>

<phone:PhoneApplicationPage.Resources>
  <local:DateConverter x:Key="DateConverter"/>
</phone:PhoneApplicationPage.Resources>

<Grid>
  <Grid.RowDefinitions>
    <RowDefinition Height="Auto"/>
    <RowDefinition Height="*"/>
  </Grid.RowDefinitions>

  <!-- The standard header -->
  <StackPanel Style="{StaticResource PhoneTitlePanelStyle}">
    <TextBlock Text="TODO LIST" Style="{StaticResource PhoneTextTitle0Style}"/>
    <TextBlock Text="{Binding Title}"
               Style="{StaticResource PhoneTextTitle1Style}"/>
  </StackPanel>

  <!-- The appropriately-colored star -->
  <Rectangle Grid.Row="2" Width="240" Height="240" Fill="{Binding Star}"
    VerticalAlignment="Bottom" HorizontalAlignment="Right" Margin="0,0,0,12">
    <Rectangle.OpacityMask>
      <ImageBrush ImageSource="Images/bigStar.png"/>
    </Rectangle.OpacityMask>
  </Rectangle>

  <ScrollViewer Grid.Row="1">
    <Grid>
      <Grid.ColumnDefinitions>
        <ColumnDefinition Width="Auto"/>
        <ColumnDefinition/>
      </Grid.ColumnDefinitions>
      <Grid.RowDefinitions>
        <RowDefinition Height="Auto"/>
        <RowDefinition Height="Auto"/>
        <RowDefinition Height="Auto"/>
        <RowDefinition Height="Auto"/>
        <RowDefinition Height="24"/>
      </Grid.RowDefinitions>
```

LISTING 26.6   Continued

```xml
        <!-- The description -->
        <TextBlock Text="{Binding Description}"
                    FontSize="{StaticResource PhoneFontSizeLarge}"
                    Grid.ColumnSpan="2" Margin="24,0,24,24" TextWrapping="Wrap"/>

        <!-- The 2-3 dates -->
        <Rectangle x:Name="AccentRectangle" Grid.Row="1" Grid.ColumnSpan="2"
                    Grid.RowSpan="4" Fill="{StaticResource PhoneAccentBrush}"/>
        <TextBlock Grid.Row="1" Text="Due:" FontWeight="Bold" Margin="24,24,24,0"
                    FontSize="{StaticResource PhoneFontSizeMedium}"/>
        <TextBlock Grid.Row="2" Text="Created:" Margin="24,0"
                    Foreground="{StaticResource PhoneSubtleBrush}"/>
        <TextBlock x:Name="ModifiedLabelTextBlock" Grid.Row="3" Text="Modified:"
                    Margin="24,0" Foreground="{StaticResource PhoneSubtleBrush}"/>
        <TextBlock Grid.Column="1" Grid.Row="1"
          Text="{Binding DueDate, Converter={StaticResource DateConverter}}"
          Margin="0,24,0,0" FontWeight="Bold"
          FontSize="{StaticResource PhoneFontSizeMediumLarge}"/>
        <TextBlock Grid.Column="1" Grid.Row="2"
          Text="{Binding CreatedDate, Converter={StaticResource DateConverter}}"
          Foreground="{StaticResource PhoneSubtleBrush}"/>
        <TextBlock x:Name="ModifiedTextBlock" Grid.Column="1" Grid.Row="3"
          Text="{Binding ModifiedDate, Converter={StaticResource DateConverter}}"
          Foreground="{StaticResource PhoneSubtleBrush}"/>
      </Grid>
    </ScrollViewer>
  </Grid>
</phone:PhoneApplicationPage>
```

LISTING 26.7   `DetailsPage.xaml.cs`—The Code-Behind for TODO List's Details Page

```csharp
using System;
using System.Windows;
using System.Windows.Navigation;
using Microsoft.Phone.Controls;
using Microsoft.Phone.Shell;

namespace WindowsPhoneApp
{
  public partial class DetailsPage : PhoneApplicationPage
  {
    IApplicationBarIconButton markUnmarkButton;

    public DetailsPage()
    {
```

LISTING 26.7   Continued

```csharp
    InitializeComponent();
    this.markUnmarkButton = this.ApplicationBar.Buttons[0]
      as IApplicationBarIconButton;
  }

  protected override void OnNavigatedTo(NavigationEventArgs e)
  {
    base.OnNavigatedTo(e);

    // Set the context for the data binding done in XAML
    this.DataContext = Settings.CurrentTask.Value;

    if (Settings.CurrentTask.Value != null)
    {
      // Only show the modified date if different from the created date
      if (Settings.CurrentTask.Value.CreatedDate ==
          Settings.CurrentTask.Value.ModifiedDate)
      {
        this.ModifiedLabelTextBlock.Visibility = Visibility.Collapsed;
        this.ModifiedTextBlock.Visibility = Visibility.Collapsed;
      }
      else
      {
        this.ModifiedLabelTextBlock.Visibility = Visibility.Visible;
        this.ModifiedTextBlock.Visibility = Visibility.Visible;
      }

      // Ensure that the application bar button correctly represents whether
      // this task is done
      if (Settings.DoneList.Value.Contains(Settings.CurrentTask.Value))
      {
        this.markUnmarkButton.IconUri =
          new Uri("/Images/appbar.unmarkDone.png", UriKind.Relative);
        this.markUnmarkButton.Text = "undo";
      }
    }
  }

  // Application bar handlers

  void MarkUnmarkButton_Click(object sender, EventArgs e)
  {
    if (this.markUnmarkButton.Text == "mark done")
    {
      this.markUnmarkButton.IconUri = new Uri("/Images/appbar.unmarkDone.png",
```

LISTING 26.7   Continued

```
          UriKind.Relative);
        this.markUnmarkButton.Text = "undo";
        // Move the item from the task list to the done list
        Settings.TaskList.Value.Remove(Settings.CurrentTask.Value);
        Settings.DoneList.Value.Add(Settings.CurrentTask.Value);
      }
      else
      {
        this.markUnmarkButton.IconUri = new Uri("/Images/appbar.markDone.png",
          UriKind.Relative);
        this.markUnmarkButton.Text = "mark done";
        // Move the item from the done list to the task list
        Settings.DoneList.Value.Remove(Settings.CurrentTask.Value);
        Settings.TaskList.Value.Add(Settings.CurrentTask.Value);
      }
    }

    void EditButton_Click(object sender, EventArgs e)
    {
      this.NavigationService.Navigate(new Uri("/AddEditPage.xaml",
        UriKind.Relative));
    }

    void DeleteButton_Click(object sender, EventArgs e)
    {
      if (MessageBox.Show(
        "Are you sure you want to permanently delete this task?", "Delete task",
        MessageBoxButton.OKCancel) == MessageBoxResult.OK)
      {
        // The task is only in one of the two lists, but just try deleting from
        // both rather than checking. One call will work, one will be a no-op.
        Settings.TaskList.Value.Remove(Settings.CurrentTask.Value);
        Settings.DoneList.Value.Remove(Settings.CurrentTask.Value);

        if (this.NavigationService.CanGoBack)
          this.NavigationService.GoBack();
      }
    }

    void AboutMenuItem_Click(object sender, EventArgs e)
    {
      this.NavigationService.Navigate(new Uri(
        "/Shared/About/AboutPage.xaml?appName=TODO List", UriKind.Relative));
    }
  }
}
```

Notes:

→ The information is placed inside a scroll viewer in case the description is really long. The big star serves as a stationary background that does not scroll with the rest of the content.

→ Data binding is used to display the various properties of the current task. A `DateConverter` value converter similar to the one in Chapter 21, "Passwords & Secrets," is used to give each `DateTimeOffset` a nice display. The only difference with this app's value converter is that it places an @ between the date and time.

→ A few display adjustments are made inside `OnNavigatedTo` so the page properly updates if the user taps the edit button to navigate to the add/edit page, makes some changes, saves them, and then navigates back. A value converter could have been written and used to avoid toggling the two text blocks' `Visibility` property in code-behind, but that seems like overkill.

The Add/Edit Page

The add/edit page acts like two distinct pages—a page for adding a new task and a page for editing an existing task—but due to their enormous similarities, it is implemented as a single page. Figure 26.6 shows this page in both of its roles.

Adding a new task

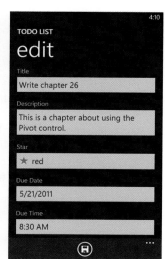

Editing an existing task

FIGURE 26.6   The add/edit page in its two different modes.

The User Interface

Listing 26.8 contains the XAML for the add/edit page.

LISTING 26.8   `AddEditPage.xaml`—The User Interface for TODO List's Add/Edit Page

```xml
<phone:PhoneApplicationPage x:Class="WindowsPhoneApp.AddItemPage"
    xmlns="http://schemas.microsoft.com/winfx/2006/xaml/presentation"
    xmlns:x="http://schemas.microsoft.com/winfx/2006/xaml"
    xmlns:phone="clr-namespace:Microsoft.Phone.Controls;assembly=Microsoft.Phone"
    xmlns:shell="clr-namespace:Microsoft.Phone.Shell;assembly=Microsoft.Phone"
    xmlns:toolkit="clr-namespace:Microsoft.Phone.Controls;
➥assembly=Microsoft.Phone.Controls.Toolkit"
    xmlns:sys="clr-namespace:System;assembly=mscorlib"
    xmlns:local="clr-namespace:WindowsPhoneApp"
    FontFamily="{StaticResource PhoneFontFamilyNormal}"
    FontSize="{StaticResource PhoneFontSizeNormal}"
    Foreground="{StaticResource PhoneForegroundBrush}"
    SupportedOrientations="PortraitOrLandscape" shell:SystemTray.IsVisible="True">

  <!-- The single-button, single-menu-item application bar -->
  <phone:PhoneApplicationPage.ApplicationBar>
    <shell:ApplicationBar>
      <shell:ApplicationBarIconButton Text="save"
        IconUri="/Shared/Images/appbar.save.png" Click="SaveButton_Click"/>
      <shell:ApplicationBar.MenuItems>
        <shell:ApplicationBarMenuItem Text="about" Click="AboutMenuItem_Click"/>
      </shell:ApplicationBar.MenuItems>
    </shell:ApplicationBar>
  </phone:PhoneApplicationPage.ApplicationBar>

  <Grid>
    <Grid.RowDefinitions>
      <RowDefinition Height="Auto"/>
      <RowDefinition Height="*"/>
    </Grid.RowDefinitions>

    <!-- The standard header -->
    <StackPanel Style="{StaticResource PhoneTitlePanelStyle}">
      <TextBlock Text="TODO LIST" Style="{StaticResource PhoneTextTitle0Style}"/>
      <TextBlock x:Name="PageTitle"
                 Style="{StaticResource PhoneTextTitle1Style}"/>
    </StackPanel>

    <ScrollViewer Grid.Row="1">
      <StackPanel Margin="{StaticResource PhoneHorizontalMargin}">
        <!-- Title -->
        <TextBlock Text="Title" Margin="11,0,0,-5"
          Foreground="{StaticResource PhoneSubtleBrush}"/>
        <TextBox x:Name="TitleTextBox" InputScope="Text"
```

LISTING 26.8   Continued

```
        TextChanged="TitleTextBox_TextChanged" KeyUp="TitleTextBox_KeyUp"/>

    <!-- Description -->
    <TextBlock Text="Description" Margin="11,11,0,-5"
      Foreground="{StaticResource PhoneSubtleBrush}"/>
    <TextBox x:Name="DescriptionTextBox" InputScope="Text" MinHeight="106"
      AcceptsReturn="True" TextWrapping="Wrap"/>

    <!-- Star -->
    <toolkit:ListPicker x:Name="StarListPicker" Header="Star">
      <toolkit:ListPicker.ItemTemplate>
        <DataTemplate>
          <StackPanel Orientation="Horizontal">
            <!-- Give each item the colored star next to its text -->
            <Rectangle Fill="{Binding}" Width="26" Height="25">
              <Rectangle.OpacityMask>
                <ImageBrush ImageSource="Images/star.png"/>
              </Rectangle.OpacityMask>
            </Rectangle>
            <TextBlock Text="{Binding}" Margin="12 0 0 0"/>
          </StackPanel>
        </DataTemplate>
      </toolkit:ListPicker.ItemTemplate>
      <sys:String>none</sys:String>
      <sys:String>red</sys:String>
      <sys:String>yellow</sys:String>
      <sys:String>green</sys:String>
      <sys:String>blue</sys:String>
    </toolkit:ListPicker>

    <!-- Due Date -->
    <TextBlock Text="Due Date" Margin="11,11,0,-5" CacheMode="BitmapCache"
               Foreground="{StaticResource PhoneSubtleBrush}"/>
    <toolkit:DatePicker x:Name="DueDatePicker" CacheMode="BitmapCache"
                        ValueChanged="DateTimePicker_ValueChanged"
                        local:Tilt.IsEnabled="True"/>
    <!-- Due Time -->
    <TextBlock Text="Due Time" Margin="11,11,0,-5" CacheMode="BitmapCache"
               Foreground="{StaticResource PhoneSubtleBrush}"/>
    <toolkit:TimePicker x:Name="DueTimePicker" CacheMode="BitmapCache"
                        ValueChanged="DateTimePicker_ValueChanged"
                        local:Tilt.IsEnabled="True"/>
  </StackPanel>
```

LISTING 26.8   Continued

```
    </ScrollViewer>
  </Grid>
</phone:PhoneApplicationPage>
```

Note:

→ This page exploits three controls from the Silverlight for Windows Phone Toolkit: list picker, date picker, and time picker. The list picker decorates each of its items with an appropriately colored star thanks to data binding that automatically works with the color strings. This is shown in Figure 26.7. For the "none" value, this app leverages the fact that an invalid string causes the binding to fail for that item and leave the rectangle with its default null fill.

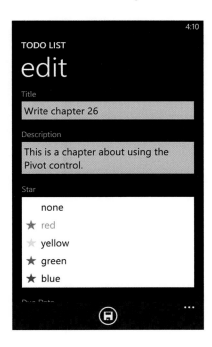

FIGURE 26.7   Each item in the list picker visually shows the star next to each color name, as seen when it is expanded.

The Code-Behind

Listing 26.9 contains the code-behind for the add/edit page.

LISTING 26.9   `AddEditPage.xaml.cs`—The Code-Behind for TODO List's Add/Edit Page

```
using System;
using System.Windows.Controls;
using System.Windows.Input;
using System.Windows.Navigation;
using Microsoft.Phone.Controls;
using Microsoft.Phone.Shell;

namespace WindowsPhoneApp
{
  public partial class AddItemPage : PhoneApplicationPage
  {
    IApplicationBarIconButton saveButton;
    DateTime? pendingChosenDate;
    DateTime? pendingChosenTime;

    public AddItemPage()
    {
      InitializeComponent();
      this.saveButton = this.ApplicationBar.Buttons[0]
        as IApplicationBarIconButton;
    }

    protected override void OnNavigatedFrom(NavigationEventArgs e)
    {
      base.OnNavigatedFrom(e);
      // Store the info in page state so it is preserved when temporarily
      // navigating away from the page. This is especially important because the
      // date picker and time picker navigate to a different page!
      this.State["Title"] = this.TitleTextBox.Text;
      this.State["Description"] = this.DescriptionTextBox.Text;
      this.State["Star"] = this.StarListPicker.SelectedItem;
      this.State["DueDate"] = this.DueDatePicker.Value;
      this.State["DueTime"] = this.DueTimePicker.Value;
    }

    protected override void OnNavigatedTo(NavigationEventArgs e)
    {
      base.OnNavigatedTo(e);

      // If we're returning from the date or time picker,
      // make sure we apply the chosen value
      if (this.pendingChosenDate.HasValue)
        this.State["DueDate"] = this.pendingChosenDate;
      if (this.pendingChosenTime.HasValue)
```

LISTING 26.9   Continued

```csharp
    this.State["DueTime"] = this.pendingChosenTime;

  // Initialize the page for either add mode or edit mode
  if (Settings.CurrentTask.Value == null)
  {
    this.PageTitle.Text = "new";
  }
  else
  {
    this.PageTitle.Text = "edit";
    this.TitleTextBox.Text = Settings.CurrentTask.Value.Title;
    this.DescriptionTextBox.Text = Settings.CurrentTask.Value.Description;
    this.StarListPicker.SelectedItem = Settings.CurrentTask.Value.Star;
    this.DueDatePicker.Value =
      Settings.CurrentTask.Value.DueDate.LocalDateTime;
    this.DueTimePicker.Value =
      Settings.CurrentTask.Value.DueDate.LocalDateTime;
  }

  // Apply any temporary values from page state
  if (this.State.ContainsKey("Title"))
    this.TitleTextBox.Text = (string)this.State["Title"];
  if (this.State.ContainsKey("Description"))
    this.DescriptionTextBox.Text = (string)this.State["Description"];
  if (this.State.ContainsKey("Star"))
    this.StarListPicker.SelectedItem = (string)this.State["Star"];
  if (this.State.ContainsKey("DueDate"))
    this.DueDatePicker.Value = (DateTime?)this.State["DueDate"];
  if (this.State.ContainsKey("DueTime"))
    this.DueTimePicker.Value = (DateTime?)this.State["DueTime"];

  // Only allow saving when there's a title
  this.saveButton.IsEnabled = (this.TitleTextBox.Text != null &&
    this.TitleTextBox.Text.Trim().Length > 0);
}

void TitleTextBox_TextChanged(object sender, TextChangedEventArgs e)
{
  // Only allow saving when there's a title
  this.saveButton.IsEnabled = (this.TitleTextBox.Text != null &&
    this.TitleTextBox.Text.Trim().Length > 0);
}

void TitleTextBox_KeyUp(object sender, KeyEventArgs e)
```

LISTING 26.9   Continued

```
{
  if (e.Key == Key.Enter)
    this.DescriptionTextBox.Focus();
}

void DateTimePicker_ValueChanged(object sender,
  DateTimeValueChangedEventArgs e)
{
  // Prevent the values from getting clobbered when navigating back
  this.pendingChosenDate = this.DueDatePicker.Value;
  this.pendingChosenTime = this.DueTimePicker.Value;
}

// Application bar handlers

void SaveButton_Click(object sender, EventArgs e)
{
  // Consolidate the due date and due time into a single DateTime.
  // First get just the date (no time) from the date picker's value
  DateTime dueDate = this.DueDatePicker.Value.Value.Date;
  // Now add the time to this date
  if (this.DueTimePicker.Value.HasValue)
    dueDate = dueDate.AddMinutes(
      this.DueTimePicker.Value.Value.TimeOfDay.TotalMinutes);

  Task item = new Task
  {
    Title = this.TitleTextBox.Text.Trim(),
    Description = this.DescriptionTextBox.Text.Trim(),
    Star = (string)this.StarListPicker.SelectedItem,
    ModifiedDate = DateTime.Now,
    DueDate = dueDate
  };

  if (Settings.CurrentTask.Value != null)
  {
    // This is an edit

    // Perform the edit differently for the task list versus done list
    if (Settings.TaskList.Value.Remove(Settings.CurrentTask.Value))
    {
      // We removed the old item, and now let's insert the new item.
      // If the due date has changed, this re-sorts the list correctly.
```

LISTING 26.9   Continued

```
          // Be sure to give this new item the original created date
          item.CreatedDate = Settings.CurrentTask.Value.CreatedDate;

          Settings.TaskList.Value.Add(item);
          Settings.CurrentTask.Value = item;
        }
        else
        {
          // We don't want to change the ordering in the done list,
          // so just update the item in-place
          Settings.CurrentTask.Value.Title = item.Title;
          Settings.CurrentTask.Value.Description = item.Description;
          Settings.CurrentTask.Value.Star = item.Star;
          Settings.CurrentTask.Value.ModifiedDate = item.ModifiedDate;
          Settings.CurrentTask.Value.DueDate = item.DueDate;
          // Don't change CreatedDate!
        }
      }
      else
      {
        // This is a new task
        item.CreatedDate = item.ModifiedDate;
        Settings.TaskList.Value.Add(item);
      }

      if (this.NavigationService.CanGoBack)
        this.NavigationService.GoBack();
    }

    void AboutMenuItem_Click(object sender, EventArgs e)
    {
      this.NavigationService.Navigate(new Uri(
        "/Shared/About/AboutPage.xaml?appName=TODO List", UriKind.Relative));
    }
  }
}
```

Notes:

→ This page stores the current value in each control in page state. This is not only a nice touch for when the user gets interrupted while filling out the page, but it is a requirement due to the way that the date and time pickers work. Because these controls navigate away from the current page, failure to save and restore the values would cause the form to get cleared out whenever the date or time picker is used!

→ If an item in the done list is being edited, its values are directly modified. If an item in the task list is being edited, the task is removed and a modified task is added.

This is done to keep the task list sorted by due date. If the due date had been changed, editing the existing task in the collection might cause the sorting to be incorrect. This is why Task's `INotifyPropertyChanged` implementation is only needed to keep the main page's "done" list box up-to-date; additions and removals are already reported by observable collections, so the property-changed notifications are only needed for direct edits.

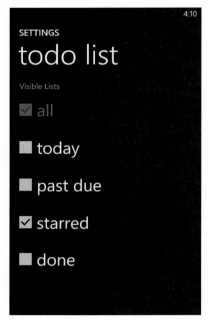

The Settings Page

The settings page, shown in Figure 26.8, enables the user to turn off any of the pivot items except for the "all" item. (The "all" check box is present but always disabled to make it clear that this item can't be hidden.) Listing 26.10 contains the XAML, and Listing 26.11 contains the code-behind.

FIGURE 26.8   The settings page enables the user to hide all but the first pivot item.

LISTING 26.10   `SettingsPage.xaml`—The User Interface for TODO List's Settings Page

```
<phone:PhoneApplicationPage x:Class="WindowsPhoneApp.SettingsPage"
    xmlns="http://schemas.microsoft.com/winfx/2006/xaml/presentation"
    xmlns:x="http://schemas.microsoft.com/winfx/2006/xaml"
    xmlns:phone="clr-namespace:Microsoft.Phone.Controls;assembly=Microsoft.Phone"
    xmlns:shell="clr-namespace:Microsoft.Phone.Shell;assembly=Microsoft.Phone"
    xmlns:local="clr-namespace:WindowsPhoneApp"
    FontFamily="{StaticResource PhoneFontFamilyNormal}"
    FontSize="{StaticResource PhoneFontSizeNormal}"
    Foreground="{StaticResource PhoneForegroundBrush}"
    SupportedOrientations="PortraitOrLandscape" shell:SystemTray.IsVisible="True">
  <Grid>
    <Grid.RowDefinitions>
      <RowDefinition Height="Auto"/>
      <RowDefinition Height="*"/>
    </Grid.RowDefinitions>
```

LISTING 26.10   Continued

```xml
    <!-- The standard header -->
    <StackPanel Grid.Row="0" Style="{StaticResource PhoneTitlePanelStyle}">
      <TextBlock Text="SETTINGS" Style="{StaticResource PhoneTextTitle0Style}"/>
      <TextBlock Text="todo list" Style="{StaticResource PhoneTextTitle1Style}"/>
    </StackPanel>
    <!-- A check box for each setting -->
    <ScrollViewer Grid.Row="1">
      <StackPanel Margin="{StaticResource PhoneHorizontalMargin}">
        <TextBlock Margin="12,12,0,0" Text="Visible Lists"
                   Foreground="{StaticResource PhoneSubtleBrush}"/>
        <CheckBox Content="all" IsEnabled="False" IsChecked="True"
                  FontSize="{StaticResource PhoneFontSizeExtraLarge}"
                  local:Tilt.IsEnabled="True"/>
        <CheckBox x:Name="TodayCheckBox" Content="today"
                  FontSize="{StaticResource PhoneFontSizeExtraLarge}"
                  local:Tilt.IsEnabled="True"/>
        <CheckBox x:Name="PastDueCheckBox" Content="past due"
                  FontSize="{StaticResource PhoneFontSizeExtraLarge}"
                  local:Tilt.IsEnabled="True"/>
        <CheckBox x:Name="StarredCheckBox" Content="starred"
                  FontSize="{StaticResource PhoneFontSizeExtraLarge}"
                  local:Tilt.IsEnabled="True"/>
        <CheckBox x:Name="DoneCheckBox" Content="done" local:Tilt.IsEnabled="True"
                  FontSize="{StaticResource PhoneFontSizeExtraLarge}"/>
      </StackPanel>
    </ScrollViewer>
  </Grid>
</phone:PhoneApplicationPage>
```

LISTING 26.11   `SettingsPage.xaml.cs`—The Code-Behind for TODO List's Settings Page

```csharp
using System.Windows.Navigation;
using Microsoft.Phone.Controls;

namespace WindowsPhoneApp
{
  public partial class SettingsPage : PhoneApplicationPage
  {
    public SettingsPage()
    {
      InitializeComponent();
    }

    protected override void OnNavigatedFrom(NavigationEventArgs e)
```

LISTING 26.11   Continued

```
  {
      base.OnNavigatedFrom(e);
      // Save the settings
      Settings.IsTodayVisible.Value = this.TodayCheckBox.IsChecked.Value;
      Settings.IsPastDueVisible.Value = this.PastDueCheckBox.IsChecked.Value;
      Settings.IsStarredVisible.Value = this.StarredCheckBox.IsChecked.Value;
      Settings.IsDoneVisible.Value = this.DoneCheckBox.IsChecked.Value;
  }

  protected override void OnNavigatedTo(NavigationEventArgs e)
  {
    base.OnNavigatedTo(e);
    // Respect the saved settings
    this.TodayCheckBox.IsChecked = Settings.IsTodayVisible.Value;
    this.PastDueCheckBox.IsChecked = Settings.IsPastDueVisible.Value;
    this.StarredCheckBox.IsChecked = Settings.IsStarredVisible.Value;
    this.DoneCheckBox.IsChecked = Settings.IsDoneVisible.Value;
  }
 }
}
```

This page is about as simple as a settings page can get. The hard part is supporting the hiding of pivot items that is done in the main page!

The Finished Product

Several things to do today

Choosing a due date with the date picker

Starred items, under the light theme

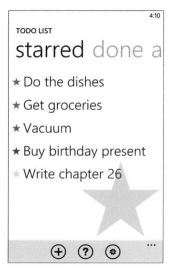

GROCERIES

Groceries is a flexible shopping list app that enables you to set up custom aisle-by-aisle lists. Name and arrange as many isles as you want to match the layout of your favorite store! This app has a lot of features to make adding items easy, such as adding in bulk, selecting favorite items, and selecting recent items.

The Groceries app showcases the panorama control, which enables the *other* signature Windows Phone user interface paradigm—the one used by every "hub" on the phone (People, Pictures, and so on). Roughly speaking, a panorama acts very similarly to a pivot: It enables horizontal swiping between multiple sections on the same page. What makes it distinct is its appearance and complex animations.

The idea of a panorama is that the user is looking at one piece of a long, horizontal canvas. The user is given several visual hints to swipe horizontally. For example, the application title is larger than what fits on the screen at a single time (unless the title is really short) and each section is a little narrower than the screen, so the left edge of the *next* section is visible even when not actively panning the page. A panorama wraps around, so panning forward from the last section goes to the first section, and panning backward from the first section goes to the last section.

Figure 27.1 demonstrates how Groceries leverages the panorama control. The first section contains the entire shopping list and the last section contains the cart (items that the user has already grabbed). In between are a

dynamic number of sections based on the user-defined aisles and whether there are any items still left to grab in each aisle.

FIGURE 27.1   The grocery panorama, shown the way panoramas are typically shown in marketing materials.

Although the viewport-on-a-long-canvas presentation in Figure 27.1 is the way panoramas are usually shown, that image does not consist of five concatenated screenshots. The reality is much more complex. A panorama consists of three separate layers that each pan at a different speeds, producing a parallax effect. The background pans at the slowest rate, followed by the title, followed by the rest of the content, which moves at the typical scrolling/swiping speed. Figure 27.2 shows what the screen really looks like when visiting each of the five sections in Figure 27.1.

FIGURE 27.2   Real screenshots when visiting each of the five panorama sections from Figure 27.1.

How should I choose between using a panorama versus using a pivot in my app?

The main consideration is your desired visual appearance. A panorama with a good background can provide a more attractive and interesting user interface than a pivot. This is true even if you use the same background for a pivot, thanks to panorama's parallax panning. A panorama also has better support for horizontal scrolling within a single section, making it easier to have variable-width sections.

In just about every other way, a pivot has advantages over a panorama. A pivot gives you more screen real estate for each section. A pivot can perform better for a large number of items and/or content for three reasons: its layout and animations are simpler, it delay-loads its items, and it provides APIs for advanced delay-loading or unloading. It's also okay to use an application bar (and status bar) with a pivot, whereas it's considered bad form to use one with a panorama. So if you want to expose several page-level actions, a pivot with an application bar is probably the best choice.

The Groceries app is actually a more natural fit for a pivot rather than a panorama, as each section is nothing more than a filtered view of the same list. A typical panorama has sections that are more varied and visually interesting than what is used in Groceries, with plenty of thumbnails (like what you see in the phone's Marketplace app). However, by using a panorama, Groceries leaves more of an impression with users and is more fun to use.

The Panorama Control

After reading about the `Pivot` control in the preceding chapter, the `Panorama` control should look familiar. `Panorama`, in the `Microsoft.Phone.Controls` namespace and `Microsoft.Phone.Controls` assembly, is an items control designed to work with content controls called `PanoramaItem`.

Although the behavior exhibited by a panorama is more complex than the behavior exhibited by a pivot, it exposes fewer APIs. Like `Pivot`, `Panorama` has `Title` and `TitleTemplate` properties and a `HeaderTemplate` property for customizing the headers of its children. Under normal circumstances, there's no need to use these template properties because the control does a good job of providing the correct look and feel.

 Because Panorama's `Title` property is of type `object`, it is possible (and acceptable) to set it to a logo rather than plain text. The Facebook app does this.

`PanoramaItem` has a `Header` property, but unlike `PivotItem`, it also exposes a `HeaderTemplate` property for customizing an individual header's appearance. (Of course, you could always directly set `Header` to a custom UI element without the need for `HeaderTemplate`.) `PanoramaItem` has also exposes an `Orientation` property that indicates the intended direction of scrolling when content doesn't fit. This property is `Vertical` by default, but setting it to `Horizontal` enables a single panorama item to extend wider than the screen. Note that you must add your own scroll viewer if you want scrolling in a vertical panorama item. In a horizontal panorama item, you *don't* want to use a scroll viewer; the panorama handles it. Each horizontal panorama item has a maximum width of two screens (960 pixels).

···

Horizontal Panorama Items and Their Headers

In the panoramas used by the built-in apps, the panorama item header scrolls more slowly than the rest of the content when the panorama item is horizontal and wider than the screen. (This ensures that you can see at least part of the item's header as long as you're viewing some of that item's content.) However, the Panorama control does not provide this behavior. Each panorama item's header always scrolls at the same rate as the rest of the panorama item's content, no matter how wide it is.

As for the layout of items inside a panorama item, you're on your own. Although certain arrangements of square images and text are commonly used in a panorama, there are no special controls that automatically give you these specific layouts. You should use the general-purpose panels such as a grid or a wrap panel.

The Main Page

The Groceries app's main page, shown earlier in Figure 27.2, is the only one that uses a panorama. It provides links to the four other pages in this app: an add-items page, an edit-items page, a settings page, and an instructions page. The code for these pages is not examined in this chapter.

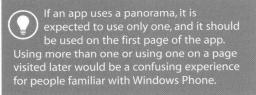

If an app uses a panorama, it is expected to use only one, and it should be used on the first page of the app. Using more than one or using one on a page visited later would be a confusing experience for people familiar with Windows Phone.

The User Interface

Listing 27.1 contains the XAML for the main page.

LISTING 27.1   `MainPage.xaml`—The Main User Interface for Groceries

```xml
<phone:PhoneApplicationPage x:Class="WindowsPhoneApp.MainPage"
    xmlns="http://schemas.microsoft.com/winfx/2006/xaml/presentation"
    xmlns:x="http://schemas.microsoft.com/winfx/2006/xaml"
    xmlns:phone="clr-namespace:Microsoft.Phone.Controls;assembly=Microsoft.Phone"
    xmlns:shell="clr-namespace:Microsoft.Phone.Shell;assembly=Microsoft.Phone"
    xmlns:controls="clr-namespace:Microsoft.Phone.Controls;
➥assembly=Microsoft.Phone.Controls"
    FontFamily="{StaticResource PhoneFontFamilyNormal}"
    FontSize="{StaticResource PhoneFontSizeNormal}"
    Foreground="White"
    SupportedOrientations="Portrait" shell:SystemTray.IsVisible="False">

  <!-- Two storyboards for animating items into and out of the cart -->
  <phone:PhoneApplicationPage.Resources>
    <Storyboard x:Name="MoveToCartStoryboard"
                Completed="MoveToCartStoryboard_Completed">
```

LISTING 27.1   Continued

```xml
      <DoubleAnimation To="-400" Duration="0:0:.2"/>
    </Storyboard>
    <Storyboard x:Name="MoveFromCartStoryboard"
                Completed="MoveFromCartStoryboard_Completed">
      <DoubleAnimation To="400" Duration="0:0:.2"/>
    </Storyboard>
  </phone:PhoneApplicationPage.Resources>


  <controls:Panorama x:Name="Panorama" Title="groceries" Foreground="White"
                     SelectionChanged="Panorama_SelectionChanged">
    <controls:Panorama.Background>
      <ImageBrush ImageSource="Images/background.jpg"/>
    </controls:Panorama.Background>


    <!-- The "list" item -->
    <controls:PanoramaItem Foreground="White">
      <!-- A complex header that contains buttons -->
      <controls:PanoramaItem.Header>
        <Grid>
          <Grid.ColumnDefinitions>
            <ColumnDefinition Width="194"/>
            <ColumnDefinition Width="Auto"/>
            <ColumnDefinition Width="Auto"/>
            <ColumnDefinition Width="Auto"/>
          </Grid.ColumnDefinitions>
          <!-- The normal header text -->
          <TextBlock Text="list"/>
          <!-- add -->
          <Button Grid.Column="1" Margin="0,20,36,0" Click="AddButton_Click"
                  Style="{StaticResource SimpleButtonStyle}">
            <Image Source="Shared/Images/normal.add.png"/>
          </Button>
          <!-- settings -->
          <Button Grid.Column="2" Margin="0,20,36,0" Click="SettingsButton_Click"
                  Style="{StaticResource SimpleButtonStyle}">
            <Image Source="Shared/Images/normal.settings.png"/>
          </Button>
          <!-- instructions -->
          <Button Grid.Column="3" Margin="0,20,36,0"
                  Click="InstructionsButton_Click"
                  Style="{StaticResource SimpleButtonStyle}">
            <Image Source="Shared/Images/normal.instructions.png"/>
          </Button>
        </Grid>
```

LISTING 27.1   Continued

```xml
    </controls:PanoramaItem.Header>
    <!-- The panorama item's content is just a list box -->
    <ListBox x:Name="MainListBox" ItemsSource="{Binding}">
      <!-- Give each item a complex template -->
      <ListBox.ItemTemplate>
        <DataTemplate>
          <!-- A horizontal stack panel with two buttons -->
          <StackPanel Orientation="Horizontal" Margin="0,0,0,16">
            <!-- The first button sends the item to the cart -->
            <Button Style="{StaticResource SimpleButtonStyle}"
                    Click="AddToCartButton_Click">
              <Button.RenderTransform>
                <CompositeTransform/>
              </Button.RenderTransform>
              <StackPanel Orientation="Horizontal">
                <Image Source="Shared/Images/normal.done.png"/>
                <TextBlock Text="{Binding Name}" Width="300" TextWrapping="Wrap"
                           Style="{StaticResource PhoneTextExtraLargeStyle}"
                           Foreground="White"/>
              </StackPanel>
            </Button>
            <!-- The second button edits the item -->
            <Button Style="{StaticResource SimpleButtonStyle}"
                    Click="EditItemButton_Click">
              <Image Source="Shared/Images/normal.edit.png"/>
            </Button>
          </StackPanel>
        </DataTemplate>
      </ListBox.ItemTemplate>
    </ListBox>
  </controls:PanoramaItem>

  <!-- The "in cart" item -->
  <controls:PanoramaItem Foreground="White">
    <!-- A complex header that contains a button -->
    <controls:PanoramaItem.Header>
      <Grid>
        <Grid.ColumnDefinitions>
          <ColumnDefinition Width="286"/>
          <ColumnDefinition Width="Auto"/>
        </Grid.ColumnDefinitions>
        <!-- The normal header text -->
        <TextBlock Text="in cart"/>
        <!-- delete -->
```

LISTING 27.1   Continued

```
              <Button Grid.Column="1" Margin="0,20,36,0" Click="DeleteButton_Click"
                      Style="{StaticResource SimpleButtonStyle}">
                <Image Source="Shared/Images/normal.delete.png"/>
              </Button>
            </Grid>
          </controls:PanoramaItem.Header>

          <!-- This panorama item's content is a list box in front of a cart image -->
          <Grid>
            <Image Source="Images/cart.png" Opacity=".3" Stretch="None"/>
            <ListBox x:Name="InCartListBox" ItemsSource="{Binding}">
              <!-- Give each item a complex template -->
              <ListBox.ItemTemplate>
                <DataTemplate>
                  <Button Margin="0,0,0,16" Style="{StaticResource SimpleButtonStyle}"
                          Click="RemoveFromCartButton_Click">
                    <Button.RenderTransform>
                      <CompositeTransform/>
                    </Button.RenderTransform>
                    <StackPanel Orientation="Horizontal">
                      <Image Source="Images/normal.outOfCart.png"/>
                      <TextBlock Text="{Binding Name}" Width="359" TextWrapping="Wrap"
                                 Style="{StaticResource PhoneTextExtraLargeStyle}"
                                 Foreground="White"/>
                    </StackPanel>
                  </Button>
                </DataTemplate>
              </ListBox.ItemTemplate>
            </ListBox>
          </Grid>
        </controls:PanoramaItem>
      </controls:Panorama>
</phone:PhoneApplicationPage>
```

Notes:

→ The `controls` XML namespace is once again used to reference the panorama.

→ This page is portrait-only, which is the expected behavior for any page with a panorama. Although the control works in the landscape orientation, there's not much room for the content!

→ This page is filled with hard-coded white foregrounds. This is necessary to ensure that the app looks the same under the light theme as it does under the dark theme. Because the background image doesn't change, we don't want the text turning black.

→ The panorama's `Background` works just like the `Background` property on other elements. You can set it to any brush, although design guidelines dictate that you use a solid color brush or an image brush. This listing sets the background to `background.jpg` with an image brush.

Be sure to test your panorama under both dark and light themes!

This is true for any app, of course, but you're more likely to make a mistake on a page with a panorama that has a fixed background image. If the background never changes, then you probably need to ensure that the color of your content never changes.

 To avoid stretching, make sure your panorama's background image is 800 pixels tall. To avoid performance problems, the image should not be much wider than about 1024 pixels, and it should be a JPEG. Groceries uses a 1024x800 JPEG.

When I decided to build this app, I anxiously went to a local grocery store with my wife's new camera because it has the ability to take panoramic photos. This was before I realized that the best background image dimensions are not panoramic at all! Figure 27.3 shows this app's `background.jpg` file.

FIGURE 27.3   The not-so-panoramic background image used by the Groceries app's panorama.

The effect of a super-wide background image is an illusion caused by the slow, parallax scrolling of the background. In fact, the amount of background scrolling depends on the number of panorama items, because the panorama ensures that you don't reach the end of the background image until you reach the end of the panorama.

In Groceries, it just so happens that the length of the "groceries" title and the length of the background image cause the title and background to scroll at roughly the same rate. To get a richer parallax effect, you could change the length of either one.

For the best results, your panorama's background image should be given a Build Action of Resource—*not* Content! This is one of those rare cases where a resource file is recommended, due to the difference between synchronous and asynchronous loading/decoding.

If the image is large and included as a content file, the panorama might appear before its background does. When included as a resource file, the panorama will never appear until the image is ready. The synchronous loading done for resource files, which is normally considered to be a problem, actually gives more desirable behavior in this case. Despite increasing the amount of time before the panorama appears, most people do not want their background image appearing later.

You can actually use live UI elements for your panorama's background! This involves a hack shared by Microsoft's Dave Relyea, the author of the Panorama control and technical editor for this book. You can read about it at http://bit.ly/panoramaxaml.

➜ Because the panorama wraps around, there is always a visible "seam" where the right edge of the background meets the left edge of the background unless you use specially crafted artwork (as in the Games hub) or a solid background (as in the People hub). The seam is okay; users are used to it, and it helps to indicate that a wraparound is occurring. (You can see this seam when wrapping around in the Pictures and Marketplace hubs, among many others.) However, the background image used by Groceries has a little bit of shading on the edges to make the transition a little smoother. This is shown in Figure 27.4.

FIGURE 27.4 Shading in the background image makes the seam less jarring when wrapping from the last panorama item to the first one.

Even when using a specially crafted image, a 1-pixel-wide background-color seam can still occasionally be seen while the user scrolls past the wraparound point. You can get rid of this seam by giving Panorama a new control template. It can be a copy of the default one, with a single negative margin added to a border named background as follows:

```
<Border x:Name="background" Background="{TemplateBinding Background}"
        CacheMode="BitmapCache" Margin="-1,0"/>
```

→ In Listing 27.1, the panorama contains the two items that are always there: the list of all items left to find, and the cart. The dynamic aisle items are added in code-behind.

→ The "list" panorama item is given a custom header with three buttons next to the typical header text: one for adding a new item, one for settings, and one for instructions. You can see these in Figure 27.2. Ordinarily, these would be application bar buttons, but because an application bar is not meant to be used with a panorama, they are placed in this available area instead.

→ The "cart" panorama item is also given a custom header with a delete button next to the header text. Whereas the other panorama items (including the ones added in code-behind) contain just a list box, the cart item contains a grid in order to place a distinguishing cart icon behind the list box.

→ Buttons are used throughout this app, and they are all marked with a custom style called SimpleButtonStyle. This style gives each button a new control template that removes the border, padding, and other behaviors, so all you see is the content. (It also adds the tilt effect used throughout this book.) It is defined in App.xaml as follows:

```
<!-- A button style that removes the border, padding, state changes for
     pressing/disabling, and ignores various properties like Foreground. It
     simply displays its content with no frills other than the tilt. -->
<Style x:Key="SimpleButtonStyle" TargetType="Button">
  <Setter Property="local:Tilt.IsEnabled" Value="True"/>
  <Setter Property="Template">
    <Setter.Value>
      <ControlTemplate TargetType="Button">
        <ContentControl x:Name="ContentContainer"
          Content="{TemplateBinding Content}"
          ContentTemplate="{TemplateBinding ContentTemplate}"
          HorizontalContentAlignment=
            "{TemplateBinding HorizontalContentAlignment}"
          VerticalContentAlignment=
            "{TemplateBinding VerticalContentAlignment}"/>
      </ControlTemplate>
```

```
      </Setter.Value>
    </Setter>
  </Style>
```

Figure 27.5 shows what the panorama looks like if each button is left with its default style (with layout adjusted so all the buttons still fit on the screen). The reason that real buttons are used in all these places is that a button's `Click` event is only raised for a real tap as opposed to a swiping motion. This enables the user to swipe the panorama on top of a button without inadvertently tapping it. If the `MouseLeftButtonUp` event were instead used to detect a tap on elements, a swipe that happens to be done on top of an element would trigger the action that's only supposed to happen on a tap.

FIGURE 27.5   Groceries is filled with buttons that easily detect non-swiping taps, which is obvious when the custom button style is removed.

> ⚠ **Avoid using raw mouse events like** MouseLeftButtonDown, MouseMove, **and** MouseLeftButtonUp **inside a panorama (or pivot)!**
>
> Because the entire control pans in response to these gestures, any extra logic you associate with these events is likely to interfere with the user's panning expectations. Find other relevant events to use instead that aren't also triggered by swiping gestures, such as a button's Click event or a list box's SelectionChanged event.

The Code-Behind

Listing 27.2 contains the code-behind for the main page.

LISTING 27.2   MainPage.xaml.cs—The Code-Behind for the Groceries App's Main Page

```
using System;
using System.Windows;
using System.Windows.Controls;
using System.Windows.Media.Animation;
using System.Windows.Threading;
using Microsoft.Phone.Controls;
```

LISTING 27.2   Continued

```
namespace WindowsPhoneApp
{
  public partial class MainPage : PhoneApplicationPage
  {
    Item pendingIntoCartItem;
    Item pendingOutOfCartItem;

    public MainPage()
    {
      InitializeComponent();
      this.Loaded += MainPage_Loaded;
    }

    void MainPage_Loaded(object sender, RoutedEventArgs e)
    {
      // Fill the two list boxes that are always there
      this.MainListBox.DataContext = FilteredLists.Need;
      this.InCartListBox.DataContext = FilteredLists.InCart;

      // Add and fill the other aisles based on the user's data
      RefreshAisles();
    }

    void RefreshAisles()
    {
      // Remove all aisles. Leave the list and cart items.
      while (this.Panorama.Items.Count > 2)
        this.Panorama.Items.RemoveAt(1);

      // Get the list of dynamic aisles
      string[] aisles = Settings.AislesList.Value;
      for (int i = aisles.Length - 1; i >= 0; i--)
      {
        string aisle = aisles[i];
        AislePanoramaItem panoramaItem = new AislePanoramaItem { Header = aisle };

        // Fill the aisle with relevant items
        panoramaItem.Items = new FilteredObservableCollection<Item>(
          Settings.AvailableItems.Value, delegate(Item item)
          {
            return (item.Status == Status.Need && item.Aisle == aisle);
          });

        // Only add aisles that contain items we still need to get
```

LISTING 27.2   Continued

```csharp
      if (panoramaItem.Items.Count > 0)
        this.Panorama.Items.Insert(1, panoramaItem);
    }
  }

  void Panorama_SelectionChanged(object sender, SelectionChangedEventArgs e)
  {
    // Check to see if the item we're leaving is now empty
    if (e.RemovedItems.Count == 1)
    {
      AislePanoramaItem aisle = e.RemovedItems[0] as AislePanoramaItem;
      if (aisle != null && aisle.Items.Count == 0)
      {
        // It's empty, so remove it.
        // But wait .5 seconds to avoid interfering with the animation!
        DispatcherTimer timer = new DispatcherTimer {
          Interval = TimeSpan.FromSeconds(.5) };
        timer.Tick += delegate(object s, EventArgs args)
        {
          this.Panorama.Items.Remove(aisle);
          timer.Stop();
        };
        timer.Start();
      }
    }
  }

  // The three "list" header button handlers

  void SettingsButton_Click(object sender, RoutedEventArgs e)
  {
    this.NavigationService.Navigate(new Uri("/SettingsPage.xaml",
      UriKind.Relative));
  }

  void AddButton_Click(object sender, RoutedEventArgs e)
  {
    this.NavigationService.Navigate(new Uri("/AddItemsPage.xaml",
      UriKind.Relative));
  }

  void InstructionsButton_Click(object sender, RoutedEventArgs e)
  {
    this.NavigationService.Navigate(new Uri("/InstructionsPage.xaml",
```

LISTING 27.2   Continued

```
      UriKind.Relative));
  }

  // The two button handlers for each item in "list"

  void AddToCartButton_Click(object sender, RoutedEventArgs e)
  {
    if (this.MoveToCartStoryboard.GetCurrentState() != ClockState.Stopped)
      return;

    this.pendingIntoCartItem = (sender as FrameworkElement).DataContext as Item;

    Storyboard.SetTarget(this.MoveToCartStoryboard,
      (sender as UIElement).RenderTransform);
    Storyboard.SetTargetProperty(this.MoveToCartStoryboard,
      new PropertyPath("TranslateX"));
    this.MoveToCartStoryboard.Begin();
  }

  void EditItemButton_Click(object sender, RoutedEventArgs e)
  {
    Item item = (sender as FrameworkElement).DataContext as Item;
    Settings.EditedItem.Value = item;
    this.NavigationService.Navigate(new Uri("/EditItemPage.xaml",
      UriKind.Relative));
  }

  // The one "in cart" header button handler

  void DeleteButton_Click(object sender, RoutedEventArgs e)
  {
    if (MessageBox.Show(
      "Are you sure you want to remove all the items from the cart?",
      "Clear cart?", MessageBoxButton.OKCancel) == MessageBoxResult.OK)
    {
      foreach (Item item in Settings.AvailableItems.Value)
      {
        // Nothing is actually deleted, just marked Unused
        if (item.Status == Status.InCart)
          item.Status = Status.Unused;
      }
    }
  }
```

LISTING 27.2   Continued

```
// The one button handler for each item in the cart

void RemoveFromCartButton_Click(object sender, RoutedEventArgs e)
{
  if (this.MoveFromCartStoryboard.GetCurrentState() != ClockState.Stopped)
    return;

  this.pendingOutOfCartItem =
    (sender as FrameworkElement).DataContext as Item;

  Storyboard.SetTarget(this.MoveFromCartStoryboard,
    (sender as UIElement).RenderTransform);
  Storyboard.SetTargetProperty(this.MoveFromCartStoryboard,
    new PropertyPath("TranslateX"));
  this.MoveFromCartStoryboard.Begin();
}


// Storyboard-completed handlers

void MoveFromCartStoryboard_Completed(object sender, EventArgs e)
{
  this.pendingOutOfCartItem.Status = Status.Need;
  // This may have caused the need to add an aisle
  RefreshAisles();
  this.MoveFromCartStoryboard.Stop();
}

void MoveToCartStoryboard_Completed(object sender, EventArgs e)
{
  this.pendingIntoCartItem.Status = Status.InCart;
  // This may have caused the need to remove an aisle
  RefreshAisles();
  this.MoveToCartStoryboard.Stop();
}
    }
  }
}
```

Notes:

→ This app maintains a single list of items (Settings.AvailableItems) that represents every item ever added by the user. Every list box in the panorama is a filtered view of this list based on properties of each item. These lists are exposed as static properties such as FilteredLists.Need (the entire grocery list in the "list" panorama item) and FilteredLists.InCart (the list of items in the cart). Unlike in the preceding chapter, where the filtering was done by the page filling the list boxes, these lists handle the filtering internally. This enables the main page to use data binding for every list box. These lists, and the `Item` type representing each grocery item, are examined in the upcoming "Supporting Data Types" section.

→ `RefreshAisles` is responsible for dynamically filling in the aisles in-between the list and cart panorama items. Each dynamic aisle is encapsulated by a custom `AislePanoramaItem` control that derives from `PanoramaItem`. This control is shown in the next section. Panorama items are only added for each user-defined aisle that has active items in it that need to be added to the cart.

→ The creation of each filtered collection for each dynamic panorama item is not very efficient, because each `FilteredObservableCollection` (whose implementation is shown later) must iterate through the passed-in list of available items. If the list of items becomes sufficiently large, a new strategy might need to be chosen.

→ This app demonstrates dynamic removal of panorama items, which happens when all of a dynamic aisle's items have been moved to the cart. Unfortunately, like a pivot, a panorama does not handle removal of its items very gracefully. There are two problems: finding a good time to remove the panorama item, and its impact on the parallax effect.

To avoid confusion, an empty panorama item is removed *after* the user has panned away from it, so the code checks for this condition inside panorama's `SelectionChanged` event handler. In this handler, the previous selection is exposed as the only item in the `RemovedItems` collection. Because removing it instantly would interfere with the panning animation that is causing the `SelectionChanged` event to be raised, the handler uses a `DispatcherTimer` to remove it half a second later. In practice, this works pretty well. The only remaining issue is that because the scrolling of the background and title is based on the total panorama width, and removing an item shortens that width, it causes a jarring jump in the placement of the background and title unless you happen to be on the first panorama item when this happens. There is no way to avoid this behavior, other than not removing panorama items!

→ Storyboards are used to animate items to/from the cart. The actual change to the lists occurs in the `Completed` event handlers, which either set the item's `Status` property to `InCart` or `Need`. This causes a property-changed notification that flows to each of the filtered lists, causing both lists to update automatically thanks to data binding.

> (!) Unlike pivot items, setting a panorama item's `Visibility` to `Collapsed` successfully hides the entire item. Listing 27.2 could leverage this to toggle an item's visibility rather than adding/removing items. However, hiding a panorama item has the same jarring impact as removing one.

⚠ Panoramas do not enable programmatic setting of the selected panorama item!

One thing conspicuously missing from Listing 27.2 is a setting that remembers the current panorama item so the page's state can be restored on the next launch or activation. Strangely, panorama's `SelectedIndex` and `SelectedItem` properties are readonly, so although you can save either value when the selection changes, you cannot restore it later.

Panorama *does* expose a read/write property called `DefaultItem` that can instantly change the panorama item on the screen, but not in the way that you'd expect. It shifts the items such that `DefaultItem` becomes the first section on the virtual canvas, as illustrated in Figure 27.6. This means that the title now aligns with the new default item and the image seam is now immediately to the left of this item! In the Groceries app, having the image seam move anywhere other than between the cart and the list sections would be a confusing experience. Therefore, the `DefaultItem` property is not suitable for attempting to return a user to where they left off.

`DefaultItem=Panorama.Items[0]` (the default value)

`DefaultItem=Panorama.Items[2]`

FIGURE 27.6 Setting `DefaultItem` shifts the panorama items, but it does not shift the title or the background image.

The `AislePanoramaItem` **Control**

`AislePanoramaItem` was added to the Visual Studio project as a user control, but then its base class was changed from `UserControl` to `PanoramaItem`. This was done to get the same kind of convenient XAML support as a user control, but applied to a `PanoramaItem` subclass. Listing 27.3 contains this control's XAML and Listing 27.4 contains its code-behind.

LISTING 27.3   `AislePanoramaItem.xaml`—The User Interface for the Custom `PanoramaItem` Subclass

```
<controls:PanoramaItem x:Class="WindowsPhoneApp.AislePanoramaItem"
    xmlns="http://schemas.microsoft.com/winfx/2006/xaml/presentation"
    xmlns:x="http://schemas.microsoft.com/winfx/2006/xaml"
    xmlns:controls="clr-namespace:Microsoft.Phone.Controls;
➥assembly=Microsoft.Phone.Controls"
    FontFamily="{StaticResource PhoneFontFamilyNormal}"
    FontSize="{StaticResource PhoneFontSizeNormal}"
    Foreground="White">

  <!-- A storyboards for animating items into the cart -->
  <controls:PanoramaItem.Resources>
    <Storyboard x:Name="MoveToCartStoryboard" Completed="Storyboard_Completed">
      <DoubleAnimation To="-400" Duration="0:0:.2"/>
    </Storyboard>
  </controls:PanoramaItem.Resources>

  <!-- The panorama item's content is just a list box -->
  <ListBox x:Name="ListBox" ItemsSource="{Binding}" >
    <ListBox.ItemTemplate>
      <DataTemplate>
        <Button Margin="0,0,0,16" Style="{StaticResource SimpleButtonStyle}"
                Click="ItemButton_Click">
          <Button.RenderTransform>
            <CompositeTransform/>
          </Button.RenderTransform>
          <StackPanel Orientation="Horizontal">
            <Image Source="Shared/Images/normal.done.png"/>
            <TextBlock Text="{Binding Name}" Width="300" TextWrapping="Wrap"
                       Style="{StaticResource PhoneTextExtraLargeStyle}"
                       Foreground="White"/>
          </StackPanel>
        </Button>
      </DataTemplate>
    </ListBox.ItemTemplate>
  </ListBox>
</controls:PanoramaItem>
```

LISTING 27.4   `AislePanoramaItem.xaml.cs`—The Code-Behind for the Custom `PanoramaItem` Subclass

```csharp
using System;
using System.Collections.Generic;
using System.Windows;
using System.Windows.Media.Animation;
using Microsoft.Phone.Controls;

namespace WindowsPhoneApp
{
  public partial class AislePanoramaItem : PanoramaItem
  {
    Item pendingItem;

    public AislePanoramaItem()
    {
      InitializeComponent();
    }

    public ICollection<Item> Items
    {
      get { return this.ListBox.DataContext as ICollection<Item>; }
      set { this.ListBox.DataContext = value; }
    }

    void ItemButton_Click(object sender, RoutedEventArgs e)
    {
      if (this.MoveToCartStoryboard.GetCurrentState() != ClockState.Stopped)
        return;

      // Animate the item when tapped
      this.pendingItem = (sender as FrameworkElement).DataContext as Item;
      Storyboard.SetTarget(this.MoveToCartStoryboard,
        (sender as UIElement).RenderTransform);
      Storyboard.SetTargetProperty(this.MoveToCartStoryboard,
        new PropertyPath("TranslateX"));
      this.MoveToCartStoryboard.Begin();
    }

    void Storyboard_Completed(object sender, EventArgs e)
    {
      // Now place the item in the cart
      this.pendingItem.Status = Status.InCart;
      this.MoveToCartStoryboard.Stop();
    }
  }
}
```

This panorama item is just like the first panorama item on the main page, but with no edit button in the item template. This convenient packaging enables it to be easily reused by main page, as is done in the `RefreshAisles` method in Listing 27.2.

Supporting Data Types

The `Item` data type that is used throughout this app is defined in Listing 27.5. It serves a similar role as the `Task` class from the preceding chapter.

LISTING 27.5   `Item.cs`—The Type of Every Item in Every List Box

```
using System.ComponentModel;

namespace WindowsPhoneApp
{
  public class Item : INotifyPropertyChanged
  {
    // The backing fields
    string name;
    string aisle;
    bool isFavorite;
    Status status;

    // The properties, which raise change notifications
    public string Name {
      get { return this.name; }
      set { this.name = value; OnPropertyChanged("Name"); } }
    public string Aisle {
      get { return this.aisle; }
      set { this.aisle = value; OnPropertyChanged("Aisle"); } }
    public bool IsFavorite {
      get { return this.isFavorite; }
      set { this.isFavorite = value; OnPropertyChanged("IsFavorite"); } }
    public Status Status {
      get { return this.status; }
      set { this.status = value; OnPropertyChanged("Status"); } }

    void OnPropertyChanged(string propertyName)
    {
      PropertyChangedEventHandler handler = this.PropertyChanged;
      if (handler != null)
        handler(this, new PropertyChangedEventArgs(propertyName));
    }

    // Treat items with the same name as equal
    public override bool Equals(object obj)
```

LISTING 27.5   Continued

```
  {
    if (!(obj is Item))
      return false;

    return (this.Name == (obj as Item).Name);
  }

  // This matches the implementation of Equals
  public override int GetHashCode()
  {
    return this.Name.GetHashCode();
  }

  public event PropertyChangedEventHandler PropertyChanged;
  }
}
```

Notes:

→ The Status enumeration is defined as follows:

```
public enum Status
{
  Need,   // In the current shopping list (but not in the cart yet)
  InCart, // In the cart
  Unused  // Added at some point in the past, but not currently used
}
```

→ The IsFavorite property is leveraged by the add-items and edit-item pages to help the user organize their entries.

→ The property-changed notifications enable the filtered collections to keep items in the appropriate filtered lists at all times. They also keep the rendering of individual items up-to-date. For example, the add-items page uses several value converters to show/hide buttons when an item's IsFavorite status changes.

The AvailableItems setting that persists the list of all items is defined as follows inside the Settings class:

```
public static readonly Setting<ObservableCollection<Item>> AvailableItems =
  new Setting<ObservableCollection<Item>>("AvailableItems",
    new ObservableCollection<Item>());
```

The filtered lists used by this app are *not* persisted but rather initialized from the single persisted list once the app runs. They are defined as follows:

```
public static class FilteredLists
{
  // A list of items in the current shopping list (but not in the cart yet)
  public static readonly ReadOnlyObservableCollection<Item> Need =
      new ReadOnlyObservableCollection<Item>(
        new FilteredObservableCollection<Item>(Settings.AvailableItems.Value,
          delegate(Item item) { return item.Status == Status.Need; }));

  // A list of items in the cart
  public static readonly ReadOnlyObservableCollection<Item> InCart =
      new ReadOnlyObservableCollection<Item>(
        new FilteredObservableCollection<Item>(Settings.AvailableItems.Value,
          delegate(Item item) { return item.Status == Status.InCart; }));

  // A list of items marked as favorites
  public static readonly ReadOnlyObservableCollection<Item> Favorites =
      new ReadOnlyObservableCollection<Item>(
        new FilteredObservableCollection<Item>(Settings.AvailableItems.Value,
          delegate(Item item) { return item.IsFavorite; }));
}
```

Each `FilteredObservableCollection` is wrapped in a `ReadOnlyObservableCollection` to prevent consumers from accidentally attempting to modify the collection directly.

Listing 27.6 contains the implementation of the custom `FilteredObservableCollection` class.

LISTING 27.6   `FilteredObservableCollection.cs`—Exposes a Subset of a Separate Observable Collection Based on a Custom Filter

```
using System;
using System.Collections.ObjectModel;
using System.Collections.Specialized;
using System.ComponentModel;

namespace WindowsPhoneApp
{
  public class FilteredObservableCollection<T> : ObservableCollection<T>
                                          where T : INotifyPropertyChanged
  {
    ObservableCollection<T> sourceCollection;
    Predicate<T> belongs;
```

LISTING 27.6   Continued

```
public FilteredObservableCollection(ObservableCollection<T> sourceCollection,
                                    Predicate<T> filter)
{
  this.sourceCollection = sourceCollection;
  this.belongs = filter;

  // Listen for any changes in the source collection
  this.sourceCollection.CollectionChanged +=
    SourceCollection_CollectionChanged;

  foreach (T item in this.sourceCollection)
  {
    // We must also listen for changes on each item, because property changes
    // are not reported through the CollectionChanged event
    item.PropertyChanged += Item_PropertyChanged;

    // Add the item to this list if it passes the filter
    if (this.belongs(item))
      this.Add(item);
  }
}

// Handler for each item's property changes
void Item_PropertyChanged(object sender, PropertyChangedEventArgs e)
{
  T item = (T)sender;
  if (this.belongs(item))
  {
    // The item belongs in this list, so add it (if it wasn't already added)
    if (!this.Contains(item))
      this.Add(item);
  }
  else
  {
    // The item does not belong in this list, so remove it if present.
    // Remove simply returns false if the item is not in this list.
    this.Remove(item);
  }
}

// Handler for collection changes
void SourceCollection_CollectionChanged(object sender,
  NotifyCollectionChangedEventArgs e)
{
```

LISTING 27.6 Continued

```
    if (e.Action == NotifyCollectionChangedAction.Add ||
        e.Action == NotifyCollectionChangedAction.Replace)
    {
      // Insert any relevant item(s) at the end of the list
      foreach (T item in e.NewItems)
      {
        // We must start tracking property changes in this item as well
        item.PropertyChanged += Item_PropertyChanged;
        if (this.belongs(item))
          this.Add(item);
      }
    }
    else if (e.Action == NotifyCollectionChangedAction.Remove ||
             e.Action == NotifyCollectionChangedAction.Replace)
    {
      // Try removing each one
      foreach (T item in e.OldItems)
      {
        // We can stop tracking property changes on this item
        item.PropertyChanged -= Item_PropertyChanged;
        this.Remove(item);
      }
    }
    else // e.Action == NotifyCollectionChangedAction.Reset
    {
      throw new NotSupportedException();
    }
    }
  }
}
```

This class is constructed with a source collection and a callback that returns whether an individual item belongs in the filtered list. This enables each instance to use a different filter, as done in the FilteredLists static class. The type of item used with this class must implement INotifyPropertyChanged, as this class tracks item-by-item property changes as well as additions and removals to the source collection. (This is a requirement for Groceries, as changing a property like Status or IsFavorite must instantly impact the filtered lists.)

The Finished Product

The add-items page uses a pivot to enable adding items in three different ways.

Assigning an aisle to an item with a full-mode list picker

Adding favorites from the add-items page

Adding recent items from the add-items page (under the light theme)

Customizing the list of aisles in the settings page

ALPHABET FLASHCARDS

Someone recently asked me how to build a flashcard app where the user could swipe between cards, much like when navigating a strip of photos in the Pictures hub or in the Facebook app. For lack of a better term, I'm referring to this as a *filmstrip* user experience.

It occurred to me that there's currently no simple panel or other element for performing this type of interaction. A simple scroll viewer doesn't work as-is because you want each item to be "magnetic" and not allow the view to rest in an unaligned position.

Although the pivot and panorama controls are much more feature-filled than what's required for this task, they provide the easiest way to create this kind of user interface. You just need to hide the title and header and make some layout tweaks. A pivot is better suited for dynamic items, thanks to its LoadingPivotItem and UnloadingPivotItem events, but a panorama is a bit better suited for faithfully mimicking a filmstrip, as it enables you to see the next or previous item in the midst of a swipe.

Therefore, Alphabet Flashcards uses a panorama to provide filmstrip-style browsing of a set of 26 flashcards, one for each letter of the alphabet. A parent can use this with a toddler to practice learning letters.

> **① Be careful about giving a panorama too many items!**
>
> A panorama was not designed to contain more than a handful of items. The performance is acceptable for this app's 27 items, but using more items or more complex items can cause noticeable performance problems and consume a lot of memory.

The User Interface

Alphabet Flashcards uses a single panorama-filled page with 27 panorama items: one for each letter in the alphabet and one that acts like a title page. Figure 28.1 shows the experience of swiping from the first item (the title page) to the second item (the letter A).

FIGURE 28.1   Swiping from the first panorama item to the second panorama item.

To get the illusion of a full-screen filmstrip experience, the panorama used by this page and its items do not use any title or headers. The items also use a slight negative top margin to consume space that would be wasted.

The right-most 48 pixels of the control are reserved for a 12-pixel margin between items and a 36-pixel preview of the next item's left side. Because we don't want the preview behavior in this app, we simply ensure the content in each item has a 36-pixel left margin. Besides keeping the next item off-screen until swiping begins, this also keeps the content centered. It does, however, force the content to have a maximum width of 384 in the portrait orientation (480 - 48×2). Figure 28.2 demonstrates this more clearly by giving the panorama an orange background, the first item a green background, the second item a blue background, and the third item a purple background.

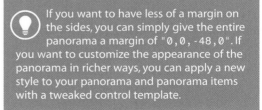

If you want to have less of a margin on the sides, you can simply give the entire panorama a margin of "0,0,-48,0". If you want to customize the appearance of the panorama in richer ways, you can apply a new style to your panorama and panorama items with a tweaked control template.

Listing 28.1 contains the XAML for this page.

FIGURE 28.2   The same sequence as in Figure 28.1, but showing where each item—and its inner content—begins and ends.

LISTING 28.1   `MainPage.xaml`—The User Interface for Alphabet Flashcards' Main Page

```
<phone:PhoneApplicationPage x:Class="WindowsPhoneApp.MainPage"
    xmlns="http://schemas.microsoft.com/winfx/2006/xaml/presentation"
    xmlns:x="http://schemas.microsoft.com/winfx/2006/xaml"
    xmlns:phone="clr-namespace:Microsoft.Phone.Controls;assembly=Microsoft.Phone"
    xmlns:controls="clr-namespace:Microsoft.Phone.Controls;
assembly=Microsoft.Phone.Controls"
    SupportedOrientations="Portrait">
  <Grid Background="White">
    <controls:Panorama x:Name="Panorama">

      <controls:Panorama.ItemTemplate>
        <DataTemplate>
          <Grid Margin="36,-24,0,0">
            <Image Source="{Binding}"/>
          </Grid>
        </DataTemplate>
      </controls:Panorama.ItemTemplate>

      <controls:Panorama.HeaderTemplate>
        <!-- Make sure the header is empty -->
        <DataTemplate><Canvas/></DataTemplate>
      </controls:Panorama.HeaderTemplate>

    </controls:Panorama>
  </Grid>
</phone:PhoneApplicationPage>
```

Notes:

→ Rather than giving the panorama 27 items in XAML, the code-behind sets its `ItemsSource` to an array of image URI strings. The panorama uses an item template to render each image inside a grid with a margin needed to get the effect shown in Figure 28.1.

→ When a panorama contains something other than a `PanoramaItem` control, such as the strings used by this app, each item's main content *and header* displays the item. Therefore, Listing 28.1 must explicitly set each item's `HeaderTemplate` to something blank to avoid each URI being rendered in a text block on top of each image.

→ The images used in this app are marked with a Build Action of Resource, so the panorama does not appear until the images are ready.

The Code-Behind

Listing 28.2 contains the code-behind for the main page. Besides filling the panorama with items, it persists and restores the selected item, so the app can resume where it left off.

LISTING 28.2   `MainPage.xaml.cs`—The Code-Behind for Alphabet Flashcards' Main Page

```
using System.Windows.Navigation;
using Microsoft.Phone.Controls;

namespace WindowsPhoneApp
{
  public partial class MainPage : PhoneApplicationPage
  {
    // Persist the selected item
    Setting<int> selectedIndex = new Setting<int>("SelectedIndex", 0);

    public MainPage()
    {
      InitializeComponent();

      this.Panorama.ItemsSource = new string[] {
        "Images/title.png",
        "Images/a.png",
        "Images/b.png",
        "Images/c.png",
        …
        "Images/x.png",
        "Images/y.png",
        "Images/z.png"
      };
```

LISTING 28.2   Continued

```
  }

  protected override void OnNavigatedTo(NavigationEventArgs e)
  {
    base.OnNavigatedTo(e);
    // Restore the selected item
    this.Panorama.DefaultItem = this.Panorama.Items[this.selectedIndex.Value];
  }

  protected override void OnNavigatedFrom(NavigationEventArgs e)
  {
    base.OnNavigatedFrom(e);
    // Remember the selected item
    this.selectedIndex.Value = this.Panorama.SelectedIndex;
  }
 }
}
```

Here, `DefaultItem` is used exactly how it was designed to be used. The problems with `DefaultItem` discussed in the preceding chapter aren't problematic in this app because there is no distinguishable panorama title or background.

The Finished Product

B is for Ball

C is for Clock

V is for Violin

WEIGHT TRACKER

Are you watching your weight? Weight Tracker enables you to weigh in as often as you like and provides several ways to visualize your progress. It is a pivot-based app with three pivot items:

→ **list**—The raw list of weigh-ins, with support for adding and deleting them. The weight trend between consecutive items is shown with up/down arrows.

→ **graph**—Plots your weight over time on a line chart, along with any number of goal weights that you can define on this app's settings page. You can view the entire range of data, or narrow it down to a custom range.

→ **progress**—Summarizes your weight loss progress compared to your final weight loss goal. This dashboard view makes use of pie charts.

Although this is a pivot-based app, the purpose of this chapter is to explain how to include charts and graphs in your apps.

Charts & Graphs

The Silverlight team has created a very rich set of open-source controls for creating seven types of interactive charts: bar charts, line charts, pie charts, bubble charts, and more. These were created several years ago for desktop Silverlight and ship in the Silverlight Toolkit. At the time of

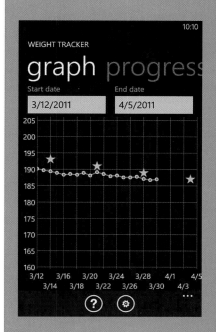

this writing, these controls are *not* included in the Silverlight *for Windows Phone* Toolkit, so you must download them separately. Where you should download them, however, has been a source of confusion.

Currently, the best place to get the chart controls is directly from David Anson's blog. David is the Microsoft developer responsible for these controls, and he was also kind enough to review this chapter. He provides "development releases" of the controls with the goal of exposing the latest functionality and bug fixes at a quicker pace than the official toolkit releases from Microsoft. His releases come with full source code as well as the compiled DLLs. The same source code can be compiled to work with Windows Phone, multiple versions of desktop Silverlight, as well as Windows Presentation Foundation (WPF). You can get "Data Visualization Development Release 4," the version used by this book, at http://bit.ly/datavis4.

If you're uncomfortable with using this unofficial release, you can instead download the chart controls from the Silverlight Toolkit (the one intended for desktop computers). However, to make matters more confusing, you must *not* use the latest version of the Silverlight Toolkit. You can download the phone-compatible version of the Silverlight Toolkit (the November 2009 release for Silverlight 3) at http://bit.ly/sl3toolkit. The downside to using this version is that it is missing performance improvements and *stacked series* support (described later) that are present in David's release.

Whichever route you take, you need to reference `System.Windows.Controls.DataVisualization.Toolkit.dll`, the assembly with all the chart-specific functionality. In David's release, use the one under `Binaries\Silverlight3` inside the `.zip` file. If you install the November 2009 Silverlight Toolkit, you can find it in `%ProgramFiles%\Microsoft SDKs\Silverlight\v3.0\Toolkit\Nov09\Bin`.

 The chart controls from the Silverlight 4 Toolkit do not work on Windows Phone at the time of this writing!

Although the latest version of the Silverlight Toolkit contains the chart controls described in this chapter, you cannot currently use them. Windows Phone OS 7.0 ships with a custom version of Silverlight that is based on Silverlight 3, despite having a few additional features that were introduced in Silverlight 4. As a result, most Silverlight 2 or Silverlight 3 code can work on Windows Phone, but code written for Silverlight 4 may not.

The Silverlight 4 version of the chart controls requires features that are not present on Windows Phone's version of Silverlight, so attempting to use this version fails at run-time in hard-to-diagnose ways. Such incompatibilities between desktop Silverlight and Silverlight for Windows Phone should hopefully fade away in the future.

 For the chart controls to work, you must reference an additional desktop Silverlight 3 assembly!

If you do not reference the *desktop Silverlight 3 version* of `System.Windows.Controls.dll`, you will get a cryptic exception when trying to use any of the chart controls. Make sure you reference the right one, which is typically installed to `%ProgramFiles%\Microsoft SDKs\Silverlight\v3.0\Libraries\Client`.

Regular Series

The primary element that enables charts is `Chart` from the `System.Windows.Controls.DataVisualization.Charting` namespace. To get different types of charts, you place different types of series in the `Chart` element. There are fifteen concrete series: seven regular ones and eight stacked ones. All of the regular ones are demonstrated in Table 29.1.

Each is shown with its default rendering under the light theme, which is decent (despite the use of phone-unfriendly gradients). The default rendering is not acceptable under the dark theme, however, as the legend text becomes white but the box's background remains a light gradient.

From code-behind, each chart in Table 29.1 is given the same data context of three simple (X,Y) points as follows:

```
this.Chart.DataContext =
  new Point[] { new Point(0, 2), new Point(1, 10), new Point(2, 6) };
```

This way, each series can bind its `ItemsSource` property to this array with simple `{Binding}` syntax then specify each X property for its *independent axis* (the X axis in most chart types) and each Y property for its *dependent axis* (the Y axis in most chart types). You can directly manipulate a series without using data binding, but doing so from code-behind is a little awkward because you can't access a series element by name.

TABLE 29.1 The Default Light-Theme Rendering of the Seven Nonstacked Chart Types, All with the Same Three-Point Data Source

Line Chart

```
<charting:Chart x:Name="Chart">
  <charting:LineSeries
    ItemsSource="{Binding}"
    IndependentValuePath="X"
    DependentValuePath="Y"/>
</charting:Chart>
```

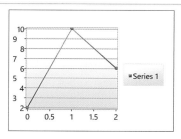

Area Chart

```
<charting:Chart x:Name="Chart">
  <charting:AreaSeries
    ItemsSource="{Binding}"
    IndependentValuePath="X"
    DependentValuePath="Y"/>
</charting:Chart>
```

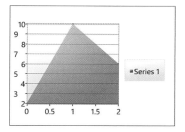

TABLE 29.1   Continued

Bar Chart

```
<charting:Chart x:Name="Chart">
  <charting:BarSeries
    ItemsSource="{Binding}"
    IndependentValuePath="X"
    DependentValuePath="Y"/>
</charting:Chart>
```

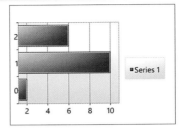

Column Chart

```
<charting:Chart x:Name="Chart">
  <charting:ColumnSeries
    ItemsSource="{Binding}"
    IndependentValuePath="X"
    DependentValuePath="Y"/>
</charting:Chart>
```

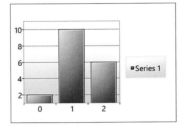

Scatter Chart

```
<charting:Chart x:Name="Chart">
  <charting:ScatterSeries
    ItemsSource="{Binding}"
    IndependentValuePath="X"
    DependentValuePath="Y"/>
</charting:Chart>
```

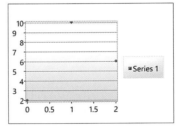

Bubble Chart

```
<charting:Chart x:Name="Chart">
  <charting:BubbleSeries
    ItemsSource="{Binding}"
    IndependentValuePath="X"
    DependentValuePath="Y"/>
</charting:Chart>
```

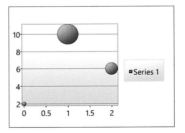

Pie Chart

```
<charting:Chart x:Name="Chart">
  <charting:PieSeries
    ItemsSource="{Binding}"
    IndependentValuePath="X"
    DependentValuePath="Y"/>
</charting:Chart>
```

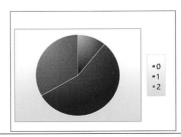

A single chart can contain multiple overlapping series, as with the following chart:

```
<charting:Chart x:Name="Chart">
  <!-- Data set #1 -->
  <charting:AreaSeries IndependentValuePath="X"
                       DependentValuePath="Y"/>
  <!-- Data set #2 -->
  <charting:AreaSeries IndependentValuePath="X"
                       DependentValuePath="Y"/>
</charting:Chart>
```

Assigning each area series the following data produces the result in Figure 29.1 (under the light theme):

```
(this.Chart.Series[0] as AreaSeries).ItemsSource =
  new Point[] { new Point(0, 2), new Point(1, 10), new Point(2, 6) };
(this.Chart.Series[1] as AreaSeries).ItemsSource =
  new Point[] { new Point(0, 8), new Point(1, 1), new Point(2, 9) };
```

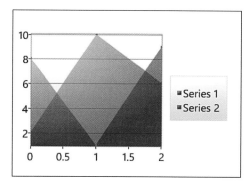

FIGURE 29.1   Using two area series in the same chart.

Each series can even be a different type. Although it's nonsensical in this case, Figure 29.2 combines all seven series from Table 29.1 into the same chart.

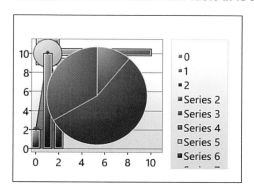

FIGURE 29.2   Using all seven types of nonstacked series in the same chart.

Stacked Series

In the Development Release 4 download of the chart controls, the first four series in Table 29.1 have two stacked counterparts: one that stacks the absolute values, and one that stacks relative values that always add up to 100%. Table 29.2 demonstrates these eight stacked series. They support multiple child series much like in Figure 29.1 but, as the name implies, each child get stacked rather than overlapped.

Each chart in Table 29.2 uses the following data context from code-behind:

```
this.Chart.DataContext = new Point[][] {
  new Point[] { new Point(0, 2), new Point(1, 10), new Point(2, 6) }, // Series 1
  new Point[] { new Point(0, 4), new Point(1, 5), new Point(2, 12) }, // Series 2
  new Point[] { new Point(0, 8), new Point(1, 2.5), new Point(2, 3) } // Series 3
};
```

A stacked series contains any number of *series definitions*. With this data context, the XAML snippets in Table 29.2 can bind three distinct series definitions to each `Point[]` element in the outermost array. When bound to an individual array of points, the assignments of `IndependentValuePath` and `DependentValuePath` work just like in the previous table.

TABLE 29.2   The Default Light-Theme Rendering of the Eight Stacked Chart Types, All with the Same Set of Three-Point Data Sources

Stacked Line Chart

```
<charting:Chart x:Name="Chart">
  <charting:StackedLineSeries>
    <charting:SeriesDefinition
      ItemsSource="{Binding [0]}"
      IndependentValuePath="X"
      DependentValuePath="Y" />
    <charting:SeriesDefinition
      ItemsSource="{Binding [1]}"
      IndependentValuePath="X"
      DependentValuePath="Y" />
    <charting:SeriesDefinition
      ItemsSource="{Binding [2]}"
      IndependentValuePath="X"
      DependentValuePath="Y" />
  </charting:StackedLineSeries>
</charting:Chart>
```

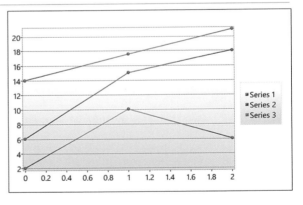

TABLE 29.2 Continued

Stacked 100% Line Chart

```
<charting:Chart x:Name="Chart">
  <charting:Stacked100LineSeries>
    <charting:SeriesDefinition
      ItemsSource="{Binding [0]}"
      IndependentValuePath="X"
      DependentValuePath="Y"/>
    <charting:SeriesDefinition
      ItemsSource="{Binding [1]}"
      IndependentValuePath="X"
      DependentValuePath="Y"/>
    <charting:SeriesDefinition
      ItemsSource="{Binding [2]}"
      IndependentValuePath="X"
      DependentValuePath="Y"/>
  </charting:Stacked100LineSeries>
</charting:Chart>
```

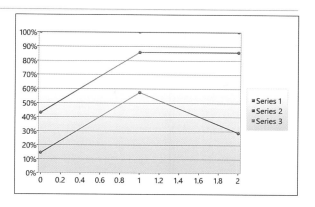

Stacked Area Chart

```
<charting:Chart x:Name="Chart">
  <charting:StackedAreaSeries>
    <charting:SeriesDefinition
      ItemsSource="{Binding [0]}"
      IndependentValuePath="X"
      DependentValuePath="Y"/>
    <charting:SeriesDefinition
      ItemsSource="{Binding [1]}"
      IndependentValuePath="X"
      DependentValuePath="Y"/>
    <charting:SeriesDefinition
      ItemsSource="{Binding [2]}"
      IndependentValuePath="X"
      DependentValuePath="Y"/>
  </charting:StackedAreaSeries>
</charting:Chart>
```

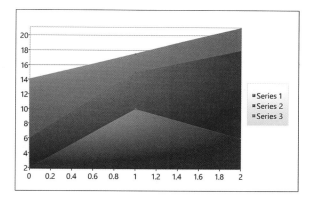

TABLE 29.2   Continued

Stacked 100% Area Chart

```
<charting:Chart x:Name="Chart">
  <charting:Stacked100AreaSeries>
    <charting:SeriesDefinition
      ItemsSource="{Binding [0]}"
      IndependentValuePath="X"
      DependentValuePath="Y"/>
    <charting:SeriesDefinition
      ItemsSource="{Binding [1]}"
      IndependentValuePath="X"
      DependentValuePath="Y"/>
    <charting:SeriesDefinition
      ItemsSource="{Binding [2]}"
      IndependentValuePath="X"
      DependentValuePath="Y"/>
  </charting:Stacked100AreaSeries>
</charting:Chart>
```

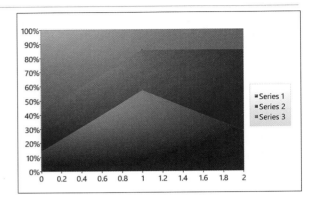

Stacked Bar Chart

```
<charting:Chart x:Name="Chart">
  <charting:StackedBarSeries>
    <charting:SeriesDefinition
      ItemsSource="{Binding [0]}"
      IndependentValuePath="X"
      DependentValuePath="Y"/>
    <charting:SeriesDefinition
      ItemsSource="{Binding [1]}"
      IndependentValuePath="X"
      DependentValuePath="Y"/>
    <charting:SeriesDefinition
      ItemsSource="{Binding [2]}"
      IndependentValuePath="X"
      DependentValuePath="Y"/>
  </charting:StackedBarSeries>
</charting:Chart>
```

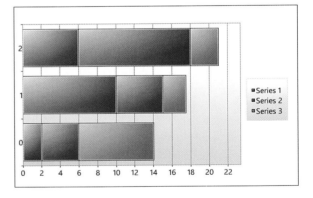

TABLE 29.2   Continued

Stacked 100% Bar Chart

```xml
<charting:Chart x:Name="Chart">
  <charting:Stacked100BarSeries>
    <charting:SeriesDefinition
      ItemsSource="{Binding [0]}"
      IndependentValuePath="X"
      DependentValuePath="Y"/>
    <charting:SeriesDefinition
      ItemsSource="{Binding [1]}"
      IndependentValuePath="X"
      DependentValuePath="Y"/>
    <charting:SeriesDefinition
      ItemsSource="{Binding [2]}"
      IndependentValuePath="X"
      DependentValuePath="Y"/>
  </charting:Stacked100BarSeries>
</charting:Chart>
```

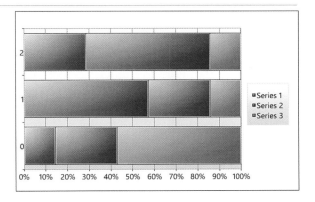

Stacked Column Chart

```xml
<charting:Chart x:Name="Chart">
  <charting:StackedColumnSeries>
    <charting:SeriesDefinition
      ItemsSource="{Binding [0]}"
      IndependentValuePath="X"
      DependentValuePath="Y"/>
    <charting:SeriesDefinition
      ItemsSource="{Binding [1]}"
      IndependentValuePath="X"
      DependentValuePath="Y"/>
    <charting:SeriesDefinition
      ItemsSource="{Binding [2]}"
      IndependentValuePath="X"
      DependentValuePath="Y"/>
  </charting:StackedColumnSeries>
</charting:Chart>
```

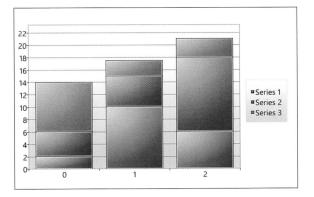

TABLE 29.2   Continued

Stacked 100% Column Chart

```
<charting:Chart x:Name="Chart">
  <charting:Stacked100ColumnSeries>
    <charting:SeriesDefinition
      ItemsSource="{Binding [0]}"
      IndependentValuePath="X"
      DependentValuePath="Y"/>
    <charting:SeriesDefinition
      ItemsSource="{Binding [1]}"
      IndependentValuePath="X"
      DependentValuePath="Y"/>
    <charting:SeriesDefinition
      ItemsSource="{Binding [2]}"
      IndependentValuePath="X"
      DependentValuePath="Y"/>
  </charting:Stacked100ColumnSeries>
</charting:Chart>
```

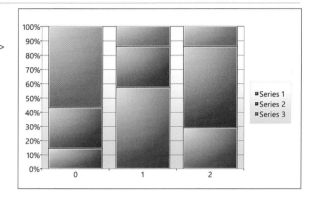

As you can see, getting reasonable-looking charts to render is fairly easy. The chart scales its axes appropriately, and even staggers axis labels if necessary (seen in Table 29.1). It applies different colors to the data automatically and has a lot of other intelligence not shown here. Chart, as well as each series object, also exposes numerous properties for formatting the chart area, legend, title, axes, data points, and more. The amount of possible customization is vast, although figuring out how to get your desired customizations (even simple-sounding things like hiding the legend or changing data colors) can be quite tricky. In the next section, Weight Tracker demonstrates how to perform several customizations on line charts and pie charts.

> Development Release 4 contains a secondary implementation of five of the non-stacked series objects (LineSeries, AreaSeries, BarSeries, ColumnSeries, and ScatterSeries). This new set resides in the System.Windows.Controls.DataVisualization.Charting.Compatible namespace. Their APIs are almost identical to the primary implementation of these controls, but internally they use the new infrastructure that was added for the stacked series objects. As a result, this secondary implementation contains several performance improvements and even works in some cases that the primary implementation does not. Although you might not notice any improved performance unless you continuously and rapidly update a chart's data, you should consider using these newer objects.

The Main Page

Weight Tracker has a main page, a settings page, an instructions page, and an about page. (The latter two pages aren't interesting and therefore aren't shown in this chapter.)

Besides the application bar and status bar, the main page contains the three-item pivot. These three items, described at the beginning of this chapter, are shown in Figure 29.3.

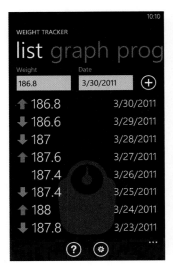 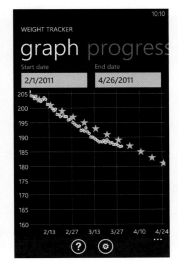 

FIGURE 29.3   The three pivot items: list, graph, and progress.

The User Interface

Listing 29.1 contains the XAML for the main page.

LISTING 29.1   `MainPage.xaml`—The User Interface for Weight Tracker's Main Page

```
<phone:PhoneApplicationPage x:Class="WindowsPhoneApp.MainPage"
    xmlns="http://schemas.microsoft.com/winfx/2006/xaml/presentation"
    xmlns:x="http://schemas.microsoft.com/winfx/2006/xaml"
    xmlns:phone="clr-namespace:Microsoft.Phone.Controls;assembly=Microsoft.Phone"
    xmlns:shell="clr-namespace:Microsoft.Phone.Shell;assembly=Microsoft.Phone"
    xmlns:controls="clr-namespace:Microsoft.Phone.Controls;
➥assembly=Microsoft.Phone.Controls"
    xmlns:toolkit="clr-namespace:Microsoft.Phone.Controls;
➥assembly=Microsoft.Phone.Controls.Toolkit"
    xmlns:charting="clr-namespace:
➥System.Windows.Controls.DataVisualization.Charting;
➥assembly=System.Windows.Controls.DataVisualization.Toolkit"
    xmlns:chartingprimitives="clr-namespace:
➥System.Windows.Controls.DataVisualization.Charting.Primitives;
➥assembly=System.Windows.Controls.DataVisualization.Toolkit"
    xmlns:datavis="clr-namespace:System.Windows.Controls.DataVisualization;
➥assembly=System.Windows.Controls.DataVisualization.Toolkit"
```

LISTING 29.1   Continued

```
  xmlns:local="clr-namespace:WindowsPhoneApp"
  FontFamily="{StaticResource PhoneFontFamilyNormal}"
  FontSize="{StaticResource PhoneFontSizeNormal}"
  Foreground="{StaticResource PhoneForegroundBrush}"
  SupportedOrientations="PortraitOrLandscape" shell:SystemTray.IsVisible="True">

<!-- The application bar, with two buttons and a menu item -->
<phone:PhoneApplicationPage.ApplicationBar>
  <shell:ApplicationBar>
    <shell:ApplicationBarIconButton Text="instructions"
      IconUri="/Shared/Images/appbar.instructions.png"
      Click="InstructionsButton_Click"/>
    <shell:ApplicationBarIconButton Text="settings"
      IconUri="/Shared/Images/appbar.settings.png"
      Click="SettingsButton_Click"/>
    <shell:ApplicationBar.MenuItems>
      <shell:ApplicationBarMenuItem Text="about" Click="AboutMenuItem_Click"/>
    </shell:ApplicationBar.MenuItems>
  </shell:ApplicationBar>
</phone:PhoneApplicationPage.ApplicationBar>


<phone:PhoneApplicationPage.Resources>
  <!-- A custom style for Chart. It's the default style from the toolkit, but
       with no title/legend, reduced margins/padding, and fewer borders. -->
  <Style x:Key="ChartStyle" TargetType="charting:Chart">
    …
  </Style>
</phone:PhoneApplicationPage.Resources>

<!-- The pivot is the root element -->
<controls:Pivot x:Name="Pivot" Title="WEIGHT TRACKER"
                SelectionChanged="Pivot_SelectionChanged">

  <!-- Item 1: list -->
  <controls:PivotItem Header="list">
    <Grid Margin="0,-24,0,0">
      <!-- A translucent foreground-colored scale image behind the list -->
      <Rectangle Opacity=".2" Margin="0,0,0,12" VerticalAlignment="Bottom"
        Width="180" Height="240" Fill="{StaticResource PhoneForegroundBrush}">
        <Rectangle.OpacityMask>
          <ImageBrush ImageSource="Images/scale.png"/>
        </Rectangle.OpacityMask>
      </Rectangle>
      <!-- The editable list, implemented as a user control -->
```

LISTING 29.1   Continued

```
      <local:WeighInEditableList x:Name="EditableList" Collection="{Binding}"/>
    </Grid>
  </controls:PivotItem>

  <!-- Item 2: graph -->
  <controls:PivotItem Header="graph">
    <Grid Margin="0,-24,0,0">
      <Grid.ColumnDefinitions>
        <ColumnDefinition/>
        <ColumnDefinition/>
      </Grid.ColumnDefinitions>
      <Grid.RowDefinitions>
        <RowDefinition Height="Auto"/>
        <RowDefinition Height="Auto"/>
        <RowDefinition/>
      </Grid.RowDefinitions>

      <!-- The start date / end date pickers -->
      <TextBlock Text="Start date" Margin="11,0,0,-5"
                 Foreground="{StaticResource PhoneSubtleBrush}"/>
      <toolkit:DatePicker x:Name="StartGraphDatePicker" Grid.Row="1"
        ValueChanged="GraphDatePicker_ValueChanged" local:Tilt.IsEnabled="True"/>

      <TextBlock Text="End date" Grid.Column="1" Margin="11,0,0,-5"
                 Foreground="{StaticResource PhoneSubtleBrush}"/>
      <toolkit:DatePicker x:Name="EndGraphDatePicker" Grid.Row="1"
        Grid.Column="1" ValueChanged="GraphDatePicker_ValueChanged"
        local:Tilt.IsEnabled="True"/>

      <!-- The line + scatter chart -->
      <charting:Chart x:Name="Chart" Style="{StaticResource ChartStyle}"
                      Grid.ColumnSpan="2" Grid.Row="2">

        <!-- Change the background of the plot area -->
        <charting:Chart.PlotAreaStyle>
          <Style TargetType="Grid">
            <Setter Property="Background"
                    Value="{StaticResource PhoneBackgroundBrush}"/>
          </Style>
        </charting:Chart.PlotAreaStyle>

        <!-- An explicit X axis, so it can be customized -->
        <charting:Chart.Axes>
          <charting:DateTimeAxis ShowGridLines="True" Orientation="X">
```

LISTING 29.1   Continued

```
        <charting:DateTimeAxis.AxisLabelStyle>
          <Style TargetType="charting:DateTimeAxisLabel">
            <Setter Property="StringFormat" Value="{}{0:M/d}" />
          </Style>
        </charting:DateTimeAxis.AxisLabelStyle>
      </charting:DateTimeAxis>
    </charting:Chart.Axes>

    <!-- The line series, for weigh-in data -->
    <charting:LineSeries ItemsSource="{Binding}"
                         IndependentValuePath="Date"
                         DependentValuePath="Weight">

      <!-- A custom style for the line -->
      <charting:LineSeries.PolylineStyle>
        <Style TargetType="Polyline">
          <Setter Property="StrokeThickness" Value="3"/>
        </Style>
      </charting:LineSeries.PolylineStyle>

      <!-- A custom style for data points -->
      <charting:LineSeries.DataPointStyle>
        <!-- A copy of the default style, but with a new background,
             border, width, height, and removal of the radial gradient -->
        <Style TargetType="charting:LineDataPoint">
          <Setter Property="Background"
                  Value="{StaticResource PhoneAccentBrush}"/>
          <Setter Property="BorderBrush"
                  Value="{StaticResource PhoneForegroundColor}"/>
          <Setter Property="Width" Value="10" />
          <Setter Property="Height" Value="10" />
          ...
        </Style>
      </charting:LineSeries.DataPointStyle>
    </charting:LineSeries>

    <!-- The scatter series, for goal weights -->
    <charting:ScatterSeries IndependentValuePath="Date"
                            DependentValuePath="Weight">

      <!-- A custom style for data points -->
      <charting:ScatterSeries.DataPointStyle>
        <Style TargetType="charting:ScatterDataPoint">
```

LISTING 29.1 Continued

```xml
                        <!-- Width and Height need to be set for the point
                             to render properly -->
                        <Setter Property="Width" Value="26"/>
                        <Setter Property="Height" Value="25"/>
                        <Setter Property="Template">
                          <Setter.Value>
                            <ControlTemplate TargetType="charting:ScatterDataPoint">
                              <!-- A star image -->
                              <Rectangle Fill="#FFC700">
                                <Rectangle.OpacityMask>
                                  <ImageBrush ImageSource="Images/star.png"/>
                                </Rectangle.OpacityMask>
                              </Rectangle>
                            </ControlTemplate>
                          </Setter.Value>
                        </Setter>
                      </Style>
                    </charting:ScatterSeries.DataPointStyle>
                  </charting:ScatterSeries>
                </charting:Chart>
              </Grid>
            </controls:PivotItem>

            <!-- Item 3: progress -->
            <controls:PivotItem Header="progress">
              <Grid>
                <TextBlock x:Name="NoDataTextBlock" Margin="22,17,0,0"
                           Style="{StaticResource PhoneTextGroupHeaderStyle}">
                  You don't have any goals set.<LineBreak/>Set one on the settings page.
                </TextBlock>
                <ScrollViewer x:Name="DataDashboard" Margin="0,-24,0,0">
                  <Grid>
                    <Grid.RowDefinitions>
                      <RowDefinition Height="Auto"/>
                      <RowDefinition/>
                      <RowDefinition Height="Auto"/>
                      <RowDefinition Height="Auto"/>
                      <RowDefinition Height="Auto"/>
                      <RowDefinition Height="Auto"/>
                      <RowDefinition Height="Auto"/>
                    </Grid.RowDefinitions>
                    <Grid.ColumnDefinitions>
                      <ColumnDefinition/>
                      <ColumnDefinition/>
```

LISTING 29.1   Continued

```xml
      </Grid.ColumnDefinitions>

      <!-- The first pie chart -->
      <charting:Chart x:Name="WeightPieChart" Grid.Row="1"
                      Style="{StaticResource ChartStyle}">

        <!-- Change the background of the plot area -->
        <charting:Chart.PlotAreaStyle>
          <Style TargetType="Grid">
            <Setter Property="Background"
                    Value="{StaticResource PhoneBackgroundBrush}"/>
          </Style>
        </charting:Chart.PlotAreaStyle>

        <!-- The pie series -->
        <charting:PieSeries ItemsSource="{Binding}">
          <!-- A custom two-color palette: the accent color for the first
               piece, and the background color for the second piece -->
          <charting:PieSeries.Palette>
            <datavis:ResourceDictionaryCollection>
              <!-- Style for the first data point -->
              <ResourceDictionary>
                <Style x:Key="DataPointStyle" TargetType="Control">
                  <Setter Property="BorderBrush"
                          Value="{StaticResource PhoneBackgroundBrush}"/>
                  <Setter Property="Background"
                          Value="{StaticResource PhoneAccentBrush}"/>
                </Style>
              </ResourceDictionary>
              <!-- Style for the second data point -->
              <ResourceDictionary>
                <Style x:Key="DataPointStyle" TargetType="Control">
                  <Setter Property="BorderBrush"
                          Value="{StaticResource PhoneBackgroundBrush}"/>
                  <Setter Property="Background"
                          Value="{StaticResource PhoneBackgroundBrush}"/>
                </Style>
              </ResourceDictionary>
            </datavis:ResourceDictionaryCollection>
          </charting:PieSeries.Palette>
        </charting:PieSeries>
      </charting:Chart>

      <!-- The second pie chart -->
```

LISTING 29.1   Continued

```xml
<charting:Chart x:Name="TimePieChart" Grid.Row="1" Grid.Column="1"
                Style="{StaticResource ChartStyle}">
  … The contents are identical to the preceding pie chart …
</charting:Chart>

<!-- Lots of text blocks -->
<TextBlock x:Name="WeightLossPercentTextBlock" Text="Weight loss"
           Margin="4" HorizontalAlignment="Center"
           Foreground="{StaticResource PhoneSubtleBrush}"/>
<TextBlock x:Name="TimePercentTextBlock" Grid.Column="1" Text="Time"
           Margin="4" HorizontalAlignment="Center"
           Foreground="{StaticResource PhoneSubtleBrush}"/>
<TextBlock x:Name="SummaryTextBlock" Grid.Row="2" Grid.ColumnSpan="2"
           HorizontalAlignment="Center" VerticalAlignment="Top"
           FontFamily="Segoe WP Black" Margin="0,0,0,8"
           Style="{StaticResource PhoneTextLargeStyle}"/>
<TextBlock Grid.Row="3" Text="Weight lost"
   HorizontalAlignment="Center" Style="{StaticResource LabelStyle}"/>
<TextBlock x:Name="WeightLostTextBlock" Grid.Row="4"
           HorizontalAlignment="Center"
           Style="{StaticResource PhoneTextExtraLargeStyle}"/>
<TextBlock Grid.Row="5" Text="Weight to lose"
   HorizontalAlignment="Center" Style="{StaticResource LabelStyle}"/>
<TextBlock x:Name="WeightRemainingTextBlock" Grid.Row="6"
   HorizontalAlignment="Center" Margin="0,0,0,24" FontSize="60"/>
<TextBlock Grid.Row="3" Grid.Column="1" Text="Days elapsed"
   HorizontalAlignment="Center" Style="{StaticResource LabelStyle}"/>
<TextBlock x:Name="DaysElapsedTextBlock" Grid.Row="4" Grid.Column="1"
           HorizontalAlignment="Center"
           Style="{StaticResource PhoneTextExtraLargeStyle}"/>
<TextBlock Grid.Row="5" Grid.Column="1" Text="Days remaining"
           HorizontalAlignment="Center"
           Style="{StaticResource LabelStyle}"/>
<TextBlock x:Name="DaysRemainingTextBlock" Grid.Row="6"
           Grid.Column="1" HorizontalAlignment="Center"
           Margin="0,0,0,24" FontSize="60"/>
          </Grid>
        </ScrollViewer>
      </Grid>
    </controls:PivotItem>
  </controls:Pivot>
</phone:PhoneApplicationPage>
```

Notes:

→ The namespace for `Chart` and the series elements is included with a `charting` prefix. The `chartingprimitives` prefix is used inside this listing's copy of `Chart`'s default style, and the `datavis` prefix is used for a `ResourceDictionaryCollection` type required by this listing's pie chart customizations.

> 💡 You can find the default style for `Chart` and all the related types in a `generic.xaml` file that ships with the Silverlight Toolkit. The source code is installed to `%ProgramFiles%\Microsoft SDKs\Silverlight\v3.0\Toolkit\Nov09\Source\Source code.zip`. Inside this file, the relevant XAML file can be found in the `Controls.DataVisualization.Toolkit\Themes` folder. You can also find an individual XAML file for each style. For example, the default style for `Chart` can also be found in `Controls.DataVisualization.Toolkit\Charting\Chart\Chart.xaml`.

→ The custom style used by all three charts on this page (`ChartStyle`) is a copy of the `Chart` control's default style with a few tweaks applied: removal of the title and legend, reduced margins and padding, and fewer borders.

→ Because each pivot item has a lot of information to fit on the page, the content in each one is given a –24 top margin to occupy some of the otherwise-blank space between the header and the content. You should be very careful when making changes such as this that violate design guidelines, as you risk having your app look "wrong" compared to other Windows Phone apps.

→ The editable list of weigh-ins in the first pivot item is implemented as a user control called `WeighInEditableList`. This control contains a list box bound to the value of its `Collection` property and includes the three controls displayed above the list box: the "Weight" text box, the "Date" text box, and the add button. The list box items also use a context menu to enable one-by-one deleting of items. This is packaged as a user control because it is also used by the settings page to enable viewing and editing of the list of goal weights. The source code for this user control is not shown in this chapter, but it is included in the Visual Studio project available to you.

→ Each weigh-in is represented by a `WeighIn` class that contains three read/write properties—`Weight`, `Date`, and `Delta`—as well as a few convenient readonly properties used by `WeighInEditableList`'s list box data template. The collection used by `WeighInEditableList` is a custom `WeighInCollection` class that derives from `ObservableCollection<WeighIn>`. It handles automatic sorting of the items in reverse chronological order, and it calculates the relevant `Delta` values (used to show the up/down arrows) whenever an item is added or removed.

→ The second pivot item contains a chart with two series: one for the list of weigh-ins, and one for the list of goal weights. The weigh-ins are shown with a line series, whereas the goal weights are shown with a scatter series (which looks just like a line series but with no lines connecting each dot). The items source for the scatter series is set in code-behind.

→ In addition to the custom `ChartStyle` style applied to the chart, several customizations are made to the chart itself as well as each series:

    → The chart is given a background that matches the page's background. (Alternatively, this could have been done inside `ChartStyle`.)

    → The chart is given an explicit X axis, so three customizations can be made: showing vertical grid lines, changing the string format of each date so the year is not shown, and restricting the range of X values (done in code-behind). Notice that the type of the axis is `DateTimeAxis`, which includes special functionality for displaying `DateTime` values. Any .NET formatting string can be used for the `StringFormat` value.

    → The style of the lines and dots used by the line series have been changed in a number of ways. The line has been made thicker, the color of both has been made to match the current theme's accent color, the radial gradient has been removed from each dot, and more.

    → The style of each data point in the scatter series has been changed to look like a star! This is done with a star-image opacity mask on a yellow rectangle.

You can pick up several prebuilt phone-friendly charting styles from David Anson at http://bit.ly/phonechartstyles.

Notice that changing visual properties on the chart or on one of its series is never as simple as setting brushes or thicknesses on these objects. Instead, you usually have to apply whole styles that may contain such settings. This allows for maximum flexibility, at the expense of some simplicity.

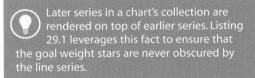
Later series in a chart's collection are rendered on top of earlier series. Listing 29.1 leverages this fact to ensure that the goal weight stars are never obscured by the line series.

→ The third and final pivot item contains two pie charts among a number of text blocks. The XAML for each pie chart looks identical, because the only difference is their data that is set in code-behind. The pie charts give themselves a page-colored background, just as the line and scatter chart does, and customizes the fills of its pie slices.

When a chart chooses colors for data points, whether in the same series or across different series, it loops through a collection of styles assigned to its `Palette` property. This collection can be changed, and each series, which also has a `Palette` property, can have its own collection. `Chart`'s default style assigns 15 brushes to `Palette` (starting with blue, red, and green gradients, as seen in Tables 29.1 and 29.2, and Figure 29.1). Because the pie charts in this listing only ever contain two slices, and because we only want the first slice to be visible, these pie series use a two-brush palette, with the second brush matching the background.

To demonstrate their impact, Figure 29.4 displays this app's line and scatter chart with various amounts of customizations removed. The second image shows the result of simply removing `Style="{StaticResource ChartStyle}"` from the chart. The first image is the result of whittling the chart down to the following simplest version that still works without changing any additional code:

```
<!-- The line + scatter chart -->
<charting:Chart x:Name="Chart"
                Grid.ColumnSpan="2" Grid.Row="2">
  <!-- An explicit X axis, so its range can be restricted from code-behind -->
  <charting:Chart.Axes>
    <charting:DateTimeAxis Orientation="X"/>
  </charting:Chart.Axes>
  <!-- The line series, for weigh-in data -->
  <charting:LineSeries ItemsSource="{Binding}"
                       IndependentValuePath="Date"
                       DependentValuePath="Weight"/>
  <!-- The scatter series, for goal weights -->
  <charting:ScatterSeries IndependentValuePath="Date"
                          DependentValuePath="Weight"/>
</charting:Chart>
```

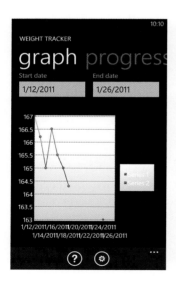

No customizations applied

All customizations applied except ChartStyle

The final result that includes ChartStyle

FIGURE 29.4   Some of the chart customizations are done by setting exposed properties, whereas others are done by changing the control template inside `ChartStyle`.

A variety of reasonable customizations (such as disabling the automatic staggering of axis labels when space is tight) can only be done by modifying the source code for the charting controls. Fortunately, because the controls are open-source, this is a viable option.

The Code-Behind

Listing 29.2 contains the code-behind for the main page, which makes the most of observable collections to keep all three pivot items up-to-date. This app manages two observable collections—one for the list of weigh-ins, and one for the list of goal weights. They are defined as follows in `Settings.cs`, along with a setting for remembering the main chart's selected start date:

```
public static class Settings
{
  public static readonly Setting<DateTime?> GraphStartDate =
    new Setting<DateTime?>("GraphStartDate", null);

  public static readonly Setting<WeighInCollection> WeighInList =
    new Setting<WeighInCollection>("WeighInList", new WeighInCollection());

  public static readonly Setting<WeighInCollection> GoalList =
    new Setting<WeighInCollection>("GoalList", new WeighInCollection());
}
```

LISTING 29.2   `MainPage.xaml.cs`—The Code-Behind for Weight Tracker's Main Page

```
using System;
using System.Collections.Specialized;
using System.Windows;
using System.Windows.Controls;
using System.Windows.Controls.DataVisualization.Charting;
using System.Windows.Navigation;
using Microsoft.Phone.Controls;

namespace WindowsPhoneApp
{
  public partial class MainPage : PhoneApplicationPage
  {
    public MainPage()
    {
      InitializeComponent();

      // Update the start/end dates of the main chart (done here so it
      // doesn't interfere with navigating back from the date pickers)
      if (Settings.WeighInList.Value.Count + Settings.GoalList.Value.Count > 0)
      {
```

LISTING 29.2   Continued

```
      // Restore the start date to the previously-used value,
      // otherwise use the earliest date with data
      if (Settings.GraphStartDate.Value != null)
        this.StartGraphDatePicker.Value = Settings.GraphStartDate.Value;
      else
        this.StartGraphDatePicker.Value = GetEarliestDataPoint().Date;

      // Don't restore any customizations to the end date. Set it to the
      // date of the last weigh-in or goal
      this.EndGraphDatePicker.Value = GetLatestDataPoint().Date;
    }

    // Update the progress dashboard (the third pivot item)
    UpdateProgress();

    // Respond to changes in the two observable collections
    Settings.WeighInList.Value.CollectionChanged += CollectionChanged;
    Settings.GoalList.Value.CollectionChanged += CollectionChanged;

    // Set the weigh-in list as the default data source for everything
    this.DataContext = Settings.WeighInList.Value;
  }

  protected override void OnNavigatedTo(NavigationEventArgs e)
  {
    base.OnNavigatedTo(e);

    // Fill out the text box with the most recent weight
    if (this.EditableList.Text.Length == 0 &&
        Settings.WeighInList.Value.Count > 0)
      this.EditableList.Text = Settings.WeighInList.Value[0].Weight.ToString();

    // When reactivated, restore the pivot selection
    if (this.State.ContainsKey("PivotSelectedIndex"))
      this.Pivot.SelectedIndex = (int)this.State["PivotSelectedIndex"];

    // Set the goal list as the source for the scatter series on the main chart
    (this.Chart.Series[1] as DataPointSeries).ItemsSource =
      Settings.GoalList.Value;
  }

  void Pivot_SelectionChanged(object sender, SelectionChangedEventArgs e)
  {
    // Remember the current pivot item for reactivation only
```

LISTING 29.2   Continued

```csharp
    this.State["PivotSelectedIndex"] = this.Pivot.SelectedIndex;
}

// Returns the earliest data point from either of the two lists
WeighIn GetEarliestDataPoint()
{
  WeighIn earliest = null;

  // Both lists are sorted in reverse chronological order
  if (Settings.WeighInList.Value.Count > 0)
    earliest = Settings.WeighInList.Value[Settings.WeighInList.Value.Count-1];

  if (Settings.GoalList.Value.Count > 0)
  {
    WeighIn earliestGoal =
      Settings.GoalList.Value[Settings.GoalList.Value.Count-1];
    if (earliest == null || earliestGoal.Date < earliest.Date)
      earliest = earliestGoal;
  }

  return earliest;
}

// Returns the latest data point from either of the two lists
WeighIn GetLatestDataPoint()
{
  WeighIn latest = null;

  // Both lists are sorted in reverse chronological order
  if (Settings.WeighInList.Value.Count > 0)
    latest = Settings.WeighInList.Value[0];

  if (Settings.GoalList.Value.Count > 0)
  {
    WeighIn latestGoal = Settings.GoalList.Value[0];
    if (latest == null || latestGoal.Date > latest.Date)
      latest = latestGoal;
  }

  return latest;
}

// Called when either of the two observable collections changes
void CollectionChanged(object sender, NotifyCollectionChangedEventArgs e)
```

LISTING 29.2   Continued

```
  {
    WeighIn earliestDataPoint = GetEarliestDataPoint();
    WeighIn latestDataPoint = GetLatestDataPoint();

    // Potentially update the range of the main chart
    if (earliestDataPoint != null && latestDataPoint != null)
    {
      // Check if a new earliest date was added. Only update start date if so.
      if ((sender == Settings.WeighInList.Value &&
           e.NewStartingIndex == Settings.WeighInList.Value.Count-1) ¦¦
          (sender == Settings.GoalList.Value &&
           e.NewStartingIndex == Settings.GoalList.Value.Count-1))
        this.StartGraphDatePicker.Value = earliestDataPoint.Date;

      // Ensure the end date matches the end of the data
      this.EndGraphDatePicker.Value = latestDataPoint.Date;
    }

    // Update the progress dashboard (the third pivot item)
    UpdateProgress();
  }

  void UpdateProgress()
  {
    // Refresh all the data on this pivot item
    this.NoDataTextBlock.Visibility = Settings.GoalList.Value.Count > 0 ?
      Visibility.Collapsed : Visibility.Visible;
    this.DataDashboard.Visibility = Settings.GoalList.Value.Count > 0 ?
      Visibility.Visible : Visibility.Collapsed;

    if (Settings.GoalList.Value.Count == 0)
      return;

    WeighIn earliestGoal =
      Settings.GoalList.Value[Settings.GoalList.Value.Count-1];
    WeighIn latestGoal = Settings.GoalList.Value[0];

    int daysRemaining = 0;
    double weightRemaining = latestGoal.Weight;
    int daysElapsed = 0;
    double weightLost = 0;

    if (Settings.WeighInList.Value.Count > 0)
    {
```

LISTING 29.2   Continued

```
      WeighIn earliestWeighIn =
        Settings.WeighInList.Value[Settings.WeighInList.Value.Count-1];
      WeighIn latestWeighIn = Settings.WeighInList.Value[0];

      daysRemaining = (latestGoal.Date - latestWeighIn.Date).Days;
      daysElapsed = (latestWeighIn.Date - earliestWeighIn.Date).Days;
      weightLost = earliestWeighIn.Weight - latestWeighIn.Weight;
      weightRemaining = latestWeighIn.Weight - latestGoal.Weight;
    }

    double weightPercent = weightLost / (weightRemaining + weightLost);
    double timePercent = (double)daysElapsed / (daysRemaining + daysElapsed);

    // Update text
    this.WeightLossPercentTextBlock.Text =
      "Weight loss: " + (weightPercent * 100).ToString("N0") + "%";
    this.TimePercentTextBlock.Text =
      "Time: " + (timePercent * 100).ToString("N0") + "%";

    this.DaysElapsedTextBlock.Text = daysElapsed.ToString("N0");
    this.DaysRemainingTextBlock.Text = daysRemaining.ToString("N0");
    this.WeightLostTextBlock.Text = weightLost.ToString("0.#");
    this.WeightRemainingTextBlock.Text = weightRemaining.ToString("0.#");

    if (weightPercent > timePercent)
      this.SummaryTextBlock.Text = "AHEAD OF SCHEDULE!";
    else if (weightPercent < timePercent)
      this.SummaryTextBlock.Text = "FALLING BEHIND";
    else
      this.SummaryTextBlock.Text = "ON TRACK";

    // Set the data for the two pie charts
    this.WeightPieChart.DataContext =
      new double[] { weightLost, weightRemaining };
    this.TimePieChart.DataContext =
      new int[] { daysElapsed, daysRemaining };
  }

  void GraphDatePicker_ValueChanged(object sender,
    DateTimeValueChangedEventArgs e)
  {
    // Minimum must be <= maximum
    if (this.StartGraphDatePicker.Value > this.EndGraphDatePicker.Value)
      this.StartGraphDatePicker.Value = this.EndGraphDatePicker.Value;
```

LISTING 29.2   Continued

```
    // Update the range of the X axis
    (this.Chart.Axes[0] as DateTimeAxis).Minimum =
      this.StartGraphDatePicker.Value;
    (this.Chart.Axes[0] as DateTimeAxis).Maximum =
      this.EndGraphDatePicker.Value;

    // Remember this new graph start date
    Settings.GraphStartDate.Value = this.StartGraphDatePicker.Value;
    }

  // Application bar handlers

  void InstructionsButton_Click(object sender, EventArgs e)
  {
    this.NavigationService.Navigate(new Uri("/InstructionsPage.xaml",
      UriKind.Relative));
  }

  void SettingsButton_Click(object sender, EventArgs e)
  {
    this.NavigationService.Navigate(new Uri("/SettingsPage.xaml",
      UriKind.Relative));
  }

  void AboutMenuItem_Click(object sender, EventArgs e)
  {
    this.NavigationService.Navigate(new Uri(
      "/Shared/About/AboutPage.xaml?appName=Weight Tracker", UriKind.Relative));
  }
  }
}
```

Notes:

→ Although the page's data context is set to the list of weigh-ins (leveraged by the first pivot item's editable list and the second pivot item's line series), this listing overrides the scatter series' items source to the list of goals at the end of OnNavigatedTo. (DataPointSeries is a common base class of the seven non-stacked series classes.)

→ This page only remembers the currently selected pivot item in page state rather than isolated storage. That's because when most users start a fresh instance, the first thing they probably want to do is record a new weigh-in.

→ At the end of UpdateProgress, each pie chart is given a simple two-number data source. The first number represents the amount of weight/time elapsed, and the second number represents the amount of weight/time remaining. This enables each pie chart to provide a visual representation of the percentages listed on the page.

→ To make the two date pickers filter the main chart, `GraphDatePicker_ValueChanged` sets the `Minimum` and `Maximum` properties on the chart's explicit X axis.

The Settings Page

The settings page, shown in Figure 29.5, enables users to view, add, and delete date-based weight goals exactly how they view, add, and delete weigh-ins on the main page. That's because it leverages the same `WeighInEditableList` user control. The page also contains a delete button for clearing all weigh-ins and all goals in bulk.

Because most of the functionality is provided by the `WeighInEditableList` user control, the implementation of the settings page is short and straightforward. Listing 29.3 contains its XAML and Listing 29.4 contains its codebehind. `WeighInEditableList`'s `IsGoalList` property being set to `true` is what makes a star appear next to each weight, rather than the up/down arrows seen on the main page.

FIGURE 29.5   The settings page enables editing a list of goal weights by hosting the same user control as the main page.

LISTING 29.3   `SettingsPage.xaml`—The User Interface for Weight Tracker's Settings Page

```
<phone:PhoneApplicationPage x:Class="WindowsPhoneApp.SettingsPage"
    xmlns="http://schemas.microsoft.com/winfx/2006/xaml/presentation"
    xmlns:x="http://schemas.microsoft.com/winfx/2006/xaml"
    xmlns:phone="clr-namespace:Microsoft.Phone.Controls;assembly=Microsoft.Phone"
    xmlns:shell="clr-namespace:Microsoft.Phone.Shell;assembly=Microsoft.Phone"
    xmlns:toolkit="clr-namespace:Microsoft.Phone.Controls;
➥assembly=Microsoft.Phone.Controls.Toolkit"
    xmlns:local="clr-namespace:WindowsPhoneApp"
    FontFamily="{StaticResource PhoneFontFamilyNormal}"
    FontSize="{StaticResource PhoneFontSizeNormal}"
    Foreground="{StaticResource PhoneForegroundBrush}"
    SupportedOrientations="PortraitOrLandscape" shell:SystemTray.IsVisible="True">
    <Grid>
```

LISTING 29.3   Continued

```xml
    <Grid.RowDefinitions>
      <RowDefinition Height="Auto"/>
      <RowDefinition Height="Auto"/>
      <RowDefinition Height="*"/>
      <RowDefinition Height="Auto"/>
    </Grid.RowDefinitions>

    <!-- The standard settings header -->
    <StackPanel Grid.Row="0" Style="{StaticResource PhoneTitlePanelStyle}">
      <TextBlock Text="SETTINGS" Style="{StaticResource PhoneTextTitle0Style}"/>
      <TextBlock Text="weight tracker"
                 Style="{StaticResource PhoneTextTitle1Style}"/>
    </StackPanel>

    <TextBlock Grid.Row="1" Margin="24,12,24,24"
               Text="Enter one or more weight goals."/>

    <!-- A translucent foreground-colored star image behind the list -->
    <Rectangle Grid.Row="2" Opacity=".2" Margin="0,0,0,12" Width="240"
               Height="240" VerticalAlignment="Bottom"
               Fill="{StaticResource PhoneForegroundBrush}">
      <Rectangle.OpacityMask>
        <ImageBrush ImageSource="Images/bigStar.png"/>
      </Rectangle.OpacityMask>
    </Rectangle>

    <!-- The editable list user control -->
    <local:WeighInEditableList Grid.Row="2" Collection="{Binding}"
                               IsGoalList="True" Margin="12,0"/>

    <!-- Delete button -->
    <Button x:Name="DeleteButton" Grid.Row="3" Content="delete all data"
            local:Tilt.IsEnabled="True" Click="DeleteButton_Click"/>
  </Grid>
</phone:PhoneApplicationPage>
```

LISTING 29.4   `SettingsPage.xaml.cs`—The Code-Behind for Weight Tracker's Settings Page

```csharp
using System.Windows;
using Microsoft.Phone.Controls;

namespace WindowsPhoneApp
{
  public partial class SettingsPage : PhoneApplicationPage
```

LISTING 29.4   Continued

```csharp
{
  public SettingsPage()
  {
    InitializeComponent();
    // This time, the data source for the editable list is the goal list
    this.DataContext = Settings.GoalList.Value;
  }

  void DeleteButton_Click(object sender, RoutedEventArgs e)
  {
    if (MessageBox.Show(
      "Are you sure you want to clear all your weigh-ins and goals?", "Delete",
      MessageBoxButton.OKCancel) == MessageBoxResult.OK)
    {
      Settings.GoalList.Value.Clear();
      Settings.WeighInList.Value.Clear();
    }
  }
}
}
```

The Finished Product

Deleting a weigh-in via the context menu

delete

Viewing the weigh-ins under the light theme

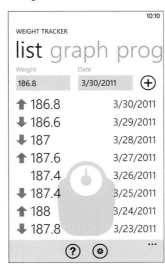

The progress section says FALLING BEHIND, ON TRACK, or AHEAD OF SCHEDULE! based on the relative progress of weight loss versus time.

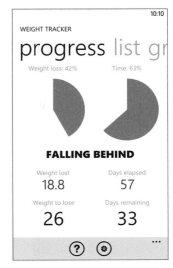

chapter 30 lessons

COWBELL

Cowbell is a simple musical instrument app. With it, you can tap the screen in any rhythm, and the app makes a cowbell noise with each tap. You can even play along with songs from your music library by switching to the Music + Videos hub, starting a song or playlist, and then switching back to Cowbell. The important aspect of Cowbell is that its sole purpose is to play sound effects.

Of all the musical instruments out there, why choose a cowbell? Many people find the idea of playing a cowbell entertaining thanks to a *Saturday Night Live* skit in 2000 with Will Ferrell and Christopher Walken. In it, Christopher Walken repeatedly asks for "more cowbell" while Will Ferrell plays it to Blue Öyster Cult's "(Don't Fear) The Reaper." With this song in your music library and this app on your phone, you can re-create the famous skit!

Playing Sound Effects

On Windows Phone, Silverlight has only one way to play audio and video: the MediaElement element. However, this element is too heavyweight for playing sound effects. When it plays, it stops any other media playback on the phone (e.g. music playing in the background from the Music + Videos hub). It can be okay to use for background music, and you must use it for playing inline video (the topic of Chapter 33, "Subservient Cat"), but do not use it for short or medium-length sounds. Instead, you should leverage XNA's support for playing sound effects. As you saw in Chapter 2, "Flashlight," Silverlight apps can use several APIs from XNA.

The relevant XNA class is called `SoundEffect`, and it lives in the `Microsoft.Xna.Framework.Audio` namespace. To use it, you must add a reference to the `Microsoft.Xna.Framework` assembly in your project. In this chapter, you'll see how to load a sound effect from an audio file and how to play it. The `SoundEffect` class provides additional richness, but the use of extra features is saved for the next chapter.

Using `MediaElement` **for sound effects could cause your app to fail marketplace certification!**

Because using `MediaElement` for sound effects results in the poor user experience of halting background media, Microsoft checks for this when certifying your app for the marketplace. If you use `MediaElement` for sound effects, your app will not be approved for publishing.

If you need sound effects for your app and are unable to make them yourself, here are a few good resources to check out:

→ The Freesound Project (freesound.org)

→ Partners in Rhyme (partnersinrhyme.com)

→ Soungle (soungle.com)

→ Sounddogs (sounddogs.com)

→ SoundLab, a pack of game-centric sounds from Microsoft (create.msdn.com/en-US/education/catalog/utility/soundlab)

The User Interface

Cowbell has a main page, an instructions page, and an about page. The latter two pages aren't interesting and therefore aren't shown in this chapter, but Listing 30.1 contains the XAML for the main page.

LISTING 30.1   `MainPage.xaml`—The User Interface for Cowbell's Main Page

```
<phone:PhoneApplicationPage
    x:Class="WindowsPhoneApp.MainPage"
    xmlns="http://schemas.microsoft.com/winfx/2006/xaml/presentation"
    xmlns:x="http://schemas.microsoft.com/winfx/2006/xaml"
    xmlns:phone="clr-namespace:Microsoft.Phone.Controls;assembly=Microsoft.Phone"
    xmlns:shell="clr-namespace:Microsoft.Phone.Shell;assembly=Microsoft.Phone"
    SupportedOrientations="Portrait">

  <!-- The application bar, with one button and one menu item -->
  <phone:PhoneApplicationPage.ApplicationBar>
    <shell:ApplicationBar Opacity=".5">
      <shell:ApplicationBarIconButton Text="instructions"
              IconUri="/Shared/Images/appbar.instructions.png"
              Click="InstructionsButton_Click"/>
    <shell:ApplicationBar.MenuItems>
```

LISTING 30.1   Continued

```
      <shell:ApplicationBarMenuItem Text="about" Click="AboutMenuItem_Click"/>
    </shell:ApplicationBar.MenuItems>
  </shell:ApplicationBar>
</phone:PhoneApplicationPage.ApplicationBar>

<!-- Just an image in a grid -->
<Grid Background="Black" MouseLeftButtonDown="Grid_MouseLeftButtonDown">
  <Image Source="Images/cowbell.png" Stretch="None"/>
</Grid>
</phone:PhoneApplicationPage>
```

This is a simple page with an application bar and a grid with a cowbell image that handles taps with its `MouseLeftButtonDown` handler. For the sake of the cowbell image that has white edges, the grid is given a hard-coded black background. Therefore, this page looks the same under both themes except for the half-opaque application bar, as seen in Figure 30.1.

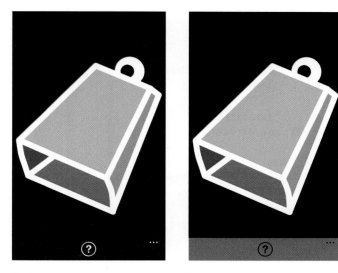

Dark theme   Light theme

FIGURE 30.1   The main page looks identical on both dark and light themes, except for the application bar.

The Code-Behind

Listing 30.2 contains the code-behind for the main page. This is where all the sound-effect logic resides.

LISTING 30.2   `MainPage.xaml.cs`—The Code-Behind for Cowbell's Main Page

```csharp
using System;
using System.Windows;
using System.Windows.Input;
using System.Windows.Media;
using System.Windows.Navigation;
using System.Windows.Resources;
using Microsoft.Phone.Controls;
using Microsoft.Phone.Shell;
using Microsoft.Xna.Framework.Audio; // For SoundEffect

namespace WindowsPhoneApp
{
  public partial class MainPage : PhoneApplicationPage
  {
    SoundEffect cowbell;

    public MainPage()
    {
      InitializeComponent();

      // Load the sound file
      StreamResourceInfo info = Application.GetResourceStream(
        new Uri("Audio/cowbell.wav", UriKind.Relative));

      // Create an XNA sound effect from the stream
      cowbell = SoundEffect.FromStream(info.Stream);

      // Subscribe to a per-frame callback
      CompositionTarget.Rendering += CompositionTarget_Rendering;

      // Required for XNA sound effects to work
      Microsoft.Xna.Framework.FrameworkDispatcher.Update();
    }

    protected override void OnNavigatedTo(NavigationEventArgs e)
    {
      base.OnNavigatedTo(e);

      // Don't let the screen auto-lock in the middle of a musical performance!
      PhoneApplicationService.Current.UserIdleDetectionMode =
        IdleDetectionMode.Disabled;
    }

    protected override void OnNavigatedFrom(NavigationEventArgs e)
```

LISTING 30.2   Continued

```
  {
    base.OnNavigatedFrom(e);

    // Restore the ability for the screen to auto-lock when on other pages
    PhoneApplicationService.Current.UserIdleDetectionMode =
      IdleDetectionMode.Enabled;
  }

  void Grid_MouseLeftButtonDown(object sender, MouseButtonEventArgs e)
  {
    // The screen was tapped, so play the sound
    cowbell.Play();
  }

  void CompositionTarget_Rendering(object sender, EventArgs e)
  {
    // Required for XNA sound effects to work.
    // Call this every frame.
    Microsoft.Xna.Framework.FrameworkDispatcher.Update();
  }

  // Application bar handlers

  void InstructionsButton_Click(object sender, EventArgs e)
  {
    this.NavigationService.Navigate(new Uri("/InstructionsPage.xaml",
      UriKind.Relative));
  }

  void AboutMenuItem_Click(object sender, EventArgs e)
  {
    this.NavigationService.Navigate(new Uri("/AboutPage.xaml",
      UriKind.Relative));
  }
  }
 }
}
```

Notes:

→ In the constructor, the stream for this app's .wav audio file is obtained with the static `Application.GetResourceStream` method. This method was first

The `SoundEffect.FromStream` method only works with PCM wave audio!

In other words, your audio files must be .wav files.

seen in Chapter 24, "Baby Name Eliminator." The cowbell.wav file is included in the project with a Build Action of Content, enabling the simple relative URI to be used. The stream is then sent to the static SoundEffect.FromStream method, which constructs an appropriate SoundEffect instance and returns it.

→ The use of the CompositionTarget.Rendering event is required for sound effects to work properly. This is explained in the following warning sidebar.

> **(!) When playing sound effects with XNA, you must continually call** Update **on XNA's framework dispatcher!**
>
> XNA's sound effect functionality, like some other functionality in XNA, only works if you frequently (as in several times a second) call the static FrameworkDispatcher.Update method from the Microsoft.Xna.Framework namespace. This is natural to do from XNA apps, because they are designed around a game loop that runs code every frame. (XNA even provides a base Game class that automatically does this, so developers don't have to.) From Silverlight apps, however, which are inherently event-based, you must go out of your way to run code on a regular schedule.
>
> To call FrameworkDispatcher.Update regularly, you could use a DispatcherTimer, as done in previous chapters. You could even use a plain System.Threading.Timer (introduced in Chapter 2) because FrameworkDispatcher.Update can be called from any thread.
>
> However, my preferred approach is to use an event Silverlight raises before every single frame is rendered. The event is called Rendering, and it is exposed on a static class called CompositionTarget. This event is useful for doing custom animations that can't easily be represented with Silverlight's animation classes from Part II, "Transforms & Animations," of this book, such as physics-based movement. In Cowbell, the event is perfect for calling FrameworkDispatcher.Update with the roughly the same frequency that an XNA app would call it. Note that the first call to FrameworkDispatcher.Update is in the page's constructor because it takes a bit of time for the first Rendering event to be raised.
>
> If you call Play without previously calling FrameworkDispatcher.Update within a short time span, an InvalidOperationException is thrown with the following helpful message:
>
> ```
> FrameworkDispatcher.Update has not been called. Regular FrameworkDispatcher.
> Update calls are necessary for fire and forget sound effects and framework
> events to function correctly. See http://go.microsoft.com/fwlink/?LinkId=193853
> for details.
> ```

→ The code in OnNavigatedTo and OnNavigatedFrom exists to ensure that the screen doesn't auto-lock. If the cowbell player has a long break during a performance, it would be very annoying if the screen automatically locked. And tapping the screen to keep it active isn't a good option, because that would make an unwanted cowbell noise!

→ The sound effect is played with a simple call to SoundEffect.Play in Grid_MouseLeftButtonDown. If Play is called before the sound effect finishes playing from a previous call, the sounds overlap.

The Audio Transport Controls

• • •

When the phone's media player plays music, this music continues playing while apps run. Users can pause, rewind, fast forward, or change songs via the 93-pixel tall top overlay that appears on top of any app when the hardware volume buttons are pressed. This functionality works great with a fun instrument app such as Cowbell. In the next release of the Windows Phone OS, due by the end of 2011, third-party apps will be able to play music in the background just like the built-in media player.

The Finished Product

The volume and audio transport controls, visible while the media player is active and the volume hardware buttons are pressed

The expanded application bar and menu

The instructions page, whose code is included with this chapter's project

chapter 31 lessons

 Sound Manipulation

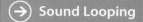 Sound Looping

SoundEffectInstance

TROMBONE

Trombone is a much more sophisticated musical instrument app than the preceding chapter's Cowbell app. You can move the slide up and down to different positions to play any note. (Other than starting at F, the slide positions bear little resemblance to real trombone slide positions!) This app supports two different sliding modes. If you use the left side of the screen, you can freely move the slide. If you use the right side of the screen, the slide snaps to the closest note line. Besides being an easier way to play this instrument, this means you could also use this app as a pitch pipe.

This trombone can play its notes in two octaves; to raise the sound by an octave, place a second finger anywhere on the screen. The most fun part about this app is that, like with a real trombone, you must actually blow on your phone to produce sound!

These last two app features require phone features discussed in later chapters (multi-touch and using the microphone) so that portion of the code is not explained in this chapter. Instead, the focus is on manipulating a single sound effect's pitch and duration to create all the audio needed by this app.

The User Interface

Trombone has a main page, an instructions page, and a settings page. The code for the settings page is not shown in this chapter because, except for its page title, it is identical to the settings page shown in Chapter 34, "Bubble

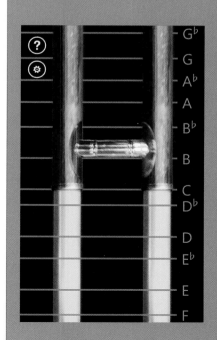

Blower." It enables the user to calibrate the microphone in case producing sounds is too hard or too easy. The code for the instructions page is not shown either because it's not interesting.

The main page, pictured in Figure 31.1 in its initial state, contains the moveable trombone slide, note guide lines, and buttons that link to the other two pages. Listing 31.1 contains the XAML.

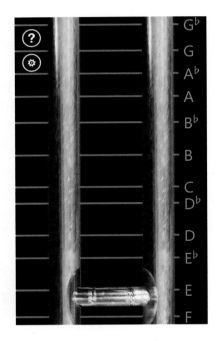

FIGURE 31.1   The main page simulates the appearance of a real trombone.

LISTING 31.1   MainPage.xaml—The User Interface for Trombone's Main Page

```xaml
<phone:PhoneApplicationPage x:Class="WindowsPhoneApp.MainPage"
    xmlns="http://schemas.microsoft.com/winfx/2006/xaml/presentation"
    xmlns:x="http://schemas.microsoft.com/winfx/2006/xaml"
    xmlns:phone="clr-namespace:Microsoft.Phone.Controls;assembly=Microsoft.Phone"
    SupportedOrientations="Portrait">
  <Canvas x:Name="LayoutRoot">

    <!-- The stationary inner slide -->
    <Image Canvas.Left="72" Source="Images/innerSlide.png"/>
    <!-- The moveable outer slide -->
    <Image x:Name="SlideImage" Canvas.Left="72" Canvas.ZIndex="1"
           Source="Images/outerSlide.png"/>
```

LISTING 31.1 Continued

```xml
      <!-- An instructions button -->
      <Rectangle Canvas.Left="18" Canvas.Top="30" Canvas.ZIndex="1"
               Width="48" Height="48" Fill="{StaticResource PhoneForegroundBrush}"
               MouseLeftButtonUp="InstructionsButton_Click">
        <Rectangle.OpacityMask>
          <ImageBrush ImageSource="/Shared/Images/normal.instructions.png"/>
        </Rectangle.OpacityMask>
      </Rectangle>

      <!-- A settings button -->
      <Rectangle Canvas.Left="18" Canvas.Top="94" Canvas.ZIndex="1"
               Width="48" Height="48" Fill="{StaticResource PhoneForegroundBrush}"
               MouseLeftButtonUp="SettingsButton_Click">
        <Rectangle.OpacityMask>
          <ImageBrush ImageSource="/Shared/Images/normal.settings.png"/>
        </Rectangle.OpacityMask>
      </Rectangle>
    </Canvas>
</phone:PhoneApplicationPage>
```

Notes:

→ The note guide lines pictured in Figure 31.1 are added in this page's code-behind.

→ An application bar would get in the way of this user interface, so two rectangles acting as buttons are used instead. They use the familiar opacity mask trick to ensure they appear as expected for any theme.

→ The trombone slide consists of two images, one on top of the other. These two images are shown in Figure 31.2.

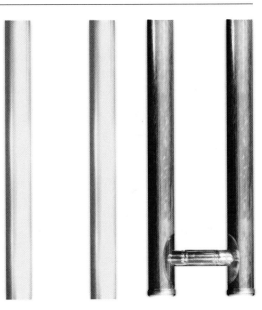

The inner slide   The outer slide

FIGURE 31.2   The slide consists of a moving image on top of a stationary image.

The Code-Behind

Listing 31.2 contains the code-behind for the main page.

LISTING 31.2   `MainPage.xaml.cs`—The Code-Behind for Trombone's Main Page

```csharp
using System;
using System.Linq;
using System.Windows;
using System.Windows.Controls;
using System.Windows.Input;
using System.Windows.Media;
using System.Windows.Navigation;
using System.Windows.Resources;
using System.Windows.Shapes;
using Microsoft.Phone.Controls;
using Microsoft.Xna.Framework.Audio; // For SoundEffect

namespace WindowsPhoneApp
{
  public partial class MainPage : PhoneApplicationPage
  {
    // The single sound effect instance
    SoundEffectInstance soundEffectInstance;

    string[] notes = { "G♭", "G",   "A♭", "A",   "B♭", "B",
                       "C",  "D♭", "D",   "E♭", "E",  "F" };

    // The relative distance of each note's pitch,
    // where 0 is the initial F and -1 is one octave lower
    double[] pitches = { -.9 /*G♭*/, -.82 /*G*/, -.75 /*A♭*/, -.68 /*A*/,
                         -.6 /*B♭*/, -.5 /*B*/, -.4 /*C*/, -.35 /*D♭*/,
                         -.25 /*D*/, -.18 /*E♭*/, -.08 /*E*/, 0 /*F*/ };

    // For microphone processing
    byte[] buffer;
    int currentVolume;

    // For several calculations
    const int TOP_NOTE_POSITION = 20;
    const int BOTTOM_NOTE_POSITION = 780;
    const int OCTAVE_RANGE = 844;

    public MainPage()
    {
      InitializeComponent();

      // Load the single sound file used by this app: the sound of F
      StreamResourceInfo info = App.GetResourceStream(
        new Uri("Audio/F.wav", UriKind.Relative));
```

LISTING 31.2   Continued

```
SoundEffect effect = SoundEffect.FromStream(info.Stream);

// Enables manipulation of the sound effect while it plays
this.soundEffectInstance = effect.CreateInstance();

// The source .wav file has a loop region, so exploit it
this.soundEffectInstance.IsLooped = true;

// Add each of the note guide lines
for (int i = 0; i < this.pitches.Length; i++)
{
  double position = BOTTOM_NOTE_POSITION + this.pitches[i] * OCTAVE_RANGE;

  // Add a line at the right position
  Line line = new Line { X2 = 410,
    Stroke = Application.Current.Resources["PhoneAccentBrush"] as Brush,
    StrokeThickness = 5, Opacity = .8 };
  Canvas.SetTop(line, position);
  this.LayoutRoot.Children.Add(line);

  // Add the note label next to the line
  TextBlock label = new TextBlock {
    Text = this.notes[i][0].ToString(), // Ignore the ♭, use 0th char only
    Foreground = Application.Current.Resources["PhoneAccentBrush"] as Brush,
    FontSize = 40 };
  Canvas.SetLeft(label, line.X2 + 12);
  Canvas.SetTop(label, position - 20);
  this.LayoutRoot.Children.Add(label);

  // Add the ♭ separately, simulating a superscript so it looks better
  if (this.notes[i].EndsWith("♭"))
  {
    TextBlock flat = new TextBlock { Text = "♭", FontSize = 25,
      FontWeight = FontWeights.Bold, Foreground =
      Application.Current.Resources["PhoneAccentBrush"] as Brush };
    Canvas.SetLeft(flat, line.X2 + label.ActualWidth + 6);
    Canvas.SetTop(flat, position - 21);
    this.LayoutRoot.Children.Add(flat);
  }
}

// Configure the microphone
Microphone.Default.BufferDuration = TimeSpan.FromSeconds(.1);
Microphone.Default.BufferReady += Microphone_BufferReady;
```

LISTING 31.2   Continued

```
    // Initialize the buffer for holding microphone data
    int size = Microphone.Default.GetSampleSizeInBytes(
      Microphone.Default.BufferDuration);
    buffer = new byte[size];

    // Start listening
    Microphone.Default.Start();

    CompositionTarget.Rendering += delegate(object sender, EventArgs e)
    {
      // Required for XNA Sound Effect API to work
      Microsoft.Xna.Framework.FrameworkDispatcher.Update();

      // Play the sound whenever the blowing into the microphone is loud enough
      if (this.currentVolume > Settings.VolumeThreshold.Value)
      {
        if (soundEffectInstance.State != SoundState.Playing)
          soundEffectInstance.Play();
      }
      else if (soundEffectInstance.State == SoundState.Playing)
      {
        // Rather than stopping immediately, the "false" makes the sound break
        // out of the loop region and play the remainder
        soundEffectInstance.Stop(false);
      }
    };

    // Call also once at the beginning
    Microsoft.Xna.Framework.FrameworkDispatcher.Update();
  }

  protected override void OnNavigatedTo(NavigationEventArgs e)
  {
    base.OnNavigatedTo(e);

    // Subscribe to the touch/multi-touch event.
    // This is application-wide, so only do this when on this page.
    Touch.FrameReported += Touch_FrameReported;
  }

  protected override void OnNavigatedFrom(NavigationEventArgs e)
  {
    base.OnNavigatedFrom(e);
```

LISTING 31.2   Continued

```
    // Unsubscribe from this application-wide event
    Touch.FrameReported -= Touch_FrameReported;
}

void Touch_FrameReported(object sender, TouchFrameEventArgs e)
{
  TouchPoint touchPoint = e.GetPrimaryTouchPoint(this);

  if (touchPoint != null)
  {
    // Get the Y position of the primary finger
    double position = touchPoint.Position.Y;

    // If the finger is on the right side of the screen, snap to the
    // closest note
    if (touchPoint.Position.X > this.ActualWidth / 2)
    {
      // Search for the current offset, expressed as a negative value from
      // 0-1, in the pitches array.
      double percentage = (-BOTTOM_NOTE_POSITION + position) / OCTAVE_RANGE;
      int index = Array.BinarySearch<double>(this.pitches, percentage);
      if (index < 0)
      {
        // An exact match wasn't found (which should almost always be the
        // case), so BinarySearch has returned a negative number that is the
        // bitwise complement of the index of the next value that is larger
        // than percentage (or the array length if there's no larger value).
        index = ~index;

        if (index < this.pitches.Length)
        {
          // Don't always use the index of the larger value. Also check the
          // closest smallest value (if there is one) and snap to it instead
          // if it's closer to the current value.
          if (index > 0 &&
              Math.Abs(percentage - this.pitches[index]) >
              Math.Abs(percentage - this.pitches[index - 1]))
              index--;

          // Snap the position to the new location, expressed in pixels
          position = BOTTOM_NOTE_POSITION +
                      this.pitches[index] * OCTAVE_RANGE;
        }
```

LISTING 31.2   Continued

```
      }
    }

    // Place the outer slide to match the finger position or snapped position
    Canvas.SetTop(this.SlideImage, position - this.ActualHeight - 40);

    // See how many fingers are in contact with the screen
    int numPoints =
      (from p in e.GetTouchPoints(this)
       where
         p.Action != TouchAction.Up
       select p).Count();

    // 1 represents one octave higher (-1 represents one octave lower)
    int startingPitch = (numPoints > 1) ? 1 : 0;

    // Express the position as a delta from the bottom position, and
    // clamp it to the valid range. This gives a little margin on both
    // ends of the screen because it can be difficult for the user to move
    // the slide all the way to either end.
    double offset = BOTTOM_NOTE_POSITION -
      Math.Max(TOP_NOTE_POSITION, Math.Min(BOTTOM_NOTE_POSITION,
      touchPoint.Position.Y));

    // Whether it's currently playing or not, change the sound's pitch based
    // on the current slide position and whether the octave has been raised
    this.soundEffectInstance.Pitch =
      (float)(startingPitch - (offset / OCTAVE_RANGE));
  }

}

void Microphone_BufferReady(object sender, EventArgs e)
{
  int size = Microphone.Default.GetData(buffer);
  if (size > 0)
    this.currentVolume = GetAverageVolume(size);
}

// Returns the average value among all the values in the buffer
int GetAverageVolume(int numBytes)
{
  long total = 0;
```

LISTING 31.2   Continued

```csharp
      // Although buffer is an array of bytes, we want to examine each
      // 2-byte value.
      // [SampleDuration for 1 sec (32000) / SampleRate (16000) = 2 bytes]
      // Therefore, we iterate through the array 2 bytes at a time.
      for (int i = 0; i < numBytes; i += 2)
      {
        // Cast from short to int to prevent -32768 from overflowing Math.Abs:
        int value = Math.Abs((int)BitConverter.ToInt16(buffer, i));
        total += value;
      }
      return (int)(total / (numBytes / 2));
    }


    // Button handlers

    void SettingsButton_Click(object sender, MouseButtonEventArgs e)
    {
      this.NavigationService.Navigate(
        new Uri("/SettingsPage.xaml", UriKind.Relative));
    }

    void InstructionsButton_Click(object sender, MouseButtonEventArgs e)
    {
      this.NavigationService.Navigate(
        new Uri("/InstructionsPage.xaml", UriKind.Relative));
    }
  }
}
```

Notes:

→ The single sound file used by this app is a recording of an F being played on a trombone. The different notes are created by dynamically altering the pitch of the F as it plays.

→ Rather than directly use the SoundEffect object, as in the preceding chapter, this app calls its CreateInstance method to get a SoundEffect**Instance** object. SoundEffectInstance provides a few more features compared to SoundEffect and, because it is tied to a single instance of the sound, it enables manipulation of the sound after it has already started to play. Trombone requires SoundEffectInstance for its looping behavior and its ability to modify the pitch of an already-playing sound.

→ SoundEffectInstance exposes an IsLooped property (false by default) that enables you to loop the audio indefinitely until Stop is called. This can behave in one of two ways, depending on the source audio file:

> → For a plain audio file, the looping applies to the entire duration, so the sound will seamlessly restart from the beginning each time it reaches the end.
>
> → For an audio file with a *loop region*, the sound will play from the beginning the first time through, but then *only the loop region* will loop indefinitely. Calling the default overload of Stop stops the sound immediately, but calling an overload and passing false for its immediate parameter *finishes the current iteration of the loop*, and then breaks out of the loop and plays the remainder of the sound.

Figure 31.3 demonstrates these two different behaviors. The latter behavior is perfect for this app, because it enables a realistic-sounding trombone note of any length, complete with a beginning and end that makes a smooth transition to and from silence. Therefore, the F.wav sound file included with this app defines a loop region. Although the sound file is less than a third of a second long, the loop region enables it to last for as long as the user can sustain his or her blowing.

> **Be careful about the length of your loop region!**
>
> If you don't want to stop a sound immediately, but want it to gracefully stop fairly quickly with Stop(false) as with this app's sound effect, your loop region (and remainder of the sound) must be very short. Otherwise, the process of finishing the current loop iteration could be too time-consuming.

> Wavosaur (www.wavosaur.com) is a free and very powerful sound editor that enables you to create a loop region inside a .wav file. Simply highlight a region of the sound; then select Tools, Loop, Create loop points. The exported .wav file will still play straight through under normal circumstances, but playing it with SoundEffectInstance and IsLooped set to true will leverage your custom loop region.

SoundEffect versus SoundEffectInstance

Whereas SoundEffect only enables you to *play* sounds, SoundEffectInstance enables you to pause/resume/stop the particular sound instance with its Pause, Resume, and Stop methods. Whereas each call to SoundEffect's Play method starts playing a fresh instance of the sound that can't be stopped (and may overlap sounds from earlier calls), a call to SoundEffectInstance's Play method does nothing if that instance of the sound is currently playing. Because SoundEffectInstance is tied to a specific sound instance, it is also able to expose a State property that reveals whether the sound is playing, paused, or stopped.

In addition to the IsLooped property, SoundEffectInstance exposes three properties for controlling the resulting sound. These can be set at any time, even in the middle of playback:

> → **Volume** (default=1)—A value from 0 (muted) to 1 (full volume).
>
> → **Pitch** (default=0)—A value from –1 (one octave lower) to 1 (one octave higher). A value of 0 plays the sound at its natural pitch.

➔ **Pan** (default=0)—A value from –1 (all the way to the left speaker) to 1 (all the way to the right speaker). A value of 0 centers the sound.

SoundEffect also enables controlling these three values with a Play overload that accepts volume, pitch, and pan parameters. However, these values always apply for the duration of the sound. (SoundEffect's parameterless Play method, used in the preceding chapter, uses a volume of 1 and a pitch and pan of 0.)

SoundEffectInstance also exposes two overloads of an Apply3D method that enables you to apply 3D positioning to the sound playback. This feature is most interesting for Xbox and PC games. For phones, 3D positioning (and even custom pan values) is likely to be overkill.

Regular Sound File

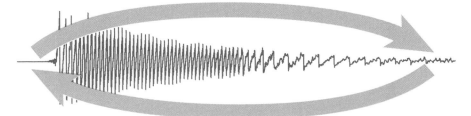

Repeat from beginning to end

Sound File with a Looping Region

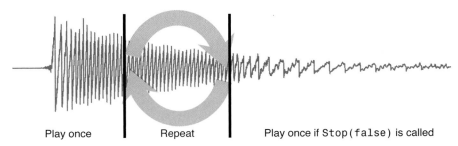

Play once   Repeat   Play once if Stop(false) is called

FIGURE 31.3   Options for looping with SoundEffectInstance.IsLooped set to true.

➔ In the CompositionTarget.Rendering event handler, the current volume from the microphone is continually compared against a threshold setting (adjustable on the settings page). If it's loud enough and the sound isn't already playing, Play is called. (The State check isn't strictly necessary because, unlike SoundEffect.Play, SoundEffectInstance.Play does nothing if the sound is already playing.) If the sound is playing and the volume is no longer loud enough, then Stop(false) is called to break out of the loop and play the end of the sound.

→ Inside `Touch_FrameReported`, which detects where the primary finger is in contact with the screen and whether a second finger is touching the screen (as discussed in Part VII, "Touch and Multi-Touch"), the sound's pitch is adjusted. The `startingPitch` variable tracks which octave the base F note is in (0 for the natural octave or 1 for an octave higher); then the distance that the finger is from the bottom of the screen determines how much lower the pitch is adjusted. As you can see from the values in the `pitches` array at

> **Can I make my audio heard when the phone's master volume is muted, or can I play audio louder than the master volume level?**
>
> No, the user is empowered to choose the maximum volume level for any sound that could be made by their phone. The 0–1 volume level of a sound effect is relative to the master volume. Note that `SoundEffect` exposes a static `MasterVolume` property that enables you to simultaneously adjust the volume of all your sounds (whether played from `SoundEffect` or `SoundEffectInstance`), but this does not enable you to get any louder than the user's chosen volume level.

the beginning of the listing, a D is produced by lowering the pitch of the F by 25% (producing a value of -.25 or .75 depending on the octave), and a B is produced by lowering the pitch of the F by half (producing a value of -.5 or .5 depending on the octave).

The Finished Product

Playing an E

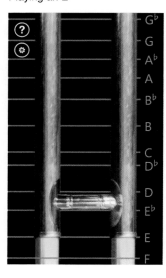

Playing under the light theme and purple accent color

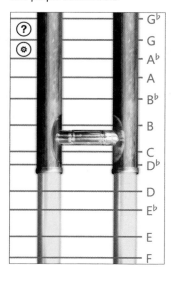

The settings page for adjusting microphone sensitivity

LOCAL FM RADIO

Local FM Radio provides a unique interface to your phone's built-in FM radio tuner. Unlike the built-in radio app in the Music + Videos hub, this app enables you to directly type the frequency of your desired station. It also shows your current signal strength, which is an interesting little validation of any static you might be experiencing.

The purpose of this app is to demonstrate the phone's simple but limited radio tuner API: the `FMRadio` class in the `Microsoft.Devices.Radio` namespace. Although the functionality exposed is very minimal, it comes with some nice perks, such as automatic integration into the Music + Video hub's history/now playing lists.

> This app requires access to the phone's media library (the `ID_CAP_MEDIALIB` capability). Without this capability, an app could still display some basic information about the phone's radio tuner, but attempting to start the radio would throw a `RadioDisabledException`.

The User Interface

As you can see from the screenshot to the right, this app's user interface is a cross between Tip Calculator and Alarm Clock. Listing 32.1 contains the XAML for this app's one and only page.

LISTING 32.1   MainPage.xaml—The User Interface for Local FM Radio

```
<phone:PhoneApplicationPage
    x:Class="WindowsPhoneApp.MainPage" x:Name="Page"
    xmlns="http://schemas.microsoft.com/winfx/2006/xaml/presentation"
    xmlns:x="http://schemas.microsoft.com/winfx/2006/xaml"
    xmlns:phone="clr-namespace:Microsoft.Phone.Controls;assembly=Microsoft.Phone"
    xmlns:shell="clr-namespace:Microsoft.Phone.Shell;assembly=Microsoft.Phone"
    xmlns:local="clr-namespace:WindowsPhoneApp"
    FontFamily="{StaticResource PhoneFontFamilyNormal}"
    FontSize="{StaticResource PhoneFontSizeNormal}"
    Foreground="{StaticResource PhoneForegroundBrush}"
    SupportedOrientations="Portrait" shell:SystemTray.IsVisible="True">

  <phone:PhoneApplicationPage.Resources>
    <!-- Style for calculator buttons -->
    <Style x:Key="CalculatorButtonStyle" TargetType="Button">
      <Setter Property="FontSize" Value="36"/>
      <Setter Property="FontFamily"
              Value="{StaticResource PhoneFontFamilySemiLight}"/>
      <Setter Property="BorderThickness" Value="0"/>
      <Setter Property="Width" Value="132"/>
      <Setter Property="Height" Value="108"/>
    </Style>
  </phone:PhoneApplicationPage.Resources>

  <StackPanel Style="{StaticResource PhoneTitlePanelStyle}">
    <TextBlock Text="FM RADIO"
                 Style="{StaticResource PhoneTextTitle0Style}"/>

    <!-- A user control much like the time display from Alarm Clock -->
    <local:FrequencyDisplay x:Name="FrequencyDisplay" Margin="0,48"
                            HorizontalAlignment="Center" FontSize="220"/>

    <!-- The same calculator buttons from Tip Calculator, but with a
         power button instead of a 00 button -->
    <Canvas x:Name="ButtonPanel" Height="396" Margin="-24,0">
      <Button Style="{StaticResource CalculatorButtonStyle}"
              Background="{Binding CalculatorMainBrush, ElementName=Page}"
              Content="7" Canvas.Left="-6" Canvas.Top="-1"/>
      <Button Style="{StaticResource CalculatorButtonStyle}"
              Background="{Binding CalculatorMainBrush, ElementName=Page}"
              Content="8" Canvas.Left="114" Canvas.Top="-1"/>
      <Button Style="{StaticResource CalculatorButtonStyle}"
              Background="{Binding CalculatorMainBrush, ElementName=Page}"
              Content="9" Canvas.Left="234" Canvas.Top="-1"/>
```

LISTING 32.1 Continued

```xml
    <Button Style="{StaticResource CalculatorButtonStyle}"
            Background="{Binding CalculatorMainBrush, ElementName=Page}"
            Content="4" Canvas.Top="95" Canvas.Left="-6"/>
    <Button Style="{StaticResource CalculatorButtonStyle}"
            Background="{Binding CalculatorMainBrush, ElementName=Page}"
            Content="5" Canvas.Top="95" Canvas.Left="114"/>
    <Button Style="{StaticResource CalculatorButtonStyle}"
            Background="{Binding CalculatorMainBrush, ElementName=Page}"
            Content="6" Canvas.Top="95" Canvas.Left="234"/>
    <Button Style="{StaticResource CalculatorButtonStyle}"
            Background="{Binding CalculatorMainBrush, ElementName=Page}"
            Content="1" Canvas.Top="191" Canvas.Left="-6"/>
    <Button Style="{StaticResource CalculatorButtonStyle}"
            Background="{Binding CalculatorMainBrush, ElementName=Page}"
            Content="2" Canvas.Top="191" Canvas.Left="114"/>
    <Button Style="{StaticResource CalculatorButtonStyle}"
            Background="{Binding CalculatorMainBrush, ElementName=Page}"
            Content="3" Canvas.Top="191" Canvas.Left="234"/>
    <Button Style="{StaticResource CalculatorButtonStyle}"
            Background="{Binding CalculatorMainBrush, ElementName=Page}"
            Content="0" Canvas.Top="287" Canvas.Left="-6"/>
    <Button Style="{StaticResource CalculatorButtonStyle}"
            Background="{Binding CalculatorMainBrush, ElementName=Page}"
            Content="power" Width="252" Canvas.Top="287" Canvas.Left="114"/>
    <Button Style="{StaticResource CalculatorButtonStyle}" FontSize="32"
            FontFamily="{StaticResource PhoneFontFamilySemiBold}"
            Background="{Binding CalculatorSecondaryBrush, ElementName=Page}"
            Content="C" Height="204" Canvas.Top="-1" Canvas.Left="354"/>
    <Button x:Name="BackspaceButton" Height="204"
            Style="{StaticResource CalculatorButtonStyle}"
            Background="{Binding CalculatorSecondaryBrush, ElementName=Page}"
            Canvas.Top="191" Canvas.Left="354">
      <!-- The "X in an arrow" backspace drawing -->
      <Canvas Width="48" Height="32">
        <Path x:Name="BackspaceXPath" Data="M24,8 39,24 M39,8 24,24"
              Stroke="{StaticResource PhoneForegroundBrush}"
              StrokeThickness="4"/>
        <Path x:Name="BackspaceBorderPath" StrokeThickness="2"
              Data="M16,0 47,0 47,31 16,31 0,16.5z"
              Stroke="{StaticResource PhoneForegroundBrush}"/>
      </Canvas>
    </Button>
  </Canvas>
```

LISTING 32.1   Continued

```
      <!-- A signal strength display -->
      <TextBlock x:Name="SignalStrengthTextBlock" Margin="24"
                 HorizontalAlignment="Center" />
    </StackPanel>
</phone:PhoneApplicationPage>
```

Notes:

→ The button style in the page's resources collection and the corresponding canvas with buttons is exactly like the XAML from Chapter 10's Tip Calculator, except that the double-zero button has been replaced with a power button.

→ The frequency display with the custom seven-segment font is implemented with a `FrequencyDisplay` user control. It is almost identical to—but simpler than—the `TimeDisplay` user control in Chapter 20, "Alarm Clock." It is not shown in this chapter, but you can view it with this app's source code.

The Code-Behind

Listing 32.2 contains the code-behind for Local FM Radio.

LISTING 32.2   `MainPage.xaml.cs`—The Code-Behind for Local FM Radio

```
using System;
using System.Windows;
using System.Windows.Controls;
using System.Windows.Input;
using System.Windows.Media;
using System.Windows.Threading;
using Microsoft.Devices.Radio;
using Microsoft.Phone.Controls;

namespace WindowsPhoneApp
{
  public partial class MainPage : PhoneApplicationPage
  {
    double frequency;
    DateTime? lastDigitButtonTap;

    // Two theme-specific custom brushes
    public Brush CalculatorMainBrush { get; set; }
    public Brush CalculatorSecondaryBrush { get; set; }

    public MainPage()
```

LISTING 32.2   Continued

```
{
  InitializeComponent();

  // Ensure the radio is on
  StartRadio();

  // Work around having no radio events by polling
  DispatcherTimer timer = new DispatcherTimer {
    Interval = TimeSpan.FromSeconds(2) };
  timer.Tick += delegate(object sender, EventArgs e) {
    // Update the signal strength every two seconds
    this.SignalStrengthTextBlock.Text = "signal strength: " +
        (FMRadio.Instance.SignalStrength * 100).ToString("##0");
  };
  timer.Start();

  // A single handler for all calculator button taps
  this.ButtonPanel.AddHandler(Button.MouseLeftButtonUpEvent,
    new MouseButtonEventHandler(CalculatorButton_MouseLeftButtonUp),
    true /* handledEventsToo */);

  // Handlers to ensure that the backspace button's vector content changes
  // color appropriately when the button is pressed
  this.BackspaceButton.AddHandler(Button.MouseLeftButtonDownEvent,
    new MouseButtonEventHandler(BackspaceButton_MouseLeftButtonDown),
    true /* handledEventsToo */);
  this.BackspaceButton.AddHandler(Button.MouseLeftButtonUpEvent,
    new MouseButtonEventHandler(BackspaceButton_MouseLeftButtonUp),
    true /* handledEventsToo */);
  this.BackspaceButton.MouseMove += BackspaceButton_MouseMove;

  // Set the colors of the two custom brushes based on whether
  // we're in the light theme or dark theme
  if ((Visibility)Application.Current.Resources["PhoneLightThemeVisibility"]
                  == Visibility.Visible)
  {
    this.CalculatorMainBrush = new SolidColorBrush(
                              Color.FromArgb(0xFF, 0xEF, 0xEF, 0xEF));
    this.CalculatorSecondaryBrush = new SolidColorBrush(
                              Color.FromArgb(0xFF, 0xDE, 0xDF, 0xDE));
  }
  else
  {
```

LISTING 32.2   Continued

```
      this.CalculatorMainBrush = new SolidColorBrush(
                               Color.FromArgb(0xFF, 0x18, 0x1C, 0x18));
      this.CalculatorSecondaryBrush = new SolidColorBrush(
                               Color.FromArgb(0xFF, 0x31, 0x30, 0x31));
    }

    // Grab the current frequency from the device's radio
    this.frequency = FMRadio.Instance.Frequency;
    UpdateFrequencyDisplay();
  }

  void StartRadio()
  {
    try
    {
      // This would throw a RadioDisabledException if the app weren't given
      // the ID_CAP_MEDIALIB capability, but we're worried instead about an
      // UnauthorizedAccessException thrown when the phone is connected to Zune
      FMRadio.Instance.PowerMode = RadioPowerMode.On;
    }
    catch
    {
      // Show a message explaining the limitation while connected to Zune
      MessageBox.Show("Be sure that your phone is disconnected from your " +
        "computer.", "Cannot turn radio on", MessageBoxButton.OK);
      return;
    }

    if (FMRadio.Instance.SignalStrength == 0)
    {
      // Show a message similar to the built-in radio app
      MessageBox.Show("This phone uses your headphones as an FM radio " +
        "antenna. To listen to radio, connect your headphones.", "No antenna",
        MessageBoxButton.OK);
    }
  }

  void StopRadio()
  {
    try { FMRadio.Instance.PowerMode = RadioPowerMode.Off; }
    catch {} // Ignore exception from being connected to Zune
  }

  // A single handler for all calculator button taps
```

LISTING 32.2   Continued

```csharp
void CalculatorButton_MouseLeftButtonUp(object sender, MouseButtonEventArgs e)
{
  // Although sender is the canvas, the OriginalSource is the tapped button
  Button button = e.OriginalSource as Button;
  if (button == null)
    return;

  string content = button.Content.ToString();

  // Determine what to do based on the string content of the tapped button
  double digit;
  if (content == "power")
  {
    if (FMRadio.Instance.PowerMode == RadioPowerMode.On)
      StopRadio();
    else
      StartRadio();
  }
  else if (double.TryParse(content, out digit)) // double so division works
  {
    // If there are already four digits (including the decimal place), or if
    // the user hasn't recently typed digits, clear the frequency first
    if (this.frequency > 100 || this.lastDigitButtonTap == null ||
        DateTime.Now - this.lastDigitButtonTap > TimeSpan.FromSeconds(3))
      this.frequency = 0;

    // Append the digit
    this.frequency *= 10;
    this.frequency += digit / 10;

    this.lastDigitButtonTap = DateTime.Now;
  }
  else if (content == "C")
  {
    // Clear the frequency
    this.frequency = 0;
  }
  else // The backspace button
  {
    // Chop off the last digit (the decimal place) with a cast
    int temp = (int)this.frequency;
    // Shift right by 1 place
    this.frequency = (double)temp / 10;
  }
```

LISTING 32.2   Continued

```csharp
      UpdateFrequencyDisplay();
  }

  void UpdateFrequencyDisplay()
  {
    try
    {
      this.FrequencyDisplay.Foreground =
        Application.Current.Resources["PhoneAccentBrush"] as Brush;

      // Update the display
      this.FrequencyDisplay.Frequency = this.frequency;
      // Update the radio
      FMRadio.Instance.Frequency = this.frequency;
    }
    catch
    {
      if (FMRadio.Instance.PowerMode == RadioPowerMode.On)
      {
        // Caused by an invalid frequency value, which easily
        // happens while typing a valid frequency
        this.FrequencyDisplay.Foreground = new SolidColorBrush(Colors.Red);
      }
    }
  }

  // Change the color of the two paths inside the backspace button when pressed
  void BackspaceButton_MouseLeftButtonDown(object sender, MouseButtonEventArgs e)
  {
    this.BackspaceXPath.Stroke =
      Application.Current.Resources["PhoneBackgroundBrush"] as Brush;
    this.BackspaceBorderPath.Stroke =
      Application.Current.Resources["PhoneBackgroundBrush"] as Brush;
  }

  // Change the color of the two paths back when no longer pressed
  void BackspaceButton_MouseLeftButtonUp(object sender, MouseEventArgs e)
  {
    this.BackspaceXPath.Stroke =
      Application.Current.Resources["PhoneForegroundBrush"] as Brush;
    this.BackspaceBorderPath.Stroke =
      Application.Current.Resources["PhoneForegroundBrush"] as Brush;
  }
```

LISTING 32.2   Continued

```
// Workaround for when the finger has not yet been released but the color
// needs to change back because the finger is no longer over the button
void BackspaceButton_MouseMove(object sender, MouseEventArgs e)
{
  // this.BackspaceButton.IsMouseOver lies when it has captured the mouse!
  // Use GetPosition instead:
  Point relativePoint = e.GetPosition(this.BackspaceButton);
  // We can get away with this simple check because
  // the button is in the bottom-right corner
  if (relativePoint.X < 0 || relativePoint.Y < 0)
    BackspaceButton_MouseLeftButtonUp(null, null); // Not over the button
  else
    BackspaceButton_MouseLeftButtonDown(null, null); // Still over the button
  }
 }
}
```

Notes:

→ Most of the code is identical to the code from Chapter 10's Tip Calculator. Besides the code that interacts with the FMRadio class and the code that handles tapping the power button, the main difference is that only one spot to the right of the decimal is maintained for the frequency value, compared to two spots for Tip Calculator's amount value.

→ You can get an instance of the FMRadio class via the static FMRadio.Instance property. The instance exposes three read-write properties that control the phone's single radio tuner exposed to all apps:

  → **Frequency**, a double value representing the current radio station.

  → **PowerMode**, which is either On or Off.

  → **CurrentRegion**, which can be UnitedStates, Japan, or Europe. The latter really means "every place in the world that isn't the U.S. or Japan."

It also exposes a read-only SignalStrength double property that exposes the received signal strength indicator (RSSI). The range of this value has not been documented, but it appears to be a value from 0 (no signal) to 1 (best signal), at least on the hardware I've tested.

Why doesn't the radio work while my phone is connected to a computer running Zune?

The Zune desktop program locks the media library, which prevents any functionality that requires the `ID_CAP_MEDIALIB` capability from working. (This is the same reason you can't use the phone's Marketplace app while your phone is connected to Zune.) If you need to debug a part of your app that depends on such functionality, you can use the Windows Phone Connect Tool that ships with the Windows Phone Developer Tools to connect to your phone without Zune running.

There's nothing that users of your app can do about this limitation other than closing Zune or disconnecting the phone, but it's a good idea to detect this situation so you can explain what's going on. Local FM Radio detects this situation inside its `StartRadio` method. It assumes that a failure to set `PowerMode` is due to the Zune connection, which is a pretty safe assumption.

Another way to detect this situation would be to see if the value of `NetworkInterface.InterfaceType` (in the `Microsoft.Phone.Net.NetworkInformation` namespace) is `Ethernet`, which should only happen when connected to Zune. However, this is a very bad property, because it performs long, blocking work before returning its value. If you decide to use it, be sure to do so on a background thread!

→ Because the signal strength can constantly vary, but there are no radio-specific events exposed, `MainPage`'s constructor uses a timer to refresh the signal strength display every two seconds. Although this kind of polling is bad for battery life, it's unlikely that a user will be running this app for very long. That's because the radio can keep playing after the app has been exited (and, importantly, this app does *not* run under the lock screen). The constructor also initializes the `frequency` variable to whatever frequency the radio was previously set.

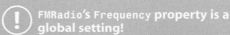 **FMRadio's Frequency property is a global setting!**

If you change the radio station, this affects the built-in radio app (and any other third-party app consuming the radio tuner). On the one hand, this is handy, because an app doesn't need to remember the last-used frequency when launched. (Indeed, the Local FM Radio app doesn't persist anything to isolated storage.) On the other hand, you must do extra work if you wish to provide any sort of isolation from the built-in radio settings.

→ The `StartRadio` and `StopRadio` methods toggle the value of the `PowerMode` property. `StartRadio` also shows a message similar to what the built-in radio app displays if the signal strength is zero, as shown in Figure 32.1. This app assumes that the user's headphones must not be plugged in when this happens, as the headphones act as the FM antenna for every current phone model.

> ! **FMRadio's `PowerMode` property is buggy in Version 7.0 of Windows Phone!**
>
> At least on some phones, setting `PowerMode` to `Off` stops the radio for a fraction of a second, but then the audio keeps playing even though the value of `PowerMode` doesn't change back! This makes it impossible to show an on/off button that is in sync with the actual state of the radio. Instead, the power button in this app ends up acting strangely. Given this state of affairs, it's only useful as a way to start the radio in case it couldn't be started when the app launched (due to being connected to Zune).

→ When the radio is on, setting the frequency to an invalid value throws an exception. Valid and invalid values are based on the current region, which would be complicated to detect with your own logic. Therefore, this app takes the easy way out and leverages the exception to turn the frequency display red. (Of course, if the current accent color is already red, then this behavior is not noticeable.)

→ After the user has left the app (or while the app is still running), he/she can still control the radio by tapping the volume-up or volume-down button. This brings up the top overlay shown in Figure 32.2. Interestingly, this overlay enables seeking to the previous/next valid station (with the rewind and fast-forward buttons), so the current station can get out-of-sync with the app's own frequency display if this is done while Local FM Radio is running. Although this app could attempt to detect and correct this situation inside its timer's `Tick` event handler, this is a minor-enough issue to warrant leaving things as-is.

FIGURE 32.1 When the phone's headphones are not connected, the phone cannot pick up any FM signal.

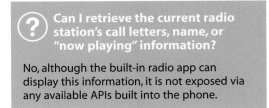

? **Can I retrieve the current radio station's call letters, name, or "now playing" information?**

No, although the built-in radio app can display this information, it is not exposed via any available APIs built into the phone.

FIGURE 32.2   In addition to changing the volume, the volume control overlay enables starting/ stopping the radio, and even seeking to the previous or next frequency with a strong-enough signal.

The Finished Product

An invalid radio frequency, shown in red

Using the light theme with the magenta accent color

Using the dark theme with the brown accent color

chapter 33

SUBSERVIENT CAT

Subservient Cat is a sort of "virtual pet" app. Unlike most cats, the subservient cat can actually obey commands! However, users have to figure out what commands the cat will respond to. It's a bit of a game, because users must keep guessing to see how many commands they can discover.

This app uses video footage of a black cat (whose real name is Boo) as its primary user interface. Therefore, this is the perfect app for learning about MediaElement, the element for playing video inside apps.

Playing Video with MediaElement

If you want to enable users to play, pause, and otherwise control videos, your best option is to use the Media Player launcher. However, if you want to play video *inline* on your own page, MediaElement enables you to do so.

MediaElement is a UI element that renders the video specified via its Source property, for example:

```
<MediaElement Source="cat.wmv"/>
```

The source URI can point to a file included in your project or to an online video. By default, MediaElement automatically starts playing the video as soon as the element is rendered (or as soon as enough of the video has been downloaded, in the online case), but you can change this by setting its AutoPlay property to false. MediaElement has

Play, Pause, and Stop methods that can be used from code-behind. It also has a Position property that reveals the current playback position (as a time span). If the video supports seeking, you can also set Position to move playback to that point in time. MediaElement can be transformed and clipped just like other Silverlight elements, and it can blended amongst other elements.

On the surface, it appears that MediaElement is straightforward to use. It has tons of caveats, however. Several warnings follow that describe some of the biggest caveats. More sidebars are placed throughout this chapter.

An app's frame can only contain one MediaElement!

Attempting to use more than one MediaElement is not supported and fails in various ways. Note that the limitation is more strict than one *per page*; only one can be attached to the *frame* at any time. (It doesn't matter if they're stopped, paused, or playing.) Therefore, multiple pages can each have a MediaElement only if they never reside on the navigation stack at the same time. Otherwise, if you need to play multiple videos, you'll either need to reuse the same MediaElement or remove the unused MediaElement from the element tree.

When including a video file in your app, make sure its Build Action is set to Content, not Resource!

This improves the performance of starting the video. When the video is embedded as a resource, it is first extracted and temporarily saved to isolated storage before it is played! (The same warning applies to audio files played by MediaElement, although this is not normally done.)

When MediaElement starts playing, any background audio (such as music playing from Zune) is paused!

This is the main reason that MediaElement should never be used for playing sound effects. Note that this is true even if your video contains no audio.

MediaElement doesn't work in the emulator under the light theme!

It's strange, but true. To test your use of a MediaElement on the emulator, you must ensure that it is running under the dark theme. Don't worry; this bug doesn't affect real phones.

MediaElement doesn't render fully opaque!

If any elements exist underneath a MediaElement, you can see them clearly through the video, even when MediaElement's Opacity property is set to 1 (as it is by default)! This is an anomaly with the composition between the phone's media player (which internally renders MediaElement's video) and the rest of Silverlight.

See "Supported Media Codecs for Windows Phone" (http://goo.gl/6NhuD) for details about the video formats supported by MediaElement and the "Recommended Video Encoding Settings" section of http://goo.gl/ttPkO for more details about what encodings work best. If you use Expression Encoder, you can encode videos with a preconfigured profile optimized for Windows Phone (and Zune HD).

The User Interface

The Subservient Cat app uses a single page—MainPage—in addition to its instructions page (not shown in this chapter). The XAML for MainPage is shown in Listing 33.1. The root grid contains three distinct pieces of user interface, all shown in Figure 33.1:

→ The MediaElement that contains the video

→ A simple "intro screen" that introduces each command done by the cat before the corresponding video clip plays

→ A panel with a text box for guessing new commands

The video   The intro screen

The command input panel

FIGURE 33.1   The three main components of the user interface on the main page.

LISTING 33.1   `MainPage.xaml`—The User Interface for Subservient Cat's Main Page

```
<phone:PhoneApplicationPage
    x:Class="WindowsPhoneApp.MainPage"
    xmlns="http://schemas.microsoft.com/winfx/2006/xaml/presentation"
    xmlns:x="http://schemas.microsoft.com/winfx/2006/xaml"
    xmlns:phone="clr-namespace:Microsoft.Phone.Controls;assembly=Microsoft.Phone"
    xmlns:shell="clr-namespace:Microsoft.Phone.Shell;assembly=Microsoft.Phone"
    FontFamily="{StaticResource PhoneFontFamilyNormal}"
    FontSize="{StaticResource PhoneFontSizeNormal}"
    Foreground="{StaticResource PhoneForegroundBrush}"
    SupportedOrientations="Landscape" Orientation="Landscape">

  <!-- The application bar-->
  <phone:PhoneApplicationPage.ApplicationBar>
    <shell:ApplicationBar Opacity=".8">
      <shell:ApplicationBarIconButton Text="command"
        IconUri="/Shared/Images/appbar.command.png"
        Click="CommandButton_Click"/>
      <shell:ApplicationBarIconButton Text="instructions"
        IconUri="/Shared/Images/appbar.instructions.png"
        Click="InstructionsButton_Click"/>
      <shell:ApplicationBarIconButton Text="discovered"
        IconUri="/Shared/Images/appbar.1.png"
        Click="DiscoveredButton_Click"/>
    </shell:ApplicationBar>
  </phone:PhoneApplicationPage.ApplicationBar>

  <Grid>
    <!-- The video, scaled to fill the page without visible letterboxing -->
    <MediaElement x:Name="MediaElement" Source="cat.wmv" Stretch="None"
      Volume="1" MediaOpened="MediaElement_MediaOpened"
              MediaFailed="MediaElement_MediaFailed">
      <MediaElement.RenderTransform>
        <CompositeTransform TranslateY="-115" TranslateX="-150"
                        ScaleX="1.68" ScaleY="1.68"/>
      </MediaElement.RenderTransform>
    </MediaElement>

    <!-- Something to show on top of the video during seeking -->
    <Border x:Name="IntroScreen" Background="#6E5962" Visibility="Collapsed">
      <Grid>
        <Image Source="Images/paw.png" Stretch="None" HorizontalAlignment="Left"
              VerticalAlignment="Top" Margin="100,100,0,0"/>
        <Image Source="Images/paw.png" Stretch="None" HorizontalAlignment="Left"
              VerticalAlignment="Top" Margin="230,50,0,0"/>
```

LISTING 33.1   Continued

```xml
            <Image Source="Images/paw.png" Stretch="None" HorizontalAlignment="Left"
                VerticalAlignment="Top" Margin="628,300,0,0"/>
            <Image Source="Images/paw.png" Stretch="None" HorizontalAlignment="Left"
                VerticalAlignment="Top" Margin="528,350,0,0"/>
            <TextBlock x:Name="NextCommandTextBlock" Foreground="Black" FontSize="40"
                    VerticalAlignment="Center" HorizontalAlignment="Center"/>
        </Grid>
    </Border>

    <!-- The user interface for typing new commands -->
    <Grid x:Name="CommandPanel"
            Background="#A000"
            Visibility="Collapsed" VerticalAlignment="Bottom">
        <Grid.RowDefinitions>
            <RowDefinition/>
            <!-- A bottom margin, so the auto-scroll while the textbox has focus
                doesn't show extra space below the video -->
            <RowDefinition Height="84"/>
        </Grid.RowDefinitions>
        <Grid.ColumnDefinitions>
            <ColumnDefinition Width="Auto"/>
            <ColumnDefinition/>
        </Grid.ColumnDefinitions>
        <Image Source="/Shared/Images/appbar.command.png" Stretch="None"
                Margin="70,0,0,0"/>
        <Rectangle Grid.Column="1" Fill="White" Margin="12,12,82,12"/>
        <TextBox x:Name="CommandTextBox" Grid.Column="1" InputScope="Text"
                Margin="0,0,70,0" TextChanged="CommandTextBox_TextChanged"
                LostFocus="CommandTextBox_LostFocus"/>
    </Grid>
  </Grid>
</phone:PhoneApplicationPage>
```

Notes:

➜ The video is landscape-oriented, so this is a landscape-only page. However, because a text box is used for guessing new commands, the code-behind temporarily changes SupportedOrientations to allow any orientation while the text box has focus. This way, phones with portrait hardware keyboards still get a good experience.

➜ The application bar has three buttons: one for revealing the command input panel, one for navigating to the instructions page, and one whose icon reveals how many commands have been discovered (updated in code-behind). Tapping this last button also tells you whether there are more commands to be discovered, as the total number is a secret. The application bar menu, dynamically filled from code-behind, contains the list of discovered commands and makes the cat perform each one when tapped. This is shown in Figure 33.2.

FIGURE 33.2   The application bar menu provides quick access to the list of already-discovered commands, such as "yawn."

→   Although the app appears to play several different short videos, it actually uses a single longer video (`cat.wmv`) for performance reasons. The code-behind is responsible for playing the appropriate segments of the video at the appropriate times.

→   The `MediaElement` is moved and enlarged with a `CompositeTransform` because the source `cat.wmv` file has black bars along the top and bottom that we don't want to see on the screen.

→   `MediaElement`'s `Volume` property (a value from 0 to 1) is set to 1 (the loudest possible volume) because the default value is .85. Although the sound can only be as loud as the user's volume level, this helps ensure that the tiny bit of audio in this app's video (a short meow) can be heard.

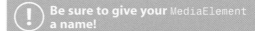

Be sure to give your `MediaElement` **a name!**

If you don't, it's possible that the marketplace publishing process won't detect your use of `MediaElement`, and therefore will not grant your app the "media library" capability that is necessary for your app to work.

The Code-Behind

Listing 33.2 contains the code-behind for the main page.

LISTING 33.2   `MainPage.xaml.cs`—The Code-Behind for Subservient Cat's Main Page

```
using System;
using System.Collections.Generic;
using System.Windows;
using System.Windows.Controls;
using System.Windows.Media;
using System.Windows.Navigation;
using System.Windows.Threading;
using Microsoft.Phone.Controls;
using Microsoft.Phone.Shell;

namespace WindowsPhoneApp
{
  public partial class MainPage : PhoneApplicationPage
  {
    // Captures the slice in the big video where each command resides
    class VideoClip
    {
      public TimeSpan Start;
      public TimeSpan End;
    }

    DispatcherTimer videoTimer = new DispatcherTimer();
    DispatcherTimer delayTimer = new DispatcherTimer();
    VideoClip pendingNewClip;

    Dictionary<string, VideoClip> possibleCommands =
      new Dictionary<string, VideoClip>();
    Dictionary<string, string> aliases = new Dictionary<string, string>();

    // Start users off with one known command: yawn
    Setting<List<string>> discoveredCommands =
      new Setting<List<string>>("DiscoveredCommands",
        new List<string>(new string[] { "yawn" }));

    IApplicationBarIconButton discoveredButton;

    public MainPage()
    {
      InitializeComponent();
```

LISTING 33.2   Continued

```csharp
    this.discoveredButton = this.ApplicationBar.Buttons[2]
                            as IApplicationBarIconButton;

    this.videoTimer.Tick += VideoTimer_Tick;
    this.delayTimer.Tick += DelayTimer_Tick;

    // All the commands and their positions in the video
    this.possibleCommands.Add("yawn", new VideoClip {
      Start = TimeSpan.FromSeconds(98.36),
      End = TimeSpan.FromSeconds(101.28) });
    this.possibleCommands.Add("meow", new VideoClip {
      Start = TimeSpan.FromSeconds(79.4),
      End = TimeSpan.FromSeconds(81.863) });
    …

    // Permitted variations for each command
    this.aliases.Add("yawn", "yawn");
    this.aliases.Add("meow", "meow");
    this.aliases.Add("speak", "meow");
    this.aliases.Add("talk", "meow");
    this.aliases.Add("say your name", "meow");
    …
  }

  protected override void OnNavigatedTo(NavigationEventArgs e)
  {
    base.OnNavigatedTo(e);

    // Fill the application bar menu with all previously-discovered commands
    this.ApplicationBar.MenuItems.Clear();
    foreach (string command in this.discoveredCommands.Value)
    {
      ApplicationBarMenuItem item = new ApplicationBarMenuItem(command);
      item.Click += ApplicationBarMenuItem_Click;
      this.ApplicationBar.MenuItems.Add(item);
    }
    // Show how many commands have been discovered on the button imag
    this.discoveredButton.IconUri = new Uri("/Shared/Images/appbar."
      + this.discoveredCommands.Value.Count + ".png", UriKind.Relative);
  }

  void MediaElement_MediaOpened(object sender, RoutedEventArgs e)
  {
    // Play a short intro clip
```

LISTING 33.2   Continued

```csharp
    this.videoTimer.Interval = TimeSpan.FromSeconds(1.48);
    this.videoTimer.Start();
  }

  void MediaElement_MediaFailed(object sender, ExceptionRoutedEventArgs e)
  {
    MessageBox.Show("To see the subservient cat, please disconnect your " +
      "phone from Zune.", "Please Disconnect", MessageBoxButton.OK);
  }

  void PlayClip(string title, TimeSpan beginTime, TimeSpan endTime)
  {
    // Set up the timer to stop playback approximately when endTime is reached
    this.videoTimer.Stop();
    this.videoTimer.Interval = endTime - beginTime;

    // Hide the video and show the intro screen
    this.MediaElement.Pause();
    this.NextCommandTextBlock.Text = title;
    this.IntroScreen.Visibility = Visibility.Visible;

    // Give the intro screen a chance to show before doing the following work
    this.Dispatcher.BeginInvoke(delegate()
    {
      // Delay the reappearance of the video until after the seek completes
      this.delayTimer.Interval = TimeSpan.FromSeconds(2);
      this.delayTimer.Start();

      // Seek to the correct spot in the video
      this.MediaElement.Position = beginTime;
    });
  }

  void VideoTimer_Tick(object sender, EventArgs e)
  {
    // We've reached the end of the current clip, so pause the video
    this.MediaElement.Pause();
    // Prevent the timer from continuing to tick
    this.videoTimer.Stop();
  }

  void DelayTimer_Tick(object sender, EventArgs e)
  {
```

LISTING 33.2   Continued

```
  // This timer is used for two reasons, either to delay the execution of a
  // new command after typing it in, or to delay the beginning of playing a
  // video clip after the intro screen is shown.

  if (this.IntroScreen.Visibility == Visibility.Collapsed)
  {
    // This is the execution of a new command
    string text = this.CommandTextBox.Text;
    this.CommandTextBox.Foreground = new SolidColorBrush(Colors.Black);
    this.CommandTextBox.Text = "";
    this.Focus(); // Closes the command input panel
    PlayClip(text.ToLowerInvariant(), this.pendingNewClip.Start,
                                      this.pendingNewClip.End);
  }
  else
  {
    // We're ready to actually play the video clip
    this.videoTimer.Start();
    this.MediaElement.Play();
    this.IntroScreen.Visibility = Visibility.Collapsed;
  }

  // Prevent the timer from continuing to tick
  this.delayTimer.Stop();
}

void CommandTextBox_LostFocus(object sender, RoutedEventArgs e)
{
  // Restore the page to landscape-only and hide the command input panel
  this.SupportedOrientations = SupportedPageOrientation.Landscape;
  this.CommandPanel.Visibility = Visibility.Collapsed;
}

void CommandTextBox_TextChanged(object sender, TextChangedEventArgs e)
{
  string text = this.CommandTextBox.Text.Trim().ToLowerInvariant();

  // Don't bother checking when the text is shorter than any valid command
  if (text.Length < 3)
    return;

  if (this.aliases.ContainsKey(text))
  {
    string commandName = this.aliases[text];
```

LISTING 33.2   Continued

```
    // Only acknowledge the command if it's not already in the list
    if (!this.discoveredCommands.Value.Contains(text))
    {
      // Signal a successful guess
      this.CommandTextBox.Foreground =
        Application.Current.Resources["PhoneAccentBrush"] as Brush;

      this.pendingNewClip = this.possibleCommands[commandName];

      // Append the new command to the application bar menu
      ApplicationBarMenuItem item = new ApplicationBarMenuItem(text);
      item.Click += ApplicationBarMenuItem_Click;
      this.ApplicationBar.MenuItems.Add(item);

      // Record the discovered command
      this.discoveredCommands.Value.Add(text);
      this.discoveredButton.IconUri = new Uri("/Shared/Images/appbar." +
        this.discoveredCommands.Value.Count + ".png", UriKind.Relative);

      // Wait a second before hiding the text box and showing the intro screen
      this.delayTimer.Interval = TimeSpan.FromSeconds(1);
      this.delayTimer.Start();
    }
  }
}

// Application bar handlers

void ApplicationBarMenuItem_Click(object sender, EventArgs e)
{
  IApplicationBarMenuItem item = sender as IApplicationBarMenuItem;

  // Grab the right clip based on the menu item's text
  VideoClip command = this.possibleCommands[this.aliases[item.Text]];

  this.Focus(); // In case the command input panel is currently showing

  PlayClip(item.Text, command.Start, command.End);
}

void CommandButton_Click(object sender, EventArgs e)
{
```

LISTING 33.2   Continued

```csharp
      // Temporarily allow a portrait orientation while the text box is in use
      this.SupportedOrientations = SupportedPageOrientation.PortraitOrLandscape;
      this.CommandPanel.Visibility = Visibility.Visible;

      // Enable automatic deployment of the software keyboard
      this.CommandTextBox.Focus();
      this.CommandTextBox.SelectAll();
    }

    void InstructionsButton_Click(object sender, EventArgs e)
    {
      this.NavigationService.Navigate(new Uri("/InstructionsPage.xaml",
        UriKind.Relative));
    }

    void DiscoveredButton_Click(object sender, EventArgs e)
    {
      // Pause, otherwise the video will keep playing while the message box is
      // shown and the timer Tick handler won't be raised to stop it!
      this.MediaElement.Pause();

      if (this.discoveredCommands.Value.Count == this.possibleCommands.Count)
      {
        MessageBox.Show("Congratulations! You have discovered all the commands!",
          "Discovered Commands", MessageBoxButton.OK);
      }
      else if (this.discoveredCommands.Value.Count == 1)
      {
        MessageBox.Show("You have discovered only one command, and it was given" +
          " to you! Keep trying! (You can see and use your command by tapping" +
          " \"...\")", "Discovered Commands", MessageBoxButton.OK);
      }
      else
      {
        MessageBox.Show("You have discovered " +
          this.discoveredCommands.Value.Count + " commands. (You can see them" +
          " and use them by tapping \"...\") There are more to discover!",
          "Discovered Commands", MessageBoxButton.OK);
      }
    }
  }
}
```

Notes:

→ The constructor populates `possibleCommands` with the list of commands along with their starting and ending times in the `cat.wmv` video. Because guessing each command by its exact name can be incredibly hard, an `aliases` dictionary is used that enables alternate forms of some commands, such as "speak" instead of "meow."

→ In `OnNavigatedTo`, the application bar menu is filled with all previously discovered commands. These are stored in `discoveredCommands`, which is a `Setting` so it always gets persisted.

→ In order to show the number of discovered commands in the application bar button's icon, several distinct images are included in this project: `appbar.1.png`, `appbar.2.png`, `appbar.3.png`, and so on. The right one is selected based on the `Count` of the `discoveredCommands` collection.

→ The video starts automatically playing when the page is loaded (because `AutoPlay` was not set to `false` in Listing 33.1), but we do not want the entire video to play and reveal all the cat's actions. Instead, only the first second and a half should play. Therefore, in `MediaElement`'s `MediaOpened` event handler (raised when the media has loaded and is ready to start playing), `videoTimer` is used to pause the video after 1.48 seconds have elapsed. The pausing is done in `videoTimer`'s `Tick` event handler, `VideoTimer_Tick`.

 You cannot call `Play` on a `MediaElement` until its `MediaOpened` event is raised!

When a `MediaElement`'s `Source` is set (either in XAML or code-behind), you cannot instantly begin interacting with the media. Instead, you must wait for `MediaOpened` to be raised. If the media cannot be loaded for some reason, a `MediaFailed` event is raised instead. Subservient Cat avoids the need to manually call `Play` because it uses the auto-play feature, but if it didn't use auto-play, then it should call `Play` inside `MediaElement_MediaOpened`.

 Why doesn't my video play on a physical phone while it is connected to a computer running Zune?

This is due to the same problem discussed in the preceding chapter. The Zune desktop program locks the media library, which prevents `MediaElement` from loading its media. Remember, if you need to debug a part of your app that depends on video actually playing, you can use the Windows Phone Connect Tool that ships with the Windows Phone Developer Tools to connect to your phone without Zune running.

Subservient Cat detects this situation by handling the `MediaFailed` event. It assumes the failure is due to the Zune connection, which is a pretty safe assumption because the source video is local to the app.

→ The `PlayClip` method ensures that the video is paused, seeks to the specified `beginTime`, and reinitializes `videoTimer` so it pauses the video at `endTime`. However, because setting `MediaElement`'s `Position` has an annoying effect of seeing the video quickly fast-forward or rewind to the desired spot (rather than an instant jump), the intro screen is shown to hide

When you set `MediaElement`'s Position, the change is not instantaneous!

Instead, you see a little bit of the video before or after the new position, as if you're watching the video in fast-forward or rewind mode. The workaround used by Subservient Cat is to temporarily obscure the video with other elements.

the video during the transition. (We don't want to reveal yet-to-be-discovered parts of the video!) The setting of `Position` is done inside a `BeginInvoke` callback so the showing of the intro screen has a chance to take effect. Without this, you still see the unwanted behavior. Two seconds is chosen as the length of the delay, during which the user can read the command text on the intro screen. We don't have a way to know when seek has actually finished, but two seconds is long enough.

In the current version of Windows Phone, `MediaElement` does not support markers. The use of markers to designate when individual clips inside `cat.wmv` begin and end would have been ideal, and would have greatly reduced the amount of code needed in Listing 33.2. However, using a `DispatcherTimer` to be notified when the relevant clip has ended is a reasonable workaround. There are two things to be aware of, however:

→ The timer doesn't give you frame-by-frame accuracy. The video used by this app has a little bit of a buffer at the end of each clip, in case `videoTimer`'s `Tick` event gets raised slightly late.

→ If you show a message box, the video will keep playing in the background but the timer's `Tick` event handler cannot be called until the message box is dismissed, no matter how much time has elapsed. (`MessageBox.Show` is a blocking operation.) This is why `DiscoveredButton_Click` in Listing 33.2 pauses the video first.

When I first wrote Subservient Cat, I called `MediaElement`'s `Stop` method inside `OnNavigatedFrom` because I was worried about the performance impact of unnecessarily playing video while the instructions page is shown and the main page is on the back stack. However, this is unnecessary because `MediaElement` is automatically paused when a page navigates away. If you don't want this behavior (perhaps because you want to hear the audio from the video continue while other pages are shown), the `MediaElement` must be attached to the frame rather than to a specific page.

•••

MediaElement and Files in Isolated Storage

If you want to play a video from isolated storage (presumably because your app downloaded it and then saved it there), you can call MediaElement's SetSource method that expects a stream rather than a URI. With this, you can pass an appropriate IsolatedStorageFileStream.

The Finished Product

The "yawn" command

The message box revealing whether there are more commands to discover

A mysterious command involving a pumpkin

BUBBLE BLOWER

Bubble Blower enables users to actually *blow* on the phone to make bubbles to appear on the screen. These bubbles grow from the bottom of the screen and pop when they reach the top. This magical effect is made possible by leveraging the phone's microphone to detect the sound of blowing, just like in Chapter 31, "Trombone." Bubble Blower has an application bar for exposing instructions, settings, and an about page, but it can be hidden (or brought back) by tapping the screen.

About the Microphone

The microphone API is technically an XNA feature; the relevant Microphone class resides in the Microsoft.Xna.Framework.Audio namespace in the Microsoft.Xna.Framework assembly. As with the sound effects APIs from the preceding part of the book, Silverlight apps can use the microphone seamlessly as long as XNA's FrameworkDispatcher.Update is called regularly.

You can get an instance of the microphone with the static Microphone.Default property. From this instance, you can call Start, Stop, and check its State at any time (which is either Started or Stopped). To retrieve the raw audio data from the microphone, you attach a handler to its BufferReady event. By default, BufferReady is raised every second, providing access to the last second of audio data, but its frequency can be changed by setting the BufferDuration property.

You need the `ID_CAP_MICROPHONE` **capability in your application manifest in order to use the microphone!**

If you have removed this from your manifest, `Microphone.Default` is always `null`, and the `Microphone.All` collection is always empty. By requesting this capability, `Microphone.Default` is guaranteed to be non-null whenever your app runs. Of course, this is only a concern at development time because marketplace certification automatically adds this capability to your manifest if needed.

 `BufferDuration` **only supports 101 distinct values!**

`BufferDuration`, defined as a `TimeSpan`, must be set to a value between 100 milliseconds and 1 second (inclusive). Furthermore, the duration must be a multiple of 10 milliseconds. If you attempt to set it to an invalid value, an `ArgumentOutOfRangeException` is thrown.

 If I plug in a headset with a microphone, does that show up as a second microphone in the `Microphone.All` **collection?**

No. Although a headset microphone can be used, it automatically takes over as the default microphone. As far as apps are concerned, there is only ever one microphone.

Inside a `BufferReady` event handler, you can call `Microphone`'s `GetData` method to fill a buffer (a byte array) with the latest audio data. If you want to capture all the audio since the last event, you must make sure the buffer is large enough. `Microphone`'s `GetSampleSizeInBytes` method can tell you how large it needs to be for any passed-in `TimeSpan`, so calling it with `Microphone.Default.BufferDuration` gives you the desired size.

 What can I do with the raw audio data once I receive it as an array of bytes? How do I interpret it?

The bytes represent the audio encoded in the *linear pulse-code modulation* (*LPCM*) format, the standard Windows format for raw and uncompressed audio. This format is used in `.wav` files, and it is often just referred to as PCM encoding rather than LPCM.

Each 2-byte value in the buffer represents an audio sample for a very small slice of time. Windows phones capture 16,000 samples per second (revealed by `Microphone`'s `SampleRate` property), so when `BufferReady` is called every second, the buffer size is 32,000 bytes (16,000 samples x 2 bytes per sample). If the audio were recorded in stereo, which does not happen on the phone, the data would be twice as long and each sample would alternate between left and right channels.

With each 2-byte value, zero represents silence. When sound occurs, it creates a waveform that oscillates between positive and negative values. The larger the *absolute value* is (no matter whether it's positive or negative), the louder the sound is.

You can do several things easily with these raw data values. For example, you can detect the relative volume of the audio over time (as this app does), and you can play back or save the audio (as done in the next two chapters). With more work, you can do advanced things like pitch detection. You could even turn the data into an actual .wav file by adding a RIFF header. See http://bit.ly/wavespec for more details.

Ignore Microphone's IsHeadset **property!**

This property was designed for the PC and Xbox and doesn't work for the phone. It is always false, even if the microphone actually belongs to a headset.

Can I process audio during a phone call?

No, you cannot receive any data from the microphone during a phone call (or while the phone is locked).

The Bubble User Control

This app needs bubbles—lots of bubbles—so it makes sense to create a user control to represent a bubble. Listing 34.1 contains the visuals for the Bubble user control. Figure 34.1 shows what Bubble looks like.

LISTING 34.1   Bubble.xaml—The User Interface for The Bubble User Control

```xml
<UserControl x:Class="WindowsPhoneApp.Bubble"
  xmlns="http://schemas.microsoft.com/winfx/2006/xaml/presentation"
  xmlns:x="http://schemas.microsoft.com/winfx/2006/xaml">
  <Canvas>
    <Ellipse Width="300" Height="300" Fill="#7FFF"/>
    <Path Width="210" Height="50" Canvas.Left="45" Canvas.Top="10" Stretch="Fill"
      Data="F1 M 358.719,138.738C 410.658,138.738 513.576,154.945
            574.107,241.833C 546.724,217.522 464.097,185.476 361.601,185.476C
            259.106,185.476 177.608,220.674 154.572,240.032C 200.667,172.503
            297.7,138.738 358.719,138.738 Z">
      <Path.Fill>
        <RadialGradientBrush RadiusX="0.5" RadiusY="1.4"
                             Center=".5,1.5" GradientOrigin=".5,1.5">
          <RadialGradientBrush.GradientStops>
            <GradientStop Color="Transparent" Offset="0.8"/>
            <GradientStop Color="#9FFF" Offset="1"/>
          </RadialGradientBrush.GradientStops>
        </RadialGradientBrush>
      </Path.Fill>
    </Path>
  </Canvas>
</UserControl>
```

Notes:

→ Although the ellipse is straightforward, the gradient-filled path
creating the arc on top of the
ellipse is something that would
most likely need to be crafted in a
tool like Expression Blend. I
certainly didn't come up with
those numbers by hand!

→ The purpose of this control is
simply to encapsulate the visuals
for a bubble. It has no built-in
behavior, so the `Bubble.xaml.cs`
code-behind file contains nothing
other than the required call to
`InitializeComponent` inside its
constructor.

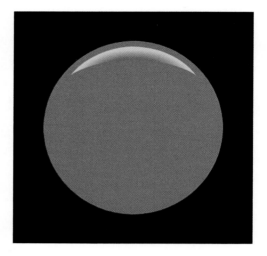

FIGURE 34.1   The `Bubble` user control, shown
against a black background.

The Main User Interface

Listing 34.2 contains the XAML for the main page. It is simple because there's nothing
other than the application bar on the page until bubbles appear.

LISTING 34.2   `MainPage.xaml`—The User Interface for Bubble Blower's Main Page

```
<phone:PhoneApplicationPage x:Class="WindowsPhoneApp.MainPage"
  xmlns="http://schemas.microsoft.com/winfx/2006/xaml/presentation"
  xmlns:x="http://schemas.microsoft.com/winfx/2006/xaml"
  xmlns:phone="clr-namespace:Microsoft.Phone.Controls;assembly=Microsoft.Phone"
  xmlns:shell="clr-namespace:Microsoft.Phone.Shell;assembly=Microsoft.Phone"
  SupportedOrientations="Portrait">

  <!-- The application bar, with 1 button and 2 menu items -->
  <phone:PhoneApplicationPage.ApplicationBar>
    <shell:ApplicationBar Opacity=".5">
      <shell:ApplicationBarIconButton
        IconUri="/Shared/Images/appbar.instructions.png"
        Text="instructions" Click="InstructionsButton_Click"/>
      <shell:ApplicationBar.MenuItems>
        <shell:ApplicationBarMenuItem Text="settings"
          Click="SettingsMenuItem_Click"/>
        <shell:ApplicationBarMenuItem Text="about" Click="AboutMenuItem_Click"/>
      </shell:ApplicationBar.MenuItems>
    </shell:ApplicationBar>
  </phone:PhoneApplicationPage.ApplicationBar>
```

LISTING 34.2   Continued

```
  </phone:PhoneApplicationPage.ApplicationBar>

  <!-- Hard-coded background! Grid is only here because
       the page can't be given a background. -->
  <Grid Background="Black">
    <!-- Size and background are there to enable tapping
         anywhere except close to the application bar -->
    <Canvas x:Name="RootCanvas" Width="480" Height="700" VerticalAlignment="Top"
            MouseLeftButtonDown="RootCanvas_MouseLeftButtonDown"
            Background="Transparent"/>
  </Grid>
</phone:PhoneApplicationPage>
```

Notes:

→ The application bar provides links to three other pages: instructions, settings, and about. The settings page is examined later in this chapter, and the instructions page is shown at the end. The about page is the standard one used throughout this book.

→ The background is hard-coded to black because the bubbles would not appear on a white background. This is set on the grid because setting the page's background property has no effect.

→ The application bar is half-opaque, so bubbles show through underneath yet the text on the button and menu items remains readable. An opacity of zero would not work (without hardcoding the application bar foreground to a color such as white) because the application bar text would be black on top of the hard-coded black background when the light theme is used. As always, you need to be careful when using any hardcoded colors in your app!

→ The canvas has a `MouseLeftButtonDown` event handler for toggling the application bar's visibility when tapped. It has an explicit transparent background, so it responds to taps anywhere within its area.

→ The canvas only covers the top 700 pixels of the screen because if it gets too close to the application bar, users might accidentally tap it (and hide the application bar) when trying to tap the bar, especially its ellipsis.

The Main Code-Behind

The code-behind in Listing 34.3 is responsible for starting the microphone, determining when to produce bubbles, producing them, and animating them from the bottom of the screen to the top. This bottom-to-top animation only makes sense if the microphone is below the screen, but that's a pretty safe assumption for all phone models considering how phones work.

The technique for determining when the user is blowing is simply checking for loud-enough sounds. (Blowing on a microphone produces a pretty loud sound.) If the sound picked up by the microphone is below a certain threshold, it assumes the sound is background noise. Of course, this approach can be fooled by just talking loud enough or making any other noises.

LISTING 34.3   `MainPage.xaml.cs`—The Code-Behind for Bubble Blower's Main Page

```csharp
using System;
using System.Windows;
using System.Windows.Controls;
using System.Windows.Input;
using System.Windows.Media;
using System.Windows.Media.Animation;
using Microsoft.Phone.Controls;
using Microsoft.Xna.Framework.Audio;

namespace WindowsPhoneApp
{
  public partial class MainPage : PhoneApplicationPage
  {
    Random random = new Random();
    byte[] buffer;
    int currentVolume;

    public MainPage()
    {
      InitializeComponent();

      // Get called on every frame
      CompositionTarget.Rendering += CompositionTarget_Rendering;

      // Prevent off-screen bubble parts from being
      // seen when animating to other pages
      this.Clip = new RectangleGeometry { Rect = new Rect(0, 0, 480, 800) };

      // Required for XNA Microphone API to work
      Microsoft.Xna.Framework.FrameworkDispatcher.Update();

      // Configure the microphone with the smallest supported BufferDuration (.1)
      Microphone.Default.BufferDuration = TimeSpan.FromSeconds(.1);
      Microphone.Default.BufferReady += Microphone_BufferReady;

      // Initialize the buffer for holding microphone data
      int size = Microphone.Default.GetSampleSizeInBytes(
                   Microphone.Default.BufferDuration);
```

LISTING 34.3   Continued

```csharp
    this.buffer = new byte[size];

    // Start listening
    Microphone.Default.Start();
}

void Microphone_BufferReady(object sender, EventArgs e)
{
  int size = Microphone.Default.GetData(this.buffer);
  if (size > 0)
    this.currentVolume = GetAverageVolume(size);
}

void CompositionTarget_Rendering(object sender, EventArgs e)
{
  // Required for XNA Microphone API to work
  Microsoft.Xna.Framework.FrameworkDispatcher.Update();

  if (this.currentVolume > Settings.VolumeThreshold.Value)
    AddBubble(false);
  if (this.currentVolume > Settings.VolumeThreshold.Value * 5)
    AddBubble(true); // Add an extra (& faster) bubble for extra-hard blowing
}

// Returns the average value among all the values in the buffer
int GetAverageVolume(int numBytes)
{
  long total = 0;

  // Buffer is an array of bytes, but we want to examine each 2-byte value.
  // [SampleDuration for 1 sec (32000) / SampleRate (16000) = 2 bytes]
  // Therefore, we iterate through the array 2 bytes at a time.
  for (int i = 0; i < numBytes; i += 2)
  {
    // Cast from short to int to prevent -32768 from overflowing Math.Abs:
    int value = Math.Abs((int)BitConverter.ToInt16(this.buffer, i));
    total += value;
  }
  return (int)(total / (numBytes / 2));
}

void AddBubble(bool fast)
{
  // Choose a scale for the bubble between .1 (10%) and 1 (100%)
```

LISTING 34.3   Continued

```
double scale = (double)random.Next(10, 100) / 100;

// Set the vertical animation duration based on the scale
// (from .55 sec for scale==.1 to 1 sec for scale==1)
double duration = .5 + scale / 2;

// If this isn't a "fast" bubble, lengthen the duration of the animation
if (!fast)
  duration *= 1.5;

// Create a new bubble, set its location/size & add it to the root canvas
Bubble bubble = new Bubble();
Canvas.SetLeft(bubble, random.Next(-100, (int)this.ActualWidth + 100));
Canvas.SetTop(bubble, this.ActualHeight + 50);
bubble.RenderTransform = new ScaleTransform { ScaleX = scale,
                                              ScaleY = scale };
bubble.RenderTransformOrigin = new Point(.5, .5);
this.RootCanvas.Children.Add(bubble);

// Dynamically create a new storyboard for the bubble with four animations
Storyboard storyboard = new Storyboard();
Storyboard.SetTarget(storyboard, bubble);
storyboard.Completed += delegate(object sender, EventArgs e)
{
  // "Pop" the bubble when the storyboard is done
  this.RootCanvas.Children.Remove(bubble);
};

// Animate the vertical position from just below the bottom of the screen
// (set earlier) to just above the top of the screen
DoubleAnimation topAnimation = new DoubleAnimation { To = -100,
  Duration = TimeSpan.FromSeconds(duration),
  EasingFunction = new QuadraticEase() };
Storyboard.SetTargetProperty(topAnimation,
  new PropertyPath("(Canvas.Top)"));

// Animate the horizontal position from the center
// to the randomly-chosen position previously set
DoubleAnimation leftAnimation = new DoubleAnimation {
  From = this.ActualWidth / 2, Duration = TimeSpan.FromSeconds(.5),
  EasingFunction = new QuadraticEase() };
Storyboard.SetTargetProperty(leftAnimation,
  new PropertyPath("(Canvas.Left)"));
```

LISTING 34.3   Continued

```
      // Animate the horizontal scale from 0 to the
      // randomly-chosen value previously set
      DoubleAnimation scaleXAnimation = new DoubleAnimation { From = 0,
        Duration = TimeSpan.FromSeconds(.5),
        EasingFunction = new QuadraticEase() };
      Storyboard.SetTargetProperty(scaleXAnimation, new PropertyPath(
        "(UserControl.RenderTransform).(ScaleTransform.ScaleX)"));

      // Animate the vertical scale from 0 to the
      // randomly-chosen value previously set
      DoubleAnimation scaleYAnimation = new DoubleAnimation { From = 0,
        Duration = TimeSpan.FromSeconds(.5),
       EasingFunction = new QuadraticEase() };
      Storyboard.SetTargetProperty(scaleYAnimation, new PropertyPath(
        "(UserControl.RenderTransform).(ScaleTransform.ScaleY)"));

      // Add the animations to the storyboad
      storyboard.Children.Add(topAnimation);
      storyboard.Children.Add(leftAnimation);
      storyboard.Children.Add(scaleXAnimation);
      storyboard.Children.Add(scaleYAnimation);

      // Start the storyboard
      storyboard.Begin();
    }

    void RootCanvas_MouseLeftButtonDown(object sender, MouseButtonEventArgs e)
    {
      // Toggle the application bar visibility
      this.ApplicationBar.IsVisible = !this.ApplicationBar.IsVisible;
    }

    // Application bar handlers

    void InstructionsButton_Click(object sender, EventArgs e)
    {
      this.NavigationService.Navigate(new Uri("/InstructionsPage.xaml",
        UriKind.Relative));
    }

    void SettingsMenuItem_Click(object sender, EventArgs e)
    {
      this.NavigationService.Navigate(new Uri("/SettingsPage.xaml",
        UriKind.Relative));
```

LISTING 34.3   Continued

```
    }

    void AboutMenuItem_Click(object sender, EventArgs e)
    {
      this.NavigationService.Navigate(new Uri(
        "/Shared/About/AboutPage.xaml?appName=Bubble Blower", UriKind.Relative));
    }
  }
}
```

Notes:

→ The constructor attaches a handler to the `Rendering` event, which is used for more than just calling `Update` on XNA's `FrameworkDispatcher`. Next, the constructor clips any off-screen content for the benefit of performance and avoiding strange artifacts when navigating away from `MainPage`. (The page's `ActualWidth` and `ActualHeight` properties can't be used until layout occurs, so this code simply hard-codes the 480x800 dimensions.) It also initializes and starts the microphone. `FrameworkDispatcher.Update` is called in the constructor to avoid occasional exceptions while debugging, complaining that `Update` hasn't been called. That can happen because during debugging, too much time can pass between starting the microphone and the first call to `CompositionTarget_Rendering`.

→ The microphone's `BufferDuration` is set to its smallest allowable value—one-tenth of a second. This is the frequency with which the `BufferReady` event handler will be called. The buffer (the array of bytes) is given the appropriate size for the time period of one-tenth of a second. (This size happens to be 3,200 bytes.)

→ Inside `Microphone_BufferReady`, the `BufferReady` event handler, `GetData` is called to fill the buffer with a fresh set of bytes representing the last .1 seconds of audio. The `currentVolume` field is then set to the average magnitude of the samples in the buffer, if the call got any data. This average is calculated in `GetAverageVolume`. This is certainly not the only approach for determining volume of the audio sample, nor is the value expressed in standard units (like decibels). But this simple technique works well enough for this app and other apps in this book.

→ `GetAverageVolume` has a few subtleties. Rather than finding the average magnitude of each *byte*, which would be meaningless, it must find the average magnitude of each 16-bit (2-byte) audio sample. Therefore, the loop increments i by 2 each time to retrieve each 2-byte chunk. The size of each sample ideally wouldn't be hard-coded, but rather calculated by dividing a 1-second `SampleDuration` by `SampleRate`. However, this would complicate the rest of the logic. `BitConverter.ToInt16` is used to convert the two bytes at the current position of the buffer array to a single numeric value. The absolute value of each sample is used because it doesn't matter whether it is positive or negative, just how large the absolute value is. And if we didn't take the absolute value of each sample, the resultant average would always be close to zero due to values cancelling each other out!

→ `CompositionTarget_Rendering`, besides calling `Update`, adds a new bubble if the average volume in the current buffer is loud enough. This means that a new bubble is added during *every frame* that the volume is loud enough. (Adding just one new bubble every relevant .1 second would not be enough.) If the average volume is greater than an even higher threshold, a second bubble is added. Note that this handler continues to get called even after navigating to another page. This is a bit wasteful processing-wise, but it is not a big deal for this app because visits to the other pages should be short-lived. `VolumeThreshold` is defined as follows with a default value of 400, arrived at by trial and error:

```
namespace WindowsPhoneApp
{
  public static class Settings
  {
    public static readonly Setting<int> VolumeThreshold =
      new Setting<int>("VolumeThreshold", 400);
  }
}
```

→ `AddBubble` creates a new `Bubble` and adds it to the canvas just below the bottom of the screen (the page's height + 50). It picks a random horizontal position for the bubble and a random size (leveraging `ScaleTransform`). It then dynamically creates and starts a storyboard with four animations. `topAnimation` moves the bubble to 100 pixels above the top of the screen using a duration relative to the size of the bubble (so smaller bubbles move faster). Therefore, bubbles smaller than 100 pixels travel all the way off the screen, but most bubbles are still partially visible when they "pop." The pop effect—removing the element when the animation is done without any kind of animated transition—is simple but effective. `leftAnimation` animates the bubble's horizontal position from the center of the screen to the randomly chosen position for a hard-coded duration shorter than the length of the vertical animation. This helps to give the effect of all bubbles being blown out of a small wand slightly below the screen. The rest of that effect comes from the last two animations, which make the bubble grow from a size of zero to the randomly chosen size with the same duration as `leftAnimation`. All animations use `QuadraticEase` to give a realistic motion, causing the bubbles to linger slightly before they pop.

The Settings Page

The settings page, shown in Figure 34.2, enables adjusting of the "microphone sensitivity." This changes the value of `VolumeThreshold`. Although the default value of 400 works well for my phone, other phones from other manufactures might have microphones with slightly different characteristics. In addition, allowing users to adjust this value is helpful to make the app work as well as possible in a variety of environments. Blowing bubbles in a car might require a higher VolumeThreshold value than normal in order to ignore background noise, and blowing bubbles at a sporting event likely requires an even-higher value.

When providing an experience based on a hardware feature—such as the microphone or accelerometer—it's a good idea to provide end-user calibration, just in case different phone models have slightly different characteristics than the phone(s) used for testing.

FIGURE 34.2   The settings page for Bubble Blower enables changing and resetting the microphone's sensitivity.

The XAML for Figure 34.2 is shown in Listing 34.4.

LISTING 34.4   SettingsPage.xaml—The Settings User Interface for Bubble Blower

```
<phone:PhoneApplicationPage x:Class="WindowsPhoneApp.SettingsPage" x:Name="Page"
  xmlns="http://schemas.microsoft.com/winfx/2006/xaml/presentation"
  xmlns:x="http://schemas.microsoft.com/winfx/2006/xaml"
  xmlns:phone="clr-namespace:Microsoft.Phone.Controls;assembly=Microsoft.Phone"
  xmlns:shell="clr-namespace:Microsoft.Phone.Shell;assembly=Microsoft.Phone"
  xmlns:local="clr-namespace:WindowsPhoneApp"
  FontFamily="{StaticResource PhoneFontFamilyNormal}"
  FontSize="{StaticResource PhoneFontSizeNormal}"
```

LISTING 34.4   Continued

```
    Foreground="{StaticResource PhoneForegroundBrush}"
    SupportedOrientations="PortraitOrLandscape"
    shell:SystemTray.IsVisible="True">
  <Grid Background="{StaticResource PhoneBackgroundBrush}">
    <Grid.RowDefinitions>
      <RowDefinition Height="Auto"/>
      <RowDefinition Height="*"/>
    </Grid.RowDefinitions>

    <!-- The standard settings header -->
    <StackPanel Grid.Row="0" Style="{StaticResource PhoneTitlePanelStyle}">
      <TextBlock Text="SETTINGS" Style="{StaticResource PhoneTextTitle0Style}"/>
      <TextBlock Text="bubble blower"
                 Style="{StaticResource PhoneTextTitle1Style}"/>
    </StackPanel>

    <!-- A stacked text block, slider, and button -->
    <StackPanel Grid.Row="1" Margin="{StaticResource PhoneMargin}">
      <TextBlock Text="Microphone sensitivity"
                 Foreground="{StaticResource PhoneSubtleBrush}"
                 Margin="{StaticResource PhoneMargin}"/>
      <Slider x:Name="SensitivitySlider" Maximum="4000" LargeChange="100"
              IsDirectionReversed="True"
              Value="{Binding Threshold, Mode=TwoWay, ElementName=Page}"/>
      <Button Content="reset" Click="ResetButton_Click"
              local:Tilt.IsEnabled="True"/>
    </StackPanel>
  </Grid>
</phone:PhoneApplicationPage>
```

Notes:

→ The concept of microphone *sensitivity* is more user-friendly than the idea of a *threshold*, so the user interface uses this terminology. However, microphone sensitivity is the inverse of the volume threshold, so the slider's behavior must be reversed by setting its `IsDirectionReversed` property to `true`. This makes the slider report its maximum value when it is "empty" (when its thumb is all the way to the left) and decrement its value as the slider fills up and reaches its minimum value.

→ The slider's value is allowed to vary from 4,000 to 0. It is given a corresponding `LargeChange` value of 100, so the value changes at a reasonable rate when the user holds a finger on the slider. Its current value is bound to a `Threshold` property on the current page instance, with two-way data binding.

→ As mentioned in previous chapters, it's always a good idea to have a reset button
  when sliders are involved.

The code-behind for the settings page is shown in Listing 34.5.

LISTING 34.5   `SettingsPage.xaml.cs`—The Settings Code-Behind for Bubble Blower

```
using System.Windows;
using Microsoft.Phone.Controls;

namespace WindowsPhoneApp
{
  public partial class SettingsPage : PhoneApplicationPage
  {
    public SettingsPage()
    {
      InitializeComponent();
    }

    // Simple property bound to the slider
    public int Sensitivity
    {
      get { return Settings.VolumeThreshold.Value; }
      set { Settings.VolumeThreshold.Value = value; }
    }

    void ResetButton_Click(object sender, RoutedEventArgs e)
    {
      this.SensitivitySlider.Value = Settings.VolumeThreshold.DefaultValue;
    }
  }
}
```

Sensitivity is not a dependency property, so changes to its value do not automatically
update the slider; changes only flow from the slider *to* the property. (The initial value is
fetched by the slider when the page loads, however.) This is why `ResetButton_Click`
updates the slider's value rather than `Sensitivity`. By doing so, it updates the user interface *and* the value of the `VolumeThreshold` setting with one line of code.

The Finished Product

Blowing lots of bubbles

The expanded application bar menu

The instructions page

TALKING PARROT

The Talking Parrot app provides more entertainment with the microphone. After greeting you with a friendly "hello," the parrot listens to what you say and then repeats it in its own voice, with a whistle or squawk thrown in. This app must not only turn the buffer collected from the microphone into a playable XNA sound effect, but it also must determine when is a good time to listen to the user and when is a good time to play the captured audio.

The Main User Interface

Listing 35.1 contains the XAML for the main page. It consists of three parts: a bunch of animations that are triggered by code-behind, an application bar, and several images (plus one ellipse) placed in specific spots on a canvas. The individual images that form the parrot are shown in Figure 35.1.

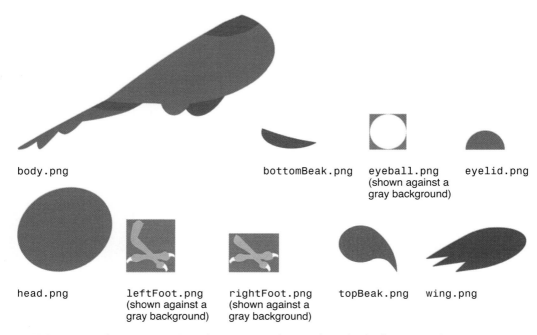

body.png   bottomBeak.png   eyeball.png   eyelid.png
                                                  (shown against a
                                                  gray background)

head.png   leftFoot.png   rightFoot.png   topBeak.png   wing.png
                  (shown against a (shown against a
                  gray background) gray background)

FIGURE 35.1   The parrot consists of nine images that can be individually animated.

LISTING 35.1   MainPage.xaml—The User Interface for Talking Parrot's Main Page

```
<phone:PhoneApplicationPage x:Class="WindowsPhoneApp.MainPage"
    xmlns="http://schemas.microsoft.com/winfx/2006/xaml/presentation"
    xmlns:x="http://schemas.microsoft.com/winfx/2006/xaml"
    xmlns:phone="clr-namespace:Microsoft.Phone.Controls;assembly=Microsoft.Phone"
    xmlns:shell="clr-namespace:Microsoft.Phone.Shell;assembly=Microsoft.Phone"
    SupportedOrientations="Portrait">

  <!-- Animations as named resources -->
  <phone:PhoneApplicationPage.Resources>
    <Storyboard x:Name="BlinkStoryboard" Duration="0:0:4" RepeatBehavior="Forever"
      Storyboard.TargetProperty=
        "(UIElement.RenderTransform).(CompositeTransform.TranslateY)">
      <DoubleAnimation Storyboard.TargetName="TopEyelidImage" To="0"
                      Duration="0:0:.1" AutoReverse="True"/>
      <DoubleAnimation Storyboard.TargetName="BottomEyelidImage" To="77"
                      Duration="0:0:.1" AutoReverse="True"/>
    </Storyboard>

    <Storyboard x:Name="HeadUpStoryboard" Storyboard.TargetProperty=
            "(UIElement.RenderTransform).(CompositeTransform.TranslateY)">
```

LISTING 35.1   Continued

```xml
    <DoubleAnimation Storyboard.TargetName="HeadCanvas" To="-7"
                     Duration="0:0:1">
      <DoubleAnimation.EasingFunction>
        <QuinticEase/>
      </DoubleAnimation.EasingFunction>
    </DoubleAnimation>
  </Storyboard>

  <Storyboard x:Name="HeadDownStoryboard" Storyboard.TargetProperty=
              "(UIElement.RenderTransform).(CompositeTransform.TranslateY)">
    <DoubleAnimation Storyboard.TargetName="HeadCanvas" To="0" Duration="0:0:1">
      <DoubleAnimation.EasingFunction>
        <QuadraticEase/>
      </DoubleAnimation.EasingFunction>
    </DoubleAnimation>
  </Storyboard>

  <Storyboard x:Name="WingFlutterStoryboard" Storyboard.TargetProperty=
              "(UIElement.RenderTransform).(CompositeTransform.Rotation)">
    <DoubleAnimation Storyboard.TargetName="WingImage" To="35" Duration="0:0:1"
                     AutoReverse="True">
      <DoubleAnimation.EasingFunction>
        <BounceEase/>
      </DoubleAnimation.EasingFunction>
    </DoubleAnimation>
  </Storyboard>

  <Storyboard x:Name="StompStoryboard" Storyboard.TargetProperty=
              "(UIElement.RenderTransform).(CompositeTransform.TranslateY)">
    <DoubleAnimation Storyboard.TargetName="LeftFootImage" To="-30"
                     Duration="0:0:.2" AutoReverse="True">
      <DoubleAnimation.EasingFunction>
        <QuinticEase/>
      </DoubleAnimation.EasingFunction>
    </DoubleAnimation>
    <DoubleAnimation Storyboard.TargetName="RightFootImage" To="-10"
                     BeginTime="0:0:.1" Duration="0:0:.2" AutoReverse="True">
      <DoubleAnimation.EasingFunction>
        <QuinticEase/>
      </DoubleAnimation.EasingFunction>
    </DoubleAnimation>
  </Storyboard>
```

LISTING 35.1   Continued

```
<Storyboard x:Name="SpeakStoryboard" Storyboard.TargetProperty=
            "(UIElement.RenderTransform).(CompositeTransform.Rotation)">
  <DoubleAnimationUsingKeyFrames x:Name="TopBeakAnimation"
                                 Storyboard.TargetName="TopBeakImage" />
  <DoubleAnimationUsingKeyFrames x:Name="BottomBeakAnimation"
                                 Storyboard.TargetName="BottomBeakImage" />
</Storyboard>
</phone:PhoneApplicationPage.Resources>

<!-- The application bar -->
<phone:PhoneApplicationPage.ApplicationBar>
  <shell:ApplicationBar Opacity=".5">
    <shell:ApplicationBarIconButton Text="instructions"
      IconUri="/Shared/Images/appbar.instructions.png"
      Click="InstructionsButton_Click"/>
    <shell:ApplicationBar.MenuItems>
      <shell:ApplicationBarMenuItem Text="settings"
                                    Click="SettingsMenuItem_Click"/>
      <shell:ApplicationBarMenuItem Text="about"
                                    Click="AboutMenuItem_Click"/>
    </shell:ApplicationBar.MenuItems>
  </shell:ApplicationBar>
</phone:PhoneApplicationPage.ApplicationBar>

<!-- Many images placed in a canvas -->
<Canvas>
  <Image Source="Images/background.png" Stretch="None"/>
  <Image x:Name="RightFootImage" Source="Images/rightFoot.png"
        Canvas.Left="159" Canvas.Top="537">
    <Image.RenderTransform>
      <CompositeTransform TranslateY="0"/>
    </Image.RenderTransform>
  </Image>
  <Image x:Name="LeftFootImage" Source="Images/leftFoot.png"
        Canvas.Left="109" Canvas.Top="532">
    <Image.RenderTransform>
      <CompositeTransform TranslateY="0"/>
    </Image.RenderTransform>
  </Image>
  <Image Source="Images/body.png" Canvas.Left="-164" Canvas.Top="346"/>
  <Canvas x:Name="HeadCanvas">
    <Canvas.RenderTransform>
      <CompositeTransform TranslateY="0"/>
    </Canvas.RenderTransform>
```

LISTING 35.1   Continued

```xml
    <Image Source="Images/head.png" Canvas.Left="155" Canvas.Top="203"/>
    <Image x:Name="BottomBeakImage" Source="Images/bottomBeak.png"
           Canvas.Left="282" Canvas.Top="294" RenderTransformOrigin=".5,0">
      <Image.RenderTransform>
        <CompositeTransform Rotation="0" CenterX="15" CenterY="15"/>
      </Image.RenderTransform>
    </Image>
    <Image x:Name="TopBeakImage" Source="Images/topBeak.png"
           Canvas.Left="279" Canvas.Top="252">
      <Image.RenderTransform>
        <CompositeTransform Rotation="0" CenterX="38" CenterY="38"/>
      </Image.RenderTransform>
    </Image>
    <Image Source="Images/eyeball.png" Canvas.Left="198" Canvas.Top="248"/>
    <Ellipse x:Name="Pupil" Fill="Black" Width="18" Height="18"
             Canvas.Left="240" Canvas.Top="275"/>
    <Image x:Name="AngryEyelidImage" Source="Images/eyelid.png"
           Visibility="Collapsed" Canvas.Left="196" Canvas.Top="246">
      <Image.RenderTransform>
        <CompositeTransform Rotation="15" CenterX="76" CenterY="39"/>
      </Image.RenderTransform>
    </Image>
    <Image x:Name="TopEyelidImage" Source="Images/eyelid.png"
           Canvas.Left="196" Canvas.Top="246">
      <Image.RenderTransform>
        <CompositeTransform TranslateY="-37" Rotation="0"
                            CenterX="76" CenterY="39"/>
      </Image.RenderTransform>
    </Image>
    <Image x:Name="BottomEyelidImage" Source="Images/eyelid.png"
           Canvas.Left="196" Canvas.Top="246">
      <Image.RenderTransform>
        <CompositeTransform ScaleY="-1" TranslateY="112"/>
      </Image.RenderTransform>
    </Image>
  </Canvas>
  <Image x:Name="WingImage" Source="Images/wing.png"
         Canvas.Left="68" Canvas.Top="414">
    <Image.RenderTransform>
      <CompositeTransform Rotation="0" CenterX="190" CenterY="26"/>
    </Image.RenderTransform>
  </Image>
  </Canvas>
</phone:PhoneApplicationPage>
```

Notes:

→ The page is portrait-only due to the exact layout required by the background and pieces of the parrot.

→ The animations are given names rather than dictionary keys, so they can be easily referenced from code-behind.

→ The animations lower, raise, and rotate various pieces of the parrot when triggered by code-behind. Every animatable piece uses a composite transform for consistency and for ease in animating multiple aspects (such as rotation *and* translation).

→ SpeakStoryboard is special. Although it has two keyframe animations to animate the top and bottom beak, they start out empty. These are continually updated from code-behind based on the audio to be spoken, so the parrot appears to mouth the actual words and sounds it speaks.

→ Any of the parrot pieces (as well as the background) could have been created as vector shapes instead of images. Instead, the black pupil is the only vector shape used in the parrot (an ellipse). This gives us the flexibility to grow/shrink the pupil without pixelation and the flexibility to change its color, although this app doesn't take advantage of these capabilities.

→ The application bar provides links to three other pages: instructions, settings, and about. The settings page is examined later in this chapter.

The Main Code-Behind

The code-behind for the main page is shown in Listing 35.2.

LISTING 35.2   `MainPage.xaml.cs`—The Code-Behind for Talking Parrot's Main Page

```
using System;
using System.IO;
using System.Windows;
using System.Windows.Input;
using System.Windows.Media;
using System.Windows.Media.Animation;
using Microsoft.Phone.Controls;
using Microsoft.Xna.Framework.Audio;

namespace WindowsPhoneApp
{
  public partial class MainPage : PhoneApplicationPage
  {
    byte[] buffer;

    // Used for capturing audio from the microphone
```

LISTING 35.2   Continued

```
MemoryStream recordedStream;
long playbackStartPosition = -1;
int consecutiveSilentSamples;
DateTime? speakingDoneTime;

// Used for playing the three included sounds: hello, whistle, and squawk
bool playingIncludedSound;
Random random = new Random();

public MainPage()
{
  InitializeComponent();

  SoundEffects.Initialize();
  CompositionTarget.Rendering += CompositionTarget_Rendering;

  // Start blinking, which runs the whole time
  this.BlinkStoryboard.Begin();

  // Prevent the off-screen tail from being seen when
  // animating to the instructions or about pages
  this.Clip = new RectangleGeometry {
    Rect = new Rect(0, 0, Constants.SCREEN_WIDTH, Constants.SCREEN_HEIGHT) };

  // Configure the microphone with the smallest supported BufferDuration (.1)
  Microphone.Default.BufferDuration = TimeSpan.FromSeconds(.1);
  Microphone.Default.BufferReady += Microphone_BufferReady;

  // Initialize the buffer for holding microphone data
  int size = Microphone.Default.GetSampleSizeInBytes(
    Microphone.Default.BufferDuration);
  this.buffer = new byte[size];

  // Initialize the stream used to record microphone data
  this.recordedStream = new MemoryStream();

  // Speak a "hello" greeting
  PrepareStoryboardForIncludedSound(SoundEffects.HelloBuffer);
  Speak(SoundEffects.Hello, 0);
}

protected override void OnMouseLeftButtonDown(MouseButtonEventArgs e)
{
  base.OnMouseLeftButtonDown(e);
```

LISTING 35.2   Continued

```
    // Get mad!
    this.AngryEyelidImage.Visibility = Visibility.Visible;
  }

  protected override void OnMouseLeftButtonUp(MouseButtonEventArgs e)
  {
    base.OnMouseLeftButtonUp(e);
    // Become happy again
    this.AngryEyelidImage.Visibility = Visibility.Collapsed;
  }

  void CompositionTarget_Rendering(object sender, EventArgs e)
  {
    // Required for XNA Microphone API to work
    Microsoft.Xna.Framework.FrameworkDispatcher.Update();

    // Check if currently-playing audio has finished
    if (this.speakingDoneTime != null && DateTime.Now > this.speakingDoneTime)
    {
      if (!this.playingIncludedSound)
      {
        // Don't restart the microphone yet! We just played audio from the
        // microphone, so add either a whistle or squawk to make it sound more
        // like a parrot. This will reset speakingDoneTime.
        int choice = random.Next(2); // A random number: either 0 or 1
        byte[] buffer = (choice == 0 ? SoundEffects.WhistleBuffer :
                                       SoundEffects.SquawkBuffer);
        SoundEffect effect = (choice == 0 ? SoundEffects.Whistle :
                                            SoundEffects.Squawk);
        PrepareStoryboardForIncludedSound(buffer);
        Speak(effect, 0); // Play at the normal speed (0)
      }
      else
      {
        // Now it's time to restart the microphone
        Microphone.Default.Start();

        // Reset state
        this.speakingDoneTime = null;
        this.playingIncludedSound = false;

        // Smoothly return the head to its resting position
        this.HeadDownStoryboard.Begin();
      }
```

LISTING 35.2   Continued

```csharp
    }
  }

  void Speak(SoundEffect effect, float speed)
  {
    // Stop listening, because it is time to talk
    Microphone.Default.Stop();

    // Determine when the audio will be done playing and it's time to either
    // add a squawk/whistle or restart the microphone.
    // The length is halved for microphone-recorded sounds to avoid extra lag
    // time seen in practice.
    this.speakingDoneTime = DateTime.Now +
      TimeSpan.FromTicks((long)(effect.Duration.Ticks *
      (speed == 0 ? 1 : speed / 2)));

    // Stop any in-progress storyboards
    this.SpeakStoryboard.Stop();
    this.WingFlutterStoryboard.Stop();
    this.HeadUpStoryboard.Stop();
    this.StompStoryboard.Stop();

    // Start the storyboards
    this.SpeakStoryboard.Begin();
    this.WingFlutterStoryboard.Begin();
    this.HeadUpStoryboard.Begin();
    this.StompStoryboard.Begin();

    // Play the audio at full volume with the passed-in speed (pitch)
    effect.Play(1, speed, 0);
  }

  // Changes the contents of TopBeakAnimation and BottomBeakAnimation
  // to match the audio in the buffer, so the beak appears to speak the sounds
  void PrepareStoryboardForIncludedSound(byte[] buffer)
  {
    ResetSpeakStoryboard();

    // Loop through the buffer in 100-millisecond chunks
    for (int i = 0; i < buffer.Length;
                  i += Constants.INCLUDED_SOUND_BYTES_PER_100_MILLISECONDS)
    {
      // Cast from short to int to prevent -32768 from overflowing Math.Abs
      int currentVolume = Math.Abs((int)BitConverter.ToInt16(buffer, i));
```

LISTING 35.2   Continued

```
    // Add a keyframe to the top & bottom beak animations based on the
    // current audio level. ANIMATION_ADJUSTMENT is a fudge factor that
    // slightly speeds-up the animation to account for lag.
    KeyTime keyTime = TimeSpan.FromSeconds(Math.Max(0,
      (double)i / Constants.INCLUDED_SOUND_BYTES_PER_SECOND
      - Constants.ANIMATION_ADJUSTMENT));
    AddSpeakKeyFrame(currentVolume, keyTime);
  }

  // Add the final keyframe 100 ms later that smoothly closes the beak
  KeyTime finalKeyTime = TimeSpan.FromSeconds(Math.Max(0, (double)
    (buffer.Length + Constants.INCLUDED_SOUND_BYTES_PER_100_MILLISECONDS) /
    Constants.INCLUDED_SOUND_BYTES_PER_SECOND));
  AddFinalSpeakKeyFrame(finalKeyTime);

  // The preceding work was computationally expensive, so it's time for
  // another update before attempting to play the sound
  Microsoft.Xna.Framework.FrameworkDispatcher.Update();

  this.playingIncludedSound = true;
}

// Stop the storyboard and empty the keyframes in its two animations
void ResetSpeakStoryboard()
{
  SpeakStoryboard.Stop();
  TopBeakAnimation.KeyFrames.Clear();
  BottomBeakAnimation.KeyFrames.Clear();
}

// Position the top and bottom beak based on the current volume.
// A louder volume results in a wider opening.
void AddSpeakKeyFrame(int currentVolume, KeyTime keyTime)
{
  // The top beak rotation should always be an angle between 0 and -50
  TopBeakAnimation.KeyFrames.Add(new DiscreteDoubleKeyFrame {
    KeyTime = keyTime, Value = Math.Max(-50, currentVolume / -15) });

  // The bottom beak rotation should always be an angle between 0 and 30
  BottomBeakAnimation.KeyFrames.Add(new DiscreteDoubleKeyFrame {
    KeyTime = keyTime, Value = Math.Min(30, currentVolume / 15) });
}

// Close the beak
```

LISTING 35.2   Continued

```csharp
void AddFinalSpeakKeyFrame(KeyTime keyTime)
{
  // Use keyframes that do a smooth quintic ease from the previous values
  TopBeakAnimation.KeyFrames.Add(new EasingDoubleKeyFrame {
    EasingFunction = new QuinticEase(), KeyTime = keyTime, Value = 0 });
  BottomBeakAnimation.KeyFrames.Add(new EasingDoubleKeyFrame {
    EasingFunction = new QuinticEase(), KeyTime = keyTime, Value = 0 });
}

void Microphone_BufferReady(object sender, EventArgs e)
{
  int size = Microphone.Default.GetData(this.buffer);
  if (size == 0)
    return;

  // Unconditionally record the audio data by writing it to the stream
  this.recordedStream.Write(this.buffer, 0, size);

  int currentVolume = SoundEffects.GetAverageVolume(this.buffer, size);
  if (currentVolume > Settings.VolumeThreshold.Value)
  {
    // The current volume is loud enough to be considered talking
    this.consecutiveSilentSamples = 0;

    if (this.playbackStartPosition == -1)
    {
      // Start a new phrase.
      // Back up half a second if we've got the data, for a smoother result.
      this.playbackStartPosition = Math.Max(0, this.recordedStream.Position
        - Constants.MICROPHONE_BYTES_PER_100_MILLISECONDS * 5);
      ResetSpeakStoryboard();
    }

    // Add a keyframe to the beak animations based on the current volume
    // ANIMATION_ADJUSTMENT is a fudge factor that slightly speeds-up the
    // animation to account for lag.
    KeyTime keyTime = TimeSpan.FromSeconds(Math.Max(0,
        Constants.SOUND_SPEED_FACTOR * (this.recordedStream.Position
      - Constants.MICROPHONE_BYTES_PER_100_MILLISECONDS
      - this.playbackStartPosition) / Constants.MICROPHONE_BYTES_PER_SECOND
      - Constants.ANIMATION_ADJUSTMENT));
    AddSpeakKeyFrame(currentVolume, keyTime);
  }
  else
```

LISTING 35.2   Continued

```
    {
      // The current volume is NOT loud enough to be considered talking
      this.consecutiveSilentSamples++; // 10 times == 1 second

      // Check for the end of a spoken phrase. This happens when we've got a
      // nonnegative playback start position followed by a second (10 samples)
      // of silence.
      if (this.playbackStartPosition != -1 &&
        this.consecutiveSilentSamples == 10)
      {
        this.consecutiveSilentSamples = 0;

        // Add the final keyframe that smoothly closes the beak
        KeyTime keyTime = TimeSpan.FromSeconds(Math.Max(0,
            Constants.SOUND_SPEED_FACTOR * (this.recordedStream.Position
          - Constants.MICROPHONE_BYTES_PER_100_MILLISECONDS
          - this.playbackStartPosition) / Constants.MICROPHONE_BYTES_PER_SECOND
          - Constants.ANIMATION_ADJUSTMENT));
        AddFinalSpeakKeyFrame(keyTime);

        // Copy the appropriate slice of audio from the recorded stream into
        // a buffer
        byte[] buffer = new byte[this.recordedStream.Position -
          this.playbackStartPosition];
        this.recordedStream.Seek(this.playbackStartPosition, SeekOrigin.Begin);
        this.recordedStream.Read(buffer, 0, buffer.Length);

        // Amplify the recorded audio, as it tends to be softer than desired
        if (Settings.VolumeMultiplier.Value > 1)
          SoundEffects.AmplifyAudio(buffer, Settings.VolumeMultiplier.Value);

        // Reset variables
        this.playbackStartPosition = -1;
        this.recordedStream.Position = 0;

        // Create a new sound effect from the buffer and speak it
        SoundEffect effect = new SoundEffect(buffer,
          Microphone.Default.SampleRate, AudioChannels.Mono);
        Speak(effect, Constants.SOUND_SPEED_FACTOR);
      }
    }
  }
```

LISTING 35.2 Continued

```
// Application bar handlers

void InstructionsButton_Click(object sender, EventArgs e)
{
  this.NavigationService.Navigate(new Uri("/InstructionsPage.xaml",
    UriKind.Relative));
}

void SettingsMenuItem_Click(object sender, EventArgs e)
{
  this.NavigationService.Navigate(new Uri("/SettingsPage.xaml",
    UriKind.Relative));
}

void AboutMenuItem_Click(object sender, EventArgs e)
{
  this.NavigationService.Navigate(
    new Uri("/Shared/About/AboutPage.xaml?appName=Talking Parrot",
      UriKind.Relative));
}
  }
}
```

Notes:

→ The constructor is nearly identical to the preceding chapter's constructor, although it doesn't start the microphone right away because the parrot speaks a greeting instead. We never use the microphone while the parrot is speaking because it might hear itself talk and begin an infinite pattern of repeating itself! Other than speaking the greeting, the other additional tasks are initializing the SoundEffects class, shown in Listing 35.3, initializing a stream for recording microphone audio, and starting the blinking animation that continuously moves the parrot's eyelids for the duration of the app. The microphone is once again given the shortest possible buffer duration, so the app can remain as responsive as possible.

→ The handlers for screen taps (OnMouseLeftButtonDown and OnMouseLeftButtonUp) toggle the visibility of an "angry eyelid" to give the parrot an annoyed appearance when touched. This could be changed to handle taps specifically on the parrot's body, but handling taps anywhere on the screen is simpler and likely good enough.

→ CompositionTarget_Rendering, besides calling Update, is responsible for taking action each time the parrot is done speaking. It determines when the parrot is done by comparing the current time to speakingDoneTime, a field set later in the code. If the parrot has just finished speaking audio recorded from the microphone, it makes the parrot speak either a whistle or a squawk (randomly chosen), which resets speakingDoneTime to the later time when the sound effect will finish. If the parrot has just finished speaking one of the included sounds (hello, whistle, or squawk), it restarts the microphone, so it can listen for something new to repeat. As with the preceding chapter, all this code continues to run when navigating forward to a different page. However, this is quite handy for this app because it enables you to aurally test the two settings in real-time as you adjust the sliders on the settings page.

→ The Speak method does the important work of stopping the microphone, setting speakingDoneTime, playing the passed-in sound effect at the passed-in speed, and animating the parrot to mouth the words, flutter its wing, raise its head, and stomp its feet. The magic of SpeakStoryboard mouthing the words in the current audio is enabled by manually updating its animation based on the raw audio data that will be played. This is done inside PrepareStoryboardForIncludedSound for the three included sounds and inside Microphone_BufferReady for the audio recorded from the microphone.

→ PrepareStoryboardForIncludedSound grabs a sample from the passed-in buffer at every 100 milliseconds (mimicking the behavior of the microphone event) and adds a keyframe to the top and bottom beak animations based on the volume of each sample. The louder the sound, the wider the beak needs to be open. The included sounds have a different bitrate than audio captured from the microphone, so the mapping of time to bytes in the buffer is handled by constants specific to these sounds. A final keyframe is added at the end to handle smoothly closing the beak. Because the three included sounds never change, the animations for each one could have been precalculated (or cached after the first time). However, this dynamic approach is done for simplicity and consistency with the code for sounds recorded from the microphone. It also means you can swap in different sound files, and things will work as expected.

→ AddSpeakKeyFrame adds each keyframe as a discrete keyframe (meaning no interpolation between each frame). This is reasonable considering the speed at which the frames advance. It manipulates the value of currentVolume to give it an appropriate range for the angle of rotation for each piece of the beak.

→ Add**Final**SpeakKeyFrame gives the final keyframe a quintic (power of five) ease from the preceding value to zero, so the beak snaps shut smoothly.

→ Microphone_BufferReady uses the same approach as the preceding chapter to determine the volume of the last .1 seconds of audio. If the audio is loud enough and we haven't started tracking the audio as a phrase to play back, we start paying attention to the audio by marking the starting position in the recorded stream and adding a keyframe to the beak animations (as done previously with the included sounds). We continue to listen to the audio (and add keyframes to the animations) until there has been a full second of silence, which equates to ten consecutive samples where the average volume was below the threshold.

→ Because human speech gradually ramps up to a volume above the threshold, simply starting playback at the point where the volume is loud enough would cut off the beginning of whatever was spoken and sound strange. Therefore, the starting position in the recorded stream is backed up half a second from the current point when set inside `Microphone_BufferReady`. This is why the microphone audio is always appended to the stream, regardless of volume.

→ When the end of relevant audio (a second of silence) has been detected inside `Microphone_BufferReady`, it copies all the data placed into the recorded stream from the chosen starting position onward into a new byte array. Although previous apps have obtained a sound effect from the static `SoundEffect.FromStream` method, this code—after potentially amplifying the audio—calls a constructor that enables passing in the raw audio data as a byte array. It then plays the dynamic sound effect (along with the appropriate animations) by calling `Speak`. It chooses a playback speed (pitch) 80% higher than normal (specified by the `SOUND_SPEED_FACTOR` constant) so it sounds more like a parrot speaking than the original person whose voice was recorded.

→ The default volume threshold used by Talking Parrot is lower than the one used by Bubble Blower. Here are the two settings used by this app, with their default values:

```
public static class Settings
{
  public static readonly Setting<int> VolumeThreshold =
    new Setting<int>("VolumeThreshold", 500);
  public static readonly Setting<int> VolumeMultiplier =
    new Setting<int>("VolumeMultiplier", 4);
}
```

Talking Parrot's `SoundEffects` class is similar to the same-named class in previous chapters, but it also exposes the `AmplifyAudio` and `GetAverageVolume` methods used by Listing 35.2. Listing 35.3 contains the implementation.

LISTING 35.3   `SoundEffects.cs`—Exposes the Built-In Sound Effects and Audio Utility Methods

```
using System;
using System.IO;
using System.Windows.Resources;
using Microsoft.Xna.Framework.Audio;

namespace WindowsPhoneApp
{
  public static class SoundEffects
  {
    public static SoundEffect Hello { get; private set; }
    public static SoundEffect Squawk { get; private set; }
```

LISTING 35.3   Continued

```csharp
public static SoundEffect Whistle { get; private set; }

public static byte[] HelloBuffer { get; private set; }
public static byte[] SquawkBuffer { get; private set; }
public static byte[] WhistleBuffer { get; private set; }

public static void Initialize()
{
  StreamResourceInfo info;

  info = App.GetResourceStream(new Uri("Audio/hello.wav", UriKind.Relative));
  HelloBuffer = GetBytes(info.Stream);
  info.Stream.Position = 0;
  Hello = SoundEffect.FromStream(info.Stream);

  info = App.GetResourceStream(
    new Uri("Audio/squawk.wav", UriKind.Relative));
  SquawkBuffer = GetBytes(info.Stream);
  info.Stream.Position = 0;
  Squawk = SoundEffect.FromStream(info.Stream);

  info = App.GetResourceStream(
    new Uri("Audio/whistle.wav", UriKind.Relative));
  WhistleBuffer = GetBytes(info.Stream);
  info.Stream.Position = 0;
  Whistle = SoundEffect.FromStream(info.Stream);

  // Required for XNA Microphone API to work
  Microsoft.Xna.Framework.FrameworkDispatcher.Update();
}

static byte[] GetBytes(Stream stream)
{
  byte[] bytes = new byte[stream.Length];
  stream.Read(SquawkBuffer, 0, (int)stream.Length);
  return bytes;
}

// Make the sound louder by modifying the raw audio samples
public static void AmplifyAudio(byte[] buffer, int multiplier)
{
  // Buffer is an array of bytes, but we want to examine each 2-byte value
  for (int i = 0; i < buffer.Length; i += 2)
  {
```

LISTING 35.3   Continued

```csharp
      int value = BitConverter.ToInt16(buffer, i);
      if (value > Settings.VolumeThreshold.Value)
      {
        // Only amplify samples that are loud enough to not
        // be considered background noise
        value *= Settings.VolumeMultiplier.Value;

        // Make sure the multiplied value stays within bounds
        if (value > short.MaxValue)
          value = short.MaxValue;
        else if (value < short.MinValue)
          value = short.MinValue;

        // Replace the two bytes with the amplified value
        byte[] newValue = BitConverter.GetBytes(value);
        buffer[i] = newValue[0];
        buffer[i + 1] = newValue[1];
      }
    }
  }

  // Returns the average value among the first numBytes in the buffer
  public static int GetAverageVolume(byte[] buffer, int numBytes)
  {
    long total = 0;

    // Buffer is an array of bytes, but we want to examine each 2-byte value
    for (int i = 0; i < numBytes; i += 2)
    {
      // Cast from short to int to prevent -32768 from overflowing Math.Abs:
      int value = Math.Abs((int)BitConverter.ToInt16(buffer, i));
      total += value;
    }
    return (int)(total / (numBytes / 2));
  }
}
}
```

Unlike in past apps, the raw audio data for each sound file is copied into a byte array exposed as a property. Listing 35.2 used these byte arrays to determine the volume over time, just like what is done for audio from the microphone.

> 💡 The audio captured from the microphone can often be much softer than desired. To combat this, the `AmplifyAudio` method in Listing 35.3 increases the volume of the recorded microphone audio by manually multiplying the value of each sample in the buffer (if the sample is louder than a threshold, to avoid amplifying background noise). Although the volume of the played-back audio is ultimately limited by the phone's volume setting, this technique can make the audio surprisingly loud. Of course, the more that the audio is amplified, the more distorted it may sound.

> 💡 You can play music from the music library while using this app to make the parrot "sing" the song. You just have to pause the music, so the parrot gets the second of silence needed to prompt it to speak! This can be controlled via the top bar that gets displayed while adjusting the phone's volume, shown in Figure 35.2.

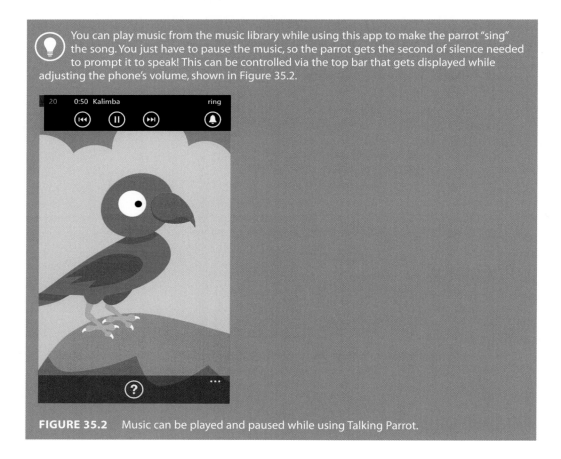

FIGURE 35.2   Music can be played and paused while using Talking Parrot.

Here are the constants (and read-only fields) used by this app:

```
public static class Constants
{
  // Screen
  public const int SCREEN_WIDTH = 480;
  public const int SCREEN_HEIGHT = 800;
```

```
    public const float SOUND_SPEED_FACTOR = .8f;
    public const float ANIMATION_ADJUSTMENT = .1f;
    public static readonly long MICROPHONE_BYTES_PER_SECOND =
        Microphone.Default.GetSampleSizeInBytes(TimeSpan.FromSeconds(1));
    public static readonly long MICROPHONE_BYTES_PER_100_MILLISECONDS =
        Constants.MICROPHONE_BYTES_PER_SECOND / 10;
    public const int INCLUDED_SOUND_BYTES_PER_SECOND = 141100;
    public const int INCLUDED_SOUND_BYTES_PER_100_MILLISECONDS = 14110;
}
```

The Settings Page

The settings page, shown in Figure
35.3, is like the settings page from the
Bubble Blower app, but with two
sliders instead of one. The first slider
adjusts the "parrot voice volume,"
which maps to the VolumeMultiplier
setting. The second slider is just like
the one from Bubble Blower, which
maps to the VolumeThreshold setting.
It is labeled as "parrot hearing sensitivity" instead of "microphone sensitivity" to be more appropriate to the
theme of this app.

The XAML for Figure 35.3 is shown in
Listing 35.4. The differences from
Bubble Blower's settings page are empha-
sized.

FIGURE 35.3 The settings page for Talking
Parrot enables changing and resetting
VolumeMultiplier and VolumeThreshold.

LISTING 35.4   SettingsPage.xaml—The Settings User Interface for Talking Parrot

```
<phone:PhoneApplicationPage x:Name="Page"
    x:Class="WindowsPhoneApp.SettingsPage"
    xmlns="http://schemas.microsoft.com/winfx/2006/xaml/presentation"
    xmlns:x="http://schemas.microsoft.com/winfx/2006/xaml"
    xmlns:phone="clr-namespace:Microsoft.Phone.Controls;assembly=Microsoft.Phone"
    xmlns:shell="clr-namespace:Microsoft.Phone.Shell;assembly=Microsoft.Phone"
    xmlns:local="clr-namespace:WindowsPhoneApp"
    FontFamily="{StaticResource PhoneFontFamilyNormal}"
    FontSize="{StaticResource PhoneFontSizeNormal}"
    Foreground="{StaticResource PhoneForegroundBrush}"
    SupportedOrientations="PortraitOrLandscape"
    shell:SystemTray.IsVisible="True">
```

LISTING 35.4   Continued

```xml
<Grid Background="{StaticResource PhoneBackgroundBrush}">
  <Grid.RowDefinitions>
    <RowDefinition Height="Auto"/>
    <RowDefinition Height="*"/>
  </Grid.RowDefinitions>

  <!-- The standard settings header: -->
  <StackPanel Grid.Row="0" Style="{StaticResource PhoneTitlePanelStyle}">
    <TextBlock Text="SETTINGS" Style="{StaticResource PhoneTextTitle0Style}"/>
    <TextBlock Text="talking parrot"
               Style="{StaticResource PhoneTextTitle1Style}"/>
  </StackPanel>

  <!-- Stacked contents inside a ScrollViewer,
       for the benefit of landscape orientation: -->
  <ScrollViewer Grid.Row="1">
    <StackPanel Margin="{StaticResource PhoneMargin}">
      <TextBlock Text="Parrot voice volume"
                 Foreground="{StaticResource PhoneSubtleBrush}"
                 Margin="{StaticResource PhoneMargin}"/>
      <Slider x:Name="VolumeSlider" Minimum="1" Maximum="18"
                 Value="{Binding Volume, Mode=TwoWay, ElementName=Page}"/>
      <TextBlock Text="Parrot hearing sensitivity"
                 Foreground="{StaticResource PhoneSubtleBrush}"
                 Margin="{StaticResource PhoneMargin}"/>
      <Slider x:Name="SensitivitySlider" Maximum="1000" LargeChange="100"
                 IsDirectionReversed="True"
                 Value="{Binding Threshold, Mode=TwoWay, ElementName=Page}"/>
      <Button Content="reset" Click="ResetButton_Click"
                 local:Tilt.IsEnabled="True"/>
    </StackPanel>
  </ScrollViewer>
</Grid>
</phone:PhoneApplicationPage>
```

Notes:

➜ Because the page is now a little too tall for the landscape orientations, the StackPanel is wrapped inside a ScrollViewer.

➜ The allowed range for VolumeMultiplier is 1–18.

➜ Although SensitivitySlider needs to be reversed to map to the underlying threshold value, VolumeSlider does not.

The code-behind for the settings page is shown in Listing 35.5.

LISTING 35.5   `SettingsPage.xaml.cs`—The Settings Code-Behind for Talking Parrot

```
using System.Windows;
using Microsoft.Phone.Controls;

namespace WindowsPhoneApp
{
  public partial class SettingsPage : PhoneApplicationPage
  {
    public SettingsPage()
    {
      InitializeComponent();
    }

    // Simple property bound to the first slider
    public int Volume
    {
      get { return Settings.VolumeMultiplier.Value; }
      set { Settings.VolumeMultiplier.Value = value; }
    }

    // Simple property bound to the second slider
    public int Threshold
    {
      get { return Settings.VolumeThreshold.Value; }
      set { Settings.VolumeThreshold.Value = value; }
    }

    private void ResetButton_Click(object sender, RoutedEventArgs e)
    {
      this.VolumeSlider.Value = Settings.VolumeMultiplier.DefaultValue;
      this.SensitivitySlider.Value = Settings.VolumeThreshold.DefaultValue;
    }
  }
}
```

The Finished Product

The parrot at rest

Angry when touched

The expanded application
bar menu

The instructions page

chapter 36

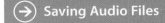
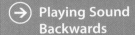

SOUND RECORDER

Sound Recorder enables you to record, manage, and play audio clips. It is named after the Sound Recorder program on Windows and reminiscent of the Voice Memos app on the iPhone. It can come in quite handy when you're away from a computer and have some thoughts that you don't want to forget, especially because it enables you to pause in the midst of a single recording.

Control your recording with simple (and large!) record, pause, and stop buttons. Rename or delete previous recordings one-by-one, or bulk-delete unwanted recordings with a check box mechanism matching the one used by the built-in Mail app. When playing a recording, you can adjust the playback speed, pause it, adjust the playback position on an interactive slider, and even reverse the sound!

The idea of adjusting the speed is that you can listen to recorded thoughts or a lecture much faster than the words were originally spoken. Playing the audio back at a faster rate can help you be more productive.

But why would you want to play recorded words *backward*? Laura Foy from Microsoft's Channel 9 has theorized that it's to "find out if you're secretly sending satanic messages" (see http://bit.ly/laurafoy), but my real motivation is to enable people to play the nerdy game my brother and I used to play as kids. Here's how you play:

1. Record yourself saying a word or phrase.

2. Play it backwards many times, so you can try to memorize what it sounds like backward.

3. Make a new recording with you mimicking the backward audio.

4. Play this new recording backward to see how close you can come to replicating the original word or phrase.

We used to play this game with Sound Recorder on Windows (the *good* version of the program, prior to Windows Vista). Now you can play it anytime and anywhere with Sound Recorder on your Windows Phone! You'll be surprised by the sounds you have to make to produce a good result!

As far as interaction with the microphone is concerned, Sound Recorder is simpler than Talking Parrot because it doesn't need to automatically determine when to start and stop collecting data. This app requires a lot more code, however, for *managing* the audio that it does capture.

Sound Recorder contains three pages in addition to its about page: the main page, which does all the recording; the list page, which shows past recordings; and the details page, which handles playback and editing.

The Main Page

The main page, shown at the beginning of this chapter, has three basic states: stopped, recording, and paused. Figure 36.1 demonstrates all three.

Stopped   Recording   Paused

FIGURE 36.1   The three possible states of the main page.

The four buttons (shown two at a time) mimic application bar buttons but are significantly bigger. Using real application bar buttons would be fine (and easier to implement), but this makes the buttons a little easier to press when the user is in a hurry.

This page's user interface, with its photograph and Volume Units (VU) meter, does a bad job of following the design guideline that Windows Phone apps should be "authentically digital." Showing a digital display similar to the phone's voice recognition overlay would fit in better. However, sometimes violating guidelines can help your app stand out in a positive way.

The User Interface

Listing 36.1 contains the XAML for the main page. It consists of two images, four custom buttons, a line for the VU meter needle, and a text block for displaying the elapsed time.

LISTING 36.1   `MainPage.xaml`—The User Interface for Sound Recorder's Main Page

```xaml
<phone:PhoneApplicationPage x:Class="WindowsPhoneApp.MainPage"
    xmlns="http://schemas.microsoft.com/winfx/2006/xaml/presentation"
    xmlns:x="http://schemas.microsoft.com/winfx/2006/xaml"
    xmlns:phone="clr-namespace:Microsoft.Phone.Controls;assembly=Microsoft.Phone"
    xmlns:shell="clr-namespace:Microsoft.Phone.Shell;assembly=Microsoft.Phone"
    xmlns:local="clr-namespace:WindowsPhoneApp"
    FontFamily="{StaticResource PhoneFontFamilyNormal}"
    FontSize="{StaticResource PhoneFontSizeNormal}"
    Foreground="{StaticResource PhoneForegroundBrush}"
    SupportedOrientations="Portrait" shell:SystemTray.IsVisible="True">
  <Canvas>
    <!-- The on-air image -->
    <Image Source="Images/background.png"/>
    <!-- The off-air image -->
    <Image x:Name="OffAirImage" Source="Images/offAir.png"/>

    <!-- The large buttons: 2 in the same left spot, 2 in the same right spot -->
    <local:ImageButton x:Name="RecordButton" Click="RecordButton_Click"
                       Text="record" Canvas.Left="16" Canvas.Top="586"
                       Source="../../Images/RecordButton.png"
                       PressedSource="../../Images/RecordButtonPressed.png"/>
    <local:ImageButton x:Name="PauseButton" Click="PauseButton_Click"
                       Text="pause" Canvas.Left="16" Canvas.Top="586"
                       Source="../../Images/PauseButton.png"
                       PressedSource="../../Images/PauseButtonPressed.png"
                       Visibility="Collapsed"/>
    <local:ImageButton x:Name="ListButton" Click="ListButton_Click"
                       Text="list" Canvas.Left="371" Canvas.Top="586"
                       Source="../../Images/ListButton.png"
                       PressedSource="../../Images/ListButtonPressed.png"/>
    <local:ImageButton x:Name="StopButton" Click="StopButton_Click"
                       Text="stop" Canvas.Left="371" Canvas.Top="586"
                       Source="../../Images/StopButton.png"
```

LISTING 36.1   Continued

```
                             PressedSource="../../Images/StopButtonPressed.png"
                             Visibility="Collapsed"/>

    <!-- The needle for the sound meter -->
    <Line Canvas.Left="240" Canvas.Top="590" Width="3" Height="110" Y2="110"
          Stroke="Black" StrokeThickness="3" StrokeStartLineCap="Triangle"
          RenderTransformOrigin=".5,1">
      <Line.RenderTransform>
        <RotateTransform x:Name="NeedleTransform" Angle="-55"/>
      </Line.RenderTransform>
    </Line>

    <!-- The elapsed time -->
    <TextBlock x:Name="TimerTextBlock" Canvas.Top="512" Width="480"
      TextAlignment="Center" Style="{StaticResource PhoneTextExtraLargeStyle}"
      Foreground="White" Visibility="Collapsed"/>
  </Canvas>
</phone:PhoneApplicationPage>
```

Notes:

→ The page is portrait-only due to the dimensions of the artwork and the exact layout of the controls surrounding it.

→ The second image, OffAirImage, is shown during the stopped and paused states. It covers the illuminated "on air" sign with one that is off, and it also dims the VU meter (whose needle still moves in response to sound). It accomplishes the dimming with a translucent region in the image, as demonstrated in Figure 36.2.

→ The four buttons are instances of a simple user control called ImageButton that is included with this app's source code. Rather than doing tricks with opacity masks to get the inverted-colors-when-pressed effect, this control simply asks for two separate image files. It displays PressedSource when pressed; otherwise it displays Source.

→ Because background.png (with fixed colors) fills the page, the text and images in this page all use a hard-coded white color.

→ The VU meter needle is implemented as a Line element whose RotateTransform is manipulated from code behind. Its RenderTransformOrigin of .5,1 rotates it around its bottom edge. It is positioned with Canvas.Left and Canvas.Top rather than solely with its X1 and Y1 properties—and it is given an explicit width and height—to make the transform work more understandably.

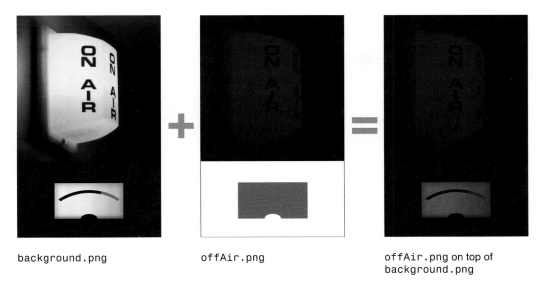

background.png   offAir.png   offAir.png on top of
                                                            background.png

FIGURE 36.2   The overlay image replaces the photo and dims the sound meter.

The Code-Behind

Listing 36.2 contains the code-behind for the main page.

LISTING 36.2   `MainPage.xaml.cs`—The Code-Behind for Sound Recorder's Main Page

```
using System;
using System.IO;
using System.Windows;
using System.Windows.Media;
using Microsoft.Phone.Controls;
using Microsoft.Xna.Framework.Audio;

namespace WindowsPhoneApp
{
  public partial class MainPage : PhoneApplicationPage
  {
    // Used for capturing audio from the microphone
    byte[] buffer;
    MemoryStream stream;

    // Needle management
    double targetNeedleAngle;
    const int MIN_ANGLE = -55;
    const int MAX_ANGLE = 55;
    const int VELOCITY_FACTOR = 10;
```

LISTING 36.2   Continued

```
const int DOWNWARD_VELOCITY = -6;
const int SMALL_ANGLE_DELTA = 6;
const int RANGE_FACTOR = 20;

// The current state (Stopped, Recording, or Paused)
AudioState currentState = AudioState.Stopped;

public MainPage()
{
  InitializeComponent();
  CompositionTarget.Rendering += CompositionTarget_Rendering;

  // Required for XNA Microphone API to work
  Microsoft.Xna.Framework.FrameworkDispatcher.Update();

  // Configure the microphone with the smallest supported BufferDuration (.1)
  Microphone.Default.BufferDuration = TimeSpan.FromSeconds(.1);
  Microphone.Default.BufferReady += Microphone_BufferReady;

  // Initialize the buffer for holding microphone data
  int size = Microphone.Default.GetSampleSizeInBytes(
    Microphone.Default.BufferDuration);
  this.buffer = new byte[size];

  // Initialize the stream used to record microphone data
  this.stream = new MemoryStream();

  // Listen the whole time so the needle moves even when not recording
  Microphone.Default.Start();
}

void Microphone_BufferReady(object sender, EventArgs e)
{
  int size = Microphone.Default.GetData(this.buffer);
  if (size == 0)
    return;

  // Calculate the target angle for the volume meter needle
  long volume = GetAverageVolume(size);
  double range = Math.Min(MAX_ANGLE - MIN_ANGLE, volume / RANGE_FACTOR);
  this.targetNeedleAngle = MIN_ANGLE + range;

  if (CurrentState == AudioState.Recording)
  {
```

LISTING 36.2   Continued

```
      // If recording, write the current buffer to the stream and
      // refresh the elapsed time
      this.stream.Write(this.buffer, 0, size);
      TimeSpan recordingLength = Microphone.Default.GetSampleDuration(
                                    (int)this.stream.Position);
      this.TimerTextBlock.Text = String.Format("{0:00}:{1:00}",
        recordingLength.Minutes, recordingLength.Seconds);
    }
  }

  void CompositionTarget_Rendering(object sender, EventArgs e)
  {
    // Required for XNA Microphone API to work
    Microsoft.Xna.Framework.FrameworkDispatcher.Update();

    double newAngle = this.targetNeedleAngle;
    double delta = this.targetNeedleAngle - this.NeedleTransform.Angle;

    // If the difference is larger than SMALL_ANGLE_DELTA°, gradually move the
    // needle rather than directly setting its angle to the target angle
    if (Math.Abs(delta) > SMALL_ANGLE_DELTA)
    {
      // Limit the downward velocity, so it returns to the
      // resting position at a constant rate (DOWNWARD_VELOCITY)
      newAngle = this.NeedleTransform.Angle +
                  Math.Max(delta / VELOCITY_FACTOR, DOWNWARD_VELOCITY);
    }

    // Update the needle's angle, restricting it
    // to a range of MIN_ANGLE° to MAX_ANGLE°
    this.NeedleTransform.Angle =
      Math.Max(MIN_ANGLE, Math.Min(MAX_ANGLE, newAngle));
  }

  // Returns the average value among all the values in the buffer
  int GetAverageVolume(int numBytes)
  {
    long total = 0;

    // Buffer is an array of bytes, but we want to examine each 2-byte value
    for (int i = 0; i < numBytes; i += 2)
    {
      // Cast from short to int to prevent -32768 from overflowing Math.Abs
      int value = Math.Abs((int)BitConverter.ToInt16(this.buffer, i));
```

LISTING 36.2   Continued

```
      total += value;
    }
    return (int)(total / (numBytes / 2));
  }


  AudioState CurrentState
  {
    get { return this.currentState; }
    set
    {
      this.currentState = value;

      // Not pretty code, but shorter than the alternatives
      switch (this.currentState)
      {
        case AudioState.Recording:
          RecordButton.Visibility = Visibility.Collapsed;
          ListButton.Visibility = Visibility.Collapsed;
          OffAirImage.Visibility = Visibility.Collapsed;
          PauseButton.Visibility = Visibility.Visible;
          StopButton.Visibility = Visibility.Visible;
          TimerTextBlock.Text = "";
          TimerTextBlock.Visibility = Visibility.Visible;
          break;
        case AudioState.Paused:
          RecordButton.Visibility = Visibility.Visible;
          OffAirImage.Visibility = Visibility.Visible;
          PauseButton.Visibility = Visibility.Collapsed;
          TimerTextBlock.Text += " (paused)";
          break;
        case AudioState.Stopped:
          RecordButton.Visibility = Visibility.Visible;
          ListButton.Visibility = Visibility.Visible;
          OffAirImage.Visibility = Visibility.Visible;
          PauseButton.Visibility = Visibility.Collapsed;
          StopButton.Visibility = Visibility.Collapsed;
          TimerTextBlock.Visibility = Visibility.Collapsed;
          break;
      }
    }
  }

  // Button click handlers
```

LISTING 36.2 Continued

```
    void RecordButton_Click(object sender, EventArgs e)
    {
      CurrentState = AudioState.Recording;
    }

    void ListButton_Click(object sender, EventArgs e)
    {
      CurrentState = AudioState.Stopped;
      this.NavigationService.Navigate(
        new Uri("/ListPage.xaml", UriKind.Relative));
    }

    void PauseButton_Click(object sender, EventArgs e)
    {
      CurrentState = AudioState.Paused;
    }

    void StopButton_Click(object sender, EventArgs e)
    {
      CurrentState = AudioState.Stopped;

      // Create a new recording with a unique filename
      Recording r = new Recording { Filename = Guid.NewGuid().ToString(),
          TimeStamp = DateTimeOffset.Now };

      // Save the recording
      r.SaveContent(this.stream);

      // Ready the stream for another recording
      this.stream.Position = 0;

      // Add the recording to the persisted list
      Settings.RecordingsList.Value.Add(r);
    }
  }
}
```

Notes:

→ The structure of this code is pretty similar to the preceding two chapters. In this app, the microphone is started from the constructor to enable the VU meter needle to move at all times, not just while recording is in progress. During development, ensure that your application manifest contains the ID_CAP_MICROPHONE capability, otherwise the call to Microsoft.Default.Start will fail due to Microphone.Default being null.

➡ In the microphone's `BufferReady` event handler, the buffer is written to the stream, but only if we're recording. (The three states of the page are indicated by the three-value `AudioState` enumeration.) The average volume of the sample is used to determine where the needle should be placed, transforming the value to a range from `MIN_ANGLE` (-55°) to `MAX_ANGLE` (55°). The `GetAverageVolume` method is identical to the one from the preceding two chapters.

➡ `CompositionTarget_Rendering` not only performs the requisite call to `FrameworkDispatcher.Update`, but it also takes the opportunity to adjust the needle based on the value of `targetNeedleAngle` calculated in `Microphone_BufferReady`. If the difference between the current angle and the target angle is small enough, the needle is directly moved to the target angle. Otherwise, the needle is moved a fraction of the necessary distance each time `CompositionTarget_Rendering` is called to provide a smooth animation. The speed of "downward" motion (decreasing the angle due to softer audio) is limited to `DOWNWARD_VELOCITY` to provide a more realistic effect of a needle that can jump to a louder volume but always smoothly returns to its resting position. This isn't meant to be an accurate simulation of VU meter ballistics, but it should look good enough to most people.

➡ `CurrentState`'s property setter updates the user interface the old-fashioned way; by touching several properties on several elements. It would look more satisfactory if the relevant elements were data-bound to a version of `CurrentState` that is either a dependency property or a property that manually raises change notifications. However, several value converters would be needed to morph the enumeration value into the variety of `Visibility` values and strings needed. The end result would involve much more code.

➡ The code that actually saves the audio data is at the end of the listing in `StopButton_Click`. To do this, the memory stream holding the data is passed to `SaveContent` on a custom `Recording` class shown in the next listing.

➡ This app uses two persisted settings, defined as follows in a separate `Settings.cs` file:

```
public static class Settings
{
  // The user's data
  public static readonly Setting<ObservableCollection<Recording>>
  RecordingsList =
    new Setting<ObservableCollection<Recording>>("RecordingsList",
      new ObservableCollection<Recording>());

  // Communicate the selection on the list page to the details page
  public static readonly Setting<int> SelectedRecordingIndex =
    new Setting<int>("SelectedRecordingIndex", -1);
}
```

The `Recording` class acts much like the `Note` class from Chapter 22, "Notepad." Each object contains metadata that includes the name of the file in isolated storage that contains the actual content. Listing 36.3 shows the implementation of `Recording`.

> Chapter 22 outlines the reasons why it doesn't make sense to rely on the isolated storage file system alone to discover, enumerate, and otherwise manage a list of files. Those same reasons apply here. The approach that works best is to have a separately persisted list of custom objects that point to any physical files, just like `Note` in Chapter 22's Notepad app and `Recording` in Sound Recorder.

LISTING 36.3   `Recording.cs`—The Object Representing Each Sound File Stored in Isolated Storage

```csharp
using System;
using System.ComponentModel;
using System.IO;
using System.IO.IsolatedStorage;
using Microsoft.Xna.Framework.Audio;

namespace WindowsPhoneApp
{
  public class Recording : INotifyPropertyChanged
  {
    // The backing fields
    string filename;
    string label;
    DateTimeOffset timeStamp;
    TimeSpan duration;

    // The properties, which raise change notifications
    public string Filename
    {
      get { return this.filename; }
      set { this.filename = value; OnPropertyChanged("Filename"); }
    }
    public string Label
    {
      get { return this.label; }
      set { this.label = value; OnPropertyChanged("Label");
          // Raise notifications for the readonly properties based on Label
          OnPropertyChanged("Title"); OnPropertyChanged("ShortTitle");
          OnPropertyChanged("Subtitle"); }
    }
    public DateTimeOffset TimeStamp
    {
```

LISTING 36.3   Continued

```
      get { return this.timeStamp; }
      set { this.timeStamp = value; OnPropertyChanged("TimeStamp");
            // Raise notifications for the readonly properties based on TimeStamp
            OnPropertyChanged("Title"); OnPropertyChanged("ShortTitle");
            OnPropertyChanged("Subtitle"); }
    }
    public TimeSpan Duration
    {
      get { return this.duration; }
      set { this.duration = value; OnPropertyChanged("Duration");
            // Raise notifications for the readonly properties based on Duration
            OnPropertyChanged("Title"); OnPropertyChanged("ShortTitle");
            OnPropertyChanged("Subtitle"); }
    }

    // A few computed properties for display purposes
    public string Title
    {
      get {
        return String.Format("{0} ({1:00}:{2:00})",
          this.label ?? this.TimeStamp.LocalDateTime.ToShortTimeString(),
          this.Duration.Minutes, Math.Floor(this.Duration.Seconds));
      }
    }
    public string ShortTitle
    {
      get {
        return this.label ?? this.TimeStamp.LocalDateTime.ToShortTimeString();
      }
    }
    public string Subtitle
    {
      get {
        if (this.label != null)
          return String.Format("{0} {1}",
            this.TimeStamp.LocalDateTime.ToShortDateString(),
            this.TimeStamp.LocalDateTime.ToShortTimeString());
        else
          return this.TimeStamp.LocalDateTime.ToShortDateString();
      }
    }

    // Save the stream to isolated storage
    public void SaveContent(MemoryStream memoryStream)
```

LISTING 36.3   Continued

```
  {
    // Store the duration of the content, used for display purposes
    this.Duration = Microphone.Default.GetSampleDuration(
                              (int)memoryStream.Position);

    using (IsolatedStorageFile userStore =
           IsolatedStorageFile.GetUserStoreForApplication())
    using (IsolatedStorageFileStream stream =
           userStore.CreateFile(this.Filename))
    {
      stream.Write(memoryStream.GetBuffer(), 0, (int)memoryStream.Position);
    }
  }

  // Get the raw bytes from the file in isolated storage
  byte[] GetBuffer()
  {
    byte[] buffer =
      new byte[Microphone.Default.GetSampleSizeInBytes(this.Duration)];

    using (IsolatedStorageFile userStore =
           IsolatedStorageFile.GetUserStoreForApplication())
    using (IsolatedStorageFileStream stream =
           userStore.OpenFile(this.Filename, FileMode.Open))
    {
      stream.Read(buffer, 0, buffer.Length);
    }
    return buffer;
  }

  // Create and return a sound effect based on the raw bytes in the file
  public SoundEffect GetContent()
  {
    return new SoundEffect(this.GetBuffer(), Microphone.Default.SampleRate,
      AudioChannels.Mono);
  }

  // Delete the file
  public void DeleteContent()
  {
    using (IsolatedStorageFile userStore =
           IsolatedStorageFile.GetUserStoreForApplication())
      userStore.DeleteFile(this.Filename);
  }
```

LISTING 36.3   Continued

```
// Overwrite the file's contents with the audio data reversed
public void Reverse()
{
  byte[] buffer = this.GetBuffer();
  using (IsolatedStorageFile userStore =
         IsolatedStorageFile.GetUserStoreForApplication())
  using (IsolatedStorageFileStream stream =
         userStore.OpenFile(this.Filename, FileMode.Open, FileAccess.Write))
  {
    // Reverse each 2-byte chunk (each 16-bit audio sample)
    for (int i = buffer.Length - 2; i >= 0; i -= 2)
      stream.Write(buffer, i, 2);
  }
}

void OnPropertyChanged(string propertyName)
{
  PropertyChangedEventHandler handler = this.PropertyChanged;
  if (handler != null)
    handler(this, new PropertyChangedEventArgs(propertyName));
}

public event PropertyChangedEventHandler PropertyChanged;
  }
}
```

Notes:

➜ Any changes to Label, TimeStamp, or Duration also raise property-changed notifications for Title, Subtitle, and ShortTitle, three readonly properties whose value is based on these read/write properties. The list page leverages Title and Subtitle in the display for each recording, and the details page leverages ShortTitle.

➜ The implementation of SaveContent is a straightforward writing of the passed-in stream's bytes to the isolated storage file indicated by the Filename property. This method also automatically sets Duration to the length of the recording (revealed by the microphone) so this information can be leveraged in other parts of the app without having to load the audio file. This is especially important for the list page, which displays the duration for every recording simultaneously.

➜ When GetBuffer reads in the data from isolated storage, it knows how big the buffer needs to be ahead of time, thanks to the stored duration (and thanks to the microphone's GetSampleSizeInBytes method). GetBuffer is not public; consumers instead call GetContent, which returns the audio data as a familiar SoundEffect object.

➔ `DeleteContent` deletes the file containing the audio data, just like the same-named method from the Notepad app.

➔ The `Reverse` method does the trick of reversing the audio file. It's simply a matter of reversing the bytes, *except* that this needs to be done in 2-byte chunks to keep each 16-bit audio sample intact.

The List Page

The list page, shown in Figure 36.3, contains a list box with recordings that link to the details page. However, this is not a regular list box—it is a custom subclass called `CheckableListBox` that mimics the Mail app's mechanism for bulk-selecting items. To enter bulk-selection mode, you can either tap the application bar button or tap the left-most edge of any item in the list. The latter approach has the advantage of automatically selecting the tapped item. The code to `CheckableListBox` is not covered in this chapter, but it is included with this chapter's source code.

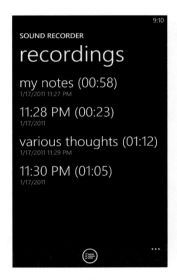

The list of recordings

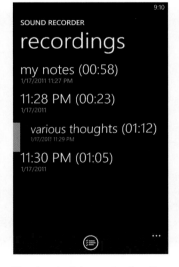

Tapping the left margin of an item makes a special glyph appear

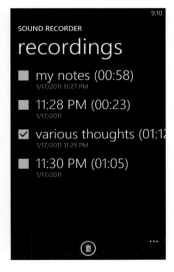

The item is now the first selection in bulk-selection mode

FIGURE 36.3   The `CheckableListBox` supports multi-select interaction the same way as the phone's built-in Mail app.

The only thing you can do with bulk-selected items is delete them. Notice in Figure 36.3 that the application bar changes to show a delete button at the same time that the check boxes appear.

The XAML for the list page is shown in Listing 36.4, and the code-behind is shown in Listing 36.5.

LISTING 36.4   `ListPage.xaml`—The User Interface for Sound Recorder's List of Recordings

```
<phone:PhoneApplicationPage x:Class="WindowsPhoneApp.ListPage"
    xmlns="http://schemas.microsoft.com/winfx/2006/xaml/presentation"
    xmlns:x="http://schemas.microsoft.com/winfx/2006/xaml"
    xmlns:phone="clr-namespace:Microsoft.Phone.Controls;assembly=Microsoft.Phone"
    xmlns:shell="clr-namespace:Microsoft.Phone.Shell;assembly=Microsoft.Phone"
    xmlns:local="clr-namespace:WindowsPhoneApp"
    FontFamily="{StaticResource PhoneFontFamilyNormal}"
    FontSize="{StaticResource PhoneFontSizeNormal}"
    Foreground="{StaticResource PhoneForegroundBrush}"
    SupportedOrientations="PortraitOrLandscape" shell:SystemTray.IsVisible="True">

  <!-- The application bar, with one button and one menu item -->
  <phone:PhoneApplicationPage.ApplicationBar>
    <shell:ApplicationBar>
      <shell:ApplicationBarIconButton Text="select" Click="SelectButton_Click"
                                  IconUri="/Shared/Images/appbar.select.png"/>
      <shell:ApplicationBar.MenuItems>
        <shell:ApplicationBarMenuItem Text="about" Click="AboutMenuItem_Click"/>
      </shell:ApplicationBar.MenuItems>
    </shell:ApplicationBar>
  </phone:PhoneApplicationPage.ApplicationBar>

  <Grid>
    <Grid.RowDefinitions>
      <RowDefinition Height="Auto"/>
      <RowDefinition Height="*"/>
    </Grid.RowDefinitions>
    <!-- The standard header -->
    <StackPanel Grid.Row="0" Style="{StaticResource PhoneTitlePanelStyle}">
      <TextBlock Text="SOUND RECORDER"
                 Style="{StaticResource PhoneTextTitle0Style}"/>
      <TextBlock Text="recordings" Style="{StaticResource PhoneTextTitle1Style}"/>
    </StackPanel>

    <TextBlock x:Name="NoItemsTextBlock" Grid.Row="1" Text="No recordings"
               Visibility="Collapsed" Margin="22,17,0,0"
               Style="{StaticResource PhoneTextGroupHeaderStyle}"/>

    <!-- A list box supporting check boxes for bulk selection -->
    <local:CheckableListBox x:Name="CheckableListBox" Grid.Row="1"
                            Margin="0,18,0,0"
                            SelectionMode="Multiple" ItemsSource="{Binding}"
                            SelectionChanged="ListBox_SelectionChanged">
      <local:CheckableListBox.ItemTemplate>
```

LISTING 36.4   Continued

```xml
        <DataTemplate>
          <!-- Give each recording two lines: a title and a subtitle -->
          <StackPanel>
            <TextBlock Text="{Binding Title}" Margin="-2,-13,0,0"
                       Style="{StaticResource PhoneTextExtraLargeStyle}"/>
            <TextBlock Text="{Binding Subtitle}" Margin="0,-5,0,28"
                       Style="{StaticResource PhoneTextSubtleStyle}"/>
          </StackPanel>
        </DataTemplate>
      </local:CheckableListBox.ItemTemplate>
    </local:CheckableListBox>
  </Grid>
</phone:PhoneApplicationPage>
```

LISTING 36.5   `ListPage.xaml.cs`—The Code-Behind for Sound Recorder's List of Recordings

```csharp
using System;
using System.ComponentModel;
using System.Windows;
using System.Windows.Controls;
using System.Windows.Navigation;
using Microsoft.Phone.Controls;
using Microsoft.Phone.Shell;

namespace WindowsPhoneApp
{
  public partial class ListPage : PhoneApplicationPage
  {
    bool inSelectMode;

    public ListPage()
    {
      InitializeComponent();
      // Assign the data source for the list box
      this.DataContext = Settings.RecordingsList.Value;
    }

    protected override void OnNavigatedTo(NavigationEventArgs e)
    {
      base.OnNavigatedTo(e);
      if (Settings.RecordingsList.Value.Count == 0)
        ShowListAsEmpty();
    }
```

LISTING 36.4   Continued

```
protected override void OnBackKeyPress(CancelEventArgs e)
{
  base.OnBackKeyPress(e);

  // The Back button should exit select mode
  if (this.inSelectMode)
  {
    e.Cancel = true;
    LeaveSelectMode();
  }
}

void ListBox_SelectionChanged(object sender, SelectionChangedEventArgs e)
{
  if (this.CheckableListBox.SelectedItems.Count == 1 &&
    !this.CheckableListBox.AreCheckBoxesShowing)
  {
    // This is a normal, single selection, so navigate to the details page
    Settings.SelectedRecordingIndex.Value =
      this.CheckableListBox.SelectedIndex;
    this.NavigationService.Navigate(
      new Uri("/DetailsPage.xaml", UriKind.Relative));

    // Clear the selection for next time
    this.CheckableListBox.SelectedIndex = -1;
  }
  else if (this.CheckableListBox.AreCheckBoxesShowing && !this.inSelectMode)
    this.EnterSelectMode();
  else if (!this.CheckableListBox.AreCheckBoxesShowing && this.inSelectMode)
    this.LeaveSelectMode();

  if (this.inSelectMode)
    (this.ApplicationBar.Buttons[0] as IApplicationBarIconButton).IsEnabled =
      (this.CheckableListBox.SelectedItems.Count > 0);
}

void ShowListAsEmpty()
{
  NoItemsTextBlock.Visibility = Visibility.Visible;
  this.ApplicationBar.IsVisible = false;
}

void EnterSelectMode()
{
```

LISTING 36.4   Continued

```csharp
    // Show the check boxes
    this.CheckableListBox.ShowCheckBoxes();

    // Clear the application bar and show a delete button
    this.ApplicationBar.Buttons.Clear();

    ApplicationBarIconButton deleteButton = new ApplicationBarIconButton(
      new Uri("/Shared/Images/appbar.delete.png", UriKind.Relative));
    deleteButton.Text = "delete";
    deleteButton.IsEnabled = false; // Will be enabled when >=1 item selected
    deleteButton.Click += DeleteButton_Click;
    this.ApplicationBar.Buttons.Add(deleteButton);

    this.inSelectMode = true;
  }

  void LeaveSelectMode()
  {
    // Hide the check boxes
    if (this.CheckableListBox.AreCheckBoxesShowing)
      this.CheckableListBox.HideCheckBoxes();

    // Clear the application bar and show a select button
    this.ApplicationBar.Buttons.Clear();
    ApplicationBarIconButton button = new ApplicationBarIconButton(
      new Uri("/Shared/Images/appbar.select.png", UriKind.Relative));
    button.Text = "select";
    button.Click += SelectButton_Click;
    this.ApplicationBar.Buttons.Add(button);

    this.inSelectMode = false;
  }

  // Application bar handlers

  void SelectButton_Click(object sender, EventArgs e)
  {
    EnterSelectMode();
  }

  void DeleteButton_Click(object sender, EventArgs e)
  {
    if (MessageBox.Show("Are you sure you want to delete " +
        (this.CheckableListBox.SelectedItems.Count > 1 ? "these recordings" :
```

LISTING 36.4   Continued

```
        "this recording") + "?", "Delete recording" +
        (this.CheckableListBox.SelectedItems.Count > 1 ? "s" : "") + "?",
        MessageBoxButton.OKCancel) == MessageBoxResult.OK)
    {
      Recording[] itemsToDelete =
        new Recording[this.CheckableListBox.SelectedItems.Count];
      this.CheckableListBox.SelectedItems.CopyTo(itemsToDelete, 0);

      this.CheckableListBox.SelectedIndex = -1;
      this.LeaveSelectMode();

      for (int i = 0; i < itemsToDelete.Length; i++)
      {
        // Remove it from the list
        Settings.RecordingsList.Value.Remove(itemsToDelete[i]);
        // Delete the audio file in isolated storage
        itemsToDelete[i].DeleteContent();
      }

      if (Settings.RecordingsList.Value.Count == 0)
        ShowListAsEmpty();
    }
  }

  void AboutMenuItem_Click(object sender, EventArgs e)
  {
    this.NavigationService.Navigate(new Uri(
      "/Shared/About/AboutPage.xaml?appName=Sound Recorder", UriKind.Relative));
  }
 }
}
```

Notes:

→ The checkable list box data-binds to the RecordingsList setting and stays up-to-date thanks to the observable collection and property-changed notifications from each item. Its SelectionMode property, inherited from the base list box control, is set to Multiple to enable bulk-selection to work.

→ Tapping an item navigates to the details page filled out for that item. This is communicated via the SelectedRecordingIndex setting that is set appropriately before navigating.

→ When an item is deleted, the code makes sure to call DeleteContent in addition to removing the Recording instance from the list. Otherwise, the audio file would be left behind in isolated storage.

→ The rest of the code manages the
`CheckableListBox`. Bulk-selection
mode (just called *select mode* in the
listing) can be triggered either by
tapping an item's left margin
(handled internally in code for
`CheckableListBoxItem`) or by
tapping the "select" button on the
application bar. As in the Mail app,
bulk-selection mode can be exited
either by pressing the hardware
Back button or by unchecking all
of the check boxes.

The Details Page

The details page, shown in Figure 36.4
with its application bar expanded,
enables playback, editing, and deletion
of the selected sound.

The XAML for this page is shown in
Listing 36.6, and the code-behind is
shown in Listing 36.7.

FIGURE 36.4   The details page contains several
features in addition to playing the selected
recording.

LISTING 36.6   `DetailsPage.xaml`—The User Interface for Sound Recorder's Details Page

```xaml
<phone:PhoneApplicationPage x:Class="WindowsPhoneApp.DetailsPage"
    xmlns="http://schemas.microsoft.com/winfx/2006/xaml/presentation"
    xmlns:x="http://schemas.microsoft.com/winfx/2006/xaml"
    xmlns:phone="clr-namespace:Microsoft.Phone.Controls;assembly=Microsoft.Phone"
    xmlns:shell="clr-namespace:Microsoft.Phone.Shell;assembly=Microsoft.Phone"
    xmlns:local="clr-namespace:WindowsPhoneApp"
    FontFamily="{StaticResource PhoneFontFamilyNormal}"
    FontSize="{StaticResource PhoneFontSizeNormal}"
    Foreground="{StaticResource PhoneForegroundBrush}"
    SupportedOrientations="PortraitOrLandscape" shell:SystemTray.IsVisible="True">

  <!-- The application bar, with 3 buttons and 2 menu items -->
  <phone:PhoneApplicationPage.ApplicationBar>
    <shell:ApplicationBar>
      <shell:ApplicationBarIconButton Text="pause"
        IconUri="/Shared/Images/appbar.pause.png" Click="PlayPauseButton_Click"/>
      <shell:ApplicationBarIconButton Text="edit name"
        IconUri="/Shared/Images/appbar.edit.png" Click="EditButton_Click"/>
```

LISTING 36.6   Continued

```xml
    <shell:ApplicationBarIconButton Text="delete"
      IconUri="/Shared/Images/appbar.delete.png" Click="DeleteButton_Click"/>
    <shell:ApplicationBar.MenuItems>
      <shell:ApplicationBarMenuItem Text="reverse"
                                    Click="ReverseMenuItem_Click"/>
      <shell:ApplicationBarMenuItem Text="about" Click="AboutMenuItem_Click"/>
    </shell:ApplicationBar.MenuItems>
  </shell:ApplicationBar>
</phone:PhoneApplicationPage.ApplicationBar>

<Grid>
  <Grid.RowDefinitions>
    <RowDefinition Height="Auto"/>
    <RowDefinition Height="Auto"/>
    <RowDefinition Height="Auto"/>
  </Grid.RowDefinitions>

  <!-- The standard header -->
  <StackPanel Grid.Row="0" Style="{StaticResource PhoneTitlePanelStyle}">
    <TextBlock x:Name="ApplicationTitle" Text="SOUND RECORDER"
               Style="{StaticResource PhoneTextTitle0Style}"/>
    <TextBlock Text="{Binding ShortTitle}"
               Style="{StaticResource PhoneTextTitle1Style}"/>
  </StackPanel>

  <!-- The playback slider -->
  <TextBlock x:Name="PlaybackDurationTextBlock" Grid.Row="1"
             Foreground="{StaticResource PhoneSubtleBrush}" Margin="12,58,0,0"/>
  <Slider x:Name="PlaybackSlider" SmallChange=".1" Grid.Row="1"
          Margin="0,24,0,84"/>

  <!-- The playback speed slider with its reset button -->
  <Grid Grid.Row="2">
    <Grid.ColumnDefinitions>
      <ColumnDefinition/>
      <ColumnDefinition Width="Auto"/>
    </Grid.ColumnDefinitions>
    <TextBlock Text="Playback Speed" Grid.ColumnSpan="2" Margin="12,0,0,0"
                    Foreground="{StaticResource PhoneSubtleBrush}"/>
    <Slider x:Name="SpeedSlider" Grid.Row="1" SmallChange=".1" LargeChange=".1"
            Minimum="-1" Maximum="1" Margin="0,18,0,0"
            ValueChanged="SpeedSlider_ValueChanged"/>
    <Button Grid.Row="1" Grid.Column="1" Content="reset" Margin="0,0,0,16"
            VerticalAlignment="Center" local:Tilt.IsEnabled="True"
```

LISTING 36.6   Continued

```
                Click="SpeedResetButton_Click"/>
    </Grid>

    <!-- The "edit name" dialog -->
    <local:Dialog x:Name="EditDialog" Grid.RowSpan="3" Closed="EditDialog_Closed">
      <local:Dialog.InnerContent>
        <StackPanel>
          <TextBlock Text="Choose a name" Margin="11,5,0,-5"
                      Foreground="{StaticResource PhoneSubtleBrush}"/>
          <TextBox Text="{Binding Result, Mode=TwoWay}" InputScope="Text"/>
        </StackPanel>
      </local:Dialog.InnerContent>
    </local:Dialog>
  </Grid>
</phone:PhoneApplicationPage>
```

LISTING 36.7   `DetailsPage.xaml.cs`—The Code-Behind for Sound Recorder's Details Page

```
using System;
using System.ComponentModel;
using System.Windows;
using System.Windows.Media;
using System.Windows.Navigation;
using Microsoft.Phone.Controls;
using Microsoft.Phone.Shell;
using Microsoft.Xna.Framework.Audio;

namespace WindowsPhoneApp
{
  public partial class DetailsPage : PhoneApplicationPage
  {
    Recording selectedRecording;
    SoundEffectInstance soundInstance;
    double durationScale = 1;
    double elapsedSeconds;
    DateTime lastPlayFrame;
    SoundState lastSoundState = SoundState.Stopped;
    IApplicationBarIconButton playPauseButton;

    public DetailsPage()
    {
      InitializeComponent();
      this.playPauseButton = this.ApplicationBar.Buttons[0]
        as IApplicationBarIconButton;
```

LISTING 36.7   Continued

```csharp
  }

  protected override void OnNavigatedTo(NavigationEventArgs e)
  {
    base.OnNavigatedTo(e);

    // The recording chosen from the list page
    this.selectedRecording =
      Settings.RecordingsList.Value[Settings.SelectedRecordingIndex.Value];

    // The actual sound effect instance to play
    this.soundInstance = this.selectedRecording.GetContent().CreateInstance();

    // The page title data-binds to the ShortTitle property
    this.DataContext = this.selectedRecording;

    // Adjust the playback slider based on the recording's length
    PlaybackSlider.Maximum = this.selectedRecording.Duration.TotalSeconds;

    // Start playing automatically
    Play();
  }

  void Play()
  {
    CompositionTarget.Rendering += CompositionTarget_Rendering;

    this.playPauseButton.Text = "pause";
    this.playPauseButton.IconUri = new Uri("/Shared/Images/appbar.pause.png",
      UriKind.Relative);

    this.lastPlayFrame = DateTime.Now;

    if (this.soundInstance.State == SoundState.Paused)
      this.soundInstance.Resume();
    else
    {
      // Play from the beginning
      this.soundInstance.Play();
      this.elapsedSeconds = 0;
    }
  }

  void Pause()
```

LISTING 36.7   Continued

```
  {
    this.playPauseButton.Text = "play";
    this.playPauseButton.IconUri = new Uri("/Shared/Images/appbar.play.png",
      UriKind.Relative);

    this.soundInstance.Pause();
  }

  void CompositionTarget_Rendering(object sender, EventArgs e)
  {
    if (this.soundInstance != null)
    {
      // Keep the playback slider up-to-date with the playing audio
      if (this.soundInstance.State == SoundState.Playing ||
          this.lastSoundState == SoundState.Playing
          /* So remaining time after pausing/stopping is accounted for */)
      {
        this.elapsedSeconds +=
          (DateTime.Now - lastPlayFrame).TotalSeconds / this.durationScale;
        this.lastPlayFrame = DateTime.Now;

        this.PlaybackSlider.Value = this.elapsedSeconds;

        if (this.soundInstance.State == SoundState.Stopped)
          this.PlaybackSlider.Value = this.PlaybackSlider.Maximum;

        UpdatePlaybackLabel();
      }

      // Automatically turn the pause button back into a play button when the
      // recording has finished playing
      if (this.soundInstance.State != SoundState.Playing &&
          this.playPauseButton.Text != "play")
      {
        this.playPauseButton.Text = "play";
        this.playPauseButton.IconUri =
          new Uri("/Shared/Images/appbar.play.png", UriKind.Relative);

        // Unhook this event since it gets hooked on each play
        CompositionTarget.Rendering -= CompositionTarget_Rendering;
      }
      this.lastSoundState = this.soundInstance.State;

      // Required for XNA sound effect to work
```

LISTING 36.7   Continued

```csharp
      Microsoft.Xna.Framework.FrameworkDispatcher.Update();
    }
  }

  void UpdatePlaybackLabel()
  {
    TimeSpan elapsedTime =
      TimeSpan.FromSeconds(elapsedSeconds * this.durationScale);
    TimeSpan scaledDuration =
      TimeSpan.FromSeconds(PlaybackSlider.Maximum * this.durationScale);

    PlaybackDurationTextBlock.Text = String.Format("{0:00}:{1:00}",
      elapsedTime.Minutes, Math.Floor(elapsedTime.Seconds)) + " / " +
      String.Format("{0:00}:{1:00}",
      scaledDuration.Minutes, Math.Floor(scaledDuration.Seconds));
  }

  // Speed slider handlers

  void SpeedSlider_ValueChanged(object sender,
    RoutedPropertyChangedEventArgs<double> e)
  {
    // Directly apply the -1 to 1 slider value as the pitch
    this.soundInstance.Pitch = (float)SpeedSlider.Value;

    // The duration scale used by other calculations ranges from
    // .5 for double-speed/half-length (+1 pitch) to
    // 2 for half-speed/double-length (-1 pitch)
    this.durationScale = 1 + Math.Abs(this.soundInstance.Pitch);
    if (this.soundInstance.Pitch > 0)
      this.durationScale = 1 / this.durationScale;

    UpdatePlaybackLabel();
  }

  void SpeedResetButton_Click(object sender, RoutedEventArgs e)
  {
    SpeedSlider.Value = 0;
  }

  // Handlers related to the "edit name" dialog

  protected override void OnBackKeyPress(CancelEventArgs e)
  {
```

LISTING 36.7   Continued

```
  base.OnBackKeyPress(e);

  if (EditDialog.Visibility == Visibility.Visible)
  {
    e.Cancel = true;
    EditDialog.Hide(MessageBoxResult.Cancel);
  }
}

void EditDialog_Closed(object sender, MessageBoxResultEventArgs e)
{
  this.ApplicationBar.IsVisible = true;
  if (e.Result == MessageBoxResult.OK)
  {
    this.selectedRecording.Label = EditDialog.Result.ToString();
  }
}

// Application bar handlers

void PlayPauseButton_Click(object sender, EventArgs e)
{
  if (this.soundInstance.State == SoundState.Playing)
    this.Pause();
  else
    this.Play();
}

void EditButton_Click(object sender, EventArgs e)
{
  EditDialog.Result = this.selectedRecording.Label;
  EditDialog.Show();
  this.ApplicationBar.IsVisible = false;
}

void DeleteButton_Click(object sender, EventArgs e)
{
  if (MessageBox.Show("Are you sure you want to delete this recording?",
    "Delete recording?", MessageBoxButton.OKCancel) == MessageBoxResult.OK)
  {
    // Remove it from the list
    Settings.RecordingsList.Value.Remove(this.selectedRecording);
    // Delete the audio file in isolated storage
    this.selectedRecording.DeleteContent();
```

LISTING 36.7   Continued

```
      if (this.NavigationService.CanGoBack)
        this.NavigationService.GoBack();
    }
  }

  void ReverseMenuItem_Click(object sender, EventArgs e)
  {
    this.selectedRecording.Reverse();
    // We must get the new, reversed sound effect instance
    this.soundInstance = this.selectedRecording.GetContent().CreateInstance();
    // Re-apply the chosen pitch
    this.soundInstance.Pitch = (float)SpeedSlider.Value;
    Play();
  }

  void AboutMenuItem_Click(object sender, EventArgs e)
  {
    this.NavigationService.Navigate(new Uri(
      "/Shared/About/AboutPage.xaml?appName=Sound Recorder", UriKind.Relative));
  }
  }
}
```

Notes:

→ All three rows in this page's root grid are given a height of Auto, so the content doesn't shift when the application bar is hidden during the display of the "edit name" dialog.

→ The Dialog user control used by several apps in this book is leveraged here to enable the user to rename the recording. This name is applied as the Label property on the Recording instance, which impacts the Title, ShortTitle, and Subtitle properties as shown in Listing 36.3.

→ The CompositionTarget_Rendering handler, used only while the audio is playing, keeps the slider and pause/play button in sync with the audio.

→ The speed slider uses the familiar Pitch property on SoundEffectInstance to adjust the audio as it plays. This affects speed *and* pitch, as there's unfortunately no built-in way to adjust the speed while maintaining the pitch.

→ The audio reversal is done inside ReverseMenuItem_Click. Because the reversal is done to the file in isolated storage, the sound effect instance must be retrieved again. Invoking the reversal a second time restores the audio file to its original data.

The Finished Product

The image buttons highlight and tilt when pressed, just like application bar buttons

Editing the name of a recording

Tapping the left margin to enter bulk-selection mode under the light theme with a magenta accent color

chapter 37

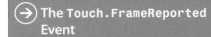

REFLEX TEST

Reflex Test is a simple game in which you see how quickly you can tap the screen when a target appears. (You can tap anywhere on the screen; the target is just a visual gimmick.) The app keeps track of your fastest time as well as your average time.

The tap detection done by this app could easily be done with a simple `MouseLeftButtonDown` event handler, but instead this app serves as an introduction to multi-touch functionality. You can easily use the multi-touch infrastructure for single touches, as this app does.

The User Interface

Reflex Test has a main page, an instructions page, and an about page. The latter two pages aren't interesting and therefore aren't shown in this chapter, but Listing 37.1 contains the XAML for the main page.

Figure 37.1 illustrates main page's user interface during the four stages of the reflex-testing process.

The page starts out mostly empty.

An indeterminate progress bar animates on the top while the user waits for the target to appear.

The target appears.

The user taps the screen and sees the results.

FIGURE 37.1 The main page goes through four stages as the app is used.

LISTING 37.1 `MainPage.xaml`—The User Interface for Reflex Test's Main Page

```xml
<phone:PhoneApplicationPage
    x:Class="WindowsPhoneApp.MainPage"
    xmlns="http://schemas.microsoft.com/winfx/2006/xaml/presentation"
    xmlns:x="http://schemas.microsoft.com/winfx/2006/xaml"
    xmlns:phone="clr-namespace:Microsoft.Phone.Controls;assembly=Microsoft.Phone"
    xmlns:shell="clr-namespace:Microsoft.Phone.Shell;assembly=Microsoft.Phone"
    FontFamily="{StaticResource PhoneFontFamilyNormal}"
    FontSize="{StaticResource PhoneFontSizeNormal}"
    Foreground="{StaticResource PhoneForegroundBrush}"
    SupportedOrientations="PortraitOrLandscape">

  <!-- Add three animations to the page's resource dictionary -->
  <phone:PhoneApplicationPage.Resources>

    <!-- Slide the best time out then back in -->
    <Storyboard x:Name="SlideBestTimeStoryboard">
      <DoubleAnimationUsingKeyFrames Storyboard.TargetName="BestTimeTransform"
                                     Storyboard.TargetProperty="TranslateX">
        <DiscreteDoubleKeyFrame KeyTime="0:0:0" Value="0"/>
        <EasingDoubleKeyFrame KeyTime="0:0:.4" Value="-800">
          <EasingDoubleKeyFrame.EasingFunction>
            <QuadraticEase/>
          </EasingDoubleKeyFrame.EasingFunction>
        </EasingDoubleKeyFrame>
        <DiscreteDoubleKeyFrame KeyTime="0:0:.4" Value="800"/>
```

LISTING 37.1   Continued

```xml
      <EasingDoubleKeyFrame KeyTime="0:0:.8" Value="0">
        <EasingDoubleKeyFrame.EasingFunction>
          <QuadraticEase/>
        </EasingDoubleKeyFrame.EasingFunction>
      </EasingDoubleKeyFrame>
    </DoubleAnimationUsingKeyFrames>
    <ObjectAnimationUsingKeyFrames Storyboard.TargetName="BestTimeTextBlock"
                                   Storyboard.TargetProperty="Visibility">
      <!-- Ensure the time is visible on the way in,
           even if collapsed on the way out -->
      <DiscreteObjectKeyFrame KeyTime="0:0:.4" Value="Visible"/>
    </ObjectAnimationUsingKeyFrames>
  </Storyboard>

  <!-- Slide the average time out then back in -->
  <Storyboard x:Name="SlideAvgTimeStoryboard">
    <DoubleAnimationUsingKeyFrames Storyboard.TargetName="AvgTimeTransform"
                                   Storyboard.TargetProperty="TranslateX">
      <DiscreteDoubleKeyFrame KeyTime="0:0:0" Value="0"/>
      <EasingDoubleKeyFrame KeyTime="0:0:.4" Value="-800">
        <EasingDoubleKeyFrame.EasingFunction>
          <QuadraticEase/>
        </EasingDoubleKeyFrame.EasingFunction>
      </EasingDoubleKeyFrame>
      <DiscreteDoubleKeyFrame KeyTime="0:0:.4" Value="800"/>
      <EasingDoubleKeyFrame KeyTime="0:0:.8" Value="0">
        <EasingDoubleKeyFrame.EasingFunction>
          <QuadraticEase/>
        </EasingDoubleKeyFrame.EasingFunction>
      </EasingDoubleKeyFrame>
    </DoubleAnimationUsingKeyFrames>
    <ObjectAnimationUsingKeyFrames Storyboard.TargetName="AvgTimeTextBlock"
                                   Storyboard.TargetProperty="Visibility">
      <!-- Ensure the time is visible on the way in,
           even if collapsed on the way out -->
      <DiscreteObjectKeyFrame KeyTime="0:0:.4" Value="Visible"/>
    </ObjectAnimationUsingKeyFrames>
  </Storyboard>

  <!-- Animate in (then out) a message, which will either say
       "CONGRATULATIONS!" or "TOO EARLY!" -->
  <Storyboard x:Name="ShowMessageStoryboard"
              Storyboard.TargetName="MessageTransform">
    <DoubleAnimationUsingKeyFrames Storyboard.TargetProperty="TranslateY">
```

LISTING 37.1   Continued

```
        <DiscreteDoubleKeyFrame KeyTime="0:0:0" Value="800"/>
        <EasingDoubleKeyFrame KeyTime="0:0:.5" Value="50">
          <EasingDoubleKeyFrame.EasingFunction>
            <QuadraticEase/>
          </EasingDoubleKeyFrame.EasingFunction>
        </EasingDoubleKeyFrame>
        <DiscreteDoubleKeyFrame KeyTime="0:0:2.5" Value="50"/>
        <EasingDoubleKeyFrame KeyTime="0:0:3" Value="-800">
          <EasingDoubleKeyFrame.EasingFunction>
            <QuadraticEase/>
          </EasingDoubleKeyFrame.EasingFunction>
        </EasingDoubleKeyFrame>
      </DoubleAnimationUsingKeyFrames>
    </Storyboard>
  </phone:PhoneApplicationPage.Resources>

  <!-- The application bar, with two buttons and one menu item -->
  <phone:PhoneApplicationPage.ApplicationBar>
    <shell:ApplicationBar>
      <shell:ApplicationBarIconButton Text="instructions"
        IconUri="/Shared/Images/appbar.instructions.png"
        Click="InstructionsButton_Click"/>
      <shell:ApplicationBarIconButton Text="delete"
        IconUri="/Shared/Images/appbar.delete.png" Click="DeleteButton_Click"/>
      <shell:ApplicationBar.MenuItems>
        <shell:ApplicationBarMenuItem Text="about" Click="AboutMenuItem_Click"/>
      </shell:ApplicationBar.MenuItems>
    </shell:ApplicationBar>
  </phone:PhoneApplicationPage.ApplicationBar>

  <Grid Background="Transparent">
    <Grid.RowDefinitions>
      <RowDefinition Height="Auto"/>
      <RowDefinition Height="*"/>
    </Grid.RowDefinitions>

    <!-- A target vector graphic and ellipse to mark where the screen
         was touched, collapsed until appropriate to show -->
    <Grid Grid.RowSpan="2">
      <Grid x:Name="TargetGrid" Visibility="Collapsed">
        <Ellipse Width="440" Height="440" StrokeThickness="35"
                 Stroke="{StaticResource PhoneAccentBrush}"/>
        <Ellipse Width="300" Height="300" StrokeThickness="35"
                 Stroke="{StaticResource PhoneAccentBrush}"/>
```

LISTING 37.1   Continued

```xml
      <Ellipse Width="160" Height="160" StrokeThickness="35"
               Stroke="{StaticResource PhoneAccentBrush}"/>
      <Ellipse x:Name="TouchEllipse" Visibility="Collapsed" Opacity=".9"
               Fill="{StaticResource PhoneForegroundBrush}" Width="100"
               Height="100" HorizontalAlignment="Left" VerticalAlignment="Top"/>
    </Grid>
  </Grid>

  <!-- Show indeterminate progress (dancing dots) while waiting for the target
       to appear (IsIndeterminate is set from code-behind for perf reasons) -->
  <ProgressBar x:Name="ProgressBar" Visibility="Collapsed"
               VerticalAlignment="Top"/>

  <!-- The standard header -->
  <StackPanel Style="{StaticResource PhoneTitlePanelStyle}">
    <TextBlock Text="REFLEX TEST"
               Style="{StaticResource PhoneTextTitle0Style}"/>
    <TextBlock x:Name="PageTitle" Text="tap to begin"
               Style="{StaticResource PhoneTextTitle1Style}"/>
  </StackPanel>

  <Grid Grid.Row="1" Margin="{StaticResource PhoneHorizontalMargin}">

    <!-- A display for the best time, average time, and # of tries -->
    <StackPanel x:Name="TimesPanel" VerticalAlignment="Bottom"
                HorizontalAlignment="Right">
      <TextBlock Text="BEST TIME" Foreground="{StaticResource PhoneSubtleBrush}"
                 HorizontalAlignment="Right"/>
      <TextBlock x:Name="BestTimeTextBlock" HorizontalAlignment="Right"
                 FontSize="{StaticResource PhoneFontSizeExtraExtraLarge}"
                 Margin="0,-15,0,30">
        <TextBlock.RenderTransform>
          <CompositeTransform x:Name="BestTimeTransform"/>
        </TextBlock.RenderTransform>
      </TextBlock>
      <TextBlock x:Name="AvgTimeHeaderTextBlock" Text="AVG TIME"
                 Foreground="{StaticResource PhoneSubtleBrush}"
                 HorizontalAlignment="Right"/>
      <TextBlock x:Name="AvgTimeTextBlock" HorizontalAlignment="Right"
                 FontSize="{StaticResource PhoneFontSizeExtraExtraLarge}"
                 Margin="0,-15,0,0">
        <TextBlock.RenderTransform>
          <CompositeTransform x:Name="AvgTimeTransform"/>
        </TextBlock.RenderTransform>
```

LISTING 37.1   Continued

```
      </TextBlock>
    </StackPanel>

    <!-- A "CONGRATULATIONS!" or "TOO EARLY!" message -->
    <TextBlock x:Name="MessageTextBlock" RenderTransformOrigin=".5,.5"
               FontWeight="Bold" HorizontalAlignment="Center"
               FontSize="{StaticResource PhoneFontSizeExtraLarge}">
      <TextBlock.RenderTransform>
        <CompositeTransform x:Name="MessageTransform" TranslateY="800"/>
      </TextBlock.RenderTransform>
    </TextBlock>
  </Grid>
 </Grid>
</phone:PhoneApplicationPage>
```

The first two animations are used to slide in the best time and average time text blocks the first time they are displayed, and to slide them out and then in when they are updated. The last animation slides a message onto and then off the screen: "CONGRATU-LATIONS!" when the user gets a new best time, or "TOO EARLY!" when the user taps the screen before the target appears.

The Code-Behind

Listing 37.2 contains the code-behind for the main page.

```
using System;
using System.Windows;
using System.Windows.Input;
using System.Windows.Navigation;
using System.Windows.Threading;
using Microsoft.Phone.Controls;

namespace WindowsPhoneApp
{
  public partial class MainPage : PhoneApplicationPage
  {
    // Persistent settings
    Setting<TimeSpan> bestTime = new Setting<TimeSpan>("BestTime",
                                             TimeSpan.MaxValue);
    Setting<TimeSpan> avgTime = new Setting<TimeSpan>("AvgTime",
                                             TimeSpan.MaxValue);
    Setting<int> numTries = new Setting<int>("NumTries", 0);
```

LISTING 37.2 Continued

```csharp
DispatcherTimer timer = new DispatcherTimer();
Random random = new Random();
DateTime beginTime;
DateTime targetShownTime;
bool tapToBegin;

public MainPage()
{
  InitializeComponent();
  this.timer.Tick += Timer_Tick;
}

protected override void OnNavigatedTo(NavigationEventArgs e)
{
  base.OnNavigatedTo(e);

  // Subscribe to the touch/multi-touch event.
  // This is application-wide, so only do this when on this page.
  Touch.FrameReported += Touch_FrameReported;

  // Respect the persisted values
  UpdateLabels(true);

  // Reset
  this.tapToBegin = true;
  this.PageTitle.Text = "tap to begin";
}

protected override void OnNavigatedFrom(NavigationEventArgs e)
{
  base.OnNavigatedFrom(e);

  // Unsubscribe from this application-wide event
  Touch.FrameReported -= Touch_FrameReported;
}

void Touch_FrameReported(object sender, TouchFrameEventArgs e)
{
  TouchPoint point = e.GetPrimaryTouchPoint(this);

  if (point != null && point.Action == TouchAction.Down)
  {
    if (this.tapToBegin)
    {
```

LISTING 37.2   Continued

```
      // Get started
      this.tapToBegin = false;
      this.PageTitle.Text = "";
      this.TargetGrid.Visibility = Visibility.Collapsed;
      this.TouchEllipse.Visibility = Visibility.Collapsed;

      // Show the indeterminate progress bar
      this.ProgressBar.IsIndeterminate = true;
      this.ProgressBar.Visibility = Visibility.Visible;

      this.beginTime = DateTime.Now;

      // Make the target appear between .5 sec and 7 sec from now
      timer.Interval = TimeSpan.FromMilliseconds(random.Next(500, 7000));
      timer.Start();
    }
    else if (this.TargetGrid.Visibility == Visibility.Visible)
    {
      // The target has been tapped
      DateTime endTime = DateTime.Now;

      // Position and show the ellipse where the screen was touched
      this.TouchEllipse.Margin = new Thickness(
        point.Position.X - this.TouchEllipse.Height / 2,
        point.Position.Y - this.TouchEllipse.Height / 2, 0, 0);
      this.TouchEllipse.Visibility = Visibility.Visible;

      // Show the elapsed time
      TimeSpan newTime = endTime - this.targetShownTime;
      this.PageTitle.Text = newTime.TotalSeconds + " sec";
      this.tapToBegin = true;

      // Record this attempt and update the UI
      double oldTotal = this.avgTime.Value.TotalSeconds * this.numTries.Value;
      // New average
      this.avgTime.Value = TimeSpan.FromSeconds(
        (oldTotal + newTime.TotalSeconds) / (this.numTries.Value + 1));
      // New total number of tries
      this.numTries.Value++;
      if (newTime < this.bestTime.Value)
      {
        // New best time
        this.bestTime.Value = newTime;
        UpdateLabels(true);
```

LISTING 37.2   Continued

```
        // Animate in a congratulations message
        this.MessageTextBlock.Text = "CONGRATULATIONS!";
        this.ShowMessageStoryboard.Begin();
      }
      else
      {
        UpdateLabels(false);
      }
    }
    else
    {
      // The screen has been tapped too early

      // Cancel the timer that would show the target
      this.timer.Stop();

      // Hide the progress bar and turn off the indeterminate
      // animation to avoid poor performance
      this.ProgressBar.Visibility = Visibility.Collapsed;
      this.ProgressBar.IsIndeterminate = false;

      // Show exactly how early the tap was
      DateTime endTime = this.beginTime + this.timer.Interval;
      this.PageTitle.Text = (DateTime.Now - endTime).TotalSeconds + " sec";
      this.tapToBegin = true;

      // Animate in an explanatory message
      this.MessageTextBlock.Text = "TOO EARLY!";
      this.ShowMessageStoryboard.Begin();
    }
  }
}

void Timer_Tick(object sender, EventArgs e)
{
  // Show the target
  this.TargetGrid.Visibility = Visibility.Visible;

  // Hide the progress bar and turn off the indeterminate
  // animation to avoid poor performance
  this.ProgressBar.Visibility = Visibility.Collapsed;
  this.ProgressBar.IsIndeterminate = false;

  this.targetShownTime = DateTime.Now;
```

LISTING 37.2   Continued

```
    // We only want the Tick once
    this.timer.Stop();
  }

  void UpdateLabels(bool animateBestTime)
  {
    if (this.numTries.Value > 0)
    {
      // Ensure the panel is visible and update the text blocks
      this.TimesPanel.Visibility = Visibility.Visible;
      this.BestTimeTextBlock.Text = this.bestTime.Value.TotalSeconds + " sec";
      this.AvgTimeTextBlock.Text = this.avgTime.Value.TotalSeconds + " sec";
      if (this.numTries.Value == 1)
        this.AvgTimeHeaderTextBlock.Text = "AVG TIME (1 TRY)";
      else
        this.AvgTimeHeaderTextBlock.Text = "AVG TIME (" + this.numTries.Value
          + " TRIES)";

      // Animate the textblocks out then in. The animations take care of
      // showing the textblocks if they are collapsed.
      this.SlideAvgTimeStoryboard.Begin();
      if (animateBestTime)
        this.SlideBestTimeStoryboard.Begin();
      else
        this.BestTimeTextBlock.Visibility = Visibility.Visible;
    }
    else
    {
      // Hide everything
      this.TimesPanel.Visibility = Visibility.Collapsed;
      this.BestTimeTextBlock.Visibility = Visibility.Collapsed;
      this.AvgTimeTextBlock.Visibility = Visibility.Collapsed;
    }
  }

  // Application bar handlers

  void InstructionsButton_Click(object sender, EventArgs e)
  {
    this.NavigationService.Navigate(new Uri("/InstructionsPage.xaml",
      UriKind.Relative));
  }

  void DeleteButton_Click(object sender, EventArgs e)
```

LISTING 37.2   Continued

```
    {
      if (MessageBox.Show("Are you sure you want to clear your times?",
        "Delete history", MessageBoxButton.OKCancel) == MessageBoxResult.OK)
      {
        this.numTries.Value = 0;
        this.bestTime.Value = TimeSpan.MaxValue;
        UpdateLabels(true);
      }
    }

    void AboutMenuItem_Click(object sender, EventArgs e)
    {
      this.NavigationService.Navigate(new Uri(
        "/Shared/About/AboutPage.xaml?appName=Reflex Text", UriKind.Relative));
    }
  }
}
```

Notes:

→ The event for capturing touch and multi-touch activity has the odd name FrameReported and is exposed on a static class called Touch (from the System.Windows.Input namespace). This event gets raised for touch activity across the entire application, so Listing 37.1 attaches a handler to this event in OnNavigatedTo but removes the handler in OnNavigatedFrom.

 Be sure to detach any FrameReported handlers as soon as possible!

In addition to the performance implication of FrameReported handlers being invoked when they don't need to be, forgetting to detach from the event can cause other problems if the page containing the handler is no longer active.

→ Inside the FrameReported event handler (Touch_FrameReported), GetPrimaryTouchPoint is called to get single-touch data, which is all this app cares about. If multiple fingers are pressed on the screen, GetPrimaryTouchPoint returns data about the **first** finger that makes contact with the screen.

→ FrameReported gets raised for three types of actions: a finger making contact with the screen, a finger moving on the screen, and a finger being released from the screen. These actions are analogous to mouse down, mouse move, and mouse up events, although here they apply per finger. This app only cares about taps, so the logic inside Touch_FrameReported only runs when the primary touch point is a touching-down action.

→ In addition to the Action property, the TouchPoint class returned by GetPrimaryTouchPoint exposes Position and Size properties. This app only makes use of the position of the touch point in order to place TouchEllipse in the spot that was tapped.

→ Notice that the progress bar's IsIndeterminate property is only set to true while it is visible. This is to avoid the performance problems discussed in Chapter 18, "Cocktails."

> **You should ignore** TouchPoint's Size **property!**
>
> The current version of Windows Phone doesn't actually support the discovery of a touch point's size, so the reported Size.Width and Size.Height are always 1. This is unfortunate, as it would be a nice touch (no pun intended) for Reflex Test to make TouchEllipse the size of the fingertip that touched the screen.

The Finished Product

Under the light theme with the magenta accent color

In a landscape orientation

The instructions page, whose code is available in this chapter's project

chapter 38

lessons

-

→ Multi-Touch

→ Tracking Individual Fingers

MUSICAL ROBOT

Musical Robot is a quirky musical instrument app that can play two-octaves-worth of robotic sounds based on where you place your fingers. Touching toward the left produces lower notes, and touching toward the right produces higher notes. You can slide your fingers around to produce interesting effects. You can use multiple fingers—as many as your phone supports simultaneously—to play chords (multiple notes at once). You're more likely to use this app to annoy your friends rather than play actual compositions, but it's fun nevertheless!

Musical Robot is structured much like the preceding chapter's Reflex Test app—a single page that leverages the multi-touch `FrameReported` event. This time, however, the multi-touch nature of this event is exploited.

The User Interface

Musical Robot's main page, pictured in Figure 38.1 in its initial state, contains a few visual elements that have nothing to do with the core functionality of this app, but provide some visual flair and simple instructions. Listing 38.1 contains the XAML.

FIGURE 38.1   The main page contains a robot image and instructions.

LISTING 38.1   `MainPage.xaml`—The User Interface for Musical Robot's Main Page

```
<phone:PhoneApplicationPage x:Class="WindowsPhoneApp.MainPage"
    xmlns="http://schemas.microsoft.com/winfx/2006/xaml/presentation"
    xmlns:x="http://schemas.microsoft.com/winfx/2006/xaml"
    xmlns:phone="clr-namespace:Microsoft.Phone.Controls;assembly=Microsoft.Phone"
    SupportedOrientations="Landscape" Orientation="Landscape">
  <Canvas>
    <!-- The dynamic mouth that is visible through the image's mouth hole -->
    <Rectangle Canvas.Left="168" Canvas.Top="127" Width="114" Height="23"
                RadiusX="10" RadiusY="10" RenderTransformOrigin=".5,.5"
                Fill="{StaticResource PhoneForegroundBrush}">
      <Rectangle.RenderTransform>
        <!-- The scale is continually changed from code-behind -->
        <ScaleTransform x:Name="MouthScale" ScaleX="0"/>
      </Rectangle.RenderTransform>
    </Rectangle>

    <!-- 5 lights representing up to 5 simultaneous fingers -->
    <Ellipse x:Name="Light1" Visibility="Collapsed" Canvas.Left="137"
            Canvas.Top="284" Width="23" Height="23" Fill="Red"/>
    <Ellipse x:Name="Light2" Visibility="Collapsed" Canvas.Left="174"
            Canvas.Top="294" Width="23" Height="23" Fill="Red"/>
    <Ellipse x:Name="Light3" Visibility="Collapsed" Canvas.Left="213"
            Canvas.Top="298" Width="23" Height="23" Fill="Red"/>
    <Ellipse x:Name="Light4" Visibility="Collapsed" Canvas.Left="252"
            Canvas.Top="294" Width="23" Height="23" Fill="Red"/>
```

LISTING 38.1   Continued

```xml
<Ellipse x:Name="Light5" Visibility="Collapsed" Canvas.Left="290"
         Canvas.Top="284" Width="23" Height="23" Fill="Red"/>

<!-- The accent-colored robot -->
<Rectangle Width="453" Height="480" Fill="{StaticResource PhoneAccentBrush}">
  <Rectangle.OpacityMask>
    <ImageBrush ImageSource="Images/robot.png"/>
  </Rectangle.OpacityMask>
</Rectangle>

<!-- Instructions -->
<TextBlock Canvas.Left="350" Canvas.Top="40" FontFamily="Segoe WP Black"
           FontSize="40" Foreground="{StaticResource PhoneAccentBrush}">
    <TextBlock.RenderTransform>
        <RotateTransform Angle="-10"/>
    </TextBlock.RenderTransform>
    TAP &amp; DRAG.
    <LineBreak/>
    USE MANY FINGERS!
</TextBlock>
  </Canvas>
</phone:PhoneApplicationPage>
```

Notes:

→ `MouthScale`'s `ScaleX` value is randomly set anywhere from 0 to 1 whenever a finger makes contact with or moves across the screen. This provides the illusion that the robot is singing as it makes its noises.

→ The circles are filled with red to indicate how many fingers are simultaneously in contact with the screen (up to 5). The limit of 5 is simply due to space constraints in the artwork. It does not reflect on multi-touch limitations of the operating system or any particular device.

 How many simultaneous touch points does Windows Phone support?

All Windows phones are guaranteed to support at least four simultaneous touch points. (Current models support exactly four.) The operating system can support up to 10, in case an ambitious device wants to support it.

The Code-Behind

Listing 38.2 contains the code-behind for the main page.

LISTING 38.2   `MainPage.xaml.cs`—The Code-Behind for Musical Robot's Main Page

```csharp
using System;
using System.Collections.Generic;
using System.Linq;
using System.Windows;
using System.Windows.Input;
using System.Windows.Navigation;
using Microsoft.Phone.Controls;
using Microsoft.Xna.Framework.Audio;

namespace WindowsPhoneApp
{
  public partial class MainPage : PhoneApplicationPage
  {
    // Store a separate sound effect instance for each unique finger
    Dictionary<int, SoundEffectInstance> fingerSounds =
      new Dictionary<int, SoundEffectInstance>();

    // For the random mouth movement
    Random random = new Random();

    public MainPage()
    {
      InitializeComponent();
      SoundEffects.Initialize();
    }

    protected override void OnNavigatedTo(NavigationEventArgs e)
    {
      base.OnNavigatedTo(e);

      // Subscribe to the touch/multi-touch event.
      // This is application-wide, so only do this when on this page.
      Touch.FrameReported += Touch_FrameReported;
    }

    protected override void OnNavigatedFrom(NavigationEventArgs e)
    {
      base.OnNavigatedFrom(e);

      // Unsubscribe from this application-wide event
      Touch.FrameReported -= Touch_FrameReported;
    }

    void Touch_FrameReported(object sender, TouchFrameEventArgs e)
```

LISTING 38.2   Continued

```csharp
{
  // Get all touch points
  TouchPointCollection points = e.GetTouchPoints(this);

  // Filter out the "up" touch points because those fingers are
  // no longer in contact with the screen
  int numPoints =
    (from p in points where p.Action != TouchAction.Up select p).Count();

  // Update up to 5 robot lights to indicate how many fingers are in contact
  this.Light1.Visibility =
    (numPoints >= 1 ? Visibility.Visible : Visibility.Collapsed);
  this.Light2.Visibility =
    (numPoints >= 2 ? Visibility.Visible : Visibility.Collapsed);
  this.Light3.Visibility =
    (numPoints >= 3 ? Visibility.Visible : Visibility.Collapsed);
  this.Light4.Visibility =
    (numPoints >= 4 ? Visibility.Visible : Visibility.Collapsed);
  this.Light5.Visibility =
    (numPoints >= 5 ? Visibility.Visible : Visibility.Collapsed);

  // If any fingers are in contact, stretch the inner mouth anywhere from
  // 0 to 100%
  if (numPoints == 0)
    this.MouthScale.ScaleX = 0;
  else
    this.MouthScale.ScaleX = this.random.NextDouble(); // Returns a # from 0-1

  // Process each touch point individually
  foreach (TouchPoint point in points)
  {
    // The "touch device" is each finger, and it has a unique ID
    int fingerId = point.TouchDevice.Id;

    if (point.Action == TouchAction.Up)
    {
      // Stop the sound corresponding to this just-lifted finger
      if (this.fingerSounds.ContainsKey(fingerId))
        this.fingerSounds[fingerId].Stop();

      // Remove the sound from the dictionary
      this.fingerSounds.Remove(fingerId);
    }
    else
    {
```

LISTING 38.2   Continued

```
            // Turn the horizontal position into a pitch from -1 to 1.
            // -1 represents 1 octave lower, 1 represents 1 octave higher.
            float pitch = (float)(2 * point.Position.X / this.ActualWidth) - 1;

            if (!this.fingerSounds.ContainsKey(fingerId))
            {
              // We haven't yet created the sound effect for this finger, so do it
              this.fingerSounds.Add(fingerId, SoundEffects.Sound.CreateInstance());
              this.fingerSounds[fingerId].IsLooped = true;
            }

            // Start playing the looped sound at the correct pitch
            this.fingerSounds[fingerId].Pitch = pitch;
            this.fingerSounds[fingerId].Play();
        }
      }

    // Work around the fact that we sometimes don't get Up actions reported
    CheckForStuckSounds(points);
  }

  void CheckForStuckSounds(TouchPointCollection points)
  {
    List<int> soundsToRemove = new List<int>();

    // Inspect each active sound
    foreach (var sound in this.fingerSounds)
    {
      bool found = false;

      // See if this sound corresponds to an active finger
      foreach (TouchPoint point in points)
      {
        if (point.TouchDevice.Id == sound.Key)
        {
          found = true;
          break;
        }
      }

      // It doesn't, so stop the sound and mark it for removal
      if (!found)
      {
        sound.Value.Stop();
        soundsToRemove.Add(sound.Key);
```

LISTING 38.2   Continued

```
        }
      }

      // Remove each orphaned sound
      foreach (int id in soundsToRemove)
        this.fingerSounds.Remove(id);
    }
  }
}
```

Notes:

→ Because this app contains only a single page, unsubscribing from the `FrameReported` event in `OnNavigatedFrom` is not necessary, but this is done to keep good hygiene in case another page is ever added (or this code is used in a different app).

→ Inside the `FrameReported` event handler (`Touch_FrameReported`), `GetTouchPoints` is called to get the entire collection of touch points. On most devices, this collection will always contain 1–4 items. It never is zero-length or `null`.

→ Because each touch point can be in the returned collection for one of three reasons (making initial contact with the screen, moving on the screen, or being released from the screen), simply counting its items does *not* tell us how many fingers are currently in contact with the screen. To do this, we must filter out any touch points whose `Action` property is set to `Up`. This could be done by manually enumerating the `points` collection, but this code instead opts for a LINQ query to set the value of `numPoints`.

→ The code responsible for starting and stopping each sound makes use of a property on `TouchPoint` not mentioned in the preceding chapter: `TouchDevice`. This odd-sounding property represents the user's finger responsible for the touch point. Each finger is assigned an integer ID, exposed as a property on `TouchDevice`, which can be used to track each finger individually. This would otherwise be impossible when multiple fingers are triggering events simultaneously. The ID assigned to any finger is guaranteed to remain unique during the lifetime of a down/move/up action cycle.

→ The `fingerSounds` dictionary leverages the unique finger IDs for its keys. This listing starts playing a looped sound as each new finger makes contact with the screen, it adjusts the pitch of the sound as the finger is moved, and it stops the sound as the finger is released.

→ The `SoundEffects` class used by this listing is just like the same-named class used by many of this book's apps, but customized to expose a single sound through its `Sound` property. The included sound is so short that it is barely audible when played by itself, but the `IsLooped` property on `SoundEffectInstance` is leveraged to produce a smooth and *very* audible sound. The pitch of each sound is varied based on the horizontal position of each touch point. The looping and pitch adjustment is much like what's done in Chapter 31, "Trombone," although the audio file used by Musical Robot doesn't define a loop region.

Occasionally, a finger-up action might not be reported!

Due to a bug in Silverlight (or perhaps in some touch drivers), a finger that has reported touching down and moving around might never report that it has been lifted up. Instead, the corresponding touch point simply vanishes from the collection returned by GetTouchPoints. In Musical Robot, this would manifest as sounds that never stop playing.

To prevent such "stuck" sounds, the CheckForStuckSounds method in Listing 38.2 looks at every active sound and attempts to find a current touch point that corresponds to it. If a sound is not associated with an active touch point, it is stopped and removed from the dictionary, just like what happens when a finger properly reports being lifted up.

Can a finger ID continue to identity a specific finger even if it temporarily leaves the screen?

No, the phone cannot continue to track a specific finger once it has broken contact with the screen. The unique ID, assigned during each *new* initial contact, is only valid until the FrameReported event reports an Up action for that touch point.

The Finished Product

Light theme, purple accent color

Dark theme, orange accent color

Light theme, green accent color

chapter 39

PAINT

Paint is a classic finger-painting app, but with several powerful options:

→ You can paint on top of any color canvas or a photo from your pictures library and paint with multiple fingers simultaneously (naturally).

→ In addition to using the rich color picker shared by many apps in this book, Paint provides many options for customizing the brush strokes.

→ You can undo and redo your strokes to get them just right.

→ A "stroke straightening" feature can help you create more precise artwork, either by straightening your diagonal lines or by snapping your lines to be completely vertical/horizontal.

→ Save your masterpieces to your phone's pictures library.

Paint uses multi-touch the same way as the preceding chapter's Musical Robot app, but it applies the data to an interesting element worth knowing about—*ink presenter*.

An ink presenter holds a collection of objects known as *strokes* that are meant to represent handwriting. Each stroke contains a collection of points that are connected to form each one. Each stroke also exposes a DrawingAttributes object with four properties: Color, OutlineColor, Width,

and `Height`. Therefore, this app's main drawing surface is simply an ink presenter whose strokes are added based on the touch data and settings chosen for the `DrawingAttributes` object.

Paint has two pages (in addition to standard instructions and about pages not shown in this chapter)—the main page containing the drawing surface and a palette page for adjusting the brush settings. This chapter begins by examining the palette page first, as it uses an ink presenter in a simpler fashion.

The Palette Page

Paint's palette page, pictured in Figure 39.1, enables changing each of the properties on the `DrawingAttributes` object. It links to this book's shared color picker for the main color as well as the optional outline color, and exposes two sliders for independently controlling a stroke's width and height.

The page has a hard-coded stroke that demonstrates how the different settings affect the resulting strokes as the user changes them. This is especially helpful for visualizing width and height changes, as shown in Figure 39.2.

FIGURE 39.1   The palette page exposes a way to change each of the four properties on `DrawingAttributes`.

Width=2, Height=2   Width=2, Height=55   Width=55, Height=2   Width=55, Height=55

FIGURE 39.2   Demonstrating every combination of the minimum and maximum brush sizes.

The User Interface

Listing 39.1 contains the XAML for the palette page.

LISTING 39.1   `PalettePage.xaml`—The User Interface for Paint's Palette Page

```xaml
<phone:PhoneApplicationPage x:Class="WindowsPhoneApp.PalettePage"
    xmlns="http://schemas.microsoft.com/winfx/2006/xaml/presentation"
    xmlns:x="http://schemas.microsoft.com/winfx/2006/xaml"
    xmlns:phone="clr-namespace:Microsoft.Phone.Controls;assembly=Microsoft.Phone"
    xmlns:shell="clr-namespace:Microsoft.Phone.Shell;assembly=Microsoft.Phone"
    xmlns:local="clr-namespace:WindowsPhoneApp"
    FontFamily="{StaticResource PhoneFontFamilyNormal}"
    FontSize="{StaticResource PhoneFontSizeNormal}"
    Foreground="{StaticResource PhoneForegroundBrush}"
    SupportedOrientations="Portrait" shell:SystemTray.IsVisible="True">
  <Canvas>
    <!-- The standard header -->
    <StackPanel Style="{StaticResource PhoneTitlePanelStyle}">
      <TextBlock Text="PAINT" Style="{StaticResource PhoneTextTitle0Style}"/>
      <TextBlock Text="palette" Style="{StaticResource PhoneTextTitle1Style}"/>
    </StackPanel>

    <!-- The translucent foreground-colored palette image -->
    <Rectangle Canvas.Left="6" Width="474" Height="632" Opacity=".6"
               Fill="{StaticResource PhoneForegroundBrush}">
      <Rectangle.OpacityMask>
        <ImageBrush ImageSource="Images/paletteBackground.png"/>
      </Rectangle.OpacityMask>
    </Rectangle>

    <!-- The InkPresenter with a single 5-point stroke -->
    <InkPresenter x:Name="PreviewInkPresenter" Canvas.Left="236" Canvas.Top="220">
      <InkPresenter.Strokes>
        <Stroke>
          <Stroke.StylusPoints>
            <StylusPoint X="100" Y="0"/>
            <StylusPoint X="0" Y="0"/>
            <StylusPoint X="80" Y="80"/>
            <StylusPoint X="0" Y="120"/>
            <StylusPoint X="0" Y="170"/>
          </Stroke.StylusPoints>
        </Stroke>
      </InkPresenter.Strokes>
    </InkPresenter>

    <!-- Paint color -->
```

LISTING 39.1   Continued

```
    <TextBlock Text="Paint color" Canvas.Left="84" Canvas.Top="431" FontSize="23"
                Foreground="{StaticResource PhoneBackgroundBrush}"/>
    <Ellipse x:Name="PaintColorEllipse" Canvas.Left="78" Canvas.Top="305"
      Width="120" Height="120" Stroke="{StaticResource PhoneBackgroundBrush}"
      StrokeThickness="10" local:Tilt.IsEnabled="True"
      MouseLeftButtonUp="PaintColorEllipse_MouseLeftButtonUp"/>

    <!-- Outline color -->
    <CheckBox x:Name="OutlineCheckBox" Canvas.Left="210" Canvas.Top="521"
      Foreground="{StaticResource PhoneBackgroundBrush}"
      local:Tilt.IsEnabled="True" Checked="OutlineCheckBox_IsCheckedChanged"
      Unchecked="OutlineCheckBox_IsCheckedChanged">
      <TextBlock FontSize="23" Foreground="{StaticResource PhoneBackgroundBrush}">
        Outline<LineBreak/>color
      </TextBlock>
    </CheckBox>
    <Ellipse x:Name="OutlineColorEllipse" Canvas.Left="213" Canvas.Top="414"
      Width="120" Height="120" Stroke="{StaticResource PhoneBackgroundBrush}"
      StrokeThickness="10" local:Tilt.IsEnabled="True"
      MouseLeftButtonUp="OutlineColorEllipse_MouseLeftButtonUp"/>

    <!-- Brush width -->
    <TextBlock Text="Brush width" Canvas.Left="35" Canvas.Top="660"
                Foreground="{StaticResource PhoneSubtleBrush}"/>
    <Slider x:Name="BrushWidthSlider" Canvas.Left="24" Canvas.Top="680"
            Minimum="2" Maximum="55" Width="203"
            ValueChanged="BrushWidthSlider_ValueChanged"/>

    <!-- Brush height -->
    <TextBlock Text="Brush height" Canvas.Left="263" Canvas.Top="660"
                Foreground="{StaticResource PhoneSubtleBrush}"/>
    <Slider x:Name="BrushHeightSlider" Canvas.Left="252" Canvas.Top="680"
            Minimum="2" Maximum="55" Width="203"
            ValueChanged="BrushHeightSlider_ValueChanged"/>
  </Canvas>
</phone:PhoneApplicationPage>
```

Notes:

→ The ink presenter's collection of strokes contains just one 5-point stroke. The stroke doesn't specify any explicit drawing attributes because those are set in code-behind. By default, a stroke is given a width and height of 3, a color of black, and an outline color of transparent.

→ The `StylusPoint` objects that must be used to define a stroke are just like `Point` objects, but they have one additional property—`PressureFactor`—that unfortunately has no effect on Windows Phone.

→ The slider-enforced minimum and maximum width/height values of 2 and 55, respectively, are arbitrary. The corresponding properties on `DrawingAttributes` can be set to any nonnegative `double`.

Can I change the thickness of a stroke's outline?

No, it is always a thin, approximately 1-pixel border. However, you could mimic a thicker border by rendering a duplicate stroke with a larger width and height behind each "real" stroke. It turns out that this is exactly how the outline color is rendered anyway, which you can see by giving the stroke a translucent or transparent color. This is demonstrated in Figure 39.3, which uses a translucent white stroke color and a green outline color.

FIGURE 39.3   A stroke outline is really just a slightly larger stroke underneath, which can be seen when a translucent paint color is used.

What's the difference between an ink presenter with strokes and a path with polylines?

Either of these two elements can be used for an app like Paint, as the differences between them are subtle. The main reason to prefer an ink presenter is that it performs better for the large number of points that are generated by finger movement. It's also slightly easier to serialize its strokes so they can be saved and then later restored.

A path is more powerful because it can express mathematical curves between any two points, whereas each stroke's stylus points are connected with straight lines. (There are just so many points when plotting finger movement that you don't normally notice the connections.) It also supports arbitrary brushes (like gradient or image brushes instead of a solid color), and you can leverage its fill and stroke properties to either fill in a closed shape or to provide a true border of any thickness.

An ink presenter is more powerful because it can contain arbitrary UI elements in addition to strokes. (That's because InkPresenter derives from Canvas.) It also holds the promise of easily enabling pressure-sensitive painting, as each stylus point exposes a PressureFactor property that can be set to a value from 0 to 1. However, given that setting this property currently has no effect on Windows Phone, *and* touch points never report how hard a finger is pressing the screen, this advantage is only a theoretical one for the future.

The Code-Behind

Listing 39.2 contains the code-behind for the palette page.

LISTING 39.2   `PalettePage.xaml.cs`—The Code-Behind for Paint's Palette Page

```
using System;
using System.Windows;
using System.Windows.Ink;
using System.Windows.Input;
using System.Windows.Media;
using System.Windows.Navigation;
using Microsoft.Phone.Controls;

namespace WindowsPhoneApp
{
  public partial class PalettePage : PhoneApplicationPage
  {
    public PalettePage()
    {
      InitializeComponent();
    }

    protected override void OnNavigatedTo(NavigationEventArgs e)
    {
      base.OnNavigatedTo(e);
```

LISTING 39.2   Continued

```csharp
    // Respect the saved settings
    this.PaintColorEllipse.Fill =
      new SolidColorBrush(Settings.PaintColor.Value);
    this.OutlineColorEllipse.Fill =
      new SolidColorBrush(Settings.OutlineColor.Value);
    this.OutlineCheckBox.IsChecked = Settings.HasOutline.Value;
    this.BrushWidthSlider.Value = Settings.BrushWidth.Value;
    this.BrushHeightSlider.Value = Settings.BrushHeight.Value;

    // Update the ink presenter with the current settings
    DrawingAttributes attributes =
      this.PreviewInkPresenter.Strokes[0].DrawingAttributes;
    attributes.Color = Settings.PaintColor.Value;
    attributes.Width = Settings.BrushWidth.Value;
    attributes.Height = Settings.BrushHeight.Value;
    if (Settings.HasOutline.Value)
      attributes.OutlineColor = Settings.OutlineColor.Value;
    else
      attributes.OutlineColor = Colors.Transparent; // Hide the outline
  }


  void PaintColorEllipse_MouseLeftButtonUp(object sender,
    MouseButtonEventArgs e)
  {
    // Get a string representation of the colors we need to pass to the color
    // picker, without the leading #
    string currentColorString =
      Settings.PaintColor.Value.ToString().Substring(1);
    string defaultColorString =
      Settings.PaintColor.DefaultValue.ToString().Substring(1);

    // The color picker works with the same isolated storage value that the
    // Setting works with, but we have to clear its cached value to pick up
    // the value chosen in the color picker
    Settings.PaintColor.ForceRefresh();

    // Navigate to the color picker
    this.NavigationService.Navigate(new Uri(
      "/Shared/Color Picker/ColorPickerPage.xaml?"
      + "&currentColor=" + currentColorString
      + "&defaultColor=" + defaultColorString
      + "&settingName=PaintColor", UriKind.Relative));
  }
```

LISTING 39.2   Continued

```
void OutlineColorEllipse_MouseLeftButtonUp(object sender,
  MouseButtonEventArgs e)
{
  // Get a string representation of the colors, without the leading #
  string currentColorString =
    Settings.OutlineColor.Value.ToString().Substring(1);
  string defaultColorString =
    Settings.OutlineColor.DefaultValue.ToString().Substring(1);

  // The color picker works with the same isolated storage value that the
  // Setting works with, but we have to clear its cached value to pick up
  // the value chosen in the color picker
  Settings.OutlineColor.ForceRefresh();

  // Navigate to the color picker
  this.NavigationService.Navigate(new Uri(
    "/Shared/Color Picker/ColorPickerPage.xaml?"
    + "showOpacity=true"
    + "&currentColor=" + currentColorString
    + "&defaultColor=" + defaultColorString
    + "&settingName=OutlineColor", UriKind.Relative));
}

void OutlineCheckBox_IsCheckedChanged(object sender, RoutedEventArgs e)
{
  // Toggle the outline
  Settings.HasOutline.Value = this.OutlineCheckBox.IsChecked.Value;
  if (Settings.HasOutline.Value)
    this.PreviewInkPresenter.Strokes[0].DrawingAttributes.OutlineColor =
      Settings.OutlineColor.Value;
  else
    this.PreviewInkPresenter.Strokes[0].DrawingAttributes.OutlineColor =
      Colors.Transparent;
}

void BrushWidthSlider_ValueChanged(object sender,
  RoutedPropertyChangedEventArgs<double> e)
{
  if (this.BrushWidthSlider != null) // Ignore during XAML parsing
  {
    Settings.BrushWidth.Value = (int)this.BrushWidthSlider.Value;
    this.PreviewInkPresenter.Strokes[0].DrawingAttributes.Width =
      Settings.BrushWidth.Value;
  }
```

LISTING 39.2   Continued

```
    }

    void BrushHeightSlider_ValueChanged(object sender,
      RoutedPropertyChangedEventArgs<double> e)
    {
      if (this.BrushHeightSlider != null) // Ignore during XAML parsing
      {
        Settings.BrushHeight.Value = (int)this.BrushHeightSlider.Value;
        this.PreviewInkPresenter.Strokes[0].DrawingAttributes.Height =
          Settings.BrushHeight.Value;
      }
    }
  }
}
```

Notes:

→ This app uses the following settings defined in a separate `Settings.cs` file:

```
public static class Settings
{
  // Drawing attributes for strokes
  public static readonly Setting<Color> PaintColor = new Setting<Color>(
    "PaintColor", (Color)Application.Current.Resources["PhoneAccentColor"]);
  public static readonly Setting<Color> OutlineColor =
    new Setting<Color>("OutlineColor", Colors.Black);
  public static readonly Setting<bool> HasOutline =
    new Setting<bool>("HasOutline", false);
  public static readonly Setting<int> BrushWidth =
    new Setting<int>("BrushWidth", 10);
  public static readonly Setting<int> BrushHeight =
    new Setting<int>("BrushHeight", 10);

  // Background color
  public static readonly Setting<Color> PageColor =
    new Setting<Color>("PageColor", Colors.White);
}
```

All but the last one are modified by this page.

→ To update the stroke with all the current values, this code simply retrieves the 0th element of the ink presenter's `Strokes` collection.

→ When the user turns off the outline color (by unchecking the check box), the outline color is set to transparent. This is the only way to prevent the outline color from interfering with the size of the stroke and even the color of the stroke if the main color is translucent.

The Main Page

Paint's main page is nothing more than a drawing surface and an application bar with several available actions. As demonstrated in Figure 39.4, although the application bar adjusts for the current orientation, the artwork remains fixed relative to the screen. Having the artwork rotate would be problematic, as the page size would effectively change. Having the application bar rotate, however, is a nice touch when doing landscape-oriented artwork.

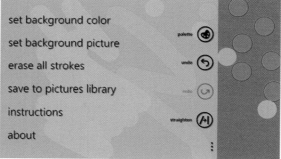

FIGURE 39.4   The application bar rotates according to the current orientation, but the artwork does not (relative to the physical screen).

When designing this app, I wanted the palette button on the application bar to be colored with the current paint color as a helpful visual aid. However, it's not currently possible to emit dynamic images to be used by application bar buttons. (If you have a reasonably small number of possible colors, you could include them in your project and swap between them, much like Chapter 33's Subservient Cat app does with its numeric images.) Therefore, I decided to update the application bar's background color with the current paint color as the next best thing. In Figure 39.4, the current paint color is a light, translucent blue.

The User Interface

Listing 39.3 contains the XAML for the main page.

LISTING 39.3   `MainPage.xaml`—The User Interface for Paint's Main Page

```xaml
<phone:PhoneApplicationPage x:Class="WindowsPhoneApp.MainPage"
    xmlns="http://schemas.microsoft.com/winfx/2006/xaml/presentation"
    xmlns:x="http://schemas.microsoft.com/winfx/2006/xaml"
    xmlns:phone="clr-namespace:Microsoft.Phone.Controls;assembly=Microsoft.Phone"
    xmlns:shell="clr-namespace:Microsoft.Phone.Shell;assembly=Microsoft.Phone"
    SupportedOrientations="PortraitOrLandscape">
  <!-- The application bar, and that's it! -->
  <phone:PhoneApplicationPage.ApplicationBar>
    <shell:ApplicationBar>
      <shell:ApplicationBarIconButton Text="palette"
        IconUri="/Images/appbar.palette.png" Click="PaletteButton_Click"/>
      <shell:ApplicationBarIconButton Text="undo"
        IconUri="/Shared/Images/appbar.undo.png" Click="UndoButton_Click"/>
      <shell:ApplicationBarIconButton Text="redo"
        IconUri="/Shared/Images/appbar.redo.png" Click="RedoButton_Click"/>
      <shell:ApplicationBarIconButton Text="straighten"
        IconUri="/Images/appbar.straighten1.png" Click="StraightenButton_Click"/>
      <shell:ApplicationBar.MenuItems>
        <shell:ApplicationBarMenuItem Text="set background color"
                                      Click="SetBackgroundColorMenuItem_Click"/>
        <shell:ApplicationBarMenuItem Text="set background picture"
                                      Click="SetBackgroundPictureMenuItem_Click"/>
        <shell:ApplicationBarMenuItem Text="erase all strokes"
                                      Click="EraseMenuItem_Click"/>
        <shell:ApplicationBarMenuItem Text="save to pictures library"
                                      Click="SaveToPicturesLibraryMenuItem_Click"/>
        <shell:ApplicationBarMenuItem Text="instructions"
                                      Click="InstructionsMenuItem_Click"/>
        <shell:ApplicationBarMenuItem Text="about"
                                      Click="AboutMenuItem_Click"/>
      </shell:ApplicationBar.MenuItems>
    </shell:ApplicationBar>
  </phone:PhoneApplicationPage.ApplicationBar>
</phone:PhoneApplicationPage>
```

This XAML file has the distinction of being the only one in this book where the page has no content! It only sets the values of its `SupportedOrientations` and `ApplicationBar` properties. That's because the content shown on main page is created from code-behind and placed in a frame-rooted popup. This is what enables the behavior demonstrated 39.4, in which the application bar rotates but the content does not.

The Code-Behind

Listing 39.4 contains the code-behind for the main page.

LISTING 39.4   `MainPage.xaml.cs`—The Code-Behind for Paint's Main Page

```
using System;
using System.Collections.Generic;
using System.IO;
using System.Linq;
using System.Windows;
using System.Windows.Controls;
using System.Windows.Controls.Primitives;
using System.Windows.Ink;
using System.Windows.Input;
using System.Windows.Media;
using System.Windows.Media.Imaging;
using System.Windows.Navigation;
using Microsoft.Phone;
using Microsoft.Phone.Controls;
using Microsoft.Phone.Shell;
using Microsoft.Phone.Tasks;

namespace WindowsPhoneApp
{
  public partial class MainPage : PhoneApplicationPage
  {
    // Undo and redo stacks
    Stack<HistoryEntry> undoStack = new Stack<HistoryEntry>();
    Stack<HistoryEntry> redoStack = new Stack<HistoryEntry>();

    // The in-progress strokes, tracked separately for each unique finger
    Dictionary<int, Stroke> fingerStrokes = new Dictionary<int, Stroke>();

    // The popup and its contents
    Popup popup = new Popup { IsOpen = true };
    Grid grid = new Grid { Width = 480, Height = 800 };
    InkPresenter inkPresenter = new InkPresenter();
    Image backgroundImage = new Image {
      Stretch = Stretch.Uniform, RenderTransformOrigin = new Point(.5, .5),
      RenderTransform = new CompositeTransform()
    };

    // Application bar buttons and a menu item that are changed by code-behind
    IApplicationBarIconButton undoButton;
    IApplicationBarIconButton redoButton;
    IApplicationBarIconButton straightenButton;
```

LISTING 39.4 Continued

```
IApplicationBarMenuItem backgroundPictureMenuItem;

public MainPage()
{
  InitializeComponent();

  // Assign the application bar items
  this.undoButton = this.ApplicationBar.Buttons[1]
    as IApplicationBarIconButton;
  this.redoButton = this.ApplicationBar.Buttons[2]
    as IApplicationBarIconButton;
  this.straightenButton = this.ApplicationBar.Buttons[3]
    as IApplicationBarIconButton;
  this.backgroundPictureMenuItem = this.ApplicationBar.MenuItems[1]
    as IApplicationBarMenuItem;

  // Restore the background image, if persisted previously
  if (IsolatedStorageHelper.FileExists("background.jpg"))
    SetBackgroundImage(IsolatedStorageHelper.LoadImageFile("background.jpg"));

  // Restore the strokes, if persisted previously.
  // These are stored in a file rather than isolated storage settings due to
  // a problem with the default serializer.
  StrokeCollection strokes =
    IsolatedStorageHelper.LoadSerializedObjectFromFile("strokes.xml",
      typeof(StrokeCollection)) as StrokeCollection;
  if (strokes != null)
    this.inkPresenter.Strokes = strokes;

  // Refresh the app bar based on the presence of a background image & strokes
  RefreshAppBarMenu();
  RefreshAppBarButtons();

  // Attach the UI to the popup, which is already showing (IsOpen=true)
  this.grid.Children.Add(this.backgroundImage);
  this.grid.Children.Add(this.inkPresenter);
  this.popup.Child = this.grid;
}

protected override void OnNavigatedFrom(NavigationEventArgs e)
{
  base.OnNavigatedFrom(e);

  // Need to hide the popup so the other page can be shown!
```

LISTING 39.4   Continued

```
    this.popup.IsOpen = false;

    // Unsubscribe from this application-wide event
    Touch.FrameReported -= Touch_FrameReported;

    // Persist the current strokes.
    // These are stored in a file rather than isolated storage settings due to
    // a problem with the default serializer.
    IsolatedStorageHelper.SaveFile("strokes.xml", this.inkPresenter.Strokes);
  }

  protected override void OnNavigatedTo(NavigationEventArgs e)
  {
    base.OnNavigatedTo(e);

    // Ensure the popup is shown, as it gets hidden when navigating away
    this.popup.IsOpen = true;

    // Reapply the background color, in case we just returned
    // from the color picker page
    this.grid.Background = new SolidColorBrush(Settings.PageColor.Value);

    // Apply the current paint color as the app bar background color
    Color paintColor = Settings.PaintColor.Value;
    // Prevent the background from getting too transparent,
    // potentialy making the buttons and menu items unreadable
    if (paintColor.A < 60)
      paintColor.A = 60;
    this.ApplicationBar.BackgroundColor = paintColor;

    // Choose a foreground color that will be visible over the background color
    if (IsLight(Settings.PaintColor.Value))
      this.ApplicationBar.ForegroundColor = Colors.Black;
    else
      this.ApplicationBar.ForegroundColor = Colors.White;

    // Subscribe to the touch/multi-touch event.
    // This is application-wide, so only do this when on this page.
    Touch.FrameReported += Touch_FrameReported;
  }

  void Touch_FrameReported(object sender, TouchFrameEventArgs e)
  {
    // Get all touch points
```

LISTING 39.4   Continued

```
TouchPointCollection points = e.GetTouchPoints(this.inkPresenter);

// Process each touch point individually
foreach (TouchPoint point in points)
{
  // The "touch device" is each finger, and it has a unique ID
  int fingerId = point.TouchDevice.Id;

  if (point.Action == TouchAction.Down)
  {
    // Start a new stroke
    Stroke stroke = new Stroke();

    // Apply all the current settings
    stroke.DrawingAttributes.Color = Settings.PaintColor.Value;
    stroke.DrawingAttributes.Width = Settings.BrushWidth.Value;
    stroke.DrawingAttributes.Height = Settings.BrushHeight.Value;
    if (Settings.HasOutline.Value)
      stroke.DrawingAttributes.OutlineColor = Settings.OutlineColor.Value;
    else
      stroke.DrawingAttributes.OutlineColor = Colors.Transparent;

    // The first point of this stroke is the current finger position
    stroke.StylusPoints.Add(
      new StylusPoint(point.Position.X, point.Position.Y));

    // Track which finger this stroke belongs to
    this.fingerStrokes[fingerId] = stroke;

    // Add it to the ink presenter's collection of strokes
    this.inkPresenter.Strokes.Add(stroke);
  }
  else if (point.Action == TouchAction.Move)
  {
    // Keep adding new points to the stroke
    if (this.fingerStrokes.ContainsKey(fingerId))
      this.fingerStrokes[fingerId].StylusPoints.Add(
        new StylusPoint(point.Position.X, point.Position.Y));
  }
  else // TouchAction.Up
  {
    // The stroke is finished
    if (this.fingerStrokes.ContainsKey(fingerId))
    {
```

LISTING 39.4   Continued

```
          // Enable this action to be undone
          this.undoStack.Push(
            new HistoryEntry { StrokeAdded = this.fingerStrokes[fingerId] });
          this.redoStack.Clear();

          // Stop tracking this stroke
          this.fingerStrokes.Remove(fingerId);

          // Refresh the state of the undo/redo/straighten buttons
          RefreshAppBarButtons();
        }
      }
    }
  }
}


bool IsLight(Color color)
{
  return ((color.R + color.G + color.B) / 3 > 127.5);
}


void SetBackgroundImage(ImageSource source)
{
  this.backgroundImage.Source = source;

  // The ImageOpened event doesn't get raised after this, but the values for
  // ActualWidth and ActualHeight aren't correct yet. The BeginInvoke enables
  // us to retrieve the values.
  this.Dispatcher.BeginInvoke(delegate()
  {
    // Rotate the image based on whether it's landscape or portrait
    if (this.backgroundImage.ActualWidth > this.backgroundImage.ActualHeight)
    {
      this.backgroundImage.Width = 800;
      this.backgroundImage.Margin = new Thickness((480 - 800) / 2, 0, 0, 0);
      (this.backgroundImage.RenderTransform as CompositeTransform).Rotation =
        90;
    }
    else
    {
      this.backgroundImage.Width = 480;
      this.backgroundImage.Margin = new Thickness(0, 0, 0, 0);
      (this.backgroundImage.RenderTransform as CompositeTransform).Rotation =
        0;
    }
```

LISTING 39.4   Continued

```
    });
  }

  // Update the state of the application bar menu
  void RefreshAppBarMenu()
  {
    if (IsolatedStorageHelper.FileExists("background.jpg"))
      this.backgroundPictureMenuItem.Text = "remove background picture";
    else
      this.backgroundPictureMenuItem.Text = "set background picture";
  }

  // Update the state of the application bar buttons
  void RefreshAppBarButtons()
  {
    this.undoButton.IsEnabled = (this.undoStack.Count > 0);
    this.redoButton.IsEnabled = (this.redoStack.Count > 0);
    this.straightenButton.IsEnabled = (this.inkPresenter.Strokes.Count > 0);

    // Customize the straighten button icon based on the last stroke's shape
    if (this.inkPresenter.Strokes.Count > 0)
    {
      Stroke lastStroke =
        this.inkPresenter.Strokes[this.inkPresenter.Strokes.Count - 1];

      if (lastStroke.StylusPoints.Count > 2)
        this.straightenButton.IconUri =
          new Uri("/Images/appbar.straighten1.png", UriKind.Relative);
      else
        this.straightenButton.IconUri =
          new Uri("/Images/appbar.straighten2.png", UriKind.Relative);
    }
  }

  // Application bar button handlers

  void PaletteButton_Click(object sender, EventArgs e)
  {
    this.NavigationService.Navigate(
      new Uri("/PalettePage.xaml", UriKind.Relative));
  }

  void UndoButton_Click(object sender, EventArgs e)
  {
```

LISTING 39.4   Continued

```csharp
  if (this.undoStack.Count == 0)
    return;

  // Get the previous action
  HistoryEntry entry = this.undoStack.Pop();

  // If a stroke was added, remove it
  if (entry.StrokeAdded != null)
    this.inkPresenter.Strokes.Remove(entry.StrokeAdded);

  // If strokes were removed, add them back
  if (entry.StrokesRemoved != null)
    foreach (Stroke s in entry.StrokesRemoved)
      this.inkPresenter.Strokes.Add(s);

  // Enable the undo to be undone
  this.redoStack.Push(entry);

  // Update the state of the undo/redo/straighten buttons
  RefreshAppBarButtons();
}

void RedoButton_Click(object sender, EventArgs e)
{
  if (this.redoStack.Count == 0)
    return;

  // Get the action that was just undone
  HistoryEntry entry = this.redoStack.Pop();

  // If a stroke was added, add it back
  if (entry.StrokeAdded != null)
    this.inkPresenter.Strokes.Add(entry.StrokeAdded);

  // If strokes were removed, remove them again
  if (entry.StrokesRemoved != null)
    foreach (Stroke s in entry.StrokesRemoved)
      this.inkPresenter.Strokes.Remove(s);

  // Enable this action to be undone
  this.undoStack.Push(entry);

  // Update the state of the undo/redo/straighten buttons
  RefreshAppBarButtons();
```

LISTING 39.4   Continued

```csharp
    }

    void StraightenButton_Click(object sender, EventArgs e)
    {
      if (this.inkPresenter.Strokes.Count == 0)
        return;

      bool straightened = false;
      Stroke lastStroke =
        this.inkPresenter.Strokes[this.inkPresenter.Strokes.Count - 1];

      // Clone the stroke before changing it, simply so the original stroke
      // can be placed in the undo stack.
      // The DrawingAttributes instance is shared by both, but we don't change it.
      Stroke newStroke = new Stroke { DrawingAttributes =
        lastStroke.DrawingAttributes };
      foreach (StylusPoint point in lastStroke.StylusPoints)
        newStroke.StylusPoints.Add(point);

      if (newStroke.StylusPoints.Count > 2)
      {
        // This is a raw stroke, so do the first round of straightening simply
        // by removing every point except its two endpoints
        while (newStroke.StylusPoints.Count > 2)
          newStroke.StylusPoints.RemoveAt(1);
        straightened = true;
      }
      else if (newStroke.StylusPoints.Count == 2)
      {
        // This is already a straight line, so make it completely horizontal or
        // completely vertical depending on which is closer
        double deltaX = newStroke.StylusPoints[0].X - newStroke.StylusPoints[1].X;
        double deltaY = newStroke.StylusPoints[0].Y - newStroke.StylusPoints[1].Y;

        if (Math.Abs(deltaX) > Math.Abs(deltaY))
        {
          // The line is more horizontal than vertical
          if (newStroke.StylusPoints[0].Y != newStroke.StylusPoints[1].Y)
          {
            // Give the horizontal line the average Y value
            double newY = (newStroke.StylusPoints[0].Y +
                           newStroke.StylusPoints[1].Y) / 2;
            newStroke.StylusPoints[0] =
              new StylusPoint(newStroke.StylusPoints[0].X, newY);
```

LISTING 39.4   Continued

```
      newStroke.StylusPoints[1] =
        new StylusPoint(newStroke.StylusPoints[1].X, newY);
      straightened = true;
    }
  }
  else
  {
    // The line is more vertical than horizontal
    if (newStroke.StylusPoints[0].X != newStroke.StylusPoints[1].X)
    {
      // Give the vertical line the average X value
      double newX = (newStroke.StylusPoints[0].X +
                     newStroke.StylusPoints[1].X) / 2;
      newStroke.StylusPoints[0] =
        new StylusPoint(newX, newStroke.StylusPoints[0].Y);
      newStroke.StylusPoints[1] =
        new StylusPoint(newX, newStroke.StylusPoints[1].Y);
      straightened = true;
    }
  }
}

if (straightened)
{
  // Remove the old stroke and swap in the cloned and modified stroke
  this.inkPresenter.Strokes.Remove(lastStroke);
  this.inkPresenter.Strokes.Add(newStroke);

  // Update the undo/redo stacks
  HistoryEntry entry = new HistoryEntry { StrokeAdded = newStroke };
  entry.StrokesRemoved = new Stroke[] { lastStroke };
  this.undoStack.Push(entry);
  this.redoStack.Clear();

  // Update the state of the undo/redo/straighten buttons
  RefreshAppBarButtons();
}
}

// Application bar menu handlers

void SetBackgroundColorMenuItem_Click(object sender, EventArgs e)
{
  // Get a string representation of the colors, without the leading #
```

LISTING 39.4   Continued

```csharp
    string currentColorString = Settings.PageColor.Value.ToString().Substring(1);
    string defaultColorString =
      Settings.PageColor.DefaultValue.ToString().Substring(1);

    // The color picker works with the same isolated storage value that the
    // Setting works with, but we have to clear its cached value to pick up
    // the value chosen in the color picker
    Settings.PageColor.ForceRefresh();

    // Navigate to the color picker
    this.NavigationService.Navigate(new Uri(
      "/Shared/Color Picker/ColorPickerPage.xaml?"
      + "showOpacity=false"
      + "&currentColor=" + currentColorString
      + "&defaultColor=" + defaultColorString
      + "&settingName=PageColor", UriKind.Relative));
  }

  void SetBackgroundPictureMenuItem_Click(object sender, EventArgs e)
  {
    if (IsolatedStorageHelper.FileExists("background.jpg"))
    {
      // "remove background picture" was tapped
      IsolatedStorageHelper.DeleteFile("background.jpg");
      this.backgroundImage.Source = null;
      RefreshAppBarMenu();
      return;
    }

    // "set background picture" was tapped
    PhotoChooserTask task = new PhotoChooserTask();
    task.ShowCamera = true;
    task.Completed += delegate(object s, PhotoResult args)
    {
      if (args.TaskResult == TaskResult.OK)
      {
        // Apply the image to the background
        SetBackgroundImage(PictureDecoder.DecodeJpeg(args.ChosenPhoto));

        // Seek back to the beginning of the stream again
        args.ChosenPhoto.Seek(0, SeekOrigin.Begin);

        // Save the file to isolated storage.
        // This overwrites the file if it already exists.
```

LISTING 39.4   Continued

```
      IsolatedStorageHelper.SaveFile("background.jpg", args.ChosenPhoto);
      RefreshAppBarMenu();
    }
  };
  task.Show();
}

void EraseMenuItem_Click(object sender, EventArgs e)
{
  // Allow this to be undone by storing all the current strokes
  HistoryEntry entry = new HistoryEntry();
  entry.StrokesRemoved = this.inkPresenter.Strokes.ToArray();
  this.undoStack.Push(entry);
  this.redoStack.Clear();

  // Erase them all
  this.inkPresenter.Strokes.Clear();

  // Update the state of the undo/redo buttons
  RefreshAppBarButtons();
}

void SaveToPicturesLibraryMenuItem_Click(object sender, EventArgs e)
{
  // Create a new bitmap with the page's dimensions
  WriteableBitmap bitmap = new WriteableBitmap((int)this.grid.ActualWidth,
      (int)this.grid.ActualHeight);

  // Render the contents to the bitmap
  bitmap.Render(grid, null);

  // We must explicitly tell the bitmap to draw its new contents
  bitmap.Invalidate();

  using (MemoryStream stream = new MemoryStream())
  {
    // Fill the stream with a JPEG representation of this bitmap
    bitmap.SaveJpeg(stream, (int)this.grid.ActualWidth,
    (int)this.grid.ActualHeight,
      0 /* orientation */, 100 /* quality */);

    // Seek back to the beginning of the stream
    stream.Seek(0, SeekOrigin.Begin);
```

LISTING 39.4   Continued

```
      // Save the image
      try
      {
        new Microsoft.Xna.Framework.Media.MediaLibrary().SavePicture(
          "paint.jpg", stream);
      }
      catch
      {
        MessageBox.Show("To do this, please disconnect your phone from Zune.",
          "Please Disconnect", MessageBoxButton.OK);
        return;
      }
    }
    MessageBox.Show(
      "Your artwork has been saved. Go to your phone's Pictures hub to view it.",
      "Success", MessageBoxButton.OK);
  }

  void InstructionsMenuItem_Click(object sender, EventArgs e)
  {
    this.NavigationService.Navigate(new Uri("/InstructionsPage.xaml",
      UriKind.Relative));
  }

  void AboutMenuItem_Click(object sender, EventArgs e)
  {
    this.NavigationService.Navigate(
      new Uri("/Shared/About/AboutPage.xaml?appName=Paint", UriKind.Relative));
  }
  }
}
```

Notes:

→ The undo/redo feature is implemented as two stacks of the following simple data
type:

```
public struct HistoryEntry
{
  public Stroke StrokeAdded { get; set; }
  public IList<Stroke> StrokesRemoved { get; set; }
}
```

The undo feature supports not just the removal of newly added strokes, but undoing the straightening of a stroke and undoing the erasure of all strokes simultaneously. If it weren't for these two extra undo cases, this app wouldn't need an undo stack at all—it could just treat the ink presenter's `Strokes` collection as the stack and remove each stroke from the end of the list.

→ The `fingerStrokes` dictionary is used just like the `fingerSounds` dictionary from the preceding chapter, tracking each in-progress stroke while associating it with the correct finger. The hack to work around missing `Up` actions is not done here, however, because the only bad effect caused by this is extra entries left behind in the dictionary.

→ Although ink presenters can contain arbitrary elements with canvas-style layout, this page uses an image *behind* the ink presenter—placing both in a one-cell grid—to take advantage of grid's automatic layout.

→ An `IsolatedStorageHelper` class like the one used in Chapter 23, "Baby Milestones," is used to save and retrieve the background image that the user may optionally place behind the ink presenter. This version of `IsolatedStorageHelper` does not do any caching, however, because this app only uses a single image file-name. This version also includes two new methods for serializing an object to/from isolated storage. These are discussed at the end of this chapter.

→ Because the application bar's background is set to whatever the user has chosen as the paint color (inside `OnNavigatedTo`), we must ensure that the buttons and text are visible on top of this color no matter what. A simple `IsLight` method is used, defined toward the end of the listing, to make the foreground white if the background is dark or to make the foreground black if the background is light. The code in `OnNavigatedTo` also prevents the application bar background from becoming too transparent, as that could cause the buttons and text to become unreadable based on whatever the artwork happened to contain underneath.

→ `Touch_FrameReported` contains the code at the heart of this app. When a finger touches down, a new stroke is created and given drawing attributes that match all of the current settings. A stylus point is then added to its `StylusPoints` collection that matches the finger's current location, and then it is added to the ink presenter's `Strokes` collection. When a finger moves, the correct stroke is retrieved based on the finger ID, and then a new stylus point is added to it based on the current location. When a finger breaks contact with the screen, no further changes need to be made to the stroke, but the undo/redo stacks are adjusted appropriately and the application bar is refreshed.

→ The stroke-straightening feature works in two phases. The first time it is tapped, all stylus points on the most recent stroke are removed except for the starting and ending points. This causes it to form a straight but likely diagonal line. The second time it is tapped, the location of both points is adjusted to make the line horizontal or vertical, whichever is a closer match. The stroke is cloned and the copy is modified, but that's only done so that the original stroke can be placed in the undo stack. If straightening did not need to be undone, the changes to the stroke's points could be done directly to the instance already in the ink presenter.

→ The straightening process is demonstrated in Figure 39.5 for two different strokes. Notice that the straighten button's icon changes to indicate which phase the most recent stroke is currently in.

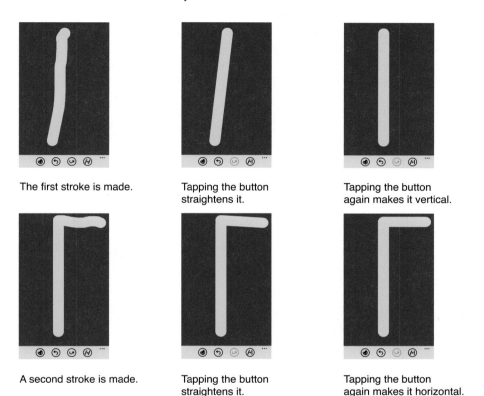

The first stroke is made.

Tapping the button straightens it.

Tapping the button again makes it vertical.

A second stroke is made.

Tapping the button straightens it.

Tapping the button again makes it horizontal.

FIGURE 39.5   The sequence of straightening two strokes.

→ XNA's `MediaLibrary.SavePicture` method is called to save the artwork to the pictures library. Similar to the Local FM Radio and Subservient Cat apps, it checks for a failure case caused when the phone is connected to Zune on a PC. There's one more failure case caused by the Zune connection: Calling `Show` on `PhotoChooserTask` causes the `Completed` event to be raised with the event-args `TaskResult` property set to `TaskResult.Cancel`. Because this isn't easily distinguishable from the user cancelling the task, this case is left alone. It's more likely to cause confusion for developers than users.

Manual Serialization and Deserialization

Although an ink presenter's `Strokes` collection is serializable, attempting to assign such a collection to an isolated storage application setting (or a page state item) does not work. The automatic serialization process throws an exception. Therefore, rather than using a

Setting object to persist and retrieve the ink presenter's strokes, Listing 39.4 uses two methods in the project's `IsolatedStorageHelper` class implemented as follows:

```
public static void SaveFile(string filename, object serializableObject)
{
  using (IsolatedStorageFile userStore =
    IsolatedStorageFile.GetUserStoreForApplication())
  using (IsolatedStorageFileStream stream = userStore.CreateFile(filename))
  using (StreamWriter writer = new StreamWriter(stream))
  {
    // Serialize the object to XML and write it to the file
    XmlSerializer serializer = new XmlSerializer(serializableObject.GetType());
    serializer.Serialize(writer, serializableObject);
  }
}


public static object LoadSerializedObjectFromFile(string filename, Type type)
{
  using (IsolatedStorageFile userStore =
    IsolatedStorageFile.GetUserStoreForApplication())
  {
    if (userStore.FileExists(filename))
    {
      using (IsolatedStorageFileStream stream =
        userStore.OpenFile(filename, FileMode.Open))
      using (StreamReader reader = new StreamReader(stream))
      {
        // Deserialize the object from the XML in the file
        XmlSerializer serializer = new XmlSerializer(type);
        return serializer.Deserialize(reader);
      }
    }
  }
  return null;
}
```

Manual serialization and deserialization is done with `System.Runtime.Serialization.XmlSerializer` from the `System.Xml.Serialization` assembly. The serialized XML it produces looks like the following for a one-point, one-stroke collection:

```
<?xml version="1.0" encoding="utf-16"?>
<ArrayOfStroke xmlns:xsi="http://www.w3.org/2001/XMLSchema-instance"
xmlns:xsd="http://www.w3.org/2001/XMLSchema">
  <Stroke>
    <StylusPoints>
```

```
      <StylusPoint>
        <X>100</X>
        <Y>0</Y>
        <PressureFactor>0.5</PressureFactor>
      </StylusPoint>
    </StylusPoints>
    <DrawingAttributes>
      <Color>
        <A>255</A>
        <R>27</R>
        <G>161</G>
        <B>226</B>
      </Color>
      <OutlineColor>
        <A>0</A>
        <R>255</R>
        <G>255</G>
        <B>255</B>
      </OutlineColor>
      <Width>10</Width>
      <Height>10</Height>
    </DrawingAttributes>
  </Stroke>
</ArrayOfStroke>
```

XmlSerializer isn't the only available option, however. Silverlight for Windows Phone also ships with System.Runtime.Serialization.DataContractSerializer (in the System.Runtime.Serialization assembly) and System.Runtime.Serialization .Json.DataContractJsonSerializer (in the System.Servicemodel.Web assembly).

DataContractSerializer serializes objects to XML, but in a different way than XmlSerializer. It also happens to support the serialization of a broader set of types and properties. The serialized XML it produces looks like the following for the same stroke collection:

```
<ArrayOfStroke xmlns:i="http://www.w3.org/2001/XMLSchema-instance" xmlns="http://s
chemas.datacontract.org/2004/07/System.Windows.Ink"><Stroke><DrawingAttributes><Co
lor xmlns:d4p1="http://schemas.datacontract.org/2004/07/System.Windows.Media"><d4p
1:A>255</d4p1:A><d4p1:B>226</d4p1:B><d4p1:G>161</d4p1:G><d4p1:R>27</d4p1:R></Color
><Height>10</Height><OutlineColor xmlns:d4p1="http://schemas.datacontract.org/2004
/07/System.Windows.Media"><d4p1:A>0</d4p1:A><d4p1:B>255</d4p1:B><d4p1:G>255</d4p1:
G><d4p1:R>255</d4p1:R></OutlineColor><Width>10</Width></DrawingAttributes><StylusP
oints xmlns:d3p1="http://schemas.datacontract.org/2004/07/System.Windows.Input"><d
3p1:StylusPoint><d3p1:PressureFactor>0.5</d3p1:PressureFactor><d3p1:X>100</d3p1:X>
<d3p1:Y>0</d3p1:Y></d3p1:StylusPoint></StylusPoints></Stroke></ArrayOfStroke>
```

Rather than pretty-printing the XML, which is not needed in this case, it produces one big line.

DataContract**Json**Serializer serializes objects to JavaScript Object Notation (JSON), the popular format that is usually much more compact than XML. Here is the serialized JSON for the same stroke collection, which again is produced as one big line:

```
[{"DrawingAttributes":{"Color":{"A":255,"B":226,"G":161,"R":27},"Height":10,"Outli
neColor":{"A":0,"B":255,"G":255,"R":255},"Width":10},"StylusPoints":[{"PressureFac
tor":0.5,"X":100,"Y":0}]}]
```

 JSON is often a great serialization format thanks to its compact representation. Although DataContractJsonSerializer is adequate for serializing and deserializing JSON, you should consider using Json.NET (available from http://json.codeplex.com) instead. This high-performance open-source library is faster.

The Finished Product

Painting on a photo, leveraging stroke straightening and outlines

The palette page under the light theme

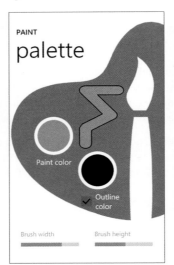

Choosing a background picture

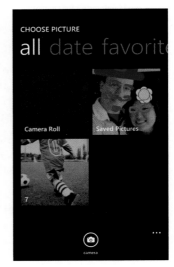

chapter 40

 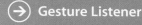
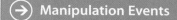

DARTS

Darts is an addictive and slick game that provides a great reason to demonstrate support for the *flick* gesture (a single-finger, rapid swipe). To make detecting flicks easy, this app leverages a feature in the Silverlight for Windows Phone Toolkit called the *gesture listener*.

In this one-player game, you throw a dart by flicking the screen. The direction and strength of your flick determines the angle and distance of the throw. Depending on where the dart lands, you could earn 0–60 points with each throw. Try to get the highest score possible with 20 darts!

 This game has a lot of potential for easy-to-add enhancements. For some examples, check out my "Hooked on Darts" version of this app in the Windows Phone Marketplace.

Detecting Gestures

The three preceding apps in this part of the book leverage touch points in a straightforward fashion. Often, however, you want to support standard gestures such as flicks, pinch-and-stretch zooming, and rotation. Detecting such gestures based on raw touch point data from the `FrameReported` event would be a major undertaking.

Fortunately, two options exist that make detecting gestures much easier: Silverlight's manipulation events and the Silverlight for Windows Phone Toolkit's gesture listener.

Manipulation Events

Silverlight defines three manipulation events on every UI element:

→ `ManipulationStarted`

→ `ManipulationDelta`

→ `ManipulationCompleted`

These events combine the information from all active touch points and package the data in an easy-to-consume form. `ManipulationStarted` gets raised when the `TouchDown` action happens for the first finger. `ManipulationDelta` gets raised for each `TouchMove`. `ManipulationCompleted` gets raised after `TouchUp` is reported for *all* fingers.

The `ManipulationDelta` event gives you information about how the relevant element is expected to be translated or scaled based on a one-finger panning gesture or a two-finger pinch or stretch. The `ManipulationDelta` and `ManipulationCompleted` events also provide translation and scale velocities in both X and Y dimensions.

Gesture Listener

Although the manipulation events are helpful for detecting gestures, the Silverlight for Windows Phone Toolkit's gesture listener raises the bar for simplicity and ease-of-use. In fact, all the remaining apps in this part of the book use the gesture listener instead of the manipulation events.

The `GestureListener` class exposes nothing but 12 events for detecting 6 types of gestures:

→ **Tap** (with the `Tap` event)

→ **Double Tap** (with the `DoubleTap` event)

→ **Touch & Hold** (with the `Hold` event)

→ **Flick** (with the `Flick` event)

→ **Pinch & Stretch** (with the `PinchStarted`, `PinchDelta`, and `PinchCompleted` events)

→ **Drag** (with the `DragStarted`, `DragDelta`, and `DragCompleted` events)

The remaining two events—
`GestureBegin` and `GestureCompleted`—
are generic events raised for any
gestures, analogous to the
`ManipulationStarted` and
`ManipulationCompleted` events.

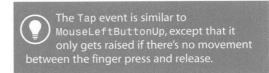

The Tap event is similar to MouseLeftButtonUp, except that it only gets raised if there's no movement between the finger press and release.

A gesture listener can be attached to any element with the `GestureService` class, which exposes a `GestureListener` attachable property. For example, the following XAML detects a touch & hold gesture (pressing an element for one second) on a text block:

```
<TextBlock …>
  <toolkit:GestureService.GestureListener>
    <toolkit:GestureListener Hold="GestureListener_Hold"/>
  </toolkit:GestureService.GestureListener>
</TextBlock>
```

> ⓘ **The gesture listener can cause performance problems!**
> As of the February 2011 version of the Silverlight for Windows Phone Toolkit, the gesture listener internally uses XNA's TouchPanel class to detect gestures. However, this can cause performance problems and can even interfere with the input received by other Silverlight controls. Therefore, until these issues are resolved in a future version of the toolkit, you should avoid using the gesture listener (or the XNA TouchPanel) in traditional apps with typical controls. Darts and the other apps in this book that use the gesture listener do not have such problems.

The User Interface

Darts has a main page, an instructions page, and an about page. The latter two pages aren't interesting and therefore aren't shown in this chapter, but Listing 40.1 contains the XAML for the main page. The main page has an "intro panel" canvas that does triple duty as a welcome screen, a game-over screen, as well as a paused screen. Underneath the intro panel is a canvas with all the game elements. Figure 40.1 shows the intro panel in its initial state and then the appearance of the page once the user flicks the screen to start the game.

The initial page appearance   Ready to play

FIGURE 40.1   The main page overlays an intro panel on top of the game canvas.

LISTING 40.1   `MainPage.xaml`—The User Interface for Darts' Main Page

```xml
<phone:PhoneApplicationPage x:Class="WindowsPhoneApp.MainPage"
    xmlns="http://schemas.microsoft.com/winfx/2006/xaml/presentation"
    xmlns:x="http://schemas.microsoft.com/winfx/2006/xaml"
    xmlns:phone="clr-namespace:Microsoft.Phone.Controls;assembly=Microsoft.Phone"
    xmlns:shell="clr-namespace:Microsoft.Phone.Shell;assembly=Microsoft.Phone"
    xmlns:toolkit="clr-namespace:Microsoft.Phone.Controls;
➥assembly=Microsoft.Phone.Controls.Toolkit"
    FontFamily="Segoe WP Black" FontSize="{StaticResource PhoneFontSizeNormal}"
    Foreground="White" SupportedOrientations="Portrait">

  <!-- Allow the gesture anywhere on the page -->
  <toolkit:GestureService.GestureListener>
    <toolkit:GestureListener Flick="GestureListener_Flick"/>
  </toolkit:GestureService.GestureListener>

  <!-- Add several animations to the page's resource dictionary -->
  <phone:PhoneApplicationPage.Resources>

    <!-- The dart-throwing animation, adjusted from code-behind based on
         the angle and velocity of the flick -->
    <Storyboard x:Name="DartThrowStoryboard"
                Completed="DartThrowStoryboard_Completed">
      <!-- Animate the horizontal position -->
      <DoubleAnimation x:Name="DartXAnimation"
                       Storyboard.TargetName="DartTransform"
                       Storyboard.TargetProperty="TranslateX" Duration="0:0:.5">
        <DoubleAnimation.EasingFunction>
          <CircleEase/>
        </DoubleAnimation.EasingFunction>
      </DoubleAnimation>
      <!-- Animate the vertical position -->
      <DoubleAnimation x:Name="DartYAnimation"
                       Storyboard.TargetName="DartTransform"
                       Storyboard.TargetProperty="TranslateY" Duration="0:0:.5">
        <DoubleAnimation.EasingFunction>
          <CircleEase/>
        </DoubleAnimation.EasingFunction>
      </DoubleAnimation>
      <!-- Animate the horizontal scale -->
      <DoubleAnimation x:Name="DartScaleXAnimation"
                       Storyboard.TargetName="DartTransform"
                       Storyboard.TargetProperty="ScaleX" By="1.2"
                       Duration="0:0:.25" AutoReverse="True">
        <DoubleAnimation.EasingFunction>
```

LISTING 40.1   Continued

```xml
          <CircleEase/>
      </DoubleAnimation.EasingFunction>
  </DoubleAnimation>
  <!-- Animate the vertical scale -->
  <DoubleAnimation x:Name="DartScaleYAnimation"
                   Storyboard.TargetName="DartTransform"
                   Storyboard.TargetProperty="ScaleY" By="4"
                   Duration="0:0:.25" AutoReverse="True">
      <DoubleAnimation.EasingFunction>
        <CircleEase/>
      </DoubleAnimation.EasingFunction>
  </DoubleAnimation>
</Storyboard>

<!-- Leave the dart in its ending position for half a second before returning
     it to the bottom of the page for another throw -->
<Storyboard x:Name="DartDelayStoryboard" Duration="0:0:.5"
            Completed="DartDelayStoryboard_Completed"/>

<!-- Move the dart back to the starting position -->
<Storyboard x:Name="DartReturnStoryboard">
  <DoubleAnimation Storyboard.TargetName="DartTransform"
                   Storyboard.TargetProperty="TranslateX" To="0"
                   Duration="0:0:.2">
    <DoubleAnimation.EasingFunction>
      <QuinticEase EasingMode="EaseInOut"/>
    </DoubleAnimation.EasingFunction>
  </DoubleAnimation>
  <DoubleAnimation Storyboard.TargetName="DartTransform"
                   Storyboard.TargetProperty="TranslateY" To="0"
                   Duration="0:0:.2">
    <DoubleAnimation.EasingFunction>
      <QuinticEase EasingMode="EaseInOut"/>
    </DoubleAnimation.EasingFunction>
  </DoubleAnimation>
</Storyboard>

<!-- Slide the dart completely off the bottom of the screen -->
<Storyboard x:Name="DartOffScreenStoryboard">
  <DoubleAnimation Storyboard.TargetName="DartTransform"
                   Storyboard.TargetProperty="TranslateY" To="130"
                   Duration="0:0:.6">
    <DoubleAnimation.EasingFunction>
      <QuinticEase EasingMode="EaseInOut"/>
```

LISTING 40.1   Continued

```xml
        </DoubleAnimation.EasingFunction>
      </DoubleAnimation>
  </Storyboard>

  <!-- Slide the intro panel off the top of the screen -->
  <Storyboard x:Name="IntroOffStoryboard"
              Completed="IntroOffStoryboard_Completed">
    <DoubleAnimation Storyboard.TargetName="IntroPanelTransform"
                     Storyboard.TargetProperty="TranslateY" To="-800"
                     Duration="0:0:1">
      <DoubleAnimation.EasingFunction>
        <QuinticEase EasingMode="EaseInOut"/>
      </DoubleAnimation.EasingFunction>
    </DoubleAnimation>
  </Storyboard>

  <!-- Slide the intro panel back onto the screen from up above -->
  <Storyboard x:Name="IntroOnStoryboard">
    <DoubleAnimation Storyboard.TargetName="IntroPanelTransform"
                     Storyboard.TargetProperty="TranslateY" To="0"
                     Duration="0:0:1">
      <DoubleAnimation.EasingFunction>
        <QuinticEase EasingMode="EaseInOut"/>
      </DoubleAnimation.EasingFunction>
    </DoubleAnimation>
  </Storyboard>

  … more storyboards …

  <!-- Animate in (then out) a message, such as the # of points just earned -->
  <Storyboard x:Name="ShowMessageStoryboard"
              Storyboard.TargetName="MessageTransform">
    <DoubleAnimationUsingKeyFrames Storyboard.TargetProperty="TranslateY">
      <DiscreteDoubleKeyFrame KeyTime="0:0:0" Value="800"/>
      <EasingDoubleKeyFrame KeyTime="0:0:.5" Value="430">
        <EasingDoubleKeyFrame.EasingFunction>
          <QuadraticEase/>
        </EasingDoubleKeyFrame.EasingFunction>
      </EasingDoubleKeyFrame>
      <DiscreteDoubleKeyFrame KeyTime="0:0:2.5" Value="430"/>
      <EasingDoubleKeyFrame KeyTime="0:0:3" Value="-800">
        <EasingDoubleKeyFrame.EasingFunction>
          <QuadraticEase/>
        </EasingDoubleKeyFrame.EasingFunction>
```

LISTING 40.1   Continued

```
        </EasingDoubleKeyFrame>
      </DoubleAnimationUsingKeyFrames>
    </Storyboard>
  </phone:PhoneApplicationPage.Resources>

  <!-- The application bar, with two buttons and one menu item -->
  <phone:PhoneApplicationPage.ApplicationBar>
    <shell:ApplicationBar BackgroundColor="#5F3000" ForegroundColor="White"
                          Opacity=".8">
      <shell:ApplicationBarIconButton Text="instructions"
        IconUri="/Shared/Images/appbar.instructions.png"
        Click="InstructionsButton_Click"/>
      <shell:ApplicationBarIconButton Text="delete"
        IconUri="/Shared/Images/appbar.delete.png" Click="DeleteButton_Click"/>
      <shell:ApplicationBar.MenuItems>
        <shell:ApplicationBarMenuItem Text="about" Click="AboutMenuItem_Click"/>
      </shell:ApplicationBar.MenuItems>
    </shell:ApplicationBar>
  </phone:PhoneApplicationPage.ApplicationBar>

  <Grid Background="#5F3000">
    <Grid.Clip>
      <RectangleGeometry Rect="0,0,480,800"/>
    </Grid.Clip>
    <!-- The game canvas -->
    <Canvas>
      <!-- The dartboard background -->
      <Ellipse Width="480" Height="480" Fill="#8000"/>
      <!-- The dartboard segments -->
      <Canvas x:Name="DartboardSegments">
        <!-- Vector art created in Expression Blend. Each region with a different
             point value is a distinct Path element (82 total) -->
        <Path x:Name="D1" Data="M268.269483095,61.50827908C287.000166325,
          64.476988515,305.148564115,70.37132529,322.042831735,
          78.980320525L240.000027675,240.000437465z" Fill="Green"
          Canvas.Left="239.417" Canvas.Top="60.925" Stretch="Fill"
          Width="83.209" Height="179.658"/>
        … 81 more paths …
      </Canvas>
      <!-- The dartboard numbers -->
      <Canvas Opacity=".5">
        <TextBlock Text="20" Canvas.Left="218" Canvas.Top="1"
                   FontFamily="Segoe WP" FontSize="40"/>
        … 19 more text blocks …
```

LISTING 40.1   Continued

```
    </Canvas>

    <!-- Each time a dart lands, a little black "hole" is placed in this
         canvas to mark the position -->
    <Canvas x:Name="HolesCanvas"/>

    <!-- The dart -->
    <Image x:Name="DartImage" Canvas.Top="675" Canvas.Left="202"
           Width="100">
      <Image.RenderTransform>
        <CompositeTransform x:Name="DartTransform" TranslateY="130"/>
      </Image.RenderTransform>
    </Image>
  </Canvas>

  <!-- A display for the current score and # of darts remaining -->
  <StackPanel x:Name="ScorePanel" Visibility="Collapsed"
              VerticalAlignment="Bottom" HorizontalAlignment="Right"
              Margin="18,64">
    <TextBlock Text="SCORE" Foreground="{StaticResource PhoneSubtleBrush}"
               HorizontalAlignment="Right"/>
    <TextBlock x:Name="ScoreTextBlock" HorizontalAlignment="Right"
               FontSize="{StaticResource PhoneFontSizeExtraExtraLarge}"
               Margin="0,-20,0,0">
      <TextBlock.RenderTransform>
        <CompositeTransform x:Name="ScoreTransform"/>
      </TextBlock.RenderTransform>
    </TextBlock>
    <TextBlock Text="DARTS REMAINING"
               Foreground="{StaticResource PhoneSubtleBrush}"
               HorizontalAlignment="Right"/>
    <TextBlock x:Name="DartsRemainingTextBlock" HorizontalAlignment="Right"
               FontSize="{StaticResource PhoneFontSizeExtraExtraLarge}"
               Margin="0,-20,0,0">
      <TextBlock.RenderTransform>
        <CompositeTransform x:Name="DartsRemainingTransform"/>
      </TextBlock.RenderTransform>
    </TextBlock>
  </StackPanel>

  <!-- The welcome/paused/game-over screen -->
  <Grid x:Name="IntroPanel">
    <Grid.RenderTransform>
      <CompositeTransform x:Name="IntroPanelTransform"/>
```

LISTING 40.1   Continued

```xml
      </Grid.RenderTransform>
      <Rectangle Fill="#5F3000" Opacity=".6"/>

      <!-- The title and subtitle -->
      <TextBlock Text="DARTS" Margin="-19,200,0,0" FontSize="140">
        <TextBlock.RenderTransform>
          <RotateTransform Angle="-20"/>
        </TextBlock.RenderTransform>
      </TextBlock>
      <TextBlock x:Name="Subtitle" Text="DO A PRACTICE FLICK TO BEGIN"
                 Margin="40,340,-40,0" FontSize="27">
        <TextBlock.RenderTransform>
          <RotateTransform Angle="-20"/>
        </TextBlock.RenderTransform>
      </TextBlock>

      <!-- A display for the best score, average score, and # of games -->
      <StackPanel x:Name="StatsPanel" VerticalAlignment="Bottom"
                  HorizontalAlignment="Right" Margin="18,64">
        <TextBlock Text="BEST SCORE" Foreground="{StaticResource PhoneSubtleBrush}"
                   HorizontalAlignment="Right"/>
        <TextBlock x:Name="BestScoreTextBlock" HorizontalAlignment="Right"
                   FontSize="{StaticResource PhoneFontSizeExtraExtraLarge}"
                   Margin="0,-20,0,0">
          <TextBlock.RenderTransform>
            <CompositeTransform x:Name="BestScoreTransform"/>
          </TextBlock.RenderTransform>
        </TextBlock>
        <TextBlock x:Name="AvgScoreHeaderTextBlock" Text="AVG SCORE"
                   Foreground="{StaticResource PhoneSubtleBrush}"
                   HorizontalAlignment="Right"/>
        <TextBlock x:Name="AvgScoreTextBlock" HorizontalAlignment="Right"
                   FontSize="{StaticResource PhoneFontSizeExtraExtraLarge}"
                   Margin="0,-20,0,0">
          <TextBlock.RenderTransform>
            <CompositeTransform x:Name="AvgScoreTransform"/>
          </TextBlock.RenderTransform>
        </TextBlock>
      </StackPanel>
    </Grid>

    <!-- An animated message -->
    <TextBlock x:Name="MessageTextBlock" RenderTransformOrigin=".5,.5"
               FontWeight="Bold" HorizontalAlignment="Center" FontSize="120">
```

LISTING 40.1   Continued

```
      <TextBlock.RenderTransform>
        <CompositeTransform x:Name="MessageTransform" TranslateY="800"/>
      </TextBlock.RenderTransform>
    </TextBlock>
  </Grid>
</phone:PhoneApplicationPage>
```

Notes:

→ To detect the flick gesture, this app handles the Flick event of a gesture listener attached to the whole page.

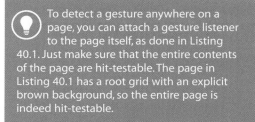

To detect a gesture anywhere on a page, you can attach a gesture listener to the page itself, as done in Listing 40.1. Just make sure that the entire contents of the page are hit-testable. The page in Listing 40.1 has a root grid with an explicit brown background, so the entire page is indeed hit-testable.

→ This page contains lots of storyboards for smoothly transitioning elements on and off the screen. (Many of them are similar or identical to the animations in Chapter 37, "Reflex Test," and are omitted here.) The most important one is DartThrowStoryboard, which makes the dart travel based on the flick data. Its first two animations, which alter the dart transform's TranslateX and TranslateY values, have their By values set in code-behind. The second two animations, which alter ScaleX and ScaleY, make the dart appear to jump out of and then back into the screen in a pseudo-3D arc motion. ScaleY is increased much more than ScaleX to make the image appear to flatten out, because the image already has Y-rotation perspective applied to it. The next section shows how the in-flight dart appears.

→ This app's dartboard is one of the more interesting chunks of XAML in the whole book. It consists of 82 path elements and 19 text blocks on top of an ellipse. (Although I usually type all my XAML by hand, I created this part in Expression Blend!) Representing each region with a unique score value as a distinct element makes it easy to figure out how many points to award the user when the dart lands. The code-behind performs hit testing to find the topmost element hit by the dart and then awards points accordingly.

Why are there 82 paths? Because there are 4 for each of the 20 wedges (the outer ring that awards double points, the outer "normal" wedge, the inner ring that awards triple points, and then the inner "normal" wedge), plus the outer and inner bull's-eyes. Figure 40.2 illustrates how these 82 elements stack to form the final dartboard, as if the elements were separated and viewed at a 3D perspective.

→ The DartImage element doesn't have its Source assigned. This is done in code-behind, because the source is continually changed between three different images.

FIGURE 40.2   A visualization of the 82 distinct dartboard segments.

→ The root grid has a clip applied to avoid a far-flung dart from causing the screen to go blank. This happens whenever Silverlight tries to render an element that is too far away.

The Code-Behind

Listing 40.2 contains the code-behind for the main page.

LISTING 40.2   `MainPage.xaml.cs`—The Code-Behind for Darts' Main Page

```
using System;
using System.ComponentModel;
using System.Windows;
using System.Windows.Controls;
using System.Windows.Media;
using System.Windows.Media.Animation;
using System.Windows.Media.Imaging;
using System.Windows.Navigation;
using System.Windows.Shapes;
using Microsoft.Phone.Controls;

namespace WindowsPhoneApp
{
  public partial class MainPage : PhoneApplicationPage
```

LISTING 40.2   Continued

```csharp
{
  // Persistent settings
  Setting<int> bestScore = new Setting<int>("BestScore", 0);
  Setting<double> avgScore = new Setting<double>("AvgScore", 0);
  Setting<int> numGames = new Setting<int>("NumGames", 0);

  // Current game state
  int dartsRemaining;
  int score;

  // Three different dart images
  BitmapImage dartStartImageSource =
    new BitmapImage(new Uri("Images/dartStart.png", UriKind.Relative));
  BitmapImage dartBigImageSource =
    new BitmapImage(new Uri("Images/dartBig.png", UriKind.Relative));
  BitmapImage dartSmallImageSource =
    new BitmapImage(new Uri("Images/dartSmall.png", UriKind.Relative));

  public MainPage()
  {
    InitializeComponent();
    // Use the starting dart image
    this.DartImage.Source = this.dartStartImageSource;
  }

  protected override void OnNavigatedTo(NavigationEventArgs e)
  {
    base.OnNavigatedTo(e);
    // Respect the persisted values
    UpdateStatsLabels();
  }

  protected override void OnBackKeyPress(CancelEventArgs e)
  {
    base.OnBackKeyPress(e);
    // If the game is in progress, pause it rather than exiting the app
    if (this.IntroPanel.Visibility == Visibility.Collapsed)
    {
      this.Subtitle.Text =
        "PAUSED.\nFLICK TO RESUME THE GAME,\nOR PRESS BACK TO EXIT.";
      ShowIntroPanel();
      e.Cancel = true;
    }
  }
```

LISTING 40.2   Continued

```csharp
  // The event handler for flicks
  void GestureListener_Flick(object sender, FlickGestureEventArgs e)
  {
    if (this.IntroPanel.Visibility == Visibility.Visible)
    {
      // Start a new game if we're out of darts
      if (this.dartsRemaining == 0)
      {
        // Remove all holes and clear the tracking variables
        this.HolesCanvas.Children.Clear();
        this.dartsRemaining = 20;
        this.score = 0;

        // Animate the off-screen dart to the starting position
        this.DartReturnStoryboard.Begin();

        // Animate a message
        this.MessageTextBlock.Text = "GO!";
        this.ShowMessageStoryboard.Begin();
      }

      // Remove the intro panel (for both new-game and unpause cases)
      HideIntroPanel();
    }
    else
    {
      // First ensure that a dart throw is not in progress
      if (this.DartThrowStoryboard.GetCurrentState() == ClockState.Active ||
          this.DartDelayStoryboard.GetCurrentState() == ClockState.Active)
        return;

      // Throw the dart!
      this.DartTransform.TranslateX = 0;
      this.DartTransform.TranslateY = 0;

      // Here is where the flick data is used
      this.DartXAnimation.By = e.HorizontalVelocity / 10;
      this.DartYAnimation.By = e.VerticalVelocity / 10;

      // The animation scales the image up by as much as 4 vertically, so
      // replace the image with a higher-resolution one
      this.DartImage.Source = this.dartBigImageSource;

      this.DartThrowStoryboard.Begin();
```

LISTING 40.2   Continued

```
      }
    }

    void IntroOffStoryboard_Completed(object sender, EventArgs e)
    {
      // The intro panel is now off-screen, so collapse it for better performance
      this.IntroPanel.Visibility = Visibility.Collapsed;
    }

    void DartThrowStoryboard_Completed(object sender, EventArgs e)
    {
      // The dart has landed, so change the image to a small one
      // that looks better that this scale (and is angled like it's sticking into
      // the wall)
      this.DartImage.Source = this.dartSmallImageSource;

      // Determine the exact point where the tip of the dart has landed
      Point point = new Point(
        // X: The tip isn't quite centered in the image, hence the slight offset
        Canvas.GetLeft(this.DartImage) + this.DartTransform.TranslateX
          + this.DartImage.Width / 2 - 11.5,
        // Y: The tip is at the top edge of the image
        Canvas.GetTop(this.DartImage) + this.DartTransform.TranslateY
      );

      // Place a "hole" where the tip of the dart landed
      Ellipse hole = new Ellipse { Fill = new SolidColorBrush(Colors.Black),
                                   Width = 5, Height = 5 };
      Canvas.SetLeft(hole, point.X - hole.Width / 2);
      Canvas.SetTop(hole, point.Y - hole.Height / 2);
      this.HolesCanvas.Children.Add(hole);

      // Calculate the score for this throw
      int pointsEarned = DetermineScoreAtPoint(point);

      // Update the game state and display
      this.score += pointsEarned;
      this.dartsRemaining--;
      UpdateScoreLabels(pointsEarned > 0);

      // Let the dart sit for a while before it animates back to the start
      this.DartDelayStoryboard.Begin();

      if (this.dartsRemaining > 0)
```

LISTING 40.2   Continued

```
    {
      // Animate in the score message
      this.MessageTextBlock.Text = pointsEarned.ToString();
      this.ShowMessageStoryboard.Begin();
    }
    else
    {
      // Game over!

      // Update the stats
      double oldTotal = this.avgScore.Value * this.numGames.Value;
      // New average
      this.avgScore.Value = (oldTotal + score) / (this.numGames.Value + 1);
      // New total number of games
      this.numGames.Value++;

      this.Subtitle.Text = "FINAL SCORE: " + this.score + ". FLICK AGAIN!";

      if (this.score > this.bestScore.Value)
      {
        // New best score
        this.bestScore.Value = this.score;

        // Animate a best-score message
        this.MessageTextBlock.Text = "BEST!";
        this.ShowMessageStoryboard.Begin();
      }

      ShowIntroPanel();
    }
  }

  void DartDelayStoryboard_Completed(object sender, EventArgs e)
  {
    // Restore the image
    this.DartImage.Source = this.dartStartImageSource;

    // Move the dart to the starting position for the next throw,
    // or off-screen if the game is over
    if (this.dartsRemaining > 0)
      this.DartReturnStoryboard.Begin();
    else
      this.DartOffScreenStoryboard.Begin();
  }
```

LISTING 40.2   Continued

```csharp
int DetermineScoreAtPoint(Point p)
{
  // Retrieve all elements inside DartboardSegments that intersect with p
  foreach (UIElement element in
          VisualTreeHelper.FindElementsInHostCoordinates(p,
                                                this.DartboardSegments))
  {
    // Fortunately, the list of elements is ordered from top-to-bottom.
    // We only care about the top-most element, so we can directly return a
    // value based on the first item in this collection.
    if (element == this.InnerBull)
      return 50;
    else if (element == this.OuterBull)
      return 25;
    else if (element is Path)
    {
      // The elements are named with a letter and a number.
      // The letter is D for double score, T for triple score, or something
      // else (A or B) for a normal region.
      // The number is the score.
      string name = (element as FrameworkElement).Name;

      // Retrieve the score from the name
      int score = int.Parse(name.Substring(1));

      // Apply a multiplier, if applicable
      if (name[0] == 'D')
        score *= 2;
      else if (name[0] == 'T')
        score *= 3;

      return score;
    }
  }

  // No relevant element was hit
  return 0;
}

void ShowIntroPanel()
{
  UpdateStatsLabels();
  this.IntroOnStoryboard.Begin();
  this.IntroPanel.Visibility = Visibility.Visible;
```

LISTING 40.2   Continued

```
    this.ScorePanel.Visibility = Visibility.Collapsed;
    this.ApplicationBar.IsVisible = true;
  }

  void HideIntroPanel()
  {
    UpdateScoreLabels(true);
    this.IntroOffStoryboard.Begin();
    this.ScorePanel.Visibility = Visibility.Visible;
    this.ApplicationBar.IsVisible = false;
  }

  void UpdateStatsLabels()
  {
    if (this.numGames.Value > 0)
    {
      this.BestScoreTextBlock.Text = this.bestScore.Value.ToString();
      this.AvgScoreTextBlock.Text = this.avgScore.Value.ToString("0.#");
      if (this.numGames.Value == 1)
        this.AvgScoreHeaderTextBlock.Text = "AVG SCORE (1 GAME)";
      else
        this.AvgScoreHeaderTextBlock.Text = "AVG SCORE (" + this.numGames.Value
          + " GAMES)";
    }
    else
    {
      this.BestScoreTextBlock.Text = "0";
      this.AvgScoreTextBlock.Text = "0";
      this.AvgScoreHeaderTextBlock.Text = "AVG SCORE";
    }

    // Animate the textblocks out then in
    this.SlideAvgScoreStoryboard.Begin();
    this.SlideBestScoreStoryboard.Begin();
  }

  void UpdateScoreLabels(bool animateScore)
  {
    this.ScoreTextBlock.Text = this.score.ToString();
    this.DartsRemainingTextBlock.Text = this.dartsRemaining.ToString();
    // Animate the textblocks out then in
    this.SlideDartsRemainingStoryboard.Begin();
    if (animateScore)
      this.SlideScoreStoryboard.Begin();
```

LISTING 40.2   Continued

```
      }

      // Application bar handlers

      void InstructionsButton_Click(object sender, EventArgs e)
      {
        this.NavigationService.Navigate(new Uri("/InstructionsPage.xaml",
          UriKind.Relative));
      }

      void DeleteButton_Click(object sender, EventArgs e)
      {
        if (MessageBox.Show("Are you sure you want to clear your scores?",
          "Delete history", MessageBoxButton.OKCancel) == MessageBoxResult.OK)
        {
          this.numGames.Value = 0;
          this.bestScore.Value = 0;
          UpdateStatsLabels();
        }
      }

      void AboutMenuItem_Click(object sender, EventArgs e)
      {
        this.NavigationService.Navigate(new Uri(
          "/Shared/About/AboutPage.xaml?appName=Darts", UriKind.Relative));
      }
    }
  }
}
```

Notes:

→ Three dart image sources are created (once) and then assigned as `DartImage`'s `Source` value at various stages of the dart-throwing procedure. Figure 40.3 shows all three. The start image looks more vertical, whereas the big and small images have a lot more perspective. The small image is used while the dart is sticking into the dartboard (or wall). The big image is used only while the dart is in flight, because otherwise the up-scaling of the small image would produce a pixelated result. The combination of `DartThrowStoryboard`'s motion and the image-swapping produces a pretty realistic pseudo-3D dart motion demonstrated in Figure 40.4.

dartStart.png   dartBig.png   dartSmall.png

FIGURE 40.3   The three dart images are swapped in and out to provide the best-looking result.

FIGURE 40.4   The dart's flight path when it hits a double 3 (6 points).

→ OnBackKeyPress is overridden to show a paused screen when the back key is pressed during a game, canceling the exiting of the app. When the intro panel is shown as a paused screen or game-over screen, the text under the "DARTS" title is updated to explain what is going on, as shown in Figure 40.5.

The paused screen   The game-over screen

FIGURE 40.5   The intro screen subtitle updates to show that the game is paused or to show the final score.

→ GestureListener_Flick is the flick handler that processes the data from FlickGestureEventArgs and adjusts the two relevant dart-throwing animations appropriately. The Flick event is described in the next section.

→ DetermineScoreAtPoint uses a static method called FindElementsInHostCoordinates on System.Windows.Media.VisualTreeHelper to find the top-most element underneath the passed-in point. (FindElementsInHostCoordinates also exposes an overload that accepts a rectangular region rather than a point.) Because of the naming scheme used by the dart-board elements, the hit element's name can be converted into the correct point value.

 Your game might fail marketplace certification if pressing the Back hardware button doesn't pause the game!

The Windows Phone 7 Certification Requirements (http://go.microsoft.com/?linkid=9730558) state:

For games, when the Back button is pressed during gameplay, the game can choose to present a pause context menu or dialog or navigate the user to the prior menu screen. Pressing the Back button again while in a paused context menu or dialog closes the menu or dialog.

Although this makes the pausing behavior seem optional, I've had a game fail certification because it chose not to provide a pausing experience. (And this was a pool game in which pausing is meaningless!) Even if you can get away without doing this, it's probably a good idea to have your app include this pausing behavior for consistency with user expectations for Windows Phone games.

> VisualTreeHelper.FindElementsInHostCoordinates is the best way to determine what element or elements are underneath a specific point or region. Unlike approaches from previous chapters that involve mapping a point into an element's coordinate space one element at a time, FindElementsInHostCoordinates examines all elements that are children of the passed-in element. (It also examines the passed-in element itself.)

The Flick Event

The FlickGestureEventArgs instance passed to the Flick event exposes the following properties:

→ **Angle**—A double value expressed in degrees

→ **Direction**—Either Horizontal or Vertical, revealing the primary direction of the flick

→ **HorizontalVelocity**—A double value expressing the horizontal magnitude of the 2D velocity vector in pixels per second

→ **VerticalVelocity**—A double value expressing the vertical magnitude of the 2D velocity vector in pixels per second

This app has no use for the Direction property, which is meant for elements whose motion should be locked to a single direction when the flick occurs. Instead, this app's dart freely moves in whatever angle the flick reports, even if it's completely horizontal or downward instead of upward.

> A flick event is not raised until the finger has broken contact with the screen. Before then, the finger motion raises drag (and other) events.

Because Listing 40.2 applies the horizontal and vertical velocities as offsets to the dart's position, it doesn't even need to check the Angle property. The ratio between the two velocities effectively gives the appropriate angle. When set as offsets to the dart's position, the velocity values are divided by 10 to give a distance range that works well for this app. This factor was arrived at by trial and error.

> If you want to detect flicks without using the gesture listener (perhaps to avoid the problems discussed at the beginning of this chapter), you can use the ManipulationCompleted event defined on all UI elements. The data passed to its handlers includes a FinalVelocities property that is equivalent to the pair of HorizontalVelocity and VerticalVelocity properties exposed to Flick event handlers.

The Finished Product

Ready to throw another dart

Getting 14 points, narrowly missing the outer bull's-eye

The instructions page, whose code is available in this chapter's project

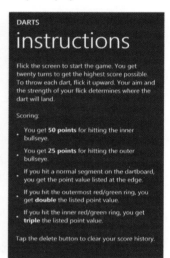

chapter 41

DEEP ZOOM VIEWER

Deep Zoom is a slick technology for creating, viewing, and manipulating huge images or collections of images. It can be used to create experiences much like Bing Maps or Google Maps, but applied to any domain. With the samples available from this app, you can explore large panoramic photographs, scanned-in artwork, a computer-generated data visualization, an example of what a deep zoom advertisement might look like, and, yes, Earth.

To maximize performance, Deep Zoom images are *multi-resolution*; the image file format includes many separate subimages—called *tiles*—at multiple zoom levels. Tiles are downloaded on-demand and rendered in a fairly seamless fashion with smooth transitions. For end users, the result is a huge image that can be loaded, zoomed, and panned extremely quickly.

Deep Zoom Viewer enables viewing and interacting with any online Deep Zoom image right on your Windows phone. You can enter a URL that points to any Deep Zoom image (or image collection), or you can browse any of the seven interesting samples that are already provided.

To render a Deep Zoom image, this app leverages Silverlight's `MultiScaleImage` control, which does all the hard work. To view a file, you just need to place a `MultiScaleImage` on a page and then set its `Source` property to an appropriate URL. However, the control does not provide any built-in gestures for manipulating the image. Therefore, this app provides a perfect opportunity to

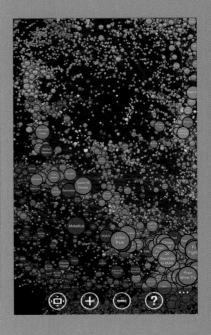

demonstrate how to implement pinch-&-stretch zooming and double-tap gestures—practically a requirement for any respectable Deep Zoom viewer.

Pinching is the standard zoom-out gesture that involves placing two fingers on the screen and then sliding them toward each other. Stretching is the standard zoom-in gesture that involves placing two fingers on the screen and then sliding them away from each other. In this app, double tapping is used to quickly zoom in, centered on the point that was tapped.

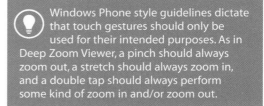

Windows Phone style guidelines dictate that touch gestures should only be used for their intended purposes. As in Deep Zoom Viewer, a pinch should always zoom out, a stretch should always zoom in, and a double tap should always perform some kind of zoom in and/or zoom out.

How do I create my own Deep Zoom images?

Currently, the quickest and easiest way is to use Microsoft's free Zoom.it service (http://zoom.it). This turns any JPG, PNG, or TIFF image into a Deep Zoom image. The service also supports SVG files, PDF files, and even *web pages* as input! You just enter an appropriate URL, and it does the conversion. It even hosts the file for you!

Alternatively, the most powerful option is to use Microsoft's Deep Zoom Composer, a free program that can be downloaded at http://bit.ly/deepzoomdownload.

Deep Zoom versus Seadragon

Although Deep Zoom refers to a Silverlight-specific feature, the underlying Seadragon technology (which Microsoft originally acquired from a company called Seadragon Software) has been exposed in other forms. For example, Microsoft has released an open-source JavaScript version called "Seadragon Ajax" in its Ajax Control Toolkit. It can view the same file types as Deep Zoom.

The User Interface

Deep Zoom Viewer is a single-page app (except for an instructions page) that dedicates all of its screen real estate to the `MultiScaleImage` control. On top of this, it layers a translucent application bar and a dialog that enables the user to type arbitrary Deep Zoom image URLs. Figure 41.1 shows the main page with its application bar menu expanded, and Figure 41.2 shows the main page with its dialog showing. The XAML for this page is in Listing 41.1.

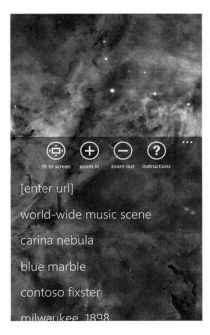

FIGURE 41.1   The application bar menu is expanded on top of the Carina Nebula.

FIGURE 41.2   Entering a custom URL is done via a dialog that appears on top of the current Deep Zoom image.

LISTING 41.1   `MainPage.xaml`—The User Interface for Deep Zoom Viewers' Main Page

```
<phone:PhoneApplicationPage x:Class="WindowsPhoneApp.MainPage"
    xmlns="http://schemas.microsoft.com/winfx/2006/xaml/presentation"
    xmlns:x="http://schemas.microsoft.com/winfx/2006/xaml"
    xmlns:phone="clr-namespace:Microsoft.Phone.Controls;assembly=Microsoft.Phone"
    xmlns:shell="clr-namespace:Microsoft.Phone.Shell;assembly=Microsoft.Phone"
    xmlns:toolkit="clr-namespace:Microsoft.Phone.Controls;
➥assembly=Microsoft.Phone.Controls.Toolkit"
    xmlns:local="clr-namespace:WindowsPhoneApp"
    FontFamily="{StaticResource PhoneFontFamilyNormal}"
    FontSize="{StaticResource PhoneFontSizeNormal}"
    Foreground="{StaticResource PhoneForegroundBrush}"
    SupportedOrientations="PortraitOrLandscape">

  <!-- The application bar -->
  <phone:PhoneApplicationPage.ApplicationBar>
    <shell:ApplicationBar Opacity=".5">
      <shell:ApplicationBarIconButton Text="fit to screen"
        IconUri="/Images/appbar.fitToScreen.png"
        Click="FitToScreenButton_Click"/>
      <shell:ApplicationBarIconButton Text="zoom in"
        IconUri="/Shared/Images/appbar.plus.png"
        Click="ZoomInButton_Click"/>
      <shell:ApplicationBarIconButton Text="zoom out"
        IconUri="/Shared/Images/appbar.minus.png"
        Click="ZoomOutButton_Click"/>
      <shell:ApplicationBarIconButton Text="instructions"
        IconUri="/Shared/Images/appbar.instructions.png"
        Click="InstructionsButton_Click"/>
      <shell:ApplicationBar.MenuItems>
        <shell:ApplicationBarMenuItem Text="[enter url]"
                                      Click="CustomUrlMenuItem_Click"/>
      </shell:ApplicationBar.MenuItems>
    </shell:ApplicationBar>
  </phone:PhoneApplicationPage.ApplicationBar>

  <Grid>
    <!-- The Deep Zoom image -->
    <MultiScaleImage x:Name="DeepZoomImage">
      <!-- Attach the gesture listener to this element -->
```

LISTING 41.1   Continued

```
      <toolkit:GestureService.GestureListener>
        <toolkit:GestureListener DoubleTap="GestureListener_DoubleTap"
                                 PinchStarted="GestureListener_PinchStarted"
                                 PinchDelta="GestureListener_PinchDelta"/>
      </toolkit:GestureService.GestureListener>
    </MultiScaleImage>

    <!-- Show a progress bar while loading an image -->
    <ProgressBar x:Name="ProgressBar" Visibility="Collapsed"/>

    <!-- A dialog for entering a URL -->
    <local:Dialog x:Name="CustomFileDialog" Closed="CustomFileDialog_Closed">
      <local:Dialog.InnerContent>
        <StackPanel>
          <TextBlock Text="Enter the URL of a Deep Zoom file" Margin="11,5,0,-5"
                     Foreground="{StaticResource PhoneSubtleBrush}"/>
          <TextBox InputScope="Url" Text="{Binding Result, Mode=TwoWay}"/>
        </StackPanel>
      </local:Dialog.InnerContent>
    </local:Dialog>
  </Grid>
</phone:PhoneApplicationPage>
```

Notes:

→ A gesture listener from the Silverlight for Windows Phone Toolkit is attached to the `MultiScaleImage` control, so we can very easily detect double taps and pinch/stretch gestures.

→ The dialog for entering custom URLs is implemented with a `Dialog` user control that has been used by other apps in this book.

→ The `MultiScaleImage` control has a lot of automatic functionality to make the viewing experience as smooth as possible. For example, as tiles are downloaded, they are smoothly blended in with a blurry-to-crisp transition, captured in Figure 41.3.

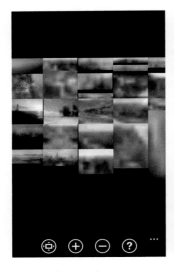 

Blurry while zooming out

Finished zooming, and the image
is now crisp

FIGURE 41.3   You can occasionally catch pieces of the view starting out blurry and then seamlessly becoming crisp.

The Code-Behind

Listing 41.2 contains the code-behind for the main page.

LISTING 41.2   `MainPage.xaml.cs`—The Code-Behind for Deep Zoom Viewers' Main Page

```
using System;
using System.ComponentModel;
using System.Windows;
using System.Windows.Input;
using System.Windows.Media;
using System.Windows.Navigation;
using Microsoft.Phone.Controls;
using Microsoft.Phone.Shell;

namespace WindowsPhoneApp
{
  public partial class MainPage : PhoneApplicationPage
  {
    // Persistent settings
    Setting<Uri> savedImageUri = new Setting<Uri>("ImageUri",
      new Uri(Data.BaseUri, "last-fm.dzi"));
    Setting<Point> savedViewportOrigin = new Setting<Point>("ViewportOrigin",
      new Point(0, -.2));
```

LISTING 41.2   Continued

```
Setting<double> savedZoom = new Setting<double>("Zoom", 1);

// Used by pinch and stretch
double zoomWhenPinchStarted;

// Used by panning and double-tapping
Point mouseDownPoint = new Point();
Point mouseDownViewportOrigin = new Point();

public MainPage()
{
  InitializeComponent();

  // Fill the application bar menu with the sample images
  foreach (File f in Data.Files)
  {
    ApplicationBarMenuItem item = new ApplicationBarMenuItem(f.Title);
    // This assignment is needed so each anonymous method gets the right value
    string filename = f.Filename;
    item.Click += delegate(object sender, EventArgs e)
    {
      OpenFile(new Uri(Data.BaseUri, filename), true);
    };
    this.ApplicationBar.MenuItems.Add(item);
  }

  // Handle success for any attempt to open a Deep Zoom image
  this.DeepZoomImage.ImageOpenSucceeded +=
    delegate(object sender, RoutedEventArgs e)
  {
    // Hide the progress bar
    this.ProgressBar.Visibility = Visibility.Collapsed;
    this.ProgressBar.IsIndeterminate = false; // Avoid a perf issue

    // Initialize the view
    this.DeepZoomImage.ViewportWidth = this.savedZoom.Value;
    this.DeepZoomImage.ViewportOrigin = this.savedViewportOrigin.Value;
  };

  // Handle failure for any attempt to open a Deep Zoom image
  this.DeepZoomImage.ImageOpenFailed +=
    delegate(object sender, ExceptionRoutedEventArgs e)
  {
    // Hide the progress bar
```

LISTING 41.2   Continued

```
    this.ProgressBar.Visibility = Visibility.Collapsed;
    this.ProgressBar.IsIndeterminate = false; // Avoid a perf issue

    MessageBox.Show("Unable to open " + this.savedImageUri.Value + ".",
      "Error", MessageBoxButton.OK);
  };

  // Load the previously-viewed (or default) image
  OpenFile(this.savedImageUri.Value, false);
}

protected override void OnNavigatedFrom(NavigationEventArgs e)
{
  base.OnNavigatedFrom(e);
  // Remember settings for next time
  this.savedViewportOrigin.Value = this.DeepZoomImage.ViewportOrigin;
  this.savedZoom.Value = this.DeepZoomImage.ViewportWidth;
}

// Attempt to open the Deep Zoom image at the specified URI
void OpenFile(Uri uri, bool resetPosition)
{
  if (resetPosition)
  {
    // Restore these settings to their default values
    this.savedZoom.Value = this.savedZoom.DefaultValue;
    this.savedViewportOrigin.Value = this.savedViewportOrigin.DefaultValue;
  }

  this.savedImageUri.Value = uri;

  // Assign the image
  this.DeepZoomImage.Source = new DeepZoomImageTileSource(uri);

  // Show a temporary progress bar
  this.ProgressBar.IsIndeterminate = true;
  this.ProgressBar.Visibility = Visibility.Visible;
}

// Three handlers (mouse down/move/up) to implement panning

protected override void OnMouseLeftButtonDown(MouseButtonEventArgs e)
{
```

LISTING 41.2   Continued

```
    base.OnMouseLeftButtonDown(e);

    // Ignore if the dialog is visible
    if (this.CustomFileDialog.Visibility == Visibility.Visible)
      return;

    this.mouseDownPoint = e.GetPosition(this.DeepZoomImage);
    this.mouseDownViewportOrigin = this.DeepZoomImage.ViewportOrigin;

    this.DeepZoomImage.CaptureMouse();
  }

  protected override void OnMouseMove(MouseEventArgs e)
  {
    base.OnMouseMove(e);

    // Ignore if the dialog is visible
    if (this.CustomFileDialog.Visibility == Visibility.Visible)
      return;

    Point p = e.GetPosition(this.DeepZoomImage);

    // ViewportWidth is the absolute zoom (2 == half size, .5 == double size)
    double scale = this.DeepZoomImage.ActualWidth /
                   this.DeepZoomImage.ViewportWidth;

    // Pan the image by setting a new viewport origin based on the mouse-down
    // location and the distance the primary finger has moved
    this.DeepZoomImage.ViewportOrigin = new Point(
      this.mouseDownViewportOrigin.X + (this.mouseDownPoint.X - p.X) / scale,
      this.mouseDownViewportOrigin.Y + (this.mouseDownPoint.Y - p.Y) / scale);
  }

  protected override void OnMouseLeftButtonUp(MouseButtonEventArgs e)
  {
    base.OnMouseLeftButtonUp(e);
    // Stop panning
    this.DeepZoomImage.ReleaseMouseCapture();
  }

  // The three gesture handlers for double tap, pinch, and stretch

  void GestureListener_DoubleTap(object sender, GestureEventArgs e)
  {
```

LISTING 41.2   Continued

```
  // Ignore if the dialog is visible
  if (this.CustomFileDialog.Visibility == Visibility.Visible)
    return;

  // Zoom in by a factor of 2 centered at the place where the double tap
  // occurred (the same place as the most recent MouseLeftButtonDown event)
  ZoomBy(2, this.mouseDownPoint);
}

// Raised when two fingers touch the screen (likely to begin a pinch/stretch)
void GestureListener_PinchStarted(object sender,
  PinchStartedGestureEventArgs e)
{
  this.zoomWhenPinchStarted = this.DeepZoomImage.ViewportWidth;
}

// Raised continually as either or both fingers move
void GestureListener_PinchDelta(object sender, PinchGestureEventArgs e)
{
  // Ignore if the dialog is visible
  if (this.CustomFileDialog.Visibility == Visibility.Visible)
    return;

  // The distance ratio is always relative to when the pinch/stretch started,
  // so be sure to apply it to the ORIGINAL zoom level, not the CURRENT
  double zoom = this.zoomWhenPinchStarted / e.DistanceRatio;
  this.DeepZoomImage.ViewportWidth = zoom;
}

void ZoomBy(double zoomFactor, Point centerPoint)
{
  // Restrict how small the image can get (don't get smaller than half size)
  if (this.DeepZoomImage.ViewportWidth >= 2 && zoomFactor < 1)
    return;

  // Convert the on-screen point to the image's coordinate system, which
  // is (0,0) in the top-left corner and (1,1) in the bottom right corner
  Point logicalCenterPoint =
    this.DeepZoomImage.ElementToLogicalPoint(centerPoint);

  // Perform the zoom
  this.DeepZoomImage.ZoomAboutLogicalPoint(
    zoomFactor, logicalCenterPoint.X, logicalCenterPoint.Y);
```

LISTING 41.2   Continued

```
  }

  // Code for the custom file dialog

  protected override void OnBackKeyPress(CancelEventArgs e)
  {
    base.OnBackKeyPress(e);

    // If the dialog is open, close it instead of leaving the page
    if (this.CustomFileDialog.Visibility == Visibility.Visible)
    {
      e.Cancel = true;
      this.CustomFileDialog.Hide(MessageBoxResult.Cancel);
    }
  }

  void CustomFileDialog_Closed(object sender, MessageBoxResultEventArgs e)
  {
    // Try to open the typed-in URL
    if (e.Result == MessageBoxResult.OK && this.CustomFileDialog.Result != null)
      OpenFile(new Uri(this.CustomFileDialog.Result.ToString()), true);
  }

  // Application bar handlers

  void FitToScreenButton_Click(object sender, EventArgs e)
  {
    this.DeepZoomImage.ViewportWidth = 1; // Un-zoom
    this.DeepZoomImage.ViewportOrigin = new Point(0, -.4); // Give a top margin
  }

  void ZoomInButton_Click(object sender, EventArgs e)
  {
    // Zoom in by 50%, keeping the current center point
    ZoomBy(1.5, new Point(this.DeepZoomImage.ActualWidth / 2,
                          this.DeepZoomImage.ActualHeight / 2));
  }

  void ZoomOutButton_Click(object sender, EventArgs e)
  {
    // Zoom out by 50%, keeping the current center point
    ZoomBy(1 / 1.5, new Point(this.DeepZoomImage.ActualWidth / 2,
                              this.DeepZoomImage.ActualHeight / 2));
```

LISTING 41.2   Continued

```csharp
    }

    void InstructionsButton_Click(object sender, EventArgs e)
    {
      this.NavigationService.Navigate(
        new Uri("/InstructionsPage.xaml", UriKind.Relative));
    }

    void CustomUrlMenuItem_Click(object sender, EventArgs e)
    {
      // Show the custom file dialog, initialized with the current URI
      if (this.savedImageUri.Value != null)
        this.CustomFileDialog.Result = this.savedImageUri.Value;
      this.CustomFileDialog.Show();
    }
  }
}
```

Notes:

→ The application bar menu is filled with a list of sample files based on the following two classes defined in a separate Data.cs file:

```csharp
public struct File
{
  public string Title { get; set; }
  public string Filename { get; set; }
}

public static class Data
{
  public static readonly Uri BaseUri =
    new Uri("http://static.seadragon.com/content/misc/");

  public static File[] Files = {
    new File { Title = "World-Wide Music Scene", Filename = "last-fm.dzi" },
    new File { Title = "Carina Nebula", Filename = "carina-nebula.dzi" },
    new File { Title = "Blue Marble", Filename = "blue-marble.dzi" },
    new File { Title = "Contoso Fixster", Filename = "contoso-fixster.dzi" },
    new File { Title = "Milwaukee, 1898", Filename = "milwaukee.dzi" },
    new File { Title = "Yosemite Panorama", Filename="yosemite-panorama.dzi" },
    new File { Title = "Angkor Wat Temple", Filename = "angkor-wat.dzi" }
  };
}
```

→ When constructing the URI for each filename, `BaseUri` is prepended to the filename using an overloaded constructor of `Uri` that accepts two arguments.

→ Much like the `Image` element, the `MultiScaleImage` element is told what to render by setting its `Source` property. This is done inside `OpenFile`. Note that the type of `Source` is `MultiScaleTileSource`, an abstract class with one concrete subclass: `DeepZoomImageTileSource`.

→ After setting `Source`, the image download is asynchronous and either results in an `ImageOpenSucceeded` or `ImageOpenFailed` event being raised. This listing leverages this fact to temporarily show an indeterminate progress bar while the initial download is occurring, although this is usually extremely fast.

Can `MultiScaleImage` work with a local image included with the app?

Surprisingly, no! Only online files are supported.

→ The current zoom level and visible region of the image are represented by two properties: `ViewportWidth` and `ViewportOrigin`.

→ **ViewportWidth** is actually the *inverse* of the zoom level. A value of .5 means that half the width is visible. (So the zoom level is 2.) A value of 2 means that the width of the viewport is double that of the image, so the image width occupies half of the visible area.

→ **ViewportOrigin** is the point in the image that is currently at the top-left corner of the visible area. The point is expressed in what Deep Zoom calls *logical coordinates*. In this system, (0,0) is the top-left corner of the image, and (1,1) is the bottom-right corner of the image.

→ This app's panning functionality is supported with traditional `MouseLeftButtonDown`, `MouseMove`, and `MouseLeftButtonUp` handlers that implement a typical drag-and-drop scheme. In `MouseMove`, the amount that the finger has moved since `MouseLeftButtonDown` is applied to the `ViewportOrigin`, but this value is scaled appropriately based on the control's width (480 or 800, depending on the phone orientation) and the zoom level. This is necessary because `ViewportOrigin` must be set to a logical point, and it also ensures that the panning gesture doesn't get magnified as the user zooms in.

Be sure to use a logical point when setting `ViewportOrigin`!

Otherwise, the image will likely pan far off-screen. Luckily, `MultiScaleImage` provides two handy methods—`ElementToLogicalPoint` and `LogicalToElementPoint`—for converting between logical points and element-relative points. (When the `MultiScaleImage` control fills the screen and has no transforms applied, as in this app, element-relative points are equivalent to points on the screen.)

→ After the three handlers that implement panning, this listing contains the three handlers for gesture listener events. The first handler (GestureListener_ DoubleTap) performs a 2x zoom each time a double tap is detected.

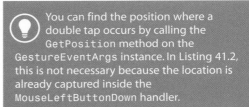

MultiScaleImage has built-in inertia effects whenever you change the zoom level or viewport origin, so the panning and zooming done by this app exhibit smooth and inertial transitions without any extra work. If you do *not* want these effects, simply set MultiScaleImage's UseSprings property to false.

→ The next two handlers (GestureListener_PinchStarted and GestureListener_PinchDelta) handle pinching *and stretching* gestures. The DistanceRatio property reveals how much further apart (>1) or closer together (<1) the two fingers are, compared to when they made contact with the screen. The key to getting the appropriate effect is to apply this ratio to the *original* zoom level captured in the PinchStarted event handler. Normally, as with a ScaleTransform or CompositeTransform, you would multiply the original value by the ratio. Because ViewportWidth is the *inverse* of the zoom level, however, this listing instead *divides* its value by the ratio.

→ GestureListener_PinchDelta directly updates ViewportWidth rather than calling the ZoomBy method used elsewhere. ZoomBy centers the zoom around a passed-in point, but MultiScaleImage doesn't work well when the viewport is continually and rapidly moved.

You can find the position where a double tap occurs by calling the GetPosition method on the GestureEventArgs instance. In Listing 41.2, this is not necessary because the location is already captured inside the MouseLeftButtonDown handler.

The same three gesture listener events—PinchStarted, PinchDelta, and PinchCompleted—can be used to detect both pinching and stretching. The key piece of data is the DistanceRatio property on PinchGestureEventArgs, which indicates how far apart or close together the two fingers are compared to when they first touched the screen. Be careful how you use this value, however. A value greater than 1 does not necessarily mean stretching is occurring, and a value less than one does not necessarily mean pinching is occurring. For example, users could stretch their fingers until the ratio is 5 and then pinch them until the ratio goes back down to 2. As long as the ratio is continually applied to the zooming element's *original* zoom level when the pinch/stretch started rather than the *current* zoom level, pinching and stretching will work as intended.

➔ ZoomBy, used by the double-tap handler and the zooming application bar button handlers, zooms the viewport by an amount relative to the current zoom level with MultiScaleImage's ZoomAboutLogicalPoint method.

 How do I determine the center point of a pinch or stretch gesture, so I can center my zoom on that point?

Although it's not done by this app (due to flakiness in constantly recentering the viewport), it's common practice to center the zoom of a pinch or stretch gesture based on the midpoint between the two fingers. Although this point is not directly exposed by the gesture listener, you can calculate it as follows:

```
void GestureListener_PinchDelta(object sender, PinchGestureEventArgs e)
{
  Point firstPoint = e.GetPosition(this, 0);  // Finger #1
  Point secondPoint = e.GetPosition(this, 1); // Finger #2

  // Calculate the midpoint
  Point pinchOrigin = new Point(
    (firstPoint.X + secondPoint.X) / 2,
    (firstPoint.Y + secondPoint.Y) / 2);
  …
}
```

Both PinchGestureEventArgs and PinchStartedGestureEventArgs expose an overload of GetPosition that enables passing 0 or 1 to get the point for either of the two relevant fingers. (The regular GetPosition overload always gives the data for the first, primary finger.) By continually calculating the midpoint in a PinchDelta event handler rather than once in a PinchStarted event handler, the center is continually updated as the two fingers move, which gives the best experience.

The Finished Product

The full Yosemite panorama

Zoomed in to a part of Yosemite

Zoomed in to a Milwaukee 1898 panoramic poster

chapter 42

JIGSAW PUZZLE

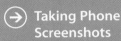
Jigsaw Puzzle enables you to turn any picture into a challenging 30-piece jigsaw puzzle. You can use one of the included pictures, or choose a photo from your camera or pictures library. You can even zoom and crop the photo to get it just right. Drag pieces up from a scrollable tray at the bottom of the screen and place them where you think they belong. As you drag a piece, it snaps to each of the 30 possible correct positions to reduce your frustration when arranging pieces. Jigsaw Puzzle also can solve the puzzle for you, or reshuffle the pieces, both with fun animations.

Other than the instructions page, Jigsaw Puzzle contains a main page and a page for cropping an imported picture. This app leverages gesture listener's drag events for a few different reasons. On the main page, dragging is used for moving puzzle pieces and for scrolling the tray of unused pieces at the bottom of the screen. On the page for cropping imported pictures, dragging is used to pan the picture. (Gesture listener's pinch/stretch events are also used for zooming the picture, just like in the preceding chapter.)

> Are you thinking of ways to increase the difficulty of the puzzles in this app? Although the puzzle pieces would become too difficult to drag if you make them much smaller (without also enabling zooming), you could enable pieces to be rotated. The next chapter demonstrates how to implement a rotation gesture.

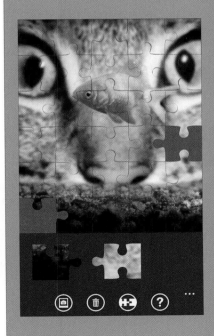

The Main Page

Jigsaw Puzzle's main page contains the 30 pieces arranged in 6 rows of 5. Each piece is a 96x96 canvas that contains a vector drawing represented as a `Path` element. 14 distinct shapes are used (4 if you consider rotated/flipped versions as equivalent), shown in Figure 42.1.

FIGURE 42.1   The 14 shapes consist of 4 corner pieces, 8 edge pieces, and 2 middle pieces.

Each piece is actually larger than 96 pixels in at least one dimension, which is fine because each `Path` can render outside the bounds of its parent 96x96 canvas. Each `Path` is given an appropriate offset inside its parent canvas to produce the appropriate interlocking pattern, as illustrated in Figure 42.2. Every puzzle presented by this app uses these exact 30 pieces in the exact same spots; only the image on the pieces changes.

The choice of a vector-based path to represent each piece is important because it enables the nonrectangular shapes to interlock and retain precise hit-testing. If puzzle-piece-shaped images were instead used as an opacity mask on rectangular elements, the bounding box of each piece would respond to gestures on the entire area that overlaps the bounding box of any pieces underneath. This would cause the wrong piece to move in many areas of the puzzle. The use of paths also enables us to apply a custom stroke to each piece to highlight its edges.

The User Interface

Listing 42.1 contains the XAML for the main page.

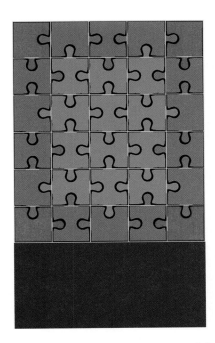

FIGURE 42.2   The 30 vector-based shapes, each shown with its parent canvas represented as a yellow square outline.

LISTING 42.1   `MainPage.xaml`—The User Interface for Jigsaw Puzzle's Main Page

```xml
<phone:PhoneApplicationPage x:Class="WindowsPhoneApp.MainPage"
    xmlns="http://schemas.microsoft.com/winfx/2006/xaml/presentation"
    xmlns:x="http://schemas.microsoft.com/winfx/2006/xaml"
    xmlns:phone="clr-namespace:Microsoft.Phone.Controls;assembly=Microsoft.Phone"
    xmlns:shell="clr-namespace:Microsoft.Phone.Shell;assembly=Microsoft.Phone"
    xmlns:toolkit="clr-namespace:Microsoft.Phone.Controls;
➥assembly=Microsoft.Phone.Controls.Toolkit"
    SupportedOrientations="Portrait">

  <!-- Listen for drag events anywhere on the page -->
  <toolkit:GestureService.GestureListener>
    <toolkit:GestureListener DragStarted="GestureListener_DragStarted"
                             DragDelta="GestureListener_DragDelta"
                             DragCompleted="GestureListener_DragCompleted"/>
  </toolkit:GestureService.GestureListener>

  <!-- The application bar, with 4 buttons and 5 menu items -->
  <phone:PhoneApplicationPage.ApplicationBar>
    <shell:ApplicationBar Opacity=".5" ForegroundColor="White"
                          BackgroundColor="#443225">
```

LISTING 42.1   Continued

```xml
    <shell:ApplicationBarIconButton Text="picture"
      IconUri="/Shared/Images/appbar.picture.png" Click="PictureButton_Click"/>
    <shell:ApplicationBarIconButton Text="start over"
      IconUri="/Shared/Images/appbar.delete.png" Click="StartOverButton_Click"/>
    <shell:ApplicationBarIconButton Text="solve" IsEnabled="False"
      IconUri="/Images/appbar.solve.png" Click="SolveButton_Click"/>
    <shell:ApplicationBarIconButton Text="instructions"
      IconUri="/Shared/Images/appbar.instructions.png"
      Click="InstructionsButton_Click"/>
    <shell:ApplicationBar.MenuItems>
      <shell:ApplicationBarMenuItem Text="cat and fish"
                                    Click="ApplicationBarMenuItem_Click"/>
      <shell:ApplicationBarMenuItem Text="city"
                                    Click="ApplicationBarMenuItem_Click"/>
      <shell:ApplicationBarMenuItem Text="statue of liberty"
                                    Click="ApplicationBarMenuItem_Click"/>
      <shell:ApplicationBarMenuItem Text="traffic"
                                    Click="ApplicationBarMenuItem_Click"/>
      <shell:ApplicationBarMenuItem Text="under water"
                                    Click="ApplicationBarMenuItem_Click"/>
    </shell:ApplicationBar.MenuItems>
  </shell:ApplicationBar>
</phone:PhoneApplicationPage.ApplicationBar>

<!-- Prevent off-screen pieces from appearing during a page transition -->
<phone:PhoneApplicationPage.Clip>
  <RectangleGeometry Rect="0,0,480,800"/>
</phone:PhoneApplicationPage.Clip>

<Canvas Background="#655">

  <!-- The tray at the bottom -->
  <Rectangle x:Name="Tray" Fill="#443225" Width="480" Height="224"
             Canvas.Top="576"/>

  <!-- All 30 pieces placed where they belong -->
  <Canvas x:Name="PiecesCanvas">

    <!-- Row 1 -->
    <Canvas Width="96" Height="96">
      <Path Data="F1M312.63,0L385.7,0C385.48,…" Height="129" Stretch="Fill"
            Width="96" Stroke="#2000">
        <Path.Fill>
          <ImageBrush Stretch="None" AlignmentX="Left" AlignmentY="Top"/>
```

LISTING 42.1 Continued

```xml
          </Path.Fill>
        </Path>
        <Canvas.RenderTransform><CompositeTransform/></Canvas.RenderTransform>
      </Canvas>

      <Canvas Canvas.Left="96" Width="96" Height="96">
        <Path Data="F1M25.12,909.28C49.47,909.27,…" Height="96"
              Canvas.Left="-33" Stretch="Fill" Width="162" Stroke="#2000">
          <Path.Fill>
            <ImageBrush Stretch="None" AlignmentX="Left" AlignmentY="Top">
              <ImageBrush.Transform>
                <TranslateTransform X="-63"/>
              </ImageBrush.Transform>
            </ImageBrush>
          </Path.Fill>
        </Path>
        <Canvas.RenderTransform><CompositeTransform/></Canvas.RenderTransform>
      </Canvas>

… 27 pieces omitted …

      <Canvas Canvas.Left="384" Canvas.Top="480" Width="96" Height="96">
        <Path Data="F1M777.45,0L800.25,0C802.63,…" Canvas.Left="-33"
              Height="96" Stretch="Fill" Width="129" Stroke="#2000">
          <Path.Fill>
            <ImageBrush Stretch="None" AlignmentX="Left" AlignmentY="Top">
              <ImageBrush.Transform>
                <TranslateTransform X="-351" Y="-480"/>
              </ImageBrush.Transform>
            </ImageBrush>
          </Path.Fill>
        </Path>
        <Canvas.RenderTransform><CompositeTransform/></Canvas.RenderTransform>
      </Canvas>
    </Canvas>

    <!-- The image without visible piece boundaries, shown when solved -->
    <Image x:Name="CompleteImage" Visibility="Collapsed" IsHitTestVisible="False"
           Stretch="None"/>
  </Canvas>
</phone:PhoneApplicationPage>
```

Notes:

→ A gesture listener is attached to the entire page to listen for the three drag events: `DragStarted`, `DragDelta`, and `DragCompleted`.

→ The path data for each piece is quite complicated and was created in Expression Blend.

> My favorite way to create vector artwork based on an illustration is with Vector Magic (http://vectormagic.com). It's not free, but it does a fantastic job of converting image files to a variety of vector formats. If you download the result as a PDF file and then rename the file extension to `.ai`, you can import it into Expression Blend, which converts it to XAML.

→ Although each piece is placed in its final "solved" position, the code-behind adjusts each position by modifying `TranslateX` and `TranslateY` properties on the `CompositeTransform` assigned to each piece. This gives us the nice property that no matter where a piece is moved, it can be returned to its solved position by setting both of these properties to zero.

→ The magic behind making each puzzle piece contain a portion of a photo is enabled by the image brush that fills each path. (The actual image is set in code-behind.) To make each piece contain the correct portion of the photo, each image brush (except the one used on the piece in the top left corner) is given a `TranslateTransform`. This shifts its rendering by the distance that the piece is from the top-left corner. (To make this work, each image brush is marked with top-left alignment, rather than its default center alignment.)

> Fortunately for apps such as Jigsaw Puzzle, using many image brushes that point to the same image is efficient. Silverlight shares the underlying image rather than creating a separate copy for each brush.

→ The scrolling tray at the bottom isn't an actual scroll viewer; it's just a simple rectangle. The code-behind manually scrolls puzzle pieces when they sufficiently overlap this rectangle. This is done for two reasons: It's convenient to keep the pieces on the same canvas at all times, and the gesture listener currently interferes with Silverlight elements such as scroll viewers.

→ The `CompleteImage` element at the bottom of the listing is used to show the complete image once the puzzle is solved, without the puzzle piece borders and tiny gaps between pieces obscuring it. Because it is aligned with the puzzle, showing this image simply makes it seem like the puzzle edges have faded away. Figure 42.3 shows what this looks like for the cat-and-fish puzzle shown at the beginning of this chapter. Because `CompleteImage` is not hit-testable, the user can still drag a piece while it is showing. As soon as any piece moves out of its correct position, the code-behind hides the image once again.

FIGURE 42.3   Once the puzzle is solved, the puzzle piece borders are no longer visible.

The Code-Behind

Listing 42.2 contains the code-behind for the main page.

LISTING 42.2   `MainPage.xaml.cs`—The Code-Behind for Jigsaw Puzzle's Main Page

```
using System;
using System.Collections.Generic;
using System.Linq;
using System.Windows;
using System.Windows.Controls;
using System.Windows.Media;
using System.Windows.Media.Animation;
using System.Windows.Media.Imaging;
using System.Windows.Navigation;
using System.Windows.Shapes;
using System.Windows.Threading;
using Microsoft.Phone.Controls;
using Microsoft.Phone.Shell;

namespace WindowsPhoneApp
{
```

LISTING 42.2   Continued

```csharp
public partial class MainPage : PhoneApplicationPage
{
  bool isDraggingTray;
  bool isDraggingPiece;
  double cumulativeDeltaX;
  double cumulativeDeltaY;
  int topmostZIndex;
  List<FrameworkElement> piecesOnTray = new List<FrameworkElement>();
  Random random = new Random();
  IApplicationBarIconButton solveButton;

  public MainPage()
  {
    InitializeComponent();
    this.solveButton = this.ApplicationBar.Buttons[2]
      as IApplicationBarIconButton;
  }

  protected override void OnNavigatedFrom(NavigationEventArgs e)
  {
    base.OnNavigatedFrom(e);

    // Persist the offset currently being applied to each piece, so
    // they can appear in the same locations next time
    Settings.PieceOffsets.Value.Clear();
    foreach (FrameworkElement piece in this.PiecesCanvas.Children)
    {
      Settings.PieceOffsets.Value.Add(new Point(
        (piece.RenderTransform as CompositeTransform).TranslateX,
        (piece.RenderTransform as CompositeTransform).TranslateY));
    }
  }

  protected override void OnNavigatedTo(NavigationEventArgs e)
  {
    base.OnNavigatedTo(e);

    RefreshPuzzleImage();

    bool arePiecesCorrect = false;
    if (Settings.PieceOffsets.Value.Count == this.PiecesCanvas.Children.Count)
    {
      // Restore the persisted position of each piece
      for (int i = 0; i < this.PiecesCanvas.Children.Count; i++)
```

LISTING 42.2   Continued

```
    {
      UIElement piece = this.PiecesCanvas.Children[i];
      CompositeTransform t = piece.RenderTransform as CompositeTransform;
      t.TranslateX = Settings.PieceOffsets.Value[i].X;
      t.TranslateY = Settings.PieceOffsets.Value[i].Y;
    }
    arePiecesCorrect = AreAllPiecesCorrect();
  }
  else
  {
    // This is the first run. After a 1-second delay, animate the pieces
    // from their solved positions to random positions on the tray.
    DispatcherTimer timer = new DispatcherTimer {
      Interval = TimeSpan.FromSeconds(1) };
    timer.Tick += delegate(object sender, EventArgs args)
    {
      StartOver();
      timer.Stop();
    };
    timer.Start();
  }

  if (arePiecesCorrect)
    ShowAsSolved();
  else
    ShowAsUnsolved();
}


// The three drag event handlers

void GestureListener_DragStarted(object sender, DragStartedGestureEventArgs e)
{
  // Determine if we're dragging the tray, a piece, or neither
  FrameworkElement source = e.OriginalSource as FrameworkElement;

  if (source == this.Tray)
  {
    // An empty spot on the tray is being dragged
    if (e.Direction == System.Windows.Controls.Orientation.Horizontal)
      this.isDraggingTray = true;
    return;
  }

  FrameworkElement piece = GetPieceFromDraggedSource(source);
```

LISTING 42.2   Continued

```
  if (piece == null)
    return;

  if (e.Direction == System.Windows.Controls.Orientation.Horizontal &&
      GetPieceTop(piece) > Constants.ON_TRAY_Y)
  {
    // Although a piece is being dragged, the piece is on the tray and the
    // drag is horizontal, so consider this to be a tray drag instead
    this.isDraggingTray = true;
  }
  else
  {
    this.isDraggingPiece = true;
    // A piece is being dragged, so record its pre-drag position
    CompositeTransform t = piece.RenderTransform as CompositeTransform;
    this.cumulativeDeltaX = t.TranslateX;
    this.cumulativeDeltaY = t.TranslateY;
  }
}

void GestureListener_DragDelta(object sender, DragDeltaGestureEventArgs e)
{
  if (this.isDraggingTray)
  {
    // Scroll the tray
    ScrollTray(e.HorizontalChange);
  }
  else if (this.isDraggingPiece)
  {
    FrameworkElement piece = GetPieceFromDraggedSource(
      e.OriginalSource as FrameworkElement);
    if (piece == null)
      return;

    CompositeTransform t = piece.RenderTransform as CompositeTransform;

    // Apply the position change caused by dragging.
    // We're keeping track of the total change from DragStarted so the piece
    // remains in the right spot after repeated snapping and unsnapping.
    this.cumulativeDeltaX += e.HorizontalChange;
    this.cumulativeDeltaY += e.VerticalChange;
    t.TranslateX = this.cumulativeDeltaX;
    t.TranslateY = this.cumulativeDeltaY;
```

LISTING 42.2   Continued

```
      // Ensure that this piece is on top of all others
      this.topmostZIndex++;
      Canvas.SetZIndex(piece, this.topmostZIndex);

      // Ensure that the puzzle is no longer in the solved state
      ShowAsUnsolved();

      // If the piece is not on the tray, snap it to a solved horizontal
      // and/or vertical boundary if it's close enough
      double left = GetPieceLeft(piece);
      double top = GetPieceTop(piece);

      if (top > Constants.ON_TRAY_Y)
        return; // The piece is on the tray, so never mind

      // Snapping to a horizontal boundary
      if (left % Constants.PIECE_WIDTH < Constants.SNAPPING_MARGIN)
        t.TranslateX -= left % Constants.PIECE_WIDTH;
      else if (left % Constants.PIECE_WIDTH >
                Constants.PIECE_WIDTH - Constants.SNAPPING_MARGIN)
        t.TranslateX += Constants.PIECE_WIDTH - left % Constants.PIECE_WIDTH;

      // Snapping to a vertical boundary
      if (top % Constants.PIECE_HEIGHT < Constants.SNAPPING_MARGIN)
        t.TranslateY -= top % Constants.PIECE_HEIGHT;
      else if (top % Constants.PIECE_HEIGHT >
                Constants.PIECE_HEIGHT - Constants.SNAPPING_MARGIN)
        t.TranslateY += Constants.PIECE_HEIGHT - top % Constants.PIECE_HEIGHT;
    }
  }


  void GestureListener_DragCompleted(object sender,
                                     DragCompletedGestureEventArgs e)
  {
    // Give the tray an extra push (simulating inertia) based on
    // the final dragging horizontal velocity
    if (this.isDraggingTray && e.HorizontalVelocity != 0)
      ScrollTray(e.HorizontalVelocity / 10);

    this.isDraggingTray = this.isDraggingPiece = false;

    if (AreAllPiecesCorrect())
      ShowAsSolved();
  }
```

LISTING 42.2   Continued

```
FrameworkElement GetPieceFromDraggedSource(FrameworkElement source)
{
  // When a piece is dragged, the source is the path,
  // but we want to return its parent canvas
  if (source == null || source.Parent == null ||
      (source.Parent as FrameworkElement).Parent == null ||
      (source.Parent as FrameworkElement).Parent != this.PiecesCanvas)
    return null;
  else
    return source.Parent as FrameworkElement;
}


double GetPieceTop(FrameworkElement piece)
{
  return Canvas.GetTop(piece) +
         (piece.RenderTransform as CompositeTransform).TranslateY;
}


double GetPieceLeft(FrameworkElement piece)
{
  return Canvas.GetLeft(piece) +
         (piece.RenderTransform as CompositeTransform).TranslateX;
}


void ScrollTray(double amount)
{
  // Retrieve the minimum and maximum horizontal positions among all
  // pieces in the tray, to provide bounds on how far it can scroll
  double minX = double.MaxValue;
  double maxX = double.MinValue;
  this.piecesOnTray.Clear();
  foreach (FrameworkElement piece in this.PiecesCanvas.Children)
  {
    if (GetPieceTop(piece) > Constants.ON_TRAY_Y)
    {
      this.piecesOnTray.Add(piece);
      double left = GetPieceLeft(piece);
      if (left < minX) minX = left;
      if (left > maxX) maxX = left;
    }
  }

  if (this.piecesOnTray.Count == 0)
    return;
```

LISTING 42.2   Continued

```
    // Change the amount if it would make the tray scroll too far
    if (amount < 0 && (maxX + amount < this.ActualWidth -
        Constants.MAX_PIECE_WIDTH || minX < Constants.NEGATIVE_SCROLL_BOUNDARY))
      amount = Math.Max(-maxX + this.ActualWidth - Constants.MAX_PIECE_WIDTH,
                        Constants.NEGATIVE_SCROLL_BOUNDARY - minX);
    if (amount > 0 && minX + amount > Constants.TRAY_LEFT_MARGIN)
      amount = Constants.TRAY_LEFT_MARGIN - minX;

    // "Scroll" the tray by moving each piece on the tray the same amount
    foreach (FrameworkElement piece in this.piecesOnTray)
      (piece.RenderTransform as CompositeTransform).TranslateX += amount;
  }

  // Move each piece to the tray in a random order
  void StartOver()
  {
    // Copy the children to an array so their order
    // in the collection is preserved
    UIElement[] pieces = this.PiecesCanvas.Children.ToArray();

    // Shuffle the children in place
    for (int i = pieces.Length - 1; i > 0; i--)
    {
      int r = this.random.Next(0, i);
      // Swap the current child with the randomly-chosen one
      UIElement temp = pieces[i]; pieces[i] = pieces[r]; pieces[r] = temp;
    }

    // Now move the pieces to the bottom in their random order
    for (int i = 0; i < pieces.Length; i++)
    {
      UIElement piece = pieces[i];
      // Alternate the pieces between two rows
      CreatePieceMovingStoryboard(piece, TimeSpan.Zero, TimeSpan.FromSeconds(1),
          (i % 2 * Constants.TRAY_2ND_ROW_HORIZONTAL_OFFSET) +
          (i / 2) * Constants.TRAY_HORIZONTAL_SPACING - Canvas.GetLeft(piece),
          (i % 2 * Constants.TRAY_VERTICAL_SPACING) + Constants.TRAY_TOP_MARGIN
          - Canvas.GetTop(piece)).Begin();
      // Reset the z-index of each piece
      Canvas.SetZIndex(piece, 0);
    }

    this.topmostZIndex = 0;
    ShowAsUnsolved();
```

LISTING 42.2   Continued

```
  }

  // Create a storyboard that animates the piece to the specified position
  Storyboard CreatePieceMovingStoryboard(UIElement piece, TimeSpan beginTime,
    TimeSpan duration, double finalX, double finalY)
  {
    DoubleAnimation xAnimation = new DoubleAnimation { To = finalX,
      Duration = duration, EasingFunction = new QuinticEase() };
    DoubleAnimation yAnimation = new DoubleAnimation { To = finalY,
      Duration = duration, EasingFunction = new QuinticEase() };
    Storyboard.SetTargetProperty(xAnimation, new PropertyPath("TranslateX"));
    Storyboard.SetTargetProperty(yAnimation, new PropertyPath("TranslateY"));

    Storyboard storyboard = new Storyboard { BeginTime = beginTime };
    Storyboard.SetTarget(storyboard, piece.RenderTransform);
    storyboard.Children.Add(xAnimation);
    storyboard.Children.Add(yAnimation);

    return storyboard;
  }

  bool AreAllPiecesCorrect()
  {
    for (int i = 0; i < this.PiecesCanvas.Children.Count; i++)
    {
      UIElement piece = this.PiecesCanvas.Children[i];
      CompositeTransform t = piece.RenderTransform as CompositeTransform;
      if (t.TranslateX != 0 || t.TranslateY != 0)
        return false; // This piece is in the wrong place
    }
    // All pieces are in the right place
    return true;
  }

  void ShowAsSolved()
  {
    this.solveButton.IsEnabled = false;

    int piecesToMove = 0;
    Storyboard storyboard = null;

    // For any piece that's out of place, animate it to the solved position
    for (int i = 0; i < this.PiecesCanvas.Children.Count; i++)
    {
```

LISTING 42.2   Continued

```csharp
    UIElement piece = this.PiecesCanvas.Children[i];
    CompositeTransform t = piece.RenderTransform as CompositeTransform;

    if (t.TranslateX == 0 && t.TranslateY == 0)
      continue; // This piece is already in the right place

    // Animate it to a (0,0) offset, which is its natural position
    storyboard = CreatePieceMovingStoryboard(piece,
      TimeSpan.FromSeconds(.3 * piecesToMove), // Spread out the animations
      TimeSpan.FromSeconds(1), 0, 0);
    storyboard.Begin();

    // Ensure each piece moves on top of pieces already in the right place
    this.topmostZIndex++;
    Canvas.SetZIndex(piece, this.topmostZIndex);

    piecesToMove++;
  }

  if (storyboard == null)
  {
    // Everything is in the right place
    this.CompleteImage.Visibility = Visibility.Visible;
  }
  else
  {
    // Delay the showing of CompleteImage until the last storyboard
    // has completed
    storyboard.Completed += delegate(object sender, EventArgs e)
    {
      // Ensure that the user didn't unsolve the puzzle during the animation
      if (!this.solveButton.IsEnabled)
        this.CompleteImage.Visibility = Visibility.Visible;
    };
  }
}

void ShowAsUnsolved()
{
  this.solveButton.IsEnabled = true;
  this.CompleteImage.Visibility = Visibility.Collapsed;
}

void RefreshPuzzleImage()
```

LISTING 42.2   Continued

```
{
  ImageSource imageSource = null;

  // Choose the right image based on the setting
  switch (Settings.PhotoIndex.Value)
  {
    // The first case is for a custom photo saved
    // from CroppedPictureChooserPage
    case -1:
      try { imageSource = IsolatedStorageHelper.LoadFile("custom.jpg"); }
      catch { imageSource = new BitmapImage(new Uri("Images/catAndFish.jpg",
            UriKind.Relative)); }
      break;
    // The remaining cases match the indices in the application bar menu
    case 0:
      imageSource = new BitmapImage(new Uri("Images/catAndFish.jpg",
                                        UriKind.Relative));
      break;
    case 1:
      imageSource = new BitmapImage(new Uri("Images/city.jpg",
                                        UriKind.Relative));
      break;
    case 2:
      imageSource = new BitmapImage(new Uri("Images/statueOfLiberty.jpg",
                                        UriKind.Relative));
      break;
    case 3:
      imageSource = new BitmapImage(new Uri("Images/traffic.jpg",
                                        UriKind.Relative));
      break;
    case 4:
      imageSource = new BitmapImage(new Uri("Images/underWater.jpg",
                                        UriKind.Relative));
      break;
  }

  if (imageSource != null)
  {
    this.CompleteImage.Source = imageSource;

    // Each of the 30 pieces needs to be filled with the right image
    foreach (Canvas piece in this.PiecesCanvas.Children)
      ((piece.Children[0] as Shape).Fill as ImageBrush).ImageSource =
        imageSource;
```

LISTING 42.2   Continued

```
    }
  }

  // Application bar handlers

  void PictureButton_Click(object sender, EventArgs e)
  {
    this.NavigationService.Navigate(new Uri("/CroppedPictureChooserPage.xaml",
      UriKind.Relative));
  }

  void StartOverButton_Click(object sender, EventArgs e)
  {
    if (MessageBox.Show("Are you sure you want to dismantle the puzzle and " +
        "start from scratch?", "Start over", MessageBoxButton.OKCancel)
        == MessageBoxResult.OK)
      StartOver();
  }

  void SolveButton_Click(object sender, EventArgs e)
  {
    if (MessageBox.Show("Do you give up? Are you sure you want the puzzle to "
        + "be solved for you?", "Solve", MessageBoxButton.OKCancel)
        != MessageBoxResult.OK)
      return;

    ShowAsSolved();
  }

  void InstructionsButton_Click(object sender, EventArgs e)
  {
    this.NavigationService.Navigate(new Uri("/InstructionsPage.xaml",
      UriKind.Relative));
  }

  void ApplicationBarMenuItem_Click(object sender, EventArgs e)
  {
    for (int i = 0; i < this.ApplicationBar.MenuItems.Count; i++)
    {
      // Set the persisted photo index to match the menu item index
      if (sender == this.ApplicationBar.MenuItems[i])
        Settings.PhotoIndex.Value = i;
    }
    RefreshPuzzleImage();
```

LISTING 42.2   Continued

```
      }
    }
}
```

Notes:

→ This app uses two settings defined in a separate `Settings.cs` file for remembering the user's chosen photo and for remembering the position of every puzzle piece:

```
public static class Settings
{
  public static Setting<int> PhotoIndex = new Setting<int>("PhotoIndex", 2);
  public static Setting<List<Point>> PieceOffsets =
    new Setting<List<Point>>("PieceOffsets", new List<Point>());
}
```

→ This app also uses many constants, defined as follows in a `Constants.cs` file:

```
public static class Constants
{
  public const int PUZZLE_WIDTH = 480;
  public const int PUZZLE_HEIGHT = 576;
  public const int PIECE_WIDTH = 96;
  public const int PIECE_HEIGHT = 96;
  public const int MAX_PIECE_WIDTH = 162;
  public const int SNAPPING_MARGIN = 15;
  public const int NEGATIVE_SCROLL_BOUNDARY = -1550;
  public const int TRAY_HORIZONTAL_SPACING = 110;
  public const int TRAY_VERTICAL_SPACING = 80;
  public const int TRAY_LEFT_MARGIN = 24;
  public const int TRAY_TOP_MARGIN = 590;
  public const int TRAY_2ND_ROW_HORIZONTAL_OFFSET = 50;
  public const int ON_TRAY_Y = 528;
}
```

→ The first time Jigsaw Puzzle is run, the pieces animate from their solved positions to a random ordering on the tray. (This condition is detected in `OnNavigatedTo` because the `PieceOffsets` list does not initially contain the same number of elements as pieces in `PiecesCanvas`.) This ordering of pieces on the tray is shown in Figure 42.4. Every other time, the pieces are placed exactly where they were previously left by reapplying their persisted `TranslateX` and `TranslateY` values.

FIGURE 42.4   The puzzle pieces are arranged on the tray once they animate away from their solved positions.

→ The three drag event handlers act differently depending on whether a puzzle piece is being dragged or the tray is being dragged. When the tray is dragged horizontally, we want it to scroll and reveal off-screen pieces. When a piece is dragged, it should move wherever the user's finger takes it.

→ The DragStarted event handler (GestureListener_DragStarted) determines which type of dragging is occurring and sets either isDraggingTray or isDraggingPiece. (This handler can be called in cases where neither is true, such as dragging on an empty upper part of the screen, because these handlers are attached to the whole page.)

DragStarted isn't raised as soon as a finger touches the screen and starts moving; the gesture listener waits for the finger to move more than 12 pixels away to ensure that the gesture is a drag rather than a tap, and to determine the primary direction of the drag. DragStartedGestureEventArgs exposes this primary direction as a Direction property that is either Horizontal or Vertical.

GestureListener_DragStarted leverages the Direction property to determine which kind of drag is happening. If the element reporting the event is the tray *and* the direction is horizontal, then it considers the gesture to be a tray drag. If a piece is being dragged horizontally and the vertical position of the piece visually makes it

look like it's on the tray, it also considers the gesture to be a tray drag. This is important to avoid the requirement that the tray can only be dragged on an empty spot.
If a piece is being dragged vertically, or if it's dragged in any direction far enough
from the tray, then it's considered to be a piece drag.

Although this scheme is easy to implement, users might find the requirement to
drag pieces off the tray in a mostly vertical fashion to be confusing and/or inconvenient. A more flexible approach would be to perform your own math and use a
wider angle range.

> ⚠ **The** Direction **property passed to drag events never changes until a new drag is initiated!**
>
> Although the Direction property exposed to DragStarted handlers is also exposed to
> DragDelta and DragCompleted handlers, its value never changes until the drag has completed
> and a new drag has started. This is true even if the actual direction of the finger motion changes
> to be completely vertical instead of horizontal, or vice versa. This makes it easy to implement
> panning or other motion that is locked to one axis, although it also means that detecting more
> flexible motion requires you to interpret the finger motion manually.
>
> In Jigsaw Puzzle, this fact can cause frustration if a user tries to drag a piece from the tray directly
> to its final position, yet the straight-line path is more horizontal than it is vertical. To help combat
> this, the instructions page explains that pieces must be dragged upward to leave the tray.

→ The DragDelta event exposes two more properties than DragStarted:
   HorizontalChange and VerticalChange. For tray dragging, the HorizontalChange
   value is passed to a ScrollTray helper method. This method provides the illusion of
   scrolling by manually updating the horizontal position of every piece whose vertical
   position makes it appear to be on the tray. Keeping all the pieces in the same canvas
   at all times (instead of moving pieces on the tray to a separate panel inside an
   actual scroll viewer) makes the logic throughout this page easier.

   For piece dragging, both HorizontalChange and VerticalChange are applied to the
   current piece's transform, and then the piece is snapped to one or two solved-piece
   boundary locations if it's close enough to a horizontal and/or vertical boundary.
   Ordinarily, the values of HorizontalChange and VerticalChange would be directly
   added to TranslateX and TranslateY, respectively, but this doesn't work well when
   snapping is done. Because each snap moves the piece by as much as 14 pixels away
   from its natural position, continued snapping would cause the piece to drift further
   away from the user's finger if we continued to add the HorizontalChange and
   VerticalChange values. Instead, by manually tracking the total cumulative distance
   from the beginning of the drag, the piece is returned to its natural position after it
   breaks free of a snapping boundary.

> **!** **The** `HorizontalChange` **and** `VerticalChange` **properties exposed by** `DragDelta` **are relative to the previous raising of** `DragDelta`**!**
>
> Unlike `PinchGestureEventArgs`, whose `DistanceRatio` and `TotalAngleDelta` properties are relative to the values when pinching or stretching started, the `HorizontalChange` and `VerticalChange` properties exposed by `DragDeltaGestureEventArgs` and `DragCompletedGestureEventArgs` do not accumulate as dragging proceeds.

→ The `DragCompleted` event exposes all the properties from `DragDelta` plus two more: `HorizontalVelocity` and `VerticalVelocity`. These values are the same ones exposed to the `Flick` event, and enable inertial flicking motion at the end of a drag. Just like in Chapter 40, "Darts," the velocity is scaled down and then used to continue the dragging motion a bit. This is done for tray dragging only, to make it better mimic a real scroll viewer. Therefore, only the horizontal component of the velocity is used. At the end of every drag action, the location of each piece is checked to see whether the puzzle has been solved. We know that the pieces are all in the correct spots if their transforms all have `TranslateX` and `TranslateY` values of zero.

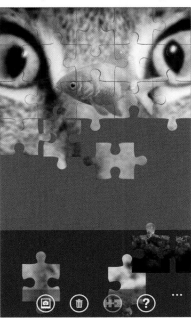

→ The "picture" and "instructions" button click handlers navigate to other pages, and the "start over" and "solve" button click handlers trigger animations that either move the pieces to random spots on the tray or to their solved positions. The solve animation is performed by the `ShowAsSolved` method, which animates each out-of-place piece to its correct position over the course of one second, spaced .3 seconds apart. The resulting effect smoothly fills in the pieces in row major order, as pictured in Figure 42.5.

FIGURE 42.5   The automatic solving animation makes the pieces float into place according to their order in the canvas.

The Cropped Picture Chooser Page

The cropped picture chooser page is responsible for launching the built-in photo chooser and then allowing the user to crop the chosen photo before returning to the main page.

Because the photo chooser can sometimes be slow to launch, and because decoding the chosen picture can be slow, this page shows a "loading" message during these actions. Figure 42.6 demonstrates the user flow through this page.

Waiting for the photo chooser to appear

Automatic navigation to the OS-provided photo chooser

Navigating back to the page and waiting for the chosen image to load

When the image loads, the cropping user interface is shown

The photo has been zoomed and panned

After pressing the done button, we return to the main page with the cropped picture now in use

FIGURE 42.6   The sequence of events when navigating to the cropped photo chooser page.

The User Interface

Listing 42.3 contains the XAML for this page.

LISTING 42.3   `CroppedPictureChooserPage.xaml`—The User Interface for Jigsaw Puzzle's Cropped Picture Chooser Page

```
<phone:PhoneApplicationPage x:Class="WindowsPhoneApp.CroppedPictureChooserPage"
    xmlns="http://schemas.microsoft.com/winfx/2006/xaml/presentation"
    xmlns:x="http://schemas.microsoft.com/winfx/2006/xaml"
    xmlns:phone="clr-namespace:Microsoft.Phone.Controls;assembly=Microsoft.Phone"
    xmlns:shell="clr-namespace:Microsoft.Phone.Shell;assembly=Microsoft.Phone"
    xmlns:toolkit="clr-namespace:Microsoft.Phone.Controls;
➥assembly=Microsoft.Phone.Controls.Toolkit"
```

LISTING 42.3   Continued

```
    FontFamily="{StaticResource PhoneFontFamilyNormal}"
    FontSize="{StaticResource PhoneFontSizeNormal}"
    Foreground="{StaticResource PhoneForegroundBrush}"
    SupportedOrientations="Portrait">

  <!-- The 2-button application bar, shown on return from the PhotoChooserTask -->
  <phone:PhoneApplicationPage.ApplicationBar>
    <shell:ApplicationBar Opacity="0" IsVisible="False" ForegroundColor="White">
      <shell:ApplicationBarIconButton Text="done"
        IconUri="/Shared/Images/appbar.done.png" Click="DoneButton_Click"/>
      <shell:ApplicationBarIconButton Text="cancel"
        IconUri="/Shared/Images/appbar.cancel.png" Click="CancelButton_Click"/>
    </shell:ApplicationBar>
  </phone:PhoneApplicationPage.ApplicationBar>

  <!-- Listen for drag events anywhere on the page -->
  <toolkit:GestureService.GestureListener>
    <toolkit:GestureListener DragDelta="GestureListener_DragDelta"
                             PinchStarted="GestureListener_PinchStarted"
                             PinchDelta="GestureListener_PinchDelta"/>
  </toolkit:GestureService.GestureListener>

  <!-- Prevent a zoomed-in photo from making the screen go blank -->
  <phone:PhoneApplicationPage.Clip>
    <RectangleGeometry Rect="0,0,480,800"/>
  </phone:PhoneApplicationPage.Clip>

  <Canvas Background="#443225">

    <!-- Shown on return from the PhotoChooserTask -->
    <Canvas x:Name="CropPanel" Visibility="Collapsed">
      <!-- Designate the puzzle boundary -->
      <Rectangle Fill="White" Canvas.Top="112" Width="480" Height="576"/>

      <!-- The canvas provides screen-centered zooming -->
      <Canvas Canvas.Top="112" Width="480" Height="576"
              RenderTransformOrigin=".5,.5">
        <Canvas.RenderTransform>
          <!-- For zooming -->
          <CompositeTransform x:Name="CanvasTransform"/>
        </Canvas.RenderTransform>
        <Image x:Name="Image" Stretch="None" CacheMode="BitmapCache">
          <Image.RenderTransform>
            <!-- For panning -->
```

LISTING 42.3   Continued

```
          <CompositeTransform x:Name="ImageTransform"/>
        </Image.RenderTransform>
      </Image>
    </Canvas>

    <!-- Top and bottom borders that let the image show through slightly -->
    <Rectangle Opacity=".8" Fill="#443225" Width="480" Height="112"/>
    <Rectangle Canvas.Top="688" Opacity=".8" Fill="#443225" Width="480"
               Height="112"/>

    <!-- The title and instructions -->
    <StackPanel Style="{StaticResource PhoneTitlePanelStyle}">
      <TextBlock Text="CROP PICTURE" Foreground="White"
                 Style="{StaticResource PhoneTextTitle0Style}"/>
      <TextBlock Foreground="White" TextWrapping="Wrap" Width="432">
        Pinch &amp; stretch your fingers to zoom.<LineBreak/>
        Drag to move the picture.
      </TextBlock>
    </StackPanel>
  </Canvas>

  <!-- Shown while launching the PhotoChooserTask -->
  <Canvas x:Name="LoadingPanel">
    <StackPanel Style="{StaticResource PhoneTitlePanelStyle}">
      <TextBlock x:Name="LoadingTextBlock" Text="LOADING..." Foreground="White"
                 Style="{StaticResource PhoneTextTitle0Style}" Width="432"
                 TextWrapping="Wrap"/>
    </StackPanel>
  </Canvas>
  </Canvas>
</phone:PhoneApplicationPage>
```

Notes:

→ Drag gestures (and pinch/stretch gestures) are detected with a page-level gesture listener, just like on the main page.

→ The white rectangle not only reveals the puzzle's dimensions if the picture doesn't completely cover the area, but it also ends up giving the puzzle a white background when this happens. This is demonstrated in Figure 42.7.

→ Two different transforms are used to make the user's gestures feel natural. Whereas drag gestures adjust ImageTransform much like the dragging of puzzle pieces on the main page, pinch and stretch gestures are applied to CanvasTransform. Because the canvas represents the puzzle area and it's marked with a centered render transform origin of (.5,.5), the user's gesture always zooms the image centered around the middle of the puzzle. If this were applied to the image instead, zooming would occur around the *image's* middle, which might be far off-screen as the image gets zoomed and panned.

→ Two subtle things on this page prevent its performance from being disastrous. The bitmap caching on the image makes the panning and zooming much smoother than it would be otherwise, as does the clip applied to the page. (The page's clip also prevents the entire screen from going blank if the photo is zoomed in to an extreme amount, caused by Silverlight failing to render a surface that is too big.)

The photo has been panned to reveal a white background

The white background appears in the puzzle

FIGURE 42.7   A white rectangle serves as the puzzle's background if the picture doesn't completely cover it.

 If an image has transparent regions, those regions are not hit-testable when used to fill a shape!

This app ensures that the picture used to fill the puzzle pieces never contains any transparency. Those transparent regions would not respond to any touch events, making it difficult or impossible to drag the affected pieces. Note that this is different behavior compared to giving an otherwise-rectangular element transparent regions with an opacity mask. With an opacity mask, the transparent regions are still hit-testable (just like an element marked with an opacity of 0).

Appropriate use of bitmap caching, covered in Chapter 19, "Animation Lab," can make a huge difference when it comes to zooming, panning, or otherwise manipulating a large element—even when the element in question is effectively already a bitmap. Be sure to experiment with different placements, however. In Listing 42.3, moving `CacheMode="BitmapCache"` to the parent canvas would preserve the smooth zooming, but it would make panning performance even worse than not using bitmap caching at all! That's because the ever-changing transform on the child image would constantly invalidate the cached canvas bitmap.

The Code-Behind

Listing 42.4 contains the code-behind for this page.

LISTING 42.4   `CroppedPictureChooserPage.xaml.cs`—The Code-Behind for Jigsaw Puzzle's Cropped Picture Chooser Page

```
using System;
using System.IO;
using System.Windows;
using System.Windows.Media;
using System.Windows.Media.Imaging;
using Microsoft.Phone;
using Microsoft.Phone.Controls;
using Microsoft.Phone.Tasks;

namespace WindowsPhoneApp
{
  public partial class CroppedPictureChooserPage : PhoneApplicationPage
  {
    bool loaded;
    double scaleWhenPinchStarted;

    public CroppedPictureChooserPage()
    {
      InitializeComponent();
      this.Loaded += CroppedPictureChooserPage_Loaded;
    }

    void CroppedPictureChooserPage_Loaded(object sender, RoutedEventArgs e)
    {
      if (this.loaded)
        return;

      this.loaded = true;

      // When navigating to this page in the forward direction only (from the
```

LISTING 42.4   Continued

```
    // main page or when reactiving the app), launch the photo chooser task
    Microsoft.Phone.Tasks.PhotoChooserTask task = new PhotoChooserTask();
    task.ShowCamera = true;
    task.Completed += delegate(object s, PhotoResult args)
    {
      if (args.TaskResult == TaskResult.OK)
      {
        WriteableBitmap imageSource = PictureDecoder.DecodeJpeg(
                                        args.ChosenPhoto);

        // Perform manual "uniform to fill" scaling by choosing the larger
        // of the two scales that make the image just fit in one dimension
        double scale = Math.Max(
            (double)Constants.PUZZLE_WIDTH / imageSource.PixelWidth,
            (double)Constants.PUZZLE_HEIGHT / imageSource.PixelHeight);
        this.CanvasTransform.ScaleX = this.CanvasTransform.ScaleY = scale;

        // Center the image in the puzzle
        this.ImageTransform.TranslateY =
          -(imageSource.PixelHeight - Constants.PUZZLE_HEIGHT) / 2;
        this.ImageTransform.TranslateX =
          -(imageSource.PixelWidth - Constants.PUZZLE_WIDTH) / 2;

        // Show the cropping user interface
        this.Image.Source = imageSource;
        this.LoadingPanel.Visibility = Visibility.Collapsed;
        this.CropPanel.Visibility = Visibility.Visible;
        this.ApplicationBar.IsVisible = true;
      }
      else
      {
        // The user cancelled from the photo chooser, but we can't automatically
        // navigate back right here, so update "LOADING..." with instructions
        this.LoadingTextBlock.Text =
          "Press the Back button again to return to the puzzle.";
      }
    };
    task.Show();
  }

  // Raised for single-finger dragging
  void GestureListener_DragDelta(object sender, DragDeltaGestureEventArgs e)
  {
    // Pan the image based on the drag
```

LISTING 42.4   Continued

```
    this.ImageTransform.TranslateX +=
      e.HorizontalChange / this.CanvasTransform.ScaleX;
    this.ImageTransform.TranslateY +=
      e.VerticalChange / this.CanvasTransform.ScaleY;
}


// Raised when two fingers touch the screen (likely to begin a pinch/stretch)
void GestureListener_PinchStarted(object sender,
  PinchStartedGestureEventArgs e)
{
  this.scaleWhenPinchStarted = this.CanvasTransform.ScaleX;
}


// Raised continually as either or both fingers move
void GestureListener_PinchDelta(object sender, PinchGestureEventArgs e)
{
  // The distance ratio is always relative to when the pinch/stretch started,
  // so be sure to apply it to the ORIGINAL zoom level, not the CURRENT
  double scale = this.scaleWhenPinchStarted * e.DistanceRatio;
  this.CanvasTransform.ScaleX = this.CanvasTransform.ScaleY = scale;
}


// Application bar handlers

void DoneButton_Click(object sender, EventArgs e)
{
  // Create a new bitmap with the puzzle's dimensions
  WriteableBitmap wb = new WriteableBitmap(Constants.PUZZLE_WIDTH,
                                           Constants.PUZZLE_HEIGHT);

  // Render the page's contents to the puzzle, but shift it upward
  // so only the region intended to be for the puzzle is used
  wb.Render(this, new TranslateTransform { Y = -112 });

  // We must explicitly tell the bitmap to draw its new contents
  wb.Invalidate();

  using (MemoryStream stream = new MemoryStream())
  {
    // Fill the stream with a JPEG representation of this bitmap
    wb.SaveJpeg(stream, Constants.PUZZLE_WIDTH, Constants.PUZZLE_HEIGHT,
      0 /* orientation */, 100 /* quality */);

    // Seek back to the beginning of the stream
```

LISTING 42.4 Continued

```
      stream.Seek(0, SeekOrigin.Begin);

      // Save the file to isolated storage.
      // This overwrites the file if it already exists.
      IsolatedStorageHelper.SaveFile("custom.jpg", stream);
    }

    // Indicate that the user has chosen to use a custom image
    Settings.PhotoIndex.Value = -1;

    // Return to the puzzle
    if (this.NavigationService.CanGoBack)
      this.NavigationService.GoBack();
  }

  void CancelButton_Click(object sender, EventArgs e)
  {
    // Don't do anything, just return to the puzzle
    if (this.NavigationService.CanGoBack)
      this.NavigationService.GoBack();
  }
}
}
```

Notes:

→ The `PhotoChooserTask` is used much like in Chapter 23, "Baby Milestones," and Chapter 39, "Paint." The image source returned by `PictureDecoder.DecodeJpeg` is a powerful subclass called `WriteableBitmap`. Inside `PhotoChooserTask`'s `Completed` event handler, `WriteableBitmap`'s `PixelWidth` and `PixelHeight` properties are leveraged to center the image and give it an appropriate initial scale to fit the puzzle's dimensions.

→ The `DragDelta` event handler and the `PinchStarted`/`PinchDelta` event handlers provide the most straightforward implementation of panning and zooming in this book.

Inside `DragDelta`, the `HorizontalChange` and `VerticalChange` values are directly added to the image transform each time; although they must be divided by any scale applied to the parent canvas so the distance that the image travels remains consistent. This direct application works well because the `TranslateX` and `TranslateY` are not changed through any other means, such as the snapping logic used on the main page.

The `PinchStarted` handler records the scale when two fingers touch the screen, arbitrarily choosing `ScaleX` because both `ScaleX` and `ScaleY` are always set to the same value. The `PinchDelta` handler multiplies the initial scale by the finger distance ratio and then applies it to the canvas transform.

→ The handler for the done button's click event, `DoneButton_Click`, leverages `WriteableBitmap`'s killer feature—the ability to capture the contents of any element

and write it to a JPEG file. A new `WriteableBitmap` is created with the puzzle's dimensions, and then `this` (the entire page) is rendered into it with a transform that shifts it 112 pixels upward. This is necessary to avoid rendering the page's header into the captured image. Figure 42.8 demonstrates what happens if `null` is passed for the second parameter of `Render`.

After refreshing the bitmap with a call to `Invalidate`, `SaveJpeg` writes the contents in JPEG format to a memory stream which can then be written to isolated storage. This is done with an `IsolatedStorageHelper` class that is identical to the one used in Chapter 23, but without the caching behavior (because the same filename is used each time, and the small file size makes it quick to retrieve).

FIGURE 42.8   If the page is rendered to the puzzle image from its top-left corner, the page header becomes part of the puzzle!

If you want to take a screenshot of your app for your marketplace submission on a real phone rather than the emulator, you can temporarily put code in your page that captures the screen and saves it to your pictures library as follows:

```
void CaptureScreen()
{
  // Create a new bitmap with the page's dimensions
  WriteableBitmap wb = new WriteableBitmap((int)this.ActualWidth,
                                           (int)this.ActualHeight);

  // Render the page's contents with no transform applied
```

```
wb.Render(this, null);

// We must explicitly tell the bitmap to draw its new contents
wb.Invalidate();

using (MemoryStream stream = new MemoryStream())
{
  // Fill the stream with a JPEG representation of this bitmap
  wb.SaveJpeg(stream, (int)this.ActualWidth, (int)this.ActualHeight,
    0 /* orientation */, 100 /* quality */);

  // Seek back to the beginning of the stream
  stream.Seek(0, SeekOrigin.Begin);

  // Requires referencing Microsoft.Xna.Framework.dll
  // and the ID_CAP_MEDIALIB capability, and only works
  // when the phone is not connected to Zune
  new Microsoft.Xna.Framework.Media.MediaLibrary().SavePicture(
    "screenshot.jpg", stream);
}
}
```

Once there, you can sync it to your desktop with Zune to retrieve the photo in its full resolution. This has a few important limitations, however:

→ It doesn't capture parts of the user interface outside of the Silverlight visual tree—the application bar, status bar, and message boxes.

→ It doesn't capture any popups, even ones that are attached to an element on the page.

→ It doesn't capture any WebBrowser instances.

→ It doesn't capture any MediaElement instances.

Also, you need to determine a way to invoke this code without impacting what you're capturing.

Listing 42.4 doesn't make any attempt to preserve the page's state in the face of deactivation and reactivation; it simply relaunches the photo chooser. There are a few strategies for preserving the state of this page. The most natural would be to persist the image to a separate temporary file in isolated storage, along with values in page state that remember the current zoom and panning values.

What's the difference between detecting dragging with gesture listener drag events versus using mouse down, mouse move, and mouse up events?

One major difference is that the drag events are only raised when one finger is in contact with the screen. With the mouse events (or with the multi-touch `FrameReported` event), you can base dragging on the primary finger and simply ignore additional touch points. This may or may not be a good thing, depending on your app. Because the preceding chapter uses the mouse events for panning, it gives the user the ability to do zooming and panning as a combined gesture, which mimics the behavior of the built-in Maps app. In Jigsaw Puzzle's cropped photo chooser page, on the other hand, the user must lift their second finger if they wish to pan right after zooming the picture.

Another difference is that the drag events are not raised until the gesture listener is sure that a drag is occurring, e.g. one finger has made contact with the screen and has already moved a little bit. In contrast, the mouse move event is raised as soon as the finger moves *at all*. For Jigsaw Puzzle, the delayed behavior of the drag events is beneficial for helping to avoid accidental dragging.

A clear benefit of the drag events, if applicable to your app, is that the finger velocity at the end of the gesture is exposed to your code. However, you could still get this information when using the mouse approach if you also attach a handler to gesture listener's `Flick` event. The `Direction` property exposed to the drag events, discussed earlier, also enables interesting behavior that is tedious to replicate on your own.

The Finished Product

The menu with included puzzle pictures

The Statue of Liberty puzzle

The Traffic puzzle

SPIN THE BOTTLE!

The Spin the Bottle! app enables you to play the classic kissing game even if you don't have a bottle handy. In this game, people sit in a circle and take turns spinning the bottle. When someone spins, he or she must kiss whomever the bottle ends up pointing toward. Even if you have no plans to play the game, you could still use this app as a fun time-waster. You could even find work-related applications for this, such as using it to assign tasks to your team members!

This app introduces a new gesture—the rotation gesture—which is a two-finger twist. It also simulates inertia (and friction), so the bottle keeps spinning once the fingers have left the screen and then gradually slows to a halt. The faster the fingers twist before releasing, the longer the bottle will continue to spin. This simulation of what happens in the real world is essential for this kind of app, otherwise the user could control exactly where the bottle would point!

The User Interface

This app contains only one page. Its user interface, shown to the right, is just an image of a bottle surrounded by two text blocks. Listing 43.1 contains the XAML.

LISTING 43.1   `MainPage.xaml`—The User Interface for Spin the Bottle!'s Main Page

```xml
<phone:PhoneApplicationPage x:Class="WindowsPhoneApp.MainPage"
    xmlns="http://schemas.microsoft.com/winfx/2006/xaml/presentation"
    xmlns:x="http://schemas.microsoft.com/winfx/2006/xaml"
    xmlns:phone="clr-namespace:Microsoft.Phone.Controls;assembly=Microsoft.Phone"
    xmlns:toolkit="clr-namespace:Microsoft.Phone.Controls;
➥assembly=Microsoft.Phone.Controls.Toolkit"
    SupportedOrientations="Portrait">

  <!-- Add two storyboards to the page's resource dictionary -->
  <phone:PhoneApplicationPage.Resources>
    <!-- The initial spin to smoothly match the angle when the two fingers first
         make contact with the screen -->
    <Storyboard x:Name="SpinStoryboard" Storyboard.TargetName="BottleTransform"
                Storyboard.TargetProperty="Angle">
      <DoubleAnimation x:Name="SpinAnimation" Duration="0:0:.2"/>
    </Storyboard>

    <!-- The inertia-simulating storyboard, whose strength is based on the
         velocity of the fingers -->
    <Storyboard x:Name="InertiaStoryboard" Storyboard.TargetName="BottleTransform"
                Storyboard.TargetProperty="Angle">
      <DoubleAnimation x:Name="InertiaAnimation">
        <DoubleAnimation.EasingFunction>
          <!-- Simulates drag -->
          <PowerEase Power="7"/>
        </DoubleAnimation.EasingFunction>
      </DoubleAnimation>
    </Storyboard>
  </phone:PhoneApplicationPage.Resources>

  <!-- Allow the rotate gesture anywhere on the page -->
  <toolkit:GestureService.GestureListener>
    <toolkit:GestureListener PinchStarted="GestureListener_PinchStarted"
                        PinchDelta="GestureListener_PinchDelta"
                        PinchCompleted="GestureListener_PinchCompleted"/>
  </toolkit:GestureService.GestureListener>

  <!-- The explicit background is important for detecting the gesture anywhere -->
  <Canvas Background="Transparent">
    <!-- The title -->
    <TextBlock Canvas.Left="-3" Canvas.Top="74" FontFamily="Segoe WP Black"
               FontSize="80" Foreground="#2EA538" LineHeight="58"
               LineStackingStrategy="BlockLineHeight">
      <TextBlock.RenderTransform>
```

LISTING 43.1   Continued

```
        <RotateTransform Angle="-10"/>
      </TextBlock.RenderTransform>
      SPIN THE<LineBreak/>BOTTLE!
    </TextBlock>

    <!-- Instructions -->
    <TextBlock Canvas.Left="-5" Canvas.Top="780" FontFamily="Segoe WP Black"
               FontSize="34" Foreground="#2EA538" Width="480" TextWrapping="Wrap"
               TextAlignment="Right" LineHeight="26"
               LineStackingStrategy="BlockLineHeight">
      <TextBlock.RenderTransform>
        <RotateTransform Angle="-10"/>
      </TextBlock.RenderTransform>
      DO A TWO-FINGERED SPIN AS FORCEFULLY AS POSSIBLE!
    </TextBlock>

    <!-- The bottle -->
    <Image Canvas.Left="166" Canvas.Top="160" Source="Images/bottle.png"
           Width="148" Height="480" RenderTransformOrigin=".5,.5">
      <Image.RenderTransform>
        <!-- The transform's angle is the target of both storyboards
             plus direct manipulation from code-behind -->
        <RotateTransform x:Name="BottleTransform"/>
      </Image.RenderTransform>
    </Image>
  </Canvas>
</phone:PhoneApplicationPage>
```

Notes:

→ The two storyboards are customized from code-behind before they are started. The inertia storyboard uses a PowerEase easing function to simulate friction by gradually slowing down the animation toward the end.

→ To detect the rotate gesture, this app uses a gesture listener to detect all three pinch/stretch events. After all, a two-finger pinch/stretch gesture is very similar to the desired rotate gesture. The code must simply pay attention to the angle formed by the two fingers rather than the distance between them.

→ This is the perfect kind of app for the gesture listener, because there are no controls on the page that could be impacted by its use.

→ The root canvas is given a transparent background, which is important for ensuring that the entire screen is hit-testable.

The Code-Behind

Listing 43.2 contains the code-behind for the main page.

LISTING 43.2   `MainPage.xaml.cs`—The Code-Behind for Spin the Bottle!'s Main Page

```
using System;
using Microsoft.Phone.Controls;

namespace WindowsPhoneApp
{
  public partial class MainPage : PhoneApplicationPage
  {
    double startingAngle;
    double previousDelta;
    DateTime previousTime;

    public MainPage()
    {
      InitializeComponent();
    }

    void GestureListener_PinchStarted(object sender,
                                      PinchStartedGestureEventArgs e)
    {
      // Normalize the current angle, which can get quite large
      // or small after the inertia animation
      this.BottleTransform.Angle %= 360;

      // Reset the velocity-tracking variables
      this.previousDelta = 0;
      this.previousTime = DateTime.Now;

      // Rather than instantly jump to the angle of the fingers, smoothly
      // animate to that angle
      this.SpinAnimation.To = startingAngle = e.Angle + 90;
      this.SpinStoryboard.Begin();
    }

    void GestureListener_PinchDelta(object sender, PinchGestureEventArgs e)
    {
      // Directly update the angle of the bottle, as this should be a small
      // incremental change
      this.BottleTransform.Angle = startingAngle + e.TotalAngleDelta;

      // Every 1/10th of a second, record the current delta and time
```

LISTING 43.2   Continued

```
    if ((DateTime.Now - this.previousTime).TotalSeconds > .1)
    {
      this.previousDelta = e.TotalAngleDelta;
      this.previousTime = DateTime.Now;
    }
  }

  void GestureListener_PinchCompleted(object sender, PinchGestureEventArgs e)
  {
    // Now compare the values from ~.1 second ago to the current values to
    // get the rotation velocity at the moment the fingers release the bottle
    double distance = e.TotalAngleDelta - this.previousDelta;
    double time = (DateTime.Now - this.previousTime).TotalSeconds;

    if (distance == 0 || time == 0)
      return;

    double velocity = distance / time;

    // Adjust the inertia animation so the length of the remaining spin
    // animation is proportional to the velocity
    this.InertiaAnimation.Duration =
      TimeSpan.FromMilliseconds(Math.Abs(velocity));

    // Choose a number of spins proportional to the length of the animation
    this.InertiaAnimation.By = 360 *
      Math.Pow(this.InertiaAnimation.Duration.TimeSpan.TotalSeconds, 5);

    // Make sure the bottle spins in the appropriate direction
    if (velocity < 0)
      this.InertiaAnimation.By *= -1;

    this.InertiaStoryboard.Begin();
    }
  }
}
```

Notes:

→ Other than the constructor, the code-behind simply consists of the three pinch/stretch event handlers.

→ In GestureListener_PinchStarted, the handy Angle property on PinchStartedGestureEventArgs is used instead of Distance. To make the angle of the bottle match the angle represented by the two fingers, the code could have simply set BottleTransform's Angle to this value. However, to avoid a jarring experience, this method uses SpinAnimation to quickly animate from the bottle's current angle to the new angle.

→ GestureListener_PinchDelta ignores the familiar DistanceRatio property passed via PinchGestureEventArgs and instead uses its TotalAngleDelta property. Adding this to the angle reported in the PinchStarted event gives an angle that matches the current position of the fingers. (The bottle ends up pointing toward the second of the two fingers.) Note that this method *does* directly set BottleTransform's Angle to this value rather than animate it, but this is perfectly acceptable because the angle only changes by a small amount between PinchStarted, PinchDelta, and subsequent PinchDelta events.

→ This app's inertia simulation is different from what was done in the preceding chapter because this app manually calculates the final velocity. Every tenth of a second, GestureListener_PinchDelta records the current time and the current angle delta. When the PinchCompleted event is raised, GestureListener_PinchCompleted again captures the current time and angle delta and then compares them to the previously recorded values to determine the velocity at the point of release. (GestureListener_PinchDelta doesn't record the values every time because the last angle delta passed to PinchDelta matches the angle delta passed to PinchCompleted, so it would always give a velocity of zero!)

→ The absolute velocity value is not very meaningful, but its relative size and direction are. The mapping of the velocity value to InertiaAnimation's duration and number of spins was derived by trial and error, looking for a realistic final effect.

The Finished Product

Under the light theme

'Round and 'round it goes…

…where it stops, nobody knows!

BOXING GLOVE

Boxing Glove is an app for people who feel like being immature (or people who simply *are* immature). With it, you can throw punches into the air and hear a variety of punching/groaning sound effects. The punching sound effects occur right when you hit your imaginary target.

Boxing Glove supports right- or left-handed punching, and has a few entertaining features, such as a button that makes a "ding ding ding" bell sound as if to signify the start of a fight.

To provide the effect of making a punching sound at the appropriate time, this app uses the phone's accelerometer.

 This app, like each remaining app in this book, requires access to your phone's sensors (`ID_CAP_SENSORS`). In version 7 of the Windows Phone OS, the accelerometer is the only applicable sensor.

The Accelerometer

Several times a second, the phone's accelerometer reports the direction and magnitude of the total force being applied to the phone. This force is expressed with three values—X, Y, and Z—where X is horizontal, Y is vertical, and Z is perpendicular to the screen. This is illustrated in Figure 44.1.

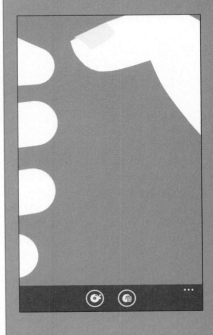

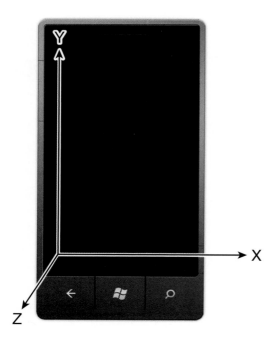

FIGURE 44.1   The three accelerometer dimensions, relative to the phone screen.

The magnitude of each value is a multiplier of g (the gravitational force on the surface of Earth). Each value is restricted to a range from -2 to 2. If the phone is resting flat on a table with the screen up, the values reported for X and Y are roughly zero, and the value of Z is roughly -1 (1 g into the screen toward the ground). That's because the only force being applied to the phone in this situation is gravity. By shifting the phone's angle and orientation and then keeping it roughly still, the values of X, Y, and Z reveal which way is down in the real world thanks to the ever-present force of gravity. When you abruptly move or shake the phone, the X, Y, and Z values are able to reveal this activity as well.

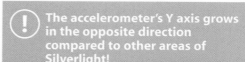

The accelerometer's Y axis grows in the opposite direction compared to other areas of Silverlight!

As shown in Figure 44.1, the Y axis grows upward rather than downward. This matches XNA's coordinate system, but not Silverlight's. You can compare Figure 44.1 to Figure 17.2 in Chapter 17, "Pick a Card Magic Trick."

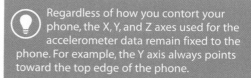

Regardless of how you contort your phone, the X, Y, and Z axes used for the accelerometer data remain fixed to the phone. For example, the Y axis always points toward the top edge of the phone.

To get the accelerometer data, you create an instance of the `Accelerometer` class from the `Microsoft.Devices.Sensors` namespace in the `Microsoft.Devices.Sensors` assembly.

This assembly is not referenced by Windows Phone projects by default, so you must add it via the Add Reference dialog in Visual Studio.

The `Accelerometer` class exposes `Start` and `Stop` methods and—most importantly—a `ReadingChanged` event. This event gets raised many times a second (after `Start` is called) and reports the data via properties on the event-args parameter passed to handlers. These properties are X, Y, Z, and `Timestamp`. The physical accelerometer is always running; `Start` and `Stop` simply start/stop the data reporting to your app.

Sounds pretty simple, right? The class is indeed simple although, as you'll see in the remaining chapters, interpreting the data in a satisfactory way can be complicated.

The User Interface

Boxing Glove has a main page, a settings page, an instructions page, and an about page. The latter two pages aren't interesting and therefore aren't shown in this chapter, but Listing 44.1 contains the XAML for the main page. The page, with its application bar menu expanded, is shown in Figure 44.2.

> To get the best performance and battery life, it's good to stop the accelerometer data reporting when you don't need the data and then restart it when you do.

FIGURE 44.2   The main page, with its application bar menu expanded.

LISTING 44.1   `MainPage.xaml`—The User Interface for Boxing Glove's Main Page

```
<phone:PhoneApplicationPage
    x:Class="WindowsPhoneApp.MainPage"
    xmlns="http://schemas.microsoft.com/winfx/2006/xaml/presentation"
    xmlns:x="http://schemas.microsoft.com/winfx/2006/xaml"
    xmlns:phone="clr-namespace:Microsoft.Phone.Controls;assembly=Microsoft.Phone"
    xmlns:shell="clr-namespace:Microsoft.Phone.Shell;assembly=Microsoft.Phone"
    SupportedOrientations="Portrait">

  <!-- The application bar, with two buttons and three menu items -->
  <phone:PhoneApplicationPage.ApplicationBar>
    <shell:ApplicationBar Opacity=".5">
```

LISTING 44.1   Continued

```
        <shell:ApplicationBarIconButton Text="ring bell"
                IconUri="/Images/appbar.bell.png" Click="RingBellButton_Click" />
        <shell:ApplicationBarIconButton Text="switch hand"
                IconUri="/Images/appbar.leftHand.png"
                Click="SwitchHandButton_Click" />
        <shell:ApplicationBar.MenuItems>
          <shell:ApplicationBarMenuItem Text="instructions"
                                        Click="InstructionsMenuItem_Click"/>
          <shell:ApplicationBarMenuItem Text="settings"
                                        Click="SettingsMenuItem_Click"/>
          <shell:ApplicationBarMenuItem Text="about"
                                        Click="AboutMenuItem_Click"/>
        </shell:ApplicationBar.MenuItems>
      </shell:ApplicationBar>
    </phone:PhoneApplicationPage.ApplicationBar>

    <Border Background="{StaticResource PhoneAccentBrush}">
      <Image Source="Images/hand.png" RenderTransformOrigin=".5,.5">
        <Image.RenderTransform>
          <!-- ScaleX is 1 for right-handed or -1 for left-handed -->
          <CompositeTransform x:Name="ImageTransform" ScaleX="1"/>
        </Image.RenderTransform>
      </Image>
    </Border>
</phone:PhoneApplicationPage>
```

Besides the application bar, this page basically contains an image that instructs the user how to hold the phone. The background takes on the theme accent color, so the screen in Figure 44.2 is from a phone whose accent color is set to red.

The application bar contains a button for performing a "ding ding ding" bell sound on demand (to mimic the start of a fight in a boxing ring), and a button for swapping between right-handed mode and left-handed mode. The composite transform flips the image horizontally (in code-behind) when left-handed mode is in use.

The Code-Behind

Listing 44.2 contains the code-behind for the main page. It makes use of two persisted settings defined in a separate Settings.cs file as follows:

```
public static class Settings
{
  public static readonly Setting<bool> IsRightHanded =
    new Setting<bool>("IsRightHanded", true);
  public static readonly Setting<double> Threshold =
```

```
    new Setting<double>("Threshold", 1.5);
}
```

LISTING 44.2   `MainPage.xaml.cs`—The Code-Behind for Boxing Glove's Main Page

```
using System;
using System.Windows;
using System.Windows.Media;
using System.Windows.Navigation;
using Microsoft.Devices.Sensors;
using Microsoft.Phone.Controls;
using Microsoft.Phone.Shell;

namespace WindowsPhoneApp
{
  public partial class MainPage : PhoneApplicationPage
  {
    Accelerometer accelerometer;
    IApplicationBarIconButton switchHandButton;
    DateTimeOffset acceleratingQuicklyForwardTime = DateTimeOffset.MinValue;
    Random random = new Random();

    double currentThreshold;

    public MainPage()
    {
      InitializeComponent();
      this.switchHandButton = this.ApplicationBar.Buttons[1]
                              as IApplicationBarIconButton;

      // Initialize the accelerometer
      this.accelerometer = new Accelerometer();
      this.accelerometer.ReadingChanged += Accelerometer_ReadingChanged;

      SoundEffects.Initialize();
    }

    protected override void OnNavigatedTo(NavigationEventArgs e)
    {
      base.OnNavigatedTo(e);

      // Start the accelerometer
      try
      {
        this.accelerometer.Start();
```

LISTING 44.2   Continued

```
    }
    catch
    {
      MessageBox.Show(
      "Unable to start your accelerometer. Please try running this app again.",
      "Accelerometer Error", MessageBoxButton.OK);
    }

    // Also ensures the threshold is updated on return from settings page
    UpdateForCurrentHandedness();
  }

  protected override void OnNavigatedFrom(NavigationEventArgs e)
  {
    base.OnNavigatedFrom(e);

    // Stop the accelerometer
    try
    {
      this.accelerometer.Stop();
    }
    catch { /* Nothing to do */ }
  }

  // Process data coming from the accelerometer
  void Accelerometer_ReadingChanged(object sender,
                                    AccelerometerReadingEventArgs e)
  {
    // Only pay attention to large-enough magnitudes in the X dimension
    if (Math.Abs(e.X) < Math.Abs(this.currentThreshold))
      return;

    // See if the force is in the same direction as the threshold
    // (forward punching motion)
    if (e.X * this.currentThreshold > 0)
    {
      // Forward acceleration
      this.acceleratingQuicklyForwardTime = e.Timestamp;
    }
    else if (e.Timestamp - this.acceleratingQuicklyForwardTime
             < TimeSpan.FromSeconds(.2))
    {
      // This is large backward force shortly after the forward force.
      // Time to make the punching noise!
```

LISTING 44.2   Continued

```
      this.acceleratingQuicklyForwardTime = DateTimeOffset.MinValue;

      // We're on a different thread, so transition to the UI thread.
      // This is a requirement for playing the sound effect.
      this.Dispatcher.BeginInvoke(delegate()
      {
        switch (this.random.Next(0, 4))
        {
          case 0: SoundEffects.Punch1.Play(); break;
          case 1: SoundEffects.Punch2.Play(); break;
          case 2: SoundEffects.Punch3.Play(); break;
          case 3: SoundEffects.Punch4.Play(); break;
        }

        switch (this.random.Next(0, 10)) // Only grunt some of the time
        {
          case 0: SoundEffects.Grunt1.Play(); break;
          case 1: SoundEffects.Grunt2.Play(); break;
          case 2: SoundEffects.Grunt3.Play(); break;
        }
      });
    }
  }

  void UpdateForCurrentHandedness()
  {
    this.currentThreshold = (Settings.IsRightHanded.Value ?
                              Settings.Threshold.Value :
                              -Settings.Threshold.Value);

    this.ImageTransform.ScaleX = (Settings.IsRightHanded.Value ? 1 : -1);

    // Show the opposite hand on the application bar button
    if (Settings.IsRightHanded.Value)
      this.switchHandButton.IconUri = new Uri("/Images/appbar.leftHand.png",
                                      UriKind.Relative);
    else
      this.switchHandButton.IconUri = new Uri("/Images/appbar.rightHand.png",
                                      UriKind.Relative);
  }

  // Application bar handlers

  void RingBellButton_Click(object sender, EventArgs e)
```

LISTING 44.2   Continued

```
    {
      SoundEffects.DingDingDing.Play();
    }

    void SwitchHandButton_Click(object sender, EventArgs e)
    {
      Settings.IsRightHanded.Value = !Settings.IsRightHanded.Value;
      UpdateForCurrentHandedness();
    }

    void InstructionsMenuItem_Click(object sender, EventArgs e)
    {
      this.NavigationService.Navigate(new Uri("/InstructionsPage.xaml",
                                      UriKind.Relative));
    }

    void SettingsMenuItem_Click(object sender, EventArgs e)
    {
      this.NavigationService.Navigate(new Uri("/SettingsPage.xaml",
                                      UriKind.Relative));
    }

    void AboutMenuItem_Click(object sender, EventArgs e)
    {
      this.NavigationService.Navigate(new Uri("/AboutPage.xaml",
                                      UriKind.Relative));
    }
  }
}
```

Notes:

→ The constructor contains the code for initializing the accelerometer. It constructs an instance of Accelerometer and attaches a handler to its ReadingChanged event. The SoundEffects class, defined in Listing 44.3, is also initialized.

→ OnNavigatedTo contains the code for starting the accelerometer, and OnNavigatedTo stops it. If it weren't stopped, the handler would still be called (and the sound effects would still be made) while the main page is on the back stack. This would happen when the user visits the settings, instructions, or about pages. Leaving the accelerometer running would not be a problem, and may even be desirable for some apps. However, Listing 44.1 stops it to avoid two threads potentially reading/writing the threshold variable at the same time, as discussed in a later sidebar.

The calls to `Accelerometer.Start` and `Accelerometer.Stop` can throw an exception!

This can happen at development-time if you omit the `ID_CAP_SENSORS` capability from your app manifest. For a published app in the marketplace (which automatically gets the appropriate capability), this should not happen unless you have previously called the `Accelerometer` instance's `Dispose` method. Of course, there's not much that many accelerometer-based apps can do when the accelerometer fails to start, so Boxing Glove simply instructs to user to try closing and reopening the app and hope for the best.

→ Inside `Accelerometer_ReadingChanged`, the handler for the `ReadingChanged` event, only two properties of the `AccelerometerReadingEventArgs` instance are examined: `X` and `Timestamp`. The algorithm is as follows: If the app detects a strong forward horizontal force followed quickly by a strong backward horizontal force, it's time to make a punching sound. Making the sound when the forward force is detected isn't good enough, because the sound would be made too early. The sound should occur when the punching motion *stops* (i.e. hits the imaginary target of the punch). The detected backward force does not result from the phone being moved backward, but rather from the fast deceleration that occurs when the user stops their flying fist in mid-air.

→ The definition of "strong" used by `Accelerometer_ReadingChanged`'s algorithm is determined by a threshold that is configurable by the user on the settings page. The absolute value of the threshold ranges from almost 0 (.1) to almost 2 (1.9). The sign of the threshold depends on whether the app is in right-handed mode or left-handed mode. In right-handed mode, forward motion means pushing to phone toward its left, so the threshold of forward force is negative. In left-handed mode, forward motion means pushing the phone toward its right, so the threshold of forward force is positive. This adjustment is made inside `UpdateForCurrentHandedness`.

→ When it's time to make a punching noise, the sound is randomly chosen, potentially along with a randomly chosen grunting sound.

→ The `Timestamp` property passed to `ReadingChanged` event handlers is not a `DateTime`, but rather a `DateTimeOffset` that captures the precise point in time. See Chapter 21, "Passwords & Secrets," for the difference between `DateTime` and `DateTimeOffset`.

 The accelerometer's `ReadingChanged` event is raised on a non-UI thread!

This is great for processing the data without creating a bottleneck on the UI thread, but it does mean that you must explicitly transition to the UI thread before performing any work that requires it. This includes updating any UI elements or, as in this app, playing a sound effect. Listing 44.2 uses the page dispatcher's `BeginInvoke` method to play the sound effect on the UI thread.

> Although you can start the accelerometer from a page's constructor, it's normally better to wait until an event such as Loaded. That's because starting it within the constructor could cause the ReadingChanged event to be raised earlier than when you're prepared to handle it. For example, it can be raised before (or during) the deserialization of persisted settings, causing a failure if a setting is accessed in the event handler. It can be raised before the CompositionTarget.Rendering event is raised, which would be a problem if the implementation of SoundEffects (shown in the next listing) waited for the first Rendering event to call XNA's FrameworkDispatcher.Update method.
>
> Boxing Glove chooses to start the accelerometer in OnNavigatedTo and stop it in OnNavigatedFrom so the ReadingChanged event-handler thread doesn't try to access the threshold member while the call to UpdateForCurrentHandedness inside OnNavigatedTo potentially updates it on the UI thread.

The SoundEffects class used by Listing 44.2 is shown in Listing 44.3. It encapsulates the work of setting up the sound effects, with code similar to the apps from Part V, "Audio & Video."

LISTING 44.3   SoundEffects.cs—Initializes and Exposes Boxing Glove's Eight Sound Effects

```
using System;
using System.Windows.Resources;
using Microsoft.Xna.Framework.Audio; // For SoundEffect

namespace WindowsPhoneApp
{
  public static class SoundEffects
  {
    public static void Initialize()
    {
      StreamResourceInfo info;

      info = App.GetResourceStream(new Uri("Audio/punch1.wav", UriKind.Relative));
      Punch1 = SoundEffect.FromStream(info.Stream);

      info = App.GetResourceStream(new Uri("Audio/punch2.wav", UriKind.Relative));
      Punch2 = SoundEffect.FromStream(info.Stream);

      info = App.GetResourceStream(new Uri("Audio/punch3.wav", UriKind.Relative));
      Punch3 = SoundEffect.FromStream(info.Stream);

      info = App.GetResourceStream(new Uri("Audio/punch4.wav", UriKind.Relative));
      Punch4 = SoundEffect.FromStream(info.Stream);

      info = App.GetResourceStream(new Uri("Audio/grunt1.wav", UriKind.Relative));
      Grunt1 = SoundEffect.FromStream(info.Stream);
```

LISTING 44.3   Continued

```
    info = App.GetResourceStream(new Uri("Audio/grunt2.wav", UriKind.Relative));
    Grunt2 = SoundEffect.FromStream(info.Stream);

    info = App.GetResourceStream(new Uri("Audio/grunt3.wav", UriKind.Relative));
    Grunt3 = SoundEffect.FromStream(info.Stream);

    info = App.GetResourceStream(new Uri("Audio/dingDingDing.wav",
                                 UriKind.Relative));
    DingDingDing = SoundEffect.FromStream(info.Stream);

    CompositionTarget.Rendering += delegate(object sender, EventArgs e)
    {
      // Required for XNA Sound Effect API to work
      Microsoft.Xna.Framework.FrameworkDispatcher.Update();
    };

    // Call also once at the beginning
    Microsoft.Xna.Framework.FrameworkDispatcher.Update();
  }

  public static SoundEffect Punch1 { get; private set; }
  public static SoundEffect Punch2 { get; private set; }
  public static SoundEffect Punch3 { get; private set; }
  public static SoundEffect Punch4 { get; private set; }
  public static SoundEffect Grunt1 { get; private set; }
  public static SoundEffect Grunt2 { get; private set; }
  public static SoundEffect Grunt3 { get; private set; }
  public static SoundEffect DingDingDing { get; private set; }
  }
}
```

The Settings Page

The settings page, shown in Figure 44.3, contains a slider and a reset button for adjusting the threshold value from .1 to 1.9. The XAML is shown in Listing 44.4 and its code-behind is in Listing 44.5.

> Because of hardware variations between different phone models (or even among the same model, depending on wear and tear), apps that use the accelerometer should often enable the user to adjust or otherwise calibrate the interpretation of the raw data. Chapter 47, "Moo Can," shows how to support calibration more generically than the threshold adjustment enabled by Boxing Glove's settings page.

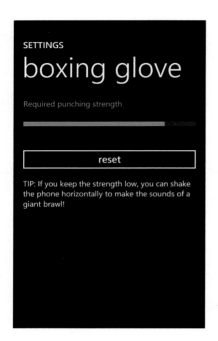

FIGURE 44.3   The settings page enables the user to adjust the accelerometer threshold, described as "required punching strength."

LISTING 44.4   `SettingsPage.xaml`—The User Interface for Boxing Glove's Settings Page

```
<phone:PhoneApplicationPage
    x:Class="WindowsPhoneApp.SettingsPage" x:Name="Page"
    xmlns="http://schemas.microsoft.com/winfx/2006/xaml/presentation"
    xmlns:x="http://schemas.microsoft.com/winfx/2006/xaml"
    xmlns:phone="clr-namespace:Microsoft.Phone.Controls;assembly=Microsoft.Phone"
    xmlns:shell="clr-namespace:Microsoft.Phone.Shell;assembly=Microsoft.Phone"
    xmlns:local="clr-namespace:WindowsPhoneApp"
    FontFamily="{StaticResource PhoneFontFamilyNormal}"
    FontSize="{StaticResource PhoneFontSizeNormal}"
    Foreground="{StaticResource PhoneForegroundBrush}"
    SupportedOrientations="PortraitOrLandscape"
    shell:SystemTray.IsVisible="True">
  <Grid Background="{StaticResource PhoneBackgroundBrush}">
    <Grid.RowDefinitions>
      <RowDefinition Height="Auto"/>
      <RowDefinition Height="*"/>
    </Grid.RowDefinitions>

    <!-- The standard settings header -->
    <StackPanel Grid.Row="0" Style="{StaticResource PhoneTitlePanelStyle}">
```

LISTING 44.4   Continued

```xml
      <TextBlock Text="SETTINGS" Style="{StaticResource PhoneTextTitle0Style}"/>
      <TextBlock Text="boxing glove"
                 Style="{StaticResource PhoneTextTitle1Style}"/>
    </StackPanel>

    <ScrollViewer Grid.Row="1">
      <StackPanel Margin="{StaticResource PhoneMargin}">
        <TextBlock Text="Required punching strength"
                   Foreground="{StaticResource PhoneSubtleBrush}"
                   Margin="{StaticResource PhoneMargin}"/>
        <Slider x:Name="StrengthSlider" Minimum=".1" Maximum="1.9"
                LargeChange=".1"
                Value="{Binding Threshold, Mode=TwoWay, ElementName=Page}"/>
        <Button Content="reset" Click="ResetButton_Click"
                local:Tilt.IsEnabled="True"/>
        <TextBlock TextWrapping="Wrap" Margin="{StaticResource PhoneMargin}"
                   Text="…"/>
      </StackPanel>
    </ScrollViewer>
  </Grid>
</phone:PhoneApplicationPage>
```

LISTING 44.5   `SettingsPage.xaml.cs`—The Code-Behind for Boxing Glove's Settings Page

```csharp
using System.Windows;
using Microsoft.Phone.Controls;

namespace WindowsPhoneApp
{
  public partial class SettingsPage : PhoneApplicationPage
  {
    public SettingsPage()
    {
      InitializeComponent();
    }

    // Simple property bound to the slider
    public double Threshold
    {
      get { return Settings.Threshold.Value; }
      set { Settings.Threshold.Value = value; }
    }

    void ResetButton_Click(object sender, RoutedEventArgs e)
```

LISTING 44.5   Continued

```
    {
      this.StrengthSlider.Value = Settings.Threshold.DefaultValue;
    }
  }
}
```

The Finished Product

Right-handed mode, with the green accent color

Left-handed mode, with the magenta accent color

The instructions page, whose code is available in this chapter's project

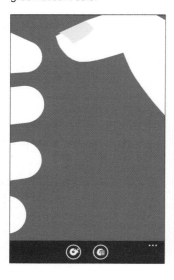

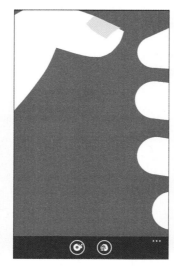

BOXING GLOVE

instructions

Hold the phone as indicated by the fingers on the screen (with your palm against the back of the phone), then make punching motions. If you punch hard enough (and your volume is high enough), you'll hear a variety of punching noises and grunts.

Tap the "switch hand" button to adjust the app for your right hand or left hand.

Tap the "settings" menu item to adjust how forcefully you must punch in order to make noises.

The screen background is your phone theme's accent color. To change the color, change your theme.

Be careful, don't overexert yourself, and be nice! Don't punch actual things or beings. Punch the air.

COIN TOSS

Coin Toss helps you with any heads-or-tails type of decision. Make an upward tossing motion with the phone in your hand, and watch the coin of your choice flip to give you an answer. You can choose between a penny, nickel, dime, or quarter, and see a neat visual history of your coin tosses.

The lesson of this chapter is detecting a tossing/throwing motion with the phone. And surprise, surprise, it's the same algorithm used in the preceding chapter for detecting punches! (I guess they call it "throwing punches" for a reason!) The only difference is that the Z axis is tracked rather than the X axis.

The Main User Interface

Coin Toss has a main page, a history page, a settings page, and an instructions page. The code for the latter two pages isn't shown in this chapter. The settings page is actually identical to the settings page from the preceding chapter, except "Required punching strength" is renamed to "Required tossing strength," and the tip textbox at the bottom is removed.

Listing 45.1 contains the XAML for the main page. It is much more complicated than the preceding chapter's main page in order to support all the animations done by this app.

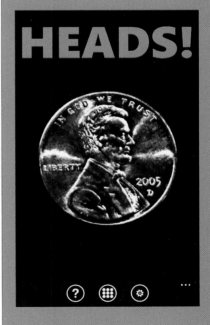

LISTING 45.1   `MainPage.xaml`—The User Interface for Coin Toss's Main Page

```
<phone:PhoneApplicationPage
    x:Class="WindowsPhoneApp.MainPage"
    xmlns="http://schemas.microsoft.com/winfx/2006/xaml/presentation"
    xmlns:x="http://schemas.microsoft.com/winfx/2006/xaml"
    xmlns:phone="clr-namespace:Microsoft.Phone.Controls;assembly=Microsoft.Phone"
    xmlns:shell="clr-namespace:Microsoft.Phone.Shell;assembly=Microsoft.Phone"
    SupportedOrientations="Portrait">
  <!-- Add three storyboards to the page's resource dictionary -->
  <phone:PhoneApplicationPage.Resources>

    <!-- The 3D flip, 90° at a time -->
    <Storyboard x:Name="FlipStoryboard" Storyboard.TargetName="CoinProjection"
                Storyboard.TargetProperty="RotationX"
                Completed="FlipStoryboard_Completed">
      <DoubleAnimation By="90" Duration="0:0:.06"/>
    </Storyboard>

    <!-- The movement up and off the screen -->
    <Storyboard x:Name="RiseAndFallStoryboard"
                Storyboard.TargetName="CoinTransform">
      <!-- Moving up then back down -->
      <DoubleAnimation x:Name="RiseAndFallAnimation1" AutoReverse="True"
                       Storyboard.TargetProperty="TranslateY" By="-300">
        <DoubleAnimation.EasingFunction>
          <QuadraticEase/>
        </DoubleAnimation.EasingFunction>
      </DoubleAnimation>
      <!-- Growing then shrinking (X) -->
      <DoubleAnimation x:Name="RiseAndFallAnimation2" AutoReverse="True"
                       Storyboard.TargetProperty="ScaleX" By="1.05">
        <DoubleAnimation.EasingFunction>
          <QuadraticEase/>
        </DoubleAnimation.EasingFunction>
      </DoubleAnimation>
      <!-- Growing then shrinking (Y) -->
      <DoubleAnimation x:Name="RiseAndFallAnimation3" AutoReverse="True"
                       Storyboard.TargetProperty="ScaleY" By="1.05">
        <DoubleAnimation.EasingFunction>
          <QuadraticEase/>
        </DoubleAnimation.EasingFunction>
      </DoubleAnimation>
    </Storyboard>

    <!-- Flip in the "HEADS!" or "TAILS!" text in 3D -->
```

LISTING 45.1   Continued

```xml
  <Storyboard x:Name="ShowResultStoryboard"
              Storyboard.TargetName="ResultProjection"
              Storyboard.TargetProperty="RotationX">
    <DoubleAnimation To="0" Duration="0:0:.4">
      <DoubleAnimation.EasingFunction>
        <BackEase/>
      </DoubleAnimation.EasingFunction>
    </DoubleAnimation>
  </Storyboard>
</phone:PhoneApplicationPage.Resources>

<!-- The application bar, with three buttons and four menu items -->
<phone:PhoneApplicationPage.ApplicationBar>
  <shell:ApplicationBar Opacity=".8">
    <shell:ApplicationBarIconButton Text="instructions"
            IconUri="/Shared/Images/appbar.instructions.png"
            Click="InstructionsButton_Click" />
    <shell:ApplicationBarIconButton Text="history"
            IconUri="/Images/appbar.history.png"
            Click="HistoryButton_Click" />
    <shell:ApplicationBarIconButton Text="settings"
            IconUri="/Shared/Images/appbar.settings.png"
            Click="SettingsButton_Click" />
    <shell:ApplicationBar.MenuItems>
      <shell:ApplicationBarMenuItem Text="penny" Click="CoinMenuItem_Click"/>
      <shell:ApplicationBarMenuItem Text="nickel" Click="CoinMenuItem_Click"/>
      <shell:ApplicationBarMenuItem Text="dime" Click="CoinMenuItem_Click"/>
      <shell:ApplicationBarMenuItem Text="quarter" Click="CoinMenuItem_Click"/>
    </shell:ApplicationBar.MenuItems>
  </shell:ApplicationBar>
</phone:PhoneApplicationPage.ApplicationBar>

<Grid>
  <!-- The grid containing the coin -->
  <Grid RenderTransformOrigin=".5,.5">
    <Grid.RenderTransform>
      <!-- Used to move and scale the coin -->
      <CompositeTransform x:Name="CoinTransform"/>
    </Grid.RenderTransform>
    <Grid.Projection>
      <!-- Used to flip the coin in 3D -->
      <PlaneProjection x:Name="CoinProjection"/>
    </Grid.Projection>
```

LISTING 45.1   Continued

```
  <!-- The tails side of the coin -->
  <Image x:Name="TailsImage" RenderTransformOrigin=".5,.5"
           Stretch="None">
    <!-- Reverse, so it looks correct when flipped over -->
    <Image.RenderTransform>
      <ScaleTransform ScaleY="-1"/>
    </Image.RenderTransform>
  </Image>

  <!-- The heads side of the coin -->
  <Image x:Name="HeadsImage" Stretch="None"/>
</Grid>

<!-- The "HEADS!" or "TAILS!" text block, which animates independently -->
<TextBlock x:Name="ResultTextBlock" FontFamily="Segoe WP Black" FontSize="120"
  Foreground="{StaticResource PhoneAccentBrush}" HorizontalAlignment="Center">
  <TextBlock.Projection>
    <!-- Used to flip the text in 3D -->
    <PlaneProjection x:Name="ResultProjection" RotationX="90"/>
  </TextBlock.Projection>
</TextBlock>
  </Grid>
</phone:PhoneApplicationPage>
```

Notes:

→ The first two storyboards create the 3D coin-flip effect, pictured in Figure 45.1. The first storyboard does the 3D part, and the second one makes it more realistic by animating the scale and position of the coin while it flips in 3D. The first storyboard is almost identical to the card-flip storyboard used in Chapter 17, "Pick a Card Magic Trick." It rotates the coin around the X axis, whereas the card-flip storyboard rotates the card around the Y axis. Just like the playing card, the coin ends up looking like a flat sheet when the rotation is almost perpendicular to the screen (seen in Figure 45.1). Silverlight's limited 3D support doesn't provide any built-in way to give the coin thickness, but fortunately the coin flipping happens so quickly that this oddity isn't easily detectable.

→ The final storyboard performs a 3D flip-in animation on the "HEADS!" or "TAILS!" result text, as shown in Figure 45.2.

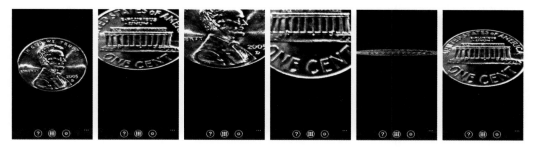

FIGURE 45.1   The coin appears to leap out from the screen as it spins in 3D.

FIGURE 45.2   The 3D text animation in action.

→ The application bar contains buttons for going to each of the other pages, and the application bar menu contains an entry for each of the four available coins, as shown in Figure 45.3. Although the settings page isn't really important enough to have a prominent spot on the application bar, a button is used rather than a menu item because mixing a settings menu item with the four coin menu items wouldn't be the cleanest presentation.

→ Much like the main playing card in Chapter 17's Pick a Card app, the coin consists of two overlapping images—one for the heads side of the coin and one for the tails side. The source for each image is set in code-behind because it changes based on the user's coin preference.

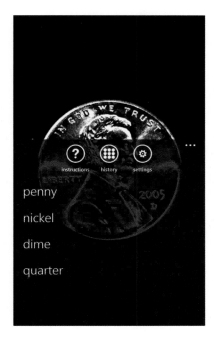

FIGURE 45.3   The application bar menu enables the choice between four coins.

The Main Code-Behind

Listing 45.2 contains the code-behind for the main page. It makes use of three persisted settings defined in a separate `Settings.cs` file as follows:

```
public static class Settings
{
  public static readonly Setting<string> ChosenCoin =
    new Setting<string>("ChosenCoin", "penny");
  public static readonly Setting<List<string>> HistoryList =
    new Setting<List<string>>("HistoryList", new List<string>());
  public static readonly Setting<double> Threshold =
    new Setting<double>("Threshold", 1);
}
```

The `Threshold` setting is like the one from the preceding chapter, but with a default value of 1 rather than 1.5, so the default strength required for performing a coin toss is less than the default strength required for punching in the Boxing Glove app.

LISTING 45.2   `MainPage.xaml.cs`—The Code-Behind for Coin Toss's Main Page

```
using System;
using System.Windows;
using System.Windows.Media.Imaging;
using System.Windows.Navigation;
using Microsoft.Devices.Sensors;
using Microsoft.Phone.Controls;
using Microsoft.Phone.Shell;

namespace WindowsPhoneApp
{
  public partial class MainPage : PhoneApplicationPage
  {
    Accelerometer accelerometer;

    int animationStep;
    int animationTotalSteps;
    bool isTails = false;
    bool isTossing = false;
    DateTimeOffset acceleratingQuicklyForwardTime = DateTime.MinValue;
    Random random = new Random();

    public MainPage()
    {
      InitializeComponent();

      // Initialize the accelerometer
```

LISTING 45.2   Continued

```
    this.accelerometer = new Accelerometer();
    this.accelerometer.ReadingChanged += Accelerometer_ReadingChanged;
}

protected override void OnNavigatedTo(NavigationEventArgs e)
{
  base.OnNavigatedTo(e);

  // Start the accelerometer
  try
  {
    this.accelerometer.Start();
  }
  catch
  {
    MessageBox.Show(
    "Unable to start your accelerometer. Please try running this app again.",
    "Accelerometer Error", MessageBoxButton.OK);
  }

  // Restore the chosen coin
  this.HeadsImage.Source = new BitmapImage(new Uri("Images/" +
    Settings.ChosenCoin.Value + "Heads.png", UriKind.Relative));
  this.TailsImage.Source = new BitmapImage(new Uri("Images/" +
    Settings.ChosenCoin.Value + "Tails.png", UriKind.Relative));
}

protected override void OnNavigatedFrom(NavigationEventArgs e)
{
  base.OnNavigatedTo(e);

  // Stop the accelerometer
  try
  {
    this.accelerometer.Stop();
  }
  catch { /* Nothing to do */ }
}

// Process data coming from the accelerometer
void Accelerometer_ReadingChanged(object sender,
                                  AccelerometerReadingEventArgs e)
{
  // We want the threshold to be negative, so
```

LISTING 45.2   Continued

```
  // forward motion is up and out of the screen
  double threshold = -Settings.Threshold.Value;

  // Only pay attention to large-enough magnitudes in the Z dimension
  if (Math.Abs(e.Z) < Math.Abs(threshold))
    return;

  // See if the force is in the same direction as the threshold
  // (forward throwing motion)
  if (e.Z * threshold > 0)
  {
    // Forward acceleration
    this.acceleratingQuicklyForwardTime = e.Timestamp;
  }
  else if (e.Timestamp - this.acceleratingQuicklyForwardTime
           < TimeSpan.FromSeconds(.2))
  {
    // This is large backward force shortly after the forward force.
    // Time to flip the coin!

    this.acceleratingQuicklyForwardTime = DateTimeOffset.MinValue;

    // We're on a different thread, so transition to the UI thread
    this.Dispatcher.BeginInvoke(delegate() { BeginToss(); });
  }
}

void BeginToss()
{
  if (this.isTossing)
    return;

  this.isTossing = true;

  this.ShowResultStoryboard.Stop();

  // Choose heads or tails
  bool willBeTails = this.random.Next(0, 2) == 0;

  // First randomly choose number of complete 360° flips
  // (multiples of 4 because the animation is done 90° at a time)
  this.animationTotalSteps = this.random.Next(3, 6) * 4;

  if (this.isTails != willBeTails)
```

LISTING 45.2   Continued

```
    {
      // It needs to land on the opposite side,
      // so add two more animation steps (180°)
      this.animationTotalSteps += 2;
    }

    // Make the duration of the rise-and-fall animations match the length
    // of time that the coin will be spinning (+ a .1 second buffer)
    this.RiseAndFallAnimation1.Duration =
    this.RiseAndFallAnimation2.Duration =
    this.RiseAndFallAnimation3.Duration =
      TimeSpan.FromSeconds(this.animationTotalSteps * .03 + .1);

    this.isTails = willBeTails;
    this.animationStep = 0;

    // Perform the first 90° of the flip and start the rise-and-fall in sync
    this.FlipStoryboard.Begin();
    this.RiseAndFallStoryboard.Begin();
  }

  void FlipStoryboard_Completed(object sender, EventArgs e)
  {
    this.animationStep++;

    if (this.animationStep == this.animationTotalSteps)
    {
      // We're done
      if (this.isTails)
      {
        this.ResultTextBlock.Text = "TAILS!";
        Settings.HistoryList.Value.Add("Images/" +
          Settings.ChosenCoin.Value + "Tails.png");
      }
      else
      {
        this.ResultTextBlock.Text = "HEADS!";
        Settings.HistoryList.Value.Add("Images/" +
          Settings.ChosenCoin.Value + "Heads.png");
      }

      this.isTossing = false;
      this.ShowResultStoryboard.Begin();
```

LISTING 45.2   Continued

```
      return;
    }

    // Each complete rotation has 4 phases (0°, 90°, 180°, 270°)
    int phase = this.animationStep % 4;

    // Check for 90° or 270°, the two points where the coin is
    // perpendicular to the screen (and therefore invisible)
    if (phase == 1 || phase == 3)
    {
      // This is when we toggle the visible image between heads and tails
      // by showing/hiding the heads image on top of the tails image
      if (this.HeadsImage.Visibility == Visibility.Collapsed)
        this.HeadsImage.Visibility = Visibility.Visible;
      else
        this.HeadsImage.Visibility = Visibility.Collapsed;
    }

    this.FlipStoryboard.Begin();
  }

  // Application bar handlers

  void InstructionsButton_Click(object sender, EventArgs e)
  {
    this.NavigationService.Navigate(new Uri("/InstructionsPage.xaml",
      UriKind.Relative));
  }

  void HistoryButton_Click(object sender, EventArgs e)
  {
    this.NavigationService.Navigate(new Uri("/HistoryPage.xaml",
      UriKind.Relative));
  }

  void SettingsButton_Click(object sender, EventArgs e)
  {
    this.NavigationService.Navigate(new Uri("/SettingsPage.xaml",
      UriKind.Relative));
  }

  void CoinMenuItem_Click(object sender, EventArgs e)
  {
    IApplicationBarMenuItem menuItem = sender as IApplicationBarMenuItem;
```

LISTING 45.2   Continued

```
      Settings.ChosenCoin.Value = menuItem.Text;
      this.HeadsImage.Source = new BitmapImage(new Uri("Images/" + menuItem.Text
        + "Heads.png", UriKind.Relative));
      this.TailsImage.Source = new BitmapImage(new Uri("Images/" + menuItem.Text
        + "Tails.png", UriKind.Relative));
    }
  }
}
```

Notes:

→ The interaction with the accelerometer is identical to the preceding chapter, except that `e.Z` is used instead of `e.X`. Notice that the threshold is made negative, which seems to contradict the description of the Z axis in Figure 44.1 from the preceding chapter. That's because when you hold a phone flat and accelerate it upward, it "feels heavier" in the opposite direction, causing the value of `e.Z` to *decrease*. You experience the same sensation when going up in a fast-moving elevator. The same behavior applies to either direction in any dimension. This is the difference between measuring g-forces (what accelerometers do) versus measuring acceleration.

→ The project includes image files named pennyHeads.png, pennyTails.png, nickelHeads.png, nickelTails.png, and so on. This is why the code is able to take the text from the menu item (or the string from the `ChosenCoin` setting) and simply prepend it to `Heads.png` or `Tails.png`.

→ The URI string from the chosen heads or tails coin image is added to the history list each time. Although this is an odd and inefficient way to store the data, it's an easy way to get the history page's experience, shown next.

The History Page

The history page, shown in Figure 45.4, uses a wrap panel from the Silverlight for Windows Phone Toolkit to display miniature versions of past coin results.

The XAML for the history page is shown in Listing 45.3 and its code-behind is in Listing 45.4. The wrap panel is placed inside a scroll viewer so the entire history can be accessed when the coins are wrapped to off-screen rows.

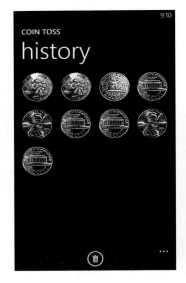

Portrait orientation

Landscape orientation

FIGURE 45.4 The history page uses a wrap panel that reflows the coins based on the current orientation.

LISTING 45.3 `HistoryPage.xaml`—The User Interface for Coin Toss's History Page

```
<phone:PhoneApplicationPage
    x:Class="WindowsPhoneApp.HistoryPage"
    xmlns="http://schemas.microsoft.com/winfx/2006/xaml/presentation"
    xmlns:x="http://schemas.microsoft.com/winfx/2006/xaml"
    xmlns:phone="clr-namespace:Microsoft.Phone.Controls;assembly=Microsoft.Phone"
    xmlns:shell="clr-namespace:Microsoft.Phone.Shell;assembly=Microsoft.Phone"
    xmlns:toolkit="clr-namespace:Microsoft.Phone.Controls;
➡assembly=Microsoft.Phone.Controls.Toolkit"
    FontFamily="{StaticResource PhoneFontFamilyNormal}"
    FontSize="{StaticResource PhoneFontSizeNormal}"
    SupportedOrientations="PortraitOrLandscape"
    shell:SystemTray.IsVisible="True">

  <!-- The application bar with a delete button -->
  <phone:PhoneApplicationPage.ApplicationBar>
    <shell:ApplicationBar Opacity=".8">
      <shell:ApplicationBarIconButton Text="delete"
             IconUri="/Shared/Images/appbar.delete.png"
             Click="DeleteButton_Click" />
    </shell:ApplicationBar>
  </phone:PhoneApplicationPage.ApplicationBar>
```

LISTING 45.3   Continued

```xml
<Grid Background="{StaticResource PhoneBackgroundBrush}">
  <Grid.RowDefinitions>
    <RowDefinition Height="Auto"/>
    <RowDefinition Height="*"/>
  </Grid.RowDefinitions>

  <!-- The standard header -->
  <StackPanel Grid.Row="0" Style="{StaticResource PhoneTitlePanelStyle}">
    <TextBlock Text="COIN TOSS" Style="{StaticResource PhoneTextTitle0Style}"/>
    <TextBlock Text="history"
               Style="{StaticResource PhoneTextTitle1Style}"/>
  </StackPanel>

  <TextBlock Name="NoItemsTextBlock" Text="No history. Start tossing!"
             Visibility="Collapsed"
             Margin="22 17 0 0"
             Style="{StaticResource PhoneTextGroupHeaderStyle}"
             Grid.Row="1"/>

  <ScrollViewer Grid.Row="1">
    <toolkit:WrapPanel x:Name="WrapPanel" Margin="12,0,0,0"/>
  </ScrollViewer>
</Grid>
</phone:PhoneApplicationPage>
```

LISTING 45.4   `HistoryPage.xaml.cs`—The Code-Behind for Coin Toss's History Page

```csharp
using System;
using System.Windows;
using System.Windows.Controls;
using System.Windows.Media.Imaging;
using System.Windows.Navigation;
using Microsoft.Phone.Controls;

namespace WindowsPhoneApp
{
  public partial class HistoryPage : PhoneApplicationPage
  {
    public HistoryPage()
    {
      InitializeComponent();
    }

    protected override void OnNavigatedTo(NavigationEventArgs e)
```

LISTING 45.4   Continued

```
  {
    base.OnNavigatedTo(e);

    foreach (string uri in Settings.HistoryList.Value)
    {
      this.WrapPanel.Children.Add(new Image {
        Source = new BitmapImage(new Uri(uri, UriKind.Relative)),
        Height = 90, Margin = new Thickness(12) });
    }

    if (Settings.HistoryList.Value.Count == 0)
      ShowListAsEmpty();
  }

  void DeleteButton_Click(object sender, EventArgs e)
  {
    if (MessageBox.Show(
      "Are you sure you want to clear your coin toss history?",
      "Delete history", MessageBoxButton.OKCancel) == MessageBoxResult.OK)
    {
      Settings.HistoryList.Value.Clear();
      this.WrapPanel.Children.Clear();
      ShowListAsEmpty();
    }
  }

  void ShowListAsEmpty()
  {
    this.NoItemsTextBlock.Visibility = Visibility.Visible;
    this.ApplicationBar.IsVisible = false;
  }
  }
}
```

The Finished Product

Finally, it landed on tails!

A long history of coin tosses

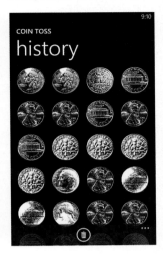

Under the white theme with the magenta accent color

chapter 46 → lessons

→ Shaking Detection

NOISE MAKER

Noise Maker makes a loud, annoying noise when you shake the phone. This app is meant for sporting events, much like the vuvuzelas that became infamous during the 2010 FIFA World Cup. You can use it to help cheer on your team, or to distract the opposition. The main lesson of this chapter—figuring out when the phone is being shaken—can be useful for many apps. You might wish to use the same shake-detection algorithm for more serious apps, perhaps as a gesture to refresh data.

The Main Page

Noise Maker has a main page, a settings page, and an about page (not shown in this chapter). Listing 46.1 contains the XAML for the main page. This produces the user interface shown to the right. Listing 46.2 contains its code-behind.

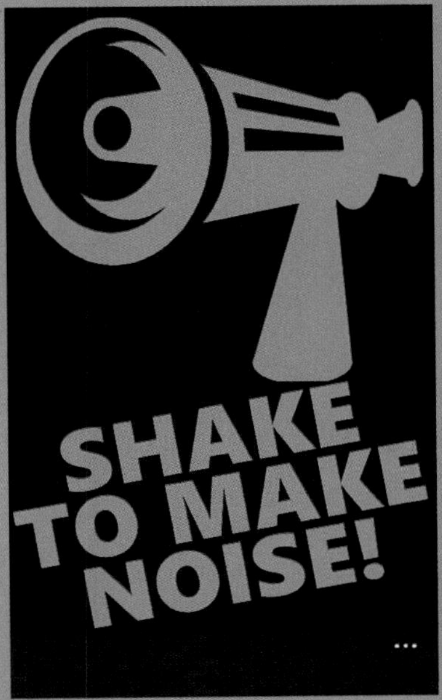

LISTING 46.1   `MainPage.xaml`—The User Interface for Noise Maker's Main Page

```
<phone:PhoneApplicationPage
    x:Class="WindowsPhoneApp.MainPage"
    xmlns="http://schemas.microsoft.com/winfx/2006/xaml/presentation"
    xmlns:x="http://schemas.microsoft.com/winfx/2006/xaml"
    xmlns:phone="clr-namespace:Microsoft.Phone.Controls;assembly=Microsoft.Phone"
    xmlns:shell="clr-namespace:Microsoft.Phone.Shell;assembly=Microsoft.Phone"
    SupportedOrientations="Portrait">

  <!-- The application bar, with two menu items -->
  <phone:PhoneApplicationPage.ApplicationBar>
    <shell:ApplicationBar>
      <shell:ApplicationBar.MenuItems>
        <shell:ApplicationBarMenuItem Text="settings"
                                      Click="SettingsMenuItem_Click"/>
        <shell:ApplicationBarMenuItem Text="about" Click="AboutMenuItem_Click"/>
      </shell:ApplicationBar.MenuItems>
    </shell:ApplicationBar>
  </phone:PhoneApplicationPage.ApplicationBar>

  <StackPanel>
    <!-- An accent-colored image -->
    <Rectangle Fill="{StaticResource PhoneAccentBrush}" Width="456" Height="423"
               Margin="{StaticResource PhoneMargin}">
      <Rectangle.OpacityMask>
        <ImageBrush ImageSource="Images/logo.png"/>
      </Rectangle.OpacityMask>
    </Rectangle>
    <!-- Accent-colored rotated text -->
    <TextBlock FontFamily="Segoe WP Black" Text="SHAKE TO MAKE NOISE!"
               FontSize="100" Foreground="{StaticResource PhoneAccentBrush}"
               TextWrapping="Wrap" TextAlignment="Center" Margin="0,20,0,0"
               LineHeight="80" LineStackingStrategy="BlockLineHeight"
               RenderTransformOrigin=".5,.5">
      <TextBlock.RenderTransform>
        <RotateTransform Angle="-10"/>
      </TextBlock.RenderTransform>
    </TextBlock>
  </StackPanel>
</phone:PhoneApplicationPage>
```

LISTING 46.2   `MainPage.xaml.cs`—The Code-Behind for Noise Maker's Main Page

```
using System;
using System.Windows;
using System.Windows.Navigation;
using Microsoft.Devices.Sensors;
using Microsoft.Phone.Controls;
using Microsoft.Phone.Shell;

namespace WindowsPhoneApp
{
  public partial class MainPage : PhoneApplicationPage
  {
    Accelerometer accelerometer;

    public MainPage()
    {
      InitializeComponent();

      // Initialize the accelerometer
      this.accelerometer = new Accelerometer();
      this.accelerometer.ReadingChanged += Accelerometer_ReadingChanged;

      SoundEffects.Initialize();

      // Allow the app to run (producing sounds) even when the phone is locked.
      // Once disabled, you cannot re-enable the default behavior!
      PhoneApplicationService.Current.ApplicationIdleDetectionMode =
        IdleDetectionMode.Disabled;
    }

    protected override void OnNavigatedTo(NavigationEventArgs e)
    {
      base.OnNavigatedTo(e);

      // Start the accelerometer
      try
      {
        this.accelerometer.Start();
      }
      catch
      {
        MessageBox.Show(
        "Unable to start your accelerometer. Please try running this app again.",
        "Accelerometer Error", MessageBoxButton.OK);
      }
```

LISTING 46.2   Continued

```csharp
    }

    protected override void OnNavigatedFrom(NavigationEventArgs e)
    {
      base.OnNavigatedTo(e);

      // Stop the accelerometer
      try
      {
        this.accelerometer.Stop();
      }
      catch { /* Nothing to do */ }
    }

    // Process data coming from the accelerometer
    void Accelerometer_ReadingChanged(object sender,
                                   AccelerometerReadingEventArgs e)
    {
      if (ShakeDetection.JustShook(e))
      {
        // We're on a different thread, so transition to the UI thread
        this.Dispatcher.BeginInvoke(delegate()
        {
          // Play each sound, which builds on top
          // of previously-playing sound effects
          if (Settings.IsLowChosen.Value)
            SoundEffects.Low.Play();
          if (Settings.IsMediumChosen.Value)
            SoundEffects.Medium.Play();
          if (Settings.IsHighChosen.Value)
            SoundEffects.High.Play();
        });
      }
    }

    // Application bar handlers

    void SettingsMenuItem_Click(object sender, EventArgs e)
    {
      this.NavigationService.Navigate(new Uri("/SettingsPage.xaml",
        UriKind.Relative));
    }

    void AboutMenuItem_Click(object sender, EventArgs e)
```

LISTING 46.2 Continued

```
    {
        this.NavigationService.Navigate(new Uri("/AboutPage.xaml",
          UriKind.Relative));
    }
  }
}
```

Notes:

→ This listing makes use of three persisted settings defined in a separate `Settings.cs` file as follows:

```
public static class Settings
{
  public static readonly Setting<bool> IsLowChosen =
    new Setting<bool>("IsLowChosen", false);
  public static readonly Setting<bool> IsMediumChosen =
    new Setting<bool>("IsMediumChosen", true);
  public static readonly Setting<bool> IsHighChosen =
    new Setting<bool>("IsHighChosen", false);
}
```

→ The `SoundEffects` class used by this app is exactly like the one used in Chapter 44, "Boxing Glove," but with `Low`, `Medium`, and `High` properties that expose the audio from three `.wav` files with the same names.

→ This app supports playing one, two, or three sounds simultaneously when a shake is detected. Any previously playing sound effects are not stopped by the calls to `Play`. The resulting additive effect means that shaking more vigorously (technically, more frequently) causes the sound to be louder.

→ The shake detection is done with a simple `JustShook` method defined in Listing 46.3.

LISTING 46.3 `ShakeDetection.cs`—The Shake Detection Algorithm

```
using System;
using Microsoft.Devices.Sensors;

namespace WindowsPhoneApp
{
  public static class ShakeDetection
  {
    static AccelerometerReadingEventArgs previousData;
    static int numShakes;
```

LISTING 46.3   Continued

```
// Two properties for controlling the algorithm
public static int RequiredConsecutiveShakes { get; set; }
public static double Threshold { get; set; }

static ShakeDetection()
{
  RequiredConsecutiveShakes = 1;
  Threshold = .7;
}

// Call this with the accelerometer data
public static bool JustShook(AccelerometerReadingEventArgs e)
{
  if (previousData != null)
  {
    if (IsShaking(previousData, e, Threshold))
    {
      numShakes++;
      if (numShakes == RequiredConsecutiveShakes)
      {
        // Just shook!
        numShakes = 0;
        return true;
      }
    }
    else if (!IsShaking(previousData, e, .2))
      numShakes = 0;
  }

  previousData = e;
  return false;
}

// It's a shake if the values in at least two dimensions
// are different enough from the previous values
static bool IsShaking(AccelerometerReadingEventArgs previous,
  AccelerometerReadingEventArgs current, double threshold)
{
  double deltaX = Math.Abs(previous.X - current.X);
  double deltaY = Math.Abs(previous.Y - current.Y);
  double deltaZ = Math.Abs(previous.Z - current.Z);

  return (deltaX > threshold && deltaY > threshold) ||
         (deltaY > threshold && deltaZ > threshold) ||
```

LISTING 46.3   Continued

```
                (deltaX > threshold && deltaZ > threshold);
    }
  }
}
```

→ The core part of the algorithm—the IsShaking method—simply checks for two out of the three data points being sufficiently different from the previous set of data points. "Sufficiently different" is determined by a threshold that defaults to .7 but can be changed by the consumer of this class.

→ JustShook keeps track of the previous data and calls IsShaking. It uses the RequiredConsecutiveShakes property to support specifying a number of consecutive shakes required before considering that a shake has happened.

→ Although it's a good idea for apps to provide calibration functionality when the accelerometer is used, it's not really necessary for something as coarse as shake detection. Any differences between phones are not likely to be noticed.

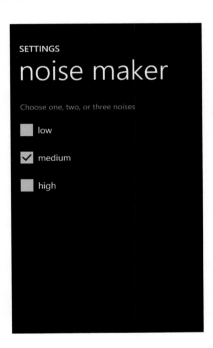

FIGURE 46.1   The settings page enables customization of the sound effects.

The Settings Page

The settings page, shown in Figure 46.1, enables the user to turn on/off any of the three noises with simple check boxes. Listing 46.4 contains the XAML, and Listing 46.5 contains the code-behind.

LISTING 46.4   SettingsPage.xaml—The User Interface for Noise Maker's Settings Page

```
<phone:PhoneApplicationPage
    x:Class="WindowsPhoneApp.SettingsPage"
    xmlns="http://schemas.microsoft.com/winfx/2006/xaml/presentation"
    xmlns:x="http://schemas.microsoft.com/winfx/2006/xaml"
    xmlns:phone="clr-namespace:Microsoft.Phone.Controls;assembly=Microsoft.Phone"
    xmlns:shell="clr-namespace:Microsoft.Phone.Shell;assembly=Microsoft.Phone"
```

LISTING 46.4   Continued

```xml
  xmlns:local="clr-namespace:WindowsPhoneApp"
  FontFamily="{StaticResource PhoneFontFamilyNormal}"
  FontSize="{StaticResource PhoneFontSizeNormal}"
  Foreground="{StaticResource PhoneForegroundBrush}"
  SupportedOrientations="PortraitOrLandscape" shell:SystemTray.IsVisible="True">
<Grid Background="{StaticResource PhoneBackgroundBrush}">
  <Grid.RowDefinitions>
    <RowDefinition Height="Auto"/>
    <RowDefinition Height="*"/>
  </Grid.RowDefinitions>

  <!-- The standard settings header -->
  <StackPanel Grid.Row="0" Style="{StaticResource PhoneTitlePanelStyle}">
    <TextBlock Text="SETTINGS" Style="{StaticResource PhoneTextTitle0Style}"/>
    <TextBlock Text="noise maker"
               Style="{StaticResource PhoneTextTitle1Style}"/>
  </StackPanel>

  <ScrollViewer Grid.Row="1">
    <StackPanel Margin="{StaticResource PhoneMargin}">
      <TextBlock Text="Choose one, two, or three noises"
                 Foreground="{StaticResource PhoneSubtleBrush}"
                 Margin="{StaticResource PhoneMargin}"/>
      <CheckBox x:Name="LowCheckBox" Content="low"
        Checked="CheckBox_IsCheckedChanged"
        Unchecked="CheckBox_IsCheckedChanged" local:Tilt.IsEnabled="True"/>
      <CheckBox x:Name="MediumCheckBox" Content="medium"
        Checked="CheckBox_IsCheckedChanged"
        Unchecked="CheckBox_IsCheckedChanged" local:Tilt.IsEnabled="True"/>
      <CheckBox x:Name="HighCheckBox" Content="high"
        Checked="CheckBox_IsCheckedChanged"
        Unchecked="CheckBox_IsCheckedChanged" local:Tilt.IsEnabled="True"/>

      <!-- A warning for when no sounds are checked -->
      <StackPanel x:Name="WarningPanel" Visibility="Collapsed"
                  Orientation="Horizontal" Margin="12,4,0,0">
        <!-- Use the image as an opacity mask for the rectangle, so the image
             visible in both dark and light themes -->
        <Rectangle Fill="{StaticResource PhoneForegroundBrush}"
                   Width="48" Height="48">
          <Rectangle.OpacityMask>
            <ImageBrush ImageSource="Shared/Images/normal.error.png"/>
          </Rectangle.OpacityMask>
        </Rectangle>
```

LISTING 46.4   Continued

```
                <TextBlock Text="No sounds will be made unless you check at least one!"
                            TextWrapping="Wrap" Width="350"
                            Margin="{StaticResource PhoneMargin}"/>
          </StackPanel>
        </StackPanel>
      </ScrollViewer>
    </Grid>
</phone:PhoneApplicationPage>
```

LISTING 46.5   SettingsPage.xaml.cs—The Code-Behind for Noise Maker's Settings Page

```
using System.Windows;
using System.Windows.Navigation;
using Microsoft.Phone.Controls;

namespace WindowsPhoneApp
{
  public partial class SettingsPage : PhoneApplicationPage
  {
    public SettingsPage()
    {
      InitializeComponent();
      ShowOrHideWarning();
    }

    protected override void OnNavigatedFrom(NavigationEventArgs e)
    {
      base.OnNavigatedFrom(e);
      // Save the settings
      Settings.IsLowChosen.Value = this.LowCheckBox.IsChecked.Value;
      Settings.IsMediumChosen.Value = this.MediumCheckBox.IsChecked.Value;
      Settings.IsHighChosen.Value = this.HighCheckBox.IsChecked.Value;
    }

    protected override void OnNavigatedTo(NavigationEventArgs e)
    {
      base.OnNavigatedTo(e);
      // Respect the settings
      this.LowCheckBox.IsChecked = Settings.IsLowChosen.Value;
      this.MediumCheckBox.IsChecked = Settings.IsMediumChosen.Value;
      this.HighCheckBox.IsChecked = Settings.IsHighChosen.Value;
    }

    void CheckBox_IsCheckedChanged(object sender, RoutedEventArgs e)
```

LISTING 46.5   Continued

```
    {
      ShowOrHideWarning();
    }

    void ShowOrHideWarning()
    {
      if (!this.LowCheckBox.IsChecked.Value &&
          !this.MediumCheckBox.IsChecked.Value &&
          !this.HighCheckBox.IsChecked.Value)
        this.WarningPanel.Visibility = Visibility.Visible;
      else
        this.WarningPanel.Visibility = Visibility.Collapsed;
    }
  }
}
```

Other than a straightforward mapping of three check boxes to three settings, this page contains a warning that gets shown when all three check boxes are unchecked. This is shown in Figure 46.2.

FIGURE 46.2   The settings page shows a warning if all check boxes are unchecked.

The Finished Product

The dark theme with the orange accent color

The light theme with the magenta accent color

The light theme with the green accent color

chapter 47 ➡

MOO CAN

Do you remember those cans that moo when you turn them upside down? The Moo Can app brings this classic children's toy back to life in digital form! Moo Can makes a moo sound when you turn your phone upside down. Gravity also affects the cow on the screen, which rotates and falls toward whatever edge of the screen is currently on the bottom.

Just like the real cans, you can shake the phone to make a harsh sound that is different from the desired "moo" caused by gently turning the phone upside down. You can also change the cow to a sheep or cat, each of which makes its own unique sounds.

The Main Page

Moo Can has a main page, a calibration page, and an instructions page (not shown in this chapter). Listing 47.1 contains the XAML for the main page, and Listing 47.2 contains its code-behind.

LISTING 47.1   `MainPage.xaml`—The User Interface for Moo Can's Main Page

```
<phone:PhoneApplicationPage x:Class="WindowsPhoneApp.MainPage"
    xmlns="http://schemas.microsoft.com/winfx/2006/xaml/presentation"
    xmlns:x="http://schemas.microsoft.com/winfx/2006/xaml"
    xmlns:phone="clr-namespace:Microsoft.Phone.Controls;assembly=Microsoft.Phone"
    xmlns:shell="clr-namespace:Microsoft.Phone.Shell;assembly=Microsoft.Phone"
    SupportedOrientations="Portrait">

  <!-- The application bar, with five menu items -->
  <phone:PhoneApplicationPage.ApplicationBar>
    <shell:ApplicationBar BackgroundColor="#9CB366" ForegroundColor="White">
      <shell:ApplicationBar.MenuItems>
        <shell:ApplicationBarMenuItem Text="cow" Click="AnimalMenuItem_Click"/>
        <shell:ApplicationBarMenuItem Text="sheep" Click="AnimalMenuItem_Click"/>
        <shell:ApplicationBarMenuItem Text="cat" Click="AnimalMenuItem_Click"/>
        <shell:ApplicationBarMenuItem Text="instructions"
                                      Click="InstructionsMenuItem_Click"/>
        <shell:ApplicationBarMenuItem Text="calibrate"
                                      Click="CalibrateMenuItem_Click"/>
      </shell:ApplicationBar.MenuItems>
    </shell:ApplicationBar>
  </phone:PhoneApplicationPage.ApplicationBar>

  <Canvas>
    <Canvas.Background>
      <ImageBrush ImageSource="Images/background.png"/>
    </Canvas.Background>
    <!-- The cow, sheep, or cat -->
    <Image x:Name="AnimalImage" RenderTransformOrigin=".5,.5"
      Canvas.Left="32" Canvas.Top="50" Width="434" Height="507">
      <Image.RenderTransform>
        <CompositeTransform x:Name="AnimalTransform"/>
      </Image.RenderTransform>
    </Image>
  </Canvas>
</phone:PhoneApplicationPage>
```

The user interface contains an animal image (whose source is set in code-behind) placed over the background image. It also uses an application bar menu, shown in Figure 47.1, for switching the animal or navigating to either of the other two pages. The application bar is given hard-coded colors, so it blends in with the grass in the background image when the menu is closed.

FIGURE 47.1   The application bar menu on the main page.

LISTING 47.2   `MainPage.xaml.cs`—The Code-Behind for Moo Can's Main Page

```
using System;
using System.Windows.Media.Imaging;
using System.Windows.Navigation;
using Microsoft.Phone.Applications.Common; // For AccelerometerHelper
using Microsoft.Phone.Controls;
using Microsoft.Phone.Shell;

namespace WindowsPhoneApp
{
  public partial class MainPage : PhoneApplicationPage
  {
    Setting<string> chosenAnimal = new Setting<string>("ChosenAnimal", "cow");

    bool upsideDown = false;

    // The start, middle, end, and length of the
    // vertical path that the animal moves along
    const double MAX_Y = 170;
    const double MIN_Y = -75;
    const double MID_Y = 47.5;
```

LISTING 47.2   Continued

```
const double LENGTH_Y = 245;

// The start, middle and end of the clockwise rotation of the animal
const double MAX_ANGLE_CW = 180;
const double MIN_ANGLE_CW = 0;
const double MID_ANGLE_CW = 90;

// The start, middle and end of the counter-clockwise rotation of the animal
const double MIN_ANGLE_CCW = -180;
const double MAX_ANGLE_CCW = 0;
const double MID_ANGLE_CCW = -90;

// The length of the rotation, regardless of which direction
const double LENGTH_ANGLE = 180;

public MainPage()
{
  InitializeComponent();

  // Use the accelerometer via Microsoft's helper
  AccelerometerHelper.Instance.ReadingChanged += Accelerometer_ReadingChanged;

  SoundEffects.Initialize();

  // Allow the app to run (producing sounds) even when the phone is locked.
  // Once disabled, you cannot re-enable the default behavior!
  PhoneApplicationService.Current.ApplicationIdleDetectionMode =
    IdleDetectionMode.Disabled;
}

protected override void OnNavigatedTo(NavigationEventArgs e)
{
  base.OnNavigatedTo(e);

  // Restore the chosen animal
  ChangeAnimal();

  // Start the accelerometer with Microsoft's helper
  AccelerometerHelper.Instance.Active = true;

  // While on this page, don't allow the screen to auto-lock
  PhoneApplicationService.Current.UserIdleDetectionMode =
    IdleDetectionMode.Disabled;
}
```

LISTING 47.2   Continued

```
protected override void OnNavigatedFrom(NavigationEventArgs e)
{
  base.OnNavigatedTo(e);

  // Restore the ability for the screen to auto-lock when on other pages
  PhoneApplicationService.Current.UserIdleDetectionMode =
    IdleDetectionMode.Enabled;
}

void ChangeAnimal()
{
  switch (this.chosenAnimal.Value)
  {
    case "cow":
      this.AnimalImage.Source = new BitmapImage(
        new Uri("Images/cow.png", UriKind.Relative));
      break;
    case "sheep":
      this.AnimalImage.Source = new BitmapImage(
        new Uri("Images/sheep.png", UriKind.Relative));
      break;
    case "cat":
      this.AnimalImage.Source = new BitmapImage(
        new Uri("Images/cat.png", UriKind.Relative));
      break;
  }
}

// Process data coming from the accelerometer
void Accelerometer_ReadingChanged(object sender,
                                  AccelerometerHelperReadingEventArgs e)
{
  // Transition to the UI thread
  this.Dispatcher.BeginInvoke(delegate()
  {
    // Move the animal vertically based on the vertical force
    this.AnimalTransform.TranslateY =
      Clamp(MID_Y - LENGTH_Y * e.AverageAcceleration.Y, MIN_Y, MAX_Y);

    // Clear the upside-down flag, only when completely upright
    if (this.AnimalTransform.TranslateY == MAX_Y)
      this.upsideDown = false;

    // Rotate the animal to always be upright
```

LISTING 47.2   Continued

```
    if (e.AverageAcceleration.X <= 0)
      this.AnimalTransform.Rotation = Clamp(MID_ANGLE_CW +
        LENGTH_ANGLE * e.AverageAcceleration.Y, MIN_ANGLE_CW, MAX_ANGLE_CW);
    else
      this.AnimalTransform.Rotation = Clamp(MID_ANGLE_CCW -
        LENGTH_ANGLE * e.AverageAcceleration.Y, MIN_ANGLE_CCW, MAX_ANGLE_CCW);

    // Play the appropriate shake sound when shaken
    if (ShakeDetection.JustShook(e.OriginalEventArgs))
    {
      switch (this.chosenAnimal.Value)
      {
        case "cow": SoundEffects.MooShake.Play(); break;
        case "sheep": SoundEffects.BaaShake.Play(); break;
        case "cat": SoundEffects.MeowShake.Play(); break;
      }
    }

    // Play the normal sound when first turned upside-down
    if (!this.upsideDown && this.AnimalTransform.TranslateY == MIN_Y)
    {
      this.upsideDown = true;
      switch (this.chosenAnimal.Value)
      {
        case "cow": SoundEffects.Moo.Play(); break;
        case "sheep": SoundEffects.Baa.Play(); break;
        case "cat": SoundEffects.Meow.Play(); break;
      }
    }
  });
}

// "Clamp" the incoming value so it's no lower than min & no larger than max
static double Clamp(double value, double min, double max)
{
  return Math.Max(min, Math.Min(max, value));
}

// Application bar handlers

void AnimalMenuItem_Click(object sender, EventArgs e)
{
  this.chosenAnimal.Value = (sender as IApplicationBarMenuItem).Text;
  ChangeAnimal();
```

LISTING 47.2   Continued

```
  }

  void InstructionsMenuItem_Click(object sender, EventArgs e)
  {
    this.NavigationService.Navigate(new Uri("/InstructionsPage.xaml",
      UriKind.Relative));
  }

  void CalibrateMenuItem_Click(object sender, EventArgs e)
  {
    this.NavigationService.Navigate(new Uri(
      "/Shared/Calibrate/CalibratePage.xaml?appName=Moo Can", UriKind.Relative));
  }
  }
}
```

Notes:

→ This app moves and rotates the animal based on the accelerometer's data, as shown in Figure 47.2. However, the raw data has a lot of noise, so using it directly would produce a jerky result. (This noise didn't matter for the previous three apps because the punch, throw, and shake detection are coarse.) Therefore, this listing makes use of an `AccelerometerHelper` class published by Microsoft that performs *data smoothing* for you. It also simplifies the starting/stopping interaction with the accelerometer.

FIGURE 47.2   The chosen animal rotates and falls as you turn the phone upside down.

→ AccelerometerHelper exposes its
functionality via a static Instance
property, so the constructor uses
this to attach a handler to its
ReadingChanged event. This event
is just like the ReadingChanged

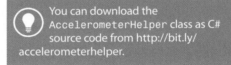

You can download the
AccelerometerHelper class as C#
source code from http://bit.ly/
accelerometerhelper.

event from the preceding chapters, but with richer data passed to handlers.

→ This project uses a SoundEffects class just like the one from previous apps but with
six properties for six possible sounds: Moo, MooShake, Baa, BaaShake, Meow, and
MeowShake.

→ This app runs while locked *and* this page prevents the screen from auto-locking.
This way, you can make the noises without keeping the phone screen on. At the
same time, you can continue to watch the cow fall up and down without having to
periodically tap the screen to keep it on.

→ To start the accelerometer, OnNavigatedTo simply sets AccelerometerHelper's
Instance's Active property to true. Internally, this calls Start (if not already
started) with the same sort of exception handling done in preceding chapters. This
app doesn't bother stopping the accelerometer, but this could be done by setting
Active to false inside OnNavigatedFrom.

→ Inside Accelerometer_ReadingChanged, the AccelerometerHelper-specific
Accelerometer**Helper**ReadingEventArgs instance is leveraged to get the *average*
acceleration in the X and Y directions. This class is different from the
AccelerometerReadingEventArgs used by the preceding apps. It exposes several
properties for getting the data with various types of smoothing applied.

Accelerometer**Helper**ReadingEventArgs exposes four properties that enable you to
choose how raw or smooth you want your data to be:

→ **RawAcceleration**—The same noisy data you would get from the Accelerometer
class's ReadingChanged event (but with calibration potentially applied, as described later
in this chapter).

→ **LowPassFilteredAcceleration**—Applies a first-order *low-pass filter* over the raw data.
The result is smoother data with a little bit of latency.

→ **OptimalyFilteredAcceleration [sic]**—This uses the same low-pass filter, but only
when the current value is close enough to a rolling average value. If the value is sufficiently greater, the raw value is reported instead. (This algorithm is done independently
for all three axes.) This gives a nice balance between having smooth results and low
latency. Small changes are handled smoothly and large changes are reported quickly.

→ **AverageAcceleration**—Reports the mean of the most recent 25 data points collected
from the "optimally filtered" algorithm. This gives the smoothest result of any of the
choices, but it also has the highest latency.

Each property exposes X, Y, Z, and Magnitude properties (but unlike AccelerometerReadingEventArgs, no Timestamp property). Magnitude reports the length of the 3D vector formed by the other three values, which is the square root of $X^2 + Y^2 + Z^2$.

For more details about the algorithms behind these properties, see http://bit.ly/accelerometerhelper.

→ This app uses the same ShakeDetection class shown in the preceding chapter. Because the JustShook method is defined to accept an instance of AccelerometerReadingEventArgs—*not* Accelerometer**Helper**ReadingEventArgs—this listing uses an OriginalEventArgs property to retrieve it. This property actually isn't exposed by the Accelerometer**Helper**ReadingEventArgs class; I added it directly to my copy of the source code.

→ A turn upside down is detected by noticing the first moment that the Y acceleration value is large enough after a point in time when it has been small enough. In other words, after the upside-down orientation has been detected, the user must turn the phone right side up to clear the value of upsideDown before another upside-down turn will be detected. Because the animal transform's TranslateY value is proportional to the Y-axis acceleration (and restricted to a range of MIN_Y to MAX_Y), the phone is completely upside down when TranslateY is MIN_Y and the phone is completely upright when TranslateY is MAX_Y.

→ This app purposely does not make any noise when turned right side up, because a real can does not either. (I didn't realize this until I bought a few of the cans and tried for myself.)

The Calibration Page

Moo Can enables users to calibrate the accelerometer in case its notion of right side up or upside down are slightly askew from reality. The process of calibration simply involves asking the user when they believe the phone is level, remembering the accelerometer's reading at that moment, and then using those values as an offset to the accelerometer data from that point onward.

One benefit of using AccelerometerHelper rather than the raw accelerometer APIs is that calibration functionality is built in. It collects the data, stores it as isolated storage application settings (named "AccelerometerCalibrationX" and "AccelerometerCalibrationY"), and automatically offsets the data it returns—even the supposedly "raw" data.

The calibration page, designed to be shared among multiple apps, shows you how to take advantage of it. Listing 47.3 contains the XAML and Listing 47.4 contains the code-behind. It produces the page shown in Figure 47.3.

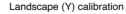

Not level enough for calibration	Portrait (X) calibration	Landscape (Y) calibration	Flat (X and Y) calibration, for when the phone is resting on a table

FIGURE 47.3   The calibration page enables calibrating just the X dimension, just the Y dimension, or both, but only when the phone is held fairly still and level.

LISTING 47.3   `CalibratePage.xaml`—The User Interface for The Accelerometer Calibration Page

```xml
<phone:PhoneApplicationPage x:Class="WindowsPhoneApp.CalibratePage"
    xmlns="http://schemas.microsoft.com/winfx/2006/xaml/presentation"
    xmlns:x="http://schemas.microsoft.com/winfx/2006/xaml"
    xmlns:phone="clr-namespace:Microsoft.Phone.Controls;assembly=Microsoft.Phone"
    xmlns:local="clr-namespace:WindowsPhoneApp"
    FontFamily="{StaticResource PhoneFontFamilyNormal}"
    FontSize="{StaticResource PhoneFontSizeNormal}"
    Foreground="{StaticResource PhoneForegroundBrush}"
    SupportedOrientations="PortraitOrLandscape">
  <Grid>
    <Grid.RowDefinitions>
      <RowDefinition Height="Auto"/>
      <RowDefinition Height="*"/>
    </Grid.RowDefinitions>

    <!-- The standard header -->
    <StackPanel Style="{StaticResource PhoneTitlePanelStyle}">
      <TextBlock x:Name="ApplicationName"
                 Style="{StaticResource PhoneTextTitle0Style}"/>
      <TextBlock Text="calibrate" Style="{StaticResource PhoneTextTitle1Style}"/>
    </StackPanel>

    <ScrollViewer Grid.Row="1">
      <StackPanel>
        <TextBlock Margin="24" TextWrapping="Wrap" Text="Tap the button …"/>
        <Button x:Name="CalibrateButton" Content="calibrate" IsEnabled="False"
```

LISTING 47.3   Continued

```
                Height="150" Click="CalibrateButton_Click"
                local:Tilt.IsEnabled="True"/>
        <TextBlock x:Name="WarningText" Visibility="Collapsed" Margin="24,0"
                TextWrapping="Wrap" FontWeight="Bold"
                Text="Your phone is not still or level enough!"/>
      </StackPanel>
    </ScrollViewer>
  </Grid>
</phone:PhoneApplicationPage>
```

LISTING 47.4   `CalibratePage.xaml.cs`—The Code-Behind for the Accelerometer Calibration Page

```
using System.Windows;
using System.Windows.Navigation;
using Microsoft.Phone.Applications.Common; // For AccelerometerHelper
using Microsoft.Phone.Controls;

namespace WindowsPhoneApp
{
  public partial class CalibratePage : PhoneApplicationPage
  {
    bool calibrateX = true, calibrateY = true;

    public CalibratePage()
    {
      InitializeComponent();

      // Use the accelerometer via Microsoft's helper
      AccelerometerHelper.Instance.ReadingChanged += Accelerometer_ReadingChanged;
      // Ensure it is active
      AccelerometerHelper.Instance.Active = true;
    }

    protected override void OnNavigatedTo(NavigationEventArgs e)
    {
      base.OnNavigatedTo(e);

      // Set the application name in the header
      if (this.NavigationContext.QueryString.ContainsKey("appName"))
      {
        this.ApplicationName.Text =
          this.NavigationContext.QueryString["appName"].ToUpperInvariant();
```

LISTING 47.4   Continued

```
    }

    // Check for calibration parameters
    if (this.NavigationContext.QueryString.ContainsKey("calibrateX"))
    {
      this.calibrateX =
        bool.Parse(this.NavigationContext.QueryString["calibrateX"]);
    }
    if (this.NavigationContext.QueryString.ContainsKey("calibrateY"))
    {
      this.calibrateY =
        bool.Parse(this.NavigationContext.QueryString["calibrateY"]);
    }
  }

  // Process data coming from the accelerometer
  void Accelerometer_ReadingChanged(object sender,
                                    AccelerometerHelperReadingEventArgs e)
  {
    this.Dispatcher.BeginInvoke(delegate()
    {
      bool canCalibrateX = this.calibrateX &&
        AccelerometerHelper.Instance.CanCalibrate(this.calibrateX, false);
      bool canCalibrateY = this.calibrateY &&
        AccelerometerHelper.Instance.CanCalibrate(false, this.calibrateY);

      // Update the enabled state and text of the calibration button
      this.CalibrateButton.IsEnabled = canCalibrateX || canCalibrateY;

      if (canCalibrateX && canCalibrateY)
        this.CalibrateButton.Content = "calibrate (flat)";
      else if (canCalibrateX)
        this.CalibrateButton.Content = "calibrate (portrait)";
      else if (canCalibrateY)
        this.CalibrateButton.Content = "calibrate (landscape)";
      else
        this.CalibrateButton.Content = "calibrate";

      this.WarningText.Visibility = this.CalibrateButton.IsEnabled ?
        Visibility.Collapsed : Visibility.Visible;
    });
  }

  void CalibrateButton_Click(object sender, RoutedEventArgs e)
```

LISTING 47.4   Continued

```
    {
      if (AccelerometerHelper.Instance.Calibrate(this.calibrateX,
                                          this.calibrateY) ||
          AccelerometerHelper.Instance.Calibrate(this.calibrateX, false) ||
          AccelerometerHelper.Instance.Calibrate(false, this.calibrateY))
      {
        // Consider it a success if we were able to
        // calibrate in either direction (or both)
        if (this.NavigationService.CanGoBack)
          this.NavigationService.GoBack();
      }
      else
      {
        MessageBox.Show("Unable to calibrate. Make sure you're holding your " +
          "phone still, even when tapping the button!", "Calibration Error",
          MessageBoxButton.OK);
      }
    }
  }
}
}
```

Notes:

→ This page enables calibration in just one dimension—or both—based on the query parameters passed when navigating to it. Listing 47.2 simply passes "appName=Moo Can" as the query string, so this app will enable any kind of calibration. Most likely, the user will be holding the phone in the portrait orientation when attempting to calibrate.

→ The calibration method— AccelerometerHelper.Instance.Calibrate—only succeeds if the phone is sufficiently still and at least somewhat-level in the relevant dimension(s). The AccelerometerHelper.Instance.CanCalibrate method tells you whether calibration will succeed, although the answer can certainly change between the time you call CanCalibrate and the time you call Calibrate, so you should always be prepared for Calibrate to fail.

→ The ReadingChanged event handler continually checks CanCalibrate so it can enable/disable the calibration button appropriately. CanCalibrate has two Boolean parameters that enable you to specify whether you care about just the X dimension, just the Y dimension, or both. (Calibrating the Z axis is not meaningful.) Listing 47.4 checks each dimension individually (if the app cares about the dimension) so it can display a helpful message to the user. The only way you can calibrate both X and Y dimensions simultaneously is by placing the phone flat on a surface parallel to the ground.

→ `CalibrateButton_Click` tries to calibrate whatever will succeed. Calibrate has the same two parameters as `CanCalibrate`, so this listing first attempts to calibrate both dimensions, but if that fails (by returning `false`), it tries to calibrate each dimension individually.

The Finished Product

The cow says, "Moo."

The sheep says, "Baa."

The cat says, "Meow."

chapter 48 lessons

→ **Determining the Phone's Angle**

LEVEL

No book covering the use of an accelerometer would be complete without showing you how to create a level! This chapter's Level app not only features four classic tubular bubble levels (one on each edge), but it also shows the current angle of the phone with little accent lines that line up with companion lines when one of the edges of the phone is parallel to the ground. This makes it even easier to visually align the phone exactly as you wish.

Getting smooth, stable results from the accelerometer is important for an app such as this that relies on slow, small movements. Therefore, as in the preceding chapter, Level makes use of Microsoft's `AccelerometerHelper` class to perform data smoothing. The key to this app is to use a little bit of trigonometry in order to determine the angle of the phone based on the accelerometer data.

The `BubbleWindow` **User Control**

The classic bubble display, shown in Figure 48.1, is implemented as a user control. That's because Level's main page uses four instances of this display. Listing 48.1 contains its XAML and Listing 48.2 contains its code-behind.

FIGURE 48.1 The `BubbleWindow` user control displays a colored bubble inside a marked rectangle.

LISTING 48.1   `BubbleWindow.xaml`—The User Interface for the `BubbleWindow` User Control

```xaml
<UserControl x:Class="WindowsPhoneApp.BubbleWindow"
    xmlns="http://schemas.microsoft.com/winfx/2006/xaml/presentation"
    xmlns:x="http://schemas.microsoft.com/winfx/2006/xaml">

  <!-- Add one storyboard to the control's resource dictionary -->
  <UserControl.Resources>
    <Storyboard x:Name="BubbleStoryboard" Storyboard.TargetName="BubbleTransform">
      <!-- Stretch the bubble horizontally -->
      <DoubleAnimation Storyboard.TargetProperty="ScaleX" By=".5"
                       Duration="0:0:.8" AutoReverse="True">
        <DoubleAnimation.EasingFunction>
          <QuadraticEase/>
        </DoubleAnimation.EasingFunction>
      </DoubleAnimation>
      <!-- Shrink the bubble horizontally -->
      <DoubleAnimation Storyboard.TargetProperty="ScaleY" By="-.2"
                       Duration="0:0:.8" AutoReverse="True">
        <DoubleAnimation.EasingFunction>
          <QuadraticEase/>
        </DoubleAnimation.EasingFunction>
      </DoubleAnimation>
    </Storyboard>
  </UserControl.Resources>

  <Canvas Background="#333">
    <Ellipse x:Name="Bubble" Width="115" Height="115" Visibility="Collapsed"
        Fill="{StaticResource PhoneAccentBrush}" RenderTransformOrigin=".5,.5">
      <Ellipse.RenderTransform>
        <!-- Used in the animations -->
        <CompositeTransform x:Name="BubbleTransform"/>
      </Ellipse.RenderTransform>
    </Ellipse>
    <Line x:Name="Line1" Stroke="White"/>
    <Line x:Name="Line2" Stroke="White"/>
    <Rectangle x:Name="Rectangle" Stroke="#A555" StrokeThickness="6"/>
  </Canvas>

</UserControl>
```

LISTING 48.2   `BubbleWindow.xaml.cs`—The Code-Behind for the `BubbleWindow` User Control

```csharp
using System.Windows;
using System.Windows.Controls;
using System.Windows.Media;
```

LISTING 48.2　Continued

```csharp
using System.Windows.Media.Animation;

namespace WindowsPhoneApp
{
  public partial class BubbleWindow : UserControl
  {
    public BubbleWindow()
    {
      InitializeComponent();
      this.Loaded += BubbleWindow_Loaded;
    }

    void BubbleWindow_Loaded(object sender, RoutedEventArgs e)
    {
      // Adjust the two centered lines and the rectangular border to fit
      // the size given to this instance of the control
      this.Line1.X1 = this.Line1.X2 =
        (this.ActualWidth / 2) - (this.Bubble.ActualWidth / 2);
      this.Line1.Y2 = this.ActualHeight;
      this.Line2.X1 = this.Line2.X2 =
        (this.ActualWidth / 2) + (this.Bubble.ActualWidth / 2);
      this.Line2.Y2 = this.ActualHeight;

      this.Rectangle.Width = this.ActualWidth;
      this.Rectangle.Height = this.ActualHeight;

      // Don't allow the bubble to render past this control's border
      this.Clip = new RectangleGeometry {
        Rect = new Rect(0, 0, this.ActualWidth, this.ActualHeight) };

      this.Bubble.Visibility = Visibility.Visible;
    }

    // Set the horizontal position of the bubble on a scale from 0 to 100
    public void SetXPercentage(double percentage)
    {
      percentage = percentage / 100;

      double left = (-this.Bubble.ActualWidth/2) + this.ActualWidth*percentage;
      Canvas.SetLeft(this.Bubble, left);
    }

    // Set the vertical position of the bubble on a scale from 0 to 100
    public void SetYPercentage(double percentage)
```

LISTING 48.2   Continued

```
  {
    percentage = percentage / 100;

    // Allow the bubble to go more off-screen with a taller possible range
    double range = this.ActualHeight + 20 * 2;

    double top = -20 + range * percentage - range / 2;
    Canvas.SetTop(this.Bubble, top);
  }

  public void Animate()
  {
    // Stretch out the bubble if the animation isn't already running
    if (this.BubbleStoryboard.GetCurrentState() != ClockState.Active)
    {
      this.BubbleStoryboard.Stop();
      this.BubbleStoryboard.Begin();
    }
  }
}
}
```

This user control has nothing to do with the accelerometer. It simply enables its consumer to do three things:

→ Set the horizontal position of the bubble from 0% (all the way to the left) to 100% (all the way to the right).

→ Set the vertical position of the bubble from 0% (all the way to the top) to 100% (all the way to the bottom).

→ Trigger an animation that stretches the bubble, appropriate to use when the bubble is moving quickly to give it more realism. This stretching is shown in Figure 48.2.

FIGURE 48.2   The stretched bubble, simulating the expected deformation from fast motion.

Note that the manual layout code in Listing 48.2 that adjusts the lines and rectangle could be eliminated by leveraging a grid's automatic layout rather than using a canvas.

The Main Page

Besides the same calibration page used by Moo Can and shown in the preceding chapter, Level only has the single main page. Listing 48.3 contains the XAML for the main page, and Listing 48.4 contains its code-behind.

LISTING 48.3   `MainPage.xaml`—The User Interface for Level's Main Page

```xaml
<phone:PhoneApplicationPage x:Class="WindowsPhoneApp.MainPage"
    xmlns="http://schemas.microsoft.com/winfx/2006/xaml/presentation"
    xmlns:x="http://schemas.microsoft.com/winfx/2006/xaml"
    xmlns:phone="clr-namespace:Microsoft.Phone.Controls;assembly=Microsoft.Phone"
    xmlns:shell="clr-namespace:Microsoft.Phone.Shell;assembly=Microsoft.Phone"
    xmlns:local="clr-namespace:WindowsPhoneApp"
    SupportedOrientations="Portrait">
  <Grid>
    <Grid.Background>
      <!-- The metallic background -->
      <ImageBrush ImageSource="Images/background.png"/>
    </Grid.Background>

    <!-- The four lines in the middle that don't move -->
    <Line Y1="240" Y2="290" X1="240" X2="240" Stroke="#555" StrokeThickness="6"/>
    <Line Y1="510" Y2="560" X1="240" X2="240" Stroke="#555" StrokeThickness="6"/>
    <Line Y1="400" Y2="400" X1="80" X2="130" Stroke="#555" StrokeThickness="6"/>
    <Line Y1="400" Y2="400" X1="350" X2="400" Stroke="#555" StrokeThickness="6"/>

    <!-- The four lines that tilt based on the phone's angle -->
    <Canvas RenderTransformOrigin=".5,.5" Width="480" Height="800">
      <Canvas.RenderTransform>
        <RotateTransform x:Name="CenterTransform" Angle="45"/>
      </Canvas.RenderTransform>
      <Line Y1="240" Y2="290" X1="240" X2="240"
            Stroke="{StaticResource PhoneAccentBrush}" StrokeThickness="6"/>
      <Line Y1="510" Y2="560" X1="240" X2="240"
            Stroke="{StaticResource PhoneAccentBrush}" StrokeThickness="6"/>
      <Line Y1="400" Y2="400" X1="80" X2="130"
            Stroke="{StaticResource PhoneAccentBrush}" StrokeThickness="6"/>
      <Line Y1="400" Y2="400" X1="350" X2="400"
            Stroke="{StaticResource PhoneAccentBrush}" StrokeThickness="6"/>
    </Canvas>

    <!-- The display for the exact angle -->
    <TextBlock x:Name="AngleTextBlock" Foreground="#555"
               HorizontalAlignment="Center" VerticalAlignment="Center"
               FontSize="{StaticResource PhoneFontSizeExtraExtraLarge}"
               RenderTransformOrigin=".5,.5">
```

LISTING 48.3   Continued

```xml
      <TextBlock.RenderTransform>
        <RotateTransform x:Name="AngleTextBlockTransform"/>
      </TextBlock.RenderTransform>
    </TextBlock>

    <!-- The circle in the center -->
    <Ellipse Width="220" Height="220" Stroke="#555" StrokeThickness="6"/>

    <!-- The four bubble level displays -->

    <local:BubbleWindow x:Name="TopWindow" Width="275" Height="75"
                        VerticalAlignment="Top"/>

    <local:BubbleWindow x:Name="BottomWindow" Width="275" Height="75"
                        VerticalAlignment="Bottom"/>

    <local:BubbleWindow x:Name="LeftWindow" Width="622" Height="75"
      HorizontalAlignment="Left" Margin="-274,0,0,0" RenderTransformOrigin=".5,.5">
      <local:BubbleWindow.RenderTransform>
        <CompositeTransform Rotation="-90"/>
      </local:BubbleWindow.RenderTransform>
    </local:BubbleWindow>

    <local:BubbleWindow x:Name="RightWindow" Width="622" Height="75"
      HorizontalAlignment="Right" Margin="0,0,-274,0" RenderTransformOrigin=".5,.5">
      <local:BubbleWindow.RenderTransform>
        <CompositeTransform Rotation="-90"/>
      </local:BubbleWindow.RenderTransform>
    </local:BubbleWindow>

    <!-- The calibrate pseudo-button that tilts based on the phone's angle -->
    <Border Margin="0,0,0,120" HorizontalAlignment="Center"
            VerticalAlignment="Bottom" local:Tilt.IsEnabled="True"
            MouseLeftButtonUp="Calibrate_MouseLeftButtonUp">
      <TextBlock Text="calibrate" Padding="36" Foreground="#555"
              FontSize="{StaticResource PhoneFontSizeExtraLarge}"
              RenderTransformOrigin=".5,.5">
      <TextBlock.RenderTransform>
        <RotateTransform x:Name="CalibrateTextBlockTransform"/>
      </TextBlock.RenderTransform>
      </TextBlock>
    </Border>
  </Grid>
</phone:PhoneApplicationPage>
```

LISTING 48.4   `MainPage.xaml.cs`—The Code-Behind for Level's Main Page

```csharp
using System;
using System.Windows.Input;
using System.Windows.Navigation;
using Microsoft.Phone.Applications.Common; // For AccelerometerHelper
using Microsoft.Phone.Controls;
using Microsoft.Phone.Shell;

namespace WindowsPhoneApp
{
  public partial class MainPage : PhoneApplicationPage
  {
    // Used to track every 5th call to Accelerometer_ReadingChanged
    double readingCount = 0;
    // The angle 5 calls ago
    double previousAngle = 0;

    public const double RADIANS_TO_DEGREES = 180 / Math.PI;

    public MainPage()
    {
      InitializeComponent();

      // Use the accelerometer via Microsoft's helper
      AccelerometerHelper.Instance.ReadingChanged += Accelerometer_ReadingChanged;
    }

    protected override void OnNavigatedTo(NavigationEventArgs e)
    {
      base.OnNavigatedTo(e);

      // Start the accelerometer with Microsoft's helper
      AccelerometerHelper.Instance.Active = true;

      // While on this page, don't allow the screen to auto-lock
      PhoneApplicationService.Current.UserIdleDetectionMode =
        IdleDetectionMode.Disabled;
    }

    protected override void OnNavigatedFrom(NavigationEventArgs e)
    {
      base.OnNavigatedTo(e);

      // Restore the ability for the screen to auto-lock when on other pages
      PhoneApplicationService.Current.UserIdleDetectionMode =
```

LISTING 48.4   Continued

```
      IdleDetectionMode.Enabled;
}

// Process data coming from the accelerometer
void Accelerometer_ReadingChanged(object sender,
                                  AccelerometerHelperReadingEventArgs e)
{
  // This is the key formula
  double rawAngle =
    Math.Atan2(e.AverageAcceleration.X, e.AverageAcceleration.Y)
    * RADIANS_TO_DEGREES;

  // Express the angle from 0-90°, used by some calculations
  double angle0to90 = Math.Abs(rawAngle) % 90;

  // Calculate the horizontal % of the left & right bubbles by
  // using the angle as an offset from the midpoint (50%)
  double landscapeXPercentage = Clamp(Math.Abs(rawAngle) > 90
                                      ? 50 + angle0to90
                                      : 50 - (90 - angle0to90), 0, 100);

  // The horizontal % of the top & bottom bubbles requires more cases
  double portraitXPercentage;
  // When the bottom bubble window is on top
  if (Math.Abs(rawAngle) <= 25)
    portraitXPercentage = Clamp(rawAngle > 0
                                ? 50 - angle0to90 * 2
                                : 50 + angle0to90 * 2, 0, 100);
  // When the top bubble window is on top
  else if (Math.Abs(rawAngle) >= 155)
    portraitXPercentage = Clamp(rawAngle > 0
                                ? 50 - (90 - angle0to90) * 2
                                : 50 + (90 - angle0to90) * 2, 0, 100);
  // When the right bubble window is on top
  else if (rawAngle < 0)
    portraitXPercentage = 100;
  // When the left bubble window is on top
  else
    portraitXPercentage = 0;

  // The Y% for the left/right bubbles is the same
  // as the X% for the top/bottom bubbles
  double landscapeYPercentage = portraitXPercentage;
  // The Y% for the top/bottom bubbles is the same
```

LISTING 48.4   Continued

```
    // as the inverse of the X% for the left/right bubbles
    double portraitYPercentage = 100 - landscapeXPercentage;

    this.Dispatcher.BeginInvoke(delegate()
    {
      // Set the primary (horizontal) position of each bubble
      this.TopWindow.SetXPercentage(portraitXPercentage);
      this.BottomWindow.SetXPercentage(portraitXPercentage);
      this.LeftWindow.SetXPercentage(landscapeXPercentage);
      this.RightWindow.SetXPercentage(landscapeXPercentage);

      // Set the vertical position of each bubble
      this.TopWindow.SetYPercentage(portraitYPercentage);
      this.BottomWindow.SetYPercentage(portraitYPercentage);
      this.LeftWindow.SetYPercentage(landscapeYPercentage);
      this.RightWindow.SetYPercentage(landscapeYPercentage);

      // On every 5th call, check to see if significant motion has occurred.
      // If the angle has changed by more than 8 degrees, trigger the
      // animation on any bubbles that are vertically close to the top
      // or bottom of their window (< 10% or > 90%).
      readingCount = (readingCount + 1) % 5;
      if (readingCount == 0)
      {
        if (Math.Abs(previousAngle - rawAngle) > 8)
        {
          if (portraitYPercentage < 10 || portraitYPercentage > 90)
          {
            this.TopWindow.Animate();
            this.BottomWindow.Animate();
          }
          if (landscapeYPercentage < 10 || landscapeYPercentage > 90)
          {
            this.LeftWindow.Animate();
            this.RightWindow.Animate();
          }
        }
        this.previousAngle = rawAngle;
      }

      // Update the exact angle display, using values from 0 to 45°
      double angle0to45 = angle0to90 <= 45 ? angle0to90 : 90 - angle0to90;
      this.AngleTextBlock.Text = angle0to45.ToString("##0.0°");
```

LISTING 48.4   Continued

```
      // Tilt the non-bubble pieces of UI accordingly
      this.AngleTextBlockTransform.Angle = rawAngle - 180;
      this.CalibrateTextBlockTransform.Angle = rawAngle - 180;
      this.CenterTransform.Angle = rawAngle - 180;
    });
  }

  void Calibrate_MouseLeftButtonUp(object sender, MouseButtonEventArgs e)
  {
    this.NavigationService.Navigate(
      new Uri("/Shared/Calibrate/CalibratePage.xaml?" +
        "appName=Level&calibrateX=true&calibrateY=true", UriKind.Relative));
  }

  // "Clamp" the incoming value so it's no lower than min & no larger than max
  static double Clamp(double value, double min, double max)
  {
    return Math.Max(min, Math.Min(max, value));
  }
}
}
```

Notes:

→ The most important calculation in this app is done as the first line of
`Accelerometer_ReadingChanged`. The X and Y acceleration vectors are perpendicular
to each other. Therefore, you can imagine the X and Y values from the accelerometer as two sides of a right triangle, as pictured in Figure 48.3. Trigonometry tells us
that the tangent of an angle is the
length of the opposite side divided
by the length of the adjacent side
(the "TOA" in the classic "SOH-
CAH-TOA" mnemonic). Therefore,
the angle equals the arctangent of
the opposite length divided by the
adjacent length. `Math.Atan2`
performs this calculation for us,
and even handles the potential
divide-by-zero case so we don't
have to.

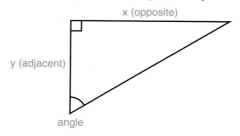

FIGURE 48.3   In a right triangle, the tangent of
an angle equals the opposite length divided by
the adjacent length.

> ⚠ **The trigonometric functions in** `System.Math` **return angles specified in radians!**
>
> This is why Listing 48.4 multiplies the result of `Math.Atan2` by the `RADIANS_TO_DEGREES` constant. This converts the value expressed in radians to a value expressed in degrees by multiplying the value by 180 / π.

➔ For the call to `Math.Atan2`, the X axis is chosen as the opposite side of the right triangle and the Y axis is chosen as the adjacent side. This choice is arbitrary, but it does impact the resultant angle. Using X as the opposite side produces the values for `rawAngle` illustrated in Figure 48.4.

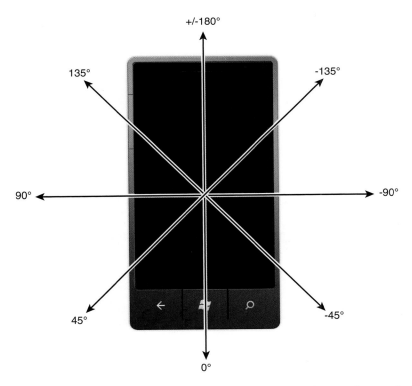

FIGURE 48.4 The raw angle reported by `Math.Atan2`, where each arrow indicates the direction that must point toward the sky.

➔ The bulk of the code in `Accelerometer_ReadingChanged` determines the appropriate horizontal percentage for the four `BubbleWindow` user controls based on the current angle. (The two "portrait" bubbles—top and bottom— always have the same values as each other, as do the two "landscape" bubbles.)

→ Because of the symmetry between the raw angle reported when the left side is facing the sky and when the right side is facing the sky, calculating the horizontal percentage for the landscape bubbles is relatively straightforward. Each degree away from 90° (or –90°) adds or subtracts one percentage point from the 50% midpoint.

→ Because of the asymmetry of the top/bottom raw angles, the horizontal percentage calculation for the portrait bubbles is more complex.

→ The angle displayed in the middle of the screen is 0.0° when any of the four sides is exactly level with the ground. Therefore, the displayed angle never gets higher than 45°. At such a point, the value starts decreasing as the next side gets closer to becoming level.

> 💡 To get even more stability in its readings, the Level app tweaks the code for AccelerometerHelper to make AverageAcceleration examine the previous *50* samples rather than 25. This was done by simply changing the value of a SamplesCount static variable from 25 to 50. This has the side effect of doubling the latency in the reported data, but this is acceptable for a level app. The latency simply makes the liquid in each bubble window act a little "thicker."

→ Rather than checking on every ReadingChanged event, this listing checks for large motion that should trigger the bubble animation every *fifth* event. This is a tradeoff between performance and latency.

The Finished Product

The reported angle is never more than 45°.

Using the magenta theme accent color

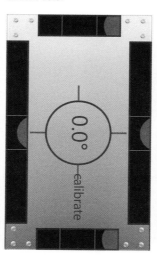

Using the lime theme accent color

BALANCE TEST

Test your hand's coordination and ability to hold your phone still in Balance Test, a fun little 2D-accelerometer-based game. You've got one minute to line up the images as many times as possible. You must keep the phone still at the correct angle for 3 seconds to earn each point. If the images become unaligned for just a moment, the hold-still time resets. This app keeps track of your best score, average score, and number of attempts, so you can keep track of your performance and watch it improve over time.

Balance Test is a lot like a 2D level app, in that you can move an image around the screen by tilting your phone in the X and Y dimensions. However, the image always "sinks" toward the corner of the screen closest to the Earth, whereas a bubble in a level would float to the highest corner.

From a code perspective, Balance Test is like a cross between the Moo Cow and Reflex Test apps. It uses Moo Cow's accelerometer-based motion extended in an additional dimension, and its scoring feature (which keeps track of the best and average scores) is almost identical to Reflex Test.

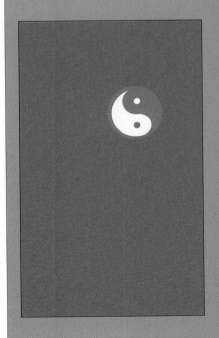

The Main Page

This app uses a single page (ignoring the standard calibration and about pages, as well as an instructions page). It features the two images that need to be aligned to earn points, shown in Figure 49.1. The one shown in white is referred to as the *target*, and gets randomly placed on the screen. The one shown in blue is referred to as the *moving piece* and is controlled by tilting the phone.

When you're not actively playing, you can see the score stats, shown in Figure 49.2. This app does something a little different—it gives the application bar a background color matching the theme accent color. The application bar is shown expanded in Figure 49.3.

Listing 49.1 contains the XAML for the main page, and Listing 49.2 contains its code-behind.

FIGURE 49.1   The images must be aligned for three seconds to get a point for your good balance.

FIGURE 49.2   The score display is just like the one used in the Reflex Test app.

FIGURE 49.3   The application bar makes a bold statement with its accent-colored background.

LISTING 49.1   `MainPage.xaml`—The User Interface for Balance Test's Main Page

```
<phone:PhoneApplicationPage x:Class="WindowsPhoneApp.MainPage"
    xmlns="http://schemas.microsoft.com/winfx/2006/xaml/presentation"
    xmlns:x="http://schemas.microsoft.com/winfx/2006/xaml"
    xmlns:phone="clr-namespace:Microsoft.Phone.Controls;assembly=Microsoft.Phone"
    xmlns:shell="clr-namespace:Microsoft.Phone.Shell;assembly=Microsoft.Phone"
    FontFamily="{StaticResource PhoneFontFamilyNormal}"
    FontSize="{StaticResource PhoneFontSizeNormal}"
    Foreground="{StaticResource PhoneForegroundBrush}"
    SupportedOrientations="Portrait">

  <!-- Add four animations to the page's resource dictionary -->
  <phone:PhoneApplicationPage.Resources>

    <!-- Move the target and scale both images -->
    <Storyboard x:Name="MoveTargetStoryboard"
                Storyboard.TargetName="TargetTransform">
      <DoubleAnimation x:Name="TargetXAnimation"
                       Storyboard.TargetProperty="TranslateX" Duration="0:0:1">
        <DoubleAnimation.EasingFunction>
          <QuarticEase/>
```

LISTING 49.1   Continued

```xml
      </DoubleAnimation.EasingFunction>
    </DoubleAnimation>
    <DoubleAnimation x:Name="TargetYAnimation"
                     Storyboard.TargetProperty="TranslateY" Duration="0:0:1">
      <DoubleAnimation.EasingFunction>
        <QuarticEase/>
      </DoubleAnimation.EasingFunction>
    </DoubleAnimation>
    <DoubleAnimation x:Name="TargetScaleXAnimation"
                     Storyboard.TargetProperty="ScaleX" Duration="0:0:1">
      <DoubleAnimation.EasingFunction>
        <QuarticEase/>
      </DoubleAnimation.EasingFunction>
    </DoubleAnimation>
    <DoubleAnimation x:Name="TargetScaleYAnimation"
                     Storyboard.TargetProperty="ScaleY" Duration="0:0:1">
      <DoubleAnimation.EasingFunction>
        <QuarticEase/>
      </DoubleAnimation.EasingFunction>
    </DoubleAnimation>
    <DoubleAnimation x:Name="MovingPieceScaleXAnimation"
                     Storyboard.TargetName="MovingPieceTransform"
                     Storyboard.TargetProperty="ScaleX" Duration="0:0:1">
      <DoubleAnimation.EasingFunction>
        <QuadraticEase/>
      </DoubleAnimation.EasingFunction>
    </DoubleAnimation>
    <DoubleAnimation x:Name="MovingPieceScaleYAnimation"
                     Storyboard.TargetName="MovingPieceTransform"
                     Storyboard.TargetProperty="ScaleY" Duration="0:0:1">
      <DoubleAnimation.EasingFunction>
        <QuadraticEase/>
      </DoubleAnimation.EasingFunction>
    </DoubleAnimation>
    <!-- Rotate the target, just for fun -->
    <DoubleAnimation Storyboard.TargetProperty="Rotation" By="360"
                     Duration="0:0:1">
      <DoubleAnimation.EasingFunction>
        <QuarticEase/>
      </DoubleAnimation.EasingFunction>
    </DoubleAnimation>
  </Storyboard>

  <!-- Slide the best score out then back in -->
```

LISTING 49.1   Continued

```xml
<Storyboard x:Name="SlideBestScoreStoryboard">
  <DoubleAnimationUsingKeyFrames Storyboard.TargetName="BestScoreTransform"
                                 Storyboard.TargetProperty="TranslateX">
    <DiscreteDoubleKeyFrame KeyTime="0:0:0" Value="0"/>
    <EasingDoubleKeyFrame KeyTime="0:0:.4" Value="-800">
      <EasingDoubleKeyFrame.EasingFunction>
        <QuadraticEase/>
      </EasingDoubleKeyFrame.EasingFunction>
    </EasingDoubleKeyFrame>
    <DiscreteDoubleKeyFrame KeyTime="0:0:.4" Value="800"/>
    <EasingDoubleKeyFrame KeyTime="0:0:.8" Value="0">
      <EasingDoubleKeyFrame.EasingFunction>
        <QuadraticEase/>
      </EasingDoubleKeyFrame.EasingFunction>
    </EasingDoubleKeyFrame>
  </DoubleAnimationUsingKeyFrames>
  <ObjectAnimationUsingKeyFrames Storyboard.TargetName="BestScoreTextBlock"
                                 Storyboard.TargetProperty="Visibility">
    <!-- Ensure the score is visible on the way in,
         even if collapsed on the way out -->
    <DiscreteObjectKeyFrame KeyTime="0:0:.4" Value="Visible"/>
  </ObjectAnimationUsingKeyFrames>
</Storyboard>

<!-- Slide the average score out then back in -->
<Storyboard x:Name="SlideAvgScoreStoryboard">
  <DoubleAnimationUsingKeyFrames Storyboard.TargetName="AvgScoreTransform"
                                 Storyboard.TargetProperty="TranslateX">
    <DiscreteDoubleKeyFrame KeyTime="0:0:0" Value="0"/>
    <EasingDoubleKeyFrame KeyTime="0:0:.4" Value="-800">
      <EasingDoubleKeyFrame.EasingFunction>
        <QuadraticEase/>
      </EasingDoubleKeyFrame.EasingFunction>
    </EasingDoubleKeyFrame>
    <DiscreteDoubleKeyFrame KeyTime="0:0:.4" Value="800"/>
    <EasingDoubleKeyFrame KeyTime="0:0:.8" Value="0">
      <EasingDoubleKeyFrame.EasingFunction>
        <QuadraticEase/>
      </EasingDoubleKeyFrame.EasingFunction>
    </EasingDoubleKeyFrame>
  </DoubleAnimationUsingKeyFrames>
  <ObjectAnimationUsingKeyFrames Storyboard.TargetName="AvgScoreTextBlock"
                                 Storyboard.TargetProperty="Visibility">
```

LISTING 49.1   Continued

```xml
        <!-- Ensure the score is visible on the way in,
             even if collapsed on the way out -->
        <DiscreteObjectKeyFrame KeyTime="0:0:.4" Value="Visible"/>
      </ObjectAnimationUsingKeyFrames>
    </Storyboard>

    <!-- Animate in (then out) a message -->
    <Storyboard x:Name="ShowMessageStoryboard"
                Storyboard.TargetName="MessageTransform">
      <DoubleAnimationUsingKeyFrames Storyboard.TargetProperty="TranslateY">
        <DiscreteDoubleKeyFrame KeyTime="0:0:0" Value="800"/>
        <EasingDoubleKeyFrame KeyTime="0:0:.5" Value="50">
          <EasingDoubleKeyFrame.EasingFunction>
            <QuadraticEase/>
          </EasingDoubleKeyFrame.EasingFunction>
        </EasingDoubleKeyFrame>
        <DiscreteDoubleKeyFrame KeyTime="0:0:2.5" Value="50"/>
        <EasingDoubleKeyFrame KeyTime="0:0:3" Value="-800">
          <EasingDoubleKeyFrame.EasingFunction>
            <QuadraticEase/>
          </EasingDoubleKeyFrame.EasingFunction>
        </EasingDoubleKeyFrame>
      </DoubleAnimationUsingKeyFrames>
    </Storyboard>
  </phone:PhoneApplicationPage.Resources>

  <!-- The application bar, with four menu items and one button -->
  <phone:PhoneApplicationPage.ApplicationBar>
    <shell:ApplicationBar Opacity=".999"
                          BackgroundColor="{StaticResource PhoneAccentColor}">
      <shell:ApplicationBarIconButton Text="start"
                                      IconUri="/Shared/Images/appbar.play.png"
                                      Click="StartButton_Click"/>
      <shell:ApplicationBar.MenuItems>
        <shell:ApplicationBarMenuItem Text="instructions"
                                      Click="InstructionsMenuItem_Click"/>
        <shell:ApplicationBarMenuItem Text="calibrate"
                                      Click="CalibrateMenuItem_Click"/>
        <shell:ApplicationBarMenuItem Text="clear scores"
                                      Click="ClearScoresMenuItem_Click"/>
        <shell:ApplicationBarMenuItem Text="about" Click="AboutMenuItem_Click"/>
      </shell:ApplicationBar.MenuItems>
    </shell:ApplicationBar>
  </phone:PhoneApplicationPage.ApplicationBar>
```

LISTING 49.1   Continued

```xml
<Grid>
  <!-- These two elements are shown while the images are aligned -->
  <ProgressBar x:Name="ProgressBar" Maximum="3000" VerticalAlignment="Top"/>
  <Rectangle x:Name="HighlightRectangle" Opacity="0"
             Fill="{StaticResource PhoneAccentBrush}"/>

  <!-- The canvas with the two images -->
  <Canvas>
    <Rectangle x:Name="Target" Fill="{StaticResource PhoneAccentBrush}"
               Width="480" Height="482">
      <Rectangle.OpacityMask>
        <ImageBrush ImageSource="Images/target.png"/>
      </Rectangle.OpacityMask>
      <Rectangle.RenderTransform>
        <CompositeTransform x:Name="TargetTransform" ScaleX="0" ScaleY="0"/>
      </Rectangle.RenderTransform>
    </Rectangle>
    <Rectangle Fill="{StaticResource PhoneForegroundBrush}"
               Width="480" Height="482">
      <Rectangle.OpacityMask>
        <ImageBrush ImageSource="Images/movingPiece.png"/>
      </Rectangle.OpacityMask>
      <Rectangle.RenderTransform>
        <CompositeTransform x:Name="MovingPieceTransform"
                            ScaleX="0" ScaleY="0"/>
      </Rectangle.RenderTransform>
    </Rectangle>
  </Canvas>

  <!-- A display for the best score, average score, and # of tries -->
  <StackPanel x:Name="ScorePanel" VerticalAlignment="Bottom"
              HorizontalAlignment="Right" Margin="12,72">
    <TextBlock Text="BEST SCORE" Foreground="{StaticResource PhoneSubtleBrush}"
               HorizontalAlignment="Right"/>
    <TextBlock x:Name="BestScoreTextBlock" HorizontalAlignment="Right"
               FontSize="{StaticResource PhoneFontSizeExtraExtraLarge}"
               Margin="0,-15,0,30">
      <TextBlock.RenderTransform>
        <CompositeTransform x:Name="BestScoreTransform"/>
      </TextBlock.RenderTransform>
    </TextBlock>
    <TextBlock x:Name="AvgScoreHeaderTextBlock" Text="AVG SCORE"
               Foreground="{StaticResource PhoneSubtleBrush}"
               HorizontalAlignment="Right"/>
```

LISTING 49.1   Continued

```
    <TextBlock x:Name="AvgScoreTextBlock" HorizontalAlignment="Right"
                FontSize="{StaticResource PhoneFontSizeExtraExtraLarge}"
                Margin="0,-15,0,0">
        <TextBlock.RenderTransform>
          <CompositeTransform x:Name="AvgScoreTransform"/>
        </TextBlock.RenderTransform>
      </TextBlock>
    </StackPanel>

    <!-- An animated message -->
    <Grid RenderTransformOrigin=".5,.5" HorizontalAlignment="Center"
          VerticalAlignment="Top">
      <Grid.RenderTransform>
        <CompositeTransform x:Name="MessageTransform" TranslateY="800"/>
      </Grid.RenderTransform>
      <TextBlock x:Name="MessageTextBlockShadow" FontWeight="Bold" FontSize="90"
        Margin="4,4,0,0" Foreground="{StaticResource PhoneBackgroundBrush}"/>
      <TextBlock x:Name="MessageTextBlock" FontWeight="Bold" FontSize="90"/>
    </Grid>
  </Grid>
</phone:PhoneApplicationPage>
```

Notes:

→ Notice that the application bar is given an opacity of .999. This is used instead of an opacity of 1 (which looks the same) to make the code-behind a little simpler. This is explained after the next listing.

→ The page isn't using two Image elements, but rather the familiar trick of using theme-colored rectangles with image brush opacity masks. This gives the target the appropriate accent color, and the moving piece the appropriate foreground color.

LISTING 49.2   MainPage.xaml.cs—The Code-Behind for Balance Test's Main Page

```
using System;
using System.Windows;
using System.Windows.Media.Animation;
using System.Windows.Navigation;
using Microsoft.Phone.Applications.Common; // For AccelerometerHelper
using Microsoft.Phone.Controls;
using Microsoft.Phone.Shell;

namespace WindowsPhoneApp
{
  public partial class MainPage : PhoneApplicationPage
```

LISTING 49.2   Continued

```csharp
{
  // The bounds for the moving piece
  double minX, maxX, lengthX, midX;
  double minY, maxY, lengthY, midY;

  DateTime? timeEntered;
  DateTime beginTime;
  Random random;

  // Persistent settings
  Setting<int> bestScore = new Setting<int>("BestScore", 0);
  Setting<double> avgScore = new Setting<double>("AvgScore", 0);
  Setting<int> numTries = new Setting<int>("NumTries", 0);

  int score;
  bool isRunning;
  const double TOLERANCE = 6;

  public MainPage()
  {
    InitializeComponent();

    // Use the accelerometer via Microsoft's helper
    AccelerometerHelper.Instance.ReadingChanged += Accelerometer_ReadingChanged;

    this.random = new Random();
  }

  protected override void OnNavigatedTo(NavigationEventArgs e)
  {
    base.OnNavigatedTo(e);

    // Respect the persisted values
    UpdateLabels(true);

    // Reset
    this.isRunning = false;

    // Start the accelerometer with Microsoft's helper
    AccelerometerHelper.Instance.Active = true;

    // While on this page, don't allow the screen to auto-lock
    PhoneApplicationService.Current.UserIdleDetectionMode =
      IdleDetectionMode.Disabled;
  }
```

LISTING 49.2   Continued

```
protected override void OnNavigatedFrom(NavigationEventArgs e)
{
  base.OnNavigatedTo(e);

  // Restore the ability for the screen to auto-lock when on other pages
  PhoneApplicationService.Current.UserIdleDetectionMode =
    IdleDetectionMode.Enabled;
}

void UpdateLabels(bool animateBestScore)
{
  if (this.numTries.Value > 0)
  {
    // Ensure the panel is visible and update the text blocks
    this.ScorePanel.Visibility = Visibility.Visible;
    this.BestScoreTextBlock.Text = this.bestScore.Value.ToString();
    this.AvgScoreTextBlock.Text = this.avgScore.Value.ToString("##0.##");
    if (this.numTries.Value == 1)
      this.AvgScoreHeaderTextBlock.Text = "AVG SCORE (1 TRY)";
    else
      this.AvgScoreHeaderTextBlock.Text = "AVG SCORE (" + this.numTries.Value
        + " TRIES)";

    // Animate the text blocks out then in. The animations take care of
    // showing the text blocks if they are collapsed.
    this.SlideAvgScoreStoryboard.Begin();
    if (animateBestScore)
      this.SlideBestScoreStoryboard.Begin();
    else
      this.BestScoreTextBlock.Visibility = Visibility.Visible;
  }
  else
  {
    // Hide everything
    this.ScorePanel.Visibility = Visibility.Collapsed;
    this.BestScoreTextBlock.Visibility = Visibility.Collapsed;
    this.AvgScoreTextBlock.Visibility = Visibility.Collapsed;
  }
}

// Process data coming from the accelerometer
void Accelerometer_ReadingChanged(object sender,
                                  AccelerometerHelperReadingEventArgs e)
{
  // Transition to the UI thread
```

LISTING 49.2   Continued

```
this.Dispatcher.BeginInvoke(delegate()
{
  if (!this.isRunning)
    return;

  // End the game after 1 minute
  if ((DateTime.Now - beginTime).TotalMinutes >= 1)
  {
    GameOver();
    return;
  }

  // Move the object based on the horizontal and vertical forces
  this.MovingPieceTransform.TranslateX =
    Clamp(this.midX + this.lengthX * e.LowPassFilteredAcceleration.X,
    this.minX, this.maxX);
  this.MovingPieceTransform.TranslateY =
    Clamp(this.midY - this.lengthY * e.LowPassFilteredAcceleration.Y,
    this.minY, this.maxY);

  // Check if the two elements are aligned, with a little bit of wiggle room
  if (Math.Abs(this.MovingPieceTransform.TranslateX
                - this.TargetTransform.TranslateX) <= TOLERANCE &&
      Math.Abs(this.MovingPieceTransform.TranslateY
                - this.TargetTransform.TranslateY) <= TOLERANCE)
  {
    if (this.timeEntered == null)
    {
      // Start tracking the time
      this.timeEntered = DateTime.Now;
      this.HighlightRectangle.Opacity = .5;
    }

    // Show the progress
    this.ProgressBar.Value =
      (DateTime.Now - this.timeEntered.Value).TotalMilliseconds;

    if (this.ProgressBar.Value >= this.ProgressBar.Maximum)
    {
      // Success!
      this.score++;

      // Animate in the score
      this.MessageTextBlock.Text = this.score.ToString();
      this.MessageTextBlockShadow.Text = this.score.ToString();
```

LISTING 49.2   Continued

```
          this.ShowMessageStoryboard.Begin();

            // Move the target to the next location
            MoveTarget();
        }
      }
      else
      {
        // The elements are not aligned, so reset everything
        this.HighlightRectangle.Opacity = 0;
        this.timeEntered = null;
        this.ProgressBar.Value = 0;
      }
    });
  }

  void GameOver()
  {
    this.isRunning = false;
    this.ApplicationBar.IsVisible = true;

    if (this.MoveTargetStoryboard.GetCurrentState() == ClockState.Active)
      this.MoveTargetStoryboard.Stop();

    // Shrink both elements to nothing
    this.TargetScaleXAnimation.To = 0;
    this.TargetScaleYAnimation.To = 0;
    this.MovingPieceScaleXAnimation.To = 0;
    this.MovingPieceScaleYAnimation.To = 0;
    this.MoveTargetStoryboard.Begin();

    // Record this attempt and update the UI
    double oldTotal = this.avgScore.Value * this.numTries.Value;
    // New average
    this.avgScore.Value = (oldTotal + this.score) / (this.numTries.Value + 1);
    // New total number of tries
    this.numTries.Value++;
    if (this.score > this.bestScore.Value)
    {
      // New best score
      this.bestScore.Value = this.score;
      UpdateLabels(true);

      // Animate in a congratulations message
      this.MessageTextBlock.Text = "NEW BEST!";
```

LISTING 49.2   Continued

```csharp
      this.MessageTextBlockShadow.Text = "NEW BEST!";
      this.ShowMessageStoryboard.Begin();
    }
    else
    {
      UpdateLabels(false);
    }
  }

  void MoveTarget()
  {
    // Choose a random scale for the images, from .1 to .5
    double scale = (random.Next(5) + 1) / 10d;

    // Adjust the horizontal bounds of the moving piece accordingly
    this.maxY = this.ActualHeight - 379 * scale;
    this.minY = -104 * scale;
    this.lengthY = Math.Abs(this.minY) + this.maxY;
    this.midY = this.minY + this.lengthY / 2;

    // Adjust the vertical bounds of the moving piece accordingly
    this.maxX = this.ActualWidth - 280 * scale;
    this.minX = -224 * scale;
    this.lengthX = Math.Abs(this.minX) + this.maxX;
    this.midX = this.minX + this.lengthX / 2;

    // Prepare and begin the animation to a new location & size
    this.TargetScaleXAnimation.To = this.TargetScaleYAnimation.To = scale;
    this.MovingPieceScaleXAnimation.To = scale;
    this.MovingPieceScaleYAnimation.To = scale;
    this.TargetXAnimation.To = this.minX + random.Next((int)this.lengthX);
    this.TargetYAnimation.To = this.minY + random.Next((int)this.lengthY);
    this.MoveTargetStoryboard.Begin();
  }

  // "Clamp" the incoming value so it's no lower than min & no larger than max
  static double Clamp(double value, double min, double max)
  {
    return Math.Max(min, Math.Min(max, value));
  }

  // Application bar handlers

  void StartButton_Click(object sender, EventArgs e)
  {
```

LISTING 49.2   Continued

```
    // Get started
    this.isRunning = true;
    this.ApplicationBar.IsVisible = false;
    this.ScorePanel.Visibility = Visibility.Collapsed;

    // Center the target before it animates to a new location
    this.TargetTransform.TranslateX = this.ActualWidth - this.Target.Width / 2;
    this.TargetTransform.TranslateY = this.ActualHeight - this.Target.Height / 2;
    MoveTarget();

    this.score = 0;
    this.beginTime = DateTime.Now;
  }

  void InstructionsMenuItem_Click(object sender, EventArgs e)
  {
    this.NavigationService.Navigate(new Uri("/InstructionsPage.xaml",
      UriKind.Relative));
  }

  void CalibrateMenuItem_Click(object sender, EventArgs e)
  {
    this.NavigationService.Navigate(new Uri(
      "/Shared/Calibrate/CalibratePage.xaml?appName=Balance Test&"
    + "calibrateX=true&calibrateY=false", UriKind.Relative));
  }

  void ClearScoresMenuItem_Click(object sender, EventArgs e)
  {
    if (MessageBox.Show("Are you sure you want to clear your scores?",
      "Clear scores", MessageBoxButton.OKCancel) == MessageBoxResult.OK)
    {
      this.numTries.Value = 0;
      this.bestScore.Value = 0;
      UpdateLabels(true);
    }
  }

  void AboutMenuItem_Click(object sender, EventArgs e)
  {
    this.NavigationService.Navigate(new Uri(
      "/Shared/About/AboutPage.xaml?appName=Balance Test", UriKind.Relative));
  }
  }
}
```

Notes:

→ This app uses the low-pass-filtered acceleration data from the `AccelerometerHelper` library. This gives a nice balance of smoothness and the right amount of latency. (Using the optimally filtered data ends up being a bit too jumpy in this case.)

→ The calculations that adjust the moving piece's position should look familiar from the Moo Can app. Notice that the acceleration-based offset is added to the X midpoint, whereas it's *subtracted* from the Y midpoint. As illustrated back in Figure 44.1, the Y-acceleration dimension grows in the opposite direction than Silverlight's typical Y dimension.

→ The page's `ActualWidth` and `ActualHeight` properties are used throughout. If the application bar had an opacity of 1, the page's `ActualHeight` would be 728 while it is visible versus 800 while it is hidden. However, in `StartButton_Click`, accessing `ActualHeight` after hiding the application bar would still report 728, as it hasn't given the layout system a chance to make the change. Thanks to the application bar's custom opacity that enables the page to extend underneath it, the timing of this is no longer a concern; `ActualHeight` reports 800 at all times.

The Finished Product

Scoring a fourth point temporarily reveals the score

A new high score has been earned

Aligned images, using the light theme with the magenta theme accent color

chapter 50

lessons

 Analyzing Walking Motion

PEDOMETER

A *pedometer* counts how many steps you take. It is a handy device for people who are interested in getting enough exercise and perhaps need a little motivation. Pedometers—especially good ones—are expensive. Thanks to the built-in accelerometer, the Pedometer app enables you to turn your phone into a pedometer without the need for a separate device.

> **(!) Current Windows phones do not report accelerometer data while the screen is turned off!**
>
> Although this app runs while the phone is locked, phones do not report accelerometer data while the screen is off. Unfortunately, this means that no steps can be registered while the screen is off. You must keep the screen on (and therefore the phone unlocked) for the entire time you use this app. This app disables the screen time-out, so you don't have to worry about your phone automatically locking in your pocket. You do, however, have to worry about accidentally bumping buttons. For the best results, the screen should face away from your body.

The Main Page

This app has a main page, a settings page, and an instructions page (not shown in this chapter). The main page shows the current number of steps and converts that

number to miles and kilometers, based on a stride-length setting customized on the settings page. It starts out in a "paused" state, shown in Figure 50.1, in which no steps are registered. This cuts down on the reporting of bogus steps. The idea is that users press the start button while the phone is close to their pocket, and then they slide the phone in carefully. (The step-detection algorithm can easily register two bogus steps with a little bit of jostling of the phone.)

This page also shows a welcome message urging the user to calibrate the pedometer, but it only shows it the first time the page is loaded (on the first run of the app).

Listing 50.1 contains the XAML for the main page, and Listing 50.2 contains its code-behind.

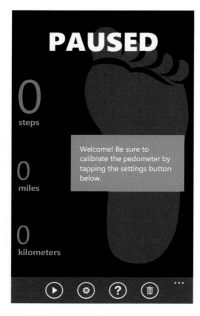

FIGURE 50.1   The app starts out in a paused state to avoid registering bogus steps.

LISTING 50.1   `MainPage.xaml`—The User Interface for Pedometer's Main Page

```xml
<phone:PhoneApplicationPage x:Class="WindowsPhoneApp.MainPage"
    xmlns="http://schemas.microsoft.com/winfx/2006/xaml/presentation"
    xmlns:x="http://schemas.microsoft.com/winfx/2006/xaml"
    xmlns:phone="clr-namespace:Microsoft.Phone.Controls;assembly=Microsoft.Phone"
    xmlns:shell="clr-namespace:Microsoft.Phone.Shell;assembly=Microsoft.Phone"
    xmlns:local="clr-namespace:WindowsPhoneApp"
    FontFamily="{StaticResource PhoneFontFamilyNormal}"
    FontSize="{StaticResource PhoneFontSizeNormal}"
    Foreground="{StaticResource PhoneForegroundBrush}"
    SupportedOrientations="Portrait" shell:SystemTray.IsVisible="True">

  <!-- The application bar, with four buttons -->
  <phone:PhoneApplicationPage.ApplicationBar>
    <shell:ApplicationBar Opacity=".5"
                        BackgroundColor="{StaticResource PhoneAccentColor}">
      <shell:ApplicationBarIconButton Text="start"
                IconUri="/Shared/Images/appbar.play.png"
                Click="StartPauseButton_Click"/>
      <shell:ApplicationBarIconButton Text="settings" Click="SettingsButton_Click"
                IconUri="/Shared/Images/appbar.settings.png"/>
```

LISTING 50.1   Continued

```
    <shell:ApplicationBarIconButton Text="instructions"
              IconUri="/Shared/Images/appbar.instructions.png"
              Click="InstructionsButton_Click"/>
    <shell:ApplicationBarIconButton Text="reset"
              IconUri="/Shared/Images/appbar.delete.png"
              Click="ResetButton_Click"/>
  </shell:ApplicationBar>
</phone:PhoneApplicationPage.ApplicationBar>

<Grid>
  <!-- The accent-colored foot -->
  <Rectangle Opacity=".5" Fill="{StaticResource PhoneAccentBrush}" Width="277"
              Height="648" Margin="0,12,12,0" VerticalAlignment="Top"
              HorizontalAlignment="Right">
    <Rectangle.OpacityMask>
      <ImageBrush ImageSource="Images/foot.png"/>
    </Rectangle.OpacityMask>
  </Rectangle>

  <StackPanel>
    <!-- PAUSED -->
    <TextBlock x:Name="PausedTextBlock" FontFamily="Segoe WP Black"
              HorizontalAlignment="Center" Text="PAUSED"
              FontSize="{StaticResource PhoneFontSizeExtraExtraLarge}"/>

    <!-- Steps -->
    <TextBlock x:Name="StepsTextBlock" Margin="12,12,0,0" Opacity=".5"
              FontSize="130"/>
    <TextBlock Text="steps" Margin="18,-24" FontWeight="Bold"
              FontSize="{StaticResource PhoneFontSizeMedium}"
              Foreground="{StaticResource PhoneSubtleBrush}"/>

    <!-- Miles -->
    <TextBlock x:Name="MilesTextBlock" Margin="12,72,0,0" Opacity=".5"
              FontSize="{StaticResource PhoneFontSizeExtraExtraLarge}"/>
    <TextBlock Text="miles" Margin="18,-12" FontWeight="Bold"
              FontSize="{StaticResource PhoneFontSizeMedium}"
              Foreground="{StaticResource PhoneSubtleBrush}"/>

    <!-- Kilometers -->
    <TextBlock x:Name="KilometersTextBlock" Margin="12,72,0,0" Opacity=".5"
              FontSize="{StaticResource PhoneFontSizeExtraExtraLarge}"/>
```

LISTING 50.1   Continued

```
        <TextBlock Text="kilometers" Margin="18,-12" FontWeight="Bold"
                   FontSize="{StaticResource PhoneFontSizeMedium}"
                   Foreground="{StaticResource PhoneSubtleBrush}"/>
      </StackPanel>

      <!-- The special one-time message -->
      <Border x:Name="FirstRunPanel" Visibility="Collapsed" Width="300"
        Margin="0,0,24,0" HorizontalAlignment="Right" VerticalAlignment="Center"
        Background="{StaticResource PhoneAccentBrush}" Padding="24">
        <TextBlock TextWrapping="Wrap" Text="Welcome! Be sure to calibrate …"/>
      </Border>
    </Grid>
</phone:PhoneApplicationPage>
```

Both the foot and the application bar are given the phone theme's accent color, but with 50% opacity to make them more subtle.

LISTING 50.2   `MainPage.xaml.cs`—The Code-Behind for Pedometer's Main Page

```
using System;
using System.ComponentModel;
using System.Windows;
using System.Windows.Navigation;
using Microsoft.Phone.Applications.Common; // For AccelerometerHelper
using Microsoft.Phone.Controls;
using Microsoft.Phone.Shell;

namespace WindowsPhoneApp
{
  public partial class MainPage : PhoneApplicationPage
  {
    IApplicationBarIconButton startPauseButton;
    IApplicationBarIconButton settingsButton;
    IApplicationBarIconButton instructionsButton;
    IApplicationBarIconButton resetButton;
    bool pastPositiveThreshold = true;

    public MainPage()
    {
      InitializeComponent();
      this.startPauseButton = this.ApplicationBar.Buttons[0]
                              as IApplicationBarIconButton;
      this.settingsButton = this.ApplicationBar.Buttons[1]
                              as IApplicationBarIconButton;
```

LISTING 50.2   Continued

```
  this.instructionsButton = this.ApplicationBar.Buttons[2]
                             as IApplicationBarIconButton;
  this.resetButton = this.ApplicationBar.Buttons[3]
                     as IApplicationBarIconButton;

  SoundEffects.Initialize();

  // Use the accelerometer via Microsoft's helper
  AccelerometerHelper.Instance.ReadingChanged
    += Accelerometer_ReadingChanged;

  // Allow the app to run when the phone is locked.
  // Once disabled, you cannot re-enable the default behavior!
  PhoneApplicationService.Current.ApplicationIdleDetectionMode =
    IdleDetectionMode.Disabled;
}

protected override void OnNavigatedTo(NavigationEventArgs e)
{
  base.OnNavigatedTo(e);

  RefreshDisplay();

  // Show the welcome message if this is the first time ever
  if (Settings.FirstRun.Value)
  {
    this.FirstRunPanel.Visibility = Visibility.Visible;
    Settings.FirstRun.Value = false;
  }
  else
  {
    this.FirstRunPanel.Visibility = Visibility.Collapsed;
  }

  // While on this page, don't allow the screen to auto-lock
  PhoneApplicationService.Current.UserIdleDetectionMode =
    IdleDetectionMode.Disabled;
}

protected override void OnNavigatedFrom(NavigationEventArgs e)
{
  base.OnNavigatedTo(e);

  // Restore the ability for the screen to auto-lock when on other pages
```

LISTING 50.2   Continued

```
      PhoneApplicationService.Current.UserIdleDetectionMode =
        IdleDetectionMode.Enabled;
    }

    protected override void OnBackKeyPress(CancelEventArgs e)
    {
      base.OnBackKeyPress(e);
      if (AccelerometerHelper.Instance.Active)
      {
        MessageBox.Show("You must pause the pedometer before leaving. …",
          "Pedometer Still Collecting Data", MessageBoxButton.OK);
        e.Cancel = true;
      }
    }

    // Process data coming from the accelerometer
    void Accelerometer_ReadingChanged(object sender,
                                      AccelerometerHelperReadingEventArgs e)
    {
      bool newStep = false;

      double magnitude = e.OptimalyFilteredAcceleration.Magnitude;

      if (!pastPositiveThreshold && magnitude > 1 + Settings.Threshold.Value)
      {
        newStep = true;
        pastPositiveThreshold = true;
      }

      if (magnitude < 1 - Settings.Threshold.Value)
        pastPositiveThreshold = false;

      if (newStep)
      {
        // We only know about one leg, so count each new step as two
        Settings.NumSteps.Value += 2;

        this.Dispatcher.BeginInvoke(delegate()
        {
          RefreshDisplay();

          if (Settings.PlaySound.Value)
            SoundEffects.Ding.Play();
        });
```

LISTING 50.2   Continued

```
    }
  }

  void RefreshDisplay()
  {
    this.StepsTextBlock.Text = Settings.NumSteps.Value.ToString("N0");
    double totalInches = Settings.NumSteps.Value * Settings.Stride.Value;
    this.MilesTextBlock.Text = (totalInches / 63360).ToString("##0.####");
    this.KilometersTextBlock.Text =
      (totalInches * 0.0000254).ToString("##0.####");
  }

  // Application bar handlers

  void StartPauseButton_Click(object sender, EventArgs e)
  {
    if (AccelerometerHelper.Instance.Active)
    {
      // Stop the accelerometer with Microsoft's helper
      AccelerometerHelper.Instance.Active = false;

      this.startPauseButton.Text = "start";
      this.startPauseButton.IconUri
        = new Uri("/Shared/Images/appbar.play.png", UriKind.Relative);
      this.PausedTextBlock.Text = "PAUSED";
      this.StepsTextBlock.Opacity = .5;
      this.MilesTextBlock.Opacity = .5;
      this.KilometersTextBlock.Opacity = .5;
      this.settingsButton.IsEnabled = true;
      this.instructionsButton.IsEnabled = true;
      this.resetButton.IsEnabled = true;
    }
    else
    {
      // Start the accelerometer with Microsoft's helper
      AccelerometerHelper.Instance.Active = true;

      this.startPauseButton.Text = "pause";
      this.startPauseButton.IconUri
        = new Uri("/Shared/Images/appbar.pause.png", UriKind.Relative);
      this.PausedTextBlock.Text = "";
      this.StepsTextBlock.Opacity = 1;
      this.MilesTextBlock.Opacity = 1;
      this.KilometersTextBlock.Opacity = 1;
```

LISTING 50.2   Continued

```
      this.settingsButton.IsEnabled = false;
      this.instructionsButton.IsEnabled = false;
      this.resetButton.IsEnabled = false;
    }
  }

  void SettingsButton_Click(object sender, EventArgs e)
  {
    this.NavigationService.Navigate(
      new Uri("/SettingsPage.xaml", UriKind.Relative));
  }

  void InstructionsButton_Click(object sender, EventArgs e)
  {
    this.NavigationService.Navigate(
      new Uri("/InstructionsPage.xaml", UriKind.Relative));
  }

  void ResetButton_Click(object sender, EventArgs e)
  {
    if (MessageBox.Show("Are you sure you want to clear your data?", "Reset",
        MessageBoxButton.OKCancel) == MessageBoxResult.OK)
    {
      Settings.NumSteps.Value = 0;
      RefreshDisplay();
    }
  }
  }
 }
}
```

Notes:

→ This listing uses the following settings defined in a separate `Settings.cs` file as follows:

```
public static class Settings
{
  // Configurable settings
  public static readonly Setting<double> Threshold =
    new Setting<double>("Threshold", .43);
  public static readonly Setting<bool> PlaySound =
    new Setting<bool>("PlaySound", true);
  public static readonly Setting<double> Stride =
    new Setting<double>("Stride", 28);
```

```
  // Current state
  public static readonly Setting<int> NumSteps =
    new Setting<int>("NumSteps", 0);

  // A special flag that is set to false during the app's first run
  public static readonly Setting<bool> FirstRun =
    new Setting<bool>("FirstRun", true);
}
```

→ The walking detection, done inside `Accelerometer_ReadingChanged`, uses the magnitude of the acceleration vector reported by the `AccelerometerHelper` library (the square root of $X^2 + Y^2 + Z^2$). Therefore, the direction of the motion doesn't matter; just the amount of motion. A phone at rest has a magnitude of 1 (pointing toward the Earth), so this algorithm looks for a sufficiently smaller magnitude followed by a sufficiently larger magnitude. This represents the motion of the single leg holding the phone, so the detection of each step is actually counted as two steps, one per leg. The definition of *sufficient* is determined by the `Threshold` setting customized on the settings page.

The Settings Page

The settings page, shown in Figure 50.2, enables the user to change the values of the `Threshold`, `PlaySound`, and `Stride` settings used in the previous listing.

Users can try different sensitivity values (which map to `Threshold`) and then manually count their steps while Pedometer runs to see if the two counts match. To make this process even easier, this app supports playing a sound every time a step is detected. When the value is correct, the user will hear a sound every other step (when the leg carrying the phone makes a step). Once a good sensitivity value is found, the user can turn off the sound.

The best sensitivity value can vary based on where the user puts the phone, the depth of the pocket containing the phone, and other factors. Therefore, a sensitivity value that works best one day may not work well the next.

FIGURE 50.2   The settings page must be visited frequently in order to calibrate the pedometer just right.

To give accurate values for miles and kilometers, users must enter their stride length at the bottom of the page. If users are unable to measure their stride length, they can multiply their height (in inches) by .413 for a woman or .415 for a man. The average stride length for a woman is 26.4 inches, and the average stride length for a man is 30 inches. This information is explained on this app's instructions page.

Listing 50.3 contains the XAML for the settings page, and Listing 50.4 contains its codebehind.

LISTING 50.3   `SettingsPage.xaml`—The User Interface for Pedometer's Settings Page

```xaml
<phone:PhoneApplicationPage
    x:Class="WindowsPhoneApp.SettingsPage" x:Name="Page"
    xmlns="http://schemas.microsoft.com/winfx/2006/xaml/presentation"
    xmlns:x="http://schemas.microsoft.com/winfx/2006/xaml"
    xmlns:phone="clr-namespace:Microsoft.Phone.Controls;assembly=Microsoft.Phone"
    xmlns:shell="clr-namespace:Microsoft.Phone.Shell;assembly=Microsoft.Phone"
    xmlns:local="clr-namespace:WindowsPhoneApp"
    xmlns:toolkit="clr-namespace:Microsoft.Phone.Controls;
➥assembly=Microsoft.Phone.Controls.Toolkit"
    FontFamily="{StaticResource PhoneFontFamilyNormal}"
    FontSize="{StaticResource PhoneFontSizeNormal}"
    Foreground="{StaticResource PhoneForegroundBrush}"
    SupportedOrientations="PortraitOrLandscape" shell:SystemTray.IsVisible="True">
  <Grid Background="Transparent">
    <Grid.RowDefinitions>
      <RowDefinition Height="Auto"/>
      <RowDefinition Height="*"/>
    </Grid.RowDefinitions>

    <!-- The standard settings header -->
    <StackPanel Grid.Row="0" Style="{StaticResource PhoneTitlePanelStyle}">
      <TextBlock Text="SETTINGS" Style="{StaticResource PhoneTextTitle0Style}"/>
      <TextBlock Text="pedometer"
                 Style="{StaticResource PhoneTextTitle1Style}"/>
    </StackPanel>

    <ScrollViewer Grid.Row="1">
      <StackPanel Margin="{StaticResource PhoneMargin}">
        <TextBlock Text="Tap &amp; hold …" TextWrapping="Wrap" Margin="12,0"/>
        <!-- The slider with three supporting text blocks -->
        <Grid Height="150">
          <TextBlock HorizontalAlignment="Right" Margin="0,12,12,0"
                     VerticalAlignment="Center" Text="report more steps"/>
          <TextBlock HorizontalAlignment="Left" Margin="12,12,0,0"
                     VerticalAlignment="Center" Text="report fewer steps"/>
```

LISTING 50.3   Continued

```
            <TextBlock x:Name="ThresholdTextBlock" Margin="12,6,0,0"
                    Foreground="{StaticResource PhoneSubtleBrush}"
                    HorizontalAlignment="Left" VerticalAlignment="Top"
                    FontSize="{StaticResource PhoneFontSizeLarge}"/>
            <Slider x:Name="ThresholdSlider" Minimum=".1" Maximum="1"
                    LargeChange=".001" IsDirectionReversed="True"
                    Value="{Binding Threshold, Mode=TwoWay, ElementName=Page}"/>
        </Grid>

        <!-- reset -->
        <Button Content="reset sensitivity" Click="ResetButton_Click"
                local:Tilt.IsEnabled="True"/>

        <!-- Play a sound toggle switch -->
        <toolkit:ToggleSwitch x:Name="PlaySoundToggleSwitch" Margin="0,30,0,0"
          Header="Play a sound every other step"
          IsChecked="{Binding PlaySound, Mode=TwoWay, ElementName=Page}"/>

        <!-- Stride length -->
        <TextBlock Style="{StaticResource LabelStyle}"
                    Text="Stride length (in inches)"/>
        <TextBox x:Name="StrideLengthTextBox" InputScope="Number"
                    Text="{Binding StrideLength, Mode=TwoWay, ElementName=Page}"/>
      </StackPanel>

    </ScrollViewer>
  </Grid>
</phone:PhoneApplicationPage>
```

LISTING 50.4   `SettingsPage.xaml.cs`—The Code-Behind for Pedometer's Settings Page

```
using System.Windows;
using Microsoft.Phone.Controls;

namespace WindowsPhoneApp
{
  public partial class SettingsPage : PhoneApplicationPage
  {
    public SettingsPage()
    {
      InitializeComponent();
      this.ThresholdTextBlock.Text =
        (Settings.Threshold.Value * 1000).ToString("N0");
```

LISTING 50.4   Continued

```
    }

    // Simple property bound to the slider
    public double Threshold
    {
      get { return Settings.Threshold.Value; }
      set { this.ThresholdTextBlock.Text = (value * 1000).ToString("N0");
            Settings.Threshold.Value = value; }
    }

    // Simple property bound to the toggle switch
    public bool PlaySound
    {
      get { return Settings.PlaySound.Value; }
      set { Settings.PlaySound.Value = value; }
    }

    // Simple property bound to the text box
    public string StrideLength
    {
      get { return Settings.Stride.Value.ToString(); }
      set
      {
        try { Settings.Stride.Value = int.Parse(value); }
        catch { }
      }
    }

    void ResetButton_Click(object sender, RoutedEventArgs e)
    {
      this.ThresholdSlider.Value = Settings.Threshold.DefaultValue;
    }
  }
}
```

The Finished Product

Dark theme with the half-opaque magenta accent color

Light theme with the half-opaque green accent color

Light theme with the half-opaque red accent color

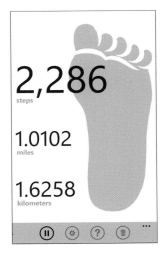

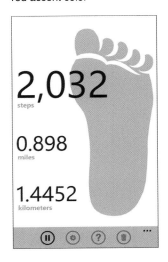

appendix a →

LESSONS INDEX

This appendix combines all the lessons listed at the start of each chapter and places them in alphabetical order. The list here is actually a superset of those lists, because

→ It includes some synonyms.

→ It includes a few minor lessons that aren't listed in their respective chapters.

→ Some lessons are listed under multiple chapters if their use is significant in all of them.

appendix b lessons

XAML REFERENCE

XAML is a relatively simple and general-purpose declarative programming language suitable for constructing and initializing objects. XAML is just XML, but with a set of rules about its elements and attributes and their mapping to objects, their properties, and the values of those properties (among other things).

Despite popular belief, XAML is not inherently about user interfaces. In Silverlight, XAML is *mostly* used to define visual elements, but it's also used for nonvisual purposes, such as the application definition inside App.xaml. Also, although an app's navigation scheme relies on XAML files, almost everything done in XAML can be done entirely in C# instead. (But note that the reverse is not true.) Practically speaking, however, XAML is heavily used in Silverlight apps for Windows Phone.

Because XAML is just a mechanism for using .NET APIs, attempts to compare it to HTML, Scalable Vector Graphics (SVG), or other domain-specific formats/languages are misguided. XAML consists of rules for how parsers/compilers must treat XML and has some keywords, but it doesn't define any interesting elements by itself. So, talking about XAML absent of any context (such as Silverlight) is like talking about C# without the .NET Framework.

This appendix explores the mechanics of XAML, examining its syntax in depth and showing how it relates to C# code.

> ⚠ **The rules for XAML vary depending on which technology you're using!**
>
> XAML parsing done in Windows Presentation Foundation (WPF) differs in a number of ways from the XAML parsing done in desktop Silverlight, which differs from the XAML parsing done for Windows Phone 7! The discussion in this appendix is specific to Windows Phone 7.
>
> Whereas desktop Silverlight 4 introduced a new parser based on the WPF parser, Windows Phone effectively uses the Silverlight 3 parser at the time of this writing. The only noticeable difference between Windows Phone's version of the parser and the desktop Silverlight 3 parser is the list of assemblies/namespaces included in the default XML namespace (http://schemas.microsoft.com/winfx/2006/xaml/presentation).

Elements and Attributes

The XAML specification defines rules that map .NET namespaces, types, properties, and events into XML namespaces, elements, and attributes. You can see this by examining the following simple (but complete) XAML file that declares a button and comparing it to the equivalent C# code:

XAML:

```
<Button xmlns="http://schemas.microsoft.com/winfx/2006/xaml/presentation"
  Content="OK"/>
```

C#:

```
System.Windows.Controls.Button b = new System.Windows.Controls.Button();
b.Content = "OK";
```

or

```
System.Windows.Controls.Button b =
  new System.Windows.Controls.Button { Content = "OK" };
```

Declaring an XML element in XAML (known as an *object element*) is equivalent to instantiating the corresponding .NET object via a default constructor. Setting an attribute on the object element is equivalent to setting a property of the same name (called a *property attribute*) or hooking up an event handler of the same name (called an *event attribute*). For example, here's an update to the button that not only sets its Content property but also attaches an event handler to its Click event:

XAML:

```
<Button xmlns="http://schemas.microsoft.com/winfx/2006/xaml/presentation"
  Content="OK" Click="Button_Click"/>
```

C#:

```
System.Windows.Controls.Button b = new System.Windows.Controls.Button();
b.Click += Button_Click;
b.Content = "OK";
```

This requires a method called Button_Click to be defined with the appropriate signature. Note that XAML, like C#, is a case-sensitive language.

 If you give an event handler an incorrect signature, a vague XamlParseException **is thrown!**

The exception's message is the unhelpful AG_E_PARSER_BAD_PROPERTY_VALUE, although it also provides the position in the XAML file where the incorrect handler is attached to the event.

• • •

Order of Property and Event Processing

At run-time, event handlers are always attached *before* any properties are set for any object declared in XAML. This enables appropriate events to be raised in response to properties being set without worrying about the order of attributes used in XAML.

The ordering of multiple property sets and multiple event handler attachments is usually performed in the relative order that property attributes and event attributes are specified on the object element. Fortunately, this ordering shouldn't matter in practice because design guidelines dictate that classes should allow properties to be set in any order, and the same holds true for attaching event handlers.

One subtlety that often confuses developers is that event handlers can get raised before the logic inside InitializeComponent assigns named XAML elements to their corresponding fields. This can lead to NullReferenceExceptions when such fields are unconditionally accessed inside certain event handlers. A slider's ValueChanged event is one such event where this behavior is commonly seen.

Namespaces

The most mysterious part about comparing the previous XAML examples with the equivalent C# examples is how the XML namespace http://schemas.microsoft.com/winfx/2006/xaml/presentation maps to the .NET namespace System.Windows.Controls. It turns out that the mapping to this and many other .NET namespaces is hard-coded. (In case you're wondering, no web page exists at the schemas.microsoft.com URL—it's just an arbitrary string like any namespace.)

The root object element in a XAML file must specify at least one XML namespace that is used to qualify itself and any child elements. You can declare additional XML namespaces (on the root or on children), but each one must be given a distinct prefix to be used on any identifiers from that namespace. For example, XAML files typically use a second namespace with the prefix x (denoted by using `xmlns:x` instead of just `xmlns`):

```
xmlns:x="http://schemas.microsoft.com/winfx/2006/xaml"
```

This is the XAML language namespace, which maps to types in the `System.Windows.Markup` namespace but also defines some special directives for the XAML parser. These directives often appear as attributes to XML elements, so they look like properties of the host element but actually are not. For a list of XAML keywords, see the "XAML Keywords" section later in this appendix.

Besides the default XML namespace used for core Silverlight elements such as `Button` and the XAML language namespace, the other XML namespaces used in Windows Phone apps do not have the same URL form. They leverage a `clr-namespace` directive that enables you to place a .NET namespace in a specific assembly directly inside XAML. For example:

```
xmlns:phone="clr-namespace:Microsoft.Phone.Controls;assembly=Microsoft.Phone"
```

The assembly specification at the end is necessary only if the desired types don't reside in the same assembly that includes the XAML file. Such types are typically used with a `local` prefix, for example:

```
xmlns:local="clr-namespace:WindowsPhoneApp"
```

Using `http://schemas.microsoft.com/winfx/2006/xaml/presentation` as a default namespace and the XAML language namespace (`http://schemas.microsoft.com/winfx/2006/xaml`) as a secondary namespace with the prefix x is just a convention, just like it's a convention to begin a C# file with a `using System;` directive. You could instead write the original XAML file as follows, and it would mean the same thing:

```
<ns:Button
  xmlns:ns="http://schemas.microsoft.com/winfx/2006/xaml/presentation"
  Content="OK"/>
```

Of course, for readability it makes sense for your most commonly used namespace (also known as the *primary* XML namespace) to be prefix free and to use short prefixes for any additional namespaces.

Property Elements

Rich composition of elements is one of the highlights of Silverlight. This can be demonstrated with a button because you can put arbitrary content inside it; you're not limited to just text! To demonstrate this, the following code embeds a simple square to make a Stop button like what might be found in a media player:

```
System.Windows.Controls.Button b = new System.Windows.Controls.Button();
System.Windows.Shapes.Rectangle r = new System.Windows.Shapes.Rectangle();
```

```
r.Width = 40;
r.Height = 40;
r.Fill = System.Windows.Media.Brushes.Red;
b.Content = r; // Make the square the content of the Button
```

A button's `Content` property is of type `System.Object`, so it can easily be set to the 40x40 `Rectangle` object.

That's pretty neat, but how can you do the same thing in XAML with property attribute syntax? What kind of string could you possibly set `Content` to that is equivalent to the preceding `Rectangle` declared in C#? There is no such string, but XAML fortunately provides an alternative (and more verbose) syntax for setting complex property values: *property elements*. It looks like the following:

```
<Button xmlns="http://schemas.microsoft.com/winfx/2006/xaml/presentation">
<Button.Content>
  <Rectangle Height="40" Width="40" Fill="Red"/>
</Button.Content>
</Button>
```

The `Content` property is now set with an XML element instead of an XML attribute, making it equivalent to the previous C# code. The period in `Button.Content` is what distinguishes property elements from object elements. Property elements always take the form `TypeName.PropertyName`, they are always contained inside a `TypeName` object element, and they can never have attributes of their own (with one exception—the `x:Uid` attribute used for localization).

Many classes designate a property (via a custom attribute) that should be set to whatever content is inside the XML element. This property is called the *content property*, and it is really just a convenient shortcut to make the XAML representation more compact.

Button's `Content` property is (appropriately) given this special designation, so the preceding button could be rewritten as follows:

```
<Button xmlns="http://schemas.microsoft.com/winfx/2006/xaml/presentation">
  <Rectangle Height="40" Width="40" Fill="Red"/>
</Button>
```

There is no requirement that the content property must actually be called `Content`; a list box uses its `Items` property as the content property.

> ! **Using property element syntax with simple string values fails at run-time!**
>
> At compile-time, property element syntax appears to work with simple property values that would normally be used with property attribute syntax, such as in the following button:
>
> ```
> <Button xmlns="http://schemas.microsoft.com/winfx/2006/xaml/presentation">
> <Button.Content>
>   OK                  <!-- This fails because it's the content property -->
> </Button.Content>
> <Button.Background>
>   Green               <!-- This works -->
> </Button.Background>
> </Button>
> ```
>
> Although the setting of Background to Green works, the setting of Content in this fashion throws a XamlParseException at run-time. It doesn't matter whether the Button.Content element is explicitly used or whether the "OK" string is used as the button's inner content. This works at design-time because Visual Studio actually uses the Silverlight 4 XAML parser! The Silverlight 3 XAML parser used at run-time does not support this.
>
> A workaround is to either use property attribute syntax (Content="OK") or place the "OK" string in an element such as a text block.

Type Converters

Let's look at the C# code equivalent to the following button:

XAML:

```
<Button xmlns="http://schemas.microsoft.com/winfx/2006/xaml/presentation"
  Content="OK" Background="Green"/>
```

C#:

```
System.Windows.Controls.Button b = new System.Windows.Controls.Button();
b.Content = "OK";
b.Background = System.Windows.Media.Brushes.Green;
```

Wait a minute. How can "Green" in XAML be equivalent to the static System.Windows.Media.Brushes.Green field (of type System.Windows.Media.SolidColorBrush) in C#? Indeed, this example exposes a subtlety with using strings to set properties in XAML that are a different data type than System.String or System.Object. In such cases, the XAML parser must look for a *type converter* that knows how to convert the string representation to the desired data type.

Silverlight provides type converters for many common data types: Brush, Color, FontWeight, Point, and so on. Unlike the XAML language, type converters generally support case-insensitive strings.

Without a type converter for `Brush`, you would have to use property element syntax to set the background in XAML, as follows:

```
<Button xmlns="http://schemas.microsoft.com/winfx/2006/xaml/presentation"
  Content="OK">
<Button.Background>
  <SolidColorBrush Color="Green"/>
</Button.Background>
</Button>
```

And even that is only possible because of a type converter for `Color` that can make sense of the `"Green"` string. If there were no `Color` type converter, you could still write the following:

```
<Button xmlns="http://schemas.microsoft.com/winfx/2006/xaml/presentation"
  Content="OK">
<Button.Background>
  <SolidColorBrush>
  <SolidColorBrush.Color>
    <Color A="255" R="0" G="128" B="0"/>
  </SolidColorBrush.Color>
  </SolidColorBrush>
</Button.Background>
</Button>
```

But *this* is only possible because of a type converter that can convert each numeric string into a `Byte` value expected by the `A`, `R`, `G`, and `B` properties of the `Color` type. Without this type converter, you would basically be stuck. Type converters don't just enhance the readability of XAML, they also enable values to be expressed that couldn't otherwise be expressed.

Children of Object Elements

A XAML file, like all XML files, must have a single root object element. Therefore, it should come as no surprise that object elements can support child object elements—not just property elements, which aren't children as far as XAML is concerned. An object element can have three types of children: a value for a content property, collection items, or a value that can be type-converted to the object element.

The Content Property

The content property, introduced in the "Property Elements" section, is leveraged in every XAML file in this book. `PhoneApplicationPage` and `UserControl` both have a content property called `Content`. (`PhoneApplicationPage` actually inherits its `Content` property from `UserControl`.) Therefore, the following page:

```
<phone:PhoneApplicationPage
  xmlns="http://schemas.microsoft.com/winfx/2006/xaml/presentation"
```

```
  xmlns:phone="clr-namespace:Microsoft.Phone.Controls;assembly=Microsoft.Phone"
  ...
>
  <Grid>
    ...
  </Grid>
</phone:PhoneApplicationPage>
```

is equivalent to this more verbose version:

```
<phone:PhoneApplicationPage
  xmlns="http://schemas.microsoft.com/winfx/2006/xaml/presentation"
  xmlns:phone="clr-namespace:Microsoft.Phone.Controls;assembly=Microsoft.Phone"
  ...
>
  <phone:PhoneApplicationPage.Content>
    <Grid>
      ...
    </Grid>
  </phone:PhoneApplicationPage.Content>
</phone:PhoneApplicationPage>
```

Visual Studio actually shows an error when you use the more verbose form, but it works fine at run-time.

 The only way to be sure your page's XAML is valid is to run your app and load the page!

At design-time, the XAML parsing done inside Visual Studio is not 100% compatible with what actually happens on Windows Phone. As mentioned earlier, this is because Visual Studio uses the Silverlight 4 XAML parser despite the fact that the Silverlight 3 XAML parser is used at run-time. Therefore, sometimes XAML that works at run-time produces design-time errors, and sometimes XAML that appears to be error-free fails to parse at run-time. The latter is much more common, as the expressiveness of XAML for Silverlight 3 is generally much more restrictive than XAML for Silverlight 4. Watch out for this, especially if you have prior XAML experience!

Running your app in the emulator is sufficient for detecting these issues, because it's using the same operating system and components that are used on a physical phone. If loading a page causes your app to exit, run your app under the debugger to see the details of the exception thrown by the call to `InitializeComponent`.

Collection Items

XAML enables you to add items to the two main types of collections that support indexing: lists and dictionaries.

Lists

A *list* is any collection that implements `System.Collections.IList`, such as `List<T>` or numerous other collection classes. For example, the following XAML adds two items to a list box whose `Items` property is an `ItemCollection` that implements `IList`:

```
<ListBox xmlns="http://schemas.microsoft.com/winfx/2006/xaml/presentation">
<ListBox.Items>
  <ListBoxItem Content="Item 1"/>
  <ListBoxItem Content="Item 2"/>
</ListBox.Items>
</ListBox>
```

This is equivalent to the following C# code:

```
System.Windows.Controls.ListBox listbox = new System.Windows.Controls.ListBox();
System.Windows.Controls.ListBoxItem item1 =
  new System.Windows.Controls.ListBoxItem();
System.Windows.Controls.ListBoxItem item2 =
  new System.Windows.Controls.ListBoxItem();
item1.Content = "Item 1";
item2.Content = "Item 2";
listbox.Items.Add(item1);
listbox.Items.Add(item2);
```

Furthermore, because `Items` is the content property for `ListBox`, you can shorten the XAML even further, as follows:

```
<ListBox xmlns="http://schemas.microsoft.com/winfx/2006/xaml/presentation">
  <ListBoxItem Content="Item 1"/>
  <ListBoxItem Content="Item 2"/>
</ListBox>
```

In all these cases, the code works because `ListBox`'s `Items` property is automatically initialized to any empty collection object. If a collection property is initially `null` instead (and is read/write, unlike `ListBox`'s read-only `Items` property), you would need to wrap the items in an explicit element that instantiates the collection. Typical elements do not act in this fashion.

Dictionaries

`System.Windows.ResourceDictionary`, a collection type used wherever resources are defined, implements `System.Collections.IDictionary`, so it supports adding, removing, and enumerating key/value pairs in procedural code, as you would do with a typical hash table. In XAML, you can add key/value pairs to any resource dictionary. For example, the following XAML adds two Colors:

```
<ResourceDictionary
  xmlns="http://schemas.microsoft.com/winfx/2006/xaml/presentation"
  xmlns:x="http://schemas.microsoft.com/winfx/2006/xaml">
  <Color x:Key="1" A="255" R="255" G="255" B="255"/>
  <Color x:Key="2" A="0" R="0" G="0" B="0"/>
</ResourceDictionary>
```

This leverages the XAML Key keyword (defined in the secondary XML namespace), which is processed specially and enables us to attach a key to each Color value. (The Color type does not define a Key property.) Therefore, the XAML is equivalent to the following C# code:

```
System.Windows.ResourceDictionary d = new System.Windows.ResourceDictionary();
System.Windows.Media.Color color1 = new System.Windows.Media.Color();
System.Windows.Media.Color color2 = new System.Windows.Media.Color();
color1.A = 255; color1.R = 255; color1.G = 255; color1.B = 255;
color2.A = 0;   color2.R = 0;   color2.G = 0;   color2.B = 0;
d.Add("1", color1);
d.Add("2", color2);
```

The value specified in XAML with x:Key is treated as a string; no type conversion is attempted.

More Type Conversion

Plain text can often be used as the child of an object element, as in the following XAML declaration of SolidColorBrush:

```
<SolidColorBrush>Green</SolidColorBrush>
```

This is equivalent to the following:

```
<SolidColorBrush Color="Green"/>
```

even though Color has not been designated as a content property. In this case, the first XAML snippet works because a type converter exists that can convert strings such as "Green" (or "green" or "#008000") into a SolidColorBrush object.

XAML Processing Rules for Object Element Children

You've now seen the three types of children for object elements. To avoid ambiguity, the XAML parser follows these rules when encountering and interpreting child elements:

1. If the type implements `IList`, call `IList.Add` for each child.

2. Otherwise, if the type implements `IDictionary`, call `IDictionary.Add` for each child, using the `x:Key` attribute value for the key and the element for the value. (For Silverlight 3, this only works for resource dictionaries.)

3. Otherwise, if the parent supports a content property (indicated by `System.Windows.Markup.ContentPropertyAttribute`) and the type of the child is compatible with that property, treat the child as its value.

4. Otherwise, if the child is plain text and a type converter exists to transform the child into the parent type (*and* no properties are set on the parent element), treat the child as the input to the type converter and use the output as the parent object instance.

5. Otherwise, treat it as unknown content and potentially raise an error.

Rules 1 and 2 enable the behavior described in the earlier "Collection Items" section, rule 3 enables the behavior described in the section "The Content Property," and rule 4 explains the often-confusing behavior described in the "More Type Conversion" section.

Loading & Parsing XAML

XAML is typically paired with a code-behind file. When you add a page or user control to a Visual Studio project, the generated XAML file contains an `x:Class` attribute on the root element that references the class defined in the code-behind file. When you reference any event handlers in XAML (via event attributes such as `Click` on `Button`), they must be defined in the class referenced by `x:Class`. The referenced class must derive from the type of the root element (such as `PhoneApplicationPage` in the case of pages).

When you compile your project, a C# source file gets generated and compiled into your assembly for each XAML file with a code-behind file. These files have a `.g.cs` suffix, where the g stands for *generated*. Each generated source file contains a partial class definition for the code-behind class. This partial class contains a field (internal by default) for every element named with `x:Name` in the XAML file, using the element name as the field name. It also defines the `InitializeComponent` method that does the work of loading the XAML, assigning the fields to the appropriate instances originally declared in XAML, and hooking up any event handlers (if any event handlers were specified in the XAML file).

If you want to dynamically load XAML yourself, you can use a very simple class called `System.Windows.Markup.XamlReader`. `XamlReader` has a single static method—Load—that accepts a XAML string, parses it, creates and initializes the appropriate .NET objects, then returns an instance of the root element. This method is the key to Chapter 11, "XAML Editor."

If XAML content in a string has a grid as its root element, the following code could be used to create live objects representing all of its contents:

```
Grid grid = (Grid)XamlReader.Load(someString);
```

You can then treat this grid just like one that was statically defined on your current page. You could change its properties, add it to the current page (perhaps by setting it as a new value for the current page's Content property), and so on.

Although there's a XAML reader, there's no built-in XAML writer!

Therefore, there's no automatic way to serialize then deserialize a live user interface.

You can retrieve child elements of this newly created grid by making use of the appropriate content properties or collection properties. The following code assumes that the grid's fifth child (a zero-based index of 4) is a button:

```
Grid grid = (Grid)XamlReader.Load(someString);
// Grab the OK button, using hard-coded knowledge
Button okButton = (Button)grid.Children[4];
```

With a reference to the button, you can again do whatever you want: Set additional properties, attach event handlers, or perform additional actions that you can't do from XAML, such as calling its methods.

Of course, code that uses a hard-coded index and other assumptions about the user interface structure isn't very satisfying, as simple changes to the XAML can break it. Fortunately, XAML supports naming of elements so they can be found and used reliably from procedural code.

Naming XAML Elements

The XAML language namespace has a Name keyword that enables you to give any element a name. For the simple OK button that we're imagining is embedded somewhere inside a Grid, the Name keyword can be used as follows:

```
<Button x:Name="okButton" Content="OK"/>
```

With this in place, you can update the preceding C# code to use the grid's FindName method that searches its children (recursively) and returns the desired instance:

```
Grid grid = (Grid)XamlReader.Load(someString);
// Grab the OK button, knowing only its name
Button okButton = (Button)grid.FindName("okButton");
```

FindName is not unique to a grid; it is defined on FrameworkElement, the base class for every visual element in Silverlight.

> **Naming Elements Without** x:Name   •••
>
> The x:Name syntax can be used to name elements, but some classes define their own Name prop-
> erty that can be treated as the element's name. On such elements, you can simply set the Name
> property to a string rather than use the x:Name syntax. Because Name doesn't exist on all relevant
> elements, and it can't be used in certain contexts, x:Name is used throughout this book. The Name
> property, however, is handy for checking an arbitrary element's name in C#.

XAML Keywords

The XAML language namespace (http://schemas.microsoft.com/winfx/2006/xaml)
defines a handful of keywords that must be treated specially by any XAML parser. They
mostly control aspects of how elements get exposed to procedural code. You've already
seen some of them (such as Key, Name, and Class), but Table B.1 lists all of the ones
supported by Windows Phone 7. They are listed with the conventional x prefix because
that is how they usually appear in XAML and in documentation.

TABLE B.1   Keywords in the XAML Language Namespace Supported By Windows Phone 7,
Assuming the Conventional x Namespace Prefix

Keyword	Valid As	Meaning
x:Class	Attribute on root element.	Defines a class for the root element that derives from the element type, optionally prefixed with a .NET namespace.
x:ClassModifier	Attribute on root element and must be used with x:Class. Does not work on pages, however, as the navigation system doesn't tolerate it.	Defines the visibility of the class speci-fied by x:Class (which is public by default). The attribute value must be specified in terms of the language being used (for example, public or internal for C#).
x:FieldModifier	Attribute on any nonroot element but must be used with x:Name (or equivalent).	Defines the visibility of the field to be generated for the element (which is internal by default). As with x:ClassModifier, the value must be specified in terms of the code-behind language (for example, public, private, ... for C#).
x:Key	Attribute on an element whose parent is a resource dictionary.	Specifies the key for the item when added to the parent dictionary.
x:Name	Attribute on any element but must be used with x:Class.	Chooses a name for the field to be generated for the element, so it can be referenced from code-behind.
x:Uid	Attribute on any element.	Marks an element with an identifier used for localization.

appendix c lessons

THEME RESOURCES REFERENCE

After you install the Windows Phone Developer Tools, you can find several ThemeResources.xaml files with resources for each theme/accent combination in %ProgramFiles%\Microsoft SDKs\Windows Phone\ v7.0\Design. The resources defined in these files are summarized in this appendix.

Brushes & Colors

	Dark Theme	Light Theme
PhoneBackgroundBrush PhoneBackgroundColor	#FF000000	#FFFFFFFF
PhoneChromeBrush PhoneChromeColor	#FF1F1F1F	#FFDDDDDD
PhoneContrastBackgroundBrush PhoneContrastBackgroundColor	#FFFFFFFF	#DE000000
PhoneContrastForegroundBrush PhoneContrastForegroundColor	#FF000000	#FFFFFFFF
PhoneDisabledBrush PhoneDisabledColor	#66FFFFFF (shown on black)	#4D000000

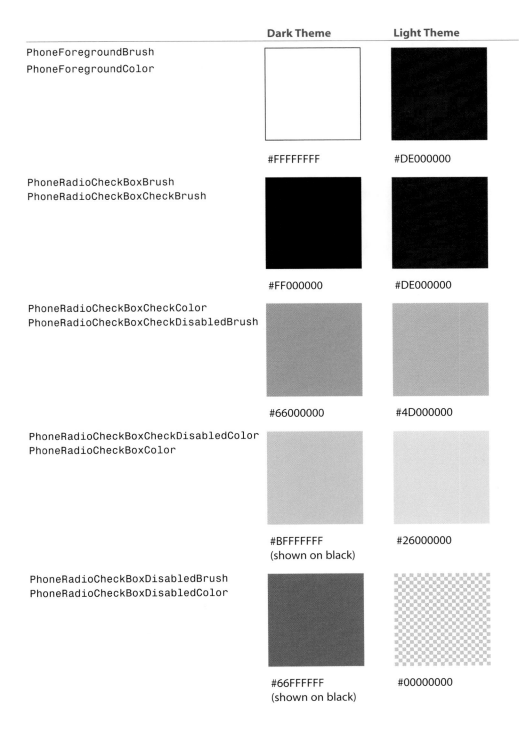

	Dark Theme	Light Theme
PhoneForegroundBrush PhoneForegroundColor	#FFFFFFFF	#DE000000
PhoneRadioCheckBoxBrush PhoneRadioCheckBoxCheckBrush	#FF000000	#DE000000
PhoneRadioCheckBoxCheckColor PhoneRadioCheckBoxCheckDisabledBrush	#66000000	#4D000000
PhoneRadioCheckBoxCheckDisabledColor PhoneRadioCheckBoxColor	#BFFFFFFF (shown on black)	#26000000
PhoneRadioCheckBoxDisabledBrush PhoneRadioCheckBoxDisabledColor	#66FFFFFF (shown on black)	#00000000

	Dark Theme	Light Theme
PhoneRadioCheckBoxPressedBorderBrush PhoneRadioCheckBoxPressedBorderColor	#FFFFFFFF	#DE000000
PhoneRadioCheckBoxPressedBrush PhoneRadioCheckBoxPressedColor	#FFFFFFFF	#00000000
PhoneSemitransparentBrush PhoneSemitransparentColor	#AA000000	#AAFFFFFF (shown on black)
PhoneSubtleBrush PhoneSubtleColor	#99FFFFFF (shown on black)	#66000000
PhoneTextBoxBrush PhoneTextBoxColor	#BFFFFFFF (shown on black)	#26000000

	Dark Theme	**Light Theme**
PhoneTextBoxEditBackgroundBrush PhoneTextBoxEditBackgroundColor	#FFFFFFFF	#00000000
PhoneTextBoxEditBorderBrush PhoneTextBoxEditBorderColor	#FFFFFFFF	#DE000000
PhoneTextBoxForegroundBrush PhoneTextBoxForegroundColor	#FF000000	#DE000000
PhoneTextBoxReadOnlyBrush PhoneTextBoxReadOnlyColor	#77000000	#2E000000
PhoneTextBoxSelectionForegroundBrush PhoneTextBoxSelectionForegroundColor	#FFFFFFFF	#FFFFFFFF

	Dark Theme	Light Theme
PhoneTextCaretBrush PhoneTextCaretColor	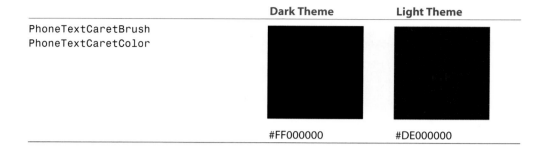	
	#FF000000	#DE000000

Possible Values for `PhoneAccentBrush` and `PhoneAccentColor`

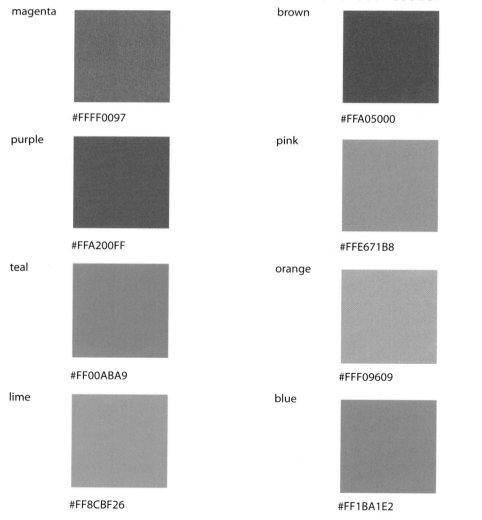

magenta
#FFFF0097

brown
#FFA05000

purple
#FFA200FF

pink
#FFE671B8

teal
#FF00ABA9

orange
#FFF09609

lime
#FF8CBF26

blue
#FF1BA1E2

red

#FFE51400

green

#FF339933

Detecting Dark Versus Light Theme

	Dark Theme	Light Theme
PhoneDarkThemeVisibility	Visible	Collapsed
PhoneDarkThemeOpacity	1	0
PhoneLightThemeVisibility	Collapsed	Visible
PhoneLightThemeOpacity	0	1

Thicknesses

PhoneTouchTargetOverhang	12
PhoneTouchTargetLargeOverhang	12,20
PhoneHorizontalMargin	12,0
PhoneVerticalMargin	0,12
PhoneMargin	12
PhoneTextBoxInnerMargin	1,2
PhonePasswordBoxInnerMargin	3,2
PhoneBorderThickness	3
PhoneStrokeThickness (type=double)	3

Fonts

Font Families

PhoneFontFamilyNormal	Segoe WP
PhoneFontFamilyLight	Segoe WP Light
PhoneFontFamilySemiLight	Segoe WP SemiLight
PhoneFontFamilySemiBold	**Segoe WP Semibold**

Font Sizes

PhoneFontSizeSmall	14pt (18.667px)
PhoneFontSizeNormal	15pt (20px)
PhoneFontSizeMedium	17pt (22.667px)
PhoneFontSizeMediumLarge	19pt (25.333px)
PhoneFontSizeLarge	24pt (32px)
PhoneFontSizeExtraLarge	32pt (42.667px)
PhoneFontSizeExtraExtraLarge	54pt (72px)
PhoneFontSizeHuge	140pt (186.667px)

Styles

PhoneTextNormalStyle
FontFamily=PhoneFontFamilyNormal (Segoe WP)
FontSize=PhoneFontSizeNormal (20px)
Foreground=PhoneForegroundBrush
Margin=PhoneHorizontalMargin (12,0)

PhoneTextSubtleStyle
FontFamily=PhoneFontFamilyNormal (Segoe WP)
FontSize=PhoneFontSizeNormal (20px)
Foreground=**PhoneSubtleBrush**
Margin=PhoneHorizontalMargin (12,0)

PhoneTextTitle1Style
FontFamily=**PhoneFontFamilySemiLight** (Segoe WP SemiLight)
FontSize=**PhoneFontSizeExtraExtraLarge** (72px)
Foreground=PhoneForegroundBrush
Margin=PhoneHorizontalMargin (12,0)

PhoneTextTitle2Style
FontFamily=**PhoneFontFamilySemiLight** (Segoe WP SemiLight)
FontSize=**PhoneFontSizeLarge** (32px)
Foreground=PhoneForegroundBrush
Margin=PhoneHorizontalMargin (12,0)

PhoneTextTitle3Style
FontFamily=**PhoneFontFamilySemiLight** (Segoe WP SemiLight)
FontSize=**PhoneFontSizeMedium** (22.667px)
Foreground=PhoneForegroundBrush
Margin=PhoneHorizontalMargin (12,0)

PhoneTextExtraLargeStyle
FontFamily=**PhoneFontFamilySemiLight** (Segoe WP SemiLight)
FontSize=**PhoneFontSizeExtraLarge** (42.667px)
Foreground=PhoneForegroundBrush
Margin=PhoneHorizontalMargin (12,0)

PhoneTextGroupHeaderStyle	FontFamily=**PhoneFontFamilySemiLight** (Segoe WP SemiLight)
	FontSize=**PhoneFontSizeLarge** (32px)
	Foreground=**PhoneSubtleBrush**
	Margin=PhoneHorizontalMargin (12,0)
PhoneTextLargeStyle	FontFamily=**PhoneFontFamilySemiLight** (Segoe WP SemiLight)
	FontSize=**PhoneFontSizeLarge** (32px)
	Foreground=PhoneForegroundBrush
	Margin=PhoneHorizontalMargin (12,0)
PhoneTextSmallStyle	FontFamily=PhoneFontFamilyNormal (Segoe WP)
	FontSize=**PhoneFontSizeSmall** (18.667px)
	Foreground=**PhoneSubtleBrush**
	Margin=PhoneHorizontalMargin (12,0)
PhoneTextContrastStyle	FontFamily=**PhoneFontFamilySemiBold** (Segoe WP Semibold)
	FontSize=PhoneFontSizeNormal (20px)
	Foreground=**PhoneContrastForegroundBrush**
	Margin=PhoneHorizontalMargin (12,0)
PhoneTextAccentStyle	FontFamily=**PhoneFontFamilySemiBold** (Segoe WP Semibold)
	FontSize=PhoneFontSizeNormal (20px)
	Foreground=**PhoneAccentBrush**
	Margin=PhoneHorizontalMargin (12,0)
PhoneFontSizeHuge	FontFamily=**PhoneFontFamilySemiLight** (Segoe WP SemiLight)
	FontSize=**PhoneFontSizeHuge** (186.667px)
	Foreground=PhoneForegroundBrush
	Margin=PhoneHorizontalMargin (12,0)

appendix d lessons

ANIMATION EASING REFERENCE

Windows Phone ships with 11 easing functions that can easily be applied to an animation or a keyframe. Each of them supports three different modes with a property called `EasingMode`. It can be set to `EaseIn`, `EaseOut` (the default value), or `EaseInOut`. Here's how you can apply one of the easing function objects—`QuadraticEase`—to a basic `DoubleAnimation`:

```
<DoubleAnimation
  Storyboard.TargetProperty="(Canvas.Top)" From="200"
  To="0" Duration="0:0:3">
<DoubleAnimation.EasingFunction>
  <QuadraticEase/>
</DoubleAnimation.EasingFunction>
</DoubleAnimation>
```

And here is how you change `EasingMode` to something other than `EaseOut`:

```
<DoubleAnimation
  Storyboard.TargetProperty="(Canvas.Top)" From="200"
  To="0" Duration="0:0:3">
<DoubleAnimation.EasingFunction>
  <QuadraticEase EasingMode="EaseIn"/>
</DoubleAnimation.EasingFunction>
</DoubleAnimation>
```

`EaseIn` inverts the interpolation done with `EaseOut`, and `EaseInOut` produces the `EaseIn` behavior for the first half of the animation and the `EaseOut` behavior for the second half.

Built-In Power Easing Functions

Table D.1 demonstrates how five of the easing functions work in all three modes by showing the path an object takes if its horizontal position animates linearly but its vertical position animates from bottom to top with each easing function and mode applied.

TABLE D.1   Five Power Easing Functions

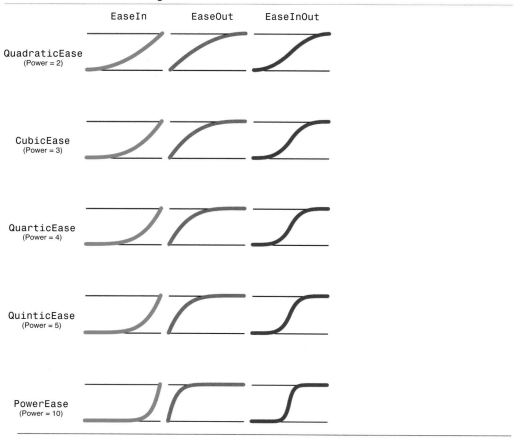

All five functions do interpolation based on a simple power function. With the default linear interpolation, when time has elapsed 50% (.5), the value has changed by 50% (.5). But with quadratic interpolation, the value has changed by 25% (.5 * .5 = .25) when time has elapsed 50%. With cubic interpolation, the value has changed by 12.5% (.5 * .5 * .5 = .125) when time has elapsed 50%. And so on. Although there are four distinct classes for powers 2 through 5, all you really need is the general-purpose PowerEase class that performs the interpolation with the value of its Power property. The default value of Power is 2 (making it the same as QuadraticEase) but Table D.1 demonstrates it with Power set to 10, just to show how the transition keeps getting sharper as Power increases. Applying PowerEase with Power set to 10 can look as follows:

```
<DoubleAnimation Storyboard.TargetProperty="(Canvas.Top)" From="200" To="0"
  Duration="0:0:3">
<DoubleAnimation.EasingFunction>
  <PowerEase Power="10"/>
</DoubleAnimation.EasingFunction>
</DoubleAnimation>
```

Other Built-In Easing Functions

Table D.2 demonstrates the remaining six easing functions in all three modes.

TABLE D.2   The Other Six Built-In Easing Functions

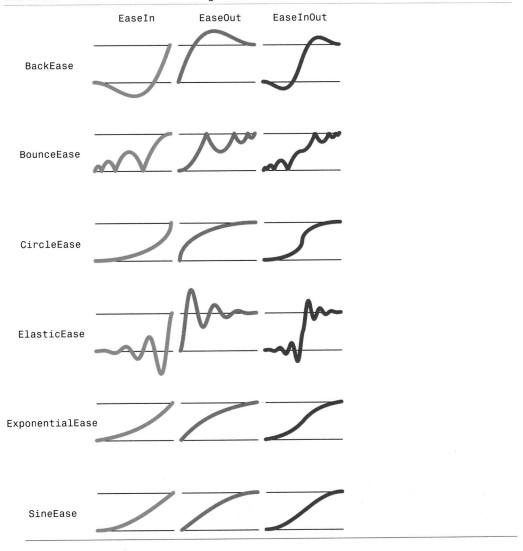

Each of these six functions has unique (and sometimes configurable) behavior:

→ **BackEase**—Moves the animated value slightly back (away from the target value) before progressing. BackEase has an Amplitude property (default=1) that controls how far back the value goes.

→ **BounceEase**—Creates what looks like a bouncing pattern (at least when used to animate position). BounceEase has two properties for controlling its behavior. Bounces (default=3) controls how many bounces occur during the animation, and Bounciness (default=2) controls how much the amplitude of each bounce changes from the previous bounce. For EaseIn, Bounciness=2 doubles the height of each bounce. For EaseOut, Bounciness=2 halves the height of each bounce. So for the more natural EaseOut case, a higher Bounciness actually makes the element appear *less* bouncy!

→ **CircleEase**—Accelerates (for EaseIn) or decelerates (for EaseOut) the value with a circular function.

→ **ElasticEase**—Creates what looks like an oscillating spring pattern (at least when used to animate position). Like BounceEase, it has two properties for controlling its behavior. Oscillations (default=3) controls how many oscillations occur during the animation, and Springiness (default=3) controls the amplitude of oscillations. The behavior of Springiness is subtle: Larger values give smaller oscillations (as if the spring is thicker and more difficult to stretch), and smaller values give larger oscillations (which, in my opinion, seems to make the motion *more* springy rather than *less*).

→ **ExponentialEase**—Interpolates the value with an exponential function, using the value of its Exponent property (default=2).

→ **SineEase**—Interpolates the value with a function based on the sine formula.

> **(!) BackEase and ElasticEase can produce unexpected negative values!**
>
> Because BackEase and ElasticEase make changes to the value outside the range of From to To, any animation starting at zero (for EaseIn or EaseInOut) or ending at zero (for EaseOut or EaseInOut) will mostly likely veer into negative territory. If such an animation is applied to a value that cannot be negative, such as an element's Width or Height, an exception will be thrown.

Writing Your Own Easing Function

Writing your own easing function is as simple as writing a class that implements IEasingFunction. The IEasingFunction interface has only one function, called Ease:

```
public double Ease(double normalizedTime)
{
  // Return a progress value, normalized from 0 to 1
  …
}
```

Ease is called throughout an animation with a value of time normalized to fall between 0 and 1. For any normalized time value, the implementation of Ease must return a progress value normalized to fall between 0 and 1. (However, the value can go outside this range, as is the case for BackEase and ElasticEase.)

Therefore, the following class successfully (although pointlessly) implements a linear easing function:

```
public class LinearEase : IEasingFunction
{
  public double Ease(double normalizedTime)
  {
    return normalizedTime; // Linear interpolation
  }
}
```

The following class implements a quadratic easing function, similar to the built-in QuadraticEase class:

```
public class SimpleQuadraticEase : IEasingFunction
{
  public double Ease(double normalizedTime)
  {
    // Only covers the EaseIn behavior:
    return normalizedTime * normalizedTime; // Quadratic interpolation
  }
}
```

What makes this SimpleQuadraticEase class different from the built-in QuadraticEase is its lack of support for EasingMode. Fortunately, an abstract EasingFunctionBase class (the base class of all 11 built-in easing functions) can give you EasingMode behavior for free.

EasingFunctionBase defines the EasingMode dependency property and implements IEasingFunction. In its implementation of Ease, it calls an abstract method, EaseInCore, that derived classes must implement the same way as they would implement Ease (if the math considers only the EaseIn case). Based on the value of EasingMode, however, EasingFunctionBase modifies the value of normalizedTime before calling EaseInCore and modifies the value returned by it. These transformations make the same EaseIn logic applicable to all three modes. This is all transparent to the derived class, so implementing an easing function with complete support for EasingMode is as simple as changing the base class and renaming Ease to EaseInCore:

```
public class CompleteQuadraticEase : EasingFunctionBase
{
  protected override double EaseInCore(double normalizedTime)
  {
    return normalizedTime * normalizedTime; // Quadratic interpolation
  }
}
```

This `CompleteQuadraticEase` class now behaves exactly like the built-in `QuadraticEase`. You can use this technique to define new and interesting easing functions, such as `SexticEase` (which would come after `QuinticEase`):

```
public class SexticEase : EasingFunctionBase
{
  protected override double EaseInCore(double normalizedTime)
  {
    return normalizedTime * normalizedTime * normalizedTime
        * normalizedTime * normalizedTime * normalizedTime;
  }
}
```

What `EaseOut` and `EaseInOut` Actually Mean

`EaseIn` is easy to understand because it corresponds exactly to the logic written inside `EaseInCore` implementations and maps to how most people think about an animated value progressing as a function of time. To understand what the `EaseOut` and `EaseInOut` modes actually do, let's examine the transformations made by `EasingFunctionBase.Ease` before and after calling the derived class's `EaseInCore` method.

For `EaseIn`, `EaseInCore` is called repeatedly with values starting at 0 and ending at 1. For `EaseOut`, however, `EaseInCore` is called repeatedly with values starting at 1 and ending at 0. (The `normalizedTime` passed to `EaseInCore` is actually 1 - `normalizedTime`.) The value returned by `EaseInCore` is then inverted in this case; the actual value returned becomes 1 - value.

For the `EaseInOut` case, the behavior is different between the first half of the animation (`normalizedTime` values from 0 up to but not including 0.5) and the second half (`normalizedTime` values from 0.5 to 1). For the first half, the `normalizedTime` value passed to `EaseInCore` is doubled (spanning the full range of 0 to 1 in half the time), but the value returned is halved. For the second half, the `normalizedTime` value passed to `EaseInCore` is doubled and inverted (spanning the full range of 1 to 0 in half the time). The value returned from `EaseInCore` is halved and inverted; then .5 is added to the value (because this is the second half of progress toward the final value). This is why every deterministic `EaseInOut` animation is symmetrical and hits 50% progress when 50% of the time has elapsed.

GEOMETRY REFERENCE

In Silverlight, a *geometry* is the simplest possible abstract representation of a shape or path. Geometries are used in two places—the value for Path.Data and the value for UIElement.Clip. These properties are of type Geometry, an abstract base class with several subclasses.

Basic Geometries

The four basic geometries are as follows:

→ **RectangleGeometry**—Has a Rect property for defining its dimensions and RadiusX and RadiusY properties for defining rounded corners

→ **EllipseGeometry**—Has RadiusX and RadiusY properties, plus a Center property

→ **LineGeometry**—Has StartPoint and EndPoint properties to define a line segment

→ **PathGeometry**—Contains a collection of PathFigure objects in its Figures content property; a general-purpose geometry

The first three geometries are really just special cases of PathGeometry, provided for convenience. You can express any rectangle, ellipse, or line segment in terms of a PathGeometry. So, let's dig a little more into the components of the powerful PathGeometry class.

Path Figures and Path Segments

Each `PathFigure` in a `PathGeometry` contains one or more connected `PathSegments` in its `Segments` content property. A `PathSegment` is simply a straight or curvy line segment, represented by one of seven derived classes:

→ **`LineSegment`**—A class for representing a line segment (of course!)

→ **`PolyLineSegment`**—A shortcut for representing a connected sequence of LineSegments

→ **`ArcSegment`**—A class for representing a segment that curves along the circumference of an imaginary ellipse

→ **`BezierSegment`**—A class for representing a cubic Bézier curve

→ **`PolyBezierSegment`**—A shortcut for representing a connected sequence of BezierSegments

→ **`QuadraticBezierSegment`**—A class for representing a quadratic Bézier curve

→ **`PolyQuadraticBezierSegment`**—A shortcut for representing a connected sequence of QuadraticBezierSegments

Bézier curves are described in Chapter 14, "Love Meter." Despite the scarier-sounding name, `QuadraticBezierSegment` is actually simpler than `BezierSegment` and computationally cheaper. A quadratic Bézier curve has only one control point, whereas a cubic Bézier curve has two. Therefore, a quadratic Bézier curve can only form a *U*-like shape (or a straight line), but a cubic Bézier curve can also take the form of an *S*-like shape.

FIGURE E.1   A path that consists of a pair of LineSegments.

The following path uses a `PathGeometry` with two simple `LineSegments` that create the *L* shape in Figure E.1:

```
<Path Stroke="Black" StrokeThickness="10">
  <Path.Data>
    <PathGeometry>
      <PathFigure>
        <LineSegment Point="0,100"/>
        <LineSegment Point="100,100"/>
      </PathFigure>
    </PathGeometry>
  </Path.Data>
</Path>
```

Notice that the definition for each `LineSegment` includes only a single `Point`. That's because it implicitly connects the previous point to the current one. The first `LineSegment` connects the default starting point of (0,0) to (0,100), and the second `LineSegment` connects (0,100) to (100,100). (The other six `PathSegments` act the same way.) If you want to provide a custom starting point, you can simply set `PathFigure`'s `StartPoint` property to a `Point` other than (0,0).

You might expect that applying a fill to this path is meaningless, but Figure E.2 shows that it actually fills it as a polygon, pretending that a line segment exists to connect the last point back to the starting point. Figure E.2 was created as follows:

FIGURE E.2   The path from Figure E.1 filled with an orange brush.

```
<Path Stroke="Black" StrokeThickness="10" Fill="Orange">
  <Path.Data>
    <PathGeometry>
      <PathFigure>
        <LineSegment Point="0,100"/>
        <LineSegment Point="100,100"/>
      </PathFigure>
    </PathGeometry>
  </Path.Data>
</Path>
```

To turn the imaginary line segment into a real one, you could add a third `LineSegment` to the `PathFigure` explicitly, or you could simply set `PathFigure`'s `IsClosed` property to true. The result of doing either is shown in Figure E.3.

FIGURE E.3   The path from Figure E.2, but with `IsClosed="True"`.

Although all `PathSegments` within a `PathFigure` must be connected, you can place multiple `PathFigures` in a `PathGeometry` if you want disjoint shapes or paths in the same geometry. You could also overlap `PathFigures` to create results that would be complicated to replicate in a single `PathFigure`. For example, the following XAML overlaps the triangle from Figure E.3 with a triangle that is given a different `StartPoint` but is otherwise identical:

```
<Path Stroke="Black" StrokeThickness="10" Fill="Orange">
  <Path.Data>
    <PathGeometry>
      <!-- Triangle #1 -->
      <PathFigure IsClosed="True">
        <LineSegment Point="0,100"/>
        <LineSegment Point="100,100"/>
      </PathFigure>
      <!-- Triangle #2 -->
```

```
    <PathFigure StartPoint="70,0" IsClosed="True">
      <LineSegment Point="0,100"/>
      <LineSegment Point="100,100"/>
    </PathFigure>
  </PathGeometry>
 </Path.Data>
</Path>
```

This dual-`PathFigure` path is displayed in Figure E.4.

The behavior of the orange fill might not be what you expected to see. `PathGeometry` enables you to control this fill behavior with its `FillRule` property.

FIGURE E.4   Overlapping triangles created by using two `PathFigures`.

FillRule

Whenever you have a geometry with intersecting points, whether via multiple overlapping `PathFigures` or overlapping `PathSegments` in a single `PathFigure`, there can be multiple interpretations of which area is *inside* a shape (and can, therefore, be filled) and which area is *outside* a shape.

With `PathGeometry`'s `FillRule` property (which can be set to a `FillRule` enumeration), you have two choices on how filling is done:

➔ **EvenOdd**—Fills a region only if you would cross an odd number of segments to travel from that region to the area outside the entire shape. This is the default.

➔ **NonZero**—Is a more complicated algorithm that takes into consideration the direction of the segments you would have to cross to get outside the entire shape. For many shapes, it is likely to fill all enclosed areas.

The difference between `EvenOdd` and `NonZero` is illustrated in Figure E.5, with the same overlapping triangles from Figure E.4.

EvenOdd   NonZero

FIGURE E.5   Overlapping triangles with different values for `PathGeometry.FillRule`.

Geometry Group

`GeometryGroup` composes one or more `Geometry` instances together. It derives from `Geometry`, so a geometry group can be used wherever a geometry is used. For example, the previously shown XAML for creating the overlapping triangles in Figure E.4 could be rewritten to use two geometries (each with a single `PathFigure`) rather than one:

```
<Path Stroke="Black" StrokeThickness="10" Fill="Orange">
  <Path.Data>
    <GeometryGroup>
      <!-- Triangle #1 -->
      <PathGeometry>
        <PathFigure IsClosed="True">
          <LineSegment Point="0,100"/>
          <LineSegment Point="100,100"/>
        </PathFigure>
      </PathGeometry>
      <!-- Triangle #2 -->
      <PathGeometry>
        <PathFigure StartPoint="70,0" IsClosed="True">
          <LineSegment Point="0,100"/>
          <LineSegment Point="100,100"/>
        </PathFigure>
      </PathGeometry>
    </GeometryGroup>
  </Path.Data>
</Path>
```

GeometryGroup, like PathGeometry, has a FillRule property that is set to EvenOdd by default. It takes precedence over any FillRule settings of its children.

This, of course, begs the question, "Why would I create a GeometryGroup when I can just as easily create a single PathGeometry with multiple PathFigures?" One minor advantage of doing this is that GeometryGroup enables you to aggregate other geometries such as RectangleGeometry and EllipseGeometry, which can be easier to use. But the major advantage of using GeometryGroup is that you can set various Geometry properties independently on each child.

For example, the following GeometryGroup composes two identical triangles but sets the Transform on one of them to rotate it 25°:

```
<Path Stroke="Black" StrokeThickness="10" Fill="Orange">
  <Path.Data>
    <GeometryGroup>
      <!-- Triangle #1 -->
      <PathGeometry>
        <PathFigure IsClosed="True">
          <LineSegment Point="0,100"/>
          <LineSegment Point="100,100"/>
        </PathFigure>
      </PathGeometry>
      <!-- Triangle #2 -->
      <PathGeometry>
        <PathGeometry.Transform>
```

```
      <RotateTransform Angle="25"/>
    </PathGeometry.Transform>
    <PathFigure IsClosed="True">
      <LineSegment Point="0,100"/>
      <LineSegment Point="100,100"/>
    </PathFigure>
  </PathGeometry>
</GeometryGroup>
  </Path.Data>
</Path>
```

The result of this is shown in Figure E.6. Creating such a geometry with a single `PathGeometry` and a single `PathFigure` would be difficult. Creating it with a single `PathGeometry` containing two `PathFigures` would be easier but would still require manually doing the math to perform the rotation. With `GeometryGroup`, however, creating it is very straightforward.

FIGURE E.6   A GeometryGroup with two identical triangles, except that one is rotated.

 Because `Stroke` and `Fill` are specified on the path rather than the geometry, GeometryGroup doesn't enable you to combine shapes with different fills or outlines.

Representing Geometries as Strings

Representing each segment in a geometry with a separate element is fine for simple shapes and paths, but for complicated artwork, it can get very verbose. Although most people use a design tool to emit XAML-based geometries rather than craft them by hand, it makes sense to keep the resultant file size as small as reasonably possible.

Therefore, Silverlight supports a flexible syntax for representing just about any `PathGeometry` as a string. For example, the `PathGeometry` representing the simple triangle displayed in Figure E.3:

```
<Path Stroke="Black" StrokeThickness="10" Fill="Orange">
  <Path.Data>
    <PathGeometry>
      <PathFigure IsClosed="True">
        <LineSegment Point="0,100"/>
        <LineSegment Point="100,100"/>
      </PathFigure>
    </PathGeometry>
  </Path.Data>
</Path>
```

can be represented with the following compact syntax:

```
<Path Stroke="Black" StrokeThickness="10" Fill="Orange"
      Data="M 0,0 L 0,100 L 100,100 Z"/>
```

Representing the overlapping triangles from Figure E.4 requires a slightly longer string:

```
<Path Stroke="Black" StrokeThickness="10" Fill="Orange"
      Data="M 0,0 L 0,100 L 100,100 Z M 70,0 L 0,100 L 100,100 Z"/>
```

These strings contain a series of commands that control properties of PathGeometry and its PathFigures, plus commands that fill one or more PathFigures with PathSegments. The syntax is pretty simple but very powerful. Table E.1 describes all the available commands.

TABLE E.1   Geometry String Commands

Command	Meaning
PathGeometry and PathFigure Properties	
F n	Set FillRule, where 0 means EvenOdd and 1 means NonZero. If you use this, it must be at the beginning of the string.
M x,y	Start a new PathFigure and set StartPoint to (x,y). This must be specified before using any other commands (excluding F). The M stands for *move*.
Z	End the PathFigure and set IsClosed to true. You can begin another disjoint PathFigure after this with an M command or use a different command to start a new PathFigure originating from the current point. If you don't want the PathFigure to be closed, you can omit the Z command entirely.
PathSegments	
L x,y	Create a LineSegment to (x,y).
A rx,ry d $f1$ $f2$ x,y	Create an ArcSegment to (x,y) based on an ellipse with radii rx and yx, rotated d degrees. The $f1$ and $f2$ flags can be set to 0 (false) or 1 (true) to control two of ArcSegment's properties: IsLargeArc and SweepDirection, respectively.
C $x1,y1$ $x2,y2$ x,y	Create a BezierSegment to (x,y) using control points ($x1,y1$) and ($x2,y2$). The C stands for *cubic* Bézier curve.
Q $x1,y1$ x,y	Create a QuadraticBezierSegment to (x,y) using control point ($x1,y1$).
Additional Shortcuts	
H x	Create a LineSegment to (x,y), where y is taken from the current point. The H stands for *horizontal line*.
V y	Create a LineSegment to (x,y), where x is taken from the current point. The V stands for *vertical line*.

TABLE E.1   Continued

Command	Meaning
S *x2,y2 x,y*	Create a `BezierSegment` to (*x*,*y*) using control points (*x1*,*y1*) and (*x2*,*y2*), where *x1* and *y1* are automatically calculated to guarantee smoothness. (This point is either the second control point of the previous segment or the current point if the previous segment is not a `BezierSegment`.) The S stands for *smooth* cubic Bézier curve.
T *x1,y1 x,y*	Create a *smooth* `QuadraticBezierSegment` to (*x*,*y*) using control point (*x1*,*y1*). Unlike Q, in which (*x1*,*y1*) determines the starting *and* ending tangents of the curve, here it only determines the starting tangent. T automatically calculates the ending tangent to guarantee smoothness. The T doesn't stand for anything; it's chosen simply to be adjacent to the S command.
Lowercase commands	Any command can be specified in lowercase to cause its relevant parameters to be interpreted as *relative* to the current point rather than absolute coordinates. This doesn't change the meaning of the F, M, and Z commands, but they can also be specified in lowercase.

• • •

Spaces and Commas in Geometry Strings

The spaces between commands and parameters are optional, and all commas are optional. But you must have at least one space or comma between parameters. Therefore, the string M 0,0 L 0,100 L 100,100 Z is equivalent to the much more confusing M0 0L0 100L100 100Z.

C

J–K

S

V

The Resources You Need to Build the Windows® Phone 7 Applications You Want

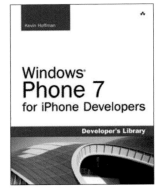

Your purchase of **101 Windows® Phone 7 Apps, Volume I,** includes access to a free online edition for 45 days through the Safari Books Online subscription service. Nearly every Sams book is available online through Safari Books Online, along with more than 5,000 other technical books and videos from publishers such as Addison-Wesley Professional, Cisco Press, Exam Cram, IBM Press, O'Reilly, Prentice Hall, and Que.

SAFARI BOOKS ONLINE allows you to search for a specific answer, cut and paste code, download chapters, and stay current with emerging technologies.

Activate your FREE Online Edition at www.informit.com/safarifree

> **STEP 1:** Enter the coupon code: IJOJZAA.

> **STEP 2:** New Safari users, complete the brief registration form.
> Safari subscribers, just log in.

If you have difficulty registering on Safari or accessing the online edition, please e-mail customer-service@safaribooksonline.com